The Ac

D0788390

9. Close the income statement accounts

8. Prepare financial statements

3. Record the transaction in a journal

7. Take an adjusted trial balance

4. Transfer to the general ledger

6. Record adjusting entries and post to the general ledger

5. Take a trial balance

The Relationships Among the Financial Statements

See Chapter 2, Exhibit 2.2, page 66.

	A	B	C	D
1	**Tara Inc.** Income Statement Month Ended April 30, 2017			
2	**Revenues**			
3	Service revenue ($7,000 + $3,000)		$ 10,000	
4	**Expenses**			
5	Salary expense	$ 1,200		
6	Rent expense	1,100		
7	Utilities expense	400		
8	Total expenses		2,700	
9	Net income		$ 7,300	
10				

	A	B	C	D
1	**Tara Inc.** Statement of Retained Earnings Month Ended April 30, 2017			
2	Retained earnings, April 1, 2017		$ 0	
3	Add: Net income for the month		7,300	
4	Subtotal		7,300	
5	Less: Dividends declared		(2,100)	
6	Retained earnings, April 30, 2017		$ 5,200	
7				

①

	A	B	C	D	E
1	**Tara Inc.** Balance Sheet April 30, 2017				
2	**Assets**		**Liabilities**		
3	Cash	$ 33,300	Accounts payable	$ 1,800	
4	Accounts receivable	2,000	**Shareholders' Equity**		
5	Office supplies	3,700	Common shares	50,000	
6	Land	18,000	Retained earnings	5,200	
7			Total shareholders' equity	55,200	
8	Total assets	$ 57,000	Total liabilities and shareholders' equity	$ 57,000	
9					

②

FINANCIAL ACCOUNTING

Dear Valued Colleagues,

Welcome to the Sixth Canadian Edition of *Financial Accounting*. We are grateful for your support as an adopter of our text as we celebrate over 15 years of success in the market. The Sixth Canadian Edition of *Financial Accounting* has been improved in many respects, as explained below.

Based on feedback from users and reviewers, some of the more advanced material in previous editions has been simplified or completely removed from the book to reduce the coverage of topics better suited to intermediate accounting courses. Also based on feedback about the Fifth Canadian Edition, some topics deemed less important by users and reviewers has been removed from the book, while other topics have been moved to more relevant chapters. As a result of these changes, the Sixth edition is more streamlined, with two fewer chapters and better-organized presentation of critical topics suitable for students in introductory financial accounting courses.

Try It in Excel®. As educators, we often have conversations with those who recruit our students. Based on these conversations, we found that students often complete their study of financial accounting without sufficient knowledge of how to use Excel to perform accounting tasks. To respond to this concern, we have adapted most of the illustrations of key accounting tasks in the book to Excel format and have added new sections in key chapters entitled "Try It in Excel," which describe line-by-line how to retrieve and prepare accounting information (such as adjusted trial balance worksheets, ratio computations, and financial statement analysis) in Excel format.

Student success. We feel we have the most advanced student learning materials in the market with MyAccountingLab. These include automatically graded homework, DemoDocs, and learning aid videos. We believe that the use of MyAccountingLab homework will greatly enhance student understanding of accounting with its instantaneous feedback. MyAccountingLab makes the study of financial accounting a more interactive and fun experience for students. In addition, we have adopted a scaffolding approach in the book and its resources. Chapter content and the end-of-chapter material builds from the basic short exercise featuring one basic single concept to more advanced problems featuring multiple learning objectives. The student can practice at the basic level and then build upon that success to advance on to more challenging problems.

Professor expectations. As professors, we know that you want a book that contains the most relevant and technically correct content available. We also know that you want excellent end-of-chapter material that is as up-to-date and error-free as possible. We reviewed and created the end-of-chapter questions, exercises, problems, and cases taking into account the types of assignments we ourselves use in class and assign as homework. Based on comments from adopters, we have thoroughly reviewed every end-of-chapter exercise and problem, with the goal of eliminating redundancy and adding relevance. The textbook and solutions manual have been put through a rigorous accuracy check to ensure that they are as complete and error-free as possible.

Bill Thomas
Wendy Tietz
Greg Berberich
Catherine Seguin

SIXTH CANADIAN EDITION

FINANCIAL ACCOUNTING

WALTER T. HARRISON, JR.
BAYLOR UNIVERSITY

CHARLES T. HORNGREN
STANFORD UNIVERSITY

C. WILLIAM (BILL) THOMAS
BAYLOR UNIVERSITY

WENDY M. TIETZ
KENT STATE UNIVERSITY

GREG BERBERICH
UNIVERSITY OF WATERLOO

CATHERINE SEGUIN
UNIVERSITY OF TORONTO

WITH CONTRIBUTIONS BY
KATHY FALK
UNIVERSITY OF TORONTO

CHRIS DERESH
DOUGLAS COLLEGE

Pearson

EDITORIAL DIRECTOR: Claudine O'Donnell
ACQUISITIONS EDITOR: Megan Farrell
MARKETING MANAGER: Claire Varley
PROGRAM MANAGER: Richard Di Santo
PROJECT MANAGER: Pippa Kennard
MANAGER OF CONTENT DEVELOPMENT: Suzanne Schaan
DEVELOPMENTAL EDITOR: Suzanne Simpson
MEDIA EDITOR: Anita Smale

MEDIA DEVELOPER: Olga Avdyeyeva
PRODUCTION SERVICES: Cenveo® Publisher Services
PERMISSIONS PROJECT MANAGER: Joanne Tang
TEXT AND PHOTO PERMISSION RESEARCH: Integra Publishing Services
INTERIOR DESIGNER: Anthony Leung
COVER DESIGNER: Anthony Leung
COVER IMAGE: © Yuji Sakai/Getty Images
VICE-PRESIDENT, CROSS MEDIA AND PUBLISHING SERVICES: Gary Bennett

Pearson Canada Inc., 26 Prince Andrew Place, Don Mills, Ontario M3C 2T8.

ISBN 978-0-13-414109-1

Library and Archives Canada Cataloguing in Publication

Harrison, Walter T., author
    Financial accounting / Walter T. Harrison Jr, Charles T. Horngren, C.
William (Bill) Thomas, Wendy M. Tietz, Greg Berberich, Catherine Seguin.
— Sixth Canadian edition.

Includes index.
ISBN 978-0-13-414109-1 (hardback)

    1. Accounting—Textbooks. I. Horngren, Charles T., 1926-, author II.
Thomas, C. William, author III. Tietz, Wendy M., author IV. Berberich,
Greg, 1968-, author V. Seguin, Catherine I., author VI. Title.

HF5635.F43095 2017   657'.044   C2016-904038-0

CONTENTS

Chapter 4
Cash and Receivables   177

Chapter 5
Inventory and Cost of
Goods Sold   230

Chapter 6

Property, Plant, and Equipment, and Intangible Assets 278

Chapter 7

Investments and the Time Value of Money 333

Chapter 11
Financial Statement Analysis   553

ABOUT THE AUTHORS

Walter T. Harrison Jr. is professor emeritus of accounting at the Hankamer School of Business, Baylor University. He received his BBA from Baylor University, his MS from Oklahoma State University, and his PhD from Michigan State University.

Professor Harrison, recipient of numerous teaching awards from student groups as well as from university administrators, has also taught at Cleveland State Community College, Michigan State University, the University of Texas, and Stanford University.

A member of the American Accounting Association and the American Institute of Certified Public Accountants, Professor Harrison has served as chairman of the Financial Accounting Standards Committee of the American Accounting Association, on the Teaching/Curriculum Development Award Committee, on the Program Advisory Committee for Accounting Education and Teaching, and on the Notable Contributions to Accounting Literature Committee.

Professor Harrison has lectured in several foreign countries and published articles in numerous journals, including *Journal of Accounting Research, Journal of Accountancy, Journal of Accounting and Public Policy, Economic Consequences of Financial Accounting Standards, Accounting Horizons, Issues in Accounting Education,* and *Journal of Law and Commerce.*

Professor Harrison has received scholarships, fellowships, and research grants or awards from PricewaterhouseCoopers, Deloitte & Touche, the Ernst & Young Foundation, and the KPMG Foundation.

Charles T. Horngren (1926–2011) was the Edmund W. Littlefield Professor of Accounting, emeritus, at Stanford University. A graduate of Marquette University, he received his MBA from Harvard University and his PhD from the University of Chicago. He was also the recipient of honourary doctorates from Marquette University and DePaul University.

A certified public accountant, Horngren served on the Accounting Principles Board for six years, the Financial Accounting Standards Board Advisory Council for five years, and the Council of the American Institute of Certified Public Accountants for three years. For six years he served as a trustee of the Financial Accounting Foundation, which oversees the Financial Accounting Standards Board and the Government Accounting Standards Board.

Horngren is a member of the Accounting Hall of Fame. As a member of the American Accounting Association, Horngren was its president and its director of research. He received its first annual Outstanding Accounting Educator Award. The California Certified Public Accountants Foundation gave Horngren its Faculty Excellence Award and its Distinguished Professor Award. He was the first person to have received both awards. The American Institute of Certified Public Accountants presented its first Outstanding Educator Award to Horngren. Horngren was named Accountant of the Year, in Education, by the national professional accounting fraternity, Beta Alpha Psi. Professor Horngren was also a member of the Institute of Management Accountants, from whom he received its Distinguished Service Award. He was a member of the institute's Board of Regents, which administers the certified management accountant examinations.

Horngren is an author of these other accounting books published by Pearson: *Cost Accounting: A Managerial Emphasis,* Fifteenth Edition, 2015 (with Srikant M. Datar and Madhav V. Rajan); *Introduction to Financial Accounting,* Eleventh Edition, 2014 (with Gary L. Sundem, John A. Elliott, and Donna Philbrick); *Introduction to Management Accounting,* Sixteenth Edition, 2014 (with Gary L. Sundem, Jeff Schatzberg, and Dave Burgstahler); *Horngren's Financial & Managerial Accounting,* Fifth Edition, 2016 (with Tracie L. Miller-Nobles, Brenda L. Mattison, and Ella Mae Matsumura); and *Horngren's Accounting,* Eleventh Edition, 2016 (with Tracie L. Miller-Nobles, Brenda L. Mattison, and Ella Mae Matsumura). Horngren was the consulting editor for Pearson's Charles T. Horngren Series in Accounting.

C. William (Bill) Thomas is the J.E. Bush Professor of Accounting and a Master Teacher at Baylor University. A Baylor University alumnus, he received both his BBA and MBA there and went on to earn his PhD from The University of Texas at Austin.

With primary interests in the areas of financial accounting and auditing, Bill Thomas has served as the J.E. Bush Professor of Accounting since 1995. He has been a member of the faculty of the Accounting and Business Law Department of the Hankamer School of Business since 1971 and served as chair of the department for 12 years. He has been recognized as an Outstanding Faculty Member of Baylor University as well as a Distinguished Professor for the Hankamer School of Business. Dr. Thomas has received many awards for outstanding teaching, including the Outstanding Professor in the Executive MBA Programs as well as the designation of Master Teacher.

Thomas is the author of textbooks in auditing and financial accounting, as well as many articles in auditing, financial accounting and reporting, taxation, ethics, and accounting education. His scholarly work focuses on the subject of fraud prevention and detection, as well as ethical issues among accountants in public practice. He presently serves as the accounting and auditing editor of *Today's CPA*, the journal of the Texas Society of Certified Public Accountants, with a circulation of approximately 28,000.

Thomas is a certified public accountant in Texas. Prior to becoming a professor, Thomas was a practicing accountant with the firms of KPMG, LLP, and BDO Seidman, LLP. He is a member of the American Accounting Association, the American Institute of Certified Public Accountants, and the Texas Society of Certified Public Accountants.

> For my wife, Mary Ann.
> *C. William (Bill) Thomas*

Wendy M. Tietz is a professor in the Department of Accounting in the College of Business Administration at Kent State University, where she has taught since 2000. She teaches introductory financial and managerial accounting in a variety of formats, including large sections, small sections, and web-based sections. She has received numerous college and university teaching awards while at Kent State University. Most recently she was named the Beta Gamma Sigma Professor of the Year for the College of Business Administration.

Dr. Tietz is a certified public accountant, a certified management accountant, and a chartered global management accountant. She is a member of the American Accounting Association (AAA), the Institute of Management Accountants (IMA), and the American Institute of Certified Public Accountants (AICPA). She has published articles in such *journals* as *Issues in Accounting Education, Accounting Education: An International Journal*, and *Journal of Accounting & Public Policy*. She received the 2014 Bea Sanders/AICPA Innovation in Teaching Award for her accounting educator blog entitled "Accounting in the Headlines." She regularly presents at AAA regional and national meetings. Dr. Tietz is also the coauthor of a managerial accounting textbook, *Managerial Accounting*, with Dr. Karen Braun.

Dr. Tietz received her PhD from Kent State University. She received both her MBA and BSA from the University of Akron. She worked in industry for several years, both as a controller for a financial institution and as the operations manager and controller for a recycled plastics manufacturer.

> To my husband, Russ, who steadfastly
> supports me in every endeavor.
> *Wendy M. Tietz*

Greg Berberich, CPA, CA, PhD, is the Director of the Masters of Accounting program in the School of Accounting and Finance at the University of Waterloo, where he has been a Lecturer since 2011. Before that, he was a faculty member at Wilfrid Laurier University for nine years. He obtained his BMath and PhD from the University of Waterloo and completed his CPA and CA in Ontario.

Berberich has taught financial accounting, auditing, and a variety of other courses at the undergraduate and graduate levels. He has presented papers at a variety of academic conferences in Canada and the United States and has served on the editorial board of the journal *Issues in Accounting Education*. Berberich was also the Treasurer of the Society for Teaching and Learning in Higher Education and the Associate Director of Teaching and Learning in Waterloo's School of Accounting and Finance. He has written a number of cases for use in university courses and professional training programs.

> For Mark, in case he ever forgets the basic
> accounting equation.
> *Greg Berberich*

Catherine I. Seguin, MBA, CGA, is Associate Professor, Teaching Stream, at the University of Toronto Mississauga. In addition to her books *Understanding Accounting for Not-for-Profit Organizations* and *Accounting for Not-for-Profit Organizations* for Carswell (Thomson-Reuters) and *Not-for-Profit Accounting*, published by CGA Canada, she revised the study guide that accompanied the third edition of this textbook. She also coauthored a practice book on management accounting and wrote a test bank for a financial accounting book for McGraw-Hill.

At the University of Toronto Mississauga, Catherine initiated, organized, and continues to run an internship course where fourth-year Bachelor of Commerce and Bachelor of Business Administration students are given an opportunity to gain practical business experience to complement their field of studies. She serves as Dean's Designate for academic offences in the Social Sciences.

In the business community, she has participated in the consultation of the reform of the Canada Corporations Act for not-for-profit organizations. In the past, she has served on several boards of not-for-profit organizations and has been a professional development speaker for CGA Ontario, Alberta, and Manitoba on the topic of not-for-profit accounting. Currently, she serves as Treasurer on the board of a small not-for-profit organization.

> To Dennis, Andrea, Allison, and Mark
> *Catherine I. Seguin*

PREFACE

HELPING STUDENTS BUILD A SOLID *FINANCIAL ACCOUNTING* FOUNDATION

Financial Accounting gives readers a solid foundation in the fundamentals of accounting and the basics of financial statements, and then builds upon that foundation to offer more advanced and challenging concepts and problems. The concepts and procedures that form the accounting cycle are also described and illustrated early in the text (Chapters 2 and 3) and are then applied consistently in the chapters that follow. This scaffolded approach helps students to better understand the meaning and relevance of financial information, see its significance within a real-world context, as well as develop the skills needed to analyze financial information in both their courses and career.

Financial Accounting has a long-standing reputation in the marketplace for being readable and easy to understand. It drives home fundamental concepts using relevant examples from real-world companies in a reader-friendly way without adding unnecessary complexity. While maintaining hallmark features of accuracy, readability, and ease of understanding, the Sixth Canadian Edition includes updated explanations, coverage, and ratio analysis with decision-making guidelines. These time-tested methodologies with the latest technology ensures that students learn basic concepts in accounting in a way that is relevant, stimulating, and fun, while exercises and examples from real-world companies help students gain a better grasp of the course material.

CHANGES TO THE SIXTH CANADIAN EDITION

Students and instructors will benefit from numerous changes incorporated into this latest edition of *Financial Accounting*. Based on feedback from users and reviewers, some of the more-advanced material in previous editions has been simplified or completely removed from the book to reduce the coverage of topics better suited to intermediate accounting courses. Also based on feedback about the Fifth Edition, some topics deemed less important by users and reviewers have been removed from the book, while other topics have been moved to more-relevant chapters. As a result of these changes, the Sixth Edition is more streamlined than previous editions, with two fewer chapters and better-organized presentation of critical topics suitable for students in introductory financial accounting courses (see the detailed chapter-by-chapter changes below for more information). All materials have been updated to reflect the IFRS and ASPE principles in effect at the time of writing (February 2016), or (in some cases) expected to be in effect by the time of the book's publication in 2017. Directly after the Learning Objectives, each chapter includes a list of relevant CPA Competencies addressed in that chapter. The visual presentation has been substantially improved to better suit what students will see in their careers, such as financial statements in spreadsheet formats. The following is a summary of the significant changes made to this edition:

Chapter 1
- The subject company has been changed to Canadian Tire from TELUS.
- The section on accounting's conceptual framework has been moved to follow the presentation of the financial statements, so students have an understanding of the financial statement elements before learning about the framework underlying them.
- The introductions to accounting fraud and the financial reporting responsibilities of management and the auditors have been moved up to Chapter 1 so students have an understanding of these concepts throughout the remainder of the book.

- Three Stop + Think exercises have been added, so there is now one for every learning objective.
- Advanced or esoteric line items were removed from the sample Canadian Tire financial statements included as exhibits so students are not overwhelmed with concepts in the very first chapter, and instead can focus their attention on easier-to-understand line items.
- Three new exercises/problems have been added to this chapter.
- Excel has been incorporated into the end-of-chapter summary problem.

Chapter 2
- Learning objectives 2, 3, and 5 have been reworded to make them more precise and distinct from each other.
- The descriptions of several common types of accounts have been changed to add clarity and better reflect common practice.
- Four Stop + Think exercises have been added, one for each of the last four learning objectives.
- Detailed instructions for how to use Excel to illustrate the impact of business transactions on the accounting equation, prepare a trial balance, and prepare financial statements have been added.
- Three new exercises/problems have been added to this chapter.
- Excel has been incorporated into the mid-chapter and end-of-chapter summary problems.

Chapter 3
- Four Stop + Think problems have been added, so now there is at least one for every learning objective in the chapter.
- Two "Try It in Excel" features have been added to illustrate how Excel can be used to simplify the preparation of accounting information.
- Three new exercises/problems have been added to this chapter.
- Excel has been incorporated into the mid-chapter and end-of-chapter summary problems.

Chapter 4
- This new chapter on Cash and Accounts Receivable combines elements of Chapter 4 from the previous edition on how to account for cash with elements from Chapter 5 on accounts receivable.
- The exposition of several accounts receivable topics has been altered to improve clarity and understanding.
- The coverage of short-term investments has been moved to Chapter 7 so it is presented alongside other investment topics.
- Four Stop + Think problems have been added, so now there is at least one for every learning objective in the chapter.
- Three new exercises/problems have been added to this chapter.
- New requirements have been added to six new exercises/problems.

Chapter 5
- This chapter on Inventory was Chapter 6 in previous editions of the book.
- Learning objectives 1, 2, 4, and 5 have been reworded to make them more precise.
- Four Stop + Think problems have been added, so now there is at least one for every learning objective in the chapter.
- The exposition of several topics has been altered to improve clarity and understanding.

Chapter 6
- This chapter on long-lived assets was Chapter 7 in previous editions of the book.
- Coverage of the DuPont model has been removed.
- Two Stop + Think problems have been added, so now there is at least one for every learning objective in the chapter.
- Three "Try It in Excel" features have been added to illustrate how Excel can be used to simplify the preparation of accounting information.

- The exposition of several topics has been altered to improve clarity and understanding.
- Six new exercises/problems have been added to the end of chapter material.
- Additional requirements added to nine exercises/problems.

Chapter 7
- This chapter on Investments was Chapter 8 in previous editions of the book.
- Coverage of foreign currency translation has been removed.
- Four Stop + Think problems have been added, so now there is at least one for every learning objective in the chapter.
- The exposition of strategic and non-strategic investments has been altered to improve clarity and understanding, and brief coverage of consolidated financial statements has been added.
- Four new exercises/problems have been added to the end of chapter material.

Chapter 8
- This chapter on Liabilities was Chapter 9 in previous editions of the book.
- Coverage of Corporate Income Taxes has been moved from Chapter 11 in the previous edition to the Current Liabilities section of this chapter.
- Three Stop + Think problems have been added, so now there is at least one for every learning objective in the chapter.
- Two "Try It in Excel" features have been added to illustrate how Excel can be used to simplify the preparation of accounting information.
- Five new exercises/problems have been added to this chapter.
- Excel has been incorporated into the mid-chapter and end-of-chapter summary problems.

Chapter 9
- This chapter on Shareholders' Equity was Chapter 10 in previous editions of the book.
- Four Stop + Think problems have been added, so now there is at least one for every learning objective in the chapter.
- The material on the Statement of Changes in Shareholders' Equity has been moved from the old Chapter 11 to this chapter, where it fits better with the other chapter concepts.
- The presentation of the material on return on assets and return on equity has been simplified to make it more understandable for students at the introductory level.
- Ten new exercises/problems have been added to this chapter.

Chapter 10
- This chapter on the Statement of Cash Flows was Chapter 12 in previous editions of the book.
- Added one Stop + Think problem, so now there is one for every learning objective in the chapter.
- The subject company has been changed from TELUS Corporation to Canadian Tire Corporation.
- One new exercise/problem has been added to this chapter.

Chapter 11
- This chapter on Financial Statement Analysis was Chapter 13 in previous editions of the book.
- A comprehensive analysis case has been added to the end of the chapter.
- Three Stop + Think problems have been added, so now there is at least one for every learning objective in the chapter.
- Two "Try It in Excel" features have been added to illustrate how Excel can be used to simplify the preparation of accounting information.
- Excel has been incorporated into the mid-chapter summary problem.
- Four new exercises/problems have been added to the end of chapter material.

VISUAL WALK-THROUGH

Try It in Excel

NEW!

Special sections called **Try It in Excel** have been added to almost every chapter, giving students explicit instructions on how to build Excel templates that streamline and simplify various accounting tasks. These tasks include preparation of the adjusted trial balance worksheet, preparation of financial statements, computation of depreciation by various methods, and computation of effective-interest bond discount and premium amortization. The presentation of most illustrative financial statements, general ledgers, and journal entries have been converted to Excel as well.

TRY IT in EXCEL® ▸ ▸ ▸

The adjusted trial balance in Exhibit 3-4 was prepared using an Excel spreadsheet. You can use it as a template to solve future problems just by changing the initial trial balance data. To prepare the Excel template, follow these steps:

1. Open a blank Excel spreadsheet. Format the spreadsheet header and column headings exactly as you see in Exhibit 3-4.
2. Enter the account titles and account balances from the "Unadjusted Trial Balance" columns.
3. Sum the debits and credits in the "Unadjusted Trial Balance" columns.
4. Enter adjusting journal entries (a) through (g) one at a time in the "Adjustments" columns. For example, for adjusting journal entry (a) enter 1,000 in the debit column on the "Rent expense" line, and 1,000 in the credit column of the "Prepaid rent" line. Do not enter the letters (a) through (g); use only the amounts.
5. In the "Adjusted Trial Balance" debit and credit columns, enter formulas as follows:
   - For asset, dividend, and expense accounts: = + (debit amounts from "Unadjusted Trial Balance" and "Adjustments" columns) − (credit amounts from "Adjustments" columns).
   - For contra asset, liability, share capital, retained earnings, and service revenue accounts: = + (credit amounts from "Unadjusted Trial Balance" and "Adjustments" columns) − (debit amounts from "Adjustments" columns).
6. Sum the "Adjustments" debit and credit columns.
7. Sum the "Adjusted Trial Balance" debit and credit columns.

	A	B	C	D
1	**Canadian Tire Corporation** Consolidated Statements of Income (Adapted) For the Years Ended January 3, 2015 and December 28, 2013*			
2	*(in millions of dollars)*	2014*	2013*	
3	Revenue	$ 12,462.9	$ 11,785.6	
4	Cost of producing revenue	(8,416.9)	(8,063.3)	
5	Gross margin	4,046.0	3,722.3	
6	Other income (expense)	11.0	(3.0)	
7	Selling, general and administrative expenses	(3,052.9)	(2,828.9)	
8	Net finance costs	(108.9)	(105.8)	
9	Change in fair value of redeemable financial instrument	(17.0)	-	
10	Income before income taxes	878.2	784.6	
11	Income taxes	(238.9)	(220.2)	
12	Net income	$ 639.3	$ 564.4	
13				

Spreadsheet Formats Used Throughout Text

NEW!

NEW DESIGN! Excel-based financial statements are used so students will familiarize themselves with the accounting information format actually used in the business world.

Stop + Think

UPDATED! Stop + Think problems offer students the opportunity to pause in their reading and apply what they've just read to basic but realistic problems. The solutions to these problems at available at the end of each chapter, so students can glance at them as they read the problems. Selected Stop + Think problems appear in MyAccountingLab.

STOP + THINK (4-3)

Neal Company had the following information relating to credit sales in 2017:

Accounts receivable, December 31, 2017	$9,500
Allowance for uncollectible accounts, credit balance, December 31, 2017 (before adjustment)	900
Sales during 2017	46,000
Collections from customers on account during 2017	49,500

The aging-of-receivables method determined the uncollectible accounts to be $1,350. How much should Neal Company record as the bad debt expense for 2017?

CPA COMPETENCIES

Competencies* addressed in this chapter:

1.2.1 Develops or evaluates appropriate accounting policies and procedures

1.2.2 Evaluates treatment for routine transactions

1.3.1 Prepares financial statements

1.4.4 Interprets financial reporting results for stakeholders (external or internal)

Competencies

NEW!

CPA Competencies provide instructors and students with clear mapping between key accounting concepts, end-of-chapter problems, and relevant competencies from the *CPA Competency Map*.

Decision Guidelines

Illustrate how financial statements are used and how accounting information aids companies in decision making.

▶ DECISION GUIDELINES

DECISION FRAMEWORK FOR MAKING ETHICAL JUDGMENTS

Making tough ethical judgments in business and accounting requires a decision framework. Answering the following four questions will help you to make ethical business decisions:

Decision	Guidelines
1. What is the issue?	1. The issue will usually deal with making a judgment about an accounting measurement or disclosure that results in economic consequences, often to numerous parties.
2. Who are the stakeholders, and what are the consequences of the decision to each of them?	2. Stakeholders include anyone who might be affected by the decision—you, your company, and potential users of the information (investors, creditors, regulatory agencies). Consequences can be economic, legal, or ethical in nature.
3. What are the decision alternatives, and how do they affect each stakeholder?	3. Analyze the impact of the decision on all stakeholders, using economic, legal, and ethical criteria. Ask, "Who will be helped or hurt, whose rights will be exercised or denied, and in what way?"
4. What decision alternative will you choose?	4. Choose the alternative that best balances your economic, legal, and ethical responsibilities to your stakeholders. Also, assess how your decision makes you feel. If it makes you feel uneasy, determine why and consider choosing another alternative.

COOKING *the* BOOKS

with Inventory

No area of accounting has a deeper ethical dimension than inventory. Managers of companies whose profits do not meet shareholder expectations are sometimes tempted to "cook the books" to increase reported income. The increase in reported income may lead investors and creditors into thinking the business is more successful than it really is.

What do managers hope to gain from fraudulent accounting? In some cases, they are trying to keep their jobs. In other cases, their bonuses are tied to reported income: the higher the company's net income, the higher the managers' bonuses.

The easiest is simply to overstate ending inventory. The two most common ways to "cook the books" with inventory are (1) inserting fictitious inventory, thus overstating quantities; and (2) deliberately overstating unit prices used in the computation of ending inventory amounts. The upward-pointing arrows in the accounting equation indicate an overstatement: reporting more assets and equity than are actually present.

ASSETS	=	LIABILITIES	+	SHAREHOLDERS' EQUITY
↑	=	0	+	↑

Cooking the Books

These boxes highlight real fraud cases in relevant sections throughout the text, giving students context to the material they are learning through real-life business situations.

IFRS/ASPE Differences

A summary of IFRS and ASPE differences is provided at the end of several chapters to identify the differences that exist between these two sets of principles.

Summary of IFRS-ASPE Differences

Concepts	IFRS	ASPE
Depreciation (p. 283)	This concept is called depreciation.	This concept is called amortization.
Significant components of an item of property, plant, or equipment (p. 298)	Significant components shall be depreciated separately.	Significant components are amortized separately only when it is practical to do so.
Impairment (p. 298)	A company shall assess at the end of each reporting period whether there are any signs that an asset may be impaired. Irrespective of any signs of impairment, a company must annually review goodwill and intangible assets with indefinite useful lives for impairment.	A company shall test an asset for impairment whenever events or circumstances indicate its carrying amount may not be recoverable.
	If an impaired asset subsequently increases in value, a company may reverse all or part of any previous write-down but not on goodwill.	A company may not reverse any write-downs, even if an impaired asset subsequently increases in value.
Revaluation (p. 299)	A company may choose to use the revaluation model to measure its property, plant, and equipment.	A company must use the cost method; no revaluation is permitted.

S6-14 In 2017, Artesia, Inc., reported $300 million in sales, $18 million in net income, and average total assets of $120 million. What is Artesia's return on assets in 2017? Assume an industry average of 16%. Did the company's return on assets improve or deteriorate? What could be some reasons for the change?

LEARNING OBJECTIVE ❻
Calculate return on assets

S6-15 Ochoa Optical, Inc., provides a full line of designer eyewear to optical dispensaries. Ochoa reported the following information for 2016 and 2017:

LEARNING OBJECTIVE ❻
Calculate return on assets

NEW!

	2017	2016
Sales revenue	$500,000	$450,000
Net income	$ 45,000	$ 42,500
Average total assets	$250,000	$240,000

Compute return on assets for 2016 and 2017. Did the return on assets improve in 2017? What would cause this ratio to change?

End-of-Chapter Problems

New and updated additional problems have been added or revised to provide instructors with updated and comprehensive testing of all learning objectives in every chapter.

DIGITAL WALK-THROUGH

 Pearson eText

The Pearson eText, available through MyAccountingLab, gives students access to their textbook anytime, anywhere. In addition to note taking, highlighting, and bookmarking, the Pearson eText offers interactive and sharing features. Instructors can share their comments or highlights, and students can add their own, creating a tight community of learners within the class.

NEW! **Auto-Graded Excel Projects**

Using proven, field-tested technology, MyAccountingLab's new auto-graded Excel Projects allow instructors to seamlessly integrate Excel content into their course without having to manually grade spreadsheets. Students have the opportunity to practice important accounting skills in Microsoft Excel, helping them to master key concepts and gain proficiency in Excel. Students simply download a spreadsheet, work live on an accounting problem in Excel, and then upload that file back into MyAccountingLab, where they receive reports on their work that provide personalized, detailed feedback to pinpoint where they went wrong on any step of the problem.

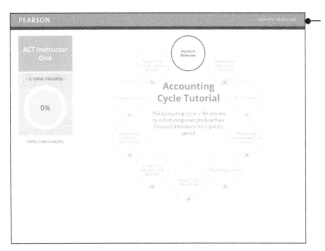

Accounting Cycle Tutorial (ACT)

MyAccountingLab's new interactive tutorial helps students master the accounting cycle for early and continued success in their introductory accounting course. The tutorial, accessed by computer, smartphone, or tablet, provides students with brief explanations of each concept of the accounting cycle. Using embedded assessments, student performance is scored and recorded in the MyAccountingLab Gradebook. Learn more at **http://www.pearsonmylabandmastering.com/northamerica/myaccountinglab/educators/features/index.html.**

Learning Catalytics

Learning Catalytics, available through MyAccountingLab, is a "bring your own device" assessment and classroom activity system that expands the possibilities for student engagement. Using Learning Catalytics, you can deliver a wide range of automatically graded or open-ended questions that test content knowledge and build critical thinking skills. The wide variety of different answer types provide great flexibility, including graphical, numerical, textual input, and more.

Try It Videos

These videos, offered only in MyAccountingLab, guide students step-by-step through select exhibits in the text.

STUDENT AND INSTRUCTOR RESOURCES

For Students

MyAccountingLab

MyAccountingLab online Homework and Assessment Manager includes:

- Pearson eText
- Student PowerPoint® Presentations
- Accounting Cycle Tutorial
- Videos
- Demo Docs
- Glossary Flashcards
- Dynamic Study Modules

For Instructors

MyAccountingLab

MyAccountingLab delivers *proven results* in helping individual students succeed.

It provides *engaging experiences* that personalize, stimulate, and measure learning for each student. And, it comes from a *trusted partner* with educational expertise and an eye on the future. MyAccountingLab is the portal to an array of learning tools for all learning styles—practice questions with guided solutions are only the beginning. Student can access MyAccountingLab at **www.pearsonmylabandmastering.com**.

MyAccountingLab can be used by itself or linked to any learning management system. MyAccountingLab provides students with a variety of resources, including a personalized study plan, tutorials, videos, glossary flashcards, and PowerPoint® Presentations.

- **NEW! Auto-Graded Excel Projects:** MyAccountingLab's new auto-graded Excel Projects allow students to practise important accounting skills in Microsoft Excel to master key accounting concepts while gaining proficiency in Excel.

- **NEW! Worked Solutions:** These provide step-by-step explanations on how to solve select problems using the exact numbers and data that were presented in the problem. Instructors will have access to the Worked Out Solutions in preview and review mode.

- **NEW! Open Response:** Open Response questions require students to type in their answers instead of choosing their answer from a drop-down menu. This helps students think critically while further preparing them for the format of their exam.

- **NEW! Accounting in the Headlines:** One of the biggest challenges for accounting instructors is that students often feel disengaged from the course material, which can seem abstract and unrelated to their personal experiences. But by incorporating real-life examples, instructors can spark student interest and engagement especially when teaching accounting at the introductory level.

  Accounting in the Headlines, an award-winning blog by renowned author Wendy Tietz, does just that with stories about real companies and events that can be used in the accounting classroom to illustrate introductory financial accounting concepts.

  Concise, tailorable, and updated on a weekly basis, these articles easily fit into the typical introductory accounting curriculum, whether the course is delivered in-person or online.

  http://accountingintheheadlines.com

  Accounting in the Headlines multiple-choice questions are available for instructors to assign in MyAccountingLab's Assignment Manager.

- **NEW!** Selected Stop + Think problems, Mid-Chapter Summary Problems, and End-of-Chapter Summary Problems appear on MyAccountingLab, along with all end-of-chapter questions that have a shaded box behind their number. All problems include three static versions for instructor flexibility.

To learn more about how MyAccountingLab combines proven learning applications with powerful assessment, instructors can visit **www.pearsonmylabandmastering.com**.

Instructor's Resource Centre

These instructor supplements are available for download from a password-protected section of Pearson Canada's online catalogue, at **www.pearsoncanada.ca/highered**. Navigate to your book's catalogue page to view a list of those supplements that are available. Speak to your local Pearson sales representative for details and access.

- **NEW!** *Flipping Your Classroom Guide:* Tips for each chapter on how to take your course from a traditional/in-class course to a hybrid, blended, or fully online format. Includes links to the discussion board prompts.
- *Instructor's Resource Manual:* This manual contains valuable resources, including chapter outlines, teaching tips, and assignment grids.
- *Instructor's Solutions Manual:* Contains solutions to all end-of-chapter questions, including short exercises, exercises, problems, and cases.
- *Computerized Test Bank:* More than 1,500 test questions, including multiple-choice, true-or-false, and essay questions, are provided in TestGen format. Pearson's computerized test banks allow instructors to filter and select questions to create quizzes, tests, or homework. Instructors can revise questions or add their own, and may be able to choose print or online options. These questions are also available in Microsoft Word format.
- *PowerPoint Presentations:* These presentations help facilitate classroom discussion.
- *Image Library:* An Image Library provides access to many of the figures and tables in the textbook.

Learning Solutions Managers

Pearson's Learning Solutions Managers work with faculty and campus course designers to ensure that Pearson technology products, assessment tools, and online course materials are tailored to meet your specific needs. This highly qualified team is dedicated to helping schools take full advantage of a wide range of educational resources, by assisting in the integration of a variety of instructional materials and media formats. Your local Pearson Canada sales representative can provide you with more details on this service program.

We hope you enjoy *Financial Accounting*.

ACKNOWLEDGMENTS

Thanks are extended to Canadian Tire for permission to include portions of their annual report in Appendix A and MyAccountingLab. Appreciation is also expressed to the following individuals and organizations:

The annual reports of a number of Canadian companies.
Professors Tom Harrison, Charles Horngren, and Bill Thomas.

Particular thanks are also due to the following instructors for reviewing the manuscript for the Sixth Canadian Edition and offering many useful suggestions:

Rob Anderson, *Thompson Rivers University*
Tammy Crowell, *Dalhousie University*
Sandra Daga, *University of Toronto*
Robert Ducharme, *University of Waterloo*
Michael Khan, *University of Toronto*
Sandra Iacobelli, *York University*
Robert Madden, *St. Francis Xavier University*
Aadil Merali, Juma *McMaster University*
Cameron Morrill, *University of Manitoba*
Seda Oz, *McGill University*
Robin Sandhawalia, *Douglas College*
Kevin Veenstra, *McMaster University*
Jenny Zhang, *Dalhousie University*

The authors acknowledge with gratitude the professional support received from Pearson Canada. In particular we thank Megan Farrell, Acquisitions Editor; Suzanne Simpson Millar, Developmental Editor; Anita Smale, Media Content Editor; Sarah Gallagher and Pippa Kennard, Project Managers; Carrie Fox, Production Editor; and Claire Varley, Marketing Manager.

A special thanks also goes out to Kathy Falk, at the University of Toronto, and Chris Deresh, from Douglas College. Kathy helped ensure our problem material was complete, accurate, and effective for the level taught in the chapter. Chris checked the coverage of CPA Competencies and provided his valuable and current knowledge on this.

PROLOGUE

Accounting Careers: Much More Than Counting Things

What kind of career can you have in accounting? Almost any kind you want. A career in accounting lets you use your analytical skills in a variety of ways, and it brings both monetary and personal rewards. Professional accountants work as executives for public companies, partners at professional services firms, and analysts at investment banks, among many other exciting positions.

Accounting as an art is widely believed to have been invented by Fra Luca Bartolomeo de Pacioli, an Italian mathematician and Franciscan friar in the sixteenth century. Pacioli was a close friend of Leonardo da Vinci and collaborated with him on many projects.

Accounting as the profession we know today has its roots in the Industrial Revolution during the eighteenth and nineteenth centuries, mostly in England. However, accounting did not attain the stature of other professions such as law, medicine, or engineering until early in the twentieth century. Professions are distinguished from trades by the following characteristics: (1) a unifying body of technical literature, (2) standards of competence, (3) codes of professional conduct, and (4) dedication to service to the public.

An aspiring accountant must obtain a university degree, pass several professional examinations, and gain three years of on-the-job training before they can receive a professional accounting designation. The most prevalent designation in Canada is the CPA, which stands for Chartered Professional Accountant. When you hold these designations, employers know what to expect about your education, knowledge, abilities, and personal attributes. They value your analytical skills and extensive training. Your CPA designation gives you a distinct advantage in the job market, and instant credibility and respect in the workplace. It's a plus when dealing with other professionals, such as bankers, lawyers, auditors, and federal regulators. In addition, your colleagues in private industry tend to defer to you when dealing with complex business matters, particularly those involving financial management.

Where Accountants Work

Where can you work as an accountant? There are four main types of employers.

Professional Accounting Firms

You can work for a professional accounting firm, which could range in size from a small local firm to a large international firm such as KPMG or Ernst & Young. These firms provide assurance, tax, and consulting services to a variety of clients, allowing you to gain a broad range of experience if you so choose. Many accountants begin their careers at a professional accounting firm and then move into more senior positions in one of the job categories described below. Others may stay on, or join one of these firms after working elsewhere, to take advantage of the many rewarding careers these firms offer.

Public or Private Companies

Rather than work for an accounting firm and provide your expertise to a variety of clients, you can work for a single company that requires your professional knowledge. Your role may be to analyze financial information and communicate that information to managers who use it to plot strategy and make decisions. Or you may be called upon to help allocate corporate resources or improve financial performance. For example, you might do a cost-benefit analysis to help decide whether to acquire a company or build a factory. Or you might describe the financial implications of choosing one business strategy over another. You might work in areas such as internal auditing, financial management, financial reporting, treasury management, and tax planning. The most senior financial position in these companies is the chief financial officer (CFO) role; some CFOs rise further to become chief executive officers (CEOs) of their companies.

Government and Not-for-Profit Entities

Federal, provincial, and local governmental bodies also require accounting expertise. You could be helping to evaluate how government agencies are being managed, or advise politicians on how to allocate resources to promote efficiency. The RCMP hires accountants to investigate the financial aspects of white-collar crime. You might find yourself working for the Canadian Revenue Agency, one of the provincial securities commissions, or a federal or provincial Auditor General.

As an accountant, you might also decide to work in the not-for-profit sector. Colleges, universities, public and private primary and secondary schools, hospitals, and charitable organizations such as churches and the United Way all have accounting functions. Accountants in the not-for-profit sector provide many of the same services as those in the for-profit sector, but their focus is less on turning a profit than on making sure the organizations spend their money wisely and operate efficiently and effectively.

Education

Finally, you can work at a college or university, advancing the thought and theory of accounting and teaching future generations of new accountants. On the research side of education, you might study how companies use accounting information. You might develop new ways of categorizing financial data, or study accounting practices in different countries. You then publish your ideas in journals and books and present them to colleagues at meetings around the world. On the education side, you can help others learn about accounting and give them the tools they need to be their best.

Regardless of which type of organization you work for, as an accountant, your knowledge will be highly valued by your clients, colleagues, and other important stakeholders. As the economy becomes increasingly global in scope, accounting standards, tax laws, and business strategies will grow more complex, so it's safe to say that the expertise provided by professional accountants will continue to be in high demand. This book could serve as the first step on your path to a challenging and rewarding career as a professional accountant!

The Financial Statements

Felix Choo/Alamy Stock Photo

1

LEARNING OBJECTIVES

1. **Explain** why accounting is the language of business
2. **Describe** the purpose of each financial statement and **explain** the elements of each one
3. **Explain** the relationships among the financial statements
4. **Explain** accounting's conceptual framework and underlying assumptions
5. **Make** ethical business decisions

CPA COMPETENCIES

Competencies* addressed in this chapter:

1.1.1 Evaluates financial reporting needs

1.1.2 Evaluates the appropriateness of the basis of financial reporting

1.1.3 Evaluates reporting processes to support reliable financial reporting

SPOTLIGHT

If you've ever shopped for a bike, garden tools, or household items, you have very likely been in a Canadian Tire store. Based in Ontario, Canadian Tire Corporation is one of Canada's largest retail companies, selling a range of products and services through its various retail banners, including Mark's, PartSource, Sport Chek, and Pro Hockey Life. The company's market reach is tremendous: over 90% of Canada's population lives within 15 minutes of a Canadian Tire store; two out of three Canadian men read the Canadian Tire flyer every week; and more than 80% of the population shops at Canadian Tire stores each year. Canadian Tire is featured throughout this textbook as a way of connecting new financial accounting concepts to the actual business activities and financial statements of a familiar Canadian corporation.

As you can see from its Consolidated Statements of Income on the next page, Canadian Tire sells a lot of goods and services—about $12.5 billion worth for the year ended January 3, 2015 (line 3). After deducting a variety of expenses incurred during 2014 (lines 4, 6–9, and 11), Canadian Tire earned net income of over $600 million for the year (line 10).

These terms—revenues, expenses, and net income—may be unfamiliar to you now, but after you read this chapter, you'll be able to explain these and many other accounting terms. Welcome to the world of accounting!

---

*© Chartered Professional Accountants of Canada.

	A	B	C	D
1	**Canadian Tire Corporation** Consolidated Statements of Income (Adapted) For the Years Ended January 3, 2015 and December 28, 2013*			
2	*(in millions of dollars)*	**2014***	**2013***	
3	Revenue	$ 12,462.9	$ 11,785.6	
4	Cost of producing revenue	(8,416.9)	(8,063.3)	
5	**Gross margin**	4,046.0	3,722.3	
6	Other income (expense)	11.0	(3.0)	
7	Selling, general and administrative expenses	(3,052.9)	(2,828.9)	
8	Net finance costs	(108.9)	(105.8)	
9	Change in fair value of redeemable financial instrument	(17.0)	-	
10	**Income before income taxes**	878.2	784.6	
11	Income taxes	(238.9)	(220.2)	
12	Net income	$ 639.3	$ 564.4	
13				

*Canadian Tire's financial year (or fiscal year) ends on the Saturday closest to December 31 each year, which is common for many retail companies, so its 2014 fiscal year actually ended on January 3, 2015. Despite the 2015 year-end date, this was still the end of its 2014 fiscal year, so it is labelled and referred to as such here and throughout the textbook.

Source: Reprinted with permission from Canadian Tire Corporation.

Each chapter of this book begins with an actual financial statement—in this chapter, it's the Consolidated Statements of Income of Canadian Tire Corporation for the years ended January 3, 2015, and December 28, 2013. The core of financial accounting revolves around the basic financial statements:

- Income statement (sometimes known as the statement of profit or loss)
- Statement of retained earnings (sometimes included in the statement of changes in owners' equity)
- Balance sheet (also known as the statement of financial position)
- Cash flow statement (also known as the statement of cash flows)
- Statement of other comprehensive income

Financial statements are the reports that companies use to convey the financial results of their business activities to various user groups, which can include managers, investors, creditors, and regulatory agencies. In turn, these parties use the reported information to make a variety of decisions, such as whether to invest in or loan money to the company. To learn accounting, you must learn to focus on decisions. In this chapter, we explain generally accepted accounting principles, their underlying assumptions and concepts, and the bodies responsible for issuing accounting standards. We discuss the judgment process that is necessary to make good accounting decisions. We also discuss the contents of the four basic financial statements that report the results of those decisions. In later chapters, we will explain in more detail how to construct the financial statements, as well as how user groups typically use the information contained in them to make business decisions.

Using Accounting Information

Canadian Tire Corporation's managers make a lot of decisions. Which bikes are selling the best? Which line of business is earning the most profit? Should Canadian Tire expand its offerings in Eastern Canada to match those in B.C. and Alberta? Accounting information helps company managers make these decisions.

MyAccountingLab

MyAccountingLab provides students with a variety of resources including a personalized study plan, videos, and an interactive Accounting Cycle Tutorial (ACT). Margin logos in Chapters 2 and 3 direct you to the appropriate ACT Steps; Steps 1 to 4 are covered in Chapter 2 and Steps 5 to 10 are covered in Chapter 3. The ACT provides brief explanations of each concept of the accounting cycle, and allows you to assess and test your mastery at each Step.

Take a look at Canadian Tire Corporation's Consolidated Statements of Income on page 2. Focus on net income (line 12). Net income is the excess of revenues over expenses. You can see that Canadian Tire earned $639 million in net income for the year ended January 3, 2015. That's good news because it means that Canadian Tire's revenues exceeded its expenses by over $600 million in 2014.

Canadian Tire's Consolidated Statements of Income convey more great news. Revenues grew from $11.8 billion in 2013 to $12.5 billion in 2014 (line 3), an increase of about 6%. Also, Canadian Tire's 2014 net income of $639 million was 13.3% higher than its 2013 net income of $564 million (line 12). Based on these key numbers, Canadian Tire's 2014 operating performance improved significantly from 2013.

There would, however, be much more accounting information to analyze before making a final assessment of Canadian Tire's 2014 financial performance. Imagine you work for a bank that Canadian Tire would like to borrow $500 million from. How would you decide whether to lend them the money? Or suppose you have $5,000 to invest. What financial information would you analyze to decide whether to invest this money in Canadian Tire? Let's see how accounting information can be used to make these kinds of decisions.

EXPLAIN WHY ACCOUNTING IS THE LANGUAGE OF BUSINESS

Accounting is an information system that measures and records business activities, processes data into reports, and reports results to decision makers. Accounting is "the language of business." The better you understand the language, the better you can make decisions using accounting information.

Accounting produces the financial statements that report information about a business entity. The financial statements report a business's financial position, operating performance, and cash flows, among other things. In this chapter, we focus on Canadian Tire's 2014 financial statements. By the end of the chapter, you will have a basic understanding of these statements.

Don't confuse bookkeeping and accounting. Bookkeeping is a mechanical part of accounting, just as arithmetic is a mechanical part of mathematics. Accounting, however, requires an understanding of the principles used to accurately report financial information, as well as the professional judgment needed to apply them and then interpret the results. Exhibit 1-1 illustrates the flow of accounting information and helps illustrate accounting's role in business. The accounting process starts and ends with people making decisions.

Who Uses Accounting Information?

Almost everyone uses accounting information! Students use it to decide how much of their income to save for next year's tuition. Managers use it to decide if they should expand their business. Let's take a closer look at how these and other groups use accounting information.

MANAGERS. Managers have to make many business decisions. Should they introduce a new product line? Should the company set up a regional sales office in Australia or South Africa? Should they consider acquiring a competitor? Should the company extend credit to a potential major customer? Accounting information helps managers make these decisions.

EXHIBIT 1-1
The Flow of Accounting Information

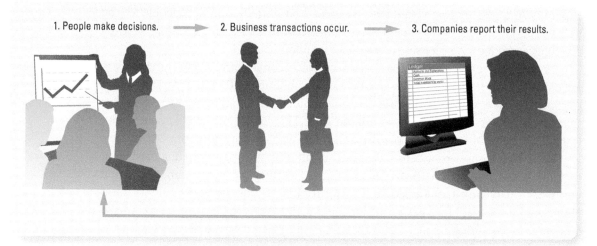

INVESTORS AND CREDITORS. Investors and creditors provide the money to finance a business's activities. Investors want to know how much income they can expect to earn on their investment. Creditors want to know if and how a business is going to pay them back. Accounting information allows investors and creditors to make these decisions.

GOVERNMENT AND REGULATORY BODIES. Many government and regulatory bodies use accounting information. For example, the federal government requires businesses, individuals, and other organizations to pay income and sales taxes. The Canada Revenue Agency uses accounting information to ensure these organizations pay the correct amount of taxes. The Ontario Securities Commission requires companies whose stock is traded publicly to provide the Commission with many kinds of periodic financial reports. All of these reports contain accounting information.

INDIVIDUALS. People like you manage bank accounts and decide whether to rent an apartment or buy a house. They also determine their monthly income and then decide how much to spend and save each month. Accounting provides the information needed to make these decisions.

NOT-FOR-PROFIT ORGANIZATIONS. Not-for-profit organizations—churches, hospitals, and charities, such as Habitat for Humanity and the Canadian Red Cross—base their decisions on accounting information. In addition, accounting information is the basis of a not-for-profit's reporting on the organization's stewardship of funds received and its compliance with the reporting requirements of the Canada Revenue Agency.

Two Kinds of Accounting: Financial Accounting and Management Accounting

Accounting information falls into two categories: financial accounting and management accounting. The distinction is based primarily on who uses the information in each category. Both *internal and external users* rely on financial accounting information, whereas management accounting information is used by *internal users only*.

Financial accounting provides information for managers inside the business and for decision makers outside the organization, such as investors, creditors, government agencies, and the public. This information must be relevant for the needs of decision makers and must provide a faithful representation of the entity's economic activities. This textbook focuses on financial accounting.

Management accounting generates inside information for the managers of the organization. Examples of management accounting information include budgets, forecasts, and projections that are used to make strategic business decisions. Internal information must be accurate and relevant for the decision needs of managers. Management accounting is covered in a separate course.

Organizing a Business

Accounting is used in every type of business. A business generally takes one of the following forms:

- Proprietorship
- Partnership
- Corporation

Exhibit 1-2 compares ways to organize a business.

EXHIBIT 1-2
The Various Forms of Business Organization

	Proprietorship	Partnership	Corporation
Owner(s)	Proprietor—one owner	Partners—two or more owners	Shareholders—generally many owners
Life of entity	Limited by owner's choice or death	Limited by owners' choices or death	Indefinite
Personal liability of owner(s) for business debts	Proprietor is personally liable	Partners are usually personally liable	Shareholders are not personally liable
Accounting status	Accounting entity is separate from proprietor	Accounting entity is separate from partners	Accounting entity is separate from shareholders

PROPRIETORSHIPS. A **proprietorship** is an unincorporated business with a single owner, called the proprietor. Dell Computer started out in the college dorm room of Michael Dell, the owner. Proprietorships tend to be small businesses, such as the vendors that set up stalls at farmers' markets, or individual professional organizations, such as physicians, lawyers, and accountants. From a legal perspective, the business is the proprietor, and the proprietor is personally liable for all business debts. But for accounting, a proprietorship is an entity separate from its proprietor. Thus, the business records do not include the proprietor's personal finances.

PARTNERSHIPS. A **partnership** is an unincorporated business with two or more parties as co-owners, and each owner is a partner. Individuals, corporations, partnerships, or other types of entities can be partners. The income (or loss) of the partnership "flows through" to the partners and they recognize it based on their agreed-upon percentage interest in the business. The partnership is not a taxpaying entity. Instead, each partner takes a proportionate share of the entity's taxable income and pays tax according to that partner's individual or corporate rate. Many retail establishments and some professional organizations of physicians, lawyers, and accountants are partnerships. Most partnerships are small or medium-sized, but some are very large, with several hundred partners. Accounting treats the partnership as a separate organization, distinct from the personal affairs of each partner. But the law views a partnership as the partners: Normally, each partner is personally liable for all the partnership's debts. For this reason, partnerships can be quite risky. Recently, professional partnerships such as public accounting firms and law firms have become limited liability partnerships (LLPs), which limits claims against the partners to their partnership assets.

CORPORATIONS. A **corporation** is an incorporated business owned by its **shareholders**, who own **shares** representing partial ownership of the corporation. One of the major advantages of a corporation is the ability to raise large sums of capital by issuing shares to the public. Individuals, partnerships, other corporations, or other types of entities may be shareholders in a corporation. Most well-known companies, such as TD Bank, Rogers, and Apple, are corporations. As with Canadian Tire Corporation, their legal names include *Corporation* or *Incorporated* (abbreviated *Corp.* and *Inc.*) to indicate they are corporations. Some, like the Ford Motor Company, bear the name *Company* to denote this fact.

A corporation is formed under federal or provincial law. From a legal perspective, unlike proprietorships and partnerships, a corporation is distinct from its owners. The corporation is like an artificial person and possesses many of the rights that a person has. Unlike proprietors and partners, the shareholders who own a corporation have no personal obligation for its debts; so we say shareholders have limited liability, as do partners in an LLP. Also, unlike other forms of organizations, a corporation pays income taxes. In the other two cases, income tax is paid personally by the proprietor or partners.

A corporation's ownership is divided into shares of stock. One becomes a shareholder by purchasing the corporation's shares. Canadian Tire, for example, has issued more than 300 million shares of stock. Any investor can become a co-owner of Canadian Tire by buying shares of its stock through the Toronto Stock Exchange (TSX).

The shares of a public corporation like Canadian Tire are widely held, which means they are owned by thousands of different shareholders who buy and sell the shares on a stock exchange. Shares of a private corporation are typically owned by a small number of shareholders, often including the founder and other family members.

The ultimate control of a corporation rests with the shareholders. They normally get one vote for each voting share they own. Shareholders also elect the members of the **board of directors**, which sets policy for the corporation and appoints officers. The board elects a chairperson, who is the most powerful person in the corporation and may also carry the title chief executive officer (CEO), the top management position. Most corporations also have vice-presidents in charge of sales, manufacturing, accounting and finance, and other key areas.

STOP + THINK (1-1)

State whether each of the following business organizations is a proprietorship, a partnership, or a corporation.

1. Farook and Ahmed each own 50% of the shares of Waterloo Motors Inc., a car dealership.

2. Jenna and James own and operate The Culinary Counter, a meal-preparation and catering business, in which they equally share the workload and profits.

3. Agata crafts handmade jewellery that she sells online and at local craft markets.

DESCRIBE THE PURPOSE OF EACH FINANCIAL STATEMENT AND EXPLAIN THE ELEMENTS OF EACH ONE

OBJECTIVE

❷ **Describe** the purpose of each financial statement and **explain** the elements of each one

The financial statements present a company's financial results to users who wish to examine the company's financial performance. What would users want to know about a company's performance? The answer to this question will vary by user, but Exhibit 1-3 presents four main questions most users would ask, as well as the financial statement that would be used to answer each question.

Each of the four financial statements reports transactions and events by grouping them into broad classes according to their economic characteristics. These broad classes are termed the *elements of financial statements*. Exhibit 1-3 presents the main elements of each financial statement. Before we examine each statement and its elements, we will introduce the principles that are used to prepare these statements.

EXHIBIT 1-3
The Financial Statements and Their Elements

Question	Financial Statement	Elements
1. How well did the company perform during the year?	Income statement	Total income (revenues + gains) − Total expenses (expenses + losses) Net income (or Net loss)
2. Why did the company's retained earnings change during the year?	Statement of retained earnings	Beginning retained earnings + Net income + Other comprehensive income (IFRS only) − Dividends Ending retained earnings
3. What is the company's financial position at the end of the year?	Balance sheet	Assets = Liabilities + Owners' equity
4. How much cash did the company generate and spend during the year?	Statement of cash flows	Operating cash flows ± Investing cash flows ± Financing cash flows Increase (or decrease) in cash

Generally Accepted Accounting Principles

Accountants prepare financial accounting information according to professional guidelines called **generally accepted accounting principles (GAAP)**. GAAP specify the standards for how accountants must record, measure, and report financial information. In Canada, GAAP are established by the Chartered Professional Accountants of Canada (CPAC), one of the country's three professional accounting bodies.

Canada actually has multiple sets of GAAP, with each set being applicable to a specific type of entity or organization. **Publicly accountable enterprises (PAEs)**, which are corporations and other organizations that have issued or plan to issue shares or debt in public markets such as the Toronto Stock Exchange, *must* apply **International Financial Reporting Standards (IFRS)**. IFRS are set by the International Accounting Standards Board and have been adopted by over 100 countries in an effort to enhance the comparability of the financial information reported by public enterprises around the world.

Private enterprises, which have not issued and do not plan to issue shares or debt on public markets, *have the option* of applying IFRS. Because IFRS are relatively complex and costly to apply, however, very few Canadian private enterprises have adopted them. Instead, they apply another set of GAAP known as **Accounting Standards for Private Enterprises (ASPE)**, which have been set by the CPAC. At the introductory financial accounting level, there are very few major differences between IFRS and ASPE, but we will discuss them where they do exist and also summarize them at the end of each chapter. In addition, all the IFRS—ASPE differences we discuss in the book have been compiled in Appendix B.

There are other sets of GAAP applicable to not-for-profit organizations, pension plans, and government entities, but they are too specialized to cover at the introductory level. If you choose to pursue accounting as a career, you will learn about them in the future.

The Income Statement Measures Operating Performance

The **income statement** (or **statement of profit or loss**) measures a company's operating performance for a *specified period of time*. The period of time covered by an income statement is typically a month, a quarter (three months), or a year, and will always be specified in the heading of the income statement. In the heading of Canadian Tire's income statement in Exhibit 1-4, we can see that it covers the years ended January 3, 2015, and December 28, 2013. Financial statements for the current year are easier to analyze and interpret when they can be compared to the prior year's statements, so you will always see the prior year's results presented beside those of the current year (unless it is an entity's first year of operations). Most companies have a *fiscal year* that ends on December 31 (known as a *calendar year-end*), but a company can choose whatever fiscal year-end date it desires. Most of Canada's big banks, for example, have a fiscal year-end of October 31. Some companies, such as Canadian Tire, have fiscal year-end dates that vary from year to year, usually because they fall on the Saturday closest to a calendar year-end date. The income statement has two main elements, income and **expenses**, which are discussed in more detail below.

INCOME. A company's **income** includes both **revenue** and **gains**. **Revenue** consists of amounts earned by a company in the course of its ordinary, day-to-day business

EXHIBIT 1-4
Consolidated Statements of Income (Adapted)

Source: Reprinted with permission from Canadian Tire Corporation.

	A	B	C
1	**Canadian Tire Corporation** Consolidated Statements of Income (Adapted) For the Years Ended January 3, 2015 and December 28, 2013		
2	*(in millions of dollars)*	2014	2013
3	Revenue	$ 12,462.9	$ 11,785.6
4	Cost of producing revenue	(8,416.9)	(8,063.3)
5	**Gross margin**	4,046.0	3,722.3
6	Other income (expense)	11.0	(3.0)
7	Selling, general and administrative expenses	(3,052.9)	(2,828.9)
8	Net finance costs	(108.9)	(105.8)
9	Change in fair value of redeemable financial instrument	(17.0)	-
10	**Income before income taxes**	878.2	784.6
11	Income taxes	(238.9)	(220.2)
12	**Net income**	$ 639.3	$ 564.4
13			

activities. The vast majority of a company's revenue is earned through the sale of its primary goods and services. Loblaws, for example, earns most of its revenue by selling groceries and other household goods. An accounting firm such as KPMG earns revenue by providing accounting, tax, and other professional services to its clients. Canadian Tire's ordinary business activities include the sale of goods and services through the various retail banners it operates. On line 3 of Canadian Tire's 2014 income statement, we see that it earned Revenues of $12,463 million in 2014. Revenue is referred to by a variety of different names, including sales, fees, interest, dividends, royalties, and rent. You will learn more about revenue and how to account for it in Chapter 3.

Gains represent other items that result in an *increase* in economic benefits to a company and may, but usually do not, occur in the course of the company's ordinary business activities. If, for example, Canadian Tire sold one of the buildings it owned for an amount that exceeded what it was last recorded at in the financial statements, the excess would be recognized as a gain on the income statement. When gains are recognized in the income statement, they are usually listed separately, either directly in the statement or in the notes to the financial statements (discussed on page 17), because knowledge of these gains is useful for making decisions. Canadian Tire does not explicitly report any gains on its 2014 income statement, but the statement of cash flows shows that the company earned $9 million in gains on the sale of property and other assets (line 8 in Exhibit 1-8) during 2014. The *other income* line on an income statement (line 6 in Exhibit 1-4) generally includes categories of revenues and gains that are not sufficiently material to report on separate lines of the statement. You will learn more about some common types of gains in Chapters 6 and 7.

EXPENSES. A company's expenses consist of **losses** as well as those expenses that are incurred in the course of its ordinary business activities. Expenses consist mainly of the costs incurred to purchase the goods and services a company needs to run its business on a day-to-day basis. For Canadian Tire, these expenses include the cost of the bikes, auto parts, and other goods it sells to customers, which is an expense commonly known as the *cost of goods sold* or *cost of sales*, an item you will learn more about in Chapter 5. Canadian Tire refers to this expense as the "Cost of producing revenue" on line 4 of its income statement. Other selling costs, as well as the wages it pays its employees, the rent it pays on its stores, and many more expenses, would be included in the $3,053 million of "Selling, general and administrative expenses" on line 7 of Canadian Tire's income statement. On line 8, we see that Canadian Tire incurred "Net finance costs" of $109 million, which consist mostly of the interest expense it paid on the money it has borrowed from banks and other lenders (less, or net of, any interest it earned on investments), a topic that will be covered in Chapter 8. The last expense on Canadian Tire's income statement is "Income taxes" of $239 million (line 11). You likely know a little bit about this kind of expense already, but it will be discussed more in Chapter 8. There are many more expenses that companies incur on a day-to-day basis but are not typically disclosed separately on the income statements of public companies, either because they are not large enough to present or because they are too sensitive to disclose to competing companies. You will encounter many of these expenses as you progress through the book.

Losses are the opposite of gains, and represent items that result in a *decrease* in economic benefits to a company. Like gains, they may, but usually do not, occur in the course of the company's ordinary business activities. If, for example, Canadian Tire sold some equipment it owned for an amount that was less than what it was last recorded at in the financial statements, the difference would be recognized as a loss on the income statement. Losses are usually listed separately in the statement or disclosed in the notes to the financial statements. Canadian Tire does not report any losses on its 2014 income statement or in the notes to the financial statements. You will learn more about some common types of losses in Chapters 6 and 7.

The income statement also reports the company's **net income**, which is calculated as follows:

Net Income = Total Revenues and Gains – Total Expenses and Losses

In accounting, the word *net* refers to the amount of something that is left after something else has been deducted from an initial total. In this case, *net income* is the amount of *income* that is left after *total expenses* (expenses + losses) have been deducted from *total income* (revenues + gains) for the period. When total expenses exceed total income, the result is called a **net loss**. Net income is sometimes known as **net earnings** or **net profit**, and is *usually considered the most important amount in a company's financial statements*. It is a key component of many financial ratios, including return on equity and earnings per share, which you will learn about in later chapters of this book.

A company whose net income is consistently increasing is usually regarded by investors and creditors as a healthy and high-quality company. In the long run, the company's value should increase. On line 12 of Canadian Tire's income statement, we see that its net income increased from $564 million in 2013 to $639 million in 2014, so Canadian Tire's managers, investors, and creditors should have been pleased with its 2014 operating performance. You will see Canadian Tire's net income of $639 million carried forward to its statement of retained earnings, which is discussed in the next section.

The Statement of Retained Earnings Reports Changes in Retained Earnings

A company's **retained earnings** represent the accumulated net income (or net earnings) of the company since the day it started business, less any net losses and dividends declared during this time. When the accumulated amount is negative, the term **deficit** is used to describe it. The **statement of retained earnings** reports the changes in a company's retained earnings during the same period covered by the income statement. Under ASPE, this statement is often added to the bottom of the income statement, although it may also be presented as a completely separate statement. Under IFRS, information on the changes in retained earnings is included in the *statement of changes in owners' equity*, which you will learn more about in Chapter 9. At the beginning of 2014, Canadian Tire had retained earnings of $4,405 million (line 3 of Exhibit 1-5). Let's look at the major changes to Canadian Tire's retained earnings during 2014.

- Because retained earnings represent a company's accumulated net income, the first addition to the opening balance is Canadian Tire's 2014 net income of $639 million (line 4), which comes directly from line 12 of the income statement in Exhibit 1-4.

- On line 5, we see that Canadian Tire declared dividends of $154 million during 2014. Dividends represent the distribution of past earnings to current shareholders of the company. You will learn more about dividends in Chapter 9.

	A	B	C
1	**Canadian Tire Corporation** Consolidated Statements of Retained Earnings (Adapted) For the Years Ended January 3, 2015 and December 28, 2013		
2	*(in millions of dollars)*	2014	2013
3	Balance, beginning of year	$ 4,405	$ 4,048
4	Net income	639	564
5	Dividends	(154)	(120)
6	Other reductions	(815)	(87)
7	Balance, end of year	$ 4,075	$ 4,405
8			

EXHIBIT 1-5
 Consolidated Statements of Retained Earnings (Adapted)

After accounting for other reductions during 2014 (line 6), Canadian Tire reports a closing retained earnings balance of $4,075 million on line 7. This balance will be carried forward to the owners' equity section of the balance sheet, which is the next financial statement we will introduce to you.

The Balance Sheet Measures Financial Position

A company's financial position consists of three elements: the assets it controls, the liabilities it is obligated to pay, and the equity its owners have accumulated in the business. These elements are reported in the **balance sheet**, which under IFRS is also known as the **statement of financial position**. (For simplicity, this financial statement will be referred to as the balance sheet throughout the textbook.) The balance sheet reports a company's financial position *as at a specific date*, which always falls on the last day of a monthly, quarterly, or annual reporting period. Because it is presented as at a specific date, you can think of the balance as a snapshot of the company's financial position at a particular point in time. The Canadian Tire balance sheet in Exhibit 1-6 reports its financial position as at the year-end dates of January 3, 2015, and December 28, 2013.

The balance sheet takes its name from the fact that the assets it reports must *always* equal—or be in balance with—the sum of the liabilities and equity it reports. This relationship is known as the **accounting equation**, and it provides the foundation for the double-entry method of accounting you will begin to learn in Chapter 2. Exhibit 1-7 illustrates the equation using the figures from Canadian Tire's 2014 balance sheet in Exhibit 1-6.

IFRS and ASPE define assets, liabilities, and equity using different terms, but the definitions are essentially equivalent. The IFRS definitions are used below, primarily because they are more concise than the ASPE definitions.

ASSETS. An **asset** is a resource controlled by the company as a result of past events and from which the company expects to receive future economic benefits. Let's use two of Canadian Tire's assets to illustrate this formal definition. One of Canadian Tire's assets is its "accounts receivable" (line 5), which arose from past sales to customers who purchased Canadian Tire's products and services on account (or on credit), with the promise to pay off the accounts at a later date. In the future, when customers do pay off their accounts, Canadian Tire will receive the economic benefit of "cash" (line 4), another asset, which it can use to fund future business activities. We classify assets into two categories on the balance sheet: **current assets** and **non-current assets**. We classify an asset as current when we expect to convert it to cash, sell it, or consume it *within one year* of the balance sheet date, or within the business's normal operating

	A	B	C	D
1	**Canadian Tire Corporation** Consolidated Balance Sheets (Adapted) As at January 3, 2015 and December 28, 2013			
2	*(in millions of dollars)*	**2014**	**2013**	
3	**Current assets**			
4	Cash	$ 662.1	$ 643.2	
5	Accounts receivable	880.2	758.5	
6	Merchandise inventories	1,623.8	1,481.0	
7	Prepaid Expenses	104.5	68.2	
8	Other current assets	5,239.6	5,026.9	
9	**Total current assets**	8,510.2	7,977.8	
10	**Non-current assets**			
11	Property & equipment	3,743.1	3,516.1	
12	Long-term receivables	684.2	686.0	
13	Long-term investments	176.0	134.7	
14	Other non-current assets	1,439.7	1,315.4	
15	**Total assets**	$ 14,553.2	$ 13,630.0	
16	**Current liabilities**			
17	Bank indebtedness	$ 14.3	$ 69.0	
18	Accounts payable	1,961.2	1,817.4	
19	Income taxes payable	54.9	57.5	
20	Other current liabilities	1,960.9	2,106.0	
21	Current portion of long-term debt	587.5	272.2	
22	**Total current liabilities**	4,578.8	4,322.1	
23	**Non-current liabilities**			
24	Long-term debt	2,131.6	2,339.1	
25	Other long-term liabilities	2,212.0	1,518.9	
26	**Total liabilities**	8,922.4	8,180.1	
27	**Shareholders' equity**			
28	Share capital	695.5	587.0	
29	Retained earnings	4,075.1	4,526.7	
30	Other equity items	860.2	336.2	
31	**Total shareholders' equity**	5,630.8	5,449.9	
32	**Total liabilities & shareholders' equity**	$ 14,553.2	$ 13,630.0	
33				

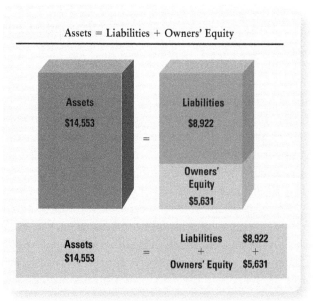

cycle if it is longer than one year. Current assets are listed in order of their **liquidity**, which is a measure of how quickly they can be converted to cash, the most liquid asset. At the end of 2014, Canadian Tire had $8,510 million in current assets (line 9). Let's look at some of Canadian Tire's major current assets, all of which will be covered in more detail in later chapters.

- Canadian Tire had "cash" of $662 million at the end of 2014 (line 4). This balance includes cash the company had in all its bank accounts at year-end, as well as any on hand in stores and other locations at that date.

- On line 5, we see that Canadian Tire had $880 million in "accounts receivable" on January 3, 2015. This balance represents the amount of money Canadian Tire expects to collect within the next year from customers who bought goods and services on account (or on credit) prior to year-end. You will read more about this asset in Chapter 4 as well.

- At the end of 2014, Canadian Tire held $1,624 million of "merchandise inventories" (line 6), which include the bikes, auto parts, and other products the company expects to sell to customers in 2015. Inventories are covered in detail in Chapter 5.

- The last major current asset on Canadian Tire's 2014 balance sheet is "prepaid expenses" of $105 million (line 7), which, as the name suggests, represent expenses that Canadian Tire has paid for but not yet consumed as at the end of the year. If, for example, on December 15, 2014, Canadian Tire paid $500,000 for TV advertising time during the Super Bowl at the end of January 2015, this amount would be included in prepaid expenses on January 3, 2015, because Canadian Tire will not realize the benefit of this expense until after year-end. Prepaid expenses are discussed in Chapter 3.

All assets that do not qualify as current are classified as non-current assets, which are also known as **long-term assets**. Canadian Tire had $6,043 million of non-current assets on January 3, 2015. We will take a brief look at the major components of this total now and revisit them in more depth later in the book.

- Canadian Tire had "property & equipment" of $3,743 million at the end of 2014 (line 11). This balance consists of the land (property) and equipment that Canadian Tire uses to carry out its business activities. Equipment assets are usually reported at their **carrying amount**, which is their original cost *net* of accumulated depreciation (or amortization). The accumulated depreciation represents the amount of the original cost of the asset that has been *used up* to generate economic benefits for the company. You will learn more about these non-current assets in Chapter 6.

- On January 3, 2015, Canadian Tire had $684 million of "long-term receivables" (line 12), which are amounts owed to the company from outside parties that will not be repaid until after the end of the next fiscal year. In Canadian Tire's case, the receivables consist primarily of loans made to other entities.

- On line 13, Canadian Tire reports "long-term investments" in the shares of other companies of $176 million. You will learn more about long-term investments like these in Chapter 7.

Between its current and non-current assets, Canadian Tire reported total assets of $14,553 at the end of 2014 (line 15). Next we will look at Canadian Tire's liabilities, the first component on the right side of the accounting equation.

LIABILITIES. A **liability** is a present obligation of the entity arising from past events, the settlement of which is expected to result in an outflow from the entity of resources embodying economic benefits. In simpler terms, a liability is a debt the entity owes as a result of a past event, and which it expects to pay off in the future using some of its assets. Canadian Tire's liabilities include "accounts payable," which are debts they owe to companies that have supplied them with goods and services in the past. Canadian Tire's largest liability is its "long-term debt" (lines 21 and 24), which represents money they have borrowed in the past from banks and other financial institutions to help them fund asset purchases and other business activities. In the future, Canadian Tire will use some of its cash to pay off both of these liabilities. Like assets, we classify liabilities as **current liabilities** or **non-current liabilities** (or **long-term liabilities**), with the distinction based on how soon after year-end the company expects to pay off the debt. Current liabilities are debts the company expects to pay off *within one year* of the balance sheet date, or within the company's normal operating cycle if it is longer than one year. Canadian Tire reported current liabilities of $4,579 million (line 22) at the end of 2014. Let's look at some of the individual liabilities that make up this total.

- Canadian Tire had "bank indebtedness" of $14 million at the end of 2014 (line 17). This amount represents temporary negative balances in some of Canadian Tire's bank accounts or amounts owing on lines of credit used to cover temporary shortfalls in the cash it needs to run its business.

- At January 3, 2015, Canadian Tire owed $1,961 million in "accounts payable" (line 18), which comprise debts related to goods and services the company has purchased on credit from its suppliers. Essentially, this liability is the opposite of the accounts receivable current asset discussed above. You will learn more about these liabilities in Chapters 3 and 8.

- Canadian Tire had $55 million of "income taxes payable" as at the end of 2014 (line 19), which represents the amount of income tax it owes at the end of the year. Income taxes will be discussed in Chapter 8.

- Canadian Tire reports a "current portion of long-term debt" totalling $588 million (line 21). This balance represents the portion of long-term debt that Canadian Tire must pay off within one year of the balance sheet date. The long-term portion of the debt is $2,132 (line 24), which will be repaid after the end of the next fiscal year. Long-term debt is discussed in more detail in Chapter 8.

In total, Canadian Tire reported $4,579 million in liabilities that it expected to pay off before the end of its next fiscal year on January 2, 2016 (line 22). It also reported total non-current (or long-term) liabilities of $4,344 million (lines 24 and 25) and total liabilities of $8,922 (line 26). Let's now examine the last major element of the balance sheet, owners' equity.

OWNERS' EQUITY. **Owners' equity** is the owners' remaining interest in the assets of the company after deducting all its liabilities. In effect, it represents the owners' claim on the company's assets *net* of the company's liabilities, so it is sometimes referred to as the **net assets** of the company. For incorporated companies like Canadian Tire, it is often called **shareholders' equity**. We can rearrange the accounting equation to clearly express the nature of this balance sheet element:

$$\text{Owners' Equity} = \text{Assets} - \text{Liabilities}$$

Let's look at two of the equity line items on Canadian Tire's 2014 balance sheet:

- Canadian Tire had "share capital" of $696 million on January 3, 2015 (line 28). This balance represents amounts contributed by shareholders in exchange for shares in Canadian Tire. You will learn more about share capital in Chapter 9.

- Canadian Tire's ending "retained earnings" of $4,075 million is carried over from the statement of retained earnings to line 29 on the balance sheet.

At January 3, 2015, Canadian Tire had total owners' equity of $5,631 (line 31). Now let's take another look at how the three main elements of Canadian Tire's balance sheet fit into the accounting equation:

Assets	=	Liabilities	+	Owners' Equity
$14,553	=	$8,922	+	$5,631

MyAccountingLab

STOP + THINK (1-2)

1. If the assets of a business are $240,000 and the liabilities are $80,000, how much is the owners' equity?

2. If the owners' equity in a business is $160,000 and the liabilities are $130,000, how much are the assets?

3. A company reported total monthly income of $129,000 and total expenses of $85,000. What is the result of operations for the month?

4. If the beginning balance of retained earnings is $100,000, total income is $75,000, expenses total $50,000, and the company pays a $10,000 dividend, what is the ending balance of retained earnings?

The Statement of Cash Flows Measures Cash Receipts and Payments

The **statement of cash flows** (or cash flow statement under ASPE) reports a company's cash receipts and cash payments for the same fiscal period covered by the income statement. This statement shows users the specific business activities that generated cash receipts or resulted in cash payments during the period. These activities are classified into three categories:

1. **Operating activities**
2. **Investing activities**
3. **Financing activities**

Exhibit 1-8 presents Canadian Tire's statements of cash flows for 2014 and 2013. Let's use it to learn more about each of these business activities.

OPERATING ACTIVITIES. These activities comprise the main revenue-producing activities of a company, and generally result from the transactions and other events that determine net income. Common operating activities include cash receipts from a company's sales of its primary goods and services as well as cash payments to suppliers and employees for the goods and services they provide to generate these sales. When Canadian Tire pays Weber for the barbeques it sells to its customers, for example, the payment is an operating activity that results in a cash outflow. Similarly, when a customer pays Canadian Tire for one of these barbeques, it results in a cash inflow from operating activities.

On line 5 of Canadian Tire's statement of cash flows, we see that the determination of cash flows from operating activities begins with the $639 million in net income it reported on line 12 of its income statement in Exhibit 1-4. In total, the

EXHIBIT 1-8
Consolidated Statements of Cash Flows (Adapted)

	A	B	C	D
1	**Canadian Tire Corporation** Consolidated Statements of Cash Flows (Adapted) For the Years Ended January 3, 2015 and December 28, 2013			
2	*(in millions of dollars)*	**2014**	**2013**	
3	Cash generated from (used for):			
4	**Operating activities**			
5	Net income	$ 639.3	$ 564.4	
6	Adjustments for:			
7	Depreciation on property & equipment & investment property	279.2	253.8	
8	Loss (gain) on disposal of property & equipment & investment property	(9.0)	(10.3)	
9	Other operating activities	(334.7)	85.1	
10	**Cash generated from operating activities**	574.8	893.0	
11	**Investing activities**			
12	Additions to property & equipment & investment property	(538.6)	(404.3)	
13	Proceeds on disposition of property & equipment & investment property	21.3	20.6	
14	Acquisition of long-term investments	(155.8)	(55.1)	
15	Proceeds from the disposition of long-term investments	7.6	0.4	
16	Other investing activities	76.0	(348.0)	
17	**Cash used for investing activities**	(589.5)	(786.4)	
18	**Financing activities**			
19	Dividends paid	(141.4)	(107.2)	
20	Issuance of long-term debt	563.7	265.8	
21	Repayment of long-term debt & finance lease liabilities	(474.0)	(659.2)	
22	Other financing activities	140.3	38.9	
23	**Cash generated from financing activities**	88.6	(461.7)	
24	**Cash generated in the year**	73.9	(355.1)	
25	**Cash, net of bank indebtedness, beginning of year**	574.2	929.5	
26	**Effect of exchange rate fluctuations on cash held**	(0.3)	(0.2)	
27	**Cash, net of bank indebtedness, end of year**	$ 647.8	$ 574.2	
28				

Source: Reprinted with permission from Canadian Tire Corporation.

company generated almost $600 million in cash inflows from operating activities in 2014 (line 10). This is a sign of excellent financial health. A company that does not regularly generate sufficient cash flows from operating activities will eventually suffer cash flow problems and may go bankrupt.

INVESTING ACTIVITIES. These activities include the purchase and sale of long-term assets and other investments that result in cash inflows or outflows related to resources used for generating future income and cash flows. Cash payments to acquire property, plant, and equipment, and the cash received upon the sale of these assets, are common investing activities. Investing activities also include cash flows from the purchase and sale of investments in other companies, and those related to loans made to other entities.

In 2014, Canadian Tire spent $539 million in cash to purchase property, equipment, and investment property (line 12) and received cash of $21 million when they sold assets of these types (line 13). They also spent $156 million to acquire other companies (line 14). Like its operating activities, Canadian Tire's 2014 investing activities indicate excellent future prospects for the company because they show that the company invested almost $600 million in new long-term assets (line 17) that will help it earn additional revenues in coming years.

FINANCING ACTIVITIES. These activities result in changes in the size and composition of a company's contributed equity and borrowings. Common financing activities include the issuance and acquisition of shares, the payment of cash dividends, the cash proceeds from borrowings, and the repayment of amounts borrowed.

In this section of Canadian Tire's statement of cash flows, we see that it paid cash dividends of $141 million to shareholders (line 19). Lines 20 and 21 report the cash inflows and outflows related to Canadian Tire's long-term borrowings during the year. In total, Canadian Tire reported total cash inflows from financing activities of $89 million for 2014.

Overall, Canadian Tire's business activities resulted in a net increase in cash of $74 million for 2014 (line 24). When this is added to its $574-million cash balance at the beginning of the year (line 25), Canadian Tire ended 2014 with $648 million in cash (line 27). IFRS and ASPE require companies to report cash net of any bank indebtedness on the statement of cash flows, as Canadian Tire does here, so to see the link between this statement and the balance sheet, we must deduct the bank indebtedness on line 17 of the balance sheet in Exhibit 1-6 from the cash balance on line 4 to arrive at the $648 million reported on the statement of cash flows.

The Notes to the Financial Statements Provide Additional Information

The notes to the financial statements are an integral part of the financial statements and should be read carefully as part of a review of the financial statements. The notes provide information that cannot be reported conveniently on the face of the financial statements. For example, the notes tell the readers information such as what accounting policies were used in preparing the financial statements, and what methods were used to account for inventories and depreciation. An example of these notes can be found in Appendix A: Annual Report for Canadian Tire Corporation. Notice that at the bottom of each of Canadian Tire's financial statements is this reminder to users: *The related notes form an integral part of these consolidated financial statements.*

Financial Reporting Responsibilities

Two parties have critical financial reporting responsibilities: a company's management and its independent outside (or external) **auditor**. Company management has the primary financial reporting duties because they are responsible for designing, maintaining, and monitoring the company's financial reporting process and for preparing the financial statements based on the information generated by this process. The auditor's responsibility is to gather evidence regarding the financial information reported by management, and then decide whether the information reported in the financial statements complies with the applicable GAAP. Upon completing its audit of a company's financial statements, the auditor provides a signed report to the board of directors and shareholders of the company that states its opinion on the fairness of the company's financial statements relative to GAAP. All publicly accountable enterprises in Canada must have their financial statements audited. Many private companies are also required by government incorporation acts, creditors, or other financial statement users to have their financial statements audited. When financial statement users see an auditor's report stating that the accompanying financial statements are fairly presented in accordance with GAAP, they have reasonable assurance they can rely on the financial information to make sound decisions.

OBJECTIVE

❸ Explain the relationships among the financial statements

EXPLAIN THE RELATIONSHIPS AMONG THE FINANCIAL STATEMENTS

Exhibit 1-9 presents summarized financial statements for the fictional Huron Ltd. This exhibit highlights the relationships among each of the four financial statements you just studied. These relationships apply to the financial statements of every

EXHIBIT 1-9
Relationships Among the Financial Statements

	A	B	C	D
1	**Huron Ltd.** Income Statement For the Year Ended December 31, 2017			
2	Income	$ 700,000		
3	Expenses	670,000		
4	Net income	$ 30,000		
5				

	A	B	C	D
1	**Huron Ltd.** Statement of Retained Earnings For the Year Ended December 31, 2017			
2	Beginning retained earnings	$ 120,000		
3	Net income	30,000		
4	Cash dividends	(10,000)		
5	Ending retained earnings	$ 140,000		
6				

	A	B	C	D
1	**Huron Ltd.** Balance Sheet As at December 31, 2017			
2	**Assets**			
3	Cash	$ 25,000		
4	All other assets	275,000		
5	Total assets	$ 300,000		
6	**Liabilities**			
7	Total liabilities	$ 120,000		
8	**Shareholders' Equity**			
9	Common shares	40,000		
10	Retained earnings	140,000		
11	Total liabilities and shareholders' equity	$ 300,000		
12				

	A	B	C	D
1	**Huron Ltd.** Statement of Cash Flows For the Year Ended December 31, 2017			
2	Net cash provided by operating activities	$ 90,000		
3	Net cash used for investing activities	(110,000)		
4	Net cash provided by financing activities	40,000		
5	Net increase in cash	20,000		
6	Beginning cash balance	5,000		
7	Ending cash balance	$ 25,000		
8				

① ② ③

organization, so examine them carefully to ensure you understand the nature of each relationship.

Specifically, note the following:

1. The income statement measures Huron's operating performance for the year ended December 31, 2017, by:

   a. Reporting all income and expenses for the year;
   b. Reporting net income if total income exceeds total expenses, or a net loss if expenses exceed income.

2. The statement of retained earnings reports changes in Huron's retained earnings balance for the year ended December 31, 2017, by:

   a. Adding the net income (or subtracting the net loss) from the income statement (link 1 in Exhibit 1-9) to the retained earnings balance at the beginning of the year; then
   b. Deducting dividends declared during the year to arrive at the retained earnings balance at the end of the year.

▶ DECISION GUIDELINES

WHAT DO DECISION MAKERS LOOK FOR WHEN EVALUATING A COMPANY?

These Decision Guidelines illustrate how people use financial statements. Decision Guidelines appear throughout the book to show how accounting information aids decision making.

Suppose you are considering an investment in Canadian Tire Corporation stock. How do you proceed? Where do you get the information you need? What do you look for?

Decision	Guidelines
1. Can the company sell its products and services?	1. Sales revenue on the income statement: Are sales growing or falling?
2. Is the company making money?	2. a. Gross profit (Sales – Cost of goods sold) b. Operating income (Gross profit – Operating expenses) c. Net income (bottom line of the income statement) All three income measures should be increasing over time.
3. What percentage of sales revenue ends up as profit?	3. Divide net income by sales revenue. Examine the trend of the net income percentage from year to year.
4. Can the company collect its accounts receivable?	4. From the balance sheet, compare the percentage increase in accounts receivable to the percentage increase in sales. If receivables are growing much faster than sales, collections may be too slow, and a cash shortage may result.

5. Can the company pay its:
  a. current liabilities?
  b. total liabilities?
	5. From the balance sheet, compare:
	  a. current assets to current liabilities. Current assets should be somewhat greater than current liabilities.
	  b. total assets to total liabilities. Total assets must be somewhat greater than total liabilities.

6. Where is the company's cash coming from? How is cash being used?	6. On the statement of cash flows, operating activities should provide the bulk of the company's cash during most years. Otherwise, the business will fail. Examine investing cash flows to see if the company is purchasing long-term assets—property, plant, and equipment and intangibles (this signals growth).

3. The balance sheet reports Huron's financial position at December 31, 2017, by:
    a. Reporting all assets, liabilities, and shareholders' equity as at the end of the year;
    b. Within the shareholders' equity section of the statement, reporting the retained earnings balance at the end of the year, which comes from the statement of retained earnings (link 2).

4. The statement of cash flows reports Huron's cash receipts and cash payments for the year ended December 31, 2017, by:

    a. Reporting cash provided by (or used in) the company's operating, investing, and financing activities during the year.
    b. Reporting the net change in the company's cash balance during the year and adding it to the beginning cash balance to arrive at the cash balance as at the end of the year, which is also reported on the balance sheet (link 3).

STOP + THINK (1-3)

On December 31, 2017, Huron Ltd. provided services to a customer for which the customer paid $1,000 in cash on that date, but the company mistakenly left this sale out of its accounting records when it prepared the financial statements in Exhibit 1-9. Given the links between the financial statements illustrated in Exhibit 1-9, what would happen to Huron Ltd.'s December 31, 2017 financial statements after they correct them to include the missing cash sale of $1,000 on December 31, 2017?

OBJECTIVE

❹ **Explain** accounting's conceptual framework and underlying assumptions

EXPLAIN ACCOUNTING'S CONCEPTUAL FRAMEWORK AND UNDERLYING ASSUMPTIONS

Accounting's Conceptual Framework

Before introducing the financial statements, we told you about IFRS and ASPE, the generally accepted accounting principles that are used to prepare most of the financial statements in Canada. We will now look at the conceptual framework and assumptions underlying IFRS and ASPE.

Exhibit 1-10 gives an overview of the joint conceptual framework of accounting developed by the IASB and the Financial Accounting Standards Board (FASB) in the United States. This conceptual framework, along with several underlying assumptions, provides the foundation for the specific accounting principles included in IFRS and ASPE, though there are some small differences between the frameworks for the two sets of standards. The overall *objective* of accounting is to provide financial information about the reporting entity that is useful to current and future investors and creditors when making investing and lending decisions and when assessing how well management is running the entity.

Fundamental Qualitative Characteristics

To be useful, information must have two *fundamental qualitative characteristics*:

- **relevance** and
- **faithful representation**.

To be **relevant**, information must have *predictive value, confirmatory value,* or both. Information has predictive value if it can be employed by users to predict an entity's future business or financial outcomes. For example, if the amount of money a company earns in the current year can be used to predict how much it will earn next

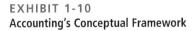

EXHIBIT 1-10
Accounting's Conceptual Framework

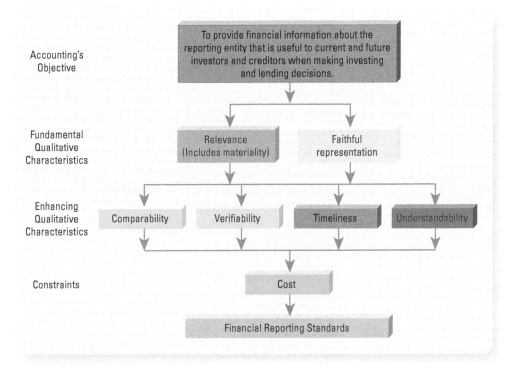

year, then the current-year amount has predictive value. It has confirmatory value if it confirms or changes prior evaluations of an entity. Therefore, if the amount of money a company earns this year can be used to confirm or update prior predictions about the company's growth prospects, then this amount would have confirmatory value. In addition, the information must be **material**, which means that it is significant enough in nature or magnitude that omitting or misstating it could affect the decisions of an informed user. In the Canadian Tire income statement at the beginning of this chapter, we noted that the company sold over $12 billion worth of goods and services in 2014, so a user of the company's financial statements would not be influenced by an error of $1,000 that occurred when determining the company's total revenues for the year. In other words, an error that small would be *immaterial* to the user's decisions about Canadian Tire. All material information must be recorded or disclosed (listed or discussed) in the financial statements.

For accounting information to provide a faithful representation to users, it must reflect the *economic substance* of a transaction or event, which may not be the same as its legal form. The information must also be complete, neutral (free of bias), and accurate (free of material error). When accounting information possesses these facets of faithful representation, it is *reliable* to users so they can have faith that the information can be relied upon to make decisions about the company and its management.

Enhancing Qualitative Characteristics

To be useful, accounting information must also possess four *enhancing qualitative characteristics*:

- **comparability**
- **verifiability**

- **timeliness**, and
- **understandability**.

For accounting information to be *comparable*, it must be reported in a way that makes it possible to compare it to similar information being reported by other companies. It must also be reported in a way that is consistent with how it was reported in previous accounting periods. For example, a company must determine the cost of its inventory at the end of the current year using the same method it used at the end of the prior year. It also must disclose in the notes which costing method it used so that users can compare its method to the methods being used by competitors or other similar businesses.

Accounting information is *verifiable* when it can be checked for accuracy, completeness, and reliability. Verifiability enhances the chance that accounting information reflects a faithful representation of the economic substance of a transaction or event. It is possible, for example, to verify the amount of cash a company reports on its balance sheet at year-end by directly confirming with its bank how much cash the company had in its accounts at that time.

Timeliness means reporting accounting information to users in time for it to influence their decisions. Accounting information tends to become less relevant as it gets older, so it should be reported to users as soon after the end of the accounting period as possible, without sacrificing the other qualitative characteristics in the process. It would not, for example, be helpful to users if a company waited until the end of 2016 to report its financial statements for the year ended December 31, 2015. Users need a company's financial information on a much more timely basis than this, which is why investors and creditors typically demand financial statements be issued within no more than three months of year-end.

Accounting information is *understandable* when it is clearly and concisely classified and presented to reasonably knowledgeable and diligent users of the information. Both IFRS and ASPE, for example, require companies to report their inventory at the lower of its cost (what they paid for it) and its net realizable value (what they could sell it for). This concept is simple enough for even novice financial statements users to understand. At times, however, even informed and careful users will require assistance in understanding certain complex transactions and events.

The Cost Constraint

Accounting information is costly to produce. A primary constraint in the decision to disclose accounting information is that the cost of disclosure should not exceed the expected benefits to users. Management of an entity is primarily responsible for preparing accounting information. Managers must exercise judgment in determining whether the information is necessary for complete understanding of underlying economic facts and not excessively costly to provide.

This book introduces you to the basic financial reporting standards that have been devised using this conceptual framework. Before we begin exposing you to these standards, let's examine the assumptions that underlie this conceptual framework.

Assumptions Underlying the Conceptual Framework

The conceptual framework has only one explicit underlying assumption: the **going-concern assumption**. There are, however, three other assumptions that are implicit in the framework, so we present them here as well. They are the **separate-entity**, **historical-cost**, and **stable-monetary-unit assumptions**.

GOING-CONCERN ASSUMPTION. We typically prepare financial information under the assumption that the reporting entity is a going concern, which means that we expect it to continue operating normally for the foreseeable future. A company that is not a going concern is at risk of going bankrupt or closing down, so it may need to significantly scale down its operations or sell some of its assets at heavily discounted rates. When this risk is present, the financial statements are typically prepared on a basis that differs from the usual standards in IFRS or ASPE. If a different basis is used in such circumstances, it must be clearly disclosed to the users of the financial statements.

SEPARATE-ENTITY ASSUMPTION. We also prepare financial statements under the assumption that the business activities of the reporting entity are separate from the activities of its owners, so we do not mix the assets, liabilities, income, or expenses of the entity with those of its owners when reporting the entity's operating performance and financial position. Consider Gerald Schwartz, the chairman, president, chief executive officer, and major shareholder of ONEX Corporation, a large Canadian public company. Mr. Schwartz personally owns a house, automobiles, and investments in various companies. His personal assets, however, would not be included among the land, buildings, vehicles, and investments reported on ONEX's financial statements because his assets are separate from those of the entity he owns and operates. The separate-entity assumption draws a clear boundary around the business activities of the reporting entity, and only the activities within this boundary are reported in the entity's financial statements.

HISTORICAL-COST ASSUMPTION. The historical-cost assumption states that assets should be recorded at their *actual cost*, measured on the date of purchase as the amount of cash paid plus the dollar value of all non-cash consideration (other assets, privileges, or rights) also given in exchange. For example, suppose Canadian Tire purchases a building for a new store. The building's current owner is asking for $600,000 for the building. The management of Canadian Tire believes the building is worth $585,000, and offers the present owner that amount. Two real estate professionals appraise the building at $610,000. The two parties compromise and agree on a price of $590,000 for the building. The historical-cost assumption requires Canadian Tire to initially record the building at its actual cost of $590,000—not at $585,000, $600,000, or $610,000—even though those amounts were what some people believed the building was worth. At the point of purchase, $590,000 is both the *relevant* amount for the building's worth and the amount that *faithfully represents* a reliable figure for the price the company paid for it.

The historical-cost and the going-concern assumptions also maintain that Canadian Tire's accounting records should continue to use historical cost to value the asset for as long as the business holds it. Why? Because cost is a *verifiable* measure that is relatively *free from bias*. Suppose that Canadian Tire owns the building for six years and that real estate prices increase during this period. As a result, at the end of the period, the building can be sold for $650,000. Should Canadian Tire increase the value of the building on the company's books to $650,000? No. According to the historical-cost assumption, the building remains on Canadian Tire's books at its historical cost of $590,000. According to the going-concern assumption, Canadian Tire intends to stay in business and keep the building, not to sell it, so its historical cost is the most relevant and the most faithful representation of its value. It is also the most easily verifiable amount. Should the company decide to sell the building later at a price above or below its recorded value, it will record the cash received, remove the value of the building from the books, and record a gain or a loss for the difference at that time.

The historical-cost assumption is not used as extensively as it once was. Accounting is moving in the direction of reporting more assets and liabilities at their fair values. **Fair value** is the amount that the business could sell the asset for, or the amount that the business could pay to settle the liability. IFRS permit certain types of assets and liabilities to be periodically adjusted to reflect their fair values rather than leaving them on the books at their historical costs. With rare exceptions, ASPE still require assets and liabilities to be kept on the books at their historical costs. Fair-value accounting is generally beyond the scope of this textbook, but in later chapters we will highlight where this option exists.

STABLE-MONETARY-UNIT ASSUMPTION. The vast majority of Canadian entities report their financial information in Canadian dollars (or monetary units), although some choose to report in U.S. dollars instead. Regardless of the reporting currency used, financial information is always reported under the assumption that the value of the currency is stable, despite the fact that its value does change due to economic factors such as inflation. By assuming that the purchasing power of the reporting currency is stable, we can add and subtract dollar values from different reporting periods without having to make adjustments for changes in the underlying value of the currency.

Now that you have an understanding of the conceptual framework and assumptions underlying the financial statements, let's take an introductory look at each of the statements that you will learn more about as you progress through this book.

STOP + THINK (1-4)

It is September 24, 2017, and your company is considering the purchase of land for future expansion. The seller is asking $50,000 for the land, which cost them $35,000 four years ago. An independent appraiser assigns the land a value of $47,000. You offer the seller $44,000 for the land and they come back with a counter-offer of $48,000. You and the seller end up settling on a purchase price of $46,000 for the land.

1. When you record the purchase of this land in your accounting records, at what value will you record it?

2. Assume that four years later someone approaches your company and offers to purchase this land, which you have yet to develop, for $60,000. You know this to be a fair price given a recent appraisal you had done on the land. You decline the offer because you have plans to begin developing the land next year. What adjustment would you make to the value of the land in your accounting records?

OBJECTIVE

⑤ Make ethical business decisions

MAKE ETHICAL BUSINESS DECISIONS

Running a business requires sound decision making, which in turn requires the exercise of good judgment, both at the individual and corporate levels. For example, you may work for or eventually run a company like Tim Hortons that devotes a percentage of its net income to a variety of charitable organizations and activities. Will this be profitable in the long run, or would it be more sensible to devote those resources to other, less-charitable activities? Making a business decision like this requires careful ethical judgment. Can that be profitable in the long run?

As an accountant, you may have to decide whether to record a $50,000 expenditure as an asset on the balance sheet or an expense on the income statement. Or, you may have to decide whether $25 million of goods delivered to customers in late 2017 should be recorded as revenue in 2017 or in 2018. As mentioned earlier, the application of IFRS and ASPE frequently requires the use of professional judgment because accounting standards contain few clear-cut rules on how to account for transactions and events. Depending on the type of business, the facts and circumstances surrounding accounting decisions may not always make them clear cut, and yet the decision may determine whether the company shows a profit or a loss in a particular period! What are the factors that influence business and accounting decisions, and how should these factors be weighed? Generally, three factors influence business and accounting decisions: *economic, legal, and ethical factors.*

The *economic* factor states that the decision being made should *maximize the economic benefits* to the decision maker. Based on economic theory, every rational person faced with a decision will choose the course of action that maximizes his or her own welfare, without regard to how that decision impacts others. In summary, the combined outcome of each person acting in his or her own self-interest will maximize the benefits to society as a whole.

The *legal* factor is based on the proposition that free societies are governed by laws. Laws are written to provide clarity and to prevent abuse of the rights of individuals or society. Democratically enacted laws both contain and express society's collective moral standards. Legal analysis involves applying the relevant laws to each decision and then choosing the action that complies with those laws. A complicating factor for a global business may be that what is legal in one country might not be legal in another. In that case, it is usually best to abide by the laws of the most restrictive country.

The *ethical* factor recognizes that while certain actions might be both economically profitable and legal, they may still not be right. Therefore, most companies, and many individuals, have established ethical standards for themselves to enforce a higher level of conduct than that imposed by law. These standards govern how we treat others and the way we restrain our selfish desires. This behaviour and its underlying beliefs are the essence of ethics. **Ethical standards** are shaped by our cultural, socioeconomic, and religious backgrounds. An *ethical analysis* is often needed to guide judgment when making business decisions.

When performing an ethical analysis, our challenge is to identify our specific ethical responsibilities and the stakeholders to whom we owe these responsibilities. As with legal issues, a complicating factor in making global ethical decisions may be that what is considered ethical in one country is not considered ethical in another.

Among the questions you may ask in making an ethical analysis are the following:

- *Which options are most honest, open, and truthful?*
- *Which options are most kind and compassionate, and build a sense of community?*
- *Which options create the greatest good for the greatest number of stakeholders?*
- *Which options result in treating others as I would want to be treated?*

Ethical training starts at home and continues throughout our lives. It is reinforced by the teaching that we receive in our church, synagogue, mosque, or other house of worship; the schools we attend; and by the persons and companies we associate with.

In addition, the Chartered Professional Accountants of Canada has a code of professional conduct that helps its members make ethical judgments and decisions. Members who violate the code are subject to a variety of disciplinary actions, including expulsion from their profession for serious violations.

Fraud and its Impact

Fraud is the intentional misrepresentation of facts done to persuade another party to act in a way that causes financial damage to that party. What are the most common types of fraud? What causes fraud? What can be done to prevent it? There are many types of fraud. Some examples are insurance fraud, cheque forgery, credit card fraud, and identity theft. The two most common types of fraud that affect financial statements are:

- **Misappropriation of assets.** This type of fraud is committed by stealing assets from a company and then covering the theft up by adjusting the accounting records or other relevant information. Examples of asset misappropriation include stealing inventory, falsifying invoices, forging or altering cheques, or overstating of expense reimbursement requests.
- **Fraudulent financial reporting.** This type of fraud is committed by company managers who make false and misleading entries in the accounting records, usually to present a more favourable financial picture than would be presented if the actual results were disclosed. The purpose of this type of fraud is to deceive investors and creditors into making decisions they might otherwise not have made if given accurate financial information.

Research has indicated that managers engage in fraudulent financial reporting for a variety of reasons, including:

- To meet profit targets set by market analysts so that the company's share price will increase (or not decrease). If, for example, analysts predicted annual net income of $10 million but it looks like the company's actual earnings will come in around $9 million, the company's managers could artificially inflate its revenues by just over one million dollars so the company exceeds the analysts' target.
- To meet loan covenants so a bank won't demand early repayment of a loan. A bank may specify that a company must have total current assets that are at least twice as high as its total current liabilities to avoid having to repay a loan before its actual due date. If it looks like the ratio of current assets to current liabilities will be only 1.9 at year end instead of the minimum of 2.0, the company's managers could fraudulently overstate the value of its inventory to increase the company's total current assets to a level that make them at least two times as high as current liabilities.
- To meet an earnings target that will result in large bonus payments to senior executives. Managers often have annual bonuses tied to meeting a specified net income level, so if it appears that net income will come in below the target, managers could deliberately exclude some expenses from the income statement to increase net income to a level beyond the bonus threshold.

Both misappropriation of assets and fraudulent financial reporting involve making false or misleading entries in the books of the company. We call this *cooking the books*. Of these two types, asset misappropriation is the most common, but fraudulent financial reporting is by far the most expensive. Livent Inc., for example, was a Canadian public company listed on the Toronto Stock Exchange. The company produced several successful musicals, such as *The Phantom of the Opera, Joseph and the Amazing Technicolor Dreamcoat, Show Boat*, and *Ragtime*. In the late 1990s, Livent declared bankruptcy in the United States, causing its shareholders and creditors to lose hundreds of millions of dollars. There were criminal investigations in Canada and the United States. Company co-founders Garth Drabinsky and Myron Gottlieb were indicted for fraud and misappropriation in the United States. In Canada, the co-founders and several other executives were charged with fraud. Drabinsky and Gottlieb were found guilty of fraud and forgery in an Ontario court for misstating the company's financial statements. In 2009, they were sentenced to time in prison. We will discuss other frauds in future chapters to illustrate how accounting principles were deliberately misapplied to "cook" the books.

Applying relevant accounting standards in a way that reports a faithful representation of the company's financial position and operating performance is always the most ethical course of action.

A thorough understanding of ethics requires more study than we can accomplish in this book. However, remember that when you are making accounting decisions, you should not check your ethics at the door!

In a business setting, sound ethical judgment begins "at the top." When employees see the top executives of their company promoting a strong ethical culture and regularly acting in a socially responsible manner, they are more likely to emulate this behaviour when making their own decisions. *Corporate Knights* magazine annually publishes a list of the most socially responsible corporations in Canada. Its 2015 list includes companies such as WestJet Airlines, Hudson's Bay, Bank of Montreal, TELUS, and Mountain Equipment Co-op. It is easier to act ethically when you work for companies that recognize the importance of ethical business practices. These companies have learned from experience that, in the long run, ethical conduct pays big rewards, not only socially, morally, and spiritually, but economically as well.

▶ DECISION GUIDELINES

DECISION FRAMEWORK FOR MAKING ETHICAL JUDGMENTS

Making tough ethical judgments in business and accounting requires a decision framework. Answering the following four questions will help you to make ethical business decisions:

Decision	Guidelines
1. What is the issue?	**1.** The issue will usually deal with making a judgment about an accounting measurement or disclosure that results in economic consequences, often to numerous parties.
2. Who are the stakeholders, and what are the consequences of the decision to each of them?	**2.** Stakeholders include anyone who might be affected by the decision—you, your company, and potential users of the information (investors, creditors, regulatory agencies). Consequences can be economic, legal, or ethical in nature.
3. What are the decision alternatives, and how do they affect each stakeholder?	**3.** Analyze the impact of the decision on all stakeholders, using economic, legal, and ethical criteria. Ask, "Who will be helped or hurt, whose rights will be exercised or denied, and in what way?"
4. What decision alternative will you choose?	**4.** Choose the alternative that best balances your economic, legal, and ethical responsibilities to your stakeholders. Also, assess how your decision makes you feel. If it makes you feel uneasy, determine why and consider choosing another alternative.

To simplify, we might ask three questions:

1. Is the action legal? If not, steer clear, unless you want to go to jail or pay monetary damages to injured parties. If the action is legal, go on to questions (2) and (3).

2. Who will be affected by the decision and how? Be as thorough about this analysis as possible, and analyze it from all three standpoints (economic, legal, and ethical).

3. How will this decision make me feel afterward? How would it make me feel if my family reads about it in the newspaper?

In later chapters we will apply this model to different accounting decisions.

STOP + THINK (1-5)

Suppose you are the chief accountant for a public company listed on the Toronto Stock Exchange. You are finalizing the company's financial statements for the 2017 year and it appears that net income will come in about $1 million below what financial analysts predicted. Your boss, the company's CEO, asks you to record $1.2 million in fictitious sales to bring net income above the analysts' target. Use the Decision Framework for Making Ethical Judgments to decide how you would respond to the CEO's request.

Summary of IFRS-ASPE Differences

Concepts	IFRS	ASPE
The income statement (p. 8)	This financial statement is called the statement of profit or loss.	This financial statement is called the income statement.
Changes in retained earnings during an accounting period (p. 10)	These changes are reported in the statement of changes in owners' equity.	These changes are reported in the statement of retained earnings.
The balance sheet (p. 11)	This financial statement is called the statement of financial position.	This financial statement is called the balance sheet.
The cash flow statement (p. 15)	This financial statement is called the statement of cash flows.	This financial statement is called the cash flow statement.
Application of IFRS and ASPE (p. 20)	Publicly accountable enterprises or those enterprises planning to become one must apply IFRS.	Private enterprises have the option of applying IFRS, but almost all apply ASPE, which is simpler and less costly for these smaller enterprises.
Historical-cost assumption (p. 23)	Certain assets and liabilities are permitted to be recorded at their fair values rather than being kept on the books at their historical costs.	With rare exceptions, assets and liabilities are carried at their historical costs for as long as the company owns or owes them.

SUMMARY

SUMMARY OF LEARNING OBJECTIVES

LEARNING OBJECTIVE	SUMMARY
1. **Explain** why accounting is the language of business	Accounting is an information system that measures and records business activities, processes data into reports, and reports results to decision makers. The better you understand the language used to prepare and report accounting information, the better you can make decisions using this information.
2. **Describe** the purpose of each financial statement and **explain** the elements of each one	The income statement (or statement of operations) measures a company's operating performance for a specified period of time. The income statement has two main elements, income and expenses, and also reports a company's net income for the period (Total Income – Total Expenses).
	The statement of retained earnings reports the changes in a company's retained earnings during the same period covered by the income statement. Under ASPE, this statement is often added to the bottom of the income statement, whereas under IFRS, information on the changes in retained earnings is included in the statement of changes in owners' equity. In its basic form, this statement adds net income to and deducts dividends from the opening retained earnings balance for the period to arrive at the ending retained earnings balance.

The balance sheet (or statement of financial position) reports a company's financial position as at a specific date, which almost always falls on the last day of a monthly, quarterly, or annual reporting period. A company's financial position consists of three elements: the assets it controls, the liabilities it is obligated to pay, and the equity its owners have accumulated in the business. The balance sheet takes its name from the fact that the assets it reports must always equal—or be in balance with—the sum of the liabilities and equity it reports. This relationship is known as the accounting equation, and it provides the foundation for the double-entry method of accounting you will begin to learn in Chapter 2.

The statement of cash flows reports the specific business activities that generated cash receipts or resulted in cash payments during the same period covered by the income statement. These business activities are classified into three categories: operating, investing, and financing activities.

3. **Explain** the relationships among the financial statements

Certain key financial statement items serve as links among the financial statements:
1. Net income from the income statement is included in the calculation of retained earnings on the statement of retained earnings (which is included as part of the statement of changes in owners' equity under IFRS).
2. The closing retained earnings balance from the statement of retained earnings is included in the calculation of owners' equity on the balance sheet.
3. The closing cash balance from the statement of cash flows appears as an asset on the balance sheet.

4. **Explain** accounting's conceptual framework and underlying assumptions

In Canada there are two main sets of GAAP. Publicly accountable enterprises (or those planning to become one) must use International Financial Reporting Standards (IFRS), whereas private enterprises have the option of applying IFRS or Accounting Standards for Private Enterprises (ASPE). Most private enterprises choose the ASPE because it is simpler and less costly to apply.

Both IFRS and ASPE rest on a conceptual framework, which helps ensure that accounting information is useful for decision-making purposes. This framework includes the fundamental qualitative characteristics of relevance and faithful representation, as well as four enhancing qualitative characteristics: comparability, verifiability, timeliness, and understandability. The cost of obtaining certain types of accounting information is sometimes a constraint on what is reported to the users of financial statements.

Underlying the conceptual framework are four assumptions: the going-concern, separate-entity, historical-cost, and stable-monetary-unit assumptions.

5. **Make** ethical business decisions

Accountants must often use professional judgment when applying IFRS and ASPE because many accounting standards do not have clear-cut rules that specify how transactions or events should be accounted for. When using professional judgment, the accountant's goal is to make a decision that fulfills their ethical responsibilities to every party with a stake in the decision. Professional accountants are governed by rules of professional conduct, which provide guidance meant to ensure that ethical standards are upheld when applying professional judgment.

MyAccountingLab

END-OF-CHAPTER SUMMARY PROBLEM

J. J. Booth and Marie Savard incorporated Tara Inc., a consulting engineering company, and began operations on April 1, 2017. During April, the business provided engineering services for clients. It is now April 30, and J. J. and Marie wonder how well Tara Inc. performed during its first month. They also want to know the business's financial position as at April 30 and cash flows during the month.

The following data are listed in alphabetical order:

Accounts payable	$ 1,800	Land	$ 18,000
Accounts receivable	2,000	Office supplies	3,700
Adjustments to reconcile net income to net cash provided by operating activities	(3,900)	Payments of cash: Acquisition of land	40,000
		Dividends	2,100
Cash balance at beginning of April	0	Rent expense	1,100
Cash balance at end of April	33,300	Retained earnings at beginning of April	0
Cash receipts:		Retained earnings at end of April	?
Issuance (sale) of shares	50,000		
Sale of land	22,000	Salary expense	1,200
Common shares	50,000	Service revenue	10,000
		Utilities expense	400

Requirements

1. Prepare the income statement, the statement of retained earnings, and the statement of cash flows for the month ended April 30, 2017, and the balance sheet as at April 30, 2017. Draw arrows linking the pertinent items in the statements.
2. Answer the investors' underlying questions.
   a. How well did Tara Inc. perform during its first month of operations?
   b. Where does Tara Inc. stand financially at the end of the first month?

ANSWERS

Requirement 1

Financial Statements of Tara Inc.

	A	B	C	D
	The title must include the name of the company, "Income Statement," and the specific period of time covered. It is critical that the time period be defined.			
1	**Tara Inc.** Income Statement For the Month Ended April 30, 2017			
2	Income:			
3	Service revenue		$ 10,000	
4	Expenses:			
5	Salary expense	$ 1,200		
6	Rent expense	1,100		
7	Utilities expense	400		
8	Total expenses		2,700	
9	Net income		$ 7,300	
10				

Side notes:

The title must include the name of the company, "Income Statement," and the specific period of time covered. It is critical that the time period be defined.

Gather all the income and expense accounts from the account listing. List the income accounts first. List the expense accounts next.

	A	B	C
1	**Tara Inc.** Statement of Retained Earnings For the Month Ended April 30, 2017		
2	Retained earnings, April 1, 2017		$ 0
3	Add: Net income for the month		7,300
4			7,300
5	Less: Dividends		(2,100)
6	Retained earnings, April 30, 2017		$ 5,200
7			

① The title must include the name of the company, "Statement of Retained Earnings," and the specific period of time covered. It is critical that the time period be defined.

The net income amount (or net loss amount) is transferred from the income statement. Retained earnings at the end of the period is the result of a calculation, and is an accumulation of the corporation's performance since it began.

	A	B	C	D
1	**Tara Inc.** Balance Sheet As at April 30, 2017			
2	**Assets**		**Liabilities**	
3	Cash	$ 33,300	Accounts payable	$ 1,800
4	Accounts receivable	2,000	**Shareholders' Equity**	
5	Office supplies	3,700	Common shares	50,000
6	Land	18,000	Retained earnings	5,200
7			Total shareholders' equity	55,200
8	Total assets	$ 57,000	Total liabilities and shareholders' equity	$ 57,000
9				

② The title must include the name of the company, "Balance Sheet," and the date of the balance sheet. It shows the financial position at the end of the day.

Gather all the asset, liability, and equity accounts from the account listing. List assets first, then liabilities, then equity accounts. The retained earnings amount is transferred from the statement of retained earnings.

It is imperative that total assets = total liabilities + shareholders' equity.

	A	B	C
1	**Tara Inc.** Statement of Cash Flows For the Month Ended April 30, 2017		
2	Cash flows from operating activities:		
3	Net income		$ 7,300
4	Adjustments to reconcile net income to net cash provided by operating activities		(3,900)
5	Net cash provided by operating activities		3,400
6	Cash flows from investing activities:		
7	Acquisition of land	$(40,000)	
8	Sale of land	22,000	
9	Net cash used for investing activities		(18,000)
10	Cash flows from financing activities:		
11	Issuance (sale) of shares	$ 50,000	
12	Payment of dividends	(2,100)	
13	Net cash provided by financing activities		47,900
14	Net increase in cash		$ 33,300
15	Cash balance, April 1, 2017		0
16	Cash balance, April 30, 2017		$ 33,300
17			

③ The title must include the name of the company, "Statement of Cash Flows," and the specific period of time covered. It is critical that the time period be defined.

Net income comes from the income statement. The adjustments amount was provided. In later chapters, you will learn how to calculate this amount.

Include all transactions that involve investing the company's cash, which involve any changes in the property, plant, and equipment.

Include all cash transactions relating to shares and long-term debt obligations.

Requirement 2

2. a. The company performed rather well in April. Net income was $7,300—very good in relation to service revenue of $10,000. Tara was able to pay cash dividends of $2,100.

Consider the net income from the income statement.

b. The business ended April with cash of $33,300. Total assets of $57,000 far exceed total liabilities of $1,800. Shareholders' equity of $55,200 provides a good cushion for borrowing. The business's financial position at April 30, 2017, is strong. The company has plenty of cash, and assets far exceed liabilities. Operating activities generated positive cash flow in the first month of operations. Lenders like to see these features before making a loan.

Consider net worth, which is total assets minus total liabilities.

TRY IT *in* EXCEL® ▶▶▶

If you've had a basic course in Excel, you can prepare financial statements easily using an Excel spreadsheet. In this chapter, you learned the accounting equation (see Exhibit 1-7 on page 12). In Exhibit 1-3 you learned the formulas for computing net income and the ending balance of retained earnings. Using the balance sheet for Tara Inc. in the End-of-Chapter Summary Problem, it is easy to prepare an Excel template for a balance sheet by programming cells for total assets (cell B8) and total liabilities and shareholders' equity (cell D8). Then, as long as you know what accounts belong in each category, you can use the insert function to insert individual assets, liabilities, and shareholders' equity accounts from a list into various cells of the spreadsheet (don't forget to include both description and amounts). You can insert subtotals for current assets, non-current assets, current liabilities, non-current liabilities, and shareholders' equity. You can also build a basic Excel template for the income statement for Tara Inc. by listing and totaling revenues and listing and totaling expenses, then subtracting total expenses from total revenues to compute net income (cell C9). You can build an Excel template for the statement of retained earnings by programming a cell for the ending balance of retained earnings (beginning balance + net income (loss) – dividends) (cell C6). Then simply insert the individual amounts and your spreadsheet does all the math for you.

Don't forget the proper order of financial statement preparation: (1) income statement, (2) statement of retained earnings, (3) balance sheet, and (4) statement of cash flows. If you have to prepare all four statements, it's best to follow that order so that you can link the income statement cell containing net income to the corresponding cell in the statement of retained earnings; link the value of the ending balance of retained earnings to the cell containing the retained earnings amount in the balance sheet; and link the ending balance of cash on the statement of cash flows to the balance of cash on the balance sheet as of the year end. These links correspond to the amounts connected by arrows (1, 2, and 3) on pages 30–31.

The beauty of this approach is that once you build a set of basic templates, you can save and use them over and over again as you progress through the course.

REVIEW

MyAccountingLab

Make the grade with MyAccountingLab: The Quick Quiz questions, Short Exercises, Exercises, and Problems (Group A) marked in #–# can be found on MyAccountingLab. You can practise them as often as you want, and most feature step-by-step guided instructions to help you find the right answer.

QUICK QUIZ   (ANSWERS APPEAR ON THE LAST PAGE OF THIS CHAPTER.)

1. The *primary* objective of financial reporting is to provide information
   a. useful for making investment and credit decisions.
   b. about the profitability of the enterprise.
   c. on the cash flows of the company.
   d. to the federal government.

2. For a business of a certain size, which type of business organization provides the least amount of protection for bankers and other creditors of the company?
   a. Proprietorship
   b. Partnership
   c. Both a and b
   d. Corporation

3. International Financial Reporting Standards (IFRS) were developed because
   a. Canadian GAAP were outdated.
   b. corporations wanted to change their reporting.
   c. different GAAP in countries of the world made global comparisons difficult.
   d. new assumptions were defined.

4. During January, assets increased by $20,000, and liabilities increased by $4,000. Shareholders' equity must have
   a. increased by $16,000.
   b. increased by $24,000.
   c. decreased by $16,000.
   d. decreased by $24,000.

5. The amount a company expects to collect from customers appears on the
   a. income statement in the expenses section.
   b. balance sheet in the current assets section.
   c. balance sheet in the shareholders' equity section.
   d. statement of cash flows.

6. All of the following are current assets except
   a. cash.
   b. accounts receivable.
   c. inventory.
   d. sales revenue.

7. Revenues are
   a. increases in share capital resulting from the owners investing in the business.
   b. increases in income resulting from selling products or performing services.
   c. decreases in liabilities resulting from paying off loans.
   d. All of the above.

8. The financial statement that reports revenues and expenses is called the
   a. statement of retained earnings.
   b. income statement.
   c. statement of cash flows.
   d. balance sheet.

9. Another name for the balance sheet is the
   a. statement of operations.
   b. statement of earnings.
   c. statement of profit and loss.
   d. statement of financial position.

10. Baldwin Corporation began the year with cash of $35,000 and a computer that cost $20,000. During the year, Baldwin earned sales revenue of $140,000 and had the following expenses: salaries, $59,000; rent, $8,000; and utilities, $3,000. At year-end, Baldwin's cash balance was down to $16,000. How much net income (or net loss) did Baldwin experience for the year?

   a. ($19,000)
   b. $70,000
   c. $107,000
   d. $140,000

11. Quartz Instruments had retained earnings of $145,000 at December 31, 2016. Net income for 2017 totalled $90,000, and dividends for 2017 were $30,000. How much retained earnings should Quartz report at December 31, 2017?
   a. $205,000
   b. $235,000
   c. $140,000
   d. $175,000

12. Net income appears on which financial statement(s)?
   a. Income statement
   b. Statement of retained earnings
   c. Both a and b
   d. Balance sheet

13. Cash paid to purchase a building appears on the statement of cash flows among the
   a. operating activities.
   b. financing activities.
   c. investing activities.
   d. shareholders' equity.

14. The shareholders' equity of Chernasky Company at the beginning and end of 2017 totalled $15,000 and $18,000, respectively. Assets at the beginning of 2017 were $25,000. If the liabilities of Chernasky Company increased by $8,000 in 2017, how much were total assets at the end of 2017? Use the accounting equation.
   a. $36,000
   b. $16,000
   c. $2,000
   d. Some other amount (fill in the blank)

15. Drexler Company had the following on the dates indicated:

	12/31/17	12/31/16
Total assets	$750,000	$520,000
Total liabilities	300,000	200,000

Drexler had no share transactions in 2017, and thus, the change in shareholders' equity for 2017 was due to net income and dividends. If dividends were $50,000, how much was Drexler's net income for 2017? Use the accounting equation and the statements of retained earnings.
   a. $100,000
   b. $130,000
   c. $180,000
   d. Some other amount (fill in the blank)

ACCOUNTING VOCABULARY

accounting An information system that measures and records business activities, processes data into reports, and reports results to decision makers.   (p. 3)

accounting equation Assets = Liabilities + Owners' Equity. Provides the foundation for the double-entry method of accounting.   (p. 11)

Accounting Standards for Private Enterprises (ASPE) Canadian accounting standards that specify the *generally accepted accounting principles* applicable to *private enterprises* that are required to follow *GAAP* and choose not to apply *IFRS*.   (p. 8)

asset A resource owned or controlled by a company as a result of past events and from which the company expects to receive future economic benefits.   (p. 11)

auditor An accountant who provides an independent opinion on whether an entity's financial statements have been prepared in accordance with generally accepted accounting principles.   (p. 17)

balance sheet Reports a company's financial position as at a specific date. In particular, it reports a company's assets, liabilities, and owners' equity. Also called the *statement of financial position*.   (p. 11)

board of directors Group elected by the shareholders to set policy for a corporation and to appoint its officers.   (p. 6)

carrying amount The historical cost of an asset net of its accumulated depreciation.   (p. 13)

comparability Investors like to compare a company's financial statements from one year to the next. Therefore, a company must consistently use the same accounting method each year.   (p. 21)

corporation An incorporated business owned by one or more *shareholders*, which according to the law is a legal "person" separate from its owners.   (p. 6)

current asset An asset that is expected to be converted to cash, sold, or consumed during the next 12 months, or within the business's normal operating cycle if longer than a year.   (p. 11)

current liability A debt due to be paid within one year or within the entity's operating cycle if the cycle is longer than a year.   (p. 14)

deficit The term used when *retained earnings* is a negative balance.   (p. 10)

ethical standards Standards that govern the way we treat others and the way we restrain our selfish desires. They are shaped by our cultural, socioeconomic, and religious backgrounds.   (p. 25)

expense A cost incurred to purchase the goods and services a company needs to run its business on a day-to-day basis. The opposite of revenue.   (p. 8)

fair value The amount that a business could sell an asset for, or the amount that a business could pay to settle a liability.   (p. 24)

faithful representation A fundamental qualitative characteristic of accounting information. Information is a faithful representation if it is complete, neutral, accurate, and reflects the economic substance of the underlying transaction or event.   (p. 20)

financial accounting The branch of accounting that provides information for managers inside a business and for decision makers outside the business.   (p. 5)

financial statements The reports that companies use to convey the financial results of their business activities to various user groups, which can include managers, investors, creditors, and regulatory agencies.   (p. 2)

financing activities Activities that result in changes in the size and composition of a company's contributed equity and borrowings.   (p. 15)

fraud The intentional misrepresentation of facts done to persuade another party to act in a way that causes financial damage to that party.   (p. 25)

fraudulent financial reporting The creation of false and misleading accounting records, usually to present a more favourable financial picture.   (p. 26)

gain A type of income other than revenue that results in an increase in economic benefits to a company, and usually occurs outside the course of the company's ordinary business activities.   (p. 8)

generally accepted accounting principles (GAAP) The guidelines of financial accounting, which specify the standards for how accountants must record, measure, and report financial information.   (p. 7)

going-concern assumption The assumption that an entity will continue operating normally for the foreseeable future.   (p. 22)

historical-cost assumption Holds that assets should be recorded at their actual cost, measured on the date of purchase as the amount of cash paid plus the dollar value of all non-cash consideration (other assets, privileges, or rights) also given in exchange.   (p. 23)

income Consists of a company's *revenues* and *gains*.   (p. 8)

income statement The financial statement that measures a company's operating performance for a specified period of time. In particular, it reports income, expenses, and net income. Also called the *statement of profit or loss*.   (p. 8)

International Financial Reporting Standards (IFRS) International accounting standards that specify the *generally accepted accounting principles* which must be applied by *publicly accountable enterprises* in Canada and over 100 other countries.   (p. 7)

investing activities Activities that include the purchase and sale of long-term assets and other investments that result in cash inflows or outflows related to resources used for generating future income and cash flows.   (p. 15)

liability An obligation (or debt) owed by a company, which it expects to pay off in the future using some of its assets.   (p. 14)

liquidity A measure of how quickly an asset can be converted to cash. The higher an asset's liquidity, the more quickly it can be converted to cash.   (p. 13)

long-term asset Another term for *non-current asset*.   (p. 13)

long-term liability Another term for *non-current liability*.   (p. 14)

loss A type of expense that results in a decrease in economic benefits to a company, and usually occurs outside the course of the company's ordinary business activities. The opposite of a gain.   (p. 9)

management accounting The branch of accounting that generates information for the internal decision makers of a business, such as top executives.   (p. 5)

material Accounting information is material if it is significant enough in nature or magnitude that omitting or misstating it could affect the decisions of an informed user.   (p. 21)

misappropriation of assets The theft of assets from a company.   (p. 26)

net assets Another name for *owners' equity*.   (p. 14)

net earnings Another name for *net income*.   (p. 10)

net income The excess of a company's total income over its total expenses. (p. 10)

net loss Occurs when a company's total expenses exceed its total income. (p. 10)

net profit Another term for *net income*. (p. 10)

non-current asset Any asset that is not classified as a current asset. (p. 11)

non-current liability A liability a company expects to pay off beyond one year from the balance sheet date. (p. 14)

operating activities Activities that comprise the main revenue-producing activities of a company, and generally result from the transactions and other events that determine net income. (p. 15)

owners' equity The company owners' remaining interest in the assets of the company after deducting all its liabilities. (p. 14)

partnership An unincorporated business with two or more parties as co-owners, with each owner being a partner in the business. (p. 5)

private enterprise An entity that has not issued and does not plan to issue shares or debt on public markets. (p. 8)

proprietorship An unincorporated business with a single owner, called the proprietor. (p. 5)

publicly accountable enterprises (PAEs) Corporations that have issued or plan to issue shares or debt in a public market. (p. 7)

relevance A fundamental qualitative characteristic of accounting information. Information is relevant if it has predictive value, confirmatory value, or both, and is *material*. (p. 20)

retained earnings Represent the accumulated net income of a company since the day it started business, less any net losses and dividends declared during this time. (p. 10)

revenue Consists of amounts earned by a company in the course of its ordinary, day-to-day business activities. The vast majority of a company's revenue is earned through the sale of its primary goods and services. (p. 8)

separate-entity assumption Holds that the business activities of the reporting entity are separate from the activities of its owners. (p. 22)

shareholder A party who owns shares of a corporation. (p. 6)

shareholders' equity Another term for *owners' equity*. (p. 14)

shares Legal units of ownership in a corporation. (p. 6)

stable-monetary-unit assumption Holds that regardless of the reporting currency used, financial information is always reported under the assumption that the value of the currency is stable, despite the fact that its value does change due to economic factors such as inflation. (p. 22)

statement of cash flows Reports cash receipts and cash payments classified according to the entity's major activities: operating, investing, and financing. (p. 15)

statement of financial position Another name for the *balance sheet*. (p. 11)

statement of profit or loss Another name for the *income statement*. (p. 8)

statement of retained earnings Summary of the changes in the retained earnings of a corporation during a specific period. (p. 10)

verifiability The ability to check financial information for accuracy, completeness, and reliability. (p. 21)

ASSESS YOUR PROGRESS

SHORT EXERCISES

S1-1 Accounting definitions are precise, and you must understand the vocabulary to properly use accounting. Sharpen your understanding of key terms by answering the following questions:

1. How do the *assets* and *shareholders' equity* of Canadian Tire differ from each other? Which one (assets or shareholders' equity) must be at least as large as the other? Which one can be smaller than the other?
2. How are Canadian Tire's *liabilities* and *shareholders' equity* similar? How are they different?

LEARNING OBJECTIVE ❷
Distinguish between assets, liabilities, and equity

S1-2 Use the accounting equation to show how to determine the amount of the missing term in each of the following situations.

LEARNING OBJECTIVE ❷
Apply the accounting equation

Total Assets	=	Total Liabilities	+	Shareholders' Equity
a. $?		$150,000		$150,000
b. 290,000		90,000		?
c. 220,000		?		120,000

S1-3 Review the accounting equation on page 12.

LEARNING OBJECTIVE ❷
Use the accounting equation

1. Use the accounting equation to show how to determine the amount of a company's owners' equity. How would your answer change if you were analyzing your own household or a single Dairy Queen restaurant?
2. If you know assets and owners' equity, how can you measure liabilities? Give the equation.

LEARNING OBJECTIVE ❷

Classify assets, liabilities, and owners' equity

S1-4 Consider Walmart, the world's largest retailer. Classify the following items as an asset (A), a liability (L), or an owners' equity (E) item for Walmart:

_____ **a.** Accounts payable
_____ **b.** Common shares
_____ **c.** Cash
_____ **d.** Retained earnings
_____ **e.** Land
_____ **f.** Prepaid expenses

_____ **g.** Accounts receivable
_____ **h.** Long-term debt
_____ **i.** Merchandise inventories
_____ **j.** Notes payable
_____ **k.** Accrued expenses payable
_____ **l.** Equipment

LEARNING OBJECTIVE ❷

Use the income statement

S1-5

1. Identify the two basic categories of items on an income statement.
2. What do we call the bottom line of the income statement?

LEARNING OBJECTIVE ❷

Prepare an income statement

S1-6 Split Second Wireless Inc. began 2017 with total assets of $110 million and ended 2017 with assets of $160 million. During 2017, Split Second earned revenues of $90 million and had expenses of $20 million. Split Second paid dividends of $10 million in 2017. Prepare the company's income statement for the year ended December 31, 2017, complete with the appropriate heading.

LEARNING OBJECTIVE ❷

Prepare a statement of retained earnings

S1-7 Mondala Ltd. began 2017 with retained earnings of $200 million. Revenues during the year were $400 million and expenses totalled $300 million. Mondala declared dividends of $40 million. What was the company's ending balance of retained earnings? To answer this question, prepare Mondala's statement of retained earnings for the year ended December 31, 2017, complete with its appropriate heading.

LEARNING OBJECTIVE ❷

Prepare a balance sheet

S1-8 At December 31, 2017, Skate Sharp Limited has cash of $13,000, receivables of $2,000, and inventory of $40,000. The company's equipment totals $75,000, and other assets amount to $10,000. Skate Sharp owes accounts payable of $10,000 and short-term notes payable of $5,000, and also has long-term debt of $70,000. Contributed capital is $15,000. Prepare Skate Sharp Limited's balance sheet at December 31, 2017, complete with its appropriate heading.

LEARNING OBJECTIVE ❷

Prepare a statement of cash flows

S1-9 Brazos Medical, Inc., ended 2016 with cash of $24,000. During 2017, Brazos earned net income of $120,000 and had adjustments to reconcile net income to net cash provided by operations totalling $20,000 (this is a negative amount).

Brazos paid $300,000 for equipment during 2017 and had to borrow half of this amount on a long-term note. During the year, the company paid dividends of $15,000 and sold old equipment, receiving cash of $60,000.

Prepare Brazos's statement of cash flows with its appropriate heading for the year ended December 31, 2017. Follow the format in the summary problem on page 31.

LEARNING OBJECTIVE ❹

Apply accounting assumptions

S1-10 John Grant is chairman of the board of The Grant Group Ltd. Suppose Grant has just founded this company, and assume that he treats his home and other personal assets as part of The Grant Group. Answer these questions about the evaluation of The Grant Group.

1. Which accounting assumption governs this situation?
2. How can the proper application of this accounting assumption give John Grant a realistic view of The Grant Group? Explain in detail.

LEARNING OBJECTIVE ❺

Make ethical judgments

S1-11 Accountants follow ethical guidelines in the conduct of their work. What are these standards of professional conduct designed to produce? Why is this goal important?

LEARNING OBJECTIVE ❷

Classify items on the financial statements

S1-12 Suppose you are analyzing the financial statements of a Canadian company. Identify each item with its appropriate financial statement, using the following abbreviations: income statement (IS), statement of retained earnings (SRE), balance sheet (BS), and statement of cash flows (SCF).

Three items appear on two financial statements, and one item shows up on three statements.

a. Dividends _____
b. Salary expense _____
c. Inventory _____
d. Sales revenue _____
e. Retained earnings _____
f. Net cash provided by operating activities _____
g. Net income _____

h. Cash _____
i. Net cash provided by financing activities _____
j. Accounts payable _____
k. Common shares _____
l. Interest revenue _____
m. Long-term debt _____
n. Net increase or decrease in cash _____

EXERCISES

E1-13 Quality Environmental Inc. needs funds, and Mary Wu, the president, has asked you to consider investing in the business. Answer the following questions about the different ways in which Wu might organize the business. Explain each answer.

a. What form of organization will enable the owners of Quality Environmental to limit their risk of loss to the amount they have invested in the business?
b. What form of business organization will give Wu the most freedom to manage the business as she wishes?
c. What form of organization will give creditors the maximum protection in the event that Quality Environmental fails and cannot pay its liabilities?

If you were Wu and could organize the business as you wish, what form of organization would you choose for Quality Environmental? Explain your reasoning.

LEARNING OBJECTIVE ❶
Organize a business

E1-14 Ed Eisler wants to open a café in Digby, Nova Scotia. In need of cash, he asks the Bank of Montreal for a loan. The bank requires financial statements to show likely results of operations for the year and the expected financial position at year-end. With little knowledge of accounting, Eisler doesn't understand the request. Explain to him the information provided by the income statement and the balance sheet. Indicate why a lender would require this information.

LEARNING OBJECTIVE ❷
Describe the purpose of the financial statements

E1-15 Identify the accounting assumption that best applies to each of the following situations.

a. Wendy's, the restaurant chain, sold a store location to Burger King. How can Wendy's determine the sale price of the store: by a professional appraisal, Wendy's cost, or the amount actually received from the sale?
b. If Trammel Crow Realtors had to liquidate its assets, their value would be less than carrying amounts of the assets.
c. Toyota Canada wants to determine which division of the company—Toyota or Lexus—is more profitable.
d. You get an especially good buy on a laptop, paying only $399 for a computer that normally costs $799. What is your accounting value for this computer?

LEARNING OBJECTIVE ❹
Apply accounting assumptions

E1-16 Compute the missing amount in the accounting equation for each company (amounts in millions):

LEARNING OBJECTIVE ❷
Use the accounting equation

	Assets	Liabilities	Shareholders' Equity
TELUS..............................	$?	$10,061	$ 6,926
Scotiabank........................	411,510	?	18,804
Shoppers Drug Mart..........	5,644	2,434	?

E1-17 Assume Maple Leaf Foods Inc. has current assets of $633.6 million, capital assets of $1,126.7 million, and other assets totalling $1,237.5 million. Current liabilities are $591.2 million and long-term liabilities total $1,245.2 million.

LEARNING OBJECTIVE ❷
Use the accounting equation; evaluating a business

Requirements

1. Use these data to write Maple Leaf Foods's accounting equation.
2. How much in resources does Maple Leaf Foods have to work with?
3. How much does Maple Leaf Foods owe creditors?
4. How much of the company's assets do the Maple Leaf Foods shareholders actually own?

LEARNING OBJECTIVE ②

Apply the accounting equation

E1-18 We Store For You Ltd.'s comparative balance sheets at December 31, 2017, and December 31, 2016, report the following (in millions):

	2017	2016
Total assets	$40	$30
Total liabilities	10	8

Requirements

Below are three situations about We Store For You's issuance of shares and payment of dividends during the year ended December 31, 2017. For each situation, use the accounting equation and statement of retained earnings to compute the amount of We Store For You's net income or loss during the year ended December 31, 2017.

1. We Store For You issued shares for $2 million and paid no dividends.
2. We Store For You issued no shares and paid dividends of $3 million.
3. We Store For You issued shares for $11 million and paid dividends of $2 million.

LEARNING OBJECTIVE ②

Apply the accounting equation

E1-19 Answer these questions about two companies:

1. Mortimer Limited began the year with total liabilities of $400,000 and total shareholders' equity of $300,000. During the year, total assets increased by 20%. How much are total assets at the end of the year?
2. Aztec Associates began a year with total assets of $500,000 and total liabilities of $200,000. Net income for the year was $100,000 and no dividends were paid. How much is shareholders' equity at the end of the year?

LEARNING OBJECTIVE ②

Identify financial statement information

E1-20 Assume MySpace Inc. is expanding into the United States. The company must decide where to locate, and how to finance the expansion. Identify the financial statement in which decision makers can find the following information about MySpace Inc. In some cases, more than one statement will report the needed data.

a. Common shares
b. Income tax payable
c. Dividends
d. Income tax expense
e. Ending balance of retained earnings
f. Total assets
g. Long-term debt
h. Revenue
i. Cash spent to acquire equipment

j. Selling, general, and administrative expenses
k. Adjustments to reconcile net income to net cash provided by operations
l. Ending cash balance
m. Current liabilities
n. Net income
o. Cost of goods sold

LEARNING OBJECTIVE ②

Apply the accounting equation; understanding the balance sheet

E1-21 Amounts of the assets and liabilities of Torrance Associates Inc., as of December 31, 2017, are given as follows. Also included are revenue and expense figures for the year ended on that date (amounts in millions):

Property and equipment, net	$ 4	Total revenue	$ 35
Investment	72	Receivables	253
Long-term liabilities	73	Current liabilities	290
Other expenses	14	Common shares	12
Cash	28	Interest expense	3
Retained earnings, beginning	19	Salary and other employee expense	9
Retained earnings, ending	?	Other assets	43

Requirement

Prepare the balance sheet of Torrance Associates Inc. at December 31, 2017. Use the accounting equation to compute ending retained earnings.

E1-22 This exercise should be worked only in connection with exercise E1-21. Refer to the data of Torrance Associates Inc. in E1-21.

LEARNING OBJECTIVE ❷

Understand the income statement

Requirements

1. Prepare the income statement of Torrance Associates Inc. for the year ended December 31, 2017.
2. What amount of dividends did Torrance declare during the year ended December 31, 2017? Hint: Prepare a statement of retained earnings.

E1-23 Groovy Limited began 2017 with $95,000 in cash. During 2017, Groovy earned net income of $300,000, and adjustments to reconcile net income to net cash provided by operations totalled $60,000, a positive amount. Investing activities used cash of $400,000, and financing activities provided cash of $70,000. Groovy ended 2017 with total assets of $250,000 and total liabilities of $110,000.

LEARNING OBJECTIVE ❷

Use the financial statements

Requirement

Prepare Groovy Limited's statement of cash flows for the year ended December 31, 2017. Identify the data items that do not appear on the statement of cash flows and indicate which financial statement reports these items.

E1-24 Assume a FedEx Kinko's at the University of Saskatchewan ended the month of July 2017 with these data:

LEARNING OBJECTIVE ❷

Prepare an income statement and a statement of retained earnings

Payments of cash:		Cash receipts:	
Acquisition of equipment	$36,000	Issuance (sale) of shares to	
Dividends	2,000	owners	$35,000
Retained earnings at July 1, 2017	0	Rent expense	700
Retained earnings at July 31, 2017	?	Common shares	35,000
Utilities expense	200	Equipment	36,000
Adjustments to reconcile net income		Office supplies expense	1,200
to cash provided by operations	3,200	Accounts payable	3,200
Salary expense	4,000	Service revenue	14,000
Cash balance July 1, 2017	0		
Cash balance July 31, 2017	8,100		

Requirement

Prepare the income statement and the statement of retained earnings of this FedEx Kinko's for the month ended July 31, 2017.

E1-25 Refer to the data in the preceding exercise. Prepare the balance sheet of the FedEx Kinko's at July 31, 2017.

LEARNING OBJECTIVE ❷

Prepare a balance sheet

E1-26 Refer to the data in exercise E1-24. Prepare the statement of cash flows of the FedEx Kinko's at the University of Saskatchewan for the month ended July 31, 2017. Draw arrows linking the pertinent items in the statements you prepared for exercises E1-24 through E1-26.

LEARNING OBJECTIVE ❷

Prepare a statement of cash flows

E1-27 This exercise should be used in conjunction with exercises E1-24 through E1-26. The owner of the FedEx Kinko's now seeks your advice as to whether the University of Saskatchewan store should cease operations or continue operating. Write a report giving the owner your opinion of operating results, dividends, financial position, and cash flows during the company's first month of operations. Cite specifics from the financial statements to support your opinion. Conclude your report with advice on whether to stay in business or cease operations.

LEARNING OBJECTIVE ❷

Use financial statements for decision making

E1-28 Apply your understanding of the relationships among the financial statements to answer these questions:

a. How can a business earn large profits but have a small balance of retained earnings?
b. Give two reasons why a business can have a steady stream of net income over a five-year period and still experience a cash shortage.
c. If you could pick a single source of cash for your business, what would it be? Why?
d. How can a business suffer net losses for several years in a row and still have plenty of cash?

PROBLEMS (GROUP A)

P1-29A Assume that the Special Contract Division of FedEx Kinko's experienced the following transactions during the year ended December 31, 2017:

a. Suppose the division provided copy services to a customer for the discounted price of $250,000. Under normal conditions, Kinko's would have provided these services for $280,000. Other revenues totalled $50,000.
b. Salaries cost the division $20,000 to provide these services. The division had to pay employees overtime. Ordinarily, the salary cost for these services would have been $18,000.
c. Other expenses totalled $240,000. Income tax expense was 30% of income before tax.
d. FedEx Kinko's has two operating divisions. Each division is accounted for separately to indicate how well each is performing. At year-end, FedEx Kinko's combines the statements of divisions to show results for FedEx Kinko's as a whole.
e. Inflation affects the amounts that FedEx Kinko's must pay for copy machines. To show the effects of inflation, net income would drop by $3,000.
f. If FedEx Kinko's were to go out of business, the sale of its assets would bring in $150,000 in cash.

Requirements

1. Prepare the Special Contracts Division income statement for the year ended December 31, 2017.
2. As CEO, identify the accounting assumption or characteristics used in accounting for the items described in a through f. State how you have applied the assumption or characteristic in preparing the division income statement.

P1-30A Compute the missing amounts (shown by a ?) for each company (in millions).

	Link Ltd.	Chain Inc.	Fence Corp.
Beginning			
Assets..	$ 78	$ 30	?
Liabilities...	47	19	$ 2
Common shares	6	1	2
Retained earnings..............................	?	10	3
Ending			
Assets..	?	$ 48	$ 9
Liabilities...	$ 48	30	?
Common shares	6	1	2
Retained earnings..............................	27	?	4
Dividends..	$ 3	$ 2	$ 0
Income statement			
Revenues...	$ 216	?	$20
Expenses	211	$144	19
Net income...	?	9	1

At the end of the year, which company has the
- highest net income?
- highest percentage of net income to revenues?

Hint: Prepare a statement of retained earnings to help with your calculations.

P1-31A Dan Shoe, the manager of STRIDES Inc., prepared the company's balance sheet while the accountant was ill. The balance sheet contains numerous errors. In particular, Shoe knew that the balance sheet should balance, so he plugged in the shareholders' equity amount needed to achieve this balance. The shareholders' equity amount is *not* correct. All other amounts are accurate.

LEARNING OBJECTIVE ❷

Understand the balance sheet

	A	B	C	D
1	**STRIDES Inc.** Balance Sheet For the Month Ended July 31, 2017			
2	Assets		Liabilities	
3	Cash	$ 25,000	Accounts receivable	$ 20,000
4	Store fixtures	10,000	Sales revenue	80,000
5	Accounts payable	16,000	Interest expense	800
6	Rent expense	4,000	Note payable	9,000
7	Salaries expense	15,000	Total	109,800
8	Land	44,000		
9	Advertising expense	3,000	**Shareholders' Equity**	
10			Shareholders' equity	7,200
11	Total assets	$ 117,000	Total liabilities and shareholders' equity	$ 117,000
12				

Requirements

1. Prepare the correct balance sheet and date it properly. Compute total assets, total liabilities, and shareholders' equity.
2. Is STRIDES Inc. actually in better or worse financial position than the erroneous balance sheet reports? Give the reason for your answer.
3. Identify the accounts listed on the incorrect balance sheet that are not reported on the balance sheet. State why you excluded them from the correct balance sheet you prepared for Requirement 1. On which financial statement should these accounts appear?

P1-32A Alexa Markowitz is a realtor. She buys and sells properties on her own, and she also earns commission as an agent for buyers and sellers. She organized her business as a corporation on March 16, 2017. The business received $60,000 cash from Markowitz and issued common shares in return. Consider the following facts as of March 31, 2017:

LEARNING OBJECTIVE ❷❹

Understand the balance sheet, entity assumption

a. Markowitz has $5,000 in her personal bank account and $14,000 in the business bank account.
b. Office supplies on hand at the real estate office total $1,000.
c. Markowitz's business spent $25,000 for a ReMax franchise, which entitles her to represent herself as an agent. ReMax is a national affiliation of independent real estate agents. This franchise is a business asset.
d. The business owes $60,000 on a note payable for some undeveloped land acquired for a total price of $110,000.
e. Markowitz owes $100,000 on a personal mortgage on her personal residence, which she acquired in 2005 for a total price of $350,000.
f. Markowitz owes $1,800 on a personal charge account with Holt Renfrew.
g. Markowitz acquired business furniture for $10,000 on March 25. Of this amount, the business owes $6,000 on accounts payable at March 31.

Requirements

1. Prepare the balance sheet of the real estate business of Alexa Markowitz Realtor Inc. at March 31, 2017.
2. Does it appear that the realty business can pay its debts? How can you tell?
3. Explain why some of the items given in the preceding facts were not reported on the balance sheet of the business.

LEARNING OBJECTIVE ❸

Prepare and use the income statement, statement of retained earnings, and balance sheet

P1-33A The assets and liabilities of Web Services Inc. as of December 31, 2017 and revenues and expenses for the year ended on that date are listed here.

Land	$ 8,000	Equipment	$ 11,000
Note payable	32,000	Interest expense	4,000
Property tax expense	2,000	Interest payable	2,000
Rent expense	15,000	Accounts payable	15,000
Accounts receivable	25,000	Salary expense	40,000
Service revenue	150,000	Building	126,000
Supplies	2,000	Cash	8,000
Utilities expense	3,000	Common shares	15,000

Beginning retained earnings were $60,000, and dividends totalled $30,000 for the year.

Requirements

1. Prepare the income statement of Web Services Inc. for the year ended December 31, 2017.
2. Prepare the company's statement of retained earnings for the year.
3. Prepare the company's balance sheet at December 31, 2017.
4. As CEO of Web Services Inc., answer the following questions and then decide if you would be pleased with Web Services's overall performance in 2017.
   a. Was Web Services profitable during 2017? By how much?
   b. Did retained earnings increase or decrease? By how much?
   c. Which is greater: total liabilities or total equity? Who owns more of Web Services's assets: creditors or Web Services's shareholders?

LEARNING OBJECTIVE ❷

Prepare a statement of cash flows

P1-34A The following data are from financial statements of Stuart Inc. for the fiscal year ended March 1, 2017 (in millions):

Purchases of capital assets and other assets	$ 144	Accounts receivable	$168
		Repurchase of common shares	177
Issuance of long-term debt	164	Payment of dividends	31
Net loss	(251)	Common shares	715
Adjustments to reconcile net income (loss) to cash provided by operations	397	Issuance of common shares	1
		Sales of capital assets and other assets	1
Revenues	1,676	Retained earnings	752
Cash, beginning of year	41	Repayment of long-term debt	1
Cash, end of year	0		
Cost of goods sold	1,370		

Requirements

1. Prepare a statement of cash flows for the fiscal year ended March 1, 2017. Follow the format of the summary problem on page 31. Not all items given are reported in the statement of cash flows.
2. What was the largest source of cash? Is this a sign of financial strength or weakness?

P1-35A Summarized versions of the Gonzales Corporation's financial statements are given below for two years.

LEARNING OBJECTIVE ❷❸

Analyze a company's financial statements; explain relationships among the financial statements

	(in thousands)	
	2017	**2016**
Statement of Income		
Revenues	$ k	$16,000
Cost of goods sold	11,500	a
Other expenses	1,300	1,200
Earnings before income taxes	4,000	3,700
Income taxes (35% tax rate)	l	1,300
Net earnings	$ m	$ b
Statement of Retained Earnings		
Beginning balance	$ n	$ 3,500
Net earnings	o	c
Dividends	(300)	(200)
Ending balance	$ p	$ d
Balance Sheet		
Assets:		
Cash	$ q	$ e
Capital assets	3,000	1,800
Other assets	r	11,200
Total assets	$ s	$15,000
Liabilities:		
Current liabilities	$ t	$ 5,600
Notes payable and long-term debt	4,500	3,200
Other liabilities	80	200
Total liabilities	$ 9,100	$ f
Shareholders' Equity:		
Common shares	$ 300	$ 300
Retained earnings	u	g
Total shareholders' equity	v	6,000
Total liabilities and shareholders' equity	$ w	$ h
Statement of Cash Flows		
Net cash provided by operating activities	$ x	$ 1,900
Net cash used for investing activities	(1,000)	(900)
Net cash used for financing activities	(700)	(1.010)
Increase (decrease) in cash	400	i
Cash at beginning of year	y	2,010
Cash at end of year	$ z	$ j

Requirements

1. Determine the missing amounts denoted by the letters.
2. As Gonzales Corporation's CEO, use the financial statements to answer these questions about the company. Explain each of your answers, and identify the financial statement where you found the information.
   a. Did operations improve or deteriorate during 2017?
   b. What is the company doing with most of its income—retaining it for use in the business or using it for dividends?
   c. How much in total resources does the company have to work with as it moves into the year 2018?

d. At the end of 2016, how much did the company owe outsiders? At the end of 2017, how much did the company owe? Is this trend good or bad in comparison to the trend in assets?

e. What is the company's major source of cash? Is cash increasing or decreasing? What is your opinion of the company's ability to generate cash?

LEARNING OBJECTIVE ❷❸

Understand the balance sheet, entity assumption

P1-36A Blackwell Services, Inc., has current assets of $240 million; property, plant, and equipment of $350 million; and other assets totaling $170 million. Current liabilities are $150 million, and long-term liabilities total $360 million.

Requirements

1. Use these data to write Blackwell Services, Inc.'s, accounting equation.
2. How much in resources does Blackwell Services have to work with?
3. How much does Blackwell Services owe creditors?
4. How much of the company's assets do the Blackwell Services shareholders actually own?

PROBLEMS (GROUP B)

LEARNING OBJECTIVE ❷❸❹

Apply assumptions and characteristics to the income statement

P1-37B Snap Fasteners Inc. experienced the following transactions during the year ended December 31, 2017:

a. All other expenses, excluding income taxes, totalled $14.9 million for the year. Income tax expense was 35% of income before tax.

b. Snap has several operating divisions. Each division is accounted for separately to show how well each division is performing. However, Snap's financial statements combine the statements of all the divisions to report on the company as a whole.

c. Inflation affects Snap's cost to manufacture goods. If Snap's financial statements were to show the effects of inflation, assume the company's reported net income would drop by $0.250 million.

d. If Snap were to go out of business, the sale of its assets might bring in over $5 million in cash.

e. Snap sold products for $56.2 million. Company management believes that the value of these products is approximately $60.5 million.

f. It cost Snap $40.0 million to manufacture the products it sold. If Snap had purchased the products instead of manufacturing them, Snap's cost would have been $43.0 million.

Requirements

1. Prepare Snap's income statement for the year ended December 31, 2017.
2. For items a through f, identify the accounting assumption or characteristic that determined how you accounted for the item described. State how you have applied the assumption or characteristic in preparing Snap's income statement.

LEARNING OBJECTIVE ❷❸❹

Apply assumptions and characteristics to the income statement

P1-38B The assets and liabilities of Beckwith Garden Supply, Inc., as of December 31, 2017, and revenues and expenses for the year ended on that date follow:

Equipment	$119,000
Interest expense...	10,200
Interest payable	2,500
Accounts payable...	24,000
Salary expense...	108,500
Building	401,000
Cash...	41,000
Common shares	12,700

Land	$ 27,000
Note payable	99,500
Property tax expense	7,300
Rent expense	40,600
Accounts receivable	84,600
Service revenue	457,600
Supplies	6,800
Utilities expense	8,500

Beginning retained earnings was $364,200, and dividends declared totaled $106,000 for the year.

Requirements

1. Prepare the income statement of Beckwith Garden Supply, Inc., for the year ended December 31, 2017.
2. Prepare the company's statement of retained earnings for the year.
3. Prepare the company's balance sheet at December 31, 2017.
4. Analyze Beckwith Garden Supply, Inc., by answering these questions:
   a. Was Beckwith Garden Supply profitable during 2017? By how much?
   b. Did retained earnings increase or decrease? By how much?
   c. Which is greater, total liabilities or total shareholders' equity? Who has a greater claim to Beckwith Garden Supply's assets, creditors of the company or the Beckwith Garden Supply shareholders?

P1-39B Compute the missing amounts (?) for each company (in millions).

LEARNING OBJECTIVE ❷❸

Apply the accounting equation; understand the financial statements

	Gas Limited	Groceries Inc.	Bottler Corp.
Beginning			
Assets	$11,200	$ 3,256	$ 909
Liabilities	4,075	1,756	564
Ending			
Assets	$12,400	$?	$1,025
Liabilities	4,400	1,699	565
Owners' Equity			
Issuance (Repurchase) of shares	$ (36)	$ (0)	$?
Dividends	341	30	0
Income Statement			
Revenues	$11,288	$11,099	$1,663
Expenses	?	10,879	1,568

Which company has the
- highest net income?
- highest percentage of net income to revenues?

Hint: Prepare a statement of owners' equity, which begins with opening shareholders' equity and adds and subtracts changes to conclude with closing shareholders' equity.

P1-40B Ned Robinson, the manager of Lunenberg Times Inc., prepared the balance sheet of the company while the accountant was ill. The balance sheet contains numerous errors. In particular, the manager knew that the balance sheet should balance, so he plugged in

LEARNING OBJECTIVE ❷

Understand the balance sheet

the shareholders' equity amount needed to achieve this balance. The shareholders' equity amount, however, is *not* correct. All other amounts are accurate.

	A	B	C	D
1	**Lunenberg Times Inc.** Balance Sheet For the Month Ended October 31, 2017			
2	Assets		Liabilities	
3	Cash	$ 25,000	Accounts receivable	$ 10,000
4	Office furniture	15,000	Sales revenue	70,000
5	Note payable	16,000	Salary expense	20,000
6	Rent expense	4,000	Accounts payable	8,000
7	Inventory	30,000		
8	Land	34,000	**Shareholders' Equity**	
9	Advertising expense	2,500	Shareholders' equity	18,500
10	Total assets	$ 126,000	Total liabilities	$ 126,500
11				

Requirements

1. Prepare the correct balance sheet, and date it properly. Compute total assets, total liabilities, and shareholders' equity.
2. Is Lunenberg Times Inc. actually in better or worse financial position than the erroneous balance sheet reports? Give the reason for your answer.
3. Identify the accounts listed in the incorrect balance sheet that are *not* reported on the corrected balance sheet. State why you excluded them from the correct balance sheet you prepared for Requirement 1. Which financial statement should these accounts appear on?

LEARNING OBJECTIVE ❷❹

Understand the balance sheet, entity assumption

P1-41B Luis Fantano is a realtor. He buys and sells properties on his own and also earns commission as an agent for buyers and sellers. Fantano organized his business as a corporation on July 10, 2017. The business received $75,000 from Fantano and issued common shares in return. Consider these facts as of July 31, 2017:

a. Fantano owes $5,000 on a personal charge account with Visa.
b. Fantano's business owes $80,000 on a note payable for some undeveloped land acquired for a total price of $135,000.
c. Fantano has $5,000 in his personal bank account and $10,000 in the business bank account.
d. Office supplies on hand at the real estate office total $1,000.
e. Fantano's business spent $35,000 for a Century 21 real estate franchise, which entitles him to represent himself as a Century 21 agent. Century 21 is a national affiliation of independent real estate agents. This franchise is a business asset.
f. Fantano owes $125,000 on a personal mortgage on his personal residence, which he acquired in 2004 for a total price of $300,000.
g. Fantano acquired business furniture for $18,000 on July 15. Of this amount, his business owes $10,000 on open account at July 31.

Requirements

1. Prepare the balance sheet of the realty business of Luis Fantano Realtor Inc. at July 31, 2017.
2. Does it appear that Fantano's realty business can pay its debts? How can you tell?
3. Identify the personal items given in the preceding facts that would not be reported on the balance sheet of the business.

P1-42B The assets and liabilities of Auto Mechanics Ltd. as of December 31, 2017, and revenues and expenses for the year ended on that date follow.

LEARNING OBJECTIVE ❷❸

Understand the income statement, statement of retained earnings, balance sheet; explain relationships among the financial statements

Interest expense	$ 4,000	Accounts receivable	$ 25,000
Land	95,000	Advertising expense	10,000
Note payable	95,000	Building	140,000
Accounts payable	21,000	Salary expense	85,000
Rent expense	6,000	Salary payable	12,000
Cash	10,000	Service revenue	210,000
Common shares	75,000	Supplies	3,000
Furniture	20,000	Property tax expense	5,000

Beginning retained earnings were $40,000, and dividends totalled $50,000 for the year.

Requirements
1. Prepare the income statement of Auto Mechanics Ltd. for the year ended December 31, 2017.
2. Prepare the Auto Mechanics Ltd. statement of retained earnings for the year.
3. Prepare Auto Mechanics's balance sheet at December 31, 2017.
4. Use the information prepared in Requirements 1 through 3 to answer the following:
   a. Was Auto Mechanics Ltd. profitable during 2017? By how much?
   b. Did retained earnings increase or decrease? By how much?
   c. Which is greater: total liabilities or total equity? Who has a claim against more of Auto Mechanics Ltd.'s assets: the creditors or the shareholders?

P1-43B The data below are adapted from the financial statements of Long Boat Ltd. at the end of a recent year (in thousands).

LEARNING OBJECTIVE ❷

Prepare a statement of cash flows

Adjustments to reconcile net income		Sales of capital assets	$ 2
to cash provided by operations	$ 65	Payment of long-term debt	26
Revenues	3,870	Cost of goods sold	3,182
Bank overdraft, beginning of year	(11)	Common shares	212
Cash, end of year	23	Accounts receivable	271
Purchases of capital assets	123	Issuance of common shares	4
Long-term debt	234	Change in bank loan	(44)
Net income	180	Payment of dividends	24
Retained earnings	1,000		

Requirements
1. Prepare Long Boat's statement of cash flows for the year. Follow the solution to the summary problem starting on page 30. Not all the items given appear on the statement of cash flows.
2. Which activities provided the bulk of Long Boat's cash? Is this a sign of financial strength or weakness?

LEARNING OBJECTIVE ❷❸

Analyze a company's financial
statements; explain relationships
among the financial statements

P1-44B Condensed versions of Your Phone Ltd.'s financial statements, with certain amounts
omitted, are given for two years.

	(thousands)	
	2017	**2016**
Statement of Income		
Revenues	$94,500	$ a
Cost of goods sold	k	65,400
Other expenses	15,660	13,550
Income before income taxes	5,645	9,300
Income taxes	1,975	3,450
Net income	$ l	$ b
Statement of Retained Earnings		
Beginning balance	$ m	$10,000
Net income	n	c
Dividends	(480)	(450)
Ending balance	$ o	$ d
Balance Sheet		
Assets:		
Cash	$ p	$ 400
Capital assets	23,790	e
Other assets	q	17,900
Total assets	$ r	$38,500
Liabilities:		
Current liabilities	$11,100	$10,000
Long-term debt and other liabilities	s	12,500
Total liabilities	24,500	f
Shareholders' Equity:		
Common shares	$ 400	$ 600
Retained earnings	t	g
Total shareholders' equity	u	16,000
Total liabilities and shareholders' equity	$ v	$ h
Statement of Cash Flows		
Net cash provided by operating activities	$ w	$ 3,600
Net cash used for investing activities	(2,700)	(4,150)
Net cash provided by financing activities	250	900
Increase (decrease) in cash	50	i
Cash at beginning of year	x	50
Cash at end of year	$ y	$ j

Requirements

1. Determine the missing amounts denoted by the letters.
2. Use Your Phone's financial statements to answer these questions about the company.
   Explain each of your answers.
   a. Did operations improve or deteriorate during 2017?
   b. What is the company doing with most of its income—retaining it for use in the business
      or using it for dividends?
   c. How much in total resources does the company have to work with as it moves into
      2018? How much in total resources did the company have at the end of 2016?
   d. At the end of 2016, how much did the company owe outsiders? At the end of 2017,
      how much did the company owe?
   e. What is the company's major source of cash? What is your opinion of the company's
      ability to generate cash? How is the company using most of its cash? Is the company
      growing or shrinking?

APPLY YOUR KNOWLEDGE

DECISION CASES

This section's material reflects CPA enabling competencies,* including:

1. Professionalism and ethical behaviour
2. Problem-solving and decision-making
3. Communication
4. Self-management
5. Teamwork and leadership

Case 1. Two businesses, Web Services and PC Providers, have sought business loans from you. To decide whether to make the loans, you have requested their balance sheets.

	A	B	C	D
1	**Web Services** Balance Sheet As at October 31, 2017			
2	**Assets**		**Liabilities**	
3	Cash	$ 11,000	Accounts payable	$ 13,000
4	Accounts receivable	4,000	Notes payable	377,000
5	Furniture	36,000	Total liabilities	390,000
6	Software	79,000	**Shareholders' Equity**	
7	Computers	300,000	Shareholders' equity	40,000
8	Total assets	$ 430,000	Total liabilities and shareholders' equity	$430,000
9				

LEARNING OBJECTIVE ❷

Evaluate business operations; use financial statements

	A	B	C	D
1	**PC Providers Inc.** Balance Sheet As at October 31, 2017			
2	**Assets**		**Liabilities**	
3	Cash	$ 9,000	Accounts payable	$ 12,000
4	Accounts receivable	24,000	Note payable	28,000
5	Merchandise inventory	85,000	Total liabilities	40,000
6	Furniture and fixtures	9,000		
7	Building	82,000	**Shareholders' Equity**	
8	Land	14,000	Shareholders' equity	183,000
9	Total assets	$ 223,000	Total liabilities and shareholders' equity	$ 223,000
10				

Requirements

1. Using only these balance sheets, to which entity would you be more comfortable lending money? Explain fully, citing specific items and amounts from the respective balance sheets.
2. Is there other financial information you would consider before making your decision? Be specific.

Case 2. After you have been out of college for a year, you have $5,000 to invest. A friend has started My Dream Inc., and she asks you to invest in her company. You obtain My Dream Inc.'s financial statements, which are summarized at the end of the first year as follows:

LEARNING OBJECTIVE ❷

Analyze a company's financial statements

	A	B	C	D
1	**My Dream Inc.** Income Statement For the Year Ended December 31, 2017			
2	Revenues	$ 80,000		
3	Expenses	60,000		
4	Net income	$ 20,000		
5				

*© Chartered Professional Accountants of Canada.

	A	B	C	D	E
1	**My Dream Inc.** Balance Sheet As at December 31, 2017				
2	Cash	$ 13,000	Liabilities	$ 35,000	
3	Other assets	67,000	Equity	45,000	
4	Total assets	$ 80,000	Total liabilities and equity	$ 80,000	
5					

Visits with your friend turn up the following facts:

a. The company owes an additional $10,000 for TV ads that was incurred in December but not recorded in the books.

b. Software costs of $20,000 were recorded as assets. These costs should have been expensed. My Dream paid cash for these expenses and recorded the cash payment correctly.

c. Revenues and receivables of $10,000 were overlooked and omitted.

Requirements

1. Prepare corrected financial statements.

2. Use your corrected statements to evaluate My Dream's results of operations and financial position.

3. Will you invest in My Dream? Give your reason.

ETHICAL ISSUES

LEARNING OBJECTIVE ⑤

Make ethical business decisions

Issue 1: You are studying frantically for an accounting exam tomorrow. You are having difficulty in this course, and the grade you make on this exam can make the difference between receiving a final grade of B or C. If you receive a C, it will lower your grade point average to the point that you could lose your academic scholarship. An hour ago, a friend, also enrolled in the course but in a different section under the same professor, called you with some unexpected news. In her sorority test files, she has just found a copy of an old exam from the previous year. In looking at the exam, it appears to contain questions that come right from the class notes you have taken, even the very same numbers. She offers to make a copy for you and bring it over.

You glance at your course syllabus and find the following: "You are expected to do your own work in this class. Although you may study with others, giving, receiving, or obtaining information pertaining to an examination is considered an act of academic dishonesty, unless such action is authorized by the instructor giving the examination. Also, divulging the contents of an essay or objective examination designated by the instructor as an examination is considered an act of academic dishonesty. Academic dishonesty is considered a violation of the student honour code and will subject the student to disciplinary procedures, which can include suspension from the university." Although you have heard a rumour that fraternities and sororities have cleared their exam files with professors, you are not sure.

Requirements

1. What is the ethical issue in this situation?

2. Who are the stakeholders? What are the possible consequences to each?

3. Analyze the alternatives from the following standpoints: (a) economic, (b) legal, and (c) ethical.

4. What would you do? How would you justify your decision? How would your decision make you feel afterward?

5. How is this similar to a business situation?

Issue 2: Jane Hill, an accountant for Stainton Hardware Inc., discovers that her supervisor, Drew Armor, made several errors last year. Overall, the errors overstated Stainton Hardware's net income by 20%. It is not clear whether the errors were deliberate or accidental. What should Jane Hill do?

FOCUS ON FINANCIALS

Canadian Tire Corporation

LEARNING OBJECTIVE ❷
Evaluate business operations

This case is based on the financial statements of Canadian Tire, which you can find in Appendix A at the back of the book and on MyAccountingLab. As you work with Canadian Tire's financial statements throughout this course, you will develop the ability to use actual financial statements.

MyAccountingLab

Requirements

1. Suppose you own shares in Canadian Tire. If you could pick one item on the company's income statement to increase year after year, what would it be? Why is this item so important? Did this item increase or decrease during the year ended January 3, 2015? Is this good news or bad news for the company?

2. What was Canadian Tire's largest expense each year? In your own words, explain the meaning of this item. Give specific examples of items that make up this expense. Why is this expense less than sales revenue?

3. Use the balance sheet as at January 3, 2015, to answer these questions. At January 3, 2015, how much in total resources did Canadian Tire have to work with? How much did the company owe? How much of its assets did the company's shareholders actually own? Use these amounts to write Canadian Tire's accounting equation at January 3, 2015 (express all items in thousands of dollars).

4. How much cash did Canadian Tire have at December 28, 2013? How much cash did it have at January 3, 2015? Where does Canadian Tire get most of its cash? How does the company spend its cash?

FOCUS ON ANALYSIS

Canadian Tire Corporation

LEARNING OBJECTIVE ❷
Evaluate a company by using
financial statements

This case is based on the financial statements of Canadian Tire, which can be found in Appendix A at the back of the book and on MyAccountingLab. As you work with Canadian Tire throughout this course, you will develop the ability to analyze financial statements of actual companies.

MyAccountingLab

Requirements

1. Does Canadian Tire's financial condition look strong or weak? How can you tell?

2. What was the result of Canadian Tire's operations during 2014? Identify both the name and the dollar value of the result of operations for 2014. Does an increase (decrease) signal good news or bad news for the company and its shareholders?

3. Which statement reports cash as part of Canadian Tire's financial position? Which statement tells why cash increased (or decreased) during the year? What items caused Canadian Tire's cash to change the most in 2014?

GROUP PROJECT

Project 1. As instructed by your professor, obtain an annual report of a Canadian company.

Requirements

1. Take the role of a loan committee of the Royal Bank of Canada. Assume the company has requested a loan from your bank. Analyze the company's financial statements and any other information you need to reach a decision regarding the largest amount of money you

would be willing to lend. Go as deeply into the analysis and the related decision as you can. Specify the following:

a. Any restrictions you would impose on the borrower.

b. The length of the loan period (that is, over what period you will allow the company to pay you back).

Note: The long-term debt note to the financial statements gives details of the company's liabilities.

2. Write your group decision in a report addressed to the bank's board of directors. Limit your report to two double-spaced word-processed pages.

3. If your professor directs you to, present your decision and analysis to the class. Limit your presentation to 10–15 minutes.

Project 1. You are the owner of a company that is about to "go public" (that is, issue its shares to outside investors). You wish to make your company look as attractive as possible to raise $1 million in cash to expand the business. At the same time, you want to give potential investors a reliable and relevant picture of your company.

Requirements

1. Design a presentation to portray your company in a way that will enable outsiders to reach an informed decision as to whether to invest in your company. The presentation should include the following:

a. Name and location of your company.

b. Nature of the company's business (be specific and detailed to provide a clear picture of the nature, history, and future goals of the business).

c. How you plan to spend the money you raise.

d. The company's comparative income statement, statement of retained earnings, balance sheet, and statement of cash flows for two years: the current year and the preceding year. Make the data as realistic as possible with the intent of receiving $1 million.

2. Prepare a word-processed presentation that does not exceed five pages.

3. If directed by your professor, distribute copies of your presentation to the class with the intent of enticing your classmates to invest in your company. Make a 10- to 15-minute investment pitch to the class. Measure your success by the amount of investment commitment you receive.

CHECK YOUR WORK

STOP + THINK ANSWERS

STOP + THINK (1-1)

1. The business is incorporated with two shareholders, so it is a corporation.

2. The business is unincorporated and the owners share the workload and profits, so it is a partnership.

3. The business is unincorporated and run by Agata alone, so it is a proprietorship.

STOP + THINK (1-2)

1. $160,000 ($240,000 − $80,000)

2. $290,000 ($160,000 + $130,000)

3. Net income of $44,000 ($129,000 − $85,000); income minus expenses.

4. $115,000 [$100,000 beginning balance + net income of $25,000 ($75,000 − $50,000) − dividends of $10,000]

STOP + THINK (1-3)

After correcting for the missing $1,000 cash sale of services on December 31, 2017, Huron Ltd.'s financial statements would change as follows:

Income Statement

- Income will increase to $701,000 due to the extra $1,000 in sales revenue.
- Net income will increase to $31,000 because of the $1,000 increase in income.

Statement of Retained Earnings

- Ending retained earnings will increase to $141,000 due to the $1,000 increase in net income.

Balance Sheet

- Cash will increase to $26,000 because of the $1,000 in cash received from the customer.
- Total assets will increase to $301,000 after the $1,000 increase in cash.
- Retained earnings will increase to $141,000 (see above).
- Total liabilities and shareholders' equity will increase to $301,000 due to the $1,000 increase in retained earnings.

Statement of Cash Flows

- Net cash provided by operating activities will increase to $91,000 as a result of the $1,000 increase in net income.
- The Net increase in cash will now be $21,000 as a result of the added $1,000 in cash from operating activities.
- The ending cash balance will now be $26,000, which agrees to the new cash balance on the balance sheet noted above.

STOP + THINK (1-4)

1. According to the historical-cost assumption, the land would be recorded at a value of $46,000, its initial actual cost.

2. According to the historical-cost and going-concern assumptions, no adjustment would be made to the value of the land despite its increase in value to $60,000. IFRS do permit companies to adjust assets such as land to their fair values, but it is rare for companies to actually make these adjustments. Even under IFRS, assets are almost always left on the books at their historical costs.

STOP + THINK (1-5)

What Is the Issue?

Your boss has asked you to engage in fraudulent financial reporting by intentionally recording $1.2 million in fictitious sales to increase net income to a level that exceeds analysts' predicted amount.

Who Are the Stakeholders, and What Are the Consequences of the Decision to Each of Them?

You: If you do what the CEO wants, the CEO will be pleased and you may be rewarded with a bonus or promotion, but you will also have committed fraud and if it is ever discovered, you will be subject to criminal charges. If you have a CPA designation, you would also lose that if the fraud is discovered. If you do not do what the CEO wants, you may be fired or demoted, the company's share price may decline as a result of missing the analysts' forecast, and the CEO's reputation as a good manager could be tarnished, but you will not have committed fraud and therefore will not have to worry about losing your designation or being criminally charged.

CEO: If you do what the CEO wants, net income will come in above analysts' predictions, so the CEO will look like a good manager of the company's affairs and may be rewarded with a bonus and stock options. The value of any shares he owns may also increase, or at least will be less likely to decrease, so his wealth will benefit, but they would also be subject to criminal charges if the fraud is uncovered. If you do not do what the CEO wants, the company's share price may decline as a result of missing the analysts' forecast, and the CEO's reputation as a good manager could be tarnished, but they will not have committed fraud and therefore will not have to worry about being criminally charged.

Shareholders: If you do what the CEO wants, the value of the company's shares may increase, or at least will be less likely to decrease, so the shareholders' wealth will benefit in the short term, but if the fraud is eventually uncovered, the share price will likely drop drastically, perhaps all the way to zero, and all the shareholders will suffer significant financial losses. If you do not do what the CEO wants, the company's share price may decline in the short term as a result of missing the analysts' forecast, but if the CEO and other company managers can improve performance in future years, the share price may turn around, so in the long run, shareholders may end up much better off financially.

What Are the Decision Alternatives and How do they Affect Each Stakeholder?

The main alternatives are to do what the CEO asks and record the fictitious sales or to decline the request and leave the records as is. See above for the impact of each of these alternatives on the key stakeholders.

What Decision Alternative will you Choose?

The best decision from an ethical, legal, and long-term economic perspective is to leave the records as is and report the truthful results for the year. While this is the obvious best response, many accountants in practice have engaged in such fraudulent financial reporting because they viewed some of the other personal and wealth-related consequences above to outweigh the legal, ethical, and economic benefits of not engaging in fraud.

QUICK QUIZ ANSWERS

1. *a*
2. *a*
3. *c*
4. *a* ($20,000 – $4,000 = $16,000)
5. *b*
6. *d*
7. *b*
8. *b*
9. *d*
10. *b* ($140,000 – $59,000 – $8,000 – $3,000 = $70,000)
11. *a* ($145,000 + $90,000 – $30,000 = $205,000)
12. *c*

13. *c*
14. *a*

	Assets	=	Liabilities	+	Shareholders' Equity
beg.	$25,000		$10,000		$15,000
change	+11,000		+8,000		+3,000
end	$36,000		$18,000		$18,000

15. *c*

	Assets	=	Liabilities	+	Shareholders' equity
2016	$520,000		$200,000		$320,000
2017	$750,000		$300,000		$450,000

$450,000 + $50,000 – 320,000 = $180,000

Recording Business Transactions

Hitoshi Yamada/ZUMA Press/Newscom

SPOTLIGHT

How do you manage information in your busy life? You may use many of thousands of apps on Apple's iPhone for texting, listening to music, or checking the weather or sports scores. You may use an iPad for reading your favourite books or playing your favourite game. The iPhone, iPad, and Apple Watch, in addition to the company's popular MacBook computers, have generated billions of dollars in profits for the company.

Apple Inc. is a U.S.-based multinational corporation that designs and manufactures consumer electronics. The company operates more than 400 retail stores worldwide and an online store where hardware and software products are sold. How does Apple determine its revenues, expenses, and net income? Like all other companies, Apple has a comprehensive accounting system. Apple's income statement is displayed on the next page. The income statement shows that during fiscal year 2014, Apple sold over $180 billion of merchandise and earned net income of almost $40 billion. Where did these figures come from? In this chapter, we'll show you.

	A	B	C
1	**Apple Inc.** Income Statement (Adapted) Fiscal Year Ended September 27, 2014		
2	*(in billions)*	**2014**	
3	Net sales	$ 182.8	
4	Cost of goods sold	112.3	
5	Gross profit	70.5	
6	Operating expenses:		
7	Research and development	6.0	
8	Selling, general, and administrative	12.0	
9	Total operating expenses	18.0	
10	Operating income	52.5	
11	Other income	1.0	
12	Income before income taxes	53.5	
13	Income tax expense	14.0	
14	Net income	$ 39.5	
15			

Source: Apple Annual Report - For the Fiscal Year Ended September 27, 2014.

Businesses engage in many different activities, and most of these activities result in transactions that must be recorded in the accounting records. A **transaction** is any event that has a financial impact on a business and that can be reliably measured. For example, Apple pays programmers to create iTunes software. Apple also sells computers, buys other companies, and repays debts. All four of these activities generate transactions that affect Apple's financial statements.

But not all activities qualify as transactions. The iPhone may be featured in TV ads, for example, which motivates some people to *consider* buying one. No transaction occurs, however, until someone *actually buys* an iPhone, which results in a positive financial impact on the company. A transaction must occur before Apple records anything in its accounting records.

Before we can record a transaction, we must also be able to reliably assign a dollar value to it, so that we have a measure of its financial impact on the business. If you were to purchase an iPhone from Apple's online store for $500, then Apple could reliably assign a dollar value to the transaction and it would then be permissible to record this sale in its accounting records.

DESCRIBE COMMON TYPES OF ACCOUNTS

OBJECTIVE

❶ **Describe** common types of accounts

Recall the accounting equation introduced in Chapter 1:

Assets = Liabilities + Shareholders' Equity

Each asset, liability, and element of shareholders' equity has its own **account**, which is used to record all the transactions affecting the related asset, liability, or element of shareholders' equity during an accounting period. Before we start learning how to record transactions in accounts, let's review some common types of accounts that companies such as Apple have in their accounting records.

Asset Accounts

Most companies have the following asset accounts in their accounting records:

CASH. Cash consists of bank account balances, paper currency and coins, and undeposited cheques.

ACCOUNTS RECEIVABLE. Accounts Receivable represent the amounts owing from customers who have purchased goods or services but not yet paid for them. In other words, they have purchased goods or services *on account* or *on credit.* The seller will *receive* payments on these *accounts* at some point in the near future. If Apple sells $1 million worth of iPads to a customer who promises to pay within 30 days, it would have an account receivable of $1 million.

INVENTORY. Inventory consists of the goods a company sells to its customers. Apple's inventory includes the iPhones, Apple Watches, and other products you see in its stores and advertisements. Companies that make the products they sell also have inventory consisting of the raw materials used to produce the finished products (e.g., the screens used to make iPhones) and any partially finished products (e.g., half-assembled MacBook computers).

PREPAID EXPENSES. Prepaid Expenses are expenses a company has paid for in advance of actually using the product or service it has purchased. If, for example, on September 15, 2017, Apple paid $2 million for TV advertising time during the Super Bowl at the end of January 2018, this amount would be included in prepaid expenses on September 30, 2017, because Apple will not realize the benefit of this expense until the ads run four months after its September year-end.

LAND. This account includes any land a company owns.

BUILDINGS. Any office buildings, factories, and other buildings owned by a company are included in the Buildings account.

EQUIPMENT, FURNITURE, AND FIXTURES. These accounts include a variety of office, computer, and manufacturing equipment, as well as any furniture and fixtures owned by a company.

Liability Accounts

You will see the following liability accounts in the accounting records of many companies:

ACCOUNTS PAYABLE. Accounts Payable represent the amounts a company owes to suppliers who have sold the company goods or services on credit. If Apple buys $1 million worth of flash drives from a supplier and promises to pay within 30 days, it would have an account payable of $1 million.

ACCRUED LIABILITIES. An accrued liability is a liability for an expense that has not been billed for or paid. Examples include interest owed on bank loans, salaries owed to employees, and amounts owed to suppliers who have not yet sent invoices requesting payment.

LOANS PAYABLE. Loans Payable include funds a company has borrowed from banks and other creditors to finance its business activities.

Shareholders' Equity Accounts

The Shareholders' Equity accounts found in a corporation's accounting records include the following:

SHARE CAPITAL. The Share Capital account includes the capital (usually in the form of cash) a company has received from its owners in exchange for shares of the company. This account is sometimes called Common Shares, which is the most basic element of equity.

RETAINED EARNINGS. The Retained Earnings account shows the cumulative net income earned by the company over its lifetime, minus its cumulative net losses and dividends.

DIVIDENDS. The Dividends account includes dividends that have been declared during the current fiscal period. Dividends are payments to shareholders that represent the distribution of a portion of the company's past earnings.

REVENUES. Revenues are a form of income that increase shareholders' equity. Companies typically earn revenue through the sale of their primary goods and services. Apple, for instance, would use an iPhone Revenue account to record its sales of that product. Scotiabank loans money to its clients and uses an Interest Revenue account to track the interest it receives on these loans.

EXPENSES. Expenses decrease shareholders' equity and consist mainly of the costs incurred to purchase the goods and services a company needs to run its business. Common types of expenses include Salary Expense, Rent Expense, Advertising Expense, and Utilities Expense.

GAINS AND LOSSES. Gains and losses also affect shareholders' equity via their impact on net income and retained earnings. Gains, which usually occur outside the course of a company's ordinary business activities, are another form of income, so they *increase* shareholders' equity. Losses, which also typically occur outside of ordinary business activities, are a type of expense, so they *reduce* shareholders' equity. If, for example, a company sells a building for more than the amount it was carried at on the balance sheet, then the company would realize a gain on the sale of this asset. If the selling price was less than the carrying amount, then the company would realize a loss. For simplicity, gains and losses are excluded from the following illustrations, but remember that when it comes to impacts on the accounting equation, gains have the same effect as revenues, whereas losses have the same impact as expenses.

MyAccountingLab

STOP + THINK (2-1)

You were reading Apple's most recent financial statements and wondered:

1. What are two distinct types of transactions that would increase Apple's shareholders' equity?

2. What are two distinct types of transactions that would decrease Apple's shareholders' equity?

OBJECTIVE

❷ Illustrate the impact of business transactions on the accounting equation

ILLUSTRATE THE IMPACT OF BUSINESS TRANSACTIONS ON THE ACCOUNTING EQUATION

To illustrate accounting for business transactions, let's return to J.J. Booth and Marie Savard. You met them in Chapter 1, when they opened a consulting engineering company on April 1, 2017, and incorporated it as Tara Inc. (Tara for short).

We will consider 11 transactions and use a spreadsheet to illustrate the effects of each one on Tara's accounting equation. In the latter part of the chapter, we will record these same 11 transactions using the formal accounting records of Tara.

TRY IT *in* EXCEL® ▸ ▸ ▸

As you review the 11 transactions, build an Excel spreadsheet. Use the accounting equation on page 56 as a model. Remember that each transaction has either an equal effect on both the left- and right-hand sides of the accounting equation, or an offsetting effect (both positive and negative) on the same side of the equation. Recreate the spreadsheet in Exhibit 2-1, Panel B (page 65), step by step, as you go along. In Excel, open a new blank spreadsheet.

Step 1   Format the worksheet. Label cell A2 "Trans." You will put transaction numbers corresponding to the transactions below in the cells in column A. Row 1 will contain the elements of the accounting equation. Enter "Assets" in cell D1. Enter an "=" sign in cell F1. Enter "Liabilities + Shareholders' equity" in cell G1. Enter "Type of SE (abbreviation for shareholders' equity) Transaction" in cell J1. Highlight cells B1 through E1 and click "merge and center" on the top toolbar. Highlight cells G1 through I1 and click "merge and center." Now you will have a spreadsheet organized around the elements of the accounting equation: "Assets = Liabilities + Shareholders' equity" and, for all transactions impacting shareholders' equity, you will be able to enter the type (common shares, revenue, expense, or dividends). This will be important for later when you construct the financial statements (Exhibit 2-2, page 66).

Step 2   Continue formatting. In cells B2 through E2, enter the asset account titles that transactions 1–11 deal with. B2: Cash; C2: AR (an abbreviation for accounts receivable); D2: Supplies; E2: Land. In cells G2 through I2, enter the liability and shareholders' equity account titles that Tara Inc.'s transactions deal with. G2: AP (an abbreviation for accounts payable); H2: C Shares (an abbreviation for common shares); and I2: RE (abbreviation for retained earnings; this is where all transactions impacting revenue, expenses, and dividends will go for now).

Step 3   In row 15, sum each column from B through E and G through I. For example, the formula in cell B15 should be "=sum(B3:B14)." In cell A15, enter "Bal." This will allow you to keep a running sum of the accounts in the balance sheet as you enter each transaction.

Step 4   In cell A16, enter "Totals." In cell C16, enter "=sum(B15:E15)." In cell H16, enter "=sum(G15:I15)." You can use the short cut symbol "Σ" followed by highlighting the respective cells. Excel allows you to keep a running sum of the column totals on each side of the equation. You should find that the running sum of the column totals on the left-hand side of the equation always equals the running sum of the column totals on the right-hand side, so the accounting equation always stays in balance. As a final formatting step, highlight cells B3 through I16. Using the "number" tab on the toolbar at the top of the spreadsheet, select "Accounting" as for format with no $ sign, and select "decrease decimal" to zero places. Now you're ready to process the transactions.

TRANSACTION 1. Booth, Savard, and several fellow engineers invest $50,000 to begin Tara, and the business issues common shares to the shareholders. The effects of this transaction on the accounting equation are as follows:

	ASSETS		LIABILITIES	+	SHAREHOLDERS' EQUITY	TYPE OF SHAREHOLDERS' EQUITY TRANSACTION
	Cash				Share Capital	
(1)	+50,000				+50,000	Issued common shares

For every transaction, the net amount on the left side of the equation must equal the net amount on the right side so that the equation stays in balance. The first transaction increases both the cash and the share capital of the business by $50,000. If you're following along in Excel, enter 1 in cell A3 of the spreadsheet you are creating. Enter 50000 in cell B3 (under Cash) and 50000 in cell H3 (under C Shares). To the right of the transaction in cell J3 write "Issued common shares" to show the reason for the increase in shareholders' equity. You don't have to enter commas; Excel will do that for you. Notice that the sum of Cash (cell B15) is now $50,000 and the sum of Common Shares (cell H15) is also $50,000. The total of accounts on the left side of the accounting equation is 50,000 (cell C16) and it equals the total of accounts on the right side of the accounting equation (cell H16).

	A	B	C	D	E
1	Tara Inc. Balance Sheet April 1, 2017				
2	Assets		Liabilities		
3	Cash	$ 50,000	None		
4			Shareholders' Equity		
5			Common shares	$ 50,000	
6			Total shareholders' equity	50,000	
7	Total assets	$ 50,000	Total liabilities and shareholders' equity	$ 50,000	
8					

Every transaction affects the financial statements, and we can prepare the statements after one, two, or any number of transactions. Tara, for example, could prepare the above balance sheet after its first transaction. This balance sheet reports that Tara has $50,000 in cash, no liabilities, and share capital of $50,000 as at April 1, 2017, its first day of operations.

As a practical matter, entities report their financial statements at the end of an accounting period, typically monthly, quarterly, and annually. An accounting system can, however, produce statements whenever managers need to know where the business stands.

TRANSACTION 2. Tara purchases land for an office location and pays cash of $40,000. The effect of this transaction on the accounting equation is:

	ASSETS				LIABILITIES	+	SHAREHOLDERS' EQUITY
	Cash	+	Land				Share Capital
Balance	50,000						50,000
(2)	−40,000		+40,000	=			
Bal.	10,000		40,000				50,000
		50,000					50,000

The purchase increases one asset (Land) and decreases another asset (Cash) by the same amount. If you're following along in Excel, enter a 2 in cell A4. Enter 240000 in cell B4 and 40000 in cell E4. The spreadsheet automatically updates, showing that after the transaction is completed, Tara has cash of $10,000, land of $40,000, total assets of $50,000, and no liabilities. Shareholders' equity is unchanged at $50,000. Note that, as shown in cells C16 and H16, total assets still equal total liabilities plus shareholders' equity.

TRANSACTION 3. Tara buys stationery and other office supplies on account, agreeing to pay $3,700 within 30 days. This transaction increases both the assets and the liabilities of the business. Its effect on the accounting equation is:

	Cash	+	Office Supplies	+	Land			Accounts Payable	+	Share Capital
	ASSETS							**LIABILITIES**	**+**	**SHAREHOLDERS' EQUITY**
Bal.	10,000				40,000					50,000
(3)			+3,700			=		+3,700		
Bal.	10,000		3,700		40,000			3,700		50,000
			53,700						53,700	

The new asset is Office Supplies (which is a prepaid expense), and the liability is Accounts Payable. If you're following along in Excel, enter 3 in cell A5, 3700 in cell D5 under the account "Supplies" and 3700 in cell G5 under "AP" (accounts payable). Notice that the spreadsheet now reflects 3 assets in row 15: cash with a balance of $10,000 (cell B15), supplies with a balance of $3,700 (cell D15), and land with a balance of $40,000 (cell E15), for total assets of $53,700 (cell C16). On the right-hand side of the accounting equation, Tara now has accounts payable (a liability) of $3,700 (cell G15) and common shares (cell H15) of $50,000, for a total of $53,700 (cell H16).

TRANSACTION 4. Tara earns service revenue by providing engineering services. Assume the business provides $7,000 in such services and collects this amount in cash. The effect on the accounting equation is an increase in the asset Cash and an increase in Retained Earnings, a shareholders' equity account:

	Cash	+	Office Supplies	+	Land			Accounts Payable	+	Share Capital	+	Retained Earnings	TYPE OF SHAREHOLDERS' EQUITY TRANSACTION
	ASSETS							**LIABILITIES**	**+**	**SHAREHOLDERS' EQUITY**			
Bal.	10,000		3,700		40,000			3,700		50,000			
(4)	+7,000					=						7,000	Service revenue
Bal.	17,000		3,700		40,000			3,700		50,000		7,000	
			60,700							60,700			

To the right we record "Service revenue" to show where the $7,000 increase in Retained Earnings came from. In the Excel spreadsheet on line 6, we enter 7000 under Cash (cell B6) and 7000 under Retained Earnings (cell I6). In cell J6, we enter "Service revenue" to show where the $7,000 increase in Retained Earnings came from. Our grand totals on the bottom of the spreadsheet now show $60,700 for total assets as well as $60,700 for total liabilities and shareholders' equity.

TRANSACTION 5. In this transaction, Tara provides $3,000 in engineering services to King Contracting Ltd., and King promises to pay Tara within one month. This promise represents an asset for Tara in the form of an account receivable. The impact of this transaction on the accounting equation is as follows:

		ASSETS				LIABILITIES +		SHAREHOLDERS' EQUITY			TYPE OF SHAREHOLDERS' EQUITY TRANSACTION
	Cash +	Accounts Receivable +	Office Supplies +	Land		Accounts Payable +		Share Capital +	Retained Earnings		
Bal.	17,000		3,700	40,000	=	3,700		50,000	7,000		
(5)		+3,000							+3,000		Service revenue
Bal.	17,000	3,000	3,700	40,000		3,700		50,000	10,000		
		63,700						63,700			

Tara records (or recognizes) revenue when it performs the service, regardless of whether it receives the cash now or later. You will learn more about revenue recognition in the next chapter. In your Excel spreadsheet, enter 3000 under Accounts Receivable on the left-hand side (cell C7) and 3000 under Retained Earnings (RE) on the right-hand side (cell I7). Also enter "Service revenue" in cell J7 to keep a record of the type of transaction (revenue) that affects shareholders' equity.

TRANSACTION 6. During the month, Tara pays for the following expenses: office rent, $1,100; employee salary, $1,200; and utilities, $400. The effect on the accounting equation is:

		ASSETS				LIABILITIES +		SHAREHOLDERS' EQUITY			TYPE OF SHAREHOLDERS' EQUITY TRANSACTION
	Cash +	Accounts Receivable +	Office Supplies +	Land		Accounts Payable +		Share Capital +	Retained Earnings		
Bal.	17,000	3,000	3,700	40,000		3,700		50,000	10,000		
(6)	−1,100				=				−1,100		Rent expense
	−1,200								−1,200		Salary expense
	− 400								− 400		Utilities expense
Bal.	14,300	3,000	3,700	40,000		3,700		50,000	7,300		
		61,000						61,000			

This transaction will take up lines 8, 9, and 10 of the Excel spreadsheet. Enter −2700 under Cash (cell B8); −1100 under Retained Earnings (cell I8); −1200 under Retained Earnings (cell I9); and −400 under Retained Earnings (cell I10). Enter the type of transaction beside each amount (rent expense, salary expense, utilities expense) to account for the type of transaction impacting shareholders' equity (SE). These expenses decrease Tara's Cash and Retained Earnings. We list each expense separately to keep track of its amount and to facilitate the preparation of the income statement later.

TRANSACTION 7. Tara pays $1,900 of the balance owing to the store from which it purchased Office Supplies in Transaction 3. The transaction decreases Cash (cell B11) and also decreases Accounts Payable (cell G11):

	ASSETS					LIABILITIES	+	SHAREHOLDERS' EQUITY		
	Cash +	Accounts + Receivable	Office + Supplies	+ Land		Accounts Payable	+	Share Capital	+	Retained Earnings
Bal.	14,300	3,000	3,700	40,000	=	3,700		50,000		7,300
(7)	−1,900					−1,900				
Bal.	12,400	3,000	3,700	40,000		1,800		50,000		7,300
		59,100						59,100		

TRANSACTION 8. J.J. Booth paid $30,000 to remodel his home. This event is a personal transaction of J.J. Booth, so according to the separate-entity assumption from Chapter 1, we do not record it in the accounting records of Tara. Business transactions must be kept separate from the personal transactions of the business's owners.

TRANSACTION 9. In Transaction 5, Tara Inc. performed services for King Contracting on account. Tara now collects $1,000 from King Contracting, which means Tara will record an increase in Cash and a decrease in Accounts Receivable. This is not service revenue now because Tara already recorded the revenue in Transaction 5. The effect of this transaction is:

	ASSETS					LIABILITIES	+	SHAREHOLDERS' EQUITY		
	Cash +	Accounts + Receivable	Office + Supplies	+ Land		Accounts Payable	+	Share Capital	+	Retained Earnings
Bal.	12,400	3,000	3,700	40,000	=	1,800		50,000		7,300
(9)	+1,000	−1,000								
Bal.	13,400	2,000	3,700	40,000		1,800		50,000		7,300
		59,100						59,100		

This transaction is entered on line 12 of the Excel spreadsheet as an increase in Cash (cell B12) and a decrease in AR (cell C12).

TRANSACTION 10. Tara sells part of the land purchased in Transaction 2 for $22,000, which is the same amount Tara paid for that part of the land. Tara receives $22,000 cash, and the effect on the accounting equation is:

	ASSETS					LIABILITIES	+	SHAREHOLDERS' EQUITY		
	Cash +	Accounts + Receivable	Office + Supplies	+ Land		Accounts Payable	+	Share Capital	+	Retained Earnings
Bal.	13,400	2,000	3,700	40,000	=	1,800		50,000		7,300
(10)	+22,000			−22,000						
Bal.	35,400	2,000	3,700	18,000		1,800		50,000		7,300
		59,100						59,100		

Note that the company did not sell all its land; Tara still owns $18,000 worth of land. This transaction is entered in the Excel spreadsheet as an increase in Cash (cell B13) and a decrease in Land (cell E13).

TRANSACTION 11. Tara pays the shareholders a $2,100 cash dividend. The effect on the accounting equation is:

		ASSETS				LIABILITIES +	SHAREHOLDERS' EQUITY			TYPE OF SHARHOLDERS' EQUITY TRANSACTION
	Cash +	Accounts Receivable +	Office Supplies	+ Land		Accounts Payable	+ Share Capital	+ Retained Earnings		
Bal.	35,400	2,000	3,700	18,000	=	1,800	50,000	7,300		
(11)	−2,100							−2,100		Dividends
Bal.	33,300	2,000	3,700	18,000		1,800	50,000	5,200		
		57,000					57,000			

The dividend decreases both Cash (cell B14) and the Retained Earnings (cell I14) of the business. *Dividends, however, are not an expense*; they directly reduce Retained Earnings. Therefore, enter "Dividend" in cell J14. We now have all the transactions affecting shareholders' equity labelled properly, which will facilitate the preparation of the financial statements later.

Transactions and Financial Statements

Exhibit 2-1 summarizes the 11 preceding transactions. Panel A gives the details of the transactions, and Panel B illustrates the impact on the accounting equation for each one that affects the business. As you study the exhibit, note that every transaction in Panel B keeps the accounting equation in balance.

Panel B in Exhibit 2-1 also provides the data needed to prepare Tara's financial statements:

- *Income statement* data appear as revenues and expenses under Retained Earnings. The revenues increase Retained Earnings; the expenses decrease Retained Earnings.

- The *balance sheet* data are composed of the ending balances of the assets, liabilities, and shareholders' equity shown at the bottom of the exhibit. The accounting equation shows that total assets ($57,000) equal total liabilities plus shareholders' equity ($57,000).

- The *statement of retained earnings* reports net income (or net loss) from the income statement. Dividends are subtracted. Ending retained earnings is the final result.

- Data for the *statement of cash flows* are aligned under the Cash account. Cash receipts increase cash, and cash payments decrease cash.

Exhibit 2-2 presents the Tara Inc. financial statements for April, the company's first month of operations. Follow the flow of data to observe the following:

1. The income statement reports revenues, expenses, and either a net income or a net loss for the period. During April, Tara earned net income of $7,300. From the transaction analysis spreadsheet in Exhibit 2-1, Panel B, service revenue consists of the sum of cells I6 and I7 ($7,000 for cash and $3,000 on account). Expenses (salary $1,200 from cell I9, rent $1,100 from cell I8, and utilities $400 from cell I10) are listed separately in the income statement. The sum of these expenses is $2,700. Net income consists of the difference between service revenue and total expenses ($10,000 − $2,700 = $7,300). This is known as a

EXHIBIT 2-1
Transaction Analysis: Tara Inc.

MyAccountingLab

Panel A—Transaction Details

(1) Received $50,000 cash and issued shares to the owners

(2) Paid $40,000 cash for land

(3) Bought $3,700 of office supplies on account

(4) Received $7,000 cash from customers for engineering services performed

(5) Performed services for customers on account, $3,000

(6) Paid cash for expenses: rent, $1,100; employee salary, $1,200; utilities, $400

(7) Paid $1,900 on the account payable from Transaction 3

(8) Shareholder uses personal funds to remodel home, which is *not* a transaction of the business

(9) Received $1,000 of the accounts receivable from Transaction 5

(10) Sold land for cash at its cost of $22,000

(11) Declared and paid a dividend of $2,100 to the shareholders

Panel B—Transaction Analysis

	A	B	C	D	E	F	G	H	I	J
1		Assets				=	Liabilities + Shareholders' Equity			Type of SE transaction
2	Trans	Cash	AR	Supplies	Land		AP	C Shares	RE	
3	1	50,000						50,000		Issued common shares
4	2	(40,000)			40,000					
5	3			3,700			3,700			
6	4	7,000							7,000	Service revenue
7	5		3,000						3,000	Service revenue
8	6	(2,700)							(1,100)	Rent expense
9									(1,200)	Salary expense
10									(400)	Utilities expense
11	7	(1,900)					(1,900)			
12	9	1,000	(1,000)							
13	10	22,000			(22,000)					
14	11	(2,100)							(2,100)	Dividend
15	Bal	33,300	2,000	3,700	18,000		1,800	50,000	5,200	
16	Totals		57,000					57,000		
17										

Statement of Cash Flows Data (bracket at left, rows 3–15)

Income Statement Data (bracket at right, rows 6–10)

Statement of Retained Earnings Data (bracket at right, rows 14–15)

Balance Sheet Data

"single-step" income statement because it includes only two types of accounts: revenues and expenses.

2. The statement of retained earnings starts with the beginning balance of retained earnings (zero for a new business). Add net income for the period from the income statement $7,300 (arrow ①), subtract dividends ($2,100 from cell I14 of the transaction analysis spreadsheet in Exhibit 2-1, Panel B), and compute the ending balance of retained earnings ($5,200).

3. The balance sheet lists the assets, liabilities, and shareholders' equity of the business at the end of the period. The assets consist of the totals of cash, accounts receivable, supplies, and land (see cells B15 through E15 in Exhibit 2-1 Panel B). Liabilities consist of only accounts payable (cell G15). Common shares carries over from cell H15. Also included in shareholders' equity is retained earnings, which comes from the statement of retained earnings (arrow ②). It has also been accumulated in cell I15 of Exhibit 2-1, Panel B.

EXHIBIT 2-2
Financial Statements of Tara Inc.

	A	B	C	D
1	**Tara Inc.** Income Statement Month Ended April 30, 2017			
2	Revenues			
3	Service revenue ($7,000 + $3,000)		$ 10,000	
4	Expenses			
5	Salary expense	$ 1,200		
6	Rent expense	1,100		
7	Utilities expense	400		
8	Total expenses		2,700	
9	Net income		$ 7,300	
10				

	A	B	C	D
1	**Tara Inc.** Statement of Retained Earnings Month Ended April 30, 2017			
2	Retained earnings, April 1, 2017		$ 0	
3	Add: Net income for the month		7,300	
4	Subtotal		7,300	
5	Less: Dividends declared		(2,100)	
6	Retained earnings, April 30, 2017		$ 5,200	
7				

①

	A	B	C	D	E
1	**Tara Inc.** Balance Sheet April 30, 2017				
2	**Assets**		**Liabilities**		
3	Cash	$ 33,300	Accounts payable	$ 1,800	
4	Accounts receivable	2,000	**Shareholders' Equity**		
5	Office supplies	3,700	Common shares	50,000	
6	Land	18,000	Retained earnings	5,200	
7			Total shareholders' equity	55,200	
8	Total assets	$ 57,000	Total liabilities and shareholders' equity	$ 57,000	
9					

②

TRY IT *in* EXCEL® ▶▶▶

If you are familiar with Excel, a quick look at Exhibit 2-2 should convince you of how easy it is to prepare the income statement, statement of retained earnings, and balance sheet in Excel. Prepare three simple templates for each of these financial statements for Tara Inc. You may use these templates again, and add to them, in Chapter 3 as you learn the adjusting-entry process. The mid-chapter summary problem will illustrate this using another small company.

STOP + THINK (2-2)

If on May 1, 2017, Tara Inc. receives a $5,000 loan from its bank, what effects would this transaction have on the assets, liabilities, and shareholders' equity of the business as reported in its April 30, 2017, balance sheet shown in Exhibit 2-2?

MyAccountingLab

MID-CHAPTER SUMMARY PROBLEM

Margaret Jarvis opens a research services business near a college campus. She names the corporation Jarvis Research Inc. During the first month of operations, July 2017, Margaret and the business engage in the following activities:

a. Jarvis Research Inc. issues common shares to Margaret Jarvis, who invests $25,000 to open the business.
b. The company purchases, on account, office supplies costing $350.
c. Jarvis Research Inc. pays cash of $20,000 to acquire a lot near the campus. The company intends to use the land as a building site for a business office.
d. Jarvis Research Inc. performs services for clients and receives cash of $1,900.
e. Jarvis Research Inc. pays $100 on the account payable from Transaction (b).
f. Margaret Jarvis pays $2,000 in personal funds for a vacation.
g. Jarvis Research Inc. pays cash expenses for office rent ($400) and utilities ($100).
h. The business sells a small parcel of the land it purchased for its cost of $5,000.
i. The business declares and pays a cash dividend of $1,200.

Requirements

1. Using Excel, build a spreadsheet to analyze the preceding transactions in terms of their effects on the accounting equation of Jarvis Research Inc. Use Exhibit 2-1, Panel B, as a guide.
2. Using Excel, prepare the income statement, statement of retained earnings, and balance sheet of Jarvis Research Inc., after recording the transactions. Draw arrows linking the statements. Use Exhibit 2-2 as a guide.

> **Name:** Jarvis Research Inc.
> **Industry:** Research services
> **Fiscal Period:** Month of July 2017
> **Key Facts:** New business

SOLUTIONS

Requirement 1

> Add all the asset balances and add all the liabilities and shareholders' equity balances. Make sure that Total assets = Total liabilities + Shareholders' equity.

	A	B	C	D	E	F	G	H	I
1			**Assets**		**=**	**Liabilities +**	**Shareholders' Equity**		**Type of SE transaction**
2	Trans	Cash	Office Supplies	Land		AP	C Shares	RE	
3	a	25,000					25,000		Issued common shares
4	b		350			350			
5	c	(20,000)		20,000					
6	d	1,900						1,900	Service revenue
7	e	(100)				(100)			
8	f(n/a)								
9	g	(400)						(400)	Rent expense
10		(100)						(100)	Utilities expense
11	h	5,000		(5,000)					
12	i	(1,200)						(1,200)	Dividend
13	Bal	10,100	350	15,000		250	25,000	200	
14	Totals		25,450				25,450		
15									

Requirement 2

The title must include the name of the company, "Income Statement," and the specific period of time covered. It is critical that the time period be defined.

	A	B	C	D
1	**Jarvis Research Inc.** Income Statement Month Ended July 31, 2017			
2	**Revenues**			
3	Service revenue		$ 1,900	
4	**Expenses**			
5	Rent expense	$ 400		
6	Utilities expense	100		
7	Total expenses		500	
8	Net income		$ 1,400	
9				

Use the revenue and expense amounts from the Retained Earnings column and names from the Type of Shareholders' Equity Transaction column.

The title must include the name of the company, "Statement of Retained Earnings," and the specific period of time covered. It is critical that the time period be defined.

	A	B	C	D
1	**Jarvis Research Inc.** Statement of Retained Earnings Month Ended July 31, 2017			
2	Retained earnings, July 1, 2017		$ 0	
3	Add: Net income for the month		1,400	
4	Subtotal		1,400	
5	Less: Dividends declared		(1,200)	
6	Retained earnings, July 31, 2017		$ 200	
7				

Beginning retained earnings is $0 because this is the first year of operations. The net income amount is transferred from the income statement. The dividends amount is from the Retained Earnings column.

The title must include the name of the company, "Balance Sheet," and the date of the balance sheet. It shows the financial position at the end of business on a specific date.

Gather the asset, liability, and shareholders' equity accounts. Insert the final balances for each account from the Balance row. The retained earnings amount is transferred from the statement of retained earnings. It is imperative that Total assets = Total liabilities + Shareholders' equity.

	A	B	C	D	E
1	**Jarvis Research Inc.** Balance Sheet July 31, 2017				
2	**Assets**		**Liabilities**		
3	Cash	$ 10,100	Accounts payable	$ 250	
4	Office supplies	350	**Shareholders' Equity**		
5	Land	15,000	Common shares	25,000	
6			Retained earnings	200	
7			Total shareholders' equity	25,200	
8	Total assets	$ 25,450	Total liabilities and shareholders' equity	$ 25,450	
9					

ANALYZE BUSINESS TRANSACTIONS USING T-ACCOUNTS

We could use the accounting equation to record all of a business's transactions, but it would be very cumbersome, even for a small business with a low volume of transactions. In this section, we introduce the **double-entry system** of accounting, which is the method that all but the smallest of businesses use to record transactions.

It is called the double-entry system because every transaction has two sides and affects two (or more) accounts. When Tara Inc. issued common shares for $50,000 in cash, for example, one side of the transaction was a $50,000 increase in the Cash account and the other side was a $50,000 increase in the Share Capital account. We must record both sides of every transaction to keep the accounting equation in balance. If we record only a single entry for the $50,000 increase in Cash, the accounting equation would be out of balance, so we must make a second entry in Share Capital to account for the $50,000 increase in equity.

Chart of Accounts

An organization uses a **chart of accounts** to keep track of all its accounts. The chart of accounts lists the name of every account and its unique account number, but it does not provide the account balances. If an accountant is unsure about what account to use when recording a transaction, they can consult the chart of accounts to help them choose the most appropriate one. If the chart of accounts does not contain an appropriate account, the accountant can add a new account to the chart and use it to record the transaction.

Exhibit 2-3 presents Tara Inc.'s chart of accounts. The gaps between account numbers leave room to insert new accounts. In the illustrations that follow, we leave out the account numbers to avoid cluttering the presentation.

EXHIBIT 2-3
Chart of Accounts—Tara Inc.

Balance Sheet Accounts

Assets	Liabilities	Shareholders' Equity
101 Cash	201 Accounts Payable	301 Share Capital
111 Accounts Receivable	231 Notes Payable	311 Dividends
141 Office Supplies		312 Retained Earnings
151 Office Furniture		
191 Land		

Income Statement Accounts
(Part of Shareholders' Equity)

Revenues	Expenses
401 Service Revenue	501 Rent Expense
	502 Salary Expense
	503 Utilities Expense

The T-Account

We can represent an account using the letter T, which we call a *T-account*. The vertical line divides the account into left (debit) and right (credit) sides, while the account title rests on the horizontal line. The Cash T-account, for example, looks like this:

Cash	
(Left side)	(Right side)
Debit	*Credit*

The left side of the account is called the **debit** side, and the right side is called the **credit** side. Students are often confused by the words *debit* and *credit*, so it may help to remember that for every account:

Debit = Left side	Credit = Right side

Using these terms, we can refine our description of a transaction as having two sides: a debit side and a credit side. The double-entry system records both sides and requires that *the debit side equals the credit side* so that the accounting equation stays in balance.

Increases and Decreases in the Accounts: The Rules of Debit and Credit

The way we record increases and decreases to an account under the double-entry system varies by account type. *The rules of debit and credit are as follows (see Exhibit 2-4 for an illustration):*

- *Increases* in assets are recorded on the *left (debit)* side of the T-account, whereas *decreases* are recorded on the *right (credit)* side. When a business receives cash, the Cash account *increases*, so we *debit* the *left side* of the Cash account to record the increase in this asset. When a business makes a cash payment, we *credit* the *right* side of the Cash account to record the *decrease* in this account.

- Conversely, *increases* in liabilities and shareholders' equity are recorded on the *right (credit)* side of the T-account, whereas *decreases* are recorded on the *left (debit)* side. When a business receives a loan, the Loan Payable account *increases*, so we *credit* the *right side* of the Loan Payable account to record the increase in this liability. When a business makes a loan payment, we *debit* the *left* side of the Loan Payable account to record the *decrease* in this account.

EXHIBIT 2-4
Accounting Equation and the Rules of Debit and Credit

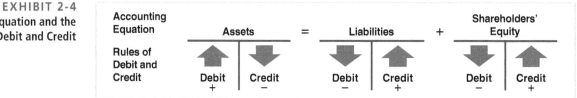

Let's use Tara Inc.'s first two transactions to apply the rules of debit and credit illustrated in Exhibit 2-4. In Transaction (1), Tara received $50,000 in cash and issued common shares in return. As a result, we debit the left side of the Cash account to record the increase in this asset and credit the right side of the Share Capital account to record the increase in shareholders' equity. These two entries are illustrated in the T-accounts in Exhibit 2-5. After recording both sides of this transaction, the debits equal the credits ($50,000 each), so the accounting equation is in balance.

Cash		
(1) Debit for increase	50,000	(2) Credit for decrease 40,000
Balance	10,000	

Land	
(2) Debit for increase	40,000
Balance	40,000

Share Capital	
	(1) Credit for increase 50,000
	Balance 50,000

EXHIBIT 2-5
T-accounts After Tara Inc.'s First Two Transactions

In Transaction (2), Tara purchased land for $40,000 in cash. To record the two sides of this transaction, we debit the left side of the Land account to record the increase in this asset and credit the right side of the Cash account to record the decrease in this asset. Again, the debits equal the credits ($40,000 each) after recording both sides of this transaction.

After both transactions, the Cash account has a $10,000 debit balance, the Land account a $40,000 debit balance, and the Share Capital account a $50,000 credit balance. The total of the debit balances ($50,000) equals the only credit balance, so the accounting equation is in balance after these transactions, as illustrated in Exhibit 2-6.

Assets	=	Liabilities	+	Shareholders' Equity
Cash $10,000 Land $40,000 $50,000				Share capital $50,000

EXHIBIT 2-6
The Accounting Equation After Tara Inc.'s First Two Transactions

The Expanded Accounting Equation

Because several accounts from three separate financial statements affect shareholders' equity, we can expand the accounting equation to explicitly reflect the impact of changes in these accounts on shareholders' equity, as shown in Exhibit 2-7. Revenues and expenses are shown in parentheses to indicate their inclusion in the calculation of net income.

Based on this expanded equation, we can express the rules of debit and credit in more detail, as shown in Exhibit 2-8. *You should not proceed until you have learned these rules*, and you must remember the following:

- To record an increase in assets, use a debit.
- To record a decrease in assets, use a credit.

For liabilities and shareholders' equity, these rules are reversed:

- To record an increase in liabilities or shareholders' equity, use a credit.
- To record a decrease in liabilities or shareholders' equity, use a debit.

EXHIBIT 2-7
The Expanded Accounting Equation

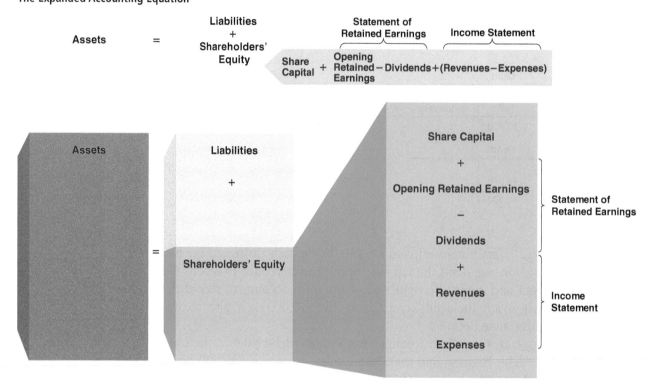

EXHIBIT 2-8
The Expanded Rules of Debit and Credit

ASSETS	=	LIABILITIES	+	SHAREHOLDERS' EQUITY			
Assets		Liabilities		Share Capital	Retained Earnings	Dividends	

Debit	Credit		Debit	Credit		Debit	Credit		Debit	Credit		Debit	Credit
+	−		−	+		−	+		−	+		+	−
Normal balance				Normal balance			Normal balance			Normal balance		Normal balance	

Revenues		Expenses	
Debit	Credit	Debit	Credit
−	+	+	−
	Normal balance	Normal Balance	

Recall that *increases* in Dividends and Expenses result in *decreases* to shareholders' equity, so applying the last rule above means that increases to Dividends and Expenses are recorded using debits, which is the opposite of the "increase = credit" rule for all other shareholders' equity accounts.

Exhibit 2-8 also highlights which side of each account the *normal balance* (debit or credit) falls on, which is the side where increases to the account are recorded (denoted by a "+" sign).

Analyzing Transactions Using Only T-Accounts

We can quickly assess the financial impact of a proposed business transaction by analyzing it informally using T-accounts. Assume, for example, that a manager is considering (a) taking out a $100,000 loan to (b) purchase $100,000 worth of equipment. The manager could record these proposed transactions in T-accounts as follows:

Cash		Equipment		Loan Payable	
(a) 100,000	(b) 100,000	(b) 100,000			(a) 100,000

This informal analysis shows the manager that the net impact of these proposed transactions will be a $100,000 increase in Equipment, with a corresponding increase in the Loan Payable account. Managers who can analyze proposed transactions this way can make business decisions with a clear idea of their impact on the company's financial statements.

STOP + THINK (2-3)

In Stop + Think 2-2, Tara Inc. received a $5,000 loan from its bank. Use debit and credit terminology to explain the effects of this transaction on Tara's accounts.

RECORD BUSINESS TRANSACTIONS IN THE JOURNAL AND POST THEM TO THE LEDGER

OBJECTIVE

④ **Record** business transactions in the journal and **post** them to the ledger

When recording transactions, accountants use a chronological record called a **journal**. The recording process follows these three steps:

1. Specify each account affected by the transaction.

2. Use the rules of debit and credit to determine whether each account is increased or decreased by the transaction.

3. Record the transaction in the journal, including a brief explanation for the entry and the date of the transaction. The debit side is entered on the left margin, and the credit side is indented slightly to the right.

Step 3 is also called "recording the journal entry" or "journalizing the transaction." Let's apply the steps to record the first transaction of Tara Inc.

Step 1 The business receives cash and issues shares. Cash and Share Capital are affected.

Step 2 Both Cash and Share Capital increase. Debit Cash to record an increase in this asset. Credit Share Capital to record an increase in this equity account.

Step 3 Record the journal entry for the transaction, as illustrated in Panel A of Exhibit 2-9.

PANEL A—Recording the Journal Entry

	A	B	C	D	E
1	Date	Accounts and Explanation	Debit	Credit	
2	Apr. 1, 2017	Cash	50,000		
3		Share Capital		50,000	
4		Issued common shares.			
5					

PANEL B—Posting it to the Ledger

Cash		Share Capital	
50,000			50,000

EXHIBIT 2-9

Recording a Journal Entry and Posting it to the Ledger

Posting from the Journal to the Ledger

The journal is a chronological record containing all of a company's transactions. The journal does not, however, indicate the balances in any of the company's accounts. To obtain these balances, we must transfer information from the journal to the **ledger**, which is an accounting process we call **posting**.

The ledger contains all of a company's accounts, along with their balances as of the most recent posting date. Posting is a simple process of directly transferring information from the journal to the ledger: debits in the journal are posted as debits in the ledger accounts, and likewise for credits. Exhibit 2-9 shows the posting of Tara Inc.'s first transaction from the journal to the ledger.

The Flow of Accounting Data

Exhibit 2-10 summarizes the flow of accounting data from the business transaction to the ledger. Let's practise using this process by revisiting Tara Inc.'s transactions for the month of April 2017. We will analyze each transaction, record it in Tara's journal (if necessary), then post it to the ledger.

EXHIBIT 2-10
Flow of Accounting Data

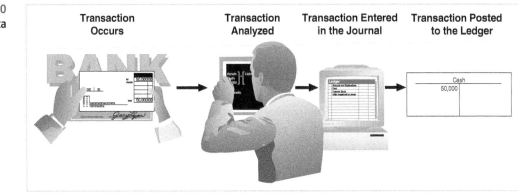

Transaction Occurs	Transaction Analyzed	Transaction Entered in the Journal	Transaction Posted to the Ledger

TRANSACTION 1 ANALYSIS. Tara received $50,000 cash from shareholders and in turn issued Share Capital to them. The accounting equation, journal entry, and posting details for this transaction are as follows:

Accounting equation

ASSETS	=	LIABILITIES	+	SHAREHOLDERS' EQUITY
+50,000	=	0	+	50,000

	A	B	C	D
1		Debit	Credit	
2	Cash	50,000		
3	Share Capital		50,000	
4	*Issued common shares.*			
5				

	Cash		Share Capital	
The ledger accounts	(1)* 50,000			(1)* 50,000

*The numbers in parentheses indicate the transaction number for purposes of this illustration.

TRANSACTION 2 ANALYSIS. The business paid $40,000 cash for land, resulting in a decrease (credit) to Cash and an increase (debit) in Land.

Accounting equation

ASSETS	=	LIABILITIES	+	SHAREHOLDERS' EQUITY
+40,000	=	0	+	0
−40,000				

	A	B	C	D
1		Debit	Credit	
2	Land	40,000		
3	Cash		40,000	
4	Paid cash for land.			
5				

The ledger accounts

Cash		Land	
(1) 50,000	(2) 40,000	(2) 40,000	

TRANSACTION 3 ANALYSIS. The business purchased $3,700 in office supplies on account. The purchase increased Office Supplies, an asset, and Accounts Payable, a liability.

Accounting equation

ASSETS	=	LIABILITIES	+	SHAREHOLDERS' EQUITY
+3,700	=	+3,700	+	0

	A	B	C	D
1		Debit	Credit	
2	Office Supplies	3,700		
3	Accounts Payable		3,700	
4	Purchased office supplies on account.			
5				

The ledger accounts

Office Supplies	Accounts Payable
(3) 3,700	(3) 3,700

TRANSACTION 4 ANALYSIS. The business performed engineering services for clients and received cash of $7,000. The transaction increased Cash and Service Revenue.

Accounting equation

ASSETS	=	LIABILITIES	+	SHAREHOLDERS' EQUITY	+	REVENUES
+7,000	=	0	+	0	+	7,000

	A	B	C	D
1		Debit	Credit	
2	Cash	7,000		
3	Service Revenue		7,000	
4	Performed services for cash.			
5				

The ledger accounts

Cash		Service Revenue	
(1) 50,000	(2) 40,000		(4) 7,000
(4) 7,000			

TRANSACTION 5 ANALYSIS. Tara performed $3,000 in services for King Contracting on account. The transaction increased Accounts Receivable and Service Revenue.

Accounting equation

ASSETS	=	LIABILITIES	+	SHAREHOLDERS' EQUITY	+	REVENUES
+3,000	=	0			+	3,000

	A	B	C	D
1		Debit	Credit	
2	Accounts Receivable	3,000		
3	Service Revenue		3,000	
4	*Performed services on account.*			
5				

	Accounts Receivable		Service Revenue	
The ledger accounts	(5) 3,000			(4) 7,000
				(5) 3,000

TRANSACTION 6 ANALYSIS. Tara paid cash for the following expenses: office rent, $1,100; employee salary, $1,200; and utilities, $400. Debit each expense account for the amount of the expense and credit Cash for the sum of these expenses.

Accounting equation	**ASSETS**	**=**	**LIABILITIES**	**+**	**SHAREHOLDERS' EQUITY**	**–**	**EXPENSES**
	−2,700	=	0			–	2,700

	A	B	C	D
1		Debit	Credit	
2	Rent Expense	1,100		
3	Salary Expense	1,200		
4	Utilities Expense	400		
5	Cash		2,700	
6	*Paid expenses.*			
7				

	Cash		Rent Expense	
The ledger accounts	(1) 50,000	(2) 40,000	(6) 1,100	
	(4) 7,000	(6) 2,700		

	Salary Expense		Utilities Expense	
	(6) 1,200		(6) 400	

TRANSACTION 7 ANALYSIS. The business paid $1,900 on the account payable created in Transaction 3. Credit Cash for the payment. The payment decreased a liability, so debit Accounts Payable.

Accounting equation	**ASSETS**	**=**	**LIABILITIES**	**+**	**SHAREHOLDERS' EQUITY**
	−1,900	=	−1,900	+	0

	A	B	C	D
1		Debit	Credit	
2	Accounts Payable	1,900		
3	Cash		1,900	
4	*Paid cash on account.*			
5				

	Cash		Accounts Payable	
The ledger accounts	(1) 50,000	(2) 40,000	(7) 1,900	(3) 3,700
	(4) 7,000	(6) 2,700		
		(7) 1,900		

TRANSACTION 8 ANALYSIS. J.J. Booth, a shareholder of Tara Inc., remodelled his personal residence. This is not a transaction of the engineering consultancy, so Tara does not record it.

TRANSACTION 9 ANALYSIS. The business collected $1,000 cash on account from the client in Transaction 5. Debit Cash for the increase in this asset, and credit Accounts Receivable for the decrease in this asset.

Accounting equation

ASSETS	=	LIABILITIES	+	SHAREHOLDERS' EQUITY
+1,000	=	0	+	0
−1,000				

	A	B	C	D
1		Debit	Credit	
2	Cash	1,000		
3	Accounts Receivable		1,000	
4	*Collected cash on account.*			
5				

The ledger accounts

	Cash			Accounts Receivable	
(1) 50,000	(2) 40,000		(5) 3,000	(9) 1,000
(4) 7,000	(6) 2,700			
(9) 1,000	(7) 1,900			

TRANSACTION 10 ANALYSIS. Tara sold a portion of its land at cost for $22,000, receiving cash in return. This transaction resulted in an increase to Cash and a decrease in Land.

Accounting equation

ASSETS	=	LIABILITIES	+	SHAREHOLDERS' EQUITY
+22,000	=	0	+	0
−22,000				

	A	B	C	D
1		Debit	Credit	
2	Cash	22,000		
3	Land		22,000	
4	*Sold land.*			
5				

The ledger accounts

	Cash			Land	
(1) 50,000	(2) 40,000		(2) 40,000	(10) 22,000
(4) 7,000	(6) 2,700			
(9) 1,000	(7) 1,900			
(10) 22,000				

TRANSACTION 11 ANALYSIS. Tara paid its shareholders cash dividends of $2,100. We credit Cash for the decrease in this asset, and debit Dividends to account for the decrease in shareholders' equity.

Accounting equation

ASSETS	=	LIABILITIES	+	SHAREHOLDERS' EQUITY	−	REVENUES
−2,100	=	0			−	2,100

	A	B	C	D
1		Debit	Credit	
2	Dividends	2,100		
3	Cash		2,100	
4	*Declared and paid dividends.*			
5				

	Cash		Dividends	
The ledger accounts	(1) 50,000	(2) 40,000	(11) 2,100	
	(4) 7,000	(6) 2,700		
	(9) 1,000	(7) 1,900		
	(10) 22,000	(11) 2,100		

Accounts After Posting to the Ledger

Exhibit 2-11 presents Tara Inc.'s ledger accounts after all transactions have been posted to them. For each account, a horizontal line separates the transaction amounts from the account balance (Bal.) at the end of the month. If the sum of an account's debits exceeds the sum of its credits, then the account will have a debit balance at the end of the period, as illustrated by the Cash debit balance of $33,300. If total credits exceed total debits, a credit balance results, as reflected in the Accounts Payable credit balance of $1,800.

EXHIBIT 2-11
Tara Inc.'s Ledger Accounts After Posting

Assets	=	Liabilities	+	Shareholders' Equity

Cash

(1)	50,000	(2)	40,000
(4)	7,000	(6)	2,700
(9)	1,000	(7)	1,900
(10)	22,000	(11)	2,100
Bal.	33,300		

Accounts Receivable

(5)	3,000	(9)	1,000
Bal.	2,000		

Office Supplies

(3)	3,700	
Bal.	3,700	

Land

(2)	40,000	(10)	22,000
Bal.	18,000		

Accounts Payable

(7)	1,900	(3)	3,700
		Bal.	1,800

Share Capital

		(1)	50,000
		Bal.	50,000

REVENUE

Service Revenue

		(4)	7,000
		(5)	3,000
		Bal.	10,000

Dividends

(11)	2,100	
Bal.	2,100	

EXPENSES

Rent Expense

(6)	1,100	
Bal.	1,100	

Salary Expense

(6)	1,200	
Bal.	1,200	

Utilities Expense

(6)	400	
Bal.	400	

STOP + THINK (2-4)

Describe a transaction that would result in a $10,000 debit to a company's Equipment ledger account and a corresponding credit to the Accounts Payable ledger account.

PREPARE AND USE A TRIAL BALANCE

A **trial balance** lists all of a business's ledger accounts and their balances. Asset accounts are listed first, followed by the liability accounts, and then all the accounts that affect shareholders' equity. We add all the debit balances and all the credit balances and place the totals at the bottom of the trial balance. If the total debits equal the total credits, we can go on to prepare the financial statements using the account balances from the trial balance. Exhibit 2-12 presents Tara Inc.'s trial balance at the end of April 2017.

EXHIBIT 2-12
Tara Inc.'s Trial Balance

	A	B	C	D
1	**Tara Inc.** Trial Balance April 30, 2017			
2		Balance		
3	Account Title	Debit	Credit	
4	Cash	$ 33,300		
5	Accounts receivable	2,000		
6	Supplies	3,700		
7	Land	18,000		
8	Accounts payable		$ 1,800	
9	Common shares		50,000	
10	Dividends	2,100		
11	Service revenue		10,000	
12	Rent expense	1,100		
13	Salary expense	1,200		
14	Utilities expense	400		
15	Total	$ 61,800	$ 61,800	
16				

MyAccountingLab

Accounting Cycle Tutorial:
Step 1: Account Balances
Step 2: Analyze and Journalize Transactions
Step 3: Post to Ledger
Step 4: Prepare Unadjusted Trial Balance

TRY IT in EXCEL® ▶ ▶ ▶

Try building Exhibit 2-12 in Excel. Open a new blank worksheet. Format the title (company name, trial balance, and date), and provide column headings (account title, debit, and credit) exactly as shown in Exhibit 2-12. Then on successive lines, enter account titles and amounts from the general ledger accounts, being careful to enter amounts in the proper debit or credit columns. Finally, sum both debit and credit columns. The total amounts of debits and credits should agree.

STOP + THINK (2-5)

If you were to prepare a trial balance for Tara Inc. on May 1, 2017, after it received the $5,000 loan from its bank, describe how it would differ from the April 30, 2017, trial balance presented in Exhibit 2-12.

▶ DECISION GUIDELINES

HOW TO MEASURE RESULTS OF OPERATIONS AND FINANCIAL POSITION

Every manager must assess their company's profitability, financial position, and cash flows, but before they can do this, the company's transactions must be recorded in the accounting records. Here are some guidelines for the manager to follow when making decisions between the transaction stage and the reporting stage of the accounting process.

Decision	Guidelines
Has a transaction occurred?	If the event affects the entity's financial position **and** it can be reliably measured—Yes
	If either condition is absent—No
Where should the transaction be recorded?	In the *journal*, the chronological record of transactions
What accounts should be used to record the transaction in the journal?	Look in the *chart of accounts* for the most appropriate accounts to use
Should the affected accounts be debited or credited?	Rules of *debit* and *credit*:

	Increase	Decrease
Assets	Debit	Credit
Liabilities	Credit	Debit
Share capital	Credit	Debit
Retained earnings	Credit	Debit
Dividends	Debit	Credit
Revenues	Credit	Debit
Expenses	Debit	Credit

Decision	Guidelines
Where are all the transactions for each account summarized?	In the *ledger*, the book of accounts
Where are all the accounts and their balances listed?	In the *trial balance*
Where are the results of operations reported?	In the *income statement* (Revenues – Expenses = Net income or net loss)
Where is the financial position reported?	In the *balance sheet* (Assets = Liabilities + Shareholders' equity)
Where are the cash flows reported?	In the *statement of cash flows*

SUMMARY

SUMMARY OF LEARNING OBJECTIVES

LEARNING OBJECTIVE	SUMMARY
1. **Describe** common types of accounts	A business transaction is any event that has a financial impact on a business and that can be reliably measured. Business transactions are recorded in the accounts affected by the transactions. An account is the record of all transactions affecting a particular asset, liability, or element of shareholders' equity. Here are the common accounts of each type: **Assets:** Cash, Accounts Receivable, Inventory, Prepaid Expenses, Land, Buildings, Equipment **Liabilities:** Accounts Payable, Accrued Liabilities, Loans Payable **Shareholders' equity:** Share Capital, Retained Earnings, Dividends, Revenues, Expenses
2. **Illustrate** the impact of business transactions on the accounting equation	Recall the accounting equation introduced in Chapter 1: $$\text{Assets} = \text{Liabilities} + \text{Shareholders' Equity}$$ Every business transaction affects at least one element of the accounting equation. When a company issues shares in exchange for $50,000 in cash, for example, the Cash asset increases by $50,000 and so does the Share Capital component of shareholders' equity. After each transaction is recorded in the accounting equation, the equation must remain in balance, as it is in our example, with $50,000 on each side of the equation. If the equation is out of balance, the transaction has been recorded incorrectly and must be revised.
3. **Analyze** business transactions using T-accounts	We can represent an account using the letter T, which we call a T-account. The vertical line divides the account into left (debit) and right (credit) sides, while the account title rests on the horizontal line. The left side of the account is called the debit side, and the right side is called the credit side. We can use these T-accounts to record transactions instead of using the cumbersome accounting equation approach. When using T-accounts to record transactions, we apply the following rules of debit and credit, which help us translate the impacts of transactions on the accounting equation into impacts on specific accounts: • To record an increase in assets, use a debit. • To record a decrease in assets, use a credit. For liabilities and shareholders' equity, these rules are reversed: • To record an increase in liabilities or shareholders' equity, use a credit. • To record a decrease in liabilities or shareholders' equity, use a debit. Recall that increases in Dividends and Expenses result in decreases to shareholders' equity, so applying the last rule above means that increases to Dividends and Expenses are recorded using debits, which is the opposite of the "increase = credit" rule for all other shareholders' equity accounts. Every transaction involves at least one debit and one credit, and after recording a transaction, the total debits must equal the total credits. This ensures that the accounting equation remains in balance after each transaction. The normal balance of each account falls on the same side as where the increases to the account are recorded. The normal balance of an asset account, for example, falls on the left (debit) side, whereas the normal balance of a liability falls on the right (credit) side of the account.

4. **Record** business transactions in the journal and **post** them to the ledger

When formally recording transactions in the accounting records, accountants use a journal, a chronological record of all a business's transactions. When making a journal entry to record a transaction, we follow these three steps:

1. Specify each account affected by the transaction.
2. Determine whether the transaction increases or decreases each account affected by the transaction, and apply the rules of debit and credit to determine whether each account should be debited or credited.
3. Record the transaction in the journal, including a brief explanation of the transaction and its date.

Before we can obtain the balance of an account at the end of an accounting period, we must post all of the transactions from the journal to the ledger. The ledger contains all of a business's accounts, and posting is a simple process of directly transferring information from the journal to the ledger. Debits in the journal are posted as debits to the ledger accounts, and likewise for credits.

5. **Prepare and use** a trial balance

A trial balance lists all of a business's ledger accounts and their balances. Asset accounts are listed first, followed by the liability accounts, and then all the accounts that affect shareholders' equity. We add all the debit balances and all the credit balances and place the totals at the bottom of the trial balance. If the total debits equal the total credits, we can go on to prepare the financial statements using the account balances from the trial balance.

There are no differences between IFRS and ASPE in this chapter.

MyAccountingLab

END-OF-CHAPTER SUMMARY PROBLEM

The trial balance of Bos Personnel Services Inc. on March 1, 2017, lists the entity's assets, liabilities, and shareholders' equity on that date.

Account Title	Balance	
	Debit	Credit
Cash	$26,000	
Accounts receivable	4,500	
Accounts payable		$ 2,000
Share capital		10,000
Retained earnings		18,500
Total	$30,500	$30,500

During March, the business completed the following transactions:
a. Borrowed $70,000 from the bank, with C. Bos signing a note payable in the name of the business.
b. Paid cash of $60,000 to a real estate company to acquire land.
c. Performed service for a customer and received cash of $5,000.
d. Purchased supplies on credit, $300.
e. Performed customer service and earned revenue on account, $4,000.

f. Paid $1,200 on account.

g. Paid the following cash expenses: salary, $3,000; rent, $1,500; and interest, $400.

h. Received $3,100 on account.

i. Received a $200 utility bill that will be paid next month.

j. Declared and paid a dividend of $300.

> **Name:** Bos Personnel Services Inc.
> **Industry:** Human Resources
> **Fiscal Period:** Month of March 2014
> **Key Fact:** An existing, ongoing business

Requirements

1. Open the following accounts, with the balances indicated, in the ledger of Bos Personnel Services Inc. Use the T-account format.
   - Assets—Cash, $26,000; Accounts Receivable, $4,500; Supplies, no balance; Land, no balance
   - Liabilities—Accounts Payable, $2,000; Note Payable, no balance
   - Shareholders' Equity—Share Capital, $10,000; Retained Earnings, $18,500; Dividends, no balance
   - Revenues—Service Revenue, no balance
   - Expenses—Salary Expense, Rent Expense, Interest Expense, Utilities Expense (none have balances)

2. Journalize the transactions listed above. Key the journal entries by transaction letter.

3. Post all transactions to the ledger and show the balance in each account after all the transactions have been posted.

4. Use Excel to prepare the trial balance of Bos Personnel Services Inc. at March 31, 2017.

5. To determine the net income or net loss of the entity during the month of March, use Excel to prepare the income statement for the month ended March 31, 2017. List expenses in order from the largest to the smallest.

> Prepare a T-account for each account name. Place the opening balance in the T-account, remembering that the normal balance in an asset account is a debit, in a liability or equity account is a credit, in a revenue account is a credit, and in an expense account is a debit.
>
> For each transaction, ensure that Debits = Credits.

> Refer to the rules of debit and credit shown in Exhibit 2-8 on page 72.

ANSWERS

Requirement 1

ASSETS	LIABILITIES	SHAREHOLDERS' EQUITY
Cash	Accounts Payable	Share Capital
Bal. 26,000	Bal. 2,000	Bal. 10,000
Accounts Receivable	Note Payable	Retained Earnings
Bal. 4,500		Bal. 18,500
Supplies		Dividends
Land		**REVENUE**
		Service Revenue

EXPENSES

Salary Expense

Rent Expense

Interest Expense

Utilities Expense

> To make sure all the account balances have been entered correctly, trace each T-account's balance back to the March 1, 2017, trial balance given on the previous page.

Requirement 2

Accounts and Explanation	Debit	Credit		Accounts and Explanation	Debit	Credit
a. Cash	70,000		**g.**	Salary Expense	3,000	
Note Payable		70,000		Rent Expense	1,500	
Borrowed cash on note payable.				Interest Expense	400	
b. Land	60,000			Cash		4,900
Cash		60,000		Paid cash expenses.		
Purchased land for cash.			**h.**	Cash	3,100	
c. Cash	5,000			Accounts Receivable		3,100
Service Revenue		5,000		Received on account.		
Performed service and received cash.			**i.**	Utilities Expense	200	
d. Supplies	300			Accounts Payable		200
Accounts Payable		300		Received utility bill.		
Purchased supplies on account.			**j.**	Dividends	300	
e. Accounts Receivable	4,000			Cash		300
Service Revenue		4,000		Declared and paid dividends.		
Performed service on account.						
f. Accounts Payable	1,200					
Cash		1,200				
Paid on account.						

> Selected transactions explained more fully:
> d. Increase Supplies (asset) and increase Accounts Payable (liability) because supplies were purchased on credit. Cash will be paid for the supplies in the future.
> e. Increase Accounts Receivable (asset) and increase Service Revenue (revenue) because the service was performed on account. Cash will be received for the service in the future.
> g. This transaction could also have been recorded with three journal entries, with a debit to the expense and a credit to Cash for each of the expenses.
> I. Increase Utilities Expense (expense) and increase Accounts Payable (liability) because cash will be paid for the utility bill in the future.

Requirement 3

ASSETS

Cash

Bal.	26,000	(b)	60,000
(a)	70,000	(f)	1,200
(c)	5,000	(g)	4,900
(h)	3,100	(j)	300
Bal.	37,700		

Accounts Receivable

Bal.	4,500	(h)	3,100
(e)	4,000		
Bal.	5,400		

Supplies

(d)	300		
Bal.	300		

Land

(b)	60,000		
Bal.	60,000		

LIABILITIES

Accounts Payable

(f)	1,200	Bal.	2,000
		(d)	300
		(i)	200
		Bal.	1,300

Note Payable

		(a)	70,000
		Bal.	70,000

SHAREHOLDERS' EQUITY

Share Capital

		Bal.	10,000

Retained Earnings

		Bal.	18,500

Dividends

(j)	300		
Bal.	300		

REVENUE

Service Revenue

		(c)	5,000
		(e)	4,000
		Bal.	9,000

EXPENSES

Salary Expense

(g)	3,000		
Bal.	3,000		

Rent Expense

(g)	1,500		
Bal.	1,500		

Interest Expense

(g)	400		
Bal.	400		

Utilities Expense

(i)	200		
Bal.	200		

> Make sure each transaction is posted to the proper T-account, and make sure no transactions were missed. Make sure that Assets = Liabilities + Shareholders' Equity for each transaction before going to the next transaction.

Requirement 4

	A	B	C	D
1	**Bos Personnel Services Inc.** Trial Balance March 31, 2017			
2		Balance		
3	Account Title	Debit	Credit	
4	Cash	$ 37,700		
5	Accounts receivable	5,400		
6	Supplies	300		
7	Land	60,000		
8	Accounts payable		$ 1,300	
9	Notes payable		70,000	
10	Share capital		10,000	
11	Retained earnings		18,500	
12	Dividends	300		
13	Service revenue		9,000	
14	Salary expense	3,000		
15	Rent expense	1,500		
16	Interest expense	400		
17	Utilities expense	200		
18	Total	$ 108,800	$ 108,800	
19				

The title must include the name of the company, "Trial Balance," and the date of the trial balance. It shows the account balances on one specific date. List all the accounts that have a balance in their T-accounts. Write the "Bal." amount for each account from Requirement 3 into the debit or credit column of the trial balance. Make sure that the total of the Debit column equals the total of the Credit column. Double-underline the totals to show that the columns have been added and the totals are final.

Requirement 5

	A	B	C	D
1	**Bos Personnel Services Inc.** Income Statement Month Ended March 31, 2017			
2	Revenues			
3	Service revenue		$ 9,000	
4				
5	Expenses			
6	Salary expense	$ 3,000		
7	Rent expense	1,500		
8	Interest expense	400		
9	Utilities expense	200		
10	Total expenses		5,100	
11	Net income		$ 3,900	
12				

The title must include the name of the company, "Income Statement," and the specific period of time covered. It is critical that the time period be defined. Prepare the income statement by listing the revenue and expense account names from the trial balance. Then transfer the amounts from the trial balance to the income statement.

REVIEW

MyAccountingLab

Make the grade with MyAccountingLab: The Quick Quiz questions, Short Exercises, Exercises, and Problems (Group A) marked in #-# can be found on MyAccountingLab. You can practise them as often as you want, and most feature step-by-step guided instructions to help you find the right answer.

QUICK QUIZ　(ANSWERS APPEAR ON THE LAST PAGE OF THIS CHAPTER.)

Test your understanding of business transactions by answering the following questions. Select the best choice from among the possible answers.

1. An investment of cash into the business will
  a. decrease total assets.
  b. decrease total liabilities.
  c. increase shareholders' equity.
  d. have no effect on total assets.

2. Purchasing a computer on account will
  a. increase total assets.
  b. increase total liabilities.
  c. have no effect on shareholders' equity.
  d. All of the above.

3. Performing a service on account will
  a. increase total assets.
  b. increase shareholders' equity.
  c. Both a and b.
  d. increase total liabilities.

4. Receiving cash from a customer on account will
  a. have no effect on total assets.
  b. increase total assets.
  c. decrease liabilities.
  d. increase shareholders' equity.

5. Purchasing computer equipment for cash will
  a. increase both total assets and total liabilities.
  b. decrease both total assets and shareholders' equity.
  c. decrease both total liabilities and shareholders' equity.
  d. have no effect on total assets, total liabilities, or shareholders' equity.

6. Purchasing a building for $100,000 by paying cash of $20,000 and signing a note payable for $80,000 will
  a. increase both total assets and total liabilities by $100,000.
  b. increase both total assets and total liabilities by $80,000.
  c. decrease total assets, and increase total liabilities by $20,000.
  d. decrease both total assets and total liabilities by $20,000.

7. What is the effect on total assets and shareholders' equity of paying the electric bill as soon as it is received each month?

	Total assets	Shareholders' equity
a.	Decrease	No effect
b.	No effect	No effect
c.	Decrease	Decrease
d.	No effect	Decrease

8. Which of the following transactions will increase an asset and increase a liability?
  a. buying equipment on account
  b. purchasing office equipment for cash
  c. issuing shares
  d. making a payment on account

9. Which of the following transactions will increase an asset and increase shareholders' equity?
  a. collecting cash from a customer on an account receivable
  b. performing a service on account for a customer
  c. borrowing money from a bank
  d. purchasing supplies on account

10. Where do we first record a transaction?
  a. ledger
  b. trial balance
  c. account
  d. journal

11. Which of the following is not an asset account?
  a. Share Capital
  b. Salary Expense
  c. Service Revenue
  d. None of the above accounts is an asset

12. Which of the following statements is false?
  a. Revenues are increased by credits.
  b. Assets are increased by debits.
  c. Dividends are increased by credits.
  d. Liabilities are decreased by debits.

13. The journal entry to record the receipt of land and a building and issuance of common shares
  a. debits Land and Building, and credits Share Capital.
  b. debits Land, and credits Share Capital.
  c. debits Share Capital, and credits Land and Building.
  d. credits Land and Building, and debits Share Capital.

14. The journal entry to record the purchase of supplies on account
  a. credits Supplies, and debits Cash.
  b. debits Supplies, and credits Accounts Payable.
  c. debits Supplies Expense, and credits Supplies.
  d. credits Supplies, and debits Accounts Payable.

15. If the credit to record the purchase of supplies on account is not posted,
  a. liabilities will be understated.
  b. expenses will be overstated.
  c. assets will be understated.
  d. shareholders' equity will be understated.

16. The journal entry to record a payment on account will
  a. debit Accounts Payable, and credit Retained Earnings.
  b. debit Cash, and credit Expenses.
  c. debit Expenses, and credit Cash.
  d. debit Accounts Payable, and credit Cash.

17. If the credit to record the payment of an account payable is not posted,
  a. liabilities will be understated.
  b. expenses will be understated.
  c. cash will be overstated.
  d. cash will be understated.

18. Which statement is false?
  a. A trial balance lists all the accounts with their current balances.
  b. A trial balance is the same as a balance sheet.
  c. A trial balance can verify the equality of debits and credits.
  d. A trial balance can be taken at any time.

19. A business's purchase of a $100,000 building with an $85,000 mortgage payable and issuance of $15,000 of common shares will
  a. increase shareholders' equity by $15,000.
  b. increase assets by $15,000.
  c. increase assets by $85,000.
  d. increase shareholders' equity by $100,000.

20. A new company completed these transactions:
  1. Shareholders invested $50,000 cash and inventory worth $25,000.
  2. Sales on account, $12,000.

  What will total assets equal?
  a. $75,000
  b. $87,000
  c. $63,000
  d. $62,000

ACCOUNTING VOCABULARY

account The record of the changes that have occurred in a particular asset, liability, or element of shareholders' equity during a period. (p. 56)

chart of accounts List of a company's accounts and their account numbers. (p. 69)

credit The right side of an account. (p. 70)

debit The left side of an account. (p. 70)

double-entry system An accounting system that uses debits and credits to record the dual effects of each business transaction. (p. 69)

journal The chronological accounting record of an entity's transactions. (p. 73)

ledger The book of accounts and their balances. (p. 74)

posting Transferring amounts from the journal to the ledger. (p. 74)

transaction An event that has a financial impact on a business and that can be reliably measured. (p. 56)

trial balance A list of all the ledger accounts with their balances. (p. 79)

ASSESS YOUR PROGRESS

SHORT EXERCISES

S2-1 Sue Deliveau opened a software consulting firm that immediately paid $2,000 for a computer. Was this event a transaction for the business?

LEARNING OBJECTIVE ❷
Analyze a transaction

S2-2 Hourglass Software began with cash of $10,000. Hourglass then bought supplies for $2,000 on account. Separately, Hourglass paid $5,000 for a computer. Answer these questions:
1. How much in total assets does Hourglass have?
2. How much in liabilities does Hourglass owe?

LEARNING OBJECTIVE ❷
Analyze the effects of transactions

LEARNING OBJECTIVE ❸

Analyze transactions using
T-accounts

S2-3 Marsha Solomon, a physiotherapist, opened a practice. The business completed the following transactions:

May	1	Solomon invested $25,000 cash to start her practice. The business issued shares to Solomon.
	1	Purchased medical supplies on account totalling $9,000.
	2	Paid monthly office rent of $4,000.
	3	Recorded $8,000 revenue for service rendered to patients, received cash of $2,000, and sent bills to patients for the remainder.

After these transactions, how much cash does the business have to work with? Use T-accounts to show your answer.

LEARNING OBJECTIVE ❸

Analyze transactions using
T-accounts

S2-4 Refer to exercise S2-3. Which of the transactions of Marsha Solomon, P.T., increased the total assets of the business? For each transaction, identify the asset or liability that was increased or decreased.

LEARNING OBJECTIVE ❸

Journalize transactions

S2-5 After operating for several months, artist Paul Marciano completed the following transactions during the latter part of June:

June	15	Borrowed $25,000 from the bank, signing a note payable.
	22	Painted a portrait for a client on account totalling $9,000.
	28	Received $5,000 cash on account from clients.
	29	Received a utility bill of $600, which will be paid during July.
	30	Paid monthly salary of $2,500 to gallery assistant.

Journalize the transactions of Paul Marciano, Artist. Include an explanation with each journal entry.

LEARNING OBJECTIVE ❹

Journalize transactions; post

S2-6 Architect Sonia Biaggi purchased supplies on account for $5,000. Later, Biaggi paid $3,000 on account.
1. Journalize the two transactions on the books of Sonia Biaggi, Architect. Include an explanation for each transaction.
2. Open a T-account for Accounts Payable and post to Accounts Payable. Compute the balance and denote it as Bal.
3. How much does Biaggi's business owe after both transactions? In which account does this amount appear?

LEARNING OBJECTIVE ❹

Journalize transactions; post

S2-7 Family Services Centre (The Centre) performed service for a client who could not pay immediately. The Centre expected to collect the $500 the following month. A month later, The Centre received $100 cash from the client.
1. Record the two transactions on the books of Family Services Centre. Include an explanation for each transaction.
2. Open these T-accounts: Cash, Accounts Receivable, and Service Revenue. Post to all three accounts. Compute each account balance and denote as Bal.
3. Answer these questions based on your analysis:
    a. How much did The Centre earn? Which account shows this amount?
    b. How much in total assets did The Centre acquire as a result of the two transactions? Show the amount of each asset.

S2-8 Assume that Lululemon Athletica Inc. reported the following summarized data at December 31, 2017. Accounts appear in no particular order; dollar amounts are in millions.

LEARNING OBJECTIVE ❺

Prepare and use a trial balance

Revenues	$275
Other liabilities	38
Other assets	101
Cash and other current assets	53
Accounts payable	5
Expenses	244
Shareholders' equity	80

Prepare the trial balance of Lululemon at December 31, 2017. List the accounts in their proper order, as on page 79. How much was Lululemon's net income or net loss?

S2-9 Blackburn Inc.'s trial balance follows:

LEARNING OBJECTIVE ❺

Use a trial balance

	A	B	C	D
1	**Blackburn Inc.** Trial Balance June 30, 2017			
2		Debit	Credit	
3	Cash	$ 6,000		
4	Accounts receivable	13,000		
5	Supplies	4,000		
6	Equipment	22,000		
7	Land	50,000		
8	Accounts payable		$ 19,000	
9	Note payable		20,000	
10	Share capital		10,000	
11	Retained earnings		8,000	
12	Service revenue		70,000	
13	Salary expense	21,000		
14	Rent expense	10,000		
15	Interest expense	1,000		
16	Total	$ 127,000	$ 127,000	
17				

Compute these amounts for Blackburn:

1. Total assets
2. Total liabilities
3. Net income or loss during June
4. Total shareholders' equity

S2-10 The accounts of Custom Pool Service, Inc., follow with their normal balances at June 30, 2017. The accounts are listed in no particular order.

LEARNING OBJECTIVE ❺

Prepare a trial balance

Account	Balance	Account	Balance
Share capital	$ 8,300	Dividends	$ 5,800
Accounts payable	4,100	Utilities expense	1,700
Service revenue	22,300	Accounts receivable	15,200
Land	29,600	Delivery expense	900
Loan payable	11,500	Retained earnings	24,700
Cash	9,200	Salary expense	8,500

Prepare the company's trial balance at June 30, 2017, listing accounts in proper sequence, as illustrated in the chapter. For example, Accounts Receivable comes before Land. List the expense with the largest balance first, the expense with the next largest balance second, and so on.

LEARNING OBJECTIVE ❶❷❸❹

Use key accounting terms

S2-11 Accounting has its own vocabulary and basic relationships. Match the accounting terms at left with the corresponding definition or meaning at right.

_____ 1. Debit
_____ 2. Expense
_____ 3. Net income
_____ 4. Ledger
_____ 5. Posting
_____ 6. Normal balance
_____ 7. Payable
_____ 8. Journal
_____ 9. Receivable
_____10. Owners' equity

A. The cost of operating a business; a decrease in shareholders' equity
B. Always a liability
C. Revenues – Expenses
D. Grouping of accounts
E. Assets – Liabilities
F. Record of transactions
G. Always an asset
H. Left side of an account
I. Side of an account where increases are recorded
J. Copying data from the journal to the ledger

LEARNING OBJECTIVE ❸

Record transactions using T-accounts

S2-12 Canadian Prairies Investments began by issuing common shares for cash of $100,000. The company immediately purchased computer equipment on account for $60,000.
1. Set up the following T-accounts for the company: Cash, Computer Equipment, Accounts Payable, Share Capital.
2. Record the transactions directly in the T-accounts without using a journal.
3. Show that total debits equal total credits.

EXERCISES

LEARNING OBJECTIVE ❸

Analyze transactions using T-accounts

E2-13 Assume The Gap has opened a store in Ottawa. Starting with cash and shareholders' equity (common shares) of $100,000, Susan Harper, the store manager, signed a note payable to purchase land for $40,000 and a building for $130,000. She also paid $50,000 for store fixtures and $40,000 for inventory to use in the business. All these were paid for in cash.

Suppose the head office of Gap requires a weekly report from store managers. Write Harper's memo to the head office to report on her borrowing and purchases. Include the store's balance sheet as the final part of your memo. Prepare a T-account to compute the balance for cash.

LEARNING OBJECTIVE ❷

Understand transactions and the accounting equation

E2-14 During April, Spokes Ltd. completed a series of transactions. For each of the following items, give an example of a business transaction that has the described effect on the accounting equation of Spokes Ltd.
a. Increase one asset, and decrease another asset.
b. Decrease an asset, and decrease shareholders' equity.
c. Decrease an asset, and decrease a liability.
d. Increase an asset, and increase shareholders' equity.
e. Increase an asset, and increase a liability.

LEARNING OBJECTIVE ❷

Analyze transactions using the accounting equation

E2-15 Fill out the following chart to show the impact on the accounting equation from each transaction.

		Assets		Liabilities		Shareholders' equity	
Date	Description	Increase	Decrease	Increase	Decrease	Increase	Decrease
Jan 2	Purchased office supplies on account for $500						
Jan 4	Issued common shares for cash for $5,000						
Jan 10	Sold services on account for $2,000						
Jan 15	Paid amount owed to vendor for the office supplies purchased on account on January 2						
Jan 18	Sold services for cash $200						
Jan 21	Received cash for payment on account from sale on January 10						
Jan 31	Paid employees for monthly payroll $1,500						

E2-16 The following selected events were experienced by either Problem Solvers Inc., a corporation, or Pierce Laflame, the major shareholder. State whether each event (1) increased, (2) decreased, or (3) had no effect on the total assets of the business. Identify any specific asset affected.

LEARNING OBJECTIVE ❷

Analyze transactions using the accounting equation

a. Received $9,000 cash from customers on account.

b. Laflame used personal funds to purchase a swimming pool for his home.

c. Sold land and received cash of $60,000 (the land was carried on the company's books at $60,000).

d. Borrowed $50,000 from the bank.

e. Made cash purchase of land for a building site, $85,000.

f. Received $20,000 cash and issued shares to a shareholder.

g. Paid $60,000 cash on accounts payable.

h. Purchased equipment and signed a $100,000 promissory note in payment.

i. Purchased supplies on account for $15,000.

j. The business paid Laflame a cash dividend of $4,000.

E2-17 Joseph Ohara opens a dental practice. During the first month of operation (March), the practice, titled Joseph Ohara Dental Clinic Ltd., experienced the following events:

LEARNING OBJECTIVE ❷

Analyze transactions using the accounting equation

March	6	Ohara invested $50,000 in the business, which in turn issued its common shares to him.
	9	The business paid cash for land costing $30,000. Ohara plans to build a professional services building on the land.
	12	The business purchased dental supplies for $3,000 on account.
	15	Joseph Ohara Dental Clinic Ltd. officially opened for business.
	15–31	During the rest of the month, Ohara treated patients and earned service revenue of $10,000, receiving cash for half the revenue earned.
	15–31	The practice paid cash expenses: employee salaries, $1,400; office rent, $1,000; utilities, $300.
	31	The practice used dental supplies with a cost of $250.
	31	The practice borrowed $10,000, signing a note payable to the bank.
	31	The practice paid $2,000 on account.

Requirements

1. Analyze the effects of these events on the accounting equation of the practice of Joseph Ohara Dental Clinic Ltd. Use a format similar to that of Exhibit 2-1, Panel B, with headings for Cash, Accounts Receivable, Dental Supplies, Land, Accounts Payable, Note Payable, Share Capital, and Retained Earnings.

2. After completing the analysis, answer these questions about the business:
   a. How much are total assets?
   b. How much does the business expect to collect from patients?
   c. How much does the business owe in total?
   d. How much of the business's assets does Ohara really own?
   e. How much net income or net loss did the business experience during its first month of operations?

E2-18 Refer to exercise E2-16. Record the transactions in the journal of Joseph Ohara Dental Clinic Ltd. List the transactions by date, and give an explanation for each transaction.

LEARNING OBVJECTIVE ❹

Journalize transactions

LEARNING OBJECTIVE ❹

Journalize transactions

E2-19 Perfect Printers Inc. completed the following transactions during October 2017, its first month of operations:

Oct.	1	Received $25,000, and issued common shares.
	2	Purchased $800 of office supplies on account.
	4	Paid $20,000 cash for land to use as a building site.
	6	Performed service for customers, and received cash of $5,000.
	9	Paid $100 on accounts payable.
	17	Performed service for Waterloo School Board on account totalling $1,500.
	23	Collected $1,000 from Waterloo School Board on account.
	31	Paid the following expenses: salary, $1,000; rent, $500.

Requirement

1. Record the transactions in the journal of Perfect Printers Inc. Key transactions by date, and include an explanation for each entry, as illustrated in the chapter.

LEARNING OBJECTIVE ❹❺

Post to the ledger and prepare and use a trial balance

E2-20 Refer to exercise E2-19.

Requirements

1. After journalizing the transactions of exercise E2-19, post the entries to the ledger using T-accounts. Key transactions by date. Date the ending balance of each account October 31, 2017.
2. Prepare the trial balance of Perfect Printers Inc., at October 31, 2017.
3. How much are total assets, total liabilities, and total shareholders' equity on October 31, 2017?

LEARNING OBJECTIVE ❹

Journalize transactions

E2-21 The first seven transactions of Splash Water Park Ltd. have been posted to the company's accounts as follows:

Cash				Supplies				Equipment		Land	
(1) 20,000	(3)	8,000		(4) 1,000	(5)	100		(6) 8,000		(3) 31,000	
(2) 7,000	(6)	8,000									
(5) 100	(7)	400									

Accounts Payable			Note Payable		Share Capital	
(7) 400	(4)	1,000		(2) 7,000		(1) 20,000
				(3) 23,000		

Requirement

Prepare the journal entries that served as the sources for the seven transactions. Include an explanation for each entry. As Splash Water Park moves into the next period, how much cash does the business have? How much does Splash Water Park owe?

LEARNING OBJECTIVE ❺

Prepare and use a trial balance

E2-22 The accounts of Victoria Garden Care Ltd. follow with their normal balances at September 30, 2017. The accounts are listed in no particular order.

Account	Balance	Account	Balance
Dividends	6,000	Share capital	8,500
Utilities expense	1,400	Accounts payable	4,300
Accounts receivable	17,500	Service revenue	24,000
Delivery expense	300	Equipment	29,000
Retained earnings	21,400	Note payable	13,000
Salary expense	8,000	Cash	9,000

Requirements

1. Prepare the company's trial balance at September 30, 2017, listing accounts in proper sequence, as illustrated in the chapter. For example, Accounts Receivable comes before Equipment. List the expense with the largest balance first, the expense with the next largest balance second, and so on.
2. Prepare the financial statement for the month ended September 30, 2017, that will tell the company's top managers the results of operations for the month.

E2-23 The trial balance of Sam's Deli Inc. at October 31, 2017, does not balance:

LEARNING OBJECTIVE ⑤

Correct errors in a trial balance

	A	B	C	D
1	Cash	$ 4,200		
2	Accounts receivable	13,000		
3	Inventory	17,000		
4	Supplies	600		
5	Land	55,000		
6	Accounts payable		$ 12,000	
7	Share capital		47,900	
8	Sales revenue		32,100	
9	Salary expense	1,700		
10	Rent expense	800		
11	Utilities expense	700		
12	Total	$ 93,000	$ 92,000	
13				

The accounting records contain the following errors:
a. Recorded a $1,000 cash revenue transaction by debiting Accounts Receivable. The credit entry was correct.
b. Posted a $1,000 credit to Accounts Payable as $100.
c. Did not record utilities expense or the related account payable in the amount of $200.
d. Understated Share Capital by $1,100.
e. Omitted insurance expense of $1,000 from the trial balance.

Requirement

Prepare the correct trial balance at October 31, 2017, complete with a heading. Journal entries are not required.

E2-24 Set up the following T-accounts: Cash, Accounts Receivable, Office Supplies, Office Furniture, Accounts Payable, Share Capital, Dividends, Service Revenue, Salary Expense, and Rent Expense.

LEARNING OBJECTIVE ③

Record transactions in T-accounts

Record the following transactions directly in the T-accounts without using a journal. Use the letters to identify the transactions. Calculate the account balances and denote as Bal.
a. In the month of May 2017, Sonia Rothesay opened an accounting firm by investing $10,000 cash and office furniture valued at $5,000. Organized as a professional corporation, the business issued common shares to Rothesay.
b. Paid monthly rent of $1,600.
c. Purchased office supplies on account, $600.
d. Paid employees' salaries of $2,000.
e. Paid $200 of the account payable created in transaction (c).
f. Performed accounting service on account, $12,100.
g. Declared and paid dividends of $2,000.

E2-25 Refer to exercise E2-24.

Requirements

1. After recording the transactions in exercise E2-24, prepare the trial balance of Sonia Rothesay, Accountant, at May 31, 2017.
2. How well did the business perform during its first month? Give the basis for your answer.

E2-26 The trial balance of 4AC, Inc., at October 31, 2017, does not balance.

Cash	$3,900	Share capital	$24,100
Accounts receivable	7,100	Retained earnings	1,700
Land	30,100	Service revenue	9,400
Accounts payable	6,200	Salary expense	2,900
Note payable	5,900	Advertising expense	1,400

Requirements

1. Prepare a trial balance for the ledger accounts of 4AC, Inc., as of October 31, 2017.
2. Determine the out-of-balance amount. The error lies in the Accounts Receivable account.

Add the out-of-balance amount to, or subtract it from, Accounts Receivable to determine the correct balance of Accounts Receivable. After correcting Accounts Receivable, advise the top management of 4AC, Inc., on the company's

a. total assets.
b. total liabilities.
c. net income or net loss for October.

E2-27 Frontland Advertising creates, plans, and handles advertising campaigns in three provinces. Recently, Frontland had to replace an inexperienced office worker in charge of bookkeeping because of some serious mistakes that had been uncovered in the accounting records. You have been hired to review these transactions to determine any corrections that might be necessary. In all cases, the bookkeeper made an accurate description of the transaction.

	A	B	C	D	E
1	May 1	Accounts receivable	100		
2		Service revenue		100	
3		*Collected an account receivable.*			
4	2	Rent expense	20,000		
5		Cash		20,000	
6		*Paid monthly rent, $2,000.*			
7	5	Cash	2,800		
8		Accounts receivable		2,800	
9		*Collected cash for services provided.*			
10	10	Supplies	3,100		
11		Accounts payable		3,100	
12		*Purchased office equipment on account.*			
13	16	Dividends	5,600		
14		Cash		5,600	
15		*Paid salaries.*			
16	25	Accounts receivable	5,400		
17		Cash		5,400	
18		*Paid for supplies purchased earlier an account.*			
19					

Requirements

1. For each of the preceding entries, indicate the effect of the error on cash, total assets, and net income. The answer for the first transaction has been provided as an example.

Date	Effect on Cash	Effect on Total Assets	Effect on Net Income
May 1	Understated $100	Overstated $100	Overstated $100

2. What is the correct balance of cash if the balance of cash on the books before correcting the preceding transactions was $6,400?
3. What is the correct amount of total assets if the total assets on the books before correcting the preceding transactions was $28,000?
4. What is the correct net income for May if the reported income before correcting the preceding transactions was $8,000?

SERIAL EXERCISE

Exercise E2-28 begins an accounting cycle that is completed in Chapter 3.

E2-28 Web Marketing Services Inc. completed these transactions during the first part of January 2017:

LEARNING OBJECTIVE ❸❹❺

Journalize and post business transactions and prepare a trial balance

Jan.	2	Received $5,000 cash from investors, and issued common shares.
	2	Paid monthly office rent, $500.
	3	Paid cash for a Dell computer, $3,000, with the computer expected to remain in service for five years.
	4	Purchased office furniture on account, $6,000, with the furniture projected to last for five years.
	5	Purchased supplies on account, $900.
	9	Performed marketing service for a client, and received cash for the full amount of $800.
	12	Paid utility expenses, $200.
	18	Performed marketing service for a client on account, $1,700.

Requirements

1. Set up T-accounts for Cash, Accounts Receivable, Supplies, Equipment, Furniture, Accounts Payable, Share Capital, Dividends, Service Revenue, Rent Expense, Utilities Expense, and Salary Expense.
2. Journalize the transactions. Explanations are not required.
3. Post to the T-accounts. Key all items by date and denote an account balance on January 18 as Bal.
4. Prepare a trial balance at January 18. In the Serial Exercise of Chapter 3, we add transactions for the remainder of January and will require a trial balance at January 31, 2017.

CHALLENGE EXERCISES

E2-29 The manager of Canadiana Gallery Ltd. needs to compute the following information:
a. Total cash paid during March. Analyze Cash.
b. Cash collections from customers during March. Analyze Accounts Receivable.
c. Cash paid on a note payable during March. Analyze Notes Payable.

LEARNING OBJECTIVE ❸

Analyze transactions using T-accounts

Here are additional data you need to analyze:

| | Balance | | |
Account	Feb. 28	Mar. 31	Additional Information for the Month of March
1. Cash...	10,000	5,000	Cash receipts, $80,000
2. Accounts Receivable	26,000	24,000	Sales on account, $50,000
3. Note Payable..	13,000	21,000	New borrowing, $25,000

Prepare a T-account to compute the amounts for (a) through (c).

LEARNING OBJECTIVE ❸❺

Analyze transactions using T-accounts; use a trial balance

E2-30 The trial balance of You Build Inc. at December 31, 2017, does not balance.

Cash..	$ 3,900	Share capital.................................	$20,000
Accounts receivable..........................	7,200	Retained earnings..........................	7,300
Land..	34,000	Service revenue	9,100
Accounts payable..............................	5,800	Salary expense..............................	3,400
Note payable	5,000	Advertising expense......................	900

Requirements

1. How much out of balance is the trial balance? Determine the out-of-balance amount. The error lies in the Accounts Receivable account. Add the out-of-balance amount to, or subtract it from, Accounts Receivable to determine the correct balance of Accounts Receivable.
2. You Build Inc. also failed to record the following transactions during December:
   a. Purchased additional land for $60,000 by signing a note payable.
   b. Earned service revenue on account, $10,000.
   c. Paid salary expense of $1,400.
   d. Purchased a TV advertisement for $1,000 on account. This account will be paid during January.

   Add these amounts to, or subtract them from, the appropriate accounts to properly include the effects of these transactions. Then prepare the corrected trial balance of You Build Inc.
3. After correcting the accounts, advise the top management of You Build Inc. on the company's:
   a. Total assets
   b. Total liabilities
   c. Net income or loss

LEARNING OBJECTIVE ❷

Analyze transactions

E2-31 This question concerns the items and the amounts that two entities, City of Regina and Public Health Organization, Inc. (PHO), should report in their financial statements.

During August, PHO provided City of Regina with medical checks for new school pupils and sent a bill for $30,000. On September 7, Regina sent a cheque to PHO for $25,000. Regina began August with a cash balance of $50,000; PHO began with cash of $0.

Requirement

For this situation, show everything that both Regina and PHO will report on their August and September income statements and on their balance sheets at August 31 and September 30. Use the following format for your answer:

Regina:		
Income statement	August	September
Balance sheet	August 31	September 30
PHO:		
Income statement	August	September
Balance sheet	August 31	September 30

After showing what each company should report, briefly explain how the City of Regina and PHO data relate to each other. Be specific.

PROBLEMS (GROUP A)

P2-32A The trial balance of Amusement Specialties Inc. follows:

LEARNING OBJECTIVE ⑤

Analyze a trial balance

	A	B	C	D
1	**Amusement Specialties Inc.** Trial Balance December 31, 2017			
2	Cash	$ 14,000		
3	Accounts receivable	11,000		
4	Prepaid expenses	4,000		
5	Equipment	171,000		
6	Building	100,000		
7	Accounts payable		$ 30,000	
8	Note payable		120,000	
9	Share capital		102,000	
10	Retained earnings		40,000	
11	Dividends	22,000		
12	Service revenue		86,000	
13	Rent expense	14,000		
14	Advertising expense	3,000		
15	Wage expense	32,000		
16	Supplies expense	7,000		
17	Total	$ 378,000	$ 378,000	
18				

Sue Sibalius, your best friend, is considering investing in Amusement Specialties Inc. She seeks your advice in interpreting this information. Specifically, she asks how to use this trial balance to compute the company's total assets, total liabilities, and net income or net loss for the year.

Requirement

Write a short note to answer Sue's questions. In your note, state the amounts of Amusement Specialties's total assets, total liabilities, and net income or net loss for the year. Also, show how you computed each amount.

P2-33A The following amounts summarize the financial position of Blythe Spirit Consulting, Inc. on May 31, 2017:

LEARNING OBJECTIVE ❷

Analyze transactions with the accounting equation and prepare the financial statements

ASSETS				=	LIABILITIES	+	SHAREHOLDERS' EQUITY	
Cash +	Accounts Receivable	+ Supplies +	Land	=	Accounts Payable	+	Common Shares	+	Retained Earnings
1,300	1,000		12,000		8,000		4,000	2,300

During June 2017, the business completed these transactions:
a. Received cash of $5,000, and issued common shares.
b. Performed services for a client, and received cash of $7,600.
c. Paid $4,000 on accounts payable.
d. Purchased supplies on account, $1,500.
e. Collected cash from a customer on account, $1,000.
f. Consulted on the design of a business report, and billed the client for services rendered, $2,500.
g. Recorded the following business expenses for the month: paid office rent, $900; paid advertising, $300.
h. Declared and paid a cash dividend of $2,000.

Requirements

1. Analyze the effects of the preceding transactions on the accounting equation of Blythe Spirit Consulting, Inc. Adapt the format of Exhibit 2-1, Panel B.
2. Prepare the income statement of Blythe Spirit Consulting, Inc. for the month ended June 30, 2017. List expenses in decreasing order by amount.
3. Prepare the entity's statement of retained earnings for the month ended June 30, 2017.
4. Prepare the balance sheet of Blythe Spirit Consulting, Inc. at June 30, 2017.

LEARNING OBJECTIVE ④

Journalize and post transactions

P2-34A Use this problem in conjunction with problem P2-33A.

Requirements

1. Journalize the transactions of Blythe Spirit Consulting, Inc. Explanations are not required.
2. Set up the following T-accounts: Cash, Accounts Receivable, Supplies, Land, Accounts Payable, Share Capital, Retained Earnings, Dividends, Service Revenue, Rent Expense, and Advertising Expense. Insert in each account its balance as given (example: Cash $1,300). Post the transactions to the accounts.
3. Compute the balance in each account. For each asset account, each liability account, and for Share Capital, compare its balance to the ending balance you obtained in problem P2-33A. Are the amounts the same or different? (In Chapter 3, we complete the accounting process. There you will learn how the Retained Earnings, Dividends, Revenue, and Expense accounts work together in the processing of accounting information.)

LEARNING OBJECTIVE ②④

Analyze transactions with the accounting equation; journalize transactions

P2-35A Mountain View Estates Ltd. experienced the following events during the organizing phase and its first month of operations. Some of the events were personal and did not affect the business. Others were business transactions.

Sept.	4	Gayland Jet, the major shareholder of the company, received $50,000 cash from an inheritance.
	5	Jet deposited $50,000 cash in a new business bank account titled Mountain View Estates Ltd. The business issued common shares to Jet.
	6	The business paid $300 cash for letterhead stationery for the new office.
	7	The business purchased office furniture. The company paid cash of $20,000 and agreed to pay the account payable for the remainder, $5,000, within three months.
	10	Jet sold Telus shares, which he had owned for several years, receiving $30,000 cash from his stockbroker.
	11	Jet deposited the $30,000 cash from the sale of the Telus shares in his personal bank account.
	12	A representative of a large company telephoned Jet and told him of the company's intention to put a down payment of $10,000 on a lot.
	18	Jet finished a real estate deal on behalf of a client and submitted his bill for services, $10,000. Jet expects to collect from this client within two weeks.
	21	The business paid half its account payable for the furniture purchased on September 7.
	25	The business paid office rent of $4,000.
	30	The business declared and paid a cash dividend of $2,000.

Requirements

1. Classify each of the preceding events as one of the following:
   a. A business-related event but not a transaction to be recorded by Mountain View Estates Ltd.
   b. A personal transaction for a shareholder, not to be recorded by Mountain View Estates Ltd.
   c. A business transaction to be recorded by the business of Mountain View Estates Ltd.

2. Analyze the effects of the preceding events on the accounting equation of Mountain View Estates Ltd. Use a format similar to that in Exhibit 2-1, Panel B.

3. At the end of the first month of operations, Jet has a number of questions about the financial standing of the business. Explain the following to him:

   a. How the business can have more cash than retained earnings.

   b. How much in total resources the business has, how much it owes, and what Jet's ownership interest is in the assets of the business.

4. Record the transactions of the business in its journal. Include an explanation for each entry.

P2-36A During October, All Pets Veterinary Clinic Ltd. completed the following transactions:

LEARNING OBJECTIVE ❹

Journalize and post transactions

Oct.	1	Dr. Squires deposited $8,000 cash in the business bank account. The business issued common shares to her.
	5	Paid monthly rent, $1,000.
	9	Paid $5,000 cash, and signed a $25,000 note payable to purchase land for an office site.
	10	Purchased supplies on account, $1,200.
	19	Paid $600 on account.
	22	Borrowed $10,000 from the bank for business use. Dr. Squires signed a note payable to the bank in the name of the business.
	31	Revenues earned during the month included $7,000 cash and $5,000 on account.
	31	Paid employees' salaries ($2,000), advertising expense ($1,500), and utilities ($1,100).
	31	Declared and paid a cash dividend of $3,000.

The clinic uses the following accounts: Cash, Accounts Receivable, Supplies, Land, Accounts Payable, Notes Payable, Share Capital, Dividends, Service Revenue, Salary Expense, Rent Expense, Utilities Expense, and Advertising Expense.

Requirements

1. Journalize each transaction of All Pets Veterinary Clinic Ltd. Explanations are not required.

2. Prepare T-accounts for Cash, Accounts Payable, and Notes Payable. Post to these three accounts.

3. After these transactions, how much cash does the business have? How much in total does it owe?

P2-37A During the first month of operations, May 2017, New Pane Windows Inc. completed the following transactions:

LEARNING OBJECTIVE ❹❺

Journalize and post transactions; prepare and use a trial balance

May	2	New Pane received $30,000 cash and issued common shares to shareholders.
	3	Purchased supplies, $1,000, and equipment, $2,600, on account.
	4	Performed services, and received cash, $1,500.
	7	Paid cash to acquire land for an office site, $22,000.
	11	Repaired a window, and billed the customer $500.
	16	Paid for the equipment purchased May 3 on account.
	17	Paid the telephone bill, $95.
	18	Received partial payment from client on account, $250.
	22	Paid the water and electricity bills, $400.
	29	Received $2,000 cash for installing a new window.
	31	Paid employee salary, $1,300.
	31	Declared and paid dividends of $1,500.

Requirements

Set up the following T-accounts: Cash, Accounts Receivable, Supplies, Equipment, Land, Accounts Payable, Share Capital, Dividends, Service Revenue, Salary Expense, and Utilities Expense.

1. Record each transaction in the journal, using the account titles given. Key each transaction by date. Explanations are not required.
2. Post the transactions to the T-accounts, using transaction dates as posting references. Label the ending balance of each account Bal., as shown in the chapter.
3. Prepare the trial balance of New Pane Windows, at May 31, 2017.
4. The manager asks you how much in total resources the business has to work with, how much it owes, and whether May 2017 was profitable (and by how much). Calculate the amounts needed to answer her questions.

LEARNING OBJECTIVE ❸❺

Record transactions in T-accounts; prepare and use a trial balance

P2-38A During the first month of operations (January 2017), Music Services Ltd. completed the following selected transactions:

a. The business has cash of $10,000 and a building valued at $50,000. The corporation issued common shares to the shareholders.
b. Borrowed $50,000 from the bank, and signed a note payable.
c. Paid $60,000 for music equipment.
d. Purchased supplies on account, $1,000.
e. Paid employees' salaries, $1,500.
f. Received $800 for service performed for customers.
g. Performed service to customers on account, $4,500.
h. Paid $100 of the account payable created in transaction (d).
i. Received a $600 utility bill that will be paid in the near future.
j. Received cash on account, $3,100.
k. Paid the following cash expenses: rent, $1,000; advertising, $800.

Requirements

1. Set up the following T-accounts: Cash, Accounts Receivable, Office Supplies, Music Equipment, Building, Accounts Payable, Note Payable, Share Capital, Service Revenue, Salary Expense, Rent Expense, Advertising Expense, and Utilities Expense.
2. Record the foregoing transactions directly in the T-accounts without using a journal. Use the letters to identify the transactions.
3. Prepare the trial balance of Music Services Ltd. at January 31, 2017.
4. The bank manager is afraid that the total liabilities of the business exceed the total assets. He also fears that the business suffered a net loss during January. Compute the amounts needed to answer his questions.

PROBLEMS (GROUP B)

LEARNING OBJECTIVE ❺

Analyze a trial balance

P2-39B The owners of Opera Tours Inc. are selling the business. They offer the trial balance that appears at the top of the next page to prospective buyers.

Your best friend is considering buying Opera Tours. She seeks your advice in interpreting this information. Specifically, she asks whether this trial balance provides the data to prepare a balance sheet and an income statement.

Requirement

Write a memo to answer your friend's questions. Indicate which accounts go on the balance sheet and which accounts go on the income statement. State the amount of net income that Opera Tours earned in 2017, and explain your computation.

	A	B	C
1	**Opera Tours Inc.** Trial Balance December 31, 2017		
2	Cash	$ 12,000	
3	Accounts receivable	45,000	
4	Prepaid expenses	4,000	
5	Equipment	231,000	
6	Accounts payable		$ 105,000
7	Note payable		92,000
8	Share capital		30,000
9	Retained earnings		32,000
10	Service revenue		139,000
11	Salary expense	69,000	
12	Tour expenses	26,000	
13	Rent expense	7,000	
14	Advertising expense	4,000	
15	Total	$ 398,000	$ 398,000
16			

P2-40B Doug Hanna operates and is the major shareholder of an interior design studio called DH Designers, Inc. The following amounts summarize the financial position of the business on April 30, 2017:

LEARNING OBJECTIVE ❷

Analyze transactions with the accounting equation and prepare the financial statements

ASSETS				=	LIABILITIES	+	SHAREHOLDERS' EQUITY	
Cash +	Accounts Receivable +	Supplies +	Land =		Accounts Payable +		Common Shares +	Retained Earnings
Bal. 1,700	2,200		24,100		5,400		10,000	12,600

During May 2017, the business completed these transactions:

a. Hanna received $30,000 as a gift and deposited the cash in the business bank account. The business issued common shares to Hanna.

b. Paid $1,000 on accounts payable.

c. Performed services for a client and received cash of $5,100.

d. Collected cash from a customer on account, $700.

e. Purchased supplies on account, $800.

f. Consulted on the interior design of a major office building and billed the client for services rendered, $15,000.

g. Received cash of $1,700 and issued common shares to a shareholder.

h. Recorded the following expenses for the month: paid office rent, $2,100; paid advertising, $1,600.

i. Declared and paid a cash dividend of $2,000.

Requirements

In order to guide Doug Hanna:

1. Analyze the effects of the preceding transactions on the accounting equation of DH Designers, Inc. Adapt the format of Exhibit 2-1, Panel B.

2. Prepare the income statement of DH Designers, Inc. for the month ended May 31, 2017. List expenses in decreasing order by amount.

3. Prepare the statement of retained earnings of DH Designers, Inc. for the month ended May 31, 2017.

4. Prepare the balance sheet of DH Designers, Inc. at May 31, 2017.

LEARNING OBJECTIVE ❹

Journalize and post transactions

P2-41B Use this problem in conjunction with problem P2-40B.

Requirements

1. Journalize the transactions of DH Designers, Inc. Explanations are not required.
2. Set up the following T-accounts: Cash, Accounts Receivable, Supplies, Land, Accounts Payable, Share Capital, Retained Earnings, Dividends, Service Revenue, Rent Expense, and Advertising Expense. Insert in each account its balance as given (example: Cash $1,700). Post to the accounts.
3. Compute the balance in each account. For each asset account, each liability account, and for Share Capital, compare its balance to the ending balance you obtained in problem P2-57B. Are the amounts the same or different? (In Chapter 3, we complete the accounting process. There you will learn how the Retained Earnings, Dividends, Revenue, and Expense accounts work together in the processing of accounting information.)

LEARNING OBJECTIVE ❷❹

Record transactions using the accounting equation and journal entries

P2-42B Lane Kohler opened a consulting practice that he operates as a corporation. The name of the new entity is Lane Kohler, Consultant, Inc. Kohler experienced the following events during the organizing phase of his new business and its first month of operations. Some of the events were personal transactions of the shareholder and did not affect the consulting practice. Others were transactions that should be accounted for by the business.

March	1	Kohler sold 1,000 shares of RIM stock and received $100,000 cash from his stockbroker.
	2	Kohler deposited in his personal bank account the $100,000 cash from sale of the RIM shares.
	3	Kohler received $150,000 cash through an inheritance from his grandfather.
	5	Kohler deposited $50,000 cash in a new business bank account titled Lane Kohler, Consultant, Inc. The business issued common shares to Kohler.
	6	A representative of a large company telephoned Kohler and told him of the company's intention to give $15,000 of consulting business to Kohler.
	7	The business paid $450 cash for letterhead stationery for the consulting office.
	9	The business purchased office furniture. Kohler paid cash of $5,000 and agreed to pay the account payable for the remainder, $10,500, within three months.
	23	Kohler finished an analysis for a client and submitted his bill for services $4,000. He expected to collect from this client within one month.
	29	The business paid $5,000 of its account payable on the furniture purchased on March 9.
	30	The business paid office rent of $2,100.
	31	The business declared and paid a cash dividend of $1,000.

Requirements

1. Classify each of the preceding events as one of the following:
   a. A personal transaction of a shareholder not to be recorded by the business of Lane Kohler, Consultant, Inc.
   b. A business transaction to be recorded by the business of Lane Kohler, Consultant, Inc.
   c. A business-related event but not a transaction to be recorded by the business of Lane Kohler, Consultant, Inc.
2. Analyze the effects of the preceding events on the accounting equation of the business of Lane Kohler, Consultant, Inc. Use a format similar to Exhibit 2-1, Panel B.
3. At the end of the first month of operations, Kohler has a number of questions about the financial standing of the business. Answer the following questions for him:
   a. How can the business have more cash than retained earnings?
   b. How much in total resources does the business have? How much does it owe? What is Kohler's ownership interest in the assets of the business?
4. Record the transactions of the business in its journal. Include an explanation for each entry.

P2-43B Wimberley Glass, Inc. has shops in the shopping malls of a major metropolitan area. The business completed the following transactions:

LEARNING OBJECTIVE ❹

Journalize and post transactions

June	1	Received cash of $25,000, and issued common shares to a shareholder.
	2	Paid $10,000 cash, and signed a $30,000 note payable to purchase land for a new glassworks site.
	7	Received $20,000 cash from sales, and deposited that amount in the bank.
	10	Purchased supplies on account, $1,000.
	15	Paid employees' salaries, $2,800, and rent on a shop, $1,800.
	15	Paid advertising expense, $1,100.
	16	Paid $1,000 on account.
	17	Declared and paid a cash dividend of $2,000.

Wimberley Glass, Inc. uses the following accounts: Cash, Supplies, Land, Accounts Payable, Note Payable, Share Capital, Dividends, Sales Revenue, Salary Expense, Rent Expense, and Advertising Expense.

Requirements

1. Journalize each transaction. Explanations are not required.
2. Prepare T-accounts for Cash, Accounts Payable, and Notes Payable. Post to these three accounts.
3. After these transactions, how much cash does the business have? How much does it owe in total?

P2-44B During the first month of operations, October 2017, Barron Environmental Services Inc. completed the following transactions:

LEARNING OBJECTIVE ❹❺

Journalize and post transactions; prepare and use a trial balance

Oct.	3	Received $20,000 cash, and issued common shares.
	4	Performed services for a client, and received $5,000 cash.
	6	Purchased supplies, $300, and furniture, $2,500, on account.
	7	Paid $15,000 cash to acquire land for an office site.
	7	Worked for a client, and billed the client $1,500.
	16	Received partial payment from a client on account, $500.
	24	Paid the telephone bill, $110.
	24	Paid the water and electricity bills, $400.
	28	Received $2,500 cash for helping a client meet environmental standards.
	31	Paid secretary's salary, $1,200.
	31	Paid $2,500 of the account payable created on October 6.
	31	Declared and paid dividends of $2,400.

Requirements

Set up the following T-accounts: Cash, Accounts Receivable, Supplies, Furniture, Land, Accounts Payable, Share Capital, Dividends, Service Revenue, Salary Expense, and Utilities Expense.

1. Record each transaction in the journal, using the account titles given. Key each transaction by date. Explanations are not required.
2. Post the transactions to the T-accounts, using transaction dates as posting references. Label the ending balance of each account Bal., as shown in the chapter.
3. Prepare the trial balance of Barron Environmental Services Inc. at October 31, 2017.
4. Report to the shareholder how much in total resources the business has to work with, how much it owes, and whether October was profitable (and by how much).

P2-45B During the first month of operations (June 2017), Schulich Graphics Service Inc. completed the following selected transactions:

LEARNING OBJECTIVE ❸❺

Record transactions directly in T-accounts; prepare and use a trial balance

a. Began the business with an investment of $20,000 cash and a building valued at $60,000. The corporation issued common shares to the shareholders.
b. Borrowed $90,000 from the bank, and signed a note payable.

c. Paid $35,000 for computer equipment.
d. Purchased office supplies on account for $1,300.
e. Performed computer graphic service on account for a client, $2,500.
f. Received $1,200 cash on account.
g. Paid $800 of the account payable created in transaction (d).
h. Received a $500 bill for advertising expense that will be paid in the near future.
i. Performed service for clients, and received $1,100 in cash.
j. Paid employees' salaries totalling $2,200.
k. Paid the following cash expenses: rent, $700; utilities, $400.

Requirements

1. Set up the following T-accounts: Cash, Accounts Receivable, Office Supplies, Computer Equipment, Building, Accounts Payable, Note Payable, Share Capital, Service Revenue, Salary Expense, Advertising Expense, Rent Expense, and Utilities Expense.
2. Record each transaction directly in the T-accounts without using a journal. Use the letters to identify the transactions.
3. Prepare the trial balance of Schulich Graphics Service Inc. at June 30, 2017.

APPLY YOUR KNOWLEDGE

DECISION CASES

This section's material reflects CPA enabling competencies,* including:

1. Professionalism and ethical behaviour
2. Problem-solving and decision-making
3. Communication
4. Self-management
5. Teamwork and leadership

LEARNING OBJECTIVE ❸❺

Record transactions directly in T-accounts, prepare a trial balance, and measure net income or loss

Case 1. A friend named Tom Tipple has asked what effect certain transactions will have on his company. Time is short, so you cannot apply the detailed procedures of journalizing and posting. Instead, you must analyze the transactions without the use of a journal. Tipple will continue the business only if he can expect to earn monthly net income of $10,000. The following transactions occurred this month:

a. Tipple deposited $10,000 cash in a business bank account, and the corporation issued common shares to him.
b. Paid $300 cash for supplies.
c. Purchased office furniture on account, $4,400.
d. Earned revenue on account, $7,000.
e. Borrowed $5,000 cash from the bank, and signed a note payable due within one year.
f. Paid the following cash expenses for one month: employee's salary, $1,700; office rent, $600.
g. Collected cash from customers on account, $1,200.
h. Paid on account, $1,000.
i. Earned revenue, and received $2,500 cash.
j. Purchased advertising in the local newspaper for cash, $800.

Requirements

1. Set up the following T-accounts: Cash, Accounts Receivable, Supplies, Furniture, Accounts Payable, Notes Payable, Share Capital, Service Revenue, Salary Expense, Advertising Expense, and Rent Expense.
2. Record the transactions directly in the accounts without using a journal. Key each transaction by letter.
3. Prepare a trial balance at the current date. List expenses with the largest amount first, the next largest amount second, and so on. The business name will be Tipple Networks, Inc.
4. Compute the amount of net income or net loss for this first month of operations. Why would you recommend that Tipple continue or not continue in business?

---

*© Chartered Professional Accountants of Canada.

LEARNING OBJECTIVE 5

Correct financial statements; decide whether to expand a business

Case 2. Barbara Boland opened a flower shop. Business has been good, and Boland is considering expanding with a second shop. A cousin has produced the following financial statements at December 31, 2017, the end of the first three months of operations:

	A	B	C	D
1	**Barbara Boland Blossoms Inc.** Income Statement Quarter Ended December 31, 2017			
2	Sales revenue	$ 36,000		
3	Share capital	10,000		
4	Total revenue	46,000		
5	Accounts payable	8,000		
6	Advertising expense	5,000		
7	Rent expense	6,000		
8	Total expenses	19,000		
9	Net income	$ 27,000		
10				

	A	B	C	D
1	**Barbara Boland Blossoms Inc.** Balance Sheet As at December 31, 2017			
2	Assets			
3	Cash	$ 6,000		
4	Cost of goods sold (expense)	22,000		
5	Flower inventory	5,000		
6	Store fixtures	10,000		
7	Total assets	$ 43,000		
8	Liabilities			
9	None			
10	Owners' Equity	$ 43,000		
11				

In these financial statements, all amounts are correct except for Owners' Equity. Boland's cousin heard that total assets should equal total liabilities plus owners' equity, so he plugged in the amount of owners' equity at $43,000 to make the balance sheet come out evenly.

Requirements

Barbara Boland has asked whether she should expand the business. Her banker says Boland may be wise to expand if (a) net income for the first quarter reaches $5,000 and (b) total assets are at least $25,000. It appears that the business has reached these milestones, but Boland doubts her cousin's understanding of accounting. Boland needs your help in making this decision. Prepare a corrected income statement and balance sheet. (Remember that Retained Earnings, which was omitted from the balance sheet, should equal net income for the period; there were no dividends.) After preparing the statements, give Boland your recommendation as to whether she should expand the flower shop.

ETHICAL ISSUES

Issue 1. Scruffy Murphy is the president and principal shareholder of Scruffy's Bar and Grill Limited. To expand, the business is applying for a $250,000 bank loan. The bank requires the company to have shareholders' equity of at least as much as the loan. Currently, shareholders' equity is $150,000. To get the loan, Murphy is considering two options for beefing up the shareholders' equity of the business:

> *Option 1.* Issue $100,000 of common shares for cash. A friend has been wanting to invest in the company. This may be the right time to extend the offer.

Option 2. Transfer $100,000 of Murphy's personal land to the business, and issue common shares to Murphy. Then, after obtaining the loan, Murphy can transfer the land back to himself and cancel the common shares.

Requirement 1

Journalize the transactions required by each option.

Requirement 2

Use the Framework for Making Ethical Judgments in Chapter 1 (p. 27) to determine which plan would be ethical.

Issue 2. Community Charities has a standing agreement with Royal Bank of Canada (RBC). The agreement allows Community Charities to overdraw its cash balance at the bank when donations are running low. In the past, Community Charities managed funds wisely and rarely used this privilege. Recently, however, Beatrice Grand has been named president of Community Charities. To expand operations, she is acquiring office equipment and spending a lot for fundraising. During Grand's presidency, Community Charities has maintained a negative bank balance of about $3,000.

Requirements

What is the ethical issue in this situation? Do you approve or disapprove of Grand's management of Community Charities's and RBC's funds? Why? Use the Framework for Making Ethical Judgments in Chapter 1 (p. 27) in answering this question.

FOCUS ON FINANCIALS

LEARNING OBJECTIVE ❹

Journalize and post transactions

MyAccountingLab

Canadian Tire Corporation

Refer to the Canadian Tire financial statements in Appendix A at the back of the book. Assume that Canadian Tire completed the following selected transactions during its 2014 fiscal year (all amounts in millions).

a. Sold goods on account, $3,101.
b. Sold goods for cash, $9,361.9.
c. Collected trade accounts receivable, $2,979.3.
d. Paid cash for inventory, $7,695.9.
e. Sold inventory that cost $7,553.1. Debit "Cost of producing revenue."
f. Purchased TV advertising on account, $4,055.
g. Paid trade accounts payable, $3,911.2.
h. Repaid long-term debt, $207.5.
i. Purchased property and equipment for cash, $227.

Requirements

1. For the following items, set up T-accounts with the given opening balances (note that the debits do not equal the credits because this is only a subset of Canadian Tire's accounts):
   • Cash and Cash Equivalents, debit balance of $643.2
   • Trade and Other Receivables, debit balance of $758.5
   • Merchandise Inventories, debit balance of $1,481.0
   • Property and Equipment, debit balance of $3,516.1
   • Trade and Other Payables, credit balance of $1,817.4
   • Long-Term Debt, credit balance of $2,339.1
   • Revenue, balance of $0
   • Selling, General and Administrative Expenses, balance of $0

2. Record Canadian Tire's transactions (a) through (i) in the journal. Explanations are not required.

3. Post the transactions in part (2) to the T-accounts (key them by letter) and compute the balance in each account.

4. For each of the following accounts, compare your balance to the actual balance in Canadian Tire's financial statements in Appendix A. Your balances should agree with the actual balances.

   a. Long-Term Debt
   b. Trade and Other Receivables
   c. Merchandise Inventories
   d. Trade and Other Payables
   e. Revenue
   f. Property and Equipment

FOCUS ON ANALYSIS

Canadian Tire Corporation

Refer to the Canadian Tire financial statements in Appendix A at the end of the book. Suppose you are an investor considering buying Canadian Tire's shares. The following questions are important:

1. Explain which of Canadian Tire's credit sales or collections from customers was the largest amount during the year ended January 3, 2015. Analyze trade receivables to answer this question.

2. A major concern of lenders, such as banks, is the amount of long-term debt a company owes. How much long-term debt does Canadian Tire owe at January 3, 2015? What must have happened to Canadian Tire's long-term debt during the 2014 fiscal year?

3. Investors are very interested in a company's revenues and profits, and its trends of revenues and profits over time. Consider Canadian Tire's operating revenues and net income during the year ended January 3, 2015. Compute the percentage change in operating revenue and also in net income or loss during this period. Which item changed more during this period, operating revenue or net income? (For convenience, show dollar amounts in millions.) Which provides a better indicator of business success? Give the reason for your answer.

LEARNING OBJECTIVE ❹

Analyze transactions and financial statements

MyAccountingLab

GROUP PROJECTS

You are promoting a concert in your area. Your purpose is to earn a profit, so you need to establish the formal structure of a business entity. Assume you organize as a corporation.

Requirements

1. Make a detailed list of 10 factors you must consider as you establish the business.

2. Describe 10 of the items your business must arrange to promote and stage the concert.

3. Identify the transactions that your business can undertake to organize, promote, and stage the concert. Journalize the transactions, and post to the relevant T-accounts. Set up the accounts you need for your business ledger.

4. Prepare the income statement, statement of retained earnings, and balance sheet immediately after the concert; that is, before you have had time to pay all the business bills and collect all receivables.

5. Assume that you will continue to promote concerts if the venture is successful. If it is unsuccessful, you will terminate the business within three months after the concert. Discuss how to evaluate the success of your venture and how to decide whether to continue in business.

CHECK YOUR WORK

STOP + THINK ANSWERS

STOP + THINK (2-1)

1. The issuance of shares and the sale of electronics products
2. The declaration and payment of dividends and the payment of expenses

STOP + THINK (2-2)

Cash would increase by $5,000 to $38,300, causing total assets to increase to $63,000.

A new account, Loan Payable, would increase by $5,000, causing liabilities to increase to $6,800.

Shareholders' equity would not change, so total liabilities and shareholders' equity would increase to $63,000.

STOP + THINK (2-3)

The loan transaction would result in a $5,000 debit (or increase) to the Cash account and a $5,000 credit (or increase) to the Loan Payable account.

STOP + THINK (2-4)

The company purchases $10,000 worth of equipment from a supplier on credit.

STOP + THINK (2-5)

Cash would have a debit balance of $38,300.

A new account, Loan payable, would appear below Accounts payable, with a credit balance of $5,000.

Total Debits and Total Credits would each equal $66,800.

QUICK QUIZ ANSWERS

1. c.	6. b.	11. d.	16. d.
2. d.	7. c.	12. c.	17. c.
3. c.	8. a.	13. a.	18. b.
4. a.	9. b.	14. b.	19. a.
5. d.	10. d.	15. a.	20. b.

Accrual Accounting and the Financial Statements

3

Mario Beauregard/CPI/The Canadian Press

LEARNING OBJECTIVES

1. **Explain** how accrual accounting differs from cash-basis accounting
2. **Apply** the revenue and expense recognition principles
3. **Record** adjusting journal entries
4. **Prepare** the financial statements
5. **Record** closing journal entries
6. **Analyze** and **evaluate** a company's debt-paying ability

CPA COMPETENCIES

Competencies* addressed in this chapter:

1.2.1 Develops or evaluates appropriate accounting policies and procedures

1.2.2 Evaluates treatment for routine transactions

1.3.1 Prepares financial statements

1.4.4 Interprets financial reporting results for stakeholders (external or internal)

SPOTLIGHT

Le Château has been selling fashion apparel, footwear, and accessories in Canada for over 50 years. What started as a single, family-owned store in Montreal in 1959 is now a global fashion brand, with its merchandise sold in 221 stores in Canada and 5 more in the Middle East. As the company's promotional materials state, Le Château's "success is built on quick identification of and response to fashion trends through our design, product development and vertically integrated operations."

As you can see from Le Château's statement of loss on the next page, the company sold just over $250 million in merchandise in its fiscal 2015 year. Unfortunately, its expenses for the year were higher, so it ended up reporting a net loss of about $38.7 million. How does Le Château determine when to recognize the revenues and expenses it reports on this statement? Read on and you will find out!

*© Chartered Professional Accountants of Canada.

	A	B	C	D
1	**Le Château Inc.** Consolidated Statement of Loss (Adapted) For the Year Ended January 31, 2015			
2	*(in thousands of dollars)*			
3	**Income**			
4	Sales	$ 250,210		
5	Finance income	18		
6	**Total income**	250,228		
7	**Expenses**			
8	Cost of sales	98,665		
9	Selling	153,853		
10	General and administrative	35,202		
11	Finance costs	2,900		
12	**Total expenses**	290,620		
13	**Loss before income taxes**	(40,392)		
14	Income tax recovery	(1,716)		
15	**Net loss**	$ (38,676)		
16				

Source: Le Château Inc. Annual Report – 2015.

Chapter 2 focused on measuring and recording transactions up to the trial balance. This chapter completes our coverage of the accounting cycle by discussing the adjustment process, the preparation of financial statements, and the closing of the books at the end of the period. It also includes a discussion of accounting principles that govern the recognition of revenue and expenses. At the end of the chapter, you will learn how to evaluate a company's debt-paying ability.

OBJECTIVE

❶ **Explain** how accrual accounting differs from cash-basis accounting

EXPLAIN HOW ACCRUAL ACCOUNTING DIFFERS FROM CASH-BASIS ACCOUNTING

Managers want to earn a profit. Investors search for companies whose share prices will increase. Banks seek borrowers who will pay their debts. Accounting provides the information these people use for decision making. Accounting information can be prepared using either the cash basis or the accrual basis of accounting.

When using **cash-basis accounting**, we record only business transactions involving the receipt or payment of cash. All other business transactions are ignored. If a business makes a $1,000 sale on account, for example, with the customer taking delivery of the goods but not paying for them until a later date, we would not record the sale transaction until we receive the cash payment from the customer. Similarly, the business would not record the purchase of $2,000 of inventory on account until it actually pays cash for the goods at some future date, despite having already received the inventory items from its supplier.

In contrast, when using **accrual accounting**, *the receipt or payment of cash is irrelevant* to deciding whether a business transaction should be recorded. What matters is whether the business has acquired an asset, earned revenue, taken on a liability, or incurred an expense. If it has, the transaction is recorded in the accounting records.

After the above sale on account, for example, the business has both gained an asset and earned revenue despite receiving no cash. Recall from Chapter 1 that an asset is a resource controlled by a company as a result of a past event and from which it expects to receive future economic benefits. The sale on account creates a $1,000 account receivable, which is an asset because it entitles the company to receive the economic benefit of cash at a future date when the customer pays off its account. The business has also earned $1,000 in revenue by delivering goods to the customer, which is a key activity in its day-to-day business operations. Because this transaction results in both an asset and revenue, we record it under the accrual basis of accounting.

Similarly, after the preceding purchase of inventory on account, the business has acquired $2,000 in assets in the form of goods it can sell to its customers in return for cash at some future date. It also has an obligation—in the form of a $2,000 account payable—that it must settle by paying cash to its supplier at some future date, so the business has also taken on a liability. Since this transaction results in an asset and a liability, we must record it under the accrual basis of accounting.

If the business were using the cash basis of accounting, neither of these initial transactions would have been recorded, leading to the following understatements in the business's financial statements: $3,000 in assets, $2,000 in liabilities, and $1,000 in revenue and net income. As a result, users relying on these cash-basis financial statements would have incomplete information about the company's financial position and results of operations, which would likely lead them to make poor business decisions.

Because the cash basis of accounting is inconsistent with the conceptual framework of accounting introduced in Chapter 1, it is not permitted by IFRS or ASPE, both of which provide extensive guidance on how to apply the accrual basis of accounting to prepare financial statements that present a relevant and faithful representation of a company's business activities.

Let's look at a simple example that illustrates the differences between the two methods of accounting. Suppose Pointz Corporation has the following transactions during July 2017:

1. Provides services to a customer for $500 in cash.
2. Provides services to a customer for $800 on account.
3. Pays employees' salaries of $450 in cash.
4. Receives a $50 hydro bill for electricity used during July.

The income statements for Pointz Corporation under the accrual basis and the cash basis of accounting appear as follows:

	A	B	C	D
1	**Pointz Corporation** Income Statement Using Accrual Accounting For the Month Ended July 31, 2017			
2	Revenue	$ 1,300		
3	Expenses:			
4	Salaries	450		
5	Hydro	50		
6	Net income	$ 800		
7	**Pointz Corporation** Income Statement Using Cash-Basis Accounting For the Month Ended July 31, 2017			
8	Revenue	$ 500		
9	Expenses:			
10	Salaries	450		
11	Hydro	0		
12	Net income	$ 50		
13				

The accrual-accounting statement reports an additional $800 in revenue because we have recorded the sale on account that is ignored in the cash-basis statement. The accrual statement also includes the $50 cost of hydro consumed during the month, which we have excluded from the cash statement because it remained unpaid at the end of the month. As a result of these differences, we report an additional $750 in net income for the month ($800 in revenue less $50 in expenses) on the accrual basis compared to the cash basis.

Next we discuss the formal principles used to determine when revenues and expenses should be recognized under accrual accounting.

STOP + THINK (3-1)

Death Valley's Little Brother (DVLB), a local independent coffee shop, sells an Americano for $3. Customers can also purchase 10 Americanos for $25 and receive a coffee card, with the card being punched every time the customer orders one of their 10 Americanos on future visits. DVLB uses accrual accounting. Briefly explain when DVLB would record revenue on the sale of a single Americano and on the sale of 10 Americanos via a coffee card.

APPLY THE REVENUE AND EXPENSE RECOGNITION PRINCIPLES

The Revenue Recognition Principle

In Chapter 1 we provided you with a basic definition of revenue, which stated that it consists of amounts earned by a company in the course of its ordinary, day-to-day business activities, primarily through the sale of goods and services. Now that you are more familiar with many fundamental accounting terms and concepts, we will provide the formal IFRS definition of revenue. IFRS define revenue as "the gross inflow of economic benefits during the period arising in the course of the ordinary activities of an entity when those inflows result in increases in equity, other than increases relating to contributions from equity participants" (ASPE has a fundamentally equivalent definition of revenue). Restating this in terms of the accounting equation, revenue is earned when ordinary business activities result in increases to both assets and shareholders' equity, other than when shareholders contribute capital to the business. When a business delivers goods to a customer who pays cash for them, the Cash asset increases and so does Shareholders' Equity (via Retained Earnings), so the business has earned revenue. But when a shareholder purchases additional shares in the business, which also increases Cash and Shareholders' Equity (via Share Capital), no revenue has been earned because the shareholder has simply injected more capital into the business.

IFRS and ASPE have revenue recognition principles which specify the conditions that must be met before a business can recognize revenue from a transaction. The principles are generally consistent across the two sets of standards, and while they both contain several criteria that must be met before recognizing revenue, we will focus on the three most fundamental criteria at this early stage in your accounting learning. A transaction must satisfy *all three* of these conditions before the business can recognize revenue:

1. The ownership (or control) and benefits of the goods have been transferred to the customer, or the services have been provided to the customer.

2. The amount of revenue can be reliably measured.

3. It is probable that the business will receive the economic benefits associated with the transaction, which usually come in the form of cash receipts.

To illustrate the application of these criteria, suppose you go shopping at Le Château and purchase a pair of pants for $75, which you pay cash for and take home with you. After this transaction, Le Château can recognize revenue because all three conditions have been met: (1) you possess the pants, along with the benefit of wearing them; (2) the pants have a price of $75; (3) Le Château received $75 in cash from you. Suppose, instead, that you find a pair of $75 pants you like but the store does not have your size in stock, so the sales clerk orders a pair in your size from another store, and tells you to come back to pick up and pay for them in three days. At this point, you do not have the pants, so you cannot benefit from wearing them, which leaves the first recognition condition unmet. In addition, after leaving the store, you may change your mind about the pants and never return to purchase them, which creates doubt about the third recognition condition. Le Château therefore cannot recognize revenue in this situation. Only if you return to the store to pick up and pay for the pants will Le Château be able to recognize any revenue.

As an example of service revenue recognition, assume a plumber comes to fix a leaky pipe under your bathroom sink, taking one hour and charging you $75, which you pay for by credit card. The plumbing company can recognize $75 in revenue here because all three recognition conditions have been met. In contrast, assume you simply call the plumbing company to arrange for a plumber to come to your home in two days to fix the leaky pipe, which the company estimates will take one hour and cost $75. In this case, none of the three conditions has been met, so the plumbing company cannot yet recognize any revenue.

A new IFRS revenue recognition standard goes into effect at the beginning of 2017 (the ASPE standard remains unchanged). The standard is based on the idea that all business transactions involve contracts that exchange goods or services for cash or claims to receive cash. The business selling the good or service must: (1) identify the contract with the customer; (2) identify the separate performance obligations in the contract; (3) determine the transaction price; (4) allocate the transaction price to the separate performance obligations in the contract; and (5) recognize revenue when (or as) the entity satisfies each performance obligation. This textbook deals mostly with the retail industry, where businesses enter into relatively simple and straightforward contracts to purchase and sell largely finished goods and to render services. In other industries, such as computer software, long-term construction, motion pictures, natural resources, or real estate, contracts can be more complex, making the issue of how and when to recognize revenue more complicated. Fortunately, the new standard has not substantially changed how revenue is recognized in the retail industry, so the three criteria stated above are sufficient to determine how and when to recognize revenue in the sales transactions used throughout this book.

The Expense Recognition Principle

In Chapter 1 we defined expenses as costs incurred to purchase the goods and services a company needs to run its business on a day-to-day basis. As with revenue recognition, IFRS and ASPE contain formal principles which set out the criteria that must be satisfied before an expense can be recognized:

1. There has been a decrease in future economic benefits caused by a decrease in an asset *or* an increase in a liability.
2. The expense can be reliably measured.

So, for example, once you have left the store with your new pants, Le Château's pants inventory (an asset) decreases by one pair, so the first expense recognition condition has been met. Le Château can check its inventory records to determine the cost of the pants it sold you, so the expense can be reliably measured. Both conditions have now been satisfied, so Le Château can recognize an expense in the form of Cost of Goods Sold. As for the situation where you are waiting for pants to be shipped from another store, Le Château cannot recognize an expense because its pants inventory will not decrease until you have actually purchased the pants.

In the case of the plumber who has fixed your leaky pipe, the plumbing company that employs him is now obligated to pay him for the one hour of work he did for you, which increases the company's Wages Payable liability. The plumber's hourly wage rate can be used to reliably measure the expense, so with both conditions satisfied, the company can recognize the wage expense associated with the plumber's work on your pipe. As for the situation where you have to wait two days for the plumber to come and fix your pipe, the plumbing company is not yet obligated to pay the plumber because he has not done the work for you. Without an increase in the Wages Payable liability, the first condition has not been met, so no expense can be recognized.

STOP + THINK (3-2)

1. A client pays Windsor Group Ltd. $900 on March 15 for consulting service to be performed April 1 to June 30. Assuming the company uses accrual accounting, has Windsor Group Ltd. earned revenue on March 15? When will Windsor Group Ltd. earn the revenue?

2. Windsor Group Ltd. pays $4,500 on July 31 for office rent for the next three months. Has the company incurred an expense on July 31?

OBJECTIVE

❸ Record adjusting journal entries

RECORD ADJUSTING JOURNAL ENTRIES

At the end of a period, the business prepares its financial statements. This process begins with the trial balance introduced in Chapter 2. We refer to this trial balance as *unadjusted* because the accounts are not yet ready for the financial statements. In most cases, the simple label "Trial Balance" means "Unadjusted Trial Balance."

Because IFRS and ASPE require accrual accounting, we must record adjusting journal entries to ensure that all assets and liabilities have been recorded at period end, and that all revenues earned and expenses incurred during the period have been included in the accounts. These entries are recorded at the end of the accounting period, just before the financial statements are prepared.

Types of Adjusting Entries

There are three main types of adjusting entries: deferrals, depreciation, and accruals. We will use a variety of transactions and related adjusting entries for the fictional Moreau Ltd. to illustrate each main type of adjustment. Other miscellaneous adjusting entries are usually required at the end of an accounting period. We will address some of these as they arise in later chapters of the book. The table below provides an overview of the main types of adjusting entries.

Main Types of Adjusting Entries

Type	Description
Deferrals	An adjusting entry must be recorded when a company receives (pays) cash in advance of providing (receiving) the related good or service that has been paid for. This type of adjusting entry results in the deferral of the recognition of the related revenue (expense) until the future period in which the economic benefit is actually provided.
Depreciation	An adjusting entry must be recorded to reflect that the future economic benefits of a tangible asset decline with age. This type of adjusting entry, which can be considered a special form of deferral, results in the depreciation (amortization under ASPE) of the value of the asset over its useful life by expensing the portion of the asset's economic benefits that has been used up during an accounting period.
Accruals	An adjusting entry must be recorded when a company delivers (or receives) a good or service in advance of it being billed and paid for. This type of adjusting entry results in the accrual of the related revenue (expense) in the period in which the good or service is actually provided, regardless of the fact that it will not be billed or paid for until a future period.

Deferrals—Prepaid Expenses

A prepaid expense is an expense a company has paid for in advance of actually using the benefit. Because it will provide a future economic benefit to the company, it is recorded as an asset when the cash payment is made. Recording the initial transaction this way results in the **deferral** of the expense to the future period in which the related benefit is realized. Let's look at the initial and adjusting entries for prepaid rent and supplies.

PREPAID RENT. Rent is usually paid in advance of the rented item being used, creating an asset for the renter, who gains the benefit of using the rented item during the future rental period. Suppose Moreau Ltd. prepays three months' office rent ($3,000) on April 1. The journal entry for the prepayment of three months' rent is as follows:

	A	B	C	D	E
1	Apr. 1	Prepaid Rent ($1,000 × 3)	3,000		
2		Cash		3,000	
3		*Paid three months' rent in advance.*			
4					

The accounting equation shows that one asset increases and another decreases. Total assets are unchanged.

ASSETS	=	LIABILITIES	+	SHAREHOLDERS' EQUITY
3,000	=	0	+	0
−3,000				

After posting, the Prepaid Rent account appears as follows:

Prepaid Rent

Apr. 1	3,000	

At the end of April, Moreau has only two months of future rental benefits remaining (2/3 of $3,000), so we must adjust the Prepaid Rent account to reflect this and to expense the $1,000 in Prepaid Rent used up during April (1/3 of $3,000).[*]

	A	B	C	D	E
1	Apr. 30	Rent Expense	1,000		
2	*Adjusting entry a*	Prepaid Rent		1,000	
3		*To record rent expense.*			
4					

Both assets and shareholders' equity decrease.

ASSETS	=	LIABILITIES	+	SHAREHOLDERS' EQUITY	
−1,000	=	0	−	1,000	Rent Expense

After posting, Prepaid Rent and Rent Expense appear as follows:

Prepaid Rent					Rent Expense		
Apr. 1	3,000	Apr. 30	1,000	→	Apr. 30	1,000	
Bal.	2,000				Bal.	1,000	

SUPPLIES. Businesses often have a stock of unused supplies on hand at the end of an accounting period, which represents an asset that will be used up in future periods. These unused supplies are another type of prepaid expense. On April 2, Moreau paid cash for $700 of office supplies, requiring the following journal entry:

	A	B	C	D	E
1	Apr. 2	Supplies	700		
2		Cash		700	
3		*Paid cash for supplies.*			
4					

---

[*]See Exhibit 3-3, page 125, for a summary of adjustments a through g.

ASSETS	=	LIABILITIES	+	SHAREHOLDERS' EQUITY
700	=	0	+	0
−700				

Moreau used some of these supplies during April, so to expense their use and adjust the Supplies asset to reflect the future benefit remaining at April 30, we need an adjusting entry. By counting and valuing the supplies on hand at April 30, we can determine the amount of the adjustment needed. If Moreau's count shows that $400 in supplies remain at April 30, then we know that $300 worth of supplies have been used during April ($700 – $400), and we can record this adjusting entry:

	A	B	C	D	E
1	Apr. 30	Supplies Expense ($700 – $400)	300		
2	*Adjusting entry b*	Supplies		300	
3		*To record supplies expense.*			
4					

ASSETS	=	LIABILITIES	+	SHAREHOLDERS' EQUITY	
−300	=	0	−	300	Supplies Expense

After posting, the Supplies and Supplies Expense accounts appear as follows:

Supplies						Supplies Expense		
Apr. 2	700	Apr. 30	300	→	Apr. 30	300		
Bal.	400				Bal.	300		

MyAccountingLab

STOP + THINK (3-3)

At the beginning of the month, supplies were $5,000. During the month, $7,000 of supplies were purchased. At month's end, $3,000 of supplies were still on hand. What adjusting entry is needed to account for the supplies, and what is the ending balance in the Supplies account?

Deferrals—Unearned Revenues

Businesses sometimes receive cash from customers before providing them with the goods or services they have paid for. Because the goods or services have not been delivered, the revenue recognition principle deems this to be **unearned revenue**. In fact, the business now has an obligation to provide the goods or services at some future date, which requires it to record a liability instead of revenue. Recording such transactions in this way results in a deferral of revenue recognition until the liability has been settled by providing the goods or services to the customer.

Suppose a customer engages Moreau Ltd. to provide consulting services over the next year, agreeing to pay Moreau $450 per month for nine hours of services ($50/hour), effective immediately. If Moreau receives the first $450 payment on April 20, it records this entry to reflect the unearned revenue:

	A	B	C	D	E
1	Apr. 20	Cash	450		
2		Unearned Service Revenue		450	
3		*Received cash in advance of providing services.*			
4					

ASSETS	=	LIABILITIES	+	SHAREHOLDERS' EQUITY
450	=	450	+	0

After posting, the liability account appears as follows:

Unearned Service Revenue

	Apr. 20	450

Unearned Service Revenue is a liability because Moreau Ltd. is obligated to perform nine hours of services for the client. During the last 10 days of April, Moreau performed three hours of services for the client, so by April 30, Moreau has settled one-third of the liability and earned one-third of the revenue ($450 × 1/3 = $150). The following adjusting entry is needed to reflect these events:

	A	B	C	D	E
1	Apr. 30	Unearned Service Revenue	150		
2	*Adjusting entry c*	Service Revenue		150	
3		*To adjust unearned service revenue that has been earned ($450 × 1/3).*			

ASSETS	=	LIABILITIES	+	SHAREHOLDERS' EQUITY	
0	=	−150	+	150	Service Revenue

This adjusting entry shifts $150 of the total amount received ($450) from liability to revenue. After posting, Unearned Service Revenue is reduced to $300, and Service Revenue is increased by $150, as follows:

Unearned Service Revenue

Apr. 30	150	Apr. 20	450
		Bal.	300

Service Revenue

			7,000
		Apr. 30	150
		Bal.	7,150

Any time a business receives cash from a customer in advance of providing the related goods or services, similar initial and adjusting entries are required to properly reflect the obligation and defer the recognition of revenue until the goods or services have been provided.

Also note that one company's unearned revenue is another company's prepaid expense. As at April 30, for example, the $300 in Unearned Service Revenue on Moreau's books would be reflected as $300 in Prepaid Consulting Services on its customer's books. Under accrual accounting, the deferral of revenue by one company will result in the deferral of an expense by another company.

Depreciation of Property, Plant, and Equipment

Property, plant, and equipment, such as buildings, furniture, and machinery, are long-term tangible assets that provide several years of economic benefits to a company. Because the future benefits of a tangible asset decline with age, however, we must reduce its carrying value each year to reflect this decline. To accomplish this, we record adjusting entries for **depreciation** (amortization under ASPE), which gradually reduce the value of the asset over its useful life by expensing the portion of the asset's economic benefits that has been used up during each accounting period. An exception is made for land, which we do not depreciate because it has an unlimited useful life, so its future economic benefits generally do not decline with age.

To illustrate depreciation, suppose that on April 3, Moreau Ltd. purchased $16,500 of office furniture, including desks, chairs, and storage cabinets, on account. The entry to record this purchase is as follows:

	A	B	C	D	E
1	Apr. 3	Furniture	16,500		
2		Accounts Payable		16,500	
3		*Purchased office furniture on account.*			

ASSETS	=	LIABILITIES	+	SHAREHOLDERS' EQUITY
16,500	=	16,500	+	0

After posting, the Furniture account appears as follows:

Furniture	
Apr. 3 16,500	

Moreau Ltd.'s furniture is expected to remain useful for five years and then be worthless. One way to *estimate* the amount of depreciation for each year is to divide the cost of the asset ($16,500 in our example) by its expected useful life (five years). This procedure—called the straight-line depreciation method—yields annual depreciation of $3,300, or monthly depreciation of $275 ($3,300/12). (Chapter 6 covers depreciation and property, plant, and equipment in more detail.)

The adjusting entry to record depreciation for April is therefore:

	A	B	C	D	E
1	Apr. 30	Depreciation Expense—Furniture	275		
2	*Adjusting entry d*	Accumulated Depreciation—Furniture		275	
3		*To record depreciation.*			

ASSETS	=	LIABILITIES	+	SHAREHOLDERS' EQUITY	
−275	=	0	−	275	Depreciation

Note that the adjusting entry does not decrease Assets by directly crediting the Furniture asset account. Instead, we decrease Assets by crediting an account called Accumulated Depreciation—Furniture, which is known as a contra asset account. A **contra account** has two distinguishing features:

1. It always has a companion account.
2. Its normal balance is opposite that of the companion account.

In this case, the Furniture account is the companion to the Accumulated Depreciation contra account. Since the Furniture account's normal balance is a debit, the normal balance of the Accumulated Depreciation account is a credit.

As its name suggests, the **Accumulated Depreciation** account accumulates all the depreciation recorded on the asset(s) included in the related companion account, so its balance increases over the life of the related assets being depreciated. A business's chart of accounts normally contains a separate Accumulated Depreciation account for each major category of depreciable asset.

After posting, the furniture-related accounts of Moreau Ltd. are as follows:

Furniture		Accumulated Depreciation—Furniture		Depreciation Expense—Furniture	
Apr. 3 16,500			Apr. 30 275	Apr. 30 275	
Bal. 16,500			Bal. 275	Bal. 275	

As at April 30, the **carrying amount** of Moreau's furniture is $16,225, which is obtained by deducting the asset's accumulated depreciation ($275) from its original cost ($16,500). All long-term tangible assets are reported at their carrying amounts on the balance sheet, with the details of their original costs and accumulated depreciation normally disclosed in a note to the financial statements.

STOP + THINK (3-4)

What will the carrying amount of Moreau Ltd.'s furniture be at the end of May 2017?

Accruals—Accrued Expenses

Businesses often incur expenses they have not yet been billed for, let alone paid. Utility bills, for example, usually arrive after the business has consumed the electricity or gas being billed. For some types of expenses, such as salaries or loan interest, no bills will ever be received. At the end of each accounting period, businesses must record adjusting entries called **accruals** to get these unbilled, unpaid expenses, which we call **accrued expenses**, into the books. By recording these accruals, we ensure the related expenses and liabilities are properly reflected in the financial statements for the period.

Let's use Salary Expense to illustrate this concept. Suppose Moreau Ltd. has one employee who receives a monthly salary of $1,900, which is paid in equal $950 amounts on the 15th and last day of each month. If a payday falls on a weekend, the salary is paid on the following Monday. The following calendar illustrates Moreau's pay days for April:

			April			
Sun.	Mon.	Tue.	Wed.	Thur.	Fri.	Sat.
					1	2
3	4	5	6	7	8	9
10	11	12	13	14	⑮	16
17	18	19	20	21	22	23
24	25	26	27	28	29	㉚

On April 15, a Friday, Moreau records this entry to account for the first half-month's salary:

	A	B	C	D	E
1	Apr. 15	Salary Expense	950		
2		Cash		950	
3		*To pay salary.*			

ASSETS	=	LIABILITIES	+	SHAREHOLDERS' EQUITY	
−950	=	0	−	950	Salary Expense

After posting, the Salary Expense account is:

Salary Expense	
Apr. 15 950	

Because April 30 falls on a Saturday, the employee will not receive the second half of the salary for April until Monday, May 2, two days after the end of the April accounting period. In this case, the business has incurred a half-month of Salary Expense that it owes the employee as at April 30. To reflect these facts, we record this accrual adjusting entry:

	A	B	C	D	E
1	Apr. 30	Salary Expense	950		
2	*Adjusting entry e*	Salary Payable		950	
3		*To accrue salary expense.*			

The accounting equation shows that an accrued expense increases liabilities and decreases shareholders' equity:

ASSETS	=	LIABILITIES	+	SHAREHOLDERS' EQUITY	
0	=	950	−	950	Salary Expense

After posting, the Salary Payable and Salary Expense accounts appear as follows:

Salary Payable		
	Apr. 30	950
	Bal.	950

Salary Expense		
Apr. 15	950	
Apr. 30	950	
Bal.	1,900	

After the accrual, Moreau's accounts contain accurate salary information for April: it incurred $1,900 in Salary Expense during the month and owed $950 of this amount as at April 30. All accrued-expense adjustments are typically recorded this way—by debiting an expense account and crediting a liability account.

Accruals—Accrued Revenues

At the end of each accounting period, we must also consider the need to record accruals to account for **accrued revenues**, which are the opposite of accrued expenses. Businesses sometimes earn revenues they have not yet billed their customers for, let alone collected cash for. Service businesses such as accounting firms, for example, often provide services to their clients prior to invoicing for the work. Some types of revenues, such as loan interest, will never be invoiced. By recording accruals for these unbilled, uncollected revenues, we ensure that the related assets and revenues are properly reflected in the financial statements for the period.

To illustrate this type of accrual, assume that during the last half of April, Moreau performed $250 worth of services for a client that were not invoiced until early May. The adjusting entry to record this accrual is as follows:

	A	B	C	D	E
1	Apr. 30	Accrued Service Revenue	250		
2	*Adjusting entry f*	Service Revenue		250	
3		*To accrue service revenue.*			

ASSETS	=	LIABILITIES	+	SHAREHOLDERS' EQUITY	
250	=	0	–	250	Service Revenues

This entry increases Assets, in the form of Accrued Service Revenue, because Moreau will receive the economic benefit of cash after it bills and collects the $250 from its client. Note that we have used Accrued Service Revenue instead of Accounts Receivable because the customer has not yet been billed, so no formal account receivable exists. This entry also increases Service Revenue by the same amount to reflect the revenue it has earned by providing the services in April. After posting, these accounts appear as follows:

Accrued Service Revenue		
	2,250	
Apr. 30	250	
Bal.	2,500	

Service Revenue		
		7,000
	Apr. 30	150
	Apr. 30	250
	Bal.	7,400

In May, when Moreau invoices the client for the work in April, it will record an entry that debits Accounts Receivable and credits Accrued Service Revenue for $250, since there is now a formal account receivable from this client.

We record similar accrual entries for other kinds of accrued revenues—an accrued revenue account is debited and a revenue account is credited.

MyAccountingLab

STOP + THINK (3-5)

Suppose Moreau Ltd. holds a loan receivable from a client. At the end of April, $125 of interest revenue has been earned but not received. Prepare the adjusting entry at April 30.

Summary of the Adjusting Process

At the end of every accounting period, we must record adjusting journal entries to ensure that we properly measure income for the period and that we accurately reflect the business's financial position as at the end of the period. Exhibit 3-1 summarizes the main types of adjusting entries, along with the types of accounts they affect.

Exhibit 3-2 details the specific deferral and accrual adjusting entries needed at the end of each accounting period, as well as the journal entries to record the transactions that precede the deferrals and succeed the accruals.

EXHIBIT 3-1
Summary of Adjusting Entries

Type of Adjusting Entry	Type of Account	
	Debit	Credit
Deferral—Prepaid Expense	Expense	Asset
Deferral—Unearned Revenue	Liability	Revenue
Depreciation	Expense	Contra asset
Accrual—Accrued Expense	Expense	Liability
Accrual—Accrued Revenue	Asset	Revenue

Adapted from material provided by Beverly Terry.

EXHIBIT 3-2
Deferral and Accrual Adjusting Entries

DEFERRALS—Cash First

	First			Later		
Prepaid expenses	Pay cash and record an asset:			→ Record an expense and decrease the asset:		
	Prepaid Expense	XXX		Expense	XXX	
	Cash		XXX	Prepaid Expense		XXX
Unearned revenues	Receive cash and record unearned revenue:			→ Record a revenue and decrease unearned revenue:		
	Cash	XXX		Unearned Revenue	XXX	
	Unearned Revenue		XXX	Revenue		XXX

(Continued)

ACCRUALS—Cash Later

	First				Later		
Accrued expenses	*Accrue expense and a payable:*			→	*Pay cash and decrease the payable:*		
	Expense..	XXX			Payable..	XXX	
	Payable..		XXX		Cash..		XXX
Accrued revenues	*Accrue revenue:*			→	*Invoice customer and record a receivable:*		
	Accrued Revenue.................................	XXX			Receivable...	XXX	
	Revenue...		XXX		Accrued Revenue.............................		XXX

COOKING *the* BOOKS

issues in Accrual Accounting

Accrual accounting provides some ethical challenges that cash accounting avoids. Suppose that on December 1, 2017, for example, Shop Online Inc. (SOI) pays $3 million in cash for an advertising campaign, which will run during December, January, and February. The ads start running immediately. If SOI properly applies the expense recognition principle discussed earlier in the chapter, it should record one-third of the expense ($1 million) during the year ended December 31, 2017, and leave the remaining $2 million as a prepaid expense that will be recognized as an expense in 2018.

But also suppose that 2017 is a great year for SOI, with its net income being much higher than expected. SOI's top managers believe, however, that 2018 will be much less profitable due to increased competition. In this case, company managers have a strong incentive to expense the full $3 million during 2017, an unethical action that would keep $2 million of advertising expense off the 2018 income statement and increase its net income by the same amount (ignoring income taxes).

Unethical managers can also exploit the revenue recognition principle to artificially improve reported liabilities, revenues, and net income. Suppose it is now December 31, 2017, and High-field Computer Products Ltd., which is having a poor fiscal year, has just received a $1 million advance cash payment for merchandise it will deliver early in January. If top managers are unethical, the company can "manufacture" revenue and net income by recording the $1 million cash payment as revenue in 2017 instead of as unearned revenue (a liability) at the end of the year.

Exhibit 3-3 summarizes the adjusting process we followed for Moreau Ltd. as at April 30, 2017. Panel A contains the information used to record each adjusting entry in Panel B, while Panel C presents all of Moreau's ledger accounts, with each adjusting entry keyed with the corresponding letter from Panel A.

Exhibit 3-3 includes an additional accrual adjustment (*entry g*) to accrue the income tax expense Moreau owes for April. This is typically the last adjusting entry a business makes at the end of an accounting period because it is based on the net income for the period, which can only be determined after all other adjusting entries have been posted to the accounts. If we assume Moreau owes $540 of income tax for April, the adjusting entry is as follows:

	A	B	C	D	E
1	Apr. 30	Income Tax Expense	540		
2	*Adjusting entry g*	Income Tax Payable		540	
3		*To accrue income tax expense.*			

EXHIBIT 3-3
The Adjusting Process of Moreau Ltd.

Panel A—Information for Adjustments at April 30, 2017

(a) Prepaid rent expired, $1,000.
(b) Supplies on hand, $400.
(c) Amount of unearned service revenue that has been earned, $150.
(d) Depreciation on furniture, $275.

(e) Accrued salary expense, $950. This entry assumes the pay period ended April 30 and the employee was paid May 2.
(f) Accrued service revenue, $250.
(g) Accrued income tax expense, $540.

Panel B—Adjusting Entries

(a) Rent Expense	1,000	
Prepaid Rent		1,000
To record rent expense.		
(b) Supplies Expense	300	
Supplies		300
To record supplies used.		
(c) Unearned Service Revenue	150	
Service Revenue		150
To record unearned revenue that has been earned.		
(d) Depreciation Expense—Furniture	275	
Accumulated Depreciation—Furniture		275
To record depreciation.		
(e) Salary Expense	950	
Salary Payable		950
To accrue salary expense.		
(f) Accrued Service Revenue	250	
Service Revenue		250
To accrue service revenue.		
(g) Income Tax Expense	540	
Income Tax Payable		540
To accrue income tax expense.		

Panel C—Ledger Accounts

Assets

Cash

Bal.	24,800		

Accrued Service Revenue

	2,250		
(f)	250		
Bal.	2,500		

Supplies

	700	(b)	300
Bal.	400		

Prepaid Rent

	3,000	(a)	1,000
Bal.	2,000		

Furniture

Bal.	16,500		

Accumulated Depreciation—Furniture

		(d)	275
		Bal.	275

Liabilities

Accounts Payable

		Bal.	13,100

Salary Payable

		(e)	950
		Bal.	950

Unearned Service Revenue

(c)	150		450
		Bal.	300

Income Tax Payable

		(g)	540
		Bal.	540

Shareholders' Equity

Share Capital

		Bal.	20,000

Retained Earnings

		Bal.	11,250

Dividends

Bal.	3,200		

Revenue

Service Revenue

			7,000
		(c)	150
		(f)	250
		Bal.	7,400

Expenses

Rent Expense

(a)	1,000		
Bal.	1,000		

Salary Expense

	950		
(e)	950		
Bal.	1,900		

Supplies Expense

(b)	300		
Bal.	300		

Depreciation Expense—Furniture

(d)	275		
Bal.	275		

Utilities Expense

Bal.	400		

Income Tax Expense

(g)	540		
Bal.	540		

The Adjusted Trial Balance

Before we prepare the financial statements, it is helpful to compile an **adjusted trial balance** listing all of the ledger accounts and their adjusted balances, which are what we need to report on the financial statements. Exhibit 3-4 contains the adjusted trial balance for Moreau Ltd. Note how clearly the adjusted trial balance presents the adjustments made to the account balances contained in the initial unadjusted trial balance. This presentation format makes it easy for us to see the impacts of all our adjusting entries on the accounts in the ledger. We see, for example, that we adjusted Supplies downward by $300 to arrive at the account's $400 balance as at April 30, 2017.

EXHIBIT 3-4
Worksheet for the Preparation of Adjusted Trial Balance

	A	B	C	D	E	F	G	
1	**Moreau Ltd.** Preparation of Adjusted Trial Balance April 30, 2017							
2		Unadjusted Trial Balance		Adjustments		Adjusted Trial Balance		
3	Account Title	Debit	Credit	Debit	Credit	Debit	Credit	
4	Cash	24,800				24,800		⎫
5	Accrued service revenue	2,250		(f) 250		2,500		
6	Supplies	700			(b) 300	400		
7	Prepaid rent	3,000			(a) 1,000	2,000		
8	Furniture	16,500				16,500		
9	Accumulated depreciation—furniture				(d) 275		275	**Balance Sheet**
10	Accounts payable		13,100				13,100	*(Exhibit 3-7)*
11	Salary payable				(e) 950		950	
12	Unearned service revenue		450	(c) 150			300	
13	Income tax payable				(g) 540		540	
14	Share capital		20,000				20,000	
15	Retained earnings		11,250				11,250	**Statement**
16	Dividends	3,200				3,200		**of Retained**
17	Service revenue		7,000		(f) 250		7,400	**Earnings**
18					(c) 150			*(Exhibit 3-6)*
19	Rent expense			(a) 1,000		1,000		
20	Salary expense	950		(e) 950		1,900		**Income**
21	Supplies expense			(b) 300		300		**Statement**
22	Depreciation expense—furniture			(d) 275		275		*(Exhibit 3-5)*
23	Utilities expense	400				400		
24	Income tax expense			(g) 540		540		
25		51,800	51,800	3,465	3,465	53,815	53,815	⎭
26								

TRY IT in EXCEL ® ▶ ▶ ▶

The adjusted trial balance in Exhibit 3-4 was prepared using an Excel spreadsheet. You can use it as a template to solve future problems just by changing the initial trial balance data. To prepare the Excel template, follow these steps:

1. Open a blank Excel spreadsheet. Format the spreadsheet header and column headings exactly as you see in Exhibit 3-4.
2. Enter the account titles and account balances from the "Unadjusted Trial Balance" columns.
3. Sum the debits and credits in the "Unadjusted Trial Balance" columns.
4. Enter adjusting journal entries (a) through (g) one at a time in the "Adjustments" columns. For example, for adjusting journal entry (a) enter 1,000 in the debit column on the "Rent expense" line, and 1,000 in the credit column of the "Prepaid rent" line. Do not enter the letters (a) through (g); use only the amounts.
5. In the "Adjusted Trial Balance" debit and credit columns, enter formulas as follows:
   - For asset, dividend, and expense accounts: = + (debit amounts from "Unadjusted Trial Balance" and "Adjustments" columns) − (credit amounts from "Adjustments" columns).
   - For contra asset, liability, share capital, retained earnings, and service revenue accounts: = + (credit amounts from "Unadjusted Trial Balance" and "Adjustments" columns) − (debit amounts from "Adjustments" columns).
6. Sum the "Adjustments" debit and credit columns.
7. Sum the "Adjusted Trial Balance" debit and credit columns.

PREPARE THE FINANCIAL STATEMENTS

OBJECTIVE

❹ **Prepare** the financial statements

The April 2017 financial statements of Moreau Ltd. can be prepared from the adjusted trial balance in Exhibit 3-4. The right side of the exhibit highlights which financial statement(s) the accounts are reported on.

- The income statement (Exhibit 3-5) reports the revenue and expense accounts.

- The statement of retained earnings (Exhibit 3-6) reports the changes in retained earnings.

- The balance sheet (Exhibit 3-7) reports assets, liabilities, and shareholders' equity.

- The arrows in Exhibits 3-5, 3-6, and 3-7 show the flow of data from one statement to the next.

TRY IT in EXCEL ® ▶ ▶ ▶

If you have already prepared Excel templates for the income statement, statement of retained earnings, and balance sheet for Tara Inc. in Chapter 2 (see Exhibit 2-2), you may use these to prepare Moreau Ltd.'s April 30, 2017, financial statements. You will have to insert and delete line items as needed because some of Moreau's accounts differ from Tara's. The value of Excel is that once you have prepared the templates for the adjusted trial balance worksheet and financial statements, you can reuse them as needed.

EXHIBIT 3-5
Income Statement

	A	B	C
1	**Moreau Ltd.** Income Statement For the Month Ended April 30, 2017		
2	Revenue:		
3	Service revenue		$ 7,400
4	Expenses:		
5	Salary	$ 1,900	
6	Rent	1,000	
7	Utilities	400	
8	Supplies	300	
9	Depreciation	275	3,875
10	Income before tax		3,525
11	Income tax expense		540
12	Net income		$ 2,985
13			

①

EXHIBIT 3-6
Statement of Retained Earnings

	A	B	C
1	**Moreau Ltd.** Statement of Retained Earnings For the Month Ended April 30, 2017		
2	Retained earnings, April 1, 2017		$ 11,250
3	Add: Net income		2,985
4			14,235
5	Less: Dividends		(3,200)
6	Retained earnings, April 30, 2017		$ 11,035
7			

EXHIBIT 3-7
Balance Sheet

	A	B	C	D	E
1	**Moreau Ltd.** Balance Sheet As at April 30, 2017				
2	**Assets**			**Liabilities**	
3	Cash		$ 24,800	Accounts payable	$ 13,100
4	Accrued service revenue		2,500	Salary payable	950
5	Supplies		400	Unearned service revenue	300
6	Prepaid rent		2,000	Income tax payable	540
7	Furniture	16,500		Total liabilities	14,890
8	Less accumulated depreciation	(275)	16,225	**Shareholders' Equity**	
9				Share capital	20,000
10				Retained earnings	11,035
11				Total shareholders' equity	31,035
12	Total assets		$ 45,925	Total liabilities and shareholders' equity	$ 45,925
13					

②

Why is the income statement prepared first and the balance sheet last?

1. The income statement is prepared first because it reports net income (revenues minus expenses), which is needed to prepare the statement of retained earnings. This link is illustrated by arrow 1 between Exhibits 3-5 and 3-6.

2. The balance sheet is prepared last because it relies on the ending balance from the statement of retained earnings to complete the shareholders' equity section of the statement. This link is illustrated by arrow 2 between Exhibits 3-6 and 3-7.

You will note that the statement of cash flows is not included in the list of statements that are prepared from the adjusted trial balance. The reason it is not included, as you will discover in Chapter 10, is that the statement of cash flows is not prepared from the adjusted trial balance, but rather from the comparative balance sheets, the income statement, and other sources.

Formats for the Financial Statements

Companies can format their balance sheets and income statements in various ways. Here we will highlight some of the most common balance sheet and income statement formats.

BALANCE SHEET FORMATS. In Chapter 1 we introduced you to the difference between current and non-current (or long-term) assets. Recall that a current asset is an asset we expect to convert to cash, sell, or consume *within one year* of the balance sheet date, or within the business's normal operating cycle if it is longer than one year. A non-current asset is any asset that does not qualify as a current asset. We make a similar distinction between current and non-current liabilities, with a current liability being one we expect to repay within one year of the balance sheet date, or within the business's normal operating cycle if it is longer than one year; while a non-current liability will be repaid beyond one year or the normal operating cycle. A **classified balance sheet** separates current assets from non-current assets and current liabilities from non-current liabilities, and it also subtotals the current assets and current liabilities. Exhibit 3-8 contains the classified balance sheet of Le Château as at January 31, 2015. An unclassified balance sheet does not separate current and non-current assets or liabilities. Regardless of which of these two formats is used, current assets are always listed in order of decreasing **liquidity**, which is a measure of how quickly they can be converted to cash, the most liquid asset. IFRS and ASPE require the use of classified balance sheets.

A balance sheet prepared in **report format** lists assets at the top, followed by liabilities, and then shareholders' equity. Le Château's balance sheet in Exhibit 3-8 is in report format.

A balance sheet prepared in **account format** uses a T-account as a framework, with assets (debits) listed on the left side and liabilities and shareholders' equity (credits) on the right. The Moreau Ltd. balance sheet in Exhibit 3-7 is in account format. Companies are free to choose the report format or the account format when preparing their balance sheets.

	A	B	C	D
1	**Le Château Inc.** Consolidated Balance Sheet (Adapted) As at January 31, 2015			
2	*(in thousands of dollars)*			
3	ASSETS			
4	**Current assets**			
5	Cash	$ 1,195		
6	Accounts receivable	2,025		
7	Income taxes refundable	619		
8	Inventories	115,357		
9	Prepaid expenses	1,079		
10	**Total current assets**	120,275		
11	Property and equipment	58,091		
12	Intangible assets	2,961		
13	**Total assets**	$ 181,327		
14	**LIABILITIES AND SHAREHOLDERS' EQUITY**			
15	**Current liabilities**			
16	Current portion of credit facility	$ 14,737		
17	Trade and other payables	16,133		
18	Deferred revenue	3,452		
19	Current portion of provisions	678		
20	Current portion of long-term debt	2,007		
21	**Total current liabilities**	37,007		
22	Credit facility	33,674		
23	Long-term debt	5,836		
24	Provisions	1,473		
25	Deferred lease credits	11,354		
26	**Total liabilities**	89,344		
27	**Shareholders' equity**			
28	Share capital	47,967		
29	Contributed surplus	4,439		
30	Retained earnings	39,577		
31	**Total shareholders' equity**	91,983		
32	**Total liabilities and shareholders' equity**	$ 181,327		
33				

INCOME STATEMENT FORMATS. A **single-step income statement** lists all the revenues together under a heading such as Revenues or Income. The expenses are also listed together in a single category titled Expenses, or Expenses and Losses. This format contains only a single step: the subtracting of Total Expenses from Total Revenues to arrive at Net Income. Le Château's statement of loss at the opening of the chapter is in single-step format.

A **multi-step income statement** contains a number of subtotals to highlight important relationships among revenues and expenses. Le Château's multi-step statement of loss in Exhibit 3-9 highlights gross profit, results from operating activities, and loss before income taxes prior to arriving at the net loss reported at the bottom of the statement. We will discuss the components of the income statement in more detail in Chapter 9.

Companies are free to use either format for their income statements, or they can use a format of their own design if it better suits their reporting needs.

EXHIBIT 3-9
Multi-Step Statement of Loss for Le Château Inc.

Source: Le Château Inc.
Annual Report - 2015.

A	B	C	D
Le Château Inc. Consolidated Statement of Loss (Adapted) For the Year Ended January 31, 2015			
(in thousands of dollars)			
Sales	$ 250,210		
Cost of sales	98,665		
Gross profit	151,545		
Operating expenses			
Selling	153,853		
General and administrative	35,202		
Total operating expenses	189,055		
Results from operating activities	(37,510)		
Finance costs	2,900		
Finance income	(18)		
Loss before income taxes	(40,392)		
Income tax recovery	(1,716)		
Net loss	$ (38,676)		

STOP + THINK (3-6)

Refer to Le Château's fiscal 2014 financial statements in Exhibits 3-8 and 3-9. Assume the company suffers a net loss of $40,000,000 in fiscal 2015. What direct impact will this have on the Shareholders' Equity section of its balance sheet at the end of the 2015 fiscal year?

MyAccountingLab

MID-CHAPTER SUMMARY PROBLEM

The trial balance of Goldsmith Inc. shown below pertains to December 31, 2017, which is the end of its fiscal year. Data needed for the adjusting entries include the following (all amounts in thousands):

a. Supplies on hand at year-end, $2.
b. Depreciation on furniture and fixtures, $20.
c. Depreciation on building, $10.
d. Salary owed but not yet paid, $5.
e. Accrued service revenue, $12.
f. Of the $45 balance of unearned service revenue, $32 was earned during the year.
g. Accrued income tax expense, $35.

Requirements

1. Open the ledger accounts with their unadjusted balances. Show dollar amounts in thousands, as shown for Accounts Receivable:

Accounts Receivable
370 |

2. Journalize the Goldsmith Inc. adjusting entries at December 31, 2017. Key entries by letter, as in Exhibit 3-3, page 125. Make entries in thousands of dollars.
3. Post the adjusting entries.
4. Using an Excel spreadsheet, prepare a worksheet for the adjusted trial balance, as shown in Exhibit 3-4.
5. Prepare the income statement, the statement of retained earnings, and the balance sheet. (At this stage, it is not necessary to classify assets or liabilities as current or long term.) Draw arrows linking these three financial statements.

Name: Goldsmith Inc.
Industry: Service corporation
Fiscal Period: Year ended December 31, 2017

	A	B	C	D
1	**Goldsmith Inc.** Trial Balance December 31, 2017			
2	*(in thousands of dollars)*			
3	Cash	$ 198		
4	Accrued service revenue	370		
5	Supplies	6		
6	Furniture and fixtures	100		
7	Accumulated depreciation—furniture and fixtures		$ 40	
8	Building	250		
9	Accumulated depreciation—building		130	
10	Accounts payable		380	
11	Salary payable			
12	Unearned service revenue		45	
13	Income tax payable			
14	Share capital		100	
15	Retained earnings		193	
16	Dividends	65		
17	Service revenue		286	
18	Salary expense	172		
19	Supplies expense			
20	Depreciation expense—furniture and fixtures			
21	Depreciation expense—building			
22	Income tax expense			
23	Miscellaneous expense	13		
24	Total	$ 1,174	$ 1,174	
25				

ANSWERS

Requirements 1 and 3 (amounts in thousands)

Assets

Cash

Bal.	198	

Accrued Service Revenue

	370	
(e)	12	
Bal.	382	

Supplies

	6	(a)	4
Bal.	2		

Furniture and Fixtures

Bal.	100	

Accumulated Depreciation—
Furniture and Fixtures

		40
	(b)	20
	Bal.	60

Liabilities

Accounts Payable

	Bal.	380

Salary Payable

	(d)	5
	Bal.	5

Unearned Service Revenue

(f)	32		45
		Bal.	13

Shareholders' Equity

Share Capital

	Bal.	100

Retained Earnings

	Bal.	193

Dividends

Bal.	65	

Expenses

Salary Expense

	172	
(d)	5	
Bal.	177	

Supplies Expense

(a)	4	
Bal.	4	

Depreciation Expense—
Furniture and Fixtures

(b)	20	
Bal.	20	

Depreciation
Expense—Building

(c)	10	
Bal.	10	

Building	
Bal.	250	

Income Tax Payable	
	(g)	35
	Bal.	35

Income Tax Expense	
(g)	35	
Bal.	35	

Miscellaneous Expense

Bal.	13	

Accumulated Depreciation—Building

		130
	(c)	10
	Bal.	140

For Requirement 1, create a T-account for each account name listed in the December 31, 2017, trial balance. Insert the opening balances into the T-accounts from the trial balance, ensuring debit and credit balances in the trial balance are debit and credit balances in the T-accounts. To make sure all the account balances have been entered correctly, trace each T-account's balance back to the December 31, 2017, trial balance.

For Requirement 3, make sure each transaction is posted to the proper T-account, and make sure no transactions were missed.

Revenue

Service Revenue

		286
(e)		12
(f)		32
	Bal.	330

Requirement 2

	A	B	C	D	E
1	2017	*(amounts in thousands of dollars)*			
2	Dec. 31	Supplies Expense	4		
3		Supplies		4	
4		*To record supplies used ($6 – $2).*			
5	Dec. 31	Depreciation Expense—Furniture and Fixtures	20		
6		Accumulated Depreciation—Furniture and Fixtures		20	
7		*To record depreciation expense on furniture and fixtures.*			
8	Dec. 31	Depreciation Expense—Building	10		
9		Accumulated Depreciation—Building		10	
10		*To record depreciation expense on building.*			
11	Dec. 31	Salary Expense	5		
12		Salary Payable		5	
13		*To accrue salary expense.*			
14	Dec. 31	Accrued Service Revenue	12		
15		Service Revenue		12	
16		*To accrue service revenue.*			
17	Dec. 31	Unearned Service Revenue	32		
18		Service Revenue		32	
19		*To record unearned service revenue that has been earned.*			
20	Dec. 31	Income Tax Expense	35		
21		Income Tax Payable		35	
22		*To accrue income tax expense.*			
23					

Refer to the rules of debit and credit shown in Chapter 2, Exhibit 2-8, on page 72.

Make sure that Assets = Liabilities + Shareholders' Equity for each transaction before going to the next transaction.

Requirement 4

	A	B	C	D	E	F	G
		Unadjusted Trial Balance		Adjustments		Adjusted Trial Balance	
1	**Goldsmith Inc.** Preparation of Adjusted Trial Balance December 31, 2017						
2		Unadjusted Trial Balance		Adjustments		Adjusted Trial Balance	
3	*(amounts in thousands of dollars)*	Debit	Credit	Debit	Credit	Debit	Credit
4	Cash	198				198	
5	Accrued service revenue	370		(e) 12		382	
6	Supplies	6			(a) 4	2	
7	Furniture and fixtures	100				100	
8	Accumulated depreciation—furniture and fixtures		40		(b) 20		60
9	Building	250				250	
10	Accumulated depreciation—building		130		(c) 10		140
11	Accounts payable		380				380
12	Salary payable				(d) 5		5
13	Unearned service revenue		45	(f) 32			13
14	Income tax payable				(g) 35		35
15	Share capital		100				100
16	Retained earnings		193				193
17	Dividends	65				65	
18	Service revenue		286		(e) 12		330
19					(f) 32		
20	Salary expense	172		(d) 5		177	
21	Supplies expense			(a) 4		4	
22	Depreciation expense—furniture and fixtures			(b) 20		20	
23	Depreciation expense—building			(c) 10		10	
24	Income tax expense			(g) 35		35	
25	Miscellaneous expense	13				13	
26		1,174	1,174	118	118	1,256	1,256
27							

Create a worksheet with columns for the unadjusted trial balance, adjustments, and the adjusted trial balance. List all the account names that have a balance in their T-accounts. Write the account balances from the December 31, 2017, trial balance in the first two columns. Write the adjustment amounts in the next two columns. Write the "Bal." amounts from the T-accounts in the Adjusted Trial Balance columns. Ensure total debits equal total credits for each pair of columns. Double-check the Adjusted Trial Balance amounts by adding the Adjustments to the Unadjusted Trial Balance amounts. Double-underline the totals to show that the columns have been added and the totals are final.

Requirement 5

	A	B	C	D
1	**Goldsmith Ltd.** Income Statement For the Year Ended December 31, 2017			
2	*(amounts in thousands of dollars)*			
3	Revenue:			
4	Service revenue		$ 330	
5	Expenses:			
6	Salary	$ 177		
7	Depreciation—furniture and fixtures	20		
8	Depreciation—building	10		
9	Supplies	4		
10	Miscellaneous	13	224	
11	Income before tax		106	
12	Income tax expense		35	
13	Net income		$ 71	
14				

The title must include the name of the company, "Income Statement," and the specific period of time covered. It is critical that the time period is defined.

Gather all the revenue and expense account names and amounts from the Debit and Credit Adjusted Trial Balance columns of the worksheet.

Notice that income tax expense is always reported separately from the other expenses, and it appears as the last item before net income (or net loss).

	A	B	C	D
1	**Goldsmith Inc.** Statement of Retained Earnings For the Year Ended December 31, 2017			
2	*(amounts in thousands of dollars)*			
3	Retained earnings, January 1, 2017		$ 193	
4	Add: Net income		71	
5			264	
6	Less: Dividends		(65)	
7	Retained earnings, December 31, 2017		$ 199	
8				

The title must include the name of the company, "Statement of Retained Earnings," and the specific period of time covered. It is critical that the time period is defined.

Beginning retained earnings and dividends are from the Adjusted Trial Balance columns of the worksheet.

The net income amount is transferred from the income statement.

	A	B	C	D	E	F
1	**Goldsmith Inc.** Balance Sheet As at December 31, 2017					
2	Assets			Liabilities		
3	*(amounts in thousands of dollars)*					
4	Cash		$ 198	Accounts payable	$ 380	
5	Accounts receivable		382	Salary payable	5	
6	Supplies		2	Unearned service revenue	13	
7	Furniture and fixtures	$ 100		Income tax payable	35	
8	Less accumulated depreciation	(60)	40	Total liabilities	433	
9				Shareholders' Equity		
10	Building	$ 250		Share capital	100	
11	Less accumulated depreciation	(140)	110	Retained earnings	199	
12				Total shareholders' equity	299	
13	Total assets		$ 732	Total liabilities and shareholders' equity	$ 732	
14						

The title must include the name of the company, "Balance Sheet," and the date of the balance sheet. It shows the financial position on one specific date.

Gather all the asset, liability, and equity accounts and amounts from the Adjusted Trial Balance columns of the worksheet. The retained earnings amount is transferred from the statement of retained earnings.

It is imperative that Total assets = Total liabilities + Shareholders' equity.

OBJECTIVE

⑤ **Record** closing journal entries

RECORD CLOSING JOURNAL ENTRIES

Recall that a business's Retained Earnings represent the accumulated net income of the business since its inception, less any net losses and dividends declared during this time. To keep track of this balance, at the end of each fiscal year we must record **closing entries**, which are journal entries that transfer the balances in all revenue, expense, and dividend accounts into the Retained Earnings account. After these entries, all the income statement and dividend accounts have zero balances, leaving them ready to begin tracking revenues, expenses, and dividends for the next fiscal year.

Because the revenue, expense, and dividend accounts are closed at the end of each year, we call them **temporary accounts**. In effect, they temporarily contain a business's revenues, expenses, and dividends for a year, and then are returned to zero balances before starting the next fiscal year. In contrast, all the asset, liability, and shareholders' equity accounts we report on the balance sheet are **permanent accounts** because their balances carry forward from year to year. The balances in these accounts at the end of one fiscal year become the beginning balances of the next fiscal year.

To record and post the closing journal entries at the end of a fiscal year, follow this process:

① Debit each revenue account for the amount of its credit balance. Credit Retained Earnings for the sum of the revenues. Now the sum of the revenues has been added to Retained Earnings.

② Credit each expense account for the amount of its debit balance. Debit Retained Earnings for the sum of the expenses. The sum of the expenses has now been deducted from Retained Earnings.

③ Credit the Dividends account for the amount of its debit balance. Debit Retained Earnings for the same amount. The dividends have now been deducted from Retained Earnings.

④ Post all of the closing journal entries to the ledger to close the accounts for the year.

Exhibit 3-10 illustrates the process of journalizing and posting the closing entries for Moreau Ltd. at the end of April. Panel A contains the closing journal entries, which have been prepared using the revenue, expense, and dividend account balances contained in Moreau's adjusted trial balance in Exhibit 3-4. Panel B shows these entries being posted to the ledger accounts. Note that after the closing entries have been posted, the ending credit balance of $11,035 in the Retained Earnings account matches the Retained Earnings balance in the statement of retained earnings in Exhibit 3-6 and the balance sheet in Exhibit 3-7. If the ending balance in the Retained Earnings account does not match the balance reported in these financial statements, then you know you have made an error in the closing process.

MyAccountingLab

Accounting Cycle Tutorial
Step 5: Adjusting Entries
Step 7: Prepare the Adjusted Trial Balance
Step 8: Prepare the Financial Statements
Step 9: Closing Entries
Step 10: Prepare the Post-Closing Trial Balance

EXHIBIT 3-10
**Journalizing and Posting
Closing Entries**

PANEL A—Journalizing the Closing Entries		
Closing Entries		

	Apr. 30	Service Revenue..	7,400	
①		Retained Earnings..		7,400
	30	Retained Earnings...	4,415	
②		Rent Expense..		1,000
		Salary Expense		1,900
		Supplies Expense...		300
		Depreciation Expense—Furniture		275
		Utilities Expense..		400
		Income Tax Expense..		540
	30	Retained Earnings...	3,200	
③		Dividends..		3,200

PANEL B—Posting to the Accounts

Rent Expense

Adj.	1,000		
Bal.	1,000	Clo.	1,000

Salary Expense

	950		
Adj.	950		
Bal.	1,900	Clo.	1,900

Supplies Expense

Adj.	300		
Bal.	300	Clo.	300

Depreciation Expense

Adj.	275		
Bal.	275	Clo.	275

Utilities Expense

	400		
Bal.	400	Clo.	400

Income Tax Expense

Adj.	540		
Bal.	540	Clo.	540

Service Revenue

			7,000
		Adj.	250
		Adj.	150
Clo.	7,400	Bal.	7,400

Retained Earnings

Clo.	4,415		11,250
Clo.	3,200	Clo.	7,400
		Bal.	11,035

Dividends

Bal.	3,200	Clo.	3,200

Adj. = Amount posted from an adjusting entry
Clo. = Amount posted from a closing entry
Bal. = Balance
As arrow ② in Panel B shows, it is not necessary to make a separate closing entry for each expense. In one closing entry, we record one debit to Retained Earnings and a separate credit to each expense account.

STOP + THINK (3-7)

Refer to Le Château's financial statements in Exhibits 3-8 and 3-9. The company reported $250,210,000 in sales for the year ended January 3, 2015. When the company opened for business on January 4, 2015, how many dollars in sales would have been recorded in the Sales account of their general ledger? Now take a look at their balance sheet. What balance would have been reported in their Cash account when they opened for business on January 4, 2015?

OBJECTIVE

❻ Analyze and evaluate a company's debt-paying ability

ANALYZE AND EVALUATE A COMPANY'S DEBT-PAYING ABILITY

As we have noted, managers, investors, and creditors use accounting information to make business decisions. A bank considering lending money must predict whether the borrower can repay the loan. If the borrower already has a lot of debt compared to its assets, the probability of repayment may be low. If the borrower owes relatively little, however, the odds of repayment are higher. To evaluate a company's debt-paying ability, decision makers examine data and ratios calculated using information in the financial statements. Let's see how this process works.

Net Working Capital

Net working capital (or simply working capital) is a figure that indicates a company's liquidity. In this context, liquidity refers to the ease with which a company will be able to use its current assets to pay off its current liabilities. The higher a company's liquidity, the easier it will be able to pay off its current liabilities. The calculation for net working capital is:

$$\text{Net working capital} = \text{Total current assets} - \text{Total current liabilities}$$

Generally, a company is considered to be liquid when its current assets sufficiently exceed its current liabilities. The sufficiency of the excess is usually evaluated using the current ratio, which we discuss below, and typically varies by industry.

Using the balance sheet data in Exhibit 3-8, we can calculate Le Château's net working capital at the end of 2015 (all dollar amounts in thousands from here on):

$$\text{Net working capital} = \$120,275 - \$37,007 = \$83,268$$

Le Château's current assets exceed its current liabilities by $83,268, meaning that after the company pays all of its current liabilities, it will still have almost $85,000 in current assets to fund other business activities. For a company of its size, Le Château would be considered highly liquid.

Current Ratio

Another means of evaluating a company's liquidity using its current assets and current liabilities is via the **current ratio**, which is calculated as follows:

$$\text{Current ratio} = \frac{\text{Total current assets}}{\text{Total current liabilities}}$$

The higher the current ratio, the better we consider the company's liquidity. As a rule of thumb, a company's current ratio should be at least 1.50, which indicates the company has $1.50 in current assets for every $1.00 in current liabilities. The threshold does, however, vary by industry, and in some cases can be as low as 1.00 or as high as 2.00. A current ratio of less than 1.00 is considered low by any standard, as it indicates that current liabilities exceed current assets, or that the net working capital is negative.

Le Château's current ratio at January 31, 2015, was:

$$\text{Current ratio} = \frac{\text{Total current assets}}{\text{Total current liabilities}} = \frac{\$120,275}{\$37,007} = 3.25$$

Le Château's current ratio of 3.25 is very strong and indicates to current and potential lenders that the company should have little trouble paying its current liabilities.

Debt Ratio

We can also evaluate a company's debt-paying ability using the **debt ratio**, which is calculated as follows:

$$\text{Debt ratio} = \frac{\text{Total liabilities}}{\text{Total assets}}$$

This ratio indicates the proportion of a company's assets that is financed with debt, which helps evaluate the company's ability to pay both current and long-term debts (total liabilities). In contrast to the current ratio, a low debt ratio is better than a high debt ratio because it indicates a company has not used an excessive amount of debt to finance its assets, which means it should be easier for the company to use its assets to generate the cash needed to pay off its liabilities. Companies with low debt ratios are less likely to encounter financial difficulty.

Le Château's debt ratio at January 31, 2015, was:

$$\text{Debt ratio} = \frac{\text{Total liabilities}}{\text{Total assets}} = \frac{\$89,344}{\$181,327} = 0.49$$

As with the current ratio, the threshold for an acceptable debt ratio varies by industry, but most companies have a ratio between 0.60 and 0.70 (60% and 70%). Le Château's debt ratio of 0.49 (49%) is therefore well below the norm, and indicates the company should have little difficulty paying down its debts. When considered along with its very high current ratio, we can say that Le Château has a very high debt-paying ability at the end of 2015.

How Do Transactions Affect the Ratios?

Companies such as Le Château are keenly aware of how transactions affect their ratios. Lending agreements often require that a company's current ratio not fall below a certain level, or that its debt ratio not rise above a specified threshold. When a company fails to meet one of these conditions, it is said to default on its lending agreements. The penalty for default can be severe, and in the extreme can require immediate repayment of the loan. As noted, Le Château's debt-paying ability is very high, so it is not in danger of default. Companies that do face this danger can pursue a variety of strategies to avoid default, including:

- Increase sales to enhance both net income and current assets.
- Decrease expenses to improve net income and reduce liabilities.
- Sell additional shares to increase cash and shareholders' equity.

Let's use Le Château Inc. to examine the effects of some transactions on the company's current ratio and debt ratio. As shown in the preceding section, Le Château's ratios are as follows:

$$\text{Current ratio} = \frac{\$120{,}275}{\$37{,}007} = 3.25 \qquad \text{Debt ratio} = \frac{\$89{,}344}{\$181{,}327} = 0.49$$

The managers of any company would be concerned about how inventory purchases, collections on account, expense accruals, and depreciation would affect its ratios. Let's see how Le Château would be affected by some typical transactions. For each transaction, the journal entry helps identify the effects on the ratios. Note that the impact of each transaction is being analyzed in isolation.

a. Issued shares and received cash of $5 million (all journal entry amounts in thousands of dollars).

	A	B	C	D
1	Cash	5,000		
2	Share Capital		5,000	
3				

The increase in Cash, a current asset, affects both ratios as follows:

$$\text{Current ratio} = \frac{\$120{,}275 + \$5{,}000}{\$37{,}007} = 3.39 \qquad \text{Debt ratio} = \frac{\$89{,}344}{\$181{,}327 + \$5{,}000} = 0.48$$

The issuance of shares slightly improves both ratios, as current assets increase while liabilities remain unchanged.

b. Paid cash to purchase buildings for $2 million.

	A	B	C	D
1	Buildings	2,000		
2	Cash		2,000	
3				

Cash, a current asset, decreases, but total assets stay the same; liabilities are unchanged.

$$\text{Current ratio} = \frac{\$120{,}275 - \$2{,}000}{\$37{,}007} = 3.20 \qquad \text{Debt ratio} = \frac{\$89{,}344}{\$181{,}327 - \$2{,}000 + \$2{,}000} = 0.49$$

The cash purchase of a building hurts the current ratio but doesn't affect the debt ratio.

c. Sold inventory that had been purchased at a cost of $20 million.

	A	B	C	D
1	Cost of Sales	20,000		
2	Inventory		20,000	
3				

This transaction causes a decrease in current and total assets but leaves liabilities unchanged:

$$\text{Current ratio} = \frac{\$120,275 - \$20,000}{\$37,007} = 2.71 \qquad \text{Debt ratio} = \frac{\$89,344}{\$181,327 - \$20,000} = 0.55$$

As a result, both ratios are worse after this entry is recorded.

   d. Collected accounts receivable of $1 million.

	A	B	C	D
1	Cash	1,000		
2	Accounts Receivable		1,000	
3				

$$\text{Current ratio} = \frac{\$120,275 + \$1,000 - \$1,000}{\$37,007} = 3.25 \quad \text{Debt ratio} = \frac{\$89,344}{\$181,327 + \$1,000 - \$1,000} = 0.49$$

This transaction has no effect on total current assets, total assets, or total liabilities, so the ratios do not change.

   e. Accrued expenses of $3 million.

	A	B	C	D
1	Operating Expenses	3,000		
2	Accrued Expenses Payable		3,000	
3				

$$\text{Current ratio} = \frac{\$120,275}{\$37,007 + \$3,000} = 3.01 \quad \text{Debt ratio} = \frac{\$89,344 + \$3,000}{\$181,327} = 0.51$$

After this entry, current and total liabilities increase while assets remain unchanged, so both ratios are slightly hurt by this accrual.

   f. Recorded depreciation of $15 million.

	A	B	C	D
1	Depreciation Expense	15,000		
2	Accumulated Depreciation		15,000	
3				

No liabilities or current assets are affected, but the credit to Accumulated Depreciation reduces total assets, so the debt ratio increases.

$$\text{Current ratio} = \frac{\$120,275}{\$37,007} = 3.25 \quad \text{Debt ratio} = \frac{\$89,344}{\$181,327 - \$15,000} = 0.54$$

   g. Made cash sales of $30 million.

	A	B	C	D
1	Cash	30,000		
2	Sales Revenue		30,000	
3				

These cash sales improve both the current ratio and the debt ratio as follows:

$$\text{Current ratio} = \frac{\$120,275 + \$30,000}{\$37,007} = 4.06 \qquad \text{Debt ratio} = \frac{\$89,344}{\$181,327 + \$30,000} = 0.42$$

STOP + THINK (3-8)

Le Château's income statement in Exhibit 3-9 reports that the company's cost of sales was $98,665,000 in fiscal 2014, which represents the cost of the inventory they sold to customers during the year. According to their balance sheet in Exhibit 3-8, they had inventory worth $115,357,000 on hand at the end of fiscal 2014. This balance represents about 95% of the company's total current assets at the end of the year. Does this information cause you any concern about Le Château's current ratio going into its 2015 fiscal year?

The following Decision Guidelines summarize the key factors to consider when evaluating a company's debt-paying ability.

▶ DECISION GUIDELINES

EVALUATE DEBT-PAYING ABILITY USING NET WORKING CAPITAL, THE CURRENT RATIO, AND THE DEBT RATIO

In general, a *larger* amount of net working capital is preferable to a smaller amount. Similarly, a *high* current ratio is preferable to a low current ratio. *Increases* in net working capital and *increases* in the current ratio improve debt-paying ability. By contrast, a *low* debt ratio is preferable to a high debt ratio. Improvement in debt-paying ability is indicated by a decrease in the debt ratio.

No single ratio gives the whole picture about a company. Therefore, lenders and investors use many ratios to evaluate a company. Let's apply what we have learned. Suppose you are a loan officer at the TD Bank, and Le Château has asked you for a $20 million loan to remodel its stores. How will you make this loan decision? The Decision Guidelines show how bankers and investors use two key ratios.

USING NET WORKING CAPITAL AND THE CURRENT RATIO

Decision	Guidelines
How can you measure a company's ability to pay current liabilities with current assets?	Net working capital = Total current assets − Total current liabilities $$\text{Current ratio} = \frac{\text{Total current assets}}{\text{Total current liabilities}}$$
Who uses net working capital and the current ratio for decision making?	*Lenders and other creditors*, who must predict whether a borrower can pay its current liabilities. *Investors*, who know that a company that cannot pay its debts is not a good investment because it may go bankrupt. *Managers*, who must have enough cash to pay the company's current liabilities.
What are good net working capital and current ratio values?	There is no correct answer for this. It depends on the industry as well as the individual entity's ability to quickly generate cash from operations. An entity with strong operating cash flow can operate successfully with a low amount of net working capital as long as cash comes in through operations at least as fast as accounts payable become due. A current ratio of, say, 1.10–1.20 is sometimes sufficient. An entity with relatively low cash flow from operations needs a higher current ratio of, say, 1.30–1.50. Traditionally, a current ratio of 2.00 was considered ideal. Recently, acceptable values have decreased as companies have been able to operate more efficiently. Today, a current ratio of 1.50 is considered strong. Although not ideal, cash-rich companies can operate with a current ratio below 1.0.

USING THE DEBT RATIO	
Decision	**Guidelines**
How can you measure a company's ability to pay total liabilities?	$$\text{Debt ratio} = \frac{\text{Total liabilities}}{\text{Total assets}}$$
Who uses the debt ratio for decision making?	*Lenders and other creditors,* who must predict whether a borrower can pay its debts.
	Investors, who know that a company that cannot pay its debts is not a good investment because it may go bankrupt.
	Managers, who must have enough assets to pay the company's debts.
What is a good debt ratio value?	Depends on the industry:
	A company with strong cash flow can operate successfully with a high debt ratio of, say, 0.70–0.80.
	A company with weak cash flow needs a lower debt ratio of, say, 0.50–0.60.
	Traditionally, a debt ratio of 0.50 was considered ideal. Recently, values have increased as companies have been able to operate more efficiently. Today, a normal value of the debt ratio is around 0.60–0.70.

SUMMARY

SUMMARY OF LEARNING OBJECTIVES

LEARNING OBJECTIVE	SUMMARY
1. **Explain** how accrual accounting differs from cash-basis accounting	When using the cash basis of accounting, we record only business transactions involving the receipt or payment of cash. All other business transactions are ignored. In contrast, when using accrual accounting, *the receipt or payment of cash is irrelevant* to deciding whether a business transaction should be recorded. What matters is whether the business has acquired an asset, earned revenue, taken on a liability, or incurred an expense. If it has, the transaction is recorded in the accounting records.
2. **Apply** the revenue and expense recognition principles	According to the revenue recognition principle, a transaction must satisfy *all three* of these conditions before the business can recognize revenue: 1. The ownership (or control) and benefits of the goods have been transferred to the customer, or the services have been provided to the customer. 2. The amount of revenue can be reliably measured. 3. It is probable that the business will receive the economic benefits associated with the transaction, which usually come in the form of cash receipts. The expense recognition principle sets out the two criteria that must be satisfied before an expense can be recognized: 1. There has been a decrease in future economic benefits caused by a decrease in an asset *or* an increase in a liability. 2. The expense can be reliably measured.

3. **Record** adjusting journal entries

Under accrual accounting, we must record adjusting journal entries at the end of each accounting period to ensure that all assets and liabilities have been recorded at period end and that all revenues earned and expenses incurred during the period have been included in the accounts.

There are three main types of adjusting entries: deferrals, depreciation (amortization under ASPE), and accruals. Deferrals include adjustments related to transactions for which a business has received or paid cash in advance of delivering or receiving goods and services. Depreciation adjustments are made to expense the benefits of capital assets that have been used up during the period. Accruals include adjustments related to revenues earned or expenses incurred prior to any cash or invoices changing hands.

4. **Prepare** the financial statements

The financial statements can be prepared using the account balances from the adjusted trial balance. The income statement is prepared first, followed by the statement of retained earnings, and then the balance sheet.

A classified balance sheet reports current assets and liabilities separately from their non-current counterparts. A balance sheet prepared using a report format lists assets first, followed by liabilities, and then shareholders' equity. A balance sheet in account format lists assets on the left and liabilities and shareholders' equity on the right.

A single-step income statement reports all revenue items together, followed by all expense items, whereas a multi-step income statement splits revenues and expenses into two or more categories to highlight important subtotals (e.g., gross profit, income from operations) useful to decision makers.

5. **Record** closing journal entries

At the end of each fiscal year we must record closing entries, which are journal entries that transfer the balances in all revenue, expense, and dividend accounts into the Retained Earnings account. After these entries, all the income statement and dividend accounts have zero balances, leaving them ready to begin tracking revenues, expenses, and dividends for the next fiscal year.

6. **Analyze** and **evaluate** a company's debt-paying ability

We can evaluate a company's debt-paying ability using net working capital, the current ratio, and the debt ratio. A business's net working capital equals its total current assets minus its total current liabilities, and this figure should be sufficiently in excess of zero for a company to avoid debt-paying troubles. The current ratio equals total current assets divided by total current liabilities, so a higher current ratio is correlated with a stronger debt-paying ability. The debt ratio is calculated by dividing total liabilities by total assets, so for this ratio, a lower ratio indicates a higher debt-paying ability.

There are no differences between IFRS and ASPE in this chapter.

MyAccountingLab

END-OF-CHAPTER SUMMARY PROBLEM

This problem follows on the mid-chapter summary problem that begins on page 131.

Requirements

1. Make Goldsmith Inc.'s closing entries at December 31, 2017. Explain what the closing entries accomplish and why they are necessary.
2. Post the closing entries to Retained Earnings and compare Retained Earnings' ending balance with the amount reported on the balance sheet on page 135. The two amounts should be the same.
3. Prepare Goldsmith Inc.'s classified balance sheet to identify the company's current assets and current liabilities. (Goldsmith Inc. has no long-term liabilities.) Then compute the company's current ratio and debt ratio at December 31, 2017.
4. The top management of Goldsmith Inc. has asked you for a $500,000 loan to expand the business. They propose to pay off the loan over a 10-year period. Recompute Goldsmith Inc.'s debt ratio assuming you make the loan.

Name: Goldsmith Inc.
Industry: Service corporation
Fiscal Period: Year ended December 31, 2017
Key Fact: Existing, ongoing business

ANSWERS

Requirement 1

2017			(in thousands)	
Dec. 31	Service Revenue		330	
	Retained Earnings			330
31	Retained Earnings		259	
	Salary Expense			177
	Depreciation Expense—Furniture and Fixtures........			20
	Depreciation Expense—Building			10
	Supplies Expense			4
	Income Tax Expense			35
	Miscellaneous Expense			13
31	Retained Earnings		65	
	Dividends			65

To close revenue accounts, debit each revenue account for the amounts reported on the income statement, and credit Retained Earnings for the total of the debits.

To close expense accounts, credit each expense account for the amounts reported on the income statement, and debit Retained Earnings for the total of the credits.

To close the dividend accounts, credit each dividend account for the amounts reported on the statement of retained earnings, and debit Retained Earnings for the total of the credits.

Explanation of Closing Entries

The closing entries set the balance of each revenue, expense, and Dividends account back to zero for the start of the next accounting period. They also add the year's net income to and deduct any dividends declared from Retained Earnings, so this account accurately reflects the earnings that have been retained by the company.

Requirement 2

Retained Earnings

Clo.	259		193
Clo.	65	Clo.	330
		Bal.	199

The balance in the Retained Earnings T-account should equal the Retained Earnings balance reported on the balance sheet.

The balance in the Retained Earnings account agrees with the amount reported on the balance sheet, as it should.

Requirement 3

	A	B	C	D	E	F
1	**Goldsmith Inc.** Balance Sheet As at December 31, 2017					
2	**Assets**			**Liabilities**		
3	*(amounts in thousands of dollars)*					
4	Current assets			Current liabilities		
5	Cash		$ 198	Accounts payable	$ 380	
6	Accounts receivable		382	Salary payable	5	
7	Supplies		2	Unearned service revenue	13	
8	Total current assets		582	Income tax payable	35	
9	Capital assets			Total current liabilities	433	
10	Furniture and fixtures	$ 100				
11	Less accumulated			**Shareholders' Equity**		
12	depreciation	(60)	40	Share capital	100	
13	Building	$ 250		Retained earnings	199	
14	Less accumulated depreciation	(140)	110	Total shareholders' equity	299	
15	Total assets		$ 732	Total liabilities and shareholders' equity	$ 732	
16						

The title must include the name of the company, "Balance Sheet," and the date of the balance sheet. It shows the financial position on one specific date.

The classified balance sheet uses the same accounts and balances as those on page 135. However, segregate current assets (assets expected to be converted to cash within one year) from capital assets, and segregate current liabilities (liabilities expected to be paid or settled within one year) from other liabilities.

$$\text{Current ratio} = \frac{\text{Current assets}}{\text{Current liabilities}}$$

$$\text{Debt ratio} = \frac{\text{Total liabilities}}{\text{Total assets}}$$

$$\text{Current ratio} = \frac{\$582}{\$433} = 1.34 \quad \text{Debt ratio} = \frac{\$433}{\$732} = 0.59$$

Requirement 4

You must add $500,000 to the current liabilities and total assets to account for the additional $500,000 loan.

$$\text{Debt ratio assuming the loan is made} = \frac{\$433 + \$500}{\$732 + \$500} = \frac{\$933}{\$1,232} = 0.76$$

REVIEW

MyAccountingLab

Make the grade with MyAccountingLab: The Quick Quiz questions, Short Exercises, Exercises, and Problems (Group A) marked in #-# can be found on MyAccountingLab. You can practise them as often as you want, and most feature step-by-step guided instructions to help you find the right answer.

QUICK QUIZ   (ANSWERS APPEAR ON THE LAST PAGE OF THIS CHAPTER.)

Questions 1 through 3 are based on the following facts:

Freddie Handel began a music business in July 2017. Handel prepares monthly financial statements and uses the accrual basis of accounting. The following transactions are Handel Company's only activities during July through October:

July	14	Bought music on account for $10, with payment to the supplier due in 90 days
Aug.	3	Performed a job on account for Joey Bach for $25, collectible from Bach in 30 days. Used up all the music purchased on July 14
Sept.	16	Collected the $25 receivable from Bach
Oct.	22	Paid the $10 owed to the supplier from the July 14 transaction

1. In which month should Handel record the cost of the music as an expense?

a. July
b. August
c. September
d. October

2. In which month should Handel report the $25 revenue on its income statement?

a. July
b. August
c. September
d. October

3. If Handel Company uses the *cash* basis of accounting instead of the accrual basis, in what month will Handel report revenue and in what month will it report expense?

	Revenue	Expense
a.	September	October
b.	September	July
c.	August	October
d.	September	August

4. In which month should revenue be recorded?
a. In the month that goods are ordered by the customer
b. In the month that goods are shipped to the customer
c. In the month that the invoice is mailed to the customer
d. In the month that cash is collected from the customer

5. On January 1 of the current year, Aladdin Company paid $600 rent to cover six months (January through June). Aladdin recorded this transaction as follows:

Prepaid Rent	600	
Cash		600

Aladdin adjusts the accounts at the end of each month. Based on these facts, the adjusting entry at the end of January should include
a. a credit to Prepaid Rent for $500.
b. a debit to Prepaid Rent for $500.
c. a debit to Prepaid Rent for $100.
d. a credit to Prepaid Rent for $100.

6. Assume the same facts as in the previous problem. Aladdin's adjusting entry at the end of February should include a debit to Rent Expense in the amount of
a. $0.
b. $500.
c. $200.
d. $100.

7. What effect does the adjusting entry in Question 3-41 have on Aladdin's net income for February?
a. increase by $100
b. increase by $200
c. decrease by $100
d. decrease by $200

8. An adjusting entry recorded March salary expense that will be paid in April. Which statement best describes the effect of this adjusting entry on the company's accounting equation at the end of March?
a. Assets are not affected, liabilities are decreased, and shareholders' equity is decreased.
b. Assets are decreased, liabilities are increased, and shareholders' equity is decreased.
c. Assets are not affected, liabilities are increased, and shareholders' equity is decreased.
d. Assets are decreased, liabilities are not affected, and shareholders' equity is decreased.

9. On April 1, 2017, Metro Insurance Company sold a one-year insurance policy covering the year ended April 1, 2018. Metro collected the full $1,200 on April 1, 2017. Metro made the following journal entry to record the receipt of cash in advance:

Cash 1,200
    Unearned Revenue 1,200

Nine months have passed, and Metro has made no adjusting entries. Based on these facts, the adjusting entry needed by Metro at December 31, 2017, is

a. Unearned Revenue 300
    Insurance Revenue 300
b. Insurance Revenue 300
    Unearned Revenue 300
c. Unearned Revenue 900
    Insurance Revenue 900
d. Insurance Revenue 900
    Unearned Revenue 900

10. The Unearned Revenue account of Dean Incorporated began 2017 with a normal balance of $5,000 and ended 2017 with a normal balance of $12,000. During 2017, the Unearned Revenue account was credited for $19,000 that Dean will earn later. Based on these facts, how much revenue did Dean earn in 2017?

a. $5,000
b. $19,000
c. $24,000
d. $12,000

11. What is the effect on the financial statements of recording depreciation on equipment?
a. Assets are decreased, but net income and shareholders' equity are not affected.
b. Net income, assets, and shareholders' equity are all decreased.
c. Net income and assets are decreased, but shareholders' equity is not affected.
d. Net income is not affected, but assets and shareholders' equity are decreased.

12. For 2017, Monterrey Company had revenues in excess of expenses. Which statement describes Monterrey's closing entries at the end of 2017?
a. Revenues will be debited, expenses will be credited, and retained earnings will be debited.
b. Revenues will be credited, expenses will be debited, and retained earnings will be debited.
c. Revenues will be debited, expenses will be credited, and retained earnings will be credited.
d. Revenues will be credited, expenses will be debited, and retained earnings will be credited.

13. Which of the following accounts would *not* be included in the closing entries?
a. Accumulated Depreciation
b. Service Revenue
c. Depreciation Expense
d. Retained Earnings

14. A major purpose of preparing closing entries is to
a. zero out the liability accounts.
b. close out the Supplies account.
c. adjust the asset accounts to their correct current balances.
d. update the Retained Earnings account.

15. Selected data for Austin Company follow:

Current assets.....	$50,000	Current liabilities	$40,000
Capital assets......	70,000	Long-term liabilities....	35,000
Total revenues.....	30,000	Total expenses	20,000

Based on these facts, what are Austin's ratios?

	Current ratio	Debt ratio
a.	2 to 1	0.5 to 1
b.	0.83 to 1	0.5 to 1
c.	1.25 to 1	0.625 to 1
d.	2 to 1	0.633 to 1

ACCOUNTING VOCABULARY

account format A balance sheet format that lists assets on the left side and liabilities above shareholders' equity on the right side. (p. 129)

accrual An adjustment related to revenues earned or expenses incurred prior to any cash or invoice changing hands. (p. 120)

accrual accounting A basis of accounting that records transactions based on whether a business has acquired an asset, earned revenue, taken on a liability, or incurred an expense, regardless of whether cash is involved. (p. 110)

accrued expense An expense that has been incurred but not yet paid or invoiced. (p. 120)

accrued revenue A revenue that has been earned but not yet collected or invoiced. (p. 122)

accumulated depreciation The account showing the sum of all depreciation expense from the date of acquiring a capital asset. (p. 120)

adjusted trial balance A list of all the ledger accounts with their adjusted balances. (p. 126)

carrying amount (of a capital asset) The asset's cost minus accumulated depreciation. (p. 120)

cash-basis accounting Accounting that records only transactions in which cash is received or paid. (p. 110)

classified balance sheet A balance sheet that shows current assets separate from long-term assets, and current liabilities separate from long-term liabilities. (p. 129)

closing entries Entries that transfer the revenue, expense, and dividend balances from these respective accounts to the Retained Earnings account. (p. 136)

contra account An account that always has a companion account and whose normal balance is opposite that of the companion account. (p. 120)

current ratio Current assets divided by current liabilities. Measures a company's ability to pay current liabilities with current assets. (p. 138)

debt ratio Ratio of total liabilities to total assets. States the proportion of a company's assets that is financed with debt. (p. 139)

deferral An adjustment related to a transaction for which a business has received or paid cash in advance of delivering or receiving goods or services. (p. 115)

depreciation An expense to recognize the portion of a capital asset's economic benefits that has been used up during an accounting period. (p. 119)

liquidity A measure of how quickly an asset can be converted to cash. The higher an asset's liquidity, the more quickly it can be converted to cash. (p. 129)

multi-step income statement An income statement that contains subtotals to highlight important relationships between revenues and expenses. (p. 130)

net working capital Current assets − current liabilities. Measures the ease with which a company will be able to use its current assets to pay off its current liabilities. (p. 138)

permanent accounts Assets, liabilities, and shareholders' equity accounts, which all have balances that carry forward to the next fiscal year. (p. 136)

report format A balance sheet format that lists assets at the top, followed by liabilities and then shareholders' equity. (p. 129)

single-step income statement Lists all revenues together and all expenses together; there is only one step in arriving at net income. (p. 130)

temporary accounts Revenue, expense, and dividend accounts, which do not have balances that carry forward to the next fiscal year. (p. 136)

unearned revenue A liability that arises when a business receives cash from a customer prior to providing the related goods or services. (p. 117)

ASSESS YOUR PROGRESS

SHORT EXERCISES

LEARNING OBJECTIVE ❶

Apply accrual accounting

S3-1 Marquis Inc. made sales of $700 million during 2017. Of this amount, Marquis Inc. collected cash for all but $30 million. The company's cost of goods sold was $300 million, and all other expenses for the year totalled $350 million. Also during 2017, Marquis Inc. paid $400 million for its inventory and $280 million for everything else. Beginning cash was $100 million. Marquis Inc.'s top management is interviewing you for a job and you are asked two questions:

a. How much was Marquis Inc.'s net income for 2017?
b. How much was Marquis Inc.'s cash balance at the end of 2017?

LEARNING OBJECTIVE ❶

Apply accrual accounting

S3-2 Great Sporting Goods Inc. began 2017 owing notes payable of $4.0 million. During 2017, the company borrowed $2.6 million on notes payable and paid off $2.5 million of notes payable from prior years. Interest expense for the year was $1.0 million, including $0.2 million of interest payable accrued at December 31, 2017. Show what Great Sporting Goods Inc. should report for these facts on the following financial statements:

- Income Statement
  Interest expense
- Balance Sheet
  Notes payable
  Interest payable

S3-3 Ford Canada sells large fleets of vehicles to auto rental companies, such as Budget and Avis. Suppose Budget is negotiating with Ford to purchase 1,000 Explorers. Write a short paragraph to explain to Ford when the company should, and should not, record this sales revenue and the related cost of goods sold.

LEARNING OBJECTIVE ❷

Apply the revenue and expense recognition principles

S3-4 Answer the following questions about prepaid expenses:

a. On November 1, World Travel Ltd. prepaid $6,000 for three months' rent. Give the adjusting entry to record rent expense at December 31. Include the date of the entry and an explanation. Then post all amounts to the two accounts involved, and show their balances at December 31. World Travel adjusts the accounts only at December 31.

b. On December 1, World Travel paid $800 for supplies. At December 31, World Travel has $500 of supplies on hand. Make the required journal entry at December 31. Post all accounts to the accounts and show their balances at December 31.

LEARNING OBJECTIVE ❸

Record adjusting journal entries

S3-5 Suppose that on January 1, Roots Ltd. paid cash of $30,000 for computers that are expected to remain useful for three years. At the end of three years, the computers' values are expected to be zero.

1. Make journal entries to record (a) the purchase of the computers on January 1, and (b) the annual depreciation on December 31. Include dates and explanations, and use the following accounts: Computer Equipment; Accumulated Depreciation—Computer Equipment; and Depreciation Expense—Computer Equipment.
2. Post to the accounts and show their balances at December 31.
3. What is the computers' carrying amount at December 31?
4. Which account(s) will Roots report on the income statement for the year? Which accounts will appear on the balance sheet of December 31? Show the amount to report for each item on both financial statements.

LEARNING OBJECTIVE ❸❹

Record depreciation and prepare financial statements

S3-6 During 2017, Many Miles Trucking paid salary expense of $40 million. At December 31, Many Miles accrued salary expense of $2 million. Many Miles paid $1.9 million to its employees on January 3, 2018, the company's next payday after the end of the 2017 year. For this sequence of transactions, show what Many Miles would include on its 2017 income statement and its balance sheet at the end of 2017.

LEARNING OBJECTIVE ❷

Apply the revenue and expense recognition principles

S3-7 Schwartz & Associates Inc. borrowed $100,000 on October 1 by signing a note payable to Scotiabank. The interest expense for each month is $500. The loan agreement requires Schwartz & Associates Inc. to pay interest on December 31.

1. Make Schwartz & Associates Inc.'s adjusting entry to accrue interest expense and interest payable at October 31, at November 30, and at December 31. Date each entry and include its explanation.
2. Post all three entries to the Interest Payable account. You need not take the balance of the account at the end of each month.
3. Record the payment of three months' interest at December 31.

LEARNING OBJECTIVE ❸

Record adjusting journal entries

S3-8 Return to the situation in S3-7. Here you are accounting for the same transactions on the books of Scotiabank, which lent the money to Schwartz & Associates Inc. Perform all three steps in S3-7 for Scotiabank using the bank's own accounts.

LEARNING OBJECTIVE ❸

Record adjusting journal entries

LEARNING OBJECTIVE ❷❸

S3-9 Write a paragraph explaining why unearned revenues are liabilities instead of revenues. In your explanation, use the following actual example: *Maclean's* magazine collects cash from

Apply the revenue recognition principle and record adjusting journal entries

subscribers in advance and later delivers magazines to subscribers over a one-year period. Explain what happens to the unearned subscription revenue over the course of a year as *Maclean's* delivers magazines to subscribers. Into what account does the unearned subscription revenue go as *Maclean's* delivers magazines?

Give the journal entries that *Maclean's* would make to:

a. Collect $40,000 of subscription revenue in advance.
b. Record earning $10,000 of subscription revenue.

LEARNING OBJECTIVE ❸

Report prepaid expenses

S3-10 Birdie Golf Ltd. prepaid three months' rent ($6,000) on January 1. At March 31, Birdie prepared a trial balance and made the necessary adjusting entry at the end of the quarter. Birdie adjusts its accounts every quarter of the fiscal year, which ends December 31.

What amount appears for Prepaid Rent on

a. Birdie's unadjusted trial balance at March 31?
b. Birdie's adjusted trial balance at March 31?

What amount appears for Rent Expense on

a. Birdie's unadjusted trial balance at March 31?
b. Birdie's adjusted trial balance at March 31?

LEARNING OBJECTIVE ❸

Record adjusting journal entries

S3-11 Josie Inc. collects cash from customers two ways:

1. Accrued Revenue. Some customers pay Josie after Josie has performed service for the customer. During 2017, Josie made sales of $50,000 on account and later received cash of $40,000 on account from these customers.
2. Unearned Revenue. A few customers pay Josie in advance, and Josie later performs service for the customer. During 2017, Josie collected $7,000 cash in advance and later earned $6,000 of this amount.

Journalize the following for Josie:

a. Earning service revenue of $50,000 on account and then collecting $40,000 on account
b. Receiving $7,000 in advance and then earning $6,000 as service revenue

LEARNING OBJECTIVE ❹

Prepare the financial statements

S3-12 Entertainment Centre Ltd. reported the following data at March 31, 2017, with amounts adapted and in thousands:

Retained earnings, March 31, 2016 ...	$ 1,300	Cost of goods sold	$126,000
Accounts receivable	27,700	Cash	900
Net revenues	174,500	Property and equipment, net	7,200
Total current liabilities	53,600	Share capital	26,000
All other expenses	45,000	Inventories	33,000
Other current assets	4,800	Long-term liabilities	13,500
Other assets	24,300	Dividends	0

You are the CFO responsible for reporting Entertainment Centre Ltd. (ECL) results. Use these data to prepare ECL's income statement for the year ended March 31, 2017, the statement of retained earnings for the year ended March 31, 2017, and the classified balance sheet at March 31, 2017. Use the report format for the balance sheet. Draw arrows linking the three statements to explain the information flows between the statements.

LEARNING OBJECTIVE ❺

Prepare closing entries

S3-13 Use the Entertainment Centre Ltd. data in S3-12 to make the company's closing entries at March 31, 2017. Then set up a T-account for Retained Earnings and post to that account. Compare Retained Earnings' ending balance to the amount reported on ECL's statement of retained earnings and balance sheet. What do you find? Why is this important?

S3-14 Use the Entertainment Centre Ltd. data in S3-12 to compute ECL's

a. Current ratio

b. Debt ratio

Round to two decimal places. Report to the CEO whether these values look strong, weak, or middle-of-the-road.

LEARNING OBJECTIVE ❻

Evaluate a company's debt-paying ability

S3-15 Use the Entertainment Centre Ltd. data in S3-12 to answer the following questions.

1. Was the net revenue high enough to cover all of ECL's costs?
2. What could you do to improve this situation?

LEARNING OBJECTIVE ❻

Use the financial statements

EXERCISES

E3-16 During 2017, Organic Foods Inc. made sales of $4,000 (assume all on account) and collected cash of $4,100 from customers. Operating expenses totalled $800, all paid in cash. At December 31, 2017, Organic Foods's customers owed the company $400. Organic Foods owed creditors $700 on account. All amounts are in millions.

1. For these facts, show what Organic Foods Inc. would report on the following 2017 financial statements:
   - Income statement
   - Balance sheet
2. Suppose Organic Foods had used cash-basis accounting. What would Organic Foods Ltd. have reported for these facts?

LEARNING OBJECTIVE ❶

Apply accrual and cash-basis accounting

E3-17 During 2017, Valley Sales Inc. earned revenues of $500,000 on account. Valley Sales collected $410,000 from customers during the year. Expenses totalled $420,000, and the related cash payments were $400,000. Show what Valley Sales would report on its 2017 income statement under the

a. Cash basis

b. Accrual basis

Compute net income under both bases of accounting. Which basis measures net income more appropriately? Explain your answer.

LEARNING OBJECTIVE ❶

Apply accrual and cash-basis accounting

E3-18 Riverside Corporation began 2016 owing notes payable of $3.5 million. During 2016, Riverside borrowed $1.7 million on notes payable and paid off $1.6 million of notes payable from prior years. Interest expense for the year was $0.4 million, including $0.2 million of interest payable accrued at December 31, 2016.

Show what Riverside should report for these facts on the following financial statements:

1. Income statement for 2016
   a. Interest expense
2. Balance sheet as of December 31, 2016
   a. Notes payable
   b. Interest payable

LEARNING OBJECTIVE ❶

Apply accrual and cash-basis accounting

E3-19 During 2017, Dish Networks Inc. earned revenues of $700 million. Expenses totalled $540 million. Dish collected all but $20 million of the revenues and paid $530 million on its expenses. Dish's top managers are evaluating the year, and they ask you the following questions:

a. Under accrual accounting, what amount of revenue should the company report for 2017? Is the $700 million revenue earned, or is it the amount of cash actually collected?

b. Under accrual accounting, what amount of total expense should Dish report for the year—$540 million or $530 million?

c. Which financial statement reports revenues and expenses? Which statement reports cash receipts and cash payments?

LEARNING OBJECTIVE ❷

Recognize revenue and record expenses under accrual basis of accounting

LEARNING OBJECTIVE ❷

Apply expense recognition principles

E3-20 Write a short paragraph to explain in your own words the concept of depreciation as used in accounting.

LEARNING OBJECTIVE ❷

Apply revenue and expense
recognition principles

E3-21 Answer each of the following questions.

a. Employees earned wages of $20,000 during the current month, but were not paid until the following month. Should the employer record any expenses at the end of the current month?

b. The current year has been a poor one, so the business is planning to delay the recording of some expenses until they are paid early the following year. Is this acceptable?

c. A dentist performs a surgical operation and bills the patient's insurance company. It may take three months to collect from the insurance company. Should the dentist record revenue now or wait until cash is collected?

d. A construction company is building a highway system, and construction will take three years. How do you think it should record the revenue it earns—over the year or over three years?

e. A utility bill is received on December 30 and will be paid next year. When should the company record utility expense?

LEARNING OBJECTIVE ❸

Record adjusting journal entries and
analyze their effects on net income

E3-22 An accountant made the following adjustments at December 31, the end of the accounting period:

a. Prepaid insurance, beginning, $700. Payments for insurance during the period, $2,100. Prepaid insurance, ending, $800.

b. Interest revenue accrued, $900.

c. Unearned service revenue, beginning, $800. Unearned service revenue, ending, $300.

d. Depreciation, $6,200.

e. Employees' salaries owed for three days of a five-day work week; weekly payroll, $9,000.

f. Income before income tax expense, $20,000. Income tax rate is 25%.

Requirements

1. Journalize the adjusting entries.
2. Suppose the adjustments were not made. Compute the overall overstatement or understatement of net income as a result of the omission of these adjustments.

LEARNING OBJECTIVE ❶

Apply accrual accounting

E3-23 Green Leaf Fertilizer Ltd. experienced four situations for its supplies. Compute the amounts indicated by question marks for each situation. For situations 1 and 2, journalize the needed transaction. Consider each situation separately.

	Situation			
	1	2	3	4
Beginning supplies	$ 500	$1,000	$ 300	$ 900
Payments for supplies during the year	?	3,100	?	1,100
Total amount to account for	$1,300	?	?	2,000
Ending supplies	400	500	700	?
Supplies expense	$ 900	$?	$ 700	$1,400

LEARNING OBJECTIVE ❸

Record adjusting entries

E3-24 Clark Motors Ltd. faced the following situations. Journalize the adjusting entry needed at year-end (December 31, 2017) for each situation. Consider each fact separately.

a. The business has interest expense of $9,000 early in January 2018.

b. Interest revenue of $3,000 has been earned but not yet received.

c. When the business collected $12,000 in advance three months ago, the accountant debited Cash and credited Unearned Revenue. The client was paying for two cars, one delivered in December, the other to be delivered in February 2018.

d. Salary expense is $1,000 per day—Monday through Friday—and the business pays employees each Friday. For example purposes, assume that this year, December 31 falls on a Tuesday.

e. The unadjusted balance of the Supplies account is $3,100. The total cost of supplies on hand is $800.

f. Equipment was purchased at the beginning of this year at a cost of $60,000. The equipment's useful life is five years. Record the depreciation for this year and then determine the equipment's carrying amount.

E3-25 The accounting records of Lalonde Ltée include the following unadjusted balances at May 31: Accounts Receivable, $1,300; Supplies, $900; Salary Payable, $0; Unearned Service Revenue, $800; Service Revenue, $14,400; Salary Expense, $4,200; Supplies Expense, $0. As Lalonde's accountant you have developed the following data for the May 31 adjusting entries:

a. Supplies on hand, $300
b. Salary owed to employees, $2,000
c. Service revenue accrued, $600
d. Unearned service revenue that has been earned, $700

LEARNING OBJECTIVE ❸

Record adjusting entries directly in T-accounts

Open the foregoing T-accounts with their beginning balances. Then record the adjustments directly in the accounts, keying each adjustment amount by letter. Show each account's adjusted balance. Journal entries are not required.

E3-26 The adjusted trial balance of Honeybee Hams Inc. follows.

LEARNING OBJECTIVE ❹

Prepare the financial statements

	A	B	C	D
1	**Honeybee Hams Inc.** Adjusted Trial Balance December 31, 2017			
2		**Adjusted Trial Balance**		
3	*(in thousands of dollars)*	Debit	Credit	
4	Cash	$ 3,300		
5	Accounts receivable	1,800		
6	Inventories	1,100		
7	Prepaid expenses	1,900		
8	Capital assets	6,600		
9	Accumulated depreciation		$ 2,400	
10	Other assets	9,900		
11	Accounts payable		7,700	
12	Income tax payable		600	
13	Other liabilities		2,200	
14	Share capital		4,900	
15	Retained earnings (December 31, 2016)		4,500	
16	Dividends	1,700		
17	Sales revenue		41,000	
18	Cost of goods sold	25,000		
19	Selling, administrative, and general expense	10,000		
20	Income tax expense	2,000		
21		$ 63,300	$ 63,300	
22				

Requirement

Prepare Honeybee Hams's income statement and statement of retained earnings for the year ended December 31, 2017, and its balance sheet on that date. Draw arrows linking the three statements.

E3-27 The adjusted trial balances of Tower Development Inc. for March 31, 2016, and March 31, 2017, include these amounts (in millions):

LEARNING OBJECTIVE ❹

Determine financial statement amounts

	2017	2016
Receivables	$300	$200
Prepaid insurance	180	110
Accrued liabilities (for other operating expenses)	700	600

Tower Development completed these transactions during the year ended March 31, 2017.

Collections from customers	$20,800
Payment of prepaid insurance	400
Cash payments for other operating expenses	4,100

Compute the amount of sales revenue, insurance expense, and other operating expense to report on the income statement for the year ended March 31, 2017.

LEARNING OBJECTIVE ❹

Report on the financial statements

E3-28 This question deals with the items and the amounts that two entities, Mountain Services Inc. (Mountain) and City of Squamish (Squamish), should report in their financial statements.

1. On March 31, 2017, Mountain collected $12,000 in advance from Squamish, a client. Under the contract, Mountain is obligated to provide consulting services for Squamish evenly during the year ended March 31, 2017. Assume you are Mountain.

   Mountain's income statement for the year ended December 31, 2017, will report _____ of $_____.

   Mountain's balance sheet at December 31, 2017, will report _____ of $_____.

2. Assume that you are Squamish. Squamish's income statement for the year ended December 31, 2017, will report _____ of $_____.

   Squamish's balance sheet at December 31, 2017, will report _____ of $_____.

LEARNING OBJECTIVE ❶

Apply accrual accounting

E3-29 This exercise builds from a simple situation to a slightly more complex situation. Rogers, a wireless phone service provider, collects cash in advance from customers. All amounts are in millions.

Assume Rogers collected $400 in advance during 2017 and at year-end still owed customers phone service worth $90.

Requirements

1. Show what Rogers will report for 2017 on its

   - Income statement
   - Balance sheet

2. Use the same facts for Rogers as in Requirement 1. Further, assume Rogers reported unearned service revenue of $80 at the end of 2016.

   Show what Rogers will report for 2017 on the same financial statements. Explain why your answer differs from your answer to Requirement 1.

LEARNING OBJECTIVE ❺

Record closing entries

E3-30 Prepare the required closing entries for the following selected accounts from the records of SouthWest Transport Inc. at December 31, 2017 (amounts in thousands):

Cost of services sold	$11,600	Service revenue	$23,600
Accumulated depreciation	17,800	Depreciation expense	4,100
Selling, general, and		Other revenue	600
administrative expense	6,900	Income tax expense	400
Retained earnings,		Dividends	400
December 31, 2016	1,900	Income tax payable	300

How much net income did SouthWest Transport Inc. earn during the year ended December 31, 2017? Prepare a T-account for Retained Earnings to show the December 31, 2017, balance of Retained Earnings.

E3-31 The unadjusted trial balance and the income statement amounts from the December 31, 2017, adjusted trial balance of Yosaf Portraits Ltd. are given below.

LEARNING OBJECTIVE ❸❺

Identify and record adjusting and closing entries

	A	B	C	D	E	F
1	**Yosaf Portraits Ltd.** Trial Balance December 31, 2017					
2	Account Title	Unadjusted Trial Balance		From the Adjusted Trial Balance		
3	Cash	10,200				
4	Prepaid rent	1,100				
5	Equipment	32,100				
6	Accumulated depreciation		3,800			
7	Accounts payable		4,600			
8	Salary payable					
9	Unearned service revenue		8,400			
10	Income tax payable					
11	Note payable, long term		10,000			
12	Share capital		8,700			
13	Retained earnings		1,300			
14	Dividends	1,000				
15	Service revenue		12,800			19,500
16	Salary expense	4,000		4,900		
17	Rent expense	1,200		1,400		
18	Depreciation expense			300		
19	Income tax expense			1,600		
20		49,600	49,600	8,200	19,500	
21	Net income			11,300		
22				19,500	19,500	
23						

Requirement

Journalize the adjusting and closing entries of Yosaf Portraits Ltd. at December 31, 2017. There was only one adjustment to Service Revenue.

E3-32 Refer to exercise E3-31.

LEARNING OBJECTIVE ❹❻

Prepare a classified balance sheet and evaluate a company's debt-paying ability

Requirements

1. After solving E3-30, use the data in that exercise to prepare Yosaf Portraits Ltd.'s classified balance sheet at December 31, 2017. Use the report format. First you must compute the adjusted balance for several balance sheet accounts.
2. Compute Yosaf Portraits Ltd.'s current ratio and debt ratio at December 31, 2017. A year ago, the current ratio was 1.55 and the debt ratio was 0.45. Indicate whether the company's ability to pay its debts—both current and total—improved or deteriorated during the current year.

E3-33 Le Gasse Inc. reported this information at December 31:

LEARNING OBJECTIVE ❻

Evaluate debt-paying ability

	2017	2016	2015
Current assets	$ 20	$ 15	$ 8
Total assets	50	57	35
Current liabilities	10	8	6
Total liabilities	20	20	10
Sales revenue	204	190	175
Net income	28	20	25

Requirements

1. Using this information, calculate the current ratio and the debt ratio for 2017, 2016, and 2015.
2. Explain whether each ratio improved or deteriorated over the three years. In each case, what does your answer indicate?

SERIAL EXERCISE

Exercise E3-34 continues the Web Marketing Services Inc. situation begun in exercise E-28 of Chapter 2 (p. 95).

LEARNING OBJECTIVE ❸❹❺❻

Adjust the accounts, prepare the financial statements, close the accounts, and use financial statements to evaluate the business

E3-34 Refer to exercise E2-28 of Chapter 2. Start from the trial balance and the posted T-accounts prepared at January 18, 2017. Later in January, the business completed these transactions:

2017

Jan. 21	Received $900 in advance for marketing work to be performed evenly over the next 30 days
21	Hired a secretary to be paid on the 15th day of each month
26	Paid $900 on account
28	Collected $600 on account
31	Declared and paid dividends of $1,000

Requirements

1. Open these T-accounts: Accumulated Depreciation—Equipment, Accumulated Depreciation—Furniture, Salary Payable, Unearned Service Revenue, Retained Earnings, Depreciation Expense—Equipment, Depreciation Expense—Furniture, and Supplies Expense. Also, use the T-accounts opened for exercise E2-28.
2. Journalize the transactions of January 21 through 31.
3. Post the January 21 to January 31 transactions to the T-accounts, keying all items by date. Denote account balances as Bal.
4. Prepare a trial balance at January 31. Also, set up columns for the adjustments and for the adjusted trial balance, as illustrated in Exhibit 3-4, on page 126.
5. At January 31, the following information is gathered for the adjusting entries:

   a. Accrued service revenue, $1,000
   b. Earned $300 of the service revenue collected in advance on January 21
   c. Supplies on hand, $300
   d. Depreciation expense—equipment, $100; furniture, $200
   e. Accrued expense for secretary's salary, $1,000

      Make these adjustments directly in the adjustments columns and complete the adjusted trial balance at January 31, 2017.
6. Journalize and post the adjusting entries. Denote each adjusting amount as Adj. and an account balance as Bal.
7. Prepare the income statement and statement of retained earnings of Web Marketing Services Inc. for the month ended January 31, 2017, and the classified balance sheet at that date. Draw arrows to link the financial statements.
8. Journalize and post the closing entries at January 31, 2017. Denote each closing amount as Clo. and an account balance as Bal.
9. Using the information you have prepared, compute the current ratio and the debt ratio of Web Marketing Services Inc. (to two decimals) and evaluate these ratio values as indicative of a strong or weak financial position.

CHALLENGE EXERCISES

E3-35 Valley Bleu Ltée reported the following current accounts at December 31, 2016 (amounts in thousands):

LEARNING OBJECTIVE ❸❹❻

Compute financial statement amounts, analyze debt-paying ability

a. Cash	$1,700
b. Receivables	5,600
c. Inventory	1,800
d. Prepaid expenses	800
e. Accounts payable	2,400
f. Unearned revenue	1,200
g. Accrued expenses payable	1,700

During 2017, Valley Bleu completes these transactions:

- Used inventory of $3,800
- Sold services on account, $6,500
- Depreciation expense, $400
- Paid for accrued expenses, $500
- Collected from customers on account, $7,500
- Accrued expenses, $1,300
- Purchased inventory of $3,500 on account
- Paid on account, $5,000
- Used up prepaid expenses, $600

Compute Valley Bleu's current ratio at December 31, 2016, and again at December 31, 2017. Did the current ratio improve or deteriorate during 2017? Comment on the company's current ratio.

E3-36 The accounts of Maritime Specialists Ltd. prior to the year-end adjustments are given below.

LEARNING OBJECTIVE ❸❹

Compute financial statement amounts

Cash	$ 4,000	Share capital	$ 10,000
Accounts receivable	7,000	Retained earnings	43,000
Supplies	4,000	Dividends	16,000
Prepaid insurance	3,000	Service revenue	155,000
Building	107,000	Salary expense	32,000
Accumulated depreciation—building	14,000	Depreciation expense—building	0
Land	51,000	Supplies expense	0
Accounts payable	6,000	Insurance expense	0
Salary payable	0	Advertising expense	7,000
Unearned service revenue	5,000	Utilities expense	2,000

Adjusting data at the end of the year include:

- **a.** Unearned service revenue that has been earned, $1,000
- **b.** Accrued service revenue, $2,000
- **c.** Supplies used in operations, $3,000
- **d.** Accrued salary expense, $3,000
- **e.** Prepaid insurance expired, $1,000
- **f.** Depreciation expense, building, $2,000

Jon Whale, the principal shareholder, has received an offer to sell Maritime Specialists. He needs to know the following information within one hour:

a. Net income for the year covered by these data
b. Total assets
c. Total liabilities
d. Total shareholders' equity
e. Proof that Total assets = Total liabilities + Total shareholders' equity, after all items are updated

Requirement

Without opening any accounts, making any journal entries, or using a worksheet, provide Whale with the requested information. The business is not subject to income tax. Show all computations.

LEARNING OBJECTIVE ⑥

Analyze and **evaluate** a company's debt-paying ability

E3-37 Satterfield Corporation reported the following current accounts at December 31, 2016 (amounts in thousands):

Cash	$1,500
Receivables	5,900
Inventory	2,700
Prepaid expenses	1,000
Accounts payable	2,600
Unearned revenue	1,600
Accrued expenses payable	1,900

During January 2017, Satterfield completed these selected transactions:
- Sold services on account, $9,000
- Depreciation expense, $400
- Paid for expenses, $7,300
- Collected from customers on account, $8,100
- Accrued expenses, $500
- Paid on account, $1,400
- Used up prepaid expenses, $700

Compute Satterfield's net working capital and current ratio at December 31, 2016, and again at January 31, 2017. Did the net working capital and current ratio improve or deteriorate during January 2017? Comment on the level of the company's net working capital and current ratio.

LEARNING OBJECTIVE ④

Prepare the financial statements

E3-38 Tidy Car, Inc., provides mobile detailing to its customers. The Income Statement for the month ended January 31, 2016, the Balance Sheet for December 31, 2015, and details of postings to the Cash account in the general ledger for the month of January 2016 follow:

	A	B	C	D
1	**Tidy Car, Inc.** Income Statement Month ended January 31, 2016			
2	Revenue			
3	Detailing revenue	$ 36,500		
4	Gift certificates redeemed	700	$ 37,200	
5	Expenses:			
6	Salary expense	$ 10,000		
7	Depreciation expense—equipment	6,800		
8	Supplies expense	3,100		
9	Advertising expense	3,000	22,900	
10	Net income		$ 14,300	
11				

	A	B	C	D	E	F
1	**Tidy Car, Inc.** Balance Sheet December 31, 2015					
2	Assets			Liabilities		
3	Cash		$ 1,900	Accounts payable	$ 3,500	
4	Accounts receivable		2,600	Salary payable	1,700	
5	Supplies		1,800	Unearned service revenue	1,200	
6	Equipment	$34,000		Total liabilities	6,400	
7	Less: Accumulated			Shareholders' Equity		
8	depreciation	(6,800)	27,200	Common shares	10,000	
9				Retained earnings	17,100	
10				Total shareholders' equity	27,100	
11				Total liabilities and		
12	Total assets		$ 33,500	shareholders' equity	$ 33,500	
13						

Cash			
Bal 12/31/2015	1,900		
Cash collections from customers	38,700	Salaries paid	11,400
Issuance of common stock	12,000	Dividends paid	1,300
		Purchase of equipment	6,000
		Payments of accounts payable	1,800
		Advertising paid	2,800
Bal 1/31/2016	?		

The following additional information is also available:

1. $1,100 of the cash collected from customers in January 2016 was for gift certificates for detailing services to be performed in the future. As of January 31, 2016, $1,600 of gift certificates were still outstanding.
2. $3,300 of supplies were purchased on account.
3. Employees are paid monthly during the first week after the end of the pay period.

Requirements

Based on these statements, prepare the Balance Sheet for January 31, 2016.

PROBLEMS (GROUP A)

P3-39A Lewitas Ltd. earned revenues of $35 million during 2017 and ended the year with income of $8 million. During 2017, Lewitas Ltd. collected $33 million from customers and paid cash for all of its expenses plus an additional $1 million for accounts payable. Answer these questions about Lewitas's operating results, financial position, and cash flows during 2017:

LEARNING OBJECTIVE ❶❹

Apply accrual accounting and prepare financial statements

Requirements

1. How much were the company's total expenses? Show your work.
2. Identify all the items that Lewitas will report on its 2017 income statement. Show each amount.
3. Lewitas began 2017 with receivables of $4 million. All sales were on account. What was the company's receivables balance at the end of 2017? Identify the appropriate financial statement, and show how Lewitas will report ending receivables in the 2017 annual report.
4. Lewitas began 2017 owing accounts payable totalling $9 million. How much in accounts payable did the company owe at the end of the year? Identify the appropriate financial statement, and show how Lewitas will report these accounts payable in its 2017 annual report.

LEARNING OBJECTIVE ❶

Apply accrual and cash-basis
accounting

P3-40A Prairies Consultants Inc. had the following selected transactions in August 2017:

Aug.	1	Prepaid insurance for August through December, $1,000
	4	Purchased software for cash, $800
	5	Performed service and received cash, $900
	8	Paid advertising expense, $300
	11	Performed service on account, $3,000
	19	Purchased computer on account, $1,600
	24	Collected for the August 11 service
	26	Paid account payable from August 19
	29	Paid salary expense, $900
	31	Adjusted for August insurance expense (see Aug. 1)
	31	Earned revenue of $800 that was collected in advance in July

Requirements

1. Show how each transaction would be handled using the cash basis and the accrual basis. Under each column, give the amount of revenue or expense for August. Journal entries are not required. Use the following format for your answer, and show your computations. Assume depreciation expense of $30 for software and $30 for the computer.

	A	B	C	D
1	**Prairies Consultants Inc.** Amount of Revenue (Expense) for August 2017			
2	Date	**Cash Basis**	**Accrual Basis**	
3				

2. Compute August income (loss) before tax under each accounting method.
3. Indicate which measure of net income or net loss is preferable. Use the transactions on August 11 and 24 to explain.

LEARNING OBJECTIVE ❶

Explain the difference between
accrual and cash accounting

P3-41A Write a memo to explain to a new employee the difference between the cash basis of accounting and the accrual basis. Mention the basis on which revenues and expenses are recorded under each method.

LEARNING OBJECTIVE ❸

Record adjusting journal entries

P3-42A Journalize the adjusting entry needed on December 31, 2017, the end of the current accounting period, for each of the following independent cases affecting Callaway Corp. Include an explanation for each entry.

a. Details of Prepaid Insurance are shown in the account:

Prepaid Insurance			
Jan. 1	Bal.	400	
Mar. 31		3,600	

Callaway prepays insurance on March 31 each year. At December 31, $900 is still prepaid.

b. Callaway pays employees each Friday. The amount of the weekly payroll is $6,000 for a five-day work week. The current accounting period ends on Wednesday.

c. Callaway has a note receivable. During the current year, the company has earned accrued interest revenue of $500 that it will receive next year.

d. The beginning balance of Supplies was $2,600. During the year, Callaway purchased supplies costing $6,100, and at December 31 the cost of supplies on hand is $2,100.

e. Callaway is providing financial services for Manatawabi Investments Inc., and the owner of Manatawabi paid Callaway $12,000 for its annual service fee. Callaway recorded this amount as Unearned Service Revenue. Callaway estimates that it has earned one-third of the total fee during the current year.

f. Depreciation for the current year includes Office Furniture, $1,000, and Equipment, $2,700. Make a compound entry.

P3-43A The unadjusted trial balance of The Rock Industries Ltd. at January 31, 2017, appears below.

LEARNING OBJECTIVE ❸❹

Prepare an adjusted trial balance and the financial statements

	A	B	C	D
1	**The Rock Industries Ltd.** Trial Balance January 31, 2017			
2	Cash	$ 8,000		
3	Accounts receivable	10,000		
4	Prepaid rent	3,000		
5	Supplies	2,000		
6	Furniture	36,000		
7	Accumulated depreciation		$ 3,000	
8	Accounts payable		10,000	
9	Salary payable			
10	Share capital		26,000	
11	Retained earnings (December 31, 2016)		13,000	
12	Dividends	4,000		
13	Service revenue		14,000	
14	Salary expense	2,000		
15	Rent expense			
16	Utilities expense	1,000		
17	Depreciation expense			
18	Supplies expense			
19	Total	$ 66,000	$ 66,000	
20				

Adjustment data:

a. Accrued service revenue at January 31, $2,000

b. Prepaid rent expired during the month. The unadjusted prepaid balance of $3,000 relates to the period January through March.

c. Supplies used during January, $2,000

d. Depreciation on furniture for the month. The estimated useful life of the furniture is three years.

e. Accrued salary expense at January 31 for Monday, Tuesday, and Wednesday. The five-day weekly payroll of $5,000 will be paid on Friday, February 2.

Requirements

1. Using Exhibit 3-4, page 126, as an example, prepare the adjusted trial balance of The Rock Industries Ltd. at January 31, 2017. Key each adjusting entry by letter.

2. Prepare the income statement, the statement of retained earnings, and the classified balance sheet. Draw arrows linking the three financial statements.

LEARNING OBJECTIVE ❸❹

Record adjusting journal entries and prepare the balance sheet

P3-44A Sundance Apartments Inc.'s unadjusted and adjusted trial balance at April 30, 2017, follow:

	A	B	C	D	E	F
1	**Sundance Apartments Inc.** Adjusted Trial Balance April 30, 2017					
2		**Trial Balance**		**Adjusted Trial Balance**		
3	Account Title	Debit	Credit	Debit	Credit	
4	Cash	$ 8,300		$ 8,300		
5	Accounts receivable	6,300		6,800		
6	Interest receivable			300		
7	Note receivable	4,100		4,100		
8	Supplies	900		200		
9	Prepaid insurance	2,400		700		
10	Building	66,400		66,400		
11	Accumulated depreciation		$ 16,000		$ 18,200	
12	Accounts payable		6,900		6,900	
13	Wages payable				400	
14	Unearned rental revenue		600		100	
15	Share capital		18,000		18,000	
16	Retained earnings		42,700		42,700	
17	Dividends	3,600		3,600		
18	Rental revenue		9,900		10,900	
19	Interest revenue				300	
20	Wages expense	1,600		2,000		
21	Insurance expense			1,700		
22	Depreciation expense			2,200		
23	Property tax expense	300		300		
24	Supplies expense			700		
25	Utilities expense	200		200		
26		$ 94,100	$ 94,100	$ 97,500	$ 97,500	
27						

Requirements

1. Make the adjusting entries that account for the differences between the two trial balances.
2. Compute Sundance Apartments Inc.'s total assets, total liabilities, total equity, and net income. Prove your answer with the accounting equation.

LEARNING OBJECTIVE ❹❻

Prepare financial statements and analyze debt-paying ability

P3-45A The adjusted trial balance of Marshall Ltd. at December 31, 2017, is given on page 163.

Requirements

1. Prepare Marshall Ltd.'s 2017 income statement, statement of retained earnings, and balance sheet. List expenses (except for income tax) in decreasing order on the income statement, and show total liabilities on the balance sheet. Draw arrows linking the three financial statements.
2. Marshall Ltd.'s lenders require that the company maintain a debt ratio no higher than 0.50. Compute Marshall Ltd.'s debt ratio at December 31, 2017, to determine whether the company is in compliance with this debt restriction. If not, suggest a way that Marshall Ltd. could have avoided this difficult situation.

	A	B	C	D
1	**Marshall Ltd.** Adjusted Trial Balance December 31, 2017			
2	Cash	$ 1,400		
3	Accounts receivable	8,900		
4	Supplies	2,300		
5	Prepaid rent	1,600		
6	Equipment	37,100		
7	Accumulated depreciation		$ 4,300	
8	Accounts payable		3,700	
9	Interest payable		800	
10	Unearned service revenue		600	
11	Income tax payable		2,100	
12	Note payable		18,600	
13	Share capital		5,000	
14	Retained earnings		1,000	
15	Dividends	24,000		
16	Service revenue		107,900	
17	Depreciation expense	1,600		
18	Salary expense	39,900		
19	Rent expense	10,300		
20	Interest expense	3,100		
21	Insurance expense	3,800		
22	Supplies expense	2,900		
23	Income tax expense	7,100		
24	Total	$ 144,000	$ 144,000	
25				

P3-46A The accounts of Marciano Services Ltd. at March 31, 2017, are listed in alphabetical order.

LEARNING OBJECTIVE ❺

Record closing entries

Accounts payable	$14,700	Note payable, long term	6,200
Accounts receivable	16,500	Other assets	14,100
Accumulated depreciation—		Prepaid expenses	5,300
equipment	7,100	Retained earnings, March 31, 2016	20,200
Advertising expense	10,900	Salary expense	17,800
Cash	7,500	Salary payable	2,400
Current portion of note payable	800	Service revenue	94,100
Depreciation expense	1,900	Share capital	9,100
Dividends	31,200	Supplies	3,800
Equipment	43,200	Supplies expense	4,600
Insurance expense	600	Unearned service revenue	2,800

Requirements

1. All adjustments have been journalized and posted, but the closing entries have not been made. Journalize Marciano Ltd.'s closing entries at March 31, 2017.
2. Set up a T-account for Retained Earnings and post to that account. Compute Marciano's net income for the year ended March 31, 2017. What is the ending balance of Retained Earnings?
3. Did retained earnings increase or decrease during the year? What caused the increase or the decrease?

LEARNING OBJECTIVE ❹❻

Prepare a balance sheet and evaluate debt-paying ability

P3-47A Refer to problem P3-46A.

1. Use the Marciano Ltd. data in problem P3-46A to prepare the company's classified balance sheet at March 31, 2017. Show captions for total assets, total liabilities, and shareholders' equity.
2. Evaluate Marciano's debt position as strong or weak, giving your reason. Assess whether Marciano's ability to pay both current and total debts improved or deteriorated during 2017. In order to complete your evaluation, compute Marciano's current and debt ratios at March 31, 2017, rounding to two decimal places. At March 31, 2016, the current ratio was 1.30 and the debt ratio was 0.30.

LEARNING OBJECTIVE ❻

Evaluate debt-paying ability

P3-48A The balance sheet at December 31, 2015, 2016, and 2017 and income statement for the years ended December 31, 2015, 2016, and 2017 for Ojibway Inc. include the following data:

Ojibway Inc.
Balance Sheet
As at December 31
(in thousands)

	2017	2016	2015
Assets			
Current assets			
Cash	$ 3.0	$ 1.0	$ 0.5
Accounts receivable	8.0	5.0	3.5
Total current assets	11.0	6.0	4.0
Furniture and equipment, net	16.0	9.5	3.0
Total assets	$ 27.0	$ 15.5	$ 7.0
Liabilities			
Current liabilities			
Accounts payable	$ 5.0	$ 4.5	$ 3.0
Salaries payable	1.5	1.0	0.5
Total current liabilities	6.5	5.5	3.5
Notes payable	9.0	5.0	3.5
Total liabilities	15.5	10.5	7.0
Shareholders' equity			
Shareholders' equity	11.5	5.0	0.0
Total liabilities and shareholders' equity	$ 27.0	$ 15.5	$ 7.0

Ojibway Inc.
Income Statement
For the year ended December 31
(in thousands)

	2017	2016	2015
Revenue			
Service revenue	$100.0	$ 90.0	$ 64.0
Expenses			
Salary	60.0	57.5	46.0
Rent	18.0	16.0	12.0
Supplies	4.0	3.0	2.0
Utilities	4.5	4.0	2.0
Depreciation	5.0	3.0	2.0
Total expenses	91.5	83.5	64.0
Income before taxes	8.5	6.5	0.0
Income tax expense	2.0	1.5	
Net income	$ 6.5	$ 5.0	$ 0.0

Requirements

Use the years of data to answer the following:
1. Calculate the current ratio for 2015, 2016, and 2017.
2. Calculate the debt ratio for 2015, 2016, and 2017.
3. Evaluate each ratio and determine if the ratio has improved or deteriorated over the three years. Explain what the changes mean.

PROBLEMS (GROUP B)

P3-49B During 2017, Schubert Inc. earned revenues of $19 million from the sale of its products. Schubert ended the year with net income of $4 million. Schubert collected cash of $20 million from customers.

Answer these questions about Schubert's operating results, financial position, and cash flows during 2017:
1. How much were Schubert's total expenses? Show your work.
2. Identify all the items that Schubert will report on its income statement for 2017. Show each amount.
3. Schubert began 2017 with receivables of $6 million. All sales are on account. What was Schubert's receivables balance at the end of 2017? Identify the appropriate financial statement and show how Schubert will report its ending receivables balance in the company's 2017 annual report.
4. Schubert began 2017 owing accounts payable of $9 million. Schubert incurs all expenses on account. During 2017, Schubert paid $18 million on account. How much in accounts payable did Schubert owe at the end of 2017? Identify the appropriate financial statement and show how Schubert will report these accounts payable in its 2017 annual report.

LEARNING OBJECTIVE ❸❹

Apply accrual accounting and prepare financial statements

P3-50B Fred's Catering Ltd. had the following selected transactions during May 2017:

May 1	Received $800 in advance for a banquet to be served later
5	Paid electricity expenses, $700
9	Received cash for the day's sales, $2,000
14	Purchased two food warmers, $1,800
23	Served a banquet, receiving a note receivable, $700
31	Accrued salary expense, $900
31	Prepaid $3,000 building rent for June and July

LEARNING OBJECTIVE ❶

Apply accrual and cash-basis accounting

Requirements

1. Show how each transaction would be handled using the cash basis and the accrual basis. Under each column, give the amount of revenue or expense for May. Journal entries are not required. Use the following format for your answer, and show your computations. Ignore depreciation expense.

	A	B	C	D
1	**Fred's Catering Ltd.** Amount of Revenue (Expense) for May 2017			
2	Date	Cash Basis	Accrual Basis	
3				

2. Compute income (loss) before tax for May under the two accounting methods.
3. Which method better measures income and assets? Use the last transaction to explain.

LEARNING OBJECTIVE ❶❷

Explain accrual accounting and expense recognition

P3-51B As the controller of Stuart Enterprises Inc. you have hired a new employee, whom you must train. She objects to making an adjusting entry for accrued utilities at the end of the period. She reasons, "We will pay the utilities soon. Why not wait until payment to record the expense? In the end, the result will be the same." Write a reply to explain to the employee why the adjusting entry is needed for accrued utility expense.

LEARNING OBJECTIVE ❸

Record adjusting journal entries

P3-52B Journalize the adjusting entry needed on December 31, 2017, the end of the current accounting period, for each of the following independent cases affecting Lee Computer Systems Inc. (LCSI). Include explanations for each entry.

a. Each Friday, LCSI pays employees for the current week's work. The amount of the payroll is $5,000 for a five-day work week. The current accounting period ends on Tuesday.

b. LCSI has received notes receivable from some clients for services. During the current year, LCSI has earned accrued interest revenue of $1,100, which will be received next year.

c. The beginning balance of Supplies was $1,800. During the year, LCSI purchased supplies costing $12,500, and at December 31 the inventory of supplies on hand is $2,900.

d. LCSI is developing software for a client and the client paid LCSI $20,000 at the start of the project. LCSI recorded this amount as Unearned Service Revenue. The software development will take several months to complete. LCSI executives estimate that the company has earned three-quarters of the total fee during the current year.

e. Depreciation for the current year includes Computer Equipment, $6,300, and Building, $3,700. Make a compound entry.

f. Details of Prepaid Insurance are shown in the Prepaid Insurance account. LCSI pays the annual insurance premium (the payment for insurance coverage is called a premium) on September 30 each year. At December 31, nine months of insurance is still prepaid.

Prepaid Insurance		
Jan. 1	Bal.	1,800
Sept. 30		3,600

LEARNING OBJECTIVE ❸❹❻

Record adjusting entries, prepare financial statements, and evaluate debt-paying ability

P3-53B Consider the unadjusted trial balance of Creative Advertising Ltd. at October 31, 2017, and the related month-end adjustment data.

	A	B	C	D
1	**Creative Advertising Ltd.** Trial Balance October 31, 2017			
2	Cash	$ 16,300		
3	Accounts receivable	7,000		
4	Prepaid rent	4,000		
5	Supplies	600		
6	Computers	36,000		
7	Accumulated depreciation		$ 3,000	
8	Accounts payable		8,800	
9	Salary payable			
10	Share capital		15,000	
11	Retained earnings (September 30, 2016)		21,000	
12	Dividends	4,600		
13	Advertising revenue		25,400	
14	Salary expense	4,400		
15	Rent expense			
16	Utilities expense	300		
17	Depreciation expense			
18	Supplies expense			
19	Total	$ 73,200	$ 73,200	
20				

Adjustment data:

a. Accrued advertising revenue at October 31, $2,900

b. Prepaid rent expired during the month: The unadjusted prepaid balance of $4,000 relates to the period October 2017 through January 2018.

c. Supplies used during October, $200

d. Depreciation on computers for the month: The computers' expected useful life is three years.

e. Accrued salary expense at October 31 for Monday through Thursday; the five-day weekly payroll is $2,000.

Requirements

1. Using Exhibit 3-4, page 126, as an example, prepare the adjusted trial balance of Creative Advertising Ltd. at October 31, 2017. Key each adjusting entry by letter.

2. Prepare the income statement, the statement of retained earnings, and the classified balance sheet. Draw arrows linking the three financial statements.

3. a. Compare the business's net income for October to the amount of dividends paid to the owners. Suppose this trend continues into November. What will be the effect on the business's financial position, as shown by its accounting equation?

   b. Will the trend make it easier or more difficult for Creative Advertising Ltd. to borrow money if the business gets in a bind and needs cash? Why?

   c. Does either the current ratio or the cash position suggest the need for immediate borrowing? Explain.

P3-54B Your Talent Agency Ltd.'s unadjusted and adjusted trial balances at December 31, 2017, are shown below.

LEARNING OBJECTIVE ❸❹

Record adjusting entries and prepare a balance sheet

	A	B	C	D	E	F
1	**Your Talent Agency Ltd.** Adjusted Trial Balance December 31, 2017					
2		**Trial Balance**		**Adjusted Trial Balance**		
3	**Account Title**	Debit	Credit	Debit	Credit	
4	Cash	$ 4,100		$ 4,100		
5	Accounts receivable	11,200		12,400		
6	Supplies	1,000		700		
7	Prepaid insurance	2,600		900		
8	Office furniture	21,600		21,600		
9	Accumulated depreciation		$ 8,200		$ 9,300	
10	Accounts payable		6,300		6,300	
11	Salary payable				900	
12	Interest payable				400	
13	Note payable		6,000		6,000	
14	Unearned commission revenue		1,500		1,100	
15	Share capital		5,000		5,000	
16	Retained earnings		3,500		3,500	
17	Dividends	18,300		18,300		
18	Commission revenue		72,800		74,400	
19	Depreciation expense			1,100		
20	Supplies expense			300		
21	Utilities expense	4,900		4,900		
22	Salary expense	26,600		27,500		
23	Rent expense	12,200		12,200		
24	Interest expense	800		1,200		
25	Insurance expense			1,700		
26		$ 103,300	$ 103,300	$ 106,900	$ 106,900	
27						

Requirements

1. Make the adjusting entries that account for the difference between the two trial balances.
2. Compute Your Talent Agency Ltd.'s total assets, total liabilities, total equity, and net income.
3. Prove your answer with the accounting equation.

LEARNING OBJECTIVE ❹❻

Prepare financial statements and
evaluate debt-paying ability

P3-55B The adjusted trial balance of Reid and Campbell Ltd. at December 31, 2017, appears below.

A	B	C	D
1 **Reid and Campbell Ltd.** Adjusted Trial Balance December 31, 2017			
2 Cash	$ 11,600		
3 Accounts receivable	41,400		
4 Prepaid rent	1,300		
5 Store furnishings	67,600		
6 Accumulated depreciation		$ 12,900	
7 Accounts payable		3,600	
8 Deposits		4,500	
9 Interest payable		2,100	
10 Salary payable		900	
11 Income tax payable		8,800	
12 Note payable		26,200	
13 Share capital		12,000	
14 Retained earnings, Dec. 31, 2016		20,300	
15 Dividends	48,000		
16 Sales		165,900	
17 Depreciation expense	11,300		
18 Salary expense	44,000		
19 Rent expense	12,000		
20 Interest expense	1,200		
21 Income tax expense	18,800		
22 Total	$ 257,200	$ 257,200	
23			

Requirements

1. Prepare Reid and Campbell Ltd.'s 2017 income statement, statement of retained earnings, and balance sheet. List expenses in decreasing order on the income statement and show total liabilities on the balance sheet. Draw arrows linking the three financial statements.
2. Compute Reid and Campbell Ltd.'s debt ratio at December 31, 2017, rounding to two decimal places. Evaluate the company's debt ratio as strong or weak.

LEARNING OBJECTIVE ❺

Record closing journal entries

P3-56B The accounts of For You eTravel Inc. at December 31, 2017, are listed in alphabetical order.

Accounts payable	$ 5,100	Other assets	3,600
Accounts receivable	6,600	Retained earnings	
Accumulated depreciation—furniture	11,600	December 31, 2016	5,300
Advertising expense	2,200	Salary expense	24,600
Cash	7,300	Salary payable	3,900
Depreciation expense	1,300	Service revenue	93,500
Dividends	47,400	Share capital	15,000
Furniture	41,400	Supplies	7,700
Interest expense	800	Supplies expense	5,700
Note payable, long term	$10,600	Unearned service revenue	3,600

Requirements

1. All adjustments have been journalized and posted, but the closing entries have not been made. Journalize For You eTravel Inc.'s closing entries at December 31, 2017.
2. Set up a T-account for Retained Earnings and post to that account. Compute For You's net income for the year ended December 31, 2017. What is the ending balance of Retained Earnings?
3. Did Retained Earnings increase or decrease during the year? What caused the increase or the decrease?

P3-57B Refer to Problem 3-56B.

LEARNING OBJECTIVE❹❻

Prepare a balance sheet and evaluate debt-paying ability

1. Use the For You eTravel Inc. data in problem P3-56B to prepare the company's classified balance sheet at December 31, 2017. Show captions for total assets, total liabilities, and total liabilities and shareholders' equity.
2. Evaluate For You's debt position as strong or weak, giving your reason. Assess whether For You's ability to pay both current and total debts improved or deteriorated during 2017. In order to complete your evaluation, compute For You's current and debt ratios at December 31, 2017, rounding to two decimal places. At December 31, 2016, the current ratio was 1.50 and the debt ratio was 0.45.

P3-58B A company's balance sheet at December 31, 2015, 2016, and 2017 and income statement for the years ended December 31, 2015, 2016, and 2017 include the data on pages 169–170.

LEARNING OBJECTIVE ❻

Evaluate debt-paying ability

Requirements

Use the years of data to answer the following:
1. Calculate the current ratio for 2015, 2016, and 2017.
2. Calculate the debt ratio for 2015, 2016, and 2017.
3. Evaluate each ratio and determine if the ratio has improved or deteriorated over the three years. Explain what the changes mean.

Balance Sheet
As at December 31
(in thousands)

	2017	2016	2015
Assets			
Current assets			
Cash	$ 6.0	$ 4.0	$ 3.5
Accounts receivable	11.0	8.0	6.5
Total current assets	17.0	12.0	10.0
Furniture and equipment, net	19.0	12.5	6.0
Total assets	$36.0	$24.5	$16.0
Liabilities			
Current liabilities			
Accounts payable	$ 8.0	$ 7.0	$ 6.0
Salaries payable	4.5	4.0	3.5
Total current liabilities	12.5	11.0	9.5
Notes payable	12.0	6.0	5.5
Total liabilities	24.5	17.0	15.0
Shareholders' equity			
Shareholders' equity	11.5	7.5	1.0
Total liabilities and shareholders' equity	$36.0	$24.5	$16.0

Income Statement
For the year ended December 31
(in thousands)

	2017	2016	2015
Revenue			
Service revenue	$110.0	$99.0	$75.0
Expenses			
Salary	65.0	59.0	48.0
Rent	20.0	18.0	17.0
Supplies	7.5	6.0	3.0
Utilities	6.0	4.5	3.5
Depreciation	6.0	3.0	2.0
Total expenses	104.5	90.5	73.5
Income before taxes	5.5	8.5	1.5
Income tax expense	1.5	2.0	.5
Net income	$ 4.0	$ 6.5	$ 1.0

APPLY YOUR KNOWLEDGE

DECISION CASES

This section's material reflects CPA enabling competencies,* including:

1. Professionalism and ethical behaviour
2. Problem-solving and decision-making
3. Communication
4. Self-management
5. Teamwork and leadership

LEARNING OBJECTIVE ❸❻

Adjust and correct the accounts; evaluating debt-paying ability

Case 1. Below is a list of accounts of Patel Consulting Ltd. at January 31, 2017. The unadjusted trial balance of Patel Consulting Ltd. at January 31, 2017, does not balance. In addition, the trial balance needs to be updated before the financial statements at January 31, 2017, can be prepared. The manager needs to know the current ratio of Patel Consulting Ltd.

	A	B	C	D
1	**Patel Consulting Ltd.** List of Accounts January 31, 2017			
2	Cash	$ 6,000		
3	Accounts receivable	2,200		
4	Supplies	800		
5	Prepaid rent	12,000		
6	Land	41,000		
7	Accounts payable		10,000	
8	Salary payable		0	
9	Unearned service revenue		1,500	
10	Note payable, due in three years		25,400	
11	Share capital		15,000	
12	Retained earnings		7,300	
13	Service revenue		9,100	
14	Salary expense	3,400		
15	Rent expense	0		
16	Advertising expense	900		
17	Supplies expense	0		
18		?	?	
19				

*© Chartered Professional Accountants of Canada.

Requirements

1. How much *out of balance* is the trial balance? The error is in the Land account.

2. Patel Consulting Ltd. needs to make the following adjustments at January 31:

    a. Supplies of $600 were used during January.

    b. The balance of Prepaid Rent was paid on January 1 and covers the rest of 2017. No adjustment was made January 31.

    c. At January 31, Patel Consulting owes employees $400.

    d. Unearned service revenue of $800 was earned during January.

    Prepare a corrected, adjusted trial balance. Give Land its correct balance.

3. After the error is corrected and after these adjustments are made, compute the current ratio of Patel Consulting Ltd. If your business had this current ratio, could you sleep at night?

Case 2. On October 1, Sue Skate opened a restaurant named Silver Skates Ltd. After the first month of operations, Skate is at a crossroads. The October financial statements paint a glowing picture of the business, and Skate has asked you whether she should expand Silver Skates. To expand the business, Sue Skate wants to be earning net income of $10,000 per month and have total assets of $35,000. Based on the financial information available to her, Skate believes she is meeting both goals.

    To start the business, she invested $20,000, not the $10,000 amount reported as "Share capital" on the balance sheet. The bookkeeper plugged the $10,000 "Share capital" amount into the balance sheet to make it come out even. The bookkeeper made other mistakes too. Skate shows you the following financial statements that the bookkeeper prepared.

LEARNING OBJECTIVE ❹

Prepare financial statements and make an expansion decision

A	B	C	D
Silver Skates Ltd. Income Statement For the Month Ended October 31, 2017			
Revenues:			
Investments by owner	$ 20,000		
Unearned banquet sales revenue	3,000		
		$ 23,000	
Expenses:			
Wages expense	$ 5,000		
Rent expense	4,000		
Dividends	3,000		
Depreciation expense—fixtures	1,000		
		13,000	
Net income (Net loss)		$ 10,000	

A	B	C	D	E
Silver Skates Ltd. Balance Sheet October 31, 2017				
Assets:		Liabilities:		
Cash	$ 6,000	Accounts payable	$ 5,000	
Prepaid insurance	1,000	Sales revenue	32,000	
Insurance expense	1,000	Accumulated depreciation—		
Food inventory	3,000	fixtures	1,000	
Cost of goods sold (expense)	14,000		38,000	
Fixtures (tables, chairs, etc.)	19,000	Owners' equity:		
Dishes and silverware	4,000	Share capital	10,000	
	$ 48,000		$ 48,000	

Requirements

Prepare a corrected income statement, statement of retained earnings, and balance sheet for Silver Skates Ltd. Then, based on your corrected statements, recommend to Sue Skate whether she should expand her business.

LEARNING OBJECTIVE ❹

Prepare financial statements and compute a purchase price

Case 3. Walter Liu has owned and operated LW Media Inc. since its beginning 10 years ago. Recently, Liu mentioned that he would consider selling the company for the right price.

Assume that you are interested in buying this business. You obtain its most recent monthly trial balance, which follows. Revenues and expenses vary little from month to month, and June is a typical month. Your investigation reveals that the trial balance does not include the effects of monthly revenues of $5,000 and expenses totalling $1,100. If you were to buy LW Media Inc., you would hire a manager so you could devote your time to other duties. Assume that your manager would require a monthly salary of $6,000.

Requirements

1. Assume that the most you would pay for the business is 20 times the monthly net income *you could expect to earn* from it. Compute this possible price.
2. Walter Liu states that the least he will take for the business is 1.5 times shareholders' equity on June 30, 2017. Compute this amount.
3. Under these conditions, how much should you offer Liu? Give your reason.

	A	B	C	D
1	**LW Media Inc.** Trial Balance June 30, 2017			
2	Cash	$ 10,000		
3	Accounts receivable	4,900		
4	Prepaid expenses	3,200		
5	Equipment	115,000		
6	Accumulated depreciation		$ 76,500	
7	Land	158,000		
8	Accounts payable		13,800	
9	Salary payable			
10	Unearned revenue		56,700	
11	Share capital		50,000	
12	Retained earnings		88,000	
13	Dividends	9,000		
14	Revenue		20,000	
15	Rent expense			
16	Salary expense	4,000		
17	Utilities expense	900		
18	Depreciation expense			
19	Supplies expense			
20	Total	$ 305,000	$ 305,000	
21				

ETHICAL ISSUES

Issue 1. ARAS Inc. is in its third year of operations and the company has grown. To expand the business, ARAS borrowed $1 million from Royal Bank of Canada. As a condition for making this loan, the bank required that ARAS maintain a current ratio of at least 1.50 and a debt ratio of no more than 0.50.

Business recently has been worse than expected. Expenses have brought the current ratio down to 1.47 and the debt ratio up to 0.51 at December 15. Shane Rollins, the general manager, is considering the implication of reporting this current ratio to the bank. Rollins is considering recording this year some revenue on account that ARAS will earn next year. The contract for this job has been signed, and ARAS will perform the service during January.

Requirements

1. Journalize the revenue transaction, omitting amounts, and indicate how recording this revenue in December would affect the current ratio and the debt ratio.

2. State whether it is ethical to record the revenue transaction in December. Identify the accounting principle relevant to this situation.

3. Propose to ARAS a course of action that is ethical.

Issue 2. The net income of Accent Photography Company Ltd. decreased sharply during 2017. Mark Smith, owner of the company, anticipates the need for a bank loan in 2018. Late in 2017, he instructed the accountant to record a $20,000 sale of portraits to the Smith family, even though the photos will not be shot until January 2018. Smith also told the accountant *not* to make the following December 31, 2017, adjusting entries:

Salaries owed to employees	$5,000
Prepaid insurance that has expired	1,000

Requirements

1. Compute the overall effect of these transactions on the company's reported income for 2017. Is income overstated or understated?

2. Why did Smith take these actions? Are they ethical? Give your reason, identifying the parties helped and the parties harmed by Smith's action.

3. As a personal friend, what advice would you give the accountant?

FOCUS ON FINANCIALS

Canadian Tire Corporation

LEARNING OBJECTIVE ❸❻

Record journal entries and evaluate debt-paying ability

Like all other businesses, Canadian Tire adjusts accounts prior to year-end to measure assets, liabilities, revenues, and expenses for the financial statements. Examine Canadian Tire's balance sheet in Appendix A, and pay particular attention to (a) Prepaid Expenses and Deposits and (b) Trade and Other Payables.

MyAccountingLab

Requirements

1. Why aren't Prepaid Expenses "true" expenses?

2. Open T-accounts for the Prepaid Expenses and Deposits account and the Trade Payables account. Insert Canadian Tire's balances (in millions) at December 28, 2013.

3. Journalize the following for the year ended January 3, 2015. Key entries by letter, and show accounts in millions. Explanations are not required.

    a. Paid the beginning balance of Trade and Other Payables.

    b. Allocated Prepaid Expenses of $68.2 to Selling, General and Administrative Expenses.

    c. Recorded Trade and Other Payables in the amount of $1,961.2. Assume this relates to Selling, General and Administrative Expenses.

    d. Recorded a prepayment of $104.5 in services to Prepaid Expenses.

4. Post these entries and show that the balances in Prepaid Expenses and in Trade and Other Payables agree with the corresponding amounts reported in the January 3, 2015, balance sheet.

5. Compute the current ratios and debt ratios for Canadian Tire at December 28, 2013, and at January 3, 2015. Did the ratio values improve, deteriorate, or hold steady during the year ended January 3, 2015? Do the ratio values indicate financial strength or weakness?

FOCUS ON ANALYSIS

LEARNING OBJECTIVE ❷

Explain revenue and expense recognition principles

MyAccountingLab

Canadian Tire Corporation

During the fiscal year ended January 3, 2015 (its 2014 fiscal year), Canadian Tire had numerous accruals and deferrals. As a new member of Canadian Tire's accounting and financial staff, it is your job to explain the effects of accruals and deferrals on Canadian Tire's net income for this year. The accrual and deferral data follow, along with questions that Canadian Tire's shareholders have raised (all amounts in millions):

1. Beginning Trade and other receivables for 2014 were $758.5. Ending receivables for 2014 are $880.2. Which of these amounts did Canadian Tire earn in 2013? Which amount did Canadian Tire earn in 2014? Which amount is included in Canadian Tire's revenue for 2014?

2. Accumulated depreciation on property, plant, and equipment stood at $2,326.5 at December 28, 2013, and at $2,529.4 as at January 3, 2015. Accumulated depreciation was reduced by $72.8 for assets sold and various other reasons during the year. Calculate the depreciation expense for the year, and compare to the depreciation expense reported in Note 16 of the 2014 financial statements in Appendix A.

GROUP PROJECT

Matt Davis formed a lawn service company as a summer job. To start the business on May 1, he deposited $1,000 in a new bank account in the name of the corporation. The $1,000 consisted of an $800 loan from his father and $200 of his own money. The corporation issued 200 common shares to Davis.

Davis rented lawn equipment, purchased supplies, and hired high-school students to mow and trim his customers' lawns. At the end of each month, Davis mailed bills to his customers. On August 31, Davis was ready to dissolve the business and return to Simon Fraser University for the fall semester. Because he had been so busy, he had kept few records other than his chequebook and a list of amounts owed by customers.

At August 31, Davis's chequebook shows a balance of $1,390, and his customers still owe him $560. During the summer, he collected $5,150 from customers. His chequebook lists payments for supplies totalling $400, and he still has gasoline, weed whacker cord, and other supplies that cost a total of $50. He paid his employees wages of $1,900, and he still owes them $200 for the final week of the summer.

Davis rented some equipment from Ludwig Tool Company. On May 1, he signed a six-month lease on mowers and paid $600 for the full lease period. Ludwig will refund the unused portion of the prepayment if the equipment is in good shape. To get the refund, Davis has kept the mowers in excellent condition. In fact, he had to pay $300 to repair a mower that ran over a hidden tree stump.

To transport equipment to jobs, Davis used a trailer that he bought for $300. He figures that the summer's work used up one-third of the trailer's service potential. The business chequebook lists an expenditure of $460 for dividends paid to Davis during the summer. Also, Davis paid his father back during the summer.

Requirements

1. Prepare the income statement of Davis Lawn Service Inc. for the four months May through August. The business is not subject to income tax.
2. Prepare the classified balance sheet of Davis Lawn Service Inc. at August 31.

CHECK YOUR WORK

STOP + THINK ANSWERS

STOP + THINK (3-1)

When a customer purchases a single Americano, DVLB would record $3 in revenue immediately upon the sale because it has both acquired an asset ($3 in cash) and earned revenue by delivering the Americano to the customer. When a customer purchases 10 Americanos via a coffee card, however, DVLB has acquired an asset ($25 in cash), but they haven't yet earned any revenue because no Americanos have been delivered to the customer. In fact, upon the sale of a coffee card, DVLB has taken on a liability because it now owes the customer 10 Americanos, which it will deliver to the customer in the future. Each time the customer orders an Americano in the future using the coffee card, DVLB will record $2.50 in revenue ($25/10 Americanos) because only then will they have delivered the Americano to the customer. DVLB's liability to this customer will go down by the same amount.

STOP + THINK (3-2)

1. No, Windsor Group has yet to perform any services, so it cannot recognize revenue. It can begin to recognize revenue as it performs the services the customer has paid for.

2. No, Windsor group has not experienced a decrease in future economic benefits, so it has not incurred an expense. This transaction results in prepaid rent, an asset that will benefit the company over the next three months.

STOP + THINK (3-3)

Supplies Expense ($5,000 + $7,000 – $3,000)	9,000	
Supplies		9,000

To adjust supplies at period end.

The ending balance in the Supplies account is $3,000, the value of supplies on hand at the end of the month.

STOP + THINK (3-4)

$16,500 – $275 – $275 = $15,950.

STOP + THINK (3-5)

Interest Receivable	125	
Interest Revenue		125

To accrue interest revenue.

STOP + THINK (3-6)

Because of the $40,000,000 net loss in fiscal 2015, Le Château's Retained Earnings in the Shareholders' Equity section of its balance sheet would be reduced by this amount, bringing it to a balance of negative $423,000 (opening balance of $39,577,000 – net loss of $40,000,000). When Retained Earnings is negative, it is referred to as a Deficit, so Le Château would report a Deficit of $423,000 in the Shareholders' Equity section of its fiscal 2015 balance sheet.

STOP + THINK (3-7)

The amount of sales in Le Château's Sales account at the open of business on January 4, 2015, would have been nil because the $250,210,000 in sales from the prior year would have been closed out to Retained Earnings at the end of fiscal 2014. Le Château would have $1,195,000 in its Cash account at the open of business on January 4, 2015, the same amount it reported at the close of business on January 3, because balance sheet balances carry forward to the next fiscal year.

STOP + THINK (3-8)

In all of fiscal 2014, Le Château sold inventory with a total cost of $98,665,000 and at the end of that year they had total inventory on hand of $115,357,000, meaning they had almost $20M more inventory in stock at the beginning of fiscal 2015 than they sold in the entire preceding year. In addition, the company sells fashion apparel, which goes out of style quickly. Therefore, given the amount and nature of their inventory, they may be unable to sell much of the inventory they have on hand at the beginning of fiscal 2015. If they are unable to sell a significant amount of this inventory, then they won't get any cash for it, which will reduce the amount of money they have available to pay off current liabilities. So, even though the current ratio looks healthy at the end of fiscal 2014, the fact that so much of the company's current assets are tied up in potentially slow-moving inventory means that they may still have trouble paying their current liabilities in fiscal 2015.

QUICK QUIZ ANSWERS

1. *b*	5. *d*	9. *c*	13. *a*
2. *b*	6. *d*	10. *d*	14. *d*
3. *a*	7. *c*	11. *b*	15. *c*
4. *b*	8. *c*	12. *c*	

Cash and Receivables

4

Paul Chiasson/The Canadian Press

SPOTLIGHT

Did you know that CGI Group Inc. is the largest independent information technology and business process services firms in the world? They provide IT services to clients in Canada, the United States, Europe, and the Asia Pacific region.

Take a look at CGI's comparative balance sheets (excerpt) for 2014 and 2013 on the following page. Notice how cash and cash equivalents are the first item reported under CGI's current assets. Cash equivalents are highly liquid short-term investments that can be converted into cash immediately. As you can see, CGI had about $535 million of cash and cash equivalents at the end of 2014.

Another category of current assets is accounts receivable. On CGI's balance sheet, accounts receivable is the largest component of their current assets. This balance represents the amount of money customers owe CGI at the end of the year. Let's see why.

*© Chartered Professional Accountants of Canada.

	A	B	C	D
1	**CGI Group Inc.** Consolidated Balance Sheets (Excerpt, Adapted) As at September 30, 2014 and 2013			
2	*(in thousands, Canadian dollars)*	**2014**	**2013**	
3	**Assets**			
4	Current Assets			
5	Cash and cash equivalents	$ 535,715	$ 106,199	
6	Short-term investments	9,397	1,344	
7	Accounts receivable	1,036,068	1,205,625	
8	Work in progress	807,989	911,848	
9	Prepaid expenses and other	174,137	218,446	
10	Income taxes	8,524	17,233	
11	Total current assets before funds held for clients	2,571,830	2,460,695	
12	Funds held for clients	295,754	222,469	
13	Total current assets	$ 2,867,584	$ 5,143,859	
14				

Source: CGI – 2014 Annual Review.

This chapter shows how to account for cash and receivables. We also examine liquidity, which measures how quickly an item can be converted to cash. We begin our discussion with cash.

ACCOUNT FOR CASH

OBJECTIVE

❶ Account for cash

Most companies have cash on hand. They use it for such things as paying bills and employees' salaries, repaying loans, and buying equipment. Most companies have numerous bank accounts, but they usually combine all cash amounts into a single total on the balance sheet called "Cash and cash equivalents," as in the CGI balance sheet above. Cash is the most liquid asset because it is the medium of exchange. Companies keep their cash in a bank for safekeeping. **Cash equivalents** include liquid assets such as treasury bills, commercial paper, and money market funds, which are interest-bearing accounts that are very close to maturity (three months or less at the time of purchase). Slightly less liquid than cash, cash equivalents are sufficiently similar to be reported along with cash.

Most public companies include additional information about cash and cash equivalents in the footnotes to their financial statements. For example, Note 3 (Summary of Significant Accounting Policies) of CGI's 2014 financial statements contains the following brief comment about cash and cash equivalents:

> **Cash and cash equivalents**
> Cash and cash equivalents consist of unrestricted cash and short-term investments having an initial maturity of three months or less.

Note 4 (Cash and Cash Equivalents) shows a schedule giving the breakdown of cash and cash equivalents for both 2013 and 2014.

When a company sells their goods or services, they either receive the cash right away or through **electronic funds transfer** (EFT) or receive cheques by mail from the customer. The company deposits the cash and cheques into their bank account. Electronic funds transfer moves cash by electronic communication through debit and credit card transactions and if the customer pays their account through online banking.

To pay cash, the company can write a cheque, which tells the bank to pay the designated party a specified amount or pay through electronic funds transfer. It is cheaper for a company to pay employees by EFT (direct deposit) than by issuing payroll cheques. Many people pay their regular bills, such as mortgage, rent, and utilities, by EFT.

PREPARE AND USE A BANK RECONCILIATION

OBJECTIVE

❷ **Prepare** and **use** a bank reconciliation

Cash is the most liquid asset because it is the medium of exchange, but it is easy to conceal and relatively easy to steal. As a result, most businesses have specific controls for cash.

Keeping cash in a bank account helps control cash. This is an important option because banks have established procedures for safeguarding customers' money. Following are the documents used to control bank accounts.

Signature Card

Banks require each person authorized to sign on an account to provide a *signature card*. This protects against forgery.

Deposit Slip

Banks supply standard account forms such as *deposit slips*. The customer fills in the amount of each deposit. As proof of the transaction, the customer keeps a deposit receipt.

Cheque

To pay cash, the depositor can write a **cheque**, which tells the bank to pay the designated party a specified amount. There are three parties to a cheque:

- the maker, who signs the cheque,
- the payee, to whom the cheque is paid, and
- the bank on which the cheque is drawn.

Exhibit 4-1 shows a cheque drawn by Nixon Partners Inc., the maker. The cheque has two parts, the cheque itself and the **remittance advice** below it. This optional attachment, which may often be scanned electronically, tells the payee the reason for the payment and is used as a source document for posting the proper accounts.

EXHIBIT 4-1
Cheque With Remittance Advice

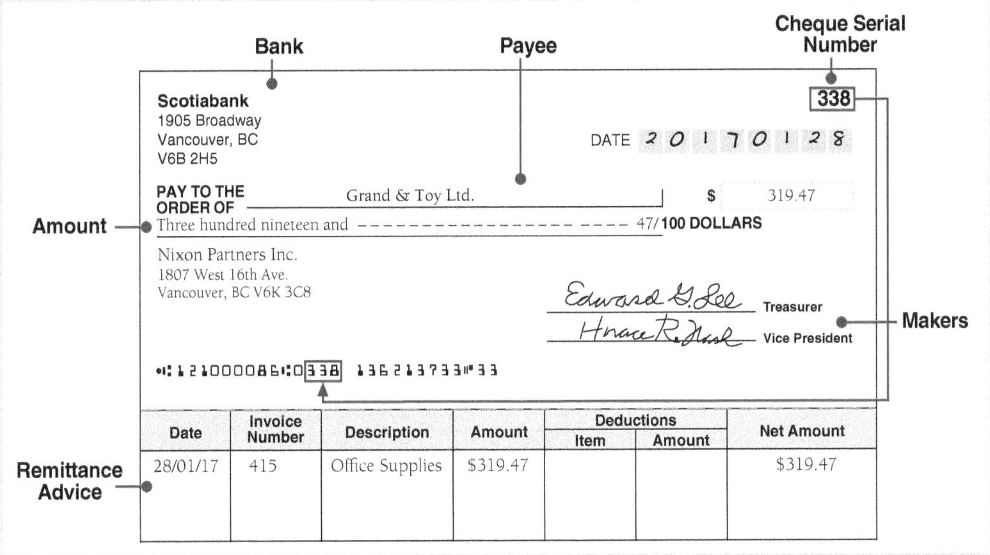

EXHIBIT 4-2
Bank Statement

ACCOUNT STATEMENT

Scotiabank
1905 Broadway Vancouver, BC V6B 2H5

Nixon Partners Inc.
1807 West 16th Avenue
Vancouver, BC V6K 3C8

BUSINESS CHEQUING ACCOUNT 136–213733

CHEQUING ACCOUNT SUMMARY AS OF 01/31/17

BEGINNING BALANCE	TOTAL DEPOSITS	TOTAL WITHDRAWALS	SERVICE CHARGES	ENDING BALANCE
6,556.12	4,352.64	4,963.00	14.25	5,931.51

BUSINESS CHEQUING ACCOUNT TRANSACTIONS

DEPOSITS	DATE	AMOUNT
Deposit	Jan04	1,000.00
Deposit	Jan04	112.00
Deposit	Jan06	194.60
EFT—Collection of rent	Jan10	904.03
Bank Collection	Jan16	2,114.00
Interest	Jan20	28.01

CHARGES	DATE	AMOUNT
Service Charge	Jan31	14.25
Cheques:		

CHEQUES			BALANCES			
Number	Date	Amount	Date	Balance	Date	Balance
332	Jan06	3,000.00	Dec31	6,556.12	Jan16	7,378.75
656	Jan06	100.00	Jan04	7,616.12	Jan20	7,045.76
333	Jan10	150.00	Jan06	4,710.72	Jan25	5,945.76
334	Jan12	100.00	Jan10	5,464.75	Jan31	5,931.51
335	Jan12	100.00	Jan12	5,264.75		
336	Jan25	1,100.00				

OTHER CHARGES	DATE	AMOUNT
NSF	Jan04	52.00
EFT—Insurance	Jan20	361.00

MONTHLY SUMMARY

Withdrawals: 8	Minimum Balance: 4,710.72	Average Balance: 6,215.00

Bank Statement

Banks send monthly statements to customers in paper form or the statements may be available on the bank's website. A **bank statement** reports the activity in a bank account. The statement shows the account's beginning and ending balances, cash receipts, payments, and electronic funds transfers. Exhibit 4-2 is the January 2017 bank statement of Nixon Partners Inc.

Bank Reconciliation

There are two records of a business's cash:

1. The Cash account in the company's general ledger. Exhibit 4-3 shows that Nixon Partners Inc.'s ending cash balance is $3,294.21.

2. The bank statement, which shows the cash receipts and payments transacted through the bank. In Exhibit 4-2, the bank shows an ending balance of $5,931.51 for Nixon Partners.

The books and the bank statement usually show different cash balances. Differences arise because of a time lag in recording transactions. Here are two examples:

- When you write a cheque, you immediately record it in your chequebook as a deduction. But the bank does not subtract the cheque from your account until

ACCOUNT Cash

EXHIBIT 4-3
Cash Records of Nixon
Partners Inc.

Date	Item	Debit	Credit	Balance
2017				
Jan. 1	Balance			6,556.12
2	Cash receipt	1,112.00		7,668.12
5	Cash receipt	194.60		7,862.72
31	Cash payments		6,160.14	1,702.58
31	Cash receipt	1,591.63		3,294.21

Cash Payments

	A	B	C	D	E
1	**Cheque No.**	**Amount**	**Cheque No.**	**Amount**	
2	332	$ 3,000.00	338	$ 319.47	
3	333	510.00	339	83.00	
4	334	100.00	340	203.14	
5	335	100.00	341	458.53	
6	336	1,100.00			
7	337	286.00	Total	$ 6,160.14	
8					

the payee cashes it at a later date. Likewise, you immediately record the cash receipts for all your deposits as additions. But it may take a day or two for the bank to add deposits to your balance.

- Your EFT payments and cash receipts are recorded by the bank before you learn of them.

To ensure accurate cash records, you need to update your cash record—either online or after you receive your bank statement. The result of this updating process allows you to prepare a **bank reconciliation**. The bank reconciliation explains all differences between your cash records and your bank statement balance.

The person who prepares a company's bank reconciliation should have no other cash duties and be independent of cash activities. Otherwise, he or she can steal cash and manipulate the reconciliation to conceal the theft.

Preparing the Bank Reconciliation

Here are the items that appear on a bank reconciliation. They all cause differences between the bank balance and the book balance to occur. We call your cash record (also known as a "chequebook") the "books."

BANK SIDE OF THE RECONCILIATION.

1. Items to show on the *Bank* side of the bank reconciliation include the following:

   a. *Deposits in transit* (outstanding deposits). You have recorded these deposits, but the bank has not. Add **deposits in transit** on the bank reconciliation.

   b. *Outstanding cheques.* You have recorded these cheques, but the payees have not yet cashed them. Subtract **outstanding cheques**.

   c. *Bank errors.* Correct all bank errors on the Bank side of the reconciliation. For example, the bank may erroneously subtract from your account a cheque written by someone else. These items are recorded in the company's books but not by the bank.

   These items are recorded on the company's books but not by the bank.

BOOK SIDE OF THE RECONCILIATION.

1. Items to show on the *Book* side of the bank reconciliation include the following:

   a. *Bank collections.* **Bank collections** are cash receipts that the bank has recorded for your account. But you haven't recorded the cash receipt yet. Many businesses have their customers pay directly to their bank. This is called a *lockbox system* and reduces theft. An example is a bank collecting an account receivable for you. Add bank collections on the bank reconciliation.

   b. *Electronic funds transfers.* The bank may receive or pay cash on your behalf. An electronic funds transfer (EFT) may be a cash receipt or a cash payment. EFTs are set up with a bank using a code and bank account number for the company. It allows electronic cheques to be sent (or received) digitally to (or from) the bank, who then disburses the money from (or deposits the money to) the company account. Add EFT receipts and subtract EFT payments.

   c. *Service charge.* This cash payment is the bank's fee for processing your transactions. Subtract service charges.

   d. *Interest income.* On certain types of bank accounts, you earn interest if you keep enough cash in your account. The bank statement tells you of this cash receipt. Add interest income.

   e. *Nonsufficient funds (NSF) cheques.* **Nonsufficient funds (NSF) cheques** are cash receipts from customers who do not have sufficient funds in their bank account to cover the amount. NSF cheques (sometimes called bad cheques) are treated as cash payments on your bank reconciliation. Subtract NSF cheques.

   f. *The cost of printed cheques.* This cash payment is handled like a service charge. Subtract this cost.

   g. *Book errors.* Correct all book errors on the Book side of the reconciliation. For example, you may have recorded a $120 cheque that you wrote as $210. These items are recorded by the bank but not by the company; therefore, journal entries must be prepared.

   These items are recorded by the bank but not by the company, therefore, journal entries must be prepared.

In a business, the bank reconciliation can be a part of internal control if it is done on a regular basis and if someone independent of the person preparing the bank reconciliation (for example, someone from another department) reviews the reconciliation.

BANK RECONCILIATION ILLUSTRATED. The bank statement in Exhibit 4-2 indicates that the January 31 bank balance of Nixon Partners Inc. is $5,931.51. However, Exhibit 4-3 shows that the company's Cash account on the books has a balance of $3,294.21. This situation calls for a bank reconciliation. Exhibit 4-4, Panel A, lists the reconciling items for easy reference, and Panel B shows the completed reconciliation.

After the reconciliation in Exhibit 4-4, the adjusted bank balance equals the adjusted book balance. This equality checks the accuracy of both the bank and the books.

RECORDING TRANSACTIONS FROM THE BANK RECONCILIATION. The bank reconciliation is an accountant's tool separate from the journals and ledgers. It does *not* account for transactions in the journal. To get the transactions into the accounts, we must record journal entries and post them to the ledger. All items on the *Book* side of the bank reconciliation require journal entries.

EXHIBIT 4-4
Bank Reconciliation

PANEL A—Reconciling Items

Bank side:

1. Deposit in transit, $1,591.63
2. Bank error: The bank deducted $100.00 on January 6 for a cheque written by another company. Add $100.00 to the bank balance.
3. Outstanding cheques—total of $1,350.14

	A	B	C
1	**Cheque No.**	**Amount**	
2	337	$ 286.00	
3	338	319.47	
4	339	83.00	
5	340	203.14	
6	341	458.53	
7			

Book side:

4. EFT receipt of your interest revenue earned on an investment, $904.03.
5. Bank collection of your note receivable, including interest of $214.00, $2,114.00.
6. Interest revenue earned on your bank balance, $28.01.
7. Book error: You recorded cheque no. 333 for $510.00. The amount you actually paid on account was $150.00. Add $360.00 to your book balance.
8. Bank service charge, $14.25.
9. NSF cheque from a customer, $52.00. Subtract $52.00 from your book balance.
10. EFT payment of insurance expense, $361.00.

PANEL B—Bank Reconciliation

	A	B	C	D	E	F
1			**Nixon Partners Inc.** Bank Reconciliation January 31, 2017			
2	**Bank**			**Books**		
3	Balance, January 31		$ 5,931.51	Balance, January 31		$3,294.21
4	Add:			Add:		
5	1. Deposit in transit		1,591.63	4. EFT receipt of interest revenue		904.03
6	2. Correction of bank error		100.00	5. Bank collection of note		
7			7,623.14	receivable		2,114.00
8				6. Interest revenue earned on		
9				bank balance		28.01
10				7. Correction of book error—		
11	Less:			overstated our cheque no. 333		360.00
12	3. Outstanding cheques					6,700.25
13	No. 337	$ 286.00				
14	No. 338	319.47		Less:		
15	No. 339	83.00		8. Service charge	$ 14.25	
16	No. 340	203.14		9. NSF cheque	52.00	
17	No. 341	458.53	(1,350.14)	10. EFT payment of insurance expense	361.00	(427.25)
18	Adjusted bank balance		$ 6,273.00	Adjusted book balance		$6,273.00
19						

These amounts should agree.

Summary of the Various Reconciling Items:

Bank Balance—Always:
- *Add* deposits in transit.
- *Subtract* outstanding cheques.
- *Add* or *subtract* corrections of bank errors.

Book Balance—Always:
- *Add* bank collections, interest revenue, and EFT receipts.
- *Subtract* service charges, NSF cheques, and EFT payments.
- *Add* or *subtract* corrections of book errors.

The bank reconciliation in Exhibit 4-4 requires Nixon Partners to make journal entries to bring the Cash account up to date. These journal entries are detailed below. Numbers in parentheses correspond to the reconciling items listed in Exhibit 4-4, Panel A.

	A	B	C	D	E	F
1	(4)	Jan. 31	Cash	904.03		
2			Interest revenue		904.03	
3			*Receipt of interest revenue.*			
4	(5)	Jan. 31	Cash	2,114.00		
5			Note receivable		1,900.00	
6			Interest revenue		214.00	
7			*Note receivable collected by bank.*			
8	(6)	Jan. 31	Cash	28.01		
9			Interest revenue		28.01	
10			*Interest earned on bank balance.*			
11	(7)	Jan. 31	Cash	360.00		
12			Accounts payable—Brown Co. Ltd.		360.00	
13			*Correction of cheque no. 333.*			
14	(8)	Jan. 31	Bank service charge expense	14.25		
15			Cash		14.25	
16			*Bank service charge.*			
17	(9)	Jan. 31	Accounts receivable—L. Ross	52.00		
18			Cash		52.00	
19			*NSF customer cheque returned by bank.*			
20	(10)	Jan. 31	Insurance expense	361.00		
21			Cash		361.00	
22			*Payment of monthly insurance.*			
23						

The entry for the NSF cheque (entry 9) needs explanation. Upon learning that a customer's $52.00 cheque to us was not good, we must credit Cash to update the Cash account. Unfortunately, we still have a receivable from the customer, so we must debit Accounts Receivable to reinstate our receivable.

Online Banking

Online banking allows you to pay bills and view your account electronically—you don't have to wait until the end of the month to get a bank statement. With online banking you can reconcile transactions at any time and keep your account current whenever you wish.

MyAccountingLab

STOP + THINK (4-1)

You have been asked to prepare a bank reconciliation and are given the following information. The bank statement balance is $4,500 and shows a service charge of $15, interest earned of $5, and an NSF cheque for $300. Deposits in transit total $1,200;

outstanding cheques are $575. You recorded as $152 a cheque of $125 in payment of an account payable.

1. What is the adjusted bank balance?

2. What was the book balance of cash before the reconciliation?

MyAccountingLab

MID-CHAPTER SUMMARY PROBLEM

The Cash account of Chima Inc. at February 28, 2017, is as follows:

			Cash				
Feb.	1	Balance	3,995	Feb.	5	400	
	6		800		12	3,100	
	15		1,800		19	1,100	
	22		1,100		26	500	
	28		2,400		27	900	
Feb.	28	Balance	4,095				

Aneil Chima deposits all cash receipts in the bank and makes all cash payments by cheque. Chima Inc. receives this bank statement on February 28, 2017 (as always, negative amounts are in parentheses):

	A	B	C	D
1	**Bank Statement for February 2017**			
2	Beginning balance		$ 3,995	
3	Deposits:			
4	Feb. 7	$ 800		
5	15	1,800		
6	23	1,100	3,700	
7	Cheques (total per day):			
8	Feb. 8	$ 400		
9	16	3,100		
10	23	1,100	(4,600)	
11	Other items:			
12	Service charge		(10)	
13	NSF cheque from M. E. Crown		(700)	
14	Bank collection of note receivable		1,000*	
15	EFT—monthly rent expense		(330)	
16	Interest on account balance		15	
17	Ending balance		$ 3,070	
18	*Includes interest of $119			

Name: Chima Inc.
Accounting Period: Month of February 2017

Requirements

1. Prepare the bank reconciliation of Chima Inc. at February 28, 2017.
2. Record the journal entries based on the bank reconciliation.

ANSWERS

Requirement 1

Before creating the bank reconciliation, compare the Cash account and the bank statement. Cross out all items that appear in both places. The items that remain are the reconciling items.

Begin with the ending balance on the bank statement.
- Add deposits (debits) from the Cash account not on the bank statement.
- Deduct cheques (credits) from the Cash account not on the bank statement.

Begin with the ending balance in the Cash general ledger account.
- Add money received by the bank on behalf of the company (increases to the bank statement balance).
- Deduct bank charges, NSF cheques, or pre-authorized payments (decreases to the bank statement balance).

	A	B	C	D
1	**Chima Inc.** Bank Reconciliation February 28, 2017			
2	**Bank:**			
3	Balance, February 28, 2017		$ 3,070	
4	Add: Deposit of February 28 in transit		2,400	
5			5,470	
6	Less: Outstanding cheques issued on			
7	Feb. 26 ($500) and Feb. 27 ($900)		(1,400)	
8	Adjusted bank balance, February 28, 2017		$ 4,070	
9	**Books:**			
10	Balance, February 28, 2017		$ 4,095	
11	Add: Bank collection of note receivable, including interest of $119		1,000	
12	Interest earned on bank balance		15	
13			5,110	
14	Less: Service charge	$ 10		
15	NSF cheque	700		
16	EFT—Rent expense	330	(1,040)	
17	Adjusted book balance, February 28, 2017		$ 4,070	
18				

Requirement 2

	A	B	C	D	E
1	Feb. 28	Cash	1,000		
2		Note receivable ($1,000 – $119)		881	
3		Interest revenue		119	
4		*Note receivable collected by bank.*			
5	28	Cash	15		
6		Interest revenue		15	
7		*Interest earned on bank balance.*			
8	28	Bank service charge expense	10		
9		Cash		10	
10		*Bank service charge.*			
11	28	Accounts receivable—M. E. Crown	700		
12		Cash		700	
13		*NSF cheque returned by bank.*			
14	28	Rent expense	330		
15		Cash		330	
16		*Monthly rent expense.*			
17					

Prepare journal entries for all reconciling items from the "Books" section of the bank reconciliation.

ACCOUNT FOR RECEIVABLES

Receivables are the third most-liquid asset after cash and short-term investments. Most of the remainder of this chapter shows how to account for receivables.

❸ Account for receivables

Types of Receivables

Receivables are monetary claims against others. They are acquired mainly by selling goods and services on account (accounts receivable) and by lending money (notes receivable). Journal entries to record receivables can be shown as follows:

Performing a Service on Account		Lending Money on a Note Receivable	
Accounts Receivable XXX		Note Receivable XXX	
Service Revenue	XXX	Cash	XXX
Performed a service on account.		Loaned money to another company.	

The two major types of receivables are accounts receivable and notes receivable. A business's *accounts receivable* are the amounts collectible from customers from the sale of goods and services. Accounts receivable, which are *current assets*, are sometimes called *trade receivables* or merely *receivables*.

The Accounts Receivable account in the general ledger serves as a *control account* that summarizes the total amount receivable from all customers. Companies also keep a *subsidiary ledger* of accounts receivable with a separate account for each customer, illustrated as follows:

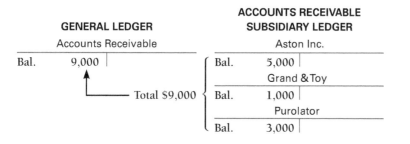

Notes receivable are more formal contracts than accounts receivable. The borrower signs a written promise to pay the creditor a definite sum at the *maturity* date. This is why notes receivable are also called *promissory notes*. The note may require the borrower to pledge *security* for the loan. This means that the borrower gives the lender permission to claim certain assets, called *collateral*, if the borrower fails to pay the amount due. We cover the details of notes receivable starting on page 195.

Other Receivables is a miscellaneous category that includes loans to employees and subsidiary companies. Some companies report other receivables under the heading Other Assets on the balance sheet.

How Do We Manage the Risk of Not Collecting?

Most companies sell on credit and thus hold accounts receivable. By selling on credit, all companies run the risk of not collecting some receivables, and unfortunately, customers sometimes don't pay their debts. The prospect that we may fail to collect from a customer provides the biggest challenge in accounting for receivables. How do we minimize this risk? The Decision Guidelines below provide some advice.

▶ **DECISION GUIDELINES**

MANAGING AND ACCOUNTING FOR ACCOUNTS RECEIVABLE

Here are the management and accounting issues a company faces when it extends credit to customers. Let's look at a business situation: Suppose you and a friend open a health club near your school. Assume you will let customers use the club and charge bills to their accounts. What challenges will you encounter by extending credit to customers?

The main issues in *managing* receivables, along with a plan of action, are the following:

Decision	Guidelines
1. What are the benefits and the costs of extending credit to customers?	**1.** Benefit—increase in sales. Cost—risk of not collecting.
2. Extend credit only to creditworthy customers.	**2.** Run a credit check on prospective customers.
3. Pursue collection from customers to maximize cash flow.	**3.** Keep a close eye on customer paying habits. Send second, and third, statements to slow-paying customers, if necessary. Do not extend credit to overdue accounts.

The main issues in accounting for receivables and the related plans of action are as follows (amounts are assumed):

Decision	Guidelines
How should receivables be reported?	Report receivables at net realizable value: **Balance sheet** Receivables $1,000 Less: Allowance for uncollectibles (80) Receivables, net $ 920 *Managers* This is the amount the company expects to collect and the appropriate amount to report for receivables. *Investors and Creditors* They are interested in seeing the net receivables because this is the amount the company actually expects to collect. They understand that legally the company is owed $1,000, but in reality, $920 is the amount expected to be collected.
How should the bad debt expense be reported?	This expense of not collecting from customers is called *bad debt expense* and is reported on the income statement. **Income statement** Sales (or service) revenue $8,000 Expenses: Bad debt expense 190 *Managers* The company measures and reports the expense associated with the failure to collect receivables. *Investors and Creditors* Because investors and creditors are interested in the profitability of the company, the bad debt expense on the income statement reflects the cost associated with selling goods on credit.

These guidelines lead to our next topic, accounting for uncollectible receivables.

MyAccountingLab

STOP + THINK (4-2)

You are considering an investment in Black Corporation and are looking at Black's June 30, 2017, financial statements, which are stated in thousands of dollars. In particular, you are focusing on Black's accounts receivable. The balance sheet includes the following:

	June 30	
	2017	2016
Accounts receivable, net of Allowance for uncollectible accounts of $3,974 as of June 30, 2017, and $2,089 as of June 30, 2016..	$134,396	$128,781

At June 30, 2017, how much did customers owe Black Corporation? How much did Black expect *not* to collect? How much of the receivables did Black expect to collect?

ESTIMATE AND ACCOUNT FOR UNCOLLECTIBLE ACCOUNTS RECEIVABLE

OBJECTIVE

❹ **Estimate** and **account for** uncollectible accounts receivable

A company gets an account receivable only when it sells its product or service on credit. You'll recall that the entry to record the earning of revenue on account is (amount assumed):

	A	B	C	D	E
1		Accounts Receivable	1,000		
2		Sales Revenue (or Service Revenue)		1,000	
3		*Earned revenue on account.*			
4					

Companies rarely collect all of their accounts receivable, so they must account for what they do not collect.

As stated above, selling on credit creates both a benefit and a cost:

- *Benefit*: Customers who cannot pay cash immediately can buy on credit, so company profits rise as sales increase.

- *Cost*: When a customer doesn't pay, the debt has gone bad, so this cost is commonly called an **uncollectible account expense**, a **doubtful account expense**, or a **bad debt expense**.

Accounts receivable are reported in the financial statements at cost minus an appropriate allowance for uncollectible accounts (that is, net realizable value). This is the amount a company expects to collect.

A company may present the allowance for uncollectible accounts in the notes to the financial statements, or disclose the information on the balance sheet as follows:

Accounts Receivable (net of allowance for
uncollectible accounts of $120,000) $2,005,234

From this information we can determine several things about the company's receivables. From the amount of its allowance for uncollectible accounts, we can see that *it does not expect to collect* $120,000 of its accounts receivable at year-end. The *net realizable value* of its receivables is $2,005,234, which is the amount it *expects to collect* from its customers. If we add the uncollectible account to the net realizable value, we get the company's *total accounts receivable* at year-end: $2,125,234.

Bad debt expense is an expense associated with the failure to collect receivables. It is usually reported as an operating expense on the income statement. To measure bad debt expense, accountants use the *allowance method*.

Allowance Method

The best way to measure bad debts is by the **allowance method**. This method records losses from failure to collect receivables. Management does not wait to see which customers will not pay. Managers estimate bad debt expense on the basis of the company's collection experience and their professional judgment. The company records the estimated amount as Bad Debt Expense and sets up an **Allowance for Uncollectible Accounts**. Other titles for this account are **Allowance for Doubtful Accounts** and **Allowance for Bad Debts**. This is a contra account to Accounts Receivable, which means that it is deducted from Accounts Receivable. The allowance shows the amount of the receivables that the business *does not expect* to collect. Management does not know yet which customer will not pay. The use of a contra account eliminates the problem of having to reduce an accounts receivable of a specific customer.

When estimating their uncollectible accounts, companies typically rely on their history of collections from customers. To estimate uncollectibles, the company uses the aging-of-receivables method.

AGING-OF-RECEIVABLES METHOD. This method is a *balance-sheet approach* because it focuses on what should be the most relevant and faithful representation of accounts receivable as of the balance sheet date. In the aging method, individual receivables from specific customers are analyzed based on how long they have been outstanding.

Accounting software packages are designed to age the company's accounts receivable. Exhibit 4-5 shows an assumed aging of receivables for Black at June 30, 2017. Black's receivables total $138,370 (in thousands of dollars). Of this amount, the aging schedule shows that the company will *not* collect $6,156, but the allowance for

EXHIBIT 4-5
Aging the Accounts Receivable of Black Corporation

Customer	Total	Dollar Amounts (in thousands) Number of Days Outstanding			
		0–30	31–60	61–90	over 90
City of Regina	$ 500	$ 500			
IBM Canada	1,000	1,000			
Keady Pipe Corp.	2,100		$ 1,000	$ 1,100	
TorBar Inc.	200			200	
Others	134,570	66,070	57,000	9,000	$2,500
	$138,370	$67,570	$58,000	$10,300	$2,500
Estimated % Uncollectible		2%	5%	10%	35%
Total Estimated Uncollectible Accounts	$ 6,156	$ 1,351	$ 2,900	$ 1,030	$ 875

uncollectible accounts is not yet up to date. Suppose Black's accounts are as follows *before the year-end adjustment* (in thousands):

Accounts Receivable	Allowance for Uncollectible Accounts
138,370	346

Using the aging method, the accounts are listed in categories based on the number of days they have been outstanding. For example, in Exhibit 4-5, the total accounts receivable is $138,370. This amount is further divided into days outstanding: 0–30 days, 31–60 days, 61–90 days, and over 90 days.

If you look under the 0–30 days category, you will see that credit sales of $67,570 were made within the last 30 days and the company is still waiting to collect cash from the customers. Management estimated that 2% or $1,351 ($67,570 × 2%) would not be collected. The estimated percentages are based on management's professional judgment and past experience with collections. The percentages could change from year to year based on industry, general economic conditions, and customer circumstances. Under the 31–60 days category, $58,000 was sold on account more than 30 days ago but less than 60 days. Management estimates that 5% of the $58,000 will not be collected. Each of the other categories has its estimated percentage of uncollectible accounts indicated as well. Adding up the total estimated uncollectible accounts for each column ($1,351 + $2,900 + $1,030 + $875), it totals $6,156. This means that Black expects *not* to collect $6,156, but the allowance for bad debts is not yet up to date. The aging method will bring the balance of the allowance account ($346) to the needed amount ($6,156) as determined by the aging schedule in Exhibit 4-5. To update the allowance, Black Corporation would make this entry:

	A	B	C	D	E
1	2017				
2	June 30	Bad Debt Expense ($6,156 – $346)	5,810		
3		Allowance for Uncollectible Accounts		5,810	
4		*Recorded expense for the year.*			
5					

Both assets and shareholders' equity decrease, as shown by the accounting equation:

ASSETS	=	LIABILITIES	+	SHAREHOLDERS' EQUITY
−5,810	=	0		−5,810 Expense

When the company uses the allowance method, expenses are properly recognized in the period they were incurred, which is the same period in which the related sales took place.

Now the balance sheet can report the amount that Black Corporation actually expects to collect from customers: $132,214 ($138,370 – $6,156). This is the net realizable value of Black's trade receivables. Black's accounts are now ready for the balance sheet, as follows:

Accounts Receivable	Allowance for Uncollectible Accounts		Bad Debt Expense
138,370		346	5,810
	Adj.	5,810	
	End. Bal.	6,156	

Net accounts receivable, $132,214

Exhibit 4-6 summarizes the aging-of-receivables method.

EXHIBIT 4-6
Summary of the Aging-of-Receivables Method for Estimating Uncollectible Accounts

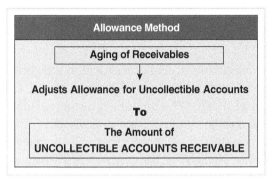

WRITING OFF UNCOLLECTIBLE ACCOUNTS. Suppose that early in July 2017, Black's credit department determines that Black cannot collect from customers Keady Pipe Corporation and TorBar Inc. (see Exhibit 4-5). Black Corporation then writes off the receivables from these two delinquent customers with the following entry (in thousands of dollars):

	A	B	C	D	E
1	2017				
2	July 12	Allowance for Uncollectible Accounts	2,300		
3		Accounts Receivable—Keady Pipe Corporation		2,100	
4		Accounts Receivable—TorBar Inc.		200	
5		*Wrote off uncollectible receivables.*			
6					

After the write-off, Black's accounts show these amounts:

Accounts Receivable—Keady Pipe Corp.	
2,100	2,100

Accounts Receivable—TorBar Inc.	
200	200

Allowance for Uncollectible Accounts	
2,300	6,156
	End Bal. 3,856

Accounts Receivable Others	
134,570	

Accounts Receivable—City of Regina	
500	

Accounts Receivable—IBM Canada	
1,000	

Total Accounts Receivable = $136,070   Allowance = $3,856

Accounts Receivable, Net = $132,214

If the write-offs are greater than the balance in the Allowance for Uncollectible Accounts, it will result in a debit balance in the Allowance account. This means that management's estimate of bad debts was too low and needs to be higher. The accounting equation shows that the write-off of uncollectibles has no effect on total assets; the net realizable value of accounts receivable is still $132,214. There is no effect on net income either, because no expense account is affected.

ASSETS	=	LIABILITIES	+	SHAREHOLDERS' EQUITY
+2,300				
−2,300	=	0	+	0

Recovery of an Uncollectible Account

Even though an account has been written off as uncollectible, the customer still owes the money and will sometimes pay off the account, at least in part.

Some companies turn delinquent receivables over to a collection agency to help recover some of their cash. This is called the *recovery of an uncollectible account*. Recall that on July 12, 2017, Black Corporation wrote off the $200 account receivable from TorBar. Suppose it is now September 1, 2017, and the company unexpectedly receives the $200 from TorBar. To account for this recovery, the company makes two journal entries to (1) reverse the earlier write-off and (2) record the cash collection, as follows:

	A	B	C	D	E
1	2017				
2	Sept. 1	Accounts Receivable—TorBar Inc.	200		
3		Allowance for Uncollectible Accounts		200	
4		*Reinstated TorBar's account receivable.*			
5		Cash	200		
6		Accounts Receivable—TorBar Inc.		200	
7		*Collected on account.*			
8					

Summary of Transactions for Accounts Receivable

Exhibit 4-7 summarizes the journal entries to record the transactions affecting accounts receivable.

During the accounting period:

Record sales on account:
Accounts receivable
   Sales revenue

Record collections from customers:
Cash
   Accounts receivable

Record write-off of uncollectible accounts:
Allowance for uncollectible accounts
   Accounts receivable

Record recovery of an uncollectible account:
Accounts receivable
   Allowance for uncollectible accounts
Cash
   Accounts receivable

At the end of the accounting period:

Estimate bad debt expense:
Bad debt expense
   Allowance for uncollectible accounts

EXHIBIT 4-7
Summary of Accounts Receivable Transactions

Computing Cash Collections from Customers

A company earns revenue and then collects the cash from customers. For Black Corporation (and most other companies), there is a time lag between earning the revenue and collecting the cash. Collections from customers are the single most important source of cash for any business. You can compute a company's collections from customers by analyzing its Accounts Receivable account. Receivables typically hold only five different items, as follows (amounts assumed):

Accounts Receivable

Beg. balance (left from last period)	200	Write-offs of uncollectible accounts	100**
		Collections from customers	$X = 1,500^†$
Sales (or service) revenue	1,800*		
End. balance (carries over to next period)	400		

*The journal entry that places revenue into the receivable account is:

	A	B	C	D
1	Accounts Receivable	1,800		
2	Sales (or Service) Revenue		1,800	
3				

**The journal entry for write-offs is:

	A	B	C	D
1	Allowance for Uncollectible Accounts	100		
2	Accounts Receivable		100	
3				

†The journal entry that places collections into the receivable account is:

	A	B	C	D
1	Cash	1,500		
2	Accounts Receivable		1,500	
3				

Suppose you know all these amounts except collections from customers. You can compute collections by solving for X in the T-account.*

Often write-offs are not known and must be omitted. Then the computation of collections becomes an approximation.

COOKING the BOOKS

shifting sales Into the Current Period

Suppose it is December 26. Late in the year a company's business dried up: Its profits are running below what everyone predicted. The company needs a loan and its banker requires financial statements to support the loan request. Unless the company acts quickly, it won't get the loan.

Fortunately, next year looks better. The company has standing orders for sales of $50,000. As soon as the company gets the merchandise, it can ship it to customers and record the sales. An old accounting trick can solve the problem. Book the $50,000 of sales in December. After all, the company will be shipping the goods on January 2 of next year. What difference does two days make?

It makes all the difference in the world. Shifting the sales into the current year will make the company look better immediately. Reported profits will rise, the current ratio will improve, and the company can then get the loan needed. Also, this false information could lead to investors making decisions that would not otherwise have been made if the information had been recorded in the proper time period. But what are the consequences? If caught, the company could be prosecuted for fraud, and lenders and investors will lose confidence in the company. Remember that the company shifted next year's sales into the current year. Next year's sales will be lower than the true amount, and profits will suffer. If next year turns out to be like this year, the company will be facing the same shortage again. Also, something may come up to keep the company from shipping the goods on January 2.

---

*An equation may help you solve for X. The equation is $\$200 + \$1,800 - X - \$100 = \$400$. $X = \$1,500$.

STOP + THINK (4-3)

Neal Company had the following information relating to credit sales in 2017:

Accounts receivable, December 31, 2017	$9,500
Allowance for uncollectible accounts, credit balance, December 31, 2017 (before adjustment)	900
Sales during 2017	46,000
Collections from customers on account during 2017	49,500

The aging-of-receivables method determined the uncollectible accounts to be $1,350. How much should Neal Company record as the bad debt expense for 2017?

ACCOUNT FOR NOTES RECEIVABLE

OBJECTIVE

⑤ **Account** for notes receivable

As stated earlier, notes receivable are more formal than accounts receivable. Notes receivable due within one year or less are current assets. Notes due beyond one year are *long-term receivables* and are reported as non-current. Some notes receivable are collected in instalments. The portion due within one year is a current asset and the remainder is a long-term asset. Assume, for example, that a company issues a $20,000 note receivable to a customer, with quarterly instalments of $2,500 due over the next two years. If six instalments are still owing at year-end, then $10,000 of the note would be a current asset (four quarterly payments of $2,500), and the remaining $5,000 would be reported as a long-term asset.

Before launching into the accounting for notes receivable, let's define some key terms:

Creditor	The party to whom money is owed. The creditor is also called the *lender*. The debt is a *note receivable* from the *borrower*.
Debtor	The party that borrowed and owes money on the note. The debtor is also called the *maker* of the note or the *borrower*. The debt is a *note payable* to the *lender*.
Interest	Interest is the cost of borrowing money. The interest is stated as an annual percentage rate.
Maturity date	The date on which the debtor must pay the note.
Principal	The amount of money borrowed by the debtor.
Term	The length of time the debtor has to repay the note.

The debtor signs the note and thereby creates a contract with the creditor. Exhibit 4-8 shows a typical promissory note.

The *principal* amount of the note ($1,000) is the amount borrowed by the debtor and lent by the creditor. This six-month note runs from July 1, 2017, to December 31, 2017, when Lauren Holland (the maker) promises to pay Canadian Western Bank (the creditor) the principal of $1,000 plus 9% interest per year. *Interest* is revenue to the creditor and an expense to the debtor.

EXHIBIT 4-8
A Promissory Note

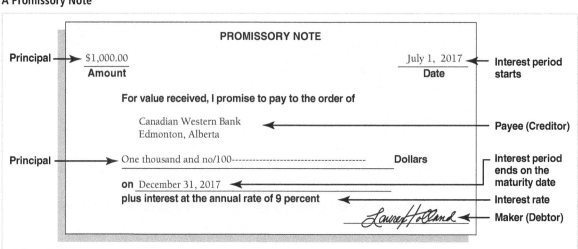

Accounting for Notes Receivable

Consider the promissory note shown in Exhibit 4-8. After Lauren Holland (the maker) signs the note, Canadian Western Bank gives her $1,000 cash. The bank would record the following journal entry:

	A	B	C	D	E
1	2017				
2	July 1	Note Receivable—L. Holland	1,000		
3		Cash		1,000	
4		*Made a loan.*			
5					

Note Receivable—L. Holland

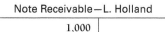

1,000

The bank gave one asset, cash, in return for another asset, a note receivable, so the total assets did not change:

ASSETS	=	LIABILITIES	+	SHAREHOLDERS' EQUITY
+1,000				
−1,000	=	0	+	0

Assume Canadian Western Bank has an October 31 year-end. The bank earns interest revenue during July, August, September, and October. At October 31, 2017, the bank accrues interest revenue for four months as follows:

	A	B	C	D	E
1	2017				
2	Oct. 31	Interest Receivable ($1,000 × 0.09 × 4/12*)	30		
3		Interest Revenue		30	
4		*Accrued interest revenue.*			
5					

*For ease of calculations, 12 months is used instead of 365 days.

The bank's assets and its revenue increase.

The bank reports these amounts in its financial statements at October 31, 2017:

Balance sheet

Current assets:

Note receivable $1,000

Interest receivable 30

Income statement

Interest revenue .... $ 30

The bank collects the note on December 31, 2017, and records:

	A	B	C	D	E
1	2017				
2	Dec. 31	Cash	1,045		
3		Note Receivable—L. Holland		1,000	
4		Interest Receivable		30	
5		Interest Revenue ($1,000 × 0.09 × 2/12)		15	
6		*Collected note at maturity.*			
7					

This entry eliminates the Note Receivable and Interest Receivable and also records the interest revenue earned from November 1 to December 31, 2017.

Note Receivable—L. Holland	
1,000	1,000

In its 2018 financial statements, the only item that Canadian Western Bank will report is the interest revenue of $15 that was earned in November and December 2017, part of its 2018 fiscal period. There's no note receivable or interest receivable on the balance sheet because those items were zeroed out when the bank collected the note at maturity.

Three aspects of these entries deserve mention:

1. Interest rates are always for an annual period unless stated otherwise. In this example, the annual interest rate is 9%. At October 31, 2017, Canadian Western Bank accrues interest revenue for the four months the bank has held the note. The interest computation is:

Principal × Interest rate × Time = Amount of Interest
$1,000 ×   0.09   × 4/12 = $30

2. The time element (4/12) is the fraction of the year that the note has been in force during the year ended October 31, 2017.

3. Interest is often completed for a number of days. For example, suppose you loaned out $10,000 on April 10. The note receivable runs for 90 days and specifies interest at 8%.

   a. Interest starts accruing on April 10, the day the money is borrowed, and continues to accrue until the note comes due 90 days later (July 8):

Month	Number of Days That Interest Accrues
April	21
May	31
June	30
July	8
Total	90

   b. The interest computation is: $10,000 × 0.08 × 90/365 = $197

Some companies sell goods and services on notes receivable (versus selling on accounts receivable). This often occurs when the payment term extends beyond the customary accounts receivable period of 30 to 60 days.

Suppose that on March 20, 2017, West Fraser Timber Co. Ltd. sells lumber for $15,000 to Darmal Const. Inc. West Fraser receives Darmal's 90-day promissory note at 10% annual interest. The entries to record the sale and collection from Darmal follow the pattern illustrated previously for Canadian Western Bank and Lauren Holland, with one exception. At the outset, West Fraser would credit Sales Revenue (instead of Cash) because West Fraser is making a sale (and not lending money to Darmal). Short-term notes receivable are valued the same way as regular accounts receivable, so we must set up an appropriate allowance for any uncollectible short-term notes. Any notes with a maturity date beyond 365 days of year-end, however, must be valued at their amortized cost by discounting them to reflect the time value of money. This topic will be addressed in more detail in Chapter 7.

A company may also accept a note receivable from a trade customer whose account receivable is past due. The customer signs a note, and the company then credits the account receivable and debits a note receivable. We would say the company "received a note receivable from a customer on account."

For example, assume that on February 1, 2017, Power Ltd. purchased $5,000 of building supplies from Piercy's Building Supplies with 60-day credit terms. Piercy's records the sale as follows:

	A	B	C	D	E
1	2017				
2	Feb. 1	Accounts Receivable—Power Ltd.	5,000		
3		Sales		5,000	
4		*To record sale to Power Ltd.*			
5					

If on April 1, 2017, Power Ltd. agrees to sign a 30-day note receivable to replace the account receivable due on that date, then Piercy's would record the following journal entry:

	A	B	C	D	E
1	2017				
2	Apr. 1	Notes Receivable	5,000		
3		Accounts Receivable—Power Ltd.		5,000	
4		*To record conversion of account receivable to note receivable*			
5					

Now let's examine some strategies to speed up cash flow.

STOP + THINK (4-4)

Saturn Company received a four-month, 5%, $4,800 note receivable on December 1. How much interest revenue should they accrue on December 31?

EXPLAIN HOW TO IMPROVE CASH FLOWS FROM SALES AND RECEIVABLES

OBJECTIVE

6 Explain how to improve cash flows from sales and receivables

Most companies strive to convert their sales to cash receipts as quickly as possible so they can use the cash to pay liabilities and invest in new products, new technology, research, and development. Thus, companies find ways to collect cash immediately. There are several ways companies can hasten their cash receipts from sales.

CREDIT CARD SALES. The merchant sells merchandise and lets the customer pay with a credit card, such as VISA, MasterCard, or a company credit card such as HBC (Hudson's Bay Company). This strategy may dramatically increase sales, but the added revenue comes at a cost. Let's see how credit cards work from the seller's perspective.

Suppose you purchase an iPhone from TELUS in Fredericton, New Brunswick, for $500 and you pay with a MasterCard. TELUS would record the sale as follows:

	A	B	C	D	E
1		Cash	485		
2		Credit Card Fee	15		
3		Sales Revenue		500	
4		*Record credit card sale.*			
5					

ASSETS	=	LIABILITIES	+	SHAREHOLDERS' EQUITY
+485	=	0	+	+500 Revenue
				−15 Expense

TELUS enters the transaction in the credit-card machine. The machine, linked to a MasterCard server, automatically credits TELUS's account for a discounted portion—say, $485—of the $500 sales amount. MasterCard gets 3%, or $15 ($500 × 0.03 = $15). To the merchant, the credit card fee is an operating expense similar to interest expense.

DEBIT CARD SALES. The merchant sells merchandise, and the customer pays by swiping a bank card such as a Scotiabank ScotiaCard or a TD Canada Trust Green Card using the Interac System. In this case, the bank card is being used as a debit card. To a merchant or service provider, a debit card is just like cash; when the card is swiped and the personal identification number (PIN) is entered, the merchant receives payment immediately as the Interac System takes money directly from the cardholder's bank account and transfers the money to the merchant's bank account less a processing fee. As with credit cards, the merchant is charged a fee. To record a sale of groceries for $65.48, Sobeys would record this entry:

	A	B	C	D	E
1		Cash	64.48		
2		Interac Fee (assumed rate)	1.00		
3		Sales Revenue		65.48	
4		*Record sale paid using Interac.*			
5				'	

ASSETS	=	LIABILITIES	+	SHAREHOLDERS' EQUITY
+64.48	=	0	+	+65.48 Revenue
				−1.00 Expense

One advantage for the merchant is that the payment is just like cash without the task of having to deposit the money. One advantage to the customer is that there is no need to carry cash. A second advantage to the cardholder is the cash-back feature (some merchants offer this service to their customers); the cardholder can ask for cash back, and the merchant will record an entry that includes the purchase plus the requested cash. Using the above date and assuming the cardholder requested $40.00 cash back, the entry would be:

	A	B	C	D	E
1		Cash	104.48		
2		Interac Fee (assumed rate)	1.00		
3		Sales Revenue		65.48	
4		Cash (to cardholder)		40.00	
5		*Record sale paid using Interac and cash back of $40.00.*			
6					

SELLING (FACTORING) RECEIVABLES. Suppose Black Corporation makes normal sales on account, debiting Accounts Receivable and crediting Sales Revenue. Black can then sell its accounts receivable to another business, called a *factor*. The factor earns revenue by paying a discounted price for the receivables and then collecting the full amount from the customers. The benefit to the company is the immediate receipt of cash.

To illustrate, suppose Black wishes to speed up cash flow and therefore sells $100,000 of accounts receivable, receiving cash of $95,000. Black would record the sale of the receivables as follows:

	A	B	C	D	E
1		Cash	95,000		
2		Financing Expense	5,000		
3		Accounts Receivable		100,000	
4		*Sold accounts receivable.*			
5					

The Financing Expense is typically reported as an operating expense, although some companies report it as a non-operating loss. Factoring a note receivable is similar to selling an account receivable; however, the credit is to Notes Receivable (instead of Accounts Receivable).

Reporting on the Statement of Cash Flows

Receivables appear on the balance sheet as current assets. We saw these in CGI Group Inc.'s balance sheet at the beginning of the chapter. We've also seen how to report the related revenue and expense on the income statement. Because receivables affect cash, their effects must also be reported on the statement of cash flows.

Receivables bring in cash when the business collects from customers. These transactions are reported as *operating activities* on the statement of cash flows because they result from sales. Chapter 10 shows how companies report their cash flows on the statement of cash flows. In that chapter, we will see exactly how to report cash flows related to receivables.

STOP + THINK (4-5)

Why is it so important for companies to convert their sales to cash receipts as quickly as possible?

EVALUATE A COMPANY'S LIQUIDITY

Managers, investors, and creditors use ratios to evaluate the financial health of a company. They care about the liquidity of assets. Liquidity is a measure of how quickly an item can be converted to cash. Remember, a balance sheet lists current assets in order of relative liquidity:

- *Cash and cash equivalents* come first because they are the most liquid assets.
- *Short-term investments* come next because they are almost as liquid as cash. They can be sold for cash whenever the owner wishes.
- *Current receivables* are less liquid than short-term investments because the company must collect the receivables.
- *Merchandise inventory* is less liquid than receivables because the goods must be sold first.
- *Prepaid expenses* are listed after inventories because they are expenses where cash has already been paid in advance.

We introduced the current ratio in Chapter 3. Recall that the current ratio is computed as follows:

$$\text{Current ratio} = \frac{\text{Total current assets}}{\text{Total current liabilities}}$$

The current ratio measures the company's ability to pay current liabilities with current assets.

Lending agreements often require the borrower to maintain a current ratio at some specified level, say 1.50 or greater. What happens when the borrower's current ratio falls below 1.50? The consequences can be severe:

- The lender can call the loan for immediate payment.
- If the borrower cannot pay, then the lender may pursue legal action to enforce collections.

Suppose it's December 10 and it looks like Black Corporation's current ratio will end the year at a value of 1.48. That would put Black in default on the lending agreement of maintaining a 1.50 or greater current ratio and create a bad situation. With three weeks remaining in the year, how can Black improve its current ratio?

There are several strategies for increasing the current ratio, such as the following:

1. Launch a major sales effort. The increase in cash and receivables will more than offset the decrease in inventory, total current assets will increase, and the current ratio will improve.

2. Pay off some current liabilities before year-end. Both current assets in the numerator and current liabilities in the denominator will decrease by the same amount. The proportionate impact on current liabilities in the denominator will be greater than the impact on current assets in the numerator, and the current ratio will increase. This strategy increases the current ratio when the current ratio is already above 1.0.

3. A third strategy, although questionable, reveals one of the accounting games that unethical companies sometimes play. Suppose Black has some long-term investments (investments that Black plans to hold for longer than a year—these are long-term assets). Before year-end, Black might choose to reclassify these long-term investments as current assets. The reclassification of these investments increases Black's current assets, and that increases the current ratio. This strategy would be acceptable if Black does in fact plan to sell the investments within the next year. But the strategy would be unethical and dishonest if Black in fact plans to keep the investments for longer than a year.

From this example you can see that accounting is not cut-and-dried or all black-and-white. It takes good judgment—which includes ethics—to become a successful accountant.

Other ratios, including the *acid-test* (or *quick ratio)* and the number of *days' sales in receivables*, also help investors measure liquidity.

Acid-Test (or Quick) Ratio

The **acid-test ratio** (or **quick ratio**) is a more stringent measure of a company's ability to pay current liabilities. The acid-test ratio is similar to the current ratio but it excludes inventory and prepaid expenses.

Inventory takes time to sell before the company is able to collect its cash. A company with lots of inventory may have an acceptable current ratio but find it hard to pay its bills. Prepaid expenses are also excluded from the acid-test ratio because the cash has already been paid for these assets that will be expensed as they are used up. The formula is:

$$\text{Acid-test ratio} = \frac{\text{Cash} + \text{Short-term investments} + \text{Net receivables}}{\text{Total current liabilities}}$$

Using CGI Group Inc.'s balance sheet in the chapter-opening story, the acid-test ratio is:

$$2014 \text{ CGI} = \frac{\$536 + \$9 + \$1,036}{\$2,778*} = 0.57$$

The higher the acid-test ratio, the easier it is to pay current liabilities. CGI's acid-test ratio of 0.57 means that CGI has $0.57 of quick assets to pay each $1.00 of current liabilities. Does this mean that CGI is in trouble? No, although CGI's quick ratio is relatively low, when analyzing ratios you might find it useful to consider other information found in the annual report. In CGI's case, over the past several years they have been busy expanding their business.

What is an acceptable acid-test ratio? The answer depends on the industry. Auto dealers can operate smoothly with an acid-test ratio of 0.20. How can auto dealers

---

*Amount taken from 2014 balance sheet in annual report.

survive with so low an acid-test ratio? GM, Toyota, and the other auto manufacturers help finance their dealers' inventory. Most dealers, therefore, have a financial safety net. In general, a quick ratio of 1.0 is considered healthy for this industry.

Days' Sales in Receivables

After a business makes a credit sale, the *next* step is collecting the receivable. **Days' sales in receivables**, also called the *collection period*, tells how long it takes to collect the average level of receivables. Shorter is better because cash is coming in quickly. The longer the collection period, the less cash is available to pay bills and expand.

Days' sales in receivables can be computed in two logical steps, as follows. First, compute accounts receivable turnover. Ideally, only credit sales should be used. Then divide 365 days by the accounts receivable turnover. We show days' sales in receivables for CGI Group Inc. as follows:

For CGI Group Inc. (in thousands)*

1. $\text{Accounts receivable turnover} = \dfrac{\text{Net sales}}{\text{Average net accounts receivable**}}$

$$\dfrac{\$10,500^*}{(\$1,036 + \$1,206)/2^*} = 9.37 \text{ times}$$

2. $\text{Days sales in receivables} = \dfrac{365 \text{ days}}{\text{Accounts receivable turnover}}$

$$= \dfrac{365}{9.37} = 39 \text{ days}$$

*Data taken from 2014 income statement and balance sheet.
**Average net accounts receivable = (Beginning net receivables + Ending net receivables)/2

Net sales come from the income statement and the receivables amounts are taken from the balance sheet. Average receivables is the simple average of the beginning and ending balances. Another approach would be to simply take Average net receivables in the numerator divided by Net sales/365 days in the denominator.

The length of the collection period depends on the credit terms of the company's sales. For example, sales on "net 30" terms should be collected within approximately 30 days. CGI's days' sales in receivables was 39 days in the 2014 financial statements, compared to an industry average of 42 days. While CGI's collections were longer than 30 days, this was shorter than other companies operating in the same industry.

Companies watch their collection periods closely. Whenever the collections get slow, the business must find other sources of financing, such as borrowing cash or factoring receivables. During recessions, customers pay more slowly, and a longer collection period may be unavoidable.

STOP + THINK (4-6)

Why are inventory and prepaid expenses excluded from the computation of the quick ratio?

▶ DECISION GUIDELINES

USING LIQUIDITY RATIOS IN DECISION MAKING

A company needs cash to pay their bills, buy more inventory, and finance new products and services. Two new ratios that measure liquidity were introduced in the chapter. Let's see how they are used in decision making.

Decision	Guidelines
How do you measure a company's ability to pay all current liabilities if they come due immediately?	$\text{Quick ratio} = \dfrac{\text{Cash} + \text{Short-term investments} + \text{Net receivables}}{\text{Current liabilities}}$
How do you determine if a company is collecting cash from their customers in a timely manner?	$\text{Days' sales in receivables} = \dfrac{\text{Average net receivables}}{\text{Net sales/365}}$
Who uses the quick ratio and days' sales in receivables for decision making and why?	*Managers* need to ensure that cash is available to pay current liabilities if they come due immediately. They know that some of this cash is tied up in accounts receivables waiting for customers to pay them. This is why companies set up policies and procedures to ensure they can receive their cash from customers quickly so it is available to pay their current debt.
	Investors know that it is important for a company to have enough cash on hand to pay back liabilities, particularly if they are due immediately. Using these ratios helps them to determine how quickly the company is able to collect what is owed them and if this cash is enough to meet current obligations.
	Creditors are expecting to be repaid and look to see how much cash the company has on hand as well as any cash the company expects to receive in the near future. They look to see if the company is able to collect from their customers quickly and if this cash is enough to pay back current liabilities if they are due immediately.

Summary of IFRS-ASPE Differences

Concepts	IFRS	ASPE

There are no differences between IFRS and ASPE in this chapter

SUMMARY

SUMMARY OF LEARNING OBJECTIVES

LEARNING OBJECTIVE	SUMMARY
1. **Account** for cash	Cash and cash equivalents are the most liquid asset and are reported as the first item under current assets on the balance sheet. Cash equivalents includes items such as treasury bills and money market funds where they will mature within three months from the date of purchase.
2. **Prepare** and **use** a bank reconciliation	To ensure accurate cash records, a bank reconciliation is prepared. It explains all differences between cash records and the bank statement.
3. **Account for** accounts receivables	Accounts receivable result from a company selling its products or services on credit. They are classified as a current asset because the company expects to collect cash from the customer within a short period of time.
4. **Estimate** and **account for** uncollectible accounts receivable	Managers use the allowance method (aging of receivables method) to estimate the uncollectible accounts. An accounts receivable is written off when a company is not able to collect from a customer. Sometimes, though, an account receivable may be recovered after it has been written off.
5. **Account** for notes receivable	Notes receivable are formal arrangements in which the debtor signs a promissory note, agreeing to pay back both the principal borrowed plus a stated percentage of interest on a certain date. The creditor has a note receivable and the debtor has a note payable.
6. **Explain** how to improve cash flows from sales and receivables	Rather than wait to collect cash from customers, a company can allow the customer to pay with a credit card or debit card, or the company can sell their receivables to another business. Collections from customers are reported as operating activities on the statement of cash flows.
7. **Evaluate** a company's liquidity	Key ratios used in decision making include the acid-test (quick ratio) and the days' sales in receivables. These ratios help managers, investors, and creditors measure the liquidity of the company. Liquidity relates to how quickly a company can obtain and pay cash.

MyAccountingLab

END-OF-CHAPTER SUMMARY PROBLEM

CHC Helicopter Corporation is Vancouver-based and is the world's largest provider of helicopter services to the global offshore oil and gas industry. Assume the company's balance sheet at April 30, 2016, adapted, reported the following:

	(in millions)
Accounts receivable	$240.6
Allowance for uncollectible accounts	(8.4)

Requirements

1. How much of the April 30, 2016, balance of accounts receivable did CHC Helicopter Corporation expect to collect? Stated differently, what was the expected net realizable value of these receivables?

2. Journalize, without explanations, 2017 entries for CHC Helicopter, assuming the following:
   a. The write-offs of uncollectible accounts receivable total $8.0 million. Prepare a T-account for Allowance for Uncollectible Accounts and post to this account.
   b. The April 30, 2017, aging of receivables indicates that $3.1 million of the total receivables of $303.4 million is uncollectible at year-end. Post to Allowance for Uncollectible Accounts as well, and show its adjusted balance at April 30, 2017
3. Show how CHC Helicopter's receivables and related allowance will appear on the April 30, 2017, balance sheet.
4. Show what CHC Helicopter's income statement will report for the foregoing transactions.

ANSWERS

Requirement 1

	(in millions)
Expected net realizable value of receivables ($240.6 — $8.4)..........................	$232.2

Requirement 2

	A	B	C	D	E
1	a.	Allowance for Uncollectible Accounts	8.0		
2		Accounts Receivable		8.0	
3					

Allowance for Uncollectible Accounts

2017 Write-offs	8.0	April 30, 2016	8.4
		2017 Balance	0.4

	A	B	C	D	E
1	b.	Bad Debt Expense ($3.1 – $0.4)	2.7		
2		Allowance for Uncollectible Accounts		2.7	
3					

Allowance for Uncollectible Accounts

	0.4
	2.7
	3.1

Requirement 3

	(in millions)
Accounts receivable (net of allowance for uncollectibe accounts of $3.1)	$300.3

Requirement 4

	(in millions)
Expenses: Bad Debt expense for 2017	$2.7

REVIEW

MyAccountingLab

Make the grade with MyAccountingLab: The Quick Quiz questions, Short Exercises, Exercises, and Problems (Group A) marked in #–# can be found on MyAccountingLab. You can practise them as often as you want, and most feature step-by-step guided instructions to help you find the right answer.

QUICK QUIZ (ANSWERS APPEAR ON THE LAST PAGE OF THIS CHAPTER.)

1. In a bank reconciliation, an EFT cash payment is
   a. added to the book balance.
   b. deducted from the book balance.
   c. added to the bank balance.
   d. deducted from the bank balance.

2. If a bookkeeper mistakenly recorded a $58 deposit as $85, the error would be shown on the bank reconciliation as a(n)
   a. $27 addition to the book balance.
   b. $85 deduction from the book balance.
   c. $27 deduction from the book balance.
   d. $85 addition to the book balance.

3. Under the allowance method for uncollectible receivables, the entry to record bad debt expense has what effect on the financial statements?
   a. Increases expenses and increases owners' equity
   b. Decreases assets and has no effect on net income
   c. Decreases owners' equity and increases liabilities
   d. Decreases net income and decreases assets

4. Snead Company uses the aging method to adjust the allowance for uncollectible accounts at the end of the period. At December 31, 2017, the balance of accounts receivable is $210,000 and the allowance for uncollectible accounts has a credit balance of $3,000 (before adjustment). An analysis of accounts receivable produced the following age groups:

Current	$150,000
60 days past due...	50,000
Over 60 days past due	10,000
	$210,000

Based on past experience, Snead estimates that the percentages of accounts that will prove to be uncollectible within the three groups are 2%, 8%, and 20%, respectively. Based on these facts, the adjusting entry for bad debt expense should be made in the amount of
   a. $3,000.   c. $9,000.
   b. $6,000.   d. $13,000.

5. Refer to question 4. The net receivables on the balance sheet are _____.

6. Accounts Receivable has a debit balance of $3,200, and the Allowance for Uncollectible Accounts has a credit balance of $300. A $100 accounts receivable is written off. What is the amount of net receivables (net realizable value) after the write off?
   a. $2,800   c. $3,000
   b. $2,900   d. $3,100

7. Refer to question 6. The balance of Allowance for Uncollectible Accounts, after adjustment, will be
   a. $100.
   b. $200.
   c. $300.
   d. impossible to determine from the information given.

8. Refer to questions 6 and 7. Early the following year, Harper wrote off $150 of old receivables as uncollectible. The balance in the Allowance account is now _____.

The next four questions use the following data:

On August 1, 2016, Maritimes Ltd. sold equipment and accepted a six-month, 9%, $10,000 note receivable. Maritimes's year-end is December 31.

9. How much interest revenue should Maritimes Ltd. accrue on December 31, 2016?
   a. $225
   b. $450
   c. $375
   d. Some other amount _____

10. If Maritimes Ltd. fails to make an adjusting entry for the accrued interest, which of the following will happen?
   a. Net income will be understated, and liabilities will be overstated.
   b. Net income will be understated, and assets will be understated.
   c. Net income will be overstated, and liabilities will be understated.
   d. Net income will be overstated, and assets will be overstated.

11. How much interest does Maritimes Ltd. expect to collect on the maturity date (February 1, 2017)?
- **a.** $450
- **b.** $280
- **c.** $75
- **d.** Some other amount _____

12. Which of the following accounts will Maritimes Ltd. credit in the journal entry at maturity on February 1, 2017, assuming collection in full?
- **a.** Interest Receivable
- **b.** Note Payable
- **c.** Interest Payable
- **d.** Cash

13. Write the journal entry for question 12.

14. Which of the following is included in the calculation of the acid-test ratio?
- **a.** Cash and accounts receivable
- **b.** Prepaid expenses and cash
- **c.** Inventory and short-term investment
- **d.** Inventory and prepaid expenses

15. A company with net sales of $1,217,000, beginning net receivables of $90,000, and ending net receivables of $110,000, has a days' sales in accounts receivable value of
- **a.** 50 days.
- **b.** 55 days.
- **c.** 30 days.
- **d.** 33 days.

16. The company in question 15 sells on credit terms of "net 30 days." Its days' sales in receivables figure is
- **a.** too high.
- **b.** too low.
- **c.** about right.
- **d.** impossible to evaluate from the data given.

ACCOUNTING VOCABULARY

acid-test ratio Ratio of the sum of cash plus short-term investments plus net receivables to total current liabilities. It is an indicator of an entity's ability to pay its current liabilities if they become due immediately. Also called the *quick ratio*. (p. 202)

aging-of-receivables method A way to estimate bad debts by analyzing accounts receivable according to the length of time they have been receivable from the customer. Also called the *balance-sheet approach* because it focuses on accounts receivable. (p. 190)

allowance for bad debts Another name for *allowance for uncollectible accounts*. (p. 190)

allowance for doubtful accounts Another name for *allowance for uncollectible accounts*. (p. 190)

allowance for uncollectible accounts A contra account, related to accounts receivable, that holds the estimated amount of collection losses. (p. 190)

allowance method A method of recording collection losses based on estimates of how much money the business will not collect from its customers. (p. 190)

bad debt expense A cost to the seller of extending credit to customers. Arises from a failure to collect an account receivable in full. (p. 189)

bank collections Collections of money by the bank on behalf of a depositor. (p. 182)

bank reconciliation A document explaining the reasons for the difference between a depositor's records and the bank's records about the depositor's cash. (p. 181)

bank statement Document showing the beginning and ending balances of a particular bank account and listing the month's transactions that affected the account. (p. 180)

cash equivalents Investments such as term deposits, guaranteed investment certificates, or high-grade government securities that are considered so similar to cash that they are combined with cash for financial disclosure on the balance sheet. (p. 178)

cheque Document instructing a bank to pay the designated person or business the specified amount of money. (p. 179)

creditor The party to whom money is owed. (p. 195)

days' sales in receivables Ratio of average net accounts receivable to one day's sales. Indicates how many days' sales remain in Accounts Receivable awaiting collection. Also called the *collection period* and *days sales outstanding*. (p. 203)

debtor The party who owes money. (p. 195)

deposits in transit A deposit recorded by the company but not yet recorded by its bank. (p. 181)

doubtful account expense Another name for *bad debt expense*. (p. 189)

electronic funds transfer System that transfers cash by electronic communication rather than by paper documents. (p. 178)

interest The borrower's cost of renting money from a lender. Interest is revenue for the lender and expense for the borrower. (p. 195)

maturity date The date on which a debt instrument must be paid. (p. 195)

nonsufficient funds (NSF) cheque A cheque for which the payer's bank account has insufficient money to pay the cheque. NSF cheques are cash receipts that turn out to be worthless. (p. 182)

outstanding cheques Cheques issued by the company and recorded on its books but not yet paid by its bank. (p. 181)

principal The amount borrowed by a debtor and lent by a creditor. (p. 195)

quick ratio Another name for *acid-test ratio*. (p. 202)

receivables Monetary claims against a business or an individual, acquired mainly by selling goods or services and by lending money. (p. 187)

remittance advice An optional attachment to a cheque (sometimes a perforated tear-off document and sometimes capable of being electronically scanned) that indicates the payer, date, and purpose of the cash payment. The remittance advice is often used as the source document for posting cash receipts or payments. (p. 179)

term The length of time from inception to maturity. (p. 195)

uncollectible account expense Another name for bad debt expense. (p. 189)

ASSESS YOUR PROGRESS

SHORT EXERCISES

S4-1 Describe the types of assets that are typically included under the heading "cash and cash equivalents" on the balance sheet. What is a "cash equivalent"?

LEARNING OBJECTIVE ❶
Report cash on the balance sheet

S4-2 At December 31, 2016, before any year-end adjustments are made, White Corporation had a $50 balance in Accounts Receivable and a $0.6 debit balance in the Allowance for Uncollectible Accounts.

LEARNING OBJECTIVE ❹
Apply the allowance method

Requirements

1. What is the normal balance in the Allowance for Uncollectible Accounts? What would cause this account to have a debit balance?
2. How does management determine the amount of uncollectible accounts?
3. The aging of receivables indicates that White Corporation will not collect $1.5 million of its accounts receivables. Prepare the journal entry to record the bad debt expense for 2016.

S4-3 Collins Woodworking accepts VISA and MasterCard at its store. Collins is charged a processing fee of 3% of the total amount of any credit card sale. Assume that Russell Knight purchases $8,000 of custom furniture and pays with a VISA card. Make the entry to record the sale to Knight. (You do not need to make the cost of goods sold entry.)

LEARNING OBJECTIVE ❻
Record a credit card sale

S4-4 The Cash account of SWITZER Ltd. reported a balance of $2,500 at August 31, 2017. Included were outstanding cheques totalling $900 and an August 31 deposit of $500 that did not appear on the bank statement. The bank statement, which came from HSBC Bank, listed an August 31, 2017, balance of $3,405. Included in the bank balance was an August 30 collection of $550 on account from a customer who pays the bank directly. The bank statement also shows a $20 service charge, $10 of interest revenue that SWITZER earned on its bank balance, and an NSF cheque for $35.

Prepare a bank reconciliation to determine how much cash SWITZER actually has at August 31, 2017.

LEARNING OBJECTIVE ❷
Prepare a bank reconciliation

S4-5 After preparing the SWITZER Ltd. bank reconciliation in exercise S4-4, make the company's journal entries for transactions that arise from the bank reconciliation. Include an explanation with each entry.

LEARNING OBJECTIVE ❷
Record transactions from a bank reconciliation

S4-6 Jordan Quinn manages the local homeless shelter. He fears that a trusted employee has been stealing from the shelter. This employee receives cash from supporters and also prepares the monthly bank reconciliation. To check on the employee, Quinn prepares his own bank reconciliation as in Exhibit 4-4 on page 183.

LEARNING OBJECTIVE ❷
Use a bank reconciliation to detect fraud

Homeless Shelter
Bank Reconciliation
August 31, 2017

Bank		Books	
Balance, August 31	$ 3,300	Balance, August 31	$2,820
Add		Add	
Deposits in transit..........................	400	Bank collections	800
		Interest revenue................	10
Less		Less	
Outstanding cheques......................	(1,100)	Service charge..................	(30)
Adjusted bank balance	$ 2,600	Adjusted book balance	$3,600

Does it appear that the employee stole from the shelter? If so, how much? Explain your answer. Which side of the bank reconciliation shows the shelter's true cash balance?

LEARNING OBJECTIVE 4

Apply the allowance method to account for uncollectibles

S4-7 During its first year of operations, Environmental Products Inc. had sales of $875,000, all on account. Industry experience suggests that Environmental Products's bad debt expense will be $17,500. At December 31, 2016, Environmental Products's accounts receivable total $80,000. The company uses the allowance method to account for uncollectibles.
1. Make Environmental Products's journal entry for bad debt expense.
2. Show how Environmental Products could report accounts receivable on its balance sheet at December 31, 2016, by disclosing the allowance for uncollectible accounts.

LEARNING OBJECTIVE 4

Apply the allowance method to account for uncollectibles

S4-8 This exercise continues the situation of exercise S4-7, in which Environmental Products ended the year 2016 with accounts receivable of $80,000 and an allowance for uncollectible accounts of $17,500. During 2017, Environmental Products completed the following transactions:
1. Credit sales, $1,000,000
2. Collections on account, $880,000
3. Write-offs of uncollectibles, $16,000
4. Bad debt expense, $15,000

Journalize the 2017 transactions for Environmental Products. Explanations are not required.

LEARNING OBJECTIVE 4

Apply the allowance method (aging-of-receivables method) to account for uncollectibles

S4-9 Use the solution to exercise S4-8 to answer these questions about Environmental Products Inc. for 2017.
1. Start with Accounts Receivable's beginning balance ($80,000) and then post to the Accounts Receivable T-account. How much do Environmental Products's customers owe the company at December 31, 2017?
2. Start with the Allowance account's beginning credit balance ($17,500) and then post to the Allowance for Uncollectible Accounts T-account. How much of the receivables at December 31, 2017, does the company expect *not* to collect?
3. At December 31, 2017, what is the net realizable value of the company's accounts receivable?

LEARNING OBJECTIVE 4

Apply the allowance method (aging-of-receivables method) to account for uncollectibles

S4-10 Gulig and Durham, a law firm, started 2017 with accounts receivable of $60,000 and an allowance for uncollectible accounts of $5,000. The 2017 service revenue on account was $400,000, and cash collections on account totalled $410,000. During 2017, Gulig and Durham wrote off uncollectible accounts receivable of $7,000. At December 31, 2017, the aging-of-receivables method indicated that Gulig and Durham will *not* collect $10,000 of its accounts receivable.

Journalize Gulig and Durham's (a) service revenue, (b) cash collections on account, (c) write-offs of uncollectible receivables, and (d) bad debt expense for the year. Explanations are not required. Prepare a T-account for Allowance for Uncollectible Accounts to show your computation of bad debt expense for the year.

LEARNING OBJECTIVE 4

Apply the allowance method (aging-of-receivables method) to account for uncollectibles

S4-11 Perform the following accounting for the receivables of Benoit, Brown & Hill, an accounting firm, at December 31, 2017.
1. Start with the beginning balances for these T-accounts:
   - Accounts Receivable, $80,000
   - Allowance for Uncollectible Accounts, $9,000
   Post the following 2017 transactions to the T-accounts:
   a. Service revenue of $850,000, all on account
   b. Collections on account, $790,000
   c. Write-offs of uncollectible accounts, $7,000
   d. Bad debt expense (allowance method), $8,000
2. What are the ending balances of Accounts Receivable and Allowance for Uncollectible Accounts?
3. Show two ways Benoit, Brown & Hill could report accounts receivable on its balance sheet at December 31, 2017.

S4-12 Metro Credit Union in Charlottetown, Prince Edward Island, loaned $90,000 to David Mann on a six-month, 8% note. Record the following for Metro Credit Union:
a. Lending the money on March 6.
b. Collecting the principal and interest at maturity. Specify the date. Explanations are not required.

LEARNING OBJECTIVE ⑤
Account for a note receivable

S4-13

1. Compute the amount of interest during 2015, 2016, and 2017 for the following note receivable: On June 30, 2015, Scotiabank loaned $100,000 to Heather Hutchison on a two-year, 8% note.
2. Which party has a (an)
   a. note receivable?
   b. note payable?
   c. interest revenue?
   d. interest expense?
3. How much in total would Scotiabank collect if Hutchison paid off the note early—say, on October 30, 2015?

LEARNING OBJECTIVE ⑤
Account for a note receivable

S4-14 On May 31, 2016, Nancy Thomas borrowed $6,000 from Assiniboine Credit Union. Thomas signed a note payable, promising to pay the credit union principal plus interest on May 31, 2017. The interest rate on the note is 8%. The accounting year of Assiniboine Credit Union ends on December 31, 2016. Journalize Assiniboine Credit Union's (a) lending money on the note receivable at May 31, 2016, (b) accruing interest at December 31, 2016, and (c) collecting the principal and interest at May 31, 2017, the maturity date of the note.

LEARNING OBJECTIVE ⑤
Account for a note receivable and interest thereon

S4-15 Using your answers to exercise S4-14, show how the Assiniboine Credit Union will report the following:
a. Whatever needs to be reported on the bank's classified balance sheet at December 31, 2016. (Ignore Cash).
b. Whatever needs to be reported on the bank's income statement for the year ended December 31, 2016.
c. Whatever needs to be reported on the bank's classified balance sheet at December 31, 2017. (Ignore Cash).
d. Whatever needs to be reported on the bank's income statement for the year ended December 31, 2017.

LEARNING OBJECTIVE ⑤
Report notes receivable

S4-16 Botany Clothiers reported the following amounts in its 2017 financial statements. The 2016 figures are given for comparison.

LEARNING OBJECTIVE ⑦
Evaluate the acid-test ratio and days' sales in receivables

	A	B	C	D	E	F
1			2017		2016	
2	**Current assets:**					
3	Cash		$ 9,000		$ 7,000	
4	Short-term investments		12,000		10,000	
5	Accounts receivable	$ 60,000		$ 54,000		
6	Less allowance for uncollectibles	(5,000)	55,000	(5,000)	49,000	
7	Inventory		170,000		172,000	
8	Prepaid insurance		1,000		1,000	
9	Total current assets		$ 247,000		$ 239,000	
10	Total current liabilities		$ 80,000		$ 70,000	
11	Net sales		$ 803,000		$ 750,000	
12						

Requirements

1. Compute Botany's acid-test ratio at the end of 2017. Round to two decimal places. How does the acid-test ratio compare with the industry average of 0.95?
2. Compare Botany's days' sales in receivables measure for 2017 with the company's credit terms of net 30 days.

LEARNING OBJECTIVE ❸,❼

Report receivables and other accounts in the financial statements and evaluate liquidity

S4-17 Victoria Medical Service reported the following selected items (amounts in thousands):

Unearned revenues (current)	$ 207	Service revenue	$8,613
Allowance for		Other assets	767
doubtful accounts	109	Property, plant, and equipment	3,316
Other expenses	2,569	Operating expense	1,620
Accounts receivable	817	Cash	239
Accounts payable	385	Notes payable (long-term)	719

1. Classify each item as (a) income statement or balance sheet and as (b) debit balance or credit balance.
2. How much net income (or net loss) did Victoria report for the year?
3. Compute Victoria's current ratio. Round to two decimal places. Evaluate the company's liquidity position.

EXERCISES

LEARNING OBJECTIVE ❶

Use the bank reconciliation

E4-18 Green Construction Inc. has poor internal control. Recently, Jean Ouimet, the owner, has suspected the bookkeeper of stealing. Here are some details of the business's cash position at June 30, 2017:

a. The Cash account shows a balance of $10,402. This amount includes a June 30 deposit of $3,794 that does not appear on the June 30 bank statement.

b. The June 30 bank statement shows a balance of $8,224. The bank statement lists a $200 bank collection, an $8 service charge, and a $36 NSF cheque. The bookkeeper has not recorded any of these items.

c. At June 30, the following cheques are outstanding:

Cheque No.	Amount
154	$116
256	150
278	853
291	990
292	206
293	145

d. The bookkeeper records all incoming cash and makes bank deposits. He also reconciles the monthly bank statement. Here is his June 30 reconciliation:

Balance per books, June 30		$10,402
Add: Outstanding cheques		1,460
Bank collection		200
Subtotal		12,062
Less: Deposits in transit	$3,794	
Service charge	8	
NSF cheque	36	(3,838)
Balance per bank, June 30		$ 8,224

Requirement

Ouimet has requested that you determine whether the bookkeeper has stolen cash from the business and, if so, how much. He also asks you to explain how the bookkeeper has attempted to conceal the theft. To make this determination, you perform your own bank reconciliation. There are no bank or book errors. Ouimet also asks you to recommend any changes needed to prevent this from happening again.

E4-19 The following items appear on a bank reconciliation:

_____ **1.** Outstanding cheques

_____ **2.** Bank error: The bank credited our account for a deposit made by another bank customer.

_____ **3.** Service charge

_____ **4.** Deposits in transit

_____ **5.** NSF cheque

_____ **6.** Bank collection of a note receivable on our behalf

_____ **7.** Book error: We debited Cash for $100. The correct debit was $1,000.

LEARNING OBJECTIVE ❷

Classify bank reconciliation items

Classify each item as (a) an addition to the bank balance, (b) a subtraction from the bank balance, (c) an addition to the book balance, or (d) a subtraction from the book balance.

E4-20 LeAnn Bryant's chequebook lists the following:

LEARNING OBJECTIVE ❷

Prepare a bank reconciliation

Date	Cheque No.	Item	Cheque	Deposit	Balance
Nov. 1					$ 705
4	622	Direct Energy	$ 19		686
9		Dividends		$116	802
13	623	Canadian Tire	43		759
14	624	Petro-Canada	58		701
18	625	Cash	50		651
26	626	St. Mark's Church	25		626
28	627	Bent Tree Apartments	275		351
30		Paycheque		846	1,197

The November bank statement shows:

Balance..			$ 705
Add deposits			116
Deduct cheques	No.	Amount	
	622	$19	
	623	43	
	624	85*	
	625	50	(197)
Other charges:			
NSF cheque...		$ 8	
Service charge		12	(20)
Balance..			$ 604

*This is the correct amount for cheque number 624.

Requirement

Prepare Bryant's bank reconciliation at November 30.

E4-21 Tim Wong operates a FedEx Kinko's store. He has just received the monthly bank statement at May 31, 2017, from Royal Bank of Canada, and the statement shows an ending balance of $595. Listed on the statement are an EFT customer collection of $300, a service charge of $12, two NSF cheques totalling $120, and a $9 charge for printed cheques. In reviewing his cash records, Wong identifies outstanding cheques totalling $603 and a May 31 deposit in transit of $1,788. During May, he recorded a $290 cheque for the salary of a part-time employee as $29. Wong's Cash account shows a May 31 cash balance of $1,882. How much cash does Wong actually have at May 31?

LEARNING OBJECTIVE ❷

Prepare a bank reconciliation

LEARNING OBJECTIVE ❷

Prepare and use a bank reconciliation

LEARNING OBJECTIVE ❹

Report uncollectible accounts by the allowance method

E4-22 Use the data from exercise E4-21 to make the journal entries that Wong should record on May 31 to update his Cash account. Include an explanation for each entry.

E4-23 At December 31, 2017, Credit Valley Nissan has an Accounts Receivable balance of $101,000. Allowance for Uncollectible Accounts has a credit balance of $2,000 before the year-end adjustment. Service revenue for 2017 was $800,000. Credit Valley estimates that bad debt expense for the year is $8,000. Make the December 31 entry to record bad debt expense. Show how the accounts receivable and the allowance for uncollectible accounts are reported on the balance sheet. Use the reporting format "Accounts receivable, net of allowance for uncollectible accounts $—" in 2017. Insert the value you've calculated for the allowance.

LEARNING OBJECTIVE ❹

Use the allowance method for uncollectible accounts

E4-24 On June 30, 2017, Perfect Party Planners (PPP) had a $40,000 balance in Accounts Receivable and a $3,000 credit balance in Allowance for Uncollectible Accounts. During July, PPP made credit sales of $75,000. July collections on account were $60,000, write-offs of uncollectible receivables totalled $2,200, and an account of $1,000 was recovered. Bad debt expense is estimated to be $1,500.

Requirements

1. Journalize sales, collections, write-offs of uncollectibles, recovery of accounts receivable, and bad debt expense by the allowance method during July. Explanations are not required.
2. Show the ending balances in Accounts Receivable, Allowance for Uncollectible Accounts, and *Net* Accounts Receivable at July 31. How much does PPP expect to collect?
3. Show how PPP will report Accounts Receivable on its July 31 balance sheet. Use the format "Accounts Receivable, net of allowance for uncollectible accounts of $—" at July 31, 2017. Insert the value you've calculated for the allowance.

LEARNING OBJECTIVE ❹

Using the allowance method for uncollectible account

E4-25 Refer to exercise E4-24.

Requirements

1. Determining bad debt expense by using the allowance method is management's estimate of uncollectible accounts and not an accurate measurement. Why not wait until a company finds out which customers can't pay and write the accounts receivable off as they occur?
2. If the allowance method is not used to estimate uncollectible accounts, what effect would this have on accounts receivable (balance sheet) and bad debt expense (income statement)?

LEARNING OBJECTIVE ❹

Use the aging method to estimate uncollectible accounts

E4-26 At December 31, 2017, before any year-end adjustments, the Accounts Receivable balance of Sunset Hills Clinic is $235,000. Allowance for Uncollectible Accounts has a $6,500 credit balance. Sunset Hills prepares the following aging schedule for accounts receivable:

	Age of Accounts			
Total Balance	0–30 Days	31–60 Days	61–90 Days	Over 90 Days
$235,000	$110,000	$60,000	$50,000	$15,000
Estimated uncollectible	0.5%	1.0%	6.0%	40%

Requirements

1. Based on the aging-of-receivables method, is the unadjusted balance of the allowance account adequate? Is it too high or too low? How does management determine what percentages to use for estimating uncollectible accounts?
2. Make the entry required by the aging schedule. Prepare a T-account for the allowance.
3. Show how Sunset Hills Clinic will report Accounts Receivable on its December 31 balance sheet.

E4-27 University Travel experienced the following revenue and accounts receivable write-offs:

LEARNING OBJECTIVE ❹

Measure and account for uncollectibles

| Month | Service Revenue | Accounts Receivable Write-Offs | | | |
		January	February	March	Total
January	$ 6,800	$53	$ 86		$139
February	7,000		105	$ 33	138
March	7,500			115	115
	$21,300	$53	$191	$148	$392

University Travel estimates bad debt expense to be $150.

Journalize service revenue (all on account), bad debt expense, and write-offs during March. Include explanations. Is the estimate of bad debts of $150 being uncollectible reasonable?

E4-28 Record the following note receivable transactions in the journal of Town & Country Realty. How much interest revenue did Town & Country earn this year? Use a 365-day year for interest computations, and round interest amounts to the nearest dollar.

LEARNING OBJECTIVE ❺

Record notes receivable and accrue interest revenue

Oct.	1	Loaned $50,000 cash to Springfield Co. on a one-year, 9% note.
Nov.	3	Performed service for Joplin Corporation, receiving a 90-day, 12% note for $10,000.
Dec.	16	Received a $2,000, six-month, 12% note on account from Afton, Inc.
	31	Accrued interest revenue for the year.

E4-29 Mattson Loan Company completed these transactions:

LEARNING OBJECTIVE ❺

Report the effects of note receivable transactions on the balance sheet and income statement

2016		
Apr.	1	Loaned $20,000 to Charlene Baker on a one-year, 5% note.
Dec.	31	Accrued interest revenue on the Baker note.
2017		
Apr.	1	Collected the maturity value of the note from Baker (principal plus interest).

Show what Mattson would report for these transactions on its 2016 and 2017 balance sheets and income statements. Mattson's accounting year ends on December 31.

E4-30 Answer these questions about receivables and uncollectibles. For the true-false questions, explain any answers that are false.

LEARNING OBJECTIVE ❹,❺

Understand receivables

1. True or false? Credit sales increase receivables. Collections and write-offs decrease receivables.
2. Which receivables figure, the *total* amount that customers *owe* the company or the *net* amount the company expects to collect, is more interesting to investors as they consider buying the company's shares? Give your reason.
3. Show how to determine net accounts receivable.
4. Caisse Desjardins lent $100,000 to Chicoutimi Ltée on a six-month, 6% note. Which party has interest receivable? Which party has interest payable? Which party has interest expense, and which has interest revenue? How much interest will these organizations record one month after Chicoutimi Ltée signs the note?
5. When Caisse Desjardins accrues interest on the Chicoutimi Ltée note, show the directional effects on the bank's assets, liabilities, and equity (increase, decrease, or no effect).

LEARNING OBJECTIVE ⑥,⑦
Use the acid-test ratio and days'
sales in receivables to evaluate a
company

E4-31 Assume Black Corporation reported the following items at year-ends 2017 and 2016.

	A	B	C	D	E	F	G
1	**Black Corporation** Consolidated Balance Sheets (Summarized)	March 1, 2017	March 3, 2016		March 1, 2017	March 3, 2016	
2	*(amounts in millions)*						
3	**Current assets:**			**Current liabilities:**			
4	Cash	$ 1,184.4	$ 677.1	Accounts payable	$ 271.1	$ 130.3	
5	Short-term investments	420.7	310.1	Other current liabilities	1,203.3	416.3	
6	Accounts receivable, net	1,174.7	572.6	Long-term liabilities	103.2	58.8	
7	Inventories	396.3	255.9				
8	Other current assets	301.3	103.6	Shareholders' equity	3,933.6	2,483.5	
9	Capital assets	2,033.8	1,169.6				
10	Total assets	$ 5,511.2	$ 3,088.9	Total liabilities and equity	$ 5,511.2	$ 3,088.9	
11	Income Statement (partial): 2017						
12	Revenue		$ 6,009.4				
13							

Requirements

1. Compute Black's (a) acid-test ratio and (b) days' sales in average receivables for 2017. Evaluate each ratio value as strong or weak. Assume Black sells on terms of net 30 days.
2. Recommend two ways the company can speed up its cash flow.

LEARNING OBJECTIVE ⑦
Analyze a company's financial
statements

E4-32 Assume Loblaw Companies Limited reported these figures in millions of dollars:

	2017	2016
Net sales	$29,384	$28,640
Receivables at end of year	885	728

Requirements

1. Compute Loblaw's average collection period during 2017.
2. Was Loblaw's collection period long or short? Potash Corporation of Saskatchewan takes 36 days to collect its average level of receivables. FedEx, the overnight shipper, takes 40 days. What causes Loblaw's collection period to be so different?

CHALLENGE EXERCISES

LEARNING OBJECTIVE ⑥
Determine whether to accept
credit cards

E4-33 Ripley Shirt Company sells on credit and manages its own receivables. Average experience for the past three years has been as follows:

	Cash	Credit	Total
Sales	$300,000	$300,000	$600,000
Cost of goods sold	165,000	165,000	330,000
Bad debt expense	—	10,000	10,000
Other expenses	84,000	84,000	168,000

John Ripley, the owner, is considering whether to accept credit cards (VISA, MasterCard). Ripley expects total sales to increase by 10% but cash sales to remain unchanged. If Ripley switches to credit cards, the business can save $8,000 on other expenses, but VISA and MasterCard charge 2% on credit card sales. Ripley figures that the increase in sales will be due to the increased volume of credit card sales.

Requirement

Should Ripley Shirt Company start accepting credit cards? Show the computations of net income under the present plan and under the credit card plan.

E4-34 Nixtel Inc. reported net receivables of $2,583 million and $2,785 million at December 31, 2017, and 2016, after subtracting allowances of $62 million and $88 million at these respective dates. Nixtel earned total revenue of $10,948 million (all on accounts) and recorded bad debt expense of $2 million for the year ended December 31, 2017.

LEARNING OBJECTIVE ❸,❹

Reconstruct receivables and uncollectible-account amounts

Requirements

Use this information to measure the following amounts for the year ended December 31, 2017:

a. Write-offs of uncollectible receivables
b. Collections from customers

PROBLEMS (GROUP A)

P4-35A The cash data of Alta Vista Toyota for June 2017 follow:

LEARNING OBJECTIVE ❷

Prepare the bank reconciliation

Cash

Date	Item	Jrnl. Ref.	Debit	Credit	Balance
June 1	Balance				5,011
30		CR6	10,578		15,589
30		CP11		10,924	4,665

Cash Receipts (CR)		Cash Payments (CP)	
Date	Cash Debit	Cheque No.	Cash Credit
June 2	$ 4,174	3113	$ 891
8	407	3114	147
10	559	3115	1,930
16	2,187	3116	664
22	1,854	3117	1,472
29	1,060	3118	1,000
30	337	3119	632
Total	$10,578	3120	1,675
		3121	100
		3122	2,413
		Total	$10,924

Alta Vista received the following bank statement on June 30, 2017:

Bank Statement for June 2017

Beginning balance		$ 5,011
Deposits and other additions		
June 4..	$ 326 EFT	
4..	4,174	
9..	407	
12..	559	
17..	2,187	
22..	1,701 BC	
23..	1,854	11,208
Cheques and other deductions		
June 7..	$ 891	
13..	1,390	
14..	903 US	
15..	147	
18..	664	
21..	219 EFT	
26..	1,472	
30..	1,000	
30..	20 SC	(6,706)
Ending balance		$ 9,513

Explanation: EFT—electronic funds transfer, BC—bank collection, US—unauthorized signature, SC—service charge

Additional data for the bank reconciliation include the following:
a. The EFT deposit was a receipt of a monthly car lease. The EFT debit was a monthly insurance payment.
b. The bank collection was of a note receivable.
c. The unauthorized signature cheque was received from a customer.
d. The correct amount of cheque number 3115, a payment on account, is $1,390. (Alta Vista's accountant mistakenly recorded the cheque for $1,930.)

Requirements
Prepare the Alta Vista Toyota bank reconciliation at June 30, 2017.

LEARNING OBJECTIVE ❷

Prepare a bank reconciliation and
the related journal entries

P4-36A The May 31 bank statement of Family Services Association (FSA) has just arrived from Scotiabank. To prepare the FSA bank reconciliation, you gather the following data:
a. FSA's Cash account shows a balance of $2,256.14 on May 31.
b. The May 31 bank balance is $4,023.05.
c. The bank statement shows that FSA earned $38.19 of interest on its bank balance during May. This amount was added to FSA's bank balance.
d. FSA pays utilities ($250) and insurance ($100) by EFT.
e. The following FSA cheques did not clear the bank by May 31:

Cheque No.	Amount
237	$ 46.10
288	141.00
291	578.05
293	11.87
294	609.51
295	8.88
296	101.63

f. The bank statement includes a donation of $850, electronically deposited to the bank for FSA.

g. The bank statement lists a $10.50 bank service charge.

h. On May 31, the FSA treasurer deposited $16.15, which will appear on the June bank statement.

i. The bank statement includes a $300 deposit that FSA did not make. The bank added $300 to FSA's account for another company's deposit.

j. The bank statement includes two charges for returned cheques from donors. One is a $395 cheque received from a donor with the imprint "Unauthorized Signature." The other is a nonsufficient funds cheque in the amount of $146.67 received from a client.

Requirements

1. Prepare the bank reconciliation for FSA.

2. Journalize the May 31 transactions needed to update FSA's Cash account. Include an explanation for each entry.

P4-37A This problem takes you through the accounting for sales, receivables, and uncollectibles for FedEx Corporation, the overnight shipper. By selling on credit, FedEx cannot expect to collect 100% of its accounts receivable. Assume that at May 31, 2017 and 2016, respectively, FedEx reported the following on its balance sheet (adapted and in millions of U.S. dollars):

LEARNING OBJECTIVE ❸,❹

Account for receivables, collections, and uncollectibles

	May 31	
	2017	**2016**
Accounts receivable	$4,517	$4,078
Less: Allowance for uncollectibles	(318)	(136)
Accounts receivable, net	$4,199	$3,942

During the year ended May 31, 2017, FedEx earned service revenue and collected cash from customers. Assume bad debt expense for the year was $380 million and that FedEx wrote off uncollectible receivables.

Requirements

1. Prepare T-accounts for Accounts Receivable and Allowance for Uncollectibles, and insert the May 31, 2016, balances as given.

2. Journalize the following assumed transactions of FedEx for the year ended May 31, 2017. Explanations are not required.

    a. Service revenue on account, $37,953 million

    b. Collections on account, $37,314 million

    c. Bad debt expense, $380 million

    d. Write-offs of uncollectible accounts receivable, $200 million

    e. Recovered an account receivable, $2 million

3. Post your entries to the Accounts Receivable and the Allowance for Uncollectibles T-accounts.

4. Compute the ending balances for the two T-accounts, and compare your balances to the actual May 31, 2017 amounts. They should be the same.

5. Show what FedEx would report on its income statement for the year ended May 31, 2017.

P4-38A The October 1, 2017, records of First Data Communications include these accounts:

LEARNING OBJECTIVE ❹

Use the aging approach for uncollectibles

Accounts Receivable	$230,000
Allowance for Uncollectible Accounts	(8,500)

At year-end, the company ages its receivables and adjusts the balance in Allowance for Uncollectible Accounts to correspond to the aging schedule. During the last quarter of 2017, the company completed the following selected transactions:

2017		
Nov.	30	Wrote off as uncollectible the $1,100 account receivable from Rainbow Carpets and the $600 account receivable from Show-N-Tell Antiques.
Dec.	31	One of its customers, Peplar Ltd., agreed to sign a 60-day note receivable to replace the $1,500 accounts receivable due on that day.
Dec.	31	Adjusted the Allowance for Uncollectible Accounts, and recorded Bad Debt Expense at year-end, based on the aging of receivables, which follows.

	Age of Accounts			
Total Balance	0–30 Days	31–60 Days	61–90 Days	Over 90 Days
$230,000	$150,000	$40,000	$14,000	$26,000
Estimated uncollectible	0.2%	0.5%	5.0%	30.0%

Requirements

1. Record the transactions in the journal. Explanations are not required.
2. Prepare a T-account for Accounts Receivable and the Allowance for Uncollectible Accounts, and post to those accounts.
3. Show how First Data would report its accounts receivable on a comparative balance sheet for 2016 and 2017. At December 31, 2016, the company's Accounts Receivable balance was $212,000 and the Allowance for Uncollectible Accounts stood at $4,200.

LEARNING OBJECTIVE ❶❹❼

Account for uncollectibles, and use ratios to evaluate a business

P4-39A Assume Deloitte & Touche, the accounting firm, advises Pappadeaux Seafood that Pappadeaux's financial statements must be changed to conform to IFRS. At December 31, 2017, Pappadeaux's accounts include the following:

Cash	$ 51,000
Short-term trading investments	17,000
Accounts receivable	37,000
Inventory	61,000
Prepaid expenses	14,000
Total current assets	$180,000
Accounts payable	$ 62,000
Other current liabilities	41,000
Total current liabilities	$103,000

Deloitte & Touche advised Pappadeaux that:
- Cash includes $20,000 that is deposited in a restricted account that is tied up until 2019.
- Pappadeaux did not estimate their uncollectible accounts but rather wrote them off when they found out that the customer could not pay them. During 2017, Pappadeaux wrote off bad receivables of $7,000. Deloitte & Touche determines that bad debt expense for the year should be for 2017 should be $15,000 based on the allowance method.
- Pappadeaux reported net income of $92,000 in 2017.

Requirements

1. Restate Pappadeaux's current accounts to conform to IFRS.
2. Compute Pappadeaux's current ratio and acid-test ratio both before and after your corrections.
3. Determine Pappadeaux's correct net income for 2017.
4. How does using the allowance method to estimate uncollectible accounts benefit the investors and creditors?

P4-40A Assume that General Mills Canada, famous for Cheerios, Chex snacks, and Yoplait yogurt, completed the following selected transactions:

LEARNING OBJECTIVE ❺

Account for notes receivable and accrued interest revenue

2016		
Nov.	30	Sold goods to Sobeys Inc., receiving a $50,000, three-month, 5% note.
Dec.	31	Made an adjusting entry to accrue interest on the Sobeys note.
2017		
Feb.	28	Collected the Sobeys note.
Mar.	1	Received a 90-day, 5%, $6,000 note from Louis Joli Goût on account.
	1	Sold the Louis note to Caisse Populaire, receiving cash of $5,900.
Dec.	16	Loaned $25,000 cash to Betty Crocker Brands, receiving a 90-day, 8% note.
	31	Accrued the interest on the Betty Crocker Brands note.

Requirements

1. Record the transactions in General Mills's journal. Round interest amounts to the nearest dollar. Explanations are not required.
2. Show what General Mills will report on its comparative classified balance sheet at December 31, 2016, and December 31, 2017.

P4-41A The comparative financial statements of Sunset Pools Inc. for 2017, 2016, and 2015 included the following selected data:

LEARNING OBJECTIVE ❼

Use ratio data to evaluate a company's financial position

	(in millions)		
	2017	2016	2015
Balance sheet:			
Current assets:			
Cash	$ 86	$ 60	$ 70
Short-term investments	130	174	112
Receivables, net of allowance for uncollectible accounts			
of $27, $21, and $15, respectively	243	245	278
Inventories	330	375	362
Prepaid expenses	10	25	26
Total current assets	$ 799	$ 879	$ 848
Total current liabilities	$ 403	$ 498	$ 413
Income statement:			
Net sales	$2,898	$2,727	$2,206

Requirements

1. Compute these ratios for 2017 and 2016:
   a. Current ratio
   b. Acid-test ratio
   c. Days' sales in receivables
2. Write a memo explaining to top management which ratio values improved from 2016 to 2017 and which ratio values deteriorated. State whether the overall trend is favourable or unfavourable, and give the reason for your evaluation.
3. Recommend two ways for Sunset Pools to improve cash flow from receivables.

PROBLEMS (GROUP B)

LEARNING OBJECTIVE ❷

Prepare a bank reconciliation

P4-42B The cash data of Navajo Products for September 2017 follow:

Cash

Date	Item	Jrnl. Ref.	Debit	Credit	Balance
Sept. 1	Balance				7,078
30		CR 10	9,106		16,184
30		CP 16		11,353	4,831

Cash Receipts (CR)		**Cash Payments (CP)**	
Date	Cash Debit	Cheque No.	Cash Credit
Sept. 1	$ 2,716	1413	$ 1,465
9	544	1414	1,004
11	1,655	1415	450
14	896	1416	8
17	367	1417	775
25	890	1418	88
30	2,038	1419	4,126
Total	$ 9,106	1420	970
		1421	200
		1422	2,267
		Total	$11,353

On September 30, 2017, Navajo received this bank statement:

Bank Statement for September 2017

Beginning balance		$ 7,078
Deposits and other additions		
Sept. 1	$ 625 EFT	
5	2,716	
10	544	
12	1,655	
15	896	
18	367	
25	890	
30	1,400 BC	9,093
Cheques and other deductions		
Sept. 8	$ 441 NSF	
9	1,465	
13	1,004	
14	450	
15	8	
19	340 EFT	
22	775	
29	88	
30	4,216	
30	25 SC	(8,812)
Ending balance		$ 7,359

Explanation: BC—bank collection, EFT—electronic funds transfer, NSF—nonsufficient funds cheque, SC—service charge

Additional data for the bank reconciliation:

a. The EFT deposit was for monthly rent revenue. The EFT deduction was for monthly insurance expense.

b. The bank collection was of a note receivable.

c. The NSF cheque was received from a customer.

d. The correct amount of cheque number 1419, a payment on account, is $4,216. (The Navajo accountant mistakenly recorded the cheque for $4,126.)

Requirements

Prepare the bank reconciliation of Navajo Products at September 30, 2017.

P4-43B The January 31 bank statement of Bed & Bath Accessories has just arrived from Royal Bank of Canada. To prepare the Bed & Bath bank reconciliation, you gather the following data:

a. The January 31 bank balance is $8,400.82.

b. Bed & Bath's Cash account shows a balance of $7,391.55 on January 31.

c. The following Bed & Bath cheques are outstanding at January 31:

LEARNING OBJECTIVE ❷
Prepare a bank reconciliation and the related journal entries

Cheque No.	Amount
616	$403.00
802	74.02
806	36.60
809	161.38
810	229.05
811	48.91

d. The bank statement includes two special deposits: $899.14, which is the amount of dividend revenue the bank collected from IBM on behalf of Bed & Bath; and $16.86, the interest revenue Bed & Bath earned on its bank balance during January.

e. The bank statement lists a $6.25 bank service charge.

f. On January 31 the Bed & Bath treasurer deposited $381.14, which will appear on the February bank statement.

g. The bank statement includes a $410.00 deduction for a cheque drawn by Bonjovi Music Company.

h. The bank statement includes two charges for returned cheques from customers. One is a nonsufficient funds cheque in the amount of $67.50 received from a customer. The other is a $195.03 cheque received from another customer. It was returned by the customer's bank with the imprint "Unauthorized Signature."

i. A few customers pay monthly bills by EFT. The January bank statement lists an EFT deposit for sales revenue of $200.23.

Requirements

1. Prepare the bank reconciliation for Bed & Bath Accessories at January 31.

2. Journalize the transactions needed to update the Cash account. Include an explanation for each entry.

P4-44B Brubacher Service Company sells for cash and on account. By selling on credit, Brubacher cannot expect to collect 100% of its accounts receivable. At December 31, 2017, and 2016, respectively, Brubacher reported the following on its balance sheet (in thousands of dollars):

LEARNING OBJECTIVE ❸❹
Account for receivables, collections, and uncollectibles

	December 31	
	2017	**2016**
Accounts receivable	$500	$400
Less: Allowance for uncollectibles	(100)	(60)
Accounts receivable, net	$400	$340

During the year ended December 31, 2017, Brubacher earned service revenue and collected cash from customers. Bad debt expense for the year was $335 thousand and Brubacher wrote off uncollectible accounts receivable.

Requirements

1. Prepare T-accounts for Accounts Receivable and Allowance for Uncollectibles, and insert the December 31, 2016, balances as given.
2. Journalize the following transactions of Brubacher for the year ended December 31, 2017. Explanations are not required.
   a. Service revenue on account, $6,700 thousand
   b. Collections from customers on account, $6,300 thousand
   c. Bad debt expense, $335 thousand
   d. Write-offs of uncollectible accounts receivable, $300 thousand
   e. Recovered an account receivable, $5 thousand
3. Post to the Accounts Receivable and Allowance for Uncollectibles T-accounts.
4. Compute the ending balances for the two T-accounts, and compare to the Brubacher Service amounts at December 31, 2017. They should be the same.
5. Show what Brubacher should report on its income statement for the year ended December 31, 2017.

LEARNING OBJECTIVE ❺

Use the aging approach for uncollectibles

P4-45B The September 30, 2017, records of Synetics Computers show:

Accounts Receivable	$110,000
Allowance for Uncollectible Accounts	(4,100)

At year-end, Synetics ages its receivables and adjusts the balance in Allowance for Uncollectible Accounts to correspond to the aging schedule. During the last quarter of 2017, Synetics completed the following selected transactions:

2017		
Oct.	31	Wrote off the following accounts receivable as uncollectible: Cisco Foods, $300; Tindall Storage, $400; and Tiffany Energy, $1,100.
Dec.	31	One of its customers, Canlon Company, agreed to sign a 60-day notes receivable to replace a $1,200 accounts receivable due on that day.
Dec.	31	Adjusted the Allowance for Uncollectible Accounts and recorded bad debt expense at year-end, based on the aging of receivables, which follows.

	Age of Accounts			
Total Balance	0–30 Days	31–60 Days	61–90 Days	Over 90 Days
$110,000	$80,000	$20,000	$4,000	$10,000
Estimated uncollectible	0.5%	1.0%	5.0%	40.0%

Requirements

1. Record the transactions in the journal. Explanations are not required.
2. Prepare a T-account for Accounts Receivable and the Allowance for Uncollectible Accounts, and post to those accounts.
3. Show how Synetics Computers would report its accounts receivable in a comparative balance sheet for 2016 and 2017. At December 31, 2016, the company's Accounts Receivable balance was $111,000 and the Allowance for Uncollectible Accounts stood at $3,700.

LEARNING OBJECTIVE ❶❹❼

Account for uncollectibles

P4-46B The top managers of Whelan Gift Stores seek the counsel of Ernst & Young, the accounting firm, and learn that Whelan must make some changes to bring its financial statements into conformity with IFRS. At December 31, 2017, Whelan Gift Stores accounts include the following:

Cash	$ 23,000
Short-term trading investments	24,000
Accounts receivable	54,000
Inventory	45,000
Prepaid expenses	17,000
Total current assets	$163,000
Accounts payable	46,000
Other current liabilities	69,000
Total current liabilities	$115,000

As the accountant from Ernst & Young, you draw the following conclusions:
- Cash includes $6,000 that is deposited in a restricted account that will be tied up until 2019.
- Whelan Gift Stores did not estimate their uncollectible accounts but rather wrote them off when they found out that the customer could not pay them. During 2017, the company wrote off bad receivables of $4,000. Ernst & Young determines that bad debt expense for 2017 should be $9,000 based on the allowance method.
- Whelan Gift Stores reported net income of $81,000 for 2017.

Requirements

1. Restate all current accounts to conform to IFRS.
2. Compute Whelan Gift Stores' current ratio and acid-test ratio both before and after your corrections.
3. Determine Whelan Gift Stores' correct net income for 2017.
4. How does using the allowance method to estimate uncollectible accounts benefit the investors and creditors?

P4-47B Lilley & Taylor, partners in an accounting practice, completed the following selected transactions:

LEARNING OBJECTIVE ❺

Account for notes receivable and accrued interest revenue

2016		
Oct.	31	Performed service for Berger Manufacturing Inc., receiving a $30,000, three-month, 5% note.
Dec.	31	Made an adjusting entry to accrue interest on the Berger note.
2017		
Jan.	31	Collected the Berger note.
Feb.	18	Received a 90-day, 8%, $10,000 note from Emerson Ltd., on account.
	19	Sold the Emerson note to a financial institution, receiving cash of $9,700.
Nov.	11	Loaned $20,000 cash to Diaz Insurance Agency, receiving a 90-day, 9% note.
Dec.	31	Accrued the interest on the Diaz note.

Requirements

1. Record the transactions in Lilley & Taylor's journal. Round all amounts to the nearest dollar. Explanations are not required.
2. Show what Lilley & Taylor will report on its comparative classified balance sheet at December 31, 2017, and December 31, 2016.

LEARNING OBJECTIVE ❼

Use ratio data to evaluate a company's financial position

P4-48B The comparative financial statements of New World Piano Company for 2017, 2016, and 2015 included the following selected data:

| | (in millions) | | |
	2017	2016	2015
Balance sheet:			
Current assets:			
Cash	$ 67	$ 66	$ 62
Short-term investments	73	81	70
Receivables, net of allowance for uncollectible accounts of $7, $6, and $4, respectively	226	174	195
Inventories	398	375	349
Prepaid expenses	22	19	16
Total current assets	$ 786	$ 715	$ 692
Total current liabilities	$ 420	$ 405	$ 388
Income statement:			
Net sales	$2,071	$2,005	$1,965

Requirements

1. As a financial advisor to an investor in New World Piano Company, compute these ratios for 2017 and 2016:
   a. Current ratio
   b. Acid-test ratio
   c. Days' sales in receivables
2. Write a memo explaining to your client which ratio values showed improvement from 2016 to 2017 and which ratio values deteriorated. State whether the overall trend is favourable or unfavourable for the company, give the reason for your evaluation, and advise your client regarding its investment.
3. Recommend two ways to improve cash flow from receivables.

APPLY YOUR KNOWLEDGE

This section's material reflects CPA enabling competencies,* including:

1. Professionalism and ethical behaviour
2. Problem-solving and decision-making
3. Communication
5. Teamwork and leadership

DECISION CASES

Case 1. A fire during 2017 destroyed most of the accounting records of Morris Financial Services Inc. The only accounting data for 2017 that Morris can come up with are the following balances at December 31, 2017. The general manager also knows that bad debt expense should be $47,000.

Accounts receivable	$180,000
Less: Allowance for uncollectibles	(22,000)
Total expenses, excluding bad debt expense	670,000
Collections from customers	840,000
Write-offs of bad receivables	30,000
Accounts receivable, December 31, 2016	110,000

LEARNING OBJECTIVE ❸❹

Account for receivables, collections, and uncollectible accounts on receivables

As the insurance claims officer, prepare a summary income statement for Morris Financial Services Inc. for the year ended December 31, 2017. The insurance claim will be affected by whether the company was profitable in 2017. Use a T-account for Accounts Receivable to compute service revenue.

*© Chartered Professional Accountants of Canada.

Case 2. Suppose you work in the loan department of CIBC. Dean Young, owner of Dean Young Sports Equipment, has come to you seeking a loan for $500,000 to expand operations. Young proposes to use accounts receivable as collateral for the loan and has provided you with the following information from the company's most recent financial statements:

LEARNING OBJECTIVE ❹❼

Estimate the collectibility of accounts receivable and evaluate liquidity

	(in thousands)		
	2017	2016	2015
Sales...	$1,475	$1,001	$902
Cost of goods sold...	876	647	605
Gross profit	599	354	297
Other expenses..	518	287	253
Net profit or (loss) before taxes....................................	$ 81	$ 67	$ 44
Accounts receivable..	$ 128	$ 107	$ 94
Allowance for uncollectible accounts.............................	13	11	9

Requirement

Analyze the trends of sales, days' sales in receivables, and cash collections from customers for 2017 and 2016. Would you make the loan to Young? Support your decision with facts and figures.

ETHICAL ISSUES

Sunnyvale Loan Company is in the consumer loan business. Sunnyvale borrows from banks and loans out the money at higher interest rates. Sunnyvale's bank requires Sunnyvale to submit quarterly financial statements to keep its line of credit. Sunnyvale's main asset is Notes Receivable. Therefore, Bad Debt Expense and Allowance for Uncollectible Accounts are important accounts for the company. Kimberly Burnham, the company's owner, prefers for net income to reflect a steady increase in a smooth pattern, rather than increase in some periods and decrease in other periods. To report smoothly increasing net income, Burnham underestimates Bad Debt Expense in some periods. In other periods, Burnham overestimates the expense. She reasons that the income overstatements roughly offset the income understatements over time.

Requirement

Is Sunnyvale Loan's practice of smoothing income ethical? Why or why not?

FOCUS ON FINANCIALS

Canadian Tire Corporation

Refer to Canadian Tire's financial statements in Appendix A at the end of the book. Suppose Canadian Tire's bank statement has just arrived at company headquarters. Further assume the bank statement shows Canadian Tire's cash balance at $664.2 million and also assume that cash and cash equivalents has a balance of $658.2 million on the books.

1. You must determine how much to report for cash and cash equivalents on the January 3, 2015 balance sheet. Suppose you uncover these reconciling items (all amounts in millions):
   a. Interest earned on bank balance, $2.2
   b. Outstanding cheques, $6.4
   c. Bank collections of various items, $4
   d. Deposits in transit, $4.3
   e. Transposition error—Canadian Tire overstated cash by $1.3
   f. Bank charges of $1

LEARNING OBJECTIVE ❶❷❸❹

Account for cash and cash equivalents and accounts receivable

Prepare a bank reconciliation to show how Canadian Tire arrived at the correct amount of cash and cash equivalents to report on its January 3, 2015, balance sheet. Journal entries are not required.

2. How much were Canadian Tire's receivables at January 3, 2015, and December 28, 2013? What can you assume from this information?

3. Assume that Canadian Tire wrote off $125 million as uncollectible. How much did Canadian Tire collect from customers during 2014?

FOCUS ON ANALYSIS

LEARNING OBJECTIVE ④⑦

Analyze accounts receivable and liquidity

MyAccountingLab

Canadian Tire Corporation

Refer to Canadian Tire's financial statements in Appendix A.

Requirements

1. Does Canadian Tire disclose the Allowance for Uncollectible Accounts in its financial statements? How can you determine what Canadian Tire expects to collect from its reported Accounts Receivable?*

2. Evaluate Canadian Tire's liquidity for 2014, and compare it with 2013. What other information might be helpful in your evaluation?

GROUP PROJECTS

Jillian Michaels and Dee Childress worked for several years as sales representatives for Xerox Corporation. During this time, they became close friends as they acquired expertise with the company's full range of copier equipment. Now they see an opportunity to put their expertise to work and fulfill lifelong desires to establish their own business. Northern Lights College has a campus in their community, Fort St. John, British Columbia, and there is no copy centre within eight kilometres of the campus. Business in the area is booming, office buildings and apartments are springing up, and the population of the city of Fort St. John is growing.

Michaels and Childress want to open a copy centre, similar to FedEx Kinko's, near the campus. A small shopping centre across the street from the college has a vacancy that would fit their needs. Michaels and Childress each have $35,000 to invest in the business, but they forecast the need for $200,000 to renovate the store and purchase some of the equipment they will need. Xerox Corporation will lease two large copiers to them at a total monthly rental of $6,000. With enough cash to see them through the first six months of operation, they are confident they can make the business succeed. The two women work very well together, and both have excellent credit ratings. Michaels and Childress must borrow $130,000 to start the business, advertise its opening, and keep it running for its first six months.

Requirements

Assume two roles: (1) Michaels and Childress, the partners who will own Fort St. John Copy Centre; and (2) loan officers at North Peace Savings and Credit Union (NPSCU).

1. As a group, visit a copy centre to familiarize yourselves with its operations. Then write a loan request that Michaels and Childress will submit to NPSCU with the intent of borrowing $130,000 to be paid back over three years. The request should specify all the details of Michaels's and Childress's plan that will motivate the bank to grant the loan. Include a budget for each of the first six months of operation of the proposed copy centre.

2. As a loan officer in a bank, write NPSCU's reply to the loan request. Specify all the details that the bank should require as conditions for making the loan.

3. If necessary, modify the loan request or the bank's reply in order to reach agreement between the two parties.

CHECK YOUR WORK

STOP + THINK ANSWERS

STOP + THINK (4-1)

1. $5,125 ($4,500 + $1,200 − $575).
2. $5,408 ($5,125 + $15 − $5 + $300 − $27)

The adjusted book and bank balances are the same. The answer can be determined by working backward from the adjusted balance.

STOP + THINK (4-2)

	(in thousands)
Customers owed Black Corporation	$138,370
Black expected not to collect	3,974
Receivables, net (or the amount Black expected to collect)	$134,396

STOP + THINK (4-3)

Aging-of-receivables: bad debt expense = $1,350 – $900 = $450

STOP + THINK (4-4)

They should accrue interest revenue on the note receivable in the amount of $20.
($4,800 × 5% × 1/12)

STOP + THINK (4-5)

Companies need cash as quickly as possible so they can use it to pay liabilities and invest in new products, new technology, and research and development.

STOP + THINK (4-6)

Inventory is excluded from the quick ratio because it takes time to sell and collect the cash. Prepaid expenses are also excluded because the cash has already been paid for these assets that will be expensed as they are used up.

QUICK QUIZ ANSWERS

1. *b*

2. *c*

3. *d*

4. *b*

5. $201,000 ($210,000 − $9,000 = $201,000)

6. *b* ($3,200 − $100) − ($300 − $100)

7. *b* $200 (300 − 100)

8. $50 ($300 − $100 − 150)

9. *c* ($10,000 × 0.09 × 5/12 = $375)

10. *b*

11. *a* ($10,000 × 0.09 × 6/12 = $450)

12. *a*

13. *Cash 10,450*

Note Receivable	10,000	
Interest Receivable	375	
Interest Revenue	75	

14. *a*

15. *c* ($1,217,000 / [$90,000 + $110,000/2] = 12.17 *times* 365/12.17 = 30 *days*)

16. *c*

5

Inventory and Cost of Goods Sold

LEARNING OBJECTIVES

1. **Account** for inventory using the perpetual and periodic inventory systems
2. **Apply** and **compare** three inventory costing methods
3. **Explain** how accounting standards apply to inventory
4. **Compute** and **evaluate** gross profit and inventory turnover
5. **Analyze** the effects of inventory errors

J.P. Moczulski/The Canadian Press

SPOTLIGHT

You have just graduated from university, taken a job, and are moving into an apartment. The place is unfurnished, so you will need a bed, dresser, sofa, table, and chairs to go with your TV and sound system. Where will you find these things? Leon's Furniture is a good source.

Leon's Furniture is known for its contemporary-styled, well-priced furnishings—just about right for a new graduate. The company operates 75 retail stores across Canada and in 2013, they bought The Brick.

Leon's Furniture Limited's balance sheet (partial) is summarized on the next page. You can see that merchandise inventory (labelled simply as inventories) is one of Leon's Furniture's biggest assets. Inventories composed about 60% of its current assets ($266.6 million/$443.3 million on December 31, 2014). That's not surprising since Leon's like other retail stores attracts customers with goods they can purchase and take home immediately.

Leon's Income Statement for the year ending December 31, 2014, shows sales of $1,974.4 million, an increase of 16.5% over the previous year ($1,694.6 million). Leon's purchased The Brick in 2013 and the effect of this acquisition is showing up in the 2014 sales. Cost of goods sold, the largest expense on the Income Statement, was $1,117.5 million, an increase of 16.5% over the previous year ($959.3 million). Gross profit (Sales minus Cost of goods sold) of $856.9 million also increased by 16.5% over 2013 ($735.3 million). This means that the company was more profitable on sales of its product in 2014 than it was in 2013.

---

*© Chartered Professional Accountants of Canada.

	A	B	C	D
1	**Leon's Furniture Limited** Consolidated Balance Sheets (partial, adapted) As at December 31			
2	*(millions)*	2014	2013	
3	**Assets**			
4	Current			
5	Cash and cash equivalents	$ 17.9	$ 5.8	
6	Marketable securities	40.7	37.4	
7	Trade receivables	112.2	104.3	
8	Inventories	266.6	277.7	
9	Other current assets	5.9	2.6	
10	**Total current assets**	443.3	427.8	
11	Other assets	786.1	784.9	
12	Property, plant, and equipment	334.1	352.7	
13	**Total Assets**	$ 1,563.5	$ 1,565.4	
14				

Source: Data taken from Leon's Furniture Limited Annual Report 2014.

We also present Leon's Furniture Limited's income statement. While sales increased in 2014, gross profit, as a percentage of sales, remained steady at 43% from 2013 to 2014.

	A	B	C	D
1	**Leon's Furniture Limited** Consolidated Income Statements (adapted) Years ending December 31			
2	*(millions)*	2014	2013	
3	Sales	$ 1,974.4	$ 1,694.6	
4	Cost of sales	1,117.5	959.3	
5	Gross profit	856.9	735.3	
6	General and administrative expenses	305.8	264.9	
7	Sales and marketing expenses	248.9	213.6	
8	Occupancy expenses	166.4	134.7	
9	Other operating expenses	15.9	14.6	
10	Operating profit	119.9	107.5	
11	Finance costs (net)	16.8	14.3	
12	Profit before income tax	103.1	93.2	
13	Income tax expense	27.6	24.9	
14	Net income	$ 75.5	$ 68.3	
15				

Source: Data taken from Leon's Furniture Limited Annual Report 2014.

You can see that the *cost of sales* (another name for **cost of goods sold**) is by far Leon's Furniture's largest expense. The account titled Cost of Sales perfectly describes that expense. In short,

- Leon's buys inventory, an asset carried on the books at cost.
- the goods that Leon's sells are no longer Leon's assets. The cost of inventory that's sold gets shifted into the expense account, Cost of Sales.

Merchandise inventory is the heart of a merchandising business, and cost of goods sold is the most important expense for a company that sells goods rather than services. This chapter covers the accounting for inventory and cost of goods sold. It also shows you how to analyze financial statements. Here, we focus on inventory, cost of goods sold, and gross profit.

OBJECTIVE

❶ Account for inventory using the perpetual and periodic inventory systems

ACCOUNT FOR INVENTORY USING THE PERPETUAL AND PERIODIC INVENTORY SYSTEMS

We begin by showing how the financial statements of a merchandiser such as Leon's Furniture Limited differ from those of service entities such as Royal LePage Real Estate. Merchandisers have two accounts that service entities don't need: Inventory on the balance sheet and Cost of Goods Sold on the income statement. The financial statements in Exhibit 5-1 highlight these differences.

EXHIBIT 5-1
Contrasting a Service Company With a Merchandiser

	A	B
1	**Service Company** **Royal LePage Real Estate** Income Statement For the Year Ended December 31, 2014	
2		
3	*Service revenue*	$ XXX
4	*Expenses*	
5	Operating and administrative	X
6	Depreciation	X
7	Income tax	X
8	Net income	$ X
9		
10		
11		

	A	B
1	**Merchandising Company** **Leon's Furniture Ltd.** Income Statement For the Year Ended December 31, 2014	
2	*(amounts in millions)*	
3	*Sales revenue*	$ 1,974.4
4	*Cost of goods sold*	1,117.5
5	Gross profit	$ 856.9
6	Operating *expenses*	
7	Operating and administrative	X
8	Depreciation	X
9	Income tax	X
10	Net income	$ 75.5
11		

	A	B
1	**Royal LePage Real Estate** Balance Sheet As at December 31, 2014	
2	Assets	
3		
4	Current assets	
5	Cash	$ X
6	Temporary investments	X
7	Accounts receivable, net	X
8	Prepaid expenses	X
9		
10		

	A	B
1	**Leon's Furniture Ltd.** Balance Sheet As at December 31, 2014	
2	Assets	
3	*(amounts in millions)*	
4	Current assets	
5	Cash	$ X
6	Temporary investments	X
7	Accounts receivable, net	X
8	*Inventory*	266.6
9	Prepaid expenses	X
10		

Accounting for Inventory

The value of inventory affects two financial statement accounts: inventory, reported as a current asset on the balance sheet; and cost of goods sold, shown as an expense on the income statement. This basic concept of accounting for merchandise inventory can be illustrated with an example. Suppose Leon's Furniture has in stock three chairs that cost $300 each. Leon's Furniture marks the chairs up by $200 and sells two of the chairs for $500 each.

- Leon's Furniture's balance sheet reports the one chair that the company still holds in inventory.
- The income statement reports the cost of the two chairs sold, as shown in Exhibit 5-2.

Balance Sheet (Partial)

Current assets

Cash	$XXX
Short-term investments	XXX
Accounts receivable	XXX
Inventory (1 chair @ cost of $300)	300
Prepaid expenses	XXX

Income Statement (Partial)

Sales revenue	
(2 chairs @ sales price of $500)	$1,000
Cost of goods sold	
(2 chairs @ cost of $300)	600
Gross profit	$ 400

Here is the basic concept of how we identify inventory, the asset, from cost of goods sold, the expense.

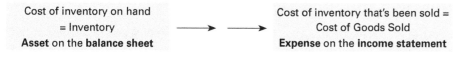

Cost of inventory on hand
= Inventory
Asset on the **balance sheet**

Cost of inventory that's been sold =
Cost of Goods Sold
Expense on the **income statement**

Inventory's cost shifts from asset to expense when the seller delivers the goods to the buyer.

Sales Price Versus Cost of Inventory

Note the difference between the sale price of inventory and the cost of inventory. In our Leon's Furniture example:

- Sales revenue is based on the *sale price* of the inventory sold ($500 per chair).
- Cost of goods sold is based on the *cost* of the inventory sold ($300 per chair).
- Inventory on the balance sheet is based on the *cost* of the inventory still on hand ($300 per chair).

Exhibit 5-2 shows these items.

Gross profit, also called **gross margin**, is the excess of sales revenue over cost of goods sold. It is called *gross profit* because operating expenses have not yet been subtracted. The actual inventory and cost of goods sold data (cost of sales) from the financial statements of Leon's Furniture Limited are:

Leon's inventory of $266.6 million represents:

$$\frac{\text{Inventory}}{\text{(balance sheet)}} = \frac{\text{Number of units of}}{\text{inventory \textit{on hand}}} \times \frac{\text{Cost per unit}}{\text{of inventory}}$$

Leon's cost of goods sold ($1,117.5) represents:

$$\frac{\text{Cost of goods sold}}{\text{(income statement)}} = \frac{\text{Number of units of}}{\text{inventory \textit{sold}}} \times \frac{\text{Cost per unit}}{\text{of inventory}}$$

Let's see what "units of inventory" and "cost per unit" mean.

NUMBER OF UNITS OF INVENTORY. This figure simply represents the number of units of inventory a business has on hand at a certain point in time. At each year-end, the business normally conducts a physical count of its inventory so it has an accurate record of the number of units on hand at that time. Leon's, for example, would conduct a physical inventory count on December 31 each year to determine the number of chairs, beds, tables, and other types of furniture it has on hand at year-end. Leon's needs an accurate count of inventory so it can properly determine the total cost of inventory to report on its year-end balance sheet.

The manager must also take into account inventory that has been shipped. Who owns it? Determining the ownership of inventory at the time of shipment depends on who has legal title. If inventory is shipped FOB (free on board) shipping point, it should be included on the books of the buyer, who has legal title, as soon as it leaves the shipper's dock. If the goods are shipped FOB destination, the inventory in transit still belongs on the books of the seller until it is delivered to the buyer.

COST PER UNIT OF INVENTORY. Determining the cost per unit of inventory poses a challenge because companies purchase goods at different prices throughout the year. Which unit costs go into the ending inventory for the balance sheet? Which unit costs go to cost of goods sold?

What Goes into Inventory Cost?

The cost of merchandise in Leon's Furniture Limited's balance sheet represents all the costs that Leon's Furniture incurred to bring the inventory to the point of sale. Both IFRS and ASPE state the following:

> The cost of inventories shall comprise all costs of purchase, costs of conversion and other costs incurred in bringing the inventories to their present location and condition.

Inventory's cost includes its basic purchase price, plus freight-in, insurance while in transit, and any costs paid to get the inventory ready to sell, less returns, allowances, and discounts.

Once a product is sitting in a Leon's Furniture showroom, other costs incurred, such as advertising and delivery costs, are not included as the cost of inventory. Advertising, sales commissions, and delivery costs are expenses.

The next section shows how the different accounting methods determine the cost of ending inventory on the balance sheet and cost of goods sold for the income statement. First, however, you need to understand how inventory accounting systems work.

Accounting for Inventory in the Perpetual System

There are two main types of inventory accounting systems: the periodic system and the perpetual system. The **periodic inventory system** is mainly used by businesses that sell inexpensive goods. A dollar store or a convenience store, for example, may not keep a running record of every one of the hundreds of items they sell. Instead, these stores count their inventory periodically—at least once a year—to determine the quantities on hand. Businesses such as some restaurants and home-town nurseries also use the periodic inventory system because the accounting cost is low.

A **perpetual inventory system** uses computer software to keep a running record of inventory on hand. This system achieves control over goods such as parts at a Ford dealer, lumber at Home Depot, furniture at Leon's, and all the various groceries and other items that a Loblaws store sells. Today, most businesses use the perpetual inventory system.

Even with a perpetual system, the business still counts the inventory on hand annually. The physical count serves as a check on the accuracy of the perpetual records and confirms the accuracy of the inventory records for preparing the financial statements. The chart below compares the perpetual and periodic systems.

Perpetual Inventory System	*Periodic Inventory System*
• Used for all types of goods	• Used for inexpensive goods
• Keeps a running record of all goods bought, sold, and on hand	• Does not keep a running record of all goods bought, sold, and on hand
• Inventory counted at least once a year	• Inventory counted at least once a year

HOW THE PERPETUAL SYSTEM WORKS. Let's use an everyday situation to show how a perpetual inventory system works. Suppose you are buying a pair of Nike cross-trainer shoes from Sport Chek. The clerk scans the bar code on the product label of your purchase. Exhibit 5-3 illustrates a typical bar code. The bar code on the product or product label holds lots of information. The optical scanner reads the bar code, and the computer records the sale and updates the inventory records.

David R. Frazier/Photolibrary, Inc./Photo Researchers, Inc./Science Source

EXHIBIT 5-3
Bar Code for Electronic Scanner

RECORDING TRANSACTIONS IN THE PERPETUAL SYSTEM. Each purchase of inventory is recorded as a debit to Inventory and a credit to Cash or Accounts Payable.

When Leon's Furniture makes a sale, two entries are needed in the perpetual system:

	A	B	C	D	E
1		The company records the sale:			
2		Dr Cash or Accounts Receivable			
3		Cr Sales Revenue			
4					
5		Leon's Furniture also records the cost of inventory sold:			
6		Dr Cost of Goods Sold			
7		Cr Inventory			
8					

RECORDING TRANSACTIONS IN THE PERIODIC SYSTEM. In the periodic inventory system, the business keeps no running record of the merchandise. Instead, at the end of the period, the business counts inventory on hand and applies the unit costs to determine the cost of ending inventory. This inventory figure appears on the balance sheet and is used to compute cost of goods sold.

In the periodic system, throughout the period the Inventory account carries the beginning balance left over from the preceding period. The business records purchases of inventory in the Purchases account (an expense). Then, at the end of the period, the Inventory account must be updated for the financial statements. A journal entry removes the beginning balance by crediting Inventory and debiting Cost of Goods Sold. A second journal entry sets up the ending Inventory balance, based on the physical count. The final entry in this sequence transfers the amount of Purchase related accounts to Cost of Goods Sold. These end-of-period entries can be made during the closing process and are shown in Exhibit 5-4, Panel A. When Leon's Furniture records a sale, the only journal entry needed in the periodic system is:

	A	B	C	D	E
1		Dr Cash or Accounts Receivable			
2		Cr Sales Revenue			
3					

Exhibit 5-4 shows the accounting for inventory in a perpetual system and a periodic system. Panel A gives the journal entries and Panel B presents the income statement and the balance sheet. All amounts are assumed.

The cost of the inventory, $560,000,* is the net amount of the purchases, determined as follows (using assumed amounts):

Purchase price of the inventory from the seller	$600,000
+ **Freight-in** (transportation cost to move the goods from the seller to the buyer)	4,000
− **Purchase returns** for unsuitable goods returned to the seller	(25,000)
− **Purchase allowances** granted by the seller	(5,000)
− **Purchase discounts** for early payment	(14,000)
= Net purchases of inventory	$560,000

Freight-in is the transportation cost paid by the buyer to move goods from the seller to the buyer. Freight-in is accounted for as part of the cost of inventory. Freight-out paid by the seller is not part of the cost of inventory. Instead, freight-out is a delivery expense. It is the seller's expense of delivering merchandise to customers. A **purchase return** is a decrease in the cost of inventory because the buyer returned the goods to the seller. A **purchase allowance** also decreases the cost of inventory because the buyer got an allowance (a deduction) from the amount owed—often because of a merchandise defect. Throughout this book, we often refer to net purchases simply as purchases.

A **purchase discount** is a decrease in the cost of inventory that is earned by paying quickly. A common arrangement states payment terms of 2/10 n/30. This means the buyer can take a 2% discount for payment within 10 days, or pay the full amount within 30 days. Another common credit term is "net 30," which directs the customer to pay the full amount within 30 days.

In summary,

NET PURCHASES = PURCHASES
−PURCHASE RETURNS AND ALLOWANCES
−PURCHASE DISCOUNTS
+FREIGHT-IN

Now study Exhibit 5-4 on the next page.

---

*The price shown does *not* include Canada's goods and services tax (GST)/harmonized sales tax (HST).

EXHIBIT 5-4

Recording and Reporting Inventory—Perpetual System and Periodic System (Amounts Assumed)

	A	B	C	D
1		Perpetual System		
2		PANEL A—Recording Transactions		
3	Jan. 2	Inventory	600,000	
4		Accounts payable		600,000
5		*Purchased 1,000 units on account.*		
6	3	Inventory	4,000	
7		Accounts payable		4,000
8		*Record freight fee on purchases.*		
9	9	Accounts payable	25,000	
10		Inventory		25,000
11		*Returned goods to supplier for credit.*		
12	11	Accounts payable	5,000	
13		Inventory		5,000
14		*Record purchase allowance.*		
15	16	Accounts payable	14,000	
16		Inventory		14,000
17		*Record purchase discount.*		
18	16	Accounts payable	560,000	
19		Cash		560,000
20		*Record payment.*		
21	31	Accounts receivable	900,000	
22		Sales revenue		900,000
23		*Record sales on account.*		
24	31	Cost of goods sold	540,000	
25		Inventory		540,000
26		*Update inventory and COGS.*		
27	31	*No adjustments required.*		
28				
29				
30				
31				
32				
33				
34				
35				
36				

	A	B	C	D
1		Periodic System		
2		PANEL A—Recording Transactions (all amounts are assumed)		
3	Jan. 2	Purchases	600,000	
4		Accounts payable		600,000
5		*Purchased 1,000 units on account.*		
6	3	Freight-in	4,000	
7		Accounts payable		4,000
8		*Record freight fee on purchases.*		
9	9	Accounts payable	25,000	
10		Purchase returns and allowance		25,000
11		*Returned goods to supplier for credit.*		
12	11	Accounts payable	5,000	
13		Purchase allowance		5,000
14		*Record purchase allowance.*		
15	16	Accounts payable	14,000	
16		Purchase discount		14,000
17		*Record purchase discount.*		
18	16	Accounts payable	560,000	
19		Cash		560,000
20		*Record payment.*		
21	31	Accounts receivable	900,000	
22		Sales revenue		900,000
23		*Record sales on account.*		
24	31	No entry.		
25				
26				
27	31	Cost of goods sold	540,000	
28		Inventory, * ending balance	120,000	
29		Purchase allowance	5,000	
30		Purchase returns and allow	25,000	
31		Purchase discount	14,000	
32		Purchases		600,000
33		Freight-in		4,000
34		Inventory, beginning		100,000
35		Close out beginning inventory, set up ending inventory and close all Purchase-related accounts including Freight in. After the process is complete, Inventory has its correct balance of $120,000 and Cost of Goods Sold shows $540,000.		
36		*Determined by physical count.		

PANEL B—Reporting in the Financial Statements (Perpetual)

Income Statement (Partial)

Sales revenue, net	$900,000
Cost of goods sold	540,000
Gross profit	$360,000

Ending Balance Sheet (Partial)

Current assets:

Cash .... $	XXX
Temporary investments......	XXX
Accounts receivable	XXX
Inventory..........................	120,000
Prepaid expenses	XXX

PANEL B—Reporting in the Financial Statements (Periodic)

Income Statement (Partial)

Sales revenue, net		$900,000
Cost of goods sold:		
Beginning inventory	$100,000	
Net Purchases..............	560,000	
Goods available for sale	660,000	
Ending inventory	(120,000)	
Cost of goods sold		540,000
Gross profit..................		$360,000

Ending Balance Sheet (Partial)

Current Assets:

Cash .... $	XXX
Temporary investments ...	XXX
Accounts receivable	XXX
Inventory	120,000
Prepaid expenses	XXX

Since the various transactions that make up the $560,000 may occur on different dates, it is instructive to now view each entry separately for both the perpetual and the periodic inventory systems with assumed dates in Exhibit 5-4.

Net sales are computed as follows:

NET SALES = SALES REVENUE
‒ SALES RETURNS AND ALLOWANCES
‒ SALES DISCOUNTS

SALES RETURNS AND ALLOWANCES. Retailers and consumers have a right to return unsatisfactory or damaged merchandise for a refund or exchange. This is called **sales returns and allowances**. In these cases, the seller is obligated to accept the returned product if the customer chooses to return it. Returned merchandise means lost profits. For example, suppose that of the goods Black Corporation sold to a customer, $9 worth of goods are returned (or Black grants them an allowance). The cost of the merchandise sold is $5. Assuming a perpetual inventory system, Black Corporation would record the following entries:

	A	B	C	D	E
1		Sales Returns and Allowances	9		
2		Accounts Receivable		9	
3					

	A	B	C	D	E
1		Dr Inventory	5		
2		Cr Cost of goods sold		5	
3					

Retailers, wholesalers, and manufacturers typically disclose sales revenue at the *net* amount, which means after the sales discounts and sales returns and allowances have been subtracted. Using hypothetical data for discounts and returns, Black Corporation's net sales (revenue) for 2017, compared with the last two years, is as follows:

Black Corporation
(2017, Adapted)

Gross revenue	$ 59,000
‒ Sales discounts	(900)
‒ Sales returns and allowances	(262)
= Net revenue	$ 57,838

	2017	2016	2015
Net revenue (in millions)	$57,838	$43,232	$43,251

SALES DISCOUNTS. Sometimes businesses offer customers **sales discounts** for early payment in order to speed up cash flow. A typical sales discount incentive might be stated as follows:

$$2/10, n/30$$

This expression means that the seller is willing to discount the order by 2% if the buyer pays the invoice within 10 days. After that time, the seller withdraws the discount offer, and the buyer is supposed to pay in full within 30 days. Assume Black Corporation sells goods to a customer and invoices them for $1,500, 2/10, n/30. If the customer pays the invoice within 10 days, it is entitled to a $30 discount, making the full amount due to settle Black Corporation's invoice $1,470 rather than $1,500. The entry to record the collection of this sale would be as follows:

	A	B	C	D	E
1		Cash	1,470		
2		Sales Discount	30		
3		Accounts Receivable		1,500	
4					

If for some reason, the customer does not pay its discounted invoice within the prescribed time period of 10 days, it forfeits its contractual right to the sales discount and would be obligated to pay Black Corporation the full amount. In that event, collection of the accounts receivable would be recorded as follows:

	A	B	C	D	E
1		Cash	1,500		
2		Accounts Receivable		1,500	
3					

STOP + THINK (5-1)

Suppose you are planning to open up a small pet food and accessories store in your neighbourhood. Would you use the perpetual inventory system or the periodic inventory system to account for inventory? Why?

APPLY AND COMPARE THREE INVENTORY COSTING METHODS

OBJECTIVE

❷ Apply and **compare** three inventory costing methods

A manager must choose one of three costing methods to apply when valuing inventory for reporting purposes. The costing method selected affects the profits to be reported, the amount of income taxes to be paid, and the values of the inventory turnover and gross profit percentage ratios derived from the financial statements.

Inventory Costing Methods

Determining the cost of inventory is easy when the unit cost remains constant, as in Exhibit 5-2, but unit cost usually changes. For example, prices often rise. Salomon snowboards that cost The Source Board Shop $150 in October may cost $160 in November and $180 in December. The Source Board Shop sells 50 snowboards in November. How many of the Salomon snowboards sold cost $150, how many cost $160, and how many cost $180?

To compute cost of goods sold and the cost of ending inventory still on hand, we must assign a unit cost to the items. Three generally accepted inventory methods are the following:

1. Specific identification cost
2. Weighted-average cost
3. First-in, first-out (FIFO) cost

As we shall see, these methods can have very different effects on reported inventory balances, cost of goods sold, income taxes, and cash flows. Therefore, companies select their inventory method with great care.

SPECIFIC IDENTIFICATION COST METHOD. Some businesses deal in unique inventory items, such as antique furniture, jewels, and real estate. These businesses cost their inventories at the specific cost of the particular unit. For instance, a Toyota dealer may have two vehicles in the showroom—a "stripped-down" model that cost $22,000 and a "loaded" model that cost $29,000. If the dealer sells the loaded model, cost of goods sold is $29,000. The stripped-down auto will be the only unit left in inventory, so ending inventory is $22,000.

The **specific identification cost method** is too expensive to use for inventory items that have common characteristics, such as metres of lumber, litres of paint, or number of automobile tires.

The other acceptable inventory accounting methods—weighted-average and FIFO—do not use the specific cost of a particular unit. Instead, they assume different flows of inventory costs.

ILLUSTRATION OF WEIGHTED-AVERAGE AND FIFO COSTING METHODS. To illustrate weighted-average and FIFO costing, we will use a common set of data, given in Exhibit 5-5.

EXHIBIT 5-5
Inventory Data Used to
Illustrate Inventory
Costing Methods

Inventory				
Begin. bal.	(10 units @ $11)	110		
Purchases:				
No. 1	(20 units @ $14)	280	Cost of goods sold	?
No. 2	(15 units @ $16)	240	(40 units @ $?)	
No. 3	(15 units @ $18)	270		
Ending bal.	(20 units @ $?)	?		

In Exhibit 5-5, Leon's began the period with 10 lamps that cost $11 each; the beginning inventory was therefore $110. During the period, Leon's bought 50 more lamps, sold 40 lamps, and ended the period with 20 lamps, summarized in the T-account in Exhibit 5-5 and as follows:

	Number of Units	Total Cost
Goods available for sale	= 10 + 20 + 15 + 15 = 60 units	$110 + $280 + $240 + $270 = $900
Cost of goods sold	= 40 units	?
Ending inventory	= 20 units	?

The big accounting questions are:

1. What is the cost of goods sold for the income statement?

2. What is the cost of the ending inventory for the balance sheet?

The answers to these questions depend on which inventory method Leon's uses. Leon's actually uses FIFO, but we will look at weighted-average costing first.

WEIGHTED-AVERAGE COST–PERPETUAL. The **weighted-average-cost method**, sometimes called the average cost method, is based on the average cost of inventory during the period. Since the inventory records are updated each time merchandise is bought and sold, *a new average cost per unit* is computed every time a purchase is made. To illustrate, we will use the data in Exhibit 5-5:

Inventory (at weighted-average cost–perpetual)

Begin. bal.	(10 units @$11)	110	
Purchases:			
No. 1	(20 units @$14)	280	
No. 2	(15 units @$16)	240	Cost of goods sold (40 units @ weighted-average cost of $14* per unit) 560
No. 3	(15 units @$18)	270	
Ending bal.	(20 units @ new weighted-average cost of $17** per unit)	340	

Since the 40 units were sold right after Purchase No. 2, the weighted-average cost per unit is based on beginning inventory, Purchase No. 1 and the units in Purchase No. 2.

The steps are:

1. Calculate the weighted-average cost per unit:

$$\frac{\text{Weighted-average}}{\text{cost per unit}} = \frac{\text{Cost of goods available*}}{\text{Number of units available}} = \overset{\text{(Beg.Inv + Purch.1 + Purch.2)}}{\frac{\$110 + \$280 + \$240}{10 + 20 + 15}}$$

$$= \frac{\$630}{45} = \$14$$

*Cost of goods available = Beginning inventory + Purchases

2. Determine the value for cost of goods sold:

$$\frac{\text{Cost of}}{\text{goods sold}} = \frac{\text{Number of}}{\text{units sold}} \times \frac{\text{weighted-average}}{\text{cost per unit}}$$

$$40 \text{ units sold} \times \$14 = \$560$$

3. Calculate the cost of ending inventory:

The cost of ending inventory is determined by taking the 5 units left over from Purchase No. 2 plus the 15 units bought from Purchase No. 3. The balance in ending inventory is:

Ending inventory = 5 units left after sale of goods @14 = $ 70
+ 15 units from Purchase No. 3 @18 = 270
20 units $340

The new weighted-average cost per unit = $340/20 units = $17 per unit.

Notice how the weighted-average cost per unit only changes after a purchase is made.

WEIGHTED-AVERAGE COST–PERIODIC. Under the periodic inventory system, the cost of inventory is based on the average cost of the inventory for the **entire period**. Using the data from Exhibit 5-5, the values for cost of goods sold and ending inventory are determined as follows:

1. Calculate the weighted-average cost per unit:

$$\frac{\text{Weighted-average}}{\text{cost per unit}} = \frac{\text{Cost of goods available*}}{\text{Number of units available}} = \frac{\$110 + \$280 + \$240 + \$270}{10 + 20 + 15 + 15}$$

$$= \frac{\$900}{60} = \$15$$

*Cost of goods available = Beginning inventory + Purchases (for the *entire period*)

2. Determine the value for cost of goods sold:

$$\frac{\text{Cost of}}{\text{goods sold}} = \frac{\text{Number of}}{\text{units sold}} \times \frac{\text{weighted-average}}{\text{cost per unit}}$$

$$40 \text{ units sold} \times \$15 = \$600$$

3. Calculate the cost of ending inventory:

$$\frac{\text{Ending}}{\text{inventory}} = \frac{\text{Number of units}}{\text{on hand}} \times \frac{\text{Weighted-average}}{\text{cost per unit}} = \$300$$

$$20 \text{ units on hand} \times \$15$$

These amounts are different from the values given under the perpetual inventory method. Why? For the perpetual inventory method, a new unit cost is computed each time a purchase is made while for the periodic inventory method; the unit cost is based on the cost of goods (and units) available for the entire period.

The following T-account shows the effects of weighted-average costing:

Inventory (at weighted-average cost–periodic)

Begin. bal.	(10 units @ $11)	110		
Purchases:				
No. 1	(20 units @ $14)	280		
No. 2	(15 units @ $16)	240	Cost of goods sold (40 units	
No. 3	(15 units @ $18)	270	@ average cost of $15 per unit)	600
Ending bal.	(20 units @ average cost of $15 per unit)	300		

FIFO COST–PERPETUAL. Under the **first-in, first-out (FIFO) cost method**, the first costs into inventory are the first costs assigned to cost of goods sold—hence, the name *first-in, first-out*. The following T-account shows how to compute FIFO cost of goods sold and ending inventory for Leon's lamps (data from Exhibit 5-5):

Inventory (at FIFO cost–perpetual)

Begin. bal.	(10 units @ $11)	110		
Purchases:				
No. 1	(20 units @ $14)	280		
No. 2	(15 units @ $16)	240	Cost of goods sold (40 units):	
			(10 units @ $11) 110 ⎫	
			(20 units @ $14) 280 ⎬ 550	
			(10 units @ $16) 160 ⎭	
No. 3	(15 units @ $18)	270		
Ending bal.	(5 units @ $16) = 80 ⎫ 350 (15 units @ $18) = 270 ⎭			

Looking at the Cost of goods sold, FIFO assumes that all of the 10 units in beginning inventory were sold along with the 20 units from Purchase No. 1 but only 10 of the 15 units from Purchase No. 2 were sold. The ending inventory contains the 5 units left from Purchase No. 2 and all of the 15 units from Purchases No. 3.

FIFO COST–PERIODIC. Just like the perpetual inventory system, the first costs into inventory are assigned to the first units sold. Using the data from Exhibit 5-5:

Inventory (at FIFO cost–periodic)

Begin. bal.	(10 units @$11)	110			
Purchases:			Cost of goods sold (40 units):		
No. 1	(20 units @$14)	280	(10 units @ $11)	110	
No. 2	(15 units @$16)	240	(20 units @ $14)	280	550
No. 3	(15 units @$18)	270	(10 units @ $16)	160	
Ending bal.	(5 units @ $16) = 80 (15 units @ $18) = 270 } 350				

Under the periodic inventory system, all of the information for the entire period is taken into account. This means that FIFO assumes that all of the 10 units in beginning inventory were sold, along with the 20 units from the No.1 purchase and 10 of the 15 units of the No. 2 purchase. The cost of ending inventory is based on the units remaining: 5 units from the No. 2 purchase and all of the 15 units from the No. 3 purchase. Notice how the amounts for cost of goods sold and ending inventory are the *same* under both the *perpetual and periodic inventory methods*.

The Effects of FIFO and Weighted-Average Cost on Cost of Goods Sold, Gross Profit, and Ending Inventory

In our Leon's example, the cost of inventory rose from $11 to $14 and up to $18. When inventory unit costs change this way, the various inventory methods produce different cost-of-goods-sold figures. Exhibit 5-6 summarizes the income effects of the two inventory methods (remember that prices are rising). Study the exhibit carefully, focusing on cost of goods sold and gross profit assuming the periodic system.

Exhibit 5-6 compares both perpetual and periodic methods. Notice how gross profit is highest under FIFO when inventory costs are increasing.

	Perpetual FIFO	Periodic FIFO	Perpetual Weighted-average	Periodic Weighted-average
Sales revenue (assumed)	$1,000	$1,000	$1,000	$1,000
Cost of goods sold	550	550	560	600
Gross profit	$ 450	$ 450	$ 440	$ 400

EXHIBIT 5-6
Effects of the FIFO and Weighted-Average Inventory Methods

Let's use the gross profit data from Exhibit 5-6 to illustrate the potential tax effects of the two methods in a period of rising prices:

	Perpetual FIFO	Periodic FIFO	Perpetual Weighted-average	Periodic Weighted-average
Gross profit	$450	$450	$440	$400
Operating expenses (assumed)	260	260	260	260
Income before income tax	$190	$190	$180	$140
Income tax expense (35%)	$ 67*	$ 67*	$ 63	$ 49

* rounded

Income tax expense is lower under weighted-average and higher under FIFO.

Exhibit 5-7 demonstrates the effect of increasing and decreasing costs of inventory on cost of goods sold and ending inventory. Study this exhibit carefully; it will help you really understand the FIFO and weighted-average inventory methods.

In a period of rising prices, FIFO will generally lead to higher profits and higher taxes than weighted-average, while the opposite is true in a period of falling prices. The difference between the two methods on profit and income taxes may be small, and each of the two methods is appropriate for certain types of inventory.

EXHIBIT 5-7
Cost of Goods Sold and Ending Inventory—FIFO and Weighted-Average; Increasing Costs and Decreasing Costs

When inventory costs are decreasing:

	Income Statement Effects Cost of Goods Sold (COGS)	Balance Sheet Effects Ending Inventory (EI)	Cash Flow Effects Income Taxes
FIFO	FIFO COGS is highest because it's based on the oldest costs, which are high. Gross profit is, therefore, the lowest.	FIFO EI is lowest because it's based on the most recent costs, which are low.	Less cash is paid for taxes, so FIFO could be used by firms seeking to minimize taxes.
Weighted-Average	Weighted-average COGS is lowest because it's based on an average of the costs for the period, which is lower than the oldest costs. Gross profit is, therefore, the highest.	Weighted-average EI is highest because the average cost for the period is higher than the most recent costs.	More cash is paid for taxes, but weighted-average may still be popular with firms seeking to maximize reported income.

When inventory costs are increasing:

	Income Statement Effects Cost of Goods Sold (COGS)	Balance Sheet Effects Ending Inventory (EI)	Cash Flow Effects Income Taxes
FIFO	FIFO COGS is lowest because it's based on oldest costs, which are low. Gross profit is, therefore, the highest.	FIFO EI is highest because it's based on the most recent costs, which are high.	More cash is paid for taxes, but FIFO may still be popular with firms seeking to maximize reported income.
Weighted-Average	Weighted-average COGS is highest because it's based on an average of the costs for the period, which is higher than the oldest costs. Gross profit is, therefore the lowest.	Weighted-average EI is lowest because the average cost for the period is lower than the most recent costs.	Less cash is paid for taxes, so weighted-average could be used by firms seeking to minimize taxes.

Comparison of the Inventory Methods

Let's compare the weighted-average and FIFO inventory methods.

1. How well does each method measure income by allocating inventory expense—cost of goods sold—against revenue? Weighted-average results in the most

realistic net income figure, it is an average that combines all costs (old costs and recent costs). In contrast, FIFO uses old inventory costs against revenue. FIFO income is therefore less realistic than weighted-average income.

2. Which method reports the most up-to-date inventory cost on the balance sheet? FIFO reports the most current inventory cost on the balance sheet. Weighted-average can value inventory at very old costs because weighted-average leaves the oldest prices in ending inventory.

3. What effects do the methods have on income taxes? As we have seen in Exhibit 5-7, in a period of rising costs, FIFO uses old inventory costs against revenue, resulting in higher income taxes. Weighted-average is an average that combines all costs (old costs and recent costs), which leads to lower profits and lower income taxes.

STOP + THINK (5-2)

King Company had 25 units @$5 in beginning inventory; bought 30 units @$6 and then sold 50 units. Assume King Company uses the FIFO perpetual inventory system. Compute the (a) cost of goods sold and the (b) cost of ending inventory.

▶ DECISION GUIDELINES

MANAGING INVENTORY

Suppose Leon's Furniture stocks two basic categories of merchandise:

- Furniture pieces, such as tables and chairs
- Small items of low value, near the checkout stations, such as flower vases and other small accent pieces

Jacob Stiles, the store manager, is considering how accounting will affect the business. Let's examine several decisions that Stiles must make to achieve his goals for his company.

Decision	Guidelines	System or Method
Which inventory system to use?	• Expensive merchandise • Keeps a running record of inventory	→ Perpetual system for the furniture
	• Cannot keep a running record of all inventory bought and sold	→ Periodic system for the vases and other small accent pieces
	• Unique inventory items	→ Specific unit cost for art objects because they are unique
Which costing method to use?	• Most current cost of ending inventory • Maximizes reported income when costs are rising	→ FIFO
	• More current measure of cost of goods sold and net income based on average costs for period	→ Weighted-average

MyAccountingLab

MID-CHAPTER SUMMARY PROBLEM

Suppose a division of DIY Building Products Inc. has these inventory records for January 2017:

Date	Item	Quantity	Unit Cost
Jan. 1	Beginning inventory	100 units	$ 8
6	Purchase	60 units	9
21	Purchase	150 units	9
24	Sales	300 units	
27	Purchase	90 units	10

Name: DIY Building Products Inc.
Industry: Building products
Fiscal Period: Month of January 2017
Key Fact: Perpetual inventory system and periodic inventory system

Operating expense for January was $1,900, and the 300 units sold on January 24 generated sales revenue of $6,770.

Requirements

1. Prepare the January income statement, showing amounts for FIFO and weighted-average cost assuming that (a) a periodic inventory system is used, and (b) a perpetual inventory system is used. Label the bottom line "Operating income." (Round figures to whole-dollar amounts.) Show your computations, and compute cost of goods sold.
2. Explain which inventory method would result in:
   a. Reporting the highest operating income
   b. Reporting inventory on the balance sheet at the most current cost
   c. Attaining the best measure of net income for the income statement

ANSWERS

Requirement 1(a) Periodic Inventory System

	A	B	C	D	E	F
1	**DIY Building Products Inc.** Income Statement for Division For the Month Ended January 31, 2017					
2			FIFO		Weighted-Average	
3	Sales revenue		$ 6,770		$ 6,770	
4	Cost of goods sold:					
5	Beginning inventory	$ 800		$ 800		
6	Purchases	2,790		2,790		
7	Cost of goods available for sale	3,590		3,590		
8	Ending inventory	(990)		(898)		
9	Cost of goods sold		2,600		2,692	
10	Gross profit		4,170		4,078	
11	Operating expenses		1,900		1,900	
12	Operating income		$ 2,270		$ 2,178	
13						

Sales revenue is given.
Beginning inventory is given.
See the Computations section.
Beginning inventory + Purchases
See the Computations section.
Cost of goods available for sale − Ending inventory
Sales revenue − Cost of goods sold
Operating expenses are given.
Gross profit − Operating expenses

Computations:

Beginning inventory:	100 × $8 = $800
Purchases:	(60 × $9) + (150 × $9) + (90 × $10) = $2,790
*Ending inventory—FIFO:	(10 × $9) + (90 × $10) = $990
Weighted-average:	100 × $8.975** = $898 (rounded from $897.50)

*Number of units in ending inventory = 100 + 60 + 150 + 90 − 300 = 100
**$3,590/400 units† = $8.975 per unit
†Number of units available = 100 + 60 + 150 + 90 = 400

Requirement 1(b) Perpetual Inventory System

	A	B	C	D
1	**DIY Building Products Inc.** Income Statement for Division For the Month Ended January 31, 2017			
2		FIFO	Weighted- Average	
3	Sales revenue	$ 6,770	$ 6,770	
4	Cost of goods sold	2,600	2,603	
5	Gross profit	4,170	4,167	
6	Operating expenses	1,900	1,900	
7	Operating income	$ 2,270	$ 2,267	
8				

Computations:

FIFO:

Cost of goods sold = (100 × $8) + (60 × $9) + (140 × $9) = $2,600

Ending inventory = (10 × $9) + (90 × $10) = $990

Weighted-average:

Cost of goods sold = (100 × $8) + (60 × $9) + (150 × $9) = $2,690

$2,690/310 units = $8.677 per unit

300 units sold × $8.677/unit = $2,603 (rounded)

Ending inventory = 10 units left after sale (310 available − 300 units sold)

        × $8.677 = $87 (rounded)

90 units bought × $10 = 900

Ending inventory   = $987 ($87 + $900)

> Use the quantities and unit costs given in the question to calculate beginning inventory and purchases. Recall that FIFO ending inventory calculations use the most current purchase prices. Weighted-average ending inventory calculations use the average purchase prices.

Requirement 2

a. Use FIFO to report the highest operating income. Income under FIFO is highest when inventory unit costs are increasing, as in this situation.

b. Use FIFO to report inventory on the balance sheet at the most current cost. The oldest inventory costs are expensed as cost of goods sold, leaving the most recent (most current) costs of the period in ending inventory.

c. Use weighted-average to attain the best measure of net income. Weighted-average inventory costs, which are expensed as part of goods sold, are closer to the most recent (most current) inventory costs than FIFO costs are.

> Because beginning inventory, purchases, and operating expense are the same for both inventory methods, use the ending inventory and operating income amounts you calculated in Requirement 1 to help you answer these questions.

EXPLAIN HOW ACCOUNTING STANDARDS APPLY TO INVENTORY

OBJECTIVE

❸ **Explain** how accounting standards apply to inventory

It is important at this point that you consider a characteristic of accounting that has special relevance to inventories:

- Comparability

Comparability

Investors like to compare a company's financial statements from one period to the next so they can use this information to make a decision. In order to do this, the company must use the same accounting method for inventory consistently from one accounting period to another.

Suppose you are analyzing Leon's Furniture's net income pattern over a two-year period. Now, suppose Leon's switched from one inventory method to another during that time and its net income increased dramatically, but only because of the change in inventory method. If you did not know about the change, you might believe that Leon's Furniture's income increased due to improved operations, which is not the case.

Recall from Chapter 1 that one of the enhancing qualitative characteristics of accounting information is **comparability**. For accounting information to be comparable, it must be reported in a way that makes it possible to compare it to similar information being reported by other companies and by comparing it with its own financial statements from one period to the next. It must also be reported in a way that is consistent with how it was reported in previous periods (**consistency principle**). This does not mean that a company is not permitted to change its accounting methods. Both IFRS and ASPE allow such a change, indicating that it is acceptable if it "results in the financial statements providing reliable and more relevant information." The change should normally be applied retrospectively, which means that prior years' financial statements should be restated to reflect the change. In addition, the effect of the change on the current financial statements should be disclosed, and would be found in the notes to the financial statements according to the disclosure principal.

Lower of Cost and Net Realizable Value

The **lower-of-cost-and-net-realizable-value (LCNRV) rule** is based on the premise that inventory can become obsolete or damaged or its selling price can decline. Both IFRS and ASPE require that inventory be reported in the financial statements at whichever is lower—the inventory's cost or its **net realizable value (NRV)**, that is, the amount the business could get if it sold the inventory, less any costs incurred to sell it. If the net realizable value of inventory falls below its historical cost, the business must write down the value of its goods to net realizable value. On the balance sheet, the business reports ending inventory at its LCNRV. How is the write-down accomplished?

Suppose Klassen Furniture Inc. paid $3,000 for inventory on September 26. By December 31, Klassen determines that it will be able to sell this inventory for only $2,000, net of selling costs. Because the inventory's net realizable value is less than its original cost, Klassen's December 31 balance sheet must report the inventory at $2,000. Exhibit 5-8 presents the effects of LCNRV on the balance sheet and the income statement. Before any LCNRV effect, cost of goods sold is $9,000.

An LCNRV write-down decreases Inventory and increases Cost of Goods Sold, as follows:

Inventory	
Sept. 26 $3,000	
	$1,000 Dec. 31
Balance $2,000	

	A	B	C	D	E
1	Dec. 31	Cost of Goods Sold	1,000		
2		Inventory		1,000	
3		*Write inventory down to net realizable value.*			
4					

Inventory that has been written down to net realizable value should be reassessed each period. If the net realizable value has increased, the previous write-down should be reversed up to the new net realizable value. Of course, the inventory cannot be written up to a value that exceeds its original cost.

Balance Sheet

Current assets:..	$ XXX
Cash..	XXX
Short-term investments	XXX
Accounts receivable..	XXX
Inventories, at net realizable value	
(which is lower than $3,000 cost)	2,000
Prepaid expenses...	XXX
Total current assets..	$X,XXX

Income Statement

Sales revenue..	$21,000
Cost of goods sold ($9,000 + $1,000)...	10,000
Gross profit	$11,000

Assume that Klassen's inventory described above was still on hand at the end of the next period and that the net realizable value had increased to $2,400. The journal entry to reverse a previous write-down would be as follows:

	A	B	C	D	E
1		Inventory	400		
2		Cost of Goods Sold		400	
3		*Write inventory up to the net realizable value.*			
4					

Companies disclose how they apply LCNRV in a note to their financial statements as shown in the following excerpt from Leon's 2014 audited annual report.

Summary of Significant Accounting Policies

Inventories

Inventories are valued at the lower of cost determined on a first-in, first-out basis, and net realizable value.... .

STOP + THINK (5-3)

Do you think it is a problem for investors trying to interpret the financial statements of companies using different methods?

COMPUTE AND EVALUATE GROSS PROFIT AND INVENTORY TURNOVER

OBJECTIVE

❹ **Compute** and **evaluate** gross profit and inventory turnover

Managers, investors, and creditors use ratios to evaluate a business. Two ratios relate directly to inventory: the gross profit percentage and the rate of inventory turnover.

Gross Profit Percentage

Gross profit—sales minus cost of goods sold—is a key indicator of a company's ability to sell inventory at a profit. Merchandisers strive to increase **gross profit percentage**, also called the *gross margin percentage*. Gross profit percentage is stated as a percentage of sales. Gross profit percentage is computed as follows for Leon's Furniture. Data (in millions) for 2014 are taken from the financial statements, page 231.

$$\text{Gross profit percentage} = \frac{\text{Gross profit}}{\text{Net sales revenue}} = \frac{\$856.9}{\$1{,}974.4} = 0.434 = 43.4\%$$

Managers and investors watch the gross profit percentage carefully. A 43.4% gross profit means that each dollar of sales generates 43.4 cents of gross profit. On average, cost of goods sold consumes 56.6 cents of each sales dollar for Leon's. For most firms, the gross profit percentage changes little from year to year, so a small downturn may signal trouble.

Leon's gross profit was 41.6%, 43.4%, and 43.4% for the years 2012 through 2014, respectively. These figures indicate that there was an increase in gross profit from 2012 to 2013, but gross profit stayed the same from 2013 to 2014. For Leon's, 2012 was another challenging year—consumers were spending less on furniture given the weak economy. However, this did not stop Leon's from opening up more stores in Canada and their acquisition of The Brick in 2013. Leon's gross profit of 43.4% in 2014 was higher than Walmart (24.2%), and slightly higher than Pier 1 (40.1%). Both Pier 1 and Leon's handle higher-priced merchandise than Walmart, which may explain their higher gross profit. Exhibit 5-9 graphs the gross profit for these three companies.

EXHIBIT 5-9
Gross Profit Percentages
of Three Leading Retailers

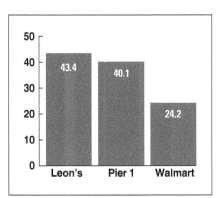

Inventory Turnover

Leon's strives to sell its inventory as quickly as possible because furniture and fixtures generate no profit until they are sold. The faster the sales, the higher the company's income; the slower the sales, the lower the company's income. **Inventory turnover**, the ratio of cost of goods sold to average inventory, indicates how rapidly inventory is sold. The 2014 computation for Leon's follows (data in millions from the financial statements, page 231):

$$\begin{array}{c}\text{Inventory} \\ \text{(balance sheet)}\end{array} = \frac{\text{Cost of goods sold}}{\text{Average inventory}} = \frac{\text{Cost of goods sold}}{\left(\begin{array}{c}\text{Beginning} \\ \text{inventory}\end{array} + \begin{array}{c}\text{Ending} \\ \text{inventory}\end{array}\right) \div 2}$$

$$= \frac{\$1{,}117.5}{(\$266.6 + \$277.7)/2} = \begin{array}{c}4.11 \text{ or } 4.1 \text{ times per year} \\ \text{(every 89 days)}\end{array}$$

The inventory turnover statistic shows how many times the company sold (or turned over) its average level of inventory during the year. Inventory turnover varies from industry to industry. To calculate how long it takes to sell inventory, take 365 days and divide by the inventory turnover. For Leon's, it would be 365/4.1 = 89 days.

Leon's and other specialty retailers turn their inventory over slowly. Retailers must keep lots of inventory on hand because visual appeal is critical in retailing. Department stores such as The Bay and discounters such as Walmart also keep a lot of inventory on hand. Exhibit 5-10 shows the inventory turnover rates for three leading retailers.

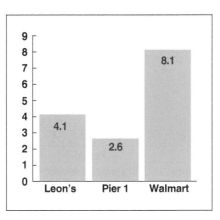

EXHIBIT 5-10
**Inventory Turnover Rates
of Three Leading Retailers**

STOP + THINK (5-4)

You have received a gift of cash from your grandparents and are considering investing in the stock market. You have carefully researched the market and have decided that you will invest in one of three companies: Leon's Furniture, Pier 1, or Walmart. Assume your analysis has resulted in Exhibits 5-9 and 5-10. What do the ratio values in the two exhibits say about the merchandising (pricing) strategies of Leon's, Pier 1, and Walmart?

▶ DECISION GUIDELINES

Companies buy and sell inventory to generate revenue. Two ratios that relate directly to inventory are the inventory turnover and the gross profit percentage. Let's see how they are used in decision making.

Decision	Guidelines
Who uses the inventory turnover and the gross profit percentage ratios for decision making and why?	*Managers* keep their eye on inventory to make sure it is selling quickly. Slow-moving inventory could be a sign that it is outdated or no longer in demand. Also, determining the selling price for inventory affects gross profit and, ultimately, net income. If the gross profit is too low, it may indicate that the inventory is costing too much or the selling price is not high enough.
	Investors want to know if inventory is selling quickly because it affects revenue and, ultimately, net income. They examine gross profit to see if it is high enough to cover all the other expenses and still provide for a reasonable profit.
	Creditors are interested in how inventory is selling because the faster inventory is sold, the sooner the cash flows in and the company can pay its debts.

⑤ Analyze the effects of inventory errors

ANALYZE THE EFFECTS OF INVENTORY ERRORS

Inventory errors sometimes occur. In Exhibit 5-11, start with period 1, in which ending inventory is *overstated* by $5,000 and cost of goods sold is therefore *understated* by $5,000. Then compare period 1 with period 3, which is correct. *Period 1 should look exactly like period 3.*

Inventory errors counterbalance in two consecutive periods. Why? Recall that period 1's ending inventory becomes period 2's beginning inventory amount. Thus, the error in period 1 carries over into period 2. Trace the ending inventory of $15,000 from period 1 to period 2. Then compare periods 2 and 3. *All periods should look exactly like period 3.* The amounts **in bold type** in Exhibit 5-11 are incorrect.

EXHIBIT 5-11
Inventory Errors: An Example

	A	B	C	D	E	F	G	H
1		Period 1		Period 2		Period 3		
2		Ending Inventory Overstated by $5,000		Beginning Inventory Overstated by $5,000		Correct		
3	Sales revenue		$ 100,000		$ 100,000		$ 100,000	
4	Cost of goods sold:							
5	Beginning inventory	$ 10,000		**$ 15,000**		$ 10,000		
6	Purchases	50,000		50,000		50,000		
7	Cost of goods available for sale	60,000		**65,000**		60,000		
8	**Ending inventory**	**(15,000)**		(10,000)		(10,000)		
9	Cost of goods sold		45,000		55,000		50,000	
10	Gross profit		$ 55,000		$ 45,000		$ 50,000	
11								

Source: The authors thank Professor Carl High for this example.

$ 100,000

Beginning inventory and ending inventory have opposite effects on cost of goods sold (beginning inventory is added; ending inventory is subtracted); therefore, after two periods, an inventory accounting error "washes out" (counterbalances) as illustrated in Exhibit 5-11. Notice that total gross profit for periods 1 and 2 combined is correct ($100,000), even though each period's gross profit is wrong by $5,000. The correct gross profit is $50,000 for each period as shown in period 3.

Note that there is a direct relationship between ending inventory (EI) and gross profit (GP), but an inverse relationship between beginning inventory (BI) and gross profit. That is, an understatement of ending inventory results in an understatement of gross profit, but an understatement of beginning inventory results in an overstatement of gross profit. (COGS = cost of goods sold)

EI↓ results in COGS↑ results in GP↓ (Direct relationship between EI and GP)

BI↓ results in COGS↓ results in GP↑ (Inverse relationship between BI and GP)

Inventory Errors

Inventory errors cannot be ignored simply because they counterbalance. Suppose you are analyzing trends in the operations of the company presented above.

Exhibit 5-11 shows a drop in gross profit from period 1 to period 2, followed by an increase in period 3. Did the company really get worse and then better again? No, that picture of operations is inaccurate because of the accounting error. The correct gross profit is $50,000 for each period. We must have accurate information for all periods. Exhibit 5-12 summarizes the effects of inventory accounting errors.

EXHIBIT 5-12
Effects of Inventory Errors

	A	B	C	D	E	F
1		Period 1		Period 2		
2	Inventory Error	Cost of Goods Sold	Gross Profit and Net Income	Cost of Goods Sold	Gross Profit and Net Income	
3	Period 1	Understated	Overstated	Overstated	Understated	
4	Ending inventory overstated					
5	Period 1					
6	Ending inventory understated	Overstated	Understated	Understated	Overstated	
7						

Reporting on the Statement of Cash Flows

Inventories appear on the balance sheet as current assets. Since inventory transactions affect cash, their effects are reported on the statement of cash flows.

Inventory transactions are *operating activities* because the purchase and sale of merchandise drives a company's operations. The purchase of inventory requires a cash payment and the sale of inventory requires a cash receipt. We will see in Chapter 10 how to report inventory transactions on the statement of cash flows.

COOKING *the* BOOKS

with Inventory

No area of accounting has a deeper ethical dimension than inventory. Managers of companies whose profits do not meet shareholder expectations are sometimes tempted to "cook the books" to increase reported income. The increase in reported income may lead investors and creditors into thinking the business is more successful than it really is.

What do managers hope to gain from fraudulent accounting? In some cases, they are trying to keep their jobs. In other cases, their bonuses are tied to reported income: the higher the company's net income, the higher the managers' bonuses.

The easiest is simply to overstate ending inventory. The two most common ways to "cook the books" with inventory are (1) inserting fictitious inventory, thus overstating quantities; and (2) deliberately overstating unit prices used in the computation of ending inventory amounts. The upward-pointing arrows in the accounting equation indicate an overstatement: reporting more assets and equity than are actually present.

ASSETS	=	LIABILITIES	+	SHAREHOLDERS' EQUITY
↑	=	0	+	↑

STOP + THINK (5-5)

It's year-end and a physical count revealed $1,500 on hand, while the accounting records indicated there should be $1,600. If this error is not corrected, what effect would this have on the year-end's (a) Cost of goods sold, (b) Net income, and (c) Shareholders' equity?

SUMMARY

SUMMARY OF LEARNING OBJECTIVES

LEARNING OBJECTIVE	SUMMARY
1. **Account** for inventory using the perpetual and periodic inventory systems	When inventory is bought, it is a current asset on the balance sheet, and when it is sold, it is an expense on the income statement. A company can use either the perpetual inventory system or the periodic inventory system to account for its inventory. A perpetual inventory system keeps a continuous record of inventory bought and sold. A periodic inventory system does not keep a continuous record of inventory; a physical count is performed to determine ending inventory. Cost of goods sold is a computation.
2. **Apply** and **compare** three inventory costing methods	The three inventory methods are the specific identification; first-in, first-out (FIFO); and the weighted-average-cost method. Specific identification is used for unique inventory items where the company identifies the specific cost of the inventory item. Under the FIFO method, the first costs into inventory are the first costs assigned to cost of goods sold. The weighted-average-cost method assigns an average cost to inventory based on the cost of the inventory for the period.
3. **Explain** how accounting standards apply to inventory	Comparability (including consistency) says that businesses should use the same accounting methods and procedures from period to period so users can compare information. The lower-of-cost-and-net-realizable-value (LCNRV) rule requires that inventory be reported in the financial statements at the lower of its cost and net realizable value. Net realizable value is the amount the business could get if it sold the inventory less any costs of selling it.
4. **Compute** and **evaluate** gross profit and inventory turnover	There are two ratios used to evaluate inventory: Gross profit percentage = Gross profit/Net sales revenue (the gross profit percentage indicates the company's ability to sell inventory at a profit) Inventory turnover = Cost of goods sold/Average inventory (inventory turnover shows how rapidly inventory is sold)
5. **Analyze** the effects of inventory errors	Inventory errors, if not corrected, can affect the values of inventory on the balance sheet, and cost of goods sold, gross profit, and net income on the income statement.

There are no differences between IFRS and ASPE in this chapter.

END-OF-CHAPTER SUMMARY PROBLEM

During February 2017, its first month of operations, Blanc Company reported the following transactions:

Feb. 1	Purchased 20,000 units on account for $2.50 each
Feb. 15	Purchased 25,000 units on account for $2.75 each
Feb. 20	Sold on account 35,000 units for $3.25 each
Feb. 23	Purchased 10,000 units on account for $2.70 each
Feb. 25	Paid for the purchases made on Feb. 1
Feb. 27	Collected $75,000 from customers on account
Feb. 28	Incurred on account $11,000 in operating expenses

The company uses the perpetual inventory method and pays 35% income tax.

Requirements

1. Prepare journal entries to record the transactions for the month of February assuming the company uses the FIFO inventory method. Explanations are not required.
2. Determine the ending inventory assuming the company uses the FIFO inventory method. (Hint: You might find it helpful to use a T-account.)
3. Prepare the company's multi-step income statement for the month of February.
4. Compute the company's gross profit percentage and the inventory turnover for the month. How does this company compare with the industry average of 17% for the gross profit and an inventory turnover of three times? Round to one decimal place.
5. Assume instead that the company uses the weighted-average method to value inventory; calculate the cost of goods sold and the ending inventory value.

Name: Blanc Company
Industry: Retail corporation
Fiscal Period: Year ended December 31, 2017
Key Fact: Perpetual inventory system

Because the company uses the perpetual inventory system, record inventory purchases and sales as they occur.

All merchandise is purchased on account.

All sales are made on account.

Use FIFO (oldest costs) to calculate cost of the 35,000 units sold:
Opening inventory: $0 (company just started)
From Feb. 1 purchase: $50,000 (20,000 units)
From Feb. 15 purchase: $68,750 (25,000 units)

Operating expenses were incurred ($11,000).

Income tax expense is 35% of net income before taxes (Sales revenue − Cost of goods sold − Operating expenses).

FIFO ending inventory:
Beginning inventory + Purchases − Cost of goods sold

ANSWERS
Requirement 1

	A	B	C	D	E
1	Feb. 1	Inventory (20,000 units × $2.50)	50,000		
2		Accounts payable		50,000	
3	Feb. 15	Inventory (25,000 units × $2.75)	68,750		
4		Accounts payable		68,750	
5	Feb. 20	Accounts receivable (35,000 × $3.25)	113,750		
6		Sales Revenue		113,750	
7		Cost of goods sold (20,000 × $2.50 + 15,000 × $2.75)	91,250		
8		Inventory		91,250	
9	Feb. 23	Inventory (10,000 units × $2.70)	27,000		
10		Accounts payable		27,000	
11	Feb. 25	Accounts payable	50,000		
12		Cash		50,000	
13	Feb. 27	Cash	75,000		
14		Accounts receivable		75,000	
15	Feb. 28	Operating expenses	11,000		
16		Accounts payable		11,000	
17	Feb. 28	Income tax expense (from Requirement 3)	4,025		
18		Tax payable		4,025	
19					

Requirement 2

FIFO − Ending inventory = $50,000 + $68,750 − $91,250 + $27,000 = $54,500

Inventory			
Feb. 1	50,000		
Feb. 15	68,750	91,250	Feb. 20
Feb. 23	27,000		
Balance			
Feb. 28	54,500		

Requirement 3

	A	B	C	D
1	**Blanc Company** Income Statement For the Month Ended February 28, 2017			
2	Sales revenue	$ 113,750		
3	Cost of goods sold	91,250		
4	Gross profit	$ 22,500		
5	Operating expenses	11,000		
6	Income before tax	$ 11,500		
7	Income tax expense (35%)	4,025		
8	Net income	$ 7,475		
9				

Beginning inventory must be the same amount as the inventory on the previous year's balance sheet.
Blanc Company just started, so there is no previous year's balance.
Ending inventory must be the same amount as the inventory on this year's balance sheet.

Sales revenue − Cost of goods sold

Gross profit − Operating expenses

IFRS require that income tax expense be presented separately from all other expenses.

Gross profit ÷ Sales revenue

Cost of goods sold ÷ Average inventory, where Average inventory = (Beginning inventory + Ending inventory) ÷ 2

Net income ÷ Sales revenue

Requirement 4

Gross profit percentage = $22,500/$113,750 = 19.8%
Inventory turnover = $91,250/$54,500* = 1.7 times
Compared to the industry averages, Blanc Company's gross profit percentage is higher, which suggests that the company is able to sell its inventory at a profit. However, the inventory turnover is low, which means that the company has too much inventory on hand.

Requirement 5

$$\text{Weighted average—calculate the unit cost} = \frac{\text{Cost of goods available for sale}}{\text{Number of units available for sale}}$$

A new unit cost must be calculated after a purchase is made.

$$\text{Feb. 15—New unit cost} = \frac{\$50,000 \text{ (Feb. 1)} + \$68,750 \text{ (Feb. 15)}}{20,000 + 25,000} = \$2.64 \text{ each}$$

Feb. 20—Cost of goods sold = 35,000 units sold × $2.64 = $92,400
Feb. 23—New unit cost is calculated as follows:
Units left after the sale on Feb. 20 (45,000 available − 35,000 sold) = 10,000 × $2.64 = $26,400
Units bought on Feb. 23 = 10,000 × $2.70 = $27,000
Total cost = $53,400 ($26,400 + $27,000) divided by 20,000 (number of units on hand) = $2.67

Therefore, ending inventory = $2.67 × 20,000 units = $53,400

---

*Since the company just started, there is no beginning inventory and, therefore, an average is not used.

REVIEW

MyAccountingLab

Make the grade with MyAccountingLab: The Quick Quiz questions, Short Exercises, Exercises, and Problems (Group A) marked in #-# can be found on MyAccountingLab. You can practise them as often as you want, and most feature step-by-step guided instructions to help you find the right answer.

QUICK QUIZ (ANSWERS APPEAR ON THE LAST PAGE OF THIS CHAPTER.)

Test your understanding of accounting for inventory by answering the following questions. Select the best choice from among the possible answers given.

1. Riverside Software began January with $3,500 of merchandise inventory. During January, Riverside made the following entries for its inventory transactions:

	A	B	C	D
1	Inventory	6,000		
2	Accounts Payable		6,000	
3	Accounts Receivable	7,200		
4	Sales Revenue		7,200	
5	Cost of Goods Sold	5,500		
6	Inventory		5,500	
7				

What was the value of Riverside's inventory at the end of January?
a. $0
b. $4,000
c. $4,500
d. $5,500

2. Use the data in question 1. What is Riverside's gross profit for January?
a. $0
b. $1,700
c. $5,500
d. $7,200

3. When does the cost of inventory become an expense?
a. When cash is collected from the customer
b. When inventory is purchased from the supplier
c. When payment is made to the supplier
d. When inventory is delivered to a customer

Questions 4 and 5 use the following facts. Leading Edge Frame Shop wants to know the effect of different inventory costing methods on its financial statements. The company uses the periodic inventory system. Inventory and purchases data for April follow.

	Units	Unit Cost	Total Cost
April 1 Beginning inventory	2,000	$10.00	$20,000
4 Purchase	1,000	10.60	10,600
9 Sale	(1,500)		

4. If Leading Edge uses the FIFO method, the cost of the ending inventory will be
a. $10,600.
b. $15,000.
c. $15,300.
d. $15,600.

5. If Leading Edge uses the weighted-average-cost method, cost of goods sold will be
a. $10,600.
b. $15,000.
c. $15,300.
d. $15,600.

6. In a period of rising prices
a. gross profit under FIFO will be higher than under weighted-average cost.
b. weighted-average-cost inventory will be greater than FIFO inventory.
c. cost of goods sold under weighted-average cost will be less than under FIFO.
d. net income under weighted-average cost will be higher than under FIFO.

7. The income statement for Heritage Health Foods shows gross profit of $144,000, operating expenses of $130,000, and cost of goods sold of $216,000. What is the amount of net sales revenue?
a. $274,000
b. $246,000
c. $360,000
d. $490,000

8. The phrase "net realizable value" as used in "the lower of cost and net realizable value" generally means
a. original cost.
b. market value.
c. retail market price.
d. liquidation price.

9. The sum of ending inventory and cost of goods sold is
a. goods available for sale.
b. net purchases.
c. gross profit.
d. beginning inventory.

10. The following data come from the inventory records of Dodge Company:

Net sales revenue	$620,000
Beginning inventory	60,000
Ending inventory	40,000
Net purchases	400,000

Based on these facts, the gross profit for Dodge Company is
a. $150,000.
b. $220,000.
c. $190,000.
d. some other amount ($_____).

11. Elizabeth Baker Cosmetics ended May with inventory of $20,000. Elizabeth Baker expects to end June with inventory of $15,000 after cost of goods sold of $90,000. How much inventory must Elizabeth Baker purchase during June to accomplish these results?
a. $85,000
b. $95,000
c. $105,000
d. Cannot be determined from the data given

12. Two financial ratios that clearly distinguish a discount chain such as Walmart from a high-end retailer such as Tiffany & Co. are the gross profit percentage and the rate of inventory turnover. Which set of relationships is most likely for Tiffany?

	Gross Profit Percentage	Inventory Turnover
a.	High	High
b.	Low	Low
c.	Low	High
d.	High	Low

13. Sales are $500,000, and cost of goods sold is $300,000. Beginning and ending inventories are $25,000 and $35,000, respectively. How many times did the company turn its inventory over during this period?
a. 16.7 times
b. 6.7 times
c. 8 times
d. 10 times

14. Tulsa Inc. reported the following data:

Freight-in	$ 20,000	Sales returns	$ 10,000
Purchases	205,000	Purchase returns	6,000
Beginning inventory	50,000	Sales revenue	490,000
Purchase discounts	4,000	Ending inventory	40,000

Tulsa's gross profit percentage is
a. 47.9%.
b. 52.1%.
c. 53.1%.
d. 54.0%.

15. Sales discounts should appear in the financial statements
a. as an addition to inventory.
b. as an addition to sales.
c. as an operating expense.
d. as a deduction from sales.

16. An error understated Rice Corporation's December 31, 2016, ending inventory by $40,000. What effect will this error have on total assets and net income for 2016?

	Assets	Net Income
a.	No effect	No effect
b.	No effect	Overstate
c.	Understate	Understate
d.	Understate	No effect

17. What is the effect of Rice Corporation's 2016 inventory error on net income for 2017?
a. No effect
b. Understate
c. Overstate

ACCOUNTING VOCABULARY

comparability Investors like to compare a company's financial statements from one year to the next. Therefore, a company must consistently use the same accounting method each year. (p. 248)

consistency principle A business must use the same accounting methods and procedures from period to period. (p. 248)

cost of goods sold Cost of the inventory the business has sold to customers. Also called *cost of sales*. (p. 231)

entire period Length of time during which beginning inventory and purchases are taken into account when calculating unit cost. (p. 241)

first-in, first-out (FIFO) cost method Inventory costing method by which the first costs into inventory are the first costs out to cost of goods sold. Ending inventory is based on the costs of the most recent purchases. (p. 242)

gross margin Another name for *gross profit*. (p. 233)

gross profit Sales revenue minus cost of goods sold. Also called *gross margin*. (p. 233)

gross profit percentage Gross profit divided by net sales revenue. Also called the *gross margin percentage*. (p. 249)

inventory turnover Ratio of cost of goods sold to average inventory. Indicates how rapidly inventory is sold. (p. 250)

lower-of-cost-and-net-realizable-value (LCNRV) rule Requires that an asset be reported in the financial statements at whichever is lower—its historical cost or its net realizable value. (p. 248)

net realizable value (NRV) The amount a business could get if it sold the inventory less the costs of selling it. (p. 248)

periodic inventory system An inventory system in which the business does not keep a continuous record of the inventory on hand. Instead, at the end of the period, the business makes a physical count of the inventory on hand and applies the appropriate unit costs to determine the cost of the ending inventory. (p. 234)

perpetual inventory system An inventory system in which the business keeps a continuous record for each inventory item to show the inventory on hand at all times. (p. 234)

purchase allowance A decrease in the cost of purchases because the seller has granted the buyer a discount (an allowance) from the amount owed. (p. 236)

purchase discount A decrease in the cost of purchases earned by making an early payment to the vendor. (p. 236)

purchase return A decrease in the cost of purchases because the buyer returned the goods to the seller. (p. 236)

sales discount Percentage reduction of sale price by the seller as an incentive for early payment before the due date. A typical way to express a sales discount is "2/10, n/30." This means the seller will grant a 2% discount if the invoice is paid within 10 days, or the full amount is due within 30 days. (p. 238)

sales returns and allowances Merchandise returned for credit or refunds for services provided. (p. 238)

specific identification cost method Inventory costing method based on the specific cost of particular units of inventory. (p. 240)

weighted-average-cost method Inventory costing method based on the average cost of inventory for the period. Weighted-average cost is determined by dividing the cost of goods available by the number of units available. Also called the *average cost method*. (p. 240)

ASSESS YOUR PROGRESS

SHORT EXERCISES

S5-1 Journalize the following assumed transactions for Shoppers Drug Mart Corporation. Show amounts in millions.

- Cash purchases of inventory, $3,900 million
- Sales on account (including credit cards), $19,400 million
- Cost of goods sold (perpetual inventory system), $4,200 million
- Collections on account, $18,900 million

LEARNING OBJECTIVE ❶
Account for inventory transactions

S5-2 Riley Kilgo Inc. purchased inventory costing $100,000 and sold 80% of the goods for $240,000. All purchases and sales were on account. Kilgo later collected 20% of the accounts receivable.

1. Journalize these transactions for Kilgo, which uses the perpetual inventory system.
2. For these transactions, show what Kilgo will report for inventory, revenues, and expenses on its financial statements. Report gross profit on the appropriate statement.

LEARNING OBJECTIVE ❶
Account for inventory transactions

S5-3 Allstate Sporting Goods started April with an inventory of 10 sets of golf clubs that cost a total of $1,500. During April, Allstate purchased 20 sets of clubs for $3,200. At the end of the month, Allstate had six sets of golf clubs on hand. The store manager must select an inventory costing method, and he asks you to tell him both cost of goods sold and ending inventory under these two accounting methods, assuming the periodic system is used.

1. **a.** Weighted-average cost
   b. FIFO
2. If the store manager wants the most current cost for ending inventory, which method should he choose?

LEARNING OBJECTIVE ❷
Apply the weighted-average-cost and FIFO methods

S5-4 University Copy Centre Ltd. uses laser printers. The company started the year with 100 containers of ink (weighted-average cost of $9.20 each, FIFO cost of $9 each). During the year, University Copy Centre purchased 700 containers of ink at $10 each and sold 600 units for $20 each. The company paid operating expenses throughout the year, to a total of $3,000. University Copy Centre is not subject to income tax. Prepare University Copy Centre Ltd.'s income statement for the year ended December 31, 2017, under the weighted-average and FIFO inventory costing methods assuming periodic system is used. Include a complete statement heading.

LEARNING OBJECTIVE ❷
Apply the weighted-average-cost and FIFO methods

S5-5 This exercise should be used in conjunction with exercise S5-4. Now assume that University Copy Centre in exercise S5-4 is a corporation subject to an 18% income tax. Compute University Copy Centre's income tax expense under the weighted-average cost and FIFO inventory costing methods. Which method would you select to (a) maximize income before tax and (b) minimize income tax expense?

LEARNING OBJECTIVE ❷
Understand income tax effects of the inventory costing methods

LEARNING OBJECTIVE ❸

Understand accounting standards related to inventory

S5-6 You are opening a new bookstore catering to the students at Queen's University. Once you have established this operation, you plan to approach investors to support an expansion to locations in other Canadian university communities. Explain to your accountant what characteristics you expect him to maintain in accounting for inventory and the reasons for your expectations.

LEARNING OBJECTIVE ❸

Apply the lower-of-cost-and-net-realizable-value rule to inventory

S5-7 It is December 31, 2017, end of year, and the controller of Garcia Corporation is applying the lower-of-cost-and-net-realizable-value (LCNRV) rule to inventories. Before any year-end adjustments Garcia has these data:

Cost of goods sold	$410,000
Historical cost of ending inventory, as determined by a physical count	60,000

Garcia determines that the net realizable value of ending inventory is $49,000. Show what Garcia should report for ending inventory and for cost of goods sold. Identify the financial statement where each item appears.

LEARNING OBJECTIVE ❹

Use ratio data to evaluate operations

S5-8 Assume Gildan Activewear Inc. made sales of $964.4 million during 2015. Cost of goods sold for the year totalled $655.3 million. At the end of 2014, Gildan's inventory stood at $200.7 million, and Gildan ended 2015 with inventory of $240 million. Compute Gildan's gross profit percentage and rate of inventory turnover for 2015.

LEARNING OBJECTIVE ❺

Assess the effect of an inventory error—one year only

S5-9 CWD Inc. reported these figures for its fiscal year (amounts in millions):

Net sales	$1,700
Cost of goods sold	1,180
Ending inventory	360

Suppose CWD later learns that ending inventory was overstated by $10 million. What are CWD's correct amounts for (a) net sales, (b) ending inventory, (c) cost of goods sold, and (d) gross profit?

LEARNING OBJECTIVE ❺

Assess the effect of an inventory error on two years

S5-10 Suppose Staples Inc.'s $1.9 million cost of inventory at its fiscal year-end on January 31, 2015, was understated by $0.5 million.
1. Would 2015 reported gross profit of $5.2 million be overstated, understated, or correct? What would be the correct amount of gross profit for 2015?
2. Will 2016's gross profit of $5.6 million be overstated, understated, or correct? What would be the correct amount of gross profit for 2016?

LEARNING OBJECTIVE ❶❸

Understand ethical implications of inventory actions

S5-11 Determine whether each of the following actions in buying, selling, and accounting for inventories is ethical or unethical. Give your reason for each answer.
1. In applying the lower-of-cost-and-net-realizable-value rule to inventories, Terre Haute Industries recorded an excessively low net realizable value for ending inventory. This allowed the company to pay less income tax for the year.
2. Laminated Photo Film purchased lots of inventory shortly before year-end to increase the weighted-average cost of goods sold and decrease reported income for the year.
3. Madison Inc. delayed the purchase of inventory until after December 31, 2017, to keep 2017's cost of goods sold from growing too large. The delay in purchasing inventory helped net income in 2017 to reach the level of profit demanded by the company's investors.
4. Dover Sales Company deliberately overstated ending inventory in order to report higher profits (net income).
5. Roberto Corporation deliberately overstated purchases to produce a high figure for cost of goods sold (low amount of net income). The real reason was to decrease the company's income tax payments to the government.

LEARNING OBJECTIVE ❶

Record inventory transactions in the periodic system

S5-12 Capital Technologies Inc. began 2017 with inventory of $20,000. During the year, Capital purchased inventory costing $100,000 and sold goods for $140,000, with all transactions on account. Capital ended the year with inventory of $30,000. Journalize all the necessary transactions under the periodic inventory system.

S5-13   Use the data in exercise S5-12 to do the following for Capital Technologies Inc.:

1. Post to the Inventory and Cost of Goods Sold accounts.
2. Compute cost of goods sold using the example given in Exhibit 5-4, Panel B.
3. Prepare the December 2017 income statement of Capital Technologies Inc. through gross profit.

LEARNING OBJECTIVE ❶

Compute cost of goods sold and prepare the income statement—periodic system

EXERCISES

E5-14 Accounting records for Red Deer Tire Ltd. yield the following data for the year ended December 31, 2017 (amounts in thousands):

LEARNING OBJECTIVE ❶❷

Account for inventory transactions—perpetual system

Inventory, December 31, 2016	$ 550
Purchases of inventory (on account)..	1,200
Sales of inventory—80% on account; 20% for cash (cost $900)	2,000
Inventory at FIFO cost, December 31, 2017...	850

Requirements

1. Journalize Red Deer Tire's inventory transactions for the year under (a) the perpetual system and (b) the periodic system. Show all amounts in thousands. Use Exhibit 5-4 as a model, on page 237.
2. What differences do you notice in the journal entries between the perpetual system and the periodic system?
3. Report ending inventory, sales, cost of goods sold, and gross profit on the appropriate financial statement (amounts in thousands), assuming the perpetual inventory system is used.

E5-15 Langley Inc. inventory records for a particular development program show the following at October 31, 2017:

LEARNING OBJECTIVE ❶❷

Analyze inventory transactions—perpetual system

Oct.	1	Beginning inventory	5 units @	$150 =	$ 750
	15	Purchase..................................	11 units @	160 =	1,760
	26	Purchase..................................	5 units @	170 =	850

At October 31, 10 of these programs are on hand. Langley uses the perpetual inventory system.

Requirements

1. Journalize for Langley:
   a. Total October purchases in one summary entry. All purchases were on credit.
   b. Total October sales and cost of goods sold in two summary entries. The selling price was $500 per unit, and all sales were on credit. Langley uses the FIFO inventory method.
2. Under FIFO, how much gross profit would Langley earn on these transactions? What is the FIFO cost of Langley's ending inventory?

E5-16 Use the data for Langley Inc. in exercise E5-15 to answer the following.

LEARNING OBJECTIVE ❷

Determine ending inventory and cost of goods sold by three methods—perpetual system

Requirements

1. Compute cost of goods sold and ending inventory, using each of the following methods:
   a. Specific unit cost, with two $150 units, three $160 units, and five $170 units still on hand at the end
   b. Weighted-average cost
   c. First-in, first-out cost
2. Which method produces the highest cost of goods sold? Which method produces the lowest cost of goods sold? What causes the difference in cost of goods sold?

LEARNING OBJECTIVE ❷

Compute the tax advantage of weighted-average cost over FIFO

E5-17 Use the data in exercise E5-15 to illustrate Langley's income tax advantage from using weighted-average cost over FIFO cost. Sales revenue is $6,000, operating expenses are $1,100, and the income tax rate is 25%. How much in taxes would Langley save by using the weighted-average-cost method versus FIFO?

LEARNING OBJECTIVE ❶❷

Determine ending inventory and cost of goods sold—FIFO versus weighted-average cost–perpetual system

E5-18 MusicBiz.net Ltd. specializes in sound equipment. Because each inventory item is expensive, MusicBiz uses a perpetual inventory system. Company records indicate the following data for a line of speakers:

Date	Item	Quantity	Unit Cost	Sale Price
June 1	Balance	6	$ 95	
8	Sale	3		$155
10	Purchase	11	100	
30	Sale	5		160

Requirements

1. Determine the amounts that MusicBiz should report for cost of goods sold and ending inventory in the following two ways:
   a. FIFO
   b. Weighted-average cost
2. MusicBiz uses the FIFO method. Prepare MusicBiz's income statement for the month ended June 30, 2017, reporting gross profit. Operating expenses totalled $319, and the income tax rate was 25%.
3. Music Biz is thinking of changing inventory costing methods from FIFO to weighted-average cost. Are they allowed to make this change? Briefly explain.

LEARNING OBJECTIVE ❶❷

Measure gross profit—FIFO versus weighted-average cost, falling prices–periodic system

E5-19 Suppose a Johnson store in Ottawa, Ontario, ended November 2017 with 800,000 units of merchandise that cost an average of $8 each. Suppose the store then sold 600,000 units for $5.0 million during December. Further, assume the store made two large purchases during December as follows:

December 6	100,000 units	@ $7	=	$ 700,000
26	400,000 units	@ 6	=	2,400,000

1. At December 31, the store manager needs to know the store's gross profit under both FIFO and weighted-average cost. Supply this information. Johnson uses the periodic inventory system.
2. What caused the FIFO and weighted-average cost gross profit figures to differ?

LEARNING OBJECTIVE ❷

Manage income taxes under the weighted-average-cost method

E5-20 Deitrick Guitar Company is nearing the end of its worst year ever. With three weeks until year-end, it appears that net income for the year will have decreased by 20% from the previous year. Jim Deitrick, the president and principal shareholder, is distressed with the year's results.

Deitrick asks you, the financial vice-president, to come up with a way to increase the business's net income. Inventory quantities are a little higher than normal because sales have been slow during the last few months. Deitrick uses the weighted-average-cost inventory method, and inventory costs have risen dramatically during the latter part of the year.

Requirement

Write a memorandum to Jim Deitrick to explain how the company can increase its net income for the year. Explain your reasoning in detail. Deitrick is a man of integrity, so your plan must be completely ethical.

LEARNING OBJECTIVE ❶❷❸

Identify effects of the inventory methods and evaluate operations

E5-21 This exercise tests your understanding of accounting for inventory. Provide a word or phrase that best fits the description. Assume that the cost of inventory is rising.

_____ 1. Generally associated with saving income taxes.

_____ 2. Results in a cost of ending inventory that is close to the current cost of replacing the inventory.

_____ **3.** Used to account for automobiles, jewellery, and art objects.

_____ **4.** Maximizes reported income.

_____ **5.** Inventory system that keeps a running record of all goods bought, sold, and on hand.

_____ **6.** Characteristic that enables investors to compare a company's financial statements from one period to the next.

_____ **7.** Writes inventory down when net realizable value drops below historical cost.

_____ **8.** Key indicator of a company's ability to sell inventory at a profit.

_____ **9.** A decrease in the buyer's cost of inventory earned by paying quickly.

E5-22 Tavistock Inc. uses a perpetual inventory system. Tavistock has these account balances at December 31, 2017, prior to making the year-end adjustments:

LEARNING OBJECTIVE ❸

Apply the lower-of-cost-and-net-realizable-value rule to inventories

Inventory		Cost of Goods Sold		Sales Revenue	
Beg. bal. 12,400					
End bal. 14,000		Bal. 78,000		Bal. 125,000	

A year ago, the net realizable value of Tavistock's ending inventory was $13,000, which exceeded cost of $12,400. Tavistock has determined that the net realizable value of the December 31, 2017, ending inventory is $12,000.

Requirement

Prepare Tavistock Inc.'s 2017 income statement through gross profit to show how the company would apply the lower-of-cost-and-net-realizable-value rule to its inventories.

E5-23 Supply the missing income statement amounts for each of the following companies (amounts in millions, at January 31, 2017):

LEARNING OBJECTIVE ❶

Determine amounts for the income statement

Company	Net Sales	Beginning Inventory	Purchases	Ending Inventory	Cost of Goods Sold	Gross Profit
Myers Confectionary	$543	$29	$470	$24	(a)	(b)
Canada Computers	74	7	(c)	8	(d)	19
Best Taste Beverages	(e)	(f)	16	2	16	19
Value for $	31	2	24	(g)	23	(h)

Prepare the income statement for Myers Confectionary Ltd., in millions of dollars, for the year ended January 31, 2017. Compute cost of goods sold using the example given in Exhibit 5-4, Panel B. Myers's operating and other expenses for the year were $204. Ignore income tax.

Note: Exercise E5-24 builds on exercise E5-23 with a profitability analysis of these actual companies.

E5-24 Refer to the data in Exercise E5-23. Compute all ratio values to answer the following questions:

LEARNING OBJECTIVE ❹

Measure profitability

- Which company has the highest gross profit percentage? Which company has the lowest?
- Which company has the highest rate of inventory turnover? Which company has the lowest?

Based on your figures, which company appears to be the most profitable?

E5-25 Suppose a company you are considering as an investment made sales of $54.8 billion in the year ended December 31, 2017. Collections from customers totalled $55 billion. The company began the year with $6.6 billion in inventories and ended with $7.9 billion. During the year, purchases of inventory added up to $39.8 billion. Of the purchases, the company paid $37.9 billion to suppliers.

LEARNING OBJECTIVE ❶❹

Measure gross profit and report cash flows

As an investor searching for a good investment, you would identify several critical pieces of information about the company's operations during the year.

Compute the company's gross profit, gross profit percentage, and rate of inventory turnover during 2017. Use the cost-of-goods-sold example as shown in Exhibit 5-4, Panel B as needed. Would the information help you make your investment decision?

LEARNING OBJECTIVE ⑤

Correct an inventory error

E5-26 Dijon Mustard Ltée. reported the following comparative income statement for the years ended September 30, 2016 and 2017:

	A	B	C	D	E	F
1	**Dijon Mustard Ltée.** Income Statement For the Years Ended September 30					
2			2017		2016	
3	Sales revenue		$ 194,000		$ 158,000	
4	Cost of goods sold					
5	Beginning inventory	$ 23,000		$ 16,000		
6	Purchases	97,000		86,000		
7	Goods available for sale	120,000		102,000		
8	Ending inventory	(21,000)		(23,000)		
9	Cost of goods sold		99,000		79,000	
10	Gross profit		95,000		79,000	
11	Operating expenses		20,000		20,000	
12	Net income		$ 75,000		$ 59,000	
13						

Dijon's shareholders are thrilled by the company's boost in sales and net income during 2017. Then they discover that the 2016 ending inventory was understated by $10,000. How well did Dijon really perform in 2017, as compared with 2016?

LEARNING OBJECTIVE ①②

Compute amounts for the inventory methods—periodic system

E5-27 Suppose a technology company's inventory records for a particular computer chip indicate the following at October 31:

Oct. 1	Beginning inventory	5 units @ $160 =	$ 800
8	Purchase	4 units @ 160 =	640
15	Purchase	11 units @ 170 =	1,870
26	Purchase	5 units @ 180 =	900

The physical count of inventory at October 31 indicates that 8 units of inventory are on hand.

Requirements

Compute ending inventory and cost of goods sold using each of the following methods, using the periodic inventory system. Round all amounts to the nearest dollar.

1. Specific unit cost, assuming four $160 units and four $170 units are on hand
2. Weighted-average cost
3. First-in, first-out cost

LEARNING OBJECTIVE ①②

Journalize inventory transactions in the periodic system; compute cost of goods sold

E5-28 Use the data in exercise E5-27 to journalize the following for the periodic system:

1. Total October purchases in one summary entry. All purchases were on credit.
2. Total October sales in a summary entry. Assume that the selling price was $300 per unit and that all sales were on credit.
3. October 31 entries for inventory. The company uses weighted-average cost. Post to the Cost of Goods Sold T-account to show how this amount is determined. Label each item in the account.
4. Show the computation of cost of goods sold using the example given in Exhibit 5-4, Panel B.

E5-29 Assume a Roots outlet store began August 2017 with 40 units of inventory that cost $30 each. The sale price of these units was $60. During August, the store completed the following inventory transactions.

		Units	Unit Cost	Unit Sale Price
Aug. 3	Sale	16	$30	$60
8	Purchase	70	31	62
11	Sale	24	30	60
19	Sale	8	31	62
24	Sale	30	31	62
30	Purchase	28	32	73
31	Sale	15	31	62

Requirements

1. Determine the store's cost of goods sold for August under the periodic inventory system. Assume the FIFO method.
2. Compute gross profit for August.
3. Last year, gross profit was $3,150. What could management do to improve gross profit?

E5-30 Accounting records for Cookies for You Ltd. yield the following data for the year ended December 31, 2017 (amounts in thousands):

Inventory, December 31, 2016	$ 410
Purchases of inventory (on account)	3,200
Sales of inventory—80% on account; 20% for cash	4,830
Inventory at the lower of FIFO cost and net realizable value, December 31, 2017	600

Requirements

1. Journalize Cookies for You's inventory transactions for the year under the periodic system. Show all amounts in thousands.
2. Report ending inventory, sales, cost of goods sold, and gross profit on the appropriate financial statement (amounts in thousands). Show the computation of cost of goods sold.

E5-31 On April 3, Parker Company sold $5,000 of merchandise to Wheeler Corporation, terms 2/10, n/30, FOB shipping point. Parker Company's cost of sales for this merchandise was $4,000. The merchandise left Parker Company's facility on April 4 and arrived at Wheeler Corporation on April 10. Wheeler Corporation paid the invoice for the merchandise on April 11.

Requirements

1. Prepare the journal entries for Parker Company for the sale of the merchandise, the cost of the sale, and the related receipt of payment from Wheeler Corporation. Assume that Wheeler Corporation takes the discount if payment is within the discount period. (You do not need to record any estimated returns/refunds for this exercise.)
2. Indicate which company (Parker Company or Wheeler Corporation) owns the merchandise at the end of each of the following dates:
   a. April 3
   b. April 4
   c. April 10

CHALLENGE EXERCISES

LEARNING OBJECTIVE ❷

Make inventory policy decisions

E5-32 For each of the following situations, identify the inventory method that you would use or, given the use of a particular method, state the strategy that you would follow to accomplish your goal:

a. Inventory costs are increasing. Your company uses weighted-average cost and is having an unexpectedly good year. It is near year-end, and you need to keep net income from increasing too much in order to save on income tax.

b. Suppliers of your inventory are threatening a labour strike, and it may be difficult for your company to obtain inventory. This situation could increase your income taxes.

c. Inventory costs are decreasing, and your company's board of directors wants to minimize income taxes.

d. Inventory costs are increasing, and the company prefers to report high income.

e. Inventory costs have been stable for several years, and you expect costs to remain stable for the indefinite future. (Give the reason for your choice of method.)

LEARNING OBJECTIVE ❶❷

Understand inventory methods

E5-33 Suppose Holt Renfrew, the specialty retailer, had these records for ladies' evening gowns during 2017.

Beginning inventory (30 @ $1,000)	$ 30,000
Purchase in February (25 @ $1,100)	27,500
Purchase in June (60 @ $1,200)	72,000
Purchase in December (25 @ $1,300)	32,500
Goods available	$162,000

Assume sales of evening gowns totalled 130 units during 2017 and that Holt uses the weighted-average-cost method under the periodic inventory system to account for inventory. The income tax rate is 30%.

Requirements

1. Compute Holt's cost of goods sold for evening gowns in 2017.
2. Compute what cost of goods sold would have been if Holt had purchased enough inventory in December—at $1,300 per evening gown—to keep year-end inventory at the same level it was at the beginning of the year, 30 units.

LEARNING OBJECTIVE ❹

Evaluate a company's profitability

E5-34 Cheri's Beauty Products Ltd. reported the figures below at December 31, 2017, 2016 and 2015. The business has declared bankruptcy. You have been asked to review the business and explain why it failed.

	A	B	C	D	E
1	**Cheri's Beauty Products Ltd.** Statement of Income For the Years Ended December 31, 2017, 2016, and 2015				
2	*(Thousands)*	**2017**	**2016**	**2015**	
3	Sales	$ 41.0	$ 39.5	$ 37.1	
4	Cost of sales	32.7	30.9	28.9	
5	Selling expenses	8.0	7.2	6.8	
6	Other expenses	0.4	1.0	0.8	
7	Net income (net loss)	$ (0.1)	$ 0.4	$ 0.6	
8	Additional data:				
9	Ending inventory	9.2	8.6	7.7	
10					

Requirement

Evaluate the trend of Cheri's Beauty Products's results of operations during 2015 through 2017. Consider the trends of sales, gross profit, and net income. Track the gross profit percentage (to three decimal places) and the rate of inventory turnover (to one decimal place) in each year—2015, 2016, and 2017. Also, discuss the role that selling expenses must have played in Cheri's Beauty Products's difficulties.

PROBLEMS (GROUP A)

P5-35A Assume a Watercrest Sports outlet store began October 2016 with 47 pairs of water skis that cost the store $38 each. The sale price of these water skis was $67. During October, the store completed these inventory transactions:

LEARNING OBJECTIVE ❷

Apply various inventory costing methods

		Units	Unit Cost	Unit Sale Price
Oct. 2	Sale	19	$38	$67
9	Purchase	83	40	
13	Sale	28	38	67
18	Sale	10	40	68
22	Sale	34	40	68
29	Purchase	24	42	

Requirements

1. The preceding data are taken from the store's perpetual inventory records. Which cost method does the store use? Explain how you arrived at your answer.
2. Determine the store's cost of goods sold for October. Also compute gross profit for October.
3. What is the cost of the store's October 31 inventory of water skis?

P5-36A Best Buy purchases merchandise inventory by the crate; each crate of inventory is a unit. The fiscal year of Best Buy ends each February 28.

Assume you are dealing with a single Best Buy store in Toronto, Ontario, and that the store experienced the following: The store began fiscal year 2017 with an inventory of 20,000 units that cost a total of $1,000,000. During the year, the store purchased merchandise on account as follows:

LEARNING OBJECTIVE ❶❷

Account for inventory in a perpetual system

April (30,000 units @ cost of $60)	$1,800,000
August (50,000 units @ cost of $64)	3,200,000
November (60,000 units @ cost of $70)	4,200,000
Total purchases	$9,200,000

Cash payments on account totalled $8,800,000.

During fiscal year 2017, the store sold 150,000 units of merchandise for $14,400,000. Cash accounted for $5,000,000 of this, and the balance was on account. Best Buy uses the FIFO method for inventories.

Operating expenses for the year were $4,000,000. The store paid 80% in cash and accrued the rest as accrued liabilities. The store accrued income tax at the rate of 33%.

Requirements

1. Make summary journal entries to record the store's transactions for the year ended February 28, 2017. Best Buy uses a perpetual inventory system.
2. Prepare a T-account to show the activity in the Inventory account.
3. Prepare the store's income statement for the year ended February 28, 2017. Show totals for gross profit, income before tax, and net income.

LEARNING OBJECTIVE ❶❷

Measure cost of goods sold and ending inventory—perpetual system

P5-37A Assume an outlet of The Runner's Store began August 2017 with 40 pairs of running shoes that cost the store $40 each. The sale price of these shoes was $70. During August, the store completed these inventory transactions:

			Units	Unit Cost	Unit Sale Price
Aug.	3	Sale	16		$70
	8	Purchase	80	41	
	11	Sale	24		70
	19	Sale	9		72
	24	Sale	30		72
	30	Purchase	18	42	

Requirement

1. Determine the store's cost of goods sold, gross profit, and ending inventory using (a) FIFO and (b) weighted-average assuming the perpetual system is used.
2. How would your answer change under (a) FIFO and (b) weighted-average cost if the periodic system was used?
3. How do you determine which inventory system to use: perpetual or periodic?

LEARNING OBJECTIVE ❶❷

Compute inventory by two methods—perpetual system

P5-38A Army-Navy Surplus Ltd. began March 2017 with 70 tents that cost $20 each. During the month, Army-Navy Surplus made the following purchases at cost:

March	4	100 tents	@ $22	=	$2,200
	19	160 tents	@ 24	=	3,840
	25	40 tents	@ 25	=	1,000

Army-Navy Surplus sold 320 tents (150 tents on March 22 and 170 tents on March 30), and at March 31 the ending inventory consists of 50 tents. The sale price of each tent was $45.

Requirements

1. Determine the cost of goods sold and ending inventory amounts for March under (a) weighted-average cost and (b) FIFO cost assuming the perpetual system is used. Round weighted-average cost per unit to four decimal places, and round all other amounts to the nearest dollar.
2. Explain why cost of goods sold is highest under weighted-average cost. Be specific.
3. Prepare Army-Navy Surplus's income statement for March 2017. Report gross profit. Operating expenses totalled $4,000. Army-Navy Surplus uses weighted-average costing for inventory. The income tax rate is 21%.

LEARNING OBJECTIVE ❶❷

Apply the different inventory costing methods—periodic system

P5-39A The records of Armstrong Aviation Supply Inc. include the following accounts for inventory of aviation fuel at December 31, 2017:

Inventory

Jan.	1	Balance	700 units @ $7.00	4,900
Mar.	6	Purchase	300 units @ 7.05	2,115
June	22	Purchase	8,400 units @ 7.50	63,000
Oct.	4	Purchase	500 units @ 8.50	4,250

Sales Revenue

Dec. 31	9,000 units	127,800

Requirements

1. Prepare a partial income statement through gross profit under the weighted-average-cost and FIFO methods assuming the periodic system is used. Round weighted-average cost per unit to four decimal places and all other amounts to the nearest dollar.

2. Which inventory method would you use to minimize income tax? Explain why this method causes income tax to be the lowest.

P5-40A AMC Trade Mart has recently had lacklustre sales. The rate of inventory turnover has dropped, and the merchandise is gathering dust. At the same time, competition has forced AMC's suppliers to lower the prices that AMC will pay when it replaces its inventory. It is now December 31, 2017, and the current net realizable value of AMC's ending inventory is $80,000 below what AMC actually paid for the goods, which was $190,000. Before any adjustments at the end of the period, the Cost of Goods Sold account has a balance of $780,000.

LEARNING OBJECTIVE ❸

Apply the lower-cost-and-net-realizable-value rule to inventories—perpetual system

What accounting action should AMC take in this situation? Give any journal entry required. At what amount should AMC report Inventory on the balance sheet? At what amount should the company report Cost of Goods Sold on the income statement? Discuss the accounting characteristic that is most relevant to this situation.

Are there circumstances that would allow AMC to increase the value of its inventory? Are there limits to which the value of the inventory may be increased?

P5-41A Chocolate Treats Ltd. and Coffee Bars Inc. are both specialty food chains. The two companies reported these figures, in thousands:

LEARNING OBJECTIVE ❹

Use gross profit percentage and inventory turnover to evaluate two companies

	A	B	C	D
1	**Chocolate Treats Ltd.** Statement of Operations			
2		Fiscal Year		
3	*(Thousands)*	2017	2016	
4	**Revenues:**			
5	Net sales	$ 543	$ 708	
6	Costs and Expenses:			
7	Cost of goods sold	475	598	
8	General and administrative expenses	68	55	
9				

	A	B	C	D
1	**Chocolate Treats Ltd.** Balance Sheet			
2		January 31,		
3	*(Thousands)*	2017	2016	
4	**Assets**			
5	Current assets:			
6	Cash and cash equivalents	$ 17	$ 28	
7	Receivables	27	30	
8	Inventories	24	29	
9				

	A	B	C	D
1	**Coffee Bars Inc.** Statement of Earnings			
2		Fiscal Year		
3	*(Thousands)*	2017	2016	
4	**Net sales**	$ 7,787	$ 6,369	
5	Cost of goods sold	3,179	2,605	
6	Selling, general, and administrative expenses	2,948	2,363	
7				

	A	B	C	D
1	**Coffee Bars Inc.** Balance Sheet			
2			Year End	
3	*(Thousands)*	2017	2016	
4	**Assets**			
5	Current assets:			
6	Cash and temporary investments	$ 313	$ 174	
7	Receivables, net	224	191	
8	Inventories	636	546	
9				

Requirements

1. Compute the gross profit percentage and the rate of inventory turnover for Chocolate Treats and for Coffee Bars for 2017.
2. Based on these statistics, which company looks more profitable? Why? What other expense category should we consider in evaluating these two companies?

LEARNING OBJECTIVE ⑤

Correct inventory errors over a three-year period

P5-42A Columbia Video Sales Ltd. reported the following data. The shareholders are very happy with Columbia's steady increase in net income.

Auditors discovered that the ending inventory for 2015 was understated by $1 million and that the ending inventory for 2016 was also understated by $1 million. The ending inventory for 2017 was correct.

	A	B	C	D	E	F	G	H
1	**Columbia Video Sales Ltd.** Income Statements for the Years Ended							
2	*(Amounts in millions)*		2017		2016		2015	
3	Net sales revenue		$ 36		$ 33		$ 30	
4	Cost of goods sold:							
5	Beginning inventory	$ 6		$ 5		$ 4		
6	Purchases	26		24		22		
7	Goods available for sale	32		29		26		
8	Less: Ending inventory	(7)		(6)		(5)		
9	Cost of goods sold		25		23		21	
10	Gross profit		11		10		9	
11	Total operating expenses		8		8		8	
12	Net income		$ 3		$ 2		$ 1	
13								

Requirements

1. Show corrected income statements for each of the three years.
2. How much did these assumed corrections add to or take away from Columbia's total net income over the three-year period? How did the corrections affect the trend of net income?
3. Will Columbia's shareholders still be happy with the company's trend of net income? Give the reason for your answer.

LEARNING OBJECTIVES ②③

Apply GAAP for sales, sales discount, and sales returns

E5-43A Chic Interiors reported the following transactions in November:

Nov.	2	Sold merchandise on account to Ella Barron, $1,300, terms 1/10, n/30.
	10	Sold merchandise on account to Amanda O'Connor, $2,500, terms 2/10, n/30.
	11	Collected payment from Ella Barron for the November 2 sale.
	15	O'Connor returned $1,700 of the merchandise purchased on November 10.
	19	Collected payment from Amanda O'Connor for the balance of the November 10 sale.

Requirements

1. Record the foregoing transactions in the journal of Chic Interiors. (Ignore cost of goods sold.)
2. Prepare a computation of net sales for the month of November.

PROBLEMS (GROUP B)

P5-44B Assume a Cross Country Sports outlet store began March 2016 with 49 pairs of running shoes that cost the store $35 each. The sale price of these shoes was $70. During March, the store completed these inventory transactions:

LEARNING OBJECTIVES ❷

Apply various inventory costing methods

		Units	Unit Cost	Unit Sale Price
Mar. 2	Sale	17	$35	$70
9	Purchase...	83	37	
13	Sale	32	35	70
18	Sale	12	37	71
22	Sale	34	37	71
29	Purchase...	18	39	

Requirements

1. The preceding data are taken from the store's perpetual inventory records. Which cost method does the store use? Explain how you arrived at your answer.
2. Determine the store's cost of goods sold for March. Also compute gross profit for March.
3. What is the cost of the store's March 31 inventory of running shoes?

P5-45B Italian Leather Goods Inc. began 2017 with an inventory of 50,000 units that cost $1,500,000. During the year, the store purchased merchandise on account as follows:

LEARNING OBJECTIVE ❶❷

Account for inventory in a perpetual system

March (40,000 units @ cost of $32)	$1,280,000
August (40,000 units @ cost of $34)	1,360,000
October (180,000 units @ cost of $35)...	6,300,000
Total purchases...	$8,940,000

Cash payments on account totalled $8,610,000.

During 2017, the company sold 260,000 units of merchandise for $12,900,000. Cash accounted for $4,700,000 of this, and the balance was on account. Italian Leather Goods uses the FIFO method for inventories.

Operating expenses for the year were $2,080,000. Italian Leather Goods paid 60% in cash and accrued the rest as accrued liabilities. The company accrued income tax at the rate of 32%.

Requirements

1. Make summary journal entries to record the Italian Leather Goods transactions for the year ended December 31, 2017. The company uses a perpetual inventory system.
2. Prepare a T-account to show the activity in the Inventory account.
3. Prepare the Italian Leather Goods Inc. income statement for the year ended December 31, 2017. Show totals for gross profit, income before tax, and net income.

P5-46B Whitewater Sports Ltd. began July 2017 with 50 backpacks that cost $19 each. The sale price of each backpack was $36. During July, Whitewater completed these inventory transactions:

LEARNING OBJECTIVE ❶❷

Measure cost of goods sold and ending inventory—perpetual system

		Units	Unit Cost	Unit Sale Price
July 2	Purchase..	12	$20	
8	Sale	37		$36
13	Sale	13		36
	Sale	4		37
17	Purchase..	24	20	
22	Sale	15		37

Requirement

1. Determine the store's cost of goods sold, gross profit, and ending inventory using (a) FIFO and (b) weighted-average assuming the perpetual system is used.
2. How would your answer change under (a) FIFO and (b) weighted-average cost if the periodic system was used?
3. How do you determine which inventory system to use: perpetual or periodic?

LEARNING OBJECTIVE ❶❷

Compute inventory by two methods—perpetual system

P5-47B Spice Inc. began October 2017 with 100 shirts that cost $76 each. During October, the store made the following purchases at cost:

Oct. 3		200 @	$81	=	$16,200
12		90 @	82	=	7,380
24		240 @	85	=	20,400

Spice sold 500 shirts (320 shirts on October 18 and 180 shirts on October 28) and ended October with 130 shirts. The sale price of each shirt was $130.

Requirements

1. Determine the cost of goods sold and ending inventory amounts by the weighted-average-cost and FIFO cost methods assuming the perpetual system is used. Round weighted-average cost per unit to three decimal places, and round all other amounts to the nearest dollar.
2. Explain why cost of goods sold is highest under weighted-average cost. Be specific.
3. Prepare Spice's income statement for October 2017. Report gross profit. Operating expenses totalled $10,000. Spice uses the weighted-average-cost method for inventory. The income tax rate is 23%.

LEARNING OBJECTIVE ❶❷

Apply the different inventory costing methods—periodic system

P5-48B The records of Sonic Sound Systems Inc. include the following for cases of CDs at December 31, 2017:

Inventory

Jan. 1 Balance	300 cases @ $300	121,500	
	100 cases @ 315		
May 19 Purchase	600 cases @ 335	201,000	
Aug. 12 Purchase	400 cases @ 350	140,000	
Oct. 4 Purchase	700 cases @ 370	259,000	

Sales Revenue

	Dec. 31	1,800 cases	910,000

Requirements

1. Prepare a partial income statement through gross profit under the weighted-average-cost and FIFO cost methods assuming the periodic system is used. Round weighted-average cost per unit to four decimal places and all other amounts to the nearest dollar.
2. Which inventory method would you use to report the highest net income? Explain why this method produces the highest reported income.

P5-49B Westside Copiers Ltd. has recently been plagued with lacklustre sales. The rate of inventory turnover has dropped, and some of the company's merchandise is gathering dust. At the same time, competition has forced some of Westside's suppliers to lower the prices that Westside will pay when it replaces its inventory. It is now December 31, 2017. The current net realizable value of Westside's ending inventory is $6,800,000, which is far less than the amount Westside paid for the goods, $8,900,000. Before any adjustments at the end of the period, Westside's Cost of Goods Sold account has a balance of $36,400,000.

What accounting action should Westside Copiers take in this situation? Give any journal entry required. At what amount should Westside report Inventory on the balance sheet? At what amount should Westside report Cost of Goods Sold on the income statement? Discuss the accounting characteristic that is most relevant to this situation.

Are there circumstances that would allow Westside Copiers to increase the value of its inventory? Are there limits to which the value of inventory may be increased?

P5-50B Trans Canada Motors Ltd. and X Country Trucks Inc. are competitors. The companies reported the following amounts, in millions. In January 2017, you wish to make an investment in one of these companies. Results for 2016 are not yet available.

LEARNING OBJECTIVE ❸

Apply the lower-of-cost-and-net-realizable-value rule to inventories—perpetual system

LEARNING OBJECTIVE ❹

Use gross profit percentage and inventory turnover to evaluate two leading companies

	A	B	C	D	E
1	**Trans Canada Motors Ltd.** Statement of Earnings				
2			Fiscal Years		
3	*(Amounts in millions)*	2015	2014	2013	
4	Net sales	$ 84.2	$ 73.6	$ 68.9	
5	Cost of sales	63.4	55.2	52.6	
6	Selling, general, and administrative expenses	12.2	11.3	11.2	
7					

	A	B	C	D	E
1	**Trans Canada Motors Ltd.** Balance Sheet				
2			Year-End		
3	*(Amounts in millions)*	2015	2014	2013	
4	Assets				
5	Cash and cash equivalents	$ 11.3	$ 16.4	$ 13.9	
6	Accounts receivable	13.4	10.9	9.9	
7	Inventories	8.0	7.8	6.9	
8					

	A	B	C	D	E
1	**X Country Trucks Inc.** Statement of Operations				
2			Fiscal Years		
3	*(Amounts in millions)*	2015	2014	2013	
4	Net sales	$ 24.0	$ 19.3	$ 13.9	
5	Cost of sales	15.9	13.7	9.9	
6	Selling, general, and administrative expenses	3.0	2.4	1.9	
7					

	A	B	C	D	E
1	**X Country Trucks Inc.** Balance Sheet				
2			Year-End		
3	*(Amounts in millions)*	2015	2014	2013	
4	Assets				
5	Cash and cash equivalents	$ 9.4	$ 6.4	$ 3.5	
6	Accounts receivable	6.0	1.3	0.9	
7	Inventories	0.4	0.3	0.2	
8					

Requirements

1. Compute both companies' gross profit percentage and their rates of inventory turnover during 2015 and 2014.
2. Can you tell from these statistics which company should be more profitable in percentage terms? Why? What other important category of expenses do the gross profit percentage and the inventory turnover ratio fail to consider?

LEARNING OBJECTIVE ⑤

Correct inventory errors over a three-year period

P5-51B The accounting records of Oriental Rugs show these data (in thousands).

As the auditor, you discovered that the ending inventory for 2015 was overstated by $100,000 and that the ending inventory for 2016 was understated by $50,000. The ending inventory at December 31, 2017, was correct.

	A	B	C	D	E	F	G	H
1	**Oriental Rugs** Income Statements for the Years Ended							
2	(*Amounts in thousands*)		2017		2016		2015	
3	Net sales revenue		$ 1,400		$ 1,200		$ 1,100	
4	Cost of goods sold:							
5	Beginning inventory	$ 400		$ 300		$ 200		
6	Purchases	800		700		600		
7	Goods available for sale	1,200		1,000		800		
8	Less ending inventory	(500)		(400)		(300)		
9	Cost of goods sold		700		600		500	
10	Gross profit		700		600		600	
11	Total operating expenses		500		430		450	
12	Net income		$ 200		$ 170		$ 150	
13								

Requirements

1. Show correct income statements for each of the three years.
2. How much did these corrections add to, or take away from, Oriental Rugs's total net income over the three-year period? How did the corrections affect the trend of net income?

LEARNING OBJECTIVES ①

Apply GAAP for sales, sales discount, and sales returns

P5-52B Wolford Interiors reported the following transactions in November:

Nov.	2	Sold merchandise on account to Maxine Holder, $1,000, terms 2/10, n/30.
	10	Sold merchandise on account to Alexis Pinney, $2,600, terms 3/10, n/30.
	11	Collected payment from Maxine Holder for November 2 sale.
	15	Pinney returned $1,500 of the merchandise purchased on November 10.
	19	Collected payment from Alexis Pinney for the balance of the November 10 sale.

Requirements

1. Record the foregoing transactions in the journal of Wolford Interiors. (Ignore cost of goods sold.)
2. Prepare a computation of net sales for the month of November.

APPLY YOUR KNOWLEDGE

DECISION CASES

Case 1. Duracraft Corporation is nearing the end of its first year of operations. Duracraft made inventory purchases of $926,000 during the year, as follows:

January	1,500 units	@	$120.00	=	$180,000
July	3,000		142.00		426,000
November	2,000		160.00		320,000
Totals	6,500				$926,000

Sales for the year are 6,000 units for $1,800,000 of revenue. Expenses other than cost of goods sold and income taxes total $425,000. The president of the company is undecided about whether to adopt the FIFO method or the weighted-average-cost method for inventories. The company uses the periodic inventory system. The income tax rate is 30%.

Requirements

1. To aid company decision making, prepare income statements under FIFO and under weighted-average cost.

2. Compare the net income under FIFO with net income under weighted-average cost. Which method produces the higher net income? What causes this difference? Be specific.

Case 2. The inventory costing method a company chooses can affect the financial statements and, thus, the decisions of the people who use those statements.

Requirements

1. Company A uses the weighted-average-cost inventory method and discloses this in notes to the financial statements. Company B uses the FIFO method to account for its inventory, but does not disclose which inventory method it uses. Company B reports a higher net income than Company A. In which company would you prefer to invest? Give your reason. Assume rising inventory costs.

2. The lower-of-cost-and-net-realizable-value rule is an accepted accounting concept. Would you want management to follow this rule in accounting for inventory if you were a shareholder or a creditor of a company? Give your reason.

3. Super Sports Company follows the lower-of-cost-and-net-realizable-value rule (LCNRV) and writes the value of its inventory of tents down to net realizable value, which has declined below cost. The following year, an unexpected camping craze results in a demand for tents that far exceeds supply, and the net realizable value increases above the previous cost. What effect will the LCNRV rule have on the income of Super Sports over the two years?

This section's material reflects CPA enabling competencies,* including:

1. Professionalism and ethical behaviour

2. Problem-solving and decision-making

3. Communication

4. Self-management

5. Teamwork and leadership

LEARNING OBJECTIVE ❶❷

Assess the impact of a year-end purchase of inventory—periodic system

LEARNING OBJECTIVE ❷❸

Assess the impact of the inventory costing method on the financial statements

ETHICAL ISSUES

During 2016, Vanguard Inc. changed to the weighted-average-cost method of accounting for inventory. Suppose that during 2017, Vanguard changes back to the FIFO method, and the following year Vanguard switches back to weighted-average cost again.

Requirements

1. What would you think of a company's ethics if it changed accounting methods every year?

2. What accounting characteristic would changing methods every year violate?

3. Who can be harmed when a company changes its accounting methods too often? How?

FOCUS ON FINANCIALS

Canadian Tire Corporation

The notes are part of the financial statements. They give details that would clutter the statements. This case will help you learn to use a company's inventory notes. Refer to Canadian Tire's statements and related notes in Appendix A at the end of the book and answer the following questions:

1. How much was Canadian Tire's inventory at January 3, 2015? What about at December 28, 2013?
2. How does Canadian Tire value its inventories? Which cost method does the company use?
3. Using the cost-of-goods-sold as shown in Exhibit 5-4, Panel B, compute Canadian Tire's purchase of inventory during the year ended January 3, 2015.
4. Did Canadian Tire's gross profit percentage and rate of inventory turnover improve or deteriorate in 2014 (versus 2013)? Ending inventory for 2012 was $1,503.3. Considering the overall effect of these two ratios, did Canadian Tire improve during 2014? How did these factors affect the net income for 2014? (Hint: Canadian Tire refers to COGS as "Cost of producing revenue.")

FOCUS ON ANALYSIS

Canadian Tire Corporation

Refer to Canadian Tire's financial statements in Appendix A at the end of the book to answer the following questions. Show amounts in millions.

1. Three important pieces of inventory information are (a) the cost of inventory on hand, (b) the cost of goods sold, and (c) the cost of inventory purchases. Identify or compute each of these items for Canadian Tire at January 3, 2015. (Hint: Canadian Tire refers to COGS as "Cost of producing revenue.")
2. Which item in Requirement 1 is most directly related to cash flow? Why?
3. Assume that all inventory purchases were made on account, and that only inventory purchases increased Accounts Payable. Compute Canadian Tire's cash payment for inventory during 2014. (Hint: Canadian Tire refers to Accounts Payable as "Trade and other payables.")

GROUP PROJECT

Obtain the annual reports of 10 companies, two from each of five different industries. Most companies' financial statements can be downloaded from their websites.

1. Compute each company's gross profit percentage and rate of inventory turnover for the most recent two years. If annual reports are unavailable or do not provide enough data for multiple-year computations, you can gather financial statement data from the System for Electronic Document Analysis and Retrieval (SEDAR).
2. For the industries of the companies you are analyzing, obtain the industry averages for gross profit percentage and inventory turnover.
3. How well does each of your companies compare to the other company in its industry? How well do your companies compare to the average for their industry? What insight about your companies can you glean from these ratios?
4. Write a memo to summarize your findings, stating whether your group would invest in each of the companies it has analyzed.

CHECK YOUR WORK

STOP + THINK ANSWERS

STOP + THINK (5-1)
The periodic inventory system would work best in this situation because of all of the small items available for sale. It would be almost impossible to keep track of inventory using the perpetual inventory system.

STOP + THINK (5-2)
a. Cost of goods sold = (25 units × $5) + (25 units × $6) = $275

b. Ending inventory = 5 units × $6 = 30

STOP + THINK (5-3)
Investors must always consider differences in methods of companies, but as long as the companies maintain a consistent method of accounting for inventory, and an investor understands the implications to cost of goods sold and inventory when prices are rising/falling, they should be able to compare and analyze different companies.

STOP + THINK (5-4)
It's obvious that both Leon's and Pier 1 sell higher-end merchandise. Leon's and Pier 1's gross profits are almost the same, and both have a much higher gross profit than Walmart. At the same time, Leon's turnover rate is higher than Pier 1 but lower than Walmart. Generally, the lower the price, the faster the turnover, and the higher the price, the slower the turnover.

STOP + THINK (5-5)
The overstatement of ending inventory in the accounting records would cause (a) Cost of goods sold to be understated, (b) Net income to be overstated, and (c) Shareholders' equity to be overstated.

QUICK QUIZ ANSWERS

1. b ($3,500 + $6,000 − $5,500 = $4,000)

2. b ($7,200 − $5,500 = $1,700)

3. d

4. d (1,000 @ $10.60 + 500 @ $10 = $15,600)

5. c $\dfrac{(\$20,000 + \$10,600)}{2,000 + 1,000} \times 1,500$
   = $10.20 × 1,500 = $15,300

6. a

7. c ($144,000 + $216,000 = $360,000)

8. b

9. a

10. d [$620,000 − ($60,000 + $400,000 − $40,000) = $200,000]

11. a ($20,000 + X − $15,000 = $90,000; X = $85,000)

12. d

13. d [$300,000 ÷ ($25,000 + $35,000) / 2] = 10 times

14. c

   Net sales = $480,000 ($490,000 − $10,000)
   COGS = $50,000 + ($205,000 + $20,000 − $4,000 − $6,000) − $40,000
   = $225,000
   GP% = ($480,000 − $225,000) / $480,000
   = 0.531 = 53.1%

15. d

16. c

17. c

6

Property, Plant, and Equipment, and Intangible Assets

David Cooper/ZUMA Press/Newscom

SPOTLIGHT

Have you ever gone to Canadian Tire to fill your car with gas? Canadian Tire has been in business for many years. As the name suggests, they began operations by selling tires. Over the years, they expanded their business by offering financial services, clothing, hardware, and gas bars.

Included in Canadian Tire's total assets are property and equipment as well as goodwill and intangible assets. A partial balance sheet along with the accompanying notes are presented on the following page. The company owns over $3,743 million of property as of January 3, 2015. Notice that over the estimated useful lives of these assets, the company has built up accumulated depreciation of about $2,529 million (Note 16) indicating that the assets are almost half used up as of that date ($2,529 million/$6,272 million). The carrying amount of Canadian Tire's property and equipment is $3,743.1 million (Note 16). The company also owns about $1,251 million (Note 14) in goodwill and other intangible assets. When you complete this chapter, you will understand better what these terms and concepts are.

	A	B	C	D
1	**Canadian Tire** Partial Balance Sheet (adapted) Long-Lived Assets			
2	*($ in millions)*	As at Jan. 3, 2015	As at Dec. 28, 2013	
3	**Non-Current Assets**			
4	Long-term receivables and other assets	$ 684.2	$ 686.0	
5	Long-term investments	176.0	134.7	
6	Goodwill and intangible assets (Note 14)	1,251.7	1,185.5	
7	Investment property	148.6	93.5	
8	Property and equipment (Note 16)	3,743.1	3,516.1	
9	Deferred income taxes	39.4	36.4	
10				

Note 14—Goodwill and Intangible Assets:

Cost	$ 2,043.2
Less: Accumulated amortization and impairment	(791.5)
Carrying amount	$ 1,251.7

Note 16—Property and Equipment:

Cost	$ 6,272.5
Less: Accumulated depreciation	(2,529.4)
Carrying amount	$ 3,743.1

Source: Reprinted with permission from Canadian Tire Corporation.

Businesses use several types of assets that are classified as long-lived, such as property, plant, and equipment, and intangible assets. These assets are used in the business and are not held for sale.

Tangible long-lived assets are also called property, plant, and equipment. For example, buildings, airplanes, and equipment are tangible long-lived assets that do not last forever. Therefore, the cost of these assets must be expensed over their useful lives, and the expense associated with this is called depreciation. Of these assets, land is unique. Land is not expensed over time because its usefulness does not decrease. Many companies report tangible long-lived assets as property, plant, and equipment on the balance sheet. Canadian Tire calls them property and equipment. Looking at the partial balance sheet above, Canadian Tire owns $3,743.1 (million) in property and equipment. To find out what is included under this category, you need to read the notes that accompany the financial statements. These notes are used to explain the numbers reported. Reading Canadian Tire's Note 16 found in their annual report reveals that these assets include land, buildings, fixtures, equipment, and leasehold improvements.

Intangible assets are useful because of the special rights they carry. They have no physical form. Patents, copyrights, and trademarks are intangible assets, as is goodwill. Accounting for intangibles, except goodwill, is similar to accounting for tangible long-lived assets. Canadian Tire has several intangible assets on its balance sheet, including goodwill. Reading Note 14 found in their annual report indicates that Canadian Tire's intangible assets include items such as their store banners, trademarks, and franchise agreements.

Not all companies have both types of assets. For example, U-Haul, a subsidiary of Amerco, is a moving and storage company that owns land, buildings, equipment, rental trucks, and trailers, but does not own any intangible assets.

Accounting for long-lived tangible assets and intangibles has its own terminology. Different names apply to the individual assets and their corresponding expense accounts, as shown in Exhibit 6-1.

EXHIBIT 6-1
Long-Lived Asset and Related
Expense Accounts

Asset Account (Balance Sheet)	Related Expense Account (Income Statement)
Tangible Long-Lived Assets	
Land	None
Buildings, machinery, and equipment	Depreciation
Furniture and fixtures	Depreciation
Computers	Depreciation
Intangible Assets	
Copyrights	Amortization
Patents	Amortization
Goodwill	Impairment losses

OBJECTIVE

❶ Measure and account for the cost of property, plant, and equipment

MEASURE AND ACCOUNT FOR THE COST OF PROPERTY, PLANT, AND EQUIPMENT

Here is a basic working rule for determining the cost of an asset:

The cost of any asset is the sum of all the costs incurred to bring the asset to its location and intended use. The cost of property, plant, and equipment includes its purchase price plus any taxes, commissions, and other amounts paid to make the asset ready for use. Because the specific costs differ for the various categories of property, plant, and equipment, we discuss the major groups individually.

Land

The cost of land includes its purchase price, real estate commission, survey fees, legal fees, and any back property taxes that the purchaser pays. Land cost also includes expenditures for grading and clearing the land and demolishing or removing unwanted buildings.

The cost of land does *not* include the cost of fencing, paving, sprinkler systems, and lighting. These are recorded in a separate account—called *land improvements*—and they are subject to depreciation.

Suppose Canadian Tire signs a $300,000 note payable to purchase 20 hectares of land for a new retail store. Canadian Tire also pays $10,000 for real estate commission, $8,000 of back taxes, $5,000 for removal of an old building, a $1,000 survey fee, and $260,000 to pave the parking lot—all in cash. What is Canadian Tire's cost of this land?

Purchase price of land		$300,000
Add related costs:		
Real estate commission	$10,000	
Back property tax	8,000	
Removal of building	5,000	
Survey fee	1,000	
Total related costs		24,000
Total cost of land		$324,000

Note that the cost to pave the parking lot, $260,000, is *not* included in the land's cost, because the pavement is a land improvement and wears out over time. Canadian Tire would record the purchase of this land as follows:

	A	B	C	D	E
1		Land	324,000		
2		Note Payable		300,000	
3		Cash		24,000	
4		*To record the purchase of land.*			
5					

ASSETS	=	LIABILITIES	+	SHAREHOLDERS' EQUITY
+324,000	=	+300,000	+	0
−24,000				

The purchase increases both assets and liabilities. There is no effect on equity.

Buildings, Machinery, and Equipment

The cost of constructing a building includes architectural fees, building permits, contractors' charges, and payments for material, labour, and overhead. The company may also include as cost the interest on money borrowed to construct a building or buy machinery and equipment for the building until the point in time when the building, machinery, and equipment are ready for their intended use.

When an existing building (new or old) is purchased, its cost includes the purchase price, brokerage commission, sales and other taxes paid, and all expenditures to repair and renovate the building for its intended purpose.

The cost of machinery and equipment includes its purchase price plus transportation, insurance while in transit, non-refundable sales and other taxes, purchase commission, installation costs, and any expenditures to test the asset before it is placed in service. The equipment cost will also include the cost of any special platforms used to support the equipment. After the asset is up and running, insurance, taxes, and maintenance costs are recorded as expenses, not as part of the asset's cost.

Land Improvements and Leasehold Improvements

For the Canadian Tire building, the cost to pave a parking lot ($260,000) would be recorded in a separate account titled Land Improvements. This account includes costs for other items such as driveways, signs, fences, and sprinkler systems. Although these assets are located on the land, they are subject to decay, and their cost should therefore be depreciated.

An airline such as WestJet leases some of its airplanes and other assets. The company customizes these assets to meet its special needs. For example, WestJet paints its logo on airplanes. These improvements are assets of WestJet Airlines Ltd., even though the company does not own the airplane. The cost of improvements to leased assets may appear under Property, Plant, and Equipment, or Other Long-Term Assets. The cost of leasehold improvements should be depreciated over the term of the lease or the life of the asset, whichever is shorter.

Lump-Sum (or Basket) Purchases of Assets

Businesses often purchase several assets as a group, or in a "basket," for a single lump-sum amount. For example, Great-West Lifeco Inc. may pay one price for land and a building. The company must identify the cost of each asset. The total cost is divided among the assets according to their relative fair values.

Suppose Great-West purchases land and a building in St. John's, Newfoundland, for a sales office. The building sits on two hectares of land, and the combined purchase price of land and building is $2,800,000. An appraisal indicates that the land's fair value is $300,000 and that the building's fair value is $2,700,000.

Great-West first calculates the ratio of each asset's fair value to the total fair value. Total appraised value is $2,700,000 + $300,000 = $3,000,000. Thus, the land, valued at $300,000, is 10% of the total fair value. The building's appraised value is 90% of the total. These percentages are then used to determine the cost of each asset, as follows:

Asset	Fair Value		Total Fair Value		Percentage of Total Fair Value		Total Cost		Cost of Each Asset
Land	$ 300,000	÷	$3,000,000	=	10%	×	$2,800,000	=	$ 280,000
Building	2,700,000	÷	3,000,000	=	90	×	2,800,000	=	2,520,000
Total	$3,000,000				100%				$2,800,000

If Great-West pays cash, the entry to record the purchase of the land and building is:

	A	B	C	D	E
1		Land	280,000		
2		Building	2,520,000		
3		Cash		2,800,000	
4					

ASSETS	=	LIABILITIES	+	SHAREHOLDERS' EQUITY
+ 280,000				
+2,520,000	=	0	+	0
−2,800,000				

Total assets don't change—merely the makeup of Great-West's assets.

Capital Expenditure Versus an Immediate Expense

When a company spends money on property, plant, and equipment, it must decide whether to record an asset or an expense. Examples of these expenditures range from WestJet Airlines's purchase of a flight simulator from CAE Electronics to replacing a tire on a plane.

Expenditures that increase the asset's productivity or extend its useful life are called **capital expenditures** (also called *betterments*). For example, the cost of a major overhaul that extends the useful life of a Canadian Tire truck is a capital expenditure. Capital expenditures are said to be *capitalized,* which means the cost is added to an asset account and not expensed immediately. A major decision in accounting for property, plant, and equipment is whether to capitalize or expense a certain cost.

Costs that do not extend the asset's productivity or its useful life, but merely maintain the asset or restore it to working order, are considered repairs and are recorded as expenses. The costs of repainting a Canadian Tire truck, repairing a dented fender, and replacing tires are also expensed immediately. Exhibit 6-2 illustrates the distinction between capital expenditures and immediate expenses for van expenditures.

Record an Asset for Capital Expenditures/Betterments	Record Repair and Maintenance Expense for an Expense
Extraordinary repairs:	*Ordinary repairs:*
Major engine overhaul	Repair of transmission or other mechanism
Modification of body for new use of van	Oil change, lubrication, and so on
Addition to storage capacity of van	Replacement tires, windshield, or a paint job

EXHIBIT 6-2
Capital Expenditure or Immediate Expense for Costs Associated With a Van

The distinction between a capital expenditure and an expense requires judgment: Does the expenditure extend the asset's productivity or its useful life? If so, capitalize it. If the cost merely repairs or maintains the asset or returns it to its prior condition, then record an expense.

Most companies expense all small costs, say, below $1,000. For higher costs, they follow the rule we gave above: they capitalize costs that extend the asset's usefulness or its useful life, and they expense all other costs. A conservative policy is one that avoids overstating assets and profits. A company that overstates its assets may get into trouble and have to defend itself in court. Whenever investors lose money because a company overstated its profits or its assets, the investors might file a lawsuit. The courts tend to be sympathetic to investor losses caused by shoddy accounting.

Accounting misstatements sometimes occur for asset costs. For example, a company may:

- Expense a cost that should have been capitalized. This error overstates expenses and understates net income in the year of the error.

- Capitalize a cost that should have been expensed. This error understates expenses and overstates net income in the year of the error.

STOP + THINK (6-1)

Why are land improvements and leasehold improvements depreciated?

MEASURE AND RECORD DEPRECIATION ON PROPERTY, PLANT, AND EQUIPMENT

OBJECTIVE

❷ Measure and record depreciation on property, plant, and equipment

As we've seen in previous chapters, property, plant, and equipment are reported on the balance sheet at carrying amount, which is:

$$\text{Carrying amount of property, plant, and equipment} = \text{Cost} - \text{Accumulated depreciation}$$

Property, plant, and equipment wears out, grows obsolete, and loses value over time. To account for this process, we allocate an asset's cost to expense over its life—a process called **depreciation**. The depreciation process begins when an asset is available for use and continues until the asset is removed. It follows the expense recognition principle discussed in Chapter 3. Depreciation apportions the cost of using property, plant, and equipment over time by allocating a portion of that cost against the revenue the asset helps earn each period. Recall that depreciation expense (not accumulated depreciation) is reported on the income statement. In the private enterprise sector, it is referred to as amortization.

Only land has an unlimited life and is not depreciated for accounting purposes. For most property, plant, and equipment, depreciation is caused by one of the following:

- **Physical wear and tear**. For example, physical deterioration takes its toll on the usefulness of WestJet's airplanes, vehicles, and buildings.

- **Obsolescence**. Computers and other electronic equipment may be *obsolete* before they deteriorate. An asset is obsolete when another asset can do the job more efficiently. An asset's useful life may be shorter than its physical life. WestJet and other companies depreciate their computers over a short period of time—perhaps four years—even though the computers will remain in working condition much longer.

Suppose WestJet buys a computer for use in scheduling flight crews. WestJet believes it will get four years of service from the computer, which will then be worthless. Under straight-line depreciation, WestJet expenses one-quarter of the asset's cost in each of its four years of use.

You've just seen what depreciation accounting is. Let's see what it is *not*.

1. **Depreciation is not a process of valuation.** Businesses do not record depreciation based on changes in the fair value of their property, plant, and equipment. Instead, businesses allocate the asset's cost to the periods of its useful life based on a specific depreciation method.

2. **Depreciation does not mean setting aside cash to replace assets as they wear out.** Any cash fund is entirely separate from depreciation.

How to Measure Depreciation

To measure depreciation for property, plant, and equipment, we must know its:

1. Cost
2. Estimated useful life
3. Estimated residual value

We have already discussed cost, which is a known amount. The other two factors must be estimated.

Estimated useful life is the length of service expected from using the asset. Useful life may be expressed in years, units of output, kilometres, or some other measure. For example, the useful life of a building is stated in years. The useful life of a WestJet airplane or van may be expressed as the total number of kilometres the aircraft or vehicle is expected to travel. Companies base such estimates on past experience and information from industry and government publications.

Estimated residual value—also called *scrap value* or *salvage value*—is the expected cash value of an asset at the end of its useful life. For example, WestJet may believe that a baggage-handling machine will be useful for seven years. After that time, WestJet may expect to sell the machine as scrap metal. The amount WestJet believes it can get for the machine is the estimated residual value. In computing depreciation, the asset's estimated residual value is *not* depreciated because WestJet expects to receive this amount from selling the asset. If there's no expected residual value, the full cost of the asset is depreciated. An asset's **depreciable cost** is measured as follows:

Depreciable cost = Asset's cost − Estimated residual value

Depreciation Methods

There are three main depreciation methods that will be discussed in this text:

- Straight-line
- Units-of-production
- Diminishing-balance—an accelerated depreciation method

These methods allocate different amounts of depreciation to each period. However, they all result in the same total amount of depreciation, which is the asset's depreciable cost. Exhibit 6-3 presents assumed data, which we will use to illustrate depreciation computations for a Canadian Tire van.

Data Item	Amount
Cost of van, January 1, 2016	$41,000
Less estimated residual value	(1,000)
Depreciable cost	$40,000
Estimated useful life:	
Years	5 years
Units of production	100,000 units [kilometres]

EXHIBIT 6-3
Data for Depreciation Computations—A Canadian Tire Van

STRAIGHT-LINE METHOD. In the **straight-line (SL) method**, an equal amount of depreciation is assigned to each year (or period) of asset use. Depreciable cost is divided by useful life in years to determine the annual depreciation expense. Applied to the Canadian Tire van data from Exhibit 6-3, straight-line depreciation is:

$$\text{Straight} - \text{line depreciation per year} = \frac{\text{Cost} - \text{Residual value}}{\text{Useful life, in years}}$$

$$= \frac{\$41,000 - \$1,000}{5}$$

$$= \$8,000$$

The entry to record depreciation is:

	A	B	C	D	E
1		Depreciation Expense	8,000		
2		Accumulated Depreciation		8,000	
3					

ASSETS	=	LIABILITIES	+	SHAREHOLDERS' EQUITY
−8,000	=	0		−8,000 Expenses

Observe that depreciation decreases the asset (through Accumulated Depreciation) and also decreases equity (through Depreciation Expense). Let's assume that Canadian Tire purchased this van on January 1, 2016; Canadian Tire's fiscal year ends on

EXHIBIT 6-4
Straight-Line Depreciation Schedule for a Canadian Tire Van

	A	B	C	D	E	F	G
1	Date	Asset Cost	Depreciation Rate	Depreciable Cost	Depreciation Expense	Accumulated Depreciation	Asset Carrying Amount
2	01-01-2016	$ 41,000					$ 41,000
3	31-12-2016		0.20*	$ 40,000	$ 8,000	$ 8,000	33,000
4	31-12-2017		0.20	40,000	8,000	16,000	25,000
5	31-12-2018		0.20	40,000	8,000	24,000	17,000
6	31-12-2019		0.20	40,000	8,000	32,000	9,000
7	31-12-2020		0.20	40,000	8,000	40,000	1,000
8							

$* \dfrac{1}{5 \text{ Years}} = 0.20 \text{ per year}$

December 31. Exhibit 6-4 gives a *straight-line depreciation schedule* for the van. The final column of the exhibit shows the *asset's carrying amount*, which is its cost less accumulated depreciation.

As an asset is used in operations, accumulated depreciation increases, and the carrying amount of the asset decreases. An asset's final carrying amount is its *residual value* ($1,000 in Exhibit 6-4). At the end of its useful life, the asset is said to be *fully depreciated*.

TRY IT *in* EXCEL® ▶ ▶ ▶

Building depreciation schedules such as the one in Exhibit 6-4 is easy with Excel. Use the information in Exhibit 6-3, the exhibit on the preceding page, and the formula on page 285 to help you program the cells. To construct Exhibit 6-4 depreciation schedule in Excel:

1. Open a new workbook. In cells A1 through G1, insert column headings to correspond to those of Exhibit 6-4, the preceding exhibit. You will have to adjust the column width of your spreadsheet to accommodate the headings.
2. In cells B2 and G2 (asset cost and carrying amount), type in the original gross cost (41,000). The remainder of the cells in column B should be blank.
3. In cell A2, type in the original purchase date (1/1/2016). In cells A3 through A7, type in the year-end dates of 12/31/2016 through 12/31/2020, respectively. Change the formatting of these cells to "date."
4. In cells C3 through C7, enter the depreciation rate for each year, which is the reciprocal of the asset's useful life (1/5, or 20%). Enter .2 in cell C3 and copy this value down through cell C7.
5. In cell D2, calculate the depreciable cost of $40,000. Enter =B2 − 1000. Copy this value down through cell D7.
6. In cell E3, enter the formula =C3*D3. The value $8,000 should appear. Copy this formula to cells E4 through E7.
7. Column F keeps a running sum of accumulated depreciation. Start with cell F3. Enter the formula =F2+E3. $8,000 (accumulated depreciation at the end of year 1) should appear. Copy cell F3 down to cells F4 through F7. You should get the same values as you see in Exhibit 6-4.
8. Column G keeps a running calculation of the declining net book value of the asset. Start with cell G3. Freeze the value of the original cost of the asset ($41,000) in cell G2 by entering "$" before both the column and row. Then subtract the value of accumulated depreciation (cell F3). The formula in cell G3 becomes =$G$2 − F3. The result should be $33,000 ($41,000 − $8,000). Copy cell G3 down through cell G7.

UNITS-OF-PRODUCTION METHOD. In the **units-of-production (UOP) method**, a fixed amount of depreciation is assigned to each *unit of output*, or service, produced by the asset. Depreciable cost is divided by useful life—in units of production—to determine this amount. This per-unit depreciation expense is then multiplied by the number of units produced each period to compute depreciation. The units-of-production depreciation for the Canadian Tire van data in Exhibit 6-3 is:

$$\frac{\text{Units-of-production}}{\text{depreciation per unit of output}} = \frac{\text{Cost} - \text{Residual value}}{\text{Useful life, in units of production}}$$

$$= \frac{\$41,000 - - \$1,000}{100,000 \text{ km}} = \$0.40/\text{km}$$

Assume that the van is driven 20,000 km during the first year, 30,000 during the second, 25,000 during the third, 15,000 during the fourth, and 10,000 during the fifth. Exhibit 6-5 shows the UOP depreciation schedule.

The amount of UOP depreciation varies with the number of units the asset produces. In our example, the total number of units produced is 100,000. UOP depreciation does not depend directly on time, as do the other methods.

EXHIBIT 6-5
Units-of-Production Depreciation Schedule for a Canadian Tire Van

	A	B	C	D	E	F	G
1	Date	Asset Cost	Depreciation Rate	Number of Units	Depreciation Expense	Accumulated Depreciation	Asset Carrying Amount
2	01-01-2016	$ 41,000					$ 41,000
3	31-12-2016		$ 0.40*	20,000	$ 8,000	$ 8,000	33,000
4	31-12-2017		0.40	30,000	12,000	20,000	21,000
5	31-12-2018		0.40	25,000	10,000	30,000	11,000
6	31-12-2019		0.40	15,000	6,000	36,000	5,000
7	31-12-2020		0.40	10,000	4,000	40,000	1,000
8							

*($41,000 – $1,000)/100,000 km = $0.40/km.

TRY IT *in* EXCEL® ▶ ▶ ▶

If you built the straight-line depreciation schedule in Exhibit 6-4 with Excel, changing the spreadsheet for units-of-production depreciation is a snap. Steps 1–3 and 6–8 are identical. Only steps 4 and 5, dealing with columns C and D, change. You might want to start by opening the straight-line schedule you prepared and saving it under another name: "units-of-production depreciation." Next, change the column headings for column C and column D. Column C should be labeled "Rate per unit." Column D should be labeled "Number Units." Assuming you do this, here are the modified steps 4 and 5 of the process we used before:

4. In column C, calculate a per-unit (rather than per-year as we did with straight-line) depreciation rate by dividing the depreciable cost ($41,000 − $1,000 in Exhibit 6-3) by the number of units (100,000 miles) to get a fixed depreciation rate per mile ($0.40). Enter .4 in cell C3 and copy down through cell C7.
5. In cells D3 through D7, respectively, enter the number of miles driven in years 1 through 5 of the asset's useful life. These are 20,000, 30,000, 25,000, 15,000, and 10,000, respectively.

    All of the other amounts in the table will automatically recalculate to reflect units-of-production depreciation, exactly as shown in Exhibit 6-5.

DIMINISHING-BALANCE METHOD. An **accelerated depreciation method** writes off a larger amount of the asset's cost near the start of its useful life than the straight-line method does. Double-diminishing-balance is the main accelerated depreciation method. The **double-diminishing-balance (DDB) method** computes annual depreciation by multiplying the asset's declining carrying amount by a constant percentage, which is two times the straight-line depreciation rate. Double-diminishing-balance amounts are computed as follows:

- *First*, compute the straight-line depreciation rate per year. A 5-year asset has a straight-line depreciation rate of 1/5, or 20% each year. A 10-year asset has a straight-line rate of 1/10, or 10%, and so on.

- *Second*, multiply the straight-line rate by 2 to compute the DDB rate. For a 5-year asset, the DDB rate is 40% (20% × 2). A 10-year asset has a DDB rate of 20% (10% × 2).

- *Third*, multiply the DDB rate by the period's beginning asset carrying amount (cost less accumulated depreciation). Under the DDB method, the residual value of the asset is ignored in computing depreciation, except during the final year. The DDB rate for the Canadian Tire van in Exhibit 6-3 (page 285) is:

$$\text{DDB depreciation rate per year} = \frac{1}{\text{Useful life, in years}} \times 2$$

$$= \frac{1}{5 \text{ years}} \times 2$$

$$= 20\% \times 2$$

$$= 40\%$$

- *Fourth*, determine the final year's depreciation amount by adjusting the depreciation expense so that the remaining carrying amount of the asset is equal to the residual value. In Exhibit 6-6, the fifth and final year's DDB depreciation is $4,314: the carrying amount of $5,314 less the $1,000 residual value. Notice how the carrying amount, $1,000, is now equal to the residual value, $1,000. *The residual value should not be depreciated* but should remain on the books until the asset is disposed of even if the asset is still being used.

EXHIBIT 6-6
Double-Diminishing-Balance Depreciation Schedule for a Canadian Tire Van

	A	B	C	D	E	F	G
1	Date	Asset Cost	DDB Rate	Asset Carrying Amount	Depreciation Expense	Accumulated Depreciation	Asset Carrying Amount
2	01-01-2016	$ 41,000					$ 41,000
3	31-12-2016		0.40	$ 41,000	$ 16,400	$ 16,400	24,600
4	31-12-2017		0.40	24,600	9,840	26,240	14,760
5	31-12-2018		0.40	14,760	5,904	32,144	8,856
6	31-12-2019		0.40	8,856	3,542	35,686	5,314
7	31-12-2020				4,314*	40,000	1,000
8							

*Last-year depreciation is the amount needed to reduce the asset's carrying amount to the residual value ($5,314 − $1,000 = $4,314).

The DDB method differs from the other methods in two ways:

1. Residual value is ignored when calculating depreciation expense; depreciation is computed on the asset's full cost.
2. Depreciation expense in the final year is whatever amount is needed to reduce the asset's carrying amount to its residual value.

TRY IT *in* EXCEL® ▶ ▶ ▶

If you built the straight-line and UOP depreciation schedules in Exhibits 6-4 and 6-5 with Excel, changing the spreadsheet for DDB depreciation is easy. Steps 1–3 and 7–8 are identical. The other steps differ only slightly. You might want to start by opening the straight-line schedule you prepared and saving it under another name: "DDB depreciation." Next, change the column heading for column C to "DDB Rate." Right-click on column D (labeled "depreciable cost" in Exhibit 6-4) and delete the entire column. This moves the "yearly expense" over to column D. Here are modified steps 4 and 5 of the process we used for the straight-line rate:

4. In column C, calculate a new depreciation rate, which is double the straight-line rate. In our example, the straight-line rate is 20% per year. The DDB rate is 40% (2 × 20%). Enter .4 in cell C3 and copy down through cell C7.
5. Column D now contains a calculated amount for yearly depreciation expense. The yearly depreciation expense is the product of the previous carrying amount of the asset (in column F) times the DDB rate (in column C). For 2016, depreciation expense is $16,400, which is calculated in Excel as =F2*C3. Enter this formula in cell D3. Your result should be $16,400. Copy this formula down through cell D6 (*not* cell D7, for reasons explained below).

All of the other amounts in the table through line 6 will automatically recalculate to reflect DDB depreciation, exactly as shown in Exhibit 6-6.

Comparing Depreciation Methods

Let's compare the three methods in terms of the yearly amount of depreciation. The yearly amount of depreciation varies by method, but the total $40,000 depreciable cost is the same under all methods.

	Amount of Depreciation Per Year		
Year	Straight-Line	Units-of-Production	Accelerated Method Double-Diminishing-Balance
1	$ 8,000	$ 8,000	$16,400
2	8,000	12,000	9,840
3	8,000	10,000	5,904
4	8,000	6,000	3,542
5	8,000	4,000	4,314
Total	$40,000	$40,000	$40,000

IFRS directs a business to choose a depreciation method that reflects the pattern in which the asset will be used. For an asset that generates revenue evenly over time, the straight-line method best meets this criterion. The units-of-production method best fits those assets that wear out because of physical use rather than obsolescence. The accelerated method (DDB) applies best to assets that generate greater amounts of revenue earlier in their useful lives and less in later years.

Exhibit 6-7 graphs annual depreciation amounts for the straight-line, units-of-production, and accelerated (DDB) methods. The graph of straight-line depreciation is flat through time because annual depreciation is the same in all periods. Units-of-production depreciation follows no particular pattern because annual depreciation depends on the use of the asset. Accelerated depreciation is greatest in the first year and less in the later years.

Recent surveys of companies in Canada and the United States indicate that straight-line depreciation is used by more than 80% of them. Around 10% of companies use some form of accelerated depreciation, and the rest use units of production and other methods. Many companies use more than one method.

EXHIBIT 6-7
Depreciation Patterns
Through Time

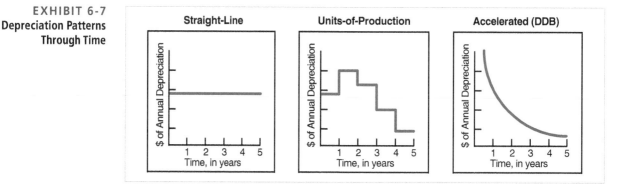

COOKING *the* BOOKS

through Depreciation

Waste Management

Since property, plant, and equipment usually involve relatively large amounts and relatively large number of assets, sometimes a seemingly subtle change in the way they are accounted for can have a tremendous impact on the financial statements. When these changes are made in order to cook the books, the results can be devastating.

Waste Management, Inc., is North America's largest integrated waste service company providing collection, transfer, recycling, disposal, and waste-to-energy services for commercial, industrial, municipal, and residential customers from coast to coast. Starting in 1992, six top executives decided that the company's profits weren't growing fast enough to meet "earnings targets," which were tied to their executive bonuses. Among several fraudulent financial tactics these top executives employed to cook the books were (1) assigning unsupported and inflated residual values to garbage trucks, (2) unjustifiably extending the estimated useful lives of their garbage trucks, and (3) assigning arbitrary residual values to other assets that previously had no residual value. All of these tactics had the effect of decreasing the amount of depreciation expense in the income statements resulting in an increase in net income of $1.7 billion. When the fraud was disclosed, Waste Management shareholders lost over $6 billion in the market value of their investments as the stock price plummeted by more than 33%. The company and these officers eventually settled civil lawsuits for approximately $700 million because of the fraud.

STOP + THINK (6-2)

Imagine a company purchased a machine for $13,000 that had a useful life of five years and residual value of $3,000. If the asset's carrying amount was $7,000, how many more years of use would the machine have assuming the company uses the straight-line method of depreciation?

MyAccountingLab

MID-CHAPTER SUMMARY PROBLEM

Suppose you are a manager at Canadian Tire. The company purchased equipment on January 1, 2015, for $44,000. The expected useful life of the equipment is 10 years or 100,000 units of production, and its residual value is $4,000. Under three depreciation methods, the annual depreciation expense and the balance of accumulated depreciation at the end of 2015 and 2016 are as follows:

	Method A		Method B		Method C	
Year	Annual Depreciation Expense	Accumulated Depreciation	Annual Depreciation Expense	Accumulated Depreciation	Annual Depreciation Expense	Accumulated Depreciation
2015	$4,000	$4,000	$8,800	$ 8,800	$1,200	$1,200
2016	4,000	8,000	7,040	15,840	5,600	6,800

Requirements

1. Your assistant has provided you with the above information. Identify the depreciation method used in each instance, and show the equation and computation for each. (Round to the nearest dollar.)
2. Assume continued use of the same method through the year 2017. Determine the annual depreciation expense, accumulated depreciation, and carrying amount of the equipment for 2015 through 2017 under each method, assuming 12,000 units of production in 2017.
3. How does a manager decide which method to use to depreciate their property, plant, and equipment?

> **Name:** Canadian Tire
> **Industry:** Retailer
> **Accounting Period:** The years 2015, 2016, 2017

ANSWERS

Requirement 1

Method A: Straight-Line

> The straight-line method assigns the same depreciation expense to each year.

Depreciable cost = $40,000 ($44,000 − $4,000)

Each year: $40,000/10 years = $4,000

Method B: Double-Diminishing-Balance

> The double-diminishing-balance method assigns an expense amount that gets smaller every year. Do not include the residual value when using this method.

$$\text{Rate} = \frac{1}{10 \text{ years}} \times 2 = 10\% \times 2 = 20\%$$

2015: 0.20 × $44,000 = $8,800

2016: 0.20 × ($44,000 − $8,800) = $7,040

Method C: Units-of-Production

With the units-of-production method, there is a direct correlation to the number of units produced.

Subtract the residual value from the original cost. Calculate the depreciation per unit. Then divide the annual depreciation expense by the unit cost to determine the number of units produced each year.

$$\text{Depreciation per unit} = \frac{\$44{,}000 - \$4{,}000}{100{,}000 \text{ units}} = \$0.40/\text{unit}$$

$$2015 : \$1{,}200 \div \$0.40 = 3{,}000 \text{ units}$$

$$2016 : \$5{,}600 \div \$0.40 = 14{,}000 \text{ units}$$

Requirement 2

Use the same $4,000 annual depreciation expense used for the prior years.

Method A: Straight-Line

Year	Annual Depreciation Expense	Accumulated Depreciation	Carrying Amount
Start			$44,000
2015	$4,000	$ 4,000	40,000
2016	4,000	8,000	36,000
2017	4,000	12,000	32,000

The depreciation expense is calculated as 20% of the prior year's carrying amount.

Method B: Double-Diminishing-Balance

Year	Annual Depreciation Expense	Accumulated Depreciation	Carrying Amount
Start			$44,000
2015	$8,800	$ 8,800	35,200
2016	7,040	15,840	28,160
2017	5,632	21,472	22,528

Use the same $0.40 per unit amount used for the prior years. Multiply by the number of units produced during 2017.

Method C: Units-of-Production

Year	Annual Depreciation Expense	Accumulated Depreciation	Carrying Amount
Start			$44,000
2015	$1,200	$ 1,200	42,800
2016	5,600	6,800	37,200
2017	4,800	11,600	32,400

Computations for 2017

Straight-line	$40,000/10 years = $4,000
Double-diminishing-balance	0.20 × $28,160 = $5,632
Units-of-production	$0.40 × 12,000 units = $4,800

Requirement 3

Managers choose the method that best reflects the way in which the asset is used up. For example, buildings normally wear out over time, so the straight-line depreciation method might be used. Equipment that produces units would wear out after continued use, so the units of production might be the best method. Diminishing balance might be used for computer equipment because of new technology advancements.

EXPLAIN ADDITIONAL TOPICS IN ACCOUNTING FOR LONG-LIVED TANGIBLE ASSETS

OBJECTIVE

❸ **Explain** additional topics in accounting for long-lived tangible assets

Depreciation for Partial Years

Companies purchase property, plant, and equipment whenever they need them. They do not wait until the beginning of a year or a month. Therefore, companies must compute *depreciation for partial years*. Suppose the County Line Bar-B-Q restaurant in Edmonton purchases a building on April 1 for $500,000. The building's estimated life is 20 years, and its estimated residual value is $80,000. The restaurant's fiscal year ends on December 31. Let's consider how the company computes depreciation for April through December:

- First compute depreciation for a full year.
- Then multiply the full year's depreciation by the fraction of the year that the company held the asset.

Assuming the straight-line method, the year's depreciation for County Line's building is $15,750, as follows:

$$\text{Full-year depreciation} = \frac{\$500,000 - \$80,000}{20} = \$21,000$$

$$\text{Partial-year depreciation: } \$21,000 \times 9/12 = \$15,750$$

What if County Line bought the asset on April 18? Many businesses record no monthly depreciation on assets purchased after the 15th of the month, and they record a full month's depreciation on an asset bought on or before the 15th.

Most companies use computerized systems to account for property, plant, and equipment. Each asset has a unique identification number that links to the asset's cost, estimated life, residual value, and depreciation method. The system will automatically calculate the depreciation expense for each period. Accumulated Depreciation is automatically updated.

Changing the Useful Life of a Depreciable Asset

Managers must decide on an asset's useful life to compute its depreciation. After an asset is put into use, managers may change its useful life on the basis of experience and new information. Such a change in accounting estimate is very rare in Canada.

An example from the United States is illustrative. Disney Enterprises, Inc., made such a change, called a *change in accounting estimate*, several years ago. The company recalculated depreciation on the basis of revised useful lives of several of its theme park assets. The following note in company's financial statements reported this change in accounting estimate:

Note 5
... [T]he Company extended the estimated useful lives of certain theme park ride and attraction assets based upon historical data and engineering studies. The effect of this change was to decrease [depreciation] by approximately $8 million (an increase in net income of approximately $4.2 million ...).

Source: From Disney Enterprises, Inc.'s Financial Statements, 2014.

Assume that a Disney hot-dog stand cost $40,000 and that the company origi-nally believed the asset had an eight-year useful life with no residual value. Using the straight-line method, the company would record $5,000 depreciation each year ($40,000/8 years = $5,000). Suppose Disney used the asset for two years. Accumulated depreciation reached $10,000, leaving a remaining depreciable carry-ing amount (cost *less* accumulated depreciation *less* residual value) of $30,000 ($40,000 − $10,000). From its experience, management believes the asset will remain useful for an additional four years. The company would spread the remaining depreciable carrying amount over the asset's remaining life as follows:

Asset's remaining depreciable carrying amount	÷	(New) Estimated useful life remaining	=	(New) Annual depreciation
$30,000	÷	10 years	=	$3,000

The yearly depreciation entry based on the new estimated useful life is:

	A	B	C	D	E
1		Depreciation Expense—Hot-Dog Stand	3,000		
2		Accumulated Depreciation—Hot-Dog Stand		3,000	
3					

ASSETS	=	LIABILITIES	+	SHAREHOLDERS' EQUITY
−3,000	=	0		−3,000 Expenses

Fully Depreciated Assets

A *fully depreciated asset* is an asset that has reached the end of its estimated useful life. Suppose Canadian Tire has fully depreciated equipment with zero residual value (cost was $40,000). Canadian Tire's accounts will appear as follows:

Equipment	−	Accumulated Depreciation	=	Carrying amount
40,000		40,000		$0

The equipment's carrying amount is zero, but that doesn't mean the equipment is worthless. Canadian Tire may continue using the equipment for a few more years but will not take any more depreciation.

When Canadian Tire disposes of the equipment, it will remove both the asset's cost ($40,000) and its accumulated depreciation ($40,000) from the books. The next section shows how to account for disposals of property, plant, and equipment.

Derecognition of Property, Plant, and Equipment

Derecognition is a term IFRS uses to refer to property, plant, and equipment that is either no longer useful or has been sold. When this occurs, the related accounts are removed from the company's books and a gain or loss is recorded.

Eventually, property, plant, and equipment cease to serve a company's needs. The asset may wear out, become obsolete, or for some other reason cease to be useful. Before accounting for the disposal of the asset, the business should bring deprecia-tion up to date to:

- Record the expense up to the date of sale
- Measure the asset's final carrying amount

To account for disposal, the asset and its related accumulated depreciation are removed from the books. Suppose the final year's depreciation expense has just been recorded to fully depreciate a machine that cost $50,000 and is estimated to have zero residual value. The machine's accumulated depreciation thus totals $50,000. Assuming that this asset is disposed of, not sold, the entry to record its disposal is:

	A	B	C	D	E
1		Accumulated Depreciation—Machinery	50,000		
2		Machinery		50,000	
3		*To dispose of a fully depreciated machine.*			
4					

ASSETS	=	LIABILITIES	+	SHAREHOLDERS' EQUITY
+50,000	=	0	+	0
−50,000				

There is no gain or loss on this disposal, so there is no effect on equity.

If assets are "junked" before being fully depreciated, the company incurs a loss on the disposal. Suppose M&M Meat Shops disposes of store fixtures that cost $4,000. Accumulated depreciation is $3,000, and the carrying amount is, therefore, $1,000. Junking these store fixtures results in a loss as follows:

	A	B	C	D	E
1		Accumulated Depreciation—Store Fixtures	3,000		
2		Loss on Disposal of Store Fixtures	1,000		
3		Store Fixtures		4,000	
4		*To dispose of store fixtures.*			
5					

ASSETS	=	LIABILITIES	+	SHAREHOLDERS' EQUITY
+3,000	=	0	+	−1,000 Loss
−4,000				

M&M Meat Shops got rid of an asset with a $1,000 carrying amount and received nothing. The result is a $1,000 loss, which decreases both total assets and equity.

The Loss on Disposal of Store Fixtures is reported as Other Income (Expense) on the income statement. Losses decrease net income exactly as expenses do. Gains increase net income in the same manner as revenues.

SELLING PROPERTY, PLANT, AND EQUIPMENT. Suppose M&M Meat Shops sells fixtures on September 30, 2017, that cost $10,000 when purchased on January 1, 2014, and have been depreciated on a straight-line basis. M&M Meat Shops originally estimated a 10-year useful life and no residual value. Prior to recording the sale, the M&M Meat Shops accountants must update the asset's depreciation. Suppose the business uses the calendar year as its accounting period. Partial-year depreciation must be recorded for the asset's expense from January 1, 2017, to the sale date. The straight-line depreciation entry at September 30, 2017, is:

	A	B	C	D	E
1	Sept. 30	Depreciation Expense ($10,000/10 years × 9/12)	750		
2		Accumulated Depreciation—Fixtures		750	
3		*To update depreciation.*			
4					

The Fixtures account and the Accumulated Depreciation—Fixtures account appear as follows. Observe that the fixtures' carrying amount is $6,250 ($10,000 − $3,750).

Fixtures			Accumulated Depreciation—Fixtures			
Jan. 1, 2014	10,000		Dec. 31, 2014	1,000		
			Dec. 31, 2015	1,000	=	Carrying amount
			Dec. 31, 2016	1,000		$6,250
			Sep. 30, 2017	750		
			Balance	3,750		

Suppose M&M Meat Shops sells the fixtures for $7,000 cash. The gain on the sale is $750, determined as follows:

Cash received from sale of the asset		$7,000
Carrying amount of asset sold:		
Cost	$10,000	
Less accumulated depreciation	(3,750)	6,250
Gain on sale of the asset		$ 750

The entry to record the sale of the fixtures for $7,000 cash is:

	A	B	C	D	E
1	Sept. 30	Cash	7,000		
2		Accumulated Depreciation—Fixtures	3,750		
3		Gain on Sale of Fixtures		750	
4		Fixtures		10,000	
5		*To sell fixtures.*			
6					

ASSETS	=	LIABILITIES	+	SHAREHOLDERS' EQUITY
+ 7,000				
+ 3,750	=	0		+ 750 Gain
− 10,000				

Gains are recorded as credits, in the same manner as revenues; losses are recorded as debits, in the same manner as expenses. Gains and losses on asset disposals appear on the income statement as Other income (expense) or Other gains (losses).

T-Accounts for Analyzing Property, Plant, and Equipment Transactions

You can perform quite a bit of analysis if you know how transactions affect the property, plant, and equipment accounts. The following are some of these accounts with descriptions of the activity in each.

Building (or Equipment)	
Beginning balance	
Cost of assets purchased	Cost of assets disposed of
Ending balance	

Accumulated Depreciation	
Accum. depreciation of assets disposed of	Beginning balance
	Depreciation expense for the current period
	Ending balance

Cash	
Cash proceeds for assets disposed of	Cash paid for assets purchased

Long-Term Debt	
	New debt incurred for assets purchased

Depreciation Expense	
Depreciation expense for the current period	

Gain on Sale of Building (or Equipment)	
	Gain on sale

Loss on Sale of Building (or Equipment)	
Loss on sale	

Example: Suppose you started the year with buildings that cost $100,000. During the year you bought another building for $150,000 and ended the year with buildings that cost $180,000. What was the cost of the building you sold?

Building		
Beginning balance	100,000	
Cost of assets purchased	150,000	Cost of assets sold ? = $70,000
Ending balance	180,000	

You can perform similar analyses to answer other interesting questions about what the business did during the period.

Special Issues in Accounting for Property, Plant, and Equipment

Long-lived assets such as property, plant, and equipment are complex because:

- Depreciation affects income taxes
- Significant components of property, plant, and equipment should be depreciated separately
- Assets should be tested regularly for impairment
- The revaluation method could be used to measure property, plant, and equipment assets

Depreciation for Tax Purposes

Many businesses use the straight-line method for reporting property, plant, and equipment on the balance sheet and depreciation expense on the income statement. However, for income tax purposes, they also keep a separate set of depreciation records. The *Income Tax Act* requires taxpayers to use accelerated and sometimes straight-line depreciation (up to specified capital cost allowance [CCA] maximums) for tax purposes. In other words, a taxpayer may use one method of depreciation for accounting purposes and another method for tax purposes.

Depreciating Significant Components

IFRS require that significant components of an item of property, plant, and equipment be depreciated separately. What does this mean? Take, for example, Air Canada or WestJet, which buy aircraft for use in their operations. Air Canada depreciates their aircraft and engines over 20–25 years, while the cabin and interior equipment are depreciated over the lesser of 5 years or the remaining useful life of the aircraft. Under ASPE, depreciating separate components is done only when practicable.

Impairment

At each reporting date, a company should review its property, plant, and equipment to see if an asset is impaired. Impairment occurs when the carrying amount exceeds its recoverable amount. Recoverable amount is determined to be the higher of an asset's fair value (less costs to sell) and its value in use. Value in use is the present value of estimated future cash flows expected to be earned from the continuing use of an asset and from its disposal at the end of its useful life.

Impairment may be caused by many factors, including obsolescence, physical damage, and loss in market value. For example, let's assume that FedEx has a long-term asset with the following information at year-end:

Carrying amount $100 million

Recoverable amount = higher of:

a. Value in use $60 million
b. Fair value $70 million

A two-stage impairment process is:

Step 1 Impairment test: Is Carrying amount > Recoverable amount? (Answer: Yes, so the asset is impaired)
Step 2 Impairment loss = Carrying amount − Higher of (a) Value in use and (b) Fair value
= $100 million − $70 million (higher of the two amounts)
= $30 million

The journal entry to record impairment is:

	A	B	C	D	E
1		Loss on Impairment	$30,000,000		
2		Accumulated Depreciation		$30,000,000	
3					

If the situation changes, IFRS do permit a company to reverse the impairment loss by writing the asset up to its carrying amount. The accounting standards for private enterprises require a company to review its property, plant, and equipment only when impairment is suspected. No reversal of the write-off is allowed.

In a note to its financial statements, Air Canada states that for its property, plant, and equipment,

> Assets that are subject to depreciation are reviewed for impairment whenever events or changes in circumstances indicate that the carrying amount may not be recoverable. An impairment test is performed by comparing the carrying amount of the asset or group of assets to their recoverable amount.

Revaluation Model

Throughout this chapter, we have shown you what IFRS refers to as the cost model. This means that a company measures property, plant, and equipment at cost less any accumulated depreciation less any accumulated impairment losses.

Another method a company could choose to measure property, plant, and equipment is called the revaluation model. Under this method, an asset would be recorded at cost when purchased but subsequently measured at its fair value less any accumulated depreciation less any accumulated impairment losses. It may be revalued at year-end or when the company believes a change in the asset value has taken place. With every new change in the asset account, depreciation has to be revised accordingly based on the new carrying amount. This topic is discussed in greater detail in an intermediate accounting course.

Example: A company chooses to use the revaluation method for a building that was bought for $1.8 million and is being depreciated over 25 years, with no residual value. Subsequently, if the appraised value is $2 million, the increase of $200,000 will be recognized through equity by the following journal entry:

	A	B	C	D	E
1		Building	200,000		
2		Revaluation surplus		200,000	
3					

Revaluation Surplus is an equity account that is reported as other comprehensive income. Only the cost model is used under ASPE.

STOP + THINK (6-3)

1. Suppose a company was having a bad year—net income was well below expectations and lower than last year's income. For depreciation purposes, the company extended the estimated useful lives of its depreciable assets. How would this accounting change affect the company's (a) depreciation expense, (b) net income, and (c) owners' equity?

2. Suppose that the company's accounting change turned a loss year into a profitable year. Without the accounting change, the company would have reported a net loss for the year. The accounting change enabled the company to report net income. Under IFRS, the company's annual report must disclose the accounting change and its effect on net income. Would investors evaluate the company as better or worse for having made this accounting change?

▶ DECISION GUIDELINES

USING PROPERTY, PLANT, AND EQUIPMENT AND RELATED EXPENSES IN DECISION MAKING

Companies must make decisions about how to account for property, plant, and equipment. Let's look at some ways property, plant, and equipment are used in decision making.

Decision	Guidelines
Capitalize or expense a cost?	*Managers*
(a) New asset	Capitalize all costs that bring the asset to its intended use, including asset purchase price, transportation charges, and taxes paid to acquire the asset.
(b) Existing asset	Capitalize only those costs that add to the asset's productivity or to its useful life.
	Expense all other costs as maintenance or repairs.
Which depreciation method to use?	*Managers*
	Use the method that best allocates the cost of an asset through depreciation expense against the revenues produced by the asset. As discussed earlier, each method will produce varying amounts of depreciation expense each year, but overall, they will result in the same total amount of depreciation. If the asset generates revenue evenly over time, the straight-line method is best; if it wears out through physical use, the units-of-production method should be used; if greater revenue is generated earlier in the asset's useful life, then diminishing-balance is the method to use.
	Investors and Creditors
	Both investors and creditors read the notes to the financial statements to see which depreciation methods management used. Why do they do this? As we have already seen, the depreciation method chosen affects both the income statement and the balance sheet. Remember, if management chooses to use the straight-line method, then depreciation expense will be the same amount each year. However, if the double-diminishing balance is used, then depreciation expense is highest in the early years of the asset's life, causing net income to be lower. This information is useful when comparing companies using different depreciation methods.

OBJECTIVE

❹ Account for intangible assets

ACCOUNT FOR INTANGIBLE ASSETS

As we saw earlier, *intangible assets* are long-lived assets with no physical form. Intangibles are valuable because they carry special rights from patents, copyrights, trademarks, franchises, and goodwill. Like buildings and equipment, an intangible asset is recorded at its acquisition cost. Intangibles are often the most valuable assets of high-tech companies and other companies that depend on research and development. The residual value of most intangibles is zero.

Intangible assets fall into two categories:

- Intangibles with *finite lives* that can be measured. We record **amortization** for these intangibles. Amortization works like depreciation and is usually computed on a straight-line basis, but one of the other methods could be used.
- Intangibles with *indefinite lives*. No amortization for these intangibles is recorded. Instead, check them annually for any loss in value (impairment), and record a loss when it occurs. Goodwill is the most prominent example of an intangible asset with an indefinite life.

The table below summarizes these categories:

	Goodwill	Indefinite life intangible	Definite life intangible
Amortized?	No	No	Yes
Annual assessment of impairment required?	Yes	Yes	No*
Reversal of impairment loss allowed in subsequent periods?	No	Yes	Yes

*Not required unless there are signs to suggest that impairment has occurred.

In the following discussions, we illustrate the accounting for both categories of intangibles.

Accounting for Specific Intangibles

Each type of intangible asset is unique, and the accounting can vary from one intangible to another.

PATENTS. **Patents** are federal government grants giving the holder the exclusive right for 20 years to produce and sell an invention. The invention may be a product or a process—for example, BlackBerry's new cellphone and IMAX's projection process. Like any other asset, a patent may be purchased. Suppose Bombardier pays $170,000 to acquire a patent on January 1, and the business believes the expected useful life of the patent is five years. Amortization expense is $34,000 per year ($170,000/5 years). Bombardier records the acquisition and amortization for this patent as follows:

	A	B	C	D	E
1	Jan. 1	Patents	170,000		
2		Cash		170,000	
3		*To acquire a patent.*			
4	Dec. 31	Amortization Expense—Patents ($170,000/5)	34,000		
5		Accumulated Amortization		34,000	
6		*To amortize the cost of a patent.*			
7					

			SHAREHOLDERS'
ASSETS	= LIABILITIES	+	EQUITY
−34,000	= 0		−34,000 Expense

Amortization for an intangible decreases both assets and equity exactly as it does for equipment.

COPYRIGHTS. **Copyrights** are exclusive rights to reproduce and sell a book, musical composition, film, or other work of art. Copyrights also protect computer software programs, such as Microsoft Word. Issued by the federal government, copyrights extend 50 years beyond the author's (composer's, artist's, or programmer's) death. The cost of obtaining a copyright from the government is low, but a company may pay a large sum to purchase an existing copyright from the owner. For example, a publisher may pay the author of a popular novel $1 million or more for the book copyright. A copyright is usually amortized over its useful life.

TRADEMARKS AND TRADE NAMES. Trademarks and trade names (or **brand names**) are distinctive identifications of products or services. You are probably familiar with McDonald's golden arches or Apple Inc.'s famous apple. Tim Hortons and Roots are names we all recognize. Advertising slogans, such as "Red Bull gives you wings," are also protected.

The cost of a trademark or trade name may be amortized over its useful life, but if the trademark is expected to generate cash flow for the indefinite future, the business should not amortize the trademark's cost.

FRANCHISES AND LICENCES. Franchises and licences are privileges granted by a private business or a government to sell a product or service in accordance with specified conditions. The Edmonton Oilers hockey organization is a franchise granted to its owner by the National Hockey League. Swiss Chalet restaurants and Canadian Tire are popular franchises. Companies purchase licences for the right to use computer software. Coca-Cola sells licences to companies around the world, which allow the companies to produce and distribute Coca-Cola beverages in specified markets. The useful lives of many franchises and licences are indefinite and, therefore, are not amortized.

GOODWILL. In accounting, **goodwill** has a very specific meaning. It is defined as the excess of the cost of purchasing another company over the sum of the market values of its net assets (assets minus liabilities). A purchaser is willing to pay for goodwill when it buys another company with abnormal earning power.

Canadian Tire expanded into another line of business when it acquired The Forzani Group in August 2011. The purchase price was $800.6 million. The fair value of the assets was $1,149.9 million, and the fair value of the liabilities was $657.7 million, so Canadian Tire paid $308.4 million for goodwill, computed as follows:

Purchase paid for The Forzani Group (FGL)	$ 800.6 million
Sum of the fair values of FGL's assets	$1,149.9 million
Less: Fair value of FGL's liabilities	657.7 million
Value of FGL's net assets	492.2 million
Excess is called *goodwill*	$ 308.4 million

Canadian Tire would consolidate The Forzani Group's financial statements, but if Canadian Tire were to combine FGL's records with its own, the entry, including goodwill, would be:

	A	B	C	D	E
1		Assets (Cash, Receivables, Inventories, Property,			
2		Plant, and Equipment, Other Assets, all at fair value)	1,149,900,000		
3		Goodwill	308,400,000		
4		Liabilities		657,700,000	
5		Cash		800,600,000	
6					

	ASSETS	=	LIABILITIES	+	SHAREHOLDERS' EQUITY
	+1,149,900,000				
	+308,400,000	=	+657,700,000	+	0
	−800,600,000				

Note that Canadian Tire has acquired both The Forzani Group's assets and its liabilities.

Goodwill has special features, as follows:

1. Goodwill is recorded *only* when it is purchased in the acquisition of another company. A purchase transaction provides objective evidence of the value of goodwill. Companies never record goodwill that they have created for their own business.

2. Goodwill is not amortized because it has an indefinite life. As you will see below, if the value of goodwill is impaired, it must be written down.

Accounting for the Impairment of an Intangible Asset

Some intangibles—such as goodwill, licences, and some trademarks—have indefinite lives and, therefore, are not subject to amortization. But all intangibles are subject to a write-down when the carrying amount exceeds its recoverable amount. Go back and reexamine the two step process for determining impairment of an asset on page 298. The 2014 annual report of Canadian Tire reported that

> The impairment on goodwill pertains to the Company's Retail operating segment and is reported in other (expense) income in the consolidated statement of income.

As a result of the impairment test, Canadian Tire recognized a goodwill impairment loss of $0.3 million. This impairment loss is recorded as an expense on the income statement.

Canadian Tire would record the write-down of goodwill as follows:

	A	B	C	D	E
1	2014				
2	Dec. 31	Loss on Goodwill Impairment	$ 0.3		
3		Goodwill		$ 0.3	
4					

ASSETS	=	LIABILITIES	+	SHAREHOLDERS' EQUITY
−0.3	=	0	+	−0.3 Expense

Under ASPE, impairment of intangible assets is tested only when there is an indication of impairment.

Accounting for Research and Development Costs

Accounting for research and development (R&D) costs is one of the most difficult issues the accounting profession has faced. R&D is the lifeblood of companies such as BlackBerry, Open Text, TELUS, and Bombardier because it is vital to the development of new products and processes. The cost of R&D activities is one of these companies' most valuable (intangible) assets.

Both IFRS and ASPE require *development costs* meeting certain criteria to be capitalized and then expensed over the life of the product, while *research costs* are to be expensed as incurred.

STOP + THINK (6-4)

Suppose the *Globe and Mail* paid $1 million for a rural newspaper in Ontario three years ago. The newspaper's assets were valued at $1,000,000 and its liabilities at $150,000. The company recorded $150,000 as goodwill at the time of purchase. What amortization expense will be recorded for the current year?

OBJECTIVE

⑤ **Analyze** a company's return on assets

ANALYZE A COMPANY'S RETURN ON ASSETS

Evaluating company performance is a key goal of financial statement analysis. Shareholders entrust managers with the responsibility of developing a business strategy that utilizes company assets in a manner that both effectively and efficiently generates a profit. In this chapter, we begin to develop a framework by which company performance can be evaluated. The most basic framework for this purpose is **return on assets (ROA)**.

ROA, also known as *rate* of return on assets, measures how profitably management has used the assets that shareholders and creditors have provided the company. The basic formula for the ROA ratio is as follows:

$$ROA = \frac{\text{Net income } + \text{ Interest Expense}}{\text{Average total assets}}$$

where Average total assets = (Beginning total assets + Ending total assets)/2

ROA measures how much the entity earned for each dollar of assets invested by both shareholders and creditors. Companies with high ROA have both selected assets and managed them more successfully than companies with low ROA. ROA is often computed on a divisional or product-line basis to help identify less profitable segments and improve their performance.

To illustrate, let's consider Masimo Corporation, a company that produces electronic instruments used in the health-care industry. The following table contains approximate financial data adapted from Masimo's income statements and balance sheets for 2016 and 2017:

Masimo Corporation
Selected (Adapted) Financial Data

	(Amounts in thousands)	
	2017	2016
Net sales	$439,000	$493,000
Net income	60,000	61,000
Interest expense	$ 4,000	$ 4,000
Average total assets	338,000	371,000

Masimo Corporation
Return on Assets

ROA

Net income + Interest expense/Average total assets

2017 = $60,000 + $4,000/$338,000 = 18.9 or 19%

2016 = $61,000 + $4,000/$371,000 = 17.5 or 18%

Overall, despite the decrease in net income from $61,000 to $60,000, the company was still able to increase the ROA from 18% to 19%. In addition, Massimo sold unproductive plant assets, reducing total average assets from $371,000 to $338,000.

STOP + THINK (6-5)

Why is interest expense added to net income in the numerator of the Return on Assets ratio?

▶ DECISION GUIDELINES

USING THE RETURN ON ASSETS IN DECISION MAKING

The fundamental goal of a company is to earn a profit. The return on asset (ROA) measures how profitably a company uses its assets. Let's see how the ROA is used in making decisions.

Decision	Guidelines
How profitable was the company?	*Managers*
	Managers try to increase the profitability of the company, whether it is through increasing sales, reducing expenses, or a combination of both. They know that investors and creditors expect them to use the assets of the company to generate a profit.
	Investors and Creditors
	Since investors and creditors provide the financing for the assets that a company owns, they are looking to see if managers were able to use these assets to generate a profit. For the investor, share prices generally react favourably when the company is profitable—and the company will be able to pay them dividends. For the creditor, profitability means the company will be able to pay back their debt.

ANALYZE THE CASH FLOW IMPACT OF LONG-LIVED ASSET TRANSACTIONS

OBJECTIVE

❻ **Analyze** the cash flow impact of long-lived asset transactions

Three main types of long-lived asset transactions appear on the statement of cash flows:

- Acquisitions
- Sales
- Depreciation and amortization

Acquisitions and sales of long-lived assets are *investing* activities. For example, a company invests in property, plant, and equipment by paying cash or incurring a liability. The purchase of buildings and equipment are investing activities that appear on the statement of cash flows. The sale of property, plant, and equipment results in a cash receipt, as illustrated in Exhibit 6-8, which excerpts data from the statement of cash flows of Canadian Tire. The acquisitions, sales, and depreciation of property, plant, and equipment and intangible assets are denoted in lines 7, 8, 12, 13, and 14.

Let's examine the investing activities first. During the year-end January 3, 2015, Canadian Tire paid $538.6 million for property and equipment and $150.1 million for intangible assets. Canadian Tire received $21.3 million from the disposal of these assets during the year. A gain or loss on the sale of these assets is not reported as an investing activity on the statement of cash flows.

Canadian Tire's statement of cash flows reports Depreciation (Amortization) in the operating activities section (line 7). You may be wondering why depreciation appears on the statement of cash flows—after all, depreciation does not affect cash. Depreciation (Amortization) decreases net income in the same way that all other expenses do, but it does not affect cash. Depreciation (Amortization) is therefore added back to net income to measure cash flows from operations under the indirect method.

Canadian Tire's cash flows are strong—cash provided by operating activities was $574.8 million. With this amount and with some financing, the company has bought property and equipment as well as other intangible assets needed to expand and run its business.

EXHIBIT 6-8
Reporting Long-lived Asset Transactions on Statement of Cash Flows

Source: Reprinted with permission from Canadian Tire Corporation.

	A	B	C	D
1	**Canadian Tire** Consolidated Statement of Cash Flows (partial, adapted) For the Year Ended January 3, 2015			
2	*(amounts in millions)*			
3	**Operating Activities:**			
4	Net earnings	$ 639.3		
5	**Adjustments to reconcile net income**			
6	**to cash provided by operating activities:**			
7	**Depreciation**	279.2		
8	**Amortization of intangible assets**	93.1		
9	Other items (summarized)	(436.8)		
10	Cash generated from operating activities	$ 574.8		
11	**Investing Activities:**			
12	**Purchases of property and equipment**	(538.6)		
13	**Additions to intangible assets**	(150.1)		
14	**Proceeds from disposals of assets**	21.3		
15	Other items (summarized)	77.9		
16	Cash used for investing activities	(589.5)		
17	**Financing Activities:**			
18	Cash generated from financing activities (summarized)	88.6		
19	Cash generated in the year	73.9		
20	Cash and cash equivalents at beginning of year	574.2		
21	Effect of exchange rate on cash	(0.3)		
22	Cash and cash equivalents at end of year	$ 647.8		
23				

STOP + THINK (6-6)

Test your ability to understand the statement of cash flows.

1. How much cash did Canadian Tire spend on purchases of property, plant, and equipment and intangibles during the year?

2. Suppose the carrying amount of the property, plant and equipment that Canadian Tire sold for $538.6 million was $539.6 million (a cost of $808.1 million minus accumulated depreciation of $268.5 million). Write a sentence to explain why the sale transaction resulted in a loss for Canadian Tire.

3. Where would Canadian Tire report any gain or loss on the sale of the capital assets—on which financial statement, under which heading?

Summary of IFRS-ASPE Differences

Concepts	IFRS	ASPE
Depreciation (p. 283)	This concept is called depreciation.	This concept is called amortization.
Significant components of an item of property, plant, or equipment (p. 298)	Significant components shall be depreciated separately.	Significant components are amortized separately only when it is practical to do so.
Impairment (p. 298)	A company shall assess at the end of each reporting period whether there are any signs that an asset may be impaired. Irrespective of any signs of impairment, a company must annually review goodwill and intangible assets with indefinite useful lives for impairment.	A company shall test an asset for impairment whenever events or circumstances indicate its carrying amount may not be recoverable.
	If an impaired asset subsequently increases in value, a company may reverse all or part of any previous write-down but not on goodwill.	A company may not reverse any write-downs, even if an impaired asset subsequently increases in value.
Revaluation (p. 299)	A company may choose to use the revaluation model to measure its property, plant, and equipment.	A company must use the cost method; no revaluation is permitted.

SUMMARY

SUMMARY OF LEARNING OBJECTIVES

LEARNING OBJECTIVE	SUMMARY
1. **Measure** and **account** for the cost of property, plant, and equipment	The cost of property, plant, and equipment is the sum of all the costs incurred to bring the asset to its location and intended use. Costs incurred after the asset has been placed in use are either capitalized (if it increases the asset's productivity or extends its useful life) or expensed (if it maintains the asset and keeps it in good working order).
2. **Measure** and **record** depreciation on property, plant, and equipment	Because assets decline in value either from wearing out, becoming obsolete, or losing value, depreciation is used to allocate their cost to the periods of their useful life. Three depreciation methods discussed include the straight-line method, the units-of-production method, and the diminishing or double-diminishing-balance method. If an asset is bought during the year, depreciation is computed for the partial year. Managers may revise their estimate of an asset's useful life and recalculate depreciation. If a fully depreciated asset is still being used, it is left on the company's records.

3. **Explain** additional topics in accounting for long-lived tangible assets

Depreciation affects income taxes because the depreciation method used for accounting purposes may be different than the depreciation method required for tax purposes. Subsequent to the acquisition of property, plant, and equipment, a company can choose to measure these assets using either the cost method or the revaluation method. The cost method uses cost as its measurement, while the revaluation method uses fair value. Significant components of property, plant, and equipment shall be depreciated separately. Property, plant, and equipment are checked annually for any impairment.

4. **Account** for intangible assets

Intangible assets are long-lived assets with no physical form and include patents, copyrights, trademarks, franchises, and licences, and goodwill. Two categories of intangibles are those with finite lives (record amortization) and those with indefinite lives (no amortization is recorded). All intangible assets are checked each year for impairment, and a loss is recorded when it occurs.

5. **Analyze** a company's return on assets

The return on assets ratio measures how profitably management has used the assets that shareholders and creditors have provided the company.

6. **Analyze** the cash flow impact of long-lived asset transactions

On the statement of cash flows, acquisitions and sales of property, plant, and equipment and intangibles are recorded under investing activities, while the depreciation and amortization expenses are added to net income under operating activities.

MyAccountingLab

END-OF-CHAPTER SUMMARY PROBLEM

The figures that follow appear in the *Answers to the Mid-Chapter Summary Problem*, Requirement 2, on page 292, for Canadian Tire.

	Method A: Straight-Line			Method B: Double-Diminishing-Balance		
Year	Annual Depreciation Expense	Accumulated Depreciation	Carrying amount	Annual Depreciation Expense	Accumulated Depreciation	Carrying Amount
Start			$44,000			$44,000
2015	$4,000	$ 4,000	40,000	$ 8,800	$ 8,800	35,200
2016	4,000	8,000	36,000	7,040	15,840	28,160
2017	4,000	12,000	32,000	5,632	21,472	22,528

Problem

Name: Canadian Tire
Industry: Retailer
Accounting Period: The years 2015, 2016, 2017

Suppose Canadian Tire purchased the equipment described in the table on January 1, 2015. Management has depreciated the equipment by using the double-diminishing-balance method. On July 1, 2017, Canadian Tire sold the equipment for $27,000 cash.

Requirement

Record depreciation for 2017 and the sale of the equipment on July 1, 2017.

ANSWERS

Problem

To record depreciation to date of sale, and then the sale of the equipment:

	A	B	C	D	E
1	2017				
2	July 1	Depreciation Expense—Equipment ($5,632 × 1/2 year)	2,816		
3		Accumulated Depreciation—Equipment		2,816	
4		*To update depreciation.*			
5					
6	July 1	Cash	27,000		
7		Accumulated Depreciation—Equipment ($15,840 + $2,816)	18,656		
8		Equipment		44,000	
9		Gain on Sale of Equipment		1,656	
10		*To record sale of equipment.*			
11					

> Depreciation expense must first be recorded for the portion of the year that the asset was used before it was sold.

> The gain on the sale is the excess of the cash received over the carrying amount of the asset.

REVIEW

MyAccountingLab

Make the grade with MyAccountingLab: The Quick Quiz questions, Short Exercises, Exercises, and Problems (Group A) marked in #-# can be found on MyAccountingLab. You can practise them as often as you want, and most feature step-by-step guided instructions to help you find the right answer.

QUICK QUIZ (ANSWERS APPEAR ON THE LAST PAGE OF THIS CHAPTER.)

1. Argyle Corp. purchased a tract of land, a small office building, and some equipment for $1,500,000. The appraised value of the land was $850,000; the building, $675,000; and the equipment, $475,000. What is the cost of the land?
a. $850,000
b. $637,500
c. $482,776
d. None of the above

2. Which of the following statements about depreciation is false?
a. Recording depreciation creates a fund to replace the asset at the end of its useful life.
b. The cost of a building minus accumulated depreciation equals the building's carrying amount.
c. Depreciation is a process of allocating the cost of property, plant, and equipment over its useful life.
d. Depreciation is caused by physical wear and tear or obsolescence.

Use the following data for Questions 3 through 6.

On August 1, 2016, Major Link Inc. purchased a new piece of equipment that cost $25,000. The estimated useful life is five years, and estimated residual value is $2,500.

3. Assume Major Link purchased the equipment on August 1, 2016. If Major Link uses the straight-line method for depreciation, what is the depreciation expense for the year ended December 31, 2016?
a. $1,875
b. $1,500
c. $2,083
d. $4,500

4. Assume Major Link purchased the equipment on January 1, 2016. If Major Link uses the straight-line method for depreciation, what is the asset's carrying amount at the end of 2017?
a. $13,500   c. $18,625
b. $15,000   d. $16,000

5. Assume Major Link purchased the equipment on January 1, 2016. If Major Link uses the double-diminishing-balance method of depreciation, what is the depreciation expense for the year ended December 31, 2017?
   a. $5,400
   b. $6,000
   c. $8,333
   d. $15,000

6. Return to Major Link's original purchase date of August 1, 2016. Assume that Major Link uses the straight-line method of depreciation and sells the equipment for $11,500 on August 1, 2020. Based on the result of the sale of the equipment, what gain (or loss) will Major Link realize?
   a. $4,500
   b. $13,500
   c. $(9,000)
   d. $0

7. A company bought a new machine for $17,000 on January 1. The machine is expected to last four years and to have a residual value of $2,000. If the company uses the double-diminishing-balance method, what is the accumulated depreciation at the end of year 2?
   a. $10,880
   b. $11,250
   c. $12,750
   d. $15,000

8. Which of the following is *not* a capital expenditure?
   a. The addition of a building wing
   b. A complete overhaul of an air-conditioning system
   c. A tune-up of a company vehicle
   d. Replacement of an old motor with a new one in a piece of equipment
   e. The cost of installing a piece of equipment

9. Which of the following assets is *not* subject to a decreasing carrying amount through amortization/depreciation?
   a. Goodwill
   b. Patents
   c. Land improvements
   d. Copyrights

10. Why would a business select an accelerated method of depreciation for reporting purposes?
   a. Accelerated depreciation results in a constant amount of depreciation.
   b. Accelerated depreciation generates a greater amount of depreciation over the life of the asset than does straight-line depreciation.
   c. Accelerated depreciation is easier to calculate because residual value is ignored.
   d. Accelerated depreciation generates higher depreciation expense immediately, and therefore lower net income in the early years of the asset's life.

11. A company sells an asset that originally cost $300,000 for $100,000 on December 31, 2017. The accumulated depreciation account had a balance of $120,000 after the current year's depreciation of $30,000 had been recorded. The company should recognize a(n)
   a. $200,000 loss on disposal.
   b. $80,000 loss on disposal.
   c. $80,000 gain on disposal.
   d. $50,000 loss on disposal.

12. Which item among the following is *not* an intangible asset?
   a. A trademark
   b. A copyright
   c. A patent
   d. Goodwill
   e. All of the above are intangible assets

13. An important measure of profitability is
   a. inventory turnover.
   b. quick (acid test) ratio.
   c. return on assets (ROA).
   d. net sales.

14. In 2017, return on assets for JBC Company has increased. This means that the
   a. company has become more effective.
   b. company has become more efficient.
   c. company has become more effective and more efficient.
   d. company has neither become more effective nor more efficient.

ACCOUNTING VOCABULARY

accelerated depreciation method A depreciation method that writes off a relatively larger amount of the asset's cost nearer the start of its useful life than the straight-line method does. (p. 288)

amortization Allocation of the cost of an intangible asset with a finite life over its useful life. (p. 301)

brand name A distinctive identification of a product or service. Also called a *trademark* or *trade name*. (p. 302)

capital expenditure Expenditure that increases an asset's capacity or efficiency, or extends its useful life. Capital expenditures are debited to an asset account. Also called *betterments*. (p. 282)

copyright Exclusive right to reproduce and sell a book, musical composition, film, other work of art, or computer program. Issued by the federal government, copyrights extend 50 years beyond the author's life. (p. 301)

depreciable cost The cost of a tangible asset minus its estimated residual value. (p. 285)

depreciation An expense to recognize the portion of a capital asset's economic benefits that has been used up during an accounting period. (p. 283)

double-diminishing-balance (DDB) method An accelerated depreciation method that computes annual depreciation by multiplying the asset's decreasing carrying amount by a constant percentage, which is two times the straight-line rate. (p. 288)

estimated residual value Expected cash value of an asset at the end of its useful life. Also called *scrap value* or *salvage value*. (p. 284)

estimated useful life Length of service that a business expects to get from an asset. May be expressed in years, units of output, kilometres, or other measures. (p. 284)

franchises and licences Privileges granted by a private business or a government to sell a product or service in accordance with specified conditions. (p. 302)

goodwill Excess of the cost of an acquired company over the sum of the market values of its net assets (assets minus liabilities). (p. 302)

intangible assets Long-lived assets with no physical form that convey a special right to current and expected future benefits. (p. 279)

obsolescence Occurs when an asset becomes outdated or no longer produces revenue for the company. (p. 284)

patent A federal government grant giving the holder the exclusive right for 20 years to produce and sell an invention. (p. 301)

physical wear and tear Occurs when the usefulness of the asset deteriorates. (p. 284)

return on assets (ROA) Measures how profitably management has used the assets that shareholders and creditors have provided the company. (p. 304)

straight-line (SL) method Depreciation method in which an equal amount of depreciation expense is assigned to each year of asset use. (p. 285)

tangible long-lived assets Also called property, plant, and equipment. (p. 279)

trademark, trade name A distinctive identification of a product or service. Also called a *brand name*. (p. 302)

units-of-production (UOP) method Depreciation method by which a fixed amount of depreciation is assigned to each unit of output produced by the plant asset. (p. 287)

ASSESS YOUR PROGRESS

SHORT EXERCISES

S6-1 Examine Riverside's assets as follows:

LEARNING OBJECTIVE ❶

Measure the cost and carrying amount of a company's property, plant, and equipment

	A	B	C	D
1	**Riverside Corporation** Consolidated Balance Sheets (Partial, Adapted)			
2		May 31,		
3	*(in millions)*	2017	2016	
4	**Assets**			
5	Current assets			
6	Cash and cash equivalents	$ 2,088	$ 257	
7	Receivables, less allowances of $144 and $125	2,770	2,623	
8	Spare parts, supplies, and fuel	4,653	4,509	
9	Prepaid expenses and other	467	423	
10	Total current assets	9,978	7,812	
11	Property and equipment, at cost			
12	Aircraft	2,392	2,392	
13	Package handling and ground support equipment	12,229	12,132	
14	Computer and electronic equipment	28,159	26,102	
15	Vehicles	581	452	
16	Facilities and other	1,432	1,589	
17	Total cost	44,793	42,667	
18	Less: Accumulated depreciation	(14,900)	(12,944)	
19	Net property and equipment	29,893	29,723	
20	Other long-term assets			
21	Goodwill	722	722	
22	Prepaid pension cost	1,340	1,271	
23	Intangible and other assets	329	333	
24	Total other long-term assets	2,391	2,326	
25	Total assets	$ 42,262	$ 39,861	
26				

1. What is Riverside's largest category of assets? List all 2017 assets in the largest category and their amounts as reported by Riverside.

2. What was Riverside's cost of property and equipment at May 31, 2017? What was the carrying amount of property and equipment on this date? Why is carrying amount less than cost?

LEARNING OBJECTIVE ❶

Measure the cost of property

S6-2 Page 280 of this chapter lists the costs included for the acquisition of land. First is the purchase price of the land, which is obviously included in the cost of the land. The reasons for including the related costs are not so obvious. For example, property tax is ordinarily an expense, not part of the cost of an asset. State why the related costs listed on page 280 are included as part of the cost of the land. After the land is ready for use, will these related costs be capitalized or expensed?

LEARNING OBJECTIVE ❶

Measure and record the lump-sum purchase of assets

S6-3 Suppose you have purchased land, a building, and some equipment. At the time of the acquisition, the land has a current fair value of $75,000, the building's fair value is $60,000, and the equipment's fair value is $15,000. Journalize the lump-sum purchase of the three assets for a total cost of $140,000. Assume you sign a note payable for this amount.

LEARNING OBJECTIVE ❶

Measure and account for equipment

S6-4 Assume WestJet repaired one of its Boeing 737 aircraft at a cost of $0.8 million, which WestJet paid in cash. Further, assume that the WestJet accountant erroneously capitalized this cost as part of the cost of the plane.

Show the effects of the accounting error on WestJet's income statement and balance sheet. To answer this question, determine whether revenues, total expenses, net income, total assets, and shareholders' equity would be overstated or understated by the accounting error.

LEARNING OBJECTIVE ❷

Compute depreciation by three methods—first year only

S6-5 Assume that at the beginning of 2017, Porter Airlines purchased a Bombardier Q400 aircraft at a cost of $25,000,000. Porter expects the plane to remain useful for five years (5,000,000 km) and to have a residual value of $5,000,000. Porter expects the plane to be flown 750,000 km the first year and 1,250,000 km each year during years 2 through 4, and 500,000 km the last year.

1. Compute Porter's first-year depreciation on the plane using the following methods:
   a. Straight-line
   b. Units-of-production
   c. Double-diminishing-balance

2. Show the airplane's carrying amount at the end of the first year under each depreciation method.

LEARNING OBJECTIVE ❷

Compute depreciation by three methods—final year only

S6-6 Use the assumed Porter Airlines data in exercise S6-5 to compute Porter's fifth-year depreciation on the plane using the following methods:

a. Straight-line

b. Units-of-production

c. Double-diminishing-balance

LEARNING OBJECTIVE ❸

Compute partial-year depreciation

S6-7 Assume that on September 30, 2017, Swiss, the national airline of Switzerland, purchased an Airbus aircraft at a cost of €40,000,000 (€ is the symbol for the euro). Swiss expects the plane to remain useful for seven years (5,000,000 km) and to have a residual value of €5,000,000. Swiss expects the plane to be flown 500,000 km during the remainder of the first year ended December 31, 2017. Compute Swiss's depreciation on the plane for the year ended December 31, 2017, using the following methods:

a. Straight-line

b. Units-of-production

c. Double-diminishing-balance

Which method would produce the highest net income for 2017? Which method produces the lowest net income?

LEARNING OBJECTIVE ❸

Compute and record depreciation after a change in useful life of the asset

S6-8 Canada's Wonderland paid $60,000 for a concession stand. Depreciation was recorded by the straight-line method over 10 years with zero residual value. Suppose that after using the concession stand for four years, Canada's Wonderland determines that the asset will remain useful for only three more years. How will this affect depreciation on the concession stand for year 5 by the straight-line method?

S6-9 On January 1, 2014, Big Rock Brewery purchased a van for $45,000. Big Rock expects the van to have a useful life of five years and a residual value of $5,000. The depreciation method used was straight-line. On December 31, 2017, the van was sold for $15,000 cash.

1. What was the carrying amount of the van on the date of sale?

2. Record the sale of the van on December 31, 2017.

LEARNING OBJECTIVE ③

Record a gain or loss on derecognition under two depreciation methods

S6-10 Define patents and goodwill, which are both intangible assets. Explain how the accounting differs between a patent and goodwill.

LEARNING OBJECTIVE ④

Account for the amortization of a company's intangible assets

S6-11 Consider the purchase of a supplier by Canadian Tire.

1. Suppose the fair value of the net assets at the date of purchase (February 1, 2017) had been $180.3 million. What would the goodwill cost have been if Canadian Tire had paid $200 million?

2. Explain how Canadian Tire will have been accounting for this goodwill up to February 1, 2019.

LEARNING OBJECTIVE ④

Analyze a company's goodwill

S6-12 This exercise summarizes the accounting for patents, which, like copyrights, trademarks, and franchises, provide the owner with a special right or privilege. It also covers research costs.

Suppose Jaguar Automobiles Ltd. paid $500,000 to research a new global positioning system. Jaguar also paid $1,200,000 to acquire a patent on a new motor. After readying the motor for production, Jaguar's sales revenue for the first year totalled $6,500,000. Cost of goods sold was $3,200,000, and selling expenses were $300,000. All these transactions occurred during fiscal 2017. Jaguar expects the patent to have a useful life of three years.

Prepare Jaguar's income statement for the fiscal year ended December 31, 2017, complete with a heading.

LEARNING OBJECTIVE ④

Account for patents and research cost

S6-13 You are reviewing the financial statements of Rising Yeast Co. During 2017, Rising Yeast purchased two other companies for $17 million. Also during fiscal 2017, Rising Yeast made capital expenditures of $2 million to expand its market share. During the year, the company sold operations, receiving cash of $25 million, and experienced a gain of $6 million on the disposal. Overall, Rising Yeast reported net income of $1 million during 2017. What would you expect the section for cash flows from investing activities on its statement of cash flows for 2017 to report? What total amount for net cash provided by (used in) investing activities do you anticipate?

LEARNING OBJECTIVE ⑥

Report investing activities on the statement of cash flows

S6-14 In 2017, Artesia, Inc., reported $300 million in sales, $17 million in net income, $1 million in interest expense, and average total assets of $120 million. What is Artesia's return on assets in 2017? Assume an industry average of 16%. Did the company's return on assets improve or deteriorate? What could be some reasons for the change?

LEARNING OBJECTIVE ⑤

Calculate return on assets

S6-15 Ochoa Optical, Inc., provides a full line of designer eyewear to optical dispensaries. Ochoa reported the following information for 2016 and 2017:

LEARNING OBJECTIVE ⑤

Calculate return on assets

	2017	2016
Sales revenue	$500,000	$450,000
Net income	$ 44,500	$ 42,000
Interest expense	$ 500	$ 500
Average total assets	$250,000	$240,000

Compute return on assets for 2016 and 2017. Did the return on assets improve in 2017? What would cause this ratio to change?

LEARNING OBJECTIVE ❶

Distinguish a capital expenditure
from an immediate expense

S6-16 Identify each of the following items as either a capital expenditure (C), expense on the income statement (E), or neither (N):

Type of Expenditure (C, E, or N)	Transaction
	1. Paid property taxes of $75,000 for the first year the new building is occupied.
	2. Paid interest on construction note for new plant building, $550,000.
	3. Repaired plumbing in main plant, paying $270,000 cash.
	4. Purchased equipment for new manufacturing plant, $6,000,000; financed with long-term note.
	5. Paid dividends of $40,000.
	6. Purchased a computer and peripheral equipment for $29,000 cash.
	7. Paved a parking lot on leased property for $300,000.
	8. Paid $90,000 in cash for installation of equipment in (4).
	9. Paid $148,000 to tear down old building on new plant site.
	10. Paid $31,000 maintenance on equipment in (4) during its first year of use.

LEARNING OBJECTIVE ❹

Measure and record goodwill

S6-17 Crunchies, Inc., dominates the snack-food industry with its Salty Chip brand. Assume that Crunchies, Inc., purchased Healthy Snacks, Inc., for $5.8 million cash. The market value of Healthy Snacks's assets is $7 million, and Healthy Snacks has liabilities with a market value of $6.0 million.

Requirements
1. Compute the cost of the goodwill purchased by Crunchies.
2. Explain how Crunchies will account for goodwill in future years.

LEARNING OBJECTIVE ❸❹

Explain the effect of asset
impairment on financial statements

S6-18 For each of the following scenarios, indicate whether a long-term asset has been impaired (Y for yes and N for no) and, if so, the amount of the loss that should be recorded.

Asset	Carrying Amount	Value in Use	Fair Value	Impaired? (Y or N)	Amount of Loss
a. Equipment	$ 180,000	$ 140,000	$ 100,000		
b. Trademark	$ 320,000	$ 460,000	$ 375,000		
c. Land	$ 52,000	$ 24,000	$ 21,000		
d. Factory building	$9 million	$9 million	$7 million		

EXERCISES

LEARNING OBJECTIVE ❶

Determine the cost of property

E6-19 Moody Inc. purchased land, paying $150,000 cash as a down payment and signing a $100,000 note payable for the balance. Moody also had to pay delinquent property tax of $5,000, title insurance costing $3,000, and $25,000 to level the land and to remove an unwanted building. The company paid $70,000 to remove earth for the foundation and then constructed an office building at a cost of $3,750,000. It also paid $100,000 for a fence around the property, $10,500 for the company sign near the property entrance, and $18,000 for lighting of the grounds. Determine the cost of the company's land, land improvements, and building.

E6-20 Assume Trois Cuisines Manufacturing bought three machines in a $100,000 lump-sum purchase. An independent appraiser valued the machines as follows:

Machine No.	Appraised Value
1	$27,000
2	45,000
3	36,000

Trois Cuisines paid one-third in cash and signed a note payable for the remainder. What is each machine's individual cost? Immediately after making this purchase, Trois Cuisines sold machine 2 for its appraised value. What is the result of the sale? Round to three decimal places.

LEARNING OBJECTIVE ❶❸

Allocate costs to assets acquired in a lump-sum purchase; derecognize equipment

E6-21 Assume Hershey Chocolate Ltd. purchased a piece of manufacturing machinery. Classify each of the following expenditures as an asset expenditure or an immediate expense related to machinery: (a) sales tax paid on the purchase price, (b) transportation and insurance while machinery is in transit from seller to buyer, (c) purchase price, (d) installation, (e) training of personnel for initial operation of the machinery, (f) special reinforcement to the machinery platform, (g) income tax paid on income earned from the sale of products manufactured by the machinery, (h) major overhaul to extend useful life by three years, (i) ordinary repairs to keep the machinery in good working order, (j) lubrication of the machinery before it is placed in service, and (k) periodic lubrication after the machinery is placed in service. What criteria differentiated an asset expenditure from an immediate expense?

LEARNING OBJECTIVE ❶

Distinguish asset expenditures from expenses

E6-22 During 2017, Roberts Inc. paid $200,000 for land and built a restaurant in Collingwood, Ontario. Prior to construction, the City of Collingwood charged Roberts Inc. $2,250 for a building permit, which Roberts Inc. paid. Roberts Inc. also paid $20,000 for architect's fees. The construction cost of $700,000 was financed by a long-term note payable issued on January 1, 2017, with interest cost of $29,000 paid at December 31, 2017. The building was completed September 30, 2017. Roberts Inc. will depreciate the building by the straight-line method over 25 years, with an estimated residual value of $60,000.

LEARNING OBJECTIVE ❶❷

Measure, depreciate, and report property and plant

1. Journalize transactions for the following (explanations are not required):
   a. Purchase of the land
   b. All the costs chargeable to the building, in a single entry
   c. Depreciation on the building

2. Report this transaction in the Property, Plant, and Equipment on the company's balance sheet at December 31, 2017.

3. What will Roberts Inc.'s income statement for the year ended December 31, 2017, report for the building?

E6-23 Assume you have a flower shop and you bought a delivery van for $30,000. You expect the van to remain in service for three years (150,000 km). At the end of its useful life, you estimate that the van's residual value will be $3,000. You estimate the van will travel 40,000 km the first year, 60,000 km the second year, and 50,000 km the third year. Prepare an estimate of the *depreciation expense* per year for the van under the three depreciation methods. Show your computations.

Which method do you think tracks the useful life cost on the van most closely? How does management determine which depreciation method to use?

LEARNING OBJECTIVE ❶❷

Determine depreciation amounts by three methods

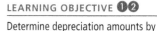

LEARNING OBJECTIVE ❶❷❻

Report property, plant, and equipment depreciation and invest cash flow

E6-24 In January 2017, suppose a Starbucks franchise in Regina purchased a building, paying $50,000 cash and signing a $100,000 note payable. The franchise paid another $50,000 to remodel the facility. Equipment and store fixtures cost $50,000; dishes and supplies—a current asset—were obtained for $10,000.

The franchise is depreciating the building over 25 years by the straight-line method, with estimated residual value of $50,000. The equipment and store fixtures will be replaced at the end of five years; these assets are being depreciated by the double-diminishing-balance method, with zero residual value. At the end of the first year, the franchise has dishes and supplies worth $2,000.

Show what the franchise will report for supplies, property, plant, and equipment and cash flows at the end of the first year on its:

- Income statement
- Balance sheet
- Statement of cash flows (investing only)

Show all computations. (*Note:* The purchase of dishes and supplies is an operating cash flow because supplies are a current asset.)

LEARNING OBJECTIVE ❺

Calculate return on assets

E6-25 Loblaws, one of the nation's largest grocery retailers, reported the following information (adapted) for its fiscal year ended January 31, 2017.

	January 31, 2017	January 31, 2016
Net sales	$48,815	$47,220
Net earnings	$ 2,000	$ 1,773
Interest expense	$ 10	$ 10
Average total assets	$33,699	$33,005

Requirements

1. Compute return on assets for the years ended January 31, 2016 and 2017.
2. Did return on assets improve or deteriorate? What are some possible causes for this change?

LEARNING OBJECTIVE ❸

Change a building's useful life

E6-26 Assume The Salvation Army purchased a building for $900,000 and depreciated it on a straight-line basis over 30 years. The estimated residual value was $100,000. After using the building for 10 years, the Salvation Army realized that the building will remain useful for only 10 more years. Starting with the 11th year, the Salvation Army began depreciating the building over the newly revised total life of 20 years and decreased the estimated residual value to $75,000. What is the effect on depreciation expense on the building for years 11 and 12?

LEARNING OBJECTIVE ❸

Record depreciation and the sale of equipment

E6-27 Assume that on January 2, 2016, a Pizza Hut franchise purchased fixtures for $15,000 cash, expecting the fixtures to remain in service five years. The restaurant has depreciated the fixtures on a double-diminishing-balance basis, with $1,000 estimated residual value. On June 30, 2017, Pizza Hut sold the fixtures for $5,000 cash. Record both the depreciation expense on the fixtures for 2017 and then the sale of the fixtures. Apart from your journal entries, also show how to compute the gain or loss on Pizza Hut's disposal of these fixtures.

LEARNING OBJECTIVE ❶❷❸

Measure equipment's cost, use UOP depreciation, and derecognize a used asset

E6-28 Bison Transport is a large trucking company that operates from Ontario to British Columbia in Canada and in the United States. Bison uses the units-of-production (UOP) method to depreciate its trucks because its managers believe UOP depreciation best measures wear and tear.

Bison Transport trades in its trucks often to keep driver morale high and maximize fuel efficiency. Assume that in 2014, the company acquired a tractor-trailer rig costing $280,000 and expected it to remain in service for five years or 1,000,000 km. Estimated residual value would be $40,000. During 2014, the truck was driven 130,000 km; during 2015, 180,000 km;

and during 2016, 180,000 km. After 90,000 km in 2017, the company wishes to trade in the tractor-trailer rig for a new rig. Determine the carrying amount of the rig and prepare the journal entry to derecognize the rig.

E6-29 Following is an excerpt from the balance sheet of On the Edge Technologies Inc.:

LEARNING OBJECTIVE ❹

Analyze intangible assets

	(in thousands)	
	2017	**2016**
Goodwill (Note 4)	$60.7	$51.8
Intangible assets (Note 4)	48.4	42.4

A potential investor in On the Edge has asked you for advice. What information would you look for in the accompanying notes to the financial statements on which to base your advice about the investment decision?

E6-30 Holze Music Company purchased for $600,000 a patent for a new sound system. Although it gives legal protection for 20 years, the patent is expected to provide the company with a competitive advantage for only six years. Make journal entries to record (a) the purchase of the patent and (b) amortization for year 1.

LEARNING OBJECTIVE ❸❹

Record intangibles, amortization, and a change in the asset's useful life

After using the patent for two years, Holze Music Company's research director learns at a professional meeting that BOSE is designing a more powerful system. On the basis of this new information, Holze Music Company determines that the patent's total useful life is only four years. Record amortization for year 3.

E6-31 BlackBerry, the manufacturer of BlackBerry smartphones, recently reported in the statement of cash flows and notes to the financial statements in its annual report that it had made acquisitions of USD $6.2 million. Assume the balance sheet reported an increase in goodwill for the year in the amount of USD $4.5 million.

LEARNING OBJECTIVE ❹❻

Understand business acquisitions and statement of cash flows

Requirements
1. What is the definition of goodwill?
2. Explain the meaning of (a) the $6.2 million that BlackBerry reported on the statement of cash flows and (b) the $4.5 million increase in goodwill on the balance sheet.
3. BlackBerry's income statement and statement of cash flows do not show any charges for amortization of goodwill during the year. Explain the reason for the lack of charges.

E6-32 Assume that Google paid $18 million to purchase MySpace.com. Assume further that MySpace had the following summarized data at the time of the Google acquisition (amounts in millions of U.S. dollars).

LEARNING OBJECTIVE ❹

Measure and record goodwill

Assets		**Liabilities and Equity**	
Current assets	$10	Total liabilities	$24
Long-term assets	20	Shareholders' equity	6
	$30		$30

MySpace's long-term assets had a current value of only $15 million.

Requirements
1. Compute the cost of the goodwill purchased by Google.
2. Record the purchase of MySpace.
3. Explain how Google will account for goodwill in the future.

LEARNING OBJECTIVE ⑥

Interpret a statement of cash flows

E6-33 The following items are excerpted from an annual report of a large retailer.

	A	B	C	D
1	Consolidated Statement of Cash Flows (Partial, Adapted) For the Year Ended December 30, 2017			
2	(amounts in millions)			
3	**Cash flow from operating activities:**			
4	Net income	$ 185.1		
5	Noncash items:			
6	Depreciation	90.9		
7	**Cash flow from investing activities:**			
8	Property, plant, and equipment	$ (233.6)		
9	Other investments	(0.6)		
10	Disposal of assets	17.0		
11				

Requirements

1. Why is depreciation listed on the statement of cash flows?
2. Explain in detail each investing activity.

LEARNING OBJECTIVE ⑥

Report cash flows for property and equipment

E6-34 Assume Flowers to Go Ltd., a chain of flower shops, completed the following transactions. For each transaction, show what the company would report for investing activities on its statement of cash flows. Show negative amounts in parentheses.

a. Sold a building for $600,000. The building had cost $1,000,000, and at the time of the sale its accumulated depreciation totalled $400,000.
b. Lost a store building in a fire. The warehouse cost $300,000 and had accumulated depreciation of $180,000. The insurance proceeds received were $120,000.
c. Renovated a store at a cost of $400,000, paying cash.
d. Purchased store fixtures for $60,000. The fixtures are expected to remain in service for five years and then be sold for $10,000. Flowers to Go uses the straight-line depreciation method.

LEARNING OBJECTIVE ⑤

Calculate return on assets

E6-35 Lowe's Companies, Inc. reported the following information (adapted) for its fiscal year ended January 31, 2017:

	January 31, 2017	January 31, 2016
Net sales	$82,189	$76,733
Net earnings	$ 1,111	$ 65
Interest expense	$ 5	$ 5
Average total assets	$23,505	$23,126

Requirements

1. Compute the return on assets for the years ended January 31, 2016 and 2017.
2. Did return on assets improve or deteriorate? What would cause this ratio to change?

LEARNING OBJECTIVE ①

Distinguish capital expenditures from expenses

E6-36 Assume Akro Products, Inc., purchased conveyor-belt machinery. Classify each of the following expenditures as a capital expenditure or an immediate expense related to machinery:

a. Major overhaul to extend the machinery's useful life by five years
b. Periodic lubrication after the machinery is placed in service
c. Purchase price
d. Training of personnel for initial operation of the machinery
e. Special reinforcement to the machinery platform

f. Transportation and insurance while machinery is in transit from seller to buyer

g. Ordinary repairs to keep the machinery in good working order

h. Lubrication of the machinery before it is placed in service

i. Sales tax paid on the purchase price

j. Installation of the conveyor-belt machinery

k. Income tax paid on income earned from the sale of products manufactured by the machinery

CHALLENGE EXERCISES

E6-37 Good Life Clubs purchased exercise equipment at a cost of $100,000 each. In addition, Good Life paid $2,000 for a special platform on which to stabilize the equipment for use. Freight costs of $2,500 to ship the equipment were paid by the equipment supplier. Good Life will depreciate the equipment by the units-of-production method, based on an expected useful life of 50,000 hours of exercise. The estimated residual value of the equipment is $10,000. How many hours of usage can Good Life expect from the equipment if budgeted depreciation expense is $10,304 for the year?

LEARNING OBJECTIVE ❶❷

Understand units-of-production depreciation

E6-38 Collicutt Energy Services Ltd. of Calgary, Alberta, reported the following for land, buildings, and equipment (in millions):

LEARNING OBJECTIVE ❸

Determine the gain or loss on sale of property and equipment

	December 31	
	2017	**2016**
Land, buildings, and equipment..	$ 544.1	$ 575.1
Accumulated depreciation...	(195.1)	(209.4)

During 2017, Collicutt Energy paid $74.2 million for new property and equipment. Depreciation for the year totalled $38.1 million. During 2017, Collicutt sold property and equipment for $20.2 million. How much was Collicutt's gain or loss on the sale of the property and equipment? How would this gain or loss be reported on the income statement?

E6-39 Rindy Inc. has a popular line of beaded jewellery. Rindy reported net earnings of $21,000 for 2017. Rindy depreciates furniture, fixtures, equipment and automotive assets on a straight-line basis over five years and assumes no residual value. Depreciation expense for the year totaled $1,000 and the assets are four years old.

LEARNING OBJECTIVE ❷❸

Determine net income after a change in depreciation method

What would net income be for 2017 if Rindy used the double-diminishing balance (DDB) instead? The company's income tax rate is 25%. How does management choose which depreciation method to use?

E6-40 Air New Zealand (ANZ) is a Star Alliance member airline. Assume that early in 2017, ANZ purchased equipment at a cost of $200,000 (NZ). Management expects the equipment to remain in service for four years and the estimated residual value to be negligible. ANZ uses the straight-line depreciation method. Through an accounting error, ANZ expensed the entire cost of the equipment at the time of purchase.

LEARNING OBJECTIVE ❶

Determine equipment capitalizing versus expensing; measure the effect of an error

Requirement

Prepare a schedule to show the overstatement or understatement in the following items at the end of each year over the four-year life of the equipment. Ignore income taxes.

1. Total current assets

2. Equipment, net

3. Net income

4. Shareholders' equity

PROBLEMS (GROUP A)

LEARNING OBJECTIVE ❶❷

Identify the elements of property and plant's cost

P6-41A Assume Milne's Moving & Storage Ltd. (MMS) of Regina, Saskatchewan, incurred the following costs in acquiring land, making land improvements, and constructing and furnishing its own storage warehouse:

a.	Purchase price of 4 acres of land, including an old building that will be used for an office (land fair value is $320,000, building fair value is $80,000)	$350,000
b.	Landscaping (additional dirt and earth moving)	8,100
c.	Fence around the land	31,600
d.	Lawyer fee for title search on the land	1,000
e.	Delinquent real estate taxes on the land to be paid by MMS	7,500
f.	Company signs at front of the company property	3,400
g.	Building permit for the warehouse	1,500
h.	Architect fee for the design of the warehouse	24,500
i.	Masonry, carpentry, roofing, and other labour to construct the warehouse	920,000
j.	Renovation of the office building	50,200
k.	Interest cost on construction loan for warehouse	9,700
l.	Landscaping (trees and shrubs)	8,200
m.	Parking lot, concrete walks, and lights on the property	57,600
n.	Concrete, wood, and other materials used in the construction of the warehouse	234,300
o.	Supervisory salary of construction supervisor (85% to warehouse, 5% to land improvements, 10% to office building)	60,000
p.	Office furniture	115,700
q.	Transportation and installation of furniture	2,300

Assume MMS depreciates buildings over 40 years, land improvements over 20 years, and furniture over 8 years, all on a straight-line basis with zero residual value.

Requirements

1. Set up columns for Land, Land Improvements, Warehouse, Office Building, and Furniture. Show how to account for each of MMS's costs by listing the cost under the correct account. Determine the total cost of each asset.
2. Assuming that all construction was complete and the assets were placed in service on September 1, 2017, record depreciation for the year ended December 31, 2017. Round to the nearest dollar.
3. Identify the management issues included in this problem and what effect they have on business operations.

LEARNING OBJECTIVE ❶❷

Record property, plant, and equipment transactions; report on the balance sheet

P6-42A Lifestyle Lighting Ltd. reported the following on its balance sheet at December 31, 2016:

Property, plant and equipment, at cost:	
Land	$ 150,000
Buildings	400,000
Less Accumulated depreciation	(87,500)
Equipment	600,000
Less Accumulated depreciation	(260,000)

In early July 2017, Lifestyle Lighting Ltd. expanded operations and purchased additional equipment at a cost of $100,000. The company depreciates buildings by the straight-line method over 20 years with residual value of $50,000. Due to obsolescence, the equipment has a useful life of only 10 years and is being depreciated by the double-diminishing-balance method with zero residual value.

Requirements

1. Journalize Lifestyle Lighting Ltd.'s property, plant, and equipment purchase and depreciation transactions for 2017.
2. Report property, plant, and equipment on the December 31, 2017, balance sheet.

P6-43A Assume that Inter-Provincial Transport Ltd.'s balance sheet includes the following assets under Property, Plant, and Equipment: Land, Buildings, and Motor-Carrier Equipment. Inter-Provincial has a separate accumulated depreciation account for each of these assets except land. Further, assume that Inter-Provincial completed the following transactions:

LEARNING OBJECTIVE ❶❷❸

Record property, plant, and equipment transactions, derecognition, and changes in useful life

2017	
Jan. 2	Sold motor-carrier equipment with accumulated depreciation of $67,000 (cost of $130,000) for $70,000 cash. Purchased similar new equipment with a cash price of $176,000.
July 3	Sold a building that had cost $650,000 and had accumulated depreciation of $145,000 through December 31 of the preceding year. Depreciation is computed on a straight-line basis. The building had a 40-year useful life and a residual value of $250,000. Inter-Provincial received $100,000 cash and a $400,000 note receivable.
Oct. 29	Purchased land and a building for a single price of $420,000. An independent appraisal valued the land at $150,000 and the building at $300,000.
Dec. 31	Recorded depreciation as follows:
	New motor-carrier equipment has an expected useful life of six years and an estimated residual value of 5% of cost. Depreciation is computed on the double-diminishing-balance method.
	Depreciation on buildings is computed by the straight-line method. The new building carries a 40-year useful life and a residual value equal to 10% of its cost.

Requirement

1. Record the transactions in Inter-Provincial Transport Ltd.'s journal.
2. How does management choose which depreciation method to use?

P6-44A The board of directors of Special Services is reviewing its 2017 annual report. A new board member—a nurse with little business experience—questions the accountant about the depreciation amounts. The nurse wonders why depreciation expense has decreased from $200,000 in 2015 to $184,000 in 2016 to $172,000 in 2017. She states that she could understand the decreasing annual amounts if the company had been disposing of buildings each year, but that has not occurred. Further, she notes that growth in the city is increasing the values of company buildings. Why is the company recording depreciation when the property values are increasing?

LEARNING OBJECTIVE ❷

Explain the concept of depreciation

Requirement

Write a paragraph or two to explain the concept of depreciation to the nurse and to answer her questions.

P6-45A On January 3, 2016, B.W. Soffer Inc. paid $224,000 for a computer system. In addition to the basic purchase price, the company paid a setup fee of $6,200, $6,700 sales tax, and $3,100 for special installation. Management estimates that the computer will remain in service for five years and have a residual value of $20,000. The computer will process 50,000 documents the first year, decreasing annually by 5,000 during each of the next four years (that is, 45,000 documents in 2017, 40,000 documents in 2018, and so on). In trying to decide which depreciation method to use, the company president has requested a depreciation schedule for each of three depreciation methods (straight-line, units-of-production, and double-diminishing-balance).

LEARNING OBJECTIVE ❶❷

Compute depreciation by three methods

Requirements

1. Prepare a depreciation schedule for each of the three depreciation methods listed, showing asset cost, depreciation expense, accumulated depreciation, and asset carrying amount.
2. B.W. Soffer Inc. reports to shareholders and creditors in the financial statements using the depreciation method that maximizes reported income in the early years of asset use. Consider the first year B.W. Soffer Inc. uses the computer system. Identify the depreciation method that meets the company's objectives. Discuss the advantages of each depreciation method.

LEARNING OBJECTIVE
❶❷❸❻

Analyze property, plant, and equipment transactions from a company's financial statements

P6-46A The excerpts that follow are adapted from financial statements of a Canadian not-for-profit organization.

(amounts in thousands)	March 31	
Balance Sheet	2017	2016
Assets		
Total current assets	$277,631	$261,015
Property, plant, and equipment	68,406	61,225
Less accumulated depreciation	(26,909)	(22,725)
Long-term investments	108,302	147,165

	For the Year Ended March 31	
Consolidated Statement of Cash Flows	2017	2016
Operating excess of revenues over expense	$13,068	$15,321
Noncash items affecting net income:		
Depreciation	4,184	3,748
Cash flows from investing activities:		
Additions to property, plant, and equipment	(7,781)	(8,623)
Reduction of (addition to) long-term investments	38,863	(96,316)

Requirements

1. How much was the entity's cost of property, plant, and equipment at March 31, 2017? How much was the carrying amount of property, plant, and equipment? Show computations.
2. The financial statements give four pieces of evidence that the entity purchased property, plant, and equipment and sold long-term investments during 2017. What is the evidence?
3. Prepare T-accounts for Property, Plant and Equipment, Accumulated Depreciation, and Long-Term Investments. Then show all the activity in these accounts during 2017. Label each increase or decrease and give its dollar amount.
4. Why is depreciation added to net income on the statement of cash flows?

LEARNING OBJECTIVE ❹

Account for intangibles and the related expenses

P6-47A **Part 1.** Sobeys Inc.'s balance sheet reports the asset Cost in Excess of Net Assets of Purchased Businesses. Assume that Sobeys acquired another company, which carried these figures:

Carrying amount of net assets	$3.8 million
Fair value of assets	4.1 million

Requirements

1. What is the term used in Canadian financial reporting for the asset Cost in Excess of Net Assets of Purchased Businesses?
2. Record Sobeys Inc.'s purchase of the other company for $5.3 million cash.
3. Assume that Sobeys determined that the asset Cost in Excess of Net Assets of Purchased Businesses increased in value by $800,000. How would this transaction be recorded?

Then, suppose Cost in Excess of Net Assets of Purchased Businesses decreased in value by $800,000. How would this transaction be recorded? Discuss the basis for your decision in each case.

Part 2. Suppose Ford paid $2.6 million for a patent related to an integrated system, including hands-free cell phone, GPS, and iPod connectivity. The company expects to install this system in its automobiles for four years. Ford will sell this as an "extra" for $1,500. In the first year, 10,000 units were sold. All costs per unit totalled $835.

Requirements

1. As the CFO, how would you record transactions relating to the patent in the first year?
2. Prepare the income statement for the integrated system's operations for the first year. Evaluate the profitability of the integrated system's operations. Use an income tax rate of 38%.
3. Explain what items were recorded as assets and why.

P6-48A At the end of 2016, Geothermal Heating Ltd. had total assets of $17.4 million and total liabilities of $9.2 million. Included among the assets were property, plant, and equipment with a cost of $4.8 million and accumulated depreciation of $3.4 million.

LEARNING OBJECTIVE ❻

Report property, plant, and equipment transactions on the statement of cash flows

Assume that Geothermal Heating completed the following selected transactions during 2017. The company earned total revenues of $26.5 million and incurred total expenses of $21.3 million, which included depreciation of $1.7 million. During the year, Geothermal Heating paid $1.4 million for new equipment and sold old equipment for $0.3 million. The cost of the assets sold was $0.8 million, and their accumulated depreciation was $0.4 million.

Requirements

1. Explain how to determine whether Geothermal Heating had a gain or loss on the sale of old equipment during the year. What was the amount of the gain or loss, if any?
2. How will Geothermal Heating report property, plant, and equipment on the balance sheet at December 31, 2017, after all the year's activity? What will the carrying amount of property, plant, and equipment be?
3. How will Geothermal Heating report operating activities and investing activities on its statement of cash flows for 2017? The company's statement of cash flows starts with net income.

P6-49A Black Corporation operates general merchandise and food discount stores in the United States. The company reported the following information for the three years ending January 31, 2017:

LEARNING OBJECTIVE ❺

Calculate return on assets

	A	B	C	D	E
1	**Black Corporation** Income Statement (Adapted) For the years ended				
2	*(in millions)*	Jan. 31, 2017	Jan. 31, 2016	Jan. 31, 2015	
3	Total net revenue	$ 67,390	$ 65,357	$ 64,948	
4	Cost of revenue	45,725	44,062	44,157	
5	Selling, general, and administrative	16,413	16,622	16,389	
6	Operating income or loss	5,252	4,673	4,402	
7	Other revenue (expense)	(757)	(801)	(866)	
8	Income before tax	4,495	3,872	3,536	
9	Income tax expense	(1,575)	(1,384)	(1,322)	
10	Net income	$ 2,920	$ 2,488	$ 2,214	
11					

	A	B	C	D	E
1	**Black Corporation** Partial Balance Sheet (Condensed)				
2	*(in millions)*	Jan. 31, 2017	Jan. 31, 2016	Jan. 31, 2015	
3	Total current assets	$ 17,213	$ 18,424	$ 17,488	
4	Property, plant, and equipment	25,493	25,280	25,756	
5	Other assets	999	829	862	
6	Total assets	$ 43,705	$ 44,533	$ 44,106	
7					

Requirements

1. Compute return on assets for Black Corporation for the years ended January 31, 2017, and January 31, 2016.
2. What factors contributed to the change in return on assets during the year?

LEARNING OBJECTIVES ❸❻

Analyze the effect of a plant asset disposal and the cash flow impact of long-lived asset transactions

P6-50A Cook Corporation reported the following related to property and equipment (all in millions):

From the balance sheets:

	12/31/16	12/31/15
Property and equipment	$26,430	$24,220
Accumulated depreciation	(16,045)	(15,210)

From the investing activities section of the 2016 cash flow statement:

Cash used to purchase property and equipment	($2,820)
Proceeds from sale of property and equipment	43

From the 2016 income statement:

Depreciation expense	$1,145
Gain or loss on the sale of equipment	??

Requirements

1. Draw T-accounts for Property and Equipment and Accumulated Depreciation. Enter information as presented and solve for the unknown in each account. (*Hint:* Recall the types of transactions that make each of the two accounts increase and decrease. You are solving for the cost of property and equipment sold and the accumulated depreciation on those assets.)
2. Based on your calculations in requirement 1, calculate the carrying amount of assets sold during 2016. What is the difference between the sales price and the carrying amount?
3. Prepare the journal entry for the sale of property and equipment during 2016. Describe the effect of this transaction on the financial statements. Compare the sales price and the carrying amount in the journal entry, and compare this to the difference you calculated in requirement 2. Describe briefly.
4. Prepare a T-account for Property and Equipment, Net. Repeat requirement 1.

PROBLEMS (GROUP B)

P6-51B McMillan Tire Inc. operates in several provinces. The head office incurred the following costs in acquiring land and a building, making land improvements, and constructing and furnishing a garage showroom:

LEARNING OBJECTIVE ❶❷

Identify the elements of property, plant, and equipment cost

a.	Purchase price of land, including a building that will be enlarged to be a warehouse (land fair value is $150,000; building fair value is $50,000)	$180,000
b.	Fence around the land	26,000
c.	Company signs near front and rear approaches to the company property	25,000
d.	Title insurance on the land acquisition	1,200
e.	Renovation of the warehouse	21,300
f.	Landscaping (additional dirt and earth moving)	3,550
g.	Architect fee for the design of the garage/showroom	45,000
h.	Building permit for the building	200
i.	Delinquent real estate taxes on the land to be paid by McMillan	3,700
j.	Concrete, wood, and other materials used in the construction of the garage/showroom	322,000
k.	Supervisory salary of construction supervisor (90% to garage/showroom 6% to land improvements, and 4% to building renovation)	55,000
l.	Landscaping (trees and shrubs)	5,350
m.	Masonry, carpentry, roofing, and other labour to construct the garage/showroom	234,000
n.	Lights for the parking lot, walkways, and company signs	8,900
o.	Parking lots and concrete walks on the property	17,450
p.	Interest cost on construction loan for garage/showroom	3,300
q.	Installation of equipment	8,000
r.	Equipment for the garage/showroom	80,000

McMillan Tire depreciates buildings over 40 years, land improvements over 10 years, and equipment over 8 years, all on a straight-line basis with zero residual value.

Requirements

1. Determine the total cost of each asset. Set up columns for Land, Land Improvements, Garage/Showroom, Warehouse, and Equipment. Decide how to account for each of McMillan's costs by listing the cost under the correct account.
2. All construction was complete and the assets were placed in service on March 29. Record depreciation for the year ended December 31. Round figures to the nearest dollar.
3. Identify the issues of this problem, and discuss how your decisions would affect the results of McMillan Tire Inc.

P6-52B Moreau Lock & Key Ltd. has a hefty investment in security equipment, as reported in the company's balance sheet at December 31, 2016:

LEARNING OBJECTIVE ❶

Record property, plant, and equipment transactions; report on the balance sheet

Property, plant, and equipment, at cost:	
Land	$ 200,000
Buildings	310,000
Less Accumulated depreciation	(40,000)
Security equipment	620,000
Less Accumulated depreciation	(370,000)

In early October 2017, Moreau Lock & Key purchased additional security equipment at a cost of $80,000. The company depreciates buildings by the straight-line method over

20 years with a residual value of $70,000. Due to obsolescence, security equipment has a useful life of only eight years and is being depreciated by the double-diminishing-balance method with zero residual value.

Requirements

1. How will Moreau Lock & Key's equipment purchase be recorded? What will the 2017 depreciation expense be?
2. Report property, plant, and equipment on the company's December 31, 2017, balance sheet.

LEARNING OBJECTIVE ❶❷❸

Record property, plant, and equipment transactions

P6-53B Schmaltz Cable Company's balance sheet reports the following assets under Property, Plant, and Equipment: Land, Buildings, Office Furniture, Communication Equipment, and Televideo Equipment. The company has a separate accumulated depreciation account for each of these assets except land. Assume that Schmaltz Cable completed the following transactions:

2017	
Jan. 4	Sold communication equipment with accumulated depreciation of $85,000 (cost of $96,000) for $18,000. Purchased new equipment for $118,000.
June 30	Sold a building that had cost $495,000 and had accumulated depreciation of $255,000 through December 31 of the preceding year. Depreciation is computed on a straight-line basis. The building has a 40-year useful life and a residual value of $95,000. The company received $50,000 cash and a $250,000 note receivable.
Nov. 4	Purchased used communication and televideo equipment from Rogers Cable Company. Total cost was $80,000 paid in cash. An independent appraisal valued the communication equipment at $75,000 and the televideo equipment at $25,000.
Dec. 31	Depreciation is recorded as follows: Equipment is depreciated by the double-diminishing-balance method over a five-year life with zero residual value. Depreciation is recorded separately on the equipment purchased on January 4 and on November 4.

Requirement

1. Record the transactions in Schmaltz Cable's journal.
2. How does management choose which depreciation method to use?

LEARNING OBJECTIVE ❷

Explain the concept of depreciation

P6-54B The board of directors of the Canadian Red Cross is having its regular quarterly meeting. Accounting policies are on the agenda, and depreciation is being discussed. A new board member, a social worker, has some strong opinions about two aspects of depreciation policy. The new board member argues that depreciation must be coupled with a fund to replace company assets. Otherwise, there is no substance to depreciation, he argues. He also challenges the three-year estimated life over which the Canadian Red Cross is depreciating association computers. He notes that the computers will last much longer and should be depreciated over at least 10 years.

Requirement

Write a paragraph or two to explain the concept of depreciation to the new board member and to answer his arguments.

LEARNING OBJECTIVE ❶❷

Compute depreciation by three methods

P6-55B On January 2, 2015, Yuki Sporting Goods Ltd. purchased branding equipment at a cost of $63,000. Before placing the equipment in service, the company spent $2,200 for delivery, $4,000 to customize the equipment, and $800 for installation. Management estimates that the equipment will remain in service for six years and have a residual value of $16,000. The equipment can be expected to brand 18,000 pieces in each of the first four years and 14,000 pieces in each of the next two years. In trying to decide which depreciation method to use, George Yuki requests a depreciation schedule for each method (straight-line, units-of-production, and double-diminishing-balance).

Requirements

1. Prepare a depreciation schedule for each of the depreciation methods listed, showing asset cost, depreciation expense, accumulated depreciation, and asset carrying amount.
2. Yuki Sporting Goods reports to its banker in the financial statements using the depreciation method that maximizes reported income in the early years of asset use. Consider the first year that Yuki Sporting Goods uses the equipment. Identify the depreciation method that meets the company's objectives. Explain your choice.

P6-56B CrossCanada Transport Inc. (CC) provides warehouse and distribution services. The excerpts that follow are adapted from CC's financial statements for fiscal year 2017.

LEARNING OBJECTIVE
❶❷❸❹❻

Analyze property, plant, and equipment transactions from a company's financial statements

(amounts in thousands)	October 31	
Balance Sheet	2017	2016
Assets		
Total current assets	$237,936	$208,530
Premises and equipment	5,941	5,246
Less Accumulated depreciation	(3,810)	(3,428)
Goodwill	4,752	4,304
	For the Year Ended October 31	
Statement of Cash Flows (in millions)	2017	2016
Cash provided from operating activities:		
Net income from continuing operations	$5,492	$4,757
Noncash items affecting net income:		
Depreciation	434	405
Cash used in investing activities:		
Acquisition of premises and equipment	(706)	(511)
Cash used in acquisitions (including $41 of premises and equipment)	(373)	(256)

Requirements

1. How much was CC's cost of property and equipment at October 31, 2017? How much was the carrying amount of premises and equipment? Show computations.
2. The financial statements give three pieces of evidence that CC purchased premises and equipment during 2017. What are they?
3. Prepare T-accounts for Premises and Equipment and Accumulated Depreciation. Then show all the activity in these accounts during 2017. Did CC dispose of any assets and, if so, what was the carrying amount?
4. Why has goodwill not been amortized?

P6-57B Part 1. The Coca-Cola Company's (CCC) balance sheet reports the asset Goodwill. Assume that CCC purchased an asset to be included in Goodwill as part of the acquisition of another company, which carried these figures (thousands of dollars):

LEARNING OBJECTIVE ❹

Account for intangibles and the related expenses

Carrying amount of long-term assets	$34,550
Fair value of assets	49,000
Liabilities	4,500

Requirements

1. Explain the terms *carrying amount of assets*, *fair value of assets*, and *goodwill*. On what would you base the purchase price of the acquisition?
2. Make the journal entry to record CCC's purchase of the other company for $50,000 cash.

Part 2. Joshua Thomas has written a new dance song which Luv Sound Inc. would like to record. Joshua is negotiating the rights to the new song. It is estimated that Luv Sound will sell about 500,000 recordings either on CD, to radio station airings, or to iPod sales. Joshua would like to receive $2,000,000 for the copyright to this song.

Requirements

1. As the CFO of Luv Sound, decide whether $2,000,000 is an appropriate amount to pay for the copyright for Joshua Thomas's song.
2. If you chose to purchase the copyright, show how you would record the transaction.
3. What would be the accumulated amortization after 300,000 copies of the song had been sold by Luv Sound Inc.?

LEARNING OBJECTIVE ⑥

Report property, plant, and equipment transactions on the statement of cash flows

P6-58B At the end of 2016, a telecommunications company had total assets of $15.3 billion and total liabilities of $10.7 billion. Included among the assets were property, plant, and equipment with a cost of $16.4 billion and accumulated depreciation of $9.1 billion.

Suppose that the company completed the following selected transactions during 2017. The company earned total revenues of $11.6 billion and incurred total expenses of $9.89 billion, which included depreciation of $1.84 billion. During the year, the company paid $1.8 billion for new property, plant, and equipment, and sold old property, plant, and equipment for $0.2 billion. The cost of the assets sold was $0.29 billion and their accumulated depreciation was $0.29 billion.

Requirements

1. Explain how to determine whether the company had a gain or a loss on the sale of the old property, plant, and equipment. What was the amount of the gain or loss, if any?
2. Show how the company would report property, plant, and equipment on the balance sheet at December 31, 2017.
3. Show how the company would report operating activities and investing activities on its statement of cash flows for 2017. The company's statement of cash flows starts with net income.

LEARNING OBJECTIVE ⑤

Calculate return on assets

P6-59B Kohl's Corporation operates family oriented department stores that sell moderately priced apparel and housewares. The company reported the following information (adapted) for the three years ending January 31, 2017:

	A	B	C	D	E
1	**Kohl's Corporation** Income Statement (Adapted)				
2		Jan. 31, 2017	Jan. 31, 2016	Jan. 31, 2015	
3	Net sales	$ 18,391	$ 17,178	$ 16,389	
4	Cost of merchandise sold	11,359	10,680	10,334	
5	Selling, general, and administrative	5,118	4,786	4,519	
6	Operating income	1,914	1,712	1,536	
7	Other revenue (expense)	(132)	(124)	(111)	
8	Income before tax	1,782	1,588	1,425	
9	Provision for income tax	(668)	(597)	(540)	
10	Net income	$ 1,114	$ 991	$ 885	
11					

Source: Based on the data from Kohl's Corporation Annual Report.

	A	B	C	D	E
1	**Kohl's Corporation** Partial Balance Sheet				
2		Jan. 31, 2017	Jan. 31, 2016	Jan. 31, 2015	
3	Total current assets	$ 5,645	$ 5,485	$ 3,728	
4	Long-term investments	386	336	333	
5	Property, plant, and equipment	7,256	7,018	6,984	
6	Other assets	277	321	318	
7	Total assets	$ 13,564	$ 13,160	$ 11,363	
8					

Requirements

1. Compute the return on assets for Kohl's for the years ended January 31, 2017, and January 31, 2016.
2. What factors contributed to the change in return on assets during the year?

P6-60B Morgan Corporation reported the following related to property and equipment (all in millions):

From the balance sheets:

LEARNING OBJECTIVES ❸❻

Analyze the effect of a plant asset disposal and the cash flow impact of long-lived asset transactions

	12/31/16	12/31/15
Property and equipment	$23,530	$21,350
Accumulated depreciation	(18,395)	(17,530)

From the investing activities section of the 2016 cash flow statement:

Cash used to purchase property and equipment	($2,820)
Proceeds from sale of property and equipment	56

From the 2016 income statement:

Depreciation expense	$1,145
Gain or loss on the sale of equipment	??

Requirements

1. Draw T-accounts for Property and Equipment and Accumulated Depreciation. Enter information as presented and solve for the unknown in each account. (*Hint:* Recall the types of transactions that make each of the two accounts increase and decrease. You are solving for the cost of Property and Equipment sold and the Accumulated Depreciation on those assets.)
2. Based on your calculations in requirement 1, calculate the carrying amount of assets sold during 2016. What is the difference between the sales price and the carrying amount?
3. Prepare the journal entry for the sale of property and equipment during 2016. Describe the effect of this transaction on the financial statements. Compare the sales price and the carrying amount in the journal entry, and compare this to the difference you calculated in requirement 2. Describe briefly.
4. Prepare a T-account for Property and Equipment, Net. Repeat requirement 1.

APPLY YOUR KNOWLEDGE

DECISION CASES

This section's material reflects CPA enabling competencies,* including:

1. Professionalism and ethical behaviour
2. Problem-solving and decision-making
3. Communication
4. Self-management
5. Teamwork and leadership

LEARNING OBJECTIVE ❷❸

Measure profitability based on different depreciation methods

Case 1. Suppose you are considering investing in two businesses, La Petite France Bakery and Burgers Ahoy Inc. The two companies are virtually identical, and both began operations at the beginning of the current year.

In early January, both companies purchased equipment costing $175,000 that had a 10-year estimated useful life and a $10,000 residual value. La Petite France uses the depreciation method that maximizes income for reporting purposes. In contrast, Burgers Ahoy uses the double-diminishing-balance method for depreciation purposes. Assume that both companies' trial balances at December 31 included the following:

Sales revenue	$350,000
Cost of goods sold	94,000
Operating expenses before depreciation	50,000

The income tax rate is 25%.

Requirements

1. Prepare both companies' income statements.
2. Write an investment newsletter to address the following questions for your clients. Which company appears to be more profitable? If prices continue rising over the long term, in which company would you prefer to invest? Why?

LEARNING OBJECTIVE ❶❹

Understand property, plant, and equipment and intangible assets

Case 2. The following questions are unrelated except that they all apply to property, plant, and equipment and intangible assets:

1. The manager of Fashion Forward Ltd. regularly buys property, plant, and equipment and debits the cost to Repairs and Maintenance Expense. Why would she do that, since she knows this action violates IFRS?
2. The manager of Greytown Express Inc. regularly debits the cost of repairs and maintenance of property, plant, and equipment to Plant and Equipment. Why would he do that, since he knows he is violating IFRS?
3. It has been suggested that because many intangible assets have no value except to the company that owns them, they should be valued at $1.00 or zero on the balance sheet. Many accountants disagree with this view. Which view do you support? Why?

ETHICAL ISSUES

Vitner's Ltd. purchased land and a building for the lump sum of $6.0 million. To report a higher net income, Mary Drink allocated 60% of the purchase price to the building and only 40% to the land. A more realistic allocation would have been 80% to the building and 20% to the land.

Requirements

1. Explain the advantage of allocating too little to the building and too much to the land.
2. Was Vitner's allocation ethical? If so, state why. If not, why not? Identify who was harmed.

---

*© Chartered Professional Accountants of Canada.

FOCUS ON FINANCIALS

Canadian Tire Corporation

LEARNING OBJECTIVE ❷❸❻

Explain property, plant, and equipment activity

Refer to Canadian Tire's financial statements in Appendix A at the end of this book, and answer the following questions.

1. Which depreciation method does Canadian Tire use for reporting to shareholders and creditors in the financial statements?
2. During 2014, Canadian Tire sold building, fixtures, and equipment (assets). What were the proceeds? What was the cost of the building, fixtures, and equipment disposed of?
3. How much did Canadian Tire pay for land, building, and fixtures during 2014? What about in 2013? Evaluate the trend in these expenditures as to whether it conveys good news for Canadian Tire.
4. During 2014, Canadian Tire added new property, plant, and equipment. Therefore, it is possible that the company's property and equipment at the end of 2014 were proportionately newer than the assets the company held at the end of 2013. Were property and equipment proportionately newer or older at the end of 2014 (versus 2013)?

FOCUS ON ANALYSIS

Canadian Tire Corporation

LEARNING OBJECTIVE
❷❸❹❻

Analyze property, plant, and equipment and intangible assets

MyAccountingLab

Refer to Canadian Tire's financial statements in Appendix A at the end of the book, and answer the following questions:

1. How much was Canadian Tire's depreciation and amortization expense during fiscal year 2014? How much was Canadian Tire's accumulated depreciation and amortization at the end of year 2013? Explain why accumulated depreciation and amortization exceeds depreciation and amortization expense for the year 2014.
2. Explain why Canadian Tire adds depreciation and amortization expenses back to net income in the computation of net cash from operating activities.
3. Does Canadian Tire have any goodwill? In 2014, was amortization on goodwill charged? Canadian Tire describes intangible assets. What are they? How much amortization of intangible assets did Canadian Tire record in 2014?

GROUP PROJECT

Obtain the annual report of two public Canadian companies from the same industry. Most annual reports can be downloaded from their websites. Examine the notes and other information that may be useful to analyze property, plant, and equipment, as well as intangible assets, including goodwill.

Requirements

1. What additions and disposals did the company make during the year? If there were any new additions, did they have to borrow money to help finance the cost of these assets? How can you tell?
2. Was there any impairment of long-lived assets? If so, what contributed to this impairment? How did it impact the financial statements?
3. Compute the return on assets for both companies for the two most recent years. Which company is using their assets more efficiently?
4. Write a memo to summarize your findings, stating which company you would invest in.

CHECK YOUR WORK

STOP + THINK ANSWERS

STOP + THINK (6-1)

These improvements wear out over time, and in the case of leasehold improvements, they expire once the terms of the lease are up.

STOP + THINK (6-2)

The yearly depreciation would be $2,000 [($13,000 − $3,000)/5]. Therefore, 2 years of use would be left [($7,000 − $3,000)/($2,000)].

STOP + THINK (6-3)

1. An accounting change that lengthens the estimated useful lives of depreciable assets

   (a) decreases depreciation expense, and

   (b, c) increases net income and owners' equity.

2. Investor reactions are not always predictable. There is research to indicate that companies cannot fool investors. In this case, investment advisors would *probably* subtract from the company's reported net income the amount added by the accounting change. Investors could then use the remaining net *loss* figure to evaluate the company's lack of progress during the year. Investors would probably view the company as worse for having made this accounting change. It is probably for this reason that such changes in accounting estimates are so rare in Canada.

STOP + THINK (6-4)

Goodwill is not amortized because it has an indefinite life. If the value of goodwill is impaired, it must be written down.

STOP + THINK (6-5)

The ROA ratio measures how profitably management has used the assets that both the shareholders and creditors have provided the company. Net income belongs to the shareholders, and the creditors earn the interest.

STOP + THINK (6-6)

1. Canadian Tire spent $538.6 million on property, plant, and equipment, and $150.1 million on intangible assets.

2. The company sold assets for $538.6 million that had a carrying amount of $539.6 million. The result of the sale was a loss of $1 million ($538.6 million received and $539.6 million carrying amount).

3. Report the loss on the *income statement* under the heading *Non-operating income (expense)*.

QUICK QUIZ ANSWERS

1. b [($850,000/[$850,000 + $675,000 + $475,000]) × $1,500,000 = $637,500]

2. a

3. a [($25,000 − $2,500)/5 × 5/12 = $1,875]

4. d [($25,000 − $2,500)/5 × 2 = $9,000; $25,000 − $9,000 = $16,000]

5. b [$25,000 × 2/5 = $10,000; ($25,000 − $10,000) × 2/5 = $6,000]

6. a [($25,000 − $2,500)/5 × 4 = $18,000; $25,000 − $18,000 = $7,000; $11,500 − $7,000 = gain of $4,500, therefore, a gain will be realized]

7. c [$17,000 × 2/4 = $8,500; ($17,000 − $8,500) × 2/4 = $4,250; $8,500 + $4,250 = $12,750]

8. c

9. a

10. d

11. b

12. e

13. c

14. c

Investments and the Time Value of Money

7

Fred Thornhill/Reuters Pictures

LEARNING OBJECTIVES

1. **Analyze** and **report** non-strategic investments
2. **Analyze** and **report** strategic investments
3. **Analyze** and **report** long-term investments in bonds
4. **Report** investing activities on the statement of cash flows
5. **Explain** the impact of the time value of money on certain types of investments

CPA COMPETENCIES

Competencies* addressed in this chapter:

1.2.2 Evaluates treatment for routine transactions

5.1.1 Evaluates the entity's financial state

SPOTLIGHT

ONEX Corporation holds several different types of investments. Have you ever wondered what you will do with all the money you will be earning once you graduate? Maybe you will start investing through a retirement or savings plan at work, and you may make some investments on your own. The reasons people invest are for current income (interest and dividends) and for appreciation of the investment's value (stocks and real estate, for example). Some very wealthy individuals invest in a wide variety of traditional and non-traditional investments in order to obtain significant influence over, or even to control, corporate entities and to maximize their wealth.

Businesses like ONEX, Canadian Tire Corporation, and TELUS invest their money for the same reasons. If you look at ONEX's balance sheet on the next page, you will see that of the $28,936 million of total assets they own, they have $5,026 million in long-term investments. This decreased from the 2013 balance of $7,564 million. In 2013, they held $754 million in short-term investments but in 2014, the balance is zero. This means they sold all of their short-term investments and some of their long-term investments. In this chapter you'll learn how to account for investments of all types.

	A	B	C	D
1	**ONEX Corporation** Consolidated Balance Sheet (Partial, Adapted) As at December 31, 2014 and 2013			
2	*(in millions of U.S. dollars)*			
3	Assets	**2014**	**2013**	
4	**Current assets**			
5	Cash and cash equivalents	$ 3,764	$ 3,191	
6	Short-term investments		754	
7	Accounts receivable	3,085	3,639	
8	Inventories	2,013	3,872	
9	Other current assets	1,483	1,478	
10	Total current assets	$ 10,345	$ 12,934	
11				
12	Property, plant, and equipment	2,902	5,105	
13	Long-term investments	5,026	7,564	
14	Other non-current assets	666	2,100	
15	Intangible assets	5,069	4,695	
16	Goodwill	4,928	4,469	
17	**Total Assets**	$ 28,936	$ 36,867	
18				

Source: ONEX Management's Discussion and Analysis and Financial Statements.

Founded in 1983, ONEX is an investment firm that buys significant interests in companies with the intention of controlling their operations. Once a company is acquired, they work with the company's management to help them become a leader in their industry. The many companies ONEX has acquired significant control of include Celestica and Cineplex. These investments are reflected in various asset accounts, such as inventory; property, plant, and equipment; and goodwill. In addition, ONEX has long-term investments.

Throughout this course, you have become increasingly familiar with the financial statements of companies such as Canadian Tire Corporation, Leon's Furniture, and CGI Group. You have seen most of the items that appear in a set of financial statements. One of your learning goals should be to develop the ability to interpret whatever you encounter in real-company statements. This chapter will help you advance toward that goal.

The first part of the chapter shows how to account for non-strategic and strategic investments, including a brief overview of consolidated financial statements. The second half of the chapter covers accounting for the time value of money.

Share Investments: A Review

Investments come in all sizes and shapes—ranging from a few shares to the acquisition of an entire company, to interests in other types of investments, such as corporate bonds. In this chapter, we will introduce you to the accounting for various types of investments from the perspective of the purchaser, or investor.

To consider investments, we need to define two key terms. The entity that owns shares in a corporation is the *investor*. The corporation that issued the shares is the *investee*. If you own ONEX common shares, you are an investor and ONEX is the investee.

Share Prices

Investors buy more shares in transactions among themselves than directly from large companies, such as ONEX. Each share is issued only once, but it may be traded

	52-Week		Stock				Net
Hi		Lo	Symbol	Div		Close	Change
$83.73		$60.02	OCX	$0.06		$79.40	+$1.57

EXHIBIT 7-1
Share Price Information for ONEX Corporation

Source: Based on the data taken from ONEX Corporation Annual Information Form.

among investors many times thereafter. You may log onto the Internet or consult a newspaper to learn ONEX's current share price.

Exhibit 7-1 presents information on ONEX common shares from a popular financial website for October 23, 2015. During the previous 52 weeks, ONEX shares reached a high price of $83.73 and a low price of $60.02 per share. The annual cash dividend is $0.06 per share. At the end of the day, the price of the shares closed at $79.40, up $1.57 from the closing price of the shares on October 22, 2015.

Reporting Investments on the Balance Sheet

An investment is an asset to the investor. The investment may be short term or long term. *Short-term investments* are current assets and are sometimes called *temporary investments* or *marketable securities*. To be listed as short term on the balance sheet,

- the investment must be *liquid* (readily convertible to cash).
- the investor must intend either to convert the investment to cash within one year or to use it to pay a current liability.

Investments that are not short term are classified as **long-term investments**, a category of non-current assets. Long-term investments include shares and bonds that the investor expects to hold for longer than one year. Exhibit 7-2 shows the positions of short-term and long-term investments on the balance sheet.

	A	B	C	D
1	**Current assets:**			
2	Cash	$ X		
3	**Short-term investments**	X		
4	Accounts receivable	X		
5	Inventories	X		
6	Prepaid expenses	X		
7	Total current assets		$ X	
8	**Long-term investments [or simply Investments]**		X	
9	Property, plant, and equipment (net)		X	
10	Intangible assets (net)		X	
11	Other assets		X	
12				

EXHIBIT 7-2
Reporting Investments on the Balance Sheet

Accounting for Investments in Shares

This topic is normally covered in an intermediate or advanced accounting course. Accordingly, the following discussion is intended to provide you with a basic understanding of investments. There are two categories of share investments: non-strategic and strategic investments.

1. *Non-strategic investments.* **Non-strategic investments** may be short-term or long-term depending on how long the company intends to hold them. For the long-term investment, if the investor owns less than but up to 20% of the voting shares

of the investee, usually the investor has little or no influence on the investee, in which case the strategy would be to hold the investment in periods beyond the end of the fiscal year. For both types of investments, the investor records the investment at the price paid and adjusts the investment account for changes in fair value either through net income (short-term or long-term investments) or through other comprehensive income (only for investments not held for short-term trading). Until January 1, 2018, if the fair value is not available, then the investment is recorded at the price paid and no adjustments are made to its value (the cost method). After this date, under IFRS 9, the investor will record the initial investment at the price paid and, at each reporting date, record any changes in fair value through either other comprehensive income (currently referred to as "Available-for-Sale Investments"[*]) or through profit or loss (net income). This chapter will illustrate IFRS 9 because Canadian companies can choose to adopt this approach early.

2. *Strategic investments.*

   a. *Investments subject to significant influence.* An investor owning between 20% and 50% of the investee's voting stock or other ownership interests may significantly influence the business activities of the investee. Significant influence allows the investor to direct the affairs of the investee. Such an investor can probably affect dividend policies, product lines, and other important matters. The investor accounts for the investment using the *equity method* by which the investor's proportionate share of the investee's profits and losses are treated as income or loss by the investor. The investor's share of dividends paid by the investee are treated as a return of investment and are credited to the investment account.

   b. *Investments in subsidiaries.* A subsidiary is a company controlled by another company (the parent), which is entitled to the rewards and bears the risks of the subsidiary. Generally a parent will own more than 50% of the voting shares of the subsidiary. Such an investment allows the investor to elect a majority of the members of the investee's board of directors and thus control the investee's policies, such as its production, distribution (supply chain), financing, and investing decisions. The financial statements of the investee are consolidated with those of the investor.

OBJECTIVE

❶ **Analyze** and **report** non-strategic investments

ANALYZE AND REPORT NON-STRATEGIC INVESTMENTS

As mentioned previously, a non-strategic investment may be short-term or long-term; the investor will hold the investment to earn dividend revenue and/or capital appreciation but has no interest in directing the affairs of the investee. In the case of a long-term investment, the investor usually holds less than 20% of the voting shares and would normally play no important role in the investee's operations.

Non-strategic investments are accounted for at fair value because the company expects to sell the investment at its current market price. The investment is recorded at the price paid and reported on the balance sheet at *fair value*.

Suppose ONEX purchases 1,000 Agrium Inc. common shares at the market price of $50.00 on July 10, 2017. Assume ONEX has no significant influence over Agrium

---

[*]The "Available for Sale" category will disappear as of January 1, 2018.

and intends to hold this investment for longer than a year. This type of investment is classified as a non-strategic investment. ONEX's entry to record the investment is:

	A	B	C	D	E
1	2017				
2	July 10	Investment in Agrium (1,000 × $50.00)	50,000		
3		Cash		50,000	
4		Purchased investment.			
5					

ASSETS	=	LIABILITIES	+	SHAREHOLDERS' EQUITY
+50,000				
−50,000	=	0	+	0

Assume on October 5, 2017 that ONEX receives a $0.14 per share cash dividend on the Agrium Inc. shares. ONEX's entry to record receipt of the dividend is:

	A	B	C	D	E
1	2017				
2	Oct. 5	Cash (1,000 × $0.14)	140		
3		Dividend Revenue		140	
4		Received cash dividend.			
5					

ASSETS	=	LIABILITIES	+	SHAREHOLDERS' EQUITY
140	=	0	+	+ 140 Revenue

The journal entries given in the example above would be the same for a short-term investment.

What Value of an Investment Is Most Relevant?

Fair value is the amount for which you can buy or sell an investment. Because of the relevance of fair values for decision making, non-strategic investments in shares are reported on the balance sheet at their fair value. On the balance sheet date we therefore adjust non-strategic investments from their last carrying amount to current fair value. Assume that the fair value of the Agrium common shares is $53,000 on December 31, 2017. As previously discussed, at initial recognition the investor can choose to report the changes in fair value in non-strategic investments either through net income or through other comprehensive income (currently referred to as "Available-for-Sale Investment"). For short-term investments, the changes in fair value are reported through net income. Shown below are the journal entries to report changes in fair value under both approaches.

Company chooses to report changes in fair value in the investment through net income:

Investment in Agrium	3,000	
Unrealized gain		3,000
Adjusted investment to fair value.		

Unrealized gains are reported under "Other Income" on the Income statement.

Company chooses to report changes in fair value in the investment (not held for trading) through other comprehensive income:

Investment in Agrium	3,000	
Other Comprehensive Income		3,000
Adjusted investment to fair value.		

Other Comprehensive Income is reported below net income on the statement of comprehensive income.

The increase in the investment's fair value creates additional equity for the investor.

ASSETS	=	LIABILITIES	+	SHAREHOLDERS' EQUITY
+3,000	=	0	+	+3,000 Unrealized gain

The Investment in Agrium account and the Other Comprehensive Income or Unrealized Gain account would appear as follows:

Investment in Agrium	Other Comprehensive Income or Unrealized Gain
50,000	
3,000	3,000

If the investment's fair value declines, the Investment in Agrium account is credited. The corresponding debit is to Other Comprehensive Income or Unrealized Loss. *Unrealized* gains and losses result from changes in fair value, not from sales of investments.

Unrealized gains and unrealized losses on non-strategic investments (not held for short-term trading) that occur in a fiscal year are reported in two places in the financial statements:

- *Other Comprehensive Income* is reported in a separate section below net income on the *statement of comprehensive income*. For example, assume the Consolidated Statement of Comprehensive Income section of Leon's Furniture Limited's 2014 annual report states:

  Other Comprehensive Income, Net of Tax
  Unrealized Gain on Financial Assets Arising
  During the Year (Net of Tax of $45)... $223

- *Accumulated Other Comprehensive Income*, which is a separate section of shareholders' equity below retained earnings on the *balance sheet*. The Shareholders' Equity section of the Leon's Furniture Limited's 2014 balance sheet reports:

  Accumulated Other Comprehensive Income .... $(142)

At December 31, 2017, ONEX would close the Other Comprehensive Income account to the shareholders' equity account Accumulated Other Comprehensive Income as follows:

	A	B	C	D	E
1	2017				
2	Dec. 31	Other Comprehensive Income	3,000		
3		Accumulated Other Comprehensive Income		3,000	
4		*To close out the unrealized gain on the investment to accumulated other comprehensive income.*			
5					

If the company chooses to recognize the changes in fair value in the investment through income (called profit or loss), unrealized gains or unrealized losses would be used instead of other comprehensive income. These unrealized gains and losses are reported under Other Income on the income statement. As mentioned previously, for short-term investments, all changes in fair value in the investment are reported through income.

Selling a Non-Strategic Investment

The sale of a non-strategic investment can result in a *realized* gain or loss. Realized gains and losses measure the difference between the amount received from the sale of the investment and the carrying amount of the investment.

Suppose ONEX sells its investment in Agrium Inc. shares for $57,000 during 2018. ONEX would record the sale as follows:

Company chooses to report changes in fair value in the investment through net income:		
Cash	57,000	
Investment in Agrium		
Investment		53,000
Gain on Sale of Investment		4,000

Realized gains and losses are reported under "Other Income" on the income statement.

Company chooses to report changes in fair value in the investment (not held for short-term trading) through other comprehensive income:		
Cash	57,000	
Investment in Agrium		53,000
Other Comprehensive Income		4,000

Realized gains are reported under Other Comprehensive Income on the statement of comprehensive income.

MyAccountingLab

STOP + THINK (7-1)

Suppose Ardnas Holdings Ltd. holds the following securities as long-term investments at March 31, 2017:

Shares	Cost	Current Fair Value
Canadian Tire Corp.	$70,000	$47,500
Quebecor	26,000	16,000
	$96,000	$63,500

Show how Ardnas Holdings will report long-term investments on its March 31, 2017, balance sheet.

ANALYZE AND REPORT STRATEGIC INVESTMENTS

OBJECTIVE

❷ **Analyze** and **report** strategic investments

An investor who holds less than 20% of the investee's voting shares usually plays no important role in the investee's operations. But an investor with a larger share holding—between 20% and 50% of the investee's voting shares—may significantly influence how the investee operates the business. Such an investor can probably affect the investee's decisions on dividend policy, product lines, and other important matters. The investor will also likely hold one or more seats on the board of directors of the investee company. We use the **equity method** to account for these types of investments.

Accounting for Investments Using the Equity Method

Investments accounted for by the equity method are recorded initially at cost. Suppose NPC Corporation paid $611 million for 32% of the common shares of Bruce Power. NPC's entry to record the purchase of this investment is (in millions):

	A	B	C	D	E
1	2017				
2	Jan. 2	Investment in Bruce Power	611		
3		Cash		611	
4		*To purchase equity investment.*			
5					

ASSETS	=	LIABILITIES	+	SHAREHOLDERS' EQUITY
+611 −611	=	0	+	0

THE INVESTOR'S PERCENTAGE OF INVESTEE INCOME. Under the equity method, NPC, as the investor, applies its percentage of ownership (32% in our example) in recording its share of the investee's net income. Suppose Bruce reports net income of $100 million for 2017; NPC would record 32% of this amount as follows (in millions):

	A	B	C	D	E
1	2017				
2	Dec. 31	Investment in Bruce Power ($100 × 0.32)	32		
3		Investment Revenue		32	
4		*To record investment revenue.*			
5					

ASSETS	=	LIABILITIES	+	SHAREHOLDERS' EQUITY
32	=	0	+	+ 32 Revenue

Because of the close relationship between NPC and Bruce, the investor increases the Investment in Bruce Power account and records Investment Revenue when the investee reports income. As Bruce's equity increases, so does the Investment account on NPC's books.

RECEIVING DIVIDENDS UNDER THE EQUITY METHOD. NPC Corporation records its proportionate part of cash dividends received from Bruce. Assume Bruce declares and pays a cash dividend of $9,375,000. NPC receives 32% of this dividend and records this entry (in millions):

	A	B	C	D	E
1	Dec. 31	Cash ($9,375,000 × 0.32)	3		
2		Investment in Bruce Power		3	
3		*To receive cash dividend on equity investment.*			
4					

ASSETS	=	LIABILITIES	+	SHAREHOLDERS' EQUITY
3 −3	=	0	+	0

The Investment in Bruce Power account is *decreased* for the receipt of a dividend on an equity method investment. Why? Because the dividend decreases the investee's equity and thus the investor's investment.

After the preceding entries are posted, NPC's Investment in Bruce Power account would include its equity in the net assets of Bruce as follows (in millions):

Investment in Bruce Power

2017	Jan. 2	Purchase	611	Dec. 31	Dividends	3
	Dec. 31	Net income	32			
	Dec. 31	Balance	640			

NPC reports Investment in Bruce Power as a long-term investment on the balance sheet and the investment revenue on the income statement as follows:

	(in millions)
Balance sheet (partial):	
Assets	
Total current assets	$XXX
Long-term investments	640
Property, plant, and equipment, net..	XXX
Income statement (partial):	
Income from operations..	$XXX
Other revenue:	
Revenue from equity investments	32
Net income..	$XXX

The gain or loss on the sale of an equity-method investment is measured as the difference between the sale proceeds and the carrying amount of the investment. For example, NPC Corporation's financial statements show that the investment in Bruce Power at December 31, 2017, was $640 million. Suppose NPC sold 10% of its interest in Bruce Power on January 10, 2018, for $62 million. The entry to record the sale would be:

	A	B	C	D	E
1	2018				
2	Jan. 10	Cash	62		
3		Loss on Sale of Investment	2		
4		Investment in Bruce Power ($640 million × 0.10)		64	
5		*Sold 10% of investment.*			
6					

ASSETS	=	LIABILITIES	+	SHAREHOLDERS' EQUITY
62				
−64	=	0	+	− 2 Loss

When there has been a loss in value in an equity investment other than a temporary decline, the investment is written down to reflect the loss. This is different than adjusting the value to fair value, which is done whether the decline is temporary or not.

SUMMARY OF THE EQUITY METHOD. The following T-account illustrates the accounting for equity-method investments.

Equity-Method Investment

Original cost	Share of losses
Share of income	Share of dividends
Balance	

Analyze and Report Controlling Interests in other Corporations Using Consolidated Financial Statements

Companies buy a significant stake in another company to *influence* the other company's operations. In this section, we cover the situation in which a corporation buys enough of another company to actually *control* that company.

Why Buy Another Company?

Most large corporations own controlling interests in other companies. A **controlling (or majority) interest** is the ownership of usually more than 50% of the investee's voting shares. Such an investment enables the investor to elect a majority of the members of the investee's board of directors and thus control the investee. The investor is called the **parent company**, and the investee company is called the **subsidiary company**. For example, ONEX Partners is a subsidiary of ONEX, the parent. Therefore, the shareholders of ONEX control ONEX Partners, as shown in Exhibit 7-3.

EXHIBIT 7-3
Ownership Structure of ONEX Partners and ONEX

Consolidation Accounting

Consolidation accounting is a method of combining the financial statements of all the companies controlled by the same parent company. This method reports a single set of financial statements for the consolidated entity, which carries the name of the parent company. Exhibit 7-4 summarizes the accounting methods used for long-term share investments.

EXHIBIT 7-4
Accounting Methods for Long-Term Investments

Percentage of Ownership	Accounting Method
Less than 20% (no influence)	Fair Value
20% to 50% (significant influence)	Equity
Greater than 50% (control)	Consolidation

Consolidated statements combine the balance sheets, income statements, and other financial statements of the parent company with those of its subsidiaries. The result is as if the parent and its subsidiaries were one company. Users can gain a better perspective on total operations than they could by examining the reports of the parent and each individual subsidiary separately.

In consolidated financial statements, the assets, liabilities, revenues, and expenses of each subsidiary are added to the parent's accounts. For example, the balance in the Cash account of ONEX Partners is added to the balance in the ONEX Cash account, and the sum of the two amounts is presented as a single amount in the ONEX consolidated balance sheet at the beginning of the chapter. Each account balance of a subsidiary loses its identity in the consolidated statements, which bear the name of the parent company, ONEX.

The Consolidated Balance Sheet and the Related Work Sheet

Suppose ONEX purchased 52% of the outstanding common shares of another Canadian company. Both ONEX and that Canadian company keep separate sets of

EXHIBIT 7-5
Work Sheet for a Consolidated Balance Sheet

	A	B	C	D	E	F	G
1		Parent Corporation	Subsidiary Corporation	Eliminations		Parent and Subsidiary Consolidated Amounts	
				Debit	Credit		
2	Assets						
3	Cash	12,000	18,000			30,000	
4	Note receivable from Subsidiary	80,000			(b) 80,000		
5	Inventory	104,000	91,000			195,000	
6	Investment in Subsidiary	150,000			(a) 150,000		
7	Other assets	218,000	138,000			356,000	
8	Total	564,000	247,000			581,000	
9	Liabilities and Shareholders' Equity						
10	Accounts payable	43,000	17,000			60,000	
11	Notes payable	190,000	80,000	(b) 80,000		190,000	
12	Common shares	176,000	100,000	(a) 100,000		176,000	
13	Retained earnings	155,000	50,000	(a) 50,000		155,000	
14	Total	564,000	247,000	230,000	230,000	581,000	
15							

books. ONEX, the parent company, uses a work sheet to prepare the consolidated statements of ONEX and its consolidated subsidiaries. Then ONEX's consolidated balance sheet shows the combined assets and liabilities of ONEX and all its subsidiaries.

Exhibit 7-5 shows the work sheet for consolidating the balance sheets of Parent Corporation and Subsidiary Corporation. We use these hypothetical entities to illustrate the consolidation process. Consider elimination entry (a) for the parent-subsidiary ownership accounts. Entry (a) credits the parent's Investment account to eliminate its debit balance. Entry (a) also eliminates the subsidiary's shareholders' equity accounts by debiting the subsidiary's Common Shares and Retained Earnings for their full balances. Without this elimination, the consolidated financial statements would include both the parent company's investment in the subsidiary and the subsidiary company's equity. But these accounts represent the same thing—Subsidiary's equity—and so they must be eliminated from the consolidated totals. If they weren't, the same resources would be counted twice.

The resulting Parent and Subsidiary consolidated balance sheet (far-right column) reports no Investment in Subsidiary account. Moreover, the consolidated totals for Common Shares and Retained Earnings are those of Parent Corporation only. Study the final column of the consolidation work sheet.

In this example, Parent Corporation has an $80,000 note receivable from Subsidiary, and Subsidiary has a note payable to Parent. The parent's receivable and the subsidiary's payable represent the same resources—all entirely within the consolidated entity. Both, therefore, must be eliminated, and entry (b) accomplishes this.

- The $80,000 credit in the Elimination column of the work sheet zeros out Parent's Note Receivable from Subsidiary.

- The $80,000 debit in the Elimination column zeros out the Subsidiary's Note Payable to Parent.

- The resulting consolidated amount for notes payable is the amount owed to creditors outside the consolidated entity, which is appropriate.

After the work sheet is complete, the consolidated amount for each account represents the total asset, liability, and equity amounts controlled by Parent Corporation.

Goodwill and Non-Controlling Interests

Goodwill and Non-Controlling Interests are two accounts that only a consolidated entity can have. *Goodwill*, which we studied in Chapter 6 (see p. 302), arises when a parent company pays more to acquire a subsidiary company than the fair value of the subsidiary's net assets. As we saw in Chapter 6, goodwill is the intangible asset that represents the parent company's excess payment to acquire the subsidiary. ONEX reports goodwill of $4,928 million on its December 31, 2014, balance sheet.

Non-controlling interest arises when a parent company purchases less than 100% of the shares of a subsidiary company. For example, ONEX owns less than 100% of some of the companies it controls. The remainder of the subsidiaries' shares is a non-controlling interest to ONEX. Non-controlling interest is included within shareholders' equity on the balance sheet of the parent company. ONEX reports non-controlling interest on its balance sheet in the amount of $1,692 (millions).

Income of a Consolidated Entity

The income of the parent company is combined with the income of each subsidiary beginning with sales revenue. All intercompany sales and expenses are eliminated, but that is a subject for an advanced accounting text. The following example is a very simplified version of a complex topic. Suppose Parent Company owns all the shares of Subsidiary S-1 and 60% of the shares of Subsidiary S-2. During the year just ended, Parent earned net income of $330,000, S-1 earned $150,000, and S-2 had a net loss of $100,000. Parent Company would report net income of $420,000, computed as follows:

	Net Income (Loss) of Each Company		Parent's Ownership of Each Company		Parent's Consolidated Net Income
Parent Company.............................	$ 330,000	×	100%	=	$330,000
Subsidiary S-1	150,000	×	100%	=	150,000
Subsidiary S-2	(100,000)	×	60%	=	(60,000)
Consolidated net income................					$420,000

MyAccountingLab

STOP + THINK (7-2)

Examine Exhibit 7-5. Why does the consolidated shareholders' equity ($176,000 + $155,000) exclude the equity of the Subsidiary Corporation?

ANALYZE AND REPORT LONG-TERM INVESTMENTS IN BONDS

Another type of non-strategic investment is when a company buys bonds. The major investors in bonds are financial institutions, pension plans, mutual funds, and insurance companies, such as Manulife Financial Corporation. The relationship between the issuing corporation and the investor (bondholder) may be diagrammed as follows:

Chapter 7
Investor (Bondholder)

Chapter 8
Issuing Corporation

Investment in bonds ⟷ Bonds payable
Interest revenue ⟷ Interest expense

An investment in bonds is classified either as short term (a current asset) or as long term. Short-term investments in bonds are rare. Here, we focus on long-term investments in bonds.

Bonds of public companies are traded on the open market, just as shares are. Bonds are usually issued in $1,000 face (par) denominations, but they typically do not sell at par value. Market prices of bonds fluctuate with market interest rates. If market rates on competing instruments are higher than the interest the company is paying on a particular bond, the bond sells at a discount (below 100% of par, or face value). For example, a quoted bond price of 96.5 means that the $1,000 bond is selling for 96.5% of par, or $965. If market rates are lower, the bond sells at a premium (above 100% of par)—a quoted bond price of 102.5 means that the bond is selling for 102.5% of par, or $1,025 (a premium over par). Bondholders receive interest, usually semi-annually.

IFRS require bond investments that are held to maturity and whose objective is to collect payments and interest to be valued at amortized cost, which determines the carrying amount. **Bond investments** are initially recorded at cost (market price as a percentage × par value of bonds issued). At each semi-annual interest payment date, the investor records interest revenue. In addition, whenever there is a premium or discount on the bond, it is amortized by adjusting the carrying amount of the bond upward or downward toward its par or face value. The amortization of the discount or premium is calculated using the effective interest method (see Chapter 8).

Suppose an investor purchases $100,000 of 5% Government of Canada bonds at a price of $95,735 on June 1, 2017. The bonds pay interest on June 1 and December 1. The investor intends to hold the bonds until their maturity on June 2, 2022. The bonds will be outstanding for five years (10 interest periods). The investor paid a discounted price for the bonds of $95,735 (an effective interest rate of 6%). The investor must amortize the bonds' carrying amount from cost of $95,735 up to $100,000 over their term to maturity. The following are the entries for this long-term investment:

	A	B	C	D	E
1	2017				
2	June 1	Long-Term Investment in Bonds ($100,000 × 95.735)	95,735		
3		Cash		95,735	
4		*To purchase bond investment.*			
5	Dec. 1	Cash ($100,000 × 0.05 × 1/2)	2,500		
6		Interest Revenue		2,500	
7		*To receive semi-annual interest.*			
8		Long-Term Investment in Bonds ([$95,735 × 0.06 × 1/2] − $2,500)	372*		
9		Interest Revenue		372*	
10		*To amortize bond investment.*			
11					

*Rounded

At December 31, the year-end adjustments are:

	A	B	C	D	E
1	Dec. 31	Interest Receivable ($100,000 × 0.05 × 1/12)	417*		
2		Interest Revenue		417*	
3		*To accrue interest revenue.*			
4	Dec. 31	Long-Term Investment in Bonds ([$96,108 × 0.06 × 1/12] − $417)	64*		
5		Interest Revenue		64*	
6		*To amortize bond investment.*			
7					

*Rounded

This amortization entry has two effects:

1. It increases the Long-Term Investment account on its march toward maturity value.
2. It increases the interest by the amount of the increase in the carrying amount of the investment.

The financial statements at December 31, 2017, report the following for this investment in bonds:

Balance sheet at December 31, 2017:

Current assets:

Interest receivable	$ 417
Long-term investments in bonds ($95,735 + $373 + $64)	96,172
Property, plant, and equipment...	X, XXX

Income statement for the year ended December 31, 2017:

Other revenues:

Interest revenue ($2,500 + $373 + $417 + $64)...	$ 3,354

STOP + THINK (7-3)

Suppose that on January 1, 2017, Microsport, Inc. purchased $120,000 face value of the 9% bonds of Service Express, Inc. at 104. The bonds mature on January 1, 2022. How much cash interest would Microsport receive on December 31, 2020?

▶ DECISION GUIDELINES

ACCOUNTING METHODS FOR INVESTMENTS

These guidelines show which accounting method to use for each type of investment. A company can have all types of investments—stock, bonds, 25% interests, and controlling interests. How should a company account for its various investments?

Type of Investment	Accounting Method
Non-strategic investments	Fair value
Significantly influenced investments	Equity method
Controlled investments	Consolidation
Investment in bonds	Amortized cost

As we have seen in this chapter, investments may be bought in order to earn either dividend revenue and/or capital appreciation (called *non-strategic*), or they are bought with the intent to significantly influence or control the company's operations (referred to as *strategic*). Let's see how investments are used in decision making.

Decision	Guidelines
Who uses investments in decision making, and why?	*Managers* buy investments with one or more of these intentions in mind. If the company has excess cash on hand, they may decide to invest this cash in a non-strategic investment rather than have it sit in a bank account where it earns little interest. On the other hand, the company may decide to buy another company's shares with a plan to be involved in the company's operations.
	Investors might consider the type of investment. If the investment was non-strategic, they would look at the statements and notes to see whether or not the investment increased or decreased in value and the amount of dividend revenue the company received. If it was a strategic investment, the investor would look to see whether or not this investment generated a reasonable profit for the company.
	Creditors are always looking to see if a company would be a good candidate for a loan and whether there was sufficient profit from operations or investment income to cover current and potentially increased interest costs.

MyAccountingLab

MID-CHAPTER SUMMARY PROBLEM

1. Identify the appropriate accounting method for each of the following long-term investment situations:
   a. Investment in 25% of investee's shares
   b. 10% investment in shares
   c. Investment in more than 50% of investee's shares
2. At what amount should the following long-term investment portfolio be reported on the June 30, 2017, balance sheet? All the investments are less than 5% of the investee's shares and are classified as non-strategic. The investor chooses to record any changes in fair value through other comprehensive income.

Shares	Investment Cost	Fair Value
Bank of Montreal	$75,000	$52,000
Canadian Tire Corp.	24,000	31,000
Jean Coutu Group	32,000	36,000

   Journalize any adjusting entry required by these data.
3. Investor Corporation paid $67,900 to acquire a 40% equity-method investment in the common shares of Investee Corporation. At the end of the first year, Investee's net income was $80,000, and Investee declared and paid cash dividends of $55,000. What is Investor's ending balance in its Equity-Method Investment account? Use a T-account to answer.

ANSWERS

1. a. Equity
   b. Fair value
   c. Consolidation

For investments:
Less than 20%→Fair value;
20% to 50%→Equity;
Greater than 50%→Consolidation

2. Report the investments at fair value ($119,000) as follows:

<table>
<tr><td>Determine the fair value for each investment in the portfolio. Then create the journal entry for any change from investment cost to current fair value.</td></tr>
</table>

Shares	Investment Cost	Fair Value
Bank of Montreal	$ 75,000	$ 52,000
Canadian Tire	24,000	31,000
Jean Coutu Group	32,000	36,000
Totals	$131,000	$119,000

Adjusting entry:

Other Comprehensive Income ($131,000 – $119,000)	12,000	
Long-Term Investments		12,000
To adjust investments to current fair value.		

3. Equity-Method Investment

<table>
<tr><td>The Equity-Method Investment T-account includes:
100% of the cost of the investment
+40% of the investee's net income
−40% of the investee's cash dividends</td></tr>
</table>

Equity-Method Investment

Cost	67,900	Dividends	22,000**
Income	32,000*		
Balance	77,900		

*$80,000 × 0.40 = $32,000
**$55,000 × 0.40 = $22,000

---

❹ **Report** investing activities on the statement of cash flows

REPORT INVESTING ACTIVITIES ON THE STATEMENT OF CASH FLOWS

Investing activities include many types of transactions. In Chapter 6, we covered investing transactions in which companies purchase and sell long-lived assets, such as property, plant, and equipment. In this chapter, we examined long-term investments in shares and bonds. These are also investing activities reported on the statement of cash flows.

Investing activities are usually reported on the statement of cash flows as the second category, after operating activities and before financing activities. Exhibit 7-6

EXHIBIT 7-6
ONEX Corporation Consolidated Statement of Cash Flows

Source: ONEX Management's Discussion and Analysis and Financial Statements.

	A	B	C	D
1	**ONEX Corporation** Consolidated Statement of Cash Flows (Partial, Adapted) For the Year Ended December 31, 2014			
2	*(in millions of U.S. dollars)*			
3	**Investing Activities**			
4	Acquisition of operating companies	$ (1,315)		
5	Purchase of property, plant, and equipment	(526)		
6	Cash interest received	125		
7	Increase due to other investing activities	3,648		
8	Cash flows used in investing activities of discontinued operations	(696)		
9		$ 1,236		
10				

provides excerpts from ONEX's statement of cash flows. During 2014, ONEX spent $526 million on new property, plant, and equipment and $1,315 million to acquire other companies. They also received $125 million in interest from their investments. Alternatively, ONEX could also have reported the interest and dividends as an operating activity. Overall, cash flows provided from investing activities was $1,236 million.

STOP + THINK (7-4)

Examine Exhibit 7-6. Where did the company spend most of its cash?

EXPLAIN THE IMPACT OF THE TIME VALUE OF MONEY ON CERTAIN TYPES OF INVESTMENTS

OBJECTIVE

5 **Explain** the impact of the time value of money on certain types of investments

Future Value

Which would you rather receive: $1,000 today, or $1,000 a year from today? A logical person would answer: "I'd rather have the cash now, because if I get it now, I can invest it so that a year from now I'll have more." The term **future value** means the amount of money that a given current investment will be worth at a specified time in the future, assuming a certain interest rate. The term *time value of money* refers to the fact that money earns interest over time. *Interest* is the cost of using money. To borrowers, interest is the fee paid to the lender for the period of the loan. To lenders, interest is the revenue earned from allowing someone else to use our money for a period of time.

Whether making investments or borrowing money, we must always recognize the interest we receive or pay. Otherwise, we overlook an important part of the transaction. Suppose you invest $4,545 in corporate bonds that pay 10% interest each year. After one year, the value of your investment has grown to $5,000, as shown in the following diagram:

End of Year	Interest	Future Value
0	—	$4,545
1	$4,545 × 0.10 = $455	5,000
2	5,000 × 0.10 = 500	5,500
3	5,500 × 0.10 = 550	6,050
4	6,050 × 0.10 = 605	6,655
5	6,655 × 0.10 = 666	7,321

The difference between your original investment (present value of $4,545) and the future value of the investment ($5,000) is the amount of interest revenue you will earn during the year ($455). Interest becomes more important as the time period lengthens because the amount of interest depends on the span of time the money is invested. The time value of money plays a key role in measuring the value of certain long-term investments, as well as long-term debt.

If the money were invested for five years, you would have to perform five calculations like the one described above. You would also have to consider the compound interest that your investment is earning. *Compound interest* is not only the interest you earn on your principal amount, but also the interest you receive on the interest you have already earned. Most business applications include compound interest.

To calculate the future value of an investment, we need three inputs: (1) the *amount of initial payment (or receipt)*, (2) the length of *time* between investment and future receipt (or *payment*), and (3) the *interest rate*. The table above shows the interest revenue earned on the original $4,545 investment each year for five years at 10%. At the end of five years, your initial $4,545 investment will be worth $7,321.

Present Value

Often a person knows or is able to estimate a future amount and needs to determine the related present value (PV). The term **present value** means the value on a given date of a future payment or series of future payments, discounted to reflect the time value of money. In Exhibit 7-7, present value and future value are on opposite ends of the same timeline. Suppose an investment promises to pay you $5,000 at the *end* of one year. How much would you pay *now* to acquire this investment? You would be willing to pay the present value of the $5,000 future amount, which, at 10% interest, is $4,545.

EXHIBIT 7-7
Future Value of an Investment

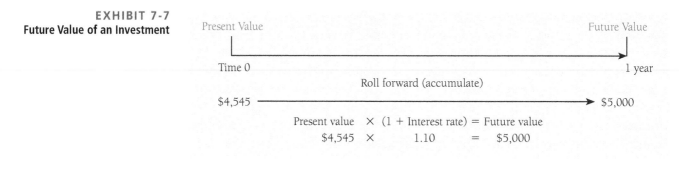

Like future value, present value depends on three factors: (1) the *amount of payment (or receipt)*, (2) the length of *time* between investment and future receipt (or *payment*), and (3) the *interest rate*. The process of computing a present value is called *discounting* because the present value is *less* than the future value.

In our investment example, the future receipt is $5,000. The investment period is one year. Assume that you demand an annual interest rate of 10% on your investment. With all three factors specified, you can compute the present value of $5,000 at 10% for one year:

$$\text{Present value} = \frac{\text{Future value}}{1 + \text{Interest rate}} = \frac{\$5,000}{1.10} = \$4,545$$

By turning the data around into a future-value problem, we can verify the present-value computation:

Amount invested (present value)	$4,545
Expected earnings ($4,545 × 0.10).......................................	455
Amount to be received one year from now (future value)	$5,000

This example illustrates that present value and future value are based on variations of the same equation:

$$\text{Future value} = \text{Present value} \times (1 + \text{Interest rate})^n$$

$$\text{Present value} = \frac{\text{Future value}}{(1 + \text{Interest rate})^n}$$

where n = number of periods

If the $5,000 is to be received two years from now, you will pay only $4,132 for the investment, as shown in Exhibit 7-8. By turning the data around, we verify that $4,132 accumulates to $5,000 at 10% for two years:

Amount invested (present value)	$4,132
Expected earnings for first year ($4,132 × 0.10)	413
Value of investment after one year	4,545
Expected earnings for second year ($4,545 × 0.10)	455
Amount to be received two years from now (future value)	$5,000

Formula: $\text{Present value} = \dfrac{\text{Future value}}{(1 + \text{Interest rate})^n}$

$$4,132 = \frac{5,000}{(1 + 0.10)^2}$$

$$\text{Future value} = \text{Present value} \times (1 + \text{Interest rate})^n$$

$$5,000 = \$4,132 \times (1 + 0.10)^2$$

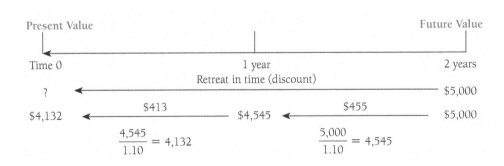

EXHIBIT 7-8
Present Value: An Example

You would pay $4,132—the present value of $5,000—to receive the $5,000 future amount at the end of two years at 10% per year. The $868 difference between the amount invested ($4,132) and the amount to be received ($5,000) is the return on the investment, the sum of the two interest receipts: $413 + $455 = $868.

Present-Value Tables

We have shown the simple formula for computing present value. However, figuring present value "by hand" for investments spanning many years is time-consuming and presents too many opportunities for arithmetic errors. Present-value tables simplify our work. Let's re-examine our examples of present value by using Exhibit 7-9, Present Value of $1.

For the 10% investment for one year, we find the junction of the 10% column and row 3 in Exhibit 7-9. The figure 0.909 is computed as follows: 1/1.10 = 0.909. This work has been done for us, and only the present values are given in the table. To figure the present value for $5,000, we multiply 0.909 by $5,000. The result is $4,545, which matches the result we obtained by hand.

EXHIBIT 7-9
Present Value of $1

	A	B	C	D	E	F	G	H	I	J	K
1					Present Value of $1						
2	Period	4%	5%	6%	7%	8%	10%	12%	14%	16%	
3	1	0.962	0.952	0.943	0.935	0.926	0.909	0.893	0.877	0.862	
4	2	0.925	0.907	0.890	0.873	0.857	0.826	0.797	0.769	0.743	
5	3	0.889	0.864	0.840	0.816	0.794	0.751	0.712	0.675	0.641	
6	4	0.855	0.823	0.792	0.763	0.735	0.683	0.636	0.592	0.552	
7	5	0.822	0.784	0.747	0.713	0.681	0.621	0.567	0.519	0.476	
8	6	0.790	0.746	0.705	0.666	0.630	0.564	0.507	0.456	0.410	
9	7	0.760	0.711	0.665	0.623	0.583	0.513	0.452	0.400	0.354	
10	8	0.731	0.677	0.627	0.582	0.540	0.467	0.404	0.351	0.305	
11	9	0.703	0.645	0.592	0.544	0.500	0.424	0.361	0.308	0.263	
12	10	0.676	0.614	0.558	0.508	0.463	0.386	0.322	0.270	0.227	
13	11	0.650	0.585	0.527	0.475	0.429	0.350	0.287	0.237	0.195	
14	12	0.625	0.557	0.497	0.444	0.397	0.319	0.257	0.208	0.168	
15	13	0.601	0.530	0.469	0.415	0.368	0.290	0.229	0.182	0.145	
16	14	0.577	0.505	0.442	0.388	0.340	0.263	0.205	0.160	0.125	
17	15	0.555	0.481	0.417	0.362	0.315	0.239	0.183	0.140	0.108	
18	16	0.534	0.458	0.394	0.339	0.292	0.218	0.163	0.123	0.093	
19	17	0.513	0.436	0.371	0.317	0.270	0.198	0.146	0.108	0.080	
20	18	0.494	0.416	0.350	0.296	0.250	0.180	0.130	0.095	0.069	
21	19	0.475	0.396	0.331	0.277	0.232	0.164	0.116	0.083	0.060	
22	20	0.456	0.377	0.312	0.258	0.215	0.149	0.104	0.073	0.051	
23											

For the two-year investment, we read down the 10% column and across row 4. We multiply 0.826 (computed as 0.909/1.10 = 0.826) by $5,000 and get $4,130, which confirms our earlier computation of $4,132 (the difference is due to rounding in the present-value table). Using the table, we can compute the present value of any single future amount.

Present Value of an Annuity

Return to Exhibit 7-8 on page 351. That investment provided the investor with only a single future receipt ($5,000 at the end of two years). *Annuity investments* provide multiple receipts of an equal amount at fixed intervals over the investment's duration.

Consider an investment that promises *annual* cash receipts of $10,000 to be received at the end of each of three years. Assume that you demand a 12% return on your investment. What is the investment's present value? That is, what would you pay today to acquire the investment? The investment spans three periods, and you would pay the sum of three present values. The computation follows.

Year	Annual Cash Receipt	Present Value of $1 at 12% (Exhibit 7-9)	Present Value of Annual Cash Receipt
1	$10,000	0.893	$ 8,930
2	10,000	0.797	7,970
3	10,000	0.712	7,120
Total present value of investment........................			$24,020

The present value of this annuity is $24,020. By paying this amount today, you will receive $10,000 at the end of each of the three years while earning 12% on your investment.

EXHIBIT 7-10
Present Value of Annuity of $1

	A	B	C	D	E	F	G	H	I	J	K
1					Present Value of Annuity of $1						
2	Period	4%	5%	6%	7%	8%	10%	12%	14%	16%	
3	1	0.962	0.952	0.943	0.935	0.926	0.909	0.893	0.877	0.862	
4	2	1.886	1.859	1.833	1.808	1.783	1.736	1.690	1.647	1.605	
5	3	2.775	2.723	2.673	2.624	2.577	2.487	2.402	2.322	2.246	
6	4	3.630	3.546	3.465	3.387	3.312	3.170	3.037	2.914	2.798	
7	5	4.452	4.329	4.212	4.100	3.993	3.791	3.605	3.433	3.274	
8	6	5.242	5.076	4.917	4.767	4.623	4.355	4.111	3.889	3.685	
9	7	6.002	5.786	5.582	5.389	5.206	4.868	4.564	4.288	4.039	
10	8	6.733	6.463	6.210	5.971	5.747	5.335	4.968	4.639	4.344	
11	9	7.435	7.108	6.802	6.515	6.247	5.759	5.328	4.946	4.608	
12	10	8.111	7.722	7.360	7.024	6.710	6.145	5.650	5.216	4.833	
13	11	8.760	8.306	7.887	7.499	7.139	6.495	5.938	5.453	5.029	
14	12	9.385	8.863	8.384	7.943	7.536	6.814	6.194	5.660	5.197	
15	13	9.986	9.394	8.853	8.358	7.904	7.103	6.424	5.842	5.342	
16	14	10.563	9.899	9.295	8.745	8.244	7.367	6.628	6.002	5.468	
17	15	11.118	10.380	9.712	9.108	8.559	7.606	6.811	6.142	5.575	
18	16	11.652	10.838	10.106	9.447	8.851	7.824	6.974	6.265	5.669	
19	17	12.166	11.274	10.477	9.763	9.122	8.022	7.120	6.373	5.749	
20	18	12.659	11.690	10.828	10.059	9.372	8.201	7.250	6.467	5.818	
21	19	13.134	12.085	11.158	10.336	9.604	8.365	7.366	6.550	5.877	
22	20	13.590	12.462	11.470	10.594	9.818	8.514	7.469	6.623	5.929	
23											

This example illustrates repetitive computations of the three future amounts, a time-consuming process. One way to ease the computational burden is to add the three present values of $1 (0.893 + 0.797 + 0.712) and multiply their sum (2.402) by the annual cash receipt ($10,000) to obtain the present value of the annuity ($10,000 × 2.402 = $24,020).

An easier approach is to use a present-value-of-an-annuity table. Exhibit 7-10 shows the present value of $1 to be received periodically for a given number of periods. The present value of a three-period annuity at 12% is 2.402 (the junction of row 5 and the 12% column). Thus, $10,000 received annually at the end of each of three years, discounted at 12%, is $24,020 ($10,000 × 2.402), which is the present value.

Using Present Value to Compute the Fair Value of Investments

Recall that, at the end of each year, investors are required to adjust the portfolio of non-strategic investments to fair values. Some types of investments (publicly traded stocks and bonds) have quoted prices in active markets. Determining fair value for these investments is easy: merely obtain the quoted price from the financial media (usually the Internet or the *Globe and Mail* on the year-end). Other types of non-traditional investments (e.g., notes, non–publicly traded bonds or stocks, contracts, annuities) may not have daily quoted market prices in active markets. Therefore, the company may use financial models that predict expected cash flows from these investments over a period of time and discount those cash flows back to the balance sheet date.

Using Microsoft Excel to Calculate Present Value

While tables such as Exhibits 7-9 and 7-10 are helpful, they are limited to the interest rates in the columns or the periods of time in the rows. Using a computer program like Microsoft Excel provides an infinite range of interest rates and periods. For that reason, most business people solve present-value problems quickly and easily using Excel rather than tables.

- *To compute the present value of a single payment*, the following formula applies:

$$= \text{Payment}/(1 + i)^n$$
$$\text{where } i = \text{interest rate}$$
$$n = \text{number of period}$$

- In Excel, we use the $^$ symbol to indicate the exponent. To illustrate, suppose you are expecting to receive a $500,000 payment four years from now, and suppose that market interest rates are 8%. You would enter the following formula in Excel:

$$= 500000/(1.08)^4$$

You should calculate a present value of $367,514.93 (rounded to $367,515).

- *To compute the present value of an annuity (stream of payments)*, open an Excel spreadsheet to a blank cell. Click the insert function button (f_x). Then select the "Financial" category from the drop-down box. The following box will appear:

© Microsoft Corporation

Scroll down the function list and select "PV." A description of the PV function will display beneath the function list, along with the following line: **PV (rate, nper, pmt, fv, type)**. Double-click PV, and the following box will appear:

© Microsoft Corporation

Enter the interest rate, the number of periods, and the payment (as a negative number). The present value of the annuity will appear at the bottom of the box after the "=" sign.

To illustrate, notice that we have assumed an investment that is expected to return $20,000 per year for 20 years and a market interest rate of 8%. The net present value of this annuity (rounded to the nearest cent) is $196,362.95, computed with Excel as follows:

MyAccountingLab

Try It in Excel: Net Present Value

Present Value of an Investment in Bonds

The present value of a bond—its market price—is the present value of the future principal amount at maturity plus the present value of the future stated interest payments. The principal is a *single amount* to be received by the investor and paid by the debtor at maturity. The interest is an *annuity* because it occurs periodically.

Let's compute the present value of 9% five-year bonds of Air Canada from the standpoint of an investor. The face value of the bonds is $100,000, and the face interest rate is 9% annually. Because bonds typically pay interest twice per year, these bonds pay 4 1/2% semi-annually. At issuance, the market interest rate is assumed to be 10% annually, but it is computed at 5% semi-annually (again, because the bonds pay interest twice a year). Therefore, the effective (market) interest rate for each of the 10 semi-annual periods is 5%. We thus use 5% in computing the present value of the maturity and of the interest. The market price of these bonds is $96,149, as follows:

	Annual Market Interest Rate ÷ 2	Number of Semi-annual Interest Payments	
PV of principal:			
$100,000 × PV of single amount at 5%		for 10 periods	
$100,000 × 0.614 (Exhibit 7-9)			$61,400
PV of stated (cash) interest:			
$100,000 × 0.045 × PV of annuity at 5%		for 10 periods	
$4,500 × 7.722 (Exhibit 7-10)			34,749
PV (market price) of bonds			$96,149

The fair value of the Air Canada bonds on the investor's balance sheet would be $96,149.*

We discuss accounting for these bonds from the debtor's point of view in Chapter 8.

---

* The process of estimating fair value using discounted cash flow models is similar for all types of investments.

STOP + THINK (7-5)

What would the present value of $5,000 be at the end of eight years if the interest was 5%?

Summary of IFRS-ASPE Differences

Concepts	IFRS	ASPE
Non-strategic investments (p. 335)	These investments are reported at fair value, with unrealized and realized gains and losses reported in net income (short-term and long-term investments), unless the company elects to report them in other comprehensive income (only for long-term investments).	These investments are reported at fair value, with unrealized and realized gains and losses reported in net income.
Strategic investments (a) Investments subject to significant influence (p. 336)	A company shall apply the equity method to account for these investments.	A company may choose to apply either the equity method or the cost method. If the share investments are quoted in an active market, then the fair value method replaces the cost method as an option, with any changes in fair value reported through net income.
(b) Investments in controlled subsidiaries (p. 342)	A company shall consolidate its financial statements with those of its subsidiaries.	A company may choose to account for its subsidiaries using the cost method, the equity method, or the consolidation method. If share investments are quoted in an active market, then the fair value method replaces the cost method, with any changes in fair value reported through net income.
Amortization of the discount or premium relating to long-term investments in bonds (p. 344)	The effective-interest method must be used to amortize discounts and premiums.	The straight-line method or the effective-interest method may be used to amortize discounts and premiums.

SUMMARY

SUMMARY OF LEARNING OBJECTIVES

LEARNING OBJECTIVE	SUMMARY
1. **Analyze** and **report** non-strategic investments	Non-strategic investments are initially recorded at cost and subsequently reported on the balance sheet at fair value. Any changes in value are recorded through net income (profit or loss, short-term and long-term investments) or under "other comprehensive income" (only long-term investments). The cost method is used for investments where the market price is not available.

2. **Analyze** and **report** strategic investments

If the company (investor) owns between 20% and 50% of the voting shares of the investee and exercises significant influence over the investee, the equity method is used to account for the investment. This means that the investor recognizes their share of the investee's net income as their own. The investor's share of dividends is treated as a return of investment. If the company (investor) owns more than 50% of the investee's shares and exercises control over the investee, the financial statements of the investee are consolidated (combined) with those of the investor. The result is as if the parent and subsidiary are one company. Goodwill and Non-controlling interest are two accounts that only a consolidated entity would have. Goodwill results when a company pays more for the subsidiary company than the fair value of the subsidiary's net assets. Non-controlling interest occurs when a company buys less than 100% of the company they control.

3. **Analyze** and **report** long-term investment in bonds

When a company buys a long-term investment in bonds, they are recorded at the price paid. When there is a premium or discount, the bonds are amortized to account for interest revenue and the bond's carrying amount. These bonds are reported on the balance sheet at its amortized cost.

4. **Report** investing activities on the statement of cash flows

Buying and selling long-term investments in shares and bonds are reported under investing activities.

5. **Explain** the impact of the time value of money on certain types of investments

Time value of money refers to the fact that money earns interest over time, and it plays a key role in measuring the value of certain long-term investments as well as long-term debt. Interest is the cost of using money. The difference between your original (present) investment and the future value of the investment is the amount of interest revenue you will earn.

MyAccountingLab

END-OF-CHAPTER SUMMARY PROBLEM

Suppose Parent Company paid $85,000 for all of the common shares of Subsidiary Company, and Parent owes Subsidiary $20,000 on a note payable.

Requirements:

Compete the following consolidation worksheet.

	A	B	C	D	E	F	G
1		Parent Corporation	Subsidiary Corporation	Eliminations		Parent and Subsidiary Consolidated Amounts	
				Debit	Credit		
2	**Assets**						
3	Cash	7,000	4,000				
4	Note receivable from Subsidiary		20,000				
5	Investment in Subsidiary	85,000					
6	Other assets	108,000	99,000				
7	Total	200,000	123,000				
8	**Liabilities and Shareholders' Equity**						
9	Accounts payable	15,000	8,000				
10	Notes payable	20,000	30,000				
11	Common shares	120,000	60,000				
12	Retained earnings	45,000	25,000				
13	Total	200,000	123,000				
14							

ANSWER

	A	B	C	D	E	F	G
1		Parent Corporation	Subsidiary Corporation	Eliminations		Parent and Subsidiary Consolidated Amounts	
1				Debit	Credit		
2	**Assets**						
3	Cash	7,000	4,000			11,000	
4	Note receivable from Subsidiary		20,000		(a) 20,000		
5	Investment in Subsidiary	85,000			(b) 85,000		
6	Other assets	108,000	99,000			207,000	
7	Total	200,000	123,000			218,000	
8	**Liabilities and Shareholders' Equity**						
9	Accounts payable	15,000	8,000			23,000	
10	Notes payable	20,000	30,000	(a) 20,000		30,000	
11	Common shares	120,000	60,000	(b) 60,000		120,000	
12	Retained earnings	45,000	25,000	(b) 25,000		45,000	
13	Total	200,000	123,000	105,000	105,000	218,000	
14							

REVIEW

MyAccountingLab

QUICK QUIZ (ANSWERS APPEAR ON THE LAST PAGE OF THIS CHAPTER.)

1. A company's investment in less than 1% of GE's shares, which it expects to hold for two years and then sell, is which type of investment?
- a. Strategic
- b. Equity
- c. Non-strategic
- d. Consolidation

2. DuBois Corporation purchased a non-strategic investment in 1,000 shares of Scotiabank (BNS) for $31 per share. On the next balance sheet date, BNS is quoted at $35 per share. DuBois's *balance sheet* should report

- a. unrealized loss of $4,000.
- b. unrealized gain of $31,000.
- c. investments of $31,000.
- d. investments of $35,000.

3. Use the DuBois Corporation data in question 2. The company reports changes in fair value through net income DuBois's *income statement* should report
- a. unrealized gain of $4,000.
- b. unrealized loss of $4,000.
- c. investments of $31,000.
- d. nothing because DuBois hasn't sold the investment.

4. Use the DuBois Corporation data in question 2. DuBois sold the Scotiabank shares for $40,000 two years later. DuBois's *income statement* should report
   a. unrealized gain of $4,000.
   b. gain on sale of $9,000.
   c. gain on sale of $5,000.
   d. investments of $40,000.

5. Alexander Moving & Storage Inc. paid $100,000 for 20% of the common shares of Sellers Ltd. Sellers earned net income of $50,000 and paid dividends of $25,000. Alexander accounts for the investment using the equity method. The carrying value of Alexander's investment in Sellers is
   a. $100,000.
   b. $105,000.
   c. $125,000.
   d. $150,000.

6. Tarrant Inc. owns 80% of Rockwall Corporation, and Rockwall owns 80% of Kaufman Company. During 2017, these companies' net incomes are as follows before any consolidations:
   - Tarrant, $100,000
   - Rockwall, $68,000
   - Kaufman, $40,000

   How much net income should Tarrant report for 2017?
   a. $100,000
   b. $164,000
   c. $180,000
   d. $204,000

7. TRULINE Inc. holds an investment in Manulife bonds that pay interest each June 30. TRULINE's *balance sheet* at December 31 should report
   a. interest receivable.
   b. interest payable.
   c. interest revenue.
   d. interest expense.

8. Consolidation accounting
   a. combines the accounts of the parent company and those of the subsidiary companies.
   b. eliminates all liabilities.
   c. reports the receivables and payables of the parent company only.
   d. All of the above.

9. On January 1, 2017, Vallée Bleue Ltée purchased $100,000 face value of the 7% bonds of Mail Frontier Inc. at 105. Interest is paid on January 1. The bonds mature on January 1, 2018. For the year ended December 31, 2017, Vallée Bleu received cash interest of
   a. $5,000.
   b. $6,000.
   c. $6,400.
   d. $7,000.

10. Return to Vallée Bleue's bond investment in question 9. Assume an effective interest rate of 6%. For the year ended December 31, 2017, Vallée Bleu earned interest revenue of
   a. $5,000.
   b. $6,300.
   c. $7,000.
   d. $7,700.

ACCOUNTING VOCABULARY

bond investments Bonds and notes are debt instruments that an investor intends to hold until maturity.   (p. 345)

consolidated statements Financial statements of the parent company plus those of majority-owned subsidiaries as if the combination were a single legal entity.   (p. 342)

controlling (majority) interest Ownership of more than 50% of an investee company's voting shares and can exercise control over the investee.   (p. 342)

equity method The method used to account for investments in which the investor has 20–50% of the investee's voting shares and can significantly influence the decisions of the investee.   (p. 339)

future value Measures the future sum of money that a given current investment is "worth" at a specified time in the future, assuming a certain interest rate.   (p. 349)

long-term investments Any investment that does not meet the criteria of a short-term investment; any investment that the investor expects to hold for longer than a year.   (p. 335)

majority interest Ownership of more than 50% of an investee company's voting shares.   (p. 342)

non-controlling interest A subsidiary company's equity that is held by shareholders other than the parent company.   (p. 344)

non-strategic investments Investments in which the investor owns less than 20% of the voting shares of the investee and is presumed to exercise no influence.   (p. 335)

parent company An investor company that owns more than 50% of the voting shares of a subsidiary company.   (p. 342)

present value The value on a given date of a future payment or series of future payments, discounted to reflect the time value of money.   (p. 350)

strategic investments Investments in which the investor owns more than 20% of the voting shares of the investee and is presumed to exercise either significant influence or control over the investee.   (p. 336)

subsidiary company An investee company in which a parent company owns more than 50% of the voting shares and can exercise control over the subsidiary.   (p. 342)

ASSESS YOUR PROGRESS

SHORT EXERCISES

LEARNING OBJECTIVE ❶

Analyze and report a non-strategic investment

S7-1 Assume Knowlton Holdings Ltd. completed these long-term non-strategic investment transactions during 2017:

2017
Feb. 10   Purchased 300 shares of BCE, paying $25 per share.
           Knowlton intends to hold the investment for the indefinite future.
Dec. 1   Received a cash dividend of $0.36 per share on the BCE shares.
Dec. 31   Adjusted the BCE investment to its current fair value of $7,000.

1. Journalize Knowlton's investment transactions assuming the company reports any changes in fair value through other comprehensive income. Explanations are not required.
2. Show how to report the investment and any unrealized gain or loss on Knowlton's balance sheet at December 31, 2017. Ignore income tax.

LEARNING OBJECTIVE ❶

Account for the sale of a non-strategic investment

S7-2 Use the data given in exercise S7-1. On May 19, 2018, Knowlton sold its investment in BCE shares for $26 per share.
1. Journalize the sale. No explanation is required.
2. How does the gain or loss that you recorded here differ from the gain or loss that was recorded at December 31, 2017?

LEARNING OBJECTIVE ❷

Analyze and report a 40% investment in another company

S7-3 Suppose on February 1, 2017, General Motors paid $41 million for a 40% investment in ABC Ltd., an auto parts manufacturer. Assume ABC earned net income of $6 million and paid cash dividends of $2 million during 2017.
1. What method should General Motors use to account for the investment in ABC? Give your reason.
2. Journalize these three transactions on the books of General Motors. Show all amounts in millions of dollars, and include an explanation for each entry.
3. Post to the Long-Term Investment T-account. What is its balance after all the transactions are posted?

LEARNING OBJECTIVE ❷

Account for the sale of an equity-method investment

S7-4 Use the data given in exercise S7-3. Assume that in November 2018, General Motors sold half its investment in ABC to Toyota. The sale price was $14 million. Compute General Motors's gain or loss on the sale.

LEARNING OBJECTIVE ❷

Understand consolidated financial statements

S7-5 Answer these questions about consolidation accounting:

1. Define *parent company*. Define *subsidiary company*.
2. How do consolidated financial statements differ from the financial statements of a single company?
3. Which company's name appears on the consolidated financial statements? How much of the subsidiary's shares must the parent own before reporting consolidated statements?

LEARNING OBJECTIVE ❷

Understand goodwill and minority interest

S7-6 Two accounts that arise from consolidation accounting are Goodwill and Non-Controlling Interest.
1. What is *goodwill*, and how does it arise? Which company reports goodwill, the parent or the subsidiary? Where is goodwill reported?
2. What is non-controlling interest and which company reports it, the parent or the subsidiary? Where is non-controlling interest reported?

S7-7 Suppose Prudential Bache (PB) buys $1,000,000 of CitiCorp bonds at a price of 101. The CitiCorp bonds pay cash interest at the annual rate of 7% and mature at the end of five years.
1. How much did PB pay to purchase the bond investment? How much will PB collect when the bond investment matures?
2. How much cash interest will PB receive each year from CitiCorp?
3. Will PB's annual interest revenue on the bond investment be more or less than the amount of cash interest received each year? Give your reason.
4. Compute PB's first-year interest revenue on this bond investment. Use the effective interest of 6.75% to amortize the investment.

LEARNING OBJECTIVE ❸

Analyze and report a bond investment

S7-8 Return to exercise S7-7, the Prudential Bache (PB) investment in CitiCorp bonds. Journalize the following on PB's books:
a. Purchase of the bond investment on January 2, 2017. PB expects to hold the investment to maturity.
b. Receipt of annual cash interest on December 31, 2017
c. Amortization of the bonds on December 31, 2017
d. Collection of the investment's face value at the maturity date on January 2, 2022. (Assume the receipt of 2021 interest and the amortization of bonds for 2021 have already been recorded, so ignore these entries.)

LEARNING OBJECTIVE ❸

Record bond investment transactions

S7-9 Calculate the present value of the following amounts:
1. $10,000 at the end of five years at 8%
2. $10,000 a year at the end of the next five years at 8%

LEARNING OBJECTIVE ❺

Calculate present value

S7-10 Arnold Financing leases airplanes to airline companies. Arnold has just signed a 10-year lease agreement that requires annual lease payments of $1,000,000. What is the present value of the lease using a 10% interest rate?

LEARNING OBJECTIVE ❺

Calculate the present value of an investment

S7-11 Companies divide their cash flows into three categories for reporting on the statement of cash flows.
1. List the three categories of cash flows in the order they appear on the statement of cash flows. Which category of cash flows is most closely related to this chapter?
2. Identify two types of transactions that companies report as cash flows from investing activities.

LEARNING OBJECTIVE ❹

Report investing activities on the statement of cash flows

S7-12 Calculate the present value of the following amounts:
1. $12,000 at the end of five years at 10%
2. $12,000 a year at the end of the next five years at 10%

LEARNING OBJECTIVE ❺

Calculate present value

S7-13 Chaplin Leasing leased a car to a customer. Chaplin will receive $150 a month for 60 months.
1. What is the present value of the lease if the annual interest rate in the lease is 12%? Use the PV function in Excel to compute the present value.
2. What is the present value of the lease if the car can likely be sold for $7,500 at the end of five years?

LEARNING OBJECTIVE ❺

Calculate the present value of an investment

EXERCISES

E7-14 Journalize the following long-term non-strategic investment transactions of Solomon Brothers Department Stores assuming the company reports changes in fair value through net income:
a. Purchased 400 shares of Royal Bank of Canada at $40 per share, with the intent of holding the shares for the indefinite future
b. Received cash dividend of $0.50 per share on the Royal Bank of Canada investment
c. At year-end, adjusted the investment account to current fair value of $35 per share
d. Sold the shares for the market price of $30 per share

LEARNING OBJECTIVE ❶

Record transactions for a non-strategic investment

E7-15 Dow-Smith Ltd. bought 3,000 common shares of Shoppers Drug Mart at $50.00 common shares of Bank of Montreal (BMO) at $42.50, and 1,400 common shares of EnCana at $93.36, all as non-strategic investments. At December 31, TSX Online reports Shoppers's shares at $48.05, BMO's shares at $31.25, and EnCana's shares at $56.96. The company reports changes in fair value through other comprehensive income

Requirements

1. Determine the cost and the fair value of the long-term investment portfolio at December 31.
2. Record Dow-Smith's adjusting entry at December 31.
3. What would Dow-Smith report on its income statement and balance sheet for the information given? Make the necessary disclosures. Ignore income tax.

E7-16 BlackBerry owns equity-method investments in several companies. Suppose BlackBerry paid $1,000,000 to acquire a 25% investment in Thai Software Company. Thai Software reported net income of $640,000 for the first year and declared and paid cash dividends of $420,000.

1. Record the following in BlackBerry's journal: (a) purchase of the investment, (b) BlackBerry's proportion of Thai Software's net income, and (c) receipt of the cash dividends.
2. What is the ending balance in BlackBerry's investment account?

E7-17 Without making journal entries, record the transactions of exercise E7-16 directly in the BlackBerry account, Long-Term Investment in Thai Software. Assume that after all the noted transactions took place, BlackBerry sold its entire investment in Thai Software for cash of $2,700,000. How much is BlackBerry's gain or loss on the sale of the investment?

E7-18 Oaktree Financial Inc. paid $500,000 for a 25% investment in the common shares of eTrav Inc. For the first year, eTrav reported net income of $200,000 and at year-end declared and paid cash dividends of $100,000. On the balance sheet date, the fair value of Oaktree's investment in eTrav shares was $384,000.

Requirements

1. Which method is appropriate for Oaktree Financial to use in accounting for its investment in eTrav? Why?
2. Show everything that Oaktree would report for the investment and any investment revenue in its year-end financial statements.

E7-19 Assume that on September 30, 2017, Manulife Financial paid 91 for 7% bonds of Hydro-Québec as a long-term bond investment. The effective interest rate was 8%. The maturity value of the bonds will be $20,000 on September 30, 2022. The bonds pay interest on March 31 and September 30.

Requirements

1. What method should Manulife use to account for its investment in the Hydro-Québec bonds?
2. Using the effective interest method of amortizing the bonds, journalize all of Manulife's transactions on the bonds for 2017.
3. Show how Manulife would report everything related to the bond investment on its balance sheet at December 31, 2017.

E7-20 Brinkman Corp. purchased ten $1,000, 5% bonds of General Electric Corporation when the market rate of interest was 4%. Interest is paid annually on the bonds, and the bonds will mature in six years. Compute the price Brinkman paid (the present value) on the bond investment.

E7-21 Alpha Inc., owns Beta Corp. The two companies' individual balance sheets follow:

LEARNING OBJECTIVE ❷

Prepare a consolidated balance sheet

	A	B	C	D	E	F
1		Alpha Inc.	Beta Corporation	Eliminations Debit	Credit	Consolidated Amounts
2	**Assets**					
3	Cash	46,000	20,000			
4	Accounts receivable, net	75,000	52,000			
5	Note receivable from Alpha		29,000			
6	Inventory	56,000	80,000			
7	Investment in Beta	113,000				
8	Plant & equipment, net	283,000	97,000			
9	Other assets	29,000	13,000			
10	Total	602,000	291,000			
11	**Liabilities and Shareholders' Equity**					
12	Accounts payable	49,000	22,000			
13	Notes payable	148,000	33,000			
14	Other liabilities	78,000	123,000			
15	Common shares	112,000	80,000			
16	Retained earnings	215,000	33,000			
17	Total	602,000	291,000			
18						

Requirements

1. Prepare a consolidated balance sheet of Alpha, Inc. It is sufficient to complete the consolidation work sheet. Use Exhibit 7-5 as a model.
2. What is the amount of shareholders' equity for the consolidated entity?

E7-22 During fiscal year 2017, Donuts 'R' Us Inc. reported net loss of $135.8 million. Donuts received $1.0 million from the sale of other businesses. Donuts made capital expenditures of $10.4 million and sold property, plant, and equipment for $7.3 million. The company purchased long-term investments at a cost of $12.2 million and sold other long-term investments for $2.5 million.

LEARNING OBJECTIVE ❹

Prepare and use a statement of cash flows

Requirement

Prepare the investing activities section of the Donuts 'R' Us statement of cash flows. Based solely on Donuts's investing activities, does it appear that the company is growing or shrinking? How can you tell?

E7-23 At the end of the year, Blue Chip Properties Ltd.'s statement of cash flows reported the following for investment activities:

LEARNING OBJECTIVE ❹

Use statement of cash flows

	A	B	C	D
1	**Blue Chip Properties Ltd.** Consolidated Statement of Cash Flows (Partial)			
2	**Cash Flows from Investing Activities**			
3	Notes receivable collected	$ 3,110,000		
4	Purchases of short-term investments	(3,457,000)		
5	Proceeds from sales of equipment	1,409,000*		
6	Proceeds from sales of investments (cost of $450,000)	461,000		
7	Expenditures for property, plant, and equipment	(1,761,000)		
8	Net cash used by investing activities	$ (238,000)		
9				

*Cost $5,100,000; Accumulated depreciation, $3,691,000

Requirement

For each item listed, make the journal entry that placed the item on Blue Chip's statement of cash flows.

CHALLENGE EXERCISES

LEARNING OBJECTIVE ⑤

Calculate the present value of competing investments

E7-24 Which option is better: receive $100,000 now or $20,000, $25,000, $30,000, $25,000, and $20,000, respectively, over the next five years?

Requirements

1. Assuming a 5% interest rate, which investment opportunity would you choose?
2. If you could earn 10%, would your choice change?
3. What would the cash flow in year 5 have to be in order for you to be indifferent to the options mentioned above?

LEARNING OBJECTIVE ①

Explain and analyze accumulated other comprehensive income

E7-25 Big-Box Retail Corporation reported shareholders' equity on its balance sheet at December 31, 2017, as follows:

Big-Box Retail Corporation
Balance Sheet (Partial)
December 31, 2017

	millions
Shareholders' Equity:	
Common shares, $0.10	
800 million shares authorized, 300 million shares issued	$1,113
Retained earnings	6,250
Accumulated other comprehensive income (loss)	(?)

Requirements

1. What one component that was discussed in this chapter is included in accumulated other comprehensive income?
2. For the component of accumulated other comprehensive income, describe the event that can cause a *positive* balance. Also describe the event that can cause a negative balance for each component.
3. At December 31, 2016, Big-Box's accumulated other comprehensive loss was $53 million. Then, during 2017, Big-Box had an unrealized loss of $16 million on non-strategic investments. Assume Big-Box chooses to record any changes in fair value through other comprehensive income. What was Big-Box's balance of accumulated other comprehensive income (loss) at December 31, 2017?

PROBLEMS (GROUP A)

LEARNING OBJECTIVE ①②

Analyze and report various long-term investment transactions on the balance sheet and income statement

P7-26A Winnipeg Exchanges Ltd. completed the following long-term investment transactions during 2017:

2017	
May 12	Purchased 20,000 shares, which make up 35% of the common shares of Fellingham Corporation at a total cost of $370,000
July 9	Received annual cash dividend of $1.26 per share on the Fellingham investment
Sept. 16	Purchased 800 common shares of Tomassini Inc. as a non-strategic investment, paying $41.50 per share
Oct. 30	Received cash dividend of $0.30 per share on the Tomassini investment
Dec. 31	Received annual report from Fellingham Corporation. Net income for the year was $510,000.

At year-end the current fair value of the Tomassini shares is $30,600. The fair value of the Fellingham shares is $652,000. The company reports changes in fair value through other comprehensive income.

Requirements

1. For which investment is current fair value used in the accounting? Why is fair value used for one investment and not the other?
2. Show what Winnipeg Exchanges Ltd. would report on its year-end balance sheet and income statement for these investment transactions. It is helpful to use a T-account for the Long-Term Investment in Fellingham Shares account. Ignore income tax.

P7-27A The beginning balance sheet of New Technology Corporation included the following:

LEARNING OBJECTIVE ❶❷

Analyze and report non-strategic and equity-method investments

Long-Term Investment in MSC Software (equity-method investment)......................... $619,000

New Technology completed the following investment transactions during the year 2017:

Mar. 16	Purchased 2,000 shares of ATI Inc. as a long-term non-strategic investment, paying $12.25 per share
May 21	Received cash dividend of $0.75 per share on the ATI investment
Aug. 17	Received cash dividend of $81,000 from MSC Software
Dec. 31	Received annual report from MSC Software. Net income for the year was $550,000. Of this amount, New Technology's proportion is 22%.

At year-end, the fair values of New Technology's investments are ATI, $25,700, and MSC, $700,000. The company reports any changes in fair value through net income.

Requirements

1. Record the transactions in the journal of New Technology Corporation.
2. Post entries to the T-account for Long-Term Investment in MSC and determine its balance at December 31, 2017.
3. Show how to report the Long-Term Non-strategic Investment and the Long-Term Investment in MSC accounts on New Technology's balance sheet at December 31, 2017.

P7-28A This problem demonstrates the dramatic effect that consolidation accounting can have on a company's ratios. ABC Company owns 100% of ABC Credit Corporation, its financing subsidiary. ABC's main operations consist of manufacturing automotive products. ABC Credit Corporation mainly helps people finance the purchase of automobiles from ABC and its dealers. The two companies' individual balance sheets are adapted and summarized as follows (amounts in billions):

LEARNING OBJECTIVE ❷

Analyze consolidated financial statements

	ABC (Parent)	ABC Credit (Subsidiary)
Total assets	$94.8	$179.0
Total liabilities	$68.4	$164.7
Total shareholders' equity	26.4	14.3
Total liabilities and equity...	$94.8	$179.0

Requirements

1. Compute the debt ratio of ABC Company considered alone.
2. Determine the consolidated total assets, total liabilities, and shareholders' equity of ABC Company after consolidating the financial statements of ABC Credit into the totals of ABC, the parent company.

3. Recompute the debt ratio of the consolidated entity. Why do companies prefer not to consolidate their financing subsidiaries into their own financial statements?

P7-29A Insurance companies and pension plans hold large quantities of bond investments. Prairie Insurance Corp. purchased $600,000 of 5% bonds of Eaton Inc. for 104.5 on March 1, 2017, when the effective interest rate was 4%. These bonds pay interest on March 1 and September 1 each year. They mature on March 1, 2022. At February 28, 2018, the market price of the bonds is 103.5.

Requirements

1. Journalize Prairie's purchase of the bonds as a long-term investment on March 1, 2017 (to be held to maturity), receipt of cash interest and amortization of the bond investment on September 1, 2017, and accrual of interest revenue and amortization at February 28, 2018. Use the effective-interest method for amortizing the bond investment.
2. Show all financial statement effects of this long-term bond investment on Prairie Insurance Corp.'s balance sheet and income statement at February 28, 2018.

P7-30A Annual cash flows from two competing investment opportunities are given. Each investment opportunity will require the same initial investment at the end of each year.

Year	Investment A	Investment B
1	$10,000	$ 8,000
2	8,000	8,000
3	6,000	8,000
	$24,000	$24,000

Requirement

Assuming a 12% interest rate, which investment opportunity would you choose?

P7-31A Zeta, Inc., owns Theta Corp. These two companies' individual balance sheets follow:

	A	B	C	D	E	F
1		Zeta Inc.	Theta Corporation	Eliminations Debit	Credit	Consolidated Amounts
2	**Assets**					
3	Cash	48,000	18,000			
4	Accounts receivable	82,000	58,000			
5	Note receivable from Zeta		33,000			
6	Inventory	54,000	83,000			
7	Investment in Theta	119,000				
8	Plant & equipment, net	288,000	98,000			
9	Other assets	29,000	11,000			
10	Total	620,000	301,000			
11	**Liabilities and Shareholders' Equity**					
12	Accounts payable	49,000	35,000			
13	Notes payable	152,000	23,000			
14	Other liabilities	78,000	124,000			
15	Common shares	107,000	82,000			
16	Retained earnings	234,000	37,000			
17	Total	620,000	301,000			
18						

Requirements

1. Prepare a consolidated balance sheet of Zeta, Inc. It is sufficient to complete the consolidation work sheet. Use Exhibit 7-5 as a model.
2. What is the amount of shareholders' equity for the consolidated entity?

P7-32A Excerpts from Smart Pro Inc.'s statement of cash flows appear as follows:

LEARNING OBJECTIVE ④

Use the statement of cash flows

	A	B	C	D
1	**Smart Pro Inc.** Consolidated Statement of Cash Flows (Partial, Adapted) For the Years Ended December 31			
2	*(in millions)*	**2017**	**2016**	
3	Cash and cash equivalents, beginning of year	$ 2,976	$ 3,695	
4	Net cash provided by operating activities	8,654	12,827	
5	Cash flows provided by (used for) investing activities:			
6	Additions to property, plant, and equipment	(7,309)	(6,674)	
7	Acquisitions of other companies	(883)	(2,317)	
8	Purchases of investments	(7,141)	(17,188)	
9	Sales of investments	15,138	16,144	
10	Net cash (used for) investing activities	(195)	(10,035)	
11	Cash flows provided by (used for) financing activities:			
12	Borrowing	329	215	
13	Repayment of long-term debt	(10)	(46)	
14	Proceeds from issuance of shares	762	797	
15	Repurchase of common shares	(4,008)	(4,007)	
16	Payment of dividends to shareholders	(538)	(470)	
17	Net cash (used for) financing activities	(3,465)	(3,511)	
18	Net increase (decrease) in cash and cash equivalents	4,994	(719)	
19	Cash and cash equivalents, end of year	$ 7,970	$ 2,976	
20				

Source: Based on Smart Pro Inc. – Annual Report.

Requirement

As the chief executive officer of Smart Pro Inc., your duty is to write the management letter to your shareholders to explain Smart Pro's investing activities during 2017. Compare the company's level of investment with the preceding year, and indicate the major way the company financed its investments during 2017. Net income for 2017 was $1,291 million.

P7-33A This problem demonstrates the dramatic effect that consolidation accounting can have on a company's ratios. Spindler Motor Company (Spindler) owns 100% of Spindler Motor Credit Corporation (SMCC), its financing subsidiary. Spindler's main operations consist of manufacturing automotive products. SMCC mainly helps people finance the purchase of automobiles from Spindler and its dealers. The two companies' individual balance sheets are adapted and summarized as follows (amounts in billions):

LEARNING OBJECTIVE ②

Analyze consolidated financial statements

	Spindler (Parent)	SMCC (Subsidiary)
Total assets	$85.1	$169.2
Total liabilities	$65.3	$155.9
Total stockholders' equity	19.8	13.3
Total liabilities and equity	$85.1	$169.2

Assume that SMCC's liabilities include $1.3 billion owed to Spindler, the parent company.

Requirements

1. Compute the debt ratio of Spindler Motor Company considered alone.
2. Determine the consolidated total assets, total liabilities, and shareholders' equity of Spindler Motor Company after consolidating the financial statements of SMCC into the totals of Spindler, the parent company.
3. Recompute the debt ratio of the consolidated entity. Why do companies prefer not to consolidate their financing subsidiaries into their own financial statements?

PROBLEMS (GROUP B)

LEARNING OBJECTIVE ❶❷

Analyze and report various long-term investment transactions on the balance sheet and income statement

P7-34B Homestead Financial Corporation owns numerous investments in the shares of other companies. Homestead Financial completed the following long-term investment transactions:

2017		
May 1	Purchased 8,000 shares, which make up 25% of the common shares of Mars Company at total cost of $450,000	
Sept. 15	Received a cash dividend of $1.40 per share on the Mars investment	
Oct. 12	Purchased 1,000 common shares of Mercury Corporation as a non-strategic investment, paying $22.50 per share	
Dec. 14	Received a cash dividend of $0.75 per share on the Mercury investment	
31	Received annual report from Mars Company. Net income for the year was $350,000.	

At year-end the current fair value of the Mercury shares is $19,200. The fair value of the Mars shares is $740,000. The company reports changes in fair value through net income.

Requirements

1. For which investment is current fair value used in the accounting? Why is fair value used for one investment and not the other?
2. Show what Homestead Financial will report on its year-end balance sheet and income statement for these investments. (It is helpful to use a T-account for the Long-Term Investment in Mars Shares account.) Ignore income tax.

LEARNING OBJECTIVE ❶❷

Analyze and report non-strategic and equity-method investments

P7-35B The beginning balance sheet of Dealmaker Securities Limited included the following:

Long-Term Investments in Affiliates (equity-method investments)........................... $409,000

Dealmaker completed the following investment transactions during the year:

Feb. 16	Purchased 10,000 shares of BCM Software common shares as a long-term non-strategic investment, paying $9.25 per share
May 14	Received cash dividend of $0.82 per share on the BCM investment
Oct. 15	Received cash dividend of $29,000 from an affiliated company
Dec. 31	Received annual reports from affiliated companies. Their total net income for the year was $620,000. Of this amount, Dealmaker's proportion is 25%.

The fair values of Dealmaker's investments are BCM, $89,000, and affiliated companies, $947,000. The company reports changes in fair value through other comprehensive income.

Requirements

1. Record the transactions in the journal of Dealmaker Securities.
2. Post entries to the Long-Term Investments in Affiliates T-account, and determine its balance at December 31.
3. Show how to report Long-Term Non-strategic Investments and Long-Term Investments in Affiliates on Dealmaker's balance sheet at December 31.

P7-36B Financial institutions hold large quantities of bond investments. Suppose Sun Life Financial purchases $500,000 of 6% bonds of General Components Corporation for 88 on January 1, 2017, when the effective interest rate is 8%. These bonds pay interest on January 1 and July 1 each year. They mature on January 1, 2025. At December 31, 2017, the market price of the bonds is 90.

LEARNING OBJECTIVE 3
Analyze and report a bond investment

Requirements

1. Journalize Sun Life's purchase of the bonds as a long-term investment on January 1, 2017 (to be held to maturity), receipt of cash interest and amortization of the bond investment on July 1, 2017, and accrual of interest revenue and amortization at December 31, 2017. Use the effective-interest method for amortizing the bond investment.
2. Show all financial statement effects of this long-term bond investment on Sun Life's balance sheet and income statement at December 31, 2017.

P7-37B Annual cash flows from two competing investment opportunities are given. Each investment opportunity will require the same initial investment.

LEARNING OBJECTIVE 5
Explain the impact of the time value of money on the valuation of investments

	Investment	
Year	X	Y
1	$15,000	$10,000
2	10,000	10,000
3	5,000	10,000
	$30,000	$30,000

Requirement

Assuming a 10% interest rate, which investment opportunity would you choose?

P7-38B This problem demonstrates the dramatic effect that consolidation accounting can have on a company's ratios. Snider Motor Company (Snider) owns 100% of Snider Motor Credit Corporation (SMCC), its financing subsidiary. Snider's main operations consist of manufacturing automotive products. SMCC mainly helps people finance the purchase of automobiles from Snider and its dealers. The two companies' individual balance sheets are adapted and summarized as follows (amounts in billions):

LEARNING OBJECTIVE 2
Analyze consolidated financial statements

	Snider (Parent)	SMCC (Subsidiary)
Total assets	$78.8	$163.1
Total liabilities	$63.8	$155.2
Total shareholders' equity	15.0	7.9
Total liabilities and equity	$78.8	$163.1

Assume that SMCC's liabilities include $1.6 billion owed to Snider, the parent company.

Requirements

1. Compute the debt ratio of Snider Motor Company considered alone.
2. Determine the consolidated total assets, total liabilities, and shareholders' equity of Snider Motor Company after consolidating the financial statements of SMCC into the totals of Snider, the parent company.
3. Recompute the debt ratio of the consolidated entity. Why do companies prefer not to consolidate their financing subsidiaries into their own financial statements?

LEARNING OBJECTIVE ❹

Use the statement of cash flows

P7-39B Marine Transport Ltd.'s statement of cash flows, as adapted, appears as follows:

	A	B	C	D
1	**Marine Transport Ltd.** Consolidated Statement of Cash Flows For the Years Ended December 31 (Stated in thousands of Canadian dollars)			
2		2017	2016	
3	Cash flows from (used in):			
4	**Operating activities:**			
5	Net earnings	$ 192,833	$ 114,676	
6	Items not involving cash:			
7	Depreciation and amortization	127,223	111,442	
8	Amortization of other liabilities	(897)	(868)	
9	Amortization of hedge settlements	1,400	1,427	
10	Net realized loss on cash flow hedge	18	—	
11	Loss on derecognition of property and equipment and			
12	ship parts	32,773	394	
13	Stock-based compensation expense	20,058	21,205	
14	Future income tax expense	41,775	46,635	
15	Unrealized foreign exchange loss (gain)	13,813	(346)	
16	Decrease in non-cash working capital	112,069	43,707	
17		541,065	338,272	
18	**Financing activities:**			
19	Increase in long-term debt	141,178	418,581	
20	Repayment of long-term debt	(156,516)	(132,559)	
21	Decrease in obligations under capital lease	(356)	(480)	
22	Share issuance costs	—	(10)	
23	Shares repurchased	(21,250)	—	
24	Issuance of common shares	1,551	—	
25	Increase in other assets	(20,897)	(27,830)	
26	Increase in non-cash working capital	(3,000)	(1,071)	
27		(59,290)	256,631	
28	**Investing activities:**			
29	Ship additions	(191,437)	(438,906)	
30	Ship disposals	1,975	3,822	
31	Other property and equipment additions	(24,639)	(43,590)	
32	Other property and equipment disposals	13,819	1,611	
33		(200,282)	(477,063)	
34				
35	Cash flow from operating, financing, and investing activities	281,493	117,840	
36	Effect of exchange rate on cash	(5,452)	37	
37	Net change in cash	276,041	117,877	
38	Cash, beginning of year	377,517	259,640	
39	Cash, end of year	$ 653,558	$ 377,517	
40				
41	Cash is defined as cash and cash equivalents.			

Requirement

As a member of an investment club, you have been asked to review Marine Transport's major investing activities during 2017. Compare the company's level of investment with the previous year, and indicate how the company financed its investments during 2017.

LEARNING OBJECTIVE ❷

Analyze consolidated financial statements

P7-40B This problem demonstrates the dramatic effect that consolidation accounting can have on a company's ratios. Randall Motor Company (Randall) owns 100% of Randall Motor Credit Corporation (RMCC), its financing subsidiary. Randall's main operations consist of manufacturing automotive products. RMCC mainly helps people finance the purchase of automobiles from Randall and its dealers. The two companies' individual balance sheets are adapted and summarized as follows (amounts in billions):

	Randall (Parent)	RMCC (Subsidiary)
Total assets	$80.6	$164.8
Total liabilities	$63.9	$155.4
Total shareholders' equity	16.7	9.4
Total liabilities and equity	$80.6	$164.8

Assume that RMCC's liabilities include $1.6 billion owed to Randall, the parent company.

Requirements

1. Compute the debt ratio of Randall Motor Company considered alone.
2. Determine the consolidated total assets, total liabilities, and shareholders' equity of Randall Motor Company after consolidating the financial statements of RMCC into the totals of Randall, the parent company.
3. Recompute the debt ratio of the consolidated entity. Why do companies prefer not to consolidate their financing subsidiaries into their own financial statements?

APPLY YOUR KNOWLEDGE

DECISION CASES

This section's material reflects CPA enabling competencies,* including:

1. Professionalism and ethical behaviour
2. Problem-solving and decision-making
3. Communication
4. Self-management
5. Teamwork and leadership

Case 1. Infografix Corporation's consolidated sales for 2017 were $26.6 million and expenses totaled $24.8 million. Infografix operates worldwide and conducts 37% of its business outside Canada. During 2014, Infografix reported the following items in its financial statements (amounts in millions):

Unrealized holding on non-strategic investments .... (328)

As you consider an investment in Infografix shares, some concerns arise. Answer the following questions:

1. What do the parentheses around the dollar amounts signify?
2. Is this item reported as an asset, liability, shareholders' equity, revenue, or expense? Are they normal-balance accounts, or are they contra accounts?
3. Is this item reason for rejoicing or sorrow at Infografix? Are Infografix's emotions about this item deep or only moderate? Why?
4. Did Infografix include this item in net income? Did it include this item in retained earnings? In the final analysis, how much net income did Infografix report for 2017?
5. Should these items scare you away from investing in Infografix shares? Why or why not?

LEARNING OBJECTIVE ❷

Make an investment decision

Case 2. Cathy Talbert is the general manager of Barham Ltd., which provides data-management services for physicians in the Regina, Saskatchewan, area. Barham is having a rough year. Net income trails projections for the year by almost $75,000. This shortfall is especially important—Barham plans to issue shares early next year and needs to show investors that the company can meet its earnings targets.

Barham holds several investments purchased a few years ago. Even though investing in shares is outside Barham's core business of data-management services, Talbert thinks these

LEARNING OBJECTIVE ❶❷❸

Make an investment sale decision

*© Chartered Professional Accountants of Canada.

investments may hold the key to helping the company meet its net income goal for the year. She is considering what to do with the following investments:

1. Barham owns 50% of the common shares of Prairie Office Systems, which provides the business forms that Barham uses. Prairie Office Systems has lost money for the past two years but still has a retained earnings balance of $550,000. Talbert thinks she can get Prairie's treasurer to declare a $160,000 cash dividend, half of which would go to Barham.

2. Barham owns a bond investment with a 4% coupon rate and an annual interest payment. The bond was purchased eight years ago for $293,000. The purchase price represents a discount from the bonds' maturity value of $400,000 based on an effective rate of 8%. These bonds mature two years from now, and their current market value is $380,000. Ms. Talbert has checked with a Scotiabank investment representative and Talbert is considering selling the bonds. A charge of 1% commission would be made on the sale transaction.

3. Barham owns 5,000 Royal Bank of Canada (RBC) shares valued at $53 per share. One year ago, RBC was worth only $28 per share. Barham purchased the RBC shares for $37 per share. Talbert wonders whether Barham should sell the RBC shares.

Requirement

Evaluate all three actions as a way for Barham Ltd. to generate the needed amount of income. Recommend the best way for Barham to achieve its net income goal.

ETHICAL ISSUE

Media One owns 15% of the voting shares of Online Inc. The remainder of the Online shares are held by numerous investors with small holdings. Austin Cohen, president of Media One and a member of Online's board of directors, heavily influences Online's policies.

Under the fair-value method of accounting for investments, Media One's net income increases as it receives dividend revenue from Online. Media One pays President Cohen a bonus, computed as a percentage of Media One's net income. Therefore, Cohen can control his personal bonus to a certain extent by influencing Online's dividends.

A recession occurs in 2017, and Media One's income is low. Cohen uses his power to have Online pay a large cash dividend. The action requires Online to borrow in order to pay the dividend.

Requirements

1. In getting Online to pay the large cash dividend, is Cohen acting within his authority as a member of the Online board of directors? Are Cohen's actions ethical? Whom can his actions harm?

2. Discuss how using the equity method of accounting for investment would decrease Cohen's potential for manipulating his bonus.

FOCUS ON FINANCIALS

LEARNING OBJECTIVE ❷

Analyze investments, consolidated statements, and international operations

MyAccountingLab

Canadian Tire Corporation

Canadian Tire's financial statements are given in Appendix A at the end of this book.

1. Does Canadian Tire have any subsidiaries? How can you tell?

2. Is Canadian Tire expanding or contracting its operations? How can you tell?

FOCUS ON ANALYSIS

Canadian Tire

Canadian Tire's financial statements are given in Appendix A at the end of this book.

1. Canadian Tire has subsidiaries. What is Canadian Tire's percentage of ownership? How can you tell?
2. Canadian Tire reports long-term investments on its consolidated balance sheet. Did they buy or sell any of these investments during the year? How can you tell?
3. Did Canadian Tire's goodwill suffer any impairment during the year? How can you tell?

LEARNING OBJECTIVE ❷

Analyze goodwill, consolidated subsidiaries, and investments

MyAccountingLab

GROUP PROJECT

Pick a stock from the *Globe and Mail* or other database or publication. Assume that your group purchases 1,000 shares as a long-term investment and that your 1,000 shares are less than 20% of the company's outstanding shares. Research the shares to determine whether the company pays cash dividends and, if so, how much and at what intervals.

Requirements

1. Track the shares for a period assigned by your professor. Over the specified period, keep a daily record of the share price to see how well your investment has performed. Keep a record of any dividends you would have received. End the period of your analysis with a month-end, such as September 30 or December 31.
2. Journalize all transactions that you have experienced, including the share purchase, dividends received (both cash dividends and stock dividends), and any year-end adjustment required by the accounting method that is appropriate for your situation. Assume you will prepare financial statements on the ending date of your study.
3. Show what you will report on your company's balance sheet, income statement, and statement of cash flows as a result of your investment transactions.

CHECK YOUR WORK

STOP + THINK ANSWERS

STOP + THINK (7-1)

Assets

Long-term investments.................................. $63,500

STOP + THINK (7-2)

The shareholders' equity of the consolidated entity is that of the parent only. To include the shareholders' equity of the subsidiary as well as the investment in the subsidiary on the parent's books would be double counting.

STOP + THINK (7-3)

Microsport would receive cash interest of $10,800 ($120,000 × .09) on December 31, 2020.

STOP + THINK (7-4)

The company spent most of its cash acquiring other companies.

STOP + THINK (7-5)

Using the table in Exhibit 7-9, the present value at the end of eight years at 5% interest would be $3,385 ($5,000 × 0.677).

QUICK QUIZ ANSWERS

1. *c*

2. *d (1,000 shares × $35 = $35,000)*

3. *a ($35,000 − $31,000 = $4,000)*

4. *c [$40,000 − (1,000 shares × $35) = $5,000]*

5. *b [$100,000 + 0.20 ($50,000 − $25,000) = $105,000]*

6. *c ($100,000 + 0.80 [$68,000 + 0.80($40,000)]*
   = $180,000)

7. *a*

8. *a*

9. *d (100,000 × 0.07 = $7,000)*

10. *b ($105,000 × 0.06 = 6,300;*
    $7,000 − $6,300 = $700
    Interest income = $7,000 − $700 = $6,300)

Liabilities

HP Canada/Alamy Stock Photo

LEARNING OBJECTIVES

1. **Explain** and **account** for current liabilities
2. **Explain** the types, features, and pricing of bonds payable
3. **Account** for bonds payable
4. **Calculate** and **account** for interest expense on bonds payable
5. **Explain** the advantages and disadvantages of financing with debt versus equity
6. **Analyze** and **evaluate** a company's debt-paying ability
7. **Describe** other types of long-term liabilities
8. **Report** liabilities on the balance sheet

CPA COMPETENCIES

Competencies* addressed in this chapter:

1.2.2 Evaluates treatment for routine transactions

1.4.4 Interprets financial reporting results for stakeholders (external or internal)

SPOTLIGHT

WestJet Airlines: A Success Story WestJet began operations in 1996 by serving five cities in Western Canada and now flies across Canada and to many destinations in the United States, Mexico, and the Caribbean. The airline decided at its start to operate with a single type of plane, the Boeing 737, in order to reduce operating costs. WestJet also decided to encourage share ownership by employees, so the front-desk staff, pilots, and flight attendants also own part of the company. This has led to a high level of service, which encourages passengers to "fly WestJet."

Airlines have some interesting liabilities. WestJet collects fares in advance and recognizes the revenue when the passenger actually takes the trip. Thus, WestJet had a liability called "advance ticket sales" of about $625 million on its balance sheet at September 30, 2015. When passengers change or cancel flights, they receive credits that they can apply toward future WestJet flights. This "nonrefundable guest credits" liability was $37 million at September 30, 2015. In this chapter, you will learn more about these and other types of liabilities commonly found on financial statements.

---

*© Chartered Professional Accountants of Canada.

	A	B	C	D	E
1	**WestJet Airlines Ltd.** Consolidated Balance Sheet (Adapted) As at September 30, 2015 (in millions)				
2	**Assets**		**Liabilities and Shareholders' Equity**		
3	Current assets:		Current liabilities:		
4	Cash and cash equivalents	$ 1,420	Accounts payable and		
5	Other current assets	263	accrued liabilities	$ 546	
6	Total current assets	1,683	Advance ticket sales	625	
7			Deferred Rewards program	114	
8			Nonrefundable guest credits	37	
9			Current portion of maintenance provisions	70	
10			Current portion of long-term debt	150	
11			Total current liabilities	1,542	
12	Non-current assets:		Non-current liabilities:		
13	Property and equipment	3,231	Maintenance provisions	233	
14	Other long-lived assets	151	Long-term debt	1,048	
15			Other liabilities	17	
16			Deferred income tax	315	
17				3,155	
18			Shareholders' equity	1,910	
19	Total assets	$ 5,065	Total liabilities and shareholders' equity	$ 5,065	
20					

Source: Based on WestJet Consolidated Balance Sheet September 30, 2015.

EXPLAIN AND ACCOUNT FOR CURRENT LIABILITIES

Current liabilities are obligations due within one year, or within the company's normal operating cycle if it is longer than one year. Obligations due beyond that are classified as *long-term liabilities* or *non-current liabilities*, as in the WestJet balance sheet above.

Current liabilities are of two kinds:

- Known amounts
- Estimated amounts

We look first at current liabilities of known amounts.

Current Liabilities of Known Amount

SHORT-TERM BORROWINGS. Companies sometimes need to borrow money on a short-term basis to cover temporary shortfalls in cash needed to run their businesses. For example, a ski resort that earns most of its revenues during the winter months may need to temporarily borrow money to supplement the minimal cash flows it generates from operations during the summer. A **line of credit** allows a company to access credit on an as-needed basis up to a maximum amount set by the lender. The ski resort, for example, could arrange with its bank to borrow up to $250,000 to help run its business over the slow summer months.

ACCOUNTS PAYABLE. Amounts owed for products or services purchased on credit are **accounts payable**. For example, WestJet purchases on account the food and beverages it serves its passengers. We have seen many other examples of accounts payable in previous chapters. One of a merchandiser's most common transactions is the credit purchase of inventory. The Hudson's Bay Company and Sobeys, for example, buy their inventory on account.

ACCRUED LIABILITIES (OR ACCRUED EXPENSES). An *accrued liability* results from an expense the business has incurred but has not yet been billed for or paid. Because accrued liabilities often arise from expenses, they are sometimes called *accrued expenses*.

For example, WestJet's salaries and wages payable accrue as employees work for the company. Interest expense accrues with the passage of time. Common types of accrued liabilities are:

- Salaries and Wages Payable
- Interest Payable
- Income Taxes Payable

Salaries and Wages Payable is the liability for salaries, wages, and related payroll expenses not yet paid at the end of the period (see the Payroll Liabilities section on page 380 for more details on this accrual). This category also includes payroll deductions withheld from employee paycheques. *Interest Payable* is the company's interest payable on notes, loans, and bonds payable. *Income Taxes Payable* is the amount of income tax the company still owes at year-end.

SHORT-TERM NOTES PAYABLE. In Chapter 4 we introduced you to promissory notes from a lender's perspective, so we called them notes *receivable*. When we record these same notes in the borrower's books, they are notes *payable*. **Short-term notes payable** are notes payable due within one year. Robertson Construction Inc. may issue short-term notes payable to borrow cash or to purchase assets. For its notes payable, Robertson must accrue interest expense at the end of each reporting period. The following sequence of entries covers the purchase of inventory, accrual of interest expense, and payment of a short-term note payable:

	A	B	C	D	E
1	2017				
2	Oct. 1	Inventory	8,000		
3		Note Payable, Short-Term		8,000	
4		*Purchase of inventory by issuing a six-month 10% note payable.*			

This transaction increases both an asset and a liability:

ASSETS	=	LIABILITIES	+	SHAREHOLDERS' EQUITY
+8,000	=	+8,000		

Assume Robertson Construction's year-end is December 31. At year-end, Robertson must accrue interest expense at 10% per year for October through December. (For ease of exposition, accrued interest has been calculated based on months rather than days. In practice, days are typically used.)

	A	B	C	D	E
1	2017				
2	Dec. 31	Interest Expense ($8,000 × 0.10 × 3/12)	200		
3		Interest Payable		200	
4		*Adjusting entry to accrue interest expense at year-end.*			

Liabilities increase, and equity decreases because of the expense:

				SHAREHOLDERS'
ASSETS	**=**	**LIABILITIES**	**+**	**EQUITY**
0	=	+200		−200 Interest Expense

The balance sheet at year-end will report the note payable of $8,000 and the related interest payable of $200 as current liabilities. The income statement will report interest expense of $200.

The following entry records the note's payment at March 31, 2018:

	A	B	C	D	E
1	2018				
2	Mar. 31	Note Payable, Short-Term	8,000		
3		Interest Payable	200		
4		Interest Expense ($8,000 × 0.10 × 3/12)	200		
5		Cash [$8,000 + ($8,000 × 0.10 × 6/12)]		8,400	
6		*Payment of a note payable and interest at maturity.*			
7					

				SHAREHOLDERS'
ASSETS	**=**	**LIABILITIES**	**+**	**EQUITY**
−8,400	=	−8,000		−200 Interest Expense
		− 200		

The debits eliminate the two payables and also record Robertson's interest expense for January, February, and March.

SALES TAX PAYABLE. The federal government and most provinces levy taxes on the sale of goods and services. Sellers collect these taxes from customers, creating **sales tax payable** to the government levying the tax. Canada has three types of sales taxes:

- Goods and services tax (GST) is a value-added tax levied by the federal government. At the time of writing, the tax is 5%. It applies to most goods and services.
- Provincial or regional sales tax (PST) is a retail tax applied to goods and services purchased by individuals or businesses *for their own use,* not for resale, with the rates varying by province or region. At the time of writing, Alberta, the Northwest Territories, Nunavut, and Yukon do not levy a provincial or regional sales tax.
- Harmonized sales tax (HST), which combines PST and GST, is also a value-added tax. Prince Edward Island, New Brunswick, Newfoundland and Labrador, Nova Scotia, and Ontario, together with the federal government, levy an HST.

The final consumer of a GST- or HST-taxable product or service bears the tax, while entities further down the supply chain from the end consumer do pay GST or HST, but receive an input tax credit (ITC) equal to the tax they have paid. These ITCs are deducted from any GST or HST collected to arrive at the net GST or HST payable to the government. For example, if a company collected $10,000 in HST on its sales and paid $8,000 in HST on goods and services it purchased, then it would end the period with HST payable of $2,000 ($10,000 in HST collected less $8,000 in ITCs).

GST or HST payable is always a current liability, as it is payable annually, quarterly, or monthly, depending on the collector's volume of business. GST and HST are remitted to the Canada Revenue Agency (CRA), which in turn remits the provincial portion of the HST to the respective provinces, with all GST and the federal portion of the HST being remitted to the federal government.

GST and HST are accounted for in the same way, so the following illustration using GST is applicable for HST as well, except for the difference in tax rates. Assume Kitchen Hardware Ltd., of Brandon, Manitoba, purchases lawn rakes for $3,000 plus 5% GST for a total of $3,150. Subsequently, Kitchen sells the rakes for $6,000 plus GST of $300 (provincial sales tax is ignored for this example but is covered below). The entries to record the purchase of the rakes, the sale of the rakes, and the remittance of the GST payable by Kitchen are as follows:

	A	B	C	D
1	Inventory	3,000		
2	GST Recoverable	150		
3	Accounts Payable		3,150	
4	To record purchase of inventory.			
5	Accounts Receivable	6,300		
6	Cost of Goods Sold	3,000		
7	Sales		6,000	
8	Inventory		3,000	
9	GST Payable		300	
10	To record sale of inventory.			
11	GST Payable	300		
12	GST ITC		150	
13	Cash		150	
14	To record payment of GST collected less GST paid.			

PST is levied at the point of sale to the final consumer, unlike GST and HST. It would apply to Kitchen Hardware when it purchases a cash register and to Mary Fortin, a customer of Kitchen, when she purchases light bulbs. Because only the final consumer pays PST, there are no ITCs for provincial taxes (except for Quebec's QST). PST payable is always a current liability as it is payable quarterly or monthly, depending on the payer's volume of business.

With respect to Kitchen Hardware's sale of rakes for $6,000, the GST would be $300 and the PST would be $420, as Manitoba's tax rate is 7%. So the total price to the consumer would be $6,720. The entries to record the sale of the rakes (including GST and PST payable) and the remittance of the PST payable by Kitchen are as follows:

	A	B	C	D
1	Accounts Receivable	6,720		
2	Cost of Goods Sold	3,000		
3	Sales		6,000	
4	Inventory		3,000	
5	GST Payable		300	
6	PST Payable		420	
7	*To record sale of inventory.*			
8	PST Payable	420		
9	Cash		420	
10	*To record payment of PST collected.*			
11				

PAYROLL LIABILITIES. **Payroll**, also called *employee compensation*, is a major expense for most companies. For service organizations—such as law firms, real estate brokers, and accounting firms—compensation is *the* major expense, just as cost of goods sold is the major expense for a merchandising company.

Employee compensation takes different forms. A *salary* is employee pay stated at a yearly or monthly rate. A *wage* is employee pay stated at an hourly rate. Sales employees often earn a *commission*, which is a percentage of the sales the employee has made. A *bonus* is an amount over and above regular compensation. Accounting for all forms of compensation follows the same pattern, as illustrated in Exhibit 8-1 (using assumed figures).

Salary expense represents *gross pay* (that is, pay before subtractions for taxes and other deductions). Salary expense creates several payroll entries, expenses, and liabilities:

- *Salaries and Wages Payable* is the employees' net (take-home) pay.
- *Employee Withholdings Income Tax Payable* is the employees' income tax that has been withheld from paycheques.
- *Canada Pension Plan Payable* and *Employment Insurance Payable* are the employees' contributions to those two government programs that have been withheld from their paycheques, along with the employer's contributions to these programs. In Quebec, the Quebec Pension Plan replaces the CPP and employees and employers must also contribute to the Quebec Parental Insurance Plan.
- *Canada Pension Plan and Employment Insurance Expense* is the cost of the employer's contribution to these two government programs. The two credits to liabilities totalling $751 represent the liability for the employer's contribution.

EXHIBIT 8-1
Accounting for Payroll Expenses and Liabilities

	A	B	C	D
1	Salary Expense	10,000		
2	Employee Withholdings Income Tax Payable		1,350	
3	Canada Pension Plan Payable		495	
4	Employment Insurance Payable		183	
5	Salary and Wages Payable [take-home pay]		7,972	
6	*To record salary expense and employee withholdings.*			
7	Canada Pension Plan and Employment Insurance Expense	751		
8	Canada Pension Plan Payable		495	
9	Employment Insurance Payable		256	
10	*To record employer's share of Canada Pension Plan and Employment Insurance.*			

ASSETS	=	LIABILITIES	+	SHAREHOLDERS' EQUITY
		+1,350		
		+ 495		
0	=	+ 183		−10,000 Salary Expense
		+7,972		
0	=	+ 495		−751 CPP and EI Expense
		+ 256		

INCOME TAXES PAYABLE. Corporations, like individuals, must pay taxes on their incomes. Personal and corporate tax rates differ, and corporate tax rates also vary by type of company and by province.

The accounting for corporate income taxes is complicated by the fact that income for accounting purposes (or **pretax accounting income**) usually differs from income for tax purposes. We determine income for accounting purposes by applying IFRS or ASPE, whereas we determine income for tax purposes by applying the rules in federal and provincial Income Tax Acts. The differences between accounting standards and tax rules result in differences between accounting income, which is used to determine a corporation's *income tax expense*, and **taxable income**, which is the income figure used to determine a corporation's *income tax payable*.

In general, income tax expense and income tax payable can be computed as follows:*

$$\text{Income tax expense} = \text{Income before income tax (from the \textit{income statement})} \times \text{Income tax rate}$$

$$\text{Income tax payable} = \text{Taxable income (from the \textit{income tax return filed with tax authorities})} \times \text{Income tax rate}$$

Income tax expense commonly differs from income tax payable because certain revenues and expenses are treated differently for accounting purposes than they are for tax purposes. The depreciation of capital assets is one area where such differences occur. Under IFRS and ASPE, companies have some leeway to choose the methods and rates they use to depreciate their assets, whereas tax rules specify the method and rate to be used for each asset type. We will use a simple example to illustrate the accounting impact of this kind of difference.

Suppose a company reports $10 million in pretax accounting income for the year ended December 31, 2017. Its operating expenses for 2017 include $2 million of depreciation, which was calculated using the straight-line method. The tax rules, however, require the use of an accelerated depreciation method, which results in depreciation for tax purposes of $2.8 million. If we assume there are no other accounting versus tax differences, then the company's taxable income for 2017 is $9.2 million, which is lower than its pretax accounting income due to the extra $800,000 ($2.8 million − $2 million) in depreciation for tax purposes. Assuming an income tax rate of 30%, the following journal entry is needed to account for the company's 2017 income taxes (dollar amounts in millions):

---

*The authors thank Jean Marie Hudson for suggesting this presentation.

	A	B	C	D	E
1	2017				
2	Dec. 31	Income Tax Expense ($10 × 0.30)	3.00		
3		Income Tax Payable ($9.2 × 0.30)		2.76	
4		Deferred Income Tax Liability		0.24	
5		*Recorded income tax for the year.*			
6					

ASSETS	=	LIABILITIES	+	SHAREHOLDERS' EQUITY	
0	=	$2.76 + $0.24		−$3.00	Income Tax Expense

The Income Tax Payable liability of $2.76 million (30% of taxable income of $9.2 million) represents the amount of income tax the company will actually have to remit to the government in 2018, so it would be reported as a current liability. The **Deferred Income Tax Liability** of $240,000, which is the difference between the company's income tax expense of $3 million and its income tax payable of $2.76 million, represents the amount of income taxes payable in future periods as a result of differences between accounting income and taxable income in the current and prior periods. Deferred income taxes are typically reported as long-term liabilities, as in WestJet's balance sheet at the beginning of the chapter. When income tax payable exceeds income tax expense, the difference is debited to a Deferred Income Tax Asset account. Under ASPE, deferred income taxes are referred to as future income taxes. Deferred and future income taxes are covered in greater depth in intermediate accounting courses.

UNEARNED REVENUES. A business sometimes collects cash from its customers before it provides the goods or services the customer has paid for. This creates a liability called **unearned revenues** because the business owes goods or services to the customer.

WestJet, for example, sells tickets and collects cash in advance of passengers actually taking their flights. WestJet therefore reports Advance Ticket Sales for airline tickets sold in advance. At September 30, 2015, WestJet owed customers $625 million of air travel (see page 376). Let's see how WestJet accounts for unearned ticket revenue.

Assume that on September 1 WestJet collects $800 for a round-trip ticket from Vancouver to Montreal, departing September 26 and returning October 10. WestJet's entries would be as follows:

	A	B	C	D	E
1	Sept. 1	Cash	800		
2		Advance Ticket Sales		800	
3		*To record cash received for future return airfare from Vancouver to Montreal.*			
4					

Advance Ticket Sales
800

WestJet's assets and liabilities increase equally. There is no revenue yet.

ASSETS	=	LIABILITIES	+	SHAREHOLDERS' EQUITY
+800	=	+800	+	0

When the passenger flies from Vancouver to Montreal on September 26, WestJet can record $400 of revenue because it has provided half of the air travel it owes the customer:

	A	B	C	D	E
1	Sept. 26	Advance Ticket Sales	400		
2		Ticket Revenue ($800/2)		400	
3		*To record revenue earned that was collected in advance.*			
4					

The liability decreases and revenue increases:

Advance Ticket Sales		Ticket Revenue
400	800	400

At September 30, WestJet reports:

- $400 of advance ticket sales (a liability) on the balance sheet for the return flight it still owes the customer
- $400 of ticket revenue on the income statement

When the customer returns to Vancouver on October 10, WestJet has earned the remaining $400 of revenue:

	A	B	C	D	E
1	Oct. 10	Advance Ticket Sales	400		
2		Ticket Revenue ($800/2)		400	
3		*Earned revenue that was collected in advance.*			
4					

Now the liability balance is zero because WestJet has provided both of the flights it owed the customer.

CURRENT PORTION OF LONG-TERM DEBT. The **current portion of long-term debt** is the amount of long-term debt that is payable within the next year. At the end of each year, a company reclassifies (from long-term debt to a current liability) the amount of its long-term debt that must be paid during the upcoming year. We will cover the accounting for long-term debt in the second half of this chapter.

STOP + THINK (8-1)

You are thinking of purchasing WestJet shares and are concerned about WestJet's debt. You examine WestJet's balance sheet on page 376 to answer the following questions about the company's current and long-term debt:

1. At September 30, 2015, how much in total did WestJet owe on current and long-term debt?

2. How much of the long-term debt did WestJet expect to pay by September 30, 2016? How much was the company scheduled to pay after this date?

Current Liabilities That Must Be Estimated

A business may know that it has a present obligation and that it is *probable* it will have to settle this obligation in the future, but it may be uncertain of the timing or amount of the liability. Despite this uncertainty, IFRS require the business to estimate and record a **provision** for this obligation in its financial statements. A provision is a specific type of contingent liability (see page 385 for further information on contingent liabilities).

Estimated liabilities vary among companies and include such things as warranties, employee pension obligations, and corporate restructuring costs. Warranty liabilities are quite common, so we will use them to illustrate the accounting for estimated liabilities.

ESTIMATED WARRANTY PAYABLE. Many companies guarantee their products under *warranty* agreements that cover some period of time after their customers purchase them. Automobile companies accrue liabilities for vehicle warranties, which usually extend for several years. The sale of a product with a warranty attached is a past event that creates a present obligation, which will require company resources (repair or replacement) to settle at some future date. At the time of the sale, however, the company does not know which products will be defective or how much it will cost to fix or replace them. The exact amount of warranty expense cannot be known with certainty, so the business must estimate warranty expense and the related warranty liability.

Assume that Black & Decker Canada Inc., which manufactures power tools, sold 4,000 tools subject to one-year warranties. If, in past years, between 2% and 4% of products proved defective and it cost an average of $50 to replace each tool, Black & Decker could estimate that 3% of the products it sells this year will require repair or replacement. In that case, Black & Decker would estimate warranty expense of $6,000 (4,000 × 0.03 × $50) for the period and make the following entry:

	A	B	C	D	E
1		Warranty Expense	6,000		
2		Estimated Warranty Payable		6,000	
3		*To accrue warranty expense.*			
4					

Estimated Warranty Payable

	6,000

If Black & Decker actually ends up replacing 100 defective tools with new tools costing $4,800, it would record the following:

	A	B	C	D	E
1		Estimated Warranty Payable	4,800		
2		Inventory		4,800	
3		*To replace defective products sold under warranty.*			
4					

Estimated Warranty Payable

4,800	6,000
	Bal. 1,200

At the end of the year, Black & Decker will report Estimated Warranty Payable of $1,200 as a current liability. The income statement reports Warranty Expense of $6,000 for the year. Then, next year Black & Decker will repeat this process. The Estimated Warranty Payable account probably won't ever zero out.

Vacation pay is another expense that must be estimated. Income taxes must also be estimated because the final amount isn't determined until early the next year.

Contingent Liabilities

Contingent liabilities are *possible* obligations that will become *actual* obligations only if some uncertain future event occurs. They also include present obligations for which there is doubt about the need for the eventual outflow of resources to settle the obligation, or for which the amount of the obligation cannot be reliably estimated. Lawsuits in progress, debt guarantees, and audits by the Canada Revenue Agency are examples of contingent liabilities.

Under ASPE, contingent liabilities that are *likely* to occur and can be *reasonably estimated* are accrued as liabilities, similar to the above treatment for provisions under IFRS. Other less-certain contingent liabilities, under both IFRS and ASPE, are simply disclosed in the notes. Even note disclosure is not required if there is only a remote chance the contingent liability will occur. Determining the proper accounting treatment of contingent liabilities is beyond the scope of this text.

Are All Liabilities Reported on the Balance Sheet or Disclosed in the Notes?

The big danger with liabilities is that a company may fail to report a debt on its balance sheet. What is the consequence of not reporting a liability? The company would definitely understate its liabilities and would probably overstate its net income. In short, its financial statements would make the company look stronger than it really is. Any such misstatement, if significant, hurts a company's credibility.

Contingent liabilities are very easy to overlook because they aren't actual debts. How would you feel if you owned shares in a company that failed to report a contingency that put the company out of business? In this case, you would hire a lawyer to file suit against the company for negligent financial reporting. If you had known of the contingency, you could have sold the shares and avoided the loss.

COOKING *the* BOOKS

with Liabilities

CRAZY EDDIE, INC.

Accidentally understating liabilities is one thing, but doing it intentionally is quite another. When unethical management decides to cook the books in the area of liabilities, its strategy is to *deliberately understate recorded liabilities*. This can be done by intentionally under-recording the amount of existing liabilities or by omitting certain liabilities altogether.

Crazy Eddie, Inc., was a large electronics retailer that used multiple tactics to overstate its financial position over a period of four consecutive years from 1984 to 1987. In addition to overstating inventory (thus understating cost of goods sold and overstating income), the management of the company deliberately understated accounts payable by issuing fictitious debit memos from suppliers. A debit memo is issued for goods returned to a supplier, such as Sony. When a debit memo is issued, accounts payable are debited (reduced), thus reducing current liabilities and increasing the current ratio. Eventually, expenses are also decreased, and profits are correspondingly increased through reduction of expenses. Crazy Eddie, Inc., issued $3 million of fictitious debit memos in one year, making the company's current ratio and working capital look better than they actually were, as well as overstating profits.

Summary of Current Liabilities

Let's summarize what we've covered thus far. A company can report its current liabilities on the balance sheet as follows:

	A	B	C	D	E
1	**Hudson Ltd.** Balance Sheet December 31, 2017				
2	Assets		Liabilities		
3	**Current assets**		**Current liabilities**		
4	Cash		Accounts payable		
5	Short-term investments		Salary payable*		
6	Etc.		Interest payable*		
7			HST/GST payable**		
8			PST payable*		
9			CPP payable*		
10			EI payable*		
11			Income tax payable		
12	Property, plant, and equipment:		Unearned revenue		
13	Land		Estimated warranty payable		
14	Etc.		Notes payable, short-term		
15			Current portion of long-term debt		
16			**Total current liabilities**		
17	Other assets:		**Long-term liabilities**		
18			**Shareholders' Equity**		
19			Share capital		
20			Retained earnings		
21	Total assets	$ XXX	Total liabilities and shareholders' equity	$ XXX	
22					

*These items are often combined and reported in a single total as "Accrued Liabilities" or "Accrued Expenses Payable."

**ASPE requires separate disclosure of the amount payable with respect to government remittances (other than income taxes), either on the face of the balance sheet or in the notes.

MyAccountingLab

MID-CHAPTER SUMMARY PROBLEM

Assume that Korvar Plastics Inc., a manufacturer of plastic pipe for the construction industry and located in Red Deer, Alberta, faced the following liability situations at June 30, 2017, the end of the company's fiscal year:

a. Long-term debt totals $10 million and is payable in annual instalments of $1 million each. The interest rate on the debt is 7%, and interest is paid each December 31.

b. Salary expense for the last payroll period of the year was $90,000. Of this amount, employees' income tax of $12,000 was withheld, and other withholdings and employee benefits were $6,000. These payroll amounts will be paid early in July.

c. Since the last reporting period, GST of $200,000 had been collected and ITCs of $76,000 had been earned.

d. On fiscal year 2017 sales of $40 million, management estimates warranty expense of 2%. One year ago, at June 30, 2016, Estimated Warranty Liability stood at $100,000. Warranty payments were $300,000 during the year ended June 30, 2017.

Show how Korvar Plastics Inc. would report these liabilities on its balance sheet at June 30, 2017.

Name: Korvar Plastics Inc.
Industry: Manufacturing
Accounting Period: June 30, 2017

ANSWERS

a. Current liabilities:

Current portion of long-term debt..	$1,000,000
Interest payable ($10,000,000 × 0.07 × 6/12)	350,000
Long-term debt ($10,000,000 − $1,000,000)..	9,000,000

Current liabilities include the amount due to be paid within one year:
• Principal repayment
• Interest payment

b. Current liabilities:

Salary payable ($90,000 − $12,000 − $6,000).................................	$ 72,000
Employee withheld income tax payable..	12,000
Other employee withholdings and benefits payable...........................	6,000

Salaries payable to employees are net of all withholdings.

c. Current liabilities:

GST payable ($200,000 − $76,000)	$ 124,000

GST payable is net of applicable ITC credits.

d. Current liabilities:

Estimated warranty payable..	$ 600,000
[$100,000 + ($40,000,000 × 0.02) − $300,000]	

Estimated warranty liability must be reduced by any warranty payments made during the year.

EXPLAIN THE TYPES, FEATURES, AND PRICING OF BONDS PAYABLE

OBJECTIVE

❷ **Explain** the types, features, and pricing of bonds payable

Large companies, such as Bombardier, Canadian Tire, and TransCanada, cannot borrow billions of dollars from a single lender. So how do large corporations borrow huge amounts? They issue (sell) bonds to the public. **Bonds payable** are groups of notes issued to multiple lenders, called *bondholders*. Bombardier can borrow large amounts by issuing bonds to thousands of investors, who each lend a modest amount to Bombardier. Here, we treat bonds and long-term notes payable together because their accounting is similar.

Bonds: An Introduction

Each bond that is issued is, in effect, a long-term note payable. Bonds payable are debts of the issuing company.

Each bond has a *principal* amount which is typically stated in units of $1,000; principal is also called the bond's **face value** or *maturity value*. The bond obligates the issuing company to pay the debt at a specific future time called the *maturity date*.

Interest is the rental fee on money borrowed. The bond states the interest rate that the issuer will pay the holder and the dates that the interest payments are due (generally twice a year).

Issuing bonds usually requires the services of a securities firm (for example, RBC Dominion Securities) to act as the underwriter of the bond issue. The **underwriter** purchases the bonds from the issuing company and resells them to its clients, or it may hold some of the bonds for its own account and sell them at a later time.

TYPES OF BONDS. All the bonds in a particular issue may mature at a specified time (**term bonds**) or in instalments over a period of time (**serial bonds**). Serial bonds are like instalment notes payable. Some of TransCanada Corporation's long-term debts are serial in nature because they come due in instalments.

Secured, or *mortgage*, *bonds* give the bondholder the right to take specified assets of the issuer if the company *defaults*, that is, fails to pay interest or principal. *Unsecured bonds*, called **debentures**, are backed only by the good faith of the borrower. Debentures carry a higher rate of interest than secured bonds because debentures are riskier investments.

BOND PRICES. Investors buy and sell bonds through bond markets. Bond prices are quoted at a percentage of their maturity value. For example:

- A $1,000 bond quoted at 100 is bought or sold for $1,000, which is 100% of its face value.

- The same bond quoted at 101.5 has a market price of $1,015 (101.5% of face value = $1,000 × 1.015). Any excess of the bond's price over its face value is called a **bond premium**.

- A $1,000 bond quoted at 88.375 is priced at $883.75 ($1,000 × 0.88375). When the price of a bond is below its face value, the difference is called a **bond discount**.

As with stocks, bond prices are reported in a wide variety of online sources. For example, on November 6, 2015, the *Globe and Mail* website reported price information for Province of Manitoba bonds. On that day, Province of Manitoba $1,000 face value bonds with an interest rate of 4.30% and maturity date of March 1, 2016, were quoted at a price of 101.26, so it would have cost you $1,012.60 to purchase one of these bonds ($1,000 face value + bond premium of $12.60). Bond prices change regularly due to changes in market demand and supply.

BOND INTEREST RATES DETERMINE BOND PRICES. Bonds are always sold at their **market price**, which is the amount investors are willing to pay. A bond's market price is determined by its present value, which equals the present value of the future principal payment plus the present value of the future interest payments. Interest is usually paid semi-annually. Some issuers pay annually or quarterly.

Two interest rates determine the price of a bond:

- The **stated interest rate** (or *coupon rate*) is the actual interest rate of the bond. The stated interest rate determines the amount of interest the borrower pays— and the investor receives—each year. For example, the Province of Manitoba's 4.3% bonds have a stated interest rate of 4.3%. Thus, Manitoba pays $43 of interest annually on each $1,000 bond. Each semi-annual interest payment is $215 ($1,000 × 0.043 × 6/12).

- The **market interest rate**, or *effective interest rate*, is the rate that investors demand for loaning their money. The market rate varies by the minute.

An entity may issue bonds with a stated interest rate that differs from the prevailing market interest rate. In fact, the two interest rates often differ because the issuer often has to finalize details of the bond weeks or months before the bonds are actually issued.

Exhibit 8-2 shows how the stated interest rate and the market interest rate interact to determine the price of a bond payable for three separate cases. If the stated interest rate does happen to equal the market rate, the bond will be issued at face value (Case A).

Manitoba may, however, issue 6% bonds when the market rate has risen to 7%. Will the Manitoba bonds attract investors in this market? No, because investors can earn 7% on other bonds of similar risk. Therefore, investors will purchase Manitoba bonds only at a *discount* (Case B). Conversely, if the market interest rate is 5%, Manitoba's 6% bonds will be so attractive that investors will pay a *premium* for them (Case C). It is useful to remember that there is an inverse relationship between the market rate and bond prices—a market rate higher than the stated rate results in a discounted bond price, whereas a market rate lower than the stated rate results in a premium price.

EXHIBIT 8-2
How the Stated Interest Rate and the Market Interest Rate Interact to Determine the Price of a Bond

Issuance Price of Bonds Payable

Case A:

Stated interest rate on a bond payable	equals	Market interest rate	implies	Face price
Example: 6%	=	6%	→	*Face: $1,000 bond issued for $1,000*

Case B:

Stated interest rate on a bond payable	less than	Market interest rate	implies	Discount price (price *below* face value)
Example: 6%	<	7%	→	*Discount: $1,000 bond issued for a price below $1,000*

Case C:

Stated interest rate on a bond payable	greater than	Market interest rate	implies	Premium price (price *above* face value)
Example: 6%	>	5%	→	*Premium: $1,000 bond issued for a price above $1,000*

STOP + THINK (8-2)

Answer the following questions about various bonds:

1. The stated interest rate on a bond is 8% and the market rate at the time the bond was issued as issued was 9%. Would the bond have been issued at a discount or a premium?

2. The stated interest rate on a bond is 9.5% and the market rate at the time the bond was issued as issued was 7.75%. Would the bond have been issued at a discount or a premium?

3. How much would you pay for $250,000 in bonds with a market price of 89.75?

4. How much would you pay for $175,000 in bonds with a market price of 101.25?

ACCOUNT FOR BONDS PAYABLE

Issuing Bonds at Face Value

Suppose Great-West Lifeco Inc. plans to issue $50,000 in 6% bonds that mature in five years. Assume that Great-West issues these bonds at face value on January 1, 2017. The issuance entry is as follows:

	A	B	C	D	E
1	2017				
2	Jan. 1	Cash	50,000		
3		Bonds Payable		50,000	
4		*To issue 6%, five-year bonds at face value.*			
5					

Bonds Payable
—————————————
| 50,000

			SHAREHOLDERS'
ASSETS	=	**LIABILITIES**	+	**EQUITY**
+50,000	=	+50,000		

Great-West, the borrower, makes a one-time entry to record the receipt of cash and the issuance of bonds. Afterward, investors buy and sell the bonds through the bond markets. These buy-and-sell transactions between outside investors do *not* involve Great-West at all.

Interest payments occur each January 1 and July 1. Great-West's entry to record the first semi-annual interest payment is as follows:

	A	B	C	D	E
1	2017				
2	July 1	Interest Expense	1,500		
3		Cash		1,500	
4		*To pay semi-annual interest. ($50,000 × 0.06 × 6/12)*			
5					

			SHAREHOLDERS'
ASSETS	=	**LIABILITIES**	+	**EQUITY**
−1,500	=			−1,500 Interest Expense

At year-end, Great-West must accrue interest expense and interest payable for six months (July through December), as follows:

	A	B	C	D	E
1	2017				
2	Dec. 31	Interest Expense ($50,000 × 0.06 × 6/12)	1,500		
3		Interest Payable		1,500	
4		*To accrue interest.*			
5					

			SHAREHOLDERS'
ASSETS	=	**LIABILITIES**	+	**EQUITY**
0	=	+1,500		−1,500 Interest Expense

At maturity, Great-West will pay off the bonds as follows (any interest owing will be paid separately):

	A	B	C	D	E
1	2022				
2	Jan. 1	Bonds Payable	50,000		
3		Cash		50,000	
4		To pay bonds payable at maturity.			
5					

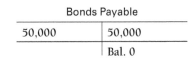

Bonds Payable

50,000	50,000
	Bal. 0

			SHAREHOLDERS'
ASSETS	=	LIABILITIES +	EQUITY
−50,000	=	−50,000	

Issuing Bonds at a Discount

Market conditions may force a company to issue bonds at a discount. Suppose Canadian Tire issues $100,000 of 9% five-year bonds when the market interest rate is 10%. The market price of the bonds drops, and Canadian Tire receives $96,149 at issuance. The transaction is recorded as follows:

	A	B	C	D	E
1	2017				
2	Jan. 1	Cash	96,149		
3		Discount on Bonds Payable	3,851		
4		Bonds Payable		100,000	
5		To issue 9%, five-year bonds at a discount.			
6					

			SHAREHOLDERS'
ASSETS	=	LIABILITIES +	EQUITY
+96,149	=	−3,851	
		+100,000	

Now the bond accounts have a net balance of $96,149 as follows:

Bonds Payable		Discount on Bonds Payable	= Net carrying amount of bonds payable
	100,000	+	3,851	= $96,149

Canadian Tire's balance sheet immediately after issuance of the bonds would report the following:

Total current liabilities...	$	XXX
Long-term liabilities		
Bonds payable, 9%, due 2022..	$100,000	
Less: Discount on bonds payable	(3,851)	96,149

Discount on Bonds Payable is a contra account to Bonds Payable, which decreases the company's liabilities. Subtracting the discount from Bonds Payable yields the *carrying amount* of the bonds. Thus, Canadian Tire's liability is $96,149, which is the amount the company borrowed.

STOP + THINK (8-3)

Suppose TD Bank issued a five-year $10,000 bond with stated interest rate of 7.25% when the market interest rate was 7.25%. TD's fiscal year ends on October 31. Journalize the following transactions (no explanations are needed):

a. Issuance of the bond, payable on May 1, 2017

b. Accrual of interest expense on October 31, 2017 (rounded to the nearest dollar)

c. Payment of cash interest on November 1, 2017

d. Payment of the bonds at maturity (give the date)

OBJECTIVE

❹ **Calculate** and **account** for interest expense on bonds payable

CALCULATE AND ACCOUNT FOR INTEREST EXPENSE ON BONDS PAYABLE

Canadian Tire pays interest on its bonds semi-annually, which is common practice. Each semi-annual interest *payment* remains the same over the life of the bonds:

$$\text{Semi-annual interest payment} = \$100{,}000 \times 0.09 \times 6/12$$

$$= \$4{,}500$$

This payment amount is fixed by the bond contract. But Canadian Tire's interest *expense* increases from period to period as the bonds march toward maturity. Remember, these bonds were issued at a discount.

Panel A of Exhibit 8-3 summarizes the Canadian Tire bond data used above. Panel B provides an amortization table that:

- determines the periodic interest expense (column C)
- shows the bond carrying amount at each semi-annual interest date (column F)

Study the exhibit carefully because the amounts we will be using come directly from the amortization table. This exhibit shows the *effective-interest method of amortization*, which is the required way of amortizing bond premiums and discounts under IFRS. ASPE permit this method, as well as the *straight-line method,* which is discussed briefly later in this section.

TRY IT *in* EXCEL® ▶ ▶ ▶

Bond amortization tables are a snap when you prepare them in Excel. Open a blank Excel spreadsheet.

- In line 1, label the columns as shown in Panel B of Exhibit 8-3.
- Column A. Starting in line 2, enter the issue date (1/1/2017) followed by each of the semiannual interest payment dates. This will continue through line 12 with the last interest payment on January 1, 2022. Highlight all cell values in rows 2 through 12 of column A, and click on the drop down box in the "number" field on the ruler at the top of the spreadsheet. Choose the "date" category and click OK to change all cell values in Column A to the date format.
- Line 2, column E. Enter 3851 in cell E2. Enter the formula =100000−E2 in cell F2. The calculated value of 96149 should appear in cell F2, representing the initial carrying value of the bond.
- Line 3, column B. Enter formula =.045*100000 in cell B3. A calculated value of 4500 should appear, representing the amount of the first cash interest payment.
- Line 3, column C. In cell C3, enter formula =.05*F2. A calculated value of 4807 should appear, representing the calculated amount of interest expense, based on the carrying amount of the bond. If the cell shows a decimal fraction, use the "decrease decimal" command in the

"number" field of the toolbar to reduce the decimals to none. This will round the value to the nearest dollar.

- Line 3, column D. In cell D3, enter formula =C3−B3. A value of 307 should appear, representing the amount of discount amortization included in interest expense on the first interest payment date.
- Line 3, column E. In cell E3, enter formula =E2−D3. A value of 3544 should appear, representing the unamortized discount remaining after the first interest payment.
- Line 3, column F. In cell F3, enter formula =100000−E3. A value of 96456 should appear, representing the adjusted carrying value of the bond after the first interest payment.
- For columns B through F, copy line 3 down through line 12. All of the numbers in the table should fill in. Line 12 will have to be adjusted for rounding by taking the remaining unamortized discount from cell E11 (461) and substituting that value in cell D12 (discount amortization). Also, substitute 4961 for interest expense in cell C12. This will adjust the final bond carrying amount to the maturity value of $100,000 and the unamortized discount to 0.
- Highlight cells B2 through F12, and insert commas to make the table easier to read. When you insert the commas, Excel automatically inserts two decimals and zeros, so use the "decrease decimal" key to format the table to whole dollars.

EXHIBIT 8-3
Debt Amortization for a Bond Discount
PANEL A—Bond Data

	A	B	C
1	Issue date—January 1, 2017	Market interest rate at time of issue—10% annually, 5% semi-annually	
2	Maturity (face) value—$100,000	Issue price—$96,149	
3	Stated interest rate—9%	Maturity date—January 1, 2022	
4	Interest paid—4½% semi-annually, $4,500 = $100,000 × 0.09 × 6/12		
5			

PANEL B—Amortization Table

	A	B	C	D	E	F	G
1	Semi-Annual Interest Date	Interest Payment (4½% of Maturity Value)	Interest Expense (5% of Preceding Bond Carrying Amount)	Bond Discount Amortization (C − B)	Bond Discount Account Balance (Preceding E − D)	Bond Carrying Amount ($100,000 − E)	
2	Jan. 1, 2017				$ 3,851	$ 96,149	
3	July 1	$ 4,500	$ 4,807	$ 307	3,544	96,456	
4	Jan. 1, 2018	4,500	4,823	323	3,221	96,779	
5	July 1	4,500	4,839	339	2,882	97,118	
6	Jan. 1, 2019	4,500	4,856	356	2,526	97,474	
7	July 1	4,500	4,874	374	2,152	97,848	
8	Jan. 1, 2020	4,500	4,892	392	1,760	98,240	
9	July 1	4,500	4,912	412	1,348	98,652	
10	Jan. 1, 2021	4,500	4,933	433	951	99,085	
11	July 1	4,500	4,954	454	461	99,539	
12	Jan. 1, 2022	4,500	4,961*	461	0	100,000	
13							

*Adjusted for the effect of rounding.

Notes
*Column B The semi-annual interest payments are constant (fixed by the bond contract).
*Column C The interest expense each period = Preceding bond carrying amount × Market interest rate.
          Interest expense increases as the bond carrying amount (F) increases.
*Column D The excess of interest expense (C) over interest payment (B) is the discount amortization (D) for the period.
*Column E The discount balance (E) decreases when amortized.
*Column F The bond carrying amount (F) increases from $96,149 at issuance to $100,000 at maturity.

Interest Expense on Bonds Issued at a Discount

In Exhibit 8-3, Canadian Tire borrowed $96,149 cash but must pay $100,000 when the bonds mature. What happens to the $3,851 balance of the discount account over the life of the bond issue?

The $3,851 is additional interest expense to Canadian Tire over and above the stated interest that Canadian Tire pays each six months. Exhibit 8-4 graphs the interest expense and the interest payment on the Canadian Tire bonds over their lifetime. Observe that the semi-annual interest payment is fixed—by contract—at $4,500 (column B in Exhibit 8-3), but the amount of interest expense (column C) increases each period as the bond carrying amount moves upward toward maturity.

EXHIBIT 8-4
Interest Expense on Bonds
Payable Issued at a Discount

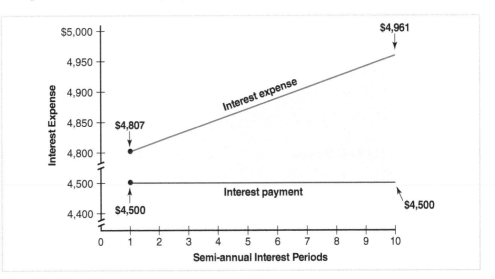

The discount is allocated to interest expense through amortization each period over the term of the bonds. Exhibit 8-5 illustrates the amortization of the bonds' carrying value from $96,149 at the start to $100,000 at maturity using the effective interest method. These amounts come from Exhibit 8-3, column F.

Now let's see how to account for the Canadian Tire bonds issued at a discount. In our example, Canadian Tire issued its bonds on January 1, 2017. On July 1, Canadian Tire made the first $4,500 semi-annual interest payment. But Canadian Tire's interest expense is greater than $4,500. Canadian Tire's journal entry to record interest expense and the interest payment for the first six months follows (with all amounts taken from Exhibit 8-3):

	A	B	C	D	E
1	2017				
2	July 1	Interest Expense	4,807		
3		Discount on Bonds Payable		307	
4		Cash		4,500	
5		To pay semi-annual interest and amortize bond discount.			
6					

The credit to Discount on Bonds Payable serves two purposes:

- It adjusts the bonds' carrying amount as the bonds approach maturity value.
- It amortizes the discount to interest expense.

ASSETS	=	LIABILITIES	+	SHAREHOLDERS' EQUITY
−4,500	=	+307		−4,807 Interest Expense

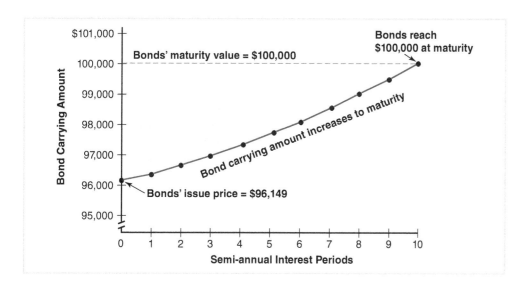

EXHIBIT 8-5
Amortizing Bonds Payable
Issued at a Discount

At December 31, 2017, Canadian Tire accrues interest and amortizes the bond discount for July through December with this entry (amounts from Exhibit 8-3):

	A	B	C	D	E
1	2017				
2	Dec. 31	Interest Expense	4,823		
3		Discount on Bonds Payable		323	
4		Interest Payable		4,500	
5		*To accrue semi-annual interest and amortize bond discount.*			
6					

ASSETS	=	LIABILITIES	+	SHAREHOLDERS' EQUITY
0	=	+323		−4,823 Interest Expense
		+4,500		

At December 31, 2017, Canadian Tire's bond accounts appear as follows:

Bonds Payable		Discount on Bonds Payable	
	100,000	3,851	307
			323
		Bal. 3,221	

Bond carrying amount, $96,779 = $100,000 − $3,221 from Exhibit 8-3

STOP + THINK (8-4)

What would you expect Canadian Tire's 2017 income statement and year-end balance sheet to report for these bonds?

Partial-Period Interest Amounts

Companies don't always issue bonds at the beginning or the end of their accounting year. They issue bonds when market conditions are most favourable, and that may be on May 16, August 1, or any other date. To illustrate partial-period interest, assume Goldcorp Inc. issues $100,000 of 8% bonds payable at 96 on August 31, 2017. The market rate of interest was 9%, and these bonds pay semi-annual interest on February 28 and August 31 each year. The first few lines of Goldcorp's amortization table are as follows:

Semi-Annual Interest Date	4% Interest Payment	4½% Interest Expense	Discount Amortization	Discount Account Balance	Bond Carrying Amount
Aug. 31, 2017				$4,000	$96,000
Feb. 28, 2018	$4,000	$4,320	$320	3,680	96,320
Aug. 31, 2018	4,000	4,334	334	3,346	96,654

Goldcorp's accounting year ends on December 31, so at year-end Goldcorp must accrue interest and amortize the bond discount for four months (September through December). At December 31, 2017, Goldcorp will make this entry:

	A	B	C	D	E
1	2017				
2	Dec. 31	Interest Expense ($4,320 × 4/6)	2,880		
3		Discount on Bonds Payable ($320 × 4/6)		213	
4		Interest Payable ($4,000 × 4/6)		2,667	
5		*To accrue interest and amortize discount at year-end.*			
6					

The year-end entry at December 31, 2017, uses 4/6 of the upcoming semi-annual amounts at February 28, 2018 because the September–December period covers four of the six months of interest to be paid on that date. This example clearly illustrates the benefit of an amortization schedule.

Issuing Bonds at a Premium

Let's modify the Canadian Tire bond example to illustrate issuance of the bonds at a premium. Assume that on January 1, 2017, Canadian Tire issues $100,000 of five-year, 9% bonds that pay interest semi-annually. If the bonds are issued when the market interest rate is 8%, their issue price is $104,100. The premium on these bonds is $4,100, and Exhibit 8-6 shows how to amortize the bonds by the effective-interest method.

Canadian Tire's entries to record issuance of the bonds on January 1, 2017, and to make the first interest payment and amortize the bonds on July 1, are as follows:

	A	B	C	D	E
1	2017				
2	Jan. 1	Cash	104,100		
3		Bonds Payable		100,000	
4		Premium on Bonds Payable		4,100	
5		*To issue 9%, five-year bonds at a premium.*			
6					

At the beginning, Canadian Tire's liability is $104,100—not $100,000. The accounting equation makes this clear.

EXHIBIT 8-6
Debt Amortization for a Bond Premium

PANEL A—Bond Data

	A	B	C
1	Issue date—January 1, 2017	Market interest rate at time of issue—8% annually, 4% semi-annually	
2	Maturity (face) value—$100,000	Issue price—$104,100	
3	Contract interest rate—9%	Maturity date—January 1, 2022	
4	Interest paid—4½% semi-annually, $4,500 = $100,000 × 0.09 × 6/12		
5			

PANEL B—Amortization Table

	A	B	C	D	E	F	G
1	Semi-Annual Interest Date	Interest Payment (4½% of Maturity Value)	Interest Expense (4% of Preceding Bond Carrying Amount)	Bond Premium Amortization (B – C)	Bond Premium Account Balance (Preceding E – D)	Bond Carrying Amount ($100,000 + E)	
2	Jan. 1, 2017				$ 4,100	$ 104,100	
3	July 1	$ 4,500	$ 4,164	$ 336	3,764	103,764	
4	Jan. 1, 2018	4,500	4,151	349	3,415	103,415	
5	July 1	4,500	4,137	363	3,052	103,052	
6	Jan. 1, 2019	4,500	4,122	378	2,674	102,674	
7	July 1	4,500	4,107	393	2,281	102,281	
8	Jan. 1, 2020	4,500	4,091	409	1,872	101,872	
9	July 1	4,500	4,075	425	1,447	101,447	
10	Jan. 1, 2021	4,500	4,058	442	1,005	101,005	
11	July 1	4,500	4,040	460	545	100,545	
12	Jan. 1, 2022	4,500	3,955*	545	0	100,000	
13							

*Adjusted for the effect of rounding.

Notes
- Column B   The semi-annual interest payments are constant (fixed by the bond contract).
- Column C   The interest expense each period = Preceding bond carrying amount × Market interest rate.
  Interest expense decreases as the bond carrying amount (F) decreases.
- Column D   The excess of each interest payment (B) over interest expense (C) is the premium amortization (D) for the period.
- Column E   The premium balance (E) decreases when amortized.
- Column F   The bond carrying amount (F) decreases from $104,100 at issuance to $100,000 at maturity.

ASSETS	=	LIABILITIES	+	SHAREHOLDERS' EQUITY
+104,100	=	+100,000		
		+4,100		

	A	B	C	D	E
1	2017				
2	July 1	Interest Expense	4,164		
3		Premium on Bonds Payable	336		
4		Cash		4,500	
5		*To pay semi-annual interest and amortize bond premium.*			

ASSETS	=	LIABILITIES	+	SHAREHOLDERS' EQUITY
−4,500	=	−336		−4,164 Interest Expense

Immediately after issuing the bonds at a premium on January 1, 2017, Canadian Tire would report the bonds payable on the balance sheet as follows:

Total current liabilities...		$ XXX
Long-term liabilities:		
Bonds payable	$100,000	
Add: Premium on bonds payable...	4,100	104,100

The premium is *added* to the balance of bonds payable to determine the carrying amount.

In Exhibit 8-6, Canadian Tire borrowed $104,100 cash but must pay only $100,000 at maturity. The $4,100 premium on the bonds results in a reduction in TELUS's interest expense over the term of the bonds. Exhibit 8-7 graphs Canadian Tire's interest payments (column B from Exhibit 8-6) and interest expense (column C).

TRY IT *in* EXCEL ▶ ▶ ▶

If you prepared a debt amortization table for bond discount with Excel (Exhibit 8-3), it's easy to prepare an amortization table for bond premium. Open a blank Excel spreadsheet.

- In line 1, label the columns as shown in Panel B of Exhibit 8-6.
- Column A. Starting in line 2, enter the issue date (1/1/2017) followed by each of the semiannual interest payment dates. This will continue through line 12 with the last interest payment on January 1, 2022. Highlight all cell values in rows 2 through 12 of column A, and click on the drop down box in the "number" field on the ruler at the top of the spreadsheet. Choose the "date" category and click OK to change all cell values in Column A to the date format.
- Line 2, column E. Enter 4100 in cell E2. Enter the formula =100000+E2 in cell F2. The calculated value of 104100 should appear in cell F2, representing the initial carrying value of the bond.
- Line 3, column B. In cell B3, enter formula =.045*100000. A calculated value of 4500 should appear, representing the first cash interest payment.
- Line 3, column C. In cell C3, enter formula =.04*F2. A calculated value of 4164 should appear, representing interest expense recognized on the first interest payment date. If the cell shows a decimal fraction, use the "decrease decimal" command in the "number" field of the toolbar to reduce the decimals to none. This will round the value to the nearest dollar.
- Line 3, column D. In cell D3, enter formula =B3−C3. A value of 336 should appear, representing the amount of premium amortization deducted from interest expense on the first interest payment date.
- Line 3, column E. In cell E3, enter formula =E2−D3. A value of 3764 should appear, representing the remaining unamortized premium after the first interest payment.
- Line 3, column F. In cell F3, enter formula =100000+E3. A value of 103764 should appear, representing the adjusted carrying value of the bond after the first interest payment.
- For columns B to F, copy line 3 down through line 12. All of the numbers in the table should fill in. Line 12 will have to be adjusted for rounding by taking the remaining unamortized premium from cell E11 (544) and substituting that value in cell D12 (premium amortization). Also, substitute 3955 for interest expense in cell C12. This will adjust the final bond carrying amount to the maturity value of $100,000 and the unamortized premium to 0. Your Excel table may be $1 off in some places because of rounding.
- Highlight cells B2 through F12 and format them for commas but no decimals, as you did for Exhibit 8-3.

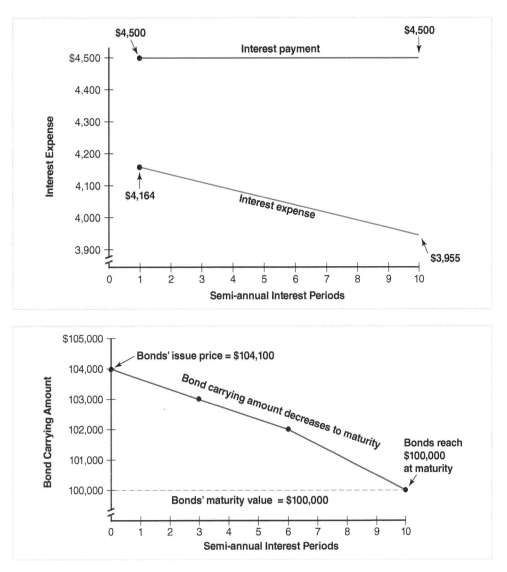

EXHIBIT 8-7
Interest Expense on Bonds
Payable Issued at a Premium

EXHIBIT 8-8
Amortizing Bonds Payable
Issued at a Premium

Through amortization, the premium decreases interest expense each period over the term of the bonds. Exhibit 8-8 diagrams the amortization of the bond carrying amount from the issue price of $104,100 to the maturity value of $100,000. All amounts are taken from Exhibit 8-6.

The Straight-Line Amortization Method

ASPE permit a simpler method of amortizing discounts and premiums. The *straight-line amortization method* divides a bond discount (or premium) into equal periodic amounts over the bond's term. The amount of interest expense is the same for each interest period.

Let's apply the straight-line method to the Canadian Tire bonds issued at a discount and illustrated in Exhibit 8-3. The amortization for each semi-annual period is calculated by dividing the total bond discount of $3,851 by 10, which is the number of semi-annual interest periods over the life of the bond. This method results in the following semi-annual interest expense:

Semi-annual cash interest payment ($100,000 × 0.09 × 6/12).............................	$4,500
+ Semi-annual amortization of discount ($3,851 ÷ 10)	385
= Semi-annual interest expense	$4,885

The straight-line amortization method uses these same amounts every period over the term of the bonds.

Canadian Tire's entry to record interest and amortization of the bond discount under the straight-line amortization method would be the same for every semi-annual interest period:

	A	B	C	D	E
1		Interest Expense	4,885		
2		Discount on Bonds Payable		385	
3		Cash		4,500	
4		*To pay semi-annual interest and amortize bond discount.*			

⑤ Explain the advantages and disadvantages of financing with debt versus equity

EXPLAIN THE ADVANTAGES AND DISADVANTAGES OF FINANCING WITH DEBT VERSUS EQUITY

Managers must decide where to get the money needed to fund acquisitions, expansion, and other operational activities. There are three main ways to finance business activities:

- By using excess cash not needed for operating activities
- By raising capital from issuing shares
- By borrowing money using loans, bonds, or notes

1. To use *excess cash*, a company must have saved enough cash and short-term investments from past profitable operations so that it can self-finance its desired business activities. This is a low-risk and low-cost option because it does not require taking on more debt or issuing more shares.

2. *Raising capital by issuing new shares* creates no new liabilities and requires no interest payments, so it does not increase a company's credit risk. Dividend payments on shares are usually optional, so they can be avoided if cash flows are poor or the company has other needs for its cash. Issuing shares, however, can cost a lot in legal and other financing fees, and can also dilute the control and earnings per share of existing shareholders.

3. *Borrowing money* does not dilute control of the company because no shares are being issued, but it can still be somewhat costly in terms of financing fees paid to arrange the debt. Taking on more debt can also increase a company's credit risk, and it requires the company to make regular principal and interest payments, which cannot be postponed when cash flows are poor. The leverage gained by borrowing money can often increase the company's earnings per share, which is beneficial to shareholders.

Earnings per share (EPS) represents the amount of net income (or loss) earned by each of a company's outstanding common shares. It is useful for evaluating the earnings performance of a company and also assessing the impact of various financing options on earnings.

Suppose Athens Corporation needs $500,000 for expansion. Assume Athens has net income of $300,000 and 100,000 common shares outstanding. Management is considering two financing plans. Plan 1 is to issue $500,000 of 6% bonds, and plan 2 is to issue 50,000 common shares for $500,000. Management believes the new cash can be invested in operations to earn income of $200,000 before interest and taxes.

Exhibit 8-9 shows the earnings-per-share advantage of borrowing. As you can see, Athens Corporation's EPS amount is higher if the company borrows by issuing bonds (compare lines 11 and 12). Athens earns more on the investment ($102,000) than the interest it pays on the bonds ($30,000).

In this case, borrowing results in higher earnings per share than issuing shares. Borrowing has its disadvantages, however. Interest expense may be high enough to eliminate net income and lead to losses. Also, borrowing creates liabilities that must be paid during bad years as well as good years. In contrast, a company that issues shares can omit its dividends during a bad year.

▶ DECISION GUIDELINES

FINANCING WITH DEBT OR WITH STOCK

Suppose you are the owner of El Taco, a regional chain of Tex-Mex restaurants in western Canada. You are planning to expand into central Canada, so you must make some key decisions about how to finance the expansion.

Decision	Guidelines
How will you finance El Taco's expansion?	Your financing plan depends on El Taco's ability to generate cash flow, your willingness to give up some control of the business, the amount of financing risk you are willing to take, and El Taco's credit rating.
Do El Taco's operations generate enough cash to meet all its financing needs?	If yes, the business needs little outside financing. There is no need to borrow.
	If no, the business will need to issue additional stock or borrow the money.
Are you willing to give up some of your control of the business?	If yes, then issue stock to other shareholders, who can vote their shares to elect the company's directors.
	If no, then borrow from bondholders, who have no vote in the management of the company.
How much leverage (financing risk) are you willing or able to take?	If much, then borrow as much as you can, and you may increase El Taco's earnings per share. But this will increase the business's debt ratio and the risk of being unable to pay its debts.
	If little, then borrow sparingly. This will hold the debt ratio down and reduce the risk of default on borrowing agreements, but El Taco's earnings per share may be lower than if you were to borrow.
How good is the business's credit rating?	The better the credit rating, the easier it is to borrow on favourable terms. A good credit rating also makes it easier to issue stock. Neither shareholders nor creditors will entrust their money to a company with a bad credit rating.

EXHIBIT 8-9
Earnings-per-Share Advantage of Borrowing

	A	B	C	D	E	F
1		Plan 1		Plan 2		
2		Borrow $500,000 at 6%		Issue 50,000 Common Shares for $500,000		
3	Net income before expansion		$ 300,000		$ 300,000	
4	Expected project income before interest and income tax	$ 200,000		$ 200,000		
5	Less interest expense ($500,000 × 0.06)	(30,000)		0		
6	Expected project income before income tax	170,000		200,000		
7	Less income tax expense (40%)	(68,000)		(80,000)		
8	Expected project net income		102,000		120,000	
9	Total company net income		$ 402,000		$ 420,000	
10	Earnings per share after expansion:					
11	Plan 1 Borrow ($402,000/100,000 shares)		$ 4.02			
12	Plan 2 ($420,000/150,000 shares)				$ 2.80	
13						

OBJECTIVE

6 Analyze and evaluate a company's debt-paying ability

ANALYZE AND EVALUATE A COMPANY'S DEBT-PAYING ABILITY

ACCOUNTS PAYABLE TURNOVER. In Chapter 3 we used working capital and the current ratio to analyze a company's liquidity. Another important measure of liquidity for a business is **accounts payable turnover (T/O)**, which measures the number of times a year a company is able to pay its accounts payable. The ratio is computed as follows:

Accounts payable turnover (T/O) = Cost of goods sold ÷ Average accounts payable
Turnover expressed in days = 365 ÷ T/O (computed above)

The average accounts payable amount is calculated using the year's opening and closing balances. Once the turnover is computed, it is usually expressed in number of days, or **days payable outstanding (DPO),** by dividing the turnover into 365. Here are recent comparative ratios for accounts payable turnover for Best Buy and RadioShack, two large consumer electronics retailers:

(In millions)	Best Buy	RadioShack
Cost of goods sold..	$37,611	$2,462
Average accounts payable	5,085	268
Accounts payable turnover (T/O)	7.40	9.19
Turnover in days (365 ÷ T/O), or days payable outstanding (DPO)	49 days	40 days

Because different industries have different business models and standard business practices, it is important to compare companies with competitors in the same industry. Since Best Buy and RadioShack are both in the consumer electronics industry, purchasing many of their products from the same vendors, it is reasonable to compare them on the basis of accounts payable turnover. RadioShack pays its accounts payable in about 40 days, whereas Best Buy takes 49 days to pay its accounts payable. If you were a supplier of these two giant companies, which would you rather do business with, on the basis of this ratio? If cash collections are important to you in order to pay your own bills, the obvious answer is RadioShack, based strictly on this ratio.

What makes an accounts payable turnover ratio strong or weak in the eyes of creditors and investors? Generally, a high turnover ratio (short period in days) is better than a low turnover ratio. Companies with shorter payment periods are generally better credit risks than those with longer payment periods. However, some companies with strong credit ratings strategically follow shrewd cash management policies, withholding payment to suppliers as long as possible, while speeding up collections, in order to conserve cash. For example, Walmart's accounts payable turnover is about 37 days, which is longer than a typical 30-day credit period. The company strategically stretches its payment period, which is tough on suppliers, but because of Walmart's size, market share, and buying power, few suppliers can afford not to do business with the company.

To be sure, credit and sales decisions are based on far more information than accounts payable turnover, so it's wise not to oversimplify. However, combined with inventory turnover (discussed in Chapter 5) and accounts receivable turnover (discussed in Chapter 4), all expressed in days, accounts payable turnover is an important ingredient in computing the *cash conversion cycle*, which is an overall measure of liquidity. Combined with the current ratio (discussed in Chapter 3) and the quick ratio (discussed in Chapter 4), studying the cash conversion cycle helps users of financial statements determine the overall liquidity of a company. We will discuss the cash conversion cycle in more depth in Chapter 11.

The Leverage Ratio

As discussed and illustrated above, financing with debt can be advantageous, but management of a company must be careful not to incur too much debt. Chapter 3 discussed the debt ratio, which measures the proportion of total liabilities to total assets, two elements of the fundamental accounting equation:

$$\text{Debt ratio} = \frac{\text{Total debt (liabilities)}}{\text{Total assets}}$$

We can rearrange this relationship between total assets, total liabilities, and shareholders' equity in a different manner to illustrate the impact that leverage can have on profitability. The **leverage ratio** is commonly calculated as follows, although other methods are sometimes used:

$$\text{Leverage ratio} = \frac{\text{Total assets}}{\text{Total shareholders' equity}}$$

This ratio shows a company's total assets per dollar of shareholders' equity. A leverage ratio of exactly 1.0 would mean a company has no debt, because total assets would exactly equal total shareholders' equity. This condition is almost nonexistent, because virtually all companies have liabilities, and, therefore, have leverage ratios in excess of 1.0. In fact, as we have shown previously, having a healthy amount of debt can actually enhance a company's profitability, in terms of the shareholders' investment. The higher the leverage ratio, the more it magnifies return on shareholders' equity (Net Income/Average Shareholders' Equity, or ROE). If net income is positive, return on assets (ROA) is positive. The leverage ratio magnifies this positive return to make return on equity (ROE) even more positive. This is because the company is using borrowed money to earn a profit (a concept known as *trading on the equity*). However, if earnings are negative (losses), ROA is negative, and the leverage ratio makes ROE even more negative. We will analyze ROE in more detail when we discuss shareholders' equity in Chapter 9. For now, let's just focus on understanding the meaning of the leverage ratio by looking at two fictional airlines, Northeast and Provincial. Here are the leverage ratios and debt ratios for the two companies:

(In millions)	Northeast	Provincial
1. Total assets	$15,463	$40,552
2. Shareholders' equity	$ 6,237	$ 1,912
3. Leverage ratio (1 ÷ 2)	2.48	21.2
4. Total debt (1 − 2)	$ 9,226	$38,640
5. Debt ratio (4 ÷ 1)	59.7%	95.3%

These figures show that Northeast has $2.48 of total assets for each dollar of shareholders' equity. This translates to a debt ratio of 59.7%, which we learned in Chapter 3 is about normal for many companies. However, Provincial has a leverage ratio of 21.2, meaning there are $21.20 of assets for each dollar of shareholders' equity. Rearranging the elements to show debt to total assets, Provincial has an astonishing ratio of 95.3%. This company is drowning in debt!

The Times-Interest-Earned Ratio

The debt ratio measures the effect of debt on the company's *financial position* but says nothing about the ability to pay interest expense. Analysts use a second ratio—the **times-interest-earned ratio**—to relate income to interest expense. To compute this ratio, we divide *income from operations* (also called *operating income* or *earnings before interest and taxes*) by interest expense. This ratio measures the number of times that operating income can *cover* interest expense. The ratio is also called the **interest-coverage ratio**. A high times-interest-earned ratio indicates ease in paying interest expense; a low value suggests difficulty. Let's see how Sobeys Inc. and Loblaw Companies Limited, two leading grocery chains, compare on the times-interest-earned ratio.

			Sobeys Inc.	**Loblaw Companies Limited**
Times-interest-earned ratio	$=$	$\dfrac{\text{Operating income}}{\text{Interest expense}}=$	$\dfrac{\$406 \text{ million}}{\$60 \text{ million}}$	$\dfrac{\$1,205 \text{ million}}{\$269 \text{ million}}$
			= 6.8 times	= 4.5 times

Sobeys's income from operations covers its interest expense 6.8 times. Loblaw's interest-coverage ratio is 4.5 times. Both companies have healthy ratios, but Sobeys's higher ratio indicates less risk relative to Loblaw's ratio.

STOP + THINK (8-5)

Suppose you are a loan officer at a bank and you must decide which of the two companies below would present a lower risk to the bank if you were to loan it money. Which company would you prefer to loan money to?

	Company A	Company B
Total assets	$4,858	$14,991
Total liabilities	$4,178	$ 8,718
Total Shareholders' equity	680	6,273
Total liabilities and Shareholders' equity	$4,858	$14,991
Operating income	$ 241	$ 1,068
Interest expense	$ 101	$ 211

DESCRIBE OTHER TYPES OF LONG-TERM LIABILITIES

OBJECTIVE

❼ **Describe** other types of long-term liabilities

Term Loans

Companies can often satisfy their long-term financing needs without resorting to the issuance of bonds in a public market. **Term loans** are a common form of long-term financing, which, like bonds, allow a company to borrow a fixed amount of money up front and repay it over a specified number of years at a stated interest rate. Unlike bonds, however, a term loan is typically arranged with a single lender, such as a bank or other financial institution. A term loan is usually secured by certain assets of the borrower, often the assets acquired using the proceeds of the loan. WestJet, for example, had $1.2 billion in term loans payable at September 30, 2015. Each of the loans comprising this balance was secured by the airplane WestJet purchased with the original loan proceeds. Term loans secured by real property, such as land and buildings, are called **mortgages**. As with other forms of long-term debt, term loans are split between their current and long-term portions on the balance sheet, and the terms of the loans, including principal repayments over the next five years, are disclosed in the notes.

Leases

A **lease** is a rental agreement in which the renter (**lessee**) agrees to make rent payments to the property owner (**lessor**) in exchange for the use of the asset for an agreed period of time. Leasing allows the lessee to acquire the use of a needed asset without having to make the large upfront payment that purchase agreements require. WestJet, for example, may lease some of its planes instead of buying them outright. Accountants distinguish between two types of leases: finance leases and operating leases. ASPE uses the term capital leases instead of finance leases. For simplicity, this section uses the term finance leases.

IFRS and ASPE are consistent in their definitions of **finance leases**: they are leases that transfer to the lessee substantially all the risks and rewards incidental to the ownership of an asset, even though formal legal title of the asset may remain with the lessor. For an **operating lease**, substantially all the risks and rewards of ownership remain with the lessor. Both sets of standards indicate that the substance of a leasing transaction determines whether it should be accounted for as a finance lease or an operating lease. Making this determination is beyond the scope of this text, so the decision criteria are not presented here. Also note that at the date of publication, a new draft IFRS lease accounting standard proposed that all leases be treated as finance leases, possibly removing the distinction between operating and finance leases under IFRS in the future.

Because a finance lease transfers to the lessee substantially all the risks and rewards incidental to the ownership of an asset, the lessee records the leased property as an asset on its financial statements, following all of the relevant accounting standards presented for property, plant, and equipment in Chapter 6. The finance lease contract also creates a formal legal obligation for the lessee, so the lessee must record a liability that reflects the future payments to be made according to the terms of the lease. Finance lease obligations are split into their current and long-term portions for balance sheet presentation purposes, just as with other forms of long-term debt. The detailed accounting for finance leases is beyond the scope of this text.

Under an operating lease, the risks and rewards of ownership do not transfer to the lessee, so they record neither an asset nor a liability. IFRS and ASPE simply require the lessee to expense the operating lease payments as they come due, and also to disclose at least the next five years of operating-lease commitments in the notes to the financial statements. In the notes to its September 30, 2015, financial statements, WestJet disclosed $1.1 billion in operating lease commitments.

Post-Employment Benefits

Employee benefits are forms of consideration given by a company in exchange for services rendered by employees. **Post-employment benefits** are a special type of employee benefits that do not become payable until after a person has completed employment with the company. They include such things as pension benefits, medical and dental insurance, and prescription drug benefits. A company's obligations for these future benefits must be recorded as liabilities on its balance sheet, split into current and long-term portions where applicable. The formal accounting for these benefits is complex and beyond the scope of this text.

OBJECTIVE

⑧ **Report** liabilities on the balance sheet

REPORT LIABILITIES ON THE BALANCE SHEET

Exhibit 8-10 again presents the liabilities of WestJet as at September 30, 2015.

Investors and creditors need the information illustrated in Exhibit 8-10 and discussed below in order to evaluate WestJet's balance sheet and the company.

Exhibit 8-10 includes Note 8 (adapted) from WestJet's financial statements, which gives additional information about the company's long-term debt. This note shows that WestJet's long-term debt consists of three tranches of term loans that have been used to finance the purchase of aircraft, as well as some unsecured notes payable. The current portion of this debt, about $150 million, can be traced to the balance sheet presented above the note.

Note 14 in Exhibit 8-10 presents the details of WestJet's operating leases and other commitments. We can see that they leased a variety of items, including aircraft, computer hardware, and inflight entertainment. Their total commitment under operating leases and other contracts was about $1.1 billion at September 30, 2015.

Working back and forth between the financial statements and the notes to the financial statements is an important part of financial analysis. You now have the tools to understand the liabilities on an actual balance sheet.

	A	B	C	D
1	**WestJet** Consolidated Balance Sheet (Partial, Adapted) As at September 30, 2015			
2	*(amounts in thousands)*			
3	Current liabilities:			
4	Accounts payable and accrued liabilities	$ 546		
5	Advance ticket sales	625		
6	Deferred Rewards program	114		
7	Nonrefundable guest credits	37		
8	Current portion of maintenance provisions	70		
9	Current portion of long-term debt	150		
10	Total current liabilities	1,542		
11	Non-current liabilities:			
12	Maintenance provisions	233		
13	Long-term debt	1,048		
14	Other liabilities	17		
15	Deferred income tax	315		
16		3,155		
17				
18	**8. LONG-TERM DEBT (Partial, Adapted)**			
19	Term loans—purchased aircraft	$ 249,286		
20	Term loan—purchased aircraft	203,106		
21	Term loan—purchased aircraft	347,649		
22	Senior unsecured notes	397,919		
23		1,197,960		
24	Current portion	(150,264)		
25		$ 1,047,696		
26				
27	**14. COMMITMENTS (Partial, Adapted)**			
28	(b) Leases and contractual commitments The Corporation has entered into operating leases and commitments for aircraft, land, buildings, equipment, computer hardware, software licences and inflight entertainment. As at September 30, 2015, the future payments under these commitments are as follows:			
29	Within 1 year	$ 313,695		
30	1–5 years	646,528		
31	Over 5 years	136,513		
32		$ 1,096,736		
33				

EXHIBIT 8-10
Reporting Liabilities of WestJet

Source: Based on WestJet Consolidated Balance Sheet September 30, 2015.

STOP + THINK (8-6)

Assume that Discount Tennis Equipment completed these selected transactions during December 2017:

a. Sales of $4,000,000 are subject to estimated warranty cost of 4%. The estimated warranty payable at the beginning of the year was $40,000, and warranty payments for the year totalled $80,000.

b. On December 1, 2014, Discount signed a $200,000 note that requires annual payments of $40,000 plus 6% interest on the unpaid balance each December 1.

c. Tennis Hut, a chain of tennis stores, ordered $150,000 of tennis equipment. With its order, Tennis Hut sent a cheque for $150,000, and Discount shipped $100,000 of the goods. Discount will ship the remainder of the goods on January 3, 2015.

d. The December payroll of $120,000 is subject to employee-withheld income tax, Canada Pension Plan and Employment Insurance, and the company's share of Canada Pension Plan and Employment Insurance totaling $35,000 and benefits of $11,000. On December 31, Discount pays employees their take-home pay and accrues all tax amounts.

Requirements

1. For each liability, classify it as current or long-term and state the amount that would appear on Discount's balance sheet at December 31, 2017.

2. Calculate the total current liabilities as at December 31, 2017.

Summary of IFRS-ASPE Differences

Concepts	IFRS	ASPE
Differences between income tax expense and income tax payable (p. 381)	Accounted for as deferred income taxes.	Accounted for as future income taxes.
Provisions and contingent liabilities (p. 385)	A contingent liability is recorded as a provision when it is probable that an outflow of economic benefits will be required to settle the liability. *Probable* is generally considered to mean that an outflow is *more likely than not* to occur.	A contingent liability is recorded as a liability when it is likely that an outflow of economic benefits will be required to settle the liability. *Likely* is generally considered to be a higher threshold to meet than *probable*, so fewer contingent liabilities will be recorded under ASPE than under IFRS.
Government remittances (p. 386)	No separate disclosure of these liabilities is required.	Government remittances (other than income taxes) such as sales taxes, Employment Insurance, and Canada Pension Plan payable must be disclosed separately, either on the balance sheet or in the notes.
Amortization of discounts and premiums (p. 393)	The effective-interest method must be used to amortize discounts and premiums.	The straight-line method is available as an amortization option.
Finance leases (p. 405)	Leases that transfer substantially all the risks and rewards incidental to the ownership of assets to the lessee are called finance leases.	The equivalent term is capital leases. There are no differences in accounting for these leases.

SUMMARY

SUMMARY OF LEARNING OBJECTIVES

LEARNING OBJECTIVE	SUMMARY
1. **Explain** and **account** for current liabilities	Current liabilities are obligations due within one year of the balance sheet date, or within the company's operating cycle if it is longer than one year. Obligations due beyond that time period are long-term liabilities.
	Current liabilities are of two kinds: (1) known amounts, such as short-term borrowings, accounts payable, short-term notes payable, sales taxes, accrued liabilities, payroll liabilities, unearned revenues, and the current portion of long-term debts; and (2) estimated amounts, such as warranties payable and contingent liabilities.
2. **Explain** the types, features, and pricing of bonds payable	Bonds payable are groups of notes issued to multiple lenders. Bonds may be term bonds, which have a fixed maturity date, or serial bonds, which mature in instalments over a certain period of time. Some bonds are secured by specific assets of the issuing company, whereas others are debentures, which are unsecured bonds.
	Bonds are bought and sold through bond markets. The price of a bond is dependent on the relationship between the stated interest rate on the bond and the current market interest rate. When the stated rate exceeds the market rate, the bond is issued at a premium above face value; when the opposite is true, the bond is issued at a discount below face value.

3. **Account** for bonds payable

Bonds payable are initially recorded as long-term liabilities at their face value less (plus) any bond discount (premium). Bond discounts and premiums are amortized to interest expense over the life of the bonds, so that by the time the bonds mature, any related discounts or premiums have been eliminated. Any bonds maturing within one year of the balance sheet date are classified as current liabilities.

4. **Calculate** and **account** for interest expense on bonds payable

Bonds pay interest semi-annually at their stated interest rate times the face value of the bonds. The interest expense is equal to the interest payment plus (minus) the amortization of any discount (premium). IFRS require interest expense to be calculated using the effective-interest method, whereas ASPE also permit use of the simpler straight-line method.

5. **Explain** the advantages and disadvantages of financing with debt versus equity

A company that wishes to fund expansion, acquisitions, or other operational activities has three main options: using excess cash, issuing new shares, or borrowing money. Each of these methods has advantages and disadvantages related to the dilution of control, the flexibility of cash payments, and impact on earnings per share.

6. **Analyze** and **evaluate** a company's debt-paying ability

Accounts payable turnover (Cost of goods sold/Average accounts payable) measures the number of times during the year a company is able to fully pay off its accounts payable. It is an important indicator of a company's liquidity, or its ability to pay off its short-term debts.

The leverage ratio (Total assets/Total shareholders' equity) shows how many dollars of assets a company has per dollar of shareholders' equity. A leverage ratio above 1.0 can enhance returns to shareholders because it means the company is using debt to invest in additional assets, which will presumably generate additional net income to be shared among the owners. An excessive leverage ratio can be dangerous, however, as it often leads to a company's inability to meet its debt payments.

The times-interest-earned ratio (Operating income/Interest expense) measures the number of times a company's operating income can cover its interest payments. The higher the ratio, the easier it is for a company to make its payments.

7. **Describe** other types of long-term liabilities

A term loan is a long-term loan at a stated interest rate, typically from a single lender such as a bank, which must be repaid over a specified number of years. It is usually secured by specific assets of the borrower, often the ones acquired using the loan proceeds. A mortgage is a term loan secured by real property such as land and buildings.

A lease is a rental agreement in which the lessee agrees to make rent payments to the lessor (property owner) in exchange for the use of property. There are two types of leases: a finance (or capital) lease that transfers to the lessee substantially all the risks and rewards incidental to the ownership of the property; and an operating lease, in which the lessor retains the risks and rewards of ownership. Finance leases are recorded as liabilities and accounted for in the same way as other long-term debts, whereas operating lease payments are expensed as they come due.

Post-employment benefits are a special type of employee benefits that do not become payable until after a person has completed employment with the company. They include such things as pension benefits, medical and dental insurance, and prescription drug benefits.

8. **Report** liabilities on the balance sheet

Financial statement users should review all of the current and long-term liabilities reported on a company's balance sheet. In order to properly interpret this information, users should also consult related information in the statement of cash flows and the notes to the financial statements.

MyAccountingLab

END-OF-CHAPTER SUMMARY PROBLEM

TransCanada Corporation has a number of bond issues outstanding in various amounts with various interest rates and maturities. Assume TransCanada has outstanding an issue of 8% bonds that mature in 2027. Suppose the bonds are dated October 1, 2017, and pay interest each April 1 and October 1.

Requirements

1. Use Excel to complete the following effective-interest amortization table through October 1, 2019:
   Bond Data
   Maturity value—$100,000
   Contract interest rate—8%
   Interest paid—4% semi-annually, $4,000 ($100,000 × 0.08 × 6/12)
   Market interest rate at the time of issue—9% annually, 4½% semi-annually
   Issue price—93.80

	A	B	C	D	E	F	G
1				Amortization Table			
2	Semi-Annual Interest Date	Interest Payment (4% of Maturity Amount)	Interest Expense (4½% of Preceding Bond Carrying Amount)	Bond Discount Amortization (C − B)	Bond Discount Account Balance (Preceding E − D)	Bond Carrying Amount ($100,000 − E)	
3	01-10-17						
4	01-04-18						
5	01-10-18						
6	01-04-19						
7	01-10-19						
8							

Name: TransCanada Corporation
Industry: Pipeline provider
Accounting Period: The years 2017, 2018, 2019

2. Using the amortization table, record the following transactions:
   a. Issuance of the bonds on October 1, 2017.
   b. Accrual of interest and amortization of the bonds on December 31, 2017.
   c. Payment of interest and amortization of the bonds on April 1, 2018.

ANSWERS

Requirement 1

The semi-annual interest payment is constant ($4,000). The interest expense is calculated as 4.5% of the previous period's carrying value. The discount account balance reflects that the issue price of $93.80 is less than $100.00.

	A	B	C	D	E	F	G
1	Semi-Annual Interest Date	Interest Payment (4% of Maturity Amount)	Interest Expense (4½% of Preceding Bond Carrying Amount)	Bond Discount Amortization (C − B)	Bond Discount Account Balance (Preceding E − D)	Bond Carrying Amount ($100,000 − E)	
2	01-10-17				$ 6,200	$ 93,800	
3	01-04-18	$ 4,000	$ 4,221	$ 221	5,979	94,021	
4	01-10-18	4,000	4,231	231	5,748	94,252	
5	01-04-19	4,000	4,241	241	5,507	94,493	
6	01-10-19	4,000	4,252	252	5,255	94,745	
7							

Requirement 2

	A	B	C	D	E
1	a. 2017				
2	Oct. 1	Cash	93,800		
3		Discount on Bonds Payable	6,200		
4		Bonds Payable		100,000	
5		To issue 8%, ten-year bonds at a discount.			
6	b. Dec. 31	Interest Expense ($4,221 × 3/6)	2,111		
7		Discount on Bonds Payable ($121 × 3/6)		111	
8		Interest Payable ($4,000 × 3/6)		2,000	
9		To accrue interest and amortize the bonds.			
10	c. 2018				
11	Apr. 1	Interest Expense	2,110		
12		Interest Payable	2,000		
13		Discount on Bonds Payable ($121 × 3/6)		110*	
14		Cash		4,000	
15		To pay semi-annual interest, part of which was accrued, and amortize the bonds.			
16					

The bonds were issued for less than $100,000, reflecting a discount. Use the amounts from columns D and E for 01-10-17 from the amortization table.

The accrued interest is calculated, and the bond discount is amortized. Use 3/6 of the amounts from columns A, B, and C for 01-04-18 from the amortization table.

The semi-annual interest payment is made ($4,000 from column A). Only the January-to-March 2018 interest expense is recorded, because the October-to-December interest expense was already recorded in Requirement 2(b). The same is true for the discount on bonds payable. Reverse Interest Payable from Requirement 2(b), because cash is paid now.

*The total amortization was $221, of which $111 was recognized at December 31, 2017.

REVIEW

MyAccountingLab

Make the grade with MyAccountingLab: The Quick Quiz questions, Short Exercises, Exercises, and Problems (Group A) marked in #–# can be found on MyAccountingLab. You can practise them as often as you want, and most feature step-by-step guided instructions to help you find the right answer.

QUICK QUIZ (ANSWERS APPEAR ON THE LAST PAGE OF THIS CHAPTER.)

1. For the purpose of classifying liabilities as current or non-current, the term *operating cycle* refers to which of the following?
   a. A period of one year
   b. The time period between date of sale and the date the related revenue is collected
   c. The time period between purchase of merchandise and the conversion of this merchandise back to cash
   d. The average time period between business recessions

2. Failure to accrue interest expense results in which of the following?
   a. An overstatement of net income and an overstatement of liabilities
   b. An understatement of net income and an overstatement of liabilities
   c. An understatement of net income and an understatement of liabilities

   d. An overstatement of net income and an understatement of liabilities

3. Sportscar Warehouse operates in a province with a 6% sales tax. For convenience, Sportscar Warehouse credits Sales Revenue for the total amount (selling price plus sales tax) collected from each customer. If Sportscar Warehouse fails to make an adjustment for sales taxes, which of the following will be true?
   a. Net income will be overstated, and liabilities will be overstated.
   b. Net income will be overstated, and liabilities will be understated.
   c. Net income will be understated, and liabilities will be overstated.
   d. Net income will be understated, and liabilities will be understated.

4. What kind of account is *Unearned Revenue*?
a. Asset account
b. Liability account
c. Revenue account
d. Expense account

5. An end-of-period adjusting entry that debits Unearned Revenue will most likely credit which of the following?
a. A revenue
b. An asset
c. An expense
d. A liability

6. Adrian Inc. manufactures and sells computer monitors with a three-year warranty. Warranty costs are expected to average 8% of sales during the warranty period. The following table shows the sales and actual warranty payments during the first two years of operations:

Year	Sales	Warranty Payments
2016	$500,000	$ 4,000
2017	700,000	32,000

Based on these facts, what amount of warranty liability should Adrian Inc. report on its balance sheet at December 31, 2017?
a. $32,000
b. $36,000
c. $60,000
d. $96,000

7. Today's Fashions has a debt that has been properly reported as a long-term liability up to the present year (2017). Some of this debt comes due in 2017. If Today's Fashions continues to report the current position as a long-term liability, the effect will be to do which of the following?
a. Overstate the current ratio
b. Overstate net income
c. Understate total liabilities
d. Understate the debt ratio

8. A bond with a face amount of $10,000 has a current price quote of 102.875. What is the bond's price?
a. $1,028,750
b. $10,200.88
c. $10,028.75
d. $10,287.50

9. Bond carrying value equals Bonds Payable
a. minus Premium on Bonds Payable.
b. plus Discount on Bonds Payable.
c. plus Premium on Bonds Payable.
d. minus Discount on Bonds Payable.
e. Both a and b
f. Both c and d

10. What type of account is *Discount on Bonds Payable*, and what is its normal balance?

Type of account	Normal balance
a. Contra liability	Debit
b. Reversing account	Debit
c. Adjusting amount	Credit
d. Contra liability	Credit

Questions Q8–11 through Q8–14 use the following data:

11. Sweetwater Company sells $100,000 of 10%, 15-year bonds for 97 on April 1, 2017. The market rate of interest on that day is 10½%. Interest is paid each year on April 1. The entry to record the sale of the bonds on April 1 would be which of the following?

a. Cash...	97,000	
Bonds Payable........................		97,000
b. Cash...	100,000	
Bonds Payable........................		100,000
c. Cash...	97,000	
Discount on Bonds Payable..........	3,000	
Bonds Payable........................		100,000
d. Cash...	100,000	
Discount on Bonds Payable......		3,000
Bonds Payable........................		97,000

12. Sweetwater Company uses the straight-line amortization method. The sale price of the bonds was $97,000. The amount of interest expense on April 1 of each year will be which of the following?
a. $4,080
b. $4,000
c. $4,200
d. $10,200
e. None of these. The interest expense is ___.

13. Write the adjusting entry required at December 31, 2017.

14. Write the journal entry required at April 1, 2018.

15. McPherson Corporation issued $100,000 of 10%, five-year bonds on January 1, 2017, for $92,280. The market interest rate when the bonds were issued was 12%. Interest is paid semi-annually on January 1 and July 1. The first interest payment is July 1, 2017. Using the effective-interest amortization method, how much interest expense will McPherson record on July 1, 2017?
a. $6,000
b. $5,228
c. $6,772
d. $5,000
e. Some other amount ($___)

16. Using the facts in the preceding question, McPherson's journal entry to record the interest expense on July 1, 2017, will include a
   a. debit to Bonds Payable.
   b. credit to Interest Expense.
   c. debit to Premium on Bonds Payable.
   d. credit to Discount on Bonds Payable.

17. Amortizing the discount on bonds payable does which of the following?
   a. Increases the recorded amount of interest expense
   b. Is necessary only if the bonds were issued at more than face value
   c. Reduces the semi-annual cash payment for interest
   d. Reduces the carrying value of the bond liability

18. The journal entry on the maturity date to record the payment of $1,000,000 of bonds payable that were issued at a $70,000 discount includes
   a. a debit to Discount on Bonds Payable for $70,000.
   b. a credit to Cash for $1,070,000.
   c. a debit to Bonds Payable for $1,000,000.
   d. All of the above.

19. The payment of the face amount of a bond on its maturity date is regarded as which of the following?
   a. An operating activity
   b. An investing activity
   c. A financing activity

ACCOUNTING VOCABULARY

account payable A liability for goods or services purchased on credit and backed by the general reputation and credit standing of the debtor. (p. 376)

accounts payable turnover (T/O) A liquidity ratio that measures the number of times per year a company was able to repay its accounts payable in full. Calculated by dividing the cost of goods sold by the average accounts payable balance for the year. (p. 402)

bond discount Excess of a bond's face (par) value over its issue price. (p. 388)

bond market price The price investors are willing to pay for the bond. It is equal to the present value of the principal payment plus the present value of the interest payments. (p. 388)

bonds payable Groups of notes payable issued to multiple lenders called *bondholders*. (p. 387)

bond premium Excess of a bond's issue price over its face value. (p. 388)

contingent liability A possible obligation that arises from past events and whose existence will be confirmed only by the occurrence or non-occurrence of one or more uncertain future events not wholly within the control of the company. (p. 385)

current portion of long-term debt The amount of the principal that is payable within one year. Also called *current instalment of long-term debt*. (p. 383)

days payable outstanding (DPO) Another way of expressing the accounts payable turnover ratio, this measure indicates how many days it will take to pay off the accounts payable balance in full. Calculated by dividing the *accounts payable turnover* into 365. (p. 402)

debentures Unsecured bonds—bonds backed only by the good faith of the borrower. (p. 388)

deferred income tax liability The amount of income taxes payable in future periods as a result of differences between accounting income and taxable income in current and prior periods. Under ASPE, this is known as a *future income tax liability*. (p. 382)

earnings per share (EPS) Amount of a company's net income per outstanding common share. (p. 400)

face value of bond The principal amount payable by the issuer. Also called *maturity value*. (p. 387)

finance lease Under IFRS, a lease that transfers substantially all the risks and rewards incidental to ownership of assets to the lessee. (p. 405)

interest-coverage ratio Another name for the *times-interest-earned ratio*. (p. 404)

lease Rental agreement in which the tenant (lessee) agrees to make rent payments to the property owner (lessor) in exchange for the use of the asset. (p. 405)

lessee Tenant in a lease agreement. (p. 405)

lessor Property owner in a lease agreement. (p. 405)

leverage ratio Shows the ratio of a company's total assets to total shareholders' equity. It is an alternative way of expressing how much debt a company has used to fund its assets, or in other words, how much leverage it has used. (p. 403)

line of credit A method of short-term borrowing that provides a company with as-needed access to credit up to a maximum amount specified by its lender. (p. 376)

market interest rate Interest rate that investors demand for loaning their money. Also called *effective interest rate*. (p. 389)

mortgage A *term loan* secured by real property, such as land and buildings. (p. 405)

operating lease A lease in which the risks and rewards of asset ownership are not transferred to the lessee. (p. 405)

payroll Employee compensation, a major expense of many businesses. (p. 380)

post-employment benefits A special type of employee benefits that do not become payable until after a person has completed employment with the company. They include such things as pension benefits, medical and dental insurance, and prescription drug benefits. (p. 406)

pretax accounting income Income before tax on the income statement; the basis for computing income tax expense. (p. 381)

provision Under IFRS, a present obligation of uncertain timing or amount that is recorded as a liability because it is probable that economic resources will be required to settle it. (p. 384)

sales tax payable The amount of HST, GST, and provincial sales tax owing to government bodies.   (p. 378)

serial bonds Bonds that mature in instalments over a period of time.   (p. 388)

short-term notes payable Notes payable due within one year.   (p. 377)

stated interest rate Interest rate printed on the bond certificate that determines the amount of cash interest the borrower pays and the investor receives each year. Also called the *coupon rate* or *contract interest rate*.   (p. 388)

taxable income The basis for computing the amount of tax to pay the government.   (p. 381)

term bonds Bonds that all mature at the same time for a particular issue.   (p. 388)

term loan A long-term loan at a stated interest rate, typically from a single lender such as a bank, which must be repaid over a specified number of years. Usually secured by specific assets of the borrower, often the ones acquired using the loan proceeds.   (p. 405)

times-interest-earned ratio Ratio of income from operations to interest expense. Measures the number of times that operating income can cover interest expense. Also called the *interest-coverage ratio*.   (p. 404)

underwriter Organization that purchases the bonds from an issuing company and resells them to its clients or sells the bonds for a commission, agreeing to buy all unsold bonds.   (p. 388)

unearned revenue A liability that arises when a business receives cash from a customer prior to providing the related goods or services.   (p. 382)

ASSESS YOUR PROGRESS

SHORT EXERCISES

LEARNING OBJECTIVE ❶

Account for a note payable

S8-1 Jasper Sports Limited purchased inventory costing $10,000 by signing a 10% short-term note payable. The purchase occurred on March 31, 2017. Jasper pays annual interest each year on March 31. Journalize Jasper's (a) purchase of inventory, (b) accrual of interest expense on December 31, 2017, and (c) payment of the note plus interest on March 31, 2018.

LEARNING OBJECTIVE ❽

Report a short-term note payable and the related interest in the financial statements

S8-2 This short exercise works with exercise S8-1.

1. Refer to the data in S8-1. Show what the company would report on its balance sheet at December 31, 2017, and on its income statement for the year ended on that date.
2. What one item will the financial statements for the year ended December 31, 2018, report? Identify the financial statement, the item, and its amount.

LEARNING OBJECTIVE ❶

Account for warranty expense and estimated warranty payable

S8-3 General Motors of Canada Limited guarantees automobiles against defects for five years or 160,000 km, whichever comes first. Suppose GM Canada can expect warranty costs during the five-year period to add up to 3% of sales.

Assume that Forbes Motors in Waterloo, Ontario, made sales of $2,000,000 on their Buick line during 2017. Forbes received cash for 10% of the sales and took notes receivable for the remainder. Payments to satisfy customer warranty claims totalled $50,000 during 2017.

1. Record the sales, warranty expense, and warranty payments for Forbes. Ignore any reimbursement that Forbes may receive from GM Canada.
2. Post to the Estimated Warranty Payable T-account. The beginning balance was $40,000. At the end of 2017, how much in estimated warranty payable does Forbes owe its customers?

LEARNING OBJECTIVE ❶❽

Report warranties in the financial statements

S8-4 Refer to the data given in exercise S8-3. What amount of warranty expense will Forbes report during 2017? Does the warranty expense for the year equal the year's cash payments for warranties? Explain the relevant accounting principle as it applies to measuring warranty expense.

LEARNING OBJECTIVE ❻

Analyze accounts payable turnover

S8-5 Wardlow Sales, Inc.'s comparative income statements and balance sheets show the following selected information for 2016 and 2017:

	2017	2016
Cost of goods sold	$2,700,000	$2,500,000
Average accounts payable	$ 300,000	$ 250,000

Requirements

1. Calculate the company's accounts payable turnover and days payable outstanding (DPO) for 2016 and 2017.
2. On the basis of this computation alone, has the company's liquidity position improved or deteriorated during 2017?

S8-6 Compute the price of the following bonds:

a. $1,000,000 quoted at 89.75
b. $500,000 quoted at 110.375
c. $100,000 quoted at 97.50
d. $400,000 quoted at 102.625

LEARNING OBJECTIVE ❷❸

Price bonds

S8-7 Determine whether the following bonds will be issued at face value, a premium, or a discount:

a. The market interest rate is 9%. Star Inc. issues bonds with a stated rate of 8½%.
b. Charger Corporation issued 7½% bonds when the market rate was 7½%.
c. Explorer Corporation issued 8% bonds when the market interest rate was 6⅞%.
d. Tundra Company issued bonds that pay cash interest at the stated interest rate of 7%. At the date of issuance, the market interest rate was 8¼%.

LEARNING OBJECTIVE ❷❸

Determine bond prices at face value, a discount, or a premium

S8-8 Suppose Scotiabank issued a six-year $10,000 bond with stated interest rate of 6.25% when the market interest rate was 6¼%. Assume that the accounting year of Scotiabank ends on October 31. Journalize the following transactions, including an explanation for each entry.

a. Issuance of the bond, payable on May 1, 2017
b. Accrual of interest expense on October 31, 2017 (rounded to the nearest dollar)
c. Payment of cash interest on November 1, 2017
d. Payment of the bonds at maturity (give the date)

LEARNING OBJECTIVE ❷❸

Journalize basic bond payable transactions

S8-9 Standard Autoparts Inc. issued $100,000 of 7%, 10-year bonds at a price of 87 on January 31, 2017. The market interest rate at the date of issuance was 9%, and the standard bonds pay interest semi-annually.

1. Prepare an effective-interest amortization table for the bonds through the first three interest payments. Use Exhibit 8-3, page 393, as a guide, and round amounts to the nearest dollar.
2. Record Standard's issuance of the bonds on January 31, 2017, and payment of the first semi-annual interest amount and amortization of the bonds on July 31, 2017. Explanations are not required.

LEARNING OBJECTIVE ❷❸

Record bond transactions and calculate interest using the effective-interest method

S8-10 Use the amortization table that you prepared for Standard Autoparts in exercise S8-9 to answer these questions about the company's long-term debt:

1. How much cash did Standard Autoparts borrow on January 31, 2017? How much cash will Standard Autoparts pay back at maturity on January 31, 2018?
2. How much cash interest will Standard Autoparts pay each six months?
3. How much interest expense will Standard Autoparts report on July 31, 2017, and on January 31, 2018? Why does the amount of interest expense increase each period? Explain in detail.

LEARNING OBJECTIVE ❹

Analyze interest on long-term debt

S8-11 Max Industries Ltd. borrowed money by issuing a $10,000 6.5%, 10-year bond. Assume the issue price was 94 on July 1, 2017.

1. How much cash did Max Industries receive when it issued the bond?
2. How much must Max Industries pay back at maturity? When is the maturity date?
3. How much cash interest will Max Industries pay each six months? Carry the interest amount to the nearest cent.
4. How much interest expense will Max Industries report each six months? Assume the straight-line amortization method, and carry the interest amount to the nearest cent.

LEARNING OBJECTIVE ❷❸❹

Determine bonds payable amounts; amortize bonds by the straight-line method

LEARNING OBJECTIVE ❸❹

Record bond transactions and calculate interest using the straight-line method

S8-12 Return to the Max Industries bond in exercise S8-11. Assume that Max Industries issued the bond on July 1, 2017, at a price of 90. Also assume that Max Industries's accounting year ends on December 31. Journalize the following transactions for Max Industries, including an explanation for each entry:

a. Issuance of the bonds on July 1, 2017.
b. Accrual of interest expense and amortization of bonds on December 31, 2017. (Use the straight-line amortization method, and round amounts to the nearest dollar.)
c. Payment of the first semi-annual interest amount on January 1, 2018.

LEARNING OBJECTIVE ❻

Calculate the leverage ratio, debt ratio, and times-interest-earned, and evaluate debt-paying ability

S8-13 Examine the following selected financial information for Best Buy Co., Inc., and Walmart Stores, Inc.:

(in millions)	Best Buy Co., Inc.	Walmart Stores, Inc.
1. Total assets	$17,849	$180,663
2. Shareholders' equity	$ 7,292	$ 71,247
3. Operating income	$ 2,114	$ 25,542
4. Interest expense	$ 87	$ 1,928
5. Leverage ratio		
6. Total debt		
7. Debt ratio		
8. Times interest earned		

1. Complete the table, calculating all the requested information for the two companies.
2. Evaluate each company's long-term debt-paying ability (strong, medium, weak).

LEARNING OBJECTIVE ❻

Compute and evaluate three ratios

S8-14 Evensen Plumbing Products Ltd. reported the following data in 2017 (in millions):

	2017
Net operating revenues	$ 29.1
Operating expenses	25.0
Operating income	4.1
Nonoperating items:	
Interest expense	(1.1)
Other	(0.2)
Net income	$ 2.8
Total assets	$100.0
Total shareholders' equity	40.0

Compute Evensen's leverage ratio, debt ratio, and times-interest-earned ratio, and write a sentence to explain what those ratio values mean. Would you be willing to lend Evensen $1 million? State your reason.

LEARNING OBJECTIVE ❽

Report liabilities, including capital lease obligations

S8-15 Trinidad Industries Inc. has the following selected accounts at December 31, 2017:

GST Payable (net of ITC)	$ 17,000
Bonds payable	300,000
Equipment	120,000
Current portion of bonds payable	40,000
Notes payable, long-term	100,000
Interest payable (due March 1, 2018)	10,000
Accounts payable	44,000
Discount on bonds payable (all long-term)	10,000
Accounts receivable	34,000

Prepare the liabilities section of Trinidad's balance sheet at December 31, 2017, to show how Trinidad would report these items. Report total current liabilities and total liabilities.

EXERCISES

E8-16 The accounting records of Audio-Video Inc. included the following balances before the year-end adjustments:

Estimated Warranty Payable	Sales Revenue	Warranty Expense
Beg. bal. 8,000	150,000	

In the past, Audio-Video's warranty expense has been 6% of sales. During the current period, the business paid $9,400 to satisfy the warranty claims of customers.

Requirements

1. Record Audio-Video's warranty expense for the period and the company's cash payments to satisfy warranty claims. Explanations are not required.
2. Show everything Audio-Video will report on its income statement and balance sheet for this situation.
3. Which data item from Requirement 2 will affect Audio-Video's current ratio? Will Audio-Video's current ratio increase or decrease as a result of this item?

E8-17 *Ontario Traveller Magazine* completed the following transactions during 2017:

Aug. 31	Sold one-year subscriptions, collecting cash of $1,500, plus HST of 13%.
Dec. 31	Remitted (paid) HST to Canada Revenue Agency (CRA).
31	Made the necessary adjustment at year-end.

Journalize these transactions (explanations are not required). Then report any liability on the company's balance sheet at December 31.

E8-18 Penske Talent Search has an annual payroll of $150,000. At December 31, Penske owes salaries of $7,600 on which employee withholdings payable are $1,200 and employee benefits payable by the company are $1,000. The company has calculated its share of Canada Pension Plan, Employment Insurance, and other employee benefits to be 6% of payroll expense. The company will pay these amounts early next year. Show what Penske will report for the foregoing on its income statement and year-end balance sheet.

E8-19 Joy's Bar and Grill completed the following note-payable transactions:

2017	
Aug. 1	Purchased kitchen equipment costing $60,000 by issuing a one-year, 5% note.
Dec. 31	Accrued interest on the note payable.
2018	
Aug. 1	Paid the note payable at maturity.

Answer these questions for Joy's Bar and Grill:

1. How much interest expense must be accrued at December 31, 2017?
2. Determine the amount of Joy's final payment on July 31, 2018.
3. How much interest expense will Joy's report for 2017 and for 2018?

E8-20 Geodesic Domes, Inc., builds environmentally sensitive structures. The company's 2017 revenues totalled $2,800 million. At December 31, 2017, and 2016, the company had $661 million and $600 million in current assets, respectively. The December 31, 2017, and 2016, balance sheets and income statements reported the following amounts:

At Year-End (in millions)	2017	2016
Liabilities and shareholders' equity		
Current liabilities		
Accounts payable..	$ 110	$ 182
Accrued expenses..	97	177
Employee compensation and benefits...	45	15
Current portion of long-term debt..	7	20
Total current liabilities..	259	394
Long-term debt	1,394	1,315
Post-retirement benefits payable	102	154
Other liabilities..	8	20
Shareholders' equity...	1,951	1,492
Total liabilities and shareholders' equity	$3,714	$3,375
Year-end (in millions)		
Cost of goods sold..	$1,656	$1,790

Requirements

1. Describe each of Geodesic Domes, Inc.'s liabilities and state how the liability arose.
2. What were the company's total assets at December 31, 2017? Evaluate the company's leverage and debt ratios at the end of 2016 and 2017. Did the company improve, deteriorate, or remain about the same over the year?
3. Accounts payable at the end of 2015 was $190 million. Calculate accounts payable turnover as a ratio and days payable outstanding (DPO) for 2016 and 2017. Calculate current ratios for 2016 and 2017 as well. Evaluate whether the company improved or deteriorated from the standpoint of ability to cover accounts payable and current liabilities over the year.

LEARNING OBJECTIVE ①⑥⑧

Analyze liabilities and debt-paying ability

E8-21 Mills Geothermal Ltd. installs environmental heating/cooling systems. The company's 2017 revenues totalled $360 million, and at December 31, 2017, the company had $65 million in current assets. The December 31, 2017, balance sheet reported the liabilities and shareholders' equity as follows:

At Year-End (in millions)	2017	2016
Liabilities and shareholders' equity		
Current liabilities		
Accounts payable..	$ 29	$ 26
Accrued expenses..	16	20
Employee compensation and benefits...	9	11
Current portion of long-term debt..	5	—
Total current liabilities..	59	57
Long-term debt	115	115
Post-retirement benefits payable	31	27
Other liabilities..	21	17
Shareholders' equity...	73	70
Total liabilities and shareholders' equity	$299	$286

Requirements

1. Describe each of Mills Geothermal Ltd.'s liabilities, and state how the liability arose.
2. What were the company's total assets at December 31, 2017? Was the company's debt ratio at the end of 2017 high, low, or in a middle range?

LEARNING OBJECTIVE ⑥

Evaluate debt-paying ability

E8-22 Companies that operate in different industries may have very different financial ratio values. These differences may grow even wider when we compare companies located in different countries.

Compare three leading companies on their current ratio, debt ratio, leverage ratio, and times-interest-earned ratio. Compute the ratios for Company B, Company N, and Company V.

(amounts in millions or billions)	Company B	Company N	Company V
Income data			
Total revenues	$9,732	¥7,320	€136,146
Operating income...	295	230	5,646
Interest expense..	41	27	655
Net income..	22	7	450
Balance sheet data **(amounts in millions or billions)**			
Total current assets..	429	5,321	144,720
Long-term assets...	81	592	65,828
Total current liabilities....................................	227	2,217	72,000
Long-term liabilities	77	2,277	111,177
Shareholders' equity	206	1,419	27,371

Note: ¥ is the symbol for a Japanese yen; € for a euro.

Based on your computed ratio values, which company looks the least risky?

E8-23 Assume that Premium Golf Equipment completed these selected transactions during December 2017:

LEARNING OBJECTIVE ❶❽
Report current and long-term liabilities

a. Sales of $3,000,000 are subject to estimated warranty cost of 3%. The estimated warranty payable at the beginning of the year was $30,000, and warranty payments for the year totalled $60,000.
b. On December 1, 2017, Premium signed a $150,000 note that requires annual payments of $30,000 plus 5% interest on the unpaid balance each December 1.
c. Golf Town, a chain of golf stores, ordered $125,000 of golf equipment. With its order, Golf Town sent a cheque for $125,000, and Premium shipped $100,000 of the goods. Premium will ship the remainder of the goods on January 3, 2018.
d. The December payroll of $100,000 is subject to employee-withheld income tax, Canada Pension Plan and Employment Insurance, and the company's share of Canada Pension Plan and Employment Insurance totalling $25,000 and benefits of $9,000. On December 31, Premium pays employees their take-home pay and accrues all tax amounts.

Requirement

Classify each liability as current or long-term and report the liability and its amount that would appear on the Premium Golf Equipment balance sheet at December 31, 2017. Show a total for current liabilities.

E8-24 On January 31, 2017, Triumph Sports Cars issued 10-year, 6% bonds with a face value of $100,000. The bonds were issued at 97 and pay interest on January 31 and July 31. Triumph amortizes bonds by the straight-line method. Record (a) issuance of the bonds on January 31, (b) the semi-annual interest payment and discount amortization on July 31, and (c) the interest accrual and discount amortization on December 31.

LEARNING OBJECTIVE ❷❸❹
Record bond transactions and calculate interest using the straight-line method

E8-25 Moreau Manufacturing Inc. has $200,000 of 8% debenture bonds outstanding. The bonds were issued at 102 in 2017 and mature in 2037.

LEARNING OBJECTIVE ❷❸❹
Measure cash amounts for a bond; amortize the bonds by the straight-line method

Requirements

1. How much cash did Moreau receive when it issued these bonds?
2. How much cash *in total* will Moreau pay the bondholders through the maturity date of the bonds?

3. Take the difference between your answers to Requirements 1 and 2. This difference represents Moreau's total interest expense over the life of the bonds. (Challenge)

4. Compute Moreau's annual interest expense by the straight-line amortization method. Multiply this amount by 20. Your 20-year total should be the same as your answer to Requirement 3. (Challenge)

LEARNING OBJECTIVE ❷❸❹

Record bond transactions and calculate interest using the effective-interest method

E8-26 Family General Stores Inc. is authorized to issue $500,000 of 7%, 10-year bonds. On December 31, 2017, when the market interest rate is 8%, the company issues $400,000 of the bonds and receives cash of $372,660. Family General amortizes bonds by the effective-interest method. The semi-annual interest dates are January 31 and July 31.

Requirements

1. Prepare a bond amortization table for the first four semi-annual interest periods.

2. Record issuance of the bonds on December 31, 2017, and the semi-annual interest payments on January 31, 2018, and on July 31, 2018.

LEARNING OBJECTIVE ❷❸❹

Record bond transactions and calculate interest using the effective-interest method

E8-27 On June 30, 2017, the market interest rate is 7%. Dellaca Enterprises issues $500,000 of 8%, 20-year bonds at 110.625. The bonds pay interest on June 30 and December 31. Dellaca amortizes bonds by the effective-interest method.

Requirements

1. Prepare a bond amortization table for the first four semi-annual interest periods.

2. Record issuance of the bonds on June 30, 2017, the payment of interest at December 31, 2017, and the semi-annual interest payment on June 30, 2018.

LEARNING OBJECTIVE ❸❹

Create a debt payment and bond amortization schedule

E8-28 Carlson Candies issued $300,000 of 8⅜%, five-year bonds on January 1, 2017, when the market interest rate was 9½%. The company pays interest annually at year-end. The issue price of the bonds was $287,041.

Requirement

Create a spreadsheet model to prepare a schedule to amortize the bonds. Use the effective-interest method of amortization. Round to the nearest dollar, and format your answer as shown here.

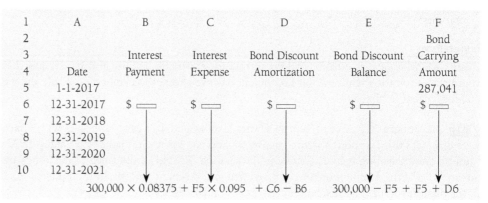

	A	B	C	D	E	F
1						
2						Bond
3		Interest	Interest	Bond Discount	Bond Discount	Carrying
4	Date	Payment	Expense	Amortization	Balance	Amount
5	1-1-2017					287,041
6	12-31-2017	$ ⟶	$ ⟶	$ ⟶	$ ⟶	$ ⟶
7	12-31-2018					
8	12-31-2019					
9	12-31-2020					
10	12-31-2021					

$300,000 \times 0.08375$ + $F5 \times 0.095$ + $C6 - B6$ $300,000 - F5$ + $F5 + D6$

LEARNING OBJECTIVE ❶❻❽

Analyze current and long-term liabilities; evaluate debt-paying ability

E8-29 Green Earth Homes, Inc., builds environmentally sensitive structures. The company's 2017 revenues totalled $2,785 million. At December 31, 2017 and 2016, the company had $643 million and $610 million in current assets, respectively. The December 31, 2017 and 2016 balance sheets and income statements reported the following amounts:

At Year-End (in millions)	2017	2016
Liabilities and shareholders' equity		
Current liabilities..		
Accounts payable..	$ 137	$ 181
Accrued expenses	163	169
Employee compensation and benefits............................	51	16
Current portion of long-term debt.................................	17	10
Total current liabilities..	368	376
Long-term debt	1,497	1,326
Post-retirement benefits payable	138	112
Other liabilities..	20	22
Shareholders' equity	2,027	1,492
Total liabilities and shareholders' equity	$4,050	3,328
Year-end (in millions)		
Cost of goods sold	$1,885	$2,196

Requirements

1. Describe each of Green Earth Homes, Inc.'s liabilities and state how the liability arose.

2. What were the company's total assets at December 31, 2017? Evaluate the company's leverage and debt ratios at the end of 2016 and 2017. Did the company improve, deteriorate, or remain about the same over the year?

3. Accounts payable at the end of 2015 was $195. Calculate accounts payable turnover as a ratio and days payable outstanding (DPO) for 2016 and 2017. Calculate current ratios for 2016 and 2017 as well. Evaluate whether the company improved or deteriorated from the standpoint of ability to cover accounts payable and current liabilities over the year.

E8-30 Companies that operate in different industries may have very different financial ratio values. These differences may grow even wider when we compare companies located in different countries.

    Compare three leading companies on their current ratio, debt ratio, and times-interest-earned ratio. Compute three ratios for Sobeys (the Canadian grocery chain), Sony (the Japanese electronics manufacturer), and Daimler (the German auto company).

LEARNING OBJECTIVE ❻

Use ratios to compare companies

	(amounts in millions or billions)		
Income data	**Sobeys**	**Sony**	**Daimler**
Total revenues	$12,853	¥7,475	€151,589
Operating income...................................	332	191	2,072
Interest expense.....................................	35	29	913
Net income...	197	124	3,227
Asset and liability data			
Total current assets...............................	$1,235	¥3,770	€93,131
Long-term assets....................................	2,504	6,838	96,891
Total current liabilities..........................	1,230	3,200	59,977
Long-term liabilities	674	4,204	95,890
Shareholders' equity..............................	1,835	3,204	34,155

    Based on your computed ratio values, which company looks the least risky? (Challenge)

E8-31 Companies that operate in different industries may have very different financial ratio values. These differences may grow even wider when we compare companies located in different countries.

    Compare three leading companies on their current ratio, debt ratio, leverage ratio, and times-interest-earned ratio. Compute the ratios for Company F, Company K, and Company R.

LEARNING OBJECTIVE ❻

Evaluate debt-paying ability

Income data	(amounts in millions or billions)		
	Company F	Company K	Company R
Total revenues	$9,724	¥7,307	€136,492
Operating income	292	224	5,592
Interest expense	46	33	736
Net income	23	15	448
Assets and liability data			
Total current assets	434	5,383	148,526
Long-term assets	96	405	49,525
Total current liabilities	207	2,197	72,100
Long-term liabilities	107	2,318	110,107
Shareholders' equity	216	1,273	15,844

Based on your computed ratio values, which company looks the least risky?

CHALLENGE EXERCISES

LEARNING OBJECTIVE ❶❻❽

Report current and long-term liabilities; evaluate leverage

E8-32 The top management of Marquis Marketing Services examines the following company accounting records at August 29, immediately before the end of the year, August 31:

Total current assets	$ 324,500
Non-current assets	1,098,500
	$1,423,000
Total current liabilities	$ 173,800
Non-current liabilities	247,500
Shareholders' equity	1,001,700
	$1,423,000

1. Suppose Marquis's management wants to achieve a current ratio of 2. How much in current liabilities should Marquis pay off within the next two days in order to achieve its goal?
2. Calculate Marquis's leverage ratio and debt ratio. Evaluate the company's debt position. Is it low, high, or about average? What other information might help you to make a decision?

LEARNING OBJECTIVE ❺❻

Understand how structuring debt transactions can affect a company

E8-33 The Cola Company reported the following comparative information at December 31, 2017, and December 31, 2016 (amounts in millions and adapted):

	2017	2016
Current assets	$21,579	$17,551
Total assets	72,921	48,671
Current liabilities	18,508	13,721
Total stockholders' equity	31,317	25,346
Net sales	35,119	30,990
Net income	11,809	6,824

Requirements
1. Calculate the following ratios for 2017 and 2016:
   a. Current ratio
   b. Debt ratio
2. At the end of 2017, The Cola Company issued $1,590 million of long-term debt that was used to retire short-term debt. What would the current ratio and debt ratio have been if this transaction had not been made?

3. The Cola Company reports that its lease payments under operating leases will total $965 million in the future and $205 million will occur in the next year (2018). What would the current ratio and debt ratio have been if these leases had been capitalized?

E8-34 Mark IV Industries Inc. issued $100 million 13% debentures due March 15, 2022, with interest payable March 15 and September 15; the price was 96.5.

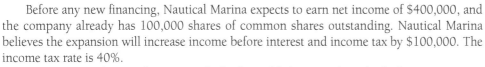

LEARNING OBJECTIVE ❷❸❹
Analyze bond transactions

Requirements
Answer these questions:

1. Journalize Mark IV Industries Inc.'s issuance of these bonds on March 15, 2017. No explanation is required, but describe the transaction in detail, indicating who received cash, who paid cash, and how much.
2. Why is the stated interest rate on these bonds so high?
3. Compute the semi-annual cash interest payment on the bonds.
4. Compute the semi-annual interest expense under the straight-line amortization method.
5. Compute both the first-year (from March 15, 2017, to March 15, 2018) and the second-year interest expense (March 15, 2018, to March 15, 2019) under the effective-interest amortization method. The market rate of interest at the date of issuance was 14%. Why is interest expense greater in the second year?

E8-35 Nautical Marina needs to raise $1.0 million to expand the company. Nautical Marina is considering the issuance of either

- $1,000,000 of 8% bonds payable to borrow the money, or
- 100,000 shares of common stock at $10 per share.

LEARNING OBJECTIVE ❺
Explain the advantages and disadvantages of financing with debt versus equity

Before any new financing, Nautical Marina expects to earn net income of $400,000, and the company already has 100,000 shares of common shares outstanding. Nautical Marina believes the expansion will increase income before interest and income tax by $100,000. The income tax rate is 40%.

Prepare an analysis to determine which plan is likely to result in the higher earnings per share. Based solely on the earnings-per-share comparison, which financing plan would you recommend for Nautical Marina?

PROBLEMS (GROUP A)

P8-36A Sea Spray Marina experienced these events during 2017.

a. December revenue totalled $110,000 and, in addition, Sea Spray collected sales tax of 7%. The sales tax amount will be remitted to the province of British Columbia early in January.

b. On October 31, Sea Spray signed a six-month, 7% note to purchase a boat costing $90,000. The note requires payment of principal and interest at maturity.

c. On August 31, Sea Spray received cash of $1,800 in advance for service revenue. This revenue will be earned evenly over six months.

d. Revenues of $900,000 were covered by Sea Spray's service warranty. At January 1, estimated warranty payable was $11,300. During the year, Sea Spray recorded warranty expense of $31,000 and paid warranty claims of $34,700.

e. Sea Spray owes $100,000 on a long-term note payable. At December 31, 6% interest for the year plus $20,000 of this principal are payable within one year.

LEARNING OBJECTIVE ❶❽
Measure current liabilities

Requirement
For each item, indicate the account and the related amount to be reported as a *current* liability on the Sea Spray Marina balance sheet at December 31, 2017.

LEARNING OBJECTIVE ❶

Record liability-related transactions

P8-37A The following transactions of Smooth Sounds Music Company occurred during 2017 and 2018:

2017		
Mar.	3	Purchased a Steinway piano (inventory) for $40,000, signing a six-month, 5% note.
Apr.	30	Borrowed $50,000 on a 9% note payable that calls for annual instalment payments of $25,000 principal plus interest. Record the short-term note payable in a separate account from the long-term note payable.
Sept.	3	Paid the six-month, 5% note at maturity.
Dec.	31	Accrued warranty expense, which is estimated at 2% of sales of $190,000.
	31	Accrued interest on the outstanding note payable.
2018		
Apr.	30	Paid the first instalment plus interest for one year on the outstanding note payable.

Requirement

Record the transactions in Smooth Sounds's journal. Explanations are not required.

LEARNING OBJECTIVE ❷❸❹❽

Issue bonds at face value, record accrual and payment of interest, and report bonds payable on the balance sheet

P8-38A The board of directors of Circuits Plus authorizes the issue of $9,000,000 of 8%, 25-year bonds payable. The semiannual interest dates are May 31 and November 30. The bonds are issued on May 31, 2016, at face value.

Requirements

1. Journalize the following transactions:
   a. Issuance of half of the bonds on May 31, 2016
   b. Payment of interest on November 30, 2016
   c. Accrual of interest on December 31, 2016
   d. Payment of interest on May 31, 2017
2. Report interest payable and bonds payable as they would appear on the Circuits Plus Balance sheet at December 31, 2016.

LEARNING OBJECTIVE ❷❸❹❽

Issue bonds at a discount, amortize by the straight-line method, and report bonds payable on the balance sheet

P8-39A On February 28, 2017, ETrade Inc. issues 8½%, 20-year bonds with a face value of $200,000. The bonds pay interest on February 28 and August 31. ETrade amortizes bonds by the straight-line method.

Requirements

1. If the market interest rate is 7⅜% when ETrade issues its bonds, will the bonds be priced at face value, a premium, or a discount? Explain.
2. If the market interest rate is 9% when ETrade issues its bonds, will the bonds be priced at face value, a premium, or a discount? Explain.
3. Assume that the issue price of the bonds is 97. Journalize the following bond transactions:
   a. Issuance of the bonds on February 28, 2017
   b. Payment of interest and amortization of the bonds on August 31, 2017
   c. Accrual of interest and amortization of the bonds on December 31, 2017
   d. Payment of interest and amortization of the bonds on February 28, 2018
4. Report interest payable and bonds payable as they would appear on the ETrade balance sheet at December 31, 2017.

LEARNING OBJECTIVE ❷❸❹

Account for bonds payable at a discount and amortize by the straight-line method

P8-40A

1. Journalize the following transactions of Trekker Boot Company:

2017		
Jan.	1	Issued $600,000 of 8%, 10-year bonds at 97.
July	1	Paid semi-annual interest and amortized bonds by the straight-line method on the 8% bonds payable.
Dec.	31	Accrued semi-annual interest expense and amortized bonds by the straight-line method on the 8% bonds payable.
2018		
Jan.	1	Paid semi-annual interest.
2027		
Jan.	1	Paid the 8% bonds at maturity.

2. At December 31, 2017, after all year-end adjustments, determine the carrying amount of Trekker's bonds payable, net.

3. For the six months ended July 1, 2017, determine the following for Trekker:

  a. Interest expense

  b. Cash interest paid

What causes interest expense on the bonds to exceed cash interest paid?

P8-41A Summit Medical Goods is embarking on a massive expansion. Assume the plans call for opening 20 new stores during the next two years. Each store is scheduled to be 30% larger than the company's existing locations, offering more items of inventory and with more elaborate displays. Management estimates that company operations will provide $1.0 million of the cash needed for expansion. Summit Medical must raise the remaining $4.75 million from outsiders.

LEARNING OBJECTIVE ❺

Explain the advantages and disadvantages of financing with debt versus equity

The board of directors is considering obtaining the $4.75 million either through borrowing at 3% or by issuing an additional 100,000 shares of common shares. This year the company has earned $1.5 million before interest and taxes and has 100,000 shares of $1-par common stock outstanding. The market price of the company's stock is $47.50 per share. Assume that income before interest and taxes is expected to grow by 10% each year for the next two years. The company's marginal income tax rate is 20%.

Requirements

1. Use Excel to evaluate the effect of the above projected alternatives on net income and earnings per share two years from now.

2. Write a memo to Summit's management discussing the advantages and disadvantages of borrowing and of issuing common shares to raise the needed cash. Which method of raising the funds would you recommend?

P8-42A Notes to the Maritime Industries Ltd. financial statements reported the following data on December 31, 2017 (the end of the fiscal year):

LEARNING OBJECTIVE ❷❸❹❽

Analyze a company's long-term debt and report long-term debt on the balance sheet (effective-interest method)

Note 6, Indebtedness

Bonds payable 5% due in 2022	$600,000	
Less Discount	(25,274)	$574,726
Notes payable 8.3% payable in $50,000		
annual instalments starting in Year 2021		250,000

Maritime Industries amortizes bonds by the effective-interest method.

Requirements

1. Answer the following questions about Maritime's long-term liabilities:

  a. What is the maturity value of the 5% bonds?

  b. What are Maritime's annual cash interest payments on the 5% bonds?

  c. What is the carrying amount of the 5% bonds at December 31, 2017?

2. Prepare an amortization table through December 31, 2020, for the 5% bonds. The market interest rate for these bonds was 6%. Maritime pays interest annually on December 31. How much is Maritime's interest expense on the 5% bonds for the year ended December 31, 2020?

3. Show how Maritime Industries would report the bonds payable and notes payable at December 31, 2020.

P8-43A On December 31, 2017, Digital Connections issued 8%, 10-year bonds payable with a maturity value of $500,000. The semi-annual interest dates are June 30 and December 31. The market interest rate is 9%, and the issue price of the bonds is 94. Digital Connections amortizes bonds by the effective-interest method.

LEARNING OBJECTIVE ❷❸❹❽

Issuing bonds at a discount, amortizing by the effective-interest method, and reporting the bonds payable on the balance sheet

Requirements

1. Prepare an effective-interest-method amortization table for the first four semi-annual interest periods.

2. Journalize the following transactions:
   a. Issuance of the bonds on December 31, 2017. Credit Bonds Payable.
   b. Payment of interest and amortization of the bonds on June 30, 2018
   c. Payment of interest and amortization of the bonds on December 31, 2018
3. Show how Digital Connections would report the remaining bonds payable on its balance sheet at December 31, 2018.

LEARNING OBJECTIVE ⑤

Finance operations with debt or with shares

P8-44A Outback Sporting Goods is embarking on a massive expansion. Assume plans call for opening 20 new stores during the next two years. Each store is scheduled to be 50% larger than the company's existing locations, offering more items of inventory, and with more elaborate displays. Management estimates that company operations will provide $1 million of the cash needed for expansion. Outback must raise the remaining $6 million from outsiders. The board of directors is considering obtaining the $6 million either through borrowing or by issuing common shares.

Requirement

Write a memo to Outback's management discussing the advantages and disadvantages of borrowing and of issuing common shares to raise the needed cash. Which method of raising the funds would you recommend?

LEARNING OBJECTIVE ①⑥⑧

Report liabilities on the balance sheet; calculate the leverage ratio, debt ratio, and times-interest-earned ratio

P8-45A The accounting records of Brighton Foods, Inc., include the following items at December 31, 2017:

Mortgage note payable, current portion	$ 92,000	Total assets	$4,500,000
Accumulated pension benefit obligation	450,000	Accumulated depreciation equipment	166,000
Bonds payable, long-term	200,000	Discount on bonds payable (all long-term)	25,000
Mortgage note payable, long-term	318,000	Operating income	370,000
Bonds payable, current portion	500,000	Equipment	744,000
Interest expense	229,000	Pension plan assets (market value)	420,000
		Interest payable	75,000

Requirements

1. Show how each relevant item would be reported on the Brighton Foods, Inc., classified balance sheet, including headings and totals for current liabilities and long-term liabilities.
2. Answer the following questions about Brighton's financial position at December 31, 2017:
   a. What is the carrying amount of the bonds payable? (Combine the current and long-term amounts.)
   b. Why is the interest-payable amount so much less than the amount of interest expense?
3. How many times did Brighton cover its interest expense during 2017?
4. Assume that all of the existing liabilities are included in the information provided. Calculate the leverage ratio and debt ratio of the company. Evaluate the health of the company from a leverage point of view. What other information would be helpful in making your evaluation?
5. Independent of your answer to (4), assume that Footnote 8 of the financial statements includes commitments for operating leases over the next 15 years in the amount of $3,000,000. If the company had to capitalize these leases in 2017, how would it change the leverage ratio and the debt ratio? How would this change impact your assessment of the company's health from a leverage point of view?

P8-46A The accounting records of Pacer Foods Inc. include the following items at December 31, 2017.

LEARNING OBJECTIVE ❻❽

Report liabilities on the balance sheet; calculate times-interest-earned ratio

Mortgage note payable		Accumulated depreciation	
current	$ 50,000	equipment	$219,000
Bonds payable, long-term	490,000	Discount on bonds payable	
Mortgage note payable		(all long-term)	7,000
long-term	150,000	Operating income......................	291,000
Bonds payable, current portion	70,000	Equipment	487,000
Interest expense.............................	67,000	Interest payable	9,000

Requirements

1. Show how each relevant item would be reported on the Pacer Foods Inc. classified balance sheet, including headings and totals for current liabilities and long-term liabilities.
2. Answer the following questions about Pacer's financial position at December 31, 2017:
   a. What is the carrying amount of the bonds payable? (Combine the current and long-term amounts.)
   b. Why is the interest-payable amount so much less than the amount of interest expense?
3. How many times did Pacer cover its interest expense during 2017?

P8-47A The board of directors of Harmony Electronics authorizes the issue of $8,000,000 of 10%, 25-year bonds payable. The semiannual interest dates are May 31 and November 30. The bonds are issued on May 31, 2016, at par.

LEARNING OBJECTIVES ❶❷

Record bond transactions [at par]; report bonds payable on the balance sheet

Requirements

1. Journalize the following transactions:
   a. Issuance of the bonds on May 31, 2016
   b. Payment of interest on November 30, 2016
   c. Accrual of interest on December 31, 2016
   d. Payment of interest on May 31, 2017
2. Report interest payable and bonds payable as they would appear on the Harmony Electronics balance sheet at December 31, 2016

PROBLEMS (GROUP B)

P8-48B Goldwater Corporation experienced these five events during 2017:

LEARNING OBJECTIVE ❶❽

Measure current liabilities

a. December sales totalled $50,000, and Goldwater collected harmonized sales tax (HST) of 13%. The HST will be remitted to CRA in January 2018. Reporting requirements are the segregation of the provincial portion (8%) and federal portion (5%).
b. On November 30, Goldwater received rent of $6,000 in advance for a lease on unused store space. This rent will be earned evenly over three months.
c. On September 30, Goldwater signed a six-month, 9% note to purchase store fixtures costing $12,000. The note requires payment of principal and interest at maturity.
d. Sales of $400,000 were covered by Goldwater's product warranty. At January 1, estimated warranty payable was $12,400. During the year, Goldwater recorded warranty expense of $22,300 and paid warranty claims of $24,600.
e. Goldwater owes $100,000 on a long-term note. At December 31, 5% interest since July 31 and $20,000 of this principal are payable within one year.

Requirement

For each item, indicate the account and the related amount to be reported as a *current* liability on the Goldwater Corporation balance sheet at December 31, 2017.

LEARNING OBJECTIVE ❶

Record liability-related transactions

P8-49B Assume that the following transactions of Sleuth Book Store occurred during 2017 and 2018:

2017

Jan.   9   Purchased store fixtures at a cost of $50,000, signing an 8%, six-month note for that amount.

June 30   Borrowed $200,000 on a 9% note that calls for annual instalment payments of $50,000 principal plus interest. Record the short-term note payable in a separate account from the long-term note payable.

July   9   Paid the six-month, 8% note at maturity.

Dec. 31   Accrued warranty expense, which is estimated at 3% of sales of $600,000.

       31   Accrued interest on the outstanding note payable.

2018

June 30   Paid the first instalment and interest for one year on the outstanding note payable.

Requirement

Record the transactions in the company's journal. Explanations are not required.

LEARNING OBJECTIVE ❷❸❹❽

Record bond transactions (at face value) and report bonds payable on the balance sheet

P8-50B Assume the board of directors of The Saddledome Foundation authorizes the issue of $1 million of 8%, 20-year bonds. The semi-annual interest dates are March 31 and September 30. The bonds are issued on March 31, 2017, at face value.

Requirements

1. Journalize the following transactions:
    a. Issuance of the bonds on March 31, 2017
    b. Payment of interest on September 30, 2017
    c. Accrual of interest on December 31, 2017
    d. Payment of interest on March 31, 2018
2. Report interest payable and bonds payable as they would appear on the Saddledome Foundation balance sheet at December 31, 2017.

LEARNING OBJECTIVE ❷❸❹❽

Record bond transactions and calculate interest using the straight-line method; report notes payable on the balance sheet

P8-51B On February 28, 2017, Panorama Ltd. issues 7%, 10-year notes with a face value of $300,000. The notes pay interest on February 28 and August 31, and Panorama amortizes notes by the straight-line method.

Requirements

1. If the market interest rate is 6% when Panorama issues its notes, will the notes be priced at face value, a premium, or a discount? Explain.
2. If the market interest rate is 8% when Panorama issues its notes, will the notes be priced at face value, a premium, or a discount? Explain.
3. Assume that the issue price of the notes is 96. Journalize the following note payable transactions:
    a. Issuance of the notes on February 28, 2017
    b. Payment of interest and amortization of the bonds on August 31, 2017
    c. Accrual of interest and amortization of the bonds on December 31, 2017
    d. Payment of interest and amortization of the bonds on February 28, 2018
4. Report interest payable and notes payable as they would appear on Panorama's balance sheet at December 31, 2017.

LEARNING OBJECTIVE ❷❸❹

Account for bonds payable at a discount and amortize by the straight-line method

P8-52B

1. Journalize the following transactions of Farm Equipment Limited:

2017

Jan.   1   Issued $100,000 of 8%, five-year bonds at 94.

July   1   Paid semi-annual interest and amortized the bonds by the straight-line method on our 8% bonds payable.

Dec. 31   Accrued semi-annual interest expense and amortized the bonds by the straight-line method on our 8% bonds payable.

2018
Jan. 1   Paid semi-annual interest.

2022
Jan. 1   Paid the 8% bonds at maturity.

2. At December 31, 2017, after all year-end adjustments, determine the carrying amount of Farm Equipment Limited's bonds payable, net.

3. For the six months ended July 1, 2017, determine the following for Farm Equipment Limited:

a. Interest expense

b. Cash interest paid

What causes interest expense on the bonds to exceed cash interest paid?

P8-53B The notes to the Community Charities financial statements reported the following data on December 31, 2017 (end of the fiscal year):

LEARNING OBJECTIVE ❷❸❹❽

Analyze a company's long-term debt and report the long-term debt on the balance sheet (effective-interest method)

Note D—Long-Term Debt

7% bonds payable, due in 2023	$ 500,000	
Less: Discount..	(26,032)	$473,968
6½% notes payable; principal due in annual amounts of		
$50,000 in 2021 through 2026		300,000

Community Charities amortizes bonds by the effective-interest method and pays all interest amounts at December 31.

Requirements

1. Answer the following questions about Community Charities's long-term liabilities:

a. What is the maturity value of the 7% bonds?

b. What is Community Charities's annual cash interest payment on the 7% bonds?

c. What is the carrying amount of the 7% bonds at December 31, 2017?

2. Prepare an amortization table through December 31, 2020, for the 7% bonds. The market interest rate on the bonds was 8%. Round all amounts to the nearest dollar. How much is Community Charities's interest expense on the 7% bonds for the year ended December 31, 2020?

3. Show how Community Charities would report the 7% bonds payable and the 6½% notes payable at December 31, 2020.

P8-54B Two businesses in very different circumstances are pondering how to raise $2 million.

HighTech.com has fallen on hard times. Net income has been low for the last three years, even falling by 10% from last year's level of profits, and cash flow also took a nose dive. Top management has experienced some turnover and has stabilized only recently. To become competitive again, High Tech needs $2 million to invest in new technology.

Decorator Services is in the midst of its most successful period since it began operations in 2015. Net income has increased by 25%. The outlook for the future is bright with new markets opening up and competitors unable to compete with Decorator. As a result, Decorator is planning a large-scale expansion.

LEARNING OBJECTIVE ❺

Finance operations with debt or shares

Requirement

Propose a plan for each company to raise the needed cash. Which company should borrow? Which company should issue shares? Consider the advantages and disadvantages of raising money by borrowing and by issuing shares, and discuss them in your answer.

LEARNING OBJECTIVE ❶❻❽

Report liabilities on the balance sheet; calculate the leverage ratio, debt ratio, and times-interest-earned ratio

P8-55B The accounting records of Braintree Foods, Inc., include the following items at December 31, 2017:

Mortgage note payable current portion	$ 97,000	Total assets	$4,200,000
Accumulated pension benefit obligation	470,000	Accumulated depreciation equipment	162,000
Bonds payable, long-term	1,680,000	Discount on bonds payable (all long-term)	22,000
Mortgage note payable long-term	314,000	Operating income	390,000
		Equipment	745,000
Bonds payable, current portion	420,000	Pension plan assets (market value)	425,000
Interest expense	227,000	Interest payable	74,000

Requirements

1. Show how each relevant item would be reported on the Braintree Foods, Inc., classified balance sheet, including headings and totals for current liabilities and long-term liabilities.
2. Answer the following questions about Braintree's financial position at December 31, 2017:
   a. What is the carrying amount of the bonds payable? (Combine the current and long-term amounts.)
   b. Why is the interest-payable amount so much less than the amount of interest expense?
3. How many times did Braintree cover its interest expense during 2017?
4. Assume that all of the existing liabilities are included in the information provided. Calculate the leverage ratio and debt ratio of the company. Evaluate the health of the company from a leverage point of view. What other information would be helpful in making your evaluation?
5. Independent of your answer to (4), assume that Footnote 8 of the financial statements includes commitments for operating leases over the next 15 years in the amount of $3,000,000. If the company had to capitalize these leases in 2017, how would it change the leverage ratio and the debt ratio? How would this change impact your assessment of the company's health from a leverage point of view?

LEARNING OBJECTIVE ❻❽

Report liabilities on the balance sheet; calculate times-interest-earned ratio

P8-56B The accounting records of Toronto Financial Services include the following items at December 31, 2017:

Premium on bonds payable (all long-term)	$ 13,000
Interest payable	3,900
Operating income	104,000
Interest expense	39,000
Bonds payable, current portion	50,000
Accumulated depreciation, building	70,000
Mortgage note payable, long-term	215,000
Bonds payable, long-term	250,000
Building	160,000

Requirements

1. Show how each relevant item would be reported on Toronto Financial Services's classified balance sheet. Include headings and totals for current liabilities and long-term liabilities.
2. Answer the following questions about the financial position of Toronto Financial Services at December 31, 2017:
   a. What is the carrying amount of the bonds payable? (Combine the current and long-term amounts.)
   b. Why is the interest payable amount so much less than the amount of interest expense? (Challenge)
3. How many times did Toronto cover its interest expense during 2017?

P8-57B The board of directors of Laptops Plus authorizes the issue of $9,000,000 of 7%, 15-year bonds payable. The semiannual interest dates are May 31 and November 30. The bonds are issued on May 31, 2016, at face value.

Requirements

1. Journalize the following transactions:
   a. Issuance of half of the bonds on May 31, 2016
   b. Payment of interest on November 30, 2016
   c. Accrual of interest on December 31, 2016
   d. Payment of interest on May 31, 2017
2. Report interest payable and bonds payable as they would appear on the Laptops Plus balance sheet at December 31, 2016.

LEARNING OBJECTIVES ①②

Record bond transactions [at par]; report bonds payable on the balance sheet)

APPLY YOUR KNOWLEDGE

DECISION CASES

This section's material reflects CPA enabling competencies,* including:

1. Professionalism and ethical behaviour
2. Problem-solving and decision-making
4. Self-management
5. Teamwork and leadership

Case 1. In 2001, Enron Corporation filed for Chapter 11 bankruptcy protection, shocking the business community: How could a company this large and this successful go bankrupt? This case explores the causes and the effects of Enron's bankruptcy.

At December 31, 2000, and for the four years ended on that date, Enron reported the following (amounts in millions):

Balance Sheet (summarized)

Total assets	$65,503
Total liabilities	54,033
Total shareholders' equity	11,470

Income Statements (excerpts)

	2000	1999	1998	1997
Net income	$ 979*	$893	$703	$105
Revenues	100,789			

*Operating Income = $1,953
Interest expense = $838

LEARNING OBJECTIVE ⑥

Explore an actual bankruptcy; calculate leverage ratio, ROA debt ratio, and times-interest-earned ratio

Unknown to investors and lenders, Enron also controlled hundreds of partnerships that owed vast amounts of money. These special-purpose entities (SPEs) did not appear on the Enron financial statements. Assume that the SPEs' assets totalled $7,000 million and their liabilities stood at $6,900 million; assume a 10% interest rate on these liabilities.

During the four-year period up to December 31, 2000, Enron's stock price shot up from $17.50 to $90.56. Enron used its escalating stock price to finance the purchase of the SPEs by guaranteeing lenders that Enron would give them Enron stock if the SPEs could not pay their loans.

In 2002, the SEC launched an investigation into Enron's accounting practices. It was alleged that Enron should have been including the SPEs in its financial statements all along. Enron then restated net income for years up to 2000, wiping out nearly $600 million of total net income (and total assets) for this four-year period. Assume that $300 million of this loss applied to 2000. Enron's stock price tumbled, and the guarantees to the SPEs' lenders added millions to Enron's liabilities (assume the full amount of the SPEs' debt). To make matters worse, the assets of the SPEs lost much of their value; assume that their market value is only $500 million.

Requirements

1. Compute the debt ratio that Enron reported at the end of 2000. Compute Enron's return on total assets (ROA) for 2000. For this purpose, use only total assets at the end of 2000, rather than the average of 1999 and 2000.

*© Chartered Professional Accountants of Canada.

2. Compute Enron's leverage ratio. Now compute Enron's return on equity (ROE) by multiplying the ROA computed in part 1 by the leverage ratio. Can you see anything unusual in these ratios that might have caused you to question them? Why or why not?

3. Add the asset and liability information about the SPEs to the reported amounts provided in the table. Recompute all ratios after including the SPEs in Enron's financial statements. Also, compute Enron's times-interest-earned ratio both ways for 2000. Assume that the changes to Enron's financial position occurred during 2000.

4. Why does it appear that Enron failed to include the SPEs in its financial statements? How do you view Enron after including the SPEs in the company's financial statements? (Challenge)

LEARNING OBJECTIVE ❺

Analyze alternative ways of raising $5 million

Case 2. Business is going well for Park'N Fly, the company that operates remote parking lots near major airports. The board of directors of this family-owned company believes that Park'N Fly could earn an additional $2 million income before interest and taxes by expanding into new markets. However, the $5 million that the business needs for growth cannot be raised within the family. The directors, who strongly wish to retain family control of the company, must consider issuing securities to outsiders. The directors are considering three financing plans.

Plan A is to borrow at 6%. Plan B is to issue 100,000 common shares. Plan C is to issue 100,000 non-voting, $3.75 preferred shares ($3.75 is the annual dividend paid on each preferred share).* Park'N Fly currently has net income of $3.5 million and 1 million common shares outstanding. The company's income tax rate is 25%.

Requirements

1. Prepare an analysis to determine which plan will result in the highest earnings per common share.

2. Recommend one plan to the board of directors. Give your reasons.

ETHICAL ISSUES

Issue 1: Microsoft Corporation is the defendant in numerous lawsuits claiming unfair trade practices. Microsoft has strong incentives not to disclose these contingent liabilities; however, IFRS and ASPE generally require that companies disclose their contingent liabilities in the notes to their financial statements.

Requirements

1. Why would a company prefer not to disclose its contingent liabilities?

2. Describe how a bank could be harmed if a company seeking a loan did not disclose its contingent liabilities.

3. What is the ethical tightrope that companies must walk when they report their contingent liabilities?

Issue 2: The top managers of Medtech.com borrowed heavily to develop a prescription-medicine distribution system. Medtech's outlook was bright, and investors poured millions into the company. Sadly, Medtech never lived up to its potential, and the company is in bankruptcy. It can't pay about half of its liabilities.

Requirement

Is it unethical for managers to saddle a company with a high level of debt? Or, is it just risky? Who could be hurt by a company's taking on too much debt? Discuss.

---

*For a discussion of preferred shares, see Chapter 9.

FOCUS ON FINANCIALS

Canadian Tire Corporation

Refer to Canadian Tire's financial statements in Appendix A at the end of this book.

1. Canadian Tire's balance sheet reports a current portion of long-term debt under current liabilities. Why is this portion of long-term debt reported as a current liability?
2. Canadian Tire's Notes to the Financial Statements include note 36, "Operating leases." What information does this provide to the user of these financial statements?

LEARNING OBJECTIVE ❶❽
Report current and long-term liabilities
MyAccountingLab

FOCUS ON ANALYSIS

Canadian Tire Corporation

How would you rate Canadian Tire's debt-paying ability at the end of 2014: excellent, neutral, or poor? Support your conclusion with relevant ratios.

LEARNING OBJECTIVE ❶❻❽
Record and analyze liabilities
MyAccountingLab

GROUP PROJECTS

Project 1. Use the Internet to locate financial statements for a company in each of the following industries:

1. A bank
2. A magazine publisher
3. A department store

For each business, list all its liabilities—both current and long-term. Then compare the three lists to identify the liabilities that the three businesses have in common. Also, identify the liabilities that are unique to each type of business.

CHECK YOUR WORK

STOP + THINK ANSWERS

STOP + THINK (8-1)

1. $1,198 million ($150 current portion + $1,048 long-term portion)
2. Pay by September 30, 2016: $150 million; pay thereafter: $1,048 million

STOP + THINK (8-2)

1. The bond would be issued at a discount because the market rate is less than the stated rate.
2. The bond would be issued at a premium because the market rate is greater than the stated rate.
3. You would pay $224,375 ($250,000 * .8975).
4. You would pay $177,187.50 ($175,000 * 1.0125).

STOP + THINK (8-3)

Date	Account Titles and Explanation	Debit	Credit
2017			
a. May 1	Cash..............................	10,000	
	Bonds Payable..............		10,000
	To issue bond at face value.		
2017			
b. Oct. 31	Interest Expense ($10,000 × 0.0725 × 6/12)	363	
	Interest Payable.............		363
	To accrue interest expense.		

Date	Account Titles and Explanation	Debit	Credit
2017			
c. Nov. 1	Interest Payable..................	363	
	Cash.............................		363
	To pay semiannual interest on bonds.		
2022			
d. May 1	Bonds Payable	10,000	
	Cash.............................		10,000
	To pay bonds at maturity.		

STOP + THINK (8-4)

Income Statement for 2017

Interest expense ($4,807 + $4,823)	$9,630

Balance Sheet at December 31, 2017

Current liabilities:		
Interest payable		$4,500
Long-term liabilities:		
Bonds payable	$100,000	
Less: Discount on bonds payable	(3,221)	96,779

STOP + THINK (8-5)

	Company A	Company B
Debt ratio	86.0%	58.2%
Leverage ratio	7.14	2.39
Times-interest-earned ratio	2.39	5.06

Based on the ratios above, Company B shows a higher debt-paying ability, so it would present a lower risk to the bank than Company A. B's debt ratio is within the comfort range of 60%–70%, whereas A's is well above this range at 86%. A is also more highly leveraged than B (7.14 vs. 2.39) and has a much lower interest-coverage ratio, at only 2.39 compared to B's much more comfortable ratio of 5.06. I would therefore prefer to loan money to the less-risky Company B.

STOP + THINK (8-6)

1. **a.** Current liability: Estimated warranty payable [$40,000 + ($4,000,000 × 0.04) − $80,000]........................... 120,000
   b. Current liability: Current portion of long-term note payable. 40,000
   Current liability: Interest payable ($200,000 × 0.06 × 1/12) 1,000
   Long-term liability: Note payable ($200,000 − $40,000)......................... 160,000
   c. Current liability: Unearned sales revenue ($150,000 − $100,000)....................... 50,000
   d. Current liability: Employee withholdings and company CPP & EI....................... 35,000
   Current liability: Employee Benefits Payable 11,000

2. Total current liabilities: $257,000

QUICK QUIZ ANSWERS

1. *a*
2. *d*
3. *b*
4. *b*
5. *a*
6. *c* [($500,000 + $700,000) × 0.08] − $4,000 − $32,000 = $60,000
7. *a*
8. *d*
9. *f*
10. *a*
11. *c*
12. *d* ($100,000 × 0.10) + [($100,000 − $97,000) / 15] = $10,200

13. Interest Expense 7,650
    Discount on Bonds Payable ($3,000/15 × 9/12)................................. 150
    Interest Payable ($100,000 × 0.10 × 9/12).. 7,500

14. Interest Payable 7,500
    Interest Expense 2,550
    Discount on Bonds Payable ($3,000/15 × 3/12)................................ 50
    Cash ($100,000 × 0.10) 10,000

15. *e* ($92,280 × 0.12 × 6/12 = $5,537)
16. *d*
17. *a*
18. *c*
19. *c*

Shareholders' Equity

Kevin Brine - Editorial/Alamy Stock Photo

CPA COMPETENCIES

Competencies* addressed in this chapter:

1.1.1 Evaluates financial reporting needs

1.2.2 Evaluates treatment for routine transactions

1.4.4 Interprets financial reporting results for stakeholders (external or internal)

SPOTLIGHT

Canadian Tire Corporation was founded in Toronto in 1923 by John W. and Alfred J. Billes. In its early days, the Billes brothers were the company's only shareholders. Canadian Tire is now a widely held public company with tens of thousands of shareholders. During 2014, there were several changes in Canadian Tire's shareholders' equity accounts. By the end of this chapter, you should be able to explain and account for many of these changes.

In this chapter, we'll show you how companies like Canadian Tire account for the issuance of shares to investors. We'll also discuss other major components of shareholders' equity, such as Contributed Surplus and Retained Earnings, plus dividends and stock splits. In addition, you will learn how to interpret information about a company's share price and performance to decide if you'd want to buy shares in a company like Canadian Tire. On the next page, you'll find details on the company's shareholders' equity as at January 3, 2015.

	A	B	C	D
1	**Canadian Tire Corporation** Shareholders' Equity (Adapted)			
2	*(in millions)*	January 3, 2015*	December 28, 2013*	

3	Class A non-voting share capital
	  Authorized: 100,000,000 Class A non-voting shares
	  without par value; issued and outstanding: 74,023,208
	  and 76,560,851 shares at January 3, 2015 and
	  December 28, 2013, respectively; fixed cumulative
	  preferential dividend of $0.01 per share per annum
		695.3	712.7	

4	Common share capital
	  Authorized: 3,423,366 common shares without par value;
	  issued and outstanding: 3,423,366 shares at
	  January 3, 2015 and December 28, 2013
		0.2	0.2	

5	Contributed surplus	2.9	2.4	
6	Accumulated other comprehensive income	82.0	47.4	
7	Retained earnings	4,075.1	4,404.6	
8	Non-controlling interests	775.3	282.6	
9		5,630.8	5,449.9	
10				

*Recall that Canadian Tire's fiscal year ends on the Saturday closest to December 31, so its 2014 fiscal year ended on January 3, 2015, and its 2013 year on December 28, 2013. Within this chapter, these years will be referred to as 2014 and 2013, respectively.

Source: Reprinted with permission from Canadian Tire Corporation.

Chapters 4 to 8 discussed accounting for assets and liabilities. By this time, you should be familiar with most of the assets and liabilities listed on Canadian Tire's balance sheet, so we will now focus on the major components of shareholders' equity. In this chapter, we discuss some of the issues a company faces when issuing shares and paying dividends.

Let's begin by looking at the key features of a corporation.

OBJECTIVE

❶ **Explain** the main features of a corporation

EXPLAIN THE MAIN FEATURES OF A CORPORATION

Anyone starting a business must decide how to organize the company. Corporations differ from proprietorships and partnerships in several ways.

SEPARATE LEGAL ENTITY. A corporation is a business entity formed under federal or provincial law. The federal or provincial government grants *articles of incorporation*, which consist of documents giving the governing body permission to form a corporation. A corporation is a distinct entity, an artificial person that exists apart from its owners, the shareholders. The corporation has many of the same rights as a person. For example, a corporation may buy, own, and sell property. Assets and liabilities in the business belong to the corporation, not to its owners. The corporation may also enter into contracts, sue, and be sued.

Nearly all well-known companies, including Canadian Tire, WestJet, and Loblaws, are corporations. Their legal names include *Limited*, *Corporation*, or *Incorporated* at the end (abbreviated *Ltd.*, *Corp.*, and *Inc.*) to indicate that they are corporations.

CONTINUOUS LIFE AND TRANSFERABILITY OF OWNERSHIP. Corporations have *continuous lives* regardless of changes in their ownership. The shareholders of a corporation may transfer shares as they wish. They may sell or trade the shares to another person, give them away, bequeath them in a will, or dispose of them in any other way. The transfer of the shares from one person to another does not affect the continuity of the corporation. In contrast, proprietorships and partnerships terminate when ownership changes.

LIMITED LIABILITY. Shareholders have **limited liability** for the corporation's debts, so they have no personal obligation to repay the company's liabilities. The most that a shareholder can lose on an investment in a corporation's shares is the cost of the investment. Limited liability is one of the most attractive features of the corporate form of organization. It enables corporations to raise more capital from a wider group of investors than proprietorships and partnerships. In contrast, proprietors and partners are personally liable for all the debts of their businesses (unless the business is organized as a limited liability partnership [LLP] or a limited liability company [LLC]).

SEPARATION OF OWNERSHIP AND MANAGEMENT. Shareholders own the corporation, but a *board of directors*—elected by the shareholders—appoints officers to manage the business. Thus, shareholders may invest $1,000 or $1 million in the corporation without having to manage it.

Company managers should run the business in the best interests of its shareholders, who rightfully own the company, but the separation between owners and managers may create problems. Corporate officers may run the business for their own benefit and not for the shareholders'. For example, the chief financial officer of Enron Corporation set up deals between Enron and several partnerships that he personally owned, enriching himself in the process, but harming the company and shareholders he worked for.

Some managers believe that their goal is to maximize the firm's value. Other managers believe that they should consider some or all of the other stakeholders of the corporation, such as employees, customers, the community where the company is located, and the environment.

CORPORATE TAXATION. Because corporations are separate legal entities, they must pay income taxes separate from those borne by their individual shareholders. Sole proprietors and partners pay individual income taxes based on their share of the business's income.

GOVERNMENT REGULATION. Because shareholders have only limited liability for corporation debts, outsiders doing business with the corporation can look no further than the corporation if it fails to pay. To protect a corporation's creditors and the shareholders, both federal and provincial governments monitor corporations. This regulation consists mainly of ensuring that corporations disclose the information in financial statements that investors and creditors need to make informed decisions.

Exhibit 9-1 summarizes the advantages and disadvantages of the corporate form of business organization.

EXHIBIT 9-1
Advantages and
Disadvantages of a
Corporation

Advantages	Disadvantages
1. Can raise more capital than a proprietorship or partnership	1. Separation of ownership and management
2. Continuous life	2. Corporate taxation
3. Ease of transferring ownership	3. Government regulation
4. Limited liability of shareholders	

Controlling and Managing a Corporation

The ultimate control of a corporation rests with the shareholders. The shareholders elect a *board of directors*, which sets the company policy and appoints officers. The board elects a **chairperson**, who usually is the most powerful person in the organization. The board also appoints the chief executive officer (CEO), who often also acts as the **president** in charge of day-to-day operations. Large corporations may also have vice-presidents in charge of sales, manufacturing, accounting and finance (the chief financial officer, or CFO), and other key areas. Exhibit 9-2 shows the authority structure in a large corporation.

EXHIBIT 9-2
Authority Structure in
a Large Corporation

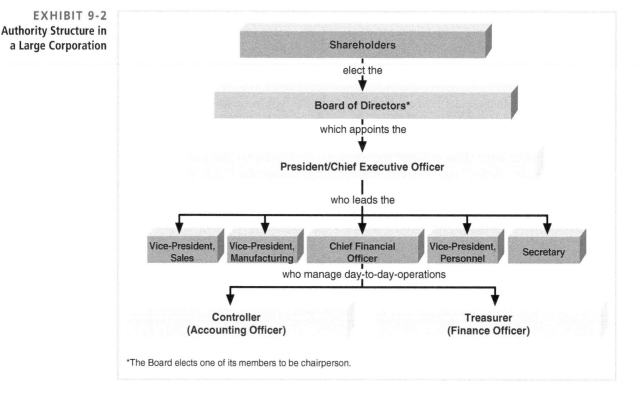

Shareholders' Rights

Ownership of shares entitles shareholders to four basic rights, unless specific rights are withheld by agreement with the shareholders:

1. *The right to sell the shares.* Shareholders have the right to sell their shares to other parties when they no longer wish to own them.

2. *The right to vote.* Shareholders have the right to participate in management by voting on matters that come before them. This is the shareholder's sole voice in the management of the corporation. A shareholder is normally entitled to one vote for each common share owned. There are some classes of common shares that give the holder multiple votes or no vote.

3. *The right to receive dividends.* Shareholders have the right to receive a proportionate share of any distributions from the company's retained earnings. Each share in a particular class receives an equal dividend.

4. *The right to receive a residual interest upon liquidation.* Shareholders have the right to receive a proportionate share of any assets remaining after the corporation pays all liabilities upon liquidation. When a company goes out of business, it sells its assets, pays its liabilities, and distributes any residual (or remaining) assets to shareholders.

Shareholders' Equity

As we saw in Chapter 1, *shareholders' equity* represents the shareholders' ownership interest in the assets of a corporation. Shareholders' equity has four common and separate components:

1. *Share capital*—amounts contributed by shareholders in exchange for shares in the corporation.

2. *Contributed surplus*—any amounts contributed by shareholders in excess of amounts allocated to share capital.

3. *Accumulated other comprehensive income*—IFRS require companies to report Accumulated Other Comprehensive Income, which is an accumulation of past earnings not included in retained earnings. This equity item requires an advanced understanding of accounting concepts, so it will not be covered in this textbook. ASPE do not require companies to account for this item.

4. *Retained earnings*—the accumulated balance of a corporation's net income since inception, less any net losses and dividends declared during this time. When the accumulation is a negative number, the term *deficit* is used to describe it.

A corporation issues *share certificates* to its owners in exchange for their investment in the business—usually cash. The basic unit of share capital is called a *share*. A corporation may issue a share certificate for any number of shares it wishes—one share, 100 shares, or any other number—but the total number of *authorized* shares is limited by charter. Shares are sometimes referred to as *stock*, particularly in the United States, but owning stock in a company means the same thing as owning shares in that company.

The terms *authorized*, *issued*, and *outstanding* are frequently used to describe a corporation's shares. *Authorized* refers to the maximum number of shares a corporation is allowed to distribute to shareholders. Companies incorporated under the *Canada Business Corporations Act* are permitted to issue an unlimited number of shares. *Issued* refers to the number of shares sold or transferred to shareholders. *Outstanding shares* are those actually in the hands of shareholders. Sometimes a company repurchases shares it has previously issued so that the number of shares outstanding will be less than the number of shares issued. For example, if a corporation issued 100,000 shares and later repurchased 20,000 shares, then the number of shares outstanding would be 80,000. The total number of shares outstanding at any time represents 100% ownership of the corporation.

Classes of Shares

Corporations issue different types of shares to appeal to a variety of investors. Every corporation issues *common shares*, which IFRS also refer to as *ordinary shares*, meaning they are subordinate to all other classes of shares a company is authorized to issue.

Unless designated otherwise, the word *share* is understood to mean "common share." Common shareholders have the four basic rights of share ownership, unless a right is specifically withheld. For example, some companies, including Canadian Tire, issue voting and non-voting common shares. In describing a corporation, we would say the common shareholders are the owners of the business. They stand to benefit the most if the corporation succeeds because they take the most risk by investing in common shares. The shares of a corporation may be either common shares or preferred shares.

Preferred shares give their owners certain advantages over common shareholders. Preferred shareholders receive dividends before the common shareholders and receive assets before the common shareholders if the corporation liquidates. Preferred shares are typically non-voting shares, but they have the other three basic shareholder rights. Companies may issue different classes of preferred shares (Class A and Class B or Series A and Series B, for example). Each class is recorded in a separate account.

Preferred shares are a hybrid of common shares and long-term debt. Like debt, preferred shares pay a fixed amount to the investor in the form of a dividend. Like common shares, the dividend does not have to be paid unless the board of directors has declared the dividend. Also, companies have no obligation to pay back true preferred shares. Preferred shares that must be redeemed (paid back) by the corporation are a liability masquerading as a stock and must be accounted for as such.

Preferred shares are much less frequently issued than common shares. A recent survey of over 600 companies found that fewer than 10% of them had issued preferred shares. TELUS, for example, is authorized to issue 2 billion preferred shares, but as at the end of 2014, none of them have actually been issued.

PAR VALUE AND STATED VALUE. **Par value shares** are shares of stock that have a value assigned to them by the articles of incorporation, which specify the legal details associated with a company's incorporation. *The Canada Business Corporations Act* and most provincial incorporating acts now require common and preferred shares to be issued without par value. Neither Canadian Tire's common nor its non-voting shares have a par value. Instead, the shares are assigned a value when they are issued; this value is known as the **stated value**.

STOP + THINK (9-1)

At the end of its 2014 fiscal year, Canadian Tire had 3.4 million voting regular common shares outstanding and 74 million non-voting Class A common shares outstanding. Why would so many investors be interested in owning Canadian Tire's Class A shares, given they do not get to vote on how the company is governed and managed?

OBJECTIVE

❷ **Account** for the issuance of shares

ACCOUNT FOR THE ISSUANCE OF SHARES

Large corporations, such as Hudson's Bay Company and EnCana Corp., need huge amounts of money to operate. Such corporations usually sell their newly issued shares though an *underwriter*, such as the brokerage firms ScotiaMcLeod and BMO Nesbitt Burns.

ISSUING SHARES FOR CASH. Suppose that on January 8, 2017, George Weston Ltd. issued 100,000 common shares for cash for $50 each. The entry to record the issuance of these shares is:

	A	B	C	D	E
1	2017				
2	Jan. 8	Cash	5,000,000		
3		Common Share Capital		5,000,000	
4		To issue common shares at $50.00 per share (100,000 × $50.00).			
5					

ASSETS	=	LIABILITIES	+	SHAREHOLDERS' EQUITY	
+5,000,000	=		+	5,000,000	Share Capital

After this transaction, the number of common shares outstanding would increase by 100,000, and the company's common share capital would increase by $5,000,000.

It is important to note that when one shareholder of a company sells some of their shares to another shareholder, there is no impact on the accounts of the company due to the separate-entity concept, which was introduced in Chapter 1. Only when a company is party to a share transaction are its accounts affected.

STOP + THINK (9-2)

Examine the details of Canadian Tire's Shareholders' Equity on page 436, then answer these questions:

1. How many more Class A non-voting shares is Canadian Tire legally allowed to issue if it wants to raise more capital?

2. Assuming no shares were repurchased in 2014, how many common shares did Canadian Tire issue in 2014?

3. What is the average issue price of each of the two types of Canadian Tire shares outstanding?

ISSUING SHARES FOR ASSETS OTHER THAN CASH. Companies sometimes issue shares in return for assets other than cash. When a transaction like this occurs, the company is required to measure the transaction based on the fair value of the assets received. If that fair value cannot be determined, the fair value of the shares given up will be the value assigned to the transaction.

For example, if on November 12, 2017, Kahn Corporation issued 15,000 common shares in return for equipment worth $4,000 and a building worth $120,000, it would record this entry:

	A	B	C	D	E
1	2017				
2	Nov. 12	Equipment	4,000		
3		Building	120,000		
4		Common Share Capital		124,000	
5		To issue common shares in exchange for equipment and a building.			
6					

ASSETS	=	LIABILITIES	=	SHAREHOLDERS' EQUITY	
+4,000 +120,000	=			+124,000	Share capital

Accounting for the issuance of preferred shares (or other kinds of non-voting shares) for cash or other assets is the same as that for common shares, except for the name of the share capital account used, which will match the type of shares being issued.

COOKING *the* BOOKS

with Share Capital

The issuance of shares for *cash* poses no ethical challenge. There is no difficulty in valuing shares issued for cash because the value of the cash—and therefore the shares—is obvious.

Issuing shares for *assets other than cash*, however, can pose an ethical challenge. The company issuing the shares often wishes to record a large amount for the non-cash asset received (such as land or a building) and for the shares that it is issuing. Why? Because large asset and shareholders' equity amounts on the balance sheet make the business look more prosperous and more creditworthy.

A company is supposed to record an asset received at its current fair value. But one person's perception of a particular asset's fair value can differ from another person's opinion. One person may appraise land at a fair value of $400,000. Another may honestly believe the land is worth only $300,000. A company receiving land in exchange for its shares must decide whether to record the land received and the shares issued at $300,000, at $400,000, or at some amount in between.

The ethical course of action is to record the asset at its current fair value, as determined by a good-faith estimate of fair value from independent appraisers. It is rare for a corporation to be found guilty of *understating* the asset values on its balance sheet, but companies have been embarrassed by *overstating* these values. Investors who rely on the financial statements may be able to prove in court that an overstatement of asset values caused them to pay too much for the company's shares. Creditors who rely on financial statements may also be able to prove in court that an overstatement of asset values caused them to loan the corporation more than if the asset values were correctly stated. In both cases, the court may render a judgment against the company. For this reason, companies often value assets conservatively.

MyAccountingLab

MID-CHAPTER SUMMARY PROBLEM

1. Test your understanding of the first half of this chapter by deciding whether each of the following statements is true or false.
   a. The policy-making body in a corporation is called the board of directors.
   b. The owner of 100 preferred shares has greater voting rights than the owner of 100 common shares.
   c. Issuance of 1,000 common shares at $12 per share increases share capital by $12,000.
   d. A corporation issues its preferred shares in exchange for land and a building with a combined fair value of $200,000. This transaction increases the corporation's owners' equity by $200,000 regardless of the assets' prior book values.
   e. Preferred shares are a riskier investment than common shares.

2. Adolfo Inc., an auto parts manufacturer, has two classes of common shares. Class A shares are entitled to one vote, whereas Class B shares are entitled to 100 votes. The two classes rank equally for dividends. The following is extracted from a recent annual report:

Shareholders' Equity

Share capital	
Class A common shares, no stated value (authorized and issued 1,260 shares)....	$ 1,260
Class B common shares, no stated value (authorized and issued 46,200 shares)....	11,000
	12,260
Retained earnings	872,403
	$884,663

Requirements

a. Record the issuance of the Class A common shares. Use the Adolfo Inc. account titles.

b. Record the issuance of the Class B common shares. Use the Adolfo Inc. account titles.

c. How much of Adolfo Inc.'s shareholders' equity was contributed by the shareholders? How much was provided by profitable operations? Does this division of equity suggest that the company has been successful? Why or why not?

d. Write a sentence to describe what Adolfo Inc.'s shareholders' equity balance means.

ANSWERS

1. a. True   b. False (preferred shares typically do not have voting rights)   c. True
   d. True   e. False (preferred shares typically have a fixed dividend right and first claim to residual assets upon dissolution or liquidation of the company)

2. a. Cash.. 1,260

       Class A Common Shares... 1,260

       To record issuance of Class A common shares.

   b. Cash 11,000

       Class B Common Shares 11,000

       To record issuance of Class B common shares.

   c. Contributed by the shareholders: $12,260 ($1,260 + $11,000).
   Provided by profitable operations: $872,403.
   This division suggests that the company has been successful because almost all of its shareholders' equity has come from profitable operations.

   d. The total of Adolfo's shareholders' equity indicates that the shareholders have a claim to $884,663 of the company's assets.

> a. and b. Share issuances increase assets (cash) and shareholders' equity.

> Compare the fraction of shareholders' equity contributed by shareholders to the fraction contributed by retained earnings. A greater retained earnings fraction is positive.

> Shareholders' equity is the net worth of the company (Assets – Liabilities).

EXPLAIN WHY A COMPANY REPURCHASES SHARES

OBJECTIVE

3 **Explain** why a company repurchases shares

Corporations may repurchase their own shares for several reasons:

1. The company needs the **repurchased shares** to fulfill future share issuance commitments, such as those related to share option plans and conversions of bonds and preferred shares into common shares.

2. The purchase may help support the share's current **market price** by decreasing the supply of shares available to the public, which will usually result in an increase in the market price per share.

3. Management wants to avoid a takeover by an outside party, so it repurchases a significant proportion of its own shares to prevent the other party from acquiring them.

In basic terms, when a company repurchases shares, share capital and total shareholders' equity decrease, but the actual IFRS guidance on accounting for share repurchases is vague and sometimes difficult to interpret. In addition, ASPE offer two choices for how to account for repurchases, both of which differ from IFRS guidance. Given the complex and differing treatments of share repurchases, accounting for them will be left for those students who take intermediate financial accounting.

STOP + THINK (9-3)

During the fiscal years 2014 through 2016, Canadian Tire repurchased millions of its Class A non-voting shares. Search the Web to find out why Canadian Tire regularly repurchased these Class A shares. Is the reason consistent with any of the reasons cited above?

ACCOUNT FOR RETAINED EARNINGS, DIVIDENDS, AND STOCK SPLITS

The Retained Earnings account carries the accumulated balance of the corporation's net income less its net losses and any dividends declared over its lifetime. *The Retained Earnings account is not a reservoir of cash available for paying dividends or investing in other business activities.* In fact, the corporation may have a large balance in Retained Earnings, but not have any cash for dividends or investing. *Cash and Retained Earnings are two entirely separate accounts with no relationship to each other.* A $500,000 balance in Retained Earnings says nothing about the company's Cash balance.

A *credit* balance in Retained Earnings is normal, indicating that the corporation's lifetime earnings exceed its lifetime losses and dividends. A *debit* balance in Retained Earnings arises when a corporation's lifetime losses and dividends exceed its lifetime earnings. Called a **deficit**, this amount is subtracted from the sum of the other equity accounts to determine total shareholders' equity. Deficits are not uncommon.

Declaring and Paying Dividends

Corporations distribute past earnings to shareholders by declaring and then paying *dividends*. The majority of dividends are paid in cash, but companies sometimes pay stock dividends as well. In this section, we first present the accounting for cash dividends and then show you how to account for stock dividends.

Cash Dividends

Before a company can pay a cash dividend, it must have:

1. retained Earnings in excess of the desired dividend and
2. enough Cash to pay the dividend.

A corporation *declares* a dividend before paying it, and only the board of directors has the authority to declare a dividend. The corporation has no obligation to pay a dividend until the board declares one, but once declared, the dividend becomes a legal liability of the corporation. There are three relevant dates for dividends: the *date of declaration*, the *date of record*, and the *date of payment*. The following example illustrates the distinction between these dates.

1. The **date of declaration** is the date on which the board of directors officially declares the payment of a dividend, creating a liability for the amount declared. If the board declares a dividend of $50,000 on June 19, 2017, the entry to account for it is:

	A	B	C	D	E
1	June 19	Retained Earnings*	50,000		
2		Dividends Payable		50,000	
3		*Declared a cash dividend.*			
4					

*In Chapter 2, we debited a Dividends account to clearly identify the purpose of the payment. From here on, we follow the more common practice of debiting the Retained Earnings account for dividend declarations.

ASSETS = **LIABILITIES** + **SHAREHOLDERS' EQUITY**
    0   =   +50,000   −50,000 Retained Earnings

2. The **date of record** follows the declaration date. In order to receive the declared dividend, one must be officially registered as a shareholder of the company on this date. Let's assume the date of record in our illustration is July 1. This date has no accounting implications, so no entry is needed.

3. The **date of payment** is the date on which the dividend is actually paid to shareholders. If the $50,000 dividend declared on June 19 to shareholders of record on July 1 is paid on July 10, the entry would be:

	A	B	C	D	E
1	July 10	Dividends Payable	50,000		
2		Cash		50,000	
3		*Paid cash dividend.*			
4					

ASSETS = **LIABILITIES** + **SHAREHOLDERS' EQUITY**
  −50,000   =   −50,000

The preceding illustration applies to cash dividends declared and paid on any type of shares.

Stock Dividends

When a company declares a **stock dividend**, it eventually pays the dividend by issuing additional shares of the company instead of by distributing cash. The total dollar value of a stock dividend is determined by multiplying the number of shares to be issued by the market price of the shares on the date of declaration. For example, if a stock dividend totalling 100,000 shares is declared on a day when the shares are valued at $10 each, then the amount of the dividend would be $1,000,000.

The relevant dates for stock dividends are the same as those for cash dividends, but the journal entries differ. On the date of declaration, we debit Retained Earnings and credit Stock Dividends Distributable (a contra-equity account). On the date of payment, we debit Stock Dividends Distributable and credit the relevant Share Capital account. A stock dividend, therefore, has no impact on the total shareholders' equity balance because Share Capital increases and Retained Earnings decreases by the same amount.

The corporation distributes stock dividends to shareholders in proportion to the number of shares they already own. If you own 300 common shares of TELUS, for example, and TELUS distributes a 10% common shares dividend, you will receive

30 (300 × 0.10) additional shares. You would then own 330 common shares. All other TELUS shareholders would also receive additional shares equal to 10% of their prior holdings.

Why would a company issue a stock dividend instead of a cash dividend? A corporation may choose to distribute stock dividends for the following reasons:

1. **To continue dividends but conserve cash.** A company may wish to conserve cash to fund its business activities while still distributing dividends to its shareholders. It can achieve these goals by issuing a stock dividend. Shareholders pay tax on stock dividends the same way they pay tax on cash dividends.

2. **To reduce the per-share market price of its shares.** When a company issues a stock dividend, the number of shares issued and outstanding increases, but the market value of the company does not change. As a result, the market value of each outstanding share will be lower after the distribution of a stock dividend. This makes the company's shares less expensive, and therefore more affordable to some investors. Assume, for example, that a company with 100,000 common shares outstanding and a market value of $1,000,000 declares and pays a 10% stock dividend. Before the dividend, the market value per share is $10 ($1,000,000/100,000 shares), but after the dividend it is only $9.09 ($1,000,000/110,000 shares).

STOP + THINK (9-4)

Company A and Company B both have 200,000 common shares outstanding. On June 30, Company A declares a 10% stock dividend and Company B declares a 20% stock dividend.

The common shares of both companies have a $10 market value per share on this date.

1. Which company's shareholders' equity will decrease the most after distributing these stock dividends?

2. Which company will have a lower market value per share after distributing these dividends?

Dividends on Preferred Shares

EXPRESSING THE DIVIDEND ON PREFERRED SHARES. Dividends on preferred shares are expressed as an annual dollar figure or as a percentage of the share's stated value. Scotiabank, for example, had some $1.40 preferred shares outstanding in October 2015, indicating that the holder of one of these shares could receive $1.40 in dividends per year.

DIVIDENDS ON PREFERRED AND COMMON SHARES. When a company has issued both preferred and common shares, the preferred shareholders receive their dividends first. The common shareholders receive dividends only if the total declared dividend is large enough to pay the preferred shareholders in full.

Pinecraft Industries Inc. has 100,000 shares of $1.50 cumulative preferred shares outstanding in addition to its common shares. Assume that in 2017, Pinecraft declares an annual dividend of $1,000,000. The allocation to preferred and common shareholders is as follows:

Preferred dividend (100,000 shares × $1.50 per share)	$ 150,000
Common dividend (remainder: $1,000,000 − $150,000)	850,000
Total dividend	$1,000,000

If Pinecraft declares only a $200,000 dividend, preferred shareholders receive $150,000, and the common shareholders receive the remaining, $50,000 ($200,000 − $150,000). A dividend of $150,000 or less would result in the common shareholders receiving no dividend.

DIVIDENDS ON CUMULATIVE AND NON-CUMULATIVE PREFERRED SHARES. The allocation of dividends may be complex if the preferred shares are *cumulative*. Corporations sometimes fail to pay a dividend to preferred shareholders. This is called *passing the dividend*, and any passed dividends on cumulative preferred shares are said to be *in arrears*. The owners of **cumulative preferred shares** must receive all dividends in arrears plus the current year's dividend before the corporation can pay dividends to the common shareholders. Preferred shares are assumed to be non-cumulative, unless otherwise stated.

The preferred shares of Pinecraft Industries Inc. are cumulative. Suppose the company passed the 2016 preferred dividend of $150,000. Before paying dividends to its common shareholders in 2017, the company must first pay preferred dividends of $150,000 for both 2016 and 2017, a total of $300,000. Assume that Pinecraft declared a dividend of $500,000 on September 6, 2017. The entry to record this declaration is:

	A	B	C	D	E
1	2017				
2	Sep. 6	Retained Earnings	500,000		
3		Dividends Payable, Preferred ($150,000 × 2)		300,000	
4		Dividends Payable, Common ($500,000 − $300,000)		200,000	
5		*To declare a cash dividend.*			
6					

Note that even though dividends of $150,000 were in arrears at the end of 2016, no liability for these dividends is recorded until the board declares a dividend. If the preferred shares are *non-cumulative*, the corporation is not obligated to pay preferred dividends in arrears.

Stock Splits

When a company wishes to increase or decrease its market value per share without altering its assets, liabilities, or shareholders' equity, it can declare a **stock split**, which results in an increase or decrease in the number of issued and outstanding shares of the company, but does not affect any financial statement balances. On October 15, 2015, for example, Skechers U.S.A., Inc. (SKX) executed a 3-for-1 stock split, which resulted in its shareholders receiving three company shares in exchange for each one they already owned. As a result of this split, the number of SKX shares issued and outstanding doubled from 41.9M to 125.7M. Just prior to the split, SKX shares were trading at around $125. With three times as many shares outstanding after the split, the price per share immediately declined to about $42 because neither the total market value nor the book value of Skechers changed as a result of the stock split.

Companies typically split their stock when they think their share price has become too expensive or if the stock is trading too far above similar companies' stock. If a company wishes to alter its share price by something other than the 66% decrease seen in the Skechers example, it merely has to change the split ratio. If, for example, a company wanted to decrease its share price from $400 to $200, it would execute a

2-for-1 stock split, which would result in there being twice times as many shares issued and outstanding after the split.

Sometimes, companies want to *increase* their share price because a very low share price often deters investors from buying the stock. Assume, for instance, that a company wants to increase its share price from $0.50 to $1.50 so it is no longer considered a penny stock (an unflattering term for a stock trading below $1 per share). It could do this by executing a 1-for-3 stock split, which means the company would issue one share in exchange for every three shares owned by a shareholder. After this split, there would be one-third as many shares issued and outstanding, resulting in a tripling of the share price. Splits like this, where the number of shares issued and outstanding decreases, are often called *reverse stock splits*.

Regardless of whether a company executes a normal stock split or a reverse split, there is no impact *on the accounts of the company*, so no journal entries are needed in the event of a stock split. From a record-keeping perspective, the only change is the number of shares issued and outstanding, and this change, along with a description of the stock split, would be disclosed in the statement of owners' equity and the notes to the financial statements.

Summary of the Effects on Assets, Liabilities, and Shareholders' Equity

We've seen how to account for the basic shareholders' equity transactions and events:

- Issuance of shares (pp. 440–442)
- Cash dividends (pp. 444–445)
- Stock dividends (pp. 445–446)
- Stock splits (pp. 447–448)

How do these transactions and events affect assets, liabilities, and equity? Exhibit 9-3 provides a helpful summary.

EXHIBIT 9-3
Effects of Share-Related Transactions and Events on Assets, Liabilities, and Equity

Transaction	Assets	=	Liabilities	+	Shareholders' Equity
Issuance of shares—common and preferred	Increase		No effect		Increase
Declaration of cash dividend	No effect		Increase		Decrease
Payment of cash dividend	Decrease		Decrease		No effect
Declaration and distribution of stock dividend	No effect		No effect		No effect
Stock split	No effect		No effect		No effect

OBJECTIVE

❺ **Distinguish** between fair value and book value per share

DISTINGUISH BETWEEN FAIR VALUE AND BOOK VALUE PER SHARE

Investors commonly use two share values to assist with investment decisions—*fair value* and *book value*. It is important to understand the distinction between these two share values and how they can affect investing decisions.

Fair Value

The **fair value** (or market price) of a share of a company's stock is the price that a willing buyer would pay a willing seller to acquire the share. The fair values of the shares of companies that are traded on public stock exchanges, such as the Toronto Stock Exchange (TSX), are easily determined by examining the prices at which the shares trade on these exchanges. On October 8, 2015, for example, one common share of Canadian Tire had a fair value of $114.43 based on the closing price of the stock on the TSX that day. Shares of private companies do not trade on public exchanges, so their fair values must generally be determined with the assistance of professional business valuators.

Book Value

The **book value** of a share of a company's common stock indicates the dollar value of net assets a common shareholder would receive for each share *after* any preferred shareholders have received their share of the company's net assets. If the company has only common shares outstanding, its book value is computed by dividing the total shareholders' equity by the number of common shares *outstanding*. For example, a company with shareholders' equity of $180,000 and 5,000 common shares outstanding has a book value of $36 per share ($180,000 ÷ 5,000 shares).

If the company has both preferred shares and common shares outstanding, the preferred shareholders have the first claim to the company's net assets, so their equity in the net assets, *including any cumulative dividends in arrears*, must be deducted from shareholders' equity before computing the book value per common share. In general, the formula for calculating book value per common share is:

$$\text{Book value per common share} = \frac{\text{Total shareholders equity} - \text{Preferred shareholders' equity}}{\text{Number of common shares outstanding}}$$

To illustrate the use of this formula, assume a company's shareholders' equity consists of the following:

	A	B	C
1	**Shareholders' Equity**		
2	Preferred shares, 400 shares issued	$ 40,000	
3	Common shares, 5,000 shares issued	131,000	
4	Retained earnings	70,000	
5	Total shareholders' equity	$ 241,000	
6			

Its book value per common share would then be $40.20 ([$241,000 – $40,000]/ 5,000 shares).

STOP + THINK (9-5)

Using the information in the following Shareholders' Equity section of the balance sheet (as at December 31, 2017), respond to the questions below. If the information you need to answer a question is not provided, answer "unknown." Consider each question to be independent of the others, unless otherwise stated.

Shareholders' Equity	2017
Authorized shares	
1,000,000 non-voting preferred shares, no par value, non-cumulative dividend of $1.00 per share	
Unlimited number of common shares, no par value	
Issued and outstanding shares	
50,000 preferred shares	$ 500,000
500,000 common shares	6,750,000
Retained earnings	3,250,000
Total Shareholders' Equity	$10,500,000

1. How much equity financing has the company received from shareholders since it was incorporated?

2. Assuming the company has paid $1,650,000 in dividends over its life to date, what is its total net income since inception?

3. At the end of 2017, how much cash does the company have available to pay dividends or otherwise fund its operations?

4. What is the book value of the assets owned by the company's common shareholders?

5. If the company paid dividends totalling $310,000 in 2017, how much of this total did the common shareholders receive (in dollars)?

6. If on January 1, 2018, the company implemented a 3-for-2 stock split of its common shares, how many common shares would be issued and outstanding after the split? If the shares had a market price of $20 on that date, what impact would the split have on shareholders' equity (in dollars)?

OBJECTIVE

❻ **Evaluate** a company's return on assets and return on equity

EVALUATE A COMPANY'S RETURN ON ASSETS AND RETURN ON EQUITY

Investors search for companies whose stocks are likely to increase in value. They're constantly comparing companies, but a comparison of Canadian Tire with a start-up company is not meaningful. Canadian Tire's revenues run into the billions, far exceeding a new company's revenues. In addition, management of the company has spent years investing in assets and managing both borrowed resources and shareholders' invested capital. Does this automatically make Canadian Tire a better investment? Not necessarily. To compare profitability of companies of different size, investors use standard profitability measures, including return on assets and return on equity.

Return on Assets

The **rate of return on total assets**, or simply **return on assets (ROA)**, measures a company's success in using its assets to earn income for the two groups who finance the business:

- Creditors to whom the corporation owes money (creditors want interest)
- Shareholders who own the corporation's shares (shareholders want net income)

The sum of net income and interest expense is the return to the two groups who finance a corporation. This sum is the numerator of the return-on-assets ratio. The denominator of the ratio is average total assets, which is computed by taking the average of the company's total assets at each of the last two fiscal year-ends. Return on assets is computed as follows, using data from Canadian Tire's 2014 financial statements (dollar amounts in millions):

$$\text{Return on assets} = \frac{\text{Net income} + \text{Interest expense}}{\text{Average total assets}}$$

$$= \frac{604.0 + 127.8}{(14{,}553.2 + 13{,}630.0)/2} = 5.2\%$$

What is a good rate of return on total assets? Ten percent is considered a strong benchmark in most industries. Rates of return on assets vary by industry, however, because the components of ROA are different across industries. Some high-technology companies earn much higher returns than do utility companies, retailers, and manufacturers of consumer goods such as toothpaste and paper towels. Companies that are efficient, generating a large amount of sales per dollar of assets invested, or companies that can differentiate their products and earn higher margins on them, have higher ROA than companies that do not have these attributes.

Return on Equity

The **rate of return on common shareholders' equity**, usually called simply **return on equity (ROE)**, shows the relationship between net income and common shareholders' equity. Return on equity is computed only on common share capital because the return to preferred shareholders is usually limited to a specified dividend (for example, 5%).

The numerator of ROE is net income minus preferred dividends, if any. The denominator is *average common shareholders' equity*—total shareholders' equity minus preferred shareholders' equity, if any. Since most companies do not have preferred shares, adjustments for preferred dividends and preferred equity are usually not necessary. Canadian Tire's ROE for 2014 is computed as follows (dollar amounts in millions):

$$\text{Return on equity} = \frac{\text{Net income} - \text{Preferred dividends}}{\text{Average common shareholders' equity}}$$

$$= \frac{604.0 - 0.0}{(4{,}855.5 + 5{,}167.3)/2} = 12.1\%$$

Because Canadian Tire has no preferred shares, preferred dividends are zero. With no preferred shares outstanding, average common shareholders' equity is the same as average total equity—the average of the beginning and ending amounts.

Canadian Tire's return on equity of 12.1% is higher than its return on assets of 5.2%. This difference results from the interest-expense component of return on assets. Companies such as Canadian Tire borrow at one rate (say, 6%) and invest the funds to earn a higher rate (say, 12%). Borrowing at a lower rate than the company's return on investments is called using leverage. Leverage increases net income as long as operating income exceeds the interest expense from borrowing.

ROE is always higher than ROA for a successful company. This also makes sense from an economic standpoint. Shareholders take a lot more investment risk than creditors, so the shareholders demand that ROE exceed ROA. They expect the return on their investment to exceed the amount they have to pay their creditors for borrowed funds. Investors and creditors use ROE in much the same way they use

ROA—to compare companies. The higher the rate of return, the more successful the company is. In many industries, 15% is considered a good ROE.

Are Canadian Tire's ROA and ROE strong, weak, or somewhere in between? To answer these questions, it is necessary to have other information, such as:

- comparative returns for Canadian Tire from prior years and
- comparative returns for other companies in the same industry.

The Decision Guidelines that follow offer suggestions for what to consider when investing in stock. You will also use all of these ratios more in Chapter 11.

STOP + THINK (9-6)

Suppose you recently sold some shares in your Tax-Free Savings Account for proceeds of $5,000. You plan to reinvest these proceeds and have narrowed your choice down to the common shares of two companies in the same industry that have a history of paying steadily increasing dividends and rising share prices. Company A had a return on assets of 10.1% and a return on equity of 18.3% in its most recent fiscal year, while Company B had an ROA of 6.7% and an ROE of 13.4%. If you were to invest all $5,000 in only one of these companies, which one would you choose and why?

▶ DECISION GUIDELINES

INVESTING IN STOCK

Suppose you've saved $5,000 to invest. You visit a nearby Edward Jones office, where the broker probes for your risk tolerance. Are you investing mainly for dividends or for growth in the stock price? You must make some key decisions.

Investor Decision	Guidelines
Which category of stock to buy for:	
• A safe investment?	Preferred shares are safer than common shares, but for even more safety, invest in high-grade corporate bonds or government securities.
• Steady dividends?	Consider cumulative preferred shares. But remember, the company is not obligated to declare preferred dividends, and the dividends are unlikely to increase.
• Increasing dividends?	Consider common shares, as long as the company's net income is increasing and the company has adequate cash flow to pay a dividend after meeting all obligations and other cash demands.
• Increasing stock price?	Consider common shares, but again only if the company's net income and cash flow are increasing.
How to identify a good stock to buy?	There are many ways to pick stock investments. One strategy that works reasonably well is to invest in companies that consistently earn higher rates of return on assets and on equity than competing firms in the same industry. Also, select industries that are expected to grow.

REPORT EQUITY TRANSACTIONS AND EVENTS IN THE FINANCIAL STATEMENTS

Reporting Changes in Shareholders' Equity

The **statement of changes in shareholders' equity** reports the details of all the changes in the shareholders' equity section of the balance sheet during the period. Exhibit 9-4 presents Canadian Tire's statement for the year ended January 3, 2015. The statement contains a column for each major element of equity, starting with Share Capital on the left and ending with a column summarizing the total changes for the period. The top row (line 3) reports the beginning balance for each element as at December 28, 2013, while the next eight rows (lines 4–11) detail the causes of the changes in each element during the 2014 fiscal year.

	A	B	C	D	E	F
1	**Canadian Tire Corporation** Consolidated Statement of Changes in Shareholders' Equity (Adapted) For the Year Ended January 3, 2015					
2	*(in millions)*	Share Capital	Contri-buted Surplus	Accumu-lated Compre-hensive Income	Retained Earnings	Total
3	**Balance as at December 28, 2013**	$ 712.9	$ 2.4	$ 47.4	$ 4,404.6	$ 5,167.3
4	Net income				604.0	604.0
5	Other comprehensive income (loss)			34.6	(13.1)	21.5
6	Issuance of Class A non-voting shares	6.9				6.9
7	Repurchase of Class A non-voting shares	(290.6)				(290.6)
8	Excess of repurchase price over average cost	266.3			(266.3)	0.0
9	Dividends				(154.1)	(154.1)
10	Issuance of redeemable financial instruments				(500.0)	(500.0)
11	Contributed surplus arising on sale of property		0.5			0.5
12	**Balance as at January 3, 2015**	$ 695.5	$ 2.9	$ 82.0	$ 4,075.1	$ 4,855.5
13						

EXHIBIT 9-4
Canadian Tire Corporation – Statement of Changes in Shareholders' Equity (Adapted)

Source: Reprinted with permission from Canadian Tire Corporation.

Let's briefly examine some of the changes in Canadian Tire's shareholders' equity during 2014. On line 4, we see the year's net income of $604 million being added to Retained Earnings, just as it would be in a stand-alone statement of retained earnings. Line 5 reports the components of comprehensive income that affect Retained Earnings and Accumulated Other Comprehensive Income. Line 6 reports that an additional $6.9 million in non-voting share capital was issued during 2014, while lines 7 and 8 show that the company repurchased some non-voting shares for a total cost that was $266.3 million higher (line 8) than the $290.6 million (line 7) they were originally issued for. On line 9, we see dividends of $154.1 million being deducted from Retained Earnings—again, just like they would be in a separate statement of retained earnings. Line 11 reports that the company generated $500,000 of contributed surplus when they sold some property during the year.

	A	B	C
1	**Canadian Tire Corporation** Consolidated Balance Sheet (Partial) As at January 3, 2015		
2	*(in millions)*		
3	**Shareholders' equity**		
4	Share capital	$ 695.5	
5	Contributed surplus	2.9	
6	Accumulated other comprehensive income	82.0	
7	Retained earnings	4075.1	
8	**Total shareholders' equity**	**$ 4,855.5**	
9			

The statement ends with the closing balances for each element as at January 3, 2015 (line 12). All of the closing balances are carried forward to the shareholders' equity section of the balance sheet, which is reported in Exhibit 9-5.

ASPE require only a statement of retained earnings, which you have seen in previous chapters. Such a statement for Canadian Tire would contain only the information in the Retained Earnings column of Exhibit 9-4.

Reporting in the Balance Sheet and Notes

Businesses often use terminology and formats in reporting shareholders' equity that differ from our examples. We use a more detailed format in this book to help you learn the main components of shareholders' equity.

One of the most important skills you will take from this textbook is the ability to understand the financial statements of real companies. Exhibit 9-6 presents a

EXHIBIT 9-6
Formats for Reporting Shareholders' Equity

	A	B	C	D	E
1	**General Textbook Format**		**Common Real-World Format**		
2	**Shareholders' equity**		**Shareholders' equity**		
3	Share capital:				
4	Preferred shares, $0.80, cumulative, 30,000 shares authorized and outstanding	$ 300,000	Contributed capital Share capital (Note 9)	$ 2,500,000	
5	Common shares, 100,000 shares authorized, 60,000 shares outstanding	2,200,000	Contributed surplus Retained earnings	11,000 1,542,000	
6			Accumulated other comprehensive income	15,000	
7	Contributed surplus from retirement of preferred shares	8,000	Total shareholders' equity	$ 4,068,000	
8	Contributed surplus from repurchase of common shares	3,000	**Notes to the Financial Statements** 1.		
9	Total capital stock	2,511,000	.		
10	Retained earnings	1,542,000	.		
11	Accumulated other comprehensive income	15,000	.		
12	Total shareholders' equity	$ 4,068,000	**9. Share capital**		
13			Preferred shares, $0.80 cumulative 30,000 shares authorized and outstanding	$ 300,000	
14			Common shares, 100,000 shares authorized, 60,000 outstanding	2,200,000	
15			Total share capital	$ 2,500,000	
16					

side-by-side comparison of our general textbook format for reporting shareholders' equity and a format you will commonly encounter in the real world.

In general, the following are a few of the key pieces of equity information that must be disclosed in the balance sheet, statement of changes in owners' equity, or the notes:

- Number of authorized, issued, and outstanding shares, and changes in these amounts during the year, for each class of share capital; their par value, if any; dividend rights and preferences; and other restrictions and features.
- Contributed surplus.
- Accumulated other comprehensive income (IFRS only).
- Retained earnings.

STOP + THINK (9-7)

Using the information in Canadian Tire's Statement of Changes in Equity in Exhibit 9-4, determine the total original cost of the Class A non-voting shares that Canadian Tire repurchased during 2014.

Summary of IFRS-ASPE Differences

Concept	IFRS	ASPE
Accumulated other comprehensive income (p. 439)	Included as a component of shareholders' equity.	No accounting or reporting of this component is required.
Statement of changes in shareholders' (or owners') equity (p. 453)	Companies must report this statement.	Companies must report only a statement of retained earnings, which contains only a subset of the information reported in the statement of changes in shareholders' equity.

SUMMARY

SUMMARY OF LEARNING OBJECTIVES

LEARNING OBJECTIVE	SUMMARY
1. **Explain** the main features of a corporation	1. A corporation is a separate legal entity that exists apart from its shareholders. 2. A corporation has a continuous life regardless of changes in ownership, and its shareholders may buy and sell their shares as they wish. 3. A corporation's shareholders have limited liability for the company's debts. The most they can lose is the amount of their initial investment.

4. Shareholders own the corporation, but company policy is set by the board of directors and implemented by company management.
5. Corporations pay income taxes separate from those borne by their shareholders.
6. Corporations are regulated by the government to ensure they report and disclose the information in their financial statements that investors and creditors need to make informed decisions.

2. **Account** for the issuance of shares

Shares are normally issued for cash, but they can also be issued in exchange for other assets, such as land or equipment. When shares are issued, the relevant Asset account is debited and the relevant Share Capital account is credited.

3. **Explain** why a company repurchases shares

Corporations repurchase their shares for several reasons:
1. To fulfill future share issuance commitments, such as those related to stock option plans.
2. To help support the corporation's market price per share by reducing the number of shares outstanding.
3. To avoid a takeover by an outside party.

4. **Account** for retained earnings, dividends, and stock splits

Retained earnings are the accumulation of a corporation's net income since inception less any net losses and dividends distributed.

Dividends are commonly paid in cash, but they can also be distributed in the form of additional stock in the corporation, which is known as a stock dividend. On the date of declaration, Retained Earnings is debited and Dividends Payable is credited for the amount of the cash dividend declared. Parties officially registered as shareholders of the corporation on the date of record will receive the dividend when it is paid (no journal entry is needed in connection with the date of record). On the date of payment of a cash dividend, Dividends Payable is debited and Cash is credited. For a stock dividend, on the date of declaration, we debit Retained Earnings and credit Stock Dividends Distributable (a contra-equity account). On the date of payment, we debit Stock Dividends Distributable and credit the relevant Share Capital account.

Stock splits are executed to increase or decrease the number of shares issued and outstanding, thereby decreasing or increasing the market price per share. An X-for-Y stock split, when X is greater than Y, increases the number of shares issued and outstanding and reduces the market price per share. If X is less than Y, the number of shares issued and outstanding decreases, and the market price per share increases. Stock splits have no effect on the corporation's shareholders' equity balances.

5. **Distinguish** between fair value and book value per share

The fair value (or market price) of a share of a company's stock is the price that a willing buyer would pay a willing seller to acquire the share.

The book value of a share of a company's common stock indicates the dollar value of net assets a common shareholder would receive for each share *after* the preferred shareholders (if any) have received their share of the net assets.

6. **Evaluate** a company's return on assets and return on equity

A company's return on assets (ROA) indicates how well it has used its assets to earn money for its creditors and shareholders. It is calculated as follows:

$$\text{ROA} = \frac{\text{Net income} + \text{Interest expense}}{\text{Average total assets}}$$

A company's return on equity (ROE) indicates how much profit it has generated for each dollar of common shareholders' equity it has. It is calculated as follows:

$$\text{ROE} = \frac{\text{Net income} - \text{Preferred dividends}}{\text{Average common shareholders' equity}}$$

Generally, the higher a company's ROA and ROE, the better its profitability. A company's ROA and ROE are best evaluated by comparing them to prior years' returns and to the returns of major competitors.

7. **Report** equity transactions and events in the financial statements

The statement of changes in shareholders' equity reports the details of all the changes in the shareholders' equity section of the balance sheet during the period. It typically reports changes in the following equity items:

- Share capital
- Contributed surplus
- Retained earnings
- Accumulated other comprehensive income

A corporation must also disclose the following equity information in its balance sheet, statement of changes in owners' equity, or the notes:

- Number of authorized, issued, and outstanding shares and changes in these amounts during the year for each class of share capital; their par value, if any; dividend rights and preferences; and other restrictions and features
- Contributed surplus
- Accumulated other comprehensive income (IFRS only)
- Retained earnings

MyAccountingLab

END-OF-CHAPTER SUMMARY PROBLEM

1. The balance sheet of Quetico Inc. reported the following at December 31, 2017:

	A	B	C
1	**Shareholders' Equity**		
2	Preferred shares, $0.40, 10,000 shares authorized and issued	$ 100,000	
3	Common shares, 100,000 shares authorized*	400,000	
4	Accumulated other comprehensive income	224,000	
5	Retained earnings	476,500	
6	Total shareholders' equity	$ 1,200,500	
7			

*The common shares were issued at a stated value of $8.00 per share.

Requirements

a. Are the preferred shares cumulative or non-cumulative? How can you tell?

b. What is the total amount of the annual preferred dividend?

c. How many common shares are outstanding?

d. Compute the book value per share of the common shares. No preferred dividends are in arrears, and Quetico Inc. has not yet declared the 2017 dividend.

2. Use the following accounts and related balances to prepare the classified balance sheet of Gandhi Ltd. at September 30, 2017. Use the account format of the balance sheet.

Common shares, 50,000 shares authorized, 20,000 shares issued $100,000	Property, plant, and equipment, net $266,000
Dividends payable 4,000	Accounts receivable, net 23,000
Cash 9,000	Preferred shares, $3.75, 10,000 shares authorized,
Accounts payable........................ 28,000	2,000 shares issued 24,000
Long-term note payable.............. 80,000	Accrued liabilities........................ 3,000
Inventory..................................... 85,000	Retained earnings 104,000
Accumulated other comprehensive income 40,000	

All features must be specified in the financial statements.

Details should be given on the balance sheet.

Each common share was sold for the $8 stated value.

Book value per common share must exclude any amounts pertaining to preferred shares.

The classified balance sheet must specify current assets and current liabilities. Make sure that Total assets = Total liabilities + Shareholders' equity.

ANSWERS

1. **a.** The preferred shares are not cumulative because they are not specifically labelled cumulative.
   b. Total annual preferred dividend: $4,000 (10,000 × $0.40).
   c. Common shares outstanding: 50,000 shares ($400,000 ÷ $8 stated value).
   d. Book value per common share:

Common:

Total shareholders' equity	$1,200,500
Less shareholders' equity allocated to preferred	(100,000)
Shareholders' equity allocated to common	$1,100,500
Book value per share ($1,100,500 ÷ 50,000 shares)	$ 22.01

2.

	A	B	C	D	E	F
1			**Gandhi Ltd.** Balance Sheet As at September 30, 2017			
2	**Assets**		**Liabilities**			
3	Current		Current			
4	Cash	$ 9,000	Accounts payable	$ 28,000		
5	Accounts receivable, net	23,000	Dividends payable	4,000		
6	Inventory	85,000	Accrued liabilities	3,000		
7	Total current assets	117,000	Total current liabilities	35,000		
8	Property, plant, and equipment, net	266,000	Long-term note payable	80,000		
9			Total liabilities		$115,000	
10						
11			**Shareholders' Equity**			
12			Preferred shares, $3.75,			
13			10,000 shares authorized,			
14			2,000 shares issued	$ 24,000		
15			Common shares,			
16			50,000 shares authorized,			
17			20,000 shares issued	100,000		
18			Retained earnings	104,000		
19			Accumulated other			
20			comprehensive income	40,000		
21			Total shareholders' equity		268,000	
22			Total liabilities and			
23	Total assets	$ 383,000	shareholders' equity		$383,000	
24						

REVIEW

MyAccountingLab

Make the grade with MyAccountingLab: The Quick Quiz questions, Short Exercises, Exercises, and Problems (Group A) marked in #–# can be found on MyAccountingLab. You can practise them as often as you want, and most feature step-by-step guided instructions to help you find the right answer.

QUICK QUIZ (ANSWERS APPEAR ON THE LAST PAGE OF THIS CHAPTER.)

1. Which of the following is a characteristic of a corporation?
a. Mutual agency
b. No income tax
c. Limited liability of shareholders
d. Both a and b

2. Team Spirit Inc. issues 240,000 common shares for $5 per share. The journal entry is:

a. Cash	240,000	
Common Shares		240,000
b. Cash	1,200,000	
Common Shares		240,000
Gain on the Sale of Shares....		960,000
c. Cash	1,200,000	
Common Shares		1,200,000
d. Cash	1,200,000	
Common Shares		480,000
Contributed Surplus on Common Shares		720,000

3. Which of the following is true about stated value?
a. It represents what a share is worth.
b. It represents the original selling price for a share.
c. It is established for a share after it is issued.
d. It is an arbitrary amount assigned by a company to a share at the time of issue.
e. It may exist for common shares but not for preferred shares.

4. The contributed capital portion of shareholders' equity does not include
a. preferred shares.
b. contributed surplus.
c. retained earnings.
d. common shares.

5. Preferred shares are *least* likely to have which of the following characteristics?
a. Preference as to assets on liquidation of the corporation
b. Extra liability for the preferred shareholders
c. The right of the holder to convert to common shares
d. Preference as to dividends

6. Which of the following classifications represents the largest quantity of common shares?
a. Issued shares
b. Outstanding shares
c. Unissued shares
d. Authorized shares

Use the following information for questions 7 through 12:
These account balances at December 31 relate to Sportaid Inc.:

Accounts Payable	$ 51,700	Preferred shares,	
Accounts Receivable	81,350	$0.10, 890,000 shares issued	89,000
Common Shares	593,000	Retained Earnings	71,800
Bonds Payable	3,400	Notes Receivable	12,500

7. What is total share capital for Sportaid Inc.?
a. $682,000
b. $701,345
c. $694,445
d. $753,800
e. None of the above

8. What is total shareholders' equity for Sportaid Inc.?
a. $766,300
b. $758,800
c. $753,800
d. $764,735
e. None of the above

9. Sportaid's net income for the period is $119,600 and beginning common shareholders' equity is $681,400. What is Sportaid's return on common shareholders' equity?
a. 15.7%
b. 16.4%
c. 17.5%
d. 18.6%

10. If the average issue price of Sportaid's outstanding common shares is $11.86, how many common shares are issued and outstanding?
a. 50,000
b. 100,000
c. 593,000
d. Unknown

11. If Sportaid's board of directors decided to declare a dividend on December 31, what is the largest dividend it could declare?
a. $753,800
b. $71,800
c. $8,900
d. $593,000

12. If the board of directors declare a dividend of $20,000 on December 31, how much of this total would the common shareholders receive? No other dividends have been declared during the year.
a. $8,900
b. $0
c. $20,000
d. $11,100

13. Shareholders are eligible for a dividend if they own the shares on the date of
a. declaration.
b. record.
c. payment.
d. issuance.

14. Mario's Foods has outstanding 500 $7.00 preferred shares and 1,200 common shares. Mario's declares dividends of $14,300. The correct entry is:

a. Retained Earnings............................ 14,300
    Dividends Payable, Preferred............   3,500
    Dividends Payable, Common...........   10,800
b. Dividends Expense 14,300
    Cash   14,300
c. Retained Earnings............................ 14,300
    Dividends Payable, Preferred............   7,150
    Dividends Payable, Common...........   7,150
d. Dividends Payable, Preferred 3,500
    Dividends Payable, Common.............. 10,800
    Cash   14,300

15. A corporation has 20,000 $8.00 preferred shares outstanding with a stated value of $2,000,000. Also, there are 20,000 common shares outstanding. If a $350,000 dividend is paid, how much goes to the preferred shareholders?
a. $0
b. $350,000

c. $160,000
d. $120,000
e. $320,000

16. Assume the same facts as in question 15. What is the amount of dividends per share on common shares?
a. $9.50
b. $8.00
c. $17.50
d. $1.50
e. None of the above

17. Which of the following is *not* true about a 10% stock dividend?
a. Shareholders do not receive additional shares.
b. No assets are affected.
c. Retained Earnings decreases.
d. The market price of the share is needed to record the stock dividend.
e. Total shareholders' equity remains the same.

18. A company declares a 5% stock dividend. The debit to Retained Earnings is an amount equal to the
a. stated value of original shares.
b. excess of the market price over the original issue price of the shares to be issued.
c. book value of the shares to be issued.
d. fair value of the shares to be issued.

19. Which of the following statements is *not* true about a 3-for-1 stock split?
a. Stated value is reduced to one-third of what it was before the split.
b. Total shareholders' equity increases.
c. The market price of each share will decrease.
d. A shareholder with 10 shares before the split owns 30 shares after the split.
e. Retained Earnings remains the same.

20. Franco Company's net income and preferred dividends are $44,000 and $4,000, respectively, and average total common shareholders' equity is $384,000. How much is Franco's return on equity?
a. 10.4%
b. 11.5%
c. 12.5%
d. 13.1%

ACCOUNTING VOCABULARY

book value (of a share) Amount of owners' equity on the company's books for each share of its stock. (p. 449)
chairperson Elected by a corporation's board of directors, usually the most powerful person in the corporation. (p. 438)
cumulative preferred shares Preferred shares whose owners must receive all dividends in arrears plus the current year's

dividend before the corporation can pay dividends to the common shareholders. (p. 447)
date of declaration The date on which the Board of Directors declares a dividend to shareholders. (p. 444)
date of payment The date on which a dividend is actually paid to shareholders. (p. 445)

date of record The date on which a person must be recorded as a shareholder in order to receive a dividend. (p. 445)

deficit The term used when *retained earnings* is a negative balance. (p. 444)

fair value (of a share) The price that a willing buyer would pay a willing seller to acquire a share. (p. 449)

limited liability No personal obligation of a shareholder for corporation debts. A shareholder can lose no more on an investment in a corporation's shares than the cost of the investment. (p. 437)

market price (of a share) The price that a willing buyer would pay a willing seller to acquire a share. (p. 443)

par value shares Shares of stock that do not have a value assigned to them by articles of the corporation. (p. 440)

preferred shares Shares that give their owners certain advantages, such as the priority to receive dividends before the common shareholders and the priority to receive assets before the common shareholders if the corporation liquidates. (p. 440)

president Chief executive officer in charge of managing the day-to-day operations of a corporation. (p. 438)

repurchased shares A corporation's own shares that it has issued and later reacquired. (p. 443)

return on assets (ROA) Measures how profitably management has used the assets that shareholders and creditors have provided the company. (p. 450)

return on equity (ROE) Net income divided by average total assets. This ratio measures how profitably management has used the assets that shareholders and creditors have provided the company. (p. 451)

stated value An arbitrary amount assigned by a company to a share of its stock at the time of issue. (p. 440)

statement of changes in shareholders' equity Reports the changes in all categories of shareholders' equity during the period. (p. 453)

stock dividend A proportional distribution by a corporation of its own shares to its shareholders. (p. 445)

stock split An increase in the number of authorized, issued, and outstanding shares of stock coupled with a proportionate reduction in the share's book value. (p. 447)

ASSESS YOUR PROGRESS

SHORT EXERCISES

S9-1 What are two main advantages that a corporation has over a proprietorship and a partnership? What are two main disadvantages of a corporation?

LEARNING OBJECTIVE ❶

Understand the advantages and disadvantages of a corporation

S9-2 Consider the authority structure in a corporation, as diagrammed in Exhibit 9-2, page 438.

LEARNING OBJECTIVE ❶

Summarize the characteristics of authority structure in a corporation

1. What group holds the ultimate power in a corporation?
2. Who is the most powerful person in the corporation? What's the abbreviation of this person's title?
3. Who is in charge of day-to-day operations? What's the abbreviation of this person's title?
4. Who is in charge of accounting and finance? What's the abbreviation of this person's title?

S9-3 Answer the following questions about the characteristics of a corporation's shares:

LEARNING OBJECTIVE ❶

Identify the characteristics of preferred and common shares

1. Who are the real owners of a corporation?
2. What privileges do preferred shareholders have over common shareholders?
3. Which class of shareholders reaps greater benefits from a highly profitable corporation? Explain.

S9-4 Study George Weston Ltd.'s January 8, 2017, share issuance entry given on pages 440–441, and answer these questions about the nature of the transaction:

LEARNING OBJECTIVE ❷

Understand the effect of a share issuance on net income

1. If George Weston had sold the shares for $80, would the $30 ($80 – $50) be profit for George Weston?
2. Suppose the shares had been issued at different times and different prices. Will shares issued at higher prices have more rights than those issued at lower prices? Give the reason for your answer.

S9-5 On December 31, 2017, shareholders' equity accounts of Green Products Inc. (GPI) had the balances shown below. GPI paid dividends of $4,096 on December 1, 2017.

LEARNING OBJECTIVE ❷❹

Issue shares and analyze retained earnings

	2017	2016
Common shares	$ 82,968	$ 64,968
Retained earnings	80,435	78,881
Total shareholders' equity	$163,403	$143,849

1. GPI sold 10,000 common shares on June 30, 2017. What was the average selling price of these shares if this was the only common-shares transaction during 2017?
2. Journalize GPI's sale of the common shares on June 30, 2017.
3. Based only on the above information, did GPI earn a profit or suffer a loss during 2017? Calculate the profit or loss.

LEARNING OBJECTIVE ②

Issue shares to finance the purchase of assets

S9-6 This Short Exercise demonstrates the similarity and the difference between two ways to acquire capital assets.

Case A—Issue shares and buy the assets in separate transactions:	Case B—Issue shares to acquire the assets in a single transaction:
Longview Corporation issued 10,000 common shares for cash of $200,000. In a separate transaction, Longview used the cash to purchase a warehouse building for $160,000 and equipment for $40,000. Journalize the two transactions.	Tyler Corporation issued 10,000 common shares to acquire a warehouse valued at $160,000 and equipment worth $40,000. Journalize this transaction.

Compare the balances in all the accounts after making both sets of entries. Are the account balances the same or different?

LEARNING OBJECTIVE ②④

Prepare the shareholders' equity section of a balance sheet

S9-7 The financial statements of Eppley Employment Services Inc. reported the following accounts (adapted, with dollar amounts in thousands):

Common shares:			Total revenues	$1,390
600 shares issued	$600		Accounts payable	420
Long-term debt	25		Retained earnings	646
			Other current liabilities	2,566
			Total expenses	805

Prepare the shareholders' equity section of Eppley's balance sheet. Net income has already been closed to Retained Earnings.

LEARNING OBJECTIVE ②④

Use shareholders' equity data

S9-8 Use the Eppley Employment Services data in exercise S9-7 to compute Eppley's:
a. Net income
b. Total liabilities
c. Total assets (use the accounting equation)

LEARNING OBJECTIVE ③

Explain the repurchase of shares to fight off a takeover of the corporation

S9-9 Karen Knox Exports, Inc., is located in Clancy, New Mexico. Knox is the only company with reliable sources for its imported gifts. The company does a brisk business with specialty stores such as Neiman Marcus. Knox's recent success has made the company a prime target for a takeover. An investment group in Alberton is attempting to buy 52% of Knox's outstanding shares against the wishes of Knox's board of directors. Board members are convinced that the Alberton investors would sell the most desirable pieces of the business and leave little of value.

At the most recent board meeting, several suggestions were advanced to fight off the hostile takeover bid. The suggestion with the most promise is to repurchase a significant quantity of outstanding shares. Knox has the cash to carry out this plan.

Requirement

Suppose you are a significant shareholder of Karen Knox Exports, Inc. Write a memorandum to explain to the board how the repurchase of shares would make it difficult for the Alberton group to take over Knox. Include in your memo a discussion of the effect that repurchasing shares would have on shares outstanding and on the size of the corporation.

LEARNING OBJECTIVE ④

Account for cash dividends

S9-10 Gleneagles Corporation earned net income of $70,000 during the year ended December 31, 2017. On December 15, Gleneagles had declared the annual cash dividend on its $0.50 preferred shares (10,000 shares issued for $100,000) and a $0.60 per share cash dividend on its common shares (25,000 shares issued for $50,000). Gleneagles then paid the dividends on January 4, 2018.

Journalize the following for Gleneagles Corporation:

a. Declaring the cash dividends on December 15, 2017
b. Paying the cash dividends on January 4, 2018

Did Retained Earnings increase or decrease during 2017? If so, by how much?

S9-11 Refer to the allocation of dividends for Pinecraft Industries Inc. on page 446. Answer these questions about Pinecraft's cash dividends:

LEARNING OBJECTIVE ④
Divide cash dividends between preferred and common shares

1. How much in dividends must Pinecraft declare each year before the common shareholders receive any cash dividends for the year?
2. Suppose Pinecraft declares cash dividends of $300,000 for 2017. How much of the dividends go to preferred? How much go to common?
3. Are Pinecraft's preferred shares cumulative or non-cumulative? How can you tell?
4. Pinecraft passed the preferred dividend in 2015 and 2016. Then in 2017, Pinecraft declares cash dividends of $800,000. How much of the dividends go to preferred? How much go to common?

S9-12 On May 1, Fidelity Software Ltd. has 80,000 common shares issued and outstanding. Suppose Fidelity distributes a 10% stock dividend on May 11 when the market price (fair value) of its shares is $10.50 per share.

LEARNING OBJECTIVE ④
Record a small stock dividend

1. Journalize Fidelity's declaration of the shares dividend. An explanation is not required.
2. What was the overall effect of the stock dividend on Fidelity's total assets? What about on its total liabilities and its total shareholders' equity?

S9-13 Refer to the real-world format of shareholders' equity in Exhibit 9-6, page 454. That company has passed its preferred dividends for three years including the current year. Compute the book value of one of the company's common shares.

LEARNING OBJECTIVE ⑤
Compute book value per share

S9-14 Use the statement of changes in shareholders' equity in Exhibit 9-4 (p. 453) to answer the following questions:

LEARNING OBJECTIVE ⑦
Use the statement of changes in shareholders' equity

1. How much additional share capital did the issuance of shares raise during 2014?
2. What effect did the payment of dividends have on shareholders' equity during 2014?

S9-15 POLA Corporation's 2018 financial statements reported the following items, with 2017 figures given for comparison (adapted and in millions):

LEARNING OBJECTIVE ⑥
Compute return on assets and return on equity

	2018	2017
Balance sheet		
Total assets	¥10,632	¥9,523
Total liabilities	¥ 7,414	¥6,639
Total shareholders' equity (all common)	3,218	2,884
Total liabilities and shareholders' equity	¥10,632	¥9,523
Income statement		
Revenues and other income	¥ 7,632	
Operating expense	7,289	
Interest expense	31	
Other expense	194	
Net income	¥ 118	

Compute POLA's return on assets and return on common equity for 2018. Evaluate the rates of return as being strong or weak. What additional information would be helpful in making this decision? ¥ is the symbol for the Japanese yen.

S9-16 At December 31, 2016, Lake Air Mall Inc. reported shareholders' equity as follows:

LEARNING OBJECTIVE ⑦
Prepare a statement of changes in shareholders' equity

Common shares, 500,000 shares authorized, 300,000 shares issued	$ 870,000
Retained earnings	680,000
	$1,550,000

During 2017, Lake Air Mall completed these transactions (listed in chronological order):

a. Declared and issued a 5% stock dividend on the outstanding shares. At the time, Lake Air Mall shares were quoted at a market price of $10 per share.

b. Issued 20,000 common shares at the price of $12 per share.

c. Net income for the year, $320,000.

d. Declared cash dividends of $100,000.

Requirement

Prepare Lake Air Mall's statement of changes in shareholders' equity for 2017, using the format of Exhibit 9-4 (p. 453) as a model.

EXERCISES

LEARNING OBJECTIVE 6

Evaluate return on equity

E9-17 Lofty Inns reported these figures for 2017 and 2016 (in millions):

	2017	2016
Balance sheet		
Total assets	$27,000	$18,400
Common share capital	43	389
Retained earnings	11,525	16,523
Other shareholders' equity	(3,008)	(9,300)
Income statement		
Net sales	$30,500	$28,200
Operating income	4,022	3,819
Net income	2,100	1,546

Requirements

1. Compute Lofty's return on assets and return on equity for 2017.

2. Do these rates of return suggest strength or weakness? Give your reason.

3. What additional information do you need to make the decision in requirement 2?

LEARNING OBJECTIVE 2 4

Issue shares and report shareholders' equity

E9-18 Burgers & Fries, Inc., is authorized to issue an unlimited number of common shares and 10,000 preferred shares. During its first year, the business completed the following share issuance transactions:

July	19	Issued 10,000 common shares for cash of $6.50 per share.
Oct.	3	Issued 500 $1.50 preferred shares for $50,000 cash.
	11	Received inventory valued at $11,000 and equipment with fair value of $8,500 for 3,300 common shares.

Requirements

1. Journalize the transactions. Explanations are not required.

2. Prepare the shareholders' equity section of Burgers & Fries's balance sheet. The ending balance of Retained Earnings is a deficit of $42,000.

LEARNING OBJECTIVE 2 4

Prepare the shareholders' equity section of a balance sheet

E9-19 Citadel Sporting Goods is authorized to issue 5,000 preferred shares and 10,000 common shares. During a two-month period, Citadel completed these share-issuance transactions:

Sept.	23	Issued 1,000 common shares for cash of $16 per share.
Oct.	2	Issued 300 $4.50 preferred shares for $20,000 cash.
	12	Received inventory valued at $15,000 and equipment with fair value of $43,000 for 4,000 common shares.

Requirement

Prepare the shareholders' equity section of the Citadel Sporting Goods balance sheet for the transactions given in this exercise. Retained Earnings has a balance of $49,000. Journal entries are not required.

E9-20 Trans World Publishing Inc. was recently organized. The company issued common shares to a lawyer who provided legal services of $15,000 to help organize the corporation. Trans World also issued common shares to an inventor in exchange for his patent with a fair value of $80,000. In addition, Trans World received cash both for the issuance of 5,000 of its preferred shares at $110 per share and for the issuance of 20,000 common shares at $20 per share. During the first year of operations, Trans World earned net income of $55,000 and declared a cash dividend of $20,000. Without making journal entries, determine the total share capital created by these transactions.

LEARNING OBJECTIVE ❷❹

Measure the share capital of a corporation

E9-21 Sagebrush Software Ltd. had the following selected account balances at December 31, 2017 (in thousands). Prepare the shareholders' equity section of Sagebrush Software's balance sheet (in thousands).

LEARNING OBJECTIVE ❷❹

Prepare shareholders' equity section of a balance sheet

Inventory	$ 653	Class A common shares, unlimited number authorized, 3,600 shares issued	$ 90
Property, plant, and equipment, net	857		
Contributed surplus	901		
Class B common shares, unlimited number authorized, 5,000 shares issued	1,380	Deficit	2,400
		Accounts receivable, net	600
		Notes payable	1,122

Explain what is meant by "deficit."

E9-22 Journalize the following transactions of Concilio Video Productions Inc.:

LEARNING OBJECTIVE ❷❹

Record share transactions and measure their effects on shareholders' equity

April	19	Issued 2,000 common shares at $10 per share.
July	22	Declared and paid a cash dividend of $0.50 per common share (21,000 common shares outstanding).
Nov.	11	Issued 800 common shares at $12 per share.

What was the overall effect of these transactions on Concilio's shareholders' equity?

E9-23 At December 31, 2017, Blumenthall Corporation reported the shareholders' equity accounts shown here (as adapted, with dollar amounts in millions):

LEARNING OBJECTIVE ❷❹

Record share issuance and dividend transactions

Common shares	
1,800 million shares issued	$2,700
Retained earnings	1,200
Total shareholders' equity	$3,900

Blumenthall's 2017 transactions included the following:

a. Net income, $350 million
b. Issuance of 6 million common shares for $12.50 per share
c. Declaration and payment of cash dividends of $25 million

Journalize Blumenthall's transactions. Explanations are not required.

LEARNING OBJECTIVE ❷❹

Report shareholders' equity after a sequence of transactions

E9-24 Use the Blumenthall Corporation data in exercise E9-23 to prepare the shareholders' equity section of the company's balance sheet at December 31, 2017.

LEARNING OBJECTIVE ❷❸❹

Infer transactions from a company's shareholders' equity

E9-25 Optical Products Company reported the following shareholders' equity on its balance sheet:

Shareholders' Equity (dollars and shares in millions)	December 31, 2017	2016
Preferred shares; authorized 20 shares; Convertible Preferred shares; issued and outstanding: 2017 and 2016—0 and 2 shares, respectively......................................	$ 0	$ 12
Common shares; authorized unlimited shares; issued: 2017 and 2016—564 and 364 shares, respectively.............................	3,270	1,900
Retained earnings...	6,280	5,006
Total shareholders' equity...	$ 9,550	$ 6,918
Total liabilities and shareholders' equity	$48,918	$45,549

Requirements

1. What caused Optical Products's preferred shares to decrease during 2017? Cite all the possible causes.
2. What caused Optical Products's common shares to increase during 2017? Identify all the possible causes.
3. How many shares of Optical Products were outstanding at December 31, 2017?
4. Optical Products's net income during 2017 was $1,410 million. How much were Optical Products's dividends during the year?

LEARNING OBJECTIVE ❹

Compute dividends on preferred and common shares

E9-26 Great Lakes Manufacturing Inc. reported the following:

Shareholders' Equity	
Preferred shares, cumulative, $0.10, 80,000 shares issued..........................	$ 80,000
Common shares, 8,130,000 shares issued	813,000

Great Lakes Manufacturing has paid all preferred dividends through 2013.

Requirement

Compute the total amounts of dividends to both preferred and common shareholders for 2016 and 2017 if total dividends are $50,000 in 2016 and $100,000 in 2017.

LEARNING OBJECTIVE ❹

Record a stock dividend and report shareholders' equity

E9-27 The shareholders' equity for Best in Show Cinemas Ltd. (BSC) (adapted) at December 31, 2016, appears as follows:

Shareholders' Equity	
Common shares, 2,000,000 shares authorized, 500,000 shares issued	$1,012,000
Retained earnings	7,122,000
Total shareholders' equity...	$8,134,000

On April 15, 2017, the market price of BSC common shares was $17 per share. Assume BSC declared a 10% stock dividend on this date and distributed the stock dividend on April 30.

Requirements

1. Journalize the declaration and distribution of the stock dividend.
2. Prepare the shareholders' equity section of the balance sheet after the stock dividend.
3. Why is total shareholders' equity unchanged by the stock dividend?
4. Suppose BSC had a cash balance of $540,000 on April 16, 2017. What is the maximum amount of cash dividends BSC can declare?

E9-28 Identify the effects—both the direction and the dollar amount—of the following assumed transactions on the total shareholders' equity of a large corporation. Each transaction is independent.

LEARNING OBJECTIVE ❷❹

Measure the effects of share issuance, dividends, and share transactions

a. Declaration of cash dividends of $80 million
b. Payment of the cash dividend declared
c. 10% stock dividend. Before the dividend, 69 million common shares were outstanding; the market price was $7.625 at the time of the dividend.
d. A 50% stock dividend. Before the dividend, 69 million common shares were outstanding; the market price was $13.75 at the time of the dividend.
e. Sale of 600 common shares for $5.00 per share
f. A 3-for-1 stock split. Prior to the split, 69 million common shares were outstanding.

E9-29 Solartech Inc. had the following shareholders' equity at January 31 (dollars in millions):

LEARNING OBJECTIVE ❹

Report shareholders' equity after a stock split

Common shares, 500 million shares authorized, 440 million shares issued	$ 318
Contributed surplus	44
Retained earnings	2,393
Total shareholders' equity	$2,755

Assume that on March 7, Solartech split its common shares 2 for 1. Prepare the shareholders' equity section of the balance sheet immediately after the split.

E9-30 The balance sheet of Oriental Rug Company reported the following:

LEARNING OBJECTIVE ❺

Measure the book value per share of common shares

Cumulative preferred shares, $0.06, outstanding 6,000 shares	$10,000
Common shareholders' equity: 8,000 shares issued and outstanding	87,200
Total shareholders' equity	$97,200

Requirements

1. Compute the book value per share for the common shares, assuming all preferred dividends are fully paid up (none in arrears).
2. Compute the book value per share of the common shares, assuming that three years' preferred dividends, including the current year, are in arrears.
3. Oriental Rug's common shares recently traded at a market price of $7.75 per share. Does this mean that Oriental Rug's shares are a good buy at $7.75?

E9-31 Lexington Inns reported these figures for 2017 and 2016 (in millions):

LEARNING OBJECTIVE ❻

Evaluate profitability

	2017	2016
Balance sheet		
Total assets	$15,702	$13,728
Common share capital	80	680
Retained earnings	11,519	16,499
Other shareholders' equity	(3,005)	(9,095)
Income statement		
Net sales	$25,500	$27,500
Operating income	4,025	3,813
Net income	1,500	1,550

Requirements

1. Compute Lexington's return on assets and return on equity for 2017.
2. Do these rates of return suggest strength or weakness? Give your reason.
3. What additional information do you need to make the decision in requirement 2?

LEARNING OBJECTIVE ⑥

Evaluate profitability

E9-32 Easton Company included the following items in its financial statements for 2017, the current year (amounts in millions):

Payment of long-term debt	$17,200	Dividends paid	$ 195
Proceeds from issuance		Net sales:	
of common shares	8,405	Current year	65,000
Total liabilities:		Preceding year	62,000
Current year-end	32,309	Net income:	
Preceding year-end	38,033	Current year	2,200
Total shareholders' equity:		Preceding year	1,995
Current year-end	23,471	Operating income:	
Preceding year-end	14,037	Current year	9,125
Borrowings.....................................	6,585	Preceding year	4,002

Requirements

1. Compute Easton's return on assets and return on equity during 2017 (the current year). Easton has no preferred stock outstanding.
2. Do the company's rates of return look strong or weak? Give your reason.

CHALLENGE EXERCISES

LEARNING OBJECTIVE ❷❹

Reconstruct transactions from the financial statements

E9-33 A-1 Networking Solutions Inc. began operations on January 1, 2017, and immediately issued its shares, receiving cash. A-1's balance sheet at December 31, 2017, reported the following shareholders' equity:

Common shares	$253,500
Retained earnings..	38,000
Total shareholders' equity...	$291,500

During 2017, A-1:

a. Issued 50,000 common shares for $5 per share.
b. Issued common shares for $7 each.
c. Earned net income of $56,000 and declared and paid cash dividends. Revenues were $171,000 and expenses totalled $115,000.

Requirement

Journalize all A-1's shareholders' equity transactions during the year. A-1's entry in part (c) to close net income to Retained Earnings was:

Revenues	171,000	
Expenses		115,000
Retained Earnings...		56,000

LEARNING OBJECTIVE ❷❹

Explain the changes in shareholders' equity

E9-34 Startech Limited reported the following shareholders' equity data (all dollars in millions):

	December 31,	
	2017	**2016**
Preferred shares...	$ 604	$ 740
Common shares	2,390	2,130
Retained earnings..	20,661	19,108

Startech earned net income of $2,960 during 2017. Common shares were issued for $20.00 each. For each account except Retained Earnings, one transaction explains the change from the December 31, 2016, balance to the December 31, 2017, balance. Two transactions affected Retained Earnings. Give a full explanation, including the dollar amount, for the change in each account.

E9-35 Fun City Inc. ended 2016 with 8 million common shares issued and outstanding. The average issue price was $1.50. Beginning retained earnings totalled $40 million.

LEARNING OBJECTIVE ❷❹

Account for changes in shareholders' equity

- In March 2017, Fun City issued 2 million common shares at a price of $2 per share.
- In May, the company declared and distributed a 10% stock dividend at a time when Fun City's common shares had a fair value of $3 per share.
- Then in October, Fun City's stock price dropped to $1 per share and the company executed a 1-for-2 stock split.
- For the year, Fun City earned net income of $26 million and declared cash dividends of $17 million.

Determine what Fun City should report for shareholders' equity at December 31, 2017. Journal entries are not required.

PROBLEMS (GROUP A)

P9-36A The board of directors of Freestroke Swim Centres Inc. is meeting to address the concerns of shareholders. Shareholders have submitted the following questions for discussion at the board meeting. Answer each question.

LEARNING OBJECTIVE ❶❹

Explain the features of a corporation's shares

1. Why did Freestroke organize as a corporation if a corporation must pay an additional layer of income tax?
2. How are preferred shares similar to common shares? How are preferred shares similar to debt?
3. Would Freestroke investors prefer to receive cash dividends or stock dividends? Explain your reasoning.

P9-37A The articles of incorporation from the province of Ontario authorize Challenger Canoes Inc. to issue 10,000 shares of $6 preferred shares and 100,000 common shares. In its first month, Challenger completed the following transactions:

LEARNING OBJECTIVE ❷❹

Record corporate transactions and prepare the shareholders' equity section of the balance sheet

2017

Oct.   6   Issued 300 common shares to the lawyer for assistance with chartering the corporation. The lawyer's fee was $1,500. Debit Organization Expense.

        9   Issued 9,000 common shares to Jerry Spence and 12,000 shares to Sheila Markle in return for cash equal to the shares, market price of $5 per share. Spence and Markle are executives of the company.

      10   Issued 400 preferred shares to acquire a patent with a fair value of $40,000.

      26   Issued 2,000 common shares for cash of $12,000.

Requirements

1. Record the transactions in the journal.
2. Prepare the shareholders' equity section of the Challenger balance sheet at October 31, 2017. The ending balance of Retained Earnings is $49,000.

P9-38A Samuells' Sportswear's articles of incorporation authorize the company to issue 5,000 $5 preferred shares and 500,000 common shares. Samuells' issued 1,000 preferred shares at $100 per share. It issued 100,000 common shares for $427,000. The company's Retained Earnings balance at the beginning of 2017 was $61,000. Net income for 2017 was $80,000, and the company declared a $5 cash dividend on preferred shares for 2017.

LEARNING OBJECTIVE ❷❹

Prepare the shareholders' equity section of the balance sheet

Requirement

Prepare the shareholders' equity section of Samuells' Sportswear Inc.'s balance sheet at December 31, 2017. Show the computation of all amounts. Journal entries are not required.

LEARNING OBJECTIVE ❸

Fight off a takeover of the corporation

P9-39A Calpak Winter Sports Ltd. is positioned ideally in the winter business. Located in Whistler, B.C., Calpak is the only company with a distribution network for its imported goods. The company did a brisk business around the 2010 Winter Olympics held in Whistler. Calpak's recent success has made the company a prime target for a takeover. Against the wishes of Calpak's board of directors, an investment group from Vancouver is attempting to buy 51% of Calpak's outstanding shares. Board members are convinced that the Vancouver investors would sell off the most desirable pieces of the business and leave little of value. At the most recent board meeting, several suggestions were advanced to fight off the hostile takeover bid.

Requirement

Suppose you are a significant shareholder of Calpak Winter Sports. Write a short memo to the board to propose an action that would make it difficult for the investor group to take over Calpak. Include in your memo a discussion of the effect your proposed action would have on the company's assets, liabilities, and total shareholders' equity.

LEARNING OBJECTIVE ❷❹

Measure the effects of share issuance and dividend transactions on shareholders' equity

P9-40A Wholegrain Health Foods Inc. is authorized to issue 5,000,000 common shares. In its initial public offering during 2013, Wholegrain issued 500,000 common shares for $7.00 per share. Over the next year, Wholegrain's share price increased and the company issued 400,000 more shares at an average price of $8.50.

During the five years from 2013 through 2017, Wholegrain earned net income of $920,000 and declared and paid cash dividends of $140,000. A 10% stock dividend was declared and distributed to the shareholders in 2017 on the shares outstanding. The market price was $8.00 per share when the stock dividend was distributed. At December 31, 2017, the company has total assets of $14,500,000 and total liabilities of $6,820,000.

Requirement

Show the computation of Wholegrain's total shareholders' equity at December 31, 2017. Present a detailed computation of each element of shareholders' equity.

LEARNING OBJECTIVE ❷❹

Analyze the shareholders' equity and dividends of a corporation

P9-41A Steeltrap Security Inc. included the following shareholders' equity on its balance sheet at December 31, 2017:

Shareholders' Equity	($ millions)
Preferred Shares:	
Authorized 20,000 shares in each class:	
$5.00 Cumulative Preferred Shares, 2,500 shares issued	$ 125,000
$2.50 Cumulative Preferred Shares, 4,000 shares issued	100,000
Common Shares:	
Authorized 80,000 shares, issued 48,000 shares..............................	384,000
Retained earnings...	529,000
	$1,138,000

Requirements

1. Identify the different issues of shares Steeltrap Security has outstanding.
2. What was the value at which the $2.50 Cumulative Preferred Shares were issued?
3. Suppose Steeltrap decided not to pay its preferred dividends for one year. Would the company have to pay these dividends in arrears before paying dividends to the common shareholders? Why?

4. What amount of preferred dividends must Steeltrap declare and pay each year to avoid having preferred dividends in arrears?
5. Assume preferred dividends are in arrears for 2016. Journalize the declaration of a $50,000 cash dividend for 2017. No explanation is needed.

P9-42A Exquisite Jewellery Limited reported the following summarized balance sheet at December 31, 2016:

LEARNING OBJECTIVE ❷❹

Account for share issuance and dividends

Assets	
Current assets	$33,400
Property and equipment, net	51,800
Total assets	$85,200
Liabilities and Equity	
Liabilities	$37,800
Shareholders' equity:	
$0.50 cumulative preferred shares, 400 shares issued	2,000
Common shares, 6,000 shares issued	23,400
Retained earnings	22,000
Total liabilities and equity	$85,200

During 2017, Exquisite completed these transactions that affected shareholders' equity:

Feb.	13	Issued 5,000 common shares for $4 per share.
June	7	Declared the regular cash dividend on the preferred shares.
July	24	Paid the cash dividend.
Aug.	9	Declared a 10% stock dividend on the common shares. Market price of the common shares was $5 per share.
Aug.	23	Distributed the stock dividend.
Nov.	20	Issued 200 common shares for $8 per share.

Requirements
1. Journalize Exquisite's transactions. Explanations are not required.
2. Report Exquisite Jewellery Limited's shareholders' equity at December 31, 2017. Net income for 2017 was $27,000.

P9-43A Niles Corporation completed the following selected transactions during the current year:

LEARNING OBJECTIVE ❷❹

Measure the effects of dividend and share transactions on a company

Mar.	3	Declared and distributed a 10% stock dividend on the 90,000 common shares outstanding. The market price of the common shares was $25 per share.
May	16	Declared a cash dividend on the $5 preferred shares (5,000 shares outstanding).
	30	Paid the cash dividends.
Dec.	8	Issued 1,500 common shares for $27 per share.
	19	Issued 10,000 common shares for $28 per share.

Requirement
Analyze each transaction in terms of its effect (in dollars) on the accounting equation of Niles Corporation.

LEARNING OBJECTIVE ❷❹❻

Prepare a corporation's balance sheet; measure profitability

P9-44A The following accounts and related balances of Bluebird Designers, Inc., as of December 31, 2017, are arranged in no particular order.

Cash	$ 45,000	Interest expense	$ 16,300
Accounts receivable, net	25,000	Property, plant, and	
Contributed surplus	53,800	equipment, net	359,000
Accrued liabilities	22,000	Common shares	
Long-term note payable	97,000	500,000 shares authorized,	
Inventory	89,000	110,000 shares issued	197,000
Dividends payable	9,000	Prepaid expenses	14,000
Retained earnings	?	Common shareholders'	
Accounts payable	135,000	equity, December 31, 2016	220,000
Trademarks, net	9,000	Net income	90,000
Goodwill	18,000	Total assets,	
		December 31, 2016	500,000
		Net sales	750,000

Requirements

1. Prepare Bluebird's classified balance sheet in the account format at December 31, 2017.
2. Compute Bluebird's rate of return on total assets and rate of return on equity for the year ended December 31, 2017.
3. Do these rates of return suggest strength or weakness? Give your reason.

LEARNING OBJECTIVE ❼

Use a statement of changes in shareholders' equity

P9-45A Asian Food Specialties Inc. reported the following statement of changes in shareholders' equity for the year ended June 30, 2017. The company was founded in 2014 and issued 455 million common shares. There had been no further share transactions until 2017.

Asian Food Specialties Inc.
Statement of Changes in Shareholders' Equity
For the Year Ended June 30, 2017

(in millions)	Common Shares	Retained Earnings	Total
Balance, June 30, 2016			
455 shares outstanding	$2,275	$1,702	$3,977
Net income		540	540
Cash dividends		(117)	(117)
Issuance of shares (5 shares)	50		50
Stock dividend (36 shares)	186	(186)	–
Issuance of shares (2 shares)	20		20
Balance, June 30, 2017	$2,531	$1,939	$4,470

Requirements

Answer these questions about Asian Food Specialties's shareholders' equity transactions:

1. The income tax rate is 33%. How much income before income tax did Asian Food Specialties report on the income statement?
2. What is the stated value of a common share at June 30, 2016?
3. At what price per share did Asian Food Specialties issue its common shares during the year?
4. Asian Food Specialties's statement of changes in shareholders' equity lists the share transactions in the order in which they occurred. What was the percentage of the stock dividend? Round to the nearest percentage.

PROBLEMS (GROUP B)

P9-46B Reinhart Industries Limited is conducting a special meeting of its board of directors to address some concerns raised by the shareholders. Shareholders have submitted the following questions. Answer each question.

1. Why are common shares and retained earnings shown separately in the shareholders' equity section of the balance sheet?
2. Lou Harris, a Reinhart shareholder, proposes to give some land she owns to the company in exchange for company shares. How should Reinhart Industries Limited determine the number of shares to issue for the land?
3. Preferred shares generally are preferred with respect to dividends and in the event of a liquidation. Why would investors buy *common* shares when *preferred* shares are available?
4. One of the Reinhart shareholders owns 100 shares of Reinhart, and someone has offered to buy her shares for their book value. What formula should be used to compute the book value of her shares?

LEARNING OBJECTIVE ❶❷❺

Explain the features of a corporation's shares

P9-47B The partners who own Bassett Furniture Co. wished to avoid the unlimited personal liability of the partnership form of business, so they incorporated as BFC Inc. The articles of incorporation from the province of Manitoba authorize the corporation to issue 10,000 $6 preferred shares and 250,000 common shares. In its first month, BFC completed the following transactions:

LEARNING OBJECTIVE ❷❹

Record corporate transactions and prepare the shareholders' equity section of the balance sheet

2017		
Jan.	3	Issued 1,000 common shares to the promoter for assistance with issuance of the common shares. The promotional fee was $10,000. Debit Organization Expense.
	6	Issued 5,000 common shares to Jo Bassett, and 3,800 shares to Mel Bassett in return for cash equal to the market price of $11 per share. (The Bassetts were partners in Bassett Furniture Co.)
	12	Issued 1,000 preferred shares to acquire a patent with a fair value of $110,000.
	22	Issued 1,500 common shares for $12 cash per share.

Requirements

1. Record the transactions in the journal.
2. Prepare the shareholders' equity section of the BFC Inc. balance sheet at January 31. The ending balance of Retained Earnings is $89,000.

P9-48B Northwest Territories Inc. has the following shareholders' equity information:

Northwest's incorporation authorizes the company to issue 10,000 $5 cumulative preferred shares and 400,000 common shares. The company issued 1,000 preferred shares at $100 per share. It issued 100,000 common shares for a total of $370,000. The company's Retained Earnings balance at the beginning of 2017 was $40,000, and net income for the year was $90,000. During 2017, Northwest declared the specified dividend on preferred shares and a $0.50 per-share dividend on common shares. Preferred dividends for 2016 were in arrears.

LEARNING OBJECTIVE ❷❹

Prepare the shareholders' equity section of the balance sheet

Requirement

Prepare the shareholders' equity section of Northwest Territories Inc.'s balance sheet at December 31, 2017. Show the computation of all amounts. Journal entries are not required.

P9-49B Gary Swan Imports Inc. is located in Stratford, Ontario. Swan is the only company with reliable sources for its imported gifts. The company does a brisk business with specialty stores such as Bowring. Swan's recent success has made the company a prime target for a takeover. An investment group from Toronto is attempting to buy 51% of Swan's

LEARNING OBJECTIVE ❸

Repurchase common shares to fight off a takeover of the corporation

outstanding shares against the wishes of Swan's board of directors. Board members are convinced that the Toronto investors would sell the most desirable pieces of the business and leave little of value.

At the most recent board meeting, several suggestions were made to fight off the hostile takeover bid. The suggestion with the most promise is to repurchase a huge quantity of common shares. Swan has the cash to carry out this plan.

Requirement

Suppose you are a significant shareholder of Gary Swan Imports Inc. Write a memorandum to explain to the board how the repurchase of common shares would make it difficult for the Toronto group to take over Swan. Include in your memo a discussion of the effect that repurchasing common shares would have on shares outstanding and on the size of the corporation.

LEARNING OBJECTIVE ②④

Measure the effects of share issuance, net income and dividend transactions on shareholders' equity

P9-50B Western Agriculture Industries Ltd. is authorized by the province of Saskatchewan to issue 500,000 common shares.

In its initial public offering during 2013, Western Agriculture issued 200,000 of its common shares for $12 per share. Over the next year, Western Agriculture's common share price increased, and the company issued 100,000 more shares at an average price of $14.50.

During the five years from 2013 to 2017, Western Agriculture earned net income of $395,000 and declared and paid cash dividends of $119,000. Stock dividends of $135,000 were declared and distributed to the shareholders in 2016 when the share market price was $10. At December 31, 2017, total assets of the company are $7,030,000, and liabilities add up to $2,904,000.

Requirement

Show the computation of Western Agriculture Industries Ltd.'s total shareholders' equity at December 31, 2017. Present a detailed computation of each element of shareholders' equity.

LEARNING OBJECTIVE ②④

Analyze the shareholders' equity and dividends of a corporation

P9-51B Teak Outdoor Furniture Limited included the following shareholders' equity on its year-end balance sheet at February 28, 2017:

Shareholders' Equity	
Preferred shares, $1.10 cumulative; authorized 100,000 shares in each class	
Class A—issued 75,000 shares	$ 1,500,000
Class B—issued 92,000 shares	1,840,000
Common shares; authorized 1,000,000 shares, issued 280,000 shares	6,940,000
Retained earnings	8,330,000
	$18,610,000

Requirements

1. Identify the different issues of shares that Teak Outdoor Furniture Limited has outstanding.
2. Give the summary entries to record issuance of all the Teak shares. Assume that all the shares were issued for cash. Explanations are not required.
3. Suppose Teak did not pay its preferred dividends for three years. Would the company have to pay those dividends in arrears before paying dividends to the common shareholders? Give your reason.

4. What amount of preferred dividends must Teak declare and pay each year to avoid having preferred dividends in arrears?

5. Assume that preferred dividends are in arrears for 2016. Record the declaration of an $800,000 dividend on February 28, 2017. An explanation is not required.

P9-52B Winnipeg Enterprises Inc. reported the following summarized balance sheet at December 31, 2016:

LEARNING OBJECTIVE ❷❹

Account for share issuance and dividends

Assets

Current assets	$18,200
Property and equipment, net	34,700
Total assets	$52,900

Liabilities and Equity

Liabilities	$ 6,200
Shareholders' equity:	
$5 cumulative preferred shares, 180 shares issued	1,800
Common shares, 2,400 shares issued	25,900
Retained earnings	19,000
Total liabilities and equity	$52,900

During 2017, Winnipeg Enterprise completed these transactions that affected shareholders' equity:

Feb.	22	Issued 1,000 common shares for $16 per share.
May	4	Declared the regular cash dividend on the preferred shares.
	24	Paid the cash dividend.
July	9	Declared 10% stock dividend on the common shares. Market price of the common shares was $18 per share.
July	23	Distributed the stock dividend.
Dec.	8	Issued 600 common shares for $15 per share.

Requirements

1. Journalize Winnipeg Enterprise's transactions. Explanations are not required.

2. Report Winnipeg Enterprise's shareholders' equity at December 31, 2017. Net income for 2017 was $62,000.

P9-53B Cones Inc. of Baie-Comeau completed the following transactions during 2017, the company's tenth year of operations:

LEARNING OBJECTIVE ❷❹

Measure the effects of dividend and share transactions on a company

Feb.	2	Issued 10,000 common shares for cash of $250,000.
Apr.	22	Sold 700 common shares for $26 per share.
Aug.	6	Declared a cash dividend on the 10,000 $0.60 preferred shares.
Sept.	1	Paid the cash dividends.
Nov.	18	Declared and distributed a 10% stock dividend on the 30,000 common shares outstanding. The market value of the common shares was $25 per share.

Requirement

Analyze each transaction in terms of its effect (in dollars) on the accounting equation of Cones Inc.

LEARNING OBJECTIVE ❷❹❻

Prepare a corporation's balance sheet; measure profitability

P9-54B The following accounts and related balances of Dove Designers, Inc., as of December 31, 2017, are arranged in no particular order.

Cash	$ 53,000	Interest expense	$ 16,200
Accounts receivable, net	27,000	Property, plant, and	
Contributed surplus	75,600	equipment, net	355,000
Accrued liabilities	25,000	Common shares,	
Long-term note payable	95,000	1,250,000 shares authorized,	
Inventory	98,000	118,000 shares issued	211,000
Dividends payable	6,000	Prepaid expenses	14,000
Retained earnings	?	Common shareholders'	
Accounts payable	130,000	equity, December 31, 2013	233,000
Trademark net	3,000	Net income	71,000
Goodwill	18,000	Total assets,	
		December 31, 2013	495,000
		Net sales	800,000

Requirements

1. Prepare Dove's classified balance sheet in the account format at December 31, 2017.
2. Compute Dove's rate of return on total assets and rate of return on equity for the year ended December 31, 2017.
3. Do these rates of return suggest strength or weakness? Give your reason.

LEARNING OBJECTIVE ❼

Use a statement of shareholders' equity

P9-55B Datacom Services Inc. reported the following statement of changes in shareholders' equity for the year ended October 31, 2017.

Datacom Services Inc.
Statement of Changes in Shareholders' Equity
For the Year Ended October 31, 2017

(in millions)	Common Shares	Retained Earnings	Total
Balance, Oct. 31, 2016,			
675 shares outstanding	$2,025	$904	$2,929
Net income		360	360
Cash dividends		(194)	(194)
Issuance of shares (13 shares)	49		49
Stock dividend (55 shares)	166	(166)	–
Balance, Oct. 31, 2017	$2,240	$904	$3,144

Requirements

Answer these questions about Datacom Services's shareholders' equity transactions:

1. The income tax rate is 33%. How much income before income tax did Datacom report on the income statement?
2. What is the stated value of a common share at October 31, 2017?
3. At what price per share did Datacom Services issue its common shares during the year?
4. Datacom Services's statement lists the share transactions in the order they occurred. What was the percentage of the stock dividend?

APPLY YOUR KNOWLEDGE

DECISION CASES

Case 1. Nate Smith and Darla Jones have written a smartphone app. They need additional capital to market the app, so they plan to incorporate their business. Smith and Jones are considering alternative capital structures for the corporation. Their primary goal is to raise as much capital as possible without giving up control of the business. Smith and Jones plan to receive 50,000 common shares of the corporation in return for the net assets of their old business. After the old company's books are closed and the assets adjusted to current fair value, Smith's and Jones's capital balances will each be $25,000.

The company's incorporation plans include an authorization to issue 10,000 preferred shares and 500,000 common shares. Smith and Jones are uncertain about the most desirable features for the preferred shares. Prior to incorporating, Smith and Jones are discussing their plans with two investment groups. The corporation can obtain capital from outside investors under either of the following plans:

- **Plan 1.** Group 1 will invest $80,000 to acquire 800 $6, non-voting preferred shares.
- **Plan 2.** Group 2 will invest $55,000 to acquire 500 $5 preferred shares and $35,000 to acquire 35,000 common shares. Each preferred share receives 50 votes on matters that come before the shareholders.

Requirements

Assume that the company is incorporated.

1. Journalize the issuance of common shares to Smith and Jones. Debit each person's capital account for its balance.
2. Journalize the issuance of shares to the outsiders under both plans.
3. Assume that net income for the first year is $120,000 and total dividends are $30,000. Prepare the shareholders' equity section of the corporation's balance sheet under both plans.
4. Recommend one of the plans to Smith and Jones. Give your reasons.

Case 2. Suppose the balance sheet of the financial statements you are analyzing had the following shareholders' equity amounts on December 31, 2017 (adapted, in millions):

Common Shares; 1,135 shares issued	$ 278
Retained earnings	$9,457
Total shareholders' equity	$9,735

During 2017, the corporation paid a cash dividend of $0.715 per share. Assume that, after paying the cash dividends, the corporation distributed a 10% dividend. Assume further that the following year, the corporation declared and paid a cash dividend of $0.65 per share. Suppose you own 10,000 of this corporation's common shares acquired three years ago, prior to the 10% stock dividend. The market price of the shares was $61.02 per share before the stock dividend.

Requirements

1. How does the stock dividend affect your proportionate ownership in the corporation? Explain.
2. What amount of cash dividends did you receive last year? What amount of cash dividends will you receive after the above dividend action?

This section's material reflects CPA enabling competencies,* including:

1. Professionalism and ethical behaviour
2. Problem-solving and decision-making
4. Self-management
5. Teamwork and leadership

LEARNING OBJECTIVE ❶❷❹
Evaluate alternative ways of raising capital

LEARNING OBJECTIVE ❹
Analyze cash dividends and stock dividends

3. Assume that immediately after the stock dividend was declared and distributed, the market price of the corporation's shares decreased from $61.02 per share to $55.473 per share. Does this decrease represent a loss to you? Explain.

4. Suppose the corporation announces at the time of the stock dividend that the company will continue to pay the annual $0.715 cash dividend per share, even after distributing the stock dividend. Would you expect the market price of the common shares to decrease to $55.473 per share as in Requirement 3? Explain.

ETHICAL ISSUE

Ethical Issue 1. *Note:* This case is based on a real situation.

George Campbell paid $50,000 for a franchise that entitled him to market Success Associates software programs in the countries of the European Union. Campbell intended to sell individual franchises for the major language groups of Western Europe: German, French, English, Spanish, and Italian. Naturally, investors considering buying a franchise from Campbell asked to see the financial statements of his business.

Believing the value of the franchise to be greater than $50,000, Campbell sought to capitalize his own franchise at $500,000. The law firm of McDonald & LaDue helped Campbell form a corporation chartered to issue 500,000 common shares. Attorneys suggested the following chain of transactions:

a. A third party borrows $500,000 and purchases the franchise from Campbell.

b. Campbell pays the corporation $500,000 to acquire all its shares.

c. The corporation buys the franchise from the third party, who repays the loan.

In the final analysis, the third party is debt-free and out of the picture. Campbell owns all the corporation's shares, and the corporation owns the franchise. The corporation's balance sheet lists a franchise acquired at a cost of $500,000. This balance sheet is Campbell's most valuable marketing tool.

Requirements

1. What is unethical about this situation?

2. Who can be harmed in this situation? How can they be harmed? What role does accounting play here?

Ethical Issue 2. St. Genevieve Petroleum Corp. is a public, independent oil producer. St. Genevieve's year-end is June 30. In February 2017, company geologists discovered a pool of oil that tripled the company's proven reserves. The March 31, 2017, interim financial statements did not disclose the new pool of oil. During February and March 2017, St. Genevieve's managers quietly purchased most of its shares. The June 30, 2017, annual financial statements did disclose the new pool of oil, and the company's share price increased from $6 to $48.

Requirements

1. Did St. Genevieve's managers behave ethically? Explain your answer.

2. Identify the fundamental qualitative characteristic relevant to this situation.

3. Who was helped and who was harmed by management's actions?

FOCUS ON FINANCIALS

Canadian Tire Corporation

LEARNING OBJECTIVE ❷❹❼

Analyze common shares and retained earnings

MyAccountingLab

Canadian Tire financial statements appear in Appendix A at the end of this book. Use information in the financial statements and the notes to the financial statements to answer the following:

1. Describe the classes of shares that Canadian Tire has authorized? How many of each class are issued and outstanding at the end of 2014?

2. Did Canadian Tire issue any new shares during 2014? If so, how many did it issue and what was the average issue price? (Challenge)

3. What was the total dollar value of dividends that Canadian Tire declared in 2014? How much cash did it use to pay dividends in 2014? Why are these figures different? (Challenge)

FOCUS ON ANALYSIS

Canadian Tire Corporation

LEARNING OBJECTIVE ❻

Compute return on assets and return on equity

MyAccountingLab

Using Canadian Tire's financial statements that appear in Appendix A at the end of this book, answer the following: (Note: Canadian Tire's total assets were $13,228.6 and its common shareholders' equity was $4,764.3 at the end of 2012.)

1. Compute Canadian Tire's return on assets and return on equity for 2014 and 2013. For simplicity, treat the non-voting share capital as a component of common shareholders' equity. Based on this information, what is your assessment of Canadian Tire's performance in 2014 compared to 2013?

GROUP PROJECT

LEARNING OBJECTIVE ❻

Evaluate companies' return on assets and equity

Obtain the most recent financial statements of three Canadian companies operating in the same industry. Using the information in these statements, calculate the ROA and ROE for each company for each of the past two years. Based on this analysis, which company would you invest in and why?

CHECK YOUR WORK

STOP + THINK ANSWERS

STOP + THINK (9-1)

Despite being unable to vote, the Class A shareholders of Canadian Tire still have the other three main rights of shareholders: the right to sell the shares (hopefully for a gain), the right to receive dividends (which they currently receive each quarter), and the right to receive a residual interest in the company if it is ever liquidated. These benefits are more than enough to entice investors in the absence of the right to vote.

STOP + THINK (9-2)

1. 25,976,792 shares (100,000,000 authorized – 74,023,208 issued and outstanding)

2. No common shares were issued in 2014, as indicated by there being the same number of common shares issued and outstanding at the end of 2013 and 2014.

3. Average issue price per Class A non-voting share = $9.39 ($695.3 million of non-voting share capital/74,023,208 shares outstanding).

   Average issue price per common share = $0.06 ($200,000 of common share capital/3,423,366 shares outstanding).

STOP + THINK (9-3)

Canadian Tire earnings releases during 2014–2016 indicate that they regularly repurchased Class A shares to offset the dilutive effect of the issuance of Class A shares pursuant to its stock option and dividend reinvestment plans. Because the issuance of Class A shares upon the cashing in of stock options or the reinvestment of dividends increases the number of Class A shares outstanding, this reduces—or dilutes—the market value of the already-outstanding Class A shares. To avoid this reduction (or dilution), Canadian Tire repurchases some of the Class A shares to maintain the market value of the shares at a level roughly consistent with what it was prior to the issuance of the Class A shares. This is consistent with reason #2 on page 443.

STOP + THINK (9-4)

1. There will be no decrease in shareholders' equity for either company because stock dividends have no net impact on this total. Share capital increases and retained earnings decrease by the same amount, regardless of the size of the stock dividend.

2. Company A's market value per share after stock dividend = $9.09 ($2,000,000 total market value/220,000 shares issued and outstanding).

   Company B's market value per share after stock dividend = $8.33 ($2,000,000 total market value/240,000 shares issued and outstanding).

   Company B will have a lower market value per share after the stock dividends are distributed.

STOP + THINK (9-5)

1. $7,250,000 ($500,000 from preferred shareholders + $6,750,000 from common shareholders)

2. $4,900,000 (Retained Earnings of $3,250,000 + Dividends Paid of $1,650,000)

3. Unknown (Cash balance not provided; *Retained Earnings does not equal cash*)

4. $10,000,000 or $20/share (Total shareholders' equity of $10,500,000 – Preferred shareholders' equity of $500,000 = Common shareholders' equity of $10,000,000/500,000 shares = $20/share)

5. $260,000 ($310,000 total – $50,000 to preferred shareholders)

6. 750,000 (500,000 common shares outstanding divided by 2, then multiplied by 3). The split would have no effect on shareholders' equity, as only the number of shares issued and outstanding changes.

STOP + THINK (9-6)

Given that the two companies are comparable in terms of their industry, dividend history, and share price increases, it would make sense to focus on their relative ROA and ROE ratios. Because Company A has the healthier ROA and ROE compared to Company B (both ratios are higher than Company B's and both are higher than their benchmarks of 10% and 15%, respectively), it would make sense to invest in Company A.

STOP + THINK (9-7)

On Line 7 of the statement in Exhibit 9-4 we see that the company paid a total of $290.6 million to repurchase the Class A shares during 2014 and on Line 8 we see that this repurchase price exceeded the average cost of the repurchased shares by $266.3 million. We can therefore subtract the excess of $266.3 from the total repurchase price of $290.6 to get the total original cost of the repurchased shares, which is $24.3 million.

QUICK QUIZ ANSWERS

1. *c*

2. *c*

3. *d*

4. *c*

5. *b*

6. *d*

7. *a ($593,000 + $89,000 = $682,000)*

8. *c ($682,000 + $71,800 = $753,800)*

9. *b {($119,600 − $8,900)/[($681,400 + $664,800*)/2] = .164}*
   ($593,000 + $71,800 = $664,800)

10. *a 593,000/$11.86 = 50,000*

11. *b (providing that sufficient cash was available)*

12. *d*

13. *b*

14. *a*

15. *c 20,000 × $8.00 = $160,000*

16. *a ($350,000 − $160,000)/20,000 = $9.50*

17. *a*

18. *d*

19. *b*

20. *a [($44,000 − $4,000)/$384,000 = .104]*

The Statement of Cash Flows

Club4traveler/Shutterstock

LEARNING OBJECTIVES

1. **Explain** the uses of the statement of cash flows

2. **Explain** and **classify** cash flows from operating, investing, and financing activities

3. **Prepare** a statement of cash flows using the indirect method of determining cash flows from operating activities

A-1. **Prepare** a statement of cash flows using the direct method of determining cash flows from operating activities

CPA COMPETENCIES

Competencies* addressed in this chapter:

1.2.2 Evaluates treatment for routine transactions

1.3.1 Prepares financial statements

SPOTLIGHT

Canadian Tire Corporation's statement of cash flows on the next page shows how much cash the company generated from and used in its operating, investing, and financing activities during 2014. The company generated about $575 million in cash from its operating activities, which include the selling of bikes, gas, and financial services. During 2014, Canadian Tire also used about $590 million in cash to perform investing activities, such as purchasing property and equipment. Canadian Tire's financing activities, including the issuance of long-term debt and payment of dividends, resulted in net cash inflows of almost $90 million. Combined, these cash flow activities netted the company $74 million in cash during 2014, leaving Canadian Tire with $648 million in cash and cash equivalents at the end of the year.

	A	B
1	**Canadian Tire Corporation** Consolidated Statement of Cash Flows (Adapted) For the Year Ended January 3, 2015	
2	*(in millions)*	**January 3, 2015**
3	**Cash generated from (used for):**	
4	**Operating activities**	
5	Net income	$ 639.3
6	Adjustments for:	
7	Depreciation on property & equipment & investment property	279.2
8	Income tax expense	238.9
9	Net finance costs	108.9
10	Amortization of intangible assets	93.1
11	Change in fair value of redeemable financial instrument	17.0
12	Changes in fair value of derivative instruments	(33.9)
13	Loss (gain) on disposal of property & equipment, investment property & assets held for sale	(9.0)
14	Interest paid	(122.0)
15	Interest received	10.4
16	Income taxes paid	(256.5)
17	Other operating activities	25.3
18	**Cash flow before changes in non-cash working capital &** **other operating activities**	990.7
19	Trade & other receivables	(38.1)
20	Merchandise inventories	(146.6)
21	Income taxes	(1.9)
22	Prepaid expenses & deposits	(36.1)
23	Trade & other payables	86.9
24	Provisions	17.1
25	Long-term provisions	(3.2)
26	Other long-term liabilities	38.4
27	Change in loans receivable	(332.4)
28	**Cash generated from operating activities**	574.8
29		
30	**Investing activities**	
31	Additions to property & equipment & investment property	(538.6)
32	Additions to intangible assets	(150.1)
33	Acquisition of short-term investments	(431.6)
34	Proceeds from the maturity & disposition of short-term investments	665.3
35	Acquisition of long-term investments	(155.8)
36	Proceeds from the disposition of long-term investments	7.6
37	Proceeds on disposition of property & equipment, investment property & assets held for sale	21.3
38	Long-term receivables & other assets	3.1
39	Purchases of stores	(10.7)
40	**Cash used for investing activities**	(589.5)
41		
42	**Financing activities**	
43	Dividends paid	(141.4)
44	Distributions paid to non-controlling interests	(19.5)
45	Net issuance (repayment) of short-term borrowings	79.4
46	Issuance of loans payable	235.6
47	Repayment of loans payable	(242.4)
48	Issuance of long-term debt	563.7
49	Repayment of long-term debt & finance lease liabilities	(474.0)

	A	B
50	Payment of transaction costs related to long-term debt	(2.0)
51	Proceeds on sale of ownership interests in the financial services business	500.0
52	Transaction costs on sale of ownership interests in the financial services business	(23.2)
53	Repurchase of share capital	(290.6)
54	Change in deposits	(97.0)
55	**Cash generated from financing activities**	88.6
56		
57	**Cash generated in the year**	73.9
58	**Cash & cash equivalents, net of bank indebtedness, beginning of year**	574.2
59	**Effect of exchange rate fluctuations on cash held**	(0.3)
60	**Cash & cash equivalents, net of bank indebtedness, end of year**	$ 647.8
61		

Source: Reprinted with permission from Canadian Tire Corporation.

In Chapter 1 we introduced you to the statement of cash flows, and in later chapters we briefly discussed cash flows from a variety of operating, investing, and financing activities, such as accounts receivable, long-lived assets, and long-term debt. In this chapter, we provide you with more detailed guidance on how to prepare and use the statement of cash flows. We begin by discussing how managers, investors, and creditors use the statement of cash flows to make business decisions. Following this introduction, we provide additional guidance on how to classify many of the common operating, investing, and financing activities performed by a company. We end the chapter by offering detailed instruction on how to prepare the statement of cash flows using *the indirect method* of determining cash flows from operating activities, which is the method used by the vast majority of companies to prepare their statements of cash flows. The chapter's Appendix provides details on how to prepare the statement of cash flows using *the direct method* of determining cash flows from operating activities, which is actually the method preferred (but not required) by IFRS and ASPE. This method is rarely used in practice, however, because the indirect method gained prominence in the past and now continues to be used for reasons of comparability and user familiarity. After working through this chapter, you will be able to prepare, analyze, and interpret a company's statement of cash flows.

EXPLAIN THE USES OF THE STATEMENT OF CASH FLOWS

OBJECTIVE

❶ **Explain** the uses of the statement of cash flows

A company's balance sheet reports its cash position at a specific date, and its balance sheets from consecutive financial periods show whether its cash balance increased or decreased over the interim period. But the balance sheet doesn't tell us *what caused the cash balance to change.* The income statement reports a company's revenues, expenses, and net income, but because it is prepared on an accrual basis, it provides limited information about *how cash flows were affected by the company's business activities* during the reporting period. To gain insight into how a company's cash flows affected its cash position during a reporting period, we need another financial statement: the statement of cash flows.

IFRS and ASPE, which provide similar guidance on the statement of cash flows, explain that the information disclosed by a company about its cash flows provides decision-relevant information to users of the company's financial statements. This statement includes details about a company's cash receipts and cash disbursements from operating, investing, and financing activities and permits a user to determine exactly what caused the company's cash balance to increase or decrease during the period. Because the statement describes cash flow activities *during a particular fiscal period* and not at a specific point in time, it is dated the same way as the income statement and the statement of changes in shareholders' equity. The Canadian Tire statement of cash flows at the beginning of the chapter, for example, is dated "For the year ended January 3, 2015." Exhibit 10-1 illustrates the relative timing of the four basic financial statements.

EXHIBIT 10-1
Timing of the Financial Statements

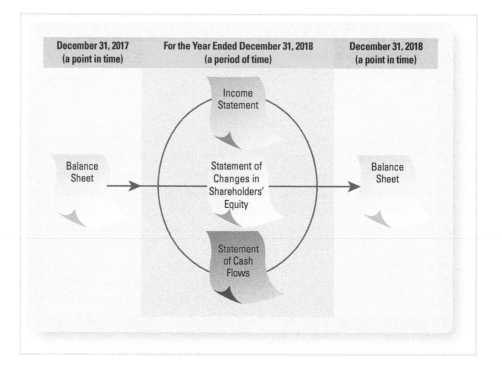

The statement of cash flows helps managers, investors, and creditors perform the following functions:

1. **Predict future cash flows.**   Past cash receipts and payments are reasonably good predictors of future cash flows.

2. **Evaluate management decisions.**   Businesses that make wise investment decisions prosper, and those that make unwise decisions suffer losses. The statement of cash flows reports how managers got cash and how they used cash to run the business.

3. **Determine ability to pay dividends and interest.**   Shareholders want dividends on their investments. Creditors collect interest and principal on their loans. The statement of cash flows reports on the ability to make these payments.

4. **Assess the relationship of net income to cash flows.**   Usually, cash and net income move together. High levels of income tend to lead to increases in cash, and low levels of income tend to lead to decreases in cash. A company's cash flow can, however, suffer even when net income is high, or improve when it suffers a net loss.

5. **Compare the operating performance of different companies.**   Because it eliminates the effects of using different accounting treatments for the same types of transactions and events, the statement of cash flows allows users to better compare the operating performance of multiple companies.

On a statement of cash flows, *cash* means more than just cash in the bank. It includes **cash equivalents**, which are short-term investments that are readily convertible to known amounts of cash, and which are very unlikely to change in value. Generally, only investments with maturities of three months or less meet these criteria. Examples include money-market investment accounts and three-month government Treasury bills. *Bank overdraft* balances should also be netted against the cash and cash equivalents total, as you can see on the last line of the Canadian Tire statement of cash flows presented at the beginning of this chapter. Throughout this chapter, the term *cash* refers to cash and cash equivalents.

STOP + THINK (10-1)

Examine the "Operating Activities" section of Canadian Tire's Statement of Cash Flows on page 482. In that section, you can see the depreciation on property and equipment and investment property, as well as the amortization of intangible assets, being added back to net income. Why are these two expenses being added back to net income in the process of calculating the company's cash flows from operating activities?

How Healthy Is a Company's Cash Flow? Telltale Signs of Financial Difficulty

Companies want to earn net income because profit measures success. Without net income, a business sinks. There will be no dividends, and the share price will likely suffer. High net income helps attract investors, but companies can't pay bills with net income—that requires cash.

A company needs both net income and strong cash flow. Income and cash flow usually move together because net income generates cash. Sometimes, however, net income and cash flow follow different patterns. To illustrate, consider Fastech Company Ltd.:

	A	B	C	D	E	F	G
1	**Fastech Company Ltd.** Income Statement For the Year Ended December 31, 2017		**Fastech Company Ltd.** Balance Sheet As at December 31, 2017				
2	Sales revenue	$ 100,000	Cash	$ 3,000	Total current liabilities	$ 50,000	
3	Cost of goods sold	30,000	Receivables	37,000	Long-term liabilities	20,000	
4	Operating expenses	10,000	Inventory	40,000			
5			PPE, net	60,000	Shareholders' equity	70,000	
6	Net income	$ 60,000	Total assets	$ 140,000	Total liabilities and equity	$ 140,000	
7							

What can we glean from Fastech's income statement and balance sheet?

- Fastech is profitable. Net income is 60% of revenue. Fastech's profitability looks outstanding.

- The current ratio is 1.6, and the debt ratio is only 50%. These measures suggest little trouble in paying bills.

- But Fastech is on the verge of bankruptcy. Can you spot the problems? Three trouble spots leap out to a financial analyst:

1. The cash balance is very low. Three thousand dollars isn't enough cash to pay the bills of a company with sales of $100,000.

2. Fastech isn't selling inventory fast enough. Fastech turned over its inventory only 0.75 times during the year. As we saw in Chapter 5, many companies have inventory turnover rates of 3 to 8 times a year. A turnover ratio of 0.75 times means it takes a very long time to sell inventory, and that delays cash collections.

3. Fastech's days' sales in receivables ratio is 135 days. Very few companies can wait that long to collect from customers. With standard credit terms of net 30 days, Fastech should collect cash within around 45 days. Fastech cannot survive with a collection period of 135 days.

The take-away lesson from this discussion is this: A company needs both net income and strong cash flow to succeed in business.

Let's now examine the three types of cash flow activities.

OBJECTIVE

❷ **Explain** and **classify** cash flows from operating, investing, and financing activities

EXPLAIN AND CLASSIFY CASH FLOWS FROM OPERATING, INVESTING, AND FINANCING ACTIVITIES

A business engages in three types of business activities:

- Operating activities
- Investing activities
- Financing activities

Operating activities comprise the main revenue-producing activities of a company and generally result from the transactions and other events that determine net income. Other activities that are not *investing* or *financing* activities are also classified as operating activities.[1] Common operating activities include cash receipts from a company's sales of its primary goods and services and cash payments to suppliers and employees for the goods and services they provide to generate these sales. When Canadian Tire pays suppliers for the goods it sells to its customers, for example, the payment is an operating activity that results in a cash outflow. Similarly, when a customer pays Canadian Tire for something they have purchased, a cash inflow from operating activities results. If a company is in the business of buying and selling long-lived assets, such as buildings or equipment, or trading investments, such as bonds and stocks, the cash flows from these transactions are classified as investing activities.

In Canadian Tire's statement of cash flows on page 482, we see that the company generated $575 million in cash flows from operating activities in 2014, and earned $639 million in net income on an accrual basis. The fact that Canadian Tire

---

[1]A simplifying assumption was made throughout Chapter 10 that all current asset accounts and all current liability accounts and their related cash flows should be classified as operating activities on the statement of cash flows.

There are, in fact, a number of current asset and current liability accounts that reflect investing and financing activities, respectively. For example, current assets may include short-term investments and short-term notes receivable. The cash flows from these accounts should be classified as investing activities on the statement of cash flows. Current liabilities may include short-term loans payable, and their related cash flows should be classified as financing activities on the statement of cash flows.

generated almost as much cash from operating activities as it earned in net income is a sign of excellent financial health because it indicates Canadian Tire has generated enough cash from its operating activities to fund capital expenditures, pay dividends, and finance its day-to-day operations without the aid of outside financing. A company that does not regularly generate sufficient cash flows from operating activities will eventually suffer liquidity and solvency problems.

Investing activities include the purchase and sale of long-term assets and other investments that do not qualify as cash equivalents. They generally consist of transactions that result in cash inflows or outflows related to resources used for generating future income and cash flows. IFRS and ASPE state that only expenditures related to assets that are recognized on the balance sheet qualify as investing activities. Cash payments to acquire tangible and intangible long-lived assets, and the cash received on the sale of these assets, are common investing activities. Investing activities also include cash flows from the purchase and sale of equity and debt instruments of other companies, and those related to both short-term and long-term advances and loans made to other entities. Any short-term investments that qualify as cash equivalents are excluded from investing activities.

In 2014, Canadian Tire spent almost $700 million on tangible and intangible assets and another $156 million on long-term investments. It also received $32 million in cash proceeds from the sale of property and other long-term assets. Like its operating activities, Canadian Tire's 2014 investing activities indicate excellent future prospects for the company because they show that the company invested almost $850 million in new long-term assets that will help it earn additional revenues in coming years.

Financing activities result in changes in the size and composition of a company's contributed equity and borrowings. Common financing activities include the issuance and acquisition of the company's shares; the payment of cash dividends; the cash proceeds from loans, bonds, and notes; and the repayment of amounts borrowed. With the exception of bank overdrafts, which are included in cash and cash equivalents, both short-term and long-term borrowings are included in financing activities.

The Financing Activities section of Canadian Tire's 2014 statement of cash flows contains more good news for the company's investors: it was able to pay them $141 million in cash dividends without having to issue any new shares (there are no proceeds from the issuance of share capital) or take on sizable amounts of new debt (net cash inflows from short-term borrowings, loans, and long-term debt were only $160 million).

In sum, Canadian Tire's 2014 statement of cash flows portrays a company with very high cash flows from operating activities, which it used to make significant investments in assets that will hopefully produce more income and cash in the future, while also having enough cash left over to pay a dividend to current shareholders without taking on much new debt or equity. In fact, even after net cash outflows from investing activities of almost $600 million, Canadian Tire ended 2014 with $648 million in cash and cash equivalents, which was $74 million more than the $574 million it had at the end of 2013.

Classifying Interest and Dividends

IFRS and ASPE offer different guidance on classifying cash flows related to interest and dividends. IFRS note that there is no consensus on the classification of interest paid or interest and dividends received. Under IFRS, interest paid and interest and dividends received may be classified as operating cash flows because they enter into the determination of net income. Alternatively, interest paid may be classified as a financing cash flow because it is a cost of obtaining financial resources, while interest and dividends received may be classified as investing cash flows because they represent returns on investments. Under IFRS, a company is free to choose either classification scheme but must use it consistently from then onward. ASPE require that all interest paid and all interest and dividends received and included in the determination of net income be classified as operating activities.

IFRS also offer a choice when classifying dividends paid: they may either be classified as a financing cash flow because they are a cost of obtaining financial resources, or they may be classified as cash flows from operating activities so that users may determine the company's ability to pay dividends out of operating cash flows. ASPE, however, require that any dividends paid and charged against retained earnings be classified as a financing activity.

For the sake of simplicity and consistency, this text classifies all interest paid and interest and dividends received as operating activities, while classifying dividends paid as a financing activity. All questions and problems in this chapter should be answered using this convention.

MyAccountingLab

STOP + THINK (10-2)

Classify each of the following as an operating activity, an investing activity, or a financing activity on the statement of cash flows prepared by the *indirect* method.

a. Issuance of shares

b. Borrowing

c. Sales revenue

d. Payment of dividends

e. Purchase of land

f. Repurchase of shares

g. Paying bonds payable

h. Interest expense

i. Sale of equipment

j. Cost of goods sold

k. Purchase of another company

l. Making a loan

Two Methods of Determining Cash Flows from Operating Activities

There are two methods of determining cash flows from operating activities on the statement of cash flows:

- **Indirect method**, in which net income is adjusted for non-cash transactions, for any deferrals or accruals of past or future operating cash receipts or payments, and for items of income or expense associated with investing or financing cash flows. (pp. 489 to 496)

- **Direct method**, which reports all cash receipts and cash payments from operating activities. (pp. 528 to 535)

The two methods use different computations, but they produce the same figure for cash from *operating activities*. IFRS and ASPE suggest that the direct method provides the most useful information to users, but this method is rarely used in practice because of the historical prominence of the indirect method. We present the indirect method below and detail the direct method in the Appendix to this chapter. The two methods do not affect *investing* or *financing* activities.

PREPARE A STATEMENT OF CASH FLOWS USING THE INDIRECT METHOD OF DETERMINING CASH FLOWS FROM OPERATING ACTIVITIES

OBJECTIVE

❸ **Prepare** a statement of cash flows using the indirect method of determining cash flows from operating activities

To illustrate the statement of cash flows we use Bradshaw Corporation, a dealer in playground equipment. Proceed as shown in the following steps to prepare the statement of cash flows by the indirect method.

Step 1 Lay out the template as shown in Exhibit 10-2. The exhibit is comprehensive. The diagram in Exhibit 10-3 (p. 490) gives a visual picture of the statement.

Step 2 Use the comparative balance sheet to determine the increase or decrease in cash during the period. The change in cash is the "check figure" for the statement of cash flows. Exhibit 10-4 (p. 491) gives Bradshaw Corporation's comparative balance sheet with cash highlighted. Bradshaw's cash decreased by $20,000 during 2017. *Why* did cash decrease? The statement of cash flows provides the answer.

	A	B
1	**Bradshaw Corporation** Statement of Cash Flows For the Year Ended December 31, 2017	
2	**Cash flows from operating activities:**	
3	Net income	
4	Adjustments to reconcile net income to net cash provided by (used for) operating activities:	
5	+ Depreciation and amortization expense	
6	+ Loss on sale of investing assets	
7	– Gain on sale of investing assets	
8	– Increases in operating current assets other than cash	
9	+ Decreases in operating current assets other than cash	
10	+ Increases in operating current liabilities	
11	– Decreases in operating current liabilities	
12	Net cash provided by (used for) operating activities	
13	**Cash flows from investing activities:**	
14	+ Proceeds from sales of tangible and intangible assets	
15	– Purchase of tangible and intangible assets	
16	+ Sales of investments that are not cash equivalents	
17	– Purchase of investments that are not cash equivalents	
18	+ Collecting on loans and advances to others	
19	– New loans and advances to others	
20	Net cash provided by (user for) investing activities	
21	**Cash flows from financing activities:**	
22	+ Proceeds from issuance of shares	
23	– Repurchase of shares	
24	+ Borrowing money (loans, bonds, notes)	
25	– Repaying debts (loans, bonds, notes)	
26	– Payment of dividends	
27	Net cash provided by (used for) financing activities	
28	**Net increase (decrease) in cash and cash equivalents during the year**	
29	+ Cash and cash equivalents at December 31, 2016	
30	= Cash and cash equivalents at December 31, 2017	
31		

EXHIBIT 10-2
Template of the Statement of Cash Flows: Indirect Method

EXHIBIT 10-3
Positive and Negative Items on the Statement of Cash Flows: Indirect Method

Positive Items	Business Activity	Negative Items
Net income		Net loss
Depreciation and amortization		Gain on sale of investing assets
Loss on sale of investing assets	Operating Activities	Increases in operating current assets other than cash
Decreases in operating current assets other than cash		Decreases in operating current liabilities
Increases in operating current liabilities		
Sale of tangible and intangible assets		Acquisition of tangible and intangible assets
Sale of investments that are not cash equivalents	Investing Activities	Purchase of investments that are not cash equivalents
Collecting on loans and advances to others		Making loans and advances to others
Issuing shares		Payment of dividends
Borrowing money	Financing Activities	Repurchase of shares
		Repaying debts

Step 3 From the income statement, take net income, depreciation and amortization expense, and any gains or losses on the sale of long-term assets. Print these items on the statement of cash flows. Exhibit 10-5 (p. 491) gives Bradshaw Corporation's income statement, with relevant items highlighted.

Step 4 Use the income statement and the balance sheet data to prepare the statement of cash flows. The statement of cash flows is complete only after you have explained the year-to-year changes in all the balance sheet accounts.

Cash Flows from Operating Activities

Operating activities comprise the main revenue-producing activities of a company, and generally result from the transactions and other events that determine net income.

The operating section of the statement of cash flows begins with net income, taken from the income statement (Exhibit 10-5), and is followed by "Adjustments to reconcile net income to net cash provided by (used for) operating activities" (Exhibit 10-6). Let's discuss these adjustments.

Ⓐ **DEPRECIATION AND AMORTIZATION EXPENSES.** When we record these expenses, we debit depreciation/amortization expense and credit accumulated depreciation/

EXHIBIT 10-4

Comparative Balance Sheet for Bradshaw Corporation

	A	B	C	D
1	**Bradshaw Corporation** Comparative Balance Sheet As at December 31, 2017 and 2016			
2	*(in thousands)*	**2017**	**2016**	**Increase (Decrease)**
3	**Assets**			
4	Current:			
5	Cash	$ 22	$ 42	$ (20)
6	Accounts receivable	93	80	13
7	Interest receivable	3	1	2
8	Inventory	135	138	(3)
9	Prepaid expenses	8	7	1
10	Long-term note receivable from another company	11	—	11
11	Property, plant, and equipment assets, net of depreciation	353	219	134
12	Total	$ 625	$ 487	$ 138
13	**Liabilities**			
14	Current:			
15	Accounts payable	$ 91	$ 57	$ 34
16	Salary and wages payable	4	6	(2)
17	Accrued liabilities	1	3	(2)
18	Long-term debt	160	77	83
19	**Shareholders' Equity**			
20	Share capital	259	258	1
21	Retained earnings	110	86	24
22	Total	$ 625	$ 487	$ 138
23				

Changes in current assets—Operating

Changes in non-current assets—Investing

Changes in current liabilities—Operating

Change in long-term liabilities and contributed capital accounts—Financing

Change due to net income—Operating
Change due to dividends—Financing

EXHIBIT 10-5

Income Statement for Bradshaw Corporation

	A	B	C	D
1	**Bradshaw Corporation** Income Statement For the Year Ended December 31, 2017			
2	*(in thousands)*			
3	Revenues and gains:			
4	Sales revenue	$ 284		
5	Interest revenue	12		
6	Dividend revenue	9		
7	Gain on sale of property, plant, and equipment	8		
8	Total revenues and gains		$ 313	
9	Expenses:			
10	Cost of goods sold	150		
11	Salary and wages expense	56		
12	Depreciation expense	18		
13	Other operating expense	17		
14	Interest expense	16		
15	Income tax expense	15		
16	Total expenses		272	
17	Net income		$ 41	
18				

		A	B	C	D
1		**Bradshaw Corporation** Statement of Cash Flows For the Year Ended December 31, 2017			
2		*(in thousands)*			
3		**Cash flows from operating activities:**			
4		Net income		$ 41	
5		Adjustments to reconcile net income to net cash provided by operating activities:			
6	Ⓐ	Depreciation	$ 18		
7	Ⓑ	Gain on sale of property, plant, and equipment	(8)		
8		Increase in accounts receivable	(13)		
9		Increase in interest receivable	(2)		
10		Decrease in inventory	3		
11	Ⓒ	Increase in prepaid expenses	(1)		
12		Increase in accounts payable	34		
13		Decrease in salary and wages payable	(2)		
14		Decrease in accrued liabilities	(2)	27	
15		Net cash provided by operating activities		$ 68	
16					

amortization. As a result, net income decreases, but there is no corresponding out-flow of cash. To reverse these non-cash expenses, we add them back to net income when determining operating cash flows.

Example: Suppose you had only two transactions during the period, a $1,000 cash sale and depreciation expense of $300. Net income is $700 ($1,000 − $300). Cash flow from operations is $1,000. To go from net income ($700) to cash flow ($1,000), we must add back the depreciation ($300).

Ⓑ **GAINS AND LOSSES ON THE SALE OF INVESTING ASSETS.** Sales of tangible and intangible assets and investments other than cash equivalents are *investing* activities, and there is often a gain or loss on these sales. On the statement of cash flows, a gain or loss on the sale is an adjustment to net income. Exhibit 10-6 includes an adjust-ment for a gain. During 2017, Bradshaw sold equipment for $62,000. The carrying amount was $54,000 (see calculation of carrying amount on page 497), so there was a gain of $8,000.

The $62,000 of cash received from the sale, which includes the $8,000 gain, is an investing activity. Net income also includes the gain, so we must subtract the gain from net cash provided from operations, as shown in Bradshaw Corporation's statement of cash flows (Exhibit 10-6). (We explain investing activities in the next section.)

A loss on the sale of investing assets also creates an adjustment in the operating section. Losses are *added back* to net income to compute cash flow from operations, because the amount of the loss does not represent an actual outflow of cash. Assume, for example, that the asset with the $54,000 carrying amount was sold for $50,000 instead of $62,000, yielding a loss of $4,000. The only cash involved in this transac-tion is the receipt of the $50,000 proceeds, which is recorded as an inflow in the investing section, just like the $62,000 above. The $4,000 loss is added back to net income in the operating section, because there is no corresponding outflow of cash.

Ⓒ **CHANGES IN NON-CASH OPERATING WORKING CAPITAL ACCOUNTS.** A com-pany's operating activities affect many of its non-cash current asset and liability accounts. When a company sells goods on credit, for example, accounts receivable increase and inventory decreases. Similarly, when a company incurs an expense but doesn't pay for it until later, accounts payable increase. As in Canadian Tire's statement of cash flows at the beginning of the chapter, these accounts are commonly referred to as **non-cash operating working capital accounts**. In this case, *non-cash* does not necessarily mean the underlying activity did not involve cash, because it often does. Instead, it simply means that the *account* itself (e.g., accounts receivable, unearned revenue) is not one that is included in the *cash and cash equivalents* balance on the statement of cash flows. These accounts are described as *operating* accounts because they derive from *operating activities*, and they are all components of a company's *working capital* balance (current assets – current liabilities). Let's examine how transactions and events in some of the common non-cash operating working capital accounts affect the operating section of the statement of cash flows.

Accounts receivable When a company makes a sale on credit, net income increases via the increase in revenue, but there is no corresponding increase in cash. So, to reconcile net income to cash flows from operations (CFO), we must *deduct* any *increase* in accounts receivable during the year. When a customer pays down its account, however, cash increases but net income is not affected. In this case, any *decrease* in accounts receivable during the year must be *added* to net income to reconcile it with CFO. Changes in other types of *non-investing* receivables (e.g., income taxes receivable) are treated the same way.

Inventory When a company purchases inventory, cash decreases but there is no impact on net income. So, to reconcile net income to CFO, we must *deduct* an *increase* in inventory from net income. Adjustments to CFO for inventory purchased on account are made via the change in *accounts payable and accrued liabilities*, which is discussed below. When inventory is sold, net income decreases via an increase in cost of goods sold, but there is no corresponding decrease in cash. Any *decrease* in inventory is therefore *added* to net income to arrive at CFO.

Prepaid expenses If a company prepays an expense, there is a cash outflow with no consequent decrease in net income, so an *increase* in prepaid expenses must be *deducted* from net income to get CFO. When we adjust prepaid expenses at the end of a reporting period to recognize the expenses related to the period, expenses increase and net income decreases, but cash is not affected. We must therefore *add* a *decrease* in prepaids to net income to reconcile it with CFO.

Accounts payable and accrued liabilities When a company incurs an expense but does not pay for it until later, net income decreases via an increase in the affected expense account, but cash does not decrease. So we must *add* any *increases* in accounts payable and accrued liabilities to net income to get CFO. When the company eventually pays the debt, cash decreases but net income is not affected, so *decreases* in accounts payable and accrued liabilities are *deducted* from net income to reconcile it with CFO. Changes in similar types of *non-financing* liabilities (e.g., provisions) are treated the same way.

Unearned revenue If a customer pays a company before receiving the related goods or services, then cash increases, but there is no impact on net income. Any *increases* in unearned revenue must therefore be *added* to net income when reconciling it with CFO. When the company eventually provides the related goods or services, net income increases via the increase in revenue, but cash is not affected. So we must *deduct* any *decrease* in unearned revenue from net income to get CFO.

As a rule, increases (decreases) in non-cash operating current asset accounts result in decreases (increases) to net income when determining CFO—*the account impact is the opposite of the CFO impact.* In contrast, increases (decreases) in non-cash operating current liability accounts result in increases (decreases) to net income when reconciling to CFO—*the account impact is consistent with the CFO impact.* Exhibit 10-7 summarizes the impacts of these changes in non-cash operating working capital accounts on cash and net income, as well as the adjustments needed to reconcile net income to CFO. We can apply these rules to Bradshaw's balance sheet data in Exhibit 10-4, which results in the CFO impacts disclosed in the Operating Activities section of its statement of cash flows in Exhibit 10-6.

EXHIBIT 10-7
Impacts of Changes in Non-cash Operating Working Capital Accounts on Cash Flows from Operations

Account	Transaction or Event	Account Impact	Cash Impact	Non-cash Net Income Impact	Cash Flows From Operations Impact
Current assets					
Accounts receivable	Sale on account	**Increase**	None	Increase	**Decrease**
Accounts receivable	Collection of account	**Decrease**	Increase	None	**Increase**
Inventory	Purchase	**Increase**	Decrease	None	**Decrease**
Inventory	Sale	**Decrease**	Increase	Decrease	**Increase**
Prepaid expenses	Prepayment of expense	**Increase**	Decrease	None	**Decrease**
Prepaid expenses	Recognition of expense	**Decrease**	None	Decrease	**Increase**
Current liabilities					
Payables and accruals	Purchase on account or accrual of expense	**Increase**	None	Decrease	**Increase**
Payables and accruals	Payment	**Decrease**	Decrease	None	**Decrease**
Unearned revenue	Cash received in advance of sale	**Increase**	Increase	None	**Increase**
Unearned revenue	Goods or services delivered	**Decrease**	None	Increase	**Decrease**

EVALUATING CASH FLOWS FROM OPERATING ACTIVITIES. Let's step back and evaluate Bradshaw's operating cash flows during 2017. Bradshaw generated $68,000 in cash flows from operating activities, which is $27,000 more than it reported in net income. This is a sign that Bradshaw has a high quality of earnings and is not using accruals and other estimates to inflate its net income. Now let's examine Bradshaw's investing and financing activities, as reported in Exhibit 10-8.

EXHIBIT 10-8
Statement of Cash Flows—
Indirect Method

	A	B	C	D
1	**Bradshaw Corporation** Statement of Cash Flows For the Year Ended December 31, 2017			
2	*(in thousands)*			
3	**Cash flows from operating activities:**			
4	Net income		$ 41	
5	Adjustments to reconcile net income to net cash provided by operating activities:			
6	Ⓐ Depreciation	$ 18		
7	Ⓑ Gain on sale of property, plant, and equipment	(8)		
8	Increase in accounts receivable	(13)		
9	Increase in interest receivable	(2)		
10	Decrease in inventory	3		
11	Ⓒ Increase in prepaid expenses	(1)		
12	Increase in accounts payable	34		
13	Decrease in salary and wages payable	(2)		
14	Decrease in accrued liabilities	(2)	27	
15	Net cash provided by operating activities		68	
16	**Cash flows from financing activities:**			
17	Acquisition of property, plant, and equipment	(206)		
18	Loan to another company	(11)		
19	Proceeds from sale of property, plant, and equipment	62		
20	Net cash used for investing activities		(155)	
21	**Cash flows from financing activities:**			
22	Proceeds from issuance of common shares	1		
23	Proceeds from issuance of long-term debt	94		
24	Repayment of long-term debt	(11)		
25	Payment of dividends	(17)		
26	Net cash provided by financing activities		67	
27	**Net decrease in cash**		(20)	
28	Cash balance, December 31, 2016		42	
29	Cash balance, December 31, 2017		$ 22	
30				

MyAccountingLab

MID-CHAPTER SUMMARY PROBLEM

Lucas Corporation reported the following income statement and comparative balance sheets, along with transaction data for 2017:

	A	B	C	D
1	**Lucas Corporation** Income Statement Year Ended December 31, 2017			
2	Sales revenue		$ 662,000	
3	Cost of goods sold		560,000	
4	Gross profit		102,000	
5	Operating expenses			
6	Salary expenses	$ 46,000		
7	Depreciation expense—equipment	7,000		
8	Amortization expense—patent	3,000		
9	Rent expense	2,000		
10	Total operating expenses		58,000	
11	Income from operations		44,000	

(Continued)

	A	B	C	D
12	Other items:			
13	Loss on sale of equipment		(2,000)	
14	Income before income tax		42,000	
15	Income tax expense		16,000	
16	Net income		$ 26,000	
17				

	A	B	C	D	E	F	G
1	**Lucas Corporation** Comparative Balance Sheets December 31, 2017 and 2016						
2	**Assets**	**2017**	**2016**	**Liabilities and Shareholders' Equity**	**2017**	**2016**	
3	Current:			Current:			
4	Cash and equivalents	$ 19,000	$ 3,000	Accounts payable	$ 35,000	$ 26,000	
5	Accounts receivable	22,000	23,000	Accrued liabilities	7,000	9,000	
6	Inventories	34,000	31,000	Income tax payable	10,000	10,000	
7	Prepaid expenses	1,000	3,000	Total current liabilities	52,000	45,000	
8	Total current assets	76,000	60,000	Long-term note payable	44,000	—	
9	Long-term investments	18,000	10,000	Bonds payable	40,000	53,000	
10	Equipment, net	67,000	52,000	Shareholders' equity:			
11	Patent, net	44,000	10,000	Share capital	52,000	20,000	
12				Retained earnings	27,000	19,000	
13				Less: Treasury stock	(10,000)	(5,000)	
14	Total assets	$ 205,000	$ 132,000	Total liabilities and equity	$ 205,000	$ 132,000	
15							

Requirement

Use the indirect method to prepare the Operating Activities section of Lucas Corporation's 2017 statement of cash flows.

ANSWER

	A	B	C	D
1	**Lucas Corporation** Statement of Cash Flows Year Ended December 31, 2017			
2	**Cash flows from operating activities:**			
3	Net income		$ 26,000	
4	Adjustments to reconcile net income to net cash provided by operating activities:			
5	Depreciation	$ 7,000		
6	Amortization	3,000		
7	Loss on sale of equipment	2,000		
8	Changes in non-cash operating working capital			
9	Decrease in accounts receivable	1,000		
10	Increase in inventories	(3,000)		
11	Decrease in prepaid expenses	2,000		
12	Increase in accounts payable	9,000		
13	Decrease in accrued liabilities	(2,000)	19,000	
14	Net cash provided by operating activities		45,000	
15				

Cash Flows from Investing Activities

Investing activities include the purchase and sale of long-term assets and other investments that do not qualify as cash equivalents. Purchases result in cash outflows from investing activities, whereas sales yield cash inflows. Cash inflows and outflows related to the same type of investing activity must be reported separately in the statement of cash flows.

ACQUISITIONS AND SALES OF TANGIBLE AND INTANGIBLE ASSETS. Companies with significant quantities of tangible assets typically keep track of them in a subledger, which details the cost, accumulated depreciation, and carrying amount of each item of property, plant, and equipment. When an asset is sold, its carrying amount can be deducted from the cash sale proceeds to determine the gain or loss on the sale of the asset. These details on individual asset sales can be accumulated to arrive at the total cash sale proceeds and net gain or loss on sales to be reported on the statement of cash flows for a given fiscal period. Without the detailed information from a company's asset subledger, we can use an alternative method to calculate this information.

To illustrate, we will use information from Bradshaw's balance sheet and income statement in Exhibits 10-4 and 10-5.

- At the beginning of 2017, Bradshaw's balance sheet shows that its carrying amount of property, plant, and equipment was $219,000. By the end of the year, it had increased to $353,000 (Exhibit 10-4).

- Bradshaw's income statement discloses depreciation expense of $18,000 and a gain on sale of property, plant, and equipment of $8,000 for 2017 (Exhibit 10-5).

Bradshaw's purchases of property, plant, and equipment total $206,000 (take this amount as given; see Exhibit 10-8). How much, then, are the proceeds from the sale of property, plant, and equipment? First, we must determine the carrying amount of property, plant, and equipment sold, as follows:

Property, plant, and equipment (net)

Beginning balance	+	Acquisitions	−	Depreciation	−	Carrying amount of assets sold	=	Ending balance
$219,000	+	$206,000	−	$18,000	−	−X	=	$353,000
						−X	=	$353,000 − $219,000 − $206,000 + $18,000
						X	=	$54,000

The sale proceeds are $62,000, determined as follows:

Sale proceeds	=	Carrying amount of assets sold	+	Gain	−	Loss
	=	$54,000	+	$8,000	−	$0
	=	$62,000				

Trace the sale proceeds of $62,000 to the statement of cash flows in Exhibit 10-8.

The Property, Plant, and Equipment T-account provides another look at the computation of the carrying amount of the assets sold.

Property, Plant, and Equipment, Net

Beginning balance	219,000	Depreciation	18,000
Acquisitions	206,000	Carrying amount of assets sold	54,000
Ending balance	353,000		

If the sale had resulted in a loss of $3,000, the sale proceeds would have been $51,000 ($54,000 − $3,000), and the statement would report $51,000 as a cash receipt from this investing activity.

The same process can be used to determine cash proceeds from the sale of intangible assets, although there would be no amortization to deal with in the case of intangibles with indefinite useful lives.

ACQUISITIONS AND SALES OF INVESTMENTS OTHER THAN CASH EQUIVALENTS. The carrying amount of investments sold can be computed in the manner illustrated for property, plant, and equipment. Investment carrying amounts are easier to calculate because there is no depreciation to account for, as shown in the following equation (Bradshaw has no investments, so the information below is for illustration only):

Investments

Beginning balance	+	Purchases	−	Carrying amount of investments sold	=	Ending balance
$100,000	+	$50,000		−X	=	$140,000
				−X	=	$140,000 − $100,000 − $50,000
				X	=	$10,000

The Investments T-account provides another look:

Investments			
Beginning balance	100		
Purchases	50	Carrying amount of investments sold	10
Ending balance	140		

If Bradshaw had realized a $15,000 gain on the sale of these investments, then the cash sale proceeds would have been $25,000 ($10,000 carrying amount + $15,000 gain), which we would report as a cash inflow in the Investing Activities section. The investment purchases of $50,000 in the illustration above would be reported as a cash outflow in the Investing section.

MAKING AND COLLECTING LOANS AND ADVANCES TO OTHERS. The beginning and ending balances of (short-term and long-term) Loans or Notes Receivable can be found on the balance sheet. If the amount of either the new loans/advances or the collections of loans/advances is known, the other amount can be computed. Bradshaw has a long-term note receivable of $11,000 at the end of 2017; this balance was zero at the end of 2016 (Exhibit 10-4; assume there were no collections during 2017). Using this information, we can determine the amount of loans/advances made during 2017 as follows:

Notes Receivable

Beginning balance	+	New loans made	−	Collections	=	Ending balance
$0	+	$X		−0	=	$11,000
		X			=	$11,000

Notes Receivable

Beginning balance	0		
New loans made	11	Collections	0
Ending balance	11		

This $11,000 loan to another company can be seen as a cash outflow in the Investing Activities section of Bradshaw's statement of cash flows in Exhibit 10-8.

Cash Flows from Financing Activities

Financing activities result in changes in the size and composition of a company's contributed equity and borrowings. The issuance of equity or borrowings results in a cash inflow; the repurchase of equity and repayment of borrowings are cash outflows. Cash inflows and outflows related to the same type of financing activity must be reported separately in the statement of cash flows.

BORROWING MONEY AND REPAYING DEBTS. The beginning and ending balances of (short-term and long-term) borrowings, such as Loans, Bonds, and Notes Payable, can be found on the balance sheet. If the amount of either the new borrowings or the repayment of debts is known, the other amount can be computed. Bradshaw's long-term debt increased from $77,000 at the end of 2016 to $160,000 by the end of 2017 (Exhibit 10-4; assume new borrowings of long-term debt were $94,000 in 2017). Using this information, we can determine the amount of long-term debt repayments made during 2017 as follows:

Long-Term Debt

Beginning balance	+	Borrowing of new debt	−	Repayments of debt	=	Ending balance
$77,000	+	$94,000		−X	=	$160,000
				−X	=	$160,000 − $77,000 − $94,000
				X	=	$11,000

This same information can be determined using a T-account as follows:

Long-Term Debt

		Beginning balance	77,000
Payments	11,000	Issuance of new debt	94,000
		Ending balance	160,000

The $94,000 cash inflow from new borrowing and the $11,000 cash outflow from the repayment of debts can be seen in the Financing Activities section in Exhibit 10-8.

Common Shares

Beginning balance	+	Issuance of new shares	−	Repurchase of shares	=	Ending balance
$258,000	+	$X	−	$0	=	$259,000
					=	$1,000

Here is the same information presented in a T-account:

Common Shares

		Beginning balance	258,000
		Issuance of new shares	1,000
		Ending balance	259,000

The $1,000 cash inflow from issuing new shares can also be seen in the Financing Activities section of Exhibit 10-8.

PAYMENT OF DIVIDENDS. Dividend payments can usually be found in the Statement of Retained Earnings (or Statement of Changes in Owners' Equity), but they can also be determined as follows, using information from Bradshaw's balance sheet (Exhibit 10-4) and income statement (Exhibit 10-5):

Retained Earnings

Beginning balance	+	Net income	−	Dividends declared	=	Ending balance
$86,000	+	$41,000		−X	=	$110,000
				−X	=	$110,000 − $86,000 − $41,000
				X	=	$17,000

The T-account provides another view of the dividend payment computation:

Retained Earnings

Dividend declarations	17,000	Beginning balance	86,000
		Net income	41,000
		Ending balance	110,000

The $17,000 dividend payment can be seen as a cash outflow in the Financing Activities section in Exhibit 10-8. Any increase or decrease in a Dividend Payable account is treated the same way as a change in a non-cash operating current liability account, except that the adjustment to cash flows is included in the Financing Activities section. If, for example, Bradshaw had a Dividends Payable account that had increased by $5,000 during 2017, then we would add this increase as a *Change in non-cash financing working capital* to the Financing Activities section of its statement of cash flows.

STOP + THINK (10-3)

Midwest Airlines
Statement of Cash Flows

(in millions)	2018	2017	2016
Cash Flows from Operating Activities			
Net income	548	313	442
Items not affecting cash:			
Depreciation and amortization	502	467	417
Loss (gain) on disposal of equipment	(25)	101	-
Changes in non-cash operating working capital items:			
(Increase) decrease in accounts receivable	(9)	(75)	43
(Increase) decrease in inventory	(13)	6	(19)
Increase (decrease) in accounts payable	855	231	129
Net Cash Inflow (Outflow) from Operating Activities	1,858	1,043	1,012

Midwest Airlines
Statement of Cash Flows

(in millions)	2018	2017	2016
Cash Flows from Investing Activities			
Business acquisitions	-	(400)	-
Proceeds from sale of investments	6	-	23
Purchase of property, plant, and equipment	(1,316)	(1,505)	(1,261)
Proceeds from disposal of equipment	100	55	-
Net Cash Inflow (Outflow) from Investing Activities	(1,210)	(1,850)	(1,238)
Cash Flows from Financing Activities			
Payment of dividends	(14)	(14)	(14)
Proceeds from sale of capital stock	132	88	93
Repurchase of capital stock	(55)	(246)	-
Proceeds from long-term debt	300	520	-
Repayment of long-term debt	(150)	(215)	(127)
Net Cash Inflow (Outflow) from Financing Activities	213	133	(48)
Increase (Decrease) in Cash and Cash Equivalents	861	(674)	(274)
Cash and Cash Equivalents, Beginning of Year	3	677	951
Cash and Cash Equivalents, End of Year	864	3	677

Based on the information in Midwest Airlines' statements of cash flows for 2016–2018, answer the following questions:

1. Has Midwest been expanding or down-sizing its business?

2. What was the carrying amount of the equipment Midwest sold in 2017?

3. If you were a financial analyst following Midwest, would you be pleased with its operating cash flows?

4. Has Midwest been relying more on debt or equity financing in recent years? Cite information about both debt and equity to support your conclusion.

5. Overall, does Midwest have a strong or poor cash position? Cite two pieces of information to support your conclusion.

Non-Cash Investing and Financing Activities

Companies sometimes engage in financing and investing activities that do not involve cash flows. An example of a non-cash transaction that involves both investing and financing is the acquisition of a subsidiary company in exchange for shares of the acquiring company. In this transaction, the acquiring company has *invested* in a new asset, the subsidiary company, and *financed* it with its own shares, but because the transaction does not involve cash, these activities are not included in the statement of cash flows. IFRS and ASPE do, however, require note disclosure of non-cash investing and financing activities. A sample disclosure of the above transaction and two other non-cash transactions is included in Exhibit 10-9.

	A	B	C
1	*(amounts in thousands)*		
2	**Note 22: Non-Cash Investing and Financing Activities**		
3	Acquisition of subsidiary by issuing common shares	$ 320	
4	Acquisition of equipment by finance lease	70	
5	Conversion of bonds payable to common shares	150	
6	Total non-cash investing and financing activities	$ 540	
7			

EXHIBIT 10-9
Sample Disclosure on Non-cash Investing and Financing Activities

Measuring Cash Adequacy: Free Cash Flow

Throughout this chapter, we have focused on cash flows from operating, investing, and financing activities. Some investors, creditors, and managers want to know how much cash a company can "free up" for new opportunities. The business world changes so quickly that new possibilities arise almost daily. A company with a significant free cash flow is better able to respond to new opportunities. **Free cash flow** is the amount of cash available from operations after paying for property, plant, and equipment. Free cash flow can be computed as follows:

$$\text{Free cash flow} = \frac{\text{Net cash flow provided by}}{\text{operating activities}} - \frac{\text{Capital expenditures on}}{\substack{\text{property, plant,} \\ \text{and equipment}}}$$

Using information from Canadian Tire's statement of cash flows on page 482, we can calculate its free cash flow for 2014. It generated cash from operating activities of $575 million and spent $539 million on capital expenditures, leaving $36 million in free cash flow for 2014. This information suggests that Canadian Tire is well poised to take advantage of new business opportunities—even after spending over $500 million on property and equipment in 2014, it still had almost $50 million of free cash flow to spend on other things.

It is important to note, however, that a negative free cash flow is not necessarily a bad sign for investors. It could mean that the company has made a significant investment in property, plant, and equipment that will pay off in the form of increased future revenues and profits.

▶ DECISION GUIDELINES

INVESTORS' AND CREDITORS' USE OF CASH-FLOW AND RELATED INFORMATION

Jan Childres is a private investor. Through years of experience she has devised some guidelines for evaluating both stock investments and bond investments. Childres uses a combination of accrual-accounting data and cash-flow information. Here are her decision guidelines for both investors and creditors.

INVESTORS

Questions	Factors to Consider	Financial Statement Predictor*
1. How much in dividends can I expect to receive from an investment in stock?	Expected future net income	Income from continuing operations
	Expected future cash balance	Net cash flows from (in order): • operating activities • investing activities • financing activities
	Future dividend policy	Current and past dividend policy
2. Is the stock price likely to increase or decrease?	Expected future income from continuing operations	Income from continuing operations
	Expected future cash flows from operating activities	Income from continuing operations Net cash flow from operating activities

CREDITORS

Question	Factors to Consider	Financial Statement Predictor*
Can the company pay the interest and principal at the maturity of a loan?	Expected future net cash flow from operating activities	Income from continuing operations Net cash flow from operating activities

*There are many other factors to consider in making these decisions. These are some of the more common ones.

Summary of IFRS-ASPE Differences

Concepts	IFRS	ASPE
Classification of interest paid and interest and dividends received (p. 487)	Interest paid may be classified as either an operating activity or a financing activity.	Interest paid must be classified as an operating activity.
Classification of interest and dividends received (p. 488)	Interest and dividends received may be classified as either operating activities or investing activities.	Interest and dividends received must be classified as operating activities.
Classification of dividends paid (p. 488)	Dividends paid may be classified as either an operating activity or a financing activity. *Note: Once a classification scheme has been chosen for each of the above items, it must be used consistently thereafter.*	Dividends paid must be classified as a financing activity.

SUMMARY

SUMMARY OF LEARNING OBJECTIVES

LEARNING OBJECTIVE	SUMMARY
1. **Explain** the uses of the statement of cash flows	The information disclosed by a company in its statement of cash flows provides decision-relevant information to users of the company's financial statements. This statement includes details about a company's cash receipts and cash disbursements from operating, investing, and financing activities, and permits a user to determine exactly what caused the company's cash balance to increase or decrease during the period.

Specifically, the statement of cash flows helps users do the following:

1. Predict future cash flows.
2. Evaluate management decisions.
3. Determine ability to pay interest and dividends.
4. Assess the relationship of net income to cash flows.
5. Compare the operating performance of different companies.

Cash includes cash equivalents, which are short-term investments that are readily convertible to known amounts of cash, and which are very unlikely to change in value.

2. **Explain** and **classify** cash flows from operating, investing, and financing activities

Operating activities comprise the main revenue-producing activities of a company, and generally result from the transactions and other events that determine net income. Other activities that are not *investing* or *financing* activities are also classified as operating activities.

There are two methods of determining cash flows from operating activities, both resulting in the same net cash flows from operating activities:

- Indirect method, in which net income is adjusted for non-cash transactions, any deferrals or accruals of past or future operating cash receipts or payments, and items of income or expense associated with investing or financing cash flows
- Direct method, which explicitly reports all cash receipts and cash payments from operating activities

Investing activities include the purchase and sale of long-term assets and other investments that do not qualify as cash equivalents. They generally consist of transactions that result in cash inflows or outflows related to resources used for generating future income and cash flows. Only expenditures related to assets that are recognized on the balance sheet qualify as investing activities.

Financing activities result in changes in the size and composition of a company's contributed equity and borrowings.

3. **Prepare** a statement of cash flows using the indirect method of determining cash flows from operating activities

To determine cash flows from operating activities using the indirect method, begin with net income and adjust it as follows:

- Add non-cash expenses, such as depreciation and amortization
- Add losses (deduct gains) on sales of tangible and intangible assets and investments
- Add decreases (deduct increases) in non-cash operating current asset accounts
- Add increases (deduct decreases) in non-cash operating current liability accounts

To determine cash flows from investing activities:

- Add sales (deduct purchases) of tangible and intangible assets and investments other than cash equivalents
- Add collection (deduct issuance) of loans and advances to others

To determine cash flows from financing activities:

- Add issuance (deduct repurchase) of shares
- Add borrowing (deduct repayment) of short-term and long-term debts
- (Deduct payment) of dividends

Non-cash investing and financing activities, such as the acquisition of a business using common shares, are excluded from the statement of cash flows, but must be disclosed in the notes to the financial statements.

MyAccountingLab

END-OF-CHAPTER SUMMARY PROBLEM

Lucas Corporation, a private company, reported the following income statement and comparative balance sheet, along with transaction data for 2017:

	A	B	C	D
1	**Lucas Corporation** Income Statement For the Year Ended December 31, 2017			
2	Sales revenue		$ 662,000	
3	Cost of goods sold		560,00	
4	Gross margin		102,00	
5	Operating expenses:			
6	Salary expenses	$ 46,000		
7	Depreciation expense, equipment	7,000		
8	Amortization expense, patent	3,000		
9	Rent expense	2,000		
10	Total operating expenses		58,000	
11	Income from operations		44,000	
12	Other items:			
13	Loss on sale of equipment		(2,000)	
14	Income before income tax		42,000	
15	Income tax expense		16,000	
16	Net income		$ 26,000	
17				

	A	B	C	D	E	F	G
1	**Lucas Corporation** Balance Sheet As at December 31, 2017 and 2016						
2	**Assets**	**2017**	**2016**	**Liabilities and Shareholders' Equity**	**2017**	**2016**	
3	Current:			Current:			
4	Cash and equivalents	$ 19,000	$ 3,000	Accounts payable	$ 35,000	$ 26,000	
5	Accounts receivable	22,000	23,000	Accrued liabilities	7,000	9,000	
6	Inventories	34,000	31,000	Income tax payable	10,000	10,000	
7	Prepaid expenses	1,000	3,000	Total current liabilities	52,000	45,000	
8	Total current assets	76,000	60,000	Long-term note payable	44,000	—	
9	Long-term investments	18,000	10,000	Bonds payable	40,000	53,000	
10	Equipment, net	67,000	52,000	Shareholders' equity:			
11	Patent, net	44,000	10,000	Share capital	42,000	15,000	
12				Retained earnings	27,000	19,000	
13				Total liabilities and			
14	Total assets	$ 205,000	$ 132,000	shareholders' equity	$ 205,000	$ 132,000	
15							

	A	B	C
1	**Transaction Data for 2017:**		
2	Purchase of equipment	$ 98,000	
3	Payment of cash dividends	18,000	
4	Issuance of common shares to repay bonds payable	13,000	
5	Purchase of long-term investment	8,000	
6	Issuance of long-term note payable to purchase patent	37,000	
7	Issuance of long-term note payable to borrow cash	7,000	
8	Issuance of common shares for cash	19,000	
9	Proceeds on sale of equipment (carrying amount, $76,000)	74,000	
10	Repurchase of common shares	5,000	
11			

Requirements

Prepare Lucas Corporation's statement of cash flows for the year ended December 31, 2017. Determine operating cash flows by the indirect method. Follow the four steps outlined below. For Step 4, prepare a T-account to show the transaction activity in each long-term balance sheet account. For each capital asset, use a single account, net of accumulated depreciation or amortization (for example: Equipment, net).

Name: Lucas Corporation
Fiscal Period: Year ended
December 31, 2017

Step 1 Lay out the template of the statement of cash flows.
Step 2 From the comparative balance sheet, determine the increase in cash during the year.
Step 3 From the income statement, take net income, depreciation and amortization, and the loss on sale of equipment, to the statement of cash flows.
Step 4 Complete the statement of cash flows. Account for the year-to-year change in each balance sheet account.

ANSWER

The title must include the name of the company, "Statement of Cash Flows," and the specific period of time covered. There are three sections: Cash flows from operating, investing, and financing activities.

Add back non-cash items: depreciation, amortization; and deduct gains/add loss from sales of long-term assets.

$2,000 = $76,000 − $74,000

Any changes in current assets and current liabilities are included in the operating activities section. Calculate as 2017 balance − 2016 balance from the balance sheets.

Any cash changes in the long-term assets are included in the investing activities section. Check "Transaction Data for 2017."

	A	B	C
1	**Lucas Corporation** Statement of Cash Flows For the Year Ended December 31, 2017		
2	**Cash flows from operating activities:**		
3	Net income		$ 26,000
4	Adjustments to reconcile net income to net cash provided by operating activities:		
5	Depreciation	$ 7,000	
6	Amortization	3,000	
7	Loss on sale of equipment	2,000	
8	Changes in non-cash operating working capital accounts:		
9	Decrease in accounts receivable	1,000	
10	Increase in inventories	(3,000)	
11	Decrease in prepaid expenses	2,000	
12	Increase in accounts payable	9,000	
13	Decrease in accrued liabilities	(2,000)	19,000
14	Net cash provided by operating activities		45,000
15			
16	**Cash flows from investing activities:**		
17	Purchase of equipment	(98,000)	
18	Sale of equipment	74,000	
19	Purchase of long-term investment	(8,000)	
20	Net cash used for investing activities		(32,000)
21			

	A	B	C
22	**Cash flows from financing activities:**		
23	Issuance of common shares	19,000	
24	Payment of cash dividends	(18,000)	
25	Issuance of long-term note payable	7,000	
26	Repurchase of common shares	(5,000)	
27	Net cash provided by financing activities		3,000
28			
29	**Net increase in cash**		16,000
30	**Cash balance, December 31, 2016**		3,000
31	**Cash balance, December 31, 2017**		$ 19,000
32			
33	**Non-cash investing and financing activities:**		
34	Issuance of long-term note payable to purchase patent		$ 37,000
35	Issuance of common shares to repay bonds payable		13,000
36	Total non-cash investing and financing activities		$ 50,000

Any cash changes in the long-term liabilities and contributed capital accounts are included in the financing activities section. Check "Transaction Data for 2017."

This result should equal the Dec. 31, 2017, balance sheet Cash amount.

Check "Transaction Data for 2017."

Long-Term Investments

Bal.	10,000	
	8,000	
Bal.	18,000	

Equipment, Net

Bal.	52,000	
	98,000	76,000
		7,000
Bal.	67,000	

Patent, Net

Bal.	10,000	
	37,000	3,000
Bal.	44,000	

Long-Term Note Payable

		Bal.	0
			37,000
			7,000
		Bal.	44,000

Bonds Payable

		Bal.	53,000
13,000			
		Bal.	40,000

Share Capital

		Bal.	15,000
			13,000
5,000			19,000
		Bal.	42,000

Retained Earnings

		Bal.	19,000
18,000			26,000
		Bal.	27,000

Use the 2016 and 2017 balance sheet amounts and the transaction data for 2017 to complete these T-accounts.

REVIEW

MyAccountingLab

Make the grade with MyAccountingLab: The Quick Quiz questions, Short Exercises, Exercises, and Problems (Group A) marked in #–# can be found on MyAccountingLab. You can practise them as often as you want, and most feature step-by-step guided instructions to help you find the right answer.

QUICK QUIZ (ANSWERS APPEAR ON THE LAST PAGE OF THIS CHAPTER.)

Test your understanding of the statement of cash flows by answering the following questions.

1. Paying off bonds payable is reported on the statement of cash flows under
   a. operating activities.
   b. investing activities.
   c. financing activities.
   d. non-cash investing and financing activities.

2. The sale of inventory for cash is reported on the statement of cash flows under
   a. operating activities.
   b. investing activities.
   c. financing activities.
   d. non-cash investing and financing activities.

3. Selling equipment is reported on the statement of cash flows under
   a. operating activities.
   b. investing activities.
   c. financing activities.
   d. non-cash investing and financing activities.

4. Which of the following terms appears on a statement of cash flows—indirect method?
   a. Payments to suppliers
   b. Amortization expense
   c. Collections from customers
   d. Cash receipt of interest revenue

5. On an indirect-method statement of cash flows, an increase in prepaid insurance would be
   a. included in payments to suppliers.
   b. added to net income.
   c. added to increases in current assets.
   d. deducted from net income.

6. On an indirect-method statement of cash flows, an increase in accounts payable would be
   a. reported in the investing activities section.
   b. reported in the financing activities section.
   c. added to net income in the operating activities section.
   d. deducted from net income in the operating activities section.

7. On an indirect-method statement of cash flows, a gain on the sale of plant assets would be
   a. ignored, because the gain did not generate any cash.
   b. reported in the investing activities section.
   c. deducted from net income in the operating activities section.
   d. added to net income in the operating activities section.

8. Paying cash dividends is a/an _____ activity.
   Receiving cash dividends is a/an _____ activity.

9. Matlock Camera Co. sold equipment with a cost of $20,000 and accumulated depreciation of $8,000 for an amount that resulted in a gain of $3,000. What amount should Matlock report on the statement of cash flows as "proceeds from sale of plant and equipment"?
   a. $9,000
   b. $17,000
   c. $15,000
   d. Some other amount ($_____)

Questions 10 through 18 use the following data. Trudeau Corporation determines operating cash flows by the indirect method.

	A	B	C	D
1	**Trudeau Corporation** Income Statement For the Year Ended December 31, 2017			
2	Sales revenue	$ 180,000		
3	Gain on sale of equipment	8,000	$ 188,000	
4	Cost of goods sold	110,000		
5	Depreciation	6,000		
6	Other operating expenses	25,000	141,000	
7	Net income		$ 47,000	
8				

	A	B	C	D	E	F	G
1				**Trudeau Corporation** Comparative Balance Sheet As at December 31, 2017 and 2016			
2	**Assets**	**2017**	**2016**	**Liabilities and Shareholders' Equity**	**2017**	**2016**	
3	Cash	$ 4,000	$ 1,000	Accounts payable	$ 6,000	$ 7,000	
4	Accounts receivable	7,000	11,000	Accrued liabilities	7,000	3,000	
5	Inventories	10,000	9,000	Common shares	20,000	10,000	
6	Plant and equipment, net	93,000	69,000	Retained earnings	81,000	70,000	
7		$ 114,000	$ 90,000		$ 114,000	$ 90,000	

10. How many items enter into the computation of Trudeau's net cash provided by operating activities?
a. 2
b. 3
c. 5
d. 7

11. How do Trudeau's accrued liabilities affect the company's statement of cash flows for 2017?
a. They don't because the accrued liabilities are not yet paid
b. Increase in cash provided by operating activities
c. Increase in cash used by investing activities
d. Increase in cash used by financing activities

12. How do accounts receivable affect Trudeau's cash flows from operating activities for 2017?
a. Increase in cash provided by operating activities
b. Decrease in cash provided by operating activities
c. They don't because accounts receivable result from investing activities
d. Decrease in cash used by investing activities

13. Trudeau's net cash provided by operating activities during 2017 was
a. $3,000.
b. $47,000.
c. $51,000.
d. $58,000.

14. How many items enter into the computation of Trudeau's net cash flow from investing activities for 2017?
a. 2
b. 3
c. 5
d. 7

15. The carrying amount of equipment sold during 2017 was $20,000. Trudeau's net cash flow from investing activities for 2017 was
a. net cash used of $22,000.
b. net cash used of $28,000.

c. net cash used of $50,000.
d. net cash provided of $28,000.

16. How many items enter into the computation of Trudeau's net cash flow from financing activities for 2017?
a. 2
b. 3
c. 5
d. 7

17. Trudeau's largest financing cash flow for 2017 resulted from the
a. sale of equipment.
b. purchase of equipment.
c. issuance of common shares.
d. payment of dividends.

18. Trudeau's net cash flow from financing activities for 2017 was
a. net cash used of $25,000.
b. net cash used of $20,000.
c. net cash provided of $10,000.
d. net cash used of $26,000.

19. Sales totalled $800,000, accounts receivable increased by $40,000, and accounts payable decreased by $35,000. How much cash did this company collect from customers?
a. $760,000
b. $795,000
c. $800,000
d. $840,000

20. Income Tax Payable was $5,000 at the end of the year and $2,800 at the beginning. Income tax expense for the year totalled $59,100. What amount of cash did this company pay for income tax during the year?
a. $56,900
b. $59,100
c. $61,300
d. $61,900

ACCOUNTING VOCABULARY

cash equivalents Investments such as term deposits, guaranteed investment certificates, or high-grade government securities that are considered so similar to cash that they are combined with cash for financial disclosure on the balance sheet.   (p. 485)

direct method A method of determining cash flows from operating activities in which all cash receipts and cash payments from operating activities are directly reported on the statement of cash flows.   (p. 488)

financing activities Activities that result in changes in the size and composition of a company's contributed equity and borrowings.   (p. 487)

free cash flow A measure of how much cash a company has available to pursue new business opportunities. Calculated by deducting capital expenditures from cash flow from operating activities.   (p. 502)

indirect method A method of determining cash flows from operating activities in which net income is adjusted for non-cash

transactions, any deferrals or accruals of past or future operating cash receipts or payments, and items of income or expense associated with investing or financing cash flows.   (p. 488)

investing activities Activities that include the purchase and sale of long-term assets and other investments that result in cash inflows or outflows related to resources used for generating future income and cash flows.   (p. 487)

non-cash operating working capital account A current asset or current liability account that derives from an operating activity and is not included in cash and cash equivalents. (p. 493)

operating activities Activities that comprise the main revenue-producing activities of a company, and generally result from the transactions and other events that determine net income. (p. 486)

ASSESS YOUR PROGRESS

Recall that for the sake of simplicity and consistency, this text classifies all interest paid and interest and dividends received as operating activities, and classifies dividends paid as a financing activity. All questions and problems in this chapter should be answered using this convention.

SHORT EXERCISES

LEARNING OBJECTIVE ❶

Understand purposes of the statement of cash flows

S10-1 State how the statement of cash flows helps investors and creditors perform each of the following functions:
a. Predict future cash flows.
b. Evaluate management decisions.

LEARNING OBJECTIVE ❷

Evaluate operating cash flows—indirect method

S10-2 Examine the Canadian Tire statement of cash flows on page 482. Suppose Canadian Tire's operating activities *used*, rather than *provided*, cash. Identify three things under the indirect method that could cause operating cash flows to be negative.

LEARNING OBJECTIVE ❸

Report cash flows from operating activities—indirect method

S10-3 Canada Wide Transportation (CWT) began 2017 with accounts receivable, inventory, and prepaid expenses totalling $65,000. At the end of the year, CWT had a total of $78,000 for these current assets. At the beginning of 2017, CWT owed current liabilities of $42,000, and at year-end, current liabilities totalled $40,000.

Net income for the year was $80,000. Included in net income were a $4,000 gain on the sale of land and depreciation expense of $9,000.

Show how CWT should report cash flows from operating activities for 2017. CWT uses the *indirect* method. Use Exhibit 10-6 (p. 492) as a guide.

LEARNING OBJECTIVE ❷

Identify items for reporting cash flows from operations—indirect method

S10-4 Bewell Clinic Inc. is preparing its statement of cash flows (indirect method) for the year ended November 30, 2017. Consider the following items in preparing the company's statement of cash flows. Identify each item as an operating activity—addition to net income (O+), or subtraction from net income (O–); an investing activity (I); a financing activity (F); or an activity that is not used to prepare the statement of cash flows by the indirect method (N). Place the appropriate symbol in the blank space.

_____	**a.** Loss on sale of land	_____	**h.** Increase in accounts payable
_____	**b.** Depreciation expense	_____	**i.** Net income
_____	**c.** Increase in inventory	_____	**j.** Payment of dividends
_____	**d.** Decrease in prepaid expense	_____	**k.** Decrease in accrued liabilities
_____	**e.** Decrease in accounts receivable	_____	**l.** Issuance of common shares
_____	**f.** Purchase of equipment	_____	**m.** Gain on sale of building
_____	**g.** Collection of cash from customers	_____	**n.** Retained earnings

S10-5 (Exercise S10-6 is an alternative exercise.) Edwards Corporation Inc. accountants have assembled the following data for the year ended June 30, 2017:

LEARNING OBJECTIVE ❸

Compute operating cash flows—indirect method

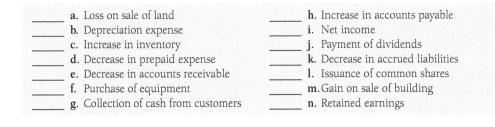

Payment of dividends.........................	$ 6,000	Other operating expenses.................	35,000
Proceeds from issuance		Purchase of equipment.....................	40,000
of common shares	20,000	Decrease in operating current	
Sales revenue.....................................	224,000	liabilities......................................	5,000
Increase in operating current		Payment of note payable...................	30,000
assets other than cash....................	30,000	Proceeds from sale of land................	60,000
Repurchase of common shares..........	5,000	Depreciation expense	8,000
Cost of goods sold.............................	$100,000		

Prepare the *operating activities section* of Edwards's statement of cash flows for the year ended June 30, 2017. Edwards uses the *indirect* method for operating cash flows.

S10-6 Use the data in exercise S10-5 to prepare Edwards Corporation's statement of cash flows for the year ended June 30, 2017. Edwards uses the *indirect* method for operating activities. Use Exhibit 10-8, page 495, as a guide, but you may stop after determining the net increase (or decrease) in cash.

LEARNING OBJECTIVE ❸

Prepare a statement of cash flows—indirect method

S10-7 Williams Corporation accountants have assembled the following data for the year ended June 30, 2016:

LEARNING OBJECTIVE ❸

Prepare a statement of cash flows using the indirect method

Net income...	$?
Cost of goods sold...	$116,000
Payment of dividends..	6,100
Other operating expenses...	34,000
Proceeds from the issuance of common shares	18,000
Purchase of equipment with cash	42,000
Sales revenue...	225,000
Increase in current liabilities...	10,000
Increase in current assets other than cash...	29,000
Payment of note payable...	30,000
Proceeds from sale of land..	27,000
Repurchase of common shares..	7,000
Depreciation expense	5,000

Prepare Williams Corporation's statement of cash flows for the year ended June 30, 2016. Williams uses the indirect method for operating activities.

LEARNING OBJECTIVE ❸

Compute investing cash flows

S10-8 Autos of Red Deer Inc. reported the following financial statements for 2017:

	A	B	C
1	**Autos of Red Deer Inc.** Income Statement For the Year Ended December 31, 2017		
2	*(in thousands)*		
3	Sales revenue	$ 710	
4	Cost of goods sold	340	
5	Salary expense	70	
6	Depreciation expense	20	
7	Other expenses	130	
8	Total expenses	560	
9	Net income	$ 150	
10			

	A	B	C	D	E	F	G
1	**Autos of Red Deer Inc.** Comparative Balance Sheet As at December 31, 2017 and 2016						
2	*(in thousands)*						
3	**Assets**	**2017**	**2016**	**Liabilities**	**2017**	**2016**	
4	Current:			Current:			
5	Cash	$ 19	$ 16	Accounts payable	$ 47	$ 42	
6	Accounts receivable	59	48	Salary payable	23	21	
7	Inventories	75	84	Accrued liabilities	8	11	
8	Prepaid expenses	3	2	Long-term notes payable	68	58	
9	Long-term investments	55	75	**Shareholders' Equity**			
10	Property, plant, and equipment	225	185	Common shares Retained earnings	40 250	32 246	
11	Total	$ 436	$ 410	Total	$ 436	$ 410	
12							

Compute the following investing cash flows:

a. Acquisitions of plant and equipment (all were for cash). Autos of Red Deer sold no plant and equipment.

b. Proceeds from the sale of investments. Autos of Red Deer purchased no investments.

LEARNING OBJECTIVE ❸

Compute financing cash flows

S10-9 Use the Autos of Red Deer data in exercise S10-8 to compute:

a. New borrowing or payment of long-term notes payable. Autos of Red Deer had only one long-term note payable transaction during the year.

b. Issuance of common shares or repurchase of common shares. Autos of Red Deer had only one common share transaction during the year.

c. Payment of cash dividends (same as dividends declared).

EXERCISES

LEARNING OBJECTIVE ❶

Identify the purposes of the statement of cash flows

E10-10 B.C. Plating Inc. has experienced an unbroken string of 10 years of growth in net income. Nevertheless, the company is facing bankruptcy. Creditors are calling all B.C. Plating's loans for immediate payment, and the cash is simply not available. It is clear that the company's top managers overemphasized profits and gave too little attention to cash flow.

Requirement

Write a brief memo, in your own words, to explain to the managers of B.C. Plating the purposes of the statement of cash flows.

E10-11 Carter-Pierce Investments specializes in low-risk government bonds. Identify each of Carter-Pierce's transactions as operating (O), investing (I), financing (F), non-cash investing and financing (NIF), or a transaction that is not reported on the statement of cash flows (N). Indicate whether each item increases (+) or decreases (–) cash. The *indirect* method is used for operating activities.

LEARNING OBJECTIVE ❷

Identify activities for the statement of cash flows—indirect method

_____	a. Acquisition of building by cash payment	_____	j. Acquisition of equipment by issuance of note payable
_____	b. Decrease in merchandise inventory	_____	k. Sale of long-term investment
_____	c. Depreciation of equipment	_____	l. Issuance of common share for cash
_____	d. Decrease in accrued liabilities	_____	m. Increase in accounts payable
_____	e. Payment of cash dividend	_____	n. Amortization of intangible assets
_____	f. Purchase of long-term investment	_____	o. Loss on sale of equipment
_____	g. Issuance of long-term note payable to borrow cash	_____	p. Payment of long-term debt
_____	h. Increase in prepaid expenses	_____	q. Cash sale of land
_____	i. Accrual of salary expense	_____	r. Repurchase of common shares
		_____	s. Net income

E10-12 Indicate whether each of the following transactions affects an operating activity, an investing activity, a financing activity, or a non-cash investing and financing activity:

LEARNING OBJECTIVE ❷

Classify transactions for the statement of cash flows—indirect method

a.	Cash	61,000	**g.**	Equipment	11,000
	Common Shares	61,000		Cash	11,000
b.	Furniture and Fixtures	18,000	**h.**	Dividends Payable	13,000
	Cash	18,000		Cash	13,000
c.	Cash	52,000	**i.**	Salary Expense	14,000
	Accounts Receivable	11,000		Cash	14,000
	Service Revenue	63,000	**j.**	Building	105,000
d.	Cash	7,000		Note Payable—Long-Term	105,000
	Long-Term Investment	7,000	**k.**	Common Shares	12,000
e.	Loss on Disposal of Equipment	1,000		Cash	12,000
	Equipment, Net	1,000	**l.**	Depreciation Expense	5,000
f.	Land	15,000		Accumulated Depreciation	5,000
	Cash	15,000	**m.**	Bonds Payable	35,000
				Cash	35,000

E10-13 The accounting records of South Central Distributors, Inc., reveal the following:

LEARNING OBJECTIVE ❸

Compute cash flows from operating activities—indirect method

Net income	$ 42,000	Depreciation	$ 6,000
Collection of dividend revenue	7,100	Decrease in current liabilities	25,000
Payment of interest	12,000	Increase in current assets other	
Sales revenue	307,000	than cash	29,000
Gain on sale of land	26,000	Payment of dividends	7,700
Acquisition of land	35,000	Payment of income tax	14,000

Requirement

Compute cash flows from operating activities by the *indirect* method. Use the format of the operating activities section of Exhibit 10-6. Also evaluate the operating cash flow of South Central Distributors. Give the reason for your evaluation.

LEARNING OBJECTIVE ❸

Compute cash flows from operating activities—indirect method

E10-14 The accounting records of Ashby Fur Traders include these accounts:

Cash			
Aug. 1	80,000		
Receipts	418,000	Payments	450,000
Aug. 31	48,000		

Accounts Receivable			
Aug. 1	8,000		
Receipts	522,000	Collections	418,000
Aug. 31	112,000		

Inventory			
Aug. 1	6,000		
Purchases	433,000	Cost of Sales	333,000
Aug. 31	106,000		

Equipment			
Aug. 1	181,000		
Acquisition	4,000		
Aug. 31	185,000		

Accumulated Depreciation—Equipment			
		Aug. 1	45,000
		Depreciation	5,000
		Aug. 31	50,000

Accounts Payable			
		Aug. 1	15,000
Payments	334,000	Purchases	433,000
		Aug. 31	114,000

Accrued Liabilities			
		Aug. 1	14,000
Payments	35,000	Receipts	30,000
		Aug. 31	9,000

Retained Earnings			
Quarterly		Aug. 1	63,000
Dividend	20,000	Net Income	25,000
		Aug. 31	68,000

Requirement

Compute Ashby's net cash provided by (used for) operating activities during August. Use the *indirect* method. Do you see any potential problems in Ashby's cash flows from operations? How can you tell?

LEARNING OBJECTIVE ❸

Prepare the statement of cash flows—indirect method

E10-15 The income statement and additional data of Breen Travel Products, Inc., follow:

	A	B	C	D
1	**Breen Travel Products, Inc.** Income Statement Year Ended December 31, 2017			
2	Revenues:			
3	Sales revenue	$ 283,000		
4	Dividend revenue	8,700	$ 291,700	
5	Expenses:			
6	Cost of goods sold	96,000		
7	Salary expense	54,000		
8	Depreciation expense	27,000		
9	Advertising expense	4,300		
10	Interest expense	2,100		
11	Income tax expense	6,000	189,400	
12	Net income		$ 102,300	
13				

Additional data:

a. Acquisition of plant assets was $200,000. Of this amount, $160,000 was paid in cash and $40,000 by signing a note payable.

b. Proceeds from sale of land totalled $23,000.

c. Proceeds from issuance of common share totalled $60,000.

d. Payment of long-term note payable was $13,000.

e. Payment of dividends was $10,000.

f. From the balance sheets:

| | December 31, | |
	2017	2016
Current assets:		
Cash	$150,000	$138,900
Accounts receivable	44,000	57,000
Inventory	104,000	72,000
Prepaid expenses	9,500	8,300
Current liabilities:		
Accounts payable	$ 38,000	$ 23,000
Accrued liabilities	11,000	24,000

Requirements

1. Prepare Breen's statement of cash flows for the year ended December 31, 2017, using the *indirect* method.
2. Evaluate Breen's cash flows for the year. In your evaluation, mention all three categories of cash flows and give the reason for your evaluation.

E10-16 Consider three independent cases for the cash flows of Texas Tires Corp. For each case, identify from the statement of cash flows how Texas Tires Corp. generated the cash to acquire new plant assets. Rank the three cases from the most healthy financially to the least healthy.

LEARNING OBJECTIVE ❸

Interpret a statement of cash flows—indirect method

	Case A	Case B	Case C
Cash flows from operating activities:			
Net income	$ 14,000	$ 14,000	$ 14,000
Depreciation and amortization	17,000	17,000	17,000
Increase in operating current assets	(1,000)	(7,000)	(3,000)
Decrease in operating current liabilities	(3,000)	(27,000)	(4,000)
	27,000	(3,000)	24,000
Cash flows from investing activities:			
Acquisition of plant assets	(141,000)	(141,000)	(141,000)
Sales of plant assets	148,000	28,000	47,000
	7,000	(113,000)	(94,000)
Cash flows from financing activities:			
Issuance of share	26,000	149,000	104,000
Payment of debt	(38,000)	(28,000)	(45,000)
	(12,000)	121,000	59,000
Net increase (decrease) in cash	$ 22,000	$ 5,000	$(11,000)

E10-17 Compute the following items for the statement of cash flows:
a. Beginning and ending Plant Assets, Net, are $125,000 and $115,000, respectively. Depreciation for the period was $19,000, and purchases of new plant assets were $45,000. Plant assets were sold at a $10,000 gain. What were the cash proceeds of the sale?
b. Beginning and ending Retained Earnings are $44,000 and $69,000, respectively. Net income for the period was $61,000, and stock dividends were $10,000. How much were cash dividends?

LEARNING OBJECTIVE ❸

Compute investing and financing amounts for the statement of cash flows

CHALLENGE EXERCISES

LEARNING OBJECTIVE ❸

Use the balance sheet and the statement of cash flows together

E10-18 Crown Specialties Ltd. reported the following at December 31, 2017 (in thousands):

	2017	2016
From the comparative balance sheet:		
Property and equipment, net	$11,150	$9,590
Long-term notes payable	4,400	3,080
From the statement of cash flows:		
Depreciation	$ 1,920	
Capital expenditures	(4,130)	
Proceeds from sale of property and equipment	770	
Proceeds from issuance of long-term note payable	1,190	
Payment of long-term note payable	(110)	
Issuance of common shares	383	

Determine the following items for Crown Specialties during 2017:

1. Gain or loss on the sale of property and equipment

2. Amount of long-term debt issued for something other than cash

LEARNING OBJECTIVE ❷❸

Infer information about cash flows using the income statement and balance sheet

E10-19 Top Notch, Inc., reported the following in its financial statements for the year ended May 31, 2016 (in thousands):

	A	B	C	D
1		**2016**	**2015**	
2	Income Statement			
3	Net sales	$ 23,984	$ 21,115	
4	Cost of sales	18,088	15,333	
5	Depreciation	259	234	
6	Other operating expenses	3,880	4,248	
7	Income tax expense	536	485	
8	Net income	$ 1,221	$ 815	
9	Balance Sheet			
10	Cash and cash equivalents	$ 15	$ 14	
11	Accounts receivable	597	609	
12	Inventory	3,060	2,790	
13	Property and equipment, net	4,345	3,425	
14	Accounts payable	1,549	1,366	
15	Accrued liabilities	942	639	
16	Income tax payable	201	190	
17	Long-term liabilities	476	463	
18	Common stock	520	446	
19	Retained earnings	4,329	3,734	
20				

Requirement

Determine the following cash receipts and payments for Top Notch, Inc., during 2016 (enter all amounts in thousands):

    a. Collections from customers

    b. Payments for inventory

    c. Payments for other operating expenses

    d. Payment of income tax

    e. Proceeds from issuance of common stock

    f. Payment of cash dividends

E10-20 The December 31, 2015, balance sheet and the 2016 statement of cash flows for Northtown, Inc., follow:

LEARNING OBJECTIVE ❷❸

Interpret information in the statement of cash flows for use in preparing the balance sheet

	A	B	C
1	**Northtown, Inc.** **Balance Sheet** December 31, 2015		
2	**Assets:**		
3	Cash	$ 14,000	
4	Accounts receivable (net)	95,000	
5	Inventory	60,500	
6	Prepaid expenses	2,600	
7	Land	99,800	
8	Machinery and equipment (net)	73,600	
9	Total assets	$ 345,500	
10	**Liabilities:**		
11	Accounts payable	$ 40,300	
12	Unearned revenue	9,000	
13	Income taxes payable	6,000	
14	Long-term debt	84,100	
15	**Total liabilities:**	139,400	
16	**Shareholders' equity:**		
17	Common shares	47,300	
18	Retained earnings	158,800	
19	Total shareholders' equity	206,100	
20	Total liabilities and shareholders' equity	$ 345,500	
21			

Requirement

Prepare the December 31, 2016, balance sheet for Northtown, Inc.

PROBLEMS (GROUP A)

P10-21A Top managers of Relax Inns are reviewing company performance for 2017. The income statement reports a 20% increase in net income over 2016. However, most of the increase resulted from a gain on insurance proceeds from fire damage to a building. The balance sheet shows a large increase in receivables. The statement of cash flows, in summarized form, reports the following:

LEARNING OBJECTIVE ❶❷

Use cash-flow data to evaluate performance

Net cash used for operating activities	$(80,000)
Net cash provided by investing activities	40,000
Net cash provided by financing activities	50,000
Increase in cash during 2017	$ 10,000

Requirement

Write a memo giving Relax Inns' managers your assessment of 2017 operations and your outlook for the future. Focus on the information content of the cash-flow data.

P10-22A Vintage Automobiles of Orangeville Ltd. was formed on January 1, 2017, when Vintage issued common shares for $300,000. Early in January 2017, Vintage made the following cash payments:
a. $150,000 for equipment
b. $120,000 for inventory (four cars at $30,000 each)
c. $20,000 for 2017 rent on a store building

LEARNING OBJECTIVE ❷❸

Prepare an income statement, balance sheet, and statement of cash flows—indirect method

In February 2017, Vintage purchased six cars for inventory on account. Cost of this inventory was $260,000 ($43,333.33 each). Before year-end, Vintage paid $208,000 of this debt. Vintage uses the FIFO method to account for inventory.

During 2017, Vintage sold eight vintage autos for a total of $500,000. Before year-end, Vintage collected 80% of this amount.

The business employs three people. The combined annual payroll is $95,000, of which Vintage owes $4,000 at year-end. At the end of the year, Vintage paid income tax of $10,000.

Late in 2017, Vintage declared and paid cash dividends of $11,000.

For equipment, Vintage uses the straight-line depreciation method over five years with zero residual value.

Requirements

1. Prepare Vintage Automobiles of Orangeville Ltd.'s income statement for the year ended December 31, 2017. Use the single-step format, with all revenues listed together and all expenses listed together.
2. Prepare Vintage's balance sheet at December 31, 2017.
3. Prepare Vintage's statement of cash flows for the year ended December 31, 2017. Format cash flows from operating activities by using the *indirect* method.
4. Comment on the business performance based on the statement of cash flows.

LEARNING OBJECTIVE ❷❸

Prepare the statement of cash flows—indirect method

P10-23A Primrose Software Inc. has assembled the following data for the year ended December 31, 2017.

	December 31	
	2017	**2016**
Current Accounts:		
Current assets:		
Cash and cash equivalents	$38,700	$22,700
Accounts receivable	69,700	64,200
Inventories	88,600	83,000
Prepaid expenses	5,300	4,100
Current liabilities:		
Accounts payable	57,200	55,800
Income tax payable	18,600	16,700
Accrued liabilities	15,500	27,200

Transaction Data for 2017:

Acquisition of land by issuing		Repurchase of common shares	$14,300
long-term note payable	$ 95,000	Loss on sale of equipment	11,700
Stock dividends	31,800	Payment of cash dividends	18,300
Collection of loan	8,700	Issuance of long-term note	
Depreciation expense	27,100	payable to borrow cash	34,400
Purchase of building	125,300	Net income	45,100
Repayment of bonds payable by		Issuance of common shares	
issuing common shares	65,000	for cash	41,200
Purchase of long-term investment	31,600	Proceeds from sale of equipment	58,000

Requirement

Prepare Primrose Software Inc.'s statement of cash flows using the *indirect* method to report operating activities. Include an accompanying schedule of non-cash investing and financing activities. How much of the cash used for investing activities was provided by operations?

P10-24A The comparative balance sheet of Northern Movie Theatre Company at March 31, 2017, reported the following:

LEARNING OBJECTIVE ❷❸

Prepare the statement of cash flows—indirect method

	March 31,	
	2017	2016
Current assets:		
Cash and cash equivalents	$ 9,900	$14,000
Accounts receivable	14,900	21,700
Inventories	63,200	60,600
Prepaid expenses	1,900	1,700
Current liabilities:		
Accounts payable	30,300	27,600
Accrued liabilities	10,700	11,100
Income tax payable	8,000	4,700

Northern's transactions during the year ended March 31, 2017, included the following:

Acquisition of land by issuing note payable	$101,000	Sale of long-term investment	$13,700
		Depreciation expense	17,300
Payment of cash dividend	30,000	Cash purchase of building	47,000
Cash purchase of equipment	78,700	Net income	50,000
Issuance of long-term note payable to borrow cash	50,000	Issuance of common shares for cash	11,000
		Stock dividend	18,000

Requirements

1. Prepare Northern Movie Theatre Company's statement of cash flows for the year ended March 31, 2017, using the *indirect* method to report cash flows from operating activities. Report non-cash investing and financing activities in an accompanying schedule.
2. Evaluate Northern's cash flows for the year. Mention all three categories of cash flows and give the reason for your evaluation.

P10-25A The 2017 comparative balance sheet and income statement of 4 Seasons Supply Corp. follow. 4 Seasons had no non-cash investing and financing transactions during 2017. During the year, there were no sales of land or equipment, no issuance of notes payable, and no repurchase of shares transactions.

LEARNING OBJECTIVE ❷❸

Prepare the statement of cash flows—indirect method

	A	B	C	D
1	**4 Seasons Supply Corp.** Comparative Balance Sheet As at December 31, 2017 and 2016			
2		**December 31**		
3		**2017**	**2016**	**Increase (Decrease)**
4	Current assets:			
5	Cash and cash equivalents	$ 17,600	$ 5,300	$ 12,300
6	Accounts receivable	27,200	27,600	(400)
7	Inventories	83,600	87,200	(3,600)
8	Prepaid expenses	2,500	1,900	600
9	Property, plant, and equipment:			
10	Land	89,000	60,000	29,000
11	Equipment, net	53,500	49,400	4,100
12	Total assets	$ 273,400	$ 231,400	$ 42,000

	A	B	C	D
13	Current liabilities:			
14	Accounts payable	$ 35,800	$ 33,700	$ 2,100
15	Salary payable	3,100	6,600	(3,500)
16	Other accrued liabilities	22,600	23,700	(1,100)
17	Long-term liabilities:			
18	Notes payable	75,000	100,000	(25,000)
19	Shareholders' equity:			
20	Common shares	88,300	64,700	23,600
21	Retained earnings	48,600	2,700	45,900
22	Total liabilities and shareholders' equity	$ 273,400	$ 231,400	$ 42,000
23				

	A	B	C	D
1	**4 Seasons Supply Corp.** Income Statement For the Year Ended December 31, 2017			
2	Revenues:			
3	Sales revenue		$ 228,700	
4	Expenses:			
5	Cost of goods sold	$ 70,600		
6	Salary expense	27,800		
7	Depreciation expense	4,000		
8	Other operating expense	10,500		
9	Interest expense	11,600		
10	Income tax expense	29,100		
11	Total expenses		153,600	
12	Net income		$ 75,100	
13				

Requirements

1. Prepare the 2017 statement of cash flows, formatting operating activities by using the *indirect* method.
2. How will what you learned in this problem help you evaluate an investment?

PROBLEMS (GROUP B)

LEARNING OBJECTIVE ❶❷

Use cash-flow information to
evaluate performance

P10-26B Top managers of Culinary Imports Limited are reviewing company performance for 2017. The income statement reports a 15% increase in net income, the fourth consecutive year showing an income increase above 10%. The income statement includes a non-recurring loss without which net income would have increased by 16%. The balance sheet shows modest increases in assets, liabilities, and shareholders' equity. The assets posting the largest increases are plant and equipment because the company is halfway through a five-year expansion program. No other asset and no liabilities are increasing dramatically. A summarized version of the statement of cash flows reports the following:

Net cash provided by operating activities	$ 310,000
Net cash used for investing activities	(290,000)
Net cash provided by financing activities...	50,000
Increase in cash during 2017..	$ 70,000

Requirement

Write a memo giving top managers of Culinary Imports Limited your assessment of 2017 operations and your outlook for the future. Focus on the net income and the cash-flow data.

P10-27B Cruise Canada Motorhomes Inc. (CCM) was formed on January 1, 2017, when the company issued its common shares for $200,000. Early in January, CCM made the following cash payments:

a. For showroom fixtures, $50,000
b. For inventory, two motorhomes at $60,000 each, a total of $120,000
c. For rent on a store building, $12,000

LEARNING OBJECTIVE ❷❸
Prepare an income statement, balance sheet, and statement of cash flows—indirect method

In February, CCM purchased three motorhomes on account. Cost of this inventory was $160,000 ($53,333.33 each). Before year-end, CCM paid $140,000 of this debt. CCM uses the FIFO method to account for inventory.

During 2017, CCM sold four motorhomes for a total of $560,000. Before year-end, CCM collected 90% of this amount.

The store employs three people. The combined annual payroll is $90,000, of which CCM owes $3,000 at year-end. At the end of the year, CCM paid income tax of $64,000.

Late in 2017, CCM declared and paid cash dividends of $40,000.

For showroom fixtures, CCM uses the straight-line depreciation method over five years with zero residual value.

Requirements

1. Prepare CCM's income statement for the year ended December 31, 2017. Use the single-step format, with all revenues listed together and all expenses listed together.
2. Prepare CCM's balance sheet at December 31, 2017.
3. Prepare CCM's statement of cash flows for the year ended December 31, 2017. Format cash flows from operating activities by the indirect method.
4. Comment on the business performance based on the statement of cash flows.

P10-28B Accountants for Crowne Plaza Products Inc. have assembled the following data for the year ended December 31, 2017:

LEARNING OBJECTIVE ❷❸
Prepare the statement of cash flows—indirect method

	December 31	
	2017	2016
Current Accounts:		
Current assets:		
Cash and cash equivalents	$29,100	$34,800
Accounts receivable	70,100	73,700
Inventories	90,600	96,500
Prepaid expenses	3,200	2,100
Current liabilities:		
Accounts payable	71,600	67,500
Income tax payable	5,900	6,800
Accrued liabilities	28,300	23,200

Transaction Data for 2017:

Payment of cash dividends	$48,300	Stock dividends	$ 12,600
Issuance of long-term note payable to borrow cash	71,000	Collection of loan	10,300
		Purchase of equipment	69,000
Net income	31,000	Payment of note payable by issuing common shares	89,400
Issuance of preferred shares for cash	36,200		
Sale of long-term investment	12,200	Purchase of long-term investment	44,800
Depreciation expense	30,300	Acquisition of building by issuing	
Payment of long-term note payable	47,800	long-term note payable	201,000
Gain on sale of investment	3,500		

Requirement

Prepare Crowne Plaza Products's statement of cash flows using the *indirect* method to report operating activities. Include an accompanying schedule of non-cash investing and financing activities. How much of the cash used for investing activities was provided by operations?

LEARNING OBJECTIVE ❷❸

Prepare the statement of cash flows—indirect method

P10-29B The comparative balance sheet of Crossbow Novelties Corp. at December 31, 2017, reported the following:

	December 31	
	2017	2016
Current Assets:		
Cash and cash equivalents	$28,800	$12,500
Accounts receivable	28,600	29,300
Inventories	51,600	53,000
Prepaid expenses	4,200	3,700
Current Liabilities:		
Accounts payable	31,100	28,000
Accrued liabilities	14,300	16,800
Income tax payable	11,000	14,300

Crossbow's transactions during 2017 included the following:

Cash purchase of building	$124,000	Depreciation expense	$17,800
Net income	52,000	Payment of cash dividends	17,000
Issuance of common shares		Cash purchase of equipment	55,000
for cash	105,600	Issuance of long-term note	
Stock dividend	13,000	payable to borrow cash	32,000
Sale of long-term investment	6,000	Repayment of note payable by	
		issuing common shares	30,000

Requirements

1. Prepare the statement of cash flows of Crossbow Novelties Corp. for the year ended December 31, 2017. Use the *indirect* method to report cash flows from operating activities. Report non-cash investing and financing activities in an accompanying schedule.
2. Evaluate Crossbow's cash flows for the year. Mention all three categories of cash flows, and give the reason for your evaluation.

LEARNING OBJECTIVE ❷❸

Prepare the statement of cash flows—indirect method

P10-30B The 2017 comparative balance sheet and income statement of Riverbend Pools Inc. follow. Riverbend had no non-cash investing and financing transactions during 2017. During the year, there were no sales of land or equipment, no issuances of notes payable, and no share repurchase transactions.

	A	B	C	D	E
1	**Riverbend Pools Inc.** Comparative Balance Sheet As at December 31, 2017 and 2016				
2		**2017**	**2016**	**Increase (Decrease)**	
3	Current assets:				
4	Cash and cash equivalents	$ 28,700	$ 15,600	$ 13,100	
5	Accounts receivable	47,100	44,000	3,100	
6	Inventories	94,300	89,900	4,400	
7	Prepaid expenses	1,700	2,200	(500)	
8	Property, plant, and equipment:				
9	Land	35,100	10,000	25,100	
10	Equipment, net	100,900	93,700	7,200	
11	Total assets	$ 307,800	$ 255,400	$ 52,400	
12	Current liabilities:				
13	Accounts payable	$ 22,700	$ 24,600	$ (1,900)	
14	Salary payable	2,100	1,400	700	
15	Other accrued liabilities	24,400	22,500	1,900	
16	Long-term liabilities:				
17	Notes payable	55,000	65,000	(10,000)	
18	Shareholders' equity:				
19	Common shares	131,100	122,300	8,800	
20	Retained earnings	72,500	19,600	52,900	
21	Total liabilities and shareholder's equity	$ 307,800	$ 255,400	$ 52,400	
22					

	A	B	C	D
1	**Riverbend Pool Inc.** Income Statement For the Year Ended December 31, 2017			
2	Revenues:			
3	Sales revenue		$ 438,000	
4	Interest revenue		$ 11,700	
5	Total revenues		449,700	
6	Expenses:			
7	Cost of goods sold	$ 185,200		
8	Salary expense	76,400		
9	Depreciation expense	15,300		
10	Other operating expense	49,700		
11	Interest expense	24,600		
12	Income tax expense	16,900		
13	Total expenses		368,100	
14	Net income		$ 81,600	
15				

Requirements

1. Prepare the statement of cash flows of Riverbend Pools Inc. for the year ended December 31, 2017. Determine cash flows from operating activities by the indirect method.
2. How will what you learned in this problem help you evaluate an investment?

APPLY YOUR KNOWLEDGE

This section's material reflects CPA enabling competencies,* including:

2. Problem-solving and decision-making

DECISION CASES

Case 1. The 2017 income statement and the 2017 comparative balance sheet of T-Bar-M Camp Inc. have just been distributed at a meeting of the camp's board of directors. The directors raise a fundamental question: Why is the cash balance so low? This question is especially troublesome because 2017 showed record profits. As the controller of the company, you must answer the question.

LEARNING OBJECTIVE ❸

Prepare and use the statement of cash flows to evaluate operations

	A	B	C
1	**T-Bar-M Camp Inc.** Income Statement For the Year Ended December 31, 2017		
2	*(in thousands)*		
3	Revenue:		
4	Sales revenue	$ 436	
5	Expenses:		
6	Cost of goods sold	$ 221	
7	Salary expense	48	
8	Depreciation expense	57	
9	Interest expenses	13	
10	Total expenses	339	
11	Net income	$ 97	
12			

	A	B	C	D
1	**T-Bar-M Camp Inc.** Comparative Balance Sheet As at December 31, 2017 and 2016			
2	*(in thousands)*	**2017**	**2016**	
3	**Assets**			
4	Cash	$ 17	$ 63	
5	Accounts receivable, net	72	61	
6	Inventories	194	181	
7	Long-term investments	31	0	
8	Property, plant, and equipment	369	259	
9	Accumulated depreciation	(244)	(198)	
10	Patents, net	177	188	
11	Totals	$ 616	$ 554	
12	**Liabilities and Shareholders' Equity**			
13	Accounts payable	$ 63	$ 56	
14	Accrued liabilities	12	17	
15	Notes payable, long-term	179	264	
16	Common shares	149	61	
17	Retained earnings	213	156	
18	Totals	$ 616	$ 554	
19				

*© Chartered Professional Accountants of Canada.

Requirements

1. Prepare a statement of cash flows for 2017 in the format that best shows the relationship between net income and operating cash flow. The company sold no plant and equipment or long-term investments and issued no notes payable during 2017. There were *no* non-cash investing and financing transactions during the year. Show all amounts in thousands.

2. Answer the board members' question: Why is the cash balance so low? Point out the two largest cash payments during 2017.

3. Considering net income and the company's cash flows during 2017, was it a good year or a bad year? Give your reasons. Explain the format you chose for the statement of cash flows.

Case 2. Applied Technology Inc. and Four-Star Catering Ltd. are asking you to recommend their shares to your clients. Because Applied and Four-Star earn about the same net income and have similar financial positions, your decision depends on their statements of cash flows, which are summarized as follows:

LEARNING OBJECTIVE ❶❷

Use cash-flow data to evaluate an investment

	Applied Technology Inc.		Four-Star Catering Ltd.	
Net cash provided by operating activities		$ 30,000		$ 70,000
Cash provided by (used for) investing activities:				
Purchase of property, plant, and equipment	$(20,000)		$(100,000)	
Sale of property, plant, and equipment	40,000	20,000	10,000	(90,000)
Cash provided by (used for) financing activities:				
Issuance of common shares		—		30,000
Paying off long-term debt	(40,000)		—	
Net increase in cash...		$ 10,000		$ 10,000

Based on their cash flows, which company looks better? Give your reasons.

ETHICAL ISSUE

Columbia Industries is having a bad year. Net income is only $37,000. Also, two important overseas customers are falling behind in their payments to Columbia, and Columbia's accounts receivable are ballooning. The company desperately needs a loan. The Columbia board of directors is considering ways to put the best face on the company's financial statements. Columbia's bank closely examines cash flow from operations. Daniel Peavey, Columbia's controller, suggests reclassifying the receivables from the slow-paying clients as long-term. He explains to the board that removing the $80,000 rise in accounts receivable from current assets will increase net cash provided by operations. This approach may help Columbia get the loan.

Requirements

1. Identify the ethical issue(s) in this situation.
2. Who are the stakeholders in this situation?
3. What is the potential impact of this reporting issue on each stakeholder?
4. What should the board do?
5. Under what conditions would the reclassification of the receivables be considered ethical?

FOCUS ON FINANCIALS

Canadian Tire Corporation

Use Canadian Tire's statement of cash flows along with the company's other financial statements, all in Appendix A at the end of the book, to answer the following questions.

Requirements

1. By which method does Canadian Tire report cash flows from operating activities? Explain your answer.
2. Evaluate Canadian Tire's change in cash in fiscal year 2014 compared with 2013.

FOCUS ON ANALYSIS

Canadian Tire Corporation

Refer to the Canadian Tire's financial statements in Appendix A at the end of this book. Focus on the fiscal year 2014.

Requirements

1. What was Canadian Tire's main source of cash? Is this a positive result? What was Canadian Tire's main use of cash? What sources of information contributed to your analysis?
2. Explain in detail the three main reasons why net cash from operations differs from net income.
3. There are two statements on which companies report declaration of dividends. Identify the two statements, review these statements, and determine what dividends Canadian Tire paid shareholders in 2014.

GROUP PROJECT

Project 1. Each member of the group should obtain the annual report of a different company. Select companies in different industries. Evaluate each company's trend of cash flows for the most recent two years. In your evaluation of the companies' cash flows, you may use any other information that is publicly available—for example, the other financial statements (income statement, balance sheet, statement of shareholders' equity, and the related notes) and news stories from magazines and newspapers. Rank the companies' cash flows from best to worst and write a two-page report on your findings.

Project 2. Select a company, and obtain its annual report, including all the financial statements. Focus on the statement of cash flows and, in particular, the cash flows from operating activities. Specify whether the company uses the direct method or the indirect method to report operating cash flows. As necessary, use the other financial statements (income statement, balance sheet, and statement of shareholders' equity) and the notes to prepare the company's cash flows from operating activities by using the *other* method.

CHECK YOUR WORK

STOP + THINK ANSWERS

STOP + THINK (10-1)

Depreciation and amortization are non-cash expenses that reduce net income, so to determine Canadian Tire's cash flows from operating activities, they must be added back to net income. Essentially, the Operating Activities section of the statement of cash flows converts accrual-based net income to a figure approximate to what net income would have been had it been determined using the cash basis of accounting.

STOP + THINK (10-2)

a. Financing
b. Financing
c. Operating
d. Financing
e. Investing
f. Financing
g. Financing
h. Operating
i. Investing
j. Operating
k. Investing
l. Investing

STOP + THINK (10-3)

1. Midwest has been expanding. It has acquired new business(es) for $400, with no significant disposals over three years. It also has total property, plant, and equipment purchases of $4,082 over the three years, with no significant disposals.

2. $156 (Proceeds of $55 − Carrying amount = loss of $101)

3. Yes, I would be pleased with Midwest's operating cash flows, as they are consistently higher than net income, which indicates a high quality of earnings. The company also has net cash inflows from operations of over $1,000 in each year, with a significant increase in 2018.

4. Midwest has been relying more on debt, as its net proceeds from equity issuances are only $10 over the three years, whereas its net proceeds from borrowing are $330 during this period.

5. Midwest has a strong cash position. It has over $850 in cash at the end of 2018, which is almost $200 more than it had at the end of 2016. Also, its cash flows from operations are its most significant source of cash in all three years.

QUICK QUIZ ANSWERS

1. c
2. a
3. b
4. b
5. d
6. c
7. c
8. Paying dividends *financing*
   Earning dividends *operating*
9. c [Carrying value = $12,000 ($20,000 − $8,000; Gain = $3,000; Proceeds = $15,000 ($12,000 + $3,000)]
10. d
11. b
12. a
13. c

$$\text{Gain} \quad \text{Amort.} \quad \text{A/Rec.}$$
[$47,000 − $8,000 + $6,000 + ($11,000 − $7,000)

$$\text{Invy.} \quad \text{A/Pay.}$$
− ($10,000 − $9,000) − ($7,000 − $6,000)

$$\text{Accr. Liab.}$$
+ ($7,000 − $3,000) = $51,000]

14. a
15. a *Cash received* = $28,000 ($20,000 + $8,000)

Cash paid = $50,000 ($69,000 − $20,000 − $6,000 + $X = $93,000; X = $50,000)

Net cash used = $22,000 ($50,000 − $28,000)

16. a
17. d
18. d *Cash received from issuance of shares* = $10,000 ($20,000 − $10,000)

Cash paid for dividends (X) = $36,000 ($70,000 + net income $47,000 − $X = $81,000; Dividends = $36,000)

Net cash used = $26,000 ($36,000 − $10,000)

19. a ($800,000 − $40,000 = $760,000)
20. a [$59,100 − ($5,000 − $2,800) = $56,900]

Appendix 10A

Preparing the Statement of Cash Flows: Direct Method

A-1 **Prepare** a statement of cash flows using the direct method of determining cash flows from operating activities

PREPARE A STATEMENT OF CASH FLOWS USING THE DIRECT METHOD OF DETERMINING CASH FLOWS FROM OPERATING ACTIVITIES

IFRS and ASPE encourage companies to prepare the statement of cash flows using the direct method because it provides clearer information about the sources and uses of cash. Very few companies use this method, however, because the indirect method gained prominence in the past and now continues to be used for reasons of comparability and user familiarity. Investing and financing cash flows are unaffected by the chosen method of reporting operating cash flows.

To illustrate the statement of cash flows, we use Bradshaw Corporation, a dealer in playground equipment. To prepare the statement of cash flows by the direct method, proceed as follows:

Step 1 Lay out the template of the *operating activities* section of the statement of cash flows by the direct method, as shown in Exhibit 10A-1.

Step 2 Use the comparative balance sheet to determine the increase or decrease in cash during the period. The change in cash is the "check figure" for the statement of cash flows. Bradshaw Corporation's comparative balance sheet indicates that Bradshaw's cash decreased by $20,000 during 2017 (Exhibit 10-4, p. 491). *Why* did Bradshaw's cash fall during 2017? The statement of cash flows explains.

Step 3 Use the available data to prepare the statement of cash flows. Bradshaw's transaction data appear in Exhibit 10A-2. These transactions affected both the income statement (Exhibit 10-5, p. 491) and the statement of cash flows. Some transactions affect one statement and some, the other.

EXHIBIT 10A-1
Template of the Operating Activities Section of the Statement of Cash Flows: Direct Method

	A
1	**Bradshaw Corporation** Statement of Cash Flows For the Year Ended December 31, 2017
2	**Cash flows from operating activities:**
3	Receipts:
4	Collections from customers
5	Interest received on notes receivable
6	Dividends received on investments in shares
7	Other operating receipts
8	Total cash receipts
9	Payments:
10	To suppliers
11	To employees
12	For interest
13	For income tax
14	Other operating payments
15	Total cash payments
16	Net cash provided by (used for) operating activities
17	

	A
1	**Operating Activities**
2	1. Sales on credit, $284,000
3	*2. Collections from customers, $271,000
4	3. Interest revenue on notes receivable, $12,000
5	*4. Collection of interest receivable, $10,000
6	*5. Cash receipt of dividend revenue on investments in shares, $9,000
7	6. Cost of goods sold, $150,000
8	7. Purchases of inventory on credit, $147,000
9	*8. Payments to suppliers, $133,000
10	9. Salary and wages expense, $56,000
11	*10. Payments of salary and wages, $58,000
12	11. Depreciation expense, $18,000
13	12. Other operating expense, $17,000
14	*13. Interest expense and payments, $16,000
15	*14. Income tax expense and payments, $15,000
16	

EXHIBIT 10A-2
Summary of Bradshaw Corporation's 2017 Operating Activities Transactions

*Indicates a cash flow to be reported on the statement of cash flows.
Note: Income statement data are taken from Exhibit 10-A6, page 532.

For example, sales (item 1) are reported on the income statement. Cash collections (item 2) go on the statement of cash flows. Other transactions, such as the cash receipt of dividend revenue (item 5), affect both statements. *The statement of cash flows reports only those transactions with cash effects* (those with an asterisk in Exhibit 10A-2). Exhibit 10A-3 gives Bradshaw Corporation's statement of cash flows for 2017.

	A	B	C	D
1	**Bradshaw Corporation** Statement of Cash Flows For the Year Ended December 31, 2017			
2	*(in thousands)*			
3	**Cash flows from operating activities:**			
4	Receipts:			
5	Collections from customers	$ 271		
6	Interest received on notes receivable	10		
7	Dividends received on investments in shares	9		
8	Total cash receipts		$ 290	
9	Payments:			
10	To suppliers	(133)		
11	To employees	(58)		
12	For interest	(16)		
13	For income tax	(15)		
14	Total cash payments		(222)	
15	Net cash provided by operating activities		(68)	
16				

EXHIBIT 10A-3
Statement of Cash Flows—Direct Method

Cash Flows from Operating Activities

Operating cash flows are listed first because they are the most important. Exhibit 10A-3 shows that Bradshaw is sound; operating activities were the largest source of cash.

CASH COLLECTIONS FROM CUSTOMERS. Both cash sales and collections of accounts receivable are reported on the statement of cash flows as "Collections from customers … $271,000" in Exhibit 10A-3.

CASH RECEIPTS OF INTEREST. The income statement reports interest revenue. Only the cash receipts of interest appear on the statement of cash flows—$10,000 in Exhibit 10A-3.

CASH RECEIPTS OF DIVIDENDS. Dividends are earned on investments in shares. Dividend revenue is reported on the income statement, and only cash receipts are reported on the statement of cash flows—$9,000 in Exhibit 10A-3. (Dividends *received* are operating activities, but dividends *paid* are financing activities.)

PAYMENTS TO SUPPLIERS. Payments to suppliers include all payments for inventory and operating expenses except employee compensation, interest, and income taxes. *Suppliers* are those entities that provide the business with its inventory and essential services. For example, a clothing store's suppliers may include Arrow Shirts, Gildan Activewear, and Levi Strauss. Other suppliers provide advertising, utilities, and various services that are operating expenses. Exhibit 10A-3 shows that Bradshaw Corporation paid suppliers $133,000.

PAYMENTS TO EMPLOYEES. This category includes payments for salaries, wages, commissions, and other forms of employee compensation. Accrued amounts are excluded because they have not yet been paid. The statement of cash flows in Exhibit 10A-3 reports only the cash payments ($58,000).

PAYMENTS FOR INTEREST EXPENSE AND INCOME TAX EXPENSE. Interest and income tax payments are reported separately. Bradshaw Corporation paid all its interest and income tax expenses in cash. Therefore, the same amount appears on the income statement and the statement of cash flows. Interest payments are operating cash flows because the interest is an expense.

DEPRECIATION EXPENSE. This expense is *not* listed on the statement of cash flows in Exhibit 10A-3 because it does not affect cash.

GAIN ON SALE OF PROPERTY, PLANT, AND EQUIPMENT. This gain is not listed on the statement of cash flows in Exhibit 10A-3 because it does not affect cash. The proceeds from selling the property, plant, and equipment will be included as a cash inflow under investing activities.

MyAccountingLab

STOP + THINK (10A-1)

Classify each of the following as an operating activity, an investing activity, or a financing activity. Also identify those items that are not reported on the statement of cash flows prepared by the *direct* method.

a. Net income

b. Payment of dividends

c. Borrowing

d. Payment of cash to suppliers

e. Making a loan

f. Receipt of cash dividends

g. Depreciation expense

h. Purchase of equipment

i. Issuance of shares

j. Purchase of another company

k. Payment of a note payable

l. Payment of income taxes

m. Collections from customers

n. Accrual of interest revenue

o. Expiration of prepaid expense

Now let's see how to compute the amounts of the operating cash flows by the direct method.

Computing Operating Cash Flows by the Direct Method

To compute operating cash flows by the direct method, we use the income statement and the *changes* in the related balance sheet accounts. Exhibit 10A-4 diagrams the process. Exhibit 10A-5 is Bradshaw Corporation's income statement and Exhibit 10A-6 (page 532) is the comparative balance sheet.

EXHIBIT 10A-4
Direct Method of Computing Cash Flows From Operating Activities

RECEIPTS/PAYMENTS	From Income Statement Account	Change in Related Balance Sheet Account	
RECEIPTS:			
From customers	Sales Revenue ————————	+ Decrease in Accounts Receivable – Increase in Accounts Receivable	
Of interest	Interest Revenue ————————	+ Decrease in Interest Receivable – Increase in Interest Receivable	
PAYMENTS:			
To suppliers	Cost of Goods Sold ————————	+ Increase in Inventory – Decrease in Inventory	+ Decrease in Accounts Payable – Increase in Accounts Payable
	Operating Expense ————————	+ Increase in Prepaids – Decrease in Prepaids	+ Decrease in Accrued Liabilities – Increase in Accrued Liabilities
To employees	Salary (Wages) Expense ————	+ Decrease in Salary (Wages) Payable – Increase in Salary (Wages) Payable	
For interest	Interest Expense ————————	+ Decrease in Interest Payable – Increase in Interest Payable	
For income tax	Income Tax Expense ————————	+ Decrease in Income Tax Payable – Increase in Income Tax Payable	

We thank Barbara Gerrity for suggesting this exhibit.

EXHIBIT 10A-5
Income Statement for the Bradshaw Corporation

	A	B	C	D
1	**Bradshaw Corporation** Income Statement For the Year Ended December 31, 2017			
2	**(in thousands)**			
3	Revenues and gains:			
4	Sales revenue	$ 284		
5	Interest revenue	12		
6	Dividend revenue	9		
7	Gain on sale of property, plant, and equipment	8		
8	Total revenues and gains		$ 313	
9	Expenses:			
10	Cost of goods sold	150		
11	Salary and wages expense	56		
12	Depreciation expense	18		
13	Other operating expense	17		
14	Interest expense	16		
15	Income tax expense	15		
16	Total expenses		272	
17	Net income		$ 41	
18				

EXHIBIT 10A-6
Comparative Balance Sheet for Bradshaw Corporation

	A	B	C	D	
				Increase (Decrease)	
1	**Bradshaw Corporation** Comparative Balance Sheet As at December 31, 2017 and 2016				
2	*(amounts in thousands)*	**2017**	**2016**	**Increase (Decrease)**	
3	**Assets**				
4	Current:				
5	Cash	$ 22	$ 42	$ (20)	
6	Accounts receivable	93	80	13	Changes in current assets—Operating
7	Interest receivable	3	1	2	
8	Inventory	135	138	(3)	
9	Prepaid expenses	8	7	1	
10	Long-term note receivable from another company	11	—	11	Changes in non-current assets—Investing
11	Property, plant, and equipment assets, net of depreciation	353	219	134	
12	Total	$ 625	$ 487	$ 138	
13	**Liabilities**				
14	Current:				
15	Accounts payable	$ 91	$ 57	$ 34	Changes in current liabilities—Operating
16	Salary and wages payable	4	6	(2)	
17	Accrued liabilities	1	3	(2)	
18	Long-term debt	160	77	83	Change in long-term liabilities and contributed capital accounts—Financing
19	**Shareholders' Equity**				
20	Share capital	259	258	1	Change due to net income—Operating
21	Retained earnings	110	86	24	Change due to dividends—Financing
22	Total	$ 625	$ 487	$ 138	
23					

COMPUTING CASH COLLECTIONS FROM CUSTOMERS. Collections start with sales revenue (an accrual-basis amount). Bradshaw Corporation's income statement (Exhibit 10A-5) reports sales of $284,000. Accounts Receivable increased from $80,000 at the beginning of the year to $93,000 at year-end, a $13,000 increase (Exhibit 10A-6). Based on those amounts, Cash Collections equal $271,000. We must solve for cash collections (X).

Accounts Receivable

Beginning balance	+	Sales	−	Collections	=	Ending balance
$80,000	+	$284,000		−X	=	$93,000
				−X	=	$93,000 − $80,000 − $284,000
				−X	=	$271,000

The T-account for Accounts Receivable provides another view of the same computation:

Accounts Receivable			
Beginning balance	80,000		
Sales	284,000	Collections	271,000
Ending balance	93,000		

Accounts Receivable increased, so collections must be less than sales.

All collections of receivables are computed in this way. Let's turn now to other cash receipts. In our example, Bradshaw Corporation earned interest revenue. Interest Receivable's balance increased by $2,000 (Exhibit 10A-6). Cash receipts of interest were $10,000 (Interest Revenue of $12,000 minus the $2,000 increase in Interest Receivable). Exhibit 10A-4 shows how to make this computation.

COMPUTING PAYMENTS TO SUPPLIERS. This computation includes two parts:

- Payments for inventory
- Payments for operating expenses (other than interest and income tax)

Payments for inventory are computed by converting cost of goods sold to the cash basis. We use Cost of Goods Sold, Inventory, and Accounts Payable. First, we must solve for purchases. All amounts come from Exhibits 10A-5 and 10A-6.

Cost of Goods Sold							
Beginning inventory	+	Purchases	−	Ending inventory	=	Cost of goods sold	
$138,000	+	X	−	$135,000	=	$150,000	
		X			=	$150,000 − $138,000 + $135,000	
		X			=	$147,000	

Now we can compute cash payments for inventory (Y), as follows:

Accounts Payable						
Beginning balance	+	Purchases	−	Payments for inventory	=	Ending balance
$57,000	+	$147,000		−Y	=	$91,000
				−Y	=	$91,000 − $57,000 − $147,000
				−Y	=	$113,000

The T-accounts show where the data come from:

Inventory					Accounts Payable		
Beg. Inventory	138,000	Cost of goods sold	150,000	Payments for		Beg. bal.	57,000
Purchases	147,000			inventory	113,000	Purchases	147,000 ◄
End. Inventory	$135,000					End bal.	91,000

Accounts Payable increased, so payments are less than purchases.

COMPUTING PAYMENTS FOR OPERATING EXPENSES. Payments for operating expenses other than interest and income tax can be computed from three accounts: Prepaid Expenses, Accrued Liabilities, and Other Operating Expenses. All Bradshaw Corporation data come from Exhibits 10A-5 and 10A-6.[2]

Prepaid Expenses

Beginning balance	+	Payments	−	Expiration of prepaid expense	=	Ending balance
$7,000	+	X		$7,000	=	$8,000
		X			=	$8,000 − $7,000 + $7,000
		X			=	$8,000

Accrued Liabilities

Beginning balance	+	Accrual of expense at year-end	−	Payments	=	Ending balance
$3,000	+	$1,000		−X	=	$1,000
				−X	=	$1,000 − $3,000 − $1,000
				−X	=	$3,000

Other Operating Expenses

Accrual of expense at year-end	+	Expiration of prepaid expense	+	Payments	=	Ending balance
$1,000	+	$7,000	+	X	=	$17,000
				X	=	$17,000 − $1,000 − $7,000
				X	=	$9,000
		Total payments for operating expenses			=	$8,000 + $3,000 + $9,000
					=	$20,000

The T-accounts give another picture of the same data:

Prepaid Expenses				Accrued Liabilities				Operating Expenses		
Beg. bal.	7,000	Expiration of prepaid expense	7,000	Payment 3,000	Beg. bal. 3,000	Accrual of expense at year-end	1,000	Accrual of expense at year-end	1,000	
Payments	8,000				Accrual of expense at year-end 1,000			Expiration of prepaid expense	7,000	
End. bal.	8,000				End. bal. 1,000			Payments	9,000	
								End. bal.	17,000	

---

[2]A simplifying assumption has been made in this example that the entire opening prepaid expenses will expire during the year and that all opening accrued liabilities will be paid during the year.

COMPUTING PAYMENTS TO EMPLOYEES. It is convenient to combine all payments to employees into one account, Salary and Wages Expense. We then adjust the expense for the change in Salary and Wages Payable, as shown here:

Salary and Wages Payable

Beginning balance	+	Salary and wages expense	−	Payments	=	Ending balance
$6,000	+	$56,000		−X	=	$4,000
				−X	=	$4,000 − $6,000 − $56,000
				−X	=	$58,000

The T-account gives another picture of the same data:

	Salary and Wages Payable	
	Beginning balance	6,000
Payments to employees 58,000	Salary and wages expense	56,000
	Ending balance	4,000

COMPUTING PAYMENTS OF INTEREST AND INCOME TAXES. Bradshaw Corporation's expense and payment amounts are the same for interest and income tax, so no analysis is required. If the expense and the payment differ, the payment can be computed as shown in Exhibit 10A-4.

Cash Flows from Investing and Financing Activities

Investing and financing cash flows are explained on pages 486–487. These computations are the same for both the direct and indirect methods.

MyAccountingLab

STOP + THINK (10A-2)

Fidelity Company reported the following for 2017 and 2016 (in millions):

As at December 31,	2017	2016
Receivables, net	$ 3,500	$3,900
Inventory	5,200	5,000
Accounts payable	900	1,200
Income taxes payable	600	700

Year Ended December 31,	2017
Revenues	$23,000
Cost of goods sold	14,100
Income tax expense	900

Based on these figures, how much cash did

- Fidelity collect from customers during 2017?
- Fidelity pay for inventory during 2017?
- Fidelity pay for income taxes during 2017?

SUMMARY

SUMMARY OF LEARNING OBJECTIVES

LEARNING OBJECTIVE	SUMMARY
A-1. **Prepare** a statement of cash flows using the direct method of determining cash flows from operating activities	To determine cash flows from operating activities using the direct method, sum cash receipts from operating activities and deduct cash payments for operating activities.
	Cash receipts from operating activities include:
	• Collections from customers • Interest received from loans and advances to others and from investments • Dividends received
	Cash payments for operating activities include:
	• Payments to suppliers • Payments to employees • Payments of interest • Payment of income taxes
	The net cash flows from operating activities determined using the direct method will always equal the net cash flows from operating activities determined using the indirect method.
	Cash flows from investing and financing activities are not affected by the method used to determine cash flows from operating activities.

MyAccountingLab

END-OF-APPENDIX SUMMARY PROBLEM

Kapoor Products Inc. reported the following comparative balance sheet and income statement for 2017:

	A	B	C	D
1	**Kapoor Products Inc.** Balance Sheet As at December 31, 2017 and 2016			
2		**2017**	**2016**	
3	Cash	$ 19,000	$ 3,000	
4	Accounts receivable	22,000	23,000	
5	Inventories	34,000	31,000	
6	Prepaid expenses	1,000	3,000	
7	Equipment (net)	90,000	79,000	
8	Intangible assets	9,000	9,000	
9		$ 175,000	$ 148,000	
10	Accounts payable	$ 14,000	$ 9,000	
11	Accrued liabilities	16,000	19,000	
12	Income tax payable	14,000	12,000	
13	Long-term debt	45,000	50,000	
14	Share capital	22,000	18,000	
15	Retained earnings	64,000	40,000	
16		$ 175,000	$ 148,000	
17				

	A	B	C	D
1	**Kapoor Products Inc.** Income Statement For the Years Ended December 31, 2017 and 2016			
2		**2017**	**2016**	
3	Sales revenue	$ 190,000	$ 165,000	
4	Gain on sale of equipment	6,000	—	
5	Total revenue and gains	196,000	165,000	
6	Cost of goods sold	85,000	70,000	
7	Depreciation expense	19,000	17,000	
8	Other operating expenses	36,000	33,000	
9	Total expenses	140,000	120,000	
10	Income before income tax	56,000	45,000	
11	Income tax expense	18,000	15,000	
12	Net income	$ 38,000	$ 30,000	
13				

Assume that you are an investment analyst for Canmore Investments Ltd. and have been tasked with analyzing Kapoor Products Inc. as Canmore is considering purchasing it. You determine that you need the following Kapoor cash-flow data for 2017. There were no non-cash investing and financing activities.

a. Collections from customers
b. Cash payments for inventory
c. Cash payments for operating expenses
d. Cash payment for income tax
e. Cash received from the sale of equipment, with Kapoor Products Inc. paying $40,000 for new equipment during the year
f. Issuance of common shares
g. Issuance of long-term debt, with Kapoor Products Inc. paying off $20,000 of long-term debt during the year
h. Cash dividends, with no stock dividends

Name: Kapoor Products Inc.
Fiscal Period: Year ended December 31, 2017

Provide your colleagues with the needed data. Show your work.

ANSWER

a. Analyze Accounts Receivable (let X = Collections from customers):

The change in Accounts Receivable of $1,000 ($22,000 – $23,000) is a result of sales and collections from customers.

Beginning	+	Sales	–	Collections	=	Ending
$23,000	+	$190,000	–	X	=	$22,000
				X	=	$191,000

b. Analyze Inventory and Accounts Payable (let X = Purchases, and let Y = Payments for inventory):

First calculate the amount of purchases. Then calculate the change in Accounts Payable that relates to cash payments.

Beginning Inventory	+	Purchases	–	Ending Inventory	=	Cost of Goods Sold
$31,000	+	X	–	$34,000	=	$85,000
		X			=	$88,000

Beginning Accounts Payable	+	Purchases	–	Payments	=	Ending Accounts Payable
$9,000	+	$88,000	–	Y	=	$14,000
				Y	=	$83,000

> Cash payments for operating expenses must account for the changes that relate to prepaid expenses and accrued liabilities.

c. Start with Other Operating Expenses, and adjust for the changes in Prepaid Expenses and Accrued Liabilities:

Other Operating Expenses		+ Increase, or − Decrease in Prepaid Expenses		− Increase, or + Decrease in Accrued Liabilities	=	Payments for Operating Expenses
$36,000	−	$2,000	+	3,000	=	$37,000

> The change in Income Tax Payable of $2,000 ($14,000 − $12,000) is a result of income tax expense and income tax payments made.

d. Analyze Income Tax Payable (let X = Payments of income tax):

Beginning	+	Income Tax Expense	−	Payments	=	Ending
$12,000	+	$18,000	−	X	=	$14,000
				X	=	$16,000

> Cash received from the sale of equipment is the carrying amount of the equipment plus the gain or minus the loss on the sale. First determine the carrying amount of the equipment sold.

e. Analyze Equipment (Net) (Let X = Carrying amount of equipment sold. Then combine with gain or loss on sale to compute cash received from sale.)

Beginning	+	Acquisitions	−	Depreciation	−	Carrying Amount Sold	=	Ending
$79,000	+	$40,000	−	$19,000	−	X	=	$90,000
						X	=	$10,000

Cash received from sale	=	Carrying Amount Sold	+	Gain, or − Loss on Sale
$16,000	=	$10,000	+	$6,000

> The change in Common Shares of $4,000 ($22,000 − $18,000) is a result of issuing shares.

f. Analyze Common Shares (let X = issuance):

Beginning	+	Issuance	=	Ending
$18,000	+	X	=	$22,000
		X	=	$ 4,000

> Long-Term Debt declined by $5,000 ($45,000 − $50,000). However, because a $20,000 payment was made during the year, $15,000 of long-term debt must have been issued.

g. Analyze Long-Term Debt (let X = issuance):

Beginning	+	Issuance	−	Payment	=	Ending
$50,000	+	X	−	$20,000	=	$45,000
		X			=	$15,000

> The change in Retained Earnings of $24,000 ($64,000 − $40,000) is a result of net income ($38,000 from the 2017 income statement) and the payment of cash dividends. The same information is shown on the statement of retained earnings.

h. Analyze Retained Earnings (let X = dividends):

Beginning	+	Net Income	−	Dividends	=	Ending
$40,000	+	$38,000	−	X	=	$64,000
				X	=	$14,000

ASSESS YOUR PROGRESS

Recall that for the sake of simplicity and consistency, this text classifies all interest paid and interest and dividends received as operating activities, and classifies dividends paid as a financing activity. All questions and problems in this chapter should be answered using this convention.

SHORT EXERCISES

S10A-1 Tally-Ho Horse Farm Inc. began 2017 with cash of $44,000. During the year, Tally-Ho earned service revenue of $500,000 and collected $510,000 from customers. Expenses for the year totalled $420,000, with $400,000 paid in cash to suppliers and employees. Tally-Ho also paid $100,000 to purchase equipment and a cash dividend of $50,000 to shareholders. During 2017, Tally-Ho borrowed $20,000 by issuing a note payable.

Prepare the company's statement of cash flows for the year. Format operating activities by the direct method.

LEARNING OBJECTIVE A-1
Prepare a statement of cash flows—direct method

S10A-2 (Exercise S10A-3 is an alternative exercise.) Maritime Fisheries Ltd. provides the following data for the year ended June 30, 2017:

LEARNING OBJECTIVE A-1
Compute operating cash flows—direct method

Cost of goods sold	$100,000	Payment of dividends	$ 6,000
Payments to suppliers	87,000	Proceeds from issuance of	
Purchase of equipment	40,000	common shares	20,000
Payments to employees	70,000	Sales revenue	210,000
Payment of note payable	30,000	Collections from customers	180,000
Proceeds from sale of land	60,000	Payment of income tax	10,000
Depreciation expense	8,000	Repurchase of common shares	5,000

Prepare the *operating activities section* of Maritime Fisheries Ltd.'s statement of cash flows for the year ended June 30, 2017. Maritime Fisheries uses the *direct* method for operating cash flows. Use Exhibit 10A-3 on page 529 as a guide.

S10A-3 Use your response and other data from exercise S10A-2 to prepare the rest of Maritime Fisheries Ltd.'s statement of cash flows for the year ended June 30, 2017. Maritime Fisheries uses the *direct* method for operating activities.

LEARNING OBJECTIVE A-1
Prepare a statement of cash flows—direct method

S10A-4 Autos of Red Deer Inc. reported the following financial statements for 2017:

LEARNING OBJECTIVE A-1
Compute operating cash flows—direct method

	A	B	C
1	**Autos of Red Deer Inc.** Income Statement For the Year Ended December 31, 2017		
2	*(in thousands)*		
3	Sales revenue	$ 710	
4	Cost of goods sold	340	
5	Salary expense	70	
6	Depreciation expense	20	
7	Other expenses	130	
8	Total expenses	560	
9	Net income	$ 150	
10			

	A	B	C	D	E	F	G
1	Autos of Red Deer Inc. Comparative Balance Sheet As at December 31, 2017 and 2016						
2	*(in thousands)*						
3	**Assets**	**2017**	**2016**	**Liabilities**	**2017**	**2016**	
4	Current:			Current:			
5	Cash	$ 19	$ 16	Accounts payable	$ 47	$ 42	
6	Accounts receivable	59	48	Salary payable	23	21	
7	Inventories	75	84	Accrued liabilities	8	11	
8	Prepaid expenses	3	2	Long-term notes payable	68	58	
9	Long-term investments	55	75	**Shareholders' Equity**			
10	Property, plant, and equipment	225	185	Share capital Retained earnings	40 250	32 246	
11	Totals	$ 436	$ 410	Total	$ 436	$ 410	
12							

Compute the following:

a. Collections from customers

b. Payments for inventory

LEARNING OBJECTIVE (A-1)

Compute operating cash flows—direct method

S10A-5 Use the Autos of Red Deer data in exercise S10A-4 to compute the following:

a. Payments to employees

b. Payments of other expenses

EXERCISES

LEARNING OBJECTIVE ❷(A-1)

Identify activities for the statement of cash flows—direct method

E10A-6 Identify each of the following transactions as operating (O), investing (I), financing (F), non-cash investing and financing (NIF), or not reported on the statement of cash flows (N). Indicate whether each transaction increases (+) or decreases (−) cash. The *direct* method is used for operating activities.

_____ a. Repurchase of common shares

_____ b. Issuance of common shares for cash

_____ c. Payment of accounts payable

_____ d. Issuance of preferred shares for cash

_____ e. Payment of cash dividend

_____ f. Sale of long-term investment

_____ g. Amortization of patent

_____ h. Collection of accounts receivable

_____ i. Issuance of long-term note payable to borrow cash

_____ j. Depreciation of equipment

_____ k. Acquisition of equipment by issuance of note payable

_____ l. Payment of long-term debt

_____ m. Acquisition of building by payment of cash

_____ n. Accrual of salary expense

_____ o. Purchase of long-term investment

_____ p. Payment of wages to employees

_____ q. Collection of cash interest

_____ r. Cash sale of land

_____ s. Distribution of stock dividend

LEARNING OBJECTIVE ❷(A-1)

Classify transactions for the statement of cash flows—direct method

E10A-7 Indicate where, if at all, each of the following transactions would be reported on a statement of cash flows prepared by the *direct* method and the accompanying schedule of non-cash investing and financing activities.

a. Equipment 18,000
     Cash.. 18,000

b. Cash.. 7,200
     Long-Term Investment 7,200

c. Bonds Payable 45,000
     Cash.................................... 45,000

d. Building 164,000
     Cash...................................... 164,000

e. Cash.. 1,400
     Accounts Receivable 1,400

f. Dividends Payable 16,500
     Cash...................................... 16,500

g.	Furniture and Fixtures	22,100		**k.**	Accounts Payable	8,300
	Note Payable, Short-Term		22,100		Cash		8,300
h.	Retained Earnings	36,000		**l.**	Salary Expense	4,300
	Common Shares		36,000		Cash		4,300
i.	Cash	2,000		**m.**	Cash	81,000
	Interest Revenue		2,000		Common Shares		81,000
j.	Land	87,700		**n.**	Common Shares	13,000
	Cash		87,700		Cash		13,000

E10A-8 The accounting records of Jasmine Pharmaceuticals Inc. reveal the following:

LEARNING OBJECTIVE Ⓐ-1

Compute cash flows from operating activities—direct method

Payment of salaries and wages	$34,000	Net income	$34,000
Depreciation	22,000	Payment of income tax	13,000
Decrease in current liabilities	20,000	Collection of dividend revenue	7,000
Increase in current assets		Payment of interest	16,000
other than cash	27,000	Cash sales	38,000
Payment of dividends	12,000	Loss on sale of land	5,000
Collection of		Acquisition of land	37,000
accounts receivable	93,000	Payment of accounts payable	54,000

Requirement

Compute cash flows from operating activities by the *direct* method. Use the format of the operating activities section of Exhibit 10A-3. Also, evaluate Jasmine's operating cash flow. Give the reason for your evaluation.

E10A-9 Selected accounts of Fishbowl Antiques Inc. show the following:

LEARNING OBJECTIVE ❷Ⓐ-1

Identify items for the statement of cash flows—direct method

Salary Payable

		Beginning balance	9,000
Payments	40,000	Salary expense	38,000
		Ending balance	7,000

Buildings

Beginning balance	90,000	Depreciation	18,000
Acquisitions	145,000	Carrying amount of	
		building sold	109,000*
Ending balance	108,000		

*Sale price was 140,000

Notes Payable

		Beginning balance	273,000
Payments	69,000	Issuance of note payable	
		for cash	83,000
		Ending balance	287,000

Requirement

For each account, identify the item or items that should appear on a statement of cash flows prepared by the *direct* method. State where to report the item.

LEARNING OBJECTIVE ⒶⒶ

Prepare the statement of cash
flows—direct method

E10A-10 The income statement and additional data of Floral World Ltd. follow:

	A	B	C	D
1	**Floral World Ltd.** Income Statement For the Year Ended December 31, 2017			
2	Revenues:			
3	Sales revenue	$ 229,000		
4	Dividend revenue	15,000	$ 244,000	
5	**Expenses:**			
6	Cost of goods sold	103,000		
7	Salary expense	45,000		
8	Depreciation expense	29,000		
9	Advertising expense	11,000		
10	Interest expense	2,000		
11	Income tax expense	9,000	199,000	
12	Net income		$ 45,000	
13				

Additional data:

a. Collections from customers are $30,000 more than sales.
b. Payments to suppliers are $1,000 more than the sum of cost of goods sold plus advertising expense.
c. Payments to employees are $1,000 more than salary expense.
d. Dividend revenue, interest expense, and income tax expense equal their cash amounts.
e. Acquisition of plant and equipment is $150,000. Of this amount, $101,000 is paid in cash and $49,000 by signing a note payable.
f. Proceeds from sale of land total $24,000.
g. Proceeds from issuance of common shares total $30,000.
h. Payment of long-term note payable is $15,000.
i. Payment of dividends is $11,000.
j. Cash balance, June 30, 2016, was $20,000.

Requirements

1. Prepare Floral World Ltd.'s statement of cash flows and accompanying schedule of non-cash investing and financing activities. Report operating activities by the *direct* method.
2. Evaluate Floral World's cash flows for the year. In your evaluation, mention all three categories of cash flows and give the reason for your evaluation.

LEARNING OBJECTIVE ⒶⒶ

Compute amounts for the statement
of cash flows—direct method

E10A-11 Compute the following items for the statement of cash flows:

a. Beginning and ending Accounts Receivable are $22,000 and $32,000, respectively. Credit sales for the period total $60,000. How much are cash collections from customers?
b. Cost of goods sold is $111,000. Beginning Inventory was $25,000, and ending Inventory is $21,000. Beginning and ending Accounts Payable are $14,000 and $8,000, respectively. How much are cash payments for inventory?

CHALLENGE EXERCISE

LEARNING OBJECTIVE ⒶⒶ

Compute cash-flow amounts

E10A-12 Morgan Industries Inc. reported the following in its financial statements for the year ended August 31, 2017 (in thousands):

	2017	2016
Income Statement		
Net sales	$24,623	$21,207
Cost of sales	18,048	15,466
Depreciation	269	230
Other operating expenses	3,883	4,248
Income tax expense	537	486
Net income	$ 1,886	$ 777
Balance Sheet		
Cash and cash equivalents	$ 17	$ 13
Accounts receivable	601	615
Inventory	3,100	2,831
Property and equipment, net	4,345	3,428
Accounts payable	1,547	1,364
Accrued liabilities	938	631
Income tax payable	201	194
Long-term liabilities	478	464
Common shares	519	446
Retained earnings	4,380	3,788

Determine the following cash receipts and payments for Morgan Industries Inc. during 2017:
a. Collections from customers
b. Payments for inventory
c. Payments for other operating expenses
d. Payment of income tax
e. Proceeds from issuance of common shares
f. Payment of cash dividends

PROBLEMS (GROUP A)

P10A-13A World Mosaic Furniture Gallery Inc. provided the following data from the company's records for the year ended April 30, 2017:

LEARNING OBJECTIVE ② A-1
Prepare the statement of cash flows—direct method

a. Credit sales, $583,900
b. Loan to another company, $12,500
c. Cash payments to purchase property, plant, and equipment, $59,400
d. Cost of goods sold, $382,600
e. Proceeds from issuance of common shares, $8,000
f. Payment of cash dividends, $48,400
g. Collection of interest, $4,400
h. Acquisition of equipment by issuing short-term note payable, $16,400
i. Payments of salaries, $93,600
j. Proceeds from sale of property, plant, and equipment, $22,400, including $6,800 loss
k. Collections on accounts receivable, $428,600
l. Interest revenue, $3,800
m. Cash receipt of dividend revenue, $4,100
n. Payments to suppliers, $368,500
o. Cash sales, $171,900
p. Depreciation expense, $59,900
q. Proceeds from issuance of note payable, $19,600
r. Payments of long-term notes payable, $50,000
s. Interest expense and payments, $13,300
t. Salary expense, $95,300
u. Loan collections, $12,800
v. Proceeds from sale of investments, $9,100, including $2,000 gain
w. Payment of short-term note payable by issuing long-term note payable, $63,000
x. Depreciation expense, $2,900
y. Income tax expense and payments, $37,900
z. Cash balance: April 30, 2016, $39,300; April 30, 2017, $36,600

Requirements
1. Prepare World Mosaic Furniture Gallery Inc.'s statement of cash flows for the year ended April 30, 2017. Use the *direct* method for cash flows from operating activities. Follow the format of Exhibit 10A-3 (p. 529), but do *not* show amounts in thousands. Include an accompanying schedule of non-cash investing and financing activities.
2. Evaluate 2017 from a cash-flow standpoint. Give your reasons.

LEARNING OBJECTIVE ❷ A-1

Prepare an income statement, balance sheet, and statement of cash flows—direct method

P10A-14A Vintage Automobiles of Orangeville Ltd. was formed on January 1, 2017, when Vintage issued common shares for $300,000. Early in January 2017, Vintage made the following cash payments:

a. $150,000 for equipment

b. $120,000 for inventory (four cars at $30,000 each)

c. $20,000 for 2017 rent on a store building

In February 2017, Vintage purchased six cars for inventory on account. Cost of this inventory was $260,000 ($43,333.33 each). Before year-end, Vintage paid $208,000 of this debt. Vintage uses the FIFO method to account for inventory.

During 2017, Vintage sold eight vintage autos for a total of $500,000. Before year-end, Vintage collected 80% of this amount.

The business employs three people. The combined annual payroll is $95,000, of which Vintage owes $4,000 at year-end. At the end of the year, Vintage paid income tax of $10,000.

Late in 2017, Vintage declared and paid cash dividends of $11,000.

For equipment, Vintage uses the straight-line depreciation method over five years with zero residual value.

Requirements

1. Prepare Vintage's income statement for the year ended December 31, 2017. Use the single-step format, with all revenues listed together and all expenses listed together.
2. Prepare Vintage's balance sheet at December 31, 2017.
3. Prepare Vintage's statement of cash flows for the year ended December 31, 2017. Format cash flows from operating activities by using the *direct* method.

LEARNING OBJECTIVE ❷ A-1

Prepare the statement of cash flows—direct method

P10A-15A The 2017 comparative balance sheet and income statement of 4 Seasons Supply Corp. follow. 4 Seasons had no non-cash investing and financing transactions during 2017. During the year, there were no sales of land or equipment, no issuance of notes payable, and no repurchase of shares transactions.

	A	B	C	D
1	**4 Seasons Supply Corp.** Comparative Balance Sheet As at December 31, 2017 and 2016			
2		**December 31**		
3		**2017**	**2016**	**Increase (Decrease)**
4	Current assets:			
5	Cash and cash equivalents	$ 17,600	$ 5,300	$ 12,300
6	Accounts receivable	27,200	27,600	(400)
7	Inventories	83,600	87,200	(3,600)
8	Prepaid expenses	2,500	1,900	600
9	Property, plant, and equipment:			
10	Land	89,000	60,000	29,000
11	Equipment, net	53,500	49,400	4,100
12	Total assets	$ 273,400	$ 231,400	$ 42,000
13	Current liabilities:			
14	Accounts payable	$ 35,800	$ 33,700	$ 2,100
15	Salary payable	3,100	6,600	(3,500)
16	Other accrued liabilities	22,600	23,700	(1,100)
17	Long-term liabilities:			
18	Notes payable	75,000	100,000	(25,000)
19	Shareholders' equity:			
20	Common shares	88,300	64,700	23,600
21	Retained earnings	48,600	2,700	45,900
22	Total liabilities and shareholders' equity	$ 273,400	$ 231,400	$ 42,000
23				

	A	B	C	D
1	**4 Seasons Supply Corp.** Income Statement For the Year Ended December 31, 2017			
2	Revenues:			
3	Sales revenue		$ 228,700	
4	Expenses:			
5	Cost of goods sold	$ 70,600		
6	Salary expense	27,800		
7	Depreciation expense	4,000		
8	Other operating expense	10,500		
9	Interest expense	11,600		
10	Income tax expense	29,100		
11	Total expenses		153,600	
12	Net income		$ 75,100	
13				

Requirements

1. Prepare the 2017 statement of cash flows using the *direct* method.
2. How will what you learned in this problem help you evaluate an investment?

P10A-16A To prepare the statement of cash flows, accountants for Franklin Electric Limited have summarized 2017 activity in two accounts as follows:

LEARNING OBJECTIVE Ⓐ①
Prepare the statement of cash flows—direct method

Cash

Beginning balance	53,600	Payments on accounts payable	399,100
Sale of long-term investment	21,200	Payments of dividends	27,200
Collections from customers	661,700	Payments of salaries and wages	143,800
Issuance of common shares	47,300	Payments of interest	26,900
Receipts of dividends	17,100	Purchase of equipment	31,400
		Payments of operating expenses	34,300
		Payment of long-term note payable	41,300
		Repurchase of common shares	26,400
		Payment of income tax	18,900
Ending balance	51,600		

Common Shares

Repurchase of common shares for cancellation	26,400	Beginning balance	110,800
		Issuance for cash	47,300
		Issuance to acquire land	80,100
		Issuance to retire note payable	19,000
		Ending balance	230,800

Requirement

Prepare the statement of cash flows of Franklin Electric Limited for the year ended December 31, 2017, using the *direct* method to report operating activities. Also prepare the accompanying schedule of non-cash investing and financing activities.

	A	B	C	D
1	**Franklin Electric Limited** Income Statement For the Year Ended December 31, 2017			
2	Revenues:			
3	Sales revenue		$ 689,300	
4	Dividend revenue		17,100	
5	Total revenue		706,400	

(Continued)

	A	B	C	D
6	Expenses and losses:			
7	Cost of goods sold	$ 402,600		
8	Salary and wage expense	150,800		
9	Depreciation expense	19,300		
10	Other operating expense	44,100		
11	Interest expense	28,800		
12	Income tax expense	16,200		
13	Loss on sale of investments	1,100		
14	Total expenses and losses		662,900	
15	Net income		$ 43,500	
16				

	A	B	C
1	**Franklin Electric Limited** Selected Balance Sheet Data		
2		**2017** **Increase** **(Decrease)**	
3	Current assets:		
4	Cash and cash equivalents	$ (2,000)	
5	Accounts receivable	27,600	
6	Inventories	(11,800)	
7	Prepaid expenses	600	
8	Long-term investments	(22,300)	
9	Equipment, net	12,100	
10	Land	80,100	
11	Current liabilities:		
12	Accounts payable	(8,300)	
13	Interest payable	1,900	
14	Salary payable	7,000	
15	Other accrued liabilities	10,400	
16	Income tax payable	(2,700)	
17	Long-term note payable	(60,300)	
18	Share capital	120,000	
19	Retained earnings	16,300	
20			

LEARNING OBJECTIVE Ⓐ①

Prepare the statement of cash flows—direct method

P10A-17A The comparative balance sheet of Graphic Design Studio Inc. at June 30, 2017, included these amounts:

	A	B	C	D	E
1	**Graphic Design Studio Inc.** Balance Sheet As at June 30, 2017 and 2016				
2		**2017**	**2016**	**Increase** **(Decrease)**	
3	Current assets:				
4	Cash	$ 28,600	$ 8,600	$ 20,000	
5	Accounts receivable	48,800	51,900	(3,100)	
6	Inventories	68,600	60,200	8,400	
7	Prepaid expenses	3,700	2,800	900	
8	Long-term investment	10,100	5,200	4,900	
9	Equipment, net	74,500	73,600	900	
10	Land	42,400	96,000	(53,600)	
11		$ 276,700	$ 298,300	$ (21,600)	

	A	B	C	D	E
12	Current liabilities:				
13	Notes payable, short-term	$ 13,400	$ 18,100	$ (4,700)	
14	Accounts payable	42,400	40,300	2,100	
15	Income tax payable	13,800	14,500	(700)	
16	Accrued liabilities	8,200	9,700	(1,500)	
17	Interest payable	3,700	2,900	800	
18	Salary payable	900	2,600	(1,700)	
19	Long-term note payable	47,400	94,100	(46,700)	
20	Share capital	59,800	51,200	8,600	
21	Retained earnings	87,100	64,900	22,200	
22		$ 276,700	$ 298,300	$ (21,600)	
23					

Transaction data for the year ended June 30, 2017, were:

a. Net income, $60,300
b. Depreciation expense on equipment, $13,400
c. Purchased long-term investment, $4,900
d. Sold land for $46,900, including $6,700 loss
e. Acquired equipment by issuing long-term note payable, $14,300
f. Paid long-term note payable, $61,000
g. Received cash for issuance of common shares, $3,900
h. Paid cash dividends, $38,100
i. Paid short-term note payable by issuing common shares, $4,700

Requirement

Prepare the statement of cash flows of Graphic Design Studio Inc. for the year ended June 30, 2017, using the *direct* method to report operating activities. Also, prepare the accompanying schedule of non-cash investing and financing activities. All current accounts except short-term notes payable result from operating transactions. The accounting records provide the following: collections from customers, $261,800; interest received, $1,300; payments to suppliers, $133,500; payments to employees, $40,500; payments for income tax, $10,600; payment of interest, $5,300.

PROBLEMS (GROUP B)

P10A-18B Rocco's Gourmet Foods Inc. provides the following data from the company's records for the year ended July 31, 2017:

LEARNING OBJECTIVE Ⓐ⓵

Prepare the statement of cash flows—direct method

a. Salary expense, $105,300
b. Cash payments to purchase property, plant, and equipment, $181,000
c. Proceeds from issuance of note payable, $44,100
d. Payments of long-term note payable, $18,800
e. Proceeds from sale of property, plant, and equipment, $59,700, including $10,600 gain
f. Interest revenue, $12,100
g. Cash receipt of dividend revenue on investments, $2,700
h. Payments to suppliers, $673,300
i. Interest expense and payments, $37,800
j. Cost of goods sold, $481,100

k. Collection of interest revenue, $11,700
l. Acquisition of equipment by issuing short-term note payable, $35,500
m. Payments of salaries, $104,000
n. Credit sales, $768,100
o. Loan to another company, $35,000
p. Income tax expense and payments, $56,400
q. Advertising expense, $27,700
r. Collections on accounts receivable, $741,100
s. Loan collections, $74,400
t. Proceeds from sale of investments, $34,700, including $3,800 loss
u. Payment of long-term note payable by issuing preferred shares, $107,300

v. Depreciation expense, $23,900
w. Cash sales, $146,000
x. Proceeds from issuance of common shares, $50,000

y. Payment of cash dividends, $50,500
z. Cash balance: July 31, 2016—$23,800; July 31, 2017—$31,400

Requirements

1. Prepare Rocco's Gourmet Foods Inc.'s statement of cash flows for the year ended July 31, 2017. Use the *direct* method for cash flows from operating activities. Follow the format of Exhibit 10A-3, but do *not* show amounts in thousands. Include an accompanying schedule of non-cash investing and financing activities.
2. Evaluate 2017 in terms of cash flow. Give reasons for your evaluation.

P10A-19B Cruise Canada Motorhomes Inc. (CCM) was formed on January 1, 2017, when the company issued its common shares for $200,000. Early in January, CCM made the following cash payments:

a. For showroom fixtures, $50,000
b. For inventory, two motorhomes at $60,000 each, a total of $120,000
c. For rent on a store building, $12,000

In February, CCM purchased three motorhomes on account. Cost of this inventory was $160,000 ($53,333.33 each). Before year-end, CCM paid $140,000 of this debt. CCM uses the FIFO method to account for inventory.

During 2017, CCM sold four motorhomes for a total of $560,000. Before year-end, CCM collected 90% of this amount.

The store employs three people. The combined annual payroll is $90,000, of which CCM owes $3,000 at year-end. At the end of the year, CCM paid income tax of $64,000.

Late in 2017, CCM declared and paid cash dividends of $40,000.

For showroom fixtures, CCM uses the straight-line depreciation method over five years with zero residual value.

Requirements

1. Prepare CCM's income statement for the year ended December 31, 2017. Use the single-step format, with all the revenues listed together and all expenses listed together.
2. Prepare CCM's balance sheet at December 31, 2017.
3. Prepare CCM's statement of cash flows for the year ended December 31, 2017. Format cash flows from operating activities by using the *direct* method.

P10A-20B The 2017 comparative balance sheet and income statement of Riverbend Pools Inc. follow. Riverbend had no non-cash investing and financing transactions during 2017. During the year, there were no sales of land or equipment, no issuances of notes payable, and no share repurchase transactions.

	A	B	C	D	E
1	**Riverbend Pools Inc.** Comparative Balance Sheet As at December 31, 2017 and 2016				
2		**2017**	**2016**	**Increase (Decrease)**	
3	Current assets:				
4	Cash and cash equivalents	$ 28,700	$ 15,600	$ 13,100	
5	Accounts receivable	47,100	44,000	3,100	
6	Inventories	94,300	89,900	4,400	
7	Prepaid expenses	1,700	2,200	(500)	

	A	B	C	D	E
8	Property, plant, and equipment:				
9	Land	35,100	10,000	25,100	
10	Equipment, net	100,900	93,700	7,200	
11	Total assets	$ 307,800	$ 255,400	$ 52,400	
12	Current liabilities:				
13	Accounts payable	$ 22,700	$ 24,600	$ (1,900)	
14	Salary payable	2,100	1,400	700	
15	Other accrued liabilities	24,400	22,500	1,900	
16	Long-term liabilities:				
17	Notes payable	55,000	65,000	(10,000)	
18	Shareholder's equity:				
19	Common shares	131,100	122,300	8,800	
20	Retained earnnings	72,500	19,600	52,900	
21	Total liabilities and shareholders' equity	$ 307,800	$ 255,400	$ 52,400	
22					

	A	B	C	D
1	**Riverbend Pools Inc.** Income Statement For the Year Ended December 31, 2017			
2	Revenues:			
3	Sales revenue		$ 438,000	
4	Interest revenue		11,700	
5	Total revenues		449,700	
6	Expenses:			
7	Cost of goods sold	$ 185,200		
8	Salary expense	76,400		
9	Depreciation expense	15,300		
10	Other operating expense	49,700		
11	Interest expense	24,600		
12	Income tax expense	16,900		
13	Total expenses		368,100	
14	Net income		$ 81,600	
15				

Requirements

1. Prepare the 2017 statement of cash flows by using the *direct* method.
2. How will what you learned in this problem help you evaluate an investment?

P10A-21B To prepare the statement of cash flows, accountants for Powers Art Gallery Inc. have summarized 2017 activity in two accounts as follows:

LEARNING OBJECTIVE A·1

Prepare the statement of cash flows—direct method

Cash			
Beginning balance	87,100	Payments of operating expenses	46,100
Issuance of common shares	60,800	Payment of long-term note payable	78,900
Receipts of dividends	1,900	Repurchase of common shares	10,400
Collection of loan	18,500	Payment of income tax	8,000
Sale of long-term investments	9,900	Payments on accounts payable	101,600
Receipts of interest	12,200	Payments of dividends	1,800
Collections from customers	308,100	Payments of salaries and wages	67,500
		Payments of interest	21,800
		Purchase of equipment	79,900
Ending balance	82,500		

	Common Shares	
	Beginning balance	103,500
	Issuance for cash	60,800
	Issuance to acquire land	62,100
	Issuance to retire long-term	
	note payable	21,100
	Ending balance	247,500

Requirement

Prepare Powers's statement of cash flows for the year ended December 31, 2017, using the *direct* method to report operating activities. Also, prepare the accompanying schedule of non-cash investing and financing activities. Powers's 2017 income statement and selected balance sheet data follow.

	A	B	C	D
1	**Power Art Gallery Inc.** Income Statement For the Year Ended December 31, 2017			
2	Revenues and gains:			
3	Sales revenue		$ 291,800	
4	Interest revenue		12,200	
5	Dividend revenue		1,900	
6	Gain on sale of investments		700	
7	Total revenues and gains		306,600	
8	Expenses:			
9	Cost of goods sold	$ 103,600		
10	Salary and wage expense	66,800		
11	Depreciation expense	20,900		
12	Other operating expense	44,700		
13	Interest expense	24,100		
14	Income tax expense	2,600		
15	Total expenses		262,700	
16	Net income		$ 43,900	
17				

	A	B	C
1	**Power Art Gallery Inc.** Selected Balance Sheet Data		
2		**2017 Increase (Decrease)**	
3	Current assets:		
4	Cash and cash equivalents	$ (4,600)	
5	Accounts receivable	(16,300)	
6	Inventories	5,700	
7	Prepaid expenses	(1,900)	
8	Loan receivable	(18,500)	
9	Long-term investments	(9,200)	
10	Equipment, net	59,000	
11	Land	62,100	

	A	B	C
12	Current liabilities:		
13	Accounts payable	$ 7,700	
14	Interest payable	2,300	
15	Salary payable	(700)	
16	Other accrued liabilities	(3,300)	
17	Income tax payable	(5,400)	
18	Long-term note payable	(100,000)	
19	Share capital	133,600	
20	Retained earnings	42,100	
21			

P10A-22B Arts de France Ltée's comparative balance sheet at September 30, 2017, included the following balances:

LEARNING OBJECTIVE A-1

Prepare the statement of cash flows—direct method

	A	B	C	D	E
1	**Arts de France Ltée** Balance Sheet As at September 30, 2017 and 2016				
2		**2017**	**2016**	**Increase (Decrease)**	
3	Current assets:				
4	Cash	$ 21,700	$ 17,600	$ 4,100	
5	Accounts receivable	46,000	46,800	(800)	
6	Inventories	121,700	116,900	4,800	
7	Prepaid expenses	8,600	9,300	(700)	
8	Long-term investment	51,100	13,800	37,300	
9	Equipment, net	131,900	92,100	39,800	
10	Land	47,100	74,300	(27,200)	
11		$ 428,100	$ 370,800	$ 57,300	
12	Current liabilities:				
13	Notes payable, short-term	$ 22,000	$ 0	$ 22,000	
14	Accounts payable	88,100	98,100	(10,000)	
15	Accrued liabilities	17,900	29,100	(11,200)	
16	Salary payable	1,500	1,100	400	
17	Long-term note payable	123,000	121,400	1,600	
18	Common shares	113,900	62,000	51,900	
19	Retained earnings	61,700	59,100	2,600	
20		$ 428,100	$ 370,800	$ 57,300	
21					

Transaction data for the year ended September 30, 2017, were:
a. Net income, $66,900
b. Depreciation expense on equipment, $8,500
c. Purchased long-term investments, $37,300
d. Sold land for $38,100, including $10,900 gain
e. Acquired equipment by issuing long-term note payable, $26,300
f. Paid long-term note payable, $24,700

g. Received cash of $51,900 for issuance of common shares
h. Paid cash dividends, $64,300
i. Acquired equipment by issuing short-term note payable, $22,000

Requirement

Prepare Arts de France's statement of cash flows for the year ended September 30, 2017, using the *direct* method to report operating activities. Also, prepare the accompanying schedule of non-cash investing and financing activities. All current accounts except short-term notes payable result from operating transactions. Prepare a supplementary schedule showing cash flows from operations by using the *direct* method. The accounting records provide the following: collections from customers, $343,100; interest received, $8,600; payments to suppliers, $216,400; payments to employees, $63,000; payment of income tax, $21,200; payment of interest, $10,700.

CHECK YOUR WORK

STOP + THINK ANSWERS

STOP + THINK (10A-1)

a. Not reported	d. Operating	g. Not reported	j. Investing	m. Operating
b. Financing	e. Investing	h. Investing	k. Financing	n. Not reported
c. Financing	f. Operating	i. Financing	l. Operating	o. Not reported

STOP + THINK (10A-2)

		Beginning receivables	+	Revenues	−	Collections	=	Ending receivable
Collections from customers	=$23,400:	$3,900	+	$23,000	−	$23,400	=	$3,500

		Cost of goods sold	+	Increase in inventory	+	Decrease in accounts payable	=	Payments
Payments for inventory	=$14,600:	$14,100	+	($5,200 − $5,000)	+	($1,200− $900)	=	$14,600

		Beginning income taxes payable	+	Income tax expense	−	Payment	=	Ending income taxes payable
Payment of income taxes	=$1,000:	$700	+	$900	−	$1,000	=	$600

Financial Statement Analysis

Bernard Weil/ZUMA Press/Newscom

11

LEARNING OBJECTIVES

1 **Perform** horizontal analysis

2 **Perform** vertical analysis

3 **Prepare** common-size financial statements

4 **Analyze** the statement of cash flows

5 **Use** ratios to make business decisions

CPA COMPETENCIES

Competencies* addressed in this chapter:

1.3.1 Prepares financial statements

1.4.4 Interprets financial reporting results for stakeholders (external or internal)

SPOTLIGHT

This book began with the financial statements of Canadian Tire, a company that sells many things, including hardware, gas, and financial services. Throughout this book we have shown you how to account for the financial position, results of operations, and cash flows of a variety of companies, such as Apple, CGI, Le Chateau, Leon's, WestJet, and ONEX. Only one aspect of the course remains: financial statement analysis. In the first half of this chapter, armed with information about the industry, the company, and its business strategy, we use horizontal, vertical, and cash flow analysis to help analyze the statements of Empire Company Ltd. When you finish this chapter, you should be able to understand the relationships among the data that reflect the financial position, results of operations, and cash flows of two different companies. The skills you learn in this chapter are transferrable, allowing you to deeply understand and interpret the financial statements of any other company of your choosing.

Empire Company Limited, which owns Sobeys, is one of Canada's leading grocery chains. Empire's revenues and net earnings look good, but how good *are* they? The analytical tools you learn in this chapter will help you answer this question.

---

*© Chartered Professional Accountants of Canada.

	A	B	C	D
1	**Empire Company Limited** Consolidated Statements of Earnings (Adapted) For the Years Ended May 2, 2015 and May 3, 2014			
2	*(in millions of dollars)*	2015	2014	
3	Sales	$ 23,928.8	$ 20,957.8	
4	Other revenue	185.3	99.5	
5	Operating expenses			
6	Cost of sales	17,966.7	15,941.3	
7	Selling & administrative expenses	5,403.8	4,787.5	
8	**Operating income**	743.6	328.5	
9	Finance costs, net	156.3	133.2	
10	**Earnings before income taxes**	587.3	195.3	
11	Income taxes	150.4	36.3	
12	Net earnings from continuing operations	$ 436.9	$ 159.0	
13	Net earnings from discontinued operations	0.0	84.4	
14	**Net earnings**	$ 436.9	$ 243.4	
15				

Source: Empire Company Limited - 2015 Annual Report.

This chapter covers the basic tools of financial analysis. The first part of the chapter shows how to evaluate Empire Company Limited from year to year and also how to compare Empire to its competitor, Metro, another of Canada's leading grocery chains. The second part of the chapter discusses the most widely used financial ratios. You have seen many of these ratios in earlier chapters; however, we have yet to use all of them in a comprehensive analysis of a company. We will use the financial statements of Apple Inc. to perform this analysis.

By studying all these ratios together, you will do the following:

- Learn the basic tools of financial analysis.

- Enhance your business education.

Regardless of your chosen field—marketing, management, finance, entrepreneurship, or accounting—you will find these analytical tools useful as you move through your career.

How Is a Company Evaluated?

Investors and creditors for both public and private corporations cannot evaluate a company by examining only one year's numerical data. That is why most financial statements cover at least two periods, like Empire's statement of earnings that begins this chapter. In fact, most financial analysis covers periods of three to five years. The goal of financial analysis is to predict the future by examining the past.

Financial analysis involves more than just doing the math. Thorough analysis of the financial position and results of operations of a company begins with understanding the business and industry of the company—the big picture. This usually entails quite a bit of reading and research, using all kinds of media—the business press, trade journals and other publications. You can often gain free access to this information on websites such as www.google.ca/finance. There are also some excellent paid sources, such as Hoovers Inc. (www.hoovers.com), where you can purchase industry and company analyses. Learning about what's happening in the industry, the markets, and the economy, along with trends in product development and specific company strategies help you put the accounting numbers in context and understand why they turned out as they did. After all, accounting data should paint a picture of the results of implementing a particular business strategy.

For example, Empire's Consolidated Statement of Earnings on page 554 reveals that operating income more than doubled, increasing from $328.5 million in 2014 to $743.6 million in 2015. Net earnings also increased from $243.4 million in 2014 to $436.9 million in 2015. Looking at these trends in isolation, without knowing some additional facts, the company appears to be operating very profitably in the food retail sector. We can, however, gain additional insight into these numbers by reading industry and company analyses. After reading Empire's annual report, for example, we learn that in fiscal 2014, the company acquired Canada Safeway and sold 30 of its grocery stores and 46 of its movie theatres. In the media, it was disclosed that the acquisition of Safeway required approval from the Canadian government whereby Empire agreed to sell some of the Safeway stores in western Canada. This additional information allows us to more clearly interpret year-over-year changes in Empire's financial numbers.

Reading the Management's Discussion and Analysis (MD&A) in a company's annual report gives management's perspectives on its operations and lends insight into why they made certain strategic decisions. For example, in the MD&A section of Empire's annual report, you will read that buying Canada Safeway allows Empire to grow and gives them access to the western Canada market. It also provides management's explanation of the effects the acquisition had on the company's sales, expenses, and net earnings in the most recent fiscal year.

Once we have an understanding of the big picture, we can dig more deeply into the numbers and they begin to make sense. Public companies' financial statements are comparative, that is, they cover at least two periods. Since one of the goals of financial analysis is to predict the future, it makes sense to start by mapping the trends of the past. This is particularly true of income statement data such as net sales and the various expenses that make up reported net income.

The graphs in Exhibit 11-1 show Empire's three-year trends in sales and operating income. Both are trending upward, which is a good sign. How would you predict Empire's sales and operating income for 2016 and beyond? Based on the recent past, you would probably extend the sales line and the operating income line upward.

Let's examine some of the tools of financial analysis. We begin with horizontal analysis.

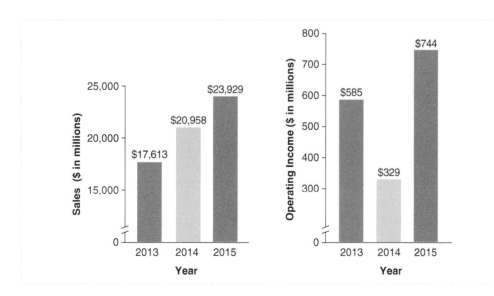

EXHIBIT 11-1
Sales and Operating Income of Empire Company Limited (Adapted)

PERFORM HORIZONTAL ANALYSIS

Many decisions hinge on the trends of a company's sales, expenses, operating income, net income, and other key financial statement figures. Has the sales figure risen from last year? If so, by how much? Suppose that sales have increased by $200,000. Considered alone, this fact is not very informative, but the *percentage change* in sales over time helps a lot. It is better to know that sales have increased by 20% than to know only that the increase is $200,000.

The study of percentage changes from year to year is called **horizontal analysis**. Computing a percentage change requires two steps:

1. Compute the dollar amount of the change from one period (the base period) to the next.

2. Divide the dollar amount of change by the base-period amount.

Illustration: Empire Company Limited

Horizontal analysis is illustrated for Empire as follows (dollars in millions):

	2015	2014	Increase (Decrease) Amount	Increase (Decrease) Percentage
Sales	$23,929	$20,958	$2,971	14.2%

Empire's sales increased by 14.2% during 2015, computed as follows:

Step 1   Compute the dollar amount of change in sales from 2014 to 2015:

$$2015 - 2014 = \text{Increase}$$

$$\$23,929 - \$20,958 = \$2,971$$

Step 2   Divide the dollar amount of change by the base-period amount. This computes the percentage change for the period:

$$\text{Percentage change} = \frac{\text{Dollar amount of change}}{\text{Base-year amount}} \times 100$$

$$= \frac{\$2,971}{\$20,958} \times 100 = 0.1417 \times 100 = 14.2\%$$

Exhibits 11-2 and 11-3 present horizontal analyses of Empire Company Ltd. The comparative statement of earnings shows that sales increased by 14.2% during 2015, while cost of sales grew by only 12.7%, resulting in a higher gross profit (Sales less cost of sales) for the year. Selling and administrative expenses increased by 12.9% and finance costs increased by 17.3%. Operating income increased by 126.4% even though sales increased by only 14.2% and various expenses were also higher for the year. Why was there such a large increase in operating income in 2015? Other revenue increased by 86.2%. In Note 19 of Empire's financial statements, we are told that most of the other revenue came from the sale of assets and lease revenue. Because of this large increase in other revenue, net earnings increased by 79.5%. Also, you will note that the difference between operating income and net earnings is caused by finance costs and income taxes, and in 2014, it includes $84.4 million in net earnings from discontinued operations. When a company sells or discontinues a component of its business, the income and expenses related to the component must be reported separately. Overall, management was able to increase the company's revenues in 2015 while limiting expenses to a lower rate of increase, resulting in the business operating more efficiently and more profitably for the year.

	A	B	C	D	E	F
1	**Empire Company Limited** Consolidated Statements of Earnings (Adapted) For the Years Ended May 2, 2015 and May 3, 2014					
2				Increase (Decrease)		
3	*(in millions of dollars)*	2015	2014	Amount	Percentage	
4	Sales	$ 23,928.8	$ 20,957.8	$ 2,971.0	14.2	
5	Other revenue	185.3	99.5	85.8	86.2	
6	Operating expenses					
7	Cost of sales	17,966.7	15,941.3	2,025.4	12.7	
8	Selling & administrative expenses	5,403.8	4,787.5	616.3	12.9	
9	**Operating income**	743.6	328.5	415.1	126.4	
10	Finance costs, net	156.3	133.2	23.1	17.3	
11	**Earnings before income taxes**	587.3	195.3	392.0	200.7	
12	Income taxes	150.4	36.3	114.1	314.3	
13	Net earnings from continuing operations	$ 436.9	$ 159.0	277.9	174.8	
14	Net earnings from discontinued operations	0.0	84.4	(84.4)	(100.0)	
15	**Net earnings**	$ 436.9	$ 243.4	$ 193.5	79.5	
16						

EXHIBIT 11-2
Comparative Income Statement—Horizontal Analysis

Source: Empire Company Limited - 2015 Annual Report.

Note: Any increase from zero to a positive number is treated as an increase of 100%; any decrease to zero is treated as a decrease of 100%. Any decrease in a negative number is treated as an increase; any increase in a negative number is treated as a decrease.

TRY IT *in* EXCEL ► ► ►

Formatting comparative financial statements for horizontal analysis when the financial statements are in Excel format is quite easy. Try reconstructing Exhibit 11-2 in Excel.

1. Start with the Consolidated Statements of Operations in the opening figure of the chapter.
2. Change the labels to correspond with Exhibit 11-2. Your spreadsheet might be slightly different from Exhibit 11-2, so the cells in which you start to enter formulas might have to be modified accordingly.
3. Insert one column between the 2015 and 2014 columns. Label this "% change".
4. Compute the percentage change as follows. We start in cell E4 (blank). Change the format of the data in the cell to % by clicking on the % box in the number field in the top toolbar. In cell E4, type the following: =(B4-C4)/C4. The result of 14.2% should appear in the cell. Copy this cell formula through line 15 of the sheet to perform this computation for all other income and expenses.

STOP + THINK (11-1)

Assume you are a financial analyst for an investment bank and have been charged with gathering information about Empire Company Limited for a client. You have performed a horizontal analysis of Empire's statements of earnings for 2015 and 2014, similar to that in Exhibit 11-2. What do you think is the single most important information for your analysis?

EXHIBIT 11-3
Comparative Balance Sheet—
Horizontal Analysis

Source: Empire Company
Limited - 2015 Annual Report.

	A	B	C	D	E	F
1	**Empire Company Limited** Consolidated Balance Sheets (Adapted) As at May 2, 2015 and May 3, 2014			**Increase (Decrease)**		
2	*(in millions of dollars)*	**2015**	**2014**	**Amount**	**Percentage**	
3	**Assets**					
4	**Current assets**					
5	Cash and cash equivalents	$ 295.9	$ 429.3	$ (133.4)	(31.1)	
6	Receivables	507.4	459.3	48.1	10.5	
7	Inventories	1,260.6	1,310.2	(49.6)	(3.8)	
8	Prepaid expenses	120.5	113.7	6.8	6.0	
9	Loans and other receivables	24.8	35.7	(10.9)	(30.5)	
10	Income taxes receivable	18.9	39.7	(20.8)	(52.4)	
11	Assets held for sale	47.8	204.8	(157.0)	(76.7)	
12		$ 2,275.9	$ 2,592.7	(316.8)	(12.2)	
13	Loans and other receivables	88.5	63.2	25.3	40.0	
14	Investments	25.1	24.8	0.3	1.2	
15	Investments, at equity	577.8	554.2	23.6	4.3	
16	Other assets	48.4	29.2	19.2	65.8	
17	Property and equipment	3,500.4	3,685.6	(185.2)	(5.0)	
18	Investment property	104.2	104.5	(0.3)	(0.3)	
19	Intangibles	943.0	993.6	(50.6)	(5.1)	
20	Goodwill	3,799.2	4,069.7	(270.5)	(6.6)	
21	Deferred tax assets	110.9	126.2	(15.3)	(12.1)	
22		$ 11,473.4	$ 12,243.7	(770.3)	(6.3)	
23	**Liabilities and Shareholders' Equity**					
24	**Current liabilities**					
25	Accounts payable and accrued liabilities	2,265.8	2,244.9	20.9	0.9	
26	Income taxes payable	40.9	21.0	19.9	94.8	
27	Current portion of long-term debt	53.9	218.0	(164.1)	(75.3)	
28	Other liabilities	122.1	82.4	39.7	48.2	
29		2,482.7	2,566.3	(83.6)	(3.3)	
30	Long-term debt	2,242.0	3,282.1	(1,040.1)	(31.7)	
31	Deferred tax liabilities	110.9	123.8	(12.9)	(10.4)	
32	Other long-term liabilities	600.9	530	70.9	13.4	
33		5,436.5	6,502.2	(1,065.7)	(16.4)	
34	**Shareholders' Equity**					
35	Capital Stock	2,109.4	2,108.6	0.8	0.04	
36	Contributed surplus	8.2	5.0	3.2	64.0	
37	Retained earnings	3,859.9	3,585.9	274.0	7.6	
38	Accumulated other comprehensive income	6.3	1.0	5.3	530.0	
39		5,983.8	5,700.5	283.3	5.0	
40	Non-controlling interest	53.1	41.0	12.1	29.5	
41		6,036.9	5,741.5	295.4	5.1	
42	**Total Liabilities and Shareholders' Equity**	$ 11,473.4	$ 12,243.7	(770.3)	(6.3)	
43						

Studying changes in the balance sheet accounts can enhance our understanding of the current and long-term financial position of the entity. Let's look at a few of the balance sheet changes in Exhibit 11-3. First, cash decreased by 31.1%. While the statement of cash flow would show why cash decreased, we are reserving that discussion for later. Reviewing the balance sheet, we can see that cash was used to prepay expenses (increase of 6%) and pay back long-term debt (decrease of 31.7%). Current Loans and other receivables decreased by 30.5%, while long-term Loans and other receivables increased by 40%. Income taxes receivable decreased by 52.4%, meaning that the company is expecting to receive a smaller refund compared to 2014, from the Canada Revenue Agency.

Accounts receivable increased by 10.5%, less than sales (14.2%). This is a good sign because if accounts receivable was growing faster than sales, collections may be too slow and a cash shortage may result. Accounts payable also increased less than sales (0.9%), indicating that the company's payments of short-term debt are keeping pace with its overall rate of growth in sales. On the whole, current assets decreased by 12.2%, while current liabilities decreased by 3.3%, resulting in negative working capital for 2015.

Property, plant, and equipment decreased by 5%, meaning the company either disposed of some assets and/or wrote them down due to impairment. Other assets grew by 65.8%, but there is no indication what they are without reading the notes. Note 8 provides a schedule of the components of this category: the major items include deferred lease assets and restricted cash, which the company is reserving for future use. While long-term debt decreased by 31.7% (the company has paid back some debt), other long-term liabilities increased by 13.4%, indicating the company borrowed more money. There was a slight increase in share capital of less than 0.5% because the company converted some Class B common shares to non-voting common shares (Note 18); this may have resulted in an increase in contributed surplus. Net earnings of $436.9 contributed to the increase in retained earnings.

Trend Percentages

Trend percentages are a form of horizontal analysis. Trends indicate the direction a business is taking. How have sales changed over a five-year period? What trend does operating income show? These questions can be answered by trend percentages over a representative period, such as the most recent five years.

Trend percentages are computed by selecting a base year whose amounts are set equal to 100%. The amount for each following year is expressed as a percentage of the base amount. To compute a trend percentage, divide an item for a later year by the base-year amount:

$$\text{Trend \%} = \frac{\text{Any-year \$}}{\text{Base-year \$}}$$

Operating income represents a company's best predictor of the future net inflows from its core business units. Empire showed operating income from continuing operations for the past five years as follows:

(in millions)	2015	2014	2013	2012	2011
Operating income	$744	$329	$573	$534	$526

We would like to calculate trend percentages for the four-year period 2012 to 2015. The base year is 2011. Trend percentages are computed by dividing each year's amount by the 2011 amount. The trend percentages for the past five years are:

	2015	2014	2013	2012	2011
Operating income	141%	63%	109%	102%	100%

Looking at the trend percentages for Empire, we can see that operating income increased steadily in 2012 and 2013, but dropped dramatically in 2014 before rising significantly in 2015. According to the Management Discussion and Analysis from the Annual Report in 2014 and 2015, operating income dropped in 2014 due to costs relating to the acquisition of Canada Safeway. In 2015, operating income grew from factors which included food inflation and store closures mandated by the Government of Canada in order for Empire to purchase Safeway Canada.

You can perform a trend analysis on any item you consider important. Trend analysis is widely used for predicting the future.

Horizontal analysis highlights changes in an item over time. However, no single technique gives a complete picture of a business.

OBJECTIVE

❷ Perform vertical analysis

PERFORM VERTICAL ANALYSIS

Vertical analysis shows the relationship of a financial statement item to its base, which is the 100% figure. All items on the particular financial statement are reported as a percentage of that base. For the income statement, total revenue (sales) is usually the base while total assets is the base for the balance sheet. One use of vertical analysis is to reveal items that need to be investigated further. For example, if cost of goods sold as a percentage of sales is 50% in the previous year and 55% in the current year, management is now aware that expenses have increased in a particular area and can take measures to reduce these costs. You can also use a form of vertical analysis by preparing common-size financial statements and using them to compare one company with another. This will be discussed further in the next section.

To perform a vertical analysis using the income statement, total revenue is usually the base. Suppose that investors have come to expect a company's net income to be greater than 8% of net sales revenue. A drop to 4% over a period of two years while general economic conditions are improving may cause investors to become disappointed in the performance of company management. Thus, they might sell the company's shares in favour of companies with more attractive earnings potential.

Illustration: Empire Company Limited

Exhibit 11-4 shows the vertical analysis of Empire's statement of earnings as a percentage of sales. In this case,

$$\text{Vertical analysis } \% = \frac{\text{Each income statement item}}{\text{Sales}}$$

For Empire, the vertical-analysis percentage for cost of sales is 74.5% ($17,966.7/$24,114.1) in 2015, which is only a slight decrease from 75.7% in 2014. Even though it is only a slight decrease, this is a good sign as it indicates that management was able to keep costs down while sales and other revenue increased. Operating income, as a percentage of sales, increased from 1.6% to 3.1%, and net earnings as a percentage of sales increased from 1.2% in 2014 to 1.8% in 2015. This indicates to management that overall net earnings improved because they were able to control their expenses.

	A	B	C	D	E	F
1	**Empire Company Limited** Consolidated Statements of Earnings (Adapted) For the Years Ended May 2, 2015 and May 3, 2014					
2	*(in millions of dollars)*	2015		2014		
3		Amount	Percentage of Sales	Amount	Percentage of Sales	
4	Sales and other revenue	$ 24,114.1	100.0%	$ 21,057.3	100.0%	
5	Operating expenses					
6	Cost of sales	17,966.7	74.5	15,941.3	$ 75.7	
7	Selling & administrative expenses	5,403.8	22.4	4,787.5	22.7	
8	Operating income	743.6	3.1	328.5	1.6	
9	Finance costs, net	156.3	0.6	133.2	0.6	
10	Earnings before income taxes	587.3	2.4	195.3	0.9	
11	Income taxes	150.4	0.6	36.3	0.2	
12	Net earnings from continuing operations	$ 436.9	1.8	$ 159.0	0.8	
13	Net earnings from discontinued operations	$0.0	0.0	$84.4	0.4	
14	Net earnings	$ 436.9	1.8	$ 243.4	1.2	
15						

*differences due to rounding

EXHIBIT 11-4
Comparative Statement of Earnings—Vertical Analysis

Source: Empire Company Limited - 2015 Annual Report.

TRY IT *in* EXCEL® ▶ ▶ ▶

Formatting comparative financial statements for vertical analysis when the financial statements are in Excel format is just as easy as it was for horizontal analysis. Try reconstructing Exhibit 11-4 in Excel.

1. Start with the Consolidated Statements of Earnings in the opening figure of the chapter. You will be ahead of the game if you have already prepared this in Excel.
2. Change the labels to correspond with Exhibit 11-4. Your spreadsheet might be slightly different than Exhibit 11-4, so the cells in which you start to enter formulas might have to be modified accordingly.
3. We are preparing two years of comparative data, so insert columns after each of the 2015 and 2014 financial columns. In our example, these become columns C and E with blank cells; label these "% of total."
4. Common-sized income statements set net sales at 100% and express all other income and expenses as percentages of net sales. To set net sales at 100%, we start in cell C3 (blank). In the cell, type the following: =B3/$B$3. It is very important to insert the $ signs in the denominator both before and after the letter B. This "freezes" cell B3 to make it a constant denominator for the values in all other cells in the column. You may also use theF4 function key to freeze the cell value. The result of 100% should appear in the cell. To increase precision, use the "increase decimal" tab in the "number" field in the toolbar. We have adjusted to a precision of two decimal places. Copy this cell formula through line 14 of the sheet to perform this computation for all other income and expenses.
5. Repeat the process in (4) for the 2014 figures columns by entering corresponding formulas in column E. Copy these formulas through line 14. Use the"borders" tab (under "font" in the toolbar) to format the cells to extend the proper underscoring as shown in Exhibit 11-4.
6. Pat yourself on the back. You're learning to use Excel for the very valuable function of vertical analysis! Now let's dig into the numbers to interpret and what they mean.

Exhibit 11-5 shows the vertical analysis of Empire's consolidated balance sheets. The base amount is total assets. The vertical analysis of Empire's balance sheet reveals several things about Empire's financial position at December 31, 2015, relative to 2014:

EXHIBIT 11-5
Comparative Balance Sheet—Vertical Analysis

Source: Empire Company Limited - 2015 Annual Report.

	A	B	C	D	E	F
1	**Empire Company Limited** Consolidated Balance Sheets (Adapted) As at May 2, 2015 and May 3, 2014					
2	*(in millions of dollars)*	2015		2014		
3		Amount	Percentage of Total	Amount	Percentage of Total	
4	**Assets**					
5	**Current assets**					
6	Cash and cash equivalents	$ 295.9	2.6	$ 429.3	3.5	
7	Receivables	507.4	4.4	459.3	3.8	
8	Inventories	1,260.6	11.0	1,310.2	10.7	
9	Prepaid expenses	120.5	1.1	113.7	0.9	
10	Loans and other receivables	24.8	0.2	35.7	0.3	
11	Income taxes receivable	18.9	0.2	39.7	0.3	
12	Assets held for sale	47.8	0.4	204.8	1.7	
13		$ 2,275.9	19.8	$ 2,592.7	21.2	
14	Loans and other receivables	88.5	0.8	63.2	0.5	
15	Investments	25.1	0.2	24.8	0.2	
16	Investments, at equity	577.8	5.0	554.2	4.5	
17	Other assets	48.4	0.4	29.2	0.2	
18	Property and equipment	3,500.4	30.5	3,685.6	30.1	
19	Investment property	104.2	0.9	104.5	0.9	
20	Intangibles	943.0	8.2	993.6	8.1	
21	Goodwill	3,799.2	33.1	4,069.7	33.2	
22	Deferred tax assets	110.9	1.0	126.2	1.0	
23		$ 11,473.4	100.0	$ 12,243.7	100.0	
24	**Liabilities and Shareholders' Equity**					
25	**Current liabilities**					
26	Accounts payable and accrued liabilities	2,265.8	19.7	2,244.9	18.3	
27	Income taxes payable	40.9	0.4	21.0	0.2	
28	Current portion of long-term debt	53.9	0.5	218.0	1.8	
29	Other liabilities	122.1	1.1	82.4	0.7	
30		2,482.7	21.6	2,566.3	21.0	
31	Long-term debt	2,242.0	19.5	3,282.1	26.8	
32	Deferred tax liabilities	110.9	1.0	123.8	1.0	
33	Other long-term liabilities	600.9	5.2	530.0	4.3	
34		5,436.5	47.4	6,502.2	53.1	
35	**Shareholders' Equity**					
36	Capital Stock	2,109.4	18.4	2,108.6	17.2	
37	Contributed surplus	8.2	0.1	5.0	0.0	
38	Retained earnings	3,859.9	33.6	3,585.9	29.3	
39	Accumulated other comprehensive income	6.3	0.1	1.0	0.0	
40		5,983.8	52.2	5,700.5	46.6	
41	Non-controlling interest	53.1	0.5	41.0	0.3	
42		6,036.9	52.6	5,741.5	46.9	
43	**Total Liabilities & Shareholders' Equity**	$ 11,473.4	100.0	$ 12,243.7	100.0	
44						

- While cash decreased by 31.1% from 2014, it also decreased as a percentage of total assets from 3.5% to 2.6%. At the same time, receivables increased slightly from 3.8% to 4.4%.
- Inventories as a percentage of total assets increased from 10.7% to 11.0%.
- The company's debt to total assets of 47.4% in 2015 decreased from 53.1% in 2014. Of the total debt, current liabilities increased slightly from 21% in 2014 to 21.6% in 2015, and long-term liabilities decreased from 32.1% to 25.7%. These debt ratios are still comfortably within reasonable limits for a retail concern.

STOP + THINK (11-2)

Using Empire's data in Exhibit 11-4, did cost of sales increase or decrease from the previous year? Is this a good sign or a bad sign?

PREPARE COMMON-SIZE FINANCIAL STATEMENTS

OBJECTIVE

❸ **Prepare** common-size financial statements

The percentages in Exhibits 11-4 and 11-5 can be presented as separate statements that report only percentages (no dollar amounts). These statements are called **common-size financial statements**.

On a common-size income statement, each item is expressed as a percentage of the net sales amount. Net sales is the *common size* to which we relate the other amounts. In the balance sheet, the common size is total assets. A common-size statement aids the comparison of different companies because their amounts are stated in percentages, thus expressing the financial results of each comparative company in terms of a common denominator.

Benchmarking

Benchmarking is the comparison of a company to a standard set by others. The goal of benchmarking is improvement. Suppose you are a financial analyst for ScotiaMcLeod. You are considering an investment in the shares of a grocery chain, and you are choosing between Empire Company Limited and Metro Inc. A direct comparison of their financial statements in dollar amounts is not meaningful because the companies differ greatly in size. We can, however, convert the income statements to common size and compare the percentages. The comparison is meaningful, as we shall see.

Benchmarking Against a Key Competitor

Exhibit 11-6 presents the common-size income statements of Empire Company Limited and Metro Inc. Metro serves as an excellent benchmark because it and Empire are both large, successful Canadian grocery chains. Empire's cost of goods sold, operating and other expenses as a percentage of sales are 2.8% (97.6% − 94.8%) higher than Metro's. Metro's net income as a percentage of sales is 2.1% (3.9% − 1.8%) is higher than Empire. When compared to Empire, it would appear that Metro is able to keep their costs down resulting in a higher percentage of net income to sales.

		A	B	C	D
1		**Empire Company Limited** Common-Size Income Statement (Adapted) for Comparison With a Key Competitor For the Years Ended as Indicated			
2			**Empire Company Limited (Adapted) May 2, 2015**	**Metro Inc. (Adapted) September 27, 2014**	
3		Sales	100.0%	100.0%	
4					
5		Cost of goods sold, operating and other expenses	97.6	94.8	
6		Income before income tax	2.4	5.2	
7		Income tax expense	0.6	1.3	
8		Net earnings	1.8%	3.9%	
9					

MyAccountingLab

STOP + THINK (11-3)

Assume you are a financial analyst for an investment bank and have been charged with gathering information about K-M Inc. for a client. You have been provided with the following 2017 income statement by K-M and have decided to calculate the common-size percentages. What does this tell you about the company? Show your calculations.

Net sales	$150,000
Cost of goods sold	60,000
Gross profit	90,000
Operating expense	40,000
Operating income	50,000
Income tax expense	15,000
Net income	$ 35,000

ANALYZE THE STATEMENT OF CASH FLOWS

So far, this chapter has focused on the income statement and balance sheet. Let's now move on to examine the consolidated statements of cash flows for Empire, which are presented in Exhibit 11-7. While the operating income is a key figure to use when analyzing a company's performance, it is also critical to examine its cash flow from operating activities, which gives us a different view of the company's operating performance. Because we record operating revenues and expenses using the accrual method, operating income may differ from operating cash flows, which are based solely on cash receipts and cash payments. A company may report significant operating income, for example, but have poor operating cash flows because it cannot sell its inventory or collect cash from its customers on a timely basis. The reverse may also be true: a company may generate significant operating cash flows but report little or no operating income. Generally, the higher the ratio of a company's cash flow from operations to its operating income, the better its quality of earnings.

The income statement and the statement of cash flows can therefore paint different pictures of the same company, so we must analyze both of them, along with the balance sheet, to gain an overall picture of a company's operating performance and financial position.

	A	B	C	D
1	**Empire Company Limited** Consolidated Statements of Cash Flows (Adapted) For the Years Ended May 2, 2015 and May 3, 2014			
2	*(in millions of dollars)*	**2015**	**2014**	
3	**Operating Activities**			
4	Net earnings	436.9	243.4	
5	Adjustments for:			
6	Depreciation	397.8	362.5	
7	Income taxes	150.4	49.6	
8	Finance costs, net	156.3	134.0	
9	Amortization of intangibles	84.7	68.1	
10	Gain on disposal of assets	(67.0)	(137.5)	
11	Impairment of non-financial assets	1.5	(7.0)	
12	Amortization of deferred items	12.7	7.1	
13	Equity in earnings of other entities	33.3	27.5	
14	Employee future benefits obligation	(0.5)	2.9	
15	Increase in long-term lease obligation	5.8	1.2	
16	Losses on remeasurement of assets and restructuring costs	0.0	34.8	
17	Stock option plan	4.0	4.8	
18	Restructuring	103.0	169.8	
19	Decrease in long-term provisions	(52.5)	(0.6)	
20	Net change in non-cash working capital	(15.7)	36.3	
21	Income taxes, paid, net	(90.2)	(211.6)	
22	Cash flows from operating activities	1,160.5	785.3	
23	*Operating cash as a % of net income*	*266%*	*323%*	
24	**Investing Activities**			
25	Net increase in investments	(40.7)	(151.6)	
26	Property, equipment and investment property	(497.2)	(563.1)	
27	Proceeds on disposal of property, equipment and investment property	781.2	1,644.4	
28	Additions to intangibles	(44.8)	(18.5)	
29	Loans and other receivables	(14.4)	21.2	
30	Other assets and long-term liabilities	(21.4)	(5.1)	
31	Proceeds on sale of asset backed commercial paper	0.0	26.0	
32	Business acquisitions	(11.7)	(5,825.0)	
33	Interest received	1.4	4.4	
34	Non-controlling interest	(5.8)	1.7	
35	Cash flows from (used) in investing activities	146.6	(4,865.6)	
36	**Financing Activities**			
37	Decrease in bank indebtedness	0.0	(6.0)	
38	Issue of long-term debt	414.4	3,337.6	
39	Deferred debt financing costs	(0.9)	(50.6)	
40	Repayment of long-term debt	(1,635.5)	(798.6)	
41	Stock option purchases	0.0	(9.1)	
42	Interest paid	(118.8)	(102.3)	
43	Issue of Non-Voting Class A shares	0.0	1,842.6	
44	Share issue costs	0.0	(75.9)	
45	Dividends paid, common shares	(99.7)	(83.3)	
46	Cash flows from (used) in financing activities	(1,440.5)	4,054.4	
47	Decrease in cash and cash equivalents	(133.4)	(25.9)	
48	Cash and cash equivalents, beginning of year	429.3	455.2	
49	Cash and cash equivalents, end of year	$ 295.9	$ 429.3	
50				

EXHIBIT 11-7
Consolidated Statements of Cash Flows—Empire Company Limited

Source: Empire Company Limited - 2015 Annual Report.

For 2015, net cash provided by operating activities was the largest source of cash for the company. Net cash provided by operations increased by 47.8% ($1,160.5 − 785.5/785.5) in 2015 over 2014. Also, for both 2015 and 2014, net cash provided by operating activities exceeded net income. Both of these relationships are signs of a healthy company. For 2014, net cash provided by financing activities was the company's largest source of cash. The company issued additional shares and borrowed heavily, which was probably used to finance the business acquisitions ($5,825) under investing activities.

The next thing to look at is how the company used this cash generated from operations. Under investing activities, it shows that in 2015 and 2014, they bought and sold property and equipment. In 2014, the company spent $5,825 million in acquiring another business, Canada Safeway. How did they pay for this? Look under financing activities and you will notice that Long-term debt ($3,337.6) Non-Voting Class A shares ($1,842.6) were used to finance this business acquisition. In 2015, the company paid back a significant amount of debt and still continued to pay dividends to the shareholders.

Analysts find that the statement of cash flows is more helpful for spotting weakness than for gauging success. Why? Because a *shortage* of cash can throw a company into bankruptcy, but lots of cash doesn't ensure success. Let's now take a look at the cash flow statement for SK Corporation—see if you can find signals of cash flow weakness.

	A	B	C	D
1	**SK Corporation** Statements of Cash Flows For the Year Ended June 30, 2017			
2	(in millions)			
3	**Operating activities:**			
4	Net income		$ 35,000	
5	Adjustments for non-cash items:			
6	Depreciation	$ 14,000		
7	Net increase in current assets other than cash	(24,000)		
8	Net increase in current liabilities	8,000	(2,000)	
9	Net cash provided by operating activities		33,000	
10	**Investing activities:**			
11	Sale of property, plant, and equipment	91,000		
12	Net cash provided by investing activities		91,000	
13	**Financing activities:**			
14	Borrowing	22,000		
15	Payment of long-term debt	(90,000)		
16	Repurchase of shares	(9,000)		
17	Payment of dividends	(23,000)		
18	Net cash used for financing activities		(100,000)	
19	Increase in cash		$ 24,000	
20				

- SK Corporation's net cash provided by operations is less than net income. Ordinarily, cash provided by operations exceeds net income because of the add-back of depreciation and amortization. The increases in current assets and current liabilities should cancel out over time. For SK, current assets increased far more than current liabilities during the year. This may be harmless, or it may signal difficulty in collecting receivables or selling inventory. Either event may cause trouble.

- The sale of property, plant, and equipment is SK's major source of cash. This is okay if it is a one-time situation. SK may be shifting from one line of business to another, and it may be selling off old assets. But, if the sale of property, plant, and equipment is the major source of cash for several periods, SK will face a cash shortage. A company cannot continue to sell off its property, plant, and equipment forever. Soon, it will go out of business.

- The only strength shown by the statement of cash flows is that SK paid off more long-term debt than it took on in new borrowing. This will improve the debt ratio and SK's credit standing.

Here are some cash flow signs of a healthy company:

- Operations are a major *source* of cash (not a *use* of cash).

- Investing activities include more purchases than sales of long-term assets.

- Financing activities are not dominated by borrowing.

STOP + THINK (11-4)

Simpson Company's net income for the year was $40,000 yet the overall increase in cash was only $3,000. The statement of cash flow revealed the following:

Net cash flow used for operating activities	($ 7,000)
Net cash flow provided by investing activities	$15,000
Net cash flow used for financing activities	($ 5,000)

Is this a sign of a healthy company? How can you tell?

MyAccountingLab

MID-CHAPTER SUMMARY PROBLEM

You, an employee at a bank lending office, are deciding whether to grant Jamate Corporation, which makes metal detectors, a large loan. You decide to perform a horizontal analysis and a vertical analysis of the comparative income statement of Jamate Corporation. State whether 2017 was a good year or a bad year and give your reasons. We encourage you to use Excel as a tool to perform your analysis.

	A	B	C	D
1	**Jamate Corporation** Comparative Income Statement For the Years Ended December 31, 2017 and 2016			
2		**2017**	**2016**	
3	Total revenues	$ 275,000	$ 225,000	
4	Expenses:			
5	Cost of products sold	194,000	165,000	
6	Engineering, selling, and administrative expenses	54,000	48,000	
7	Interest expense	5,000	5,000	
8	Income tax expense	9,000	3,000	
9	Other expense (income)	1,000	(1,000)	
10	Total expenses	263,000	220,000	
11	Net earnings	$ 12,000	$ 5,000	
12				

Name: Jamate Corporation
Fiscal Period: Years ended December 31, 2017 and 2016

ANSWER

The horizontal analysis shows that total revenues increased 22.2%. This was greater than the 19.5% increase in total expenses, resulting in a 140% increase in net earnings.

	A	B	C	D	E	F
1	**Jamate Corporation** Horizontal Analysis of Comparative Income Statement For the Years Ended December 31, 2017 and 2016				Increase (Decrease)	
2		2017	2016	Amount	Percent	
3	Total revenues	$ 275,000	$ 225,000	$ 50,000	22.2%	
4	Expenses:					
5	Cost of products sold	194,000	165,000	29,000	17.6	
6	Engineering, selling, and administrative expenses	54,000	48,000	6,000	12.5	
7	Interest expense	5,000	5,000	—	—	
8	Income tax expense	9,000	3,000	6,000	200.0	
9	Other expense (income)	1,000	(1,000)	2,000	—*	
10	Total expenses	263,000	220,000	43,000	19.5	
11	Net earnings	$ 12,000	$ 5,000	$ 7,000	140.0%	
12						

*Percentage changes are typically not computed for shifts from a negative to a positive amount, and vice versa.

Horizontal analysis compares 2017 with 2016 to determine the changes in each income statement item in dollar amounts and percent ($ and %). Large or unusual changes in $ or % should be investigated.

The net earnings increase of 140% occurred because the dollar amounts are quite small. Income tax expense increased 200%; this would be investigated.

The vertical analysis shows decreases in the percentages of net sales consumed by the cost of products sold (from 73.3% to 70.5%) and by the engineering, selling, and administrative expenses (from 21.3% to 19.6%). Because these two items are Jamate's largest dollar expenses, their percentage decreases are quite important. The relative reduction in expenses raised 2017's net earnings to 4.4% of sales, compared with 2.2% the preceding year. The overall analysis indicates that 2017 was significantly better than 2016.

	A	B	C	D	E	F
1	**Jamate Corporation** Vertical Analysis of Comparative Income Statement For the Years Ended December 31, 2017 and 2016					
2		2017		2016		
3		Amount	Percent	Amount	Percent	
4	Total revenues	$ 275,000	100.0%	$ 225,000	100.0%	
5	Expenses:					
6	Cost of products sold	194,000	70.5	165,000	73.3	
7	Engineering, selling, and administrative expenses	54,000	19.6	48,000	21.3	
8	Interest expense	5,000	1.8	5,000	2.2	
9	Income tax expense	9,000	3.3	3,000	1.4*	
10	Other expense (income)	1,000	0.4	(1,000)	(0.4)	
11	Total expenses	263,000	95.6	220,000	97.8	
12	Net earnings	$ 12,000	4.4%	$ 5,000	2.2%	
13						

*Number rounded up.

Vertical analysis expresses net earnings and expenses as a percentage of total revenues. The percentages for 2017 are compared with those of 2016. Any large or unexpected differences would be reviewed.

USE RATIOS TO MAKE BUSINESS DECISIONS

Ratios are a major tool of financial analysis. We have discussed the use of many ratios in financial analysis in various chapters throughout the book. A ratio expresses the relationship between various types of financial information. In this section, we review how ratios are computed and used to make business decisions, using Apple Inc.

⑤ **Use** ratios to make business decisions

Many companies include ratios in a special section of their annual reports. Exhibit 11-8 shows a summary of selected data from previous Apple Inc. annual reports.

The ratios we discuss in this chapter are classified as follows:

1. Measuring the ability to pay current liabilities
2. Measuring turnover and cash conversion cycle
3. Measuring leverage: overall ability to pay debts
4. Measuring profitability
5. Analyzing stock as an investment

	A	B	C	D	E
1	**Apple Inc.** Results of operations				
2	*(dollar amounts in millions):*	**FY2014**	**FY2013**	**FY2012**	
3	Net sales	$ 182,795	$ 170,910	$ 156,508	
4	Gross profit	$ 70,537	$ 64,304	$ 68,662	
5	Gross profit as percent of net sales	38.6%	37.6%	43.9%	
6	Operating income	$ 52,503	$ 48,999	$ 55,241	
7	Operating income as percent of net sales	28.7%	28.7%	35.3%	
8	Net income after provision for income taxes	$ 39,510	$ 37,037	$ 41,733	
9	Net income as percent of sales	21.6%	21.7%	26.7%	
10	Earnings per weighted-average common share, basic	$ 6.49	$ 5.72	$ 6.38	
11	Return on average stockholders' equity	34%	31%	43%	
12	Cash dividends	$ 11,126	$ 10,564	$ 2,523	
13	**Financial position (dollar amounts in millions):**				
14	Current assets	$ 68,531	$ 73,286	$ 57,653	
15	Current liabilities	63,448	43,658	38,542	
16	Working capital	5,083	29,628	19,111	
17	Current ratio	1.08	1.68	1.5	
18	Quick ratio	0.67	1.23	1.04	
19	Total assets	231,839	207,000	176,064	
20	Total liabilities	120,292	83,451	57,854	
21	Debt ratio	0.52	0.40	0.33	
22					

EXHIBIT 11-8
Financial Summary—Apple Inc.

Source: Based on the content taken from Apple Annual Report - For the Fiscal Year Ended September 27, 2014 and for the Fiscal Year Ended September 29, 2012.

Remember to Start at the Beginning: Company and Industry Information

As stated at the beginning of the chapter, financial analysis is just massaging numbers unless we give the numbers a context. That comes from understanding the company and the industry and from knowing not only its history but where it appears to be headed in the future. Apple is known as perhaps the world's most innovative company. The company was founded in 1976 and went public in 1977. For more than two decades, Apple was predominately a manufacturer of personal computers. It faced intense competition and low market share during the 1990s.

With the introduction of the successful iPod music player in 2001 and iTunes Music Store in 2003, Apple established itself as a leader in the consumer electronics and media sales industries. The company is also known for its iOS range of smart phone, media player, and tablet computer products that began with the iPhone, followed by the iPod Touch and then iPad. In 2015, the company launched both Apple TV and the Apple Watch.

As of September 29, 2012 fiscal year, Apple was the largest publicly traded corporation in the world, with an estimated value of $626 billion, larger than that of Google and Microsoft combined. As of the end of 2012 fiscal year, the company had generated an enormous stockpile of liquidity in cash and marketable securities, and had never paid a dollar of dividends to its shareholders.

Under pressure from the shareholders, the company's board of directors voted to pay Apple's first dividend at the end of fiscal 2012, as well as to engage in an aggressive share repurchase program over a period of several years. In addition, the company declared a 7-for-1 stock split in 2014, distributing 7 shares for each share owned by its existing shareholders. This reduced the market price of the share from over $700 per share to less than $100 per share. The impact of these decisions on the company's liquidity and profitability ratios over the past two years has been significant, as you will see in the discussion that follows.

NOW LET'S DO THE NUMBERS Once you gain knowledge about a company and its industry, how do you determine whether the company's performance has been strong or weak, based on its current-period ratios? You can only make that decision if you have the following ratios to compare the current period against: (1) prior-year ratios; and (2) industry comparables, either in the form of an industry average or the ratios of a strong competitor. In the case of all the ratios in the following sections, we compare Apple's current-year ratios with (1) its prior years' ratios and (2) ratios for the industry (if available) or ratios of one of Apple Inc.'s competitors.

Measuring the Ability to Pay Current Liabilities

Working capital is defined as follows:

$$\textbf{Working capital} = \textbf{Current assets} - \textbf{Current liabilities}$$

Working capital measures the ability to pay current liabilities with current assets. In general, the larger the working capital, the better the ability to pay debts. Recall that capital is total assets minus total liabilities. Working capital is like a "current" version of total capital. Consider two companies with equal working capital:

	Company	
	Jones	Smith
Current assets	$100,000	$200,000
Current liabilities	50,000	150,000
Working capital	$ 50,000	$ 50,000

Both companies have working capital of $50,000, but Jones's working capital is as large as its current liabilities. Smith's working capital is only one-third as large as current liabilities. Jones is in a better position because its working capital is a higher percentage of current liabilities. As shown in Exhibit 11-8, Apple's working capital as of September 27, 2014 (the end of its 2014 fiscal year), was $5,083 million. This compares with $29,628 million and $19,111 million at the end of its 2013 and 2012 fiscal years, respectively. Why the dramatic change in working capital? The company's reduction in working capital reflects its strategic decision to return cash to its shareholders starting in 2013. The company returned $11.1 billion more cash to shareholders in the form of cash dividends in 2014. Also, in their annual report, Apple stated that they doubled their payment to shareholders in the form of stock repurchases from $22.9 billion in fiscal 2013 to $45 billion in fiscal 2014. This left Apple Inc.'s working capital substantially lower, but still not depleted to a critical level, because the company continues to generate billions of dollars in sales monthly, mostly for cash. Let's look at two key ratios that help tell the rest of the story.

CURRENT RATIO. The most common ratio for evaluating current assets and current liabilities is the **current ratio**, which is current assets divided by current liabilities. As discussed in Chapter 3, the current ratio measures the ability to pay current liabilities with current assets. Exhibit 11-9 and Exhibit 11-10 show the consolidated statements of operations and the consolidated balance sheets of Apple Inc.

Using figures from Exhibit 11-10, the following are current ratios of Apple at September 27, 2014, and September 28, 2013.

	Formula	Apple Inc.'s Current Ratio	
		2014	2013
Current ratio $=$	$\dfrac{\text{Current assets}}{\text{Current liabilities}}$	$\dfrac{\$68,531}{\$63,448} = 1.08$	$\dfrac{\$73,286}{\$43,658} = 1.68$

Apple's current ratio decreased during 2014, from 1.68 to 1.08, for the same reason that its working capital decreased: use of excess cash to pay dividends and

	A	B	C	D	E
1	**Apple Inc.** Consolidated Statements of Operations (USD $) For the Years Ended 2014, 2013, 2012				
2	*(in millions, except share data in thousands, and per share amounts)*	**Sept. 27, 2014**	**Sept. 28, 2013**	**Sept. 29, 2012**	
3	Net sales	$ 182,795	$ 170,910	$ 156,508	
4	Cost of Sales	112,258	106,606	87,846	
5	Gross profit	70,537	64,304	68,662	
6	**Operating expenses:**				
7	Research and development	6,041	4,475	3,381	
8	Selling, general, and administrative	11,993	10,830	10,040	
9	Total operating expenses	18,034	15,305	13,421	
10	Operating income	52,503	48,999	55,241	
11	Other income/(expense), net	980	1,156	522	
12	Income before provision for income taxes	53,483	50,155	55,763	
13	Provision for income taxes	13,973	13,118	14,030	
14	Net income	$ 39,510	$ 37,037	$ 41,733	
15	**Earning per common share:**				
16	Basic	$ 6.49	$ 5.72	$ 6.38	
17	Diluted	$ 6.45	$ 5.68	$ 6.31	
18	**Shares used in computing earnings per share:**				
19	Basic	6,085,572	6,477,320	6,543,726	
20	Diluted	6,122,663	6,521,634	6,617,483	
21					

EXHIBIT 11-9
Comparative Consolidated Statements of Operations— Apple Inc.

Source: Apple Annual Report - for the Fiscal Year Ended September 27, 2014.

EXHIBIT 11-10
Comparative Consolidated Balance Sheets—Apple Inc.

Source: Apple Annual Report - for the Fiscal Year Ended September 27, 2014.

	A	B	C	D
1	**Apple Inc.** Consolidated Balance Sheets (USD $) As at September 27, 2014 and September 28, 2013			
2	*(in millions)*	Sept. 27, 2014	Sept. 28, 2013	
3	**Current assets:**			
4	Cash and cash equivalents	$ 13,844	$ 14,259	
5	Short-term marketable securities	11,233	26,287	
6	Accounts receivable, less allowance of $86 and $99, respectively	17,460	13,102	
7	Inventories	2,111	1,764	
8	Deferred tax assets	4,318	3,453	
9	Vendor non-trade receivables	9,759	7,539	
10	Other current assets	9,806	6,882	
11	Total current assets	68,531	73,286	
12	Long-term marketable securities	130,162	106,215	
13	Property, plant, and equipment, net	20,624	16,597	
14	Goodwill	4,616	1,577	
15	Acquired intangible assets, net	4,142	4,179	
16	Other assets	3,764	5,146	
17	**Total assets**	231,839	207,000	
18	**Current liabilities:**			
19	Accounts payable	30,196	22,367	
20	Accrued expenses	18,453	13,856	
21	Deferred revenue	8,491	7,435	
22	Commercial paper	6,308	0	
23	Total current liabilities	63,448	43,658	
24	Deferred revenue-non-current	3,031	2,625	
25	Long-term debt	28,987	16,960	
26	Other non-current liabilities	24,826	20,208	
27	Total liabilities	120,292	83,451	
28	Commitments and contingencies			
29	**Shareholders' equity:**			
30	Common stock and additional paid-in capital, $0.00001 par value; 12,600,000 shares authorized; 5,866,161 and 6,294,494 shares issued and outstanding, respectively	23,313	19,764	
31	Retained earnings	87,152	104,256	
32	Accumulated other comprehensive income/(loss)	1,082	(471)	
33	Total shareholders' equity	111,547	123,549	
34	**Total liabilities and shareholders' equity**	$ 231,839	$ 207,000	
35				

repurchase shares from shareholders. Further examination of current assets and current liabilities in Exhibit 11-10 shows that current liabilities increased by 45% ($63,448 − $43,658/43,658) during 2014, while current assets decreased by 6.5% ($68,531 − $73,286/$73,286). Accounts payable increased by 35% ($30,196 − $22,367/$22,367) in 2014 over 2013. This is a natural consequence of the growth the company has experienced. It is hardly a sign of trouble, especially since the current ratio is within the bounds of what is considered healthy from the standpoint of the ability to pay current liabilities. In general, a higher current ratio indicates a stronger financial position. Apple certainly has more than sufficient current assets to maintain its operations. Apple's current ratio of 1.08 is comparable to the current ratios of two competitors: Hewlett-Packard Company and Acer.

Company	Current Ratio
Hewlett-Packard Company	1.15
Acer	1.30

Note: These figures show that ratio values vary widely from one company to another in the same industry.

What is an acceptable current ratio? The answer depends on the industry. The norm for companies in most industries is around 1.50, as reported by the Risk Management Association. Apple Inc.'s current ratio of 1.08 is less than average.

QUICK (ACID-TEST) RATIO. As discussed in Chapter 4, the **quick (acid-test) ratio** tells us whether the entity could pass the acid test of paying all its current liabilities if they came due immediately (quickly). The quick ratio uses a narrower base to measure liquidity than the current ratio does.

To compute the quick ratio, we add cash, short-term investments, and accounts receivable (net of allowances), and divide by current liabilities. Inventory and prepaid expenses are excluded because they are less liquid. A business may be unable to convert inventory to cash immediately.

Using the information in Exhibit 11-10, Apple's quick ratios for 2014 and 2013 follow:

		Apple Inc.'s Quick Ratio	
Formula		2014	2013
Quick ratio $=$ $\dfrac{\text{Cash and cash equivalents} + \text{Short-term investments} + \text{Net current receivables}}{\text{Current liabilities}}$		$\dfrac{\$13,844 + \$11,233 + \$17,460}{\$63,448} = 0.67$	$\dfrac{\$14,259 + \$26,287 + \$13,102}{\$43,658} = 1.23$

Like the current ratio, the company's quick ratio declined somewhat during 2014. However, because of Apple's ability to generate cash quickly, a low quick ratio doesn't spell liquidity problems. In addition, Apple is still competitive with other major companies in its industry. Compare Apple Inc.'s quick ratio with the values of its competitors:

Company	Quick (Acid-Test) Ratio
Hewlett-Packard Company	0.73
Acer	0.90

A quick ratio of 0.90 to 1.00 is acceptable in most industries. How can many retail companies function with low quick ratios? Because they price their inventories to turn over (sell) quickly and because they collect most of the revenues in cash. This points us to the next group of ratios, which measure turnover.

Measuring Turnover and the Cash Conversion Cycle

The ability to sell inventory and collect receivables, as well as pay accounts payable, is the lifeblood of any retail, wholesale, or manufacturing concern. In this section, we discuss three ratios that measure this ability—inventory turnover, accounts receivable turnover, and accounts payable turnover—as well as the relationship between them, called the *cash conversion cycle*.

INVENTORY TURNOVER. Companies generally strive to sell their inventory as quickly as possible. The faster inventory sells, the sooner cash comes in.

Inventory turnover, discussed in Chapter 5, measures the number of times a company sells its average level of inventory during a year. A fast turnover indicates ease in selling inventory; a low turnover indicates difficulty. A value of 6 means that the company's average level of inventory has been sold six times during the year, and that's usually better than a turnover of three times. But too high a value can mean that the business is not keeping enough inventory on hand, which can lead to lost sales if the company can't fill orders. Therefore, a business strives for the most *profitable* rate of turnover, not necessarily the *highest* rate.

To compute inventory turnover, divide cost of goods sold by the average inventory for the period. We use the cost of goods sold—*not sales*—in the computation because both cost of goods sold and inventory are stated *at cost*. Apple Inc.'s inventory turnover for 2014 is as follows:

Formula		Apple Inc.'s Inventory Turnover	Competitor (Hewlett-Packard)
Inventory turnover $= \dfrac{\text{Cost of goods sold}}{\text{Average inventory}}$		$\dfrac{\$112,258}{\$1,937.5} = 57.9$	9.06
Days' inventory outstanding (DIO) $= \dfrac{365}{\text{Turnover}}$		$\dfrac{365}{57.9} = 6$ days	40 days

Cost of goods sold comes from the consolidated statement of operations (Exhibit 11-9). Average inventory is the average of beginning ($1,764) and ending inventory ($2,111). (See the balance sheet, Exhibit 11-10.) If inventory levels vary greatly from month to month, you should compute the average by adding the 12 monthly balances and dividing the sum by 12.

Inventory turnover varies widely with the nature of the business. For example, Apple's inventory turned over 57.9 times in 2014. On a daily basis (days' inventory outstanding), that means once every six days (365/57.9)! In 2013, Apple's inventory turned over 83 times. Hewlett-Packard's inventory turnover for 2014 was 9.06 times (once every 40 days). Computer and electronics manufacturers purposely keep very low inventory levels because of their ability to manufacture inventory quickly and because technology is subject to rapid obsolescence.

To evaluate inventory turnover, compare the ratio over time as well as with industry averages or competitors. Steadily increasing inventory turnover is a positive sign particularly if gross profits are also increasing. A sharp decline in inventory turnover suggests the need to take action to increase sales, usually by lowering prices. Unfortunately, this will reduce gross profits until excess inventory can be disposed of.

ACCOUNTS RECEIVABLE TURNOVER. **Accounts receivable turnover** measures the ability to collect cash from customers. In general, the higher the ratio, the better. However, a receivable turnover that is too high may indicate that credit is too tight, and that may cause a company to lose sales to good customers.

To compute accounts receivable turnover, divide net sales by average net accounts receivable. Ideally, net credit sales should be used but it cannot always be obtained. The ratio tells how many times during the year average receivables were turned into cash. Apple's accounts receivable turnover ratio for 2014 was as follows:

Formula		Apple Inc.'s Accounts Receivable Turnover	Competitor (Hewlett-Packard)
Accounts receivable turnover	$= \dfrac{\text{Net sales}}{\text{Average net accounts receivable}}$	$\dfrac{\$182{,}795}{\$15{,}281} = 11.9$	7.5
Days' sales outstanding (DSO) (or days'-sales-in-receivables)	$= \dfrac{365}{\text{Turnover}}$	$\dfrac{365}{11.9} = 31$ days	49 days

Net sales comes from Exhibit 11-9. Average net accounts receivable (Exhibit 11-10) is figured by adding beginning ($13,102) and ending receivables ($17,460), then dividing by 2. If accounts receivable vary widely during the year, compute the average by using the 12 monthly balances. Apple collected its average accounts receivable 11.9 times during 2014. Hewlett-Packard's accounts receivable turnover for 2014 was 7.5.

Apple's accounts receivable turnover of 11.9 times per year is faster than the industry average. Apple owns and operates a large number of retail stores, and much of its sales are for cash, which makes the receivables balance very low relative to the sales balance.

DAYS' SALES IN RECEIVABLES. Businesses must convert accounts receivable to cash. All else being equal, the lower the receivable balance, the better the cash flow.

The *days' sales outstanding (DSO)* or **days' sales in receivables ratio**, discussed in Chapter 4, shows how many days' sales remain in accounts receivable. First, if you have already calculated receivables turnover (see the previous section), simply divide the turnover into 365. For Apple, days' sales in receivables works out to 30.7 (rounded to 31) days (365/11.9).

In comparison, Hewlett-Packard's DSO in 2014 was 49 days (365/7.5 turnover). Hewlett-Packard sells fewer types of products than Apple and owns no retail outlets.

ACCOUNTS PAYABLE TURNOVER. Discussed in Chapter 8, *accounts payable turnover* measures the number of times per year that the entity pays off its accounts payable. To compute accounts payable turnover, divide cost of goods sold by average accounts payable. For Apple, this ratio is as follows:

Formula		Apple Inc.'s Accounts Payable Turnover	Competitor (Hewlett-Packard)
Accounts payable turnover	$= \dfrac{\text{Cost of goods sold}}{\text{Average accounts payable}}$	$\dfrac{\$112{,}258}{\$26{,}282} = 4.27$	4.93
Days payable outstanding (DPO)	$= \dfrac{365}{\text{Turnover}}$	$\dfrac{365}{4.27} = 85$ days	74 days

On average, Apple pays off its accounts payable 4.27 times per year, which is about every 85 days. To convert accounts payable turnover to days' payable outstanding (DPO), divide the turnover into 365 (365 ÷ 4.27 = 85 days). In comparison, Hewlett-Packard's accounts payable turnover is 4.93 times per year, or about every 74 days.

CASH CONVERSION CYCLE. By expressing the three turnover ratios in days, we can compute a company's **cash conversion cycle** as follows:

Formula		Apple Inc.'s Cash Conversion Cycle	Competitor (Hewlett-Packard)
Cash conversion cycle	$= \; $ DIO + DSO − DPO	6 + 31 − 85 = −48 days	15 days
where DIO	= Days' inventory outstanding		
DSO	= Days' sales outstanding		
DPO	= Days' payable outstanding		

At first glance, a negative amount for the cash conversion cycle looks odd. What does it mean? Apple is in the enviable position of being able to sell inventory and collect from its customers 48 days before it has to pay its suppliers who provided the parts and materials to produce those inventories. This means that Apple can stock less inventory and hold on to cash longer than other companies. It also helps explain why the company could afford to keep over $11 billion in short-term marketable securities (Exhibit 11-10)—to "sop up" its excess cash—and using it to make still more money while waiting to pay off suppliers. Apple's competitor Hewlett-Packard has a positive cash conversion cycle of 15 days in 2014. Retail companies that have a more "normal" inventory turnover (about four times per year, or about every 90 days) have cash conversion cycles in the range of 30 to 60 days, depending on how long it takes to collect from customers. The cash conversion cycle for service-oriented businesses consists only of (DSO − DPO) because service businesses typically do not carry inventory.

Measuring Leverage: Overall Ability to Pay Debts

The ratios discussed so far relate to current assets and current liabilities. They measure the ability to sell inventory, collect receivables, and pay current bills. Two indicators of the ability to pay total liabilities are the *debt ratio* and the *times-interest-earned ratio*.

DEBT RATIO. Suppose you are a bank loan officer and you have received loan applications for $500,000 from two similar companies. The first company already owes $600,000, and the second owes only $250,000. Which company gets the loan? Company 2 may look like the stronger candidate, because it owes less.

This relationship between total liabilities and total assets is called the **debt ratio**. Discussed in Chapters 3 and 8, the debt ratio tells us the proportion of assets financed with debt. A debt ratio of 1 reveals that debt has financed all the assets. A debt ratio of 0.50 means that debt finances half the assets. The higher the debt ratio, the greater the pressure to pay interest and principal. The lower the debt ratio, the lower the company's credit risk.

The debt ratios for Apple in 2014 and 2013 follow:

Formula	Apple Inc.'s Debt Ratio		Competitor (Hewlett-Packard)
	2014	2013	
Debt ratio $= \dfrac{\text{Total liabilities}}{\text{Total assets}}$	$\dfrac{\$120,292}{\$231,839} = 0.52$	$\dfrac{\$83,451}{\$207,000} = 0.40$	0.73

Although Apple's debt ratio increased during 2014, it is still low compared to its competitors and compared with many other public companies. The Risk Management

Association reports that the average debt ratio for most companies ranges around 0.62, with relatively little variation from company to company. However, companies in certain industries such as airlines usually have higher debt ratios. The debt ratio is related to the leverage ratio discussed in the next section.

TIMES-INTEREST-EARNED RATIO. Analysts use a second ratio—the **times-interest-earned ratio** (introduced in Chapter 8)—to relate income to interest expense. To compute the times interest-earned ratio, divide income from operations (operating income) by interest expense. This ratio measures the number of times operating income can *cover* interest expense, and is also called the *interest-coverage ratio*. A high ratio indicates ease in paying interest; a low value suggests difficulty.

Formula	Apple Inc.'s Times-Interest-Earned Ratio		Competitor (Hewlett-Packard)
	2014	2013	
Times-interest-earned ratio $= \dfrac{\text{Income from operations}}{\text{Interest expense}}$	$\dfrac{\$52,503}{\$384^*} = 136.7$	$\dfrac{\$48,999}{\$136^*} = 360.3$	12

*Interest expense is given in Note 3.

Apple's interest expense for fiscal 2014 was $384 million, up from $136 million in 2013. Income from operations covered these amounts by 137 times and 360 times, respectively. Apple has more than enough operating income to cover the costs of interest on its debt. Although Apple's competitor Hewlett-Packard has a relatively high debt ratio (0.73), its times-interest-earned ratio is quite a bit lower (12), meaning that Hewlett-Packard is quite capable of servicing its interest payments. In summary, the judgment about the adequacy of interest coverage, like so many other factors of financial statement analysis, is very much dependent on the industry, as well as the company being studied.

Measuring Profitability

The fundamental goal of business is to earn a profit, and so the ratios that measure profitability are reported widely in the media.

GROSS PROFIT PERCENTAGE. In Chapter 5, we defined gross profit as net sales − cost of goods sold. That is, gross profit is the amount of profit that the entity makes from merely selling a product before other operating costs are subtracted. Let's look at Apple's gross profit percentages:

Formula	Apple Inc.'s Gross Profit %		Competitor (Hewlett-Packard)
	2014	2013	
Gross profit % $= \dfrac{\text{Gross profit}}{\text{Net sales}}$	38.6%	37.6%	24.1%

Apple is known as *the* innovator in the technology field. The company is constantly inventing new technology that everyone literally stands in line to purchase! Do you remember the last time you visited an Apple store (perhaps when a new version of the iPhone was introduced)? How much were you willing to pay for your new iPhone, iPad, or iMac? Do you remember how crowded the store was? As we discussed in Chapter 6, because of the creative talents of their people, some companies have been able to adopt a "product differentiation" business strategy, which allows them to sell their products for more than their competitors. When everyone wants the product, they are usually willing to pay more for it. As shown in Exhibit 11-8, Apple's gross profit percentage of 38.6% in 2014 is 1% greater than it was in 2013. However, Apple's gross profit percentage in 2014 is 5% less than it was in fiscal 2012 (shown in Exhibit 11-9). Although Apple is the recognized industry leader, it does not have a monopoly on smart computing devices. In recent years, competitive pressures from other smart phone and handheld-device companies like Samsung have forced Apple to lower prices, thus affecting gross profit. However, in comparison, Hewlett-Packard has only a 24.1% gross profit percentage on its products.

OPERATING INCOME (PROFIT) PERCENTAGE. Operating income (profit) percentage is net income from operations as a percentage of net sales. It is a function of all of its individual elements: sales revenue, cost of goods sold, gross profit, and operating expenses. It is an important statistic because it measures the percentage of profit earned from each sales dollar in a company's core business operations. The first component of high operating earnings is a high gross profit percentage. After that, maximizing operating income depends on keeping operating costs as low as possible, given the level of desired product quality and customer service. Apple's operating income percentages, compared with Hewlett-Packard follow:

Formula	Apple Inc.'s Operating Income %		Competitor (Hewlett-Packard)
	2014	2013	
Operating income % $= \dfrac{\text{Operating income}}{\text{Net sales}}$	28.7%	28.7%	6.4%

Apple is far ahead of the competition on earnings from its core operations. However according to Exhibit 11-8, because of a decline in gross profit percentage in recent years, the company's operating income percentage has declined from a high of 35.3% in 2012 to 28.7% in both 2013 and 2014.

RETURN (NET PROFIT MARGIN) ON SALES. In business, *return* refers to profitability. Consider the **return on net sales**, or simply *return on sales* (ROS). (The word *net* is usually omitted for convenience.) It measures how much each sales dollar generates net income. Recall that net income can be increased in one of three ways: (1) increasing sales volume, or the amount of goods or services sold or performed; (2) increasing sales prices; or (3) decreasing cost of goods sold and operating expenses. The return-on-sales ratios for Apple are as follows:

Formula	Apple Inc.'s Return on Sales		Competitor (Hewlett-Packard)
	2014	2013	
Return on sales (Net profit margin) $= \dfrac{\text{Net income}}{\text{Net sales}}$	$\dfrac{\$39,510}{\$182,795} = 21.6\%$	$\dfrac{\$37,037}{\$170,910} = 21.7\%$	4.5%

Companies strive for a high return on sales. The higher the percentage, the more profit is being generated by sales dollars. Apple's return on sales is high in 2014 and has only decreased slightly from where it was in 2013. Compare Apple's return on sales with other leading companies such as Hewlett-Packard (4.5%), PepsiCo (9.77%), and FedEx (4.6%).

ASSET TURNOVER. **Asset turnover** measures the amount of net sales generated for each dollar invested in assets. This is a measure of how effectively and efficiently the company manages its assets. Asset turnover can be increased by (1) increasing sales in the ways just described above; (2) keeping less inventory on hand; or (3) closing unproductive facilities, selling idle assets, and consolidating operations to fewer places to reduce the amount of plant assets needed. Companies with high asset turnover tend to be more productive than companies with low asset turnover. Let's examine Apple's asset turnover for 2014 compared with 2013, and then compare it to competitor Hewlett-Packard's asset turnover:

	Formula	Apple Inc.'s Asset Turnover		Competitor (Hewlett-Packard)
		2014	2013	
Asset turnover $=$	$\dfrac{\text{Net sales}}{\text{Average total assets}}$	$\dfrac{\$182{,}795}{\$219{,}420} = 0.83$	$\dfrac{\$170{,}910}{\$191{,}532} = 0.89$	1.07

Compared to Hewlett-Packard, Apple has invested more in assets per dollar of sales. This is often the case with innovative companies, as opposed to companies that focus on low cost. To make major product innovations requires a significant investment in both tangible and intangible assets. So, while Apple is significantly more profitable than Hewlett-Packard, it is less efficiently managed, at least by this measure.

RETURN ON TOTAL ASSETS (ROA). **Return on assets (ROA)** measures how much the entity earned for each dollar of assets invested by both shareholders and creditors. Companies with high ROA have both selected assets and managed them more successfully than companies with low ROA.

Return on assets (ROA)	Apple Inc.'s ROA		Competitor (Hewlett-Packard)
	2014	2013	
$\dfrac{\text{Net income} + \text{Interest expense}}{\text{Average total assets}}$	$\dfrac{\$39{,}510 + \$384}{\$219{,}420} = 18.2\%$	$\dfrac{\$37{,}037 + \$136}{\$191{,}532} = 19.4\%$	4.8%

Successful manufacturing firms often choose between a mixture of two different strategies: product differentiation or low-cost. We see from these computations that for Apple, ROA is driven principally by its high profitability based on product differentiation, rather than efficiency. In contrast, Hewlett-Packard's ROA is based more on efficiency than profitability. Hewlett-Packard is a low-margin provider of basic computer technology, and as the low-cost provider, it is more efficient, generating more sales per dollar invested in total assets than Apple.

LEVERAGE (EQUITY MULTIPLIER) RATIO. **Leverage** measures the impact of debt financing on profitability. You learned in Chapters 8 and 9 that it can be advantageous to use borrowed capital to finance a business. Earlier, we expressed the debt ratio as the ratio of total liabilities to total assets. The **leverage ratio**, or equity multiplier, measures the proportion of each dollar of assets financed with shareholders' equity. Because total assets − shareholders' equity = total liabilities, the leverage ratio is a way of inversely expressing the debt ratio—it merely looks at financing from the other side of the fundamental accounting equation. Let's examine Apple's leverage ratios for 2014 and 2013, compared with those of its competitor, Hewlett-Packard.

	Formula	Apple Inc.'s Leverage Ratios		Competitor (Hewlett-Packard)
		2014	2013	
Leverage ratio =	$\dfrac{\text{Average total assets}}{\substack{\text{Average common}\\\text{shareholders' equity}}}$	$\dfrac{\$219,420}{\$117,548} = 1.87$	$\dfrac{\$191,532}{\$120,880} = 1.58$	3.81

As we pointed out in a previous section, Apple has a comparatively low debt ratio (52% and 40% for 2014 and 2013, respectively). This translates to very low leverage ratios for Apple (1.87 and 1.58 for 2014 and 2013, respectively). In comparison, Hewlett-Packard has a comparatively high debt ratio (73% for 2014). Therefore, Hewlett-Packard uses much more borrowed capital than equity capital to finance its operations, and its leverage ratio is much higher (3.81).

RETURN ON COMMON SHAREHOLDERS' EQUITY (ROE). A popular measure of profitability is **return on common shareholders' equity**, often shortened to *return on equity* (ROE). Also discussed in Chapter 9, this ratio shows the relationship between net income and common shareholders' investment in the company—how much income is earned for every $1 invested.

To compute this ratio, first subtract preferred dividends, if any, from net income to measure income available to the common shareholders. Then divide income available to common shareholders' by average common equity during the year. Common equity is total equity minus preferred equity. The 2014 return on common shareholders' equity for Apple is as follows:

	Formula	Apple Inc.'s 2014 Return on Common Shareholders' Equity	Competitor (Hewlett-Packard)
Rate of return on common shareholders' equity =	$\dfrac{\text{Net income} - \substack{\text{Preferred}\\\text{dividends}}}{\substack{\text{Average common}\\\text{shareholders' equity}}}$	$\dfrac{\$39,510 - \$0}{\$117,548} = 33.6\%$	18.3%

Here we see that Apple's ROE (33.6%) is higher than Hewlett-Packard's ROE (18.3%). Apple has beaten its competitor (Hewlett-Packard) on virtually every measure. Now, let's consider the impact of leverage by analyzing the components of ROE:

Rate of Return on Shareholders' Equity (ROE)	Apple Inc.'s ROE		Competitor (Hewlett-Packard)
	2014	2013	
ROA	18.2%	19.4%	4.8%
×	×	×	×
Leverage ratio	1.87	1.58	3.81
=	=	=	=
ROE	(rounded) 34%	(rounded) 31%	18.3

Apple is by far the more profitable company. However, Hewlett-Packard is slightly more efficient in terms of asset turnover and more highly leveraged than Apple, having an asset turnover ratio of 1.07, a 73% debt ratio, and a leverage ratio of $3.81 of assets per dollar of shareholders' equity.

To be sure, the use of leverage by a company is often a good thing, as long as it is kept within reasonable limits. The practice of using leverage is called **trading on the equity**. Companies like Hewlett-Packard that finance operations with debt are said to *leverage* their positions.

As we pointed out in Chapter 9, leverage can hurt ROE as well as help. If profits and cash flows drop, debts still must be paid. Therefore, leverage is a double-edged sword. It increases profits during good times but also compounds losses during bad times.

EARNINGS PER SHARE OF COMMON STOCK. Discussed in Chapters 8 and 9, *earnings per share of common stock,* or simply **earnings per share (EPS)**, is the amount of net income earned for each share of outstanding *common* stock. EPS is the most widely quoted of all financial statistics. It's the only ratio that appears on the income statement of a publicly traded company. For private companies that follow ASPE, EPS is not required to be reported.

Earnings per share is computed by dividing net income available to common shareholders by the average number of common shares outstanding during the year. Preferred dividends are subtracted from net income because the preferred shareholders have a prior claim to their dividends. Apple Inc. has no preferred stock and thus has no preferred dividends. The firm's EPS for 2014 and 2013 follows (based on Exhibit 11-9):

	Formula	Apple Inc.'s Earnings Per Share (Basic)	
		2014	2013
Earnings per share of common stock	$= \dfrac{\text{Net income} - \text{Preferred dividends (in thousands)}}{\text{Average number of common shares outstanding (in thousands)}}$	$\dfrac{\$39{,}510{,}000 - \$0}{6{,}085{,}572} = \$6.49$	$\dfrac{\$37{,}037{,}000 - \$0}{6{,}477{,}320} = \$5.72$

Apple's EPS increased 13.5% ($6.49 – $5.72/$5.72) during 2014, and that's good news. Such moderate increases in earnings have certainly had an impact on the company's stock price. In mid 2012, the stock was selling for over $500 per share! In 2014, the company announced a 7 to 1 stock split that resulted in the stock selling as low as $93. By 2015, the stock was trading at over $100. But is it still a good buy at this price? That's the relevant question a prospective shareholder wants to know. The next section gives you some information on how analysts make this decision.

Analyzing Shares as an Investment

Investors buy shares to earn a return on their investment. This return consists of two parts: (1) gains (or losses) from selling the shares, and (2) dividends.

PRICE/EARNINGS RATIO (MULTIPLE). The **price/earnings ratio (multiple)** is the ratio of common share price to earnings per share. This ratio, abbreviated P/E, appears in stock listings of many newspapers and online. It shows the market price of $1 of earnings.

Calculations for the P/E ratios of Apple follow. The market price of Apple's common stock was $100.75 at September 27, 2014 (the end of its 2014 fiscal year), and $482.75 at September 28, 2013 (the end of its 2013 fiscal year). Stock prices can be obtained from a company's website or various other financial websites.

	Formula	*Apple Inc.'s Price/Earnings Ratio*	
		2014	2013 (before restatement for 7:1 stock split in 2014)
P/E ratio =	$\dfrac{\text{Market price per share of common stock}}{\text{Earnings per share}}$	$\dfrac{\$100.75}{\$6.49} = 15.5$	$\dfrac{\$482.75}{\$40.03} = \$12.1$

Given Apple's 2014 P/E ratio of 15.5, we would say that the company's stock is selling at about 15.5 times earnings. Each $1 of Apple's earnings is worth 15.5 to the stock market. Stocks trade in ranges, and public companies report updated EPS quarterly. These earnings are annualized and projected for the upcoming year (quarterly earnings multiplied by 4). Because Apple's yearly earnings were reported in 2014, its stock has traded in the range of $100 to $131 per share. As of June 30, 2015, the latest quarterly (annualized) EPS for Apple was around $7 and the stock closed at $124.86. As of June 30, 2015, therefore, the P/E ratio for Apple was 17.8. Things change fast in the technology industry. New competitors, like Samsung and Motorola (a subsidiary of Google, Inc.), are threatening Apple with smart devices that perform comparably for a lower price. Market prices of stocks are based on consensus estimations of what may happen in the future—business cycles, government policies, new product announcements, foreign trade deals, currency fluctuations—even the health of key company executives may significantly impact the estimates. Markets run on sentiment and are very difficult to predict. Some analysts study past trends in P/E multiples and try to estimate future trading ranges. If the P/E multiple of a particular stock drifts toward the low end of a range, and if its projected earnings are increasing, it means that the price of the stock is becoming more attractive, which may be a signal to buy. As P/E multiples drift higher given projected earnings, the stock becomes too expensive, and the analyst would recommend a "hold" or "sell." Would you buy it?

DIVIDEND YIELD. **Dividend yield** is the ratio of dividends per share of stock to the stock's market price. This ratio measures the percentage of a stock's market value returned annually to the shareholders as dividends. Although dividends are never guaranteed, some well-established companies have continued to pay dividends even through turbulent economic times. *Preferred* shareholders pay special attention to this ratio because they invest primarily to receive dividends. However, certain companies, such as TELUS, Bank of Montreal, or Rogers Communications, also pay attractive dividends on their common stock. In periods of low interest rates on certificates of deposit or money-market funds, dividend-paying stocks become more attractive alternatives for conservative investors.

Apple Inc. has never paid dividends (in the technology industry, dividends are rare), but in 2012, Apple paid the first quarterly dividend in history ($2.65) per share on August 16, 2012. For the year ended September 27, 2014, Apple's stock paid $1.82 per share in dividends. So, Apple's dividend yield on its common stock was as follows:

	Formula	Dividend Yield on Apple Common Stock 2014
Dividend yield on common stock* $=$	Dividend per share of common stock / Market price per share of common stock	$\dfrac{\$1.82}{\$100.75} = 0.018$

*Dividend yields may also be calculated for preferred stock.

An investor who buys Apple common shares for $100.75 can expect to receive around 1.8% of the investment annually in the form of cash dividends. You might think that's a very low rate, but compared to current yields on certificates of deposit or bonds, it's pretty attractive. Dividend yields vary widely among companies. They are generally higher for older, established firms and lower to nonexistent for young, growth-oriented companies.

BOOK VALUE PER SHARE OF COMMON STOCK. **Book value per share of common stock** is simply common shareholders' equity divided by the number of shares of common stock outstanding. Common equity equals total equity less preferred equity. Apple has no preferred stock outstanding. Calculations of its book value per common share follow. Numbers are based on Exhibits 11-9 and 11-10, using weighted-average number of shares outstanding.

	Formula (figures in thousands)	Book Value Per Share of Apple Inc. 2014	2013
Book value per common share $=$	Total shareholders' equity − Preferred equity / Weighted-average number of common shares outstanding(basic)	$\dfrac{\$111,547,000 - \$0}{6,085,572} = \$18.33$	$\dfrac{\$123,549,000 - \$0}{6,477,320} = \$19.07$

Book value per share indicates the recorded accounting amount for each share of common stock outstanding. Many experts believe book value is not useful for invest-ment analysis because it bears no relationship to market value and provides little information beyond what's reported on the balance sheet. But some investors base their investment decisions on book value. For example, some investors rank stocks by the ratio of market price per share to book value per share. The lower the ratio, the more attractive the stock. These investors are called "value" investors, as contrasted with "growth" investors, who focus more on trends in net income.

What does the outlook for the future look like for Apple? If the company can stay on the same path it has followed for the past several years, it looks bright. Its earnings per share are solid, and its ROS, ROA, and ROE lead the industry. From the stand-point of liquidity and leverage, the company is in stellar shape. It has a negative cash conversion cycle, meaning that it sells out inventory and collects cash weeks before accounts payable are due. It has no interest-bearing debt and virtually no long-term debt. The company's recent P/E ratio of 15.5 is relatively low. Beyond that, Apple is one of the most innovative companies in the world, continually putting out personal electronics products that everyone wants. All of these factors make Apple Inc. stock look like a good investment.

STOP + THINK (11-5)

Ratios can be a useful tool when analyzing a company but it doesn't tell you everything you need to know. What other kinds of information can you gather to aid you in your analysis?

The Limitations of Ratio Analysis

Business decisions are made in a world of uncertainty. As useful as ratios are, they aren't a cure-all. Consider a physician's use of a thermometer. A reading of 38.9° Celsius tells a doctor that something is wrong with the patient but doesn't indicate what the problem is or how to cure it.

In financial analysis, a sudden drop in the current ratio signals that *something* is wrong, but it doesn't identify the problem. A manager must analyze the figures to learn what caused the ratio to fall. A drop in current assets may mean a cash shortage or that sales are slow. The manager must evaluate all the ratios in the light of factors such as increased competition or a slowdown in the economy.

Legislation, international affairs, scandals, and other factors can turn profits into losses. To be useful, ratios should be analyzed over a period of years to consider all relevant factors. Any one year, or even any two years, may not represent the company's performance over the long term. The investment decision, whether in stocks, bonds, real estate, cash, or more exotic instruments, depends on one's tolerance for risk, and risk is the one factor that is always a certainty!

Red Flags in Financial Statement Analysis

Recent accounting scandals have highlighted the importance of being alert when analyzing financial statements. Signs of trouble that may raise red flags include:

- **Earnings Problems.** Has income from continuing operations and net income decreased significantly for several years in a row? Has income turned into a loss? This may be okay for a company in a cyclical industry, such as an airline or a home builder, but most companies cannot survive consecutive loss years.

- **Decreased Cash Flow.** Cash flow validates earnings. Is cash flow from operations consistently lower than net income? Are the sales of property, plant, and equipment a major source of cash? If so, the company may be facing a cash shortage.

- **Too Much Debt.** How does the company's debt ratio compare to that of major competitors and to the industry average? If the debt ratio is much higher than average, the company may be unable to pay debts during tough times.

- **Inability to Collect Receivables.** Are days' sales in receivables growing faster than for other companies in the industry? A cash shortage may be looming.

- **Buildup of Inventories.** Is inventory turnover slowing down? If so, the company may be unable to move products, or it may be overstating inventory. Recall that one of the easiest ways to overstate net income is to overstate ending inventory.

- **Trends of Sales, Inventory, and Receivables.** Sales, receivables, and inventory generally move together. Increased sales lead to higher receivables and require more inventory to meet demand. Strange movements among these items may spell trouble.

The Decision Guidelines summarize the most widely used ratios.

▶ DECISION GUIDELINES

USING RATIOS IN FINANCIAL STATEMENT ANALYSIS

As we have seen in this chapter, ratio analysis is one tool that managers, investors, and creditors use when analyzing a company. How do they determine if a company is able to pay its bills, sell inventory, collect receivables, and so on? They use the standard ratios discussed in this book.

Ratio	Computation	Information Provided
Measuring ability to pay current liabilities:		
Managers must make sure there is enough cash on hand to pay the company's current liabilities.		
Investors know that a company that cannot pay its debts is not a good investment because it could go bankrupt.		
Creditors want to make sure they will be repaid if they loan the company money.		
1. Current ratio	$\dfrac{\text{Current assets}}{\text{Current liabilities}}$	Measures ability to pay current liabilities with current assets
2. Quick (acid-test) ratio	$\dfrac{\text{Cash} + \text{Short-term investments} + \text{Net current receivables}}{\text{Current liabilities}}$	Shows ability to pay all current liabilities if they come due immediately

Ratio	Computation	Information Provided
Measuring turnover and cash conversion:		
Managers need to know if there is too much or too little inventory on hand. This helps them decide how much inventory to buy. They also need to monitor their accounts receivable and accounts payable to ensure that cash is being received soon after sales and bills are being paid in a timely fashion.		
Investors like to see inventory being sold quickly because unsold inventory generates no profit. The time it takes to turn accounts receivable into cash and then use it to pay bills can be used to evaluate the company's liquidity.		
Creditors know that collecting cash soon after the sale enables the company to pay its bills and loans on time.		
3. Inventory turnover and days' inventory outstanding (DIO)	$$\text{Inventory turnover} = \frac{\text{Cost of goods sold}}{\text{Average inventory}}$$ $$\text{Days' inventory outstanding (DIO)} = \frac{365}{\text{Inventory turnover}}$$	Indicates saleability of inventory—the number of times a company sells its average level of inventory during a year
4. Accounts receivable turnover	$$\frac{\text{Net credit sales}}{\text{Average net accounts receivable}}$$	Measures ability to collect cash from credit customers
5. Days' sales in receivables or days' sales outstanding (DSO)	$$\frac{365}{\text{Accounts receivable turnover}}$$	Shows how many days' sales remain in Accounts Receivable—how many days it takes to collect the average level of receivables
6. Payables turnover and days' payable outstanding (DPO)	$$\text{Accounts payable turnover} = \frac{\text{Cost of goods sold}}{\text{Average accounts payable}}$$ $$\text{Days' payable outstanding (DPO)} = \frac{365}{\text{Accounts payable turnover}}$$	Shows how many times a year accounts payable turn over, and how many days it takes the company to pay off accounts payable

Ratio	Computation	Information Provided
7. Cash conversion cycle	Cash conversion cycle $=$ DIO $+$ DSO $-$ DPO where DIO $=$ Days' inventory outstanding DSO $=$ Days' sales outstanding DPO $=$ Days' payable outstanding	Shows overall liquidity by computing the total days it takes to convert inventory to receivables and back to cash, less the days to pay off creditors

Measuring ability to pay *long-term debt:*

Managers must make sure they have enough assets on hand to pay the company's debts.

Investors know that a business may be generating a profit but still be low on cash. They want to be sure they are investing in a company that can pay back its debts.

Creditors loan the company money with the anticipation of being paid back. If a company is not able to pay its debts as they come due, they could face serious financial difficulty, and even be forced into bankruptcy.

Ratio	Computation	Information Provided
8. Debt ratio	$\dfrac{\text{Total liabilities}}{\text{Total assets}}$	Indicates percentage of assets financed with debt
9. Times-interest-earned ratio	$\dfrac{\text{Income from operations}}{\text{Interest expense}}$	Measures the number of times operating income can cover interest expense

Measuring profitability:

Managers are evaluated based on how well a company has performed financially.

Investors look to see if a company is able to generate a profit, which could mean an increase in the price of their shares.

Creditors know that a profitable company is able to pay back their debt.

Ratio	Computation	Information Provided
10. Gross profit %	$$\frac{\text{Gross profit}}{\text{Net sales}}$$	Shows the percentage of profit that a company makes from merely selling the product, before any other operating costs are subtracted
11. Operating income %	$$\frac{\text{Income from operations}}{\text{Net sales}}$$	Shows the percentage of profit earned from each dollar in the company's core business, after operating costs have been subtracted
12. Return on net sales	$$\frac{\text{Net income}}{\text{Net sales}}$$	Shows the percentage of each sales dollar earned as net income
13. Asset turnover	$$\frac{\text{Net sales}}{\text{Average total assets}}$$	Measures the amount of net sales generated for each dollar invested in assets
14. Return on total assets (ROA)	$$\frac{\text{Net income} + \text{Interest expense}}{\text{Average total assets}}$$	Measures how profitably a company uses its assets
15. Leverage ratio	$$\frac{\text{Average total assets}}{\text{Average common shareholders' equity}}$$	Otherwise known as the *equity multiplier,* measures the ratio of average total assets to average common shareholders' equity
16. Return on common shareholders' equity (ROE)	$$\frac{\text{Net income} - \text{Preferred dividends}}{\text{Average common shareholders' equity}}$$	Measures how much income is earned for every dollar invested by the company's common shareholders
17. Earnings per share of common stock	$$\frac{\text{Net income} - \text{Preferred dividends}}{\text{Average number of common shares outstanding}}$$	Measures the amount of net income earned for each share of the company's common stock outstanding

Analyzing shares as an investment:

Investors purchase shares to earn a return on their investment. This return consists of two parts: (1) gains (or losses) from selling their shares, and (2) dividends (if any). They want to know if the shares are a worthwhile investment.

Ratio	Computation	Information Provided
18. Price/earnings ratio	$$\frac{\text{Market price per common share}}{\text{Earnings per share}}$$	Indicates the market price of $1 of earnings
19. Dividend yield	$$\frac{\text{Dividend per share of common (or preferred) stock}}{\text{Market price per share of common (or preferred) stock}}$$	Shows the percentage of a stock's market value returned as dividends to stockholders each period
20. Book value per share of common stock	$$\frac{\text{Total shareholders' equity} - \text{Preferred equity}}{\text{Number of shares of common stock outstanding}}$$	Indicates the recorded accounting amount for each share of common stock outstanding

SUMMARY

SUMMARY OF LEARNING OBJECTIVES

LEARNING OBJECTIVE	SUMMARY
1. **Perform** horizontal analysis	A horizontal analysis is used to study percentage changes in financial statement items, such as sales or net income, from year to year. The dollar amount of the change from one period to the next is divided by the base-year amount. A form of horizontal analysis is a trend percentage that shows how something (such as sales or net income, for example) has changed over a period of time.
2 **Perform** vertical analysis	Vertical analysis reveals the relationship of a financial statement item to a specified base. For example, using the income statement, total revenue is usually the base when analyzing income statement relationships.
3. **Prepare** common-size financial statements	A common-size statement reports only percentages (no dollar amounts). For example, on a common-size balance sheet, each item is expressed as a percentage of total assets. A common-size statement eases the comparison of different companies because their amounts are stated as percentages.
4. **Analyze** the statement of cash flows	Analyzing a cash flow statement helps to reveal whether or not the company is experiencing cash problems. Generally speaking, a company's main source of cash should come from its operations. If the major source of cash over several periods is from investing (for example, selling property, plant, and equipment), it may signal a cash shortage.
5. **Use** ratios to make business decisions	Ratios discussed in this chapter to measure the "well being" of a business include: ability to pay current liabilities, ability to sell inventory and collect receivables, ability to pay long-term debt, profitability, and analysis of shares as an investment. Ratios are an important tool of financial analysis, but should be considered as only one source of information when analyzing a company.

There are no differences between IFRS and ASPE in this chapter.

MyAccountingLab

END-OF-CHAPTER SUMMARY PROBLEM

The following financial data are adapted from the annual reports of Lampeer Corporation:

	A	B	C	D	E	F
1	**Lampeer Corporation** Four-Year Select Financial Data Years Ended January 31, 2017, 2016, 2015, 2014					
2	**Operating Results***	2017	2016	2015	2014	
3	Net Sales	$ 13,848	$ 13,673	$ 11,635	$ 9,054	
4	Cost of goods sold and occupancy expenses, excluding depreciation and amortization	9,704	8,599	6,775	5,318	
5	Interest expense	109	75	45	46	
6	Income from operations	338	1,445	1,817	1,333	
7	Net earnings (net loss)	(8)	877	1,127	824	
8	Cash dividends	76	75	76	77	
9	**Financial Position:**					
10	Merchandise inventory	1,677	1,904	1,462	1,056	
11	Total assets	7,591	7,012	5,189	3,963	
12	Current ratio	1.48:1	0.95:1	1.25:1	1.20:1	
13	Shareholders' equity	3,010	2,928	2,630	1,574	
14	Average number of shares of common stock outstanding (in thousands)	860	879	895	576	
15						

*Dollar amounts are in thousands.

Requirement

1. Compute the following ratios for 2015 through 2017, and evaluate Lampeer's operating results. Are operating results strong or weak? Did they improve or deteriorate during the three-year period? Your analysis will reveal a clear trend.
   a. Inventory turnover (assume occupancy expenses are included in cost of goods sold)
   b. Gross profit percentage
   c. Operating income (profit) percentage
   d. Return on sales
   e. Asset turnover
   f. Return on assets
   g. Leverage ratio
   h. Return on shareholders' equity
   i. Times-interest-earned ratio
   j. Earnings per share

ANSWER

	2017	2016	2015
a. Inventory turnover	$\dfrac{\$9{,}704}{(\$1{,}677 + \$1{,}904)/2} = 5.4$ times	$\dfrac{\$8{,}599}{(\$1{,}904 + \$1{,}462)/2} = 5.1$ times	$\dfrac{\$6{,}775}{(\$1{,}462 + \$1{,}056)/2} = 5.4$ times
b. Gross profit percentage	$\dfrac{\$13{,}848 - \$9{,}704}{\$13{,}848} = 29.9\%$	$\dfrac{\$13{,}673 - \$8{,}599}{\$13{,}673} = 37.1\%$	$\dfrac{\$11{,}635 - \$6{,}775}{\$11{,}635} = 41.8\%$
c. Operating income percentage	$\dfrac{\$338}{\$13{,}848} = 2.4\%$	$\dfrac{\$1{,}445}{\$13{,}673} = 10.6\%$	$\dfrac{\$1{,}817}{\$11{,}635} = 15.6\%$
d. Return on sales	$\dfrac{\$(8)}{\$13{,}848} = (0.06)\%$	$\dfrac{\$877}{\$13{,}673} = 6.4\%$	$\dfrac{\$1{,}127}{\$11{,}635} = 9.7\%$
e. Asset turnover	$\dfrac{\$13{,}848}{(\$7{,}591 + \$7{,}012)/2} = 1.897$	$\dfrac{\$13{,}673}{(\$7{,}012 + \$5{,}189)/2} = 2.241$	$\dfrac{\$11{,}635}{(\$5{,}189 + \$3{,}963)/2} = 2.543$
f. Return on assets	$[(8) + 109]/(7{,}591 + 7{,}012)/2$ $= 1.38$	$(877 + 75)/(7{,}012 + 5{,}189)/2$ $= 15.6\%$	$1{,}127 + 45/(5{,}189 + 3{,}963)/2$ $= 25.6\%$
g. Leverage ratio	$\dfrac{(\$7{,}591 + \$7{,}012)/2}{(\$3{,}010 + \$2{,}928)/2} = 2.459$	$\dfrac{(\$7{,}012 + \$5{,}189)/2}{(\$2{,}928 + \$2{,}630)/2} = 2.195$	$\dfrac{(\$5{,}189 + \$3{,}963)/2}{(\$2{,}630 + \$1{,}574)/2} = 2.176$
h. Return on shareholders' equity	$\dfrac{(8)}{(3{,}010 + 2{,}928)/2} = (0.27)$	$\dfrac{877}{(2{,}928 + 2{,}630)/2} = 31.6\%$	$\dfrac{1{,}127}{(2{,}630 + 1{,}574)/2} = 53.6\%$
i. Times-interest-earned ratio	$\dfrac{\$338}{\$109} = 3.1$ times	$\dfrac{\$1{,}445}{\$75} = 19.3$ times	$\dfrac{\$1{,}817}{\$45} = 40.4$ times
j. Earnings per share	$\dfrac{\$(8)}{860} = \$(0.01)$	$\dfrac{\$877}{879} = \$1.00$	$\dfrac{\$1{,}127}{895} = \$1.26$

Evaluation:

During this period, Lampeer's operating results deteriorated on all these measures except inventory turnover. The gross profit percentage is down sharply, as are the times-interest-earned ratio and all the return measures. From these data it is clear that Lampeer could sell its merchandise, but not at the markups the company enjoyed in the past. The final result, in 2017, was a net loss for the year. This yielded a low ROA, and because of leverage, a negative ROE.

REVIEW

MyAccountingLab

Make the grade with MyAccountingLab: The Quick Quiz questions, Short Exercises, Exercises, and Problems (Group A) marked in #–# can be found on MyAccountingLab. You can practise them as often as you want, and most feature step-by-step guided instructions to help you find the right answer.

QUICK QUIZ   (ANSWERS APPEAR ON THE LAST PAGE OF THIS CHAPTER.)

Test your understanding of financial statement analysis by answering the following questions. Select the best choice from among the possible answers given. Use the Canada Technology Corporation (CTC) financial statements to answer the questions that follow.

	A	B	C	D
1	**Canada Technology Corporation** Consolidated Statements of Financial Position	**December 31,**		
2	*(in millions)*	2017	2016	
3	Assets			
4	Current assets:			
5	Cash and cash equivalents	$ 4,317	$ 4,232	
6	Short-term investments	835	406	
7	Accounts receivable, net	3,635	2,586	
8	Inventories	327	306	
9	Other	1,519	1,394	
10	Total current assets	10,633	8,924	
11	**Property, plant, and equipment, net**	1,517	913	
12	Investments	6,770	5,267	
13	Other non-current assets	391	366	
14	Total assets	$ 19,311	$ 15,470	
15	**Liabilities and Shareholders' Equity**			
16	**Current liabilities:**			
17	Accounts payable	$ 7,316	$ 5,989	
18	Accrued and other	3,580	2,944	
19	Total current liabilities	10,896	8,933	
20	Long-term debt	505	506	
21	Other non-current liabilities	1,630	1,158	
22	Commitments and contingent liabilities	—	—	
23	Total liabilities	13,031	10,597	
24	**Shareholders' equity:**			
25	Preferred shares; shares issued: 0	—	—	
26	Common share; shares authorized: 7,000; shares issued: 2,556 and 2,579, respectively	284	1,479	
27	Retained earnings	6,131	3,486	
28	Other comprehensive loss	(83)	(33)	
29	Other	(52)	(59)	
30	Total shareholders' equity	6,280	4,873	
31	Total liabilities and shareholders' equity	$ 19,311	$ 15,470	
32				

	A	B	C	D	E
1	**Canada Technology Corporation** Consolidated Statements of Income (in millions, except per share amounts)	**Years Ended December 31,**			
2		**2017**	**2016**	**2015**	
3	Net revenue	$ 41,444	$ 35,404	$ 31,168	
4	Cost of goods sold	33,892	29,055	25,661	
5	Gross profit	7,552	6,349	5,507	
6	**Operating expenses:**				
7	Selling, general, and administrative	3,544	3,050	2,784	
8	Research, development, and engineering	464	455	452	
9	Special charges	—	—	482	
10	Total operating expenses	4,008	3,505	3,718	
11	Operating income	3,544	2,844	1,789	
12	Investment and other income (loss), net	180	183	(58)	
13	Income before income taxes	3,724	3,027	1,731	
14	Income tax expense	1,079	905	485	
15	Net income	$ 2,645	$ 2,122	$ 1,246	
16	**Earnings per common share:**				
17	Basic	$ 1.03	$ 0.82	$ 0.48	
18					

1. During 2017, CTC's total assets
  a. increased by $8,341 million.
  b. increased by 24.8%.
  c. Both a and b.
  d. increased by 19.9%.

2. CTC's current ratio at year-end 2017 is closest to
  a. 1.2.
  b. 1.1.
  c. 1.0.
  d. 0.8.

3. CTC's quick (acid-test) ratio at year-end 2017 is closest to
  a. 0.80.
  b. 0.65.
  c. 0.47.
  d. $8,787 million.

4. What is the largest single item included in CTC's debt ratio at December 31, 2017?
  a. Cash and cash equivalents
  b. Accounts payable
  c. Investments
  d. Common shares

5. Using the earliest year available as the base year, the trend percentage for CTC's net revenue during 2017 was
  a. 117%.
  b. up by $10,276 million.
  c. up by 17.1%.
  d. 133%.

6. CTC's common-size income statement for 2017 would report cost of goods sold as
  a. $33,892 million.
  b. up by 16.6%.
  c. 81.8%.
  d. 132.1%.

7. CTC's days' sales in receivables during 2017 was
  a. 22 days.
  b. 27 days.
  c. 32 days.
  d. 114 days.

8. CTC's inventory turnover during fiscal year 2017 was
  a. very slow.
  b. 54 times.
  c. 107 times.
  d. 129 times.

9. CTC's long-term debt bears interest at 6%. During the year ended December 31, 2017, CTC's times-interest-earned ratio was
  a. 117 times.
  b. 110 times.
  c. 100 times.
  d. 125 times.

10. CTC's trend of return on sales is
  a. improving.
  b. declining.
  c. stuck at 6%.
  d. worrisome.

11. How many common shares did CTC have outstanding, on average, during 2017? Hint: Use the earnings per share formula.
   a. 2,721 million
   b. 2,701 million
   c. 2,645 million
   d. 2,568 million

12. Book value per common share of CTC outstanding at December 31, 2017, was
   a. $2.72.
   b. $4.37.
   c. $6,280.
   d. $2.46.

ACCOUNTING VOCABULARY

accounts receivable turnover Measures a company's ability to collect cash from credit customers. To compute accounts receivable turnover, divide net credit sales by average net accounts receivable. (p. 574)

acid-test ratio Ratio of the sum of cash plus short-term investments plus net current receivables to total current liabilities. Tells whether the entity can pay all its current liabilities if they come due immediately. Also called the *quick ratio*. (p. 573)

asset turnover The dollars of sales generated per dollar of assets invested. Net sales divided by Average total assets. (p. 579)

benchmarking The comparison of a company to a standard set by other companies, with a view toward improvement. (p. 563)

book value per share of common stock Common stockholders' equity divided by the number of shares of common stock outstanding. The recorded amount for each share of common stock outstanding. (p. 583)

cash conversion cycle The number of days it takes to convert cash into inventory, inventory to receivables, and receivables back into cash, after paying off payables. Days inventory outstanding + days sales outstanding − days payables outstanding. (p. 575)

common-size statement A financial statement that reports only percentages (no dollar amounts). (p. 563)

current ratio Current assets divided by current liabilities. Measures a company's ability to pay current liabilities with current assets. (p. 571)

days' sales in receivables Ratio of average net accounts receivable to one day's sales. Indicates how many days' sales remain in Accounts Receivable awaiting collection. Also called the *collection period* and *days sales outstanding*. (p. 575)

debt ratio Ratio of total liabilities to total assets. States the proportion of a company's assets that is financed with debt. (p. 576)

dividend yield Ratio of dividends per share of stock to the stock's market price per share. Tells the percentage of a stock's market value that the company returns to shareholders as dividends. (p. 582)

earnings per share (EPS) Amount of a company's net income per outstanding common share. (p. 581)

horizontal analysis Study of percentage changes over time through comparative financial statements. (p. 556)

inventory turnover Ratio of cost of goods sold to average inventory. Indicates how rapidly inventory is sold. (p. 574)

leverage Earning more income on borrowed money than the related interest expense, thereby increasing the earnings for the owners of the business. Also called *trading on the equity*. (p. 579)

leverage ratio Ratio of average total assets to average common shareholders' equity. Measures the proportion of average total assets actually owned by the shareholders. (p. 579)

price/earnings ratio (multiple) Ratio of the market price of a common to the company's earnings per share. Measures the value that the stock market places on $1 of a company's earnings. (p. 581)

quick ratio Another name for *acid-test ratio*. (p. 573)

return on assets Net income divided by average total assets. This ratio measures how profitably management has used the assets that shareholders and creditors have provided the company. (p. 579)

return on common shareholders' equity Net income minus preferred dividends, divided by average common shareholders' equity. A measure of profitability. Also called *return on equity (ROE)*. (p. 580)

return on net sales Ratio of net income to net sales. A measure of profitability. Also called *return on sales*. (p. 578)

times-interest-earned ratio Ratio of income from operations to interest expense. Measures the number of times that operating income can cover interest expense. Also called the *interest-coverage ratio*. (p. 577)

trading on the equity Another name for *leverage*. (p. 581)

trend percentages A form of horizontal analysis that indicates the direction a business is taking. (p. 559)

vertical analysis Analysis of a financial statement that reveals the relationship of each statement item to a specified base, which is the 100% figure. (p. 560)

working capital Current assets minus current liabilities; measures a business's ability to meet its short-term obligations with its current assets. Also called *net working capital*. (p. 570)

ASSESS YOUR PROGRESS

SHORT EXERCISES

S11-1 Cannes Corporation reported the following amounts on its 2017 comparative income statement:

LEARNING OBJECTIVE ❶

Perform a horizontal analysis of revenues and net income

(in thousands)	2017	2016	2015
Revenues	$10,889	$10,095	$9,777
Total expenses	5,985	5,604	5,194

Perform a horizontal analysis of revenues and net income—both in dollar amounts and in percentages—for 2017 and 2016.

S11-2 Zoobilee Inc. reported the following sales and net income amounts:

LEARNING OBJECTIVE ❶

Perform a trend analysis of sales and net income

(in thousands)	2017	2016	2015	2014
Sales	$9,180	$8,990	$8,770	$8,550
Net income	520	500	460	400

Show Zoobilee's trend percentages for sales and net income. Use 2014 as the base year.

S11-3 Vision Software Limited reported the following amounts on its balance sheets at December 31, 2017, 2016, and 2015:

LEARNING OBJECTIVE ❷

Perform a vertical analysis to understand a cash shortage

	2017	2016	2015
Cash	$ 6,000	$ 6,000	$ 5,000
Receivables, net	30,000	22,000	19,000
Inventory	148,000	106,000	74,000
Prepaid expenses	2,000	2,000	1,000
Property, plant, and equipment, net	96,000	88,000	87,000
Total assets	$282,000	$224,000	$186,000

Sales and profits are high. Nevertheless, Vision is experiencing a cash shortage. Perform a vertical analysis of Vision Software's assets at the end of years 2017, 2016, and 2015. Use the analysis to explain the reason for the cash shortage.

S11-4 Porterfield Inc. and Beasley Ltd. are competitors. Compare the two companies by converting their condensed income statements to common size.

LEARNING OBJECTIVE ❸

Compare common-size income statements of two companies

(in millions)	Porterfield	Beasley
Net sales	$9,489	$19,536
Cost of goods sold	5,785	14,101
Selling and administrative expenses	2,690	3,846
Interest expense	59	16
Other expense	34	38
Income tax expense	331	597
Net income	$ 590	$ 938

Which company earned more net income? Which company's net income was a higher percentage of its net sales? Which company is more profitable? Explain your answer.

	A	B	C	D	E
1	**Black Corporation**				
2		Years Ended December 31			
3	*(dollar amounts in millions)*	**2017**	**2016**	**2015**	
4	Consolidated Financial Measures and Ratios				
5	**Operating results**				
6	Net earnings	$ 769	$ 675	$ 656	
7	Per common share	$ 2.73	$ 2.43	$ 2.39	
8	Operating income	1,312	$ 1,239	$ 1,205	
9	Operating margin	4.4%	4.4%	3.9%	
10	Gross profit percentage	22.2%	22.4%	23.4%	
11	Return on net assets	12%	12%	12%	
12	Return on shareholders' equity	13.2%	12.6%	10.9%	
13	Interest coverage	4.2 times	4.2 times	4.2 times	
14	**Financial position**				
15	Working capital	$ 1,744	$ 1,061	$ 972	
16	Current assets	$ 6,462	$ 6,092	$ 5,995	
17	Current liabilities	$ 4,718	$ 5,031	$ 5,023	
18					

LEARNING OBJECTIVE ❺

Evaluate the trend in a company's current ratio

S11-5 Examine the financial data of Black Corporation above. Show how to compute Black's current ratio from 2015 to 2017. Is the company's ability to pay its current liabilities improving or deteriorating?

LEARNING OBJECTIVE ❺

Evaluate a company's quick (acid-test) ratio

S11-6 Use the Allstott, Inc., balance sheet data below.

1. Compute Allstott, Inc.'s quick (acid-test) ratio at December 31, 2017 and 2016.
2. Use the comparative information from the table on page 597 for Baker, Inc., Calvin Company, and Dunn Companies Limited. Is Allstott's quick (acid-test) ratio for 2017 and 2016 strong, average, or weak in comparison?

	A	B	C	D	E	F
1	**Allstott, Inc.** Balance Sheets (Adapted) As at December 31, 2017 and 2016					
2				Increase (Decrease)		
3	*(dollar amounts in millions)*	**2017**	**2016**	**Amount**	**Percentage**	
4	**Assets**					
5	Current assets:					
6	Cash and cash equivalents	$ 1,200	$ 900	$ 300	33.3%	
7	Short-term investments	6	70	(64)	(91.4)	
8	Receivables, net	240	250	(10)	(4.0)	
9	Inventories	96	81	15	18.5	
10	Prepaid expenses and other assets	243	363	(120)	(33.1)	
11	Total current assets	1,785	1,664	121	7.3	
12	Property, plant, and equipment, net	3,611	3,376	235	7.0	
13	Intangible assets	1,011	878	133	15.1	
14	Other assets	828	722	106	14.7	
15	Total assets	$ 7,235	$ 6,640	$ 595	9.0%	
16	**Liabilities and Shareholders' Equity**					
17	Current liabilities:					
18	Accounts payable	$ 1,000	$ 900	$ 100	11.1%	
19	Income tax payable	39	61	(22)	(36.1)	
20	Short-term debt	118	111	7	6.3	
21	Other	70	73	(3)	(4.1)	
22	Total current liabilities	1,227	1,145	82	7.2	
23	Long-term debt	3,500	2,944	556	18.9	
24	Other liabilities	1,117	1,036	81	7.8	
25	Total liabilities	5,844	5,125	719	14.0	

	A	B	C	D	E	F
26	Shareholders' equity:					
27	Common shares	2	2	—	—	
28	Retained earnings	1,543	1,689	(146)	(8.6)	
29	Accumulated other comprehensive (loss)	(154)	(176)	22	12.5	
30	Total shareholders' equity	1,391	1,515	(124)	(8.2)	
31	Total liabilities and shareholders' equity	$ 7,235	$ 6,640	$ 595	9.0%	

Company	Quick (Acid-Test) Ratio
Baker, Inc. (Utility)...	0.71
Calvin Company (Department store)...	1.01
Dunn Companies Limited (Grocery store)	1.05

S11-7 Use the Allstott 2017 income statement that follows and the balance sheet from exercise S11-6 to compute the following:

LEARNING OBJECTIVE ⑤
Compute and evaluate turnover and the cash conversion cycle

	A	B	C	D
1	**Allstott, Inc.** Statements of Income (Adapted) Year Ended December 31, 2017 and 2016			
2	*(dollar amounts in millions)*	**2017**	**2016**	
3	Revenues	$ 9,500	$ 9,309	
4	Expenses:			
5	Food and paper (Cost of goods sold)	2,509	2,644	
6	Payroll and employee benefits	2,138	2,211	
7	Occupancy and other operating expenses	2,413	2,375	
8	General and administrative expenses	1,217	1,148	
9	Interest expense	184	117	
10	Other expense (income), net	19	(34)	
11	Income before income taxes	1,020	848	
12	Income tax expense	285	267	
13	Net income	$ 735	$ 581	
14				

a. Allstott's rate of inventory turnover and days inventory outstanding for 2017
b. Days' sales in average receivables (days sales outstanding) during 2017 (round dollar amounts to one decimal place)
c. Accounts payable turnover and days' payables outstanding
d. Length of cash conversion cycle in days

Do these measures look strong or weak? Give the reason for your answer.

S11-8 Use the financial statements of Allstott, Inc., in exercises S11-6 and S11-7.

LEARNING OBJECTIVE ⑤
Measure ability to pay long-term debt

1. Compute the company's debt ratio at December 31, 2017.
2. Compute the company's times-interest-earned ratio for 2017. For operating income, use income before both interest expense and income taxes. You can simply add interest expense back to income before taxes.
3. Is Allstott's ability to pay liabilities and interest expense strong or weak? Comment on the value of each ratio computed for questions 1 and 2.

S11-9 Use the financial statements of Allstott, Inc., in exercises S11-6 and S11-7 to compute the following profitability measures for 2017. Show each computation.

LEARNING OBJECTIVE ⑤
Measure profitability

a. Return on sales
b. Asset turnover
c. Return on assets

d. Leverage (equity multiplier) ratio

e. Return on common shareholders' equity

f. Is Allstott, Inc.'s profitability strong, medium, or weak?

LEARNING OBJECTIVE ⑤

Compute EPS and the price/earnings ratio

S11-10 The annual report of Classic Cars Inc. for the year ended December 31, 2017, included the following items (in thousands):

Preferred shares outstanding, $4; 5,000 issued......................................	$500
Net income..	$990
Number of common shares outstanding...	200

1. Compute earnings per share (EPS) and the price/earnings ratio for Classic Cars's common shares. Round to the nearest cent. The price of a common share of Classic Cars is $77.60.
2. How much does the stock market say $1 of Classic Cars's net income is worth?

LEARNING OBJECTIVE ⑤

Use ratio data to reconstruct an income statement

S11-11 A skeleton of Hill Country Florist Limited's income statement appears as follows (amounts in thousands):

	A	B	C	D
1	**Income Statement**			
2	Net sales	$ 7,278		
3	Cost of goods sold	(a)		
4	Selling expenses	1,510		
5	Administrative expenses	351		
6	Interest expense	(b)		
7	Other expenses	126		
8	Income before taxes	1,042		
9	Income tax expense	(c)		
10	Net income	$ (d)		
11				

Use the following ratio data to complete Hill Country Florist's income statement:

a. Inventory turnover was 5 (beginning inventory was $775, ending inventory was $767).

b. Return on sales is 0.12.

LEARNING OBJECTIVE ⑤

Use ratio data to reconstruct a balance sheet

S11-12 A skeleton of Hill Country Florist Limited's balance sheet appears as follows (amounts in thousands):

	A	B	C	D
1	**Balance Sheet**			
2	Cash	$ 253	Total current liabilities	$ 1,164
3	Receivables	(a)	Long-term debt	(e)
4	Inventories	555	Other long-term liabilities	826
5	Prepaid expenses	(b)		
6	Total current assets	(c)		
7	Property, plant, and equipment, net	(d)	Common shares	185
			Retained earnings	2,846
8	Other assets	1,150	Total liabilities and	
9	Total assets	$ 6,315	shareholders' equity	$ (f)
10				

Use the following ratio data to complete Hill Country Florist's balance sheet:

a. Debt ratio is 0.52.

b. Current ratio is 1.20.

c. Acid-test ratio is 0.70.

EXERCISES

E11-13 Using the given balance sheet data, what were the dollar amount of change and the percentage of each change in Rocky Mountain Lodge Limited's working capital during 2017 and 2016? Is this trend favourable or unfavourable?

LEARNING OBJECTIVE ❶
Compute year-to-year changes in working capital

Rocky Mountain Lodge Limited	2017	2016	2015
Total current assets..	$326,000	$290,000	$280,000
Total current liabilities......................................	170,000	167,000	150,000

E11-14 Prepare a horizontal analysis of the comparative income statement of Stamps Music Ltd. Round percentage changes to the nearest one-tenth percent (three decimal places).

LEARNING OBJECTIVE ❶
Prepare a horizontal analysis of an income statement

	A	B	C	D
1	**Stamps Music Ltd.** Comparative Income Statement For the Years Ended December 31, 2017 and 2016			
2		2017	2016	
3	Total revenue	$ 403,000	$ 430,000	
4	Expenses:			
5	Cost of goods sold	$ 188,000	$ 202,000	
6	Selling and general expenses	93,000	90,000	
7	Interest expense	4,000	10,000	
8	Income tax expense	37,000	42,000	
9	Total expenses	322,000	344,000	
10	Net income	$ 81,000	$ 86,000	
11				

E11-15 Compute trend percentages for Carmel Valley Sales & Service Ltd.'s total revenue and net income for the following five-year period, using year 0 as the base year. Round to the nearest full percent.

LEARNING OBJECTIVE ❶
Compute trend percentages

(in thousands)	Year 4	Year 3	Year 2	Year 1	Year 0
Total revenue......................................	$1,418	$1,287	$1,106	$1,009	$1,043
Net income..	125	104	93	81	85

Which grew faster during the period, total revenue or net income?

E11-16 Cobra Golf Limited has requested that you perform a vertical analysis of its balance sheet to determine the component percentages of its assets, liabilities, and shareholders' equity.

LEARNING OBJECTIVE ❷
Perform a vertical analysis of a balance sheet

	A	B	C	D
1	**Cobra Golf Limited** Balance Sheet As at December 31, 2017			
2	**Assets**			
3	Total current assets			
4	Property, plant, and equipment, net	$ 92,000		
5	Other assets	247,000		
6	Total assets	35,000		
7		$ 374,000		
8	**Liabilities**			
9	Total current liabilities	$ 48,000		
10	Long-term debt	108,000		
11	Total liabilities	156,000		

(Continued)

	A	B	C	D
12	**Shareholders' Equity**			
13	Total shareholders' equity	218,000		
14	Total liabilities and shareholders' equity	$ 374,000		
15				

LEARNING OBJECTIVE ❸

Prepare a common-size income statement

E11-17 Prepare a comparative common-size income statement for Stamps Music Ltd. using the 2017 and 2016 data of exercise E11-14 and rounding percentages to one-tenth percent (three decimal places).

LEARNING OBJECTIVE ❹

Analyze the statement of cash flows

E11-18 Identify any weaknesses revealed by the following statement of cash flows of Holland Marsh Farms Limited.

	A	B	C	D
1	**Holland Marsh Farms Limited** Statement of Cash Flows For the Current Year			
2	**Operating activities:**			
3	Income from operations		$ 42,000	
4	Add (subtract) non-cash items:			
5	Depreciation	$ 23,000		
6	Net increase in current assets other than cash	(45,000)		
7	Net decrease in current liabilities exclusive of short-term debt	(7,000)	(29,000)	
8	Net cash provided by operating activities		13,000	
9	**Investing activities:**			
10	Sale of property, plant, and equipment		101,000	
11	**Financing activities:**			
12	Issuance of bonds payable	$ 102,000		
13	Payment of short-term debt	(159,000)		
14	Payment of long-term debt	(79,000)		
15	Payment of dividends	(42,000)		
16	Net cash used for financing activities		(178,000)	
17	Increase (decrease) in cash		$ (64,000)	
18				

LEARNING OBJECTIVE ❺

Compute five ratios

E11-19 The financial statements of National News Inc. include the following items:

	Current Year	Preceding Year
Balance Sheet:		
Cash	$ 17,000	$ 22,000
Short-term investments	11,000	26,000
Net receivables	64,000	73,000
Inventory	77,000	71,000
Prepaid expenses	16,000	8,000
Total current assets	$185,000	$200,000
Total current liabilities	$111,000	$ 91,000
Income Statement:		
Net credit sales	$654,000	
Cost of goods sold	327,000	

Requirement

Compute the following ratios for the current year:

a. Current ratio

b. Quick (acid-test) ratio

c. Inventory turnover

d. Accounts receivable turnover

e. Days' sales in receivables

E11-20 Patio Furniture Inc. has asked you to determine whether the company's ability to pay its current liabilities and long-term debts improved or deteriorated during 2017. To answer this question, compute the following ratios for 2017 and 2016.

LEARNING OBJECTIVE ⑤

Analyze the ability to pay current liabilities

a. Current ratio
b. Quick (acid-test) ratio
c. Debt ratio
d. Times-interest-earned ratio

Summarize the results of your analysis of the following financial statement data in a written report.

	2017	2016
Cash	$ 61,000	$ 47,000
Short-term investments	28,000	—
Net receivables	142,000	116,000
Inventory	286,000	263,000
Prepaid expenses	11,000	9,000
Total assets	643,000	489,000
Total current liabilities	255,000	221,000
Long-term debt	46,000	52,000
Income from operations	165,000	158,000
Interest expense	40,000	39,000

E11-21 Compute four ratios that measure ability to earn profits for PGI Decor Inc., whose comparative income statement follows:

LEARNING OBJECTIVE ⑤

Analyze profitability

	A	B	C	D
1	**PGI Decor Inc.** Comparative Income Statement For the Years Ended December 31, 2017 and 2016			
2	(in thousands)	2017	2016	
3	Net sales	$ 174,000	$ 158,000	
4	Cost of goods sold	93,000	86,000	
5	Gross profit	81,000	72,000	
6	Selling and general expenses	46,000	41,000	
7	Income from operations	35,000	31,000	
8	Interest expense	9,000	10,000	
9	Income before income tax	26,000	21,000	
10	Income tax expense	9,000	8,000	
11	Net income	$ 17,000	$ 13,000	
12				

Additional data:

	2017	2016	2015
Total assets	$204,000	$191,000	$171,000
Common shareholders' equity	$ 96,000	$ 89,000	$ 79,000
Preferred dividends	$ 3,000	$ 3,000	$ 0
Average common shares outstanding during the year	21,000	20,000	18,000

Did the company's operating performance improve or deteriorate during 2017?

E11-22 Evaluate the common shares of Phillips Distributing Limited as an investment. Specifically, use the three share ratios to determine whether the common shares increased or decreased in attractiveness during the past year.

LEARNING OBJECTIVE ⑤

Evaluate shares as an investment

	2017	2016
Net income...	$112,000	$ 96,000
Common share dividends...	25,000	20,000
Total shareholders' equity at year-end (includes 80,000 common shares)...	580,000	500,000
Preferred shares, $8; 1,000 shares issued.................................	100,000	100,000
Market price per common share at year-end................................	$ 22.50	$ 16.75

CHALLENGE EXERCISES

LEARNING OBJECTIVE ⑤

Use ratio data to reconstruct a company's balance sheet

E11-23 The following data (dollar amounts in millions) are taken from the financial statements of Phase 1 Industries Inc.:

Total liabilities...	$11,800
Preferred shares...	$ 0
Total current assets..	$10,200
Accumulated depreciation	$ 1,400
Debt ratio..	59%
Current ratio	1.50

Requirement

Complete the following condensed balance sheet. Report amounts to the nearest million dollars.

Current assets...		$?
Property, plant, and equipment	$?	
Less accumulated depreciation	(?)	?
Total assets		$?
Current liabilities...		$?
Long-term liabilities		?
Shareholders' equity		?
Total liabilities and shareholders' equity		$?

LEARNING OBJECTIVE ⑤

Use ratio data to reconstruct a company's income statement

E11-24 The following data (dollar amounts in millions) are from the financial statements of Provincial Industry Limited:

Average shareholders' equity...	$3,600
Interest expense...	$ 400
Preferred shares...	$ 0
Operating income as a percent of sales	25%
Return on equity	20%
Income tax rate..	40%

Requirement

Complete the following condensed income statement. Report amounts to the nearest million dollars.

Sales..	$?
Operating expense...	?
Operating income..	?
Interest expense..	?
Pretax income..	?
Income tax expense	?
Net income..	$?

E11-25 An incomplete comparative income statement and balance sheet for Emore Corporation follow:

LEARNING OBJECTIVES ❶❷❸❹
Use trend percentages, common-size percentages, and ratios to reconstruct financial statements

	A	B	C	D
1	**Emore Corporation** Comparative Income Statements Years Ended December 31, 2016 and 2015			
2		2016	2015	
3	Sales revenue	$ 2,100,000	$ 2,000,000	
4	Cost of goods sold	?	1,100,000	
5	Gross profit	?	900,000	
6	Operating expense	?	700,000	
7	Operating income	?	200,000	
8	Interest expense	20,000	20,000	
9	Income before income tax	?	180,000	
10	Income tax expense (30%)	?	54,000	
11	Net income	?	$ 126,000	
12				

	A	B	C	D
1	**Emore Corporation** Balance Sheet December 31, 2016 and 2015			
2		2016	2015	
3	**Assets**			
4	Current:			
5	Cash	$?	$ 28,000	
6	Accounts receivable, net	?	145,000	
7	Inventory	?	180,000	
8	Total current assets	?	353,000	
9	Plant and equipment, net	?	447,000	
10	Total assets	$?	$ 800,000	
11	**Liabilities**			
12	Current liabilities	$ 160,000	$ 160,000	
13	10% Bonds payable	?	240,000	
14	Total liabilities	?	400,000	
15	Shareholders' Equity			
16	Common shares	?	203,200	
17	Retained earnings	?	196,800	
18	Total shareholders' equity	?	400,000	
19	Total liabilities and shareholders' equity	$?	$ 800,000	
20				

Requirement

Using the ratios, common-size percentages, and trend percentages given, complete the income statement and balance sheet for Emore for 2016. Additional information:

	A	B	C	D
1	**Additional information:**	2016	2015	
2	Common size cost of goods sold %:	75%	55%	
3	Common size common share %:	27%	25.4%	
4	Trend percentage, Operating income	130%	100%	
5	Asset turnover	2		
6	Accounts receivable turnover	15		
7	Quick (acid-test) ratio	1.30		
8	Current ratio	2.25		
9	Return on equity	35%		
10				

PROBLEMS (GROUP A)

LEARNING OBJECTIVE ❶❺

Compute trend percentages, return on sales, asset turnover, and ROA, and compare with industry

P11-26A Net sales, net income, and total assets for Aaron Shipping, Inc., for a five-year period follow:

(in thousands)	2017	2016	2015	2014	2013
Net sales...	$900	$400	$352	$314	$296
Net income..	50	39	46	37	24
Total assets	308	269	252	231	209

Requirements

1. Compute trend percentages for each item for 2014 through 2017. Use 2013 as the base year and round to the nearest percent.
2. Compute the return on net sales for 2015 through 2017, rounding to three decimal places. Explain what this means.
3. Compute asset turnover for 2015 through 2017. Explain what this means.
4. Compute the return on average total assets (ROA) for 2015 through 2017.
5. How does Aaron Shipping's return on net sales for 2017 compare with previous years? How does it compare with that of the industry? In the shipping industry, rates above 5% are considered good, and rates above 7% are outstanding.
6. Evaluate Aaron Shipping, Inc.'s ROA for 2017, compared with previous years, and against a 15% benchmark for the industry.

LEARNING OBJECTIVE ❶❺

Prepare common size financial statements and analyze ratios

P11-27A Top managers of Medical Products Inc. have asked for your help in comparing the company's profit performance and financial position with the average for the industry. The accountant has given you the company's income statement and balance sheet and also the following data for the industry:

	A	B	C	D
1	**Medical Products Inc.** Income Statement Compared With Industry Average For the Year Ended December 31, 2017			
2		Medical Products	Industry Average	
3	Net sales	$ 957,000	100.0%	
4	Cost of goods sold	652,000	55.9	
5	Gross profit	305,000	44.1	
6	Operating expenses	200,000	28.1	
7	Operating income	105,000	16.0	
8	Other expenses	3,000	2.4	
9	Net income	$ 102,000	13.6%	
10				

	A	B	C	D
1	**Medical Products Inc.** Balance Sheet Compared With Industry Average As at December 31, 2017			
2		Medical Products	Industry Average	
3	Current assets	$ 486,000	74.4%	
4	Property and equipment, net	117,000	20.0	
5	Intangible assets, net	24,000	0.6	
6	Other assets	3,000	5.0	
7	Total	$ 630,000	100.0%	

	A	B	C	D
8	Current liabilities	$ 245,000	45.6%	
9	Long-term liabilities	114,000	19.0	
10	Shareholders' equity	271,000	35.4	
11	Total	$ 630,000	100.0%	
12				

Requirements

1. Prepare a common-size income statement and balance sheet for Medical Products. The first column of each statement should present Medical Products's common-size statement, and the second column should show the industry averages.
2. For the profitability analysis, compute Medical Products's (a) ratio of gross profit to net sales, (b) ratio of operating income to net sales, and (c) ratio of net income to net sales. Compare these figures with the industry average. Is Medical Products's profit performance better or worse than the average for the industry?
3. For the analysis of financial position, compute Medical Products's (a) ratios of current assets and current liabilities to total assets and (b) ratio of shareholders' equity to total assets. Compare these ratios with the industry averages. Is Medical Products's financial position better or worse than the average for the industry?

P11-28A You are evaluating two companies as possible investments. The two companies, similar in size, are commuter airlines that fly passengers up and down the West Coast. All other available information has been analyzed and your investment decision depends on the statement of cash flows.

LEARNING OBJECTIVE ❹

Use the statement of cash flows for decision making

	A	B	C	D	E	F
1	**Commonwealth Airlines (Comair) Limited** Statement of Cash Flows For the Years Ended November 30, 2017 and 2016					
2			2017		2016	
3	**Operating activities:**					
4	Net income (net loss)		$ (67,000)		$ 154,000	
5	Adjustments for non-cash items:					
6	Total		84,000		(23,000)	
7	Net cash provided by operating activities		17,000		131,000	
8	**Investing activities:**					
9	Purchase of property, plant, and equipment	$ (50,000)		$ (91,000)		
10	Sale of long-term investments	52,000		4,000		
11	Net cash provided by (used for) investing activities		2,000		(87,000)	
12	**Financing activities:**					
13	Issuance of short-term notes payable	122,000		143,000		
14	Payment of short-term notes payable	(179,000)		(134,000)		
15	Payment of cash dividends	(45,000)		(64,000)		
16	Net cash used for financing activities		(102,000)		(55,000)	
17	Increase (decrease) in cash		(83,000)		(11,000)	
18	Cash balance at beginning of year		92,000		103,000	
19	Cash balance at end of year		$ 9,000		$ 92,000	
20						

	A	B	C	D	E	F
1	**Jetway Inc.** Statement of Cash Flows For the Years Ended November 30, 2017 and 2016					
2			2017		2016	
3	**Operating activities:**					
4	Net income		$ 184,000		$ 131,000	
5	Adjustments for non-cash items:					
6	Total		64,000		62,000	
7	Net cash provided by operating activities		248,000		193,000	
8	**Investing activities:**					
9	Purchase of property, plant, and equipment	$ (303,000)		$ (453,000)		
10	Sale of property, plant, and equipment	46,000		72,000		
11	Net cash used for investing activities		(257,000)		(381,000)	
12	**Financing activities:**					
13	Issuance of long-term notes payable	174,000		118,000		
14	Payment of short-term notes payable	(66,000)		(18,000)		
15	Net cash provided by financing activities		108,000		100,000	
16	Increase (decrease) in cash		99,000		(88,000)	
17	Cash balance at beginning of year		116,000		204,000	
18	Cash balance at end of year		$ 215,000		$ 116,000	
19						

Requirement

Discuss the relative strengths and weaknesses of Comair and Jetway. Conclude your discussion by recommending one of the companies' shares as an investment.

LEARNING OBJECTIVE ⑤

Understand the effects of business transactions on selected ratios

P11-29A Financial statement data of Metro Engineering Limited include the following items:

Cash..	$ 47,000	Accounts payable........................	$142,000
Short-term investments	21,000	Accrued liabilities......................	50,000
Accounts receivable, net	102,000	Long-term notes payable	146,000
Inventories	274,000	Other long-term liabilities	78,000
Prepaid expenses........................	15,000	Net income.................................	104,000
Total assets	933,000	Number of common shares	
Short-term notes payable	72,000	outstanding	22,000

Requirements

1. Compute Metro's current ratio, debt ratio, and earnings per share. Use the following format for your answer (use dollar and share amounts in thousands except for EPS):

Requirement 1		
Current ratio	**Debt ratio**	**Earnings per share**

2. Compute the three ratios after evaluating the effect of each transaction that follows. Consider each transaction *separately*.
   a. Borrowed $27,000 on a long-term note payable
   b. Issued 10,000 common shares, receiving cash of $108,000

c. Paid short-term notes payable, $51,000
d. Purchased merchandise of $48,000 on account, debiting Inventory
e. Received cash on account, $6,000

Format your answer as follows:

Requirement 2

| Transaction (letter) | Current ratio | Debt ratio | Earnings per share |

P11-30A Comparative financial statement data of Hamden Optical Mart follow:

LEARNING OBJECTIVE ❺

Use ratios to evaluate a share investment

	A	B	C	D
1	**Hamden Optical Mart** Comparative Income Statement Years Ended December 31, 2017 and 2016			
2		2017	2016	
3	Net sales	$ 687,000	$ 595,000	
4	Cost of goods sold	375,000	276,000	
5	Gross profit	312,000	319,000	
6	Operating expenses	129,000	142,000	
7	Income from operations	183,000	177,000	
8	Interest expense	37,000	45,000	
9	Income before income tax	146,000	132,000	
10	Income tax expense	36,000	51,000	
11	Net income	$ 110,000	$ 81,000	
12				

	A	B	C	D	E
1	**Hamden Optical Mart** Comparative Balance Sheet December 31, 2017 and 2016				
2		2017	2016	2015*	
3	Current assets:				
4	Cash	$ 45,000	$ 49,000		
5	Current receivables, net	212,000	158,000	$ 200,000	
6	Inventories	297,000	281,000	181,000	
7	Prepaid expenses	4,000	29,000		
8	Total current assets	558,000	517,000		
9	Property, plant, and equipment, net	285,000	277,000		
10	Total assets	$ 843,000	$ 794,000	700,000	
11	Accounts payable	150,000	105,000	112,000	
12	Other current liabilities	135,000	188,000		
13	Total current liabilities	$ 285,000	$ 293,000		
14	Long-term liabilities	243,000	231,000		
15	Total liabilities	528,000	524,000		
16	Common shareholders' equity, no par	315,000	270,000	199,000	
17	Total liabilities and shareholders' equity	$ 843,000	$ 794,000		
18					

*Selected 2015 amounts.

Other information:

1. Market price of Hamden common shares: $102.17 at December 31, 2017; and $77.01 at December 31, 2016
2. Average common shares outstanding: 18,000 during 2017 and 17,500 during 2016
3. All sales on credit

Requirements

1. Compute the following ratios for 2017 and 2016:
    a. Current ratio
    b. Quick (acid-test) ratio
    c. Receivables turnover and days' sales outstanding (DSO) (round to the nearest whole day)
    d. Inventory turnover and days' inventory outstanding (DIO) (round to the nearest whole day)
    e. Accounts payable turnover and days' payable outstanding (DPO) (round to the nearest whole day)
    f. Cash conversion cycle (in days)
    g. Times-interest-earned ratio
    h. Return on assets
    i. Return on common shareholders' equity
    j. Earnings per share of common shares
    k. Price/earnings ratio
2. Decide whether (a) Hamden's financial position improved or deteriorated during 2017 and (b) the investment attractiveness of Hamden's common shares appears to have increased or decreased.
3. How will what you learned in this problem help you evaluate an investment?

LEARNING OBJECTIVE ⑤

Use ratios to decide between two share investments

P11-31A Assume that you are considering purchasing shares as an investment. You have narrowed the choice to two Internet firms, Video.com Inc. and On-Line Express Ltd., and have assembled the following data.

Selected income statement data for current year:

	Video	Express
Net sales (all on credit)	$603,000	$519,000
Cost of goods sold	454,000	387,000
Income from operations	93,000	72,000
Interest expense	—	12,000
Net income	56,000	38,000

Selected balance sheet and market price data at *end* of current year:

	Video	Express
Current assets:		
Cash	$ 2 5,000	$ 39,000
Short-term investments	6,000	13,000
Current receivables, net	189,000	164,000
Inventories	211,000	183,000
Prepaid expenses	19,000	15,000
Total current assets	$450,000	$414,000
Total assets	$974,000	$938,000

	Video	Express
Total current liabilities	366,000	338,000
Total liabilities	667,000*	691,000*
Preferred shares $4.00 (250 shares)		25,000
Common shares (150,000 shares)	150,000	
(20,000 shares)		100,000
Total shareholders' equity	307,000	247,000
Market price per common share	$ 9.00	$ 47.50

*Includes long-term debt; Video, $-0-; and Express, $350,000

Selected balance sheet data at *beginning* of current year:

	Video	Express
Current receivables, net	$142,000	$193,000
Inventories	209,000	197,000
Total assets	842,000	909,000
Long-term debt	—	303,000
Preferred shares, $4.00 (250 shares)		25,000
Common shares (150,000 shares)	150,000	
(20,000 shares)		100,000
Total shareholders' equity	263,000	215,000

Your strategy is to invest in companies that have low price/earnings ratios but appear to be in good shape financially. Assume that you have analyzed all other factors and that your decision depends on the results of ratio analysis.

Requirement

Compute the following ratios for both companies for the current year and decide which company's shares better fit your investment strategy:

- **a.** Quick (acid-test) ratio
- **b.** Inventory turnover
- **c.** Days' sales in receivables
- **d.** Debt ratio
- **e.** Times-interest-earned ratio
- **f.** Return on equity
- **g.** Earnings per share
- **h.** Price/earnings ratio

P11-32A Take the role of an investment analyst at Merrill Lynch. It is your job to recommend investments for your client. The only information you have is the following ratio values for two companies in the direct mail industry:

LEARNING OBJECTIVE ❺

Analyze a company based on its ratios

Ratio	Fast Mail Ltd.	Message Direct Inc.
Days' sales in receivables	51	43
Inventory turnover	9	7
Gross profit percentage	62%	71%
Net income as a percent of sales	16%	14%
Times interest earned	12	18
Return on equity	29%	36%
Return on assets	19%	14%

Write a report to the Merrill Lynch investment committee. Recommend one company's shares over the other. State the reasons for your recommendation.

LEARNING OBJECTIVE ❺

Compute ratios; evaluate turnover, liquidity, and current debt-paying ability

P11-33A The financial statements of Adventure News, Inc., include the following items:

	2016	2015	2014
Balance sheet:			
Cash	$ 24,000	$ 30,000	
Short-term investments	12,000	21,000	
Net receivables	58,000	71,000	40,000
Inventory	90,000	73,000	59,000
Prepaid expenses	10,000	10,000	
Total current assets	194,000	205,000	
Accounts payable	40,000	70,000	30,000
Total current liabilities	133,000	95,000	
Income statement:			
Net credit sales	$491,000	$506,000	
Cost of goods sold	277,000	288,000	

Requirements

1. Compute the following ratios for 2016 and 2015:
   a. Current ratio
   b. Quick (acid-test) ratio
   c. Inventory turnover and days' inventory outstanding (DIO)
   d. Accounts receivable turnover
   e. Days' sales in average receivables or days' sales outstanding (DSO)
   f. Accounts payable turnover and days' payable outstanding (DPO). Use cost of goods sold in the formula for accounts payable turnover
   g. Cash conversion cycle (in days)
   When computing days, round your answer to the nearest whole number.
2. Evaluate the company's liquidity and current debt-paying ability for 2016. Has it improved or deteriorated from 2015?
3. As a manager of this company, what would you try to improve next year?

PROBLEMS (GROUP B)

LEARNING OBJECTIVE ❶❺

Compute trend percentages, return on sales, asset turnover, and ROA, and compare with industry

P11-34B Net sales, net income, and total assets for Azbell Shipping, Inc., for a five-year period follow:

(in thousands)	2017	2016	2015	2014	2013
Net sales	$700	$618	$325	$309	$299
Net income	41	39	41	34	27
Total assets	300	262	253	223	201

Requirements

1. Compute trend percentages for each item for 2014 through 2017. Use 2013 as the base year and round to the nearest percent.
2. Compute the return on net sales for 2015 through 2017, rounding to three decimal places. Explain what this means.

3. Compute asset turnover for 2015 through 2017. Explain what this means.
4. Compute the return on average total assets (ROA) for 2015 through 2017.
5. How does Azbell Shipping's return on net sales compare with previous years? How does it compare with that of the industry? In the shipping industry, rates above 5% are considered good, and rates above 7% are outstanding.
6. Evaluate Azbell Shipping, Inc.'s ROA for 2017, compared with previous years, and against a 15% benchmark for the industry.

P11-35B Pathfinder Inc. has asked you to compare the company's profit performance and financial position with the industry average. The proprietor has given you the company's income statement and balance sheet as well as the industry average data for retailers.

LEARNING OBJECTIVE ❷❸❺

Prepare and evaluate common-size financial statements

	A	B	C	D
1	**Pathfinder Inc.** Income Statement Compared with Industry Average For the Year Ended December 31, 2017			
2		Pathfinder	Industry Average	
3	Net sales	$ 700,000	100.0%	
4	Cost of goods sold	497,000	65.8	
5	Gross profit	203,000	34.2	
6	Operating expenses	163,000	19.7	
7	Operating income	40,000	14.5	
8	Other expenses	3,000	0.4	
9	Net income	$ 37,000	14.1%	
10				

	A	B	C	D
1	**Pathfinder Inc.** Balance Sheet Compared with Industry Average As at December 31, 2017			
2		Pathfinder	Industry Average	
3	Current assets	$ 300,000	70.9%	
4	Property and equipment, net	74,000	23.6	
5	Intangible assets, net	4,000	0.8	
6	Other assets	22,000	4.7	
7	Total	$ 400,000	100.0%	
8	Current liabilities	$ 206,000	48.1%	
9	Long-term liabilities	64,000	16.6	
10	Shareholders' equity	130,000	35.3	
11	Total	$ 400,000	100.0%	
12				

Requirements

1. Prepare a common-size income statement and a balance sheet for Pathfinder. The first column of each statement should present Pathfinder's common-size statement, and the second column, the industry averages.
2. For the profitability analysis, compute Pathfinder's (a) ratio of gross profit to net sales, (b) ratio of operating income to net sales, and (c) ratio of net income to net sales. Compare these figures with the industry averages. Is Pathfinder's profit performance better or worse than the industry average?
3. For the analysis of financial position, compute Pathfinder's (a) ratio of current assets to total assets, and (b) ratio of shareholders' equity to total assets. Compare these ratios with the industry averages. Is Pathfinder's financial position better or worse than the industry averages?

LEARNING OBJECTIVE ❹

Use the statement of cash flows for decision making

P11-36B You have been asked to evaluate two companies as possible investments. The two companies, Norfolk Industries Inc. and Strafford Crystal Limited, are similar in size. Assume that all other available information has been analyzed, and the decision concerning which company's shares to purchase depends on their cash flow data.

	A	B	C	D	E	F
1	**Norfolk Industries Inc.** Statement of Cash Flows For the Years Ended September 30, 2017 and 2016					
2			2017		2016	
3	Operating activities:					
4	Net income		$ 17,000		$ 44,000	
5	Adjustments for non-cash items:					
6	Total		(14,000)		(4,000)	
7	Net cash provided by operating activities		3,000		40,000	
8	Investing activities:					
9	Purchase of property, plant, and equipment	$ (13,000)		$ (3,000)		
10	Sale of property, plant, and equipment	86,000		79,000		
11	Net cash provided by investing activities		73,000		76,000	
12	Financing activities:					
13	Issuance of short-term notes payable	43,000		19,000		
14	Payment of short-term notes payable	(101,000)		(108,000)		
15	Net cash used for financing activities		(58,000)		(89,000)	
16	Increase in cash		18,000		27,000	
17	Cash balance at beginning of year		31,000		4,000	
18	Cash balance at end of year		$ 49,000		$ 31,000	
19						

	A	B	C	D	E	F
1	**Strafford Crystal Limited** Statement of Cash Flows For the Years Ended September 30, 2017 and 2016					
2			2017		2016	
3	Operating activities:					
4	Net income		$ 89,000		$ 71,000	
5	Adjustments for non-cash items:					
6	Total		19,000		—	
7	Net cash provided by operating activities		108,000		71,000	
8	Investing activities:					
9	Purchase of property, plant, and equipment	$ (121,000)		$ (91,000)		
10	Net cash used for investing activities		(121,000)		(91,000)	
11	Financing activities:					
12	Issuance of long-term notes payable	46,000		43,000		
13	Payment of short-term notes payable	(15,000)		(40,000)		
14	Payment of cash dividends	(12,000)		(9,000)		
15	Net cash provided by (used for) financing activities		19,000		(6,000)	
16	Increase (decrease) in cash		6,000		(26,000)	
17	Cash balance at beginning of year		54,000		80,000	
18	Cash balance at end of year		$ 60,000		$ 54,000	
19						

Requirement

Discuss the relative strengths and weaknesses of each company. Conclude your discussion by recommending one company's shares as an investment.

P11-37B Financial statement data of HiFlite Electronics Limited include the following items (dollars in thousands):

LEARNING OBJECTIVE ⑤

Understand the effects of business transactions on selected ratios

Cash	$ 22,000
Short-term investments	39,000
Accounts receivable, net	83,000
Inventories	141,000
Prepaid expenses	8,000
Total assets	677,000
Short-term notes payable	49,000
Accounts payable	103,000
Accrued liabilities	38,000
Long-term notes payable	160,000
Other long-term liabilities	31,000
Net income	91,000
Number of common shares outstanding	40,000

Requirements

1. Compute HiFlite's current ratio, debt ratio, and earnings per share. Use the following format for your answer:

> **Requirement 1**
> **Current ratio**   **Debt ratio**   **Earnings per share**

2. Compute the three ratios after evaluating the effect of each transaction that follows. Consider each transaction *separately*.
   a. Purchased store supplies of $46,000 on account
   b. Borrowed $125,000 on a long-term note payable
   c. Issued 5,000 common shares, receiving cash of $120,000
   d. Paid short-term notes payable, $32,000
   e. Received cash on account, $19,000

   Format your answer as follows:

> **Requirement 2**
> **Transaction (letter)   Current ratio   Debt ratio   Earnings per share**

P11-38B Comparative financial statement data of Panfield Optical Mart follow:

LEARNING OBJECTIVE ⑤

Use ratios to evaluate a share investment

	A	B	C	D
1	**Panfield Optical Mart** Comparative Income Statement Years Ended December 31, 2017 and 2016			
2		2017	2016	
3	Net sales	$ 686,000	$ 592,000	
4	Cost of goods sold	380,000	281,000	
5	Gross profit	306,000	311,000	
6	Operating expenses	127,000	148,000	
7	Income from operations	179,000	163,000	
8	Interest expense	30,000	50,000	
9	Income before income tax	149,000	113,000	
10	Income tax expense	38,000	45,000	
11	Net income	$ 111,000	$ 68,000	
12				

	A	B	C	D	E
1	**Panfield Optical Mart** Comparative Balance Sheet As at December 31, 2017 and 2016				
2		2017	2016	2015*	
3	Current assets:				
4	Cash	$ 32,000	$ 82,000		
5	Current receivables, net	217,000	157,000	$ 200,000	
6	Inventories	297,000	284,000	188,000	
7	Prepaid expenses	7,000	29,000		
8	Total current assets	553,000	552,000		
9	Property, plant, and equipment, net	283,000	271,000		
10	Total assets	$ 836,000	$ 823,000	701,000	
11	Accounts payable	150,000	105,000	112,000	
12	Other current liabilities	135,000	187,000		
13	Total current liabilities	$ 285,000	$ 292,000		
14	Long-term liabilities	240,000	233,000		
15	Total liabilities	525,000	525,000		
16	Common shareholders' equity, no par	311,000	298,000	199,000	
17	Total liabilities and shareholders' equity	$ 836,000	$ 823,000		
18					

*Selected 2015 amounts.

Other information:
1. Market price of Panfield common stock: $94.38 at December 31, 2017; and $85.67 at December 31, 2016
2. Common shares outstanding: 15,000 during 2017 and 10,000 during 2016
3. All sales on credit

Requirements
1. Compute the following ratios for 2017 and 2016:
    a. Current ratio
    b. Quick (acid-test) ratio
    c. Receivables turnover and days' sales outstanding (DSO) (round to nearest whole day)
    d. Inventory turnover and days' inventory outstanding (DIO) (round to nearest whole day)
    e. Accounts payable turnover and days' payable outstanding (DPO) (round to nearest whole day).
    f. Cash conversion cycle (in days)
    g. Times-interest-earned ratio
    h. Return on assets
    i. Return on common shareholders' equity
    j. Earnings per share of common stock
    k. Price/earnings ratio
2. Decide whether (a) Panfield's financial position improved or deteriorated during 2017, and (b) the investment attractiveness of Panfield's common stock appears to have increased or decreased.
3. How will what you learned in this problem help you evaluate an investment?

LEARNING OBJECTIVE ❺

Use ratios to decide between two share investments

P11-39B Assume that you are purchasing an investment and have decided to invest in a company in the publishing business. You have narrowed the choice to Thrifty Nickel Corp. and The Village Cryer Limited and have assembled the following data.

Selected income statement data for the current year:

	Thrifty Nickel	Village Cryer
Net sales (all on credit)	$371,000	$497,000
Cost of goods sold	209,000	258,000
Income from operations	79,000	138,000
Interest expense	—	19,000
Net income	48,000	72,000

Selected balance sheet data at *beginning* of the current year:

	Thrifty Nickel	Village Cryer
Current receivables, net	$ 40,000	$ 48,000
Inventories	93,000	88,000
Total assets	259,000	270,000
Long-term debt	—	86,000
Preferred shares: $5.00 (200 shares) issued	—	20,000
Common shares: (10,000 shares)	10,000	
(5,000 shares)		12,500
Total shareholders' equity	118,000	126,000

Selected balance sheet and market price data at *end* of the current year:

	Thrifty Nickel	Village Cryer
Current assets:		
Cash	$ 22,000	$ 19,000
Short-term investments	20,000	18,000
Current receivables, net	42,000	46,000
Inventories	87,000	100,000
Prepaid expenses	2,000	3,000
Total current assets	$ 173,000	$ 186,000
Total assets	265,000	328,000
Total current liabilities	108,000	98,000
Total liabilities	108,000*	131,000*
Preferred shares: $5.00 (200 shares)		20,000
Common shares: (10,000 shares)	10,000	
(5,000 shares)		12,500
Total shareholders' equity	157,000	197,000
Market price per share of common share	$ 51	$ 112

*Includes long-term debt: Thrifty Nickel, $-0-; and Village Cryer, $86,000

Your strategy is to invest in companies that have low price/earnings ratios but appear to be in good shape financially. Assume that you have analyzed all other factors and your decision depends on the results of ratio analysis.

Requirement

Compute the following ratios for both companies for the current year, and decide which company's shares better fit your investment strategy:

a. Quick (acid-test) ratio

b. Inventory turnover

c. Days' sales in average receivables

d. Debt ratio

e. Times-interest-earned ratio

f. Return on equity

g. Earnings per share

h. Price/earnings ratio

LEARNING OBJECTIVE ⑤

Analyze a company based on its ratios

P11-40B Take the role of an investment analyst at RBC Dominion Securities. It is your job to recommend investments for your clients. The only information you have is the following ratio values for two companies in the pharmaceuticals industry:

Ratio	Pain Free Ltd.	Remedy Inc.
Days' sales in receivables	36	42
Inventory turnover	6	8
Gross profit percentage	49%	51%
Net income as a percent of sales	7.2%	8.3%
Times interest earned	16	9
Return on equity	32.3%	21.5%
Return on assets	12.1%	16.4%

Write a report to your investment committee. Recommend one company's shares over the other's. State the reasons for your recommendation.

LEARNING OBJECTIVE ⑤

Compute ratios; evaluate turnover, liquidity, and current debt-paying ability

P11-41B The financial statements of Carver News, Inc., include the following items:

	2016	2015	2014
Balance sheet:			
Cash	$ 77,000	$ 103,000	
Short-term investments	13,000	27,000	
Net receivables	81,000	84,000	30,000
Inventory	88,000	75,000	60,000
Prepaid expenses	12,000	6,000	
Total current assets	271,000	295,000	
Accounts payable	85,000	70,000	50,000
Total current liabilities	138,000	96,000	
Income statement:			
Net credit sales	$491,000	$ 505,000	
Cost of goods sold	271,000	279,000	

Requirements

1. Compute the following ratios for 2016 and 2015:

   a. Current ratio

   b. Quick (acid-test) ratio

   c. Inventory turnover and days' inventory outstanding (DIO)

   d. Accounts receivable turnover

   e. Days' sales in average receivables or days' sales outstanding (DSO)

   f. Accounts payable turnover and days' payable outstanding (DPO). Use cost of goods sold in the formula for accounts payable turnover

   g. Cash conversion cycle (in days)

   When computing days, round your answer to the nearest whole number.

2. Evaluate the company's liquidity and current debt-paying ability for 2016. Has it improved or deteriorated from 2015?

3. As a manager of this company, what would you try to improve next year?

APPLY YOUR KNOWLEDGE

DECISION CASES

This section's material reflects CPA enabling competencies,* including:

1. Professionalism and ethical behaviour
2. Problem-solving and decision-making
3. Communication
4. Self-management
5. Teamwork and leadership

Case 1. Assume a major Canadian company had a bad year in 2017, when it suffered a $4.9 billion net loss. The loss pushed most of the return measures into the negative column and the current ratio dropped below 1.0. The company's debt ratio is still only 0.27. Assume top management is pondering ways to improve the company's ratios. In particular, management is considering the following transactions:

1. Sell off a segment of the business for $30 million (receiving half in cash and half in the form of a long-term note receivable). Book value of the segment business is $27 million.
2. Borrow $100 million on long-term debt.
3. Repurchase common shares for $500 million cash.
4. Write off one-fourth of goodwill carried on the books at $128 million.
5. Sell advertising at the normal gross profit of 60%. The advertisements run immediately.
6. Purchase trademarks from a competitor, paying $20 million cash and signing a one-year note payable for $80 million.

Requirements

1. Top management wants to know the effects of these transactions (increase, decrease, or no effect) on the following ratios of the company:
   a. Current ratio
   b. Debt ratio
   c. Times-interest-earned ratio
   d. Return on equity
   e. Book value per common share
2. Some of these transactions have an immediately positive effect on the company's financial condition. Some are definitely negative. Others have an effect that cannot be judged as clearly positive or negative. Evaluate each transaction's effect as positive, negative, or unclear.

LEARNING OBJECTIVE 5

Assess the effects of transactions on a company

Case 2. Company A uses the first-in, first-out (FIFO) method to account for its inventory, and Company B uses weighted-average cost. Analyze the effect of this difference in accounting methods on the two companies' ratio values. For each ratio discussed in this chapter, indicate which company will have the higher (and the lower) ratio value. Also, identify those ratios that are unaffected by the inventory valuation difference. Ignore the effects of income taxes, and assume inventory costs are increasing. Then, based on your analysis of the ratios, summarize your conclusions as to which company looks better overall.

LEARNING OBJECTIVE 5

Analyze the effects of an accounting difference on the ratios

Case 3. Suppose you manage The Runner's Store Inc., a sporting goods store that lost money during the past year. To turn the business around, you must analyze the company and industry data for the current year to learn what is wrong. The company's and industry average data follow:

LEARNING OBJECTIVE 2 5

Identify action to cut losses and establish profitability

	A	B	C	D
1	**The Runner's Store Inc.** Common-Size Balance Sheet Data			
2		Runner's Store	Industry Average	
3	Cash and short-term investments	3.0%	6.8%	
4	Trade receivables, net	15.2	11.0	
5	Inventory	64.2	60.5	
6	Prepaid expenses	1.0	0.0	
7	Total current assets	83.4	78.3	
8	Property and equipment, net	12.6	15.2	
9	Other assets	4.0	6.5	
10	Total assets	100.0%	100.0%	

(Continued)

*© Chartered Professional Accountants of Canada.

	A	B	C	D
11				
12	Notes payable, short-term 12%	17.1%	14.0%	
13	Accounts payable	21.1	25.1	
14	Accrued liabilities	7.8	7.9	
15	Total current liabilities	46.0	47.0	
16	Long-term debt, 11%	19.7	16.4	
17	Total liabilities	65.7	63.4	
18	Common shareholders' equity	34.3	36.6	
19	Total liabilities and shareholders' equity	100.0%	100.0%	
20				

	A	B	C	D
1	**The Runner's Store Inc.** Common-Size Income Statement Data			
2		Runner's Store	Industry Average	
3	Net sales	100.0%	100.0%	
4	Cost of sales	(68.2)	(64.8)	
5	Gross profit	31.8	35.2	
6	Operating expense	(37.1)	(32.3)	
7	Operating income (loss)	(5.3)	2.9	
8	Interest expense	(5.8)	(1.3)	
9	Other revenue	1.1	0.3	
10	Income (loss) before income tax	(10.0)	1.9	
11	Income tax (expense) saving	4.4	(0.8)	
12	Net income (loss)	(5.6)%	1.1%	
13				

Requirement

On the basis of your analysis of these figures, suggest four courses of action The Runner's Store might take to reduce its losses and establish profitable operations. Give your reason for each suggestion.

ETHICAL ISSUES

Turnberry Golf Corporation's long-term debt agreements make certain demands on the business. For example, Turnberry may not repurchase common shares in excess of the balance of retained earnings. Also, long-term debt may not exceed shareholders' equity, and the current ratio may not fall below 1.50. If Turnberry fails to meet any of these requirements, the company's lenders have the authority to take over management of the company.

Changes in consumer demand have made it hard for Turnberry to attract customers. Current liabilities have mounted faster than current assets, causing the current ratio to fall to 1.47. Before releasing financial statements, Turnberry management is scrambling to improve the current ratio. The controller points out that an investment can be classified as either long-term or short-term, depending on management's intention. By deciding to convert an investment to cash within one year, Turnberry can classify the investment as short-term: a current asset. On the controller's recommendation, Turnberry's board of directors votes to reclassify long-term investments as short-term.

Requirements

1. What effect will reclassifying the investments have on the current ratio? Is Turnberry's financial position stronger as a result of reclassifying the investments?

2. Shortly after the financial statements are released, sales improve; so, too, does the current ratio. As a result, Turnberry management decides not to sell the investments it had reclassified as short-term. Accordingly, the company reclassifies the investments as long-term. Has management behaved unethically? Give the reasoning underlying your answer.

FOCUS ON FINANCIALS

Canadian Tire Corporation

Use the five-year summary of selected financial data (rounded) for Canadian Tire to answer the following questions.

	2014	2013	2012	2011	2010
Revenue...	$12,463	$11,786	$11,427	$10,387	$8,981
Net income...	639	564	499	467	454
Cash from operations	575	893	743	1,406	991
Total assets	14,533	13,630	13,181	12,339	8,764
Total long-term debt..........................	2,132	2,339	2,336	2,348	1,079

LEARNING OBJECTIVE 5

Measure profitability and analyze shares as an investment

Requirements

1. Using 2010 as the base year, perform trend analysis of Canadian Tire's selected Financial Highlights for revenue, net income, and cash from operations for each year 2010 through 2014.

2. Evaluate Canadian Tire's operating performance during 2010 through 2014. Comment on each item computed.

FOCUS ON ANALYSIS

Canadian Tire Corporation

Use the Canadian Tire's financial statements in Appendix A to address the following questions.

LEARNING OBJECTIVE 3

Prepare common-size statements

MyAccountingLab

Requirements

1. During fiscal 2014, Canadian Tire's net income increased over 2013. Prepare a common-size income statement for 2014 and 2013.

2. Discuss the results of Canadian Tire based on the common-size income statement.

3. In the Management Discussion and Analysis (MD&A), management is forecasting an annualized retail sales growth of 3+ percent at Canadian Tire; 5+ percent at Mark's and 9+ percent at FGL Sports.

Given the common-size income statement prepared in Requirement 1 and the forecast management made in the MD&A, what is the company's outlook for the future?

GROUP PROJECTS

Project 1. Select an industry in which you are interested, and use the leading company in that industry as the benchmark. Then select two other companies in the same industry. For each category of ratios in the "Decision Guidelines" on page 585, compute at least two ratios for all three companies. Write a two-page report that compares the two companies with the benchmark company.

Project 2. Select a company and obtain its financial statements. Convert the income statement and the balance sheet to common size, and compare the company you selected to the industry average. Risk Management Association's *Annual Statement Studies,* Dun & Bradstreet's *Industry Norms & Key Business Ratios*, and Prentice Hall's *Almanac of Business and Industrial Financial Ratios* by Leo Troy publish common-size statements for most industries.

CHECK YOUR WORK

STOP + THINK ANSWERS

STOP + THINK (11-1)

The most important information in the analysis is the fact that net earnings increased by 79.5%. A further examination of the statements will help to determine what might have contributed to this decrease.

STOP + THINK (11-2)

Cost of sales decreased from the previous year. This could be viewed as a good sign because sales increased from last year. This means that Empire was able to keep costs down while increasing sales.

STOP + THINK (11-3)

Net sales...................	100%	(= $150,000 ÷ $150,000)
Cost of goods sold......	40	(= $60,000 ÷ $150,000)
Gross profit	60	(= $90,000 ÷ $150,000)
Operating expense......	27	(= $40,000 ÷ $150,000)
Operating income.......	33	(= $50,000 ÷ $150,000)
Income tax expense....	10	(= $15,000 ÷ $150,000)
Net income................	23%	(= $35,000 ÷ $150,000)

The company's expenses comprise 77% of net sales (40% + 27% + 10%), leaving 23% net income as a percentage of sales. The lower the expenses, the higher the net income. To determine if this percentage is reasonable, it should be compared with other companies in the same industry.

STOP + THINK (11-4)

No, this is not a good sign. Operations should be a major source of cash. Most of the company's cash is coming from investing activities.

STOP + THINK (11-5)

Understanding the business and industry through reading and researching websites, media, journals, and other publications would be helpful in analyzing a company.

QUICK QUIZ ANSWERS

1. *b* ($19,311 − $15,470 = $3,841 increase; $3,841 / $15,470 = 0.248)

2. *c* ($10,633 / $10,896 = 0.976 ≈ 1.0)

3. *a* [($4,317 + $835 + $3,635) / $10,896 = 0.806 ≈ 0.80]

4. *b*

5. *d* ($41,444 / $31,168 = 1.330)

6. *c* ($33,892 / $41,444 = 0.818)

7. *b* $\left[\dfrac{(\$3,635 + \$2,586)/2}{\$41,444/365} = 27 \text{ days} \right]$

8. *c* $\left[\dfrac{\$33,892}{(\$327 + \$306)/2} = 107 \text{ times} \right]$

9. *a* ($3,544 / (long-term debt of $505 × 0.06) = 116.7 ≈ 117 times)

10. *a*
$$\left[\begin{array}{l} 2017: \$2,645 / \$41,444 = 0.064 \\ 2016: \$2,122 / \$35,404 = 0.060 \\ 2015: \$1,246 / \$31,168 = 0.040 \end{array} \right]$$

11. *d* $\left[\text{EPS } \$1.03 = \dfrac{\text{Net income } \$2,645}{\text{Shares outstanding}} \right.$

$\left. \text{Shares outstanding} = 2,568 \right]$

12. *d* [$6,280/2,568 = $2.46]

Comprehensive Financial Statement Analysis Project

The objective of this exercise is to develop your ability to perform a comprehensive analysis on a set of financial statements. Use the copy of the 2014 annual report of Canadian Tire Corporation (year end January 3, 2015) from Appendix A.

Requirement 1

Basic information (provide sources):

a. Using a site such as www.google.ca/finance or ca.finance.yahoo.com, look up merchandising—wholesale distributors. List three competitors of Canadian Tire Corporation.

b. Describe Canadian Tire's retail segment business risks.

c. Canadian Tire claims to be a "family of companies." What companies do they own?

d. What is Canadian Tire's largest asset? Largest liability?

e. How many common shares are they authorized to issue? How many are issued? Outstanding?

f. Did Canadian Tire repurchase any common shares during the year? If so, how many?

g. When does Canadian Tire record revenue?

h. What inventory method does Canadian Tire use?

i. Does Canadian Tire have any business interests in foreign countries? Explain your answer.

Requirement 2

Using information you have learned in the text and elsewhere, evaluate Canadian Tire's profitability for 2014 compared with 2013. In your analysis, you should compute the following ratios and then comment on what those ratios indicate. NOTE: You will have to look up the annual report for 2013 to obtain total assets and shareholders' equity for 2012. See www.sedar.com or use Canadian Tire's website.

a. Return on sales

b. Asset turnover

c. Return on assets

d. Leverage ratio

e. Return on equity

f. Gross profit percentage

g. Earnings per share (show computation)

h. Book value per share

Requirement 3

Evaluate the company's ability to sell inventory and pay debts during 2014 and 2013. In your analysis, you should compute the following ratios, and then comment on what those ratios indicate. Since the 2014 annual report only includes the balance sheets for 2014 and 2013, you will need to look up the annual report for 2013 for information about 2012 accounts receivable, inventory, and accounts payable.

a. Accounts receivable turnover and days' sales outstanding

b. Inventory turnover and days' inventory outstanding

c. Accounts payable turnover and days' payable outstanding

d. Cash conversion cycle

e. Current ratio

f. Quick (acid-test) ratio

g. Debt ratio

h. Times interest earned

Requirement 4

Evaluate Canadian Tire's cash flow.

a. For 2014, what are Canadian Tire's two main sources of cash?

b. For 2014, is Canadian Tire's net cash flow from operations greater than or less than net income? What is the primary cause of the difference?

c. For 2013 and 2014, what is the primary source of cash from investing activities? What is the primary use of cash from investing activities for 2013 and 2014?

d. For 2013 and 2014, what is the primary source of cash from financing activities? What is the primary use of cash from financing activities for 2013 and 2014?

e. What trend(s) do you detect from this analysis?

Requirement 5

Other financial analysis.

a. Compute common-size percentages for sales, gross profit, operating income, and net income for 2011−2014. Comment on your results.

b. Find the selected financial data in the annual report where Canadian Tire's reports selected information since 2011. Compute trend percentages, using 2011 as the base year, for total revenues and net earnings. Comment on your results.

Requirement 6

Evaluate Canadian Tire Corporation's shares as an investment.

a. What was the closing market price of Canadian Tire Corporation's shares on January 4, 2015, the next trading day after the balance-sheet date of January 3, 2015?

b. Compute the price-earnings ratio using your EPS calculation and the market price you just determined. Now compute the price-earnings ratio as of the date you are making this evaluation (it will be later than January 4, 2015) with the price as of that date. Canadian Tire's website gives the share price you will need or you can look it up online using the ticker symbol CTC.A.

c. Based on comparison of these two computations, would you evaluate the company's shares as a "buy," "hold," or "sell"? State your reasons.

Financial Statements from Canadian Tire Annual Report 2014

Appendix A

Index to the Consolidated Financial Statements and Notes

*Reprinted with permission from Canadian Tire Corporation.

Management's Responsibility for Financial Statements

The management of Canadian Tire Corporation, Limited is responsible for the accompanying consolidated financial statements. The financial statements have been prepared by management in accordance with International Financial Reporting Standards, which recognize the necessity of relying on some best estimates and informed judgements. All financial information in our Management's Discussion and Analysis is consistent with the consolidated financial statements.

To discharge its responsibilities for financial reporting and safeguarding of assets, management depends on the Company's systems of internal accounting control. These systems are designed to provide reasonable assurance that the financial records are reliable and form a proper basis for the timely and accurate preparation of financial statements. Management meets the objectives of internal accounting control on a cost effective basis through the prudent selection and training of personnel, adoption and communication of appropriate policies, and employment of an internal audit program.

The Board of Directors oversees management's responsibilities for the consolidated financial statements primarily through the activities of its Audit Committee, which is composed solely of directors who are neither officers nor employees of the Company. This Committee meets with management and the Company's independent auditors, Deloitte LLP, to review the consolidated financial statements and recommend approval by the Board of Directors. The Audit Committee is also responsible for making recommendations with respect to the appointment of and for approving remuneration and the terms of engagement of the Company's auditors. The Audit Committee also meets with the auditors, without the presence of management, to discuss the results of their audit, their opinion on internal accounting controls, and the quality of financial reporting.

The consolidated financial statements have been audited by Deloitte LLP, who were appointed by shareholder vote at the annual shareholders' meeting. Their report is presented below.

Michael B. Medline
President and Chief Executive Officer

Dean McCann
Executive Vice-President and
Chief Financial Officer

February 26, 2015

Consolidated Balance Sheets

As at
(C$ in millions)

	January 3, 2015	December 28, 2013
		(Note 3)
ASSETS		
Cash and cash equivalents (Note 8)	$ 662.1	$ 643.2
Short-term investments (Note 9)	289.1	416.6
Trade and other receivables (Note 10)	880.2	758.5
Loans receivable (Note 11)	4,905.5	4,569.7
Merchandise inventories	1,623.8	1,481.0
Income taxes recoverable	31.9	31.5
Prepaid expenses and deposits	104.5	68.2
Assets classified as held for sale (Note 12)	13.1	9.1
Total current assets	8,510.2	7,977.8
Long-term receivables and other assets (Note 13)	684.2	686.0
Long-term investments	176.0	134.7
Goodwill and intangible assets (Note 14)	1,251.7	1,185.5
Investment property (Note 15)	148.6	93.5
Property and equipment (Note 16)	3,743.1	3,516.1
Deferred income taxes (Note 18)	39.4	36.4
Total assets	$ 14,553.2	$ 13,630.0
LIABILITIES		
Bank indebtedness (Note 8)	$ 14.3	$ 69.0
Deposits (Note 19)	950.7	1,178.4
Trade and other payables (Note 20)	1,961.2	1,817.4
Provisions (Note 21)	206.0	196.1
Short-term borrowings (Note 23)	199.8	120.3
Loans payable (Note 24)	604.4	611.2
Income taxes payable	54.9	57.5
Current portion of long-term debt (Note 25)	587.5	272.2
Total current liabilities	4,578.8	4,322.1
Long-term provisions (Note 21)	44.1	38.2
Long-term debt (Note 25)	2,131.6	2,339.1
Long-term deposits (Note 19)	1,286.2	1,152.0
Deferred income taxes (Note 18)	93.9	100.4
Other long-term liabilities (Note 26)	787.8	228.3
Total liabilities	8,922.4	8,180.1
EQUITY		
Share capital (Note 28)	695.5	712.9
Contributed surplus	2.9	2.4
Accumulated other comprehensive income	82.0	47.4
Retained earnings	4,075.1	4,404.6
Equity attributable to owners of Canadian Tire Corporation	4,855.5	5,167.3
Non-controlling interests (Note 17)	775.3	282.6
Total equity	5,630.8	5,449.9
Total liabilities and equity	$ 14,553.2	$ 13,630.0

The related notes form an integral part of these consolidated financial statements.

Maureen J. Sabia
Director

Graham W. Savage
Director

Consolidated Statements of Income

For the years ended
(C$ in millions, except per share amounts)

	January 3, 2015	December 28, 2013
Revenue (Note 30)	$ 12,462.9	$ 11,785.6
Cost of producing revenue (Note 31)	(8,416.9)	(8,063.3)
Gross margin	4,046.0	3,722.3
Other income (expense)	11.0	(3.0)
Selling, general and administrative expenses (Note 32)	(3,052.9)	(2,828.9)
Net finance costs (Note 33)	(108.9)	(105.8)
Change in fair value of redeemable financial instrument (Note 35)	(17.0)	–
Income before income taxes	878.2	784.6
Income taxes (Note 18)	(238.9)	(220.2)
Net income	$ 639.3	$ 564.4
Net income attributable to:		
Owners of Canadian Tire Corporation	$ 604.0	$ 561.2
Non-controlling interests (Note 17)	35.3	3.2
	$ 639.3	$ 564.4
Basic earnings per share attributable to owners of Canadian Tire Corporation	$ 7.65	$ 6.96
Diluted earnings per share attributable to owners of Canadian Tire Corporation	$ 7.59	$ 6.91
Weighted average number of Common and Class A Non-Voting Shares outstanding:		
Basic	78,960,025	80,652,472
Diluted	79,612,957	81,180,863

The related notes form an integral part of these consolidated financial statements.

Consolidated Statements of Comprehensive Income

For the years ended (C$ in millions)	January 3, 2015	December 28, 2013
Net income	$ 639.3	$ 564.4
Other comprehensive income		
Items that may be reclassified subsequently to net income:		
Cash flow hedges:		
Gains, net of tax of $40.4 (2013 – $30.0)	114.0	83.1
Reclassification of gains to non-financial assets, net of tax of $27.2 (2013 – $12.2)	(77.5)	(33.7)
Reclassification of gains to income, net of tax of $0.6 (2013 – $0.1)	(1.5)	(0.4)
Available-for-sale financial assets:		
(Losses) gains, net of tax of $0.1 (2013 – $nil)	(0.1)	0.1
Reclassification of gains to income, net of tax of $nil (2013 – $nil)	(0.1)	–
Item that will not be reclassified subsequently to net income:		
Actuarial (losses) gains, net of tax of $4.7 (2013 – $3.6)	(13.2)	10.0
Other comprehensive income	21.6	59.1
Other comprehensive income attributable to:		
Owners of Canadian Tire Corporation	$ 21.5	$ 59.1
Non-controlling interests	0.1	–
	$ 21.6	$ 59.1
Comprehensive income	$ 660.9	$ 623.5
Comprehensive income attributable to:		
Owners of Canadian Tire Corporation	$ 625.5	$ 620.3
Non-controlling interests	35.4	3.2
	$ 660.9	$ 623.5

The related notes form an integral part of these consolidated financial statements.

Consolidated Statements of Cash Flows

For the years ended (C$ in millions)	January 3, 2015	December 28, 2013
		(Note 39)
Cash generated from (used for):		
Operating activities		
Net income	$ **639.3**	$ 564.4
Adjustments for:		
Depreciation on property and equipment and investment property (Notes 31 and 32)	**279.2**	253.8
Income tax expense	**238.9**	220.2
Net finance costs	**108.9**	105.8
Amortization of intangible assets (Note 32)	**93.1**	91.5
Change in fair value of redeemable financial instrument (Note 35)	**17.0**	–
Changes in fair value of derivative instruments	**(33.9)**	(37.9)
Gain on disposal of property and equipment, investment property and assets held for sale	**(9.0)**	(10.3)
Interest paid	**(122.0)**	(126.5)
Interest received	**10.4**	12.0
Income taxes paid	**(256.5)**	(191.2)
Other	**25.3**	15.1
	990.7	896.9
Change in operating working capital and other (Note 34)	**(83.5)**	270.2
Change in loans receivable	**(332.4)**	(274.1)
Cash generated from operating activities	**574.8**	893.0
Investing activities		
Additions to property and equipment and investment property	**(538.6)**	(404.3)
Additions to intangible assets	**(150.1)**	(105.9)
	(688.7)	(510.2)
Acquisition of short-term investments	**(431.6)**	(339.2)
Proceeds from the maturity and disposition of short-term investments	**665.3**	193.8
Acquisition of long-term investments	**(155.8)**	(55.1)
Proceeds from the disposition of long-term investments	**7.6**	0.4
Proceeds on disposition of property and equipment, investment property and assets held for sale	**21.3**	20.6
Long-term receivables and other assets	**3.1**	(21.5)
Acquisition of Pro Hockey Life Sporting Goods Inc. (Note 7)	**–**	(58.0)
Other	**(10.7)**	(17.2)
	99.2	(276.2)
Cash used for investing activities	**(589.5)**	(786.4)
Financing activities		
Dividends paid	**(141.4)**	(107.2)
Distributions paid to non-controlling interests	**(19.5)**	(3.6)
	(160.9)	(110.8)
Net issuance (repayment) of short-term borrowings	**79.4**	(20.4)
Issuance of loans payable	**235.6**	235.9
Repayment of loans payable	**(242.4)**	(248.5)
Issuance of long-term debt	**563.7**	265.8
Repayment of long-term debt and finance lease liabilities	**(474.0)**	(659.2)
Payment of transaction costs related to long-term debt	**(2.0)**	(1.3)
	160.3	(427.7)
Proceeds on sale of ownership interests in the Financial Services business	**500.0**	–
Transaction costs on sale of ownership interests in the Financial Services business	**(23.2)**	–
Issuance of trust units to non-controlling interests	**–**	303.0
Trust unit issue costs	**–**	(24.1)
Repurchase of share capital (Note 28)	**(290.6)**	(105.9)
	186.2	173.0
Change in deposits	**(97.0)**	(96.2)
Cash generated from (used for) financing activities	**88.6**	(461.7)
Cash generated (used) in the year	**73.9**	(355.1)
Cash and cash equivalents, net of bank indebtedness, beginning of year	**574.2**	929.5
Effect of exchange rate fluctuations on cash held	**(0.3)**	(0.2)
Cash and cash equivalents, net of bank indebtedness, end of year (Note 8)	$ **647.8**	$ 574.2

The related notes form an integral part of these consolidated financial statements.

Consolidated Statements of Changes in Equity

| (C$ in millions) | Share capital | Contributed surplus | Total accumulated other comprehensive income (loss) | | | Retained earnings | Equity attributable to owners of Canadian Tire Corporation | Equity attributable to non-controlling interests | Total equity |
			Cashflow hedges	Fair value changes in available-for-sale financial assets	Total accumulated other comprehensive income (loss)				
	(Note 3)	(Note 3)				(Note 3)			
Balance at December 28, 2013	$ 712.9	$ 2.4	$ 47.0	$ 0.4	$ 47.4	$ 4,404.6	$ 5,167.3	$ 282.6	$ 5,449.9
Net income						604.0	604.0	35.3	639.3
Other comprehensive income (loss)	–	–	34.8	(0.2)	34.6	(13.1)	21.5	0.1	21.6
Total comprehensive income (loss)	–	–	34.8	(0.2)	34.6	590.9	625.5	35.4	660.9
Contributions by and distributions to owners of Canadian Tire Corporation									
Issuance of Class A Non-Voting Shares (Note 28)	6.9						6.9		6.9
Repurchase of Class A Non-Voting Shares (Note 28)	(290.6)						(290.6)		(290.6)
Excess of repurchase price over average cost (Note 28)	266.3					(266.3)	–		–
Dividends						(154.1)	(154.1)		(154.1)
Issuance of redeemable financial instrument (Note 35)						(500.0)	(500.0)		(500.0)
Contributed surplus arising on sale of property to CT REIT		0.5					0.5		0.5
Contributions by and distributions to non-controlling interests									
Sale of ownership interests in the Financial Services business, net of transaction costs								476.8	476.8
Issuance of trust units to non-controlling interests, net of transaction costs								1.8	1.8
Distributions								(21.3)	(21.3)
Total contributions and distributions	(17.4)	0.5	–	–	–	(920.4)	(937.3)	457.3	(480.0)
Balance at January 3, 2015	$ 695.5	$ 2.9	$ 81.8	$ 0.2	$ 82.0	$ 4,075.1	$ 4,855.5	$ 775.3	$ 5,630.8
Balance at December 29, 2012	$ 718.5	$ –	$ (2.0)	$ 0.3	$ (1.7)	$ 4,047.5	$ 4,764.3	$ –	$ 4,764.3
Net income						561.2	561.2	3.2	564.4
Other comprehensive income	–	–	49.0	0.1	49.1	10.0	59.1	–	59.1
Total comprehensive income	–	–	49.0	0.1	49.1	571.2	620.3	3.2	623.5
Contributions by and distributions to owners of Canadian Tire Corporation									
Issuance of Class A Non-Voting Shares (Note 28)	5.8						5.8		5.8
Repurchase of Class A Non-Voting Shares (Note 28)	(105.9)						(105.9)		(105.9)
Excess of repurchase price over average cost (Note 28)	94.5					(94.5)	–		–
Dividends						(119.6)	(119.6)		(119.6)
Contributed surplus arising on sale of property to CT REIT		2.4					2.4		2.4
Contributions by and distributions to non-controlling interests									
Issuance of trust units to non-controlling interests, net of transaction costs								283.0	283.0
Distributions								(3.6)	(3.6)
Total contributions and distributions	(5.6)	2.4	–	–	–	(214.1)	(217.3)	279.4	62.1
Balance at December 28, 2013	$ 712.9	$ 2.4	$ 47.0	$ 0.4	$ 47.4	$ 4,404.6	$ 5,167.3	$ 282.6	$ 5,449.9

The related notes form an integral part of these condensed consolidated financial statements.

1. The Company and its operations

Canadian Tire Corporation, Limited is a Canadian public company primarily domiciled in Canada. Its registered office is located at 2180 Yonge Street, Toronto, Ontario, M4P 2V8, Canada. It is listed on the Toronto Stock Exchange (TSX – CTC, CTC.A). Canadian Tire Corporation, Limited and entities it controls are together referred to in these consolidated financial statements as the "Company". Refer to Note 17 for the Company's major subsidiaries.

The Company comprises three main business operations, which offer a range of retail goods and services, including general merchandise, apparel, sporting goods, petroleum, financial services including a bank and real estate operations. Details of its three reportable operating segments are provided in Note 6.

2. Basis of preparation

Fiscal year

The fiscal year of the Company consists of a 52 or 53-week period ending on the Saturday closest to December 31. The fiscal years for the consolidated financial statements and notes presented for 2014 and 2013 are the 53-week period ended January 3, 2015 and the 52-week period ended December 28, 2013, respectively.

Statement of compliance

These consolidated financial statements have been prepared in accordance with International Financial Reporting Standards ("IFRS") and using the accounting policies described herein.

These consolidated financial statements were authorized for issuance by the Company's Board of Directors on February 26, 2015.

Basis of presentation

These consolidated financial statements have been prepared on the historical cost basis, except for the following items, which are measured at fair value:
- financial instruments at fair value through profit or loss;
- derivative financial instruments;
- available-for-sale financial assets;
- liabilities for share-based payment plans; and
- initial recognition of assets acquired and liabilities assumed in a business combination.

In addition, the post-employment defined benefit obligation is recorded at its discounted present value.

Functional and presentation currency

These consolidated financial statements are presented in Canadian dollars ("C$"), the Company's functional currency ("the functional currency"). All financial information is presented in millions, except per share amounts, which are presented in whole dollars, and the number of shares or the weighted average number of shares, which are presented in whole numbers.

Judgments and estimates

The preparation of these consolidated financial statements in accordance with IFRS requires Management to make judgments and estimates that affect the application of accounting policies and the reported amounts of assets and liabilities and disclosures of contingent assets and liabilities at the date of these consolidated financial statements and the reported amounts of revenue and expenses during the reporting periods. Actual results may differ from estimates made in these consolidated financial statements.

Judgments are made in the selection and assessment of the Company's accounting policies. Estimates are used mainly in determining the measurement of recognized transactions and balances. Estimates are based on historical experience and other factors, including expectations of future events that are believed to be reasonable under the circumstances. Judgment and estimates are often interrelated. The Company's judgments and estimates are continually re-evaluated to ensure they remain appropriate. Revisions to accounting estimates are recognized in the period in which the estimates are revised and in future periods affected.

The following are the accounting policies that are subject to judgments and estimates that the Company believes could have the most significant impact on the amounts recognized in these consolidated financial statements.

Impairment of assets

Judgment – The Company uses judgment in determining the grouping of assets to identify its Cash Generating Units ("CGUs") for purposes of testing for impairment of property and equipment and goodwill and intangible assets. The Company has determined that its Retail CGUs comprise individual stores or groups of stores within a geographic market. In testing for impairment, goodwill acquired in a business combination is allocated to the CGUs that are expected to benefit from the synergies of the business combination. In testing for impairment of intangibles with indefinite lives, these assets are allocated to the CGUs to which they relate. Furthermore, judgment has been used in determining whether there has been an indication of impairment, which would require the completion of an impairment test.

NOTES TO THE CONSOLIDATED FINANCIAL STATEMENTS

Estimation – The Company's estimate of a CGU's or group of CGUs' recoverable amount based on value in use involves estimating future cash flows before taxes. Future cash flows are estimated based on multi-year extrapolation of the most recent historical actual results or budgets and a terminal value calculated by discounting the final year in perpetuity. The growth rate applied to the terminal value is based on the Bank of Canada's target growth rate or Management's estimate of the growth rate specific to the individual item being tested. The future cash flow estimates are then discounted to their present value using an appropriate pre-tax discount rate that incorporates a risk premium specific to each business. The Company's determination of a CGU's or group of CGUs' recoverable amount based on fair value less cost to sell uses factors such as market rental rates for comparable assets.

Fair value measurement of redeemable financial instrument

Judgment – The Company uses judgment in determining the fair value measurement of the redeemable financial instrument issued in conjunction with the sale of a 20 per cent equity interest in the Company's Financial Services business. The redeemable financial instrument is subsequently remeasured at fair value at each reporting date. In calculating the fair value, judgment is used when determining the discount and growth rates applied to the forecasted earnings in the discounted cash flow valuation. Refer to Note 35 for further information regarding this financial instrument.

Estimation – The inputs to determine the fair value are taken from observable markets where possible, but where they are unavailable, assumptions are required in establishing fair value. The fair value of the redeemable financial instrument is determined based on the Company's best estimate of forecasted normalized earnings attributable to the Financial Services business, adjusted for any undistributed earnings.

Merchandise inventories

Estimation – Merchandise inventories are carried at the lower of cost and net realizable value. The estimation of net realizable value is based on the most reliable evidence available of the amount the merchandise inventories are expected to realize. Additionally, estimation is required for inventory provisions due to shrinkage and obsolescence.

Income and other taxes

Judgment – In calculating current and deferred income and other taxes, the Company uses judgment when interpreting the tax rules in jurisdictions where the Company operates. The Company also uses judgment in classifying transactions and assessing probable outcomes of claimed deductions, which considers expectations of future operating results, the timing and reversal of temporary differences and possible audits of income tax and other tax filings by tax authorities.

Consolidation

Judgment – The Company uses judgment in determining the entities that it controls and accordingly consolidates. An entity is controlled when the Company has power over an entity, exposure, or rights, to variable returns from its involvement with the entity, and is able to use its power over the entity to affect its return from the entity. The Company has power over an entity when it has existing rights that give it the current ability to direct the relevant activities, which are the activities that significantly affect the investee's returns. Since power comes from rights, power can result from contractual arrangements. However, certain contractual arrangements contain rights that are designed to protect the Company's interest without giving it power over the entity.

Loans receivable

Estimation – The Company's estimate of allowances on loans receivable is based on a roll-rate methodology that employs statistical analysis of historical data and experience of delinquency and default to estimate the amount of loans that will eventually be written off as a result of events occurring before the reporting date, with certain adjustments for other relevant circumstances influencing the recoverability of the loans receivable. Default rates, loss rates and the expected timing of future recoveries are regularly benchmarked against actual outcomes to ensure that they remain appropriate. Future customer behaviour may be affected by a number of factors, including changes in interest and unemployment rates and program design changes.

Post-employment benefits

Estimation – The accounting for the Company's post-employment benefit plan requires the use of assumptions. The accrued benefit liability is calculated using actuarial determined data and the Company's best estimates of future salary escalations, retirement ages of employees, employee turnover, mortality rates, market discount rates and expected health and dental care costs.

Other estimates include determining the useful lives of property and equipment, investment property and intangibles assets for the purposes of depreciation and amortization; in accounting for and measuring items such as customer loyalty, deferred revenue, and provision and purchase price adjustments on business combinations; and in measuring certain fair values, including those related to the valuation of business combinations, share-based payments and financial instruments.

New standards implemented

Financial instruments: Asset and liability offsetting

In December 2011, the International Accounting Standard Board ("IASB") amended International Accounting Standards ("IAS") 32 – *Financial Instruments: Presentation* ("IAS 32") to clarify the requirements which permits offsetting a financial asset and liability in the financial statements. The IAS 32 amendments were effective for annual periods beginning on or after January 1, 2014 and were applied retrospectively. The implementation of IAS 32 amendments did not have a significant impact on the Company.

Financial Instruments: Novation of derivatives and continuation of hedge accounting

In June 2013, the IASB issued *Novation of Derivatives and Continuation of Hedge Accounting – Amendments to IAS 39*. This amendment to IAS 39 – *Financial Instruments: Recognition and Measurement* ("IAS 39") provides an exception to the requirement to discontinue hedge accounting in situations where over-the-counter derivatives designated in hedging relationships are directly or indirectly novated to a central counterparty as a consequence of laws or regulations, or the introduction of laws or regulations. The IAS 39 amendments were effective for annual periods beginning on or after January 1, 2014 and were applied retrospectively. The implementation of IAS 39 amendments did not have a significant impact on the Company.

Levies

In May 2013, the IASB issued IFRS Interpretations Committee ("IFRIC") 21 – *Levies*, which is an interpretation of IAS 37 – *Provisions, Contingent Liabilities and Contingent Assets* ("IFRIC 21"). IFRIC 21 clarifies that the obligating event that gives rise to a liability to pay a levy is the activity described in the relevant legislation that triggers the payment of the levy. IFRIC 21 was effective for annual periods beginning on or after January 1, 2014 and was applied retrospectively. The implementation of IFRIC 21 did not have a significant impact on the Company.

Standards, amendments and interpretations issued and not yet adopted

The following new standards, amendments and interpretations have been issued and are expected to have an impact on the Company, but are not effective for the fiscal year ended January 3, 2015, and, accordingly, have not been applied in preparing these consolidated financial statements.

Financial instruments

In July 2014, the IASB issued the final version of IFRS 9 – *Financial Instruments* ("IFRS 9"), which brings together the classification and measurement, impairment and hedge accounting phases of the IASB's project to replace IAS 39.

Classification and measurement – Financial assets are classified and measured based on the business model under which they are managed and the contractual cash flow characteristics of the financial assets. Financial liabilities are classified in a similar manner as under IAS 39, except that financial liabilities measured at fair value will have fair value changes resulting from changes in the entity's own credit risk recognized in Other Comprehensive Income instead of net income, unless this would create an accounting mismatch.

Impairment – The measurement of impairment of financial assets is based on an expected credit loss model. It is no longer necessary for a triggering event to have occurred before credit losses are recognized. IFRS 9 also includes new disclosure requirements about expected credit losses and credit risk.

Hedge accounting – The new general hedge accounting model more closely aligns hedge accounting with risk management activities undertaken by entities when hedging their financial and non-financial risk exposures. It will provide more opportunities to apply hedge accounting to reflect actual risk management activities.

IFRS 9 will be applied retrospectively for annual periods beginning on or after January 1, 2018. Early adoption is permitted. The Company is assessing the potential impact of this standard.

Revenue from Contracts with Customers

In May 2014, the IASB issued IFRS 15 – *Revenue from Contracts with Customers* ("IFRS 15"), which replaces IAS 11 – *Construction Contracts*, IAS 18 – *Revenue* and IFRIC 13 – *Customer Loyalty Programmes* ("IFRIC 13"), as well as various other interpretations regarding revenue. IFRS 15 outlines a single comprehensive model for entities to use in accounting for revenue arising from contracts with customers, except for contracts that are within the scope of the standards on leases, insurance contracts and financial instruments. IFRS 15 also contains enhanced disclosure requirements.

IFRS 15 will be applied retrospectively for annual periods beginning on or after January 1, 2017. Early adoption is permitted. The Company is assessing the potential impact of this standard.

Disclosure initiative

In December 2014, the IASB issued *Disclosure Initiative Amendments to IAS 1* as part of the IASB's Disclosure Initiative. These amendments encourage entities to apply professional judgment regarding disclosure and presentation in their financial statements.

These amendments are effective for annual periods beginning on or after January 1, 2016. Earlier application is permitted. The Company is assessing the potential impact of these amendments.

3. Significant accounting policies

The accounting policies set out below have been applied consistently to all periods presented in these consolidated financial statements and have been applied consistently throughout the Company.

Basis of consolidation

These consolidated financial statements include the accounts of Canadian Tire Corporation, Limited and entities it controls. An entity is controlled when the Company has the ability to direct the relevant activities of the entity, has exposure, or rights, to variable returns from its involvement with the entity, and is able to use its power over the entity to affect its returns from the entity.

The results of certain subsidiaries that have different year-ends have been included in these consolidated financial statements for the 53-weeks ended January 3, 2015 and 52-weeks ended December 28, 2013. The year-end of CTFS Holdings Limited and its subsidiaries, Franchise Trust and CT Real Estate Investment Trust ("CT REIT") is December 31.

Income or loss and each component of Other Comprehensive Income ("OCI") are attributed to the owners of the Company and to the non-controlling interests. Total comprehensive income is attributed to the owners of the Company and to the non-controlling interests even if this results in the non-controlling interests having a deficit balance on consolidation.

Business combinations

The Company applies the acquisition method in accounting for business combinations.

The Company measures goodwill as the difference between the fair value of the consideration transferred, including the recognized amount of any non-controlling interests in the acquiree, and the net recognized amount (generally fair value) of the identifiable assets acquired and liabilities assumed, all measured as at the acquisition date.

Consideration transferred includes the fair value of the assets transferred (including cash), liabilities incurred by the Company on behalf of the acquiree, the fair value of any contingent consideration and equity interests issued by the Company.

Where a business combination is achieved in stages, previously held interests in the acquired entity are remeasured to fair value at the acquisition date, which is the date control is obtained, and the resulting gain or loss, if any, is recognized in net income. Amounts arising from interests in the acquiree prior to the acquisition date that have previously been recognized in OCI are reclassified to net income.

The fair values of property and equipment recognized as a result of a business combination is based on either the cost approach or market approaches, as applicable. The market value of property is the estimated amount for which a property could be exchanged on the date of valuation between a willing buyer and a willing seller in an arm's length transaction after proper marketing wherein the parties each act knowledgeably and willingly. For the cost approach, the current replacement cost or reproduction cost for each major asset is calculated.

The fair values of banners and trademarks acquired in a business combination are determined using an income approach. The "relief from royalty" method has been applied to forecast revenue using an appropriate royalty rate. This results in an estimate of the value of the intangible assets acquired by the Company.

The fair values of franchise agreements and other intangibles, such as customer relationships, are determined using an income approach or multi-period excess earnings approach. This method is based on the discounted cash flows expected to be derived from ownership of the assets. The present value of the cash flows represents the value of the intangible asset. The fair value of off-market leases acquired in a business combination is determined based on the present value of the difference between market rates and rates in the existing leases.

The fair values of inventories acquired in a business combination is determined based on the estimated selling price in the ordinary course of business less the estimated costs of sale, and a reasonable profit margin based on the effort required to complete and sell the inventories.

Transaction costs that the Company incurs in connection with a business combination are expensed immediately.

Joint arrangement

A joint arrangement is an arrangement in which two or more parties have joint control. Joint control is the contractually agreed sharing of control whereby decisions about relevant activities require unanimous consent of the parties sharing control. A joint arrangement is classified as a joint operation when the parties that has joint control of the arrangement have rights to the assets and obligations for the liabilities related to the arrangement.

Foreign currency translation

Transactions in foreign currencies are translated into Canadian dollars at rates in effect at the date of the transaction. Monetary assets and liabilities in foreign currencies are translated into Canadian dollars at the closing exchange rate at the balance sheet date. Non-monetary items that are measured in terms of historical cost are translated into Canadian dollars at the exchange rate at the date of the original transaction. Exchange gains or losses arising from translation are recorded in other income or cost of producing revenue as applicable in the consolidated statements of income.

Financial instruments
Recognition and measurement

Financial assets and financial liabilities, including derivatives, are recognized in the consolidated balance sheets when the Company becomes a party to the contractual provisions of a financial instrument or non-financial derivative contract. All financial instruments are required to be measured at fair value on initial recognition. Subsequent measurement of these assets and liabilities is based on either fair value or amortized cost using the effective interest method, depending upon their classification.

Transaction costs that are directly attributable to the acquisition or issue of financial assets and financial liabilities (other than financial assets and financial liabilities classified as fair value through profit or loss ["FVTPL"]) are added to or deducted from the fair value of the financial assets or financial liabilities, as appropriate, on initial recognition. Transaction costs directly attributable to the acquisition of financial assets or financial liabilities classified as FVTPL are recognized immediately in net income.

The Company classifies financial instruments, at the time of initial recognition, according to their characteristics and Management's choices and intentions related thereto for the purposes of ongoing measurement. Classification choices for financial assets include a) FVTPL, b) held to maturity, c) available for sale, and d) loans and receivables. Classification choices for financial liabilities include a) FVTPL and b) other liabilities.

The Company's financial assets and financial liabilities are generally classified and measured as follows:

Asset/Liability	Category	Measurement
Cash and cash equivalents	Loans and receivables	Amortized cost
Short-term investments[1]	Available for sale	Fair value
Trade and other receivables[2]	Loans and receivables	Amortized cost
Loans receivable	Loans and receivables	Amortized cost
Deposits (recorded in prepaid expenses and deposits)	Loans and receivables	Amortized cost
Long-term receivables and other assets[2]	Loans and receivables	Amortized cost
Long-term investments[3]	Available for sale	Fair value
Bank indebtness	Other liabilities	Amortized cost
Deposits	Other liabilities	Amortized cost
Trade and other payables[2]	Other liabilities	Amortized cost
Short-term borrowings	Other liabilities	Amortized cost
Loans payable	Other liabilities	Amortized cost
Long-term debt	Other liabilities	Amortized cost
Redeemable financial instrument (recorded in other long-term liabilities)	FVTPL	Fair value

[1] Certain short-term investments are classified as FVTPL and measured at fair value.
[2] Includes derivatives that are classified as FVTPL or are effective hedging instruments, and measured at fair value .
[3] Certain long-term investments are classified as FVTPL, and measured at fair value.

Financial instruments at fair value through profit or loss (FVTPL)

Financial instruments are classified as FVTPL when the financial instrument is either held for trading or designated as such upon initial recognition. Financial instruments are classified as held for trading if acquired principally for the purpose of selling in the near future or if part of an identified portfolio of financial instruments that the Company manages together and has a recent actual pattern of short-term profit-making. Derivatives are classified as FVTPL unless they are designated as effective hedging instruments.

Financial instruments classified as FVTPL are measured at fair value, with changes in fair value recorded in net income in the period in which they arise.

Available for sale

Financial assets classified as available for sale are measured at fair value with changes in fair value recognized in OCI until realized through disposal or other than temporary impairment, at which point the change in fair value is recognized in net income. Dividend income from available-for-sale financial assets is recognized in net income when the Company's right to receive payments is established. Interest income on available-for-sale financial assets, calculated using the effective interest method, is recognized in net income.

Loans and receivables

Loans and receivables are financial assets with fixed or determinable payments that are not quoted in an active market. Subsequent to initial recognition, loans and receivables are measured at amortized cost using the effective interest method, less any impairment, with gains and losses recognized in net income in the period that the asset is derecognized or impaired.

Other liabilities

Subsequent to initial recognition, other financial liabilities are measured at amortized cost using the effective interest method with gains and losses recognized in net income in the period that the liability is derecognized.

Derecognition of financial instruments

A financial asset is derecognized when the contractual rights to the cash flows from the asset expire or when the Company transfers the financial asset to another party without retaining control or substantially all the risks and rewards of ownership of the asset. Any interest in transferred financial assets created or retained by the Company is recognized as a separate asset or liability.

A financial liability is derecognized when its contractual obligations are discharged, cancelled or expire.

Derivative financial instruments

The Company enters into various derivative financial instruments as part of the Company's strategy to manage its foreign currency and interest rate exposures. The Company also enters into equity derivative contracts to hedge certain future share-based payment expenses. The Company does not hold or issue derivative financial instruments for trading purposes.

All derivative financial instruments, including derivatives embedded in financial or non-financial contracts that are not closely related to the host contracts, are measured at fair value. The gain or loss that results from remeasurement at each reporting period is recognized in net income immediately unless the derivative is designated and effective as a hedging instrument, in which case the timing of the recognition in net income depends on the nature of the hedge relationship.

Embedded derivatives

Embedded derivatives (elements of contracts whose cash flows move independently from the host contract) are required to be separated and measured at their respective fair values unless certain criteria are met. The Company does not have any significant embedded derivatives in contracts that require separate accounting and disclosure.

Hedge accounting

Where hedge accounting can be applied, certain criteria are documented at the inception of the hedge and updated at each reporting date.

Fair-value hedges

For fair-value hedges, the carrying amount of the hedged item is adjusted for changes in fair value attributable to the hedged risk, and this adjustment is recognized in net income immediately. Changes in the fair value of the hedged item, to the extent that the hedging relationship is effective, are offset by changes in the fair value of the hedging derivative, which are also included in net income. When hedge accounting is discontinued, the carrying amount of the hedged item is no longer adjusted and the cumulative fair-value adjustments to the carrying amount of the hedged item are amortized to net income over the remaining term of the hedged item using the effective interest method.

Cash flow hedges

For cash flow hedges, the effective portion of the changes in the fair value of the hedging derivative, net of taxes, is recognized in OCI, while the ineffective and unhedged portions are recognized immediately in net income. Amounts recorded in Accumulated Other Comprehensive Income ("AOCI") are reclassified to net income in the periods when the hedged item affects net income. However, when a forecast transaction that is hedged results in the recognition of a non-financial asset or liability, the gains and losses previously recognized in AOCI are reclassified from AOCI and included in the initial measurement of the cost of the non-financial asset or liability.

When hedge accounting is discontinued, the amounts previously recognized in AOCI are reclassified to net income during the periods when the variability in the cash flows of the hedged item affects net income. Gains and losses on derivatives are reclassified immediately to net income when the hedged item is sold or terminated early. If hedge accounting is discontinued due to the hedged item no longer being expected to occur, the amount previously recognized in AOCI is reclassified immediately to net income.

The Company enters into foreign currency contracts to hedge the exposure against foreign currency risk on the future payment of foreign-currency-denominated inventory purchases and certain expenses. The changes in fair value of these contracts are included in OCI to the extent the hedges continue to be effective, excluding the time value component of foreign exchange options, which is included in net income. Once the inventory is received, the Company reclassifies the related AOCI amount to merchandise inventories and subsequent changes in the fair value of the foreign currency contracts are recorded in net income as they occur. When the expenses are incurred, the Company reclassifies the AOCI amount to the expense.

Cash and cash equivalents

Cash and cash equivalents are defined as cash plus highly liquid and rated certificates of deposit or commercial paper with an original term to maturity of three months or less.

Short-term investments

Short-term investments are investments in highly liquid and rated certificates of deposit, commercial paper or other securities, primarily Canadian and United States government securities and notes of other creditworthy parties, with an original term to maturity of more than three months and remaining term to maturity of less than one year.

Trade and other receivables

The allowance for impairment of trade and other receivables is established when there is objective evidence that the Company will not be able to collect all amounts due according to the original terms of the receivables. Significant financial difficulties of the debtor, probability that the debtor will enter bankruptcy or financial reorganization, and default or delinquency in payments are considered indicators that the trade receivable is impaired. The amount of the allowance is calculated as the difference between the asset's carrying amount and the present value of estimated future cash flows, discounted at the original effective interest rate. The carrying amount of the asset is reduced through the use of an allowance account, and the amount of the loss is recognized in selling, general and administrative expenses in the consolidated statements of income. When a trade receivable is deemed uncollectible, it is written off against the allowance account. Subsequent recoveries of amounts previously written off are recognized as a recovery in selling, general and administrative expenses in the consolidated statements of income.

Loans receivable

Credit card, personal and line of credit loans

Credit card, personal and line of credit loans are recognized when cash is advanced to a borrower. They are derecognized when the borrower repays its obligations, the loans are sold or written off or substantially all of the risks and rewards of ownership are transferred.

NOTES TO THE CONSOLIDATED FINANCIAL STATEMENTS

Losses for impaired loans are recognized when there is objective evidence that impairment of the loans has occurred. Impairment allowances are calculated on individual loans and on groups of loans assessed collectively. Impairment losses are recorded in cost of producing revenue in the consolidated statements of income. The carrying amount of impaired loans in the consolidated balance sheets is reduced through the use of impairment allowance accounts. Losses expected from future events are not recognized.

All individually significant loans receivable are assessed for specific impairment. All individually significant loans receivable found not to be specifically impaired are then collectively assessed for any impairment that has been incurred but not yet identified. Loans receivable that are not individually significant are collectively assessed for impairment by grouping together loans receivable with similar risk characteristics.

The Company uses a roll-rate methodology to calculate allowances for loans' receivables. This methodology employs statistical analysis of historical data and experience of delinquency and default to estimate the amount of loans that will eventually be written off as a result of events occurring before the reporting date, with certain adjustments for other relevant circumstances influencing the recoverability of the loans receivable. The estimated loss is the difference between the present value of the expected future cash flows, discounted at the original effective interest rate of the portfolio, and the carrying amount of the portfolio. Default rates, loss rates and the expected timing of future recoveries are regularly benchmarked against actual outcomes to ensure that they remain appropriate.

Dealer loans

Loans to Associate Dealers ("Dealers"), independent third-party operators of Canadian Tire Retail stores, are initially measured at fair value plus directly attributable transaction costs and are subsequently measured at their amortized cost using the effective interest method, less an allowance for impairment, if any.

Merchandise inventories

Merchandise inventories are carried at the lower of cost and net realizable value.

Cash consideration received from vendors is recognized as a reduction to the cost of related inventory unless the cash consideration received is either a reimbursement of incremental costs incurred by the Company or a payment for assets or services delivered to the vendor.

The cost of merchandise inventories is determined based on weighted average cost and includes costs incurred in bringing the merchandise inventories to their present location and condition. All inventories are finished goods.

Net realizable value is the estimated selling price of inventory during the normal course of business less estimated selling expenses.

Long-term investments

Investments in highly liquid and rated certificates of deposit, commercial paper or other securities with a remaining term to maturity of greater than one year are classified as long-term investments. The Company's exposure to credit, currency and interest rate risks related to other investments is disclosed in Note 5.

Intangible assets

Goodwill

Goodwill represents the excess of the cost of an acquisition over the fair value of the Company's share of the identifiable assets acquired and liabilities assumed in a business combination. Goodwill is measured at cost less any accumulated impairment and is not amortized.

Intangible assets

Intangible assets with finite useful lives are measured at cost and are amortized on a straight-line basis over their estimated useful lives, generally for a period of two to seven years. The estimated useful lives and amortization methods are reviewed annually with the effect of any changes in estimate being accounted for on a prospective basis.

Intangible assets with indefinite useful lives are measured at cost less any accumulated impairment and are not amortized.

Expenditures on research activities are expensed as incurred.

Investment property

Investment property is property held to earn rental income or for appreciation of capital or both. The Company has determined that properties it provides to its Dealers, franchisees and agents are not investment property as these relate to the Company's operating activities. This was determined based on certain criteria such as whether the Company provides significant ancillary services to the lessees of the property. The Company includes property that it leases to third parties (other than Dealers, franchisees or agents) in investment property.

Investment property is measured and depreciated in the same manner as property and equipment.

Property and equipment

Property and equipment is measured at cost less accumulated depreciation and any accumulated impairment. Land is measured at cost less any accumulated impairment. Properties in the course of construction are measured at cost less any accumulated impairment. The cost of an item of property or equipment comprises costs that can be directly attributed to its acquisition and initial estimates of the cost of dismantling and removing the item and restoring the site on which it is located.

Buildings, fixtures and equipment are depreciated using a declining balance method to their estimated residual value over their estimated useful lives. The estimated useful lives, amortization method and residual values are reviewed annually with the effect of any changes in estimate being accounted for on a prospective basis.

Leasehold improvements and lease inducements are amortized on a straight-line basis over the terms of the respective leases or useful life, if shorter.

Assets held under finance leases are depreciated on the same basis as owned assets. If there is no reasonable certainty that the Company will obtain ownership, by the end of the lease term, the asset is depreciated over the shorter of lease term and its useful life.

Depreciation and amortization rates are as follows:

Asset Category	Depreciation rate/term
Buildings	4-20%
Fixtures and equipment	5-40%
Leasehold improvements	Shorter of term of lease or useful life
Assets under finance lease	Shorter of term of lease or useful life

Leased assets

Leases are classified as finance leases whenever the terms of the lease transfer substantially all the risks and rewards of ownership to the lessee. All other leases are classified as operating leases.

Lessor

When the Company is the lessor in an operating lease, rental income and licence fees are recognized in net income on a straight-line basis over the term of the lease.

Lessee

When the Company is the lessee in an operating lease, rent payments are charged to net income on a straight-line basis over the term of the lease.

Assets under finance leases are recognized as assets of the Company at their fair value or, if lower, at the present value of the minimum lease payments, each determined at the inception of the lease. The corresponding liability is included in the consolidated balance sheets as a finance lease obligation. Lease payments are apportioned between finance costs and reduction of the lease obligations so as to achieve a constant rate of interest on the remaining balance of the liability.

Sale and leaseback

The accounting treatment of a sale and leaseback transaction is assessed based upon the substance of the transaction and whether the sale is made at the asset's fair value.

For sale and finance leasebacks, any gain or loss from the sale is deferred and amortized over the lease term. For sale and operating leasebacks, the assets are sold at fair value and, accordingly, the gain or loss from the sale is recognized immediately in net income.

Impairment of assets

The carrying amounts of property and equipment, investment property and intangible assets with finite useful lives are reviewed at the end of each reporting period to determine whether there are any indicators of impairment. If any such indicators exist, then the recoverable amount of the asset is estimated. Goodwill and intangible assets with indefinite useful lives and intangible assets not yet available for use are not amortized but are tested for impairment at least annually or whenever there is an indicator that the asset may be impaired.

Cash generating units

When it is not possible to estimate the recoverable amount of an individual asset, the Company estimates the recoverable amount of the CGU to which the asset belongs. The CGUs correspond to the smallest identifiable group of assets whose continuing use generates cash inflows that are largely independent of the cash inflows from other assets or groups of assets.

Goodwill acquired in a business combination is allocated to each of the CGUs (or groups of CGUs) expected to benefit from the synergies of the combination. Intangible assets with indefinite useful lives are allocated to the CGU to which they relate.

Determining the recoverable amount

An impairment loss is recognized when the carrying amount of an asset, or of the CGU to which it belongs, exceeds the recoverable amount. The recoverable amount of an asset or CGU is defined as the higher of its fair value less costs to sell ("FVLCS") and its value in use ("VIU").

In assessing VIU, the estimated future cash flows are discounted to their present value. Cash flows are discounted using a pre-tax discount rate that includes a risk premium specific to each line of business. The Company estimates cash flows before taxes based on the most recent actual results or budgets. Cash flows are then extrapolated over a period of up to five years, taking into account a terminal value calculated by discounting the final year in perpetuity. The growth rate applied to the terminal values is based on the Bank of Canada's target growth rate or a growth rate specific to the individual item being tested based on Management's estimate.

Recording impairments and reversal of impairments

Impairments and reversals of impairments are recognized in other income in the consolidated statements of income. Any impairment loss is allocated first to reduce the carrying amount of any goodwill allocated to the CGU and then to the other assets of the CGU. Impairments of goodwill cannot be reversed. Impairments of other assets recognized in prior periods are assessed at the end of each reporting period to determine if the indicators of impairment have reversed or no longer exist. An impairment is reversed if the estimated recoverable amount exceeds the carrying amount. The increased carrying amount of an asset attributable to a reversal of impairment may not exceed the carrying amount that would have been determined had no impairment been recognized in prior periods.

Assets classified as held for sale

Non-current assets and disposal groups are classified as assets held for sale when their carrying amount is to be recovered principally through a sale transaction rather than through continuing use. This condition is regarded as met only when the sale is highly probable and the asset (or disposal group) is available for immediate sale in its present condition. Management must be committed to the sale, and it should be expected to qualify for recognition as a completed sale within one year from the date of classification. Assets (and disposal groups) classified as held for sale are measured at the lower of the carrying amount or FVLCS. The fair value measurement of assets held for sale is categorized within Level 2 of fair value hierarchy (see Note 35.4 for definition of levels).

Borrowing costs

Borrowing costs directly attributable to the acquisition or construction of a qualifying asset are capitalized. Qualifying assets are those that require a minimum of three months to prepare for their intended use. All other borrowing costs are recognized in cost of producing revenue or in net finance costs in the consolidated statements of income in the period in which they occur.

Employee benefits

Short-term benefits

Short-term employee benefit obligations are measured on an undiscounted basis and are expensed as the related service is provided.

The Company recognizes a liability and an expense for short-term benefits such as bonuses, profit-sharing and employee stock purchases if the Company has a present legal obligation or constructive obligation to pay this amount as a result of past service provided by the employee and the obligation can be estimated reasonably.

Post-employment benefits

The Company provides certain health care, dental care, life insurance and other benefits but not pensions for certain retired employees pursuant to Company policy. The Company accrues the cost of these employee benefits over the periods in which the employees earn the benefits. The cost of employee benefits earned by employees is actuarially determined using the projected benefit method pro-rated on length of service and Management's best estimate of salary escalation, retirement ages of employees, employee turnover, life expectancy, and expected health and dental care costs. The costs are discounted at a rate that is based on market rates as at the measurement date. Actuarial gains and losses are immediately recorded in OCI.

The Company also provides post-employment benefits with respect to contributions to a Deferred Profit Sharing Plan ("DPSP").

Other long-term employee benefits include:

Termination benefits

Termination benefits are payable when employment is terminated by the Company before the normal retirement date or whenever an employee accepts voluntary redundancy in exchange for these benefits. The Company recognizes a provision for termination benefits when it is demonstrably committed to either terminating the employment of current employees according to a detailed formal plan without possibility of withdrawal or providing termination benefits as a result of an offer made to encourage voluntary redundancy.

Share-based payments

Stock options with tandem stock appreciation rights ("stock options") are granted with a feature that enables the employee to exercise the stock option or receive a cash payment equal to the difference between the market price of the Company's Class A Non-Voting Shares as at the exercise date and the exercise price of the stock option. These stock options are considered to be compound instruments. The fair value of compound instruments is measured at each reporting date, taking into account the terms and conditions on which the rights to cash or equity instruments are granted. As the fair value of the settlement in cash is the same as the fair value of the settlement as a traditional stock option, the fair value of the stock option is the same as the fair value of the debt component. The corresponding expense and liability are recognized over the respective vesting period.

The fair value of the amount payable to employees with respect to share unit plans and trust unit plans, which are settled in cash, is recorded as a liability over the period that the employees unconditionally become entitled to payment. The fair value of the liability is remeasured at each reporting date with the change in the liability being recognized in selling, general and administrative expenses in the consolidated statements of income.

Insurance reserve

Included in trade and other payables is an insurance reserve that consists of an amount determined from loss reports and individual cases and an amount, based on past experience, for losses incurred but not reported. These estimates are continually reviewed and are subject to the impact of future changes in such factors as claim severity and frequency. While Management believes that the amount is adequate, the ultimate liability may be in excess of or less than the amounts provided, and any adjustment will be reflected in net income the periods in which they become known.

The Company uses actuarial valuations in determining its reserve for outstanding losses and loss-related expenses using an appropriate reserving methodology for each line of business. The Company does not discount its liabilities for unpaid claims.

Provisions

A provision is recognized if, as a result of a past event, the Company has a present legal or constructive obligation that can be estimated reliably and it is probable that an outflow of economic benefits will be required to settle the obligation. The amount recognized as a provision is the best estimate of the consideration required to settle the present obligation at the end of the reporting period, taking into account risks and uncertainty of cash flows. Where the effect of discounting is material, provisions are determined by discounting the expected future cash flows at a pre-tax rate that reflects current market assessments of the time value of money and the risks specific to the liability.

Sales and warranty returns

The provision for sales and warranty returns relates to the Company's obligation for defective goods in current store inventories and defective goods sold to customers that have yet to be returned, as well as after sales service for replacement parts. Accruals for sales and warranty returns are estimated on the basis of historical returns and are recorded so as to allocate them to the same period the corresponding revenue is recognized. These accruals are reviewed regularly and updated to reflect Management's best estimate; however, actual returns could vary from these estimates.

Site restoration and decommissioning

Legal or constructive obligations associated with the removal of underground fuel storage tanks and site remediation costs on the retirement of certain property and equipment and with the termination of certain lease agreements are recognized in the period in which they are incurred when it is probable that an outflow of resources embodying economic benefits will be required and a reasonable estimate of the amount of the obligation can be made. The obligations are initially measured at the Company's best estimate, using an expected value approach, and are discounted to present value.

Onerous contracts

A provision for onerous contracts is recognized when the expected benefits to be derived by the Company from a contract are lower than the unavoidable costs of meeting its obligations under the contract. The provision is measured at the present value of the lower of the expected cost of terminating the contract or the expected net cost of continuing with the contract.

Customer loyalty

An obligation arises from the My Canadian Tire 'Money' customer loyalty program when the Company issues e-Canadian Tire 'Money' and when the Dealers pay the Company to acquire paper-based Canadian Tire 'Money', as the Dealers retain the right to return paper-based Canadian Tire Money to the Company for refund in cash. These obligations are measured at fair value by reference to the fair value of the awards for which they could be redeemed and based on the estimated probability of their redemption. The expense is recorded in selling, general and administrative expense in the consolidated statements of the income.

Debt

Debt is classified as current when the Company expects to settle the liability in its normal operating cycle, it holds the liability primarily for the purpose of trading, the liability is due to be settled within 12 months after the date of the consolidated balance sheets or it does not have an unconditional right to defer settlement of the liability for at least 12 months after the date of the consolidated balance sheets.

Share capital

Shares issued by the Company are recorded at the value of proceeds received. Repurchased shares are removed from equity. No gain or loss is recognized in net income on the purchase, sale, issue or cancellation of the Company's shares.

During the year, the Company changed its accounting policy relating to share repurchases, which resulted in the financial statements providing more reliable and relevant information. Under the new policy, share repurchases are charged to share capital at the average cost per share outstanding and the excess between the repurchase price and the average cost is first allocated to contributed surplus, with any remainder allocated to retained earnings. Previously, share repurchases were recorded as a reduction to share capital. As a result of this accounting policy change, equity was restated as follows:

(C$ in millions)	Increase (decrease)	
	2013	2012
Share capital	$ 125.9	30.5
Contributed surplus	(3.8)	(2.9)
Retained earnings	(122.1)	(27.6)

Dividends

Dividend distributions to the Company's shareholders are recognized as a liability in the consolidated balance sheets in the period in which the dividends are approved by the Company's Board of Directors.

Distributions

Distributions to non-controlling interests are recognized as a liability in the consolidated balance sheets in the period in which the distributions are declared.

Revenue

The Company recognizes revenue when the amount can be reliably measured, when it is probable that future economic benefits will flow to the entity and when specific criteria have been met for each of the Company's activities as described below.

Sale of goods

Revenue from the sale of goods includes merchandise sold to Dealers and Mark's Work Wearhouse Ltd. ("Mark's") and FGL Sports Ltd. ("FGL Sports") franchisees, the sale of gasoline through agents, and the sale of goods by Mark's, PartSource and FGL Sports corporate-owned stores to the general public. This revenue is recognized when the goods are delivered, less an estimate for the sales and warranty returns. Revenue from the sale of goods is measured at the fair value of the consideration received less an appropriate deduction for actual and expected returns, discounts, rebates and warranty and loyalty program costs, net of sales taxes.

Sales and warranty returns

If there is any uncertainty regarding the right of a customer to return goods, no revenue is recognized until the uncertainty is resolved. However, in the case of warranties, if warranty claims can be reasonably estimated, revenue is then recorded for the net amount.

Customer loyalty programs

Loyalty award credits issued as part of a sales transaction relating to the Company's Gas Advantage, Cash Advantage and Sport Chek MasterCard Rewards credit card programs result in revenue being deferred until the loyalty award is redeemed by the customer. The portion of the revenue that is deferred is the fair value of the award. The fair value of the award takes into account the amount for which the award credits could be sold separately, less the proportion of the award credits that are not expected to be redeemed by customers.

Interest income on loans receivable

Interest income includes interest charged on loans receivable and fees that are an integral part of the effective interest rate on financial instruments, such as annual credit card fees. Interest income on financial assets that are classified as loans and receivables is determined using the effective interest method.

Services rendered

Service revenue includes Roadside Assistance Club membership revenue; Home Services revenue; insurance premiums and reinsurance revenue; extended warranty contract fees; merchant, interchange and processing fees; cash advance fees; foreign exchange fees; and service charges on the loans receivable of the Financial Services operating segment, as well as Mark's clothing alteration revenue. Service revenue is recognized according to the contractual provisions of the arrangement, which is generally when the service is provided or over the contractual period.

Merchant, interchange and processing fees, cash advance fees and foreign exchange fees on credit card transactions are recognized as revenue at the time transactions are completed. Revenue from separately priced extended warranty contracts is recorded on a straight-line basis over the term of the contracts. Revenue from Home Services is recognized when the work order is complete.

Reinsurance premiums are recorded on an accrual basis and are included in net income on a pro rata basis over the life of the insurance contract, with the unearned portion deferred in the consolidated balance sheets. Premiums that are subject to adjustment are estimated based on available information. Any variances from the estimates are recorded in the periods in which they become known.

Royalties and licence fees

Royalties and licence fees include licence fees from petroleum agents and Dealers and royalties from Mark's and FGL Sports franchisees. Royalties and licence fee revenues are recognized as they are earned in accordance with the substance of the relevant agreement and are measured on an accrual basis.

Rental income

Rental income from operating leases where the Company is the lessor is recognized on a straight-line basis over the terms of the respective leases.

Vendor rebates

The Company records cash consideration received from vendors as a reduction in the price of vendors' products and recognizes it as a reduction to the cost of related inventory or, if the related inventory has been sold, to the cost of producing revenue. Certain exceptions apply where the cash consideration received is either a reimbursement of incremental selling costs incurred by the Company or a payment for assets or services delivered to the vendor, in which case the cost is reflected as a reduction in selling, general and administrative expenses.

The Company recognizes rebates that are at the vendor's discretion when the vendor either pays the rebates or agrees to pay them and payment is considered probable and is reasonably estimable.

Finance income and finance costs

Finance income comprises interest income on funds invested (including available-for-sale financial assets). Interest income is recognized as it accrues using the effective interest method.

Finance costs comprises interest expense on borrowings (including borrowings relating to the Dealer Loan Program), unwinding of the discount on provisions and impairment recognized on financial assets. Interest on deposits is recorded in cost of producing revenue in the consolidated statements of income.

Income taxes

The income tax expense for the year comprises current and deferred income tax. Income tax expense is recognized in net income except to the extent that it relates to items recognized either in OCI or directly in equity. In this case, the income tax expense is recognized in OCI or in equity, respectively.

The income tax expense is calculated on the basis of the tax laws enacted or substantively enacted at the date of the consolidated balance sheets in the countries where the Company operates and generates taxable income.

Deferred income taxes is recognized using the liability method on unused tax losses, unused tax benefits and temporary differences arising between the tax bases of assets and liabilities and their carrying amounts in these consolidated financial statements. However, deferred income taxes is not accounted for if it arises from initial recognition of goodwill or initial recognition of an asset or liability in a transaction other than a business combination that at the time of the transaction affects neither accounting nor taxable income. Deferred income taxes is determined using tax rates (and laws) that have been enacted or substantively enacted at the date of the consolidated balance sheets and are expected to apply when the related deferred income tax asset is realized or the deferred income tax liability is settled.

Deferred income tax assets are recognized only to the extent that it is probable that future taxable income will be available against which the temporary differences can be utilized. Deferred income tax liabilities are provided on temporary differences arising on investments in subsidiaries and associates, except where the timing of the reversal of the temporary difference is controlled by the Company and it is probable that the temporary difference will not reverse in the foreseeable future.

Earnings per share attributable to owners of Canadian Tire Corporation

Basic earnings per share attributable to owners of the Company is calculated by dividing the net income attributable to owners of the Company by the weighted average number of Common and Class A Non-Voting shares outstanding during the reporting period. Diluted earnings per share attributable to the owners of the Company are calculated by adjusting the net income attributable to owners of the Company and the weighted average number of shares outstanding for the effects of all potentially dilutive equity instruments, which comprise employee stock options. Net income attributable to owners of the Company is the same for both the basic and diluted earnings per share calculations.

Non-controlling interests

When the proportion of the equity held by non-controlling interests changes, the Company adjusts the carrying amounts of the controlling and non-controlling interests to reflect the changes in their relative interest in the subsidiary. The Company recognizes directly in equity any difference between the amount by which the non-controlling interests are adjusted and the fair value of the consideration paid or received, and attribute it to the owners of the Company.

Operating segments

An operating segment is a component of the Company that engages in business activities from which it may earn revenues and incur expenses, including revenues and expenses that relate to transactions with any of the Company's other operations, and for which discrete financial information is available. Segment operating results are reviewed regularly by the Company's Chief Operating Decision Maker ("CODM") to make decisions about resources allocated to the segment and to assess the segment's performance.

4. Capital management

The Company's objectives when managing capital are:
- ensuring sufficient liquidity to support its financial obligations and execute its operating and strategic plans;
- maintaining healthy liquidity reserves and access to capital; and
- minimizing the after-tax cost of capital while taking into consideration current and future industry, market and economic risks and conditions.

The definition of capital varies from company to company, industry to industry and for different purposes. In the process of managing the Company's capital, Management includes the following items in its definition of capital, which includes Glacier Credit Card Trust ("GCCT") indebtedness but excludes Franchise Trust indebtedness:

(C$ in millions)	2014	% of total	2013[1]	% of total
Capital components				
Deposits	$ 950.7	**9.1%**	$ 1,178.4	11.6%
Short-term borrowings	199.8	**1.9%**	120.3	1.2%
Current portion of long-term debt	587.5	**5.6%**	272.2	2.6%
Long-term debt	2,131.6	**20.4%**	2,339.1	23.0%
Long-term deposits	1,286.2	**12.3%**	1,152.0	11.3%
Total debt	$ 5,155.8	**49.3%**	$ 5,062.0	49.7%
Redeemable financial instrument	517.0	**4.9%**	–	0.0%
Share capital	695.5	**6.8%**	712.9	7.0%
Contributed surplus	2.9	**0.0%**	2.4	0.0%
Retained earnings	4,075.1	**39.0%**	4,404.6	43.3%
Total capital under management	**$ 10,446.3**	**100.0%**	$ 10,181.9	100.0%

[1] Refer to Note 3 for details of accounting policy change relating to Share capital.

The Company monitors its capital structure through measuring various debt-to-capitalization and debt-to-earnings ratios and ensures its ability to service debt and meet other fixed obligations by tracking its interest and other fixed-charge coverage ratios.

The Company manages its capital structure to maintain an investment-grade rating from two credit rating agencies. Management calculates its ratios to approximate the methodology of debt-rating agencies and other market participants on a current and prospective basis. To assess its effectiveness in managing capital, Management monitors these ratios against targeted ranges.

In order to maintain or adjust the capital structure, the Company has the flexibility to adjust the amount of dividends paid to shareholders, purchase shares for cancellation pursuant to a normal course issuer bid program ("NCIB"), issue new shares, repay debt, issue new debt, issue new debt with different characteristics to replace existing debt, engage in additional sale and leaseback transactions of real estate properties and increase or decrease the amount of sales of co-ownership interests in loans receivable to GCCT.

The Company has in place various policies to manage capital, including a leverage and liquidity policy, an interest rate risk management policy and a securities and derivatives policy. As part of the overall management of capital, Management and the Audit Committee of the Board of Directors review the Company's compliance with, and performance against, these policies. In addition, periodic reviews of the policies are performed to ensure consistency with the risk tolerances.

Key financial covenants of the existing debt agreements are reviewed by Management on an ongoing basis to monitor compliance with the agreements.

The key covenants are as follows:
- a requirement to maintain, at all times, a specified minimum ratio of consolidated net tangible assets to the outstanding principal amount of all consolidated funded obligations (as defined in the respective debt agreements, which exclude the assets and liabilities of GCCT and Franchise Trust); and
- a limit on the amount available for distribution to shareholders whereby the Company is restricted from distributions (including dividends and redemptions or purchases of shares) exceeding, among other things, its accumulated net income over a defined period.

The Company was in compliance with these key covenants as at January 3, 2015 and December 28, 2013. Under these covenants, the Company currently has sufficient flexibility to fund business growth and maintain or amend dividend rates within its existing dividend policy.

In addition, the Company is required to comply with regulatory requirements for capital associated with the operations of Canadian Tire Bank ("Bank"), a federally chartered bank, and other regulatory requirements that have an impact on its business operations.

The Bank manages its capital under guidelines established by the Office of the Superintendent of Financial Institutions of Canada ("OSFI"). OSFI's regulatory capital guidelines are based on the international Basel Committee on Banking Supervision ("BCBS") framework entitled Basel III: A Global Regulatory Framework for More Resilient Banks and Banking Systems ("Basel III"), which came into effect in Canada on January 1, 2013, and measures capital in relation to credit, market and operational risks. The Bank has various capital policies and procedures and controls, including an Internal Capital Adequacy Assessment Process ("ICAAP"), which it utilizes to achieve its goals and objectives.

The Bank's objectives include:
- providing sufficient capital to maintain the confidence of investors and depositors; and
- being an appropriately capitalized institution, as measured internally, defined by regulatory authorities and compared with the Bank's peers.

OSFI's regulatory capital guidelines under Basel III allow for two tiers of capital. As at December 31, 2014 (the Bank's fiscal year-end), Common Equity Tier 1 ("CET1") capital includes common shares, retained earnings and accumulated other comprehensive income. The Bank currently does not hold any additional Tier 1 or Tier 2 capital instruments. Therefore, the Bank's CET1 is equal to its Tier 1 and total regulatory capital. Risk-weighted assets ("RWA") include all on-balance-sheet assets weighted for the risk inherent in each type of asset, as well as an operational risk component based on a percentage of average risk-weighted revenues, and a market risk component for assets held in the trading book for on and off-balance sheet financial instruments held in a foreign currency. For the purposes of calculating RWA, securitization transactions are considered off-balance-sheet transactions and therefore securitization assets are not included in the RWA calculation. Assets are included in the trading book when they are held either with trading intent or to hedge other elements in the trading book.

During the 12 months ended December 31, 2014 and 2013, the Bank complied with all regulatory capital guidelines established by OSFI and its internal targets as determined by its ICAAP.

5. Financial risk management

5.1 Overview
The Company has exposure to the following risks from its use of financial instruments:
- credit risk;
- liquidity risk; and
- market risk (including foreign currency and interest rate risk).

This note presents information about the Company's exposure to each of the above risks and the Company's objectives, policies and processes for measuring and managing risk. Further quantitative disclosures are included throughout these consolidated financial statements and notes thereto.

5.2 Risk management framework
The Company's financial risk management policies are established to identify and analyze the risks faced by the Company, to set acceptable risk tolerance limits and controls and to monitor risks and adherence to limits. The financial risk management policies and systems are reviewed regularly to ensure they remain consistent with the objectives and risk tolerance acceptable to the Company and current market trends and conditions. The Company, through its training and management standards and procedures, aims to uphold a disciplined and constructive control environment in which all employees understand their roles and obligations.

5.3 Credit risk
Credit risk is the risk of financial loss to the Company if a customer or counterparty to a financial instrument fails to meet its contractual obligations and arises principally from the Company's credit card customers, Dealer network, investment securities and financial derivative instrument counterparties.

The Company's maximum exposure to credit risk, over and above amounts recognized in the consolidated balance sheets, include the following:

(C$ in millions)	2014	2013
Undrawn loan commitments	$ 9,463.7	$ 10,556.8
Guarantees	605.2	600.4
Total	$ 10,068.9	$ 11,157.2

Refer to Note 11 for information on the credit quality and performance of loans receivables.

5.3.1 Securities and derivatives
The Company has a Securities and Derivatives Policy in place for management of the various risks (including counterparty risk) related to investment activity and use of financial derivatives. The Company's credit exposure of its investment portfolio is spread across financial institutions, provincial and federal governments and, to a lesser extent, corporate issuers, with limitations as to the amount, term to maturity and industry concentration levels.

The Company limits its exposure to credit risk by investing only in highly liquid and rated certificates of deposit, commercial paper or other approved securities and only with counterparties that are dual rated and have a credit rating in the "A" category or better.

The Company limits its credit exposure to financial derivatives by transacting only with highly rated counterparties and managing within specific limits for credit exposure, notional amounts and term to maturity.

5.3.2 Credit enhancement and guarantees provided
The Company may be required to provide credit enhancement for individual Dealer's borrowings in the form of standby letters of credit (the "LCs") or guarantees of third-party bank debt agreements in respect of the financing programs available to the Dealers (Note 37).

5.4 Liquidity risk

Liquidity risk is the risk that the Company will encounter difficulty in meeting the obligations associated with its financial liabilities that are settled by delivering cash or another financial asset. The Company's approach to managing liquidity is to ensure, as far as possible, that it will always have sufficient liquidity to meet its liabilities when due, under both normal and reasonably stressed conditions. The Company has in place a leverage and liquidity policy to manage its exposure to liquidity risk.

In addition to the leverage and liquidity policy, the Company has in place an Asset Liability Management Board policy specific to the Bank. It is the Bank's objective to ensure the availability of adequate funds by maintaining a strong liquidity management framework and to satisfy all applicable regulatory and statutory requirements. The Company uses a detailed consolidated cash flow forecast model to regularly monitor its near-term and longer-term cash flow requirements, which assists in optimizing its short-term cash and bank indebtedness position and evaluating longer-term funding strategies.

As at January 3, 2015, the Company had $3.9 billion in committed bank lines of credit of which $1.2 billion is available to the Company under a five-year syndicated credit facility maturing July 2019, $300 million is available pursuant to 365-day bilateral credit agreements maturing December 2015, $2.25 billion is available to CT Bank through a credit card funding facility maturing October 2017, and $200 million is available to CT REIT under a four-year syndicated revolving credit facility maturing October 2017.

In addition to the bank lines of credit, the Company has access to additional funding sources. A commercial paper program and medium-term notes program for the issuance of $750 million is available to the Company to April 2015. Assets of the Bank are funded through securitization of credit card receivables through GCCT, broker guaranteed investment certificate ("GIC"), retail GIC deposits and high-interest savings ("HIS") account deposits.

The following table summarizes the Company's contractual maturity for its financial liabilities, including both principal and interest payments:

(C$ in millions)	2015	2016	2017	2018	2019	Thereafter	Total
Non-derivative financial liabilities							
Bank indebtedness	$ 14.3	$ –	$ –	$ –	$ –	$ –	$ 14.3
Deposits[1]	960.0	192.0	322.3	357.9	414.0	–	2,246.2
Trade and other payables	1,834.9	–	–	–	–	–	1,834.9
Short-term borrowings	199.8	–	–	–	–	–	199.8
Loans payable	604.4	–	–	–	–	–	604.4
Long-term debt	565.8	–	634.9	264.6	500.0	550.0	2,515.3
Finance lease obligations	20.7	17.0	14.0	12.1	10.5	78.7	153.0
Mortgages	1.2	1.2	1.2	17.1	37.6	–	58.3
Interest payments[2]	132.3	113.6	97.4	76.0	54.8	461.8	935.9
Total	$ 4,333.4	$ 323.8	$ 1,069.8	$ 727.7	$ 1,016.9	$ 1,090.5	$ 8,562.1

[1] Deposits exclude the GIC broker fee discount of $9.3 million.

[2] Includes interest payments on deposits, short-term borrowings, loans payable, long-term debt and finance lease obligations.

It is not expected that the cash flows included in the maturity analysis could occur significantly earlier or at significantly different amounts except for deposits. The cash flows from deposits are not expected to vary significantly provided the expected cash flows from customers maintain a stable or increasing balance.

5.5 Market risk

Market risk is the risk that changes in market prices, such as foreign exchange rates, interest rates and equity prices, will affect the Company's income or the value of its holdings of financial instruments. The objective of market risk management is to manage market risk exposures within acceptable parameters while optimizing the return. The Company has in place foreign exchange, interest rate and equity risk management policies to manage its exposure to market risk. These policies establish guidelines on how the Company is to manage the market risk inherent to the business and provide mechanisms to ensure business transactions are executed in accordance with established limits, processes and procedures.

All such transactions are carried out within the guidelines established in the respective financial risk management policies as approved by the Board of Directors. Generally, the Company seeks to apply hedge accounting in order to manage volatility in its net income.

5.5.1 Foreign currency risk

The Company has significant demand for foreign currencies, primarily United States ("U.S.") dollars, due to its global sourcing activities. The Company's exposure to foreign exchange rate risk is managed through a comprehensive Foreign Exchange Risk Management Policy that sets forth specific guidelines and parameters, including monthly hedge percentage guidelines, for entering into foreign exchange hedge transactions for anticipated U.S.dollar-denominated purchases. The Company enters into foreign exchange contracts, primarily in U.S. dollars, to hedge future purchases of foreign-currency-denominated goods and services. The Company's exposure to a sustained movement in the currency markets is affected by competitive forces and future prevailing market conditions.

5.5.2 Interest rate risk

The Company has a policy in place whereby a minimum of 75 per cent of its long-term debt (term greater than one year) and lease obligations must be at fixed interest rates. The Company is in compliance with this policy. The Company may enter into interest rate swap contracts to manage its current and anticipated exposure to interest rate price risk. The Company had no interest rate swap contracts outstanding at January 3, 2015.

A one per cent change in interest rates would not materially affect the Company's net income or equity as the Company has minimal floating interest rate exposure as the indebtedness of the Company is predominantly at fixed rates. The Company's exposure to interest rate changes is predominantly driven by the Financial Services business to the extent that the interest rates on future GIC deposits, HIS account deposits, tax free savings account ("TFSA") deposits and securitization transactions are market-dependent. Partially offsetting this will be rates charged on credit cards and future liquidity pool investment rates available to the Bank.

6. Operating segments

The Company has three reportable operating segments: Retail, CT REIT, and Financial Services. The reportable operating segments are strategic business units offering different products and services. They are separately managed due to their distinct nature. The following summary describes the operations in each of the Company's reportable segments:

- Retail comprises the Living, Playing, Fixing, Automotive, Seasonal, Apparel and Sporting Goods categories. The retail business is conducted through a number of banners, including Canadian Tire, Canadian Tire Gas ("Petroleum"), Mark's, PartSource, and various FGL Sports banners. Retail also includes the Dealer Loan Program (the portion [silo] of Franchise Trust that issues loans to Dealers), a financing program established to provide an efficient and cost-effective way for Dealers to access the majority of the financing required for their store operations. Non-CT REIT real estate is included in Retail.
- CT REIT is an unincorporated, closed-end real estate investment trust. CT REIT holds a geographically diversified portfolio of properties comprised largely of Canadian Tire banner stores, Canadian Tire anchored retail developments, a mixed use commercial development and two distribution centres.
- Financial Services markets a range of Canadian Tire-branded credit cards, including the Canadian Tire Options MasterCard, the Cash Advantage MasterCard, the Gas Advantage MasterCard and the Sport Chek MasterCard. Financial Services also markets insurance and warranty products and processes credit card transactions with respect to purchases made in Canadian Tire associate stores and petroleum outlets. Financial Services includes Canadian Tire Bank, a federally regulated financial institution that manages and finances the Company's consumer MasterCard, Visa and retail credit card portfolios, as well as an existing block of Canadian Tire-branded personal loan and line of credit portfolios. The Bank also offers and markets HIS account deposits, TFSA deposits and GIC deposits, both directly and through third-party brokers. Financial Services also includes GCCT, a financing program established to purchase co-ownership interests in the Company's credit card loans. GCCT issues debt to third-party investors to fund its purchases.

Performance is measured based on segment income before income taxes, as included in the internal management reports reviewed by the Company's CODM. Management has determined that this measure is the most relevant in evaluating segment results.

Information regarding the results of each reportable operating segment is as follows:

					2014
(C$ in millions)	Retail	CT REIT	Financial Services	Eliminations and adjustments	Total
External revenue	$ 11,298.9	$ 12.6	$ 1,059.6	$ 91.8	$ 12,462.9
Intercompany revenue	5.7	332.2	16.1	(354.0)	–
Total revenue	11,304.6	344.8	1,075.7	(262.2)	12,462.9
Cost of producing revenue	8,033.7	–	435.2	(52.0)	8,416.9
Gross margin	3,270.9	344.8	640.5	(210.2)	4,046.0
Other income (expense)	110.4	–	(1.6)	(97.8)	11.0
Selling, general and administrative expenses	2,861.7	85.0	300.8	(194.6)	3,052.9
Net finance (income) costs	(11.9)	82.7	(6.9)	45.0	108.9
Change in fair value of redeemable financial instrument	–	–	–	(17.0)	(17.0)
Fair value adjustment on investment properties	–	141.2	–	(141.2)	–
Income before income taxes	$ 531.5	$ 318.3	$ 345.0	(316.6)	$ 878.2
Items included in the above:					
Depreciation and amortization	$ 304.4	$ –	$ 8.8	$ 59.1	$ 372.3
Interest income	116.9	0.3	783.6	(97.3)	803.5
Interest expense	90.6	83.0	109.8	(98.0)	185.4

NOTES TO THE CONSOLIDATED FINANCIAL STATEMENTS

(C$ in millions)	Retail	CT REIT	Financial Services	Eliminations and adjustments	2013 Total
External revenue	$ 10,690.2	$ 1.7	$ 1,010.4	$ 83.3	$ 11,785.6
Intercompany revenue	1.4	61.3	15.5	(78.2)	–
Total revenue	10,691.6	63.0	1,025.9	5.1	11,785.6
Cost of producing revenue	7,679.7	–	430.5	(46.9)	8,063.3
Gross margin	3,011.9	63.0	595.4	52.0	3,722.3
Other income (expense)	15.2	–	0.4	(18.6)	(3.0)
Selling, general and administrative expenses	2,509.4	16.1	278.5	24.9	2,828.9
Net finance costs (income)	54.1	15.4	(2.7)	39.0	105.8
Fair value adjustment on investment properties	–	(0.5)	–	0.5	–
Income before income taxes	$ 463.6	$ 31.0	$ 320.0	$ (30.0)	$ 784.6
Items included in the above:					
Depreciation and amortization	$ 323.5	$ –	$ 10.3	$ 11.5	$ 345.3
Interest income	53.2	0.1	740.1	(19.2)	774.2
Interest expense	82.4	15.5	112.4	(19.2)	191.1

The eliminations and adjustments include the following items:

- reclassifications of certain revenues and costs in the Financial Services segment to finance income and finance costs;
- reclassifications of revenues and operating expenses to reflect loyalty program accounting in accordance with IFRIC 13 for the Company's Canadian Tire Money programs;
- conversion from CT REIT's fair value investment property valuation policy to the Company's cost model, including the recording of depreciation; and
- inter-segment eliminations and adjustments including intercompany rent, property management fees, credit card processing fees and the change in fair value of the redeemable financial instrument.

Capital expenditures by reportable operating segment are as follows:

(C$ in millions)	Retail	CT REIT	Financial Services	2014 Total
Capital expenditures[1]	$ 524.5	$ 183.4	$ 13.9	$ 721.8

[1] Capital expenditures are presented on an accrual basis and include software additions, but exclude acquisitions related to business combinations of $6.6 million and intellectual properties of $21.4 million.

(C$ in millions)	Retail	CT REIT	Financial Services	2013 Total
Capital expenditures[1]	$ 528.2	$ 9.0	$ 6.9	$ 544.1

[1] Capital expenditures are presented on an accrual basis and include software additions, but exclude acquisitions related to business combinations and intellectual properties of $82.7 million.

Total assets by reporting operating segment are as follows:

(C$ in millions)	2014	2013[2]
Retail	$ 11,066.5	$ 10,509.0
CT REIT	4,017.4	3,603.2
Financial Services	5,553.6	5,384.6
Eliminations and adjustments	(6,084.3)	(5,866.8)
Total assets[1]	$ 14,553.2	$ 13,630.0

[1] The Company employs a shared services model for several of its back-office functions, including finance, information technology, human resources and legal. As a result, expenses relating to these functions are allocated on a systematic and rational basis to the reportable operating segments. The associated assets and liabilities are not allocated among segments in the presented measures of segmented assets and liabilities.

[2] The prior year's figures have been reclassified to correspond with current year's presentation.

NOTES TO THE CONSOLIDATED FINANCIAL STATEMENTS

Total liabilities by reporting operating segment are as follows:

(C$ in millions)	2014	2013[2]
Retail	$ 4,137.1	$ 4,322.1
CT REIT	2,015.3	1,822.9
Financial Services	4,576.3	4,408.3
Eliminations and adjustments	(1,806.3)	(2,373.2)
Total liabilities[1]	$ 8,922.4	$ 8,180.1

[1] The Company employs a shared services model for several of its back-office functions, including finance, information technology, human resources and legal. As a result, expenses relating to these functions are allocated on a systematic and rational basis to the reportable operating segments. The associated assets and liabilities are not allocated among segments in the presented measures of segmented assets and liabilities.

[2] The prior year's figures have been reclassified to correspond with current year's presentation.

The eliminations and adjustments include the following items:
- CT REIT uses the fair value for its investment properties. The adjustment to convert to the Company's cost model is included in eliminations and adjustments; and
- inter-segment eliminations.

7. Joint arrangement and business combinations

7.1 Joint arrangement of Canada Square

On July 17, 2014, CT REIT acquired a one-third interest in Canada Square, a mixed-use commercial development in Toronto, pursuant to a co-ownership arrangement (the "Co-ownership"). The Co-ownership is a joint arrangement as the material decisions about relevant activities require unanimous consent of the co-owners. This joint arrangement is a joint operation as each co-owner has rights to the assets and obligations relating to the Co-ownership. Accordingly, CT REIT recognizes its proportionate share of the assets, liabilities, revenue and expenses of the Co-ownership in its financial statements.

7.2 Acquisition of Pro Hockey Life Sporting Goods Inc. ("PHL")

In August 2013, the Company acquired 100 per cent of the issued and outstanding shares of PHL, for total consideration of $58 million. PHL is a Canadian retailer of sporting goods, with 23 urban, high-end hockey stores operating in five provinces across Canada under various trade names. The acquisition was a natural extension of the Company's sporting goods business.

The fair value of net identifiable assets acquired and liabilities assumed as at the acquisition date were $10.4 million, which included $14.1 million of intangible assets. Goodwill of $47.6 million was recognized as at the acquisition date. The goodwill was attributable mainly to the expected growth potential of the expanded customer base of PHL stores, the network of stores and access to the urban high-end customer segment within the hockey equipment market.

7.3 Other business combinations

During the year ended January 3, 2015, the Company acquired various franchise operations for total consideration of $7.3 million, of which $1 million was payable at January 3, 2015. The fair value of the net assets acquired was $3.3 million, resulting in goodwill recognized of $4 million.

During the year ended December 28, 2013, the Company acquired various franchise operations for total consideration of $32.8 million, of which $15.5 million was payable at December 28, 2013. The fair value of the net assets acquired was $24.4 million, resulting in goodwill recognized of $8.4 million.

8. Cash and cash equivalents

Cash and cash equivalents comprise the following:

(C$ in millions)	2014	2013
Cash	$ 134.5	$ 91.5
Cash equivalents	521.0	546.1
Restricted cash and cash equivalents[1]	6.6	5.6
Total cash and cash equivalents[2]	662.1	643.2
Bank indebtedness	(14.3)	(69.0)
Cash and cash equivalents, net of bank indebtedness	$ 647.8	$ 574.2

[1] Relates to GCCT and is restricted for the purpose of paying out note holders and additional funding costs.

[2] Included in cash and cash equivalents are amounts held in reserve in support of Financial Services' liquidity and regulatory requirements. See Note 34.1.

NOTES TO THE CONSOLIDATED FINANCIAL STATEMENTS

9. Short-term investments

(C$ in millions)	2014	2013
Short-term investments[1]	$ 287.5	$ 415.0
Restricted short-term investments[2]	1.6	1.6
	$ 289.1	$ 416.6

[1] Included in short-term investments are amounts held in reserve in support of Financial Services' liquidity and regulatory requirements. See Note 34.1.
[2] Relates to GCCT and is restricted for the purpose of paying out note holders and additional funding costs.

10. Trade receivables and other

(C$ in millions)	2014	2013
Trade receivables and other	$ 736.6	$ 685.5
Derivatives	143.4	72.9
Total financial assets	880.0	758.4
Other	0.2	0.1
	$ 880.2	$ 758.5

Trade receivables are primarily from Dealers and franchisees, a large and geographically dispersed group whose receivables, individually, generally comprise less than one per cent of the total balance outstanding.

Receivables from Dealers are in the normal course of business, and include cost-sharing and financing arrangements. The net average credit period on sale of goods is between one and 120 days. Interest (ranging from 0 per cent to prime plus 5 per cent) is charged on amounts past due.

11. Loans receivable

Quantitative information about the Company's loans receivable portfolio is as follows:

	Total principal amount of receivables		Average balance[1]	
(C$ in millions)	2014	2013	2014	2013
Credit card loans	$ 4,862.9	$ 4,522.7	$ 4,563.4	$ 4,253.3
Line of credit loans	5.5	6.5	5.9	7.0
Personal loans[2]	0.3	0.1	0.2	0.2
Total Financial Services' loans receivable	4,868.7	4,529.3	$ 4,569.5	$ 4,260.5
Dealer loans[3]	604.4	611.2		
Other loans	5.5	6.4		
Total loans receivable	5,478.6	5,146.9		
Less: long-term portion[4]	573.1	577.2		
Current portion of loans receivable	$ 4,905.5	$ 4,569.7		

[1] Amounts shown are net of allowance for loan impairment.
[2] Personal loans are unsecured loans that are provided to qualified existing credit card holders for terms of one to five years. Personal loans have fixed monthly payments of principal and interest; however, the personal loans can be repaid at any time without penalty.
[3] Dealer loans issued by Franchise Trust (Note 24)
[4] The long-term portion of loans receivable is included in long-term receivables and other assets and includes Dealer Loans of $568.2 million (2013 – $571.6 million)

For the year ended January 3, 2015, cash received from interest earned on credit cards and loans was $732.4 million (2013 – $690.1 million).

The carrying amount of loans includes loans to Dealers that are secured by the assets of the respective Dealer corporations. The Company's exposure to loans receivable credit risk resides at Franchise Trust and at the Bank. Credit risk at the Bank is influenced mainly by the individual characteristics of each credit card customer. The Bank uses sophisticated credit scoring models, monitoring technology and collection modelling techniques to implement and manage strategies, policies and limits that are designed to control risk. Loans receivable are generated by a large and geographically-dispersed group of customers. Current credit exposure is limited to the loss that would be incurred if all of the Bank's counterparties were to default at the same time.

NOTES TO THE CONSOLIDATED FINANCIAL STATEMENTS

A continuity schedule of the Company's allowances for loans receivable[1] is as follows:

(C$ in millions)	2014	2013
Balance, beginning of year	$ 121.4	$ 110.7
Impairments for credit losses, net of recoveries	279.7	267.0
Recoveries	59.8	59.1
Write-offs	(347.7)	(315.4)
Balance, end of year	$ 113.2	$ 121.4

[1] Loans include credit card loans, personal loans and line of credit loans. No allowances for credit losses have been made with respect to Franchise Trust.

The Company's allowances for credit losses are maintained at levels that are considered adequate to absorb future credit losses.

The Company's aging of the loans receivable that are past due, but not impaired, is as follows:

(C$ in millions)	2014			2013		
	1-90 days	> 90 days	Total	1-90 days	> 90 days	Total
Loans receivable[1]	$ 342.9	$ 60.4	$ 403.3	$ 308.9	$ 58.0	$ 366.9

[1] No past due loans for Franchise Trust and FGL Sports.

A loan is considered past due when the counterparty has not made a payment by the contractual due date. Credit card and line of credit loan balances are written off when a payment is 180 days in arrears. Line of credit loans are considered impaired when a payment is over 90 days in arrears and are written off when a payment is 180 days in arrears. Personal loans are considered impaired when a payment is over 90 days in arrears and are written off when a payment is 365 days in arrears. No collateral is held against loans receivable, except for loans to Dealers, as discussed above.

Transfers of financial assets
Glacier Credit Card Trust

GCCT is a special purpose entity that was created to securitize credit card loans receivable. As at January 3, 2015, the Bank has transferred co-ownership interest in credit card loans receivable to GCCT but has retained substantially all of the credit risk associated with the transferred assets. Due to the retention of substantially all of the risks and rewards on these assets, the Bank continues to recognize these assets within loans receivable, and the transfers are accounted for as secured financing transactions. The associated liability as at January 3, 2015, secured by these assets, includes the commercial paper and term notes on the consolidated balance sheets and is carried at amortized cost. The Bank is exposed to the majority of ownership risks and rewards of GCCT and, hence, it is consolidated. The carrying amount of the assets approximates their fair value. The difference between the credit card loans receivable transferred and the associated liabilities is shown below:

(C$ in millions)	2014		2013	
	Carrying amount	Fair value	Carrying amount	Fair value
Credit card loans receivable transferred[1]	$ 1,785.6	$ 1,785.6	$ 1,535.5	$ 1,535.5
Associated liabilities	1,780.4	1,819.6	1,532.4	1,546.1
Net position	$ 5.2	$ (34.0)	$ 3.1	$ (10.6)

[1] The fair value measurement of credit card loans receivable is categorized within Level 2 of the fair value hierarchy (see Note 35.4 for definition of levels).

For legal purposes, the co-ownership interests in the Bank's receivables owned by GCCT have been sold at law to GCCT and are not available to the creditors of the Bank.

The Bank has not identified any factors arising from current market circumstances that could lead to a need for the Bank to extend liquidity and/or credit support to GCCT over and above the existing arrangements or that could otherwise change the substance of the Bank's relationship with GCCT. There have been no changes in the capital structure of GCCT since the Bank's assessment for consolidation.

Franchise Trust

The consolidated financial statements include a portion (silo) of Franchise Trust, a legal entity sponsored by a third-party bank that originates and services loans to Dealers for their purchases of inventory and fixed assets (the "Dealer loans"). The Company has arranged for several major Canadian banks to provide standby LCs to Franchise Trust as credit support for the Dealer loans. Franchise Trust has sold all of its rights in the LCs and outstanding Dealer loans to other independent trusts set up by major Canadian banks (the "Co-owner Trusts") that raise funds in the capital markets to finance their purchase of these undivided co-ownership interests. Due to the retention of substantially all of the risks and rewards relating to these Dealer loans, the transfers are accounted for as secured financing transactions and, accordingly, the Company continues to recognize the current portion of these assets in loans receivable and the long-term portion in long-term receivables and other assets and records the associated liability secured by these assets as loans payable, being the loans that Franchise Trust has incurred to fund the Dealer loans. The Dealer loans and loans payable are initially recorded at fair value and subsequently carried at amortized cost.

(C$ in millions)	2014		2013	
	Carrying amount	Fair value	Carrying amount	Fair value
Dealer loans[1]	$ 604.4	$ 604.4	$ 611.2	$ 611.2
Associated liabilities	604.4	604.4	611.2	611.1
Net position	$ –	$ –	$ –	$ 0.1

[1] The fair value measurement of dealer loans is categorized within Level 2 of the fair value hierarchy (see Note 35.4 for definition of levels).

The Dealer loans have been sold at law and are not available to the creditors of the Company. Loans payable are not legal liabilities of the Company.

In the event that a Dealer defaults on a loan, the Company has the right to purchase such loan from the Co-owner Trusts, at which time the Co-owner Trusts will assign such Dealer's debt instrument and related security documentation to the Company. The assignment of this documentation provides the Company with first-priority security rights over all of such Dealer's assets, subject to certain prior ranking statutory claims.

In most cases, the Company would expect to recover any payments made to purchase a defaulted loan, including any associated expenses. In the event the Company does not choose to purchase a defaulted Dealer loan, the Co-owner Trusts may draw against the LCs.

The Co-owner Trusts may also draw against the LCs to cover any shortfalls in certain related fees owing to them. In any case where a draw is made against the LCs, the Company has agreed to reimburse the bank issuing the LCs for the amount so drawn. Refer to Note 37 for further information.

12. Assets classified as held for sale

Land and buildings are transferred to assets classified as held for sale from property and equipment and investment property when they meet the criteria to be assets classified as held for sale as per the Company's accounting policy. Land and buildings previously included in assets classified as held for sale are transferred to property and equipment, investment property or goodwill and intangibles, as appropriate, when it is determined that they no longer meet the criteria to be assets classified as held for sale.

As at January 3, 2015, land, buildings and investment properties classified as held for sale were $3.2 million (2013 – $1.6 million), $4.3 million (2013 – $3.3 million) and $5.6 million (2013 – $0.5 million), respectively.

In addition, franchise agreements and buildings in the amounts of $3.4 million and $0.3 million respectively, that were acquired and classified as held for sale in the 2013 PHL acquisition, were sold to franchisees in 2014.

Land and buildings classified as assets held for sale generally relate to former stores in the Retail segment that have been relocated to newer sites. The Company is actively marketing these properties to third parties and they will be sold when terms and conditions acceptable to the Company are reached.

During the year ended January 3, 2015, the Company recorded impairment of $nil (2013 – $0.1 million) as in the current year it was determined that the recoverable amount was greater than the carrying amount for all held for sale assets. During the year ended January 3, 2015, the Company recorded reversal of impairment of $nil (2013 – $nil). Impairment and reversal of impairments are recorded in the Company's Retail operating segment, and reported in other income in the consolidated statements of income.

During the year ended January 3, 2015, the Company sold assets held for sale and recorded a gain of $8.2 million (2013 – $12.9 million), which is reported in other income in the consolidated statements of income.

13. Long-term receivables and other assets

(C$ in millions)	2014	2013
Loans receivable (Note 11)	$ 573.1	$ 577.2
Mortgages receivable	32.5	53.1
Derivatives	58.3	40.3
Other receivables[1]	4.8	3.4
Total financial assets	668.7	674.0
Other [1]	15.5	12.0
	$ 684.2	$ 686.0

[1] The prior year's figures have been reclassified to correspond to current year's presentation.

NOTES TO THE CONSOLIDATED FINANCIAL STATEMENTS

14. Goodwill and intangible assets

The following table presents the changes in cost and accumulated amortization and impairment of the Company's intangible assets:

| | Indefinite-life intangible assets and goodwill | | | Finite-life intangible assets | | 2014 |
| | Goodwill | Banners and trademarks | Franchise agreements and other intangibles | Software | Other intangibles | Total |
(C$ in millions)						
Cost						
Balance, beginning of year	$ 434.5	$ 245.2	$ 154.3	$ 1,027.1	$ 23.1	$ 1,884.2
Additions internally developed	–	–	–	134.2	–	134.2
Additions related to business combinations	4.0	–	2.5	–	–	6.6
Other additions	–	21.4	–	–	–	21.4
Disposals/retirements	–	–	–	(2.6)	–	(2.6)
Other movements and transfers	–	–	–	(0.6)	–	(0.6)
Balance, end of year	$ 438.5	$ 266.6	$ 156.8	$ 1,158.1	$ 23.1	$ 2,043.2
Accumulated amortization and impairment						
Balance, beginning of year	$ (1.6)	$ –	$ –	$ (686.9)	$ (10.2)	$ (698.7)
Amortization for the year	–	–	–	(90.9)	(2.2)	(93.1)
Impairment	(0.3)	–	–	–	–	(0.3)
Disposals/retirements	–	–	–	2.5	–	2.5
Other movements and transfers	–	–	–	–	(1.9)	(1.9)
Balance, end of year	$ (1.9)	$ –	$ –	$ (775.3)	$ (14.2)	$ (791.5)
Net carrying amount, end of year	$ 436.6	$ 266.6	$ 156.8	$ 382.8	$ 8.9	$ 1,251.7

| | Indefinite-life intangible assets and goodwill | | | Finite-life intangible assets | | 2013 |
| | Goodwill | Banners and trademarks | Franchise agreements and other intangibles | Software | Other intangibles | Total |
(C$ in millions)						
Cost						
Balance, beginning of year	$ 378.5	$ 242.2	$ 142.8	$ 910.1	$ 22.5	$ 1,696.1
Additions internally developed	–	–	–	117.6	–	117.6
Additions related to business combinations	56.0	3.0	11.5	–	0.6	71.1
Other additions	–	–	–	0.2	–	0.2
Disposals/retirements	–	–	–	(2.3)	–	(2.3)
Other movements and transfers	–	–	–	1.5	–	1.5
Balance, end of year	$ 434.5	$ 245.2	$ 154.3	$ 1,027.1	$ 23.1	$ 1,884.2
Accumulated amortization and impairment						
Balance, beginning of year	$ (1.6)	$ –	$ –	$ (598.8)	$ (5.8)	$ (606.2)
Amortization for the year			–	–	(89.3)	(2.2)	(91.5)
Disposals/retirements	–	–	–	1.2	–	1.2
Other movements and transfers	–	–	–	–	(2.2)	(2.2)
Balance, end of year	$ (1.6)	$ –	$ –	$ (686.9)	$ (10.2)	$ (698.7)
Net carrying amount, end of year	$ 432.9	$ 245.2	$ 154.3	$ 340.2	$ 12.9	$ 1,185.5

The following table presents the details of the Company's goodwill:

(C$ in millions)	2014	2013
FGL Sports	$ 356.9	$ 356.9
Mark's	56.3	52.3
Canadian Tire	23.4	23.7
Total	$ 436.6	$ 432.9

Banners and trademarks includes FGL Sports and Mark's store banners, which represent legal trademarks of the Company with expiry dates ranging from 2016 to 2025. In addition, banners and trademarks includes FGL Sports and Mark's private-label brands that have legal expiry dates. The Company

NOTES TO THE CONSOLIDATED FINANCIAL STATEMENTS

currently has no approved plans to change its store banners and intends to continue to renew all trademarks and private-label brands at each expiry date indefinitely. The Company expects these assets to generate cash flows in perpetuity. Therefore, these intangible assets are considered to have indefinite useful lives.

Franchise agreements have expiry dates with options to renew or have indefinite lives. The Company's intention is to renew these agreements at each renewal date indefinitely, and the Company expects the franchise agreements and franchise locations will generate cash flows in perpetuity. Therefore, these assets are considered to have indefinite useful lives.

Other finite-life intangible assets include FGL Sports customer relationships, certain private-label brands and off-market leases that the Company has assessed as having limited life terms. These assets are amortized over a term of two to seven years. Off-market leases are amortized over the term of the lease to which they relate.

The amount of borrowing costs capitalized in 2014 was $3.2 million (2013 – $1.7 million). The capitalization rate used to determine the amount of borrowing costs capitalized during the year was 5.7 per cent (2013 – 5.7 per cent).

The amount of research and development expenditures recognized as an expense in 2014 was $2.5 million (2013 – $4.1 million).

Amortization expense of software and other finite-life intangible assets is included in selling, general and administrative expenses in the consolidated statements of income.

Impairment of intangible assets and subsequent reversal
The Company performed its annual impairment test on goodwill and indefinite-life intangible assets for all CGUs based on VIU using pre-tax discount rates ranging from 9.5 to 14.4 per cent and growth rates ranging from 1.7 to 2.0 per cent per annum.

The amount of impairment of intangible assets in 2014 was $0.3 million (2013 – $nil). There was no reversal of impairments in 2014 or 2013. The impairment on goodwill pertains to the Company's Retail operating segment and is reported in other (expense) income in the consolidated statements of income.

For all goodwill and intangible assets, the estimated recoverable amount is based on VIU exceeded the carrying amount. There is no reasonable possible change in assumptions that would cause the carrying amount to exceed the estimated recoverable amount.

15. Investment property

The following table presents changes in the cost and accumulated depreciation and impairment on the Company's investment property:

(C$ in millions)	2014	2013
Cost		
Balance, beginning of year	$ 123.9	$ 126.0
Additions	32.9	3.9
Disposals/retirements	(3.7)	–
Reclassified to/from held for sale	(3.3)	(6.6)
Other movements and transfers	29.0	0.6
Balance, end of year	$ 178.8	$ 123.9
Accumulated depreciation and impairment		
Balance, beginning of year	$ (30.4)	$ (30.9)
Depreciation for the year	(3.5)	(2.7)
Impairment	(1.6)	(1.4)
Reversal of impairment	–	0.2
Disposals/retirements	2.3	–
Reclassified to/from held for sale	5.1	4.3
Other movements and transfers	(2.1)	0.1
Balance, end of year	$ (30.2)	$ (30.4)
Net carrying amount, end of year	$ 148.6	$ 93.5

The investment properties generated rental income of $16.9 million (2013 – $10.7 million).

Direct operating expenses (including repairs and maintenance) arising from investment property recognized in net income were $8.8 million (2013 – $5.4 million).

The estimated fair value of investment property was $230.7 million (2013 – $173 million). This recurring fair value measurement is categorized within Level 3 of the fair value hierarchy (see Note 35.4 for definition of levels). The Company determines the fair value of investment property by applying a pre-tax capitalization rate to the annual rental income for the current leases. The capitalization rate ranged from 5.8 per cent to 11 per cent (2013 – 5.8 per cent to 11 per cent). The cash flows are for a term of five years, including a terminal value. The Company has real estate management expertise that is used to perform the valuation of investment property. As such, a valuation has not been performed by an independent valuation specialist.

Impairment of investment property and subsequent reversal

Any impairment or reversals of impairment are reported in other (expense) income in the consolidated statements of income.

16. Property and equipment

The following table presents the changes in the cost and accumulated depreciation and impairment on the Company's property and equipment:

(C$ in millions)	Land	Buildings	Fixtures and equipment	Leasehold improvements	Assets under finance lease	Construction in progress	2014 Total
Cost							
Balance, beginning of year	$ 815.0	$ 2,750.8	$ 938.8	$ 882.3	$ 276.6	$ 179.1	$ 5,842.6
Additions	49.8	141.2	139.8	145.2	19.4	59.3	554.7
Disposals/retirements	–	(4.8)	(35.2)	(23.4)	(10.5)	–	(73.9)
Reclassified to/from held for sale	(3.2)	(15.9)	(0.5)	(2.5)	–	–	(22.1)
Other movements and transfers	(0.6)	(13.6)	29.0	(0.5)	(29.0)	(14.1)	(28.8)
Balance, end of year	$ 861.0	$ 2,857.7	$ 1,071.9	$ 1,001.1	$ 256.5	$ 224.3	$ 6,272.5
Accumulated depreciation and impairment							
Balance, beginning of year	$ (0.3)	$ (1,201.0)	$ (641.3)	$ (316.5)	$ (167.4)	$ –	$ (2,326.5)
Depreciation for the year	–	(102.4)	(80.1)	(74.9)	(18.3)	–	(275.7)
Impairment	(4.1)	(0.6)	(0.2)	–	(0.1)	–	(5.0)
Disposals/retirements	–	3.8	27.0	23.2	10.5	–	64.5
Reclassified to/from held for sale	–	8.3	0.3	2.5	–	–	11.1
Other movements and transfers	–	2.1	(17.7)	–	17.8	–	2.2
Balance, end of year	$ (4.4)	$ (1,289.8)	$ (712.0)	$ (365.7)	$ (157.5)	$ –	$ (2,529.4)
Net carrying amount, end of year	$ 856.6	$ 1,567.9	$ 359.9	$ 635.4	$ 99.0	$ 224.3	$ 3,743.1

(C$ in millions)	Land	Buildings	Fixtures and equipment	Leasehold improvements	Assets under finance lease	Construction in progress	2013 Total
Cost							
Balance, beginning of year	$ 744.3	$ 2,683.7	$ 880.4	$ 778.2	$ 273.2	$ 102.3	$ 5,462.1
Additions	84.4	56.7	70.3	123.7	8.4	78.4	421.9
Additions related to business combinations	–	–	12.1	–	–	–	12.1
Disposals/retirements	–	(2.5)	(23.9)	(13.8)	(5.1)	–	(45.3)
Reclassified to/from held for sale	(2.3)	(4.4)	–	0.6	–	–	(6.1)
Other movements and transfers	(11.4)	17.3	(0.1)	(6.4)	0.1	(1.6)	(2.1)
Balance, end of year	$ 815.0	$ 2,750.8	$ 938.8	$ 882.3	$ 276.6	$ 179.1	$ 5,842.6
Accumulated depreciation and impairment							
Balance, beginning of year	$ (0.1)	$ (1,102.9)	$ (591.4)	$ (271.5)	$ (152.7)	$ –	$ (2,118.6)
Depreciation for the year	–	(100.0)	(71.5)	(60.0)	(19.6)	–	(251.1)
Impairment	–	–	(0.1)	–	–	–	(0.1)
Reversal of impairment	0.1	–	–	0.1	–	–	0.2
Disposals/retirements	(2.0)	3.7	21.6	13.0	4.9	–	41.2
Reclassified to/from held for sale	–	1.0	–	(0.6)	–	–	0.4
Other movements and transfers	1.7	(2.8)	0.1	2.5	–	–	1.5
Balance, end of year	$ (0.3)	$ (1,201.0)	$ (641.3)	$ (316.5)	$ (167.4)	$ –	$ (2,326.5)
Net carrying amount, end of year	$ 814.7	$ 1,549.8	$ 297.5	$ 565.8	$ 109.2	$ 179.1	$ 3,516.1

The Company capitalized borrowing costs of $7.7 million (2013 – $2.1 million) on indebtedness related to property and equipment under construction. The rate used to determine the amount of borrowing costs capitalized during the year was 5.7 per cent (2013 – 5.7 per cent).

The carrying amount of assets under finance leases at January 3, 2015, comprises $44.9 million (2013 – $51.5 million) in buildings and $54.1 million (2013 – $57.7 million) in fixtures and equipment.

Impairment of property and equipment and subsequent reversal

The impairment of property and equipment pertain to the Company's Retail operating segment. Any impairment or reversal of impairment is reported in other (expense) income in the consolidated statements of income.

17. Subsidiaries

17.1 Control of subsidiaries and composition of the Company

These consolidated financial statements include entities controlled by Canadian Tire Corporation, Limited. Control exists when Canadian Tire Corporation, Limited has the ability to direct the relevant activities and the returns of an entity. The financial statements of entities are included in these consolidated financial statements from the date that control commences until the date that control ceases.

Details of Canadian Tire Corporation, Limited's significant entities are as follows:

			Ownership interest	
Name of subsidiary	Principal activity	Country of incorporation and operation	2014	2013
CTFS Holdings Limited[1]	Marketing of insurance products, processing credit card transactions at Canadian Tire stores, banking and reinsurance	Canada	80.0%	N/A
Canadian Tire Real Estate Limited	Real estate	Canada	100.0%	100.0%
CT Real Estate Investment Trust	Real estate	Canada	83.2%	83.1%
FGL Sports Ltd.	Retailer of sporting equipment, apparel and footwear	Canada	100.0%	100.0%
Franchise Trust[2]	Canadian Tire Dealer loan program	Canada	0.0%	0.0%
Glacier Credit Card Trust[3]	Financing program to purchase co-ownership interest in Canadian Tire Bank's credit card loans	Canada	0.0%	0.0%
Mark's Work Wearhouse Ltd.	Retailer of clothing and footwear	Canada	100.0%	100.0%

[1] Legal entity CTFS Holdings Limited, incorporated in 2014, is the parent company of Canadian Tire Bank and CTFS Bermuda Holdings Limited. Canadian Tire Bank's principal activity is banking, marketing of insurance products, and processing credit card transactions at Canadian Tire stores. CTFS Bermuda Holdings Limited owns 100 per cent of CTFS Bermuda Ltd., whose principal activity is reinsurance. In 2013, the Company owned 100 per cent of these companies.

[2] Franchise Trust is a legal entity sponsored by third-party banks that originates loans to Dealers. The Company does not have any share ownership in Franchise Trust. However, the Company has determined that it has the ability to direct the relevant activities and returns of the portion (silo of assets and liabilities) of Franchise Trust that issues loans to Dealers under the Dealer loan program and related credit enhancement funds and hedging activities. The Company has control over the silo of assets and liabilities of Franchise Trust, and is therefore consolidated in these financial statements.

[3] GCCT was formed to meet specific business needs of the Company, namely to buy co-ownership interests in the Company's credit card loans. GCCT issues debt to third-party investors to fund its purchases. The Company does not have any share ownership in GCCT. However, the Company has determined that it has the ability to direct the relevant activities and returns of GCCT and has control over GCCT. GCCT is consolidated in these financial statements

17.2 Details of non-wholly owned subsidiaries that have non-controlling interest:

The portion of net assets and income attributable to third parties is reported as non-controlling interests and net income attributable to non-controlling interests in the consolidated balance sheet and statements of income, respectively. The non-controlling interests of CT REIT and CTFS Holdings Limited were initially measured at fair value on the date of acquisition.

The following table summarizes the information relating to non-controlling interests:

				2014	2013
(C$ in millions)	CT REIT[1]	CTFS Holdings Limited[2]	Other[3]	Total	CT REIT
Non-controlling interests percentage	16.8%	20.0%	50.0%		16.9%
Current assets	$ 15.1	$ 5,326.1	$ 9.0	$ 5,350.2	$ 54.8
Non-current assets	4,002.3	222.9	34.1	4,259.3	3,548.4
Current liabilities	(310.2)	(1,846.9)	(2.8)	(2,159.9)	(22.6)
Non-current liabilities	(1,705.1)	(2,699.5)	(26.7)	(4,431.3)	(1,800.3)
Net assets	2,002.2	1,002.6	13.6	3,018.4	1,780.3
Revenue	$ 344.8	241.6	187.8	774.2	$ 63.0
Net income	318.3	58.6	8.5	385.4	30.9
Net income attributable to non-controlling interests	$ 19.9	10.3	5.1	35.3	$ 3.2
Equity attributable to non-controlling interests	284.4	487.3	3.6	775.3	282.6
Distributions to non-controlling interests	(19.8)	–	(1.5)	(21.3)	(3.6)

[1] Net income attributable to non-controlling interests is based on net income of CT REIT adjusted to convert to the Company's cost method, including recording of depreciation.

[2] Net income attributable to non-controlling interests is based on the net income of CTFS Holdings Limited adjusted for contractual requirements as stipulated in the Universal Shareholder agreement.

[3] Net income attributable to non-controlling interests is based on net income of the subsidiary adjusted for contractual requirements as stipulated in the ownership agreement.

17.3 Continuity of non-controlling interests:

(C$ in millions)	2014	2013
Balance at beginning of year	$ 282.6	$ –
Sale of ownership interests, net of transaction costs	476.8	–
Comprehensive income attributable to non-controlling interests for the year[1]	35.4	3.2
Issuance of trust units to non-controlling interests, net of transaction costs	1.8	283.0
Distributions	(21.3)	(3.6)
Balance at end of year	$ 775.3	$ 282.6

[1] Includes $0.1 million included in the consolidated statement of other comprehensive income.

18. Income taxes

18.1 Deferred income tax assets and liabilities

The amount of deferred tax assets or liabilities recognized in the consolidated balance sheet and the corresponding movement recognized in consolidated statement of income, consolidated statement of changes in equity or resulting from a business combination is as follows:

						2014
(C$ in millions)	Balance, beginning of year	Recognized in profit or loss	Recognized in other comprehensive income	Recognized in equity	Acquired in Business Combination	Balance, end of year
Reserves and deferred income	$ 119.9	$ 15.3	$ –	$ –	$ –	$ 135.2
Property and equipment	(57.0)	(2.9)	–	–	–	(59.9)
Intangible assets	(146.3)	4.0	–	–	–	(142.3)
Employee benefits	30.5	1.2	4.7	–	–	36.4
Financial instruments	(17.0)	–	(12.5)	–	–	(29.5)
Finance lease assets and obligations	10.8	3.1	–	–	–	13.9
Site restoration and decommissioning	3.6	0.5	–	–	–	4.1
Deferred items	(13.4)	(7.4)	–	–	–	(20.8)
Inventory	0.1	0.9	–	–	–	1.0
Non-capital loss	1.7	1.8	–	–	–	3.5
Transaction costs	3.8	(1.3)	–	0.5	–	3.0
Minimum tax credit	1.2	–	–	–	–	1.2
Other	(1.9)	1.6	–	–	–	(0.3)
Net deferred tax asset (liability)[1]	$ (64.0)	$ 16.8	$ (7.8)	$ 0.5	$ –	$ (54.5)

[1] Includes the net amount of deferred tax asset of $39.4 million and deferred tax liabilities of $93.9 million.

NOTES TO THE CONSOLIDATED FINANCIAL STATEMENTS

| | | | | | | 2013 |
(C$ in millions)	Balance, beginning of year	Recognized in profit or loss	Recognized in other comprehensive income	Recognized in equity	Acquired in business combination	Balance, end of year
Reserves and deferred income	$ 104.3	$ 16.0	$ –	$ –	$ (0.4)	$ 119.9
Property and equipment	(55.8)	(3.7)	–	2.2	0.3	(57.0)
Intangible assets	(142.3)	(2.4)	–	–	(1.6)	(146.3)
Employee benefits	33.1	1.2	(3.6)	(0.2)	–	30.5
Financial instruments	0.7	–	(17.7)	–	–	(17.0)
Finance lease assets and obligations	11.8	(1.0)	–	–	–	10.8
Site restoration and decommissioning	3.1	0.5	–	–	–	3.6
Deferred items	0.1	(10.6)	–	–	(2.9)	(13.4)
Inventory	0.2	0.6	–	–	(0.7)	0.1
Non-capital loss	7.9	(6.2)	–	–	–	1.7
Transaction costs	–	(0.4)	–	4.2	–	3.8
Other	(0.7)	–	–	–	–	(0.7)
Net deferred tax asset (liability)[1]	$ (37.6)	$ (6.0)	$ (21.3)	$ 6.2	$ (5.3)	$ (64.0)

[1] Includes the net amount of deferred tax asset of $36.4 million and deferred tax liabilities of $100.4 million.

No deferred tax is recognized on the amount of temporary differences arising from the difference between the carrying amount of the investment in subsidiaries, branches and associates, and interests in joint arrangements accounted for in the financial statements and the cost amount for tax purposes of the investment. The Company is able to control the timing of the reversal of these temporary differences and believes it is probable that they will not reverse in the foreseeable future. The amount of these taxable temporary differences was approximately $2.5 billion at January 3, 2015 (2013 – $2.1 billion).

18.2 Income tax expense

The following are the major components of the income tax expense:

(C$ in millions)	2014	2013
Current tax expense		
Current period	$ 248.5	$ 216.8
Adjustments in respect of prior years	7.2	(2.6)
	$ 255.7	$ 214.2
Deferred tax (benefit) expense		
Deferred income tax (benefit) expense relating to the origination and reversal of temporary differences	$ (7.9)	$ 6.0
Deferred income tax (benefit) adjustments in respect of prior years	(8.9)	–
	(16.8)	6.0
Total Income tax expense	$ 238.9	$ 220.2

NOTES TO THE CONSOLIDATED FINANCIAL STATEMENTS

Reconciliation of income tax expense

Income taxes in the consolidated statements of income vary from amounts that would be computed by applying the statutory income tax rate for the following reasons:

(C$ in millions)	2014	2013
Income before tax	$ 878.2	$ 784.6
Income taxes based on the applicable statutory tax rate of 26.50% (2013–26.49%)	$ 232.7	$ 207.8
Adjustment to income taxes resulting from:		
Non-deductibility of stock option expense	10.5	15.0
Prior years' tax settlements	(7.6)	–
Income attributable to non-controlling interest in flow-through entities	(6.6)	(0.9)
Adjustments of prior years' tax estimates	5.9	(2.6)
Non-deductibility of change in fair value of redeemable financial instrument	4.5	–
Lower income tax rates on earnings of foreign subsidiaries	(0.5)	(0.8)
Other	–	1.7
Income tax expense	$ 238.9	$ 220.2

The applicable statutory tax rate is the aggregate of the Canadian federal income tax rate of 15 per cent (2013 – 15 per cent) and Canadian provincial income tax rate of 11.50 per cent (2013 – 11.49 per cent).

In the ordinary course of business, the Company is subject to ongoing audits by tax authorities. While the Company has determined that its tax filing positions are appropriate and supportable, from time to time certain matters are reviewed and challenged by the tax authorities.

As a result of the Company's investment in and development of certain information technology Scientific Research and Experimental Development (SR&ED) projects, claims have been filed with the Canada Revenue Agency (CRA) for SR&ED tax credits relating to prior periods (which are currently under audit by the CRA).

No amounts were accrued during the year in the Company's financial statements with respect to the claim for SR&ED tax credits. The 2014 tax expense has been reduced by $7.6 million (2013 – $nil) due to prior years' tax settlements and increased by $5.9 million (2013 – decreased by $2.6 million) due to adjustments to priors years' tax estimates.

The Company regularly reviews the potential for adverse outcomes with respect to tax matters. The Company believes that the ultimate disposition of these will not have a material adverse effect on its liquidity, consolidated financial position or net income because the Company has determined that it has adequate provision for these tax matters. Should the ultimate tax liability materially differ from the provision, the Company's effective tax rate and its earnings could be affected positively or negatively in the period in which the matters are resolved.

19. Deposits

Deposits consist of broker deposits and retail deposits.

Cash from broker deposits is raised through sales of GICs through brokers rather than directly to the retail customer. Broker deposits are offered for varying terms ranging from 30 days to five years and all issued broker GICs are non-redeemable prior to maturity (except in certain rare circumstances). Total short-term and long-term broker deposits outstanding at January 3, 2015, were $1,534.6 million (2013 – $1,537.9 million).

Retail deposits consist of HIS deposits, retail GICs and TFSA deposits. Total retail deposits outstanding at January 3, 2015, were $702.3 million (2013 – $792.5 million).

For repayment requirements of deposits see Note 5.4.

The following are the effective rates of interest:

	2014	2013
GIC deposits	3.00%	3.51%
HIS account deposits	1.53%	1.60%

20. Trade and other payables

(C$ in millions)	2014	2013[1]
Trade payables and accrued liabilities[2]	$ 1,834.9	$ 1,697.8
Deferred revenue	39.3	43.2
Insurance reserve	16.8	16.7
Other	70.2	59.7
	$ 1,961.2	$ 1,817.4

[1] The prior year's figures have been reclassified to correspond to current year's presentation.
[2] Financial liabilities

Deferred revenue consists mainly of unearned insurance premiums, unearned roadside assistance revenue, unearned home services revenue and unearned revenue related to gift cards.

Other consists primarily of sales taxes payable.

The credit range period on trade payables is four to 120 days (2013 – five to 120 days).

21. Provisions

The following table presents the changes to the Company's provisions:

(C$ in millions)	Sales and warranty returns	Site restoration and decommissioning	Onerous contracts	Customer loyalty	Other	2014 Total
Balance, beginning of year	$ 109.5	$ 32.4	$ 3.2	$ 71.2	$ 18.0	$ 234.3
Charges, net of reversals	252.5	5.7	1.1	123.8	14.0	397.1
Utilizations	(247.4)	(5.8)	(3.4)	(115.1)	(16.9)	(388.6)
Unwinding of discount	1.0	0.6	0.2	–	–	1.8
Change in discount rate	–	5.5	–	–	–	5.5
Balance, end of year	$ 115.6	$ 38.4	$ 1.1	$ 79.9	$ 15.1	$ 250.1
Current provisions	112.2	6.0	0.7	79.9	7.2	206.0
Long-term provisions	$ 3.4	$ 32.4	$ 0.4	$ –	$ 7.9	$ 44.1

22. Contingencies

Legal and regulatory matters

The Company is party to a number of legal and regulatory proceedings. The Company has determined that each such proceeding constitutes a routine matter incidental to the business conducted by the Company and that the ultimate disposition of the proceedings will not have a material effect on its consolidated net income, cash flows or financial position.

23. Short-term borrowings

Short-term borrowings include commercial paper notes and bank line of credit borrowings. Short-term borrowings may bear interest payable at maturity or be sold at a discount and mature at face value.

The commercial paper notes are short-term notes issued with varying original maturities of one year or fewer, typically 90 days or fewer, at interest rates fixed at the time of each renewal and are recorded at amortized cost. As at January 3, 2015, $121.8 million of commercial paper notes were issued by the Company.

As at January 3, 2015, $78 million of bank line of credit borrowings had been drawn on CT REIT's Bank Credit Facility.

24. Loans payable

Franchise Trust, an Special Purpose Entity ("SPE"), is a legal entity sponsored by a third-party bank that originates loans to Dealers. Loans payable are the loans that Franchise Trust incurs to fund loans to Dealers. These loans are not direct legal liabilities of the Company but have been consolidated in the accounts of the Company as the Company effectively controls the silo of Franchise Trust containing the Dealer loan program.

Loans payable, which are initially recognized at fair value and are subsequently measured at amortized cost, are due within one year.

25. Long-term debt

Long-term debt includes the following:

(C$ in millions)	2014 Face value	2014 Carrying amount	2013 Face value	2013 Carrying amount
Senior notes[1]				
Series 2006-2, 4.405%, May 20, 2014	$ –	$ –	$ 238.7	$ 238.6
Series 2010-1, 3.158%, November 20, 2015	250.0	249.7	250.0	249.3
Series 2012-1, 2.807%, May 20, 2017	200.0	199.4	200.0	199.2
Series 2012-2, 2.394%, October 20, 2017	400.0	398.7	400.0	398.4
Series 2013-1, 2.755%, November 20, 2018	250.0	248.9	250.0	248.6
Series 2014-1, 2.567%, September 20, 2019	472.5	470.2	–	–
Subordinated notes[1]				
Series 2006-2, 4.765%, May 20, 2014	–	–	13.9	13.9
Series 2010-1, 4.128%, November 20, 2015	14.6	14.6	14.6	14.6
Series 2012-1, 3.827%, May 20, 2017	11.6	11.6	11.6	11.6
Series 2012-2, 3.174%, October 20, 2017	23.3	23.3	23.3	23.3
Series 2013-1, 3.275%, November 20, 2018	14.6	14.6	14.6	14.6
Series 2014-1, 3.068%, September 20, 2019	27.5	27.5	–	–
Medium-term notes				
4.95% due June 1, 2015	300.0	299.3	300.0	299.7
5.65% due June 1, 2016	–	–	200.0	199.2
6.25% due April 13, 2028	150.0	149.6	150.0	149.5
6.32% due February 24, 2034	200.0	199.5	200.0	199.2
5.61% due September 4, 2035	200.0	199.5	200.0	199.2
Finance lease obligations	153.0	153.0	151.3	151.3
Mortgages	58.3	58.5	–	–
Promissory note	1.2	1.2	1.1	1.1
Total debt	$ 2,726.6	$ 2,719.1	$ 2,619.1	$ 2,611.3
Current	$ 587.5	$ 587.5	$ 272.2	$ 272.2
Non-current	2,139.1	2,131.6	2,346.9	2,339.1
Total debt	$ 2,726.6	$ 2,719.1	$ 2,619.1	$ 2,611.3

[1] Senior and subordinated notes are those of GCCT.

The carrying amount of long-term debt is net of debt issuance costs of $7.5 million (2013 – $7.2 million) and the benefit on the effective portion of the cash flow hedges of $nil (2013 – $0.6 million).

Senior and subordinated notes

Asset-backed series senior and subordinated notes issued by the Company are recorded at amortized cost using the effective interest method.

Subject to the payment of certain priority amounts, the series senior notes have recourse on a priority basis to the related series ownership interest. The series subordinated notes have recourse to the related series ownership interests on a subordinated basis to the series senior notes in terms of the priority of payment of principal and, in some circumstances, interest. The series notes, together with certain other permitted obligations of GCCT, are secured by the assets of GCCT. The entitlement of note holders and other parties to such assets is governed by the priority and payment provisions set forth in the GCCT Indenture and the related series supplements under which these series of notes were issued.

Repayment of the principal of the series 2010-1, 2012-1, 2012-2, 2013-1 and 2014-1 notes is scheduled to commence and be completed on the expected repayment dates indicated in the preceding table. Subsequent to repayment, collections distributed to GCCT with respect to the related ownership interest will be applied to pay principal owing. This process is applied to principal owing for series subordinated notes and in some circumstances interest for the series senior notes.

Principal repayments may commence earlier than these scheduled commencement dates if certain events occur including:
• the Bank failing to make required distributions to GCCT or failing to meet covenant or other contractual terms;
• the performance of the receivables failing to achieve set criteria; and
• insufficient receivables in the pool.

None of these events occurred in the year ended January 3, 2015.

Medium-term notes

Medium-term notes are unsecured and are redeemable by the Company, in whole or in part, at any time, at the greater of par or a formula price based upon interest rates at the time of redemption.

On June 25, 2014, the Company redeemed $200 million of medium-term notes, which were to mature on June 1, 2016 and bore interest at 5.65 per cent. Upon redemption, the Company paid a redemption premium of $15 million, which is included in net finance costs.

Finance lease obligations

Finance leases relate to distribution centres, fixtures and equipment. The Company generally has the option to renew such leases or purchase the leased assets at the conclusion of the lease term. During 2014, interest rates on finance leases ranged from 0.81 per cent to 8.92 per cent. Remaining terms at January 3, 2015, were four to 145 months.

Finance lease obligations are payable as follows:

	2014			2013		
(C$ in millions)	Future minimum lease payments	Interest	Present value of minimum lease payments	Future minimum lease payments	Interest	Present value of minimum lease payments
Due in less than one year	$ 29.7	$ 9.0	$ 20.7	$ 27.9	$ 9.1	$ 18.8
Due between one year and two years	25.0	8.0	17.0	25.4	8.2	17.2
Due between two years and three years	21.0	7.0	14.0	21.0	7.3	13.7
Due between three years and four years	18.4	6.3	12.1	17.3	6.6	10.7
Due between four years and five years	16.1	5.6	10.5	15.4	6.0	9.4
More than five years	98.8	20.1	78.7	106.3	24.8	81.5
	$ 209.0	$ 56.0	$ 153.0	$ 213.3	$ 62.0	$ 151.3

Mortgages

During the year, the Company assumed secured mortgages with a fair value of $59.2 million upon the purchase of certain properties. These mortgages bear interest rates ranging from 2.95 per cent to 3.60 per cent and have maturity dates ranging from January 2018 to December 2019.

Promissory notes

Promissory notes were issued as part of franchise acquisitions (Note 7.3). These notes are non-interest-bearing.

Debt covenants

The Company has provided covenants to certain of its lenders. The Company was in compliance with all of its covenants as at January 3, 2015.

26. Other long-term liabilities

(C$ in millions)	2014	2013
Redeemable financial instrument[1]	$ 517.0	$ —
Employee benefits (Note 27)	137.5	115.4
Deferred gains	18.1	21.3
Deferred revenue	13.2	14.3
Other	102.0	77.3
	$ 787.8	$ 228.3

[1] Financial liabilities.

Deferred gains relate to the sale and leaseback of certain distribution centres. The deferred gains are amortized over the terms of the leases.

Other includes long-term portion of incentive and stock option liabilities, unearned insurance premiums, unearned roadside assistance revenue, deferred lease inducements and off-market leases.

NOTES TO THE CONSOLIDATED FINANCIAL STATEMENTS

27. Post-employment benefits

Profit-sharing plan

The Company has a profit-sharing plan for certain employees. The amount awarded to employees is contingent on the Company's profitability. A portion of the award ("Base Award") is contributed to a DPSP for the benefit of the employees. The maximum amount of the Company's Base Award contribution to the DPSP per employee per year is subject to limits set by the Income Tax Act. Each participating employee is required to invest and maintain 10 per cent of the Base Award in a Company share fund of the DPSP. The share fund holds both Common Shares and Class A Non-Voting Shares. The Company's contributions to the DPSP in respect of each employee vest 20 per cent after one year of continuous service and 100 per cent after two years of continuous service.

In 2014, the Company contributed $20.5 million (2013 – $19.8 million) under the terms of the DPSP.

Defined benefit plan

The Company provides certain health care, dental care, life insurance and other benefits for certain retired employees pursuant to Company policy. The Company does not have a pension plan. Information about the Company's defined benefit plan is as follows:

(C$ in millions)	2014	2013
Change in the present value of defined benefit obligation		
Defined benefit obligation, beginning of year	$ 115.4	$ 124.9
Current service cost	1.9	2.2
Interest cost	5.6	4.9
Actuarial (gain) loss arising from changes in demographic assumptions	(0.3)	4.1
Actuarial loss (gain) arising from changes in financial assumptions	18.6	(17.4)
Actuarial gain arising from experience adjustments	(0.4)	(0.3)
Benefits paid	(3.3)	(3.0)
Defined benefit obligation, end of year[1]	$ 137.5	$ 115.4

[1] The accrued benefit obligation is not funded because funding is provided when benefits are paid. Accordingly, there are no plan assets.

(C$ in millions)	2014	2013
Components of non-pension post-retirement benefit cost		
Amounts recognized in net income:		
Current service cost	$ 1.9	$ 2.2
Interest cost	5.6	4.9
Total recognized in net income	$ 7.5	$ 7.1
Amount recognized in other comprehensive income:		
Actuarial gain (loss) arising from changes in demographic assumptions	$ 0.3	$ (4.1)
Actuarial (loss) gain arising from changes in financial assumptions	(18.6)	17.4
Actuarial gain arising from experience adjustments	0.4	0.3
Total recognized in other comprehensive income	$ (17.9)	$ 13.6

Significant actuarial assumptions used:

	2014	2013
Defined benefit obligation, end of year:		
Discount rate	4.00%	4.90%
Net benefit plan expense for the year:		
Discount rate	4.90%	4.00%

For measurement purposes, a 6.12 per cent weighted average health care cost trend rate is assumed for 2014 (2013 – 6.20 per cent). The rate is assumed to decrease gradually to 4.50 per cent for 2032 (2013 – decrease gradually to 4.50 per cent for 2032) and remain at that level thereafter.

The most recent actuarial valuation of the obligation was performed as of December 31, 2012. The next required valuation will be as of December 31, 2015.

NOTES TO THE CONSOLIDATED FINANCIAL STATEMENTS

The cumulative amount of actuarial losses before tax recognized in equity at January 3, 2015, was $45.1 million (2013 – $27.2 million).

Sensitivity analysis:

The following tables provide the sensitivity of the defined benefit obligation and defined benefit cost relating to post-employment benefits provided by the Company to the health care cost trend rate, the discount rate, and the life expectancy assumptions. For each sensitivity test, the impact of a reasonably possible change in a single factor is shown with other assumptions left unchanged.

(C$ in millions)							2014
	Total of current service and interest cost				Accrued benefit obligation		
Sensitivity analysis	Increase		Decrease		Increase		Decrease
A one-percentage-point change in assumed health care cost trend rates	$	0.5	$	(0.4)	$ 9.6	$	(8.0)
A fifty basis point change in assumed discount rates		(0.1)		0.1	(10.8)		12.3
A one year change in assumed life expectancy		0.2		(0.2)	3.2		(3.2)

The weighted average duration of the defined benefit plan obligation at January 3, 2015 is 17.5 years (2013 – 16.5 years).

28. Share capital

(C$ in millions)	2014	2013[1]
Authorized		
3,423,366 Common Shares		
100,000,000 Class A Non-Voting Shares		
Issued		
3,423,366 Common Shares (2013 – 3,423,366)	$ 0.2	$ 0.2
74,023,208 Class A Non-Voting Shares (2013 – 76,560,851)	695.3	712.7
	$ 695.5	$ 712.9

[1] Refer to Note 3 for details of accounting policy change.

All issued shares are fully paid. The Company does not hold any of its Common or Class A Non-Voting Shares. Neither the Common nor Class A Non-Voting Shares have a par value.

During 2014 and 2013, the Company issued and repurchased Class A Non-Voting Shares. Share repurchases are charged to share capital at the average cost per share outstanding and the excess between the repurchase price and the average cost is first allocated to contributed surplus, with any remaining allocated to retained earnings.

The following transactions occurred with respect to Class A Non-Voting Shares during 2014 and 2013:

(C$ in millions)	2014		2013[1]	
	Number	$	Number	$
Shares outstanding at beginning of the year	76,560,851	$ 712.7	77,720,401	$ 718.3
Issued				
Dividend reinvestment plan	62,357	6.9	63,903	5.4
Stock option plan	–	–	5,217	0.4
Repurchased[2]	(2,600,000)	(290.6)	(1,228,670)	(105.9)
Excess of repurchase price over average cost	–	266.3	–	94.5
Shares outstanding at end of the year	74,023,208	$ 695.3	76,560,851	$ 712.7

[1] Refer to Note 3 for details of accounting policy change.
[2] Repurchased shares have been restored to the status of authorized but unissued shares. The Company records shares repurchased on a transaction date basis.

Conditions of Class A Non-Voting Shares and Common Shares

The holders of Class A Non-Voting Shares are entitled to receive a fixed cumulative preferential dividend at the rate of $0.01 per share per annum. After payment of fixed cumulative preferential dividends at the rate of $0.01 per share per annum on each of the Class A Non-Voting Shares with respect to the current year and each preceding year and payment of a non-cumulative dividend on each of the Common Shares with respect to the current year at the same rate, the holders of the Class A Non-Voting Shares and the Common Shares are entitled to further dividends declared and paid in equal amounts per share without preference or distinction or priority of one share over another.

In the event of the liquidation, dissolution or winding-up of the Company, all of the property of the Company available for distribution to the holders of the Class A Non-Voting Shares and the Common Shares shall be paid or distributed equally, share for share, to the holders of the Class A Non-Voting Shares and to the holders of the Common Shares without preference or distinction or priority of one share over another.

The holders of Class A Non-Voting Shares are entitled to receive notice of and to attend all meetings of the shareholders; however, except as provided by the *Business Corporations Act* (Ontario) and as hereinafter noted, they are not entitled to vote at those meetings. Holders of Class A Non-Voting Shares, voting separately as a class, are entitled to elect the greater of (i) three Directors or (ii) one-fifth of the total number of the Company's Directors.

The holders of Common Shares are entitled to receive notice of, to attend and to have one vote for each Common Share held at all meetings of holders of Common Shares, subject only to the restriction on the right to elect those directors who are elected by the holders of Class A Non-Voting Shares as set out above.

Common Shares can be converted, at any time and at the option of each holder of Common Shares, into Class A Non-Voting Shares on a share-for-share basis. The authorized number of shares of either class cannot be increased without the approval of the holders of at least two-thirds of the shares of each class represented and voted at a meeting of the shareholders called for the purpose of considering such an increase. Neither the Class A Non-Voting Shares nor the Common Shares can be changed in any manner whatsoever whether by way of subdivision, consolidation, reclassification, exchange or otherwise unless at the same time the other class of shares is also changed in the same manner and in the same proportion.

Should an offer to purchase Common Shares be made to all or substantially all of the holders of Common Shares or be required by applicable securities legislation or by the Toronto Stock Exchange to be made to all holders of Common Shares in Ontario (other than an offer to purchase both Class A Non-Voting Shares and Common Shares at the same price per share and on the same terms and conditions) and should a majority of the Common Shares then issued and outstanding be tendered and taken up pursuant to such offer, the Class A Non-Voting Shares shall thereupon and thereafter be entitled to one vote per share at all meetings of the shareholders and thereafter the Class A Non-Voting Shares shall be designated as Class A Shares.

The foregoing is a summary of certain conditions attached to the Class A Non-Voting Shares of the Company and reference should be made to the Company's articles of amendment dated December 15, 1983 for a full statement of such conditions.

As of January 3, 2015, the Company had dividends declared and payable to holders of Class A Non-Voting Shares and Common Shares of $40.7 million (2013 – $35 million) at a rate of $0.525 per share (2013 – $0.4375 per share).

On February 26, 2015 the Company's Board of Directors declared a dividend of $0.525 per share payable on June 1, 2015 to shareholders of record as of April 30, 2015.

Dividends per share declared were $1.9625 in 2014 (2013 – $1.4875).

Dilutive effect of employee stock options is 652,932 (2013 – 528,391).

29. Share-based payments

The fair value of employee stock options and performance share units is measured using the Black-Scholes formula. Measurement inputs include the share price on the measurement date, exercise price of the instrument, expected volatility (based on weighted average historical volatility adjusted for changes expected based on publicly available information), weighted average expected life of the instruments (based on historical experience and general option holder behaviour), expected dividends, and the risk-free interest rate (based on government bonds). Service and non-market performance conditions attached to the transactions are not taken into account in determining fair value.

The Company's share-based payment plans are described below. There were no cancellations or significant modifications to any of the plans during 2014.

Stock options

The Company has granted stock options to certain employees that enable such employees to exercise their stock options and subscribe for Class A Non-Voting Shares or receive a cash payment equal to the difference between the daily weighted average share price of the Company's Class A Non-Voting Shares on the exercise date and the exercise price of the stock option. The exercise price of each option equals the weighted average closing price of Class A Non-Voting Shares on the Toronto Stock Exchange for the 10-day period preceding the date of grant. Stock options granted from 2008 to 2011 generally vested on the third anniversary of their grant and were exercisable over a term of seven years. Stock options granted from 2012 to 2014 generally vest on a graduated basis over a three-year period and are exercisable over a term of seven years. At January 3, 2015, the aggregate number of Class A Non-Voting Shares that were authorized for issuance under the stock option plan was 3.4 million.

Compensation expense, net of hedging arrangements, recorded for stock options for the year ended January 3, 2015, was $10.7 million (2013 – $15.4 million).

NOTES TO THE CONSOLIDATED FINANCIAL STATEMENTS

Stock option transactions during 2014 and 2013 were as follows:

	2014		2013	
	Number of options	Weighted average exercise price	Number of options	Weighted average exercise price
Outstanding at beginning of year	1,986,354	$ 64.26	2,406,383	$ 60.62
Granted	330,879	99.81	737,209	69.13
Exercised	(747,768)	63.17	(1,012,039)	58.91
Forfeited	(35,810)	74.90	(121,631)	66.36
Expired	(7,312)	71.90	(23,568)	63.71
Outstanding at end of year	1,526,343	$ 72.21	1,986,354	$ 64.26
Stock options exercisable at end of year	538,667		479,363	

[1] The weighted average market price of the Company's shares when the options were exercised in 2014 was $105.37 (2013 – $83.50).

The following table summarizes information about stock options outstanding and exercisable at January 3, 2015:

	Options outstanding			Options exercisable	
Range of exercise prices	Number of outstanding options	Weighted average remaining contractual life[1]	Weighted average exercise price	Number exercisable at January 3, 2015	Weighted average exercise price
$ 84.53 to 103.61	325,321	6.18	$ 99.64	–	–
66.73 to 69.01	562,105	5.17	68.99	106,004	69.01
63.67 to 66.04	378,788	4.16	63.68	172,534	63.69
62.30 to 63.42	152,551	2.61	62.50	152,551	62.50
40.04 to 53.67	107,578	1.84	49.92	107,578	49.92
$ 40.04 to 103.61	1,526,343	4.64	$ 72.21	538,667	$ 61.65

[1] Weighted average remaining contractual life is expressed in years.

Performance share unit and performance unit plans

The Company grants performance share units ("PSUs") to certain of its employees. Each PSU entitles the participant to receive a cash payment equal to the weighted average price of Class A Non-Voting Shares of the Company traded on the Toronto Stock Exchange during the 10 calendar-day period commencing on the first business day after the last day of the performance period, multiplied by a factor determined by specific performance-based criteria, as set out in the performance share unit plan. The performance period of each PSU award is approximately three years from the date of issuance. Compensation expense, net of hedging arrangements, recorded for these PSUs for the year ended January 3, 2015, was $51.2 million (2013 – $27 million).

CT REIT grants Performance Units ("PUs") to its executives. Each PU entitles the executive to receive a cash payment equal to the weighted average price of Units of CT REIT traded on the Toronto Stock Exchange during the 10 calendar day period commencing on the first business day following the end of the performance period, multiplied by a factor determined by specific performance-based criteria, as set out in the performance unit plan. The performance period of each PU award is approximately three years from the date of issuance. Compensation expense recorded for the year ended January 3, 2015 for PUs granted to executive officers was $0.2 million (2013 – $nil).

Deferred share unit and deferred unit plans

The Company offers a Deferred Share Unit Plan ("DSUP") for members of its Board of Directors. Under this plan, directors may elect to receive all or a portion of their annual compensation, which is paid quarterly, in deferred share units ("DSUs"). The number of DSUs to be issued is determined by dividing the quarterly compensation amount the director has elected to receive in DSUs by the weighted average price at which Class A Non-Voting Shares of the Company trade on the Toronto Stock Exchange during the 10-calendar day period prior to and including the last business day before the end of the calendar quarter. The DSU account of each director includes the value of dividends, if any, which are reinvested in additional DSUs. Directors are not permitted to convert DSUs into cash until their departure from the Board. The value of DSUs when converted to cash will be equivalent to the market value of the Class A Non-Voting Shares at the time the conversion takes place pursuant to the terms of the DSUP. Compensation expense recorded for the year ended January 3, 2015, was $2.2 million (2013 – $2.4 million).

The Company also offers a DSUP for certain of its executives. Under this plan, executives may elect to receive all or a portion of their annual bonus in DSUs. The number of DSUs to be issued is determined by dividing the annual bonus amount the executive has elected to receive in DSUs by the volume weighted average price at which Class A Non-Voting Shares of the Company trade on the Toronto Stock Exchange during the five business days immediately prior to the 10th business day following the release of the Company's financial statements for the year in respect of which the annual bonus was earned. The DSU account for each employee includes the value of dividends, if any, which are reinvested in additional DSUs. The executive is not permitted to convert DSUs

NOTES TO THE CONSOLIDATED FINANCIAL STATEMENTS

into cash until his or her departure from the Company. The value of DSUs when converted to cash will be equivalent to the market value of the Class A Non-Voting Shares at the time the conversion takes place pursuant to the terms of the DSUP. Compensation expense recorded for the year ended January 3, 2015, was $0.5 million (2013 – $0.6 million).

CT REIT offers a Deferred Unit Plan ("DUP") for members of its Board of Trustees who are not employees or Officers of CT REIT or its affiliates. Under this plan, trustees may elect to receive all or a portion of their annual compensation, which is paid quarterly, in Deferred Units ("DUs"). The number of DUs to be issued is determined by dividing the quarterly compensation amount the trustee has elected to receive in DUs by the weighted average price at which Units of CT REIT trade on the Toronto Stock Exchange during the five trading days immediately preceding the end of the calendar quarter. The DU account of each trustee includes the value of distributions, if any, which are reinvested in additional DUs. DUs represent the right to receive an equivalent number of Units issued by CT REIT or, at the trustee's election, the cash equivalent thereof, upon the trustee's departure from the Board. DUs that are converted to cash will be equivalent to the market value of Units of CT REIT at the time the conversion takes place pursuant to the terms of the DUP.

The fair value of a DU is equal to the traded price of a CT REIT Unit. Compensation expense recorded for the year ended January 3, 2015, was $0.1 million (2013 – $nil).

Restricted Unit Plan

CT REIT offers a Restricted Unit Plan ("RUP") for its executives. Under this plan, executives of CT REIT may elect to receive all or a portion of their annual bonus in restricted units ("RUs") which entitle the executive to receive an equivalent number of Units issued by CT REIT or, at the executive's election, the cash equivalent thereof, at the end of the vesting period which is generally five years from the annual bonus payment date. The number of RUs to be issued is determined by dividing the annual bonus amount the executive has elected to receive in RUs by the volume weighted average price at which Units of CT REIT trade on the Toronto Stock Exchange during the five business days immediately prior to the tenth business day following the release of CT REIT's financial statements for the year in which the annual bonus was earned. The RUP also provides for discretionary grants of RUs which entitle the executive to receive an equivalent number of Units of CT REIT issued by CT REIT or, at the executive's election, the cash equivalent thereof, at the end of the vesting period which is generally three years from the date of issuance. RUs that are converted to cash will be equivalent to the market value of Units of CT REIT on the conversion date pursuant to the terms of the RUP. The RU account for each executive includes the value of distributions, if any, which are reinvested in additional RUs.

The fair value of a RU is equal to the traded price of a CT REIT Unit. Compensation expense recorded for the year ended January 3, 2015 for RUs issued to executives was $0.1 million (2013 – $0.3 million).

The fair value of stock options and PSUs at the end of the year was determined using the Black-Scholes option pricing model with the following inputs:

| | 2014 | | 2013 | |
	Stock options	PSUs	Stock options	PSUs
Share price at end of year (C$)	$ 122.22	$ 122.22	$ 99.84	$ 99.84
Weighted average exercise price[1] (C$)	$ 71.89	N/A	$ 64.18	N/A
Expected remaining life (years)	3.7	1.0	4.7	1.2
Expected dividends	1.7%	2.3%	1.8%	2.2%
Expected volatility[2]	24.5%	17.7%	26.9%	21.8%
Risk-free interest rate	1.6%	1.4%	2.0%	1.3%

[1] Reflects expected forfeitures.
[2] Reflects historical volatility over a period of time similar to the remaining life of the stock options, which may not necessarily be the actual outcome.

Service and non-market performance conditions attached to the transactions are not taken into account in determining fair value.

The expense recognized for share-based compensation is summarized as follows:

(C$ in millions)	2014	2013
Expense arising from share-based payment transactions	$ 103.8	$ 99.6
Effect of hedging arrangements	(38.8)	(54.2)
Total expense included in net income	$ 65.0	$ 45.4

The total carrying amount of liabilities for share-based payment transactions at January 3, 2015, was $170.3 million (2013 – $122.2 million).

The intrinsic value of the liability for vested benefits at January 3, 2015, was $51.3 million (2013 – $29.4 million).

30. Revenue

(C$ in millions)	2014	2013[1]
Sale of goods	$ 10,890.6	$ 10,270.9
Interest income on loans receivable	784.6	754.1
Services rendered	372.2	362.6
Royalties and licence fees	363.2	349.4
Rental income	52.3	48.6
	$ 12,462.9	$ 11,785.6

[1] The prior year's figures have been reclassified to correspond to current year's presentation.

Major customers

The Company does not rely on any one customer.

31. Cost of producing revenue

(C$ in millions)	2014	2013
Inventory cost of sales[1]	$ 8,033.2	$ 7,678.0
Net impairment loss on loans receivable	274.7	262.2
Finance costs on deposits	57.6	65.2
Other	51.4	57.9
	$ 8,416.9	$ 8,063.3

[1] Inventory cost of sales includes depreciation and amortization for the year ended January 3, 2015 of $7 million (2013 – $nil).

Inventory writedowns as a result of net realizable value being lower than cost, recognized in the year ended January 3, 2015, were $40.2 million (2013 – $76.9 million).

Inventory writedowns recognized in previous periods and reversed in the year ended January 3, 2015, were $14.5 million (2013 – $21.2 million). The reversal of writedowns was the result of actual losses being lower than previously estimated.

The writedowns and reversals are included in inventory cost of sales.

32. Selling, general and administrative expenses

(C$ in millions)	2014	2013
Personnel expenses	$ 1,140.7	$ 1,019.9
Occupancy	625.1	589.8
Marketing and advertising	381.4	378.1
Depreciation of property and equipment and investment property[1]	272.2	253.8
Amortization of intangible assets	93.1	91.5
Other	540.4	495.8
	$ 3,052.9	$ 2,828.9

[1] Refer to Note 31 for depreciation and amortization on inventory cost of sales.

33. Finance income and finance costs

(C$ in millions)	2014		2013
Finance income			
Tax instalments	$ 0.1	$	0.1
Mortgages	7.9		7.7
Short- and long-term investments	10.4		10.7
Other	0.5		1.6
Total finance income	$ 18.9	$	20.1
Finance costs			
Subordinated and senior notes	$ 40.0	$	41.3
Medium-term notes	69.3		59.2
Loans payable	12.2		13.2
Finance leases	9.4		9.9
Short-term borrowings	1.3		1.4
Other[1]	6.8		4.7
	139.0		129.7
Less: Capitalized borrowing costs	11.2		3.8
Total finance costs	$ 127.8	$	125.9
Net finance costs	$ 108.9	$	105.8

[1] Includes $2.1 million of amortization of debt issuance costs (2013 – $1.7 million).

34. Notes to the consolidated statements of cash flows

Changes in operating working capital and other comprise the following:

(C$ in millions)	2014		2013
Changes in operating working capital			
Trade and other receivables	$ (38.1)	$	68.4
Merchandise inventories	(146.6)		80.3
Income taxes	(1.9)		(1.8)
Prepaid expenses and deposits	(36.1)		(27.7)
Trade and other payables	86.9		147.8
Total	(135.8)		267.0
Change in other			
Provisions	17.1		8.8
Long-term provisions	(3.2)		(14.0)
Other long-term liabilities	38.4		8.4
Total	52.3		3.2
Changes in operating working capital and other	$ (83.5)	$	270.2

34.1 Cash and marketable investments held in reserve

Cash and marketable investments includes reserves held by the Financial Services segment in support of its liquidity and regulatory requirements. As at January 3, 2015, reserves held by Financial Services totalled $344.5 million (2013 – $385.5 million) and includes restricted cash and short-term investments disclosed in Notes 8 and 9.

34.2 Supplementary information

During the year ended January 3, 2015, the Company acquired property and equipment and investment property at an aggregate cost of $587.6 million (2013 – $426.3 million). During the year ended January 3, 2015, intangible assets were internally developed or acquired at an aggregate cost of $155.6 million (2013 – $117.8 million).

The amount related to property and equipment and investment property acquired that is included in trade and other payables at January 3, 2015, is $71.7 million (2013 – $60 million). The amount related to intangible assets that is included in trade and other payables at January 3, 2015, is $22.8 million (2013 – $17.3 million).

During the year ended January 3, 2015, the Company also included in the property and equipment, investment property and intangible assets acquired non-cash items relating to finance leases, asset retirement obligations and capitalized interest in the amount of $37.3 million (2013 – $9.6 million).

35. Financial instruments

35.1 Fair value of financial instruments

Fair values have been determined for measurement and/or disclosure purposes based on the following:

The carrying amount of the Company's cash and cash equivalents, trade and other receivables, loans receivable, bank indebtedness, trade and other payables, short-term borrowings and loans payable approximate their fair value either due to their short-term nature or because they are derivatives, which are carried at fair value.

The carrying amount of the Company's long-term receivables and other assets approximates their fair value either because the interest rates applied to measure their carrying amount approximate current market interest or because they are derivatives, which are carried at fair value.

Fair values of financial instruments reflect the credit risk of the Company and counterparties when appropriate.

Investments in equity and debt securities

The fair values of financial assets at FVTPL, held-to-maturity investments and available-for-sale financial assets that are traded in active markets are determined by reference to their quoted closing bid price or dealer price quotations at the reporting date. For investments that are not traded in active markets, the Company determines fair values using a combination of discounted cash flow models, comparison to similar instruments for which market-observable prices exist and other valuation models. The fair values of loans and receivables and held-to-maturity investments are determined for disclosure purposes only.

Derivatives

The fair value of a forward exchange contract is estimated by discounting the difference between the contractual forward price and the current forward price for the residual maturity of the contract using a risk-free interest rate (based on government bonds).

The fair value of interest rate swaps is based on counterparty confirmations tested for reasonableness by discounting estimated future cash flows derived from the terms and maturity of each contract using market interest rates for a similar instrument at the measurement date.

The fair value of equity derivatives is determined by reference to share price movement adjusted for interest using market interest rates specific to the terms of the underlying derivative contracts.

Redeemable financial instrument

On October 1, 2014, The Bank of Nova Scotia ("Scotiabank") acquired a 20 per cent interest in the Financial Services business from the Company for proceeds of $476.8 million net of $23.2 million in transaction costs. In conjunction with the transaction Scotiabank was provided an option to sell and require the Company to purchase all of the interest owned by Scotiabank at any time during the six-month period following the 10th anniversary of the transaction. This obligation gives rise to a liability for the Company (the "redeemable financial instrument") and is recorded on the Company's Consolidated Balance Sheet in Other long-term liabilities. The purchase price will be based on the fair value of the Financial Services business and Scotiabank's proportionate interest in the Financial Services business, at that time.

The redeemable financial instrument was initially recorded at $500 million and is subsequently measured at fair value with changes in fair value recorded in net income for the period in which they arise. The subsequent fair value measurements of the redeemable financial instrument are calculated based on a discounted cash flow analysis using normalized earnings attributable to the Financial Services business, adjusted for any undistributed earnings and Scotiabank's proportionate interest in the business. The Company estimates future normalized earnings based on the most recent actual results. The earnings are then forecast over a period of five years, taking into account a terminal value calculated by discounting the final year in perpetuity. The growth rate applied to the terminal value is based on an industry based estimate for the Financial Services business, with reference to growth rates in the industry. The discount rate reflects the cost of equity of the Financial Services business and is based on expected market rates adjusted to reflect the risk profile of the Business. The fair value measurement is performed quarterly using internal estimates and judgment supplemented by periodic input from a third party. This recurring fair value measurement is categorized within Level 3 of the fair value hierarchy (see Note 35.4).

35.2 Fair value measurement of debt and deposits

The fair value measurement of debt and deposits is categorized within Level 2 of the fair value hierarchy (see Note 35.4). The fair values of the Company's debt and deposits compared to the carrying amounts are as follows:

(C$ in millions)	January 3, 2015		December 28, 2013	
	Carrying Amount	Fair Value	Carrying Amount	Fair Value
Liabilities carried at amortized cost				
Debt	$ 2,719.1	$ 2,900.8	$ 2,611.3	$ 2,707.4
Deposits	$ 2,236.9	$ 2,255.4	$ 2,330.4	$ 2,341.4

The difference between the fair values and the carrying amounts (excluding transaction costs, which are included in the carrying amount of debt) is due to decreases in market interest rates for similar instruments. The fair values are determined by discounting the associated future cash flows using current market interest rates for items of similar risk.

35.3 Items of income, expense, gains or losses

The following table presents certain amounts of income, expense, gains or losses arising from financial instruments that were recognized in net income or equity:

(C$ in millions)	2014	2013
Net gain (loss) on:		
Financial instruments designated at FVTPL	$ 0.2	$ 0.7
Financial instruments classified as FVTPL[1]	18.3	36.6
(Loss)/gain on AFS financial assets recognized in other comprehensive income	(0.2)	0.1
Gain on AFS financial assets reclassified to net income	0.1	–
Interest income (expense):		
Total interest income calculated using effective interest method for financial instruments that are not at FVTPL	799.3	772.3
Total interest expense calculated using effective interest method for financial instruments that are not at FVTPL	(169.6)	(191.8)
Fee expense arising from financial instruments that are not at FVTPL:		
Other fee expense	(24.6)	(11.3)

[1] Excludes gains (losses) on foreign exchange contracts.

35.4 Fair value of financial assets and financial liabilities classified using the fair value hierarchy

The Company uses a fair value hierarchy to categorize the inputs used to measure the fair value of financial assets and financial liabilities, the levels of which are:

Level 1 – Inputs are unadjusted quoted prices of identical instruments in active markets.
Level 2 – Inputs are other than quoted prices included in Level 1 but are observable for the asset or liability, either directly or indirectly.
Level 3 – Inputs are not based on observable market data.

The following table presents the financial instruments measured at fair value classified by the fair value hierarchy:

(C$ in millions)			2014		2013
Balance sheet line	Category	Level		Level	
Short-term investments	FVTPL	2	$ 115.1	2	$ 211.9
Short-term investments	Available for sale	2	174.0	2	204.7
Long-term investments	FVTPL	2	–	2	7.6
Long-term investments	Available for sale	2	176.0	2	127.1
Trade and other receivables	FVTPL[1]	2	15.1	2	8.2
Trade and other receivables	Effective hedging instruments	2	128.3	2	64.7
Long-term receivables and other assets	FVTPL[1]	2	58.3	2	40.3
Redeemable financial instrument	FVTPL	3	517.0	3	–

[1] Includes derivatives that are classified as held for trading.

Changes in fair value measurement for instruments categorized in Level 3

Level 3 financial instruments include a redeemable financial instrument.

As of January 3, 2015, the fair value of the redeemable financial instrument is estimated to be $517 million. The determination of the fair value of the redeemable financial instrument requires significant judgment on the part of Management.

The following table presents the changes in fair value measurements for these instruments:

(C$ in millions)	2014	2013
Balance, beginning of year	$ –	$ –
Fair value at inception	500.0	–
Unrealized fair value gains, net of losses, recognized in net income	17.0	–
Balance, end of year	$ 517.0	$ –

There were no transfers in either direction between categories in 2014.

36. Operating leases

The Company as lessee

The Company leases a number of retail stores, distribution centres, petroleum sites, facilities and office equipment under operating leases with termination dates extending to 2060. Generally, the leases have renewal options, primarily at the Company's option.

The annual lease payments for property and equipment under operating leases are as follows:

(C$ in millions)	2014	2013
Less than one year	$ 326.4	$ 322.9
Between one and five years	990.2	992.8
More than five years	764.5	862.4
	$ 2,081.1	$ 2,178.1

The amounts recognized as an expense are as follows:

(C$ in millions)	2014	2013
Minimum lease payments	$ 312.4	$ 309.5
Contingent rent	3.3	3.5
Sublease payments received	(35.9)	(36.0)
	$ 279.8	$ 277.0

Due to the redevelopment or replacement of existing properties, certain leased properties are no longer needed for business operations. Where possible, the Company subleases these properties to third parties, receiving sublease payments to reduce costs. In addition, the Company has certain premises where it is on the head lease and subleases the property to franchisees. The total future minimum sublease payments expected under these non-cancellable subleases were $88.8 million as at January 3, 2015 (2013 – $99.8 million). The Company has recognized a provision of $1.1 million (2013 – $3.1 million) with respect to these leases.

The Company as lessor

The Company leases out a number of its investment properties, and has certain sublease arrangements, under operating leases (Note 15), with lease terms between one to 20 years with the majority having an option to renew after the expiry date.

The lessee does not have an option to purchase the property at the expiry of the lease period.

The future annual lease payments receivable from lessees under non-cancellable leases are as follows:

(C$ in millions)	2014	2013
Less than one year	$ 23.1	$ 26.9
Between one and five years	68.5	92.3
More than five years	10.5	46.3
	$ 102.1	$ 165.5

37. Guarantees and commitments

Guarantees

In the normal course of business, the Company enters into numerous agreements that may contain features that meet the definition of a guarantee. A guarantee is defined to be a contract (including an indemnity) that contingently requires the Company to make payments to the guaranteed party based on (i) changes in an underlying interest rate, foreign exchange rate, equity or commodity instrument, index or other variable that is related to an asset, a liability or an equity security of the counterparty; (ii) failure of another party to perform under an obligating agreement; or (iii) failure of a third party to pay its indebtedness when due.

The Company has provided the following significant guarantees and other commitments to third parties:

Standby letters of credit

Franchise Trust, a legal entity sponsored by a third-party bank, originates loans to Dealers for their purchase of inventory and fixed assets. While Franchise Trust is consolidated as part of these financial statements, the Company has arranged for several major Canadian banks to provide standby LCs to Franchise Trust to support the credit quality of the Dealer loan portfolio. The banks may also draw against the LCs to cover any shortfalls in certain related fees owing to it. In any case where a draw is made against the LCs, the Company has agreed to reimburse the banks issuing the standby LCs for the amount so drawn. The Company has not recorded any liability for these amounts due to the credit quality of the Dealer Loans and to the nature of the underlying collateral represented by the inventory and fixed assets of the borrowing Dealers. In the unlikely event that all the LCs had been fully drawn simultaneously, the maximum payment by the Company under this reimbursement obligation would have been $144.6 million at January 3, 2015, (2013 – $170.4 million).

Business and property dispositions

In connection with agreements for the sale of all or part of a business or property and in addition to indemnifications relating to failure to perform covenants and breach of representations and warranties, the Company has agreed to indemnify the purchasers against claims from its past conduct, including environmental remediation. Typically, the term and amount of such indemnification will be determined by the parties in the agreements. The nature of these indemnification agreements prevents the Company from estimating the maximum potential liability it would be required to pay to counterparties. Historically, the Company has not made any significant indemnification payments under such agreements, and no amount has been accrued in the consolidated financial statements with respect to these indemnification agreements.

Lease agreements

The Company has entered into agreements with certain of its lessors that guarantee the lease payments of certain sublessees of its facilities to lessors. Generally, these lease agreements relate to facilities the Company has vacated prior to the end of the term of its lease. These lease agreements require the Company to make lease payments throughout the lease term if the sublessee fails to make the scheduled payments. These lease agreements have expiration dates through March 2016. The Company has also guaranteed leases on certain franchise stores in the event the franchisees are unable to meet their remaining lease commitments. These lease agreements have expiration dates through March 2016. The maximum amount that the Company may be required to pay under these agreements was $6.4 million (2013 – $9.4 million). In addition, the Company could be required to make payments for percentage rents, realty taxes and common area costs. No amount has been accrued in the consolidated financial statements with respect to these lease agreements.

Third-party financial guarantees

The Company has guaranteed the debts of certain Dealers. These third-party financial guarantees require the Company to make payments if the Dealer fails to make scheduled debt payments. The majority of these third-party financial guarantees have expiration dates extending up to and including July 4, 2015. The maximum amount that the Company may be required to pay under these debt agreements was $50 million (2013 – $50 million), of which $38.5 million (2013 – $38.3 million) was issued at January 3, 2015. No amount has been accrued in the consolidated financial statements with respect to these debt agreements.

The Company has entered into agreements to buy back franchise-owned merchandise inventory should the banks foreclose on any of the franchisees. The terms of the guarantees range from less than a year to the lifetime of the particular underlying franchise agreement. The Company's maximum exposure as at January 3, 2015, was $70 million (2013 –$68.5 million).

Indemnification of lenders and agents under credit facilities

In the ordinary course of business, the Company has agreed to indemnify its lenders under various credit facilities against costs or losses resulting from changes in laws and regulations that would increase the lenders' costs and from any legal action brought against the lenders related to the use of the loan proceeds. These indemnifications generally extend for the term of the credit facilities and do not provide any limit on the maximum potential liability. Historically, the Company has not made any significant indemnification payments under such agreements, and no amount has been accrued in the consolidated financial statements with respect to these indemnification agreements.

Other indemnification commitments

In the ordinary course of business, the Company provides other additional indemnification commitments to counterparties in transactions such as leasing transactions, service arrangements, investment banking agreements, securitization agreements, indemnification of trustees under indentures for outstanding public debt, director and officer indemnification agreements, escrow agreements, price escalation clauses, sales of assets (other than dispositions of businesses discussed above) and the arrangements with Franchise Trust discussed above. These additional indemnification agreements require the Company to compensate the counterparties for certain amounts and costs incurred, including costs resulting from changes in laws and regulations (including tax legislation) or as a result of litigation claims or statutory sanctions that may be suffered by a counterparty as a consequence of the transaction.

The terms of these additional indemnification agreements vary based on the contract and do not provide any limit on the maximum potential liability. Historically, the Company has not made any significant payments under such additional indemnifications, and no amount has been accrued in the consolidated financial statements with respect to these additional indemnification commitments.

The Company's exposure to credit risks related to the above noted guarantees and commitments are disclosed in Note 5.

Capital commitments

During the year ended January 3, 2015, the Company had capital commitments for the acquisition of property and equipment, investment property and intangible assets for an aggregate cost of approximately $164.6 million (2013 – $17.1 million).

38. Related parties

The Company's majority shareholder is Ms. Martha G. Billes, who controls approximately 61 per cent of the Common Shares of the Company through two privately held companies, Tire 'N' Me Pty. Ltd. and Albikin Management Inc.

The Company has related-party relationships with members of the Board of Directors, key management personnel and other entities over which they exercise control. Key management personnel include the Board of Directors, the Company's Chief Executive Officer, Chief Financial Officer and certain other senior officers. Close family members of these key management personnel, members of the Board of Directors and any entities over which they exercise control are also defined as related parties. Transactions with members of the Company's Board of Directors who were also Dealers represented less than one per cent of the Company's total revenue and were in accordance with established Company policy applicable to all Dealers. Other transactions with related parties during the year were not significant.

Key management personnel compensation, including Directors' fees recorded comprises:

(C$ in millions)	2014	2013
Salaries and short-term employee benefits	$ 12.4	$ 12.8
Share-based payments	41.3	37.2
Other long-term benefits	2.9	1.9
	$ 56.6	$ 51.9

39. Comparative figures

Certain of the prior year figures within the consolidated statement of cash flows have been reclassified to align with Management's view of the Company's operations.

Summary of Differences Between International Financial Reporting Standards and Accounting Standards for Private Enterprises

Appendix

B

Canada has two main sets of generally accepted accounting principles: the International Financial Reporting Standards (IFRS) that must be applied by publicly accountable enterprises, and the Accounting Standards for Private Enterprises (ASPE) that are applied by most other Canadian companies. The following table provides a chapter-by-chapter summary of the IFRS-ASPE differences that appear in this textbook. There are many more differences between the two sets of standards, but they are left to be discussed in senior accounting courses.

CHAPTER 1

Summary of IFRS-ASPE Differences

Concepts	IFRS	ASPE
The income statement (p. 8)	This financial statement is called the statement of profit or loss.	This financial statement is called the income statement.
Changes in retained earnings during an accounting period (p. 10)	These changes are reported in the statement of changes in owners' equity.	These changes are reported in the statement of retained earnings.
The balance sheet (p. 11)	This financial statement is called the statement of financial position.	This financial statement is called the balance sheet.
The cash flow statement (p. 15)	This financial statement is called the statement of cash flows.	This financial statement is called the cash flow statement.
Application of IFRS and ASPE (p. 20)	Publicly accountable enterprises or those enterprises planning to become one must apply IFRS.	Private enterprises have the option of applying IFRS, but almost all apply ASPE, which is simpler and less costly for these smaller enterprises.
Historical-cost assumption (p. 23)	Certain assets and liabilities are permitted to be recorded at their fair values rather than being kept on the books at their historical costs.	With rare exceptions, assets and liabilities are carried at their historical costs for as long as the company owns or owes them.

CHAPTER 6

Summary of IFRS-ASPE Differences

Concepts	IFRS	ASPE
Depreciation (p. 283)	This concept is called depreciation.	This concept is called amortization.
Significant components of an item of property, plant, or equipment (p. 298)	Significant components shall be depreciated separately.	Significant components are amortized separately only when it is practical to do so.
Impairment (p. 298)	A company shall assess at the end of each reporting period whether there are any signs that an asset may be impaired. Irrespective of any signs of impairment, a company must annually review goodwill and intangible assets with indefinite useful lives for impairment.	A company shall test an asset for impairment whenever events or circumstances indicate its carrying amount may not be recoverable.
	If an impaired asset subsequently increases in value, a company may reverse all or part of any previous write-down but not on goodwill.	A company may not reverse any write-downs, even if an impaired asset subsequently increases in value.
Revaluation (p. 299)	A company may choose to use the revaluation model to measure its property, plant, and equipment.	A company must use the cost method; no revaluation is permitted.

CHAPTER 7

Summary of IFRS-ASPE Differences

Concepts	IFRS	ASPE
Non-strategic investments (p. 335)	These investments are reported at fair value, with unrealized and realized gains and losses reported in net income (short-term and long-term), unless the company elects to report them in other comprehensive income (only for long-term investments).	These investments are reported at fair value, with unrealized and realized gains and losses reported in net income.
Strategic investments (a) Investments subject to significant influence (p. 336)	A company shall apply the equity method to account for these investments.	A company may choose to apply either the equity method or the cost method. If the share investments are quoted in an active market, then the fair value method replaces the cost method as an option, with any changes in fair value reported through net income.
(b) Investments in controlled subsidiaries (p. 342)	A company shall consolidate its financial statements with those of its subsidiaries.	A company may choose to account for its subsidiaries using the cost method, the equity method, or the consolidation method. If share investments are quoted in an active market, then the fair value method replaces the cost method, with any changes in fair value reported through net income.
Amortization of the discount or premium relating to long-term investments in bonds (p. 344)	The effective-interest method must be used to amortize discounts and premiums.	The straight-line method or the effective-interest method may be used to amortize discounts and premiums.

CHAPTER 8

Summary of IFRS-ASPE Differences

Concepts	IFRS	ASPE
Differences between income tax expense and income tax payable (p. 381)	Accounted for as deferred income taxes.	Accounted for as future income taxes.
Provisions and contingent liabilities (p. 385)	A contingent liability is recorded as a provision when it is probable that an outflow of economic benefits will be required to settle the liability. *Probable* is generally considered to mean that an outflow is *more likely than not* to occur.	A contingent liability is recorded as a liability when it is likely that an outflow of economic benefits will be required to settle the liability. *Likely* is generally considered to be a higher threshold to meet than *probable*, so fewer contingent liabilities will be recorded under ASPE than under IFRS.
Government remittances (p. 386)	No separate disclosure of these liabilities is required.	Government remittances (other than income taxes) such as sales taxes, Employment Insurance, and Canada Pension Plan payable must be disclosed separately, either on the balance sheet or in the notes.
Amortization of discounts and premiums (p. 393)	The effective-interest method must be used to amortize discounts and premiums.	The straight-line method is available as an amortization option.
Finance leases (p. 405)	Leases that transfer substantially all the risks and rewards incidental to the ownership of assets to the lessee are called finance leases.	The equivalent term is capital leases. There are no differences in accounting for these leases.

CHAPTER 9

Summary of IFRS-ASPE Differences

Concept	IFRS	ASPE
Accumulated other comprehensive income (p. 439)	Included as a component of shareholders' equity.	No accounting or reporting of this component is required.
Statement of changes in shareholders' (or owners') equity (p. 453)	Companies must report this statement.	Companies must report only a statement of retained earnings, which contains only a subset of the information reported in the statement of changes in shareholders' equity.

CHAPTER 10

Summary of IFRS-ASPE Differences

Concepts	IFRS	ASPE
Classification of interest paid and interest and dividends received (p. 487)	Interest paid may be classified as either an operating activity or a financing activity.	Interest paid must be classified as an operating activity.
Classification of interest and dividends received (p. 488)	Interest and dividends received may be classified as either operating activities or investing activities.	Interest and dividends received must be classified as operating activities.
Classification of dividends paid (p. 488)	Dividends paid may be classified as either an operating activity or a financing activity. *Note: Once a classification scheme has been chosen for each of the above items, it must be used consistently thereafter.*	Dividends paid must be classified as a financing activity.

Check Figures

CHAPTER 1

S1-1	NCF*
S1-2	a. $300,000 b. 200,000 c. 100,000
S1-3	NCF
S1-4	NCF
S1-5	NCF
S1-6	Net income $70
S1-7	R/E, end $260
S1-8	Total assets $140,000
S1-9	CB, Dec. 31, 2017, $19,000
S1-10	NCF
S1-11	NCF
S1-12	NCF
E1-13	NCF
E1-14	NCF
E1-15	NCF
E1-16	Canadian Tire Total assets $16,987 mil.
E1-17	2. $2,997.8 mil. 3. $1,836.4 mil.
E1-18	1. No net loss 2. No net loss 3. Net loss of $1 mil.
E1-19	1. Total assets $840,000 2. SE $400,000
E1-20	NCF
E1-21	R/E $25 mil.
E1-22	1. Net inc. before tax $9 mil. 2. Dividends $3 mil.
E1-23	Net cash provided by operations $360 thou. End Cash $125,000
E1-24	R/E, July 31, 2017, $5,900
E1-25	Total assets $44,100
E1-26	Net cash provided by operations $11,100. End Cash $8,100
E1-27	NCF
E1-28	NCF
P1-29A	1. Net inc. $28,000
P1-30A	Chain Inc.
P1-31A	1. Total assets $99,000

P1-32A	1. Total assets $160,000
P1-33A	1. Net inc. $86,000 2. R/E, end. $116,000 3. Total assets $180,000
P1-34A	1. Net decrease in cash $41 mil.
P1-35A	1. b. $2,400 thou. g. $5,700 thou. m. $2,600 thou. s. $17,400 thou.
P1-36A	1. Total assets $760 mil.
P1-37B	1. Net inc. $0.8 mil.
P1-38B	1. Net inc. $282,500 2. R/E, end. $540,700 3. Total assets $679,400
P1-39B	Groceries Inc. ending assets $3,389 mil. Bottlers Corp. repurchase of shares $20 mil. Gas Limited expenses $10,036 mil.
P1-40B	1. Total assets $114,000
P1-41B	1. Total assets $199,000
P1-42B	1. Net inc. $100,000 2. R/E, end. $90,000 3. Total assets $293,400
P1-43B	1. Net increase in cash $34,000
P1-44B	1. b. $5,850 thou. g. $15,400 thou. n. $3,670 thou. v. $43,490 thou.
DC1	NCF
DC2	1. Net inc. $0; Total assets $70,000
FOF	3. Total resources: $14,553.2 mil. Amt. owed $8,922.4 mil. Equity $5,630.8 mil.
FOA	2. Net earnings of $639.3 mil. is 13% increase

CHAPTER 2

S2-1	NCF
S2-2	a. $12,000 b. $2,000
S2-3	Cash bal. $23,000
S2-4	NCF
S2-5	NCF

---

*NCF = No Check Figure.

S2-6	2. A/P bal. $2,000
S2-7	2. Cash bal. $100
	A/R bal. $400, Service Rev. bal. $500
	3. Total assets $500
S2-8	T/B total $398 mil. Net income, $31 mil.
S2-9	1. $95,000
	2. $39,000
	3. $38,000
	4. $56,000
S2-10	T/B total $70,900
S2-11	NCF
S2-12	Total debits $160,000
E2-13	Cash $10,000
	B/S Total assets $270,000
E2-14	NCF
E2-15	NCF
E2-16	NCF
E2-17	2. a. $68,300 b. $5,000 c. $11,000
	d. $57,050 ($50,000 + $7,050) e. $7,050
E2-18	NCF
E2-19	NCF
E2-20	2. T/B total $32,200
	3. Total assets $30,700
E2-21	Cash bal. $10,700; Owing $30,600
E2-22	1. T/B total $71,200
	2. Net inc. $14,300
E2-23	T/B total $94,200
E2-24	Cash bal. $4,200
E2-25	1. T/B total $27,500
	2. Net income $8,500
E2-26	1. T/B out of balance by $1,900
	2. Total assets $43,000, Total liabilities $12,100,
	Net inc. $5,100
E2-27	2. $24,500
	3. $43,300
	4. $23,100
E2-28	4. T/B total $14,400
E2-29	a. Cash paid $85,000
	b. Cash collections $52,000
	c. Cash paid on a note payable $17,000
E2-30	1. T/B out of balance by $2,200
	2. T/B total $118,200
	3. Total assets $111,500, Total liabilities
	$71,800, Net inc. $12,400
E2-31	NCF
P2-32A	Total assets $300,000, Total liabilities $150,000,
	Net inc. $30,000
P2-33A	2. Net inc. $8,900
	4. Total assets 23,700

P2-34A	3. Cash bal. $7,700; A/P bal. $5,500
P2-35A	2. Total assets $56,500
P2-36A	3. Cash bal. $10,800; Amt. owed $35,600
P2-37A	3. T/B total $35,000
	4. Net inc. $2,205
P2-38A	3. T/B total $116,800
	4. Net inc. $1,400
P2-39B	Total assets $292,000
	Net inc. $33,000
P2-40B	2. Net inc. $16,400 4. Total assets $73,900
P2-41B	3. Cash bal. $32,500; A/P bal. $5,200
P2-42B	3. b. Total assets $56,400
P2-43B	3. Cash bal. $26,300; Amt. owed $30,000
P2-44B	3. T/B total $29,300
	4. Net inc. $7,290
P2-45B	3. T/B total $174,600
DC1	3. T/B total $27,900
	4. Net inc. $6,400
DC2	Net inc. $3,000; Total assets $21,000
FOF	4. Cash $741 mil; A/R $880.2 mil.; Inventories
	$1623.8 mil.; A/P $1,759.4 mil
FOA	3. Net income increases $74.9 mil. (13.3%)
	Operating revenues increase $677.3 (5.7%)

CHAPTER 3

S3-1	a. Net inc. $50 mil.
	b. Ending cash $90 mil.
S3-2	NCF
S3-3	NCF
S3-4	1. Prepaid Rent bal. $2,000
	2. Supplies bal. $500
S3-5	3. $20,000 Carrying amount
S3-6	Income statement, $42,000,000; Balance sheet
	$2,000,000
S3-7	2. Interest Payable Dec. 31 bal. $1,500
S3-8	2. Interest Receivable Dec. 31 bal. $1,500
S3-9	NCF
S3-10	Prepaid Rent: a. $6,000 b. $0; Rent Expense:
	a. $0 b. $6,000.
S3-11	NCF
S3-12	Net inc. $3,500 thou.; R/E $4,800 thou.
	Total assets $97,900 thou.
S3-13	Retained earnings $4,800 thou.
S3-14	a. 1.24 b. 0.69
S3-15	NCF
E3-16	2. Sales $4,100; Operating expenses $800
E3-17	a. Net Inc. $10,000
	b. Net Inc. $80,000

E3-18	1. Interest expense $0.4 mil.
E3-19	NCF
E3-20	NCF
E3-21	NCF
E3-22	2. Net inc. overstated by $17,200
E3-23	NCF
E3-24	Carrying amount $48,000
E3-25	Service Revenue $15,700
E3-26	Net inc. $4,000 thou.; Total assets $22,200 thou.; R/E $6,800 thou.
E3-27	Sales rev. $20,900 mil.; Insurance expense $330 mil; other operating expense $4,200 mil.
E3-28	Mountain B/S: Unearned service rev. $3,000; Squamish I/S: Consulting expense $9,000
E3-29	1. B/S: Unearned service rev. $90 mil. I/S service rev. $310 mil. 2. B/S: Unearned service rev. $90 mil. I/S service rev. $390 mil.
E3-30	Net Inc. $1,200 thou. Dec. 31, 2017, bal. of R/E $2,700 thou.
E3-31	NCF
E3-32	1. Total assets $39,100 2. Current ratio Current Yr. 1.26 Debt ratio Current Yr. 0.48
E3-33	1. 2017 Current ratio 2.0; Debt ratio 0.40; 2016 Current ratio 1.88; Debt ratio 0.35; 2015 Current ratio 1.33; Debt ratio 0.29
E3-34	7. Net inc. $1,200; Total assets $12,800; R/E $200
E3-35	2016: 1.868; 2017: 2.174
E3-36	a. Net inc. $108,000 b. Total assets $158,000 c. Total liabilities $13,000 d. Total shareholders' equity $145,000
E3-37	2016 Current ratio 1.82; 2017 Current ratio 2.06
E3-38	Total assets $59,200
P3-39A	1. $27 mil. 3. End. rec. $6 mil. 4. End. Payable $8 mil.
P3-40A	2. Cash basis—loss $700, Accrual basis—inc. $3,240
P3-41A	NCF
P3-42A	a. Insurance Exp. $3,100 d. Supplies Exp. $6,600
P3-43A	2. Net inc. $6,000; Total assets $54,000; R/E $15,000
P3-44A	2. Total assets $68,600; Net inc. $4,100; Total Liabilities $7,400

P3-45A	1. Net inc. $39,200; Total assets $47,000; Debt ratio 0.549
P3-46A	2. March 31, 2017 bal. of R/E $47,300
P3-47A	1. Total assets $83,300 2. Current ratio 2017, 1.60, Debt ratio 2017, 0.32
P3-48A	1. Current ratio 2017, 1.69; Debt ratio 2017, 0.574
P3-49B	1. $15; 3. End. rec. $5; 4. End payable $6
P3-50B	2. Cash basis—loss $2,700, Accrual basis—inc. $1,100
P3-51B	NCF
P3-52B	c. Supplies Exp. $11,400 f. Insurance Exp. $2,700
P3-53B	2. Net inc. $19,800; Total assets $61,600; R/E $36,200
P3-54B	2. Total assets $30,400; Net inc. $25,500; Total liabilities $14,700
P3-55B	1. Net inc. $78,600; Total assets $109,000 2. Debt ratio 0.42
P3-56B	2. Dec. 31, 2017 bal. of R/E $16,800
P3-57B	1. Total assets $55,000 2. Current ratio 2017, 1.71; Debt ratio 0.42
P3-58B	1. 2017, Current ratio 1.36, 2. Debt ratio 0.681
DC1	1. $2,000 3. Current ratio 1.748
DC2	Net inc. $7,000, Total assets $32,000
DC3	1. $260,000 2. Shareholder Equity $148,000
FOF	5. 2015: Current ratio 1.86; Debt ratio 0.61
FOA	2. Deprec. Expense, $275.7 mil.

CHAPTER 4

S4-1	NCF
S4-2	3. Bad debt expense $2.1 mil.
S4-3	NCF
S4-4	Adj. bal. $3,005
S4-5	NCF
S4-6	$1,000 stolen
S4-7	2. A/R, net $62,500
S4-8	Dr Bad debt exp. $15,000 Bal. for Allowance for Uncollectible Accounts $16,500
S4-9	1. A/R bal. $184,000 2. Allowance for Uncollectible Accounts $16,500 3. A/R, net $167,500
S4-10	d. Bad debt exp. $12,000
S4-11	3. A/R, net $123,000
S4-12	b. Dr Cash $93,600
S4-13	3. $102,667

S4-14	c. Dr Cash $6,480
S4-15	a. Notes rec. $6,000; Interest rec. $280
	b. Interest rev. $280
	c. Nothing to report
	d. Interest rev. $200
S4-16	1. 0.95 2. 24 days
S4-17	2. Net Inc. $4,424 thou.
	3. 1.60
E4-18	Bookkeeper stole $1,000
E4-19	NCF
E4-20	Adj. bal. $1,150
E4-21	Adj. bal. $1,780
E4-22	NCF
E4-23	A/R, net $91,000
E4-24	3. A/R, net $49,500
E4-25	2. A/R, net $52,800
E4-26	3. A/R, net $224,850
E4-27	Bad debt exp. $150; Write-offs $148
E4-28	Dec. 31 Dr Interest rec. $1,326
E4-29	I/S: Interest rev. $750 for 2016 and $250 for 2017
E4-30	NCF
E4-31	1. a. 1.89 b. 53 days
E4-32	1. 10 days
E4-33	Expected net inc. with bank card $129,800
E4-34	a. $28 mil. b. $11,148 mil.
P4-35A	Adj. bal. $6,090
P4-36A	1. Adj. bal. $2,242.16
P4-37A	4. Allowance for Uncollectible Accounts $318; A/R $4,517
	5. I/S: Bad debt. exp. $380
P4-38A	3. A/R, net: 2017, $221,000; 2016, $207,800
P4-39A	2. Corrected ratios: Current 1.48; Acid-test 0.75;
	3. Net inc., corrected $84,000
P4-40A	2. 12/31/17 Note rec. $25,000; Interest rec. $82
P4-41A	1. ratios: a. 1.98 b. 1.14 c. 31 days
P4-42B	Adj. bal. $5,960
P4-43B	1. Adj. bal. $8,239
P4-44B	5. I/S: Bad debt. exp. $335 thou.
P4-45B	3. A/R, net: 2017, $109,200; 2016 $107,300
P4-46B	2. Corrected ratios: Current 1.32; Acid-test 0.78
	3. Net inc., corrected $76,000
P4-47B	2. 12/31/17 Note rec. $20,000; Interest rec. $247
P4-48B	1. 2017 ratios: a. 1.87 b. 0.87 c. 35 days
DC1	Net inc. $223,000
DC2	2017: Days' sales in rec. 26 days; Cash collections $1,456 thou.
FOF	1. Adj. bal. $662.1 mil.
	2. Customers owed $880.2 mil. (2014) and $758.5 mil. (2013)

	3. Collected $12,216.2 mil.
FOA	2. A/R turnover = 15.21
	Days in receivables = 24 days
	Acid-test ratio = 0.40

CHAPTER 5

S5-1	NCF
S5-2	GP $160,000
S5-3	1. a. COGS: Weighted-Avg. $3,760;
	b. FIFO $3,740
S5-4	Net inc.: Weighted-Avg. $3,060; FIFO $3,100
S5-5	Inc. tax exp: Weighted-Avg. $551; FIFO $558
S5-6	NCF
S5-7	COGS $421,000
S5-8	GP% 0.321; Inv. TO 3.0 times
S5-9	c. COGS $1,190 mil. d. GP $510 mil.
S5-10	1. Correct GP $5.7 mil.
	2. Correct GP $5.1 mil.
S5-11	NCF
S5-12	NCF
S5-13	2. $90,000 3. GP $50,000
E5-14	3. GP $1,100 thou.
E5-15	2. GP $3,790
E5-16	1. COGS: a. $1,730 b. $1,760 c. $1,710
E5-17	$12.50
E5-18	2. Net inc. $132
E5-19	1. GP: FIFO $0.2 mil.;
	Weighted-avg. $0.6 mil.
E5-20	NCF
E5-21	NCF
E5-22	GP $45,000
E5-23	a. $475 c. $56 f. $2 g. $3;
	Myers (net loss) $(136) mil.
E5-24	Myers GP% 0.125; Inv. TO 17.9 times
E5-25	GP $16.3 bil.; GP% 29.7; Inv. TO 5.3 times
E5-26	Net inc.: 2017 $65,000; 2016 $69,000
E5-27	1. Ending inv. $1,320 COGS $2,890;
	2. Ending inv. $1,347 COGS $2,863;
	3. Ending Inv. $1,410 COGS $2,800
E5-28	4. COGS $2,863
E5-29	1. COGS $2,843
	2. GP $2,843
E5-30	COGS $3,010
E5-31	1. A/R $4,900
E5-32	NCF
E5-33	1. COGS $150,410; 2. COGS $152,750
E5-34	GP 2017, $8.3 thou.; GP% 0.202, Inv. TO 3.7 times

P5-35A	2. COGS $3,546; GP $2,595
P5-36A	2. Inv. ending bal. $700,000 3. Net inc. $603,000
P5-37A	1. (a) GP $2,409 Ending Inv. $2,437 (b) GP $2,400 Ending Inv. $2,428
P5-38A	1. COGS: Weighted-Avg. $7,290; FIFO $7,200 3. Net inc. $2,457
P5-39A	1. GP: Weighted-Avg. $60,286; FIFO $60,785
P5-40A	NCF
P5-41A	1. Chocolate Treats: GP% 12.5%; Inv. TO 17.9 times
P5-42A	1. Net inc. each yr. $2 mil.
P5-43A	2. Net sales $2,071
P5-44B	2. COGS $3,417; GP $3,279
P5-45B	2. Inv. ending bal. $1,750,000 3. Net inc. $1,448,400
P5-46B	1. (a) GP $1,173 Ending inv. $340 (b) GP $1,169 Ending Inv. $336
P5-47B	1. COGS: Weighted-Avg. $40,678; FIFO $40,530 3. Net inc. $11,028
P5-48B	1. GP: Weighted-Avg. $291,571; FIFO $299,500
P5-49B	NCF
P5-50B	1. 2015: TC Motors: GP% 24.7%; Inv. TO 8.0 times; X-Country Trucks: GP% 33.8%; Inv. TO 45.4 times
P5-51B	1. Net inc. (thou): 2017, $150; 2016, $320; 2015, $50
P5-52B	2. Net sales $2,047
DC1	1. Net inc.: FIFO $370,300, Weighted-avg. $364,161
DC2	NCF
FOF	3. Purchases $8,559.7 4. 2014: GP% 32.5%; Inv. TO 5.4 times
FOA	3. Cash payments $8,415.9 mil.

CHAPTER 6

S6-1	2. Carrying amount $29,893 mil.
S6-2	NCF
S6-3	Building cost $56,000
S6-4	Net inc. overstated
S6-5	2. Carrying amount: SL $21 mil.; UOP $22 mil.; DDB $15 mil.
S6-6	a. SL $4 mil. b. UOP $2 mil. c. DDB none
S6-7	a. SL 1.25 mil. b. UOP 3.5 mil. c. DDB 2.857,143 mil.
S6-8	Dep'n. Exp. $12,000
S6-9	1. $13,000
S6-10	NCF
S6-11	1. Goodwill $19.7 mil.

S6-12	1. Net inc. $2,100,000
S6-13	Net cash provided by investing $6 mil.
S6-14	ROA 15%
S6-15	ROA 2016 17.7%, ROA 2017 18%
S6-16	NCF
S6-17	GW 4.8 mil.
S6-18	a. Equip. loss $40,000
E6-19	Land $283,000, Building $3,820,000
E6-20	Machine cost 1 $25,000; 2 $41,700; 3 $33,300
E6-21	NCF
E6-22	2. Building, net $737,160
E6-23	Yr 1: SL $9,000, UOP $7,200, DDB $19,980
E6-24	I/S: Dep. Exp.–building $6,000; B/S: Building net $194,000
E6-25	1. ROA 2017 5.96%; 2016 5.4%
E6-26	Dep'n yr. 12, $55,833
E6-27	Loss on sale $2,200
E6-28	Carrying amount $140,800
E6-29	NCF
E6-30	Amort. yr. 3, $200,000
E6-31	NCF
E6-32	1. Cost of goodwill $17,000,000
E6-33	NCF
E6-34	NCF
E6-35	1. ROA 2017 4.75%; 2016 0.3%
E6-36	NCF
E6-37	5,600 hours
E6-38	Sale price $20.2 mil.
E6-39	Expected net inc. for 2017, $21,426
E6-40	2019 Effects on: 2. Equip. $50,000 under; 3. Net inc. $50,000 over; 4. Equity $50,000 under
P6-41A	1. Land $296,600; Land Improve. $103,800; Warehouse $1,241,000
P6-42A	2. A/Dep.–Building. $105,000; A/Dep.-Equip. $338,000
P6-43A	Dec. 31 Dep. Exp.–Motor Carrier Equip. $58,667; Dep.Exp.–Building. $1,050
P6-44A	NCF
P6-45A	Dep. SL $44,000; UOP 2020, $33,000, DDB, 2020, $11,104
P6-46A	1. Carrying amount $41,497 thou. 3. PPE bal. $68,406; A/Dep. bal. $26,909; Long term investment bal. $108,302
P6-47A	Part 1. 2. Goodwill $1.2 mil. Part 2. 2. Net inc. $3,720,000
P6-48A	1. Loss on sale $0.1 mil. 2. PP&E, net $0.7 mil.
P6-49A	1. ROA 2017 6.62%; 2016 5.61%

P6-50A	2. Loss on sale $257 mil.
P6-51B	1. Land $143,450; Land Improve. $86,000; Garage $654,000
P5-52B	2. A/Dep.–Building. $52,000; A/Dep.–Equip. $437,500
P6-53B	Dec. 31 Dep. Exp.–Comm.; Equip. $4,000; Dep. Exp.–Televideo Equip. $1,333
P6-54B	NCF
P6-55B	Dep. SL $9,000; UOP 2015, $9,720; DDB, 2018, $4,741
P6-56B	1. Carrying amount $2,131 mil.; 3. Premises and Equip. bal. $5,941; A/Dep. bal. $3,810
P6-57B	Part 1. 2. Goodwill $5,500; Part 2. 3. Amort. $300,000
P6-58B	1. Gain on sale $0.02 bil. 2. PPE net $7.26 bil.
P6-59B	1. ROA 2017 8.34%; 2016 8.08%
P6-60B	2. Loss on sale $304 mil.
DC1	1. Net inc.: LPF $142,125; BA $128,250
DC2	NCF
FOF	4. Proportion of PP&E used up in 2014, 50.9%
FOA	1. Dep'n exp. $279.2 mil.; Amort. exp. $93.1 mil.

CHAPTER 7

S7-1	1. Unrealized loss on invest. $500 2. LT investment at fair value $7,000
S7-2	1. Gain on sale $800
S7-3	3. LT investment bal. $42.6 mil.
S7-4	Loss on sale $7.3 mil.
S7-5	NCF
S7-6	NCF
S7-7	2. Cash Interest $70,000 4. Interest revenue $68,175
S7-8	c. Dr. Interest Revenue $1,825
S7-9	1. PV $6,810 2. PV $39,930
S7-10	PV $6,145,000
S7-11	NCF
S7-12	1. PV $7,452 2. PV $45,492
S7-13	1. PV $6,743.26 2. PV $10,871.63
E7-14	d. Loss on sale $2,000
E7-15	2. Unrealized loss $63,560 3. LT investments $242,644
E7-16	2. Invest. end. bal. $1,055,000
E7-17	Gain on sale $1,645,000
E7-18	2. Long term investment at equity $525,000

E7-19	3. Interest rec. $350; LT investment in bonds $18,214
E7-20	PV of bond investment $10,521
E7-21	2. Shareholders' equity $327,000
E7-22	Net cash used inv. $(11.8) mil.
E7-23	NCF
E7-24	1. PV of investment at 5%, $103,890 2. PV of investment at 10%, $90,855
E7-25	Accum. other comprehensive loss Dec 31, 2017, $(69) mil.
P7-26A	2. B/S LT invest. at equity $523,300, I/S Equity method invest. rev. $178,500, Div. Rev. $240, Unrealized loss $2,600
P7-27A	2. LT invest. in MSC bal. $659,000
P7-28A	3. Consolidated debt ratio 0.898
P7-29A	2. B/S LT investment in bonds $622,031; I/S Interest rev. $25,031
P7-30A	Choose Investment A, PV $19,578
P7-31A	2. Shareholders' equity $341,000
P7-32A	NCF
P7-33A	3. Consolidated debt ratio 0.917
P7-34B	2. B/S LT invest. at equity $526,300, I/S Equity method invest. rev. $87,500, Div rev. $750, Unrealized (loss) $(3,300)
P7-35B	2. LT invest. in Affil. bal. $535,000
P7-36B	2. LT invest. in bonds $445,304; Int. rev. $35,304
P7-37B	Choose Investment X, PV $25,650
P7-38B	3. Consolidated debt ratio 0.935
P7-39B	NCF
P7-40B	3. Consolidated debt ratio 0.929
DC1	NCF
DC2	2. Gain on sale $4,200 3. Gain on sale $80,000
FOF	NCF
FOA	NCF

CHAPTER 8

S8-1	3/31/2018, Debits include interest expense $250
S8-2	2. Interest exp. $250
S8-3	2. Est. Warranty pay. bal. $50,000
S8-4	Warranty exp. $60,000
S8-5	1. 2017, A/P TO = 9; Days pay. outstanding = 41 days
S8-6	a. $897,500; b. $551,875
S8-7	NCF
S8-8	b. 10/31/2017, Interest exp. $313
S8-9	2. 07/31/2017, Interest exp. $3,915

S8-10	3. 07/31/2017, Interest exp. $3,915; 01/31/2016 Interest exp. $3,934
S8-11	1. $9,400; 2. $10,000 on July 2027; 3. $325; 4. $355
S8-12	b. 12/31/2017, Int. exp. $375
S8-13	1. Leverage ratio: Best Buy 2.45, Walmart 2.53; Debt ratio: Best Buy .59 Walmart .61
S8-14	Leverage ratio 2.5; Debt ratio .60; Time interest earned ratio 3.73 times
S8-15	Total liabilities $501,000
E8-16	2. Warranty exp. $9,000; Est. Warranty Pay. $7,600
E8-17	Unearned subscription rev. $1,000
E8-18	Payroll tax exp. $9,000; Payroll pay. $6,400
E8-19	3. 2017, Interest exp. $1,250; 2018, $1,750
E8-20	2. 2017, Leverage ratio 1.90; Debt ratio 0.47
E8-21	2. Debt ratio 0.76
E8-22	Company B: Current ratio 1.89; Debt ratio 0.60; Leverage ratio 2.48; Times interest earned ratio 7.2 times
E8-23	d. Total current liabilities $149,625
E8-24	c. 12/31/2017, Interest exp. $2,625
E8-25	4. Annual interest exp. straight-line $15,800
E8-26	1. 01/31/2018 Bond carrying amount $372,811
E8-27	1. 06/30/2017 Bond carrying amount $553,125
E8-28	01/01/2017 Bond Carrying amount $287,041
E8-29	2. 2017, Leverage ratio 2; Debt ratio 0.50
E8-30	Sobeys: Current 1; Debt 0.51; Times interest earned 9.49 times
E8-31	Company F: Current ratio 2.1; Debt ratio 0.59; Leverage ratio 2.45; Times interest earned ratio 6.4 times
E8-32	2. Leverage ratio 1.52; Debt ratio .30
E8-33	1. 2017, Current ratio 1.17; Debt ratio .571
E8-34	5. 3/15/2019 Bond Carrying amount $97,632
E8-35	Plan A, EPS $4.12
P8-36A	e. Note pay. due in 1 year $20,000; Interest pay. $6,000
P8-37A	12/31/2017, Warranty Expense $3,800; 4/30/2018 Interest exp. $1,500
P8-38A	2. Interest pay. $30,000; Bonds pay. $4,500,000
P8-39A	4. Interest pay. $5,667; Bonds pay. net $194,250
P8-40A	2. Bonds pay. net $583,800; 3. a. $24,900; b. $24,000
P8-41A	2. Alternative 1, EPS $13.38
P8-42A	3. 12/31/2020 Bond carrying amt. $589,001
P8-43A	1. 12/31/2019 Bond Carrying amt. $474,920; 3. Bond pay. net $472,352

P8-44A	NCF
P8-45A	2. Carrying amt. $675,000; 3. Time interest earned ratio 1.62 times; 4. Leverage ratio 1.36, Debt ratio 0.26
P8-46A	2. Carrying amt. $553,000; 3. Time interest earned ratio 4.3 times
P8-47B	e. Long term notes pay. due in 1 year $20,000; Interest pay. $2,083
P8-48B	12/31/2017 Warranty expense $18,000; 6/30/2018 Interest exp. $9,000
P8-49B	1. a. Bonds pay. $1,000,000; c. Interest pay. $20,000
P8-50B	4. Interest pay. $7,000; Notes pay. net $289,000
P8-51B	2. $95,200; 3. a. $4,600; b. $4,000
P8-52B	2.12/31/2020 Bond carrying amt. $483,439
P8-53B	NCF
P8-54B	1. Pension liability $45,000 2. Bonds pay. carrying amt. $2,078,000 3. Times interest earned ratio 1.72 times 4. Leverage ratio 2.63; Debt ratio 0.62
P8-55B	2. Bonds pay. carrying amt. $313,000 3. Times interest earned ratio 2.7 times
P8-56B	2. Interest pay. $26,250; Bonds pay. $4,500,000
DC1	1. Debt ratio 0.82; ROA 1.5%; 2. Leverage ratio 5.71; ROE 8.5%; 3. Debt ratio 0.92; ROA 0.1%
DC2	EPS Plan A $4.78; Plan B $4.54; Plan C $4.63
FOF	NCF
FOA	Current ratio 1.858; Debt ratio 0.613

CHAPTER 9

S9-1	NCF
S9-2	NCF
S9-3	NCF
S9-4	NCF
S9-5	1. $1.80 3. $5,650 profit
S9-6	NCF
S9-7	Total SE $1,246 thou.
S9-8	a. $585 thou. b. $3,011 thou. c. $4,257 thou.
S9-9	NCF
S9-10	R/E increased $50,000
S9-11	1. $150,000 4. Pref. $450,000
S9-12	2. No effect
S9-13	BV per share $61.60
S9-14	2. Decrease SE $154.1 mil.
S9-15	ROA 1.2%; ROE 3.96%
S9-16	Total SE $2,010,000
E9-17	1. ROA 9.3%; ROE 26%

E9-18	2. Total SE $92,500
E9-19	Total SE $143,000
E9-20	Total PIC $1,045,000
E9-21	SE $(29) deficit
E9-22	Overall increase in SE $19,100
E19-23	NCF
E9-24	Total SE $4,300 mil.
E9-25	3. 564 mil. shares 4. $136 mil.
E9-26	2016: Pref. $24,000; Com. $26,000
E9-27	2. Total SE $8,134,000
E9-28	a. Decrease SE $80 mil. e. Increase SE $3,000
E9-29	Total SE $2,755 mil.
E9-30	1. $10.90 2. $10.77
E9-31	1. ROA 10.2%; ROE 18%
E9-32	1. ROA 4.1%; ROE 11.7%
E9-33	b. Issued 500 shares
E9-34	Div. $1,407 mil.
E9-35	Total SE $65 mil.
P9-36A	NCF
P9-37A	2. Total SE $207,500
P9-38A	Total SE $663,000
P9-39A	NCF
P9-40A	Total SE $7,680,000
P9-41A	4. $22,500
P9-42A	2. Total SE $95,800
P9-43A	NCF
P9-44A	1. Total assets $559,000, Total SE $296,000 2. ROA 17%; ROE 34.9%
P9-45A	1. $806 mil. 2. $5 per share 3. $10 per share 4. 7.8%
P9-46B	NCF
P9-47B	2. Total SE $323,800
P9-48B	Total SE $540,000
P9-49B	NCF
P9-50B	Total SE $4,126,000
P9-51B	4. $183,700
P9-52B	2. Total SE $132,800
P9-53B	NCF
P9-54B	1. Total assets $568,000, Total SE $312,000 2. ROA 13.4%; ROE 26.1%
P9-55B	1. $537 mil. 2. $3.01 per share 3. $3.77 per share 4. 8%
DC1	3. Total SE: Plan 1, $220,000 Plan 2, $230,000
DC2	NCF

FOF	1. 3,423,366 common shares 2. Avg. share price $110.65
FOA	1. 2014: ROA 5.2%; ROE 12.1%

CHAPTER 10

S10-1	NCF
S10-2	NCF
S10-3	Net cash oper. $70,000
S10-4	NCF
S10-5	Net cash oper. $54,000
S10-6	Net cash oper. $54,000 Net increase in cash $53,000
S10-7	Net cash oper. $56,000 Net increase in cash $15,900
S10-8	a. $60,000; b. $20,000
S10-9	a. New borrowing $10,000 b. Issuance $8,000 c. Dividends $146,000
E10-10	NCF
E10-11	NCF
E10-12	NCF
E10-13	Net cash oper. $32,000
E10-14	Net cash oper. $80,000
E10-15	Net cash oper. $111,100 Net increase in cash $11,100
E10-16	NCF
E10-17	a. Cash proceeds of sale $46,000; b. Cash dividends $26,000
E10-18	1. Gain on sale of property and equipment $120 2. LT debt issued $240
E10-19	a. $23,996 c. $3,577 f. $626
E10-20	Total assets $376,400
P10-21A	NCF
P10-22A	1. Net inc. $56,667 2. Total assets $396,667 3. Net cash oper. $(49,000) Net increase in cash $90,000
P10-23A	Net cash oper. $63,200 Net increase in cash $16,000 Non-cash inv. and fin. $160,000
P10-24A	Net cash oper. $76,900 Net (decrease) in cash $(4,100) Non-cash inv. and fin. $101,000
P10-25A	Net cash oper. $80,000 Net increase in cash $12,300
P10-26B	NCF

P10-27B	1. Net inc. $157,333
	2. Total assets $340,333
	3. Net cash oper. $81,000
	Net increase in cash $191,000
P10-28B	Net cash oper. $74,500
	Net (decrease) in cash $(5,700)
	Non-cash inv. and fin. $290,400
P10-29B	Net cash oper. $68,700
	Net increase in cash $16,300
	Non-cash inv. and fin. $30,000
P10-30B	Net cash oper. $90,600
	Net increase in cash $13,100
DC1	1. Net cash oper. $132
	Net (decrease) in cash $(46)
DC2	NCF
FOF	NCF
FOA	NCF

APPENDIX 10A

S10A-1	Net cash oper. $110,000
	Net (decrease) in cash $(20,000)
S10A-2	Net cash oper. $13,000
S10A-3	Net cash oper. $13,000
	Net increase in cash $12,000
S10A-4	a. $699,000 b. $326,000
S10A-5	a. $68,000 b. $134,000
E10A-6	NCF
E10A-7	NCF
E10A-8	Net cash oper. $21,000
E10A-9	NCF
E10A-10	Net cash oper. $102,000
	Net increase in cash $29,000
E10A-11	a. $50,000 b. $113,000
E10A-12	(in thousands) a. $24,637; b. $18,134; c. $3,576;
	d. $530; e. $73; f. $1,294
P10A-13A	Net cash oper. $95,700
	Net (decrease) in cash $(2,700)
	Non-cash inv. and fin. $79,400
P10A-14A	1. Net inc. $51,667
	2. Total assets $396,667
	3. Net cash oper. $49,000
	Net increase in cash $90,000
P10A-15A	Net cash oper. $80,000
	Net increase in cash $12,300
P10A-16A	Net cash oper. $55,800
	Net (decrease) in cash $(2,000)
	Non-cash inv. and fin. $99,100

P10A-17A	Net cash oper. $73,200
	Net increase in cash $20,000
	Non-cash inv. and fin. $19,000
P10A-18B	Net cash oper. $30,000
	Net increase in cash $7,600
	Non-cash inv. and fin. $142,800
P10A-19B	1. Net inc. $157,333
	2. Total assets $340,333
	3. Net cash oper. $81,000
	Net increase in cash $191,000
P10A-20B	Net cash oper. $90,600
	Net increase in cash $13,100
P10A-21B	Net cash oper. $77,200
	Net (decrease) in cash $(4,600)
	Non-cash inv. and fin. $83,200
P10A-22B	Net cash oper. $40,400
	Net increase in cash $4,100
	Non-cash inv. and fin. $48,300

CHAPTER 11

S11-1	2017 Net inc. increase 9.2%
S11-2	2017 Sales trend 107%
S11-3	2017 Cash 2.13%
S11-4	Net inc. Porterfield 6.22%
S11-5	2017 Current ratio 1.37
S11-6	2017 Allstott Inc. Quick ratio 1.18
S11-7	a. 28 times; 13 days b. 9 days c. 2.6 times
	d. -118 days
S11-8	1. 80.% 2. 6.5
S11-9	a. 7.73% b. 1.369 c. 13.2% d. 4.77 e. 50.6%
S11-10	1. EPS $4.85; P/E 16
S11-11	a. $3,855 thou. d. $873 thou.
S11-12	a. $562 thou. d. $3,768 thou. e. $1,294 thou.
E11-13	2017 WC increase 26.8%
E11-14	Net inc. decreased 5.8%
E11-15	Yr.4 Net inc. trend 47%
E11-16	Current assets 24.6%; Total liabilities 41.7%
E11-17	Net inc. 20% both years
E11-18	NCF
E11-19	a. 1.67 b.0.83 c. 4.4 times d. 9.5 times e. 38 days
E11-20	2017 ratios: a. 2.07 b. 0.91 c. 0.47 d. 4.13
E11-21	2017 ratios: Return on net sales 0.098; ROA.
	0.132; ROE 0.151; EPS 0.67
E11-22	2017 ratios: P/E 17.3; Div. yield. 0.014; BV
	per common share $6

E11-23	Total liab. & S/H equity $20,000 mil.	P11-35B	1. Net inc. 5.3%, Current assets 75%
E11-24	Net inc. $720 mil.	P11-36B	NCF
E11-25	Net inc. $168,000	P11-37B	1. Current ratio 1.54; 2. a. Current ratio 1.44
P11-26A	4. 2017 17.3%	P11-38B	1. 2017 a. 1.94 f. 256 k. 13
P11-27A	1. Net inc. 10.7%, Current assets 77.1%	P11-39B	Thrifty a. 0.78 b. 2.32 c. 40 d. 0.41 f. 0.349
P11-28A	NCF	P11-40B	NCF
P11-29A	1. Current ratio 1.74; 2. a. Current ratio 1.84	P11-41B	1. 2016 a. 1.96 d. 5.95 g. 67 days
P11-30A	1. 2017 a. 1.96 f. 255 k. 17	DC1	NCF
P11-31A	Video a. 0.60 b. 2.16 c. 100 d. 0.68 f. 0.196	DC2	NCF
P11-32A	NCF	DC3	NCF
P11-33A	1. 2016 a. 1.46 d. 7.61 g. 83 days	FOF	1. Net inc. trend 2014 41%
P11-34B	4. 2017 14.6%	FOA	1. Net inc. 2014 5.1%; 2013 4.8%

Glossary

accelerated depreciation method A depreciation method that writes off a relatively larger amount of the asset's cost nearer the start of its useful life than the straight-line method does. (p. 288)

account format A balance sheet format that lists assets on the left side and liabilities above shareholders' equity on the right side. (p. 129)

account payable A liability for goods or services purchased on credit and backed by the general reputation and credit standing of the debtor. (p. 376)

account The record of the changes that have occurred in a particular asset, liability, or element of shareholders' equity during a period. (p. 56)

accounting An information system that measures and records business activities, processes data into reports, and reports results to decision makers. (p. 3)

accounting equation Assets = Liabilities + Owners' Equity. Provides the foundation for the double-entry method of accounting. (p. 11)

Accounting Standards for Private Enterprises (ASPE) Canadian accounting standards that specify the *generally accepted accounting principles* applicable to *private enterprises* that are required to follow *GAAP* and choose not to apply *IFRS*. (p. 8)

accounts payable turnover (T/O) A liquidity ratio that measures the number of times per year a company was able to repay its accounts payable in full. Calculated by dividing the cost of goods sold by the average accounts payable balance for the year. (p. 402)

accounts receivable turnover Measures a company's ability to collect cash from credit customers. To compute accounts receivable turnover, divide net credit sales by average net accounts receivable. (p. 574)

accrual accounting A basis of accounting that records transactions based on whether a business has acquired an asset, earned revenue, taken on a liability, or incurred an expense, regardless of whether cash is involved. (p. 110)

accrual An adjustment related to revenues earned or expenses incurred prior to any cash or invoice changing hands. (p. 120)

accrued expense An expense that has been incurred but not yet paid or invoiced. (p. 120)

accrued revenue A revenue that has been earned but not yet collected or invoiced. (p. 122)

accumulated depreciation The account showing the sum of all depreciation expense from the date of acquiring a capital asset. (p. 120)

acid-test ratio Ratio of the sum of cash plus short-term investments plus net receivables to total current liabilities. It is an indicator of an entity's ability to pay its current liabilities if they become due immediately. Also called the *quick ratio*. (pp. 202, 573)

adjusted trial balance A list of all the ledger accounts with their adjusted balances. (p. 126)

aging-of-receivables method A way to estimate bad debts by analyzing accounts receivable according to the length of time they have been receivable from the customer. Also called the *balance-sheet approach* because it focuses on accounts receivable. (p. 190)

allowance for bad debts Another name for *allowance for uncollectible accounts*. (p. 190)

allowance for doubtful accounts Another name for *allowance for uncollectible accounts*. (p. 190)

allowance for uncollectible accounts A contra account, related to accounts receivable, that holds the estimated amount of collection losses. (p. 190)

allowance method A method of recording collection losses based on estimates of how much money the business will not collect from its customers. (p. 190)

amortization Allocation of the cost of an intangible asset with a finite life over its useful life (p. 301)

asset turnover The dollars of sales generated per dollar of assets invested. Net sales divided by Average total assets. (p. 579)

asset A resource owned or controlled by a company as a result of past events and from which the company expects to receive future economic benefits. (p. 11)

auditor An accountant who provides an independent opinion on whether an entity's financial statements have been prepared in accordance with generally accepted accounting principles. (p. 17)

bad debt expense A cost to the seller of extending credit to customers. Arises from a failure to collect an account receivable in full. (p. 189)

balance sheet Reports a company's financial position as at a specific date. In particular, it reports a company's assets, liabilities, and owners' equity. Also called the *statement of financial position*. (p. 11)

bank collections Collections of money by the bank on behalf of a depositor. (p. 182)

bank reconciliation A document explaining the reasons for the difference between a depositor's records and the bank's records about the depositor's cash. (p. 181)

bank statement Document showing the beginning and ending balances of a particular bank account and listing the month's transactions that affected the account. (p. 180)

benchmarking The comparison of a company to a standard set by other companies, with a view towards improvement. (p. 563)

board of directors Group elected by the shareholders to set policy for a corporation and to appoint its officers. (p. 6)

bond discount Excess of a bond's face (par) value over its issue price. (p. 388)

bond investments Bonds and notes are debt instruments that an investor intends to hold until maturity.   (p. 345)

bond market price The price investors are willing to pay for the bond. It is equal to the present value of the principal payment plus the present value of the interest payments.   (p. 388)

bond premium Excess of a bond's issue price over its face value.   (p. 388)

bonds payable Groups of notes payable issued to multiple lenders called *bondholders*.   (p. 387)

book value (of a share) Amount of owners' equity on the company's books for each share of its stock.   (p. 449)

book value per share of common stock Common stockholders' equity divided by the number of shares of common stock outstanding. The recorded amount for each share of common stock outstanding.   (p. 583)

brand name A distinctive identification of a product or service. Also called a *trademark* or *trade name*.   (p. 302)

capital expenditure Expenditure that increases an asset's capacity or efficiency, or extends its useful life. Capital expenditures are debited to an asset account. Also called *betterments*.   (p. 282)

carrying amount (of a capital asset) The asset's cost minus accumulated depreciation.   (p. 120)

carrying amount The historical cost of an asset net of its accumulated depreciation.   (p. 13)

cash conversion cycle The number of days it takes to convert cash into inventory, inventory to receivables, and receivables back into cash, after paying off payables. Days inventory outstanding + days sales outstanding − days payables outstanding.   (p. 575)

cash equivalents Investments such as term deposits, guaranteed investment certificates, or high-grade government securities that are considered so similar to cash that they are combined with cash for financial disclosure on the balance sheet.   (pp. 178, 485)

cash-basis accounting Accounting that records only transactions in which cash is received or paid.   (p. 110)

chairperson Elected by a corporation's board of directors, usually the most powerful person in the corporation.   (p. 438)

chart of accounts List of a company's accounts and their account numbers.   (p. 69)

cheque Document instructing a bank to pay the designated person or business the specified amount of money   (p. 179)

classified balance sheet A balance sheet that shows current assets separate from long-term assets, and current liabilities separate from long-term liabilities.   (p. 129)

closing entries Entries that transfer the revenue, expense, and dividend balances from these respective accounts to the Retained Earnings account.   (p. 136)

common-size statement A financial statement that reports only percentages (no dollar amounts).   (p. 563)

comparability Investors like to compare a company's financial statements from one year to the next. Therefore, a company must consistently use the same accounting method each year.   (pp. 21, 248)

consistency principle A business must use the same accounting methods and procedures from period to period.   (p. 248)

consolidated statements Financial statements of the parent company plus those of majority-owned subsidiaries as if the combination were a single legal entity.   (p. 342)

contingent liability A possible obligation that arises from past events and whose existence will be confirmed only by the occurrence or non-occurrence of one or more uncertain future events not wholly within the control of the company.   (p. 385)

contra account An account that always has a companion account and whose normal balance is opposite that of the companion account.   (p. 120)

controlling (majority) interest Ownership of more than 50% of an investee company's voting shares and can exercise control over the investee.   (p. 342)

copyright Exclusive right to reproduce and sell a book, musical composition, film, other work of art, or computer program. Issued by the federal government, copyrights extend 50 years beyond the author's life.   (p. 301)

corporation An incorporated business owned by one or more *shareholders*, which according to the law is a legal "person" separate from its owners.   (p. 6)

cost of goods sold Cost of the inventory the business has sold to customers. Also called *cost of sales*.   (p. 231)

credit The right side of an account.   (p. 70)

creditor The party to whom money is owed.   (p. 195)

cumulative preferred shares Preferred shares whose owners must receive all dividends in arrears plus the current year's dividend before the corporation can pay dividends to the common shareholders.   (p. 447)

current asset An asset that is expected to be converted to cash, sold, or consumed during the next 12 months, or within the business's normal operating cycle if longer than a year.   (p. 11)

current liability A debt due to be paid within one year or within the entity's operating cycle if the cycle is longer than a year.   (p. 14)

current portion of long-term debt The amount of the principal that is payable within one year. Also called *current instalment of long-term debt*.   (p. 383)

current ratio Current assets divided by current liabilities. Measures a company's ability to pay current liabilities with current assets.   (pp. 138, 571)

date of declaration The date on which the Board of Directors declares a dividend to shareholders.   (p. 444)

date of payment The date on which a dividend is actually paid to shareholders.   (p. 445)

date of record The date on which a person must be recorded as a shareholder in order to receive a dividend.   (p. 445)

days payable outstanding (DPO) Another way of expressing the accounts payable turnover ratio, this measure indicates how many days it will take to pay off the accounts payable balance in full. Calculated by dividing the *accounts payable turnover* into 365.   (p. 402)

days' sales in receivables Ratio of average net accounts receivable to one day's sales. Indicates how many days' sales remain in Accounts Receivable awaiting collection. Also called the *collection period* and *days sales outstanding*.   (pp. 203, 574)

debentures Unsecured bonds—bonds backed only by the good faith of the borrower.   (p. 388)

debit The left side of an account.   (p. 70)

debt ratio Ratio of total liabilities to total assets. States the proportion of a company's assets that is financed with debt.   (pp. 139, 576)

debtor The party who owes money.   (p. 195)

deferral An adjustment related to a transaction for which a business has received or paid cash in advance of delivering or receiving goods or services.   (p. 115)

deferred income tax liability The amount of income taxes payable in future periods as a result of differences between accounting income and taxable income in current and prior periods. Under ASPE, this is known as a *future income tax liability*.   (p. 382)

deficit The term used when *retained earnings* is a negative balance.   (pp. 10, 444)

deposits in transit A deposit recorded by the company but not yet recorded by its bank.   (p. 181)

depreciable cost The cost of a tangible asset minus its estimated residual value.   (p. 285)

depreciation An expense to recognize the portion of a capital asset's economic benefits that has been used up during an accounting period.   (pp. 119, 283)

direct method A method of determining cash flows from operating activities in which all cash receipts and cash payments from operating activities are directly reported on the statement of cash flows.   (p. 488)

dividend yield Ratio of dividends per share of stock to the stock's market price per share. Tells the percentage of a stock's market value that the company returns to shareholders as dividends.   (p. 582)

double-diminishing-balance (DDB) method An accelerated depreciation method that computes annual depreciation by multiplying the asset's decreasing carrying amount by a constant percentage, which is two times the straight-line rate.   (p. 288)

double-entry system An accounting system that uses debits and credits to record the dual effects of each business transaction.   (p. 69)

doubtful account expense Another name for *bad debt expense*.   (p. 189)

earnings per share (EPS) Amount of a company's net income per outstanding common share.   (pp. 400, 581)

electronic funds transfer System that transfers cash by electronic communication rather than by paper documents.   (p. 178)

entire period Length of time during which beginning inventory and purchases are taken into account when calculating unit cost.   (p. 241)

equity method The method used to account for investments in which the investor has 20–50% of the investee's voting shares and can significantly influence the decisions of the investee.   (p. 339)

estimated residual value Expected cash value of an asset at the end of its useful life. Also called *scrap value* or *salvage value*.   (p. 284)

estimated useful life Length of service that a business expects to get from an asset. May be expressed in years, units of output, kilometres, or other measures.   (p. 284)

ethical standards Standards that govern the way we treat others and the way we restrain our selfish desires. They are shaped by our cultural, socioeconomic, and religious backgrounds.   (p. 25)

expense A cost incurred to purchase the goods and services a company needs to run its business on a day-to-day basis. The opposite of revenue.   (p. 8)

face value of bond The principal amount payable by the issuer. Also called *maturity value*.   (p. 427)

fair value (of a share) The price that a willing buyer would pay a willing seller to acquire a share.   (p. 449)

fair value The amount that a business could sell an asset for, or the amount that a business could pay to settle a liability.   (p. 24)

faithful representation A fundamental qualitative characteristic of accounting information. Information is a faithful representation if it is complete, neutral, accurate, and reflects the economic substance of the underlying transaction or event.   (p. 20)

finance lease Under IFRS, a lease that transfers substantially all the risks and rewards incidental to ownership of assets to the lessee.   (p. 405)

financial accounting The branch of accounting that provides information for managers inside a business and for decision makers outside the business.   (p. 5)

financial statements The reports that companies use to convey the financial results of their business activities to various user groups, which can include managers, investors, creditors, and regulatory agencies.   (p. 2)

financing activities Activities that result in changes in the size and composition of a company's contributed equity and borrowings.   (pp. 15, 487)

first-in, first-out (FIFO) cost method Inventory costing method by which the first costs into inventory are the first costs out to cost of goods sold. Ending inventory is based on the costs of the most recent purchases.   (p. 242)

franchises and licences Privileges granted by a private business or a government to sell a product or service in accordance with specified conditions.   (p. 302)

fraud The intentional misrepresentation of facts done to persuade another party to act in a way that causes financial damage to that party.   (p. 25)

fraudulent financial reporting The creation of false and misleading accounting records, usually to present a more favourable financial picture.   (p. 26)

free cash flow A measure of how much cash a company has available to pursue new business opportunities. Calculated by deducting capital expenditures from cash flow from operating activities.   (p. 502)

future value Measures the future sum of money that a given current investment is "worth" at a specified time in the future, assuming a certain interest rate.   (p. 349)

gain A type of income other than revenue that results in an increase in economic benefits to a company, and usually occurs outside the course of the company's ordinary business activities.   (p. 8)

generally accepted accounting principles (GAAP) The guidelines of financial accounting, which specify the standards for how accountants must record, measure, and report financial information.   (p. 7)

going-concern assumption The assumption that an entity will continue operating normally for the foreseeable future.   (p. 22)

goodwill Excess of the cost of an acquired company over the sum of the market values of its net assets (assets minus liabilities).   (p. 302)

gross margin Another name for *gross profit*. (p. 233)

gross profit percentage Gross profit divided by net sales revenue. Also called the *gross margin percentage*. (p. 249)

gross profit Sales revenue minus cost of goods sold. Also called *gross margin*. (p. 233)

historical-cost assumption Holds that assets should be recorded at their actual cost, measured on the date of purchase as the amount of cash paid plus the dollar value of all non-cash consideration (other assets, privileges, or rights) also given in exchange. (p. 23)

horizontal analysis Study of percentage changes over time through comparative financial statements. (p. 556)

income statement The financial statement that measures a company's operating performance for a specified period of time. In particular, it reports income, expenses, and net income. Also called the *statement of profit or loss*. (p. 8)

income Consists of a company's *revenues* and *gains*. (p. 8)

indirect method A method of determining cash flows from operating activities in which net income is adjusted for non-cash transactions, any deferrals or accruals of past or future operating cash receipts or payments, and items of income or expense associated with investing or financing cash flows. (p. 488)

intangible assets Long-lived assets with no physical form that convey a special right to current and expected future benefits. (p. 279)

interest The borrower's cost of renting money from a lender. Interest is revenue for the lender and expense for the borrower. (p. 195)

interest-coverage ratio Another name for the *times-interest-earned ratio*. (p. 404)

International Financial Reporting Standards (IFRS) International accounting standards that specify the *generally accepted accounting principles* which must be applied by *publicly accountable enterprises* in Canada and over 100 other countries. (p. 7)

inventory turnover Ratio of cost of goods sold to average inventory. Indicates how rapidly inventory is sold. (pp. 250, 574)

investing activities Activities that include the purchase and sale of long-term assets and other investments that result in cash inflows or outflows related to resources used for generating future income and cash flows. (pp. 15, 487)

journal The chronological accounting record of an entity's transactions. (p. 73)

lease Rental agreement in which the tenant (lessee) agrees to make rent payments to the property owner (lessor) in exchange for the use of the asset. (p. 405)

ledger The book of accounts and their balances. (p. 74)

lessee Tenant in a lease agreement. (p. 405)

lessor Property owner in a lease agreement. (p. 405)

leverage ratio Ratio of average total assets to average common shareholders' equity. Measures the proportion of average total assets actually owned by the shareholders. (p. 579)

leverage ratio Shows the ratio of a company's total assets to total shareholders' equity. It is an alternative way of expressing how much debt a company has used to fund its assets, or in other words, how much leverage it has used. (p. 403)

leverage Earning more income on borrowed money than the related interest expense, thereby increasing the earnings for the owners of the business. Also called *trading on the equity*. (p. 579)

liability An obligation (or debt) owed by a company, which it expects to pay off in the future using some of its assets. (p. 14)

limited liability No personal obligation of a shareholder for corporation debts. A shareholder can lose no more on an investment in a corporation's shares than the cost of the investment. (p. 437)

line of credit A method of short-term borrowing that provides a company with as-needed access to credit up to a maximum amount specified by its lender. (p. 376)

liquidity A measure of how quickly an asset can be converted to cash. The higher an asset's liquidity, the more quickly it can be converted to cash. (pp. 13, 129)

long-term asset Another term for *non-current asset*. (p. 13)

long-term investments Any investment that does not meet the criteria of a short-term investment; any investment that the investor expects to hold for longer than a year. (p. 335)

long-term liability Another term for *non-current liability*. (p. 14)

loss A type of expense that results in a decrease in economic benefits to a company, and usually occurs outside the course of the company's ordinary business activities. The opposite of a gain. (p. 9)

lower-of-cost-and-net-realizable-value (LCNRV) rule Requires that an asset be reported in the financial statements at whichever is lower—its historical cost or its net realizable value. (p. 248)

majority interest Ownership of more than 50% of an investee company's voting shares. (p. 342)

management accounting The branch of accounting that generates information for the internal decision makers of a business, such as top executives. (p. 5)

market interest rate Interest rate that investors demand for loaning their money. Also called *effective interest rate*. (p. 389)

market price (of a share) The price that a willing buyer would pay a willing seller to acquire a share. (p. 443)

material Accounting information is material if it is significant enough in nature or magnitude that omitting or misstating it could affect the decisions of an informed user. (p. 21)

maturity date The date on which a debt instrument must be paid. (p. 195)

misappropriation of assets The theft of assets from a company. (p. 26)

mortgage A *term loan* secured by real property, such as land and buildings. (p. 405)

multi-step income statement An income statement that contains subtotals to highlight important relationships between revenues and expenses. (p. 130)

net assets Another name for *owners' equity*. (p. 14)

net earnings Another name for *net income*. (p. 10)

net income The excess of a company's total income over its total expenses. (p. 10)

net loss Occurs when a company's total expenses exceed its total income. (p. 10)

net profit Another term for *net income*. (p. 10)

net realizable value The amount a business could get if it sold the inventory less the costs of selling it. (p. 248)

net working capital Current assets – current liabilities. Measures the ease with which a company will be able to use its current assets to pay off its current liabilities.   (p. 138)

non-cash operating working capital account A current asset or current liability account that derives from an operating activity and is not included in cash and cash equivalents.   (p. 493)

non-controlling interest A subsidiary company's equity that is held by shareholders other than the parent company. (p. 344)

non-current asset Any asset that is not classified as a current asset.   (p. 11)

non-current liability A liability a company expects to pay off beyond one year from the balance sheet date.   (p. 14)

non-strategic investments Investments in which the investor owns less than 20% of the voting shares of the investee and is presumed to exercise no influence.   (p. 335)

nonsufficient funds (NSF) cheque A cheque for which the payer's bank account has insufficient money to pay the cheque. NSF cheques are cash receipts that turn out to be worthless.   (p. 182)

obsolescence Occurs when an asset becomes outdated or no longer produces revenue for the company.   (p. 284)

operating activities Activities that comprise the main revenue-producing activities of a company, and generally result from the transactions and other events that determine net income.   (pp. 15, 486)

operating lease A lease in which the risks and rewards of asset ownership are not transferred to the lessee.   (p. 405)

outstanding cheques Cheques issued by the company and recorded on its books but not yet paid by its bank.   (p. 181)

owners' equity The company owners' remaining interest in the assets of the company after deducting all its liabilities.   (p. 14)

par value shares Shares of stock that do not have a value assigned to them by articles of the corporation.   (p. 440)

parent company An investor company that owns more than 50% of the voting shares of a subsidiary company.   (p. 342)

partnership An unincorporated business with two or more parties as co-owners, with each owner being a partner in the business.   (p. 5)

patent A federal government grant giving the holder the exclusive right for 20 years to produce and sell an invention.   (p. 301)

payroll Employee compensation, a major expense of many businesses.   (p. 380)

periodic inventory system An inventory system in which the business does not keep a continuous record of the inventory on hand. Instead, at the end of the period, the business makes a physical count of the inventory on hand and applies the appropriate unit costs to determine the cost of the ending inventory.   (p. 234)

permanent accounts Assets, liabilities, and shareholders' equity accounts, which all have balances that carry forward to the next fiscal year.   (p. 136)

perpetual inventory system An inventory system in which the business keeps a continuous record for each inventory item to show the inventory on hand at all times.   (p. 234)

physical wear and tear Occurs when the usefulness of the asset deteriorates.   (p. 284)

post-employment benefits A special type of employee benefits that do not become payable until after a person has completed employment with the company. They include such things as pension benefits, medical and dental insurance, and prescription drug benefits.   (p. 406)

posting Transferring amounts from the journal to the ledger.   (p. 74)

preferred shares Shares that give their owners certain advantages, such as the priority to receive dividends before the common shareholders and the priority to receive assets before the common shareholders if the corporation liquidates.   (p. 440)

present value The value on a given date of a future payment or series of future payments, discounted to reflect the time value of money (p. 350)

president Chief executive officer in charge of managing the day-to-day operations of a corporation.   (p. 438)

pretax accounting income Income before tax on the income statement; the basis for computing income tax expense.   (p. 381)

price/earnings ratio (multiple) Ratio of the market price of a common to the company's earnings per share. Measures the value that the stock market places on $1 of a company's earnings.   (p. 582)

principal The amount borrowed by a debtor and lent by a creditor.   (p. 195)

private enterprise An entity that has not issued and does not plan to issue shares or debt on public markets.   (p. 8)

proprietorship An unincorporated business with a single owner, called the proprietor.   (p. 5)

provision Under IFRS, a present obligation of uncertain timing or amount that is recorded as a liability because it is probable that economic resources will be required to settle it.   (p. 384)

publicly accountable enterprises (PAEs) Corporations that have issued or plan to issue shares or debt in a public market.   (p. 7)

purchase allowance A decrease in the cost of purchases because the seller has granted the buyer a discount (an allowance) from the amount owed.   (p. 236)

purchase discount A decrease in the cost of purchases earned by making an early payment to the vendor.   (p. 236)

purchase return A decrease in the cost of purchases because the buyer returned the goods to the seller.   (p. 236)

quick ratio Another name for *acid-test ratio*.   (pp. 202, 573)

receivables Monetary claims against a business or an individual, acquired mainly by selling goods or services and by lending money.   (p. 187)

relevance A fundamental qualitative characteristic of accounting information. Information is relevant if it has predictive value, confirmatory value, or both, and is *material*.   (p. 20)

remittance advice An optional attachment to a cheque (sometimes a perforated tear-off document and sometimes capable of being electronically scanned) that indicates the payer, date, and purpose of the cash payment. The remittance advice is often used as the source document for posting cash receipts or payments.   (p. 179)

report format A balance sheet format that lists assets at the top, followed by liabilities and then shareholders' equity.   (p. 129)

repurchased shares A corporation's own shares that it has issued and later reacquired.   (p. 443)

retained earnings Represent the accumulated net income of a company since the day it started business, less any net losses and dividends declared during this time.   (p. 10)

return on assets (ROA) Net income divided by average total assets. This ratio measures how profitably management has used the assets that shareholders and creditors have provided the company.   (pp. 304, 450, 579)

return on common shareholders' equity Net income minus preferred dividends, divided by average common shareholders' equity. A measure of profitability. Also called *return on equity (ROE)*.   (p. 580)

return on equity (ROE) Measures how well management has used equity to generate profits for shareholders.   (p. 451)

return on net sales Ratio of net income to net sales. A measure of profitability. Also called *return on sales*.   (p. 578)

revenue Consists of amounts earned by a company in the course of its ordinary, day-to-day business activities. The vast majority of a company's revenue is earned through the sale of its primary goods and services.   (p. 8)

sales discount Percentage reduction of sale price by the seller as an incentive for early payment before the due date. A typical way to express a sales discount is "2/10, n/30." This means the seller will grant a 2% discount if the invoice is paid within 10 days, or the full amount is due within 30 days.   (p. 238)

sales returns and allowances Merchandise returned for credit or refunds for services provided.   (p. 238)

sales tax payable The amount of HST, GST, and provincial sales tax owing to government bodies.   (p. 378)

separate-entity assumption Holds that the business activities of the reporting entity are separate from the activities of its owners.   (p. 22)

serial bonds Bonds that mature in instalments over a period of time.   (p. 388)

shareholder A party who owns shares of a corporation.   (p. 6)

shareholders' equity Another term for *owners' equity*.   (p. 14)

shares Legal units of ownership in a corporation.   (p. 6)

short-term notes payable Notes payable due within one year.   (p. 377)

single-step income statement Lists all revenues together and all expenses together; there is only one step in arriving at net income.   (p. 130)

specific identification cost method Inventory costing method based on the specific cost of particular units of inventory.   (p. 240)

stable-monetary-unit assumption Holds that regardless of the reporting currency used, financial information is always reported under the assumption that the value of the currency is stable, despite the fact that its value does change due to economic factors such as inflation.   (p. 22)

stated interest rate Interest rate printed on the bond certificate that determines the amount of cash interest the borrower pays and the investor receives each year. Also called the *coupon rate* or *contract interest rate*.   (p. 388)

stated value An arbitrary amount assigned by a company to a share of its stock at the time of issue.   (p. 440)

statement of cash flows Reports cash receipts and cash payments classified according to the entity's major activities: operating, investing, and financing.   (p. 15)

statement of changes in shareholders' equity Reports the changes in all categories of shareholders' equity during the period.   (p. 453)

statement of financial position Another name for the *balance sheet*.   (p. 11)

statement of profit or loss Another name for the *income statement*.   (p. 8)

statement of retained earnings Summary of the changes in the retained earnings of a corporation during a specific period.   (p. 10)

stock dividend A proportional distribution by a corporation of its own shares to its shareholders.   (p. 445)

stock split An increase in the number of authorized, issued, and outstanding shares of stock coupled with a proportionate reduction in the share's book value.   (p. 447)

straight-line (SL) method Depreciation method in which an equal amount of depreciation expense is assigned to each year of asset use.   (p. 285)

strategic investments Investments in which the investor owns more than 20% of the voting shares of the investee and is presumed to exercise either significant influence or control over the investee.   (p. 336)

subsidiary company An investee company in which a parent company owns more than 50% of the voting shares and can exercise control over the subsidiary.   (p. 342)

tangible long-lived assets Also called property, plant, and equipment.   (p. 279)

taxable income The basis for computing the amount of tax to pay the government.   (p. 381)

temporary accounts Revenue, expense, and dividend accounts, which do not have balances that carry forward to the next fiscal year.   (p. 136)

term bonds Bonds that all mature at the same time for a particular issue.   (p. 388)

term loan A long-term loan at a stated interest rate, typically from a single lender such as a bank, which must be repaid over a specified number of years. Usually secured by specific assets of the borrower, often the ones acquired using the loan proceeds.   (p. 405)

term The length of time from inception to maturity.   (p. 195)

times-interest-earned ratio Ratio of income from operations to interest expense. Measures the number of times that operating income can cover interest expense. Also called the *interest-coverage ratio*.   (pp. 404, 577)

trademark, trade name A distinctive identification of a product or service. Also called a *brand name*.   (p. 302)

trading on the equity Another name for *leverage*.   (p. 581)

transaction An event that has a financial impact on a business and that can be reliably measured.   (p. 56)

trend percentages A form of horizontal analysis that indicates the direction a business is taking.   (p. 559)

trial balance A list of all the ledger accounts with their balances.   (p. 79)

uncollectible account expense Another name for bad debt expense. (p. 189)

underwriter Organization that purchases the bonds from an issuing company and resells them to its clients or sells the bonds for a commission, agreeing to buy all unsold bonds. (p. 388)

unearned revenue A liability that arises when a business receives cash from a customer prior to providing the related goods or services. (pp. 117, 382)

units-of-production (UOP) method Depreciation method by which a fixed amount of depreciation is assigned to each unit of output produced by the plant asset. (p. 287)

verifiability The ability to check financial information for accuracy, completeness, and reliability. (p. 21)

vertical analysis Analysis of a financial statement that reveals the relationship of each statement item to a specified base, which is the 100% figure. (p. 560)

weighted-average-cost method Inventory costing method based on the average cost of inventory for the period. Weighted-average cost is determined by dividing the cost of goods available by the number of units available. Also called the *average cost method*. (p. 240)

working capital Current assets minus current liabilities; measures a business's ability to meet its short-term obligations with its current assets. Also called *net working capital*. (p. 570)

Index

Note: Page numbers with *f* indicate figures.